FINANCIAL ACCOUNTING

FINANCIAL ACCOUNTING

C. WILLIAM (BILL) THOMAS
BAYLOR UNIVERSITY

WENDY M. TIETZ
KENT STATE UNIVERSITY

WALTER T. HARRISON, JR.
BAYLOR UNIVERSITY

GREG BERBERICH
UNIVERSITY OF WATERLOO

CATHERINE SEGUIN
UNIVERSITY OF TORONTO

 Pearson

Pearson Canada Inc., 26 Prince Andrew Place, North York, Ontario M3C 2H4.

9780135222171

1 2019

Library and Archives Canada Cataloguing in Publication
Title: Financial accounting / Walter T. Harrison, Jr. (Baylor University), C. William (Bill) Thomas (Baylor University), Wendy M. Tietz (Kent State University), Greg Berberich (University of Waterloo), Catherine Seguin (University of Toronto).
Names: Harrison, Walter T., Jr., author. | Thomas, C. William, author. | Tietz, Wendy M., author. | Berberich, Greg, 1968- author. | Seguin, Catherine I., author.
Description: Seventh Canadian edition. | Previously published: Toronto, Ontario: Pearson Canada Inc., 2018. | Includes index.
Identifiers: Canadiana 20190150920 | ISBN 9780135222171 (hardcover)
Subjects: LCSH: Accounting—Textbooks. | LCGFT: Textbooks.
Classification: LCC HF5636 .H37 2019 | DDC 657/.044—dc23

CONTENTS

Chapter 4
Cash and Receivables   177

Chapter 5
Inventory and Cost of
Goods Sold   230

Chapter 6
Property, Plant, and Equipment,
and Intangible Assets   278

ABOUT THE AUTHORS

C. William (Bill) Thomas is the J.E. Bush Professor of Accounting and a Master Teacher at Baylor University. A Baylor University alumnus, he received both his BBA and MBA there and went on to earn his PhD from The University of Texas at Austin.

With primary interests in the areas of financial accounting and auditing, Dr. Thomas has served as the J.E. Bush Professor of Accounting since 1995. He has been a member of the faculty of the Accounting and Business Law Department of the Hankamer School of Business since 1971 and served as chair of the department for 12 years. He has been recognized as an Outstanding Faculty Member of Baylor University as well as a Distinguished Professor for the Hankamer School of Business. Dr. Thomas has received many awards for outstanding teaching, including the Outstanding Professor in the Executive MBA Programs as well as the designation of Master Teacher.

Thomas is the author of textbooks in auditing and financial accounting, as well as many articles in auditing, financial accounting and reporting, taxation, ethics, and accounting education. His scholarly work focuses on the subject of fraud prevention and detection, as well as ethical issues among accountants in public practice. He presently serves as the accounting and auditing editor of *Today's CPA*, the journal of the Texas Society of Certified Public Accountants, with a circulation of approximately 28,000.

Thomas is a certified public accountant in Texas. Prior to becoming a professor, Thomas was a practising accountant with the firms of KPMG, LLP, and BDO Seidman, LLP. He is a member of the American Accounting Association, the American Institute of CPAs and Association of International Certified Professional Accountants, and the Texas Society of Certified Public Accountants.

For my wife, Mary Ann.
C. William (Bill) Thomas

Wendy M. Tietz is a professor in the Department of Accounting in the College of Business Administration at Kent State University. She teaches introductory financial and managerial accounting in a variety of formats, including large sections, small sections, and online sections.

Dr. Tietz is a Certified Public Accountant (Ohio), a Certified Management Accountant, and a Chartered Global Management Accountant. She is a member of the American Accounting Association, the Institute of Management Accountants, the American Institute of CPAs and Association of International Certified Professional Accountants, and the Sustainability Accounting Standards Board Alliance. She has published articles in such journals as *Issues in Accounting Education, Accounting Education: An International Journal, IMA Educational Case Journal,* and *Journal of Accounting & Public Policy*. Dr. Tietz is also the coauthor of a managerial accounting textbook, *Managerial Accounting*, with Dr. Karen Braun. She received the 2017 Bea Sanders/AICPA Innovation in Teaching Award for her web tool for financial accounting instructors, the Accounting Case Template. In 2016, Dr. Tietz was awarded the Jim Bulloch Award for Innovations in Management Accounting Education from the American Accounting Association/Institute of Management Accountants for her accounting educator blog, *Accounting in the Headlines*. She also received the 2014 Bea Sanders/AICPA Innovation in Teaching Award for her blog. She regularly presents at AAA regional and national meetings. She is intensely interested in the power of storytelling, interactivity, and social media as educational practices to promote engagement and understanding.

Dr. Tietz received her PhD from Kent State University. She received both her MBA and BSA from the University of Akron. Prior to teaching, she worked in industry for several years, both as a controller for a financial institution and as the operations manager and controller for a recycled plastics manufacturer.

To my husband, Russ, who steadfastly supports me in every endeavor.
Wendy M. Tietz

Walter T. Harrison Jr. is professor emeritus of accounting at the Hankamer School of Business, Baylor University. He received his BBA from Baylor University, his MS from Oklahoma State University, and his PhD from Michigan State University.

Professor Harrison, recipient of numerous teaching awards from student groups as well as from university administrators, has also taught at Cleveland State Community College, Michigan State University, the University of Texas, and Stanford University.

A member of the American Accounting Association and the American Institute of CPAs and Association of International Certified Professional Accountants, Professor Harrison has served as chairman of the Financial Accounting

Standards Committee of the American Accounting Association, on the Teaching/Curriculum Development Award Committee, on the Program Advisory Committee for Accounting Education and Teaching, and on the Notable Contributions to Accounting Literature Committee.

Professor Harrison has lectured in several foreign countries and published articles in numerous journals, including *Journal of Accounting Research, Journal of Accountancy, Journal of Accounting and Public Policy, Economic Consequences of Financial Accounting Standards, Accounting Horizons, Issues in Accounting Education,* and *Journal of Law and Commerce.*

Professor Harrison has received scholarships, fellowships, and research grants or awards from PricewaterhouseCoopers, Deloitte & Touche, the Ernst & Young Foundation, and the KPMG Foundation.

Charles T. Horngren (1926–2011) was the Edmund W. Littlefield Professor of Accounting, emeritus, at Stanford University. A graduate of Marquette University, he received his MBA from Harvard University and his PhD from the University of Chicago. He was also the recipient of honourary doctorates from Marquette University and DePaul University.

A certified public accountant, Horngren served on the Accounting Principles Board for six years, the Financial Accounting Standards Board Advisory Council for five years, and the Council of the American Institute of Certified Public Accountants for three years. For six years he served as a trustee of the Financial Accounting Foundation, which oversees the Financial Accounting Standards Board and the Government Accounting Standards Board.

Horngren is a member of the Accounting Hall of Fame. As a member of the American Accounting Association, Horngren was its president and its director of research. He received its first annual Outstanding Accounting Educator Award. The California Certified Public Accountants Foundation gave Horngren its Faculty Excellence Award and its Distinguished Professor Award. He was the first person to have received both awards. The American Institute of Certified Public Accountants presented its first Outstanding Educator Award to Horngren. Horngren was named Accountant of the Year, in Education, by the national professional accounting fraternity, Beta Alpha Psi. Professor Horngren was also a member of the Institute of Management Accountants, from whom he received its Distinguished Service Award. He was a member of the institute's Board of Regents, which administers the certified management accountant examinations.

Horngren is an author of these other accounting books published by Pearson: *Cost Accounting: A Managerial Emphasis,* Fifteenth Edition, 2015 (with Srikant M. Datar and Madhav V. Rajan); *Introduction to Financial Accounting,* Eleventh Edition, 2014 (with Gary L. Sundem, John A. Elliott, and Donna Philbrick); *Introduction to Management Accounting,* Sixteenth Edition, 2014 (with Gary L. Sundem, Jeff Schatzberg, and Dave Burgstahler); *Horngren's Financial & Managerial Accounting,* Fifth Edition, 2016 (with Tracie L. Miller-Nobles, Brenda L. Mattison, and Ella Mae Matsumura); and *Horngren's Accounting,* Eleventh Edition, 2016 (with Tracie L. Miller-Nobles, Brenda L. Mattison, and Ella Mae Matsumura). Horngren was the consulting editor for Pearson's Charles T. Horngren Series in Accounting.

Greg Berberich, CPA, CA, PhD, has been a Lecturer in the School of Accounting and Finance at the University of Waterloo since 2011. While at Waterloo, he has served as the Director of the Master of Accounting program and as the Associate Director of Teaching & Learning. Before Waterloo, he was a faculty member at Wilfrid Laurier University for nine years. He obtained his BMath and PhD from the University of Waterloo and completed his CPA and CA in Ontario.

He has taught financial accounting, auditing, and a variety of other courses at the undergraduate and graduate levels. He has presented papers at a variety of academic conferences in Canada and the United States and has served on the editorial board of the journal *Issues in Accounting Education.* He was also the Treasurer of the Society for Teaching and Learning in Higher Education for several years. He has written a number of cases for use in university courses and professional training programs.

For Aggie, who helps me stay balanced.
Greg Berberich

Catherine I. Seguin, MBA, CGA, is an Associate Professor, Teaching Stream, at the University of Toronto Mississauga.

She also acts as Dean's Designate for academic offences in the Social Sciences.

She has written the following books: *Understanding Accounting for Not-for-Profit Organizations* and *Accounting for Not-for-Profit Organizations* for Carswell (Thomson-Reuters) and *Not-for-Profit Accounting,* published by CGA Canada. In the not-for-profit community, she has served as Treasurer on several different boards.

To my family, who are always cheering me on:
Dennis, Andrea, Allison, Carlos, Mark, and Caileah
Catherine I. Seguin

PREFACE

HELPING STUDENTS BUILD A SOLID *FINANCIAL ACCOUNTING* FOUNDATION

Financial Accounting gives readers a solid foundation in the fundamentals of accounting and the basics of financial statements, and then builds upon that foundation to offer more advanced and challenging concepts and problems. The concepts and procedures that form the accounting cycle are also described and illustrated early in the text (Chapters 2 and 3) and are then applied consistently in the chapters that follow. This scaffolded approach helps students to better understand the meaning and relevance of financial information, see its significance within a real-world context, as well as develop the skills needed to analyze financial information in both their courses and career.

Financial Accounting has a long-standing reputation in the marketplace for being readable and easy to understand. It drives home fundamental concepts using relevant examples from real-world companies in a reader-friendly way without adding unnecessary complexity. While maintaining hallmark features of accuracy, readability, and ease of understanding, the Seventh Canadian Edition includes updated explanations, coverage, and ratio analysis with decision-making guidelines. These time-tested methodologies with the latest technology ensures that students learn basic concepts in accounting in a way that is relevant, stimulating, and fun, while exercises and examples from real-world companies help students gain a better grasp of the course material.

CHANGES TO THE SEVENTH CANADIAN EDITION

Students and instructors will benefit from numerous changes incorporated into this latest edition of *Financial Accounting*. Based on feedback from users and reviewers, the material covering investments and the time value of money (Chapter 7 in the Sixth Edition) has been moved to Appendix B of the textbook. (Full coverage of this material continues to be available in all the supplements.) As a result of this change, the Seventh Edition is more streamlined than previous editions, with ten chapters and a better flow of the introductory financial accounting topics, while keeping the investments and time value of money material conveniently in the textbook.

All materials have been updated to reflect the IFRS and ASPE principles in effect at the time of writing. Directly after the Learning Objectives, each chapter includes a list of relevant 2019 CPA Competencies addressed in that chapter. A summary of IFRS and ASPE differences is provided at the end of several chapters to identify the differences that exist between these two sets of principles. These differences are collected by chapter in Appendix C of the textbook.

The following is a summary of the significant changes made to the Seventh Canadian Edition of *Financial Accounting*:

CRITICAL THINKING QUESTIONS

Critical Thinking questions have been added to each chapter to help students apply the chapter material to questions that are less directed and that require more thoughtful application of the chapter concepts in written answers. A new icon appears beside the Critical Thinking questions.

COMPREHENSIVE CASES

Comprehensive Cases have been added to give students the opportunity to apply the concepts from a number of chapters to one or two business situations to see how the accounting concepts work together in the real world. There are five new Comprehensive Cases, which cover Chapters 1 to 3, Chapters 4 to 6, Chapters 7 to 8, Chapter 9, and Chapter 10.

ETHICAL DECISIONS

The Ethical Decisions section in every chapter now includes scenarios that require students to apply ethical principles from the CPA Canada Code of Professional Conduct.

FOCUS ON FINANCIAL STATEMENT ANALYSIS

Focus on Financial Statement Analysis questions appear at the end of each chapter. Students use the Dollarama Inc. financial statements that appear in Appendix A in the textbook to apply the chapter's accounting concepts to a familiar company's financial statements.

AVAILABLE ON MYLAB ACCOUNTING
ACCOUNTING CYCLE TUTORIAL

This interactive tutorial in MyLab Accounting helps students master the Accounting Cycle for early and continued success in financial accounting courses. The tutorial, accessed by computer, smartphone, or tablet, provides students with brief explanations of each concept of the Accounting Cycle through engaging, interactive activities. Students are immediately assessed on their understanding, and their performance is recorded in the MyLab Accounting gradebook. Whether the Accounting Cycle Tutorial is used as a remediation self-study tool or course assignment, students have yet another resource within MyLab Accounting to help them be successful with the accounting cycle.

ACT COMPREHENSIVE PROBLEM

New! The Accounting Cycle Tutorial now includes a comprehensive problem that allows students to work with the same set of transactions throughout the accounting cycle. The comprehensive problem, which can be assigned at the beginning or the end of the full cycle, reinforces the lessons learned in the Accounting Cycle Tutorial activities by emphasizing the connections between the accounting cycle concepts.

TIME VALUE OF MONEY TUTORIAL

New! The Time Value of Money Tutorial in MyLab Accounting ensures that students understand the basic theory and formulas of the TVM, while also helping test their ability to *apply* the TVM in the measurement of financial statement items. Students work through two sections. The first is to help them understand the theory-using whatever method the instructors choose (manually, through Excel®, with tables, or via a calculator). The second is to give students the opportunity to apply the theory by giving them a number of scenarios regarding each financial statement.

DYNAMIC STUDY MODULES

New! Chapter-specific Dynamic Study Modules help students study effectively on their own by continuously assessing their activity and performance in real time. Here's how it works: students complete a set of questions with a unique answer format that also asks them to indicate their confidence level. Questions repeat until the student can answer them all correctly and confidently. Dynamic Study Modules explain the concept using materials from the text. These are available as graded assignments and are accessible on smartphones, tablets, and computers.

LEARNING CATALYTICS

Text-specific Learning Catalytics helps you generate class discussion, customize your lecture, and promote peer-to-peer learning with real-time analytics. As a student response tool, Learning Catalytics uses students' smartphones, tablets, or laptops to engage them in more interactive tasks and thinking.

- **NEW!** Upload a full PowerPoint® deck for easy creation of slide questions.
- Help your students develop critical thinking skills.
- Monitor responses to find out where your students are struggling.
- Rely on real-time data to adjust your teaching strategy.
- Automatically group students for discussion, teamwork, and peer-to-peer learning.

ACKNOWLEDGMENTS

Thanks are extended to Dollarama Inc. for permission to include portions of its annual report in Appendix A and MyLab Accounting. Appreciation is also expressed to the following individuals and organizations:

The annual reports of a number of Canadian companies.

Professors Bill Thomas, Wendy Tietz, Tom Harrison, and the late Charles Horngren.

Particular thanks are also due to the following instructors for reviewing the Sixth Canadian Edition and offering many useful suggestions for the Seventh Canadian Edition:

Shiraz Charania, *Langara College*
Liang Hsuan Chen, *University of Toronto*
Kirk Collins, *Trent University*
Megan Costiuk, *University of Regina*
Laura Dallas, *Kwantlen Polytechnic University*
Athina Hall, *University of Ontario Institute of Technology*
Kayla Macfarlane, *University of Ontario Institute of Technology*
Jaime Morales, *Trent University*
Mumsy Ullattikulam, *Langara College*

The authors acknowledge with gratitude the professional support received from Pearson Canada. In particular we thank Keara Emmett, Acquisitions Editor; Anita Smale, Developmental and Media Content Editor; Sarah Gallagher, Project Manager; Manas Roy, Production Editor; and Darcey Pepper, Marketing Manager.

A special thanks also goes out to Kathy Falk, at the University of Toronto, and Chris Deresh, from Douglas College, whose contributions to the Sixth Canadian Edition led to a stronger Seventh Canadian Edition. Kathy helped ensure our problem material was complete, accurate, and effective for the level taught in the chapter. Chris checked the coverage of CPA Competencies and provided his valuable and current knowledge on this.

PROLOGUE

Accounting Careers: Much More Than Counting Things

What kind of career can you have in accounting? Almost any kind you want. A career in accounting lets you use your analytical skills in a variety of ways, and it brings both monetary and personal rewards. Professional accountants work as executives for public companies, partners at professional services firms, and analysts at investment banks, among many other exciting positions.

Accounting as an art is widely believed to have been invented by Fra Luca Bartolomeo de Pacioli, an Italian mathematician and Franciscan friar in the sixteenth century. Pacioli was a close friend of Leonardo da Vinci and collaborated with him on many projects.

Accounting as the profession we know today has its roots in the Industrial Revolution during the eighteenth and nineteenth centuries, mostly in England. However, accounting did not attain the stature of other professions such as law, medicine, or engineering until early in the twentieth century. Professions are distinguished from trades by the following characteristics: (1) a unifying body of technical literature, (2) standards of competence, (3) codes of professional conduct, and (4) dedication to service to the public.

An aspiring accountant must obtain a university degree, pass several professional examinations, and gain three years of on-the-job training before they can receive a professional accounting designation. The most prevalent designation in Canada is the CPA, which stands for Chartered Professional Accountant. When you hold this designation, employers know what to expect about your education, knowledge, competencies, and personal attributes. They value your analytical skills and extensive training. Your CPA designation gives you a distinct advantage in the job market, and instant credibility and respect in the workplace. It's a plus when dealing with other professionals, such as bankers, lawyers, auditors, and federal regulators. In addition, your colleagues in private industry tend to defer to you when dealing with complex business matters, particularly those involving financial management.

Where Accountants Work

Where can you work as an accountant? There are four main types of employers.

Professional Accounting Firms

You can work for a professional accounting firm, which could range in size from a small local firm to a large international firm such as KPMG or EY. These firms provide assurance, tax, and consulting services to a variety of clients, allowing you to gain a broad range of experience if you so choose. Many accountants begin their careers at a professional accounting firm and then move into more senior positions in one of the job categories described below. Others may stay on, or join one of these firms after working elsewhere, to take advantage of the many rewarding careers these firms offer.

Public or Private Companies

Rather than work for an accounting firm and provide your expertise to a variety of clients, you can work for a single company that requires your professional knowledge. Your role may be to analyze financial information and communicate that information to managers who use it to plot strategy and make decisions. Or you may be called upon to help allocate corporate resources or improve financial performance. For example, you might do a cost-benefit analysis to help decide whether to acquire a company or build a factory. Or you might describe the financial implications of choosing one business strategy over another. You might work in areas such as internal auditing, financial management, financial reporting, treasury management, and tax planning. The most senior financial position in these companies is the chief financial officer (CFO) role; some CFOs rise further to become chief executive officers (CEOs) of their companies.

Government and Not-for-Profit Entities

Federal, provincial, and local governmental bodies also require accounting expertise. You could be helping to evaluate how government agencies are being managed, or advise politicians on how to allocate resources to promote efficiency. The RCMP hires accountants to investigate the financial aspects of white-collar crime. You might find yourself working for the Canadian Revenue Agency, one of the provincial securities commissions, or a federal or provincial Auditor General.

As an accountant, you might also decide to work in the not-for-profit sector. Colleges, universities, public and private primary and secondary schools, hospitals, and charitable organizations such as churches and the United Way all have accounting functions. Accountants in the not-for-profit sector provide many of the same services as those in the for-profit sector, but their focus is less on turning a profit than on making sure the organizations spend their money wisely and operate efficiently and effectively.

Education

Finally, you can work at a college or university, advancing the thought and theory of accounting and teaching future generations of new accountants. On the research side of education, you might study how companies use accounting information. You might develop new ways of categorizing financial data, or study accounting practices in different countries. You then publish your ideas in journals and books and present them to colleagues at meetings around the world. On the education side, you can help others learn about accounting and give them the tools they need to be their best.

Regardless of which type of organization you work for, as an accountant, your knowledge will be highly valued by your clients, colleagues, and other important stakeholders. As the economy becomes increasingly global in scope, accounting standards, tax laws, and business strategies will grow more complex, so it's safe to say that the expertise provided by professional accountants will continue to be in high demand. This book could serve as the first step on your path to a challenging and rewarding career as a professional accountant!

QUICK REVIEW

The Financial Statements and Their Elements

Question	Financial Statement	Elements
1. How much income did the company earn during the year?	Income statement	Total income (revenues + gains) − Total expenses (expenses + losses) Net income (or Net loss)
2. Why did the company's retained earnings change during the year?	Statement of retained earnings	Beginning retained earnings + Net income + Other comprehensive income (IFRS only) − Dividends Ending retained earnings
3. What is the company's financial position at the end of the year?	Balance sheet	Assets = Liabilities + Owners' equity
4. How much cash did the company generate and spend during the year?	Statement of cash flows	Operating cash flows ± Investing cash flows ± Financing cash flows Increase (or decrease) in cash

See Chapter 1, Exhibit 1-3, page 7.

Accounting's Conceptual Framework

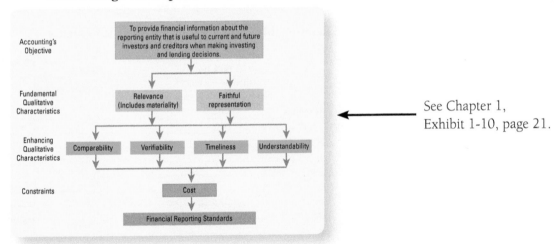

See Chapter 1, Exhibit 1-10, page 21.

The Expanded Rules of Debit and Credit

See Chapter 2, Exhibit 2-8, page 72.

Adjusting Entries

Adjusting entries are recorded at the end of the accounting period, just before the financial statements are prepared. This ensures that all assets and liabilities have been recorded at period end, and all revenues earned and expenses incurred during the period have been included in the accounts.

Type of Adjusting Entry	Debit	Credit	Example
Deferral – Prepaid Expense	Expense	Asset	Prepaid rent, insurance, supplies
Deferral – Unearned Revenue	Liability	Revenue	Cash received but goods or services to be provided in the future
Depreciation	Expense	Contra-asset	Property, plant, and equipment
Accrual – Accrued Expense	Expense	Liability	Salaries, interest
Accrual – Accrued Revenue	Asset	Revenue	Revenue earned but not yet billed

The Accounting Cycle

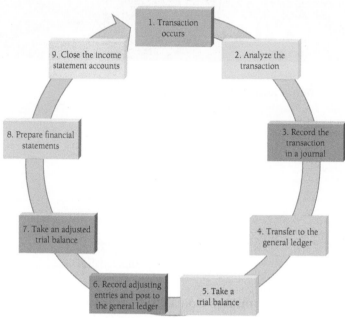

The Relationships Among the Financial Statements

See Chapter 2, Exhibit 2-2, page 65.

	A	B	C	D
1	**Tara Inc.** Income Statement For the Month Ended April 30, 2020			
2	**Revenues**			
3	Service revenue ($7,000 + $3,000)		$ 10,000	
4	**Expenses**			
5	Salary expense	$ 1,200		
6	Rent expense	1,100		
7	Utilities expense	400		
8	Total expenses		2,700	
9	Net income		$ 7,300	
10				

	A	B	C	D
1	**Tara Inc.** Statement of Retained Earnings For the Month Ended April 30, 2020			
2	Retained earnings, April 1, 2020		$ 0	
3	Add: Net income for the month		7,300	
4	Subtotal		7,300	
5	Less: Dividends declared		(2,100)	
6	Retained earnings, April 30, 2020		$ 5,200	
7				

	A	B	C	D	E
1	**Tara Inc.** Balance Sheet As at April 30, 2020				
2	**Assets**		**Liabilities**		
3	Cash	$ 33,300	Accounts payable	$ 1,800	
4	Accounts receivable	2,000	**Shareholders' Equity**		
5	Office supplies	3,700	Common shares	50,000	
6	Land	18,000	Retained earnings	5,200	
7			Total shareholders' equity	55,200	
8	Total assets	$ 57,000	Total liabilities and shareholders' equity	$ 57,000	
9					

①

②

RATIOS USED IN THIS TEXT

Ratio analysis is one tool that managers, investors, and creditors use when analyzing a company. How do they determine if a company is able to pay its bills, sell inventory, collect receivables, and so on? They use the standard ratios discussed in this book.

Ratio	Computation	Information Provided
Measuring ability to pay current liabilities:		
1. Current ratio	$$\frac{\text{Current assets}}{\text{Current liabilities}}$$	Measures ability to pay current liabilities with current assets
2. Quick (acid-test) ratio	$$\frac{\text{Cash} + \dfrac{\text{Short-term}}{\text{investments}} + \dfrac{\text{Net current}}{\text{receivables}}}{\text{Current liabilities}}$$	Shows ability to pay all current liabilities if they come due immediately
Measuring turnover and cash conversion:		
3. Inventory turnover and days' inventory outstanding (DIO)	$$\text{Inventory turnover} = \frac{\text{Cost of goods sold}}{\text{Average inventory}}$$ $$\text{Days' inventory outstanding (DIO)} = \frac{365}{\text{Inventory turnover}}$$	Indicates saleability of inventory—the number of times a company sells its average level of inventory during a year
4. Accounts receivable turnover	$$\frac{\text{Net credit sales}}{\text{Average net accounts receivable}}$$	Measures ability to collect cash from credit customers
5. Days' sales in receivables or days' sales outstanding (DSO)	$$\frac{\text{Average net accounts receivable}}{\text{Average daily sales}}$$ or $$\frac{365}{\text{Accounts receivable turnover}}$$	Shows how many days' sales remain in Accounts Receivable—how many days it takes to collect the average level of receivables
6. Payables turnover and days' payable outstanding (DPO)	$$\text{Accounts payable turnover} = \frac{\text{Cost of goods sold}}{\text{Average accounts payable}}$$ $$\text{Days' payable outstanding (DPO)} = \frac{365}{\text{Accounts payable turnover}}$$	Shows how many times a year accounts payable turn over, and how many days it takes the company to pay off accounts payable
7. Cash conversion cycle	$\text{Cash conversion cycle} = \text{DIO} + \text{DSO} - \text{DPO}$ where DIO = Days' inventory outstanding DSO = Days' sales outstanding DPO = Days' payable outstanding	Shows overall liquidity by computing the total days it takes to convert inventory to receivables and back to cash, less the days to pay off creditors

Ratio	Computation	Information Provided
Measuring ability to pay long-term debt:		
8. Debt ratio	$$\frac{\text{Total liabilities}}{\text{Total assets}}$$	Indicates percentage of assets financed with debt
9. Times-interest-earned ratio	$$\frac{\text{Income from operations}}{\text{Interest expense}}$$	Measures the number of times operating income can cover interest expense
Measuring profitability:		
10. Gross profit %	$$\frac{\text{Gross profit}}{\text{Net sales}}$$	Shows the percentage of profit that a company makes from merely selling the product, before any other operating costs are subtracted
11. Operating income %	$$\frac{\text{Income from operations}}{\text{Net sales}}$$	Shows the percentage of profit earned from each dollar in the company's core business, after operating costs have been subtracted
12. Return on net sales	$$\frac{\text{Net income}}{\text{Net sales}}$$	Shows the percentage of each sales dollar earned as net income
13. Asset turnover	$$\frac{\text{Net sales}}{\text{Average total assets}}$$	Measures the amount of net sales generated for each dollar invested in assets
14. Return on total assets	$$\frac{\text{Net income}}{\text{Average total assets}}$$	Measures how profitably a company uses its assets
15. Leverage ratio	$$\frac{\text{Average total assets}}{\text{Average common shareholders' equity}}$$	Otherwise known as the *equity multiplier,* measures the ratio of average total assets to average common shareholders' equity
16. Return on common shareholders' equity	$$\frac{\text{Net income} - \text{preferred dividends}}{\text{Average common shareholders' equity}}$$	Measures how much income is earned for every dollar invested by the company's common shareholders
17. Earnings per share of common stock	$$\frac{\text{Net income} - \text{Preferred dividends}}{\text{Average number of common shares outstanding}}$$	Measures the amount of net income earned for each share of the company's common stock outstanding
Analyzing shares as an investment:		
18. Price/earnings ratio	$$\frac{\text{Market price per common share}}{\text{Earnings per share}}$$	Indicates the market price of $1 of earnings
19. Dividend yield	$$\frac{\text{Dividend per share of common (or preferred) stock}}{\text{Market price per share of common (or preferred) stock}}$$	Shows the percentage of a stock's market value returned as dividends to stockholders each period
20. Book value per share of common stock	$$\frac{\text{Total shareholders' equity} - \text{Preferred equity}}{\text{Number of shares of common stock outstanding}}$$	Indicates the recorded accounting amount for each share of common stock outstanding

The Financial Statements

1

SPOTLIGHT

If you have ever shopped for school, party, or craft supplies, you have likely patronized a Dollarama store. Based in Montreal, Dollarama owns and operates over 1,000 stores across all ten provinces. The company is one of Canada's largest value retail companies, offering customers a wide variety of quality consumer products, general merchandise, and seasonal goods at fixed price points up to $4.00. Whether you live in a large metropolitan area, mid-sized city, or small town, you are likely only a short distance from a Dollarama store. Dollarama is featured throughout this textbook as a way of connecting new financial accounting concepts to the actual business activities and financial statements of a familiar Canadian corporation.

As you can see from its Consolidated Statements of Net Earnings on the next page, Dollarama sells a lot of goods in a year—about $3.3 billion worth for the year ended January 28, 2018 (line 3). After deducting a variety of expenses incurred during fiscal 2018 (lines 4, 6–8, and 10), Dollarama reported net earnings of over $500 million for the year (line 11). In this chapter you will begin to learn where these numbers come from and what they mean. Welcome to the world of accounting!

LEARNING OBJECTIVES

1 **Explain** why accounting is the language of business

2 **Describe** the purpose and **explain** the elements of each financial statement

3 **Prepare** financial statements and **analyze** the relationships among them

4 **Explain** and **apply** underlying accounting concepts, assumptions, and principles

5 Ethically **evaluate** business decisions

CPA COMPETENCIES

Competencies addressed in this chapter:

1.1.1 Evaluates financial reporting needs

1.1.2 Evaluates the appropriateness of the basis of financial reporting

1.1.3 Evaluates reporting processes to support reliable financial reporting

Based on Chartered Professional Accountant standards

Marc Seguin/Shutterstock

	A	B	C
1	**Dollarama Inc.** Consolidated Statements of Net Earnings (Adapted) For the Years Ended January 28, 2018 and January 29, 2017*		
2	*(in millions of dollars)*	**2018**	**2017**
3	**Sales**	$ 3,266.1	$ 2,963.2
4	Cost of sales	1,965.2	1,801.9
5	**Gross profit**	1,300.9	1,161.3
6	General, administrative and store operating expenses	474.8	458.0
7	Depreciation and amortization	70.6	57.8
8	Financing costs	39.9	33.1
9	**Earnings before income taxes**	715.6	612.4
10	Income taxes	196.2	166.8
11	Net earnings	$ 519.4	$ 445.6
12			

*Dollarama's financial year (or fiscal year) ends on the Saturday closest to January 31 each year, which is why its 2017 and 2018 year-end dates are different.

Source: Data from U.S. Securities and Exchange Commission.

Many chapters of this book begin with an actual financial statement—in this chapter, it's the Consolidated Statements of Net Earnings of Dollarama Inc. for its 2018 and 2017 fiscal years. The core of financial accounting revolves around the basic financial statements:

- Income statement (sometimes known as the statement of net earnings)
- Statement of retained earnings (sometimes included in the statement of changes in owners' equity)
- Balance sheet (also known as the statement of financial position)
- Cash flow statement (also known as the statement of cash flows)
- Statement of other comprehensive income

Financial statements are the reports that companies use to convey the financial results of their business activities to various user groups, which can include managers, investors, creditors, and regulatory agencies. In turn, these parties use the reported information to make a variety of decisions, such as whether to invest in or loan money to the company. To learn accounting, you must learn to focus on decisions. In this chapter, we explain generally accepted accounting principles, their underlying assumptions and concepts, and the bodies responsible for issuing accounting standards. We discuss the judgment process that is necessary to make good accounting decisions. We also discuss the contents of the four basic financial statements that report the results of those decisions. In later chapters, we will explain in more detail how to construct the financial statements, as well as how user groups typically use the information contained in them to make business decisions.

Using Accounting Information

Dollarama's managers make a lot of decisions. Which stores have the highest sales? Which line of business is earning the most profit? Should Dollarama expand its offerings in Eastern Canada to match those in B.C. and Alberta? Accounting information helps company managers make these decisions.

Take a look at Dollarama's Consolidated Statements of Income on page 2. Focus on net earnings (line 11). Net earnings (or net income) is the excess of sales (or revenues) over expenses. You can see that Dollarama earned $519 million in net income for the year ended January 28, 2018. That's good news because it means that Dollarama's revenues exceeded its expenses by over $500 million in fiscal 2018.

Dollarama's Consolidated Statements of Net Earnings convey more great news. Sales grew from $2.96 billion in 2017 to $3.27 billion in 2018 (line 3), an increase of 10.5%. Also, Dollarama's 2018 net earnings of $519.4 million were 16.6% higher than its 2017 net earnings of $445.6 million (line 11). Based on these key numbers, Dollarama's 2018 operating performance improved significantly from 2017.

There would, however, be much more accounting information to analyze before making a final assessment of Dollarama's 2018 financial performance. Imagine you work for a bank that Dollarama would like to borrow $500 million from. How would you decide whether to lend them the money? Or suppose you have $5,000 to invest. What financial information would you analyze to decide whether to invest this money in Dollarama? Let's see how accounting information can be used to make these kinds of decisions.

EXPLAIN WHY ACCOUNTING IS THE LANGUAGE OF BUSINESS

OBJECTIVE

❶ **Explain** why accounting is the language of business

Accounting is an information system that measures and records business activities, processes data into reports, and reports results to decision makers. Accounting is "the language of business." The better you understand the language, the better you can make decisions using accounting information.

Accounting produces the financial statements that report information about a business entity. The financial statements report a business's financial position, operating performance, and cash flows, among other things. In this chapter, we focus on Dollarama's 2018 financial statements. By the end of the chapter, you will have a basic understanding of these statements.

Don't confuse bookkeeping and accounting. Bookkeeping is a mechanical part of accounting, just as arithmetic is a mechanical part of mathematics. Accounting, however, requires an understanding of the principles used to accurately report financial information, as well as the professional judgment needed to apply them and then interpret the results. Exhibit 1-1 illustrates the flow of accounting information and helps illustrate accounting's role in business. The accounting process starts and ends with people making decisions.

Who Uses Accounting Information?

Almost everyone uses accounting information! Students use it to decide how much of their income to save for next year's tuition. Managers use it to decide if they should expand their business. Let's take a closer look at how these and other groups use accounting information.

MANAGERS. Managers have to make many business decisions. Should they introduce a new product line? Should the company set up a regional sales office in Australia or South Africa? Should they consider acquiring a competitor? Should the company extend credit to a potential major customer? Accounting information helps managers make these decisions.

EXHIBIT 1-1
The Flow of Accounting Information

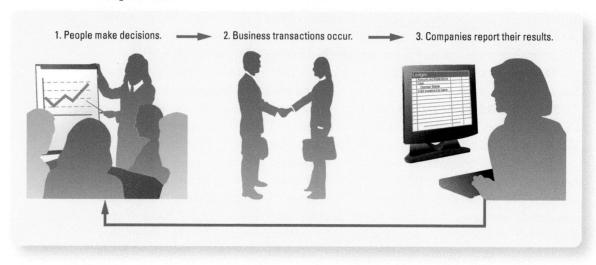

INVESTORS AND CREDITORS. Investors and creditors provide the money to finance a business's activities. Investors want to know how much income they can expect to earn on their investment. Creditors want to know if and how a business is going to pay them back. Accounting information allows investors and creditors to make these decisions.

GOVERNMENT AND REGULATORY BODIES. Many government and regulatory bodies use accounting information. For example, the federal government requires businesses, individuals, and other organizations to pay income and sales taxes. The Canada Revenue Agency uses accounting information to ensure these organizations pay the correct amount of taxes. The Ontario Securities Commission requires companies whose stock is traded publicly to provide the Commission with many kinds of periodic financial reports. All of these reports contain accounting information.

INDIVIDUALS. People like you manage bank accounts and decide whether to rent an apartment or buy a house. They also determine their monthly income and then decide how much to spend and save each month. Accounting provides the information needed to make these decisions.

NOT-FOR-PROFIT ORGANIZATIONS. Not-for-profit organizations—churches, hospitals, and charities, such as Habitat for Humanity and the Canadian Red Cross—base their decisions on accounting information. In addition, accounting information is the basis of a not-for-profit's reporting on the organization's stewardship of funds received and its compliance with the reporting requirements of the Canada Revenue Agency.

Two Kinds of Accounting: Financial Accounting and Management Accounting

Accounting information falls into two categories: financial accounting and management accounting. The distinction is based primarily on who uses the information in each category. Both *internal and external users* rely on financial accounting information, whereas management accounting information is used by *internal users only*.

Financial accounting provides information for managers inside the business and for decision makers outside the organization, such as investors, creditors, government agencies, and the public. This information must be relevant for the needs of decision makers and must provide a faithful representation of the entity's economic activities. This textbook focuses on financial accounting.

Management accounting generates inside information for the managers of the organization. Examples of management accounting information include budgets, forecasts, and projections that are used to make strategic business decisions. Internal information must be accurate and relevant for the decision needs of managers. Management accounting is covered in a separate course.

Organizing a Business

A business can be organized in one of three forms: a proprietorship, a partnership, or a corporation. Exhibit 1-2 summarizes the key features of each form. Regardless of its form, every organization must produce accounting information so its stakeholders can make decisions about it.

EXHIBIT 1-2
The Various Forms of Business Organization

	Proprietorship	Partnership	Corporation
Owner(s)	Proprietor—one owner	Partners—two or more owners	Shareholders—generally many owners
Life of entity	Limited by owner's choice or death	Limited by owners' choice or death	Limited by owners' choice, but not their death
Personal liability of owner(s) for business debts	Proprietor is personally liable	Partners are usually personally liable	Shareholders are not personally liable
Accounting status	Accounting entity is separate from proprietor	Accounting entity is separate from partners	Accounting entity is separate from shareholders

PROPRIETORSHIPS. A **proprietorship** is an unincorporated business with a single owner, called the proprietor. Dell Computer started out in the college dorm room of Michael Dell, the owner. Proprietorships tend to be small businesses, such as the vendors that set up stalls at farmers' markets, or individual professional organizations, such as physicians, lawyers, and accountants. From a legal perspective, the business *is* the proprietor, and the proprietor is personally liable for all business debts. But for accounting, a proprietorship is an entity separate from its proprietor. Thus, the business records do not include the proprietor's personal finances.

PARTNERSHIPS. A **partnership** is an unincorporated business with two or more parties as co-owners, and each owner is a partner. Individuals, corporations, partnerships, or other types of entities can be partners. The income (or loss) of the partnership "flows through" to the partners and they recognize it based on their agreed-upon percentage interest in the business. The partnership is not a taxpaying entity. Instead, each partner takes a proportionate share of the entity's taxable income and pays tax according to that partner's individual or corporate rate. Many retail establishments and some professional organizations of physicians, lawyers, and accountants are partnerships. Most partnerships are small or medium-sized, but some are very large, with several hundred partners. Accounting treats the partnership as a separate organization, distinct from the personal affairs of each partner. But the law views a partnership as the partners: Normally, each partner is personally liable for all the partnership's debts. For this reason, partnerships can be quite risky. Recently, professional partnerships such as public accounting firms and law firms have become limited liability partnerships (LLPs), which limits claims against the partners to their partnership assets.

CORPORATIONS. A **corporation** is an incorporated business owned by its **shareholders**, who own **shares** representing partial ownership of the corporation. One of the major advantages of a corporation is the ability to raise large sums of capital by issuing shares to the public. Individuals, partnerships, other corporations, or other types of entities may be shareholders in a corporation. Most well-known companies, such as TD Bank, Rogers, and Apple, are corporations. As with Dollarama Inc., their legal names include *Corporation* or *Incorporated* (abbreviated *Corp.* and *Inc.*) to indicate they are corporations. Some, like the Ford Motor Company, bear the name *Company* to denote this fact.

A corporation is formed under federal or provincial law. From a legal perspective, unlike proprietorships and partnerships, a corporation is distinct from its owners. The corporation is like an artificial person and possesses many of the rights that a person has. Unlike proprietors and partners, the shareholders who own a corporation have no personal obligation for its debts; so we say shareholders have limited liability, as do partners in an LLP. Also, unlike other forms of organizations, a corporation pays income taxes. In the other two cases, income tax is paid personally by the proprietor or partners.

A corporation's ownership is divided into shares of stock. One becomes a shareholder by purchasing the corporation's shares. Dollarama, for example, has issued more than 100 million shares of stock. Any investor can become a co-owner of Dollarama by buying shares of its stock through the Toronto Stock Exchange (TSX).

The shares of a public corporation like Dollarama are widely held, which means they are owned by thousands of different shareholders who buy and sell the shares on a stock exchange. Shares of a private corporation are typically owned by a small number of shareholders, often including the founder and other family members.

The ultimate control of a corporation rests with the shareholders. They normally get one vote for each voting share they own. Shareholders also elect the members of the **board of directors**, which sets policy for the corporation and appoints officers. The board elects a chairperson, who is the most powerful person in the corporation and may also carry the title chief executive officer (CEO), the top management position. Most corporations also have vice-presidents in charge of sales, manufacturing, accounting and finance, and other key areas.

STOP + THINK (1-1)

State whether each of the following business organizations is a proprietorship, a partnership, or a corporation.

1. Farook and Ahmed each own 50% of the shares of Waterloo Motors Inc., a car dealership.

2. Jenna and James own and operate The Culinary Counter, a meal-preparation and catering business, in which they equally share the workload and profits.

3. Agata crafts handmade jewellery that she sells online and at local craft markets.

DESCRIBE THE PURPOSE AND EXPLAIN THE ELEMENTS OF EACH FINANCIAL STATEMENT

OBJECTIVE

❷ **Describe** the purpose and **explain** the elements of each financial statement

The financial statements present a company's financial results to users who wish to examine the company's financial performance. What would users want to know about a company's performance? The answer to this question will vary by user, but Exhibit 1-3 presents four main questions most users would ask, as well as the financial statement that would be used to answer each question.

Each of the four financial statements reports transactions and events by grouping them into broad classes according to their economic characteristics. These broad classes are termed the *elements of financial statements*. Exhibit 1-3 presents the main elements of each financial statement. Before we examine each statement and its elements, we will introduce the generally accepted accounting principles that are used to prepare these statements.

EXHIBIT 1-3
The Financial Statements and Their Elements

Question	Financial Statement	Elements
1. How much income did the company earn during the year?	Income statement	Total income (revenues + gains) − Total expenses (expenses + losses) Net income (or Net loss)
2. Why did the company's retained earnings change during the year?	Statement of retained earnings	Beginning retained earnings + Net income + Other comprehensive income (IFRS only) − Dividends Ending retained earnings
3. What is the company's financial position at the end of the year?	Balance sheet	Assets = Liabilities + Owners' equity
4. How much cash did the company generate and spend during the year?	Statement of cash flows	Operating cash flows ± Investing cash flows ± Financing cash flows Increase (or decrease) in cash

Generally Accepted Accounting Principles

Accountants prepare financial accounting information according to professional guidelines called **generally accepted accounting principles (GAAP)**. GAAP specify the standards for how accountants must record, measure, and report financial information. In Canada, GAAP are established by the Chartered Professional Accountants of Canada (CPAC).

Canada actually has multiple sets of GAAP, with each set being applicable to a specific type of entity or organization. **Publicly accountable enterprises (PAEs)**, which are corporations and other organizations that have issued or plan to issue shares or debt in public markets such as the Toronto Stock Exchange, *must* apply **International Financial Reporting Standards (IFRS)**. IFRS are set by the International Accounting Standards Board and have been adopted by over 100 countries to enhance the comparability of the financial information reported by public enterprises around the world.

Private enterprises, which comprise proprietorships, partnerships, and corporations that have not issued and do not plan to issue shares or debt on public markets, *have the option* of applying IFRS. Because IFRS are relatively complex and costly to apply, however, very few Canadian private enterprises have adopted them. Instead, they apply another set of GAAP known as **Accounting Standards for Private Enterprises (ASPE)**, which have been set by the CPAC. At the introductory financial accounting level, there are very few major differences between IFRS and ASPE, but we will discuss them where they do exist and also summarize them at the end of each chapter. In addition, all the IFRS—ASPE differences we discuss in the book have been compiled in Appendix C.

There are other sets of GAAP applicable to not-for-profit organizations, pension plans, and public sector entities, but they are too specialized to cover at the introductory level. If you choose to pursue accounting as a career, you will learn about them in the future.

The Income Statement Measures Operating Performance

The **income statement** (also known by various other names such as statement of earnings, statement of net earnings, or statement of profit or loss) measures a company's operating performance for a *specified period of time*. The period of time covered by an income statement is typically a month, a quarter (three months), or a year, and will always be specified in the heading of the statement. In the heading of Dollarama's income statement (which it calls the statement of net earnings) in Exhibit 1-4, we can see that it covers the years ended January 28, 2018, and January 29, 2017. Financial statements for the current year are easier to analyze and interpret when they can be compared to the prior year's statements, so you will always see the prior year's results presented beside those of the current year (unless it is an entity's first year of operations). Most companies have a *fiscal year* that ends on December 31 (known as a *calendar year-end*), but a company can choose whatever fiscal year-end date it desires. Most of Canada's big banks, for example, have a fiscal year-end of October 31. Some companies, such as Dollarama, have fiscal year-end dates that vary from year to year, usually because they fall on the Saturday closest to a calendar year-end date. The income statement has two main elements, income and expenses, which are discussed in more detail below.

INCOME. A company's **income** includes both **revenue** and **gains**. Revenue consists of amounts earned by a company in the course of its ordinary, day-to-day business

EXHIBIT 1-4
Consolidated Statements of Net Earnings (Adapted)

Source: Data from U.S. Securities and Exchange Commission.

	A	B	C
1	**Dollarama Inc.** Consolidated Statements of Net Earnings (Adapted) For the Years Ended January 28, 2018 and January 29, 2017		
2	*(in millions of dollars)*	**2018**	**2017**
3	**Sales**	$ 3,266.1	$ 2,963.2
4	Cost of sales	1,965.2	1,801.9
5	**Gross profit**	1,300.9	1,161.3
6	General, administrative and store operating expenses	474.8	458.0
7	Depreciation and amortization	70.6	57.8
8	Financing costs	39.9	33.1
9	**Earnings before income taxes**	715.6	612.4
10	Income taxes	196.2	166.8
11	**Net earnings**	$ 519.4	$ 445.6
12			

activities. Revenue is referred to by a variety of different names, including sales, fees, interest, dividends, royalties, and rent. The vast majority of a company's revenue is earned through the sale of its primary goods and services. Loblaws, for example, earns most of its revenue by selling groceries and other household goods. An accounting firm such as KPMG earns revenue by providing accounting, tax, and other professional services to its clients. Dollarama's ordinary business activities consist of the sale of goods at the more-than 1,000 stores it operates across Canada. On line 3 of Dollarama's 2018 income statement, we see that it earned Sales revenues of $3.27 billion in 2018. You will learn more about revenue and how to account for it in Chapter 3.

Gains represent other items that result in an *increase* in economic benefits to a company and may, but usually do not, occur in the course of the company's ordinary business activities. If, for example, Dollarama sold one of the buildings it owns for an amount that exceeded what it was last recorded at in the financial statements, the excess would be recognized as a gain on the income statement. Significant gains are reported on a separate line of the income statement because knowledge of these gains is useful for making decisions. Dollarama does not report any gains on its 2018 income statement. You will learn more about some common types of gains in Chapters 6 and Appendix B.

EXPENSES. A company's expenses consist of **losses** as well as those expenses that are incurred in the course of its ordinary business activities. **Expenses** consist mainly of the costs incurred to purchase the goods and services a company needs to run its business on a day-to-day basis. For Dollarama, these expenses include the cost of the party supplies, kitchenware, and other goods it sells to customers, which is an expense commonly known as the *cost of goods sold* or *cost of sales*, an item you will learn more about in Chapter 5. Dollarama's cost of sales was $1.97 billion in 2018 (line 4). The wages it pays its employees, the rent it pays on its stores, and many more expenses, would be included in the $474.8 million of "General, administrative and store operating expenses" on line 6 of Dollarama's income statement. On line 8, we see that Dollarama incurred "Financing costs" of $39.9 million, which consist mostly of the interest expense it paid on the money it has borrowed from banks and other lenders (less, or net of, any interest it earned on investments), a topic that will be covered in Chapter 7. The last expense on Dollarama's income statement is "Income taxes" of $196.2 million (line 10). You likely know a little bit about this kind of expense already, but it will be discussed more in Chapter 7. There are many more expenses that companies incur on a day-to-day basis that are not typically disclosed separately on the income statements of public companies, either because they are not large enough to present or because they are too sensitive to disclose to competing companies. You will encounter many of these expenses as you progress through the book.

Losses are the opposite of gains, and represent items that result in a *decrease* in economic benefits to a company. Like gains, they may, but usually do not, occur in the course of the company's ordinary business activities. If, for example, Dollarama sold some equipment it owns for an amount that was less than what it was last recorded at in the financial statements, the difference would be recognized as a loss on the income statement. As with gains, significant losses are reported on a separate line of the income statement. Dollarama does not report any losses on its 2018 income statement, but in its Statement of Cash Flows in Exhibit 1-8, we can see it did suffer a very small loss on disposal of assets of $207,000. You will learn more about some common types of losses in Chapter 6.

The income statement also reports a company's **net income**, which is calculated as follows:

Net Income = Total Revenues and Gains − Total Expenses and Losses

In accounting, the word *net* refers to the amount of something that is left after something else has been deducted from an initial total. In this case, *net income* is the amount of *income* that is left after *total expenses* (expenses + losses) have been deducted from *total income* (revenues + gains) for the period. When total expenses exceed total income, the result is called a **net loss**. Net income is sometimes known as **net earnings** or **net profit**, and is *usually considered the most important amount in a company's financial statements*. It is a key component of many financial ratios, including return on equity and earnings per share, which you will learn about in later chapters of this book.

A company whose net income is consistently increasing is usually regarded by investors and creditors as a healthy and high-quality company. In the long run, the company's value should increase. On line 11 of Dollarama's income statement, we see that its net earnings increased from $445.6 million in 2017 to $519.4 million in 2018, so Dollarama's managers, investors, and creditors should have been pleased with its 2018 operating performance. You will see Dollarama's net earnings of $519.4 million carried forward to its statement of retained earnings, which is discussed in the next section.

The Statement of Retained Earnings Reports Changes in Retained Earnings

A company's **retained earnings** represent the accumulated net income (or net earnings) of the company since the day it started business, less any net losses and dividends declared during this time. When the accumulated amount is negative, the term **deficit** is used to describe it. The **statement of retained earnings** reports the changes in a company's retained earnings during the same period covered by the income statement. Under ASPE, this statement is often added to the bottom of the income statement, although it may also be presented as a completely separate statement. Under IFRS, information on the changes in retained earnings is included in the *statement of changes in shareholders' equity*, which you will learn more about in Chapter 8. At the beginning of 2018, Dollarama had a deficit of $343 million (line 3 of Exhibit 1-5). Let's look at the major changes to Dollarama's deficit during 2018.

- Because retained earnings represent a company's accumulated net income, the first addition to the opening balance is Dollarama's net earnings of $519 million (line 4), which comes directly from line 11 of the income statement in Exhibit 1-4.

- On line 5, we see that Dollarama declared dividends of $49 million during 2018. Dividends represent the distribution of past earnings to current shareholders of the company. You will learn more about dividends in Chapter 8.

After accounting for other reductions during 2018 (line 6; these reductions result from transactions covered in upper-level accounting courses), Dollarama reports a closing deficit of $663 million on line 7. This balance will be carried forward to the shareholders' equity section of the balance sheet, which is the next financial statement we will introduce to you.

	A	B	C
1	**Dollarama Inc.** Consolidated Statements of Deficit (Adapted) For the Years Ended January 28, 2018 and January 29, 2017		
2	*(in millions of dollars)*	**2018**	**2017**
3	Balance, beginning of year	$ (343)	$ (62)
4	Net earnings	519	446
5	Dividends	(49)	(48)
6	Other reductions	(790)	(679)
7	Balance, end of year	$ (663)	$ (343)
8			

EXHIBIT 1-5
Consolidated Statements of Deficit (Adapted)

Source: Data from U.S. Securities and Exchange Commission.

The Balance Sheet Measures Financial Position

A company's financial position consists of three elements: the assets it controls, the liabilities it is obligated to pay, and the equity its owners have accumulated in the business. These elements are reported in the **balance sheet**, which under IFRS is also known as the **statement of financial position**. (For simplicity, this financial statement will be referred to as the balance sheet throughout the textbook.) The balance sheet reports a company's financial position *as at a specific date*, which always falls on the last day of a monthly, quarterly, or annual reporting period. Because it is presented as at a specific date, you can think of the balance as a snapshot of the company's financial position at a particular point in time. The Dollarama balance sheet in Exhibit 1-6 reports its financial position as at the year-end dates of January 28, 2018 and January 29, 2017.

The balance sheet takes its name from the fact that the assets it reports must *always* equal—or be in balance with—the sum of the liabilities and equity it reports. This relationship is known as the **accounting equation**, and it provides the foundation for the double-entry method of accounting you will begin to learn in Chapter 2. Exhibit 1-7 illustrates the equation using the figures from Dollarama's 2018 balance sheet in Exhibit 1-6.

IFRS and ASPE define assets, liabilities, and equity using different terms, but the definitions are essentially equivalent. The IFRS definitions are used below, primarily because they are more concise than the ASPE definitions.

ASSETS. An **asset** is a resource controlled by the company as a result of past events and from which the company expects to receive future economic benefits. Let's use two of Dollarama's assets to illustrate this formal definition. One of Dollarama's assets is Accounts Receivable of $15.3 million (line 6), which represent money receivable from (or owed by) customers who purchased Dollarama's products on account (or on credit) on a past date, with the promise to pay the money owing at a later date. In the future, when customers do pay off their accounts, Dollarama will receive the economic benefit of Cash (line 4), another asset, which it can use to fund future business activities. Dollarama had $54.8 million in cash in its bank accounts and at its stores at the end of 2018.

We classify assets into two categories on the balance sheet: **current assets** and **non-current assets**. We classify an asset as current when we expect to convert it to cash, sell it, or consume it *within one year* of the balance sheet date, or within the business's normal operating cycle if it is longer than one year. Current assets are listed in order of their **liquidity**, which is a measure of how quickly they can be converted to cash, the most liquid asset. At the end of 2018, Dollarama

EXHIBIT 1-6
Consolidated Balance Sheets (Adapted)

	A	B	C
		2018	**2017**
1	**Dollarama Inc.** Consolidated Balance Sheets (Adapted) As at January 28, 2018 and January 29, 2017		
2	(millions of dollars)		
3		**2018**	**2017**
4	**Current assets**		
5	Cash	$ 54.8	$ 62.0
6	Accounts receivable	15.3	15.4
7	Prepaid expenses	8.6	7.2
8	Inventories	490.9	465.7
9	Derivative financial instruments	0.3	8.8
10		570.0	559.1
11	**Non-current assets**		
12	Property, plant and equipment	491.0	437.1
13	Intangible assets	145.6	139.5
14	Goodwill	727.8	727.8
15	**Total assets**	$ 1,934.3	$ 1,863.5
16			
17	**Current liabilities**		
18	Accounts payable and accrued liabilities	$ 228.4	$ 198.5
19	Dividend payable	12.2	11.6
20	Income taxes payable	39.5	16.6
21	Derivative financial instruments	35.7	8.1
22	Current portion of long-term debt	405.2	278.6
23		720.9	513.4
24	**Non-current liabilities**		
25	Long-term debt	1,260.5	1,050.1
26	Deferred rent and lease inducements	92.6	81.8
27	Deferred income taxes	112.7	117.8
28	**Total liabilities**	2,186.7	1,763.2
29			
30	**Shareholders' equity (deficit)**		
31	Share capital	415.8	420.3
32	Contributed surplus	27.7	24.3
33	Deficit	(663.4)	(343.0)
34	Accumulated other comprehensive loss	(32.4)	(1.3)
35	**Total shareholders' equity (deficit)**	(252.4)	100.3
36	**Total liabilities and shareholders' equity (deficit)**	$ 1,934.3	$ 1,863.5
37			

Source: Data from U.S. Securities and Exchange Commission.

EXHIBIT 1-7
The Accounting Equation (in millions of dollars)

Assets = Liabilities + Shareholders' Equity (Deficit)

For Dollarama Inc.:

Assets **$1,934.3**	**=**	**Liabilities** **$2,186.7** **+** **Shareholders'** **$(252.4)** **Equity (Deficit)**

had $570 million in current assets (line 10). Let's look at two of Dollarama's other current assets:

- A current asset on Dollarama's balance sheet is Prepaid Expenses of $8.6 million (line 7), which, as its name suggests, represent expenses that Dollarama has paid for but not yet consumed at the end of the year. If, for example, on January 15, 2018, Dollarama paid $500,000 for TV advertising time during the Super Bowl in early February (*after* its January 28 year-end date), this amount would be included in prepaid expenses on January 28, 2018, because Dollarama will not realize the benefit of this expense until after year-end.

- At the end of 2018, Dollarama held $490.9 million of Inventories (line 8), which include all the toys, gadgets, party supplies, and other products the company had in its warehouses and stores at the end of 2018 and which it expects to sell to its customers in 2019.

Any assets that do not qualify as current are classified as non-current assets, which are also known as **long-term assets**. Dollarama had three types of non-current assets on January 28, 2018. We will take a brief look at them now and revisit them in more depth later in the book.

- Dollarama had Property, Plant and Equipment of $491 million at the end of 2018 (line 12). This balance consists of the land (property), buildings (plant), and store and office equipment that Dollarama uses to carry out its business activities. Plant and equipment assets are usually reported at their **carrying amount**, which is their original cost *net* of accumulated depreciation (or amortization). The accumulated depreciation represents the amount of the original cost of the asset that has been *used up* to generate economic benefits for the company.

- Dollarama had $145.6 million of Intangible Assets (line 13) at the end of 2018. Intangible assets include things such as patents, copyrights, and trademarks that have no physical form but nonetheless provide future economic benefits to the company. Dollarama's major intangible assets are computer software and its trade name.

- On line 14, Dollarama reports Goodwill of $727.8 million. Goodwill is another type of intangible asset. It arises when one company purchases another company for a price that exceeds the fair market value of that company's net assets (its assets minus its liabilities). The Goodwill acquired represents the excess of the purchase price over the fair value of the company acquired. The Goodwill balance on Dollarama's balance sheet indicates it has purchased companies at prices that exceeded their fair values by a cumulative amount of $727.8 million.

Between its current and non-current assets, Dollarama reported total assets of $1,934.3 million at the end of 2018 (line 15). Next we will look at Dollarama's liabilities, the first component on the right side of the accounting equation.

LIABILITIES. A **liability** is a present obligation of the entity arising from past events, the settlement of which is expected to result in an outflow from the entity of resources embodying economic benefits. In simpler terms, a liability is a debt the entity owes as a result of a past event, and which it expects to pay off in the future using some of its assets. Dollarama's liabilities include $228.4 million of Accounts

Payable and Accrued Liabilities (line 18), which are debts they owe to companies that have supplied them with goods and services in the past. Dollarama's largest liability is Long-term debt (lines 22 and 25), which represents money they have borrowed from banks and other financial institutions to help them fund asset purchases and other business activities. In the future, Dollarama will use some of its cash to pay off both of these liabilities.

Like assets, we classify liabilities as **current liabilities** or **non-current liabilities** (or **long-term liabilities**), with the distinction based on how soon after year-end the company expects to pay off the debt. Current liabilities are debts the company expects to pay off *within one year* of the balance sheet date, or within the company's normal operating cycle if it is longer than one year. Dollarama reported current liabilities of $720.9 million (line 23) at the end of 2018. Let's look at some more of the individual liabilities that make up this total.

- Dollarama had Dividends Payable of $12.2 million (line 19). This balance represents dividends that the company's Board of Directors legally declared (or approved) before year-end but which will not be paid to Dollarama's shareholders until after year-end.

- Dollarama had $39.5 million of Income Taxes Payable as at the end of 2018 (line 20), which represents the amount of income tax it owes at the end of the year.

- Dollarama reports a Current Portion of Long-Term Debt of $405.2 million (line 22). This balance represents the portion of long-term debt that Dollarama must pay off within one year of the balance sheet date. The long-term portion of the debt is $1,260.5 (line 25), which will be repaid after the end of the next fiscal year.

In total, Dollarama reported $2,186.7 million in liabilities at the end of 2018 (line 28). Let's now examine the last major element of the balance sheet, owners' equity.

OWNERS' EQUITY. Owners' equity is the owners' remaining interest in the assets of the company after deducting all its liabilities. In effect, it represents the owners' claim on the company's assets *net* of the company's liabilities, so it is sometimes referred to as the **net assets** of the company. For incorporated companies like Dollarama, it is often called **shareholders' equity**. We can rearrange the accounting equation to clearly express the nature of this balance sheet element:

Owners' Equity = Assets − Liabilities

Let's look at two of the equity line items on Dollarama's 2018 balance sheet:

- Dollarama had Share Capital of $415.8 million on January 28, 2018 (line 31). This balance represents amounts paid by shareholders in exchange for shares in the company.

- Dollarama's ending Deficit of $663.4 million is carried over from the statement of retained earnings in Exhibit 1-5 to line 33 on the balance sheet.

At January 28, 2018, Dollarama had total shareholders' equity of $(252.4) (line 35). Because this balance is negative, it is formally referred to as a shareholders' deficit. Now let's take another look at how the three main elements of Dollarama's balance sheet fit into the accounting equation:

ASSETS	=	LIABILITIES	+	OWNERS' EQUITY (DEFICIT)
$1,934.3	=	$2,186.7	+	$(252.4)

MyLab Accounting

STOP + THINK (1-2)

1. If the assets of a business are $240,000 and the liabilities are $80,000, how much is the owners' equity?

2. If the owners' equity in a business is $160,000 and the liabilities are $130,000, how much are the assets?

3. A company reported total monthly income of $129,000 and total expenses of $85,000. What is the result of operations for the month?

4. If the beginning balance of retained earnings is $100,000, total income is $75,000, expenses total $50,000, and the company pays a $10,000 dividend, what is the ending balance of retained earnings?

The Statement of Cash Flows Measures Cash Receipts and Payments

The **statement of cash flows** (or cash flow statement under ASPE) reports a company's cash receipts and cash payments for the same fiscal period covered by the income statement. This statement shows users the specific business activities that generated cash receipts or resulted in cash payments during the period. These activities are classified into three categories:

1. **Operating activities**
2. **Investing activities**
3. **Financing activities**

Exhibit 1-8 presents Dollarama's statements of cash flows for 2018 and 2017. Let's use it to learn more about each of these business activities.

OPERATING ACTIVITIES. These activities comprise the main revenue-producing activities of a company, and generally result from the transactions and other events that determine net income. Common operating activities include cash receipts from a company's sales of its primary goods and services as well as cash payments to suppliers and employees for the goods and services they provide to generate these sales. When Dollarama pays a supplier for dinner plates to sell to its customers, for example, the payment is an operating activity that results in a cash outflow. Similarly, when a customer pays Dollarama for some of these plates, it results in a cash inflow from operating activities.

On line 5 of Dollarama's statement of cash flows, we see that the determination of cash flows from operating activities begins with the $519.4 million in net earnings it reported on line 11 of its income statement in Exhibit 1-4. In total, the company generated over $600 million in cash from operating activities in 2018 (line 13). This is a sign of excellent financial health. A company that does not regularly generate sufficient cash flows from operating activities will eventually suffer cash flow problems and may go bankrupt.

INVESTING ACTIVITIES. These activities include the purchase and sale of long-term assets and other investments that result in cash inflows or outflows related to resources used for generating future income and cash flows. Cash payments to acquire property, plant, and equipment, and the cash received upon the sale of these assets, are common investing activities. Investing activities also include cash flows from the purchase and sale of investments in other companies, and those related to loans made to other entities.

	A	B	C
1	**Dollarama Inc.** Consolidated Statements of Cash Flows (Adapted) For the Years Ended January 28, 2018 and January 29, 2017		
2	*(in millions of dollars)*		
3		**2018**	**2017**
4	**Operating activities**		
5	Net earnings	$ 519.4	$ 445.6
6	Adjustments to reconcile net earnings to net cash generated from operating activities:		
7	Depreciation and amortization	67.9	55.0
8	Financing costs on long-term debt	1.5	0.3
9	Loss on disposal of assets	0.2	0.0
10	Other reconciling items	22.4	7.9
11		611.5	508.8
12	Changes in non-cash working capital components	25.9	(3.6)
13	**Net cash generated from operating activities**	637.3	505.2
14			
15	**Investing activities**		
16	Additions to property, plant and equipment	(112.8)	(153.6)
17	Additions to intangible assets	(19.1)	(12.6)
18	Proceeds from disposal of property, plant and equipment	0.7	0.5
19	**Net cash used in investing activities**	(131.2)	(165.8)
20			
21	**Financing activities**		
22	Proceeds from long-term debt issued	550.0	525.0
23	Repayments of other credit facilities	(214.0)	(120.0)
24	Issuance of common shares	14.6	4.9
25	Dividends paid	(48.9)	(46.9)
26	Other financing activities	(815.0)	(699.5)
27	**Net cash used in financing activities**	(513.3)	(336.6)
28			
29	**Increase (decrease) in cash**	(7.2)	2.8
30	**Cash – beginning of year**	62.0	59.2
31	**Cash – end of year**	$ 54.8	$ 62.0
32			

In 2018, Dollarama spent $112.8 million in cash to purchase property, plant, and equipment (line 16) and received cash of $0.7 million when they sold assets of these types (line 18). Like its operating activities, Dollarama's 2018 investing activities indicate excellent future prospects for the company because they show that the company invested almost $131.2 million in new long-term assets (line 19) that will help it earn additional revenues in coming years.

FINANCING ACTIVITIES. These activities result in changes in the size and composition of a company's contributed equity and borrowings. Common financing activities include the issuance and repurchase of shares, the payment of cash dividends, the cash proceeds from borrowings, and the repayment of amounts borrowed.

In this section of Dollarama's statement of cash flows, we see that it raised $550 million in financing by issuing new long-term debt (line 22) and repaid $214 million of other borrowings during the year (line 23). The company also issued new shares for $14.6 million (line 24) and paid cash dividends of $48.9 million in 2018. In total, Dollarama reported total cash outflows from financing activities of $513.3 million for 2018 (line 27).

Overall, Dollarama's business activities resulted in a net decrease in cash of $7.2 million for 2018 (line 29). When this is subtracted from its $62-million cash balance at the beginning of the year (line 30), Dollarama ended 2018 with $54.8 million in cash (line 31), which matches the Cash balance reported on line 5 of Dollarama's balance sheet in Exhibit 1-6.

The Notes to the Financial Statements Provide Additional Information

The notes to the financial statements are an integral part of the financial statements and should be read carefully as part of a review of the financial statements. The notes provide information that cannot be reported conveniently on the face of the financial statements. For example, the notes tell the readers information such as what accounting policies were used in preparing the financial statements, and what methods were used to account for inventories and depreciation. An example of these notes can be found in Appendix A: Financial Statements for Dollarama Inc. Notice that at the bottom of each of Dollarama's financial statements is this reminder to users: *The accompanying notes are an integral part of these consolidated financial statements.*

Financial Reporting Responsibilities

Two parties have critical financial reporting responsibilities: a company's management and its independent external **auditor**. Company management has the primary financial reporting duties because they are responsible for designing, maintaining, and monitoring the company's financial reporting process and for preparing the financial statements based on the information generated by this process. The auditor's responsibility is to gather evidence regarding the financial information reported by management, and then decide whether the information reported in the financial statements complies with GAAP. Upon completing its audit of a company's financial statements, the auditor provides a signed report to the board of directors and shareholders of the company that states its opinion on the fairness of the company's financial statements relative to GAAP. All publicly accountable enterprises in Canada must have their financial statements audited. Many private enterprises are also required by government incorporation acts, creditors, or other financial statement users to have their financial statements audited. When financial statement users see an auditor's report stating that the accompanying financial statements are fairly presented in accordance with GAAP, they have reasonable assurance they can rely on the financial information to make sound decisions.

PREPARE FINANCIAL STATEMENTS AND ANALYZE THE RELATIONSHIPS AMONG THEM

OBJECTIVE

❸ **Prepare** financial statements and **analyze** the relationships among them

Exhibit 1-9 presents summarized financial statements for the fictional Huron Ltd. This exhibit highlights the relationships among each of the four financial statements you just studied. These relationships apply to the financial statements of every organization, so examine them carefully to ensure you understand the nature of each relationship.

EXHIBIT 1-9
Relationships Among the
Financial Statements

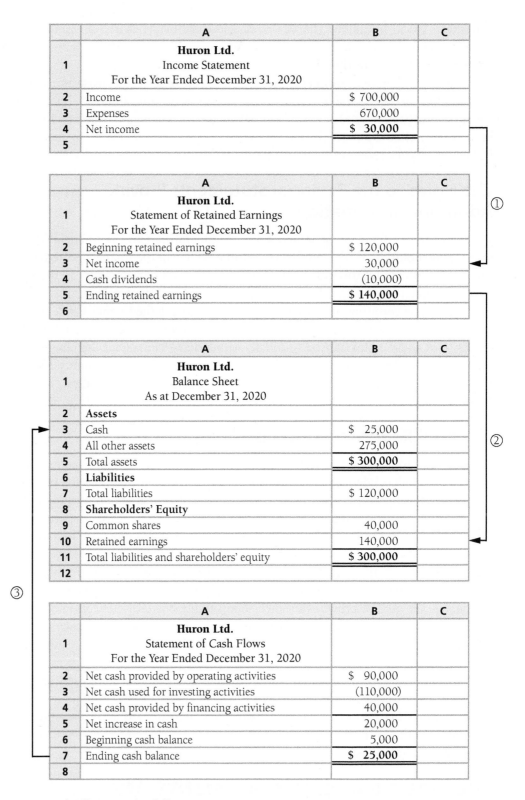

	A	B	C
1	**Huron Ltd.** Income Statement For the Year Ended December 31, 2020		
2	Income	$ 700,000	
3	Expenses	670,000	
4	Net income	$ 30,000	
5			

	A	B	C
1	**Huron Ltd.** Statement of Retained Earnings For the Year Ended December 31, 2020		
2	Beginning retained earnings	$ 120,000	
3	Net income	30,000	
4	Cash dividends	(10,000)	
5	Ending retained earnings	$ 140,000	
6			

	A	B	C
1	**Huron Ltd.** Balance Sheet As at December 31, 2020		
2	**Assets**		
3	Cash	$ 25,000	
4	All other assets	275,000	
5	Total assets	$ 300,000	
6	**Liabilities**		
7	Total liabilities	$ 120,000	
8	**Shareholders' Equity**		
9	Common shares	40,000	
10	Retained earnings	140,000	
11	Total liabilities and shareholders' equity	$ 300,000	
12			

	A	B	C
1	**Huron Ltd.** Statement of Cash Flows For the Year Ended December 31, 2020		
2	Net cash provided by operating activities	$ 90,000	
3	Net cash used for investing activities	(110,000)	
4	Net cash provided by financing activities	40,000	
5	Net increase in cash	20,000	
6	Beginning cash balance	5,000	
7	Ending cash balance	$ 25,000	
8			

Specifically, note the following:

1. The income statement measures Huron's operating performance for the year ended December 31, 2020, by:

   a. Reporting all income and expenses for the year;

   b. Reporting net income if total income exceeds total expenses, or a net loss if expenses exceed income.

2. The statement of retained earnings reports changes in Huron's retained earnings balance for the year ended December 31, 2020, by:

a. Adding the net income (or subtracting the net loss) from the income statement (link 1 in Exhibit 1-9) to the retained earnings balance at the beginning of the year; then

b. Deducting dividends declared during the year to arrive at the retained earnings balance at the end of the year.

3. The balance sheet reports Huron's financial position at December 31, 2020, by:

a. Reporting all assets, liabilities, and shareholders' equity as at the end of the year;

b. Within the shareholders' equity section of the statement, reporting the retained earnings balance at the end of the year, which comes from the statement of retained earnings (link 2).

 DECISION GUIDELINES

WHAT DO DECISION MAKERS LOOK FOR WHEN EVALUATING A COMPANY?

These Decision Guidelines illustrate how people use financial statements. Decision Guidelines appear throughout the book to show how accounting information aids decision making.

Suppose you are considering an investment in Dollarama shares. How do you proceed? Where do you get the information you need? What do you look for?

Decision	Guidelines
1. Can the company sell its products and services?	1. Sales revenue on the income statement: Are sales growing or falling?
2. Is the company making money?	2. a. Gross profit (Sales – Cost of goods sold)
	b. Operating income (Gross profit – Operating expenses)
	c. Net income (bottom line of the income statement)
	All three income measures should be increasing over time.
3. What percentage of sales revenue ends up as profit?	3. Divide net income by sales revenue. Examine the trend of the net income percentage from year to year.
4. Can the company collect its accounts receivable?	4. From the balance sheet, compare the percentage increase in accounts receivable to the percentage increase in sales. If receivables are growing much faster than sales, collections may be too slow, and a cash shortage may result.
5. Can the company pay its: a. current liabilities? b. total liabilities?	5. From the balance sheet, compare: a. current assets to current liabilities. Current assets should be somewhat greater than current liabilities. b. total assets to total liabilities. Total assets must be somewhat greater than total liabilities.
6. Where is the company's cash coming from? How is cash being used?	6. On the statement of cash flows, operating activities should provide the bulk of the company's cash during most years. Otherwise, the business will fail. Examine investing cash flows to see if the company is purchasing long-term assets—property, plant, and equipment and intangibles (this signals growth).

4. The statement of cash flows reports Huron's cash receipts and cash payments for the year ended December 31, 2020, by:

a. Reporting cash provided by (or used in) the company's operating, investing, and financing activities during the year.

b. Reporting the net change in the company's cash balance during the year and adding it to the beginning cash balance to arrive at the cash balance as at the end of the year, which is also reported on the balance sheet (link 3).

STOP + THINK (1-3)

On December 31, 2020, Huron Ltd. provided services to a customer for which the customer paid $1,000 in cash on that date, but the company mistakenly left this sale out of its accounting records when it prepared the financial statements in Exhibit 1-9. Given the links between the financial statements illustrated in Exhibit 1-9, what would happen to Huron Ltd.'s December 31, 2020 financial statements after the company corrects them to include the missing cash sale of $1,000 on December 31, 2020?

OBJECTIVE

④ Explain and apply underlying accounting concepts, assumptions, and principles

EXPLAIN AND APPLY UNDERLYING ACCOUNTING CONCEPTS, ASSUMPTIONS, AND PRINCIPLES

Accounting's Conceptual Framework

Before introducing the financial statements, we told you about IFRS and ASPE, the generally accepted accounting principles that are used to prepare most of the financial statements in Canada. We will now look at the conceptual framework and assumptions underlying IFRS and ASPE.

Exhibit 1-10 gives an overview of the joint conceptual framework of accounting developed by the IASB and the Financial Accounting Standards Board (FASB) in the United States. This conceptual framework, along with several underlying assumptions, provides the foundation for the specific accounting principles included in IFRS and ASPE, though there are some small differences between the frameworks for the two sets of standards. The overall *objective* of accounting is to provide financial information about the reporting entity that is useful to current and future investors and creditors when making investing and lending decisions and when assessing how well management is running the entity.

Fundamental Qualitative Characteristics

To be useful, information must have two *fundamental qualitative characteristics*:

- **relevance** and
- **faithful representation**.

To be relevant, information must have *predictive value, confirmatory value*, or both. Information has predictive value if it can be employed by users to predict an entity's future business or financial outcomes. For example, if the amount of money a company earns in the current year can be used to predict how much it will earn next year, then the current-year amount has predictive value. It has confirmatory value if it confirms or changes prior evaluations of an entity. Therefore, if the amount of money a company earns this year can be used to confirm or update prior predictions about the company's growth prospects, then this amount would have confirmatory value. In

EXHIBIT 1-10
Accounting's Conceptual Framework

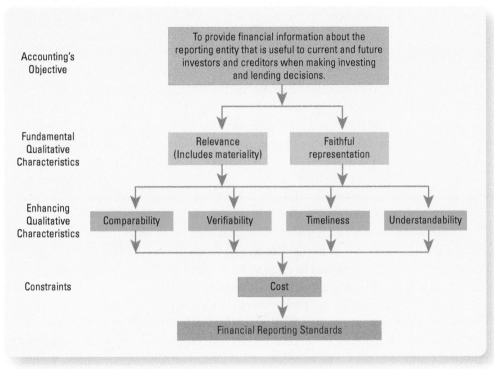

addition, the information must be **material**, which means that it is significant enough in nature or magnitude that omitting or misstating it could affect the decisions of an informed user. In the Dollarama income statement at the beginning of this chapter, we noted that the company sold over $3 billion worth of goods in 2018, so a user of the company's financial statements would not be influenced by an error of $1,000 that occurred when determining the company's total revenues for the year. In other words, an error that small would be *immaterial* to the user's decisions about Dollarama. All material information must be recorded or disclosed (listed or discussed) in the financial statements.

For accounting information to provide a faithful representation to users, it must reflect the *economic substance* of a transaction or event, which may not be the same as its legal form. The information must also be complete, neutral (free of bias), and accurate (free of material error). When accounting information possesses these facets of faithful representation, it is *reliable* to users so they can have faith that the information can be relied upon to make decisions about the company and its management.

Enhancing Qualitative Characteristics

To be useful, accounting information must also possess four *enhancing qualitative characteristics*:

- **comparability**
- **verifiability**
- **timeliness**, and
- **understandability**.

For accounting information to be *comparable*, it must be reported in a way that makes it possible to compare it to similar information being reported by other companies. It must also be reported in a way that is consistent with how it was reported in previous accounting periods. For example, a company must determine the cost of its inventory at the end of the current year using the same method it used at the end of the prior year. It also must disclose in the notes which costing method it used so that users can compare its method to the methods being used by competitors or other similar businesses.

Accounting information is *verifiable* when it can be checked for accuracy, completeness, and reliability. Verifiability enhances the chance that accounting information reflects a faithful representation of the economic substance of a transaction or event. It is possible, for example, to verify the amount of cash a company reports on its balance sheet at year-end by directly confirming with its bank how much cash the company had in its accounts at that time.

Timeliness means reporting accounting information to users in time for it to influence their decisions. Accounting information tends to become less relevant as it gets older, so it should be reported to users as soon after the end of the accounting period as possible, without sacrificing the other qualitative characteristics in the process. It would not, for example, be helpful to users if a company waited until the end of 2021 to report its financial statements for the year ended December 31, 2020. Users need a company's financial information on a much more timely basis than this, which is why investors and creditors typically demand financial statements be issued within no more than three months of year-end.

Accounting information is *understandable* when it is clearly and concisely classified and presented to reasonably knowledgeable and diligent users of the information. Both IFRS and ASPE, for example, require companies to report their inventory at the lower of its cost (what they paid for it) and its net realizable value (what they could sell it for). This concept is simple enough for even novice financial statements users to understand. At times, however, even informed and careful users will require assistance in understanding certain complex transactions and events.

The Cost Constraint

Accounting information is costly to produce. A primary constraint in the decision to disclose accounting information is that the cost of disclosure should not exceed the expected benefits to users. Management of an entity is primarily responsible for preparing accounting information. Managers must exercise judgment in determining whether the information is necessary for complete understanding of underlying economic facts and not excessively costly to provide.

This book introduces you to the basic financial reporting standards that have been devised using this conceptual framework. Before we begin exposing you to these standards, let's examine the assumptions that underlie this conceptual framework.

Assumptions Underlying the Conceptual Framework

The conceptual framework has only one explicit underlying assumption: the **going-concern assumption**. There are, however, three other assumptions that are implicit in the framework, so we present them here as well. They are the **separate-entity**, **historical-cost**, and **stable-monetary-unit assumptions**.

GOING-CONCERN ASSUMPTION. We typically prepare financial information under the assumption that the reporting entity is a going concern, which means that we expect it to continue operating normally for the foreseeable future. A company that is not a going concern is at risk of going bankrupt or closing down, so it may need to significantly scale down its operations or sell some of its assets at heavily discounted rates. When this risk is present, the financial statements are typically prepared on a basis that differs from the usual standards in IFRS or ASPE. If a different basis is used in such circumstances, it must be clearly disclosed to the users of the financial statements.

SEPARATE-ENTITY ASSUMPTION. We also prepare financial statements under the assumption that the business activities of the reporting entity are separate from the activities of its owners, so we do not mix the assets, liabilities, income, or expenses of the entity with those of its owners when reporting the entity's operating performance and financial position. Consider Gerald Schwartz, the chairman, president, chief executive officer, and major shareholder of ONEX Corporation, a large Canadian public company. Mr. Schwartz personally owns a house, automobiles, and investments in various companies. His personal assets, however, would not be included among the land, buildings, vehicles, and investments reported on ONEX's financial statements because his assets are separate from those of the entity he owns and operates. The separate-entity assumption draws a clear boundary around the business activities of the reporting entity, and only the activities within this boundary are reported in the entity's financial statements.

HISTORICAL-COST ASSUMPTION. The historical-cost assumption states that assets should be recorded at their *actual cost*, measured on the date of purchase as the amount of cash paid plus the dollar value of all non-cash consideration (other assets, privileges, or rights) also given in exchange. For example, suppose Dollarama purchases a building for a new store. The building's current owner is asking for $600,000 for the building. The management of Dollarama believes the building is worth $585,000, and offers the present owner that amount. Two real estate professionals appraise the building at $610,000. The two parties compromise and agree on a price of $590,000 for the building. The historical-cost assumption requires Dollarama to initially record the building at its actual cost of $590,000—not at $585,000, $600,000, or $610,000—even though those amounts were what some people believed the building was worth. At the point of purchase, $590,000 is both the *relevant* amount for the building's worth and the amount that *faithfully represents* a reliable figure for the price the company paid for it.

The historical-cost and the going-concern assumptions also maintain that Dollarama's accounting records should continue to use historical cost to value the asset for as long as the business holds it. Why? Because cost is a *verifiable* measure that is relatively *free from bias*. Suppose that Dollarama owns the building for six years and that real estate prices increase during this period. As a result, at the end of the period, the building can be sold for $650,000. Should Dollarama increase the value of the building on the company's books to $650,000? No. According to the historical-cost assumption, the building remains on Dollarama's books at its historical cost of $590,000. According to the going-concern assumption, Dollarama intends to stay in business and keep the building, not to sell it, so its historical cost is the most relevant and the most faithful representation of its value. It is also the most easily verifiable amount. Should the company decide to sell the building later at a price above or below its recorded value, it will record the cash received, remove the value of the building from the books, and record a gain or a loss for the difference at that time.

The historical-cost assumption is not used as extensively as it once was. Accounting is moving in the direction of reporting more assets and liabilities at their fair values. **Fair value** is the amount that the business could sell the asset for, or the amount that the business could pay to settle the liability. IFRS permit certain types of assets and liabilities to be periodically adjusted to reflect their fair values rather than leaving them on the books at their historical costs. With rare exceptions, ASPE still require assets and liabilities to be kept on the books at their historical costs. Fair-value accounting is generally beyond the scope of this textbook, but in later chapters we will highlight where this option exists.

STABLE-MONETARY-UNIT ASSUMPTION. The vast majority of Canadian entities report their financial information in Canadian dollars (or monetary units), although some choose to report in U.S. dollars instead. Regardless of the reporting currency used, financial information is always reported under the assumption that the value of the currency is stable, despite the fact that its value does change due to economic factors such as inflation. By assuming that the purchasing power of the reporting currency is stable, we can add and subtract dollar values from different reporting periods without having to make adjustments for changes in the underlying value of the currency.

Now that you have an understanding of the conceptual framework and assumptions underlying the financial statements, let's take an introductory look at each of the statements that you will learn more about as you progress through this book.

STOP + THINK (1-4)

It is September 24, 2020, and your company is considering the purchase of land for future expansion. The seller is asking $50,000 for the land, which cost them $35,000 four years ago. An independent appraiser assigns the land a value of $47,000. You offer the seller $44,000 for the land and they come back with a counter-offer of $48,000. You and the seller end up settling on a purchase price of $46,000 for the land.

1. When you record the purchase of this land in your accounting records, at what value will you record it?

2. Assume that four years later someone approaches your company and offers to purchase this land, which you have yet to develop, for $60,000. You know this to be a fair price given a recent appraisal you had done on the land. You decline the offer because you have plans to begin developing the land next year. What adjustment would you make to the value of the land in your accounting records?

OBJECTIVE

❺ Ethically **evaluate** business decisions

ETHICALLY EVALUATE BUSINESS DECISIONS

Running a business requires sound decision making, which in turn requires the exercise of good judgment, both at the individual and corporate levels. For example, you may work for or eventually run a company like Tim Hortons that devotes a percentage of its net income to a variety of charitable organizations and activities. Will this be profitable in the long run, or would it be more sensible to devote those resources to other, less-charitable activities? Making a business decision like this requires careful ethical judgment. Can that be profitable in the long run?

As an accountant, you may have to decide whether to record a $50,000 expenditure as an asset on the balance sheet or an expense on the income statement. Or, you may have to decide whether $25 million of goods delivered to customers in late 2020 should be recorded as revenue in 2020 or in 2021. As mentioned earlier, the application of IFRS and ASPE frequently requires the use of professional judgment because accounting standards contain few clear-cut rules on how to account for transactions and events. Depending on the type of business, the facts and circumstances surrounding accounting decisions may not always make them clear cut, and yet the decision may determine whether the company shows a profit or a loss in a particular period! What are the factors that influence business and accounting decisions, and how should these factors be weighed? Generally, three factors influence business and accounting decisions: *economic, legal, and ethical factors.*

The *economic* factor states that the decision being made should *maximize the economic benefits* to the decision maker. Based on economic theory, every rational person faced with a decision will choose the course of action that maximizes his or her own welfare, without regard to how that decision impacts others. In summary, the combined outcome of each person acting in his or her own self-interest will maximize the benefits to society as a whole.

The *legal* factor is based on the proposition that free societies are governed by laws. Laws are written to provide clarity and to prevent abuse of the rights of individuals or society. Democratically enacted laws both contain and express society's collective moral standards. Legal analysis involves applying the relevant laws to each decision and then choosing the action that complies with those laws. A complicating factor for a global business may be that what is legal in one country might not be legal in another. In that case, it is usually best to abide by the laws of the most restrictive country.

The *ethical* factor recognizes that while certain actions might be both economically profitable and legal, they may still not be right. Therefore, most companies, and many individuals, have established ethical standards for themselves to enforce a higher level of conduct than that imposed by law. These standards govern how we treat others and the way we restrain our selfish desires. This behaviour and its underlying beliefs are the essence of ethics. **Ethical standards** are shaped by our cultural, socioeconomic, and religious backgrounds. An *ethical analysis* is often needed to guide judgment when making business decisions.

When performing an ethical analysis, our challenge is to identify our specific ethical responsibilities and the stakeholders to whom we owe these responsibilities. As with legal issues, a complicating factor in making global ethical decisions may be that what is considered ethical in one country is not considered ethical in another.

Among the questions you may ask in making an ethical analysis are the following:

- *Which options are most honest, open, and truthful?*
- *Which options are most kind and compassionate, and build a sense of community?*
- *Which options create the greatest good for the greatest number of stakeholders?*
- *Which options result in treating others as I would want to be treated?*

Ethical training starts at home and continues throughout our lives. It is reinforced by the schools we attend; by the persons and companies we associate with; and by the teaching we receive if we attend a church, synagogue, mosque, or other house of worship.

In a business setting, sound ethical judgment begins "at the top." When employees see the top executives of their company promoting a strong ethical culture and regularly acting in a socially responsible manner, they are more likely to emulate this behaviour when making their own decisions. *Corporate Knights* magazine annually publishes a list of the most socially responsible corporations in Canada. Its 2018 list includes companies such as the Royal Canadian Mint, Toronto Hydro, IGM Financial, and Suncor Energy. It is easier to act ethically when you work for companies that recognize the importance of ethical business practices. These companies have learned from experience that, in the long run, ethical conduct pays big rewards, not only socially, morally, and spiritually, but economically as well.

Applying relevant accounting standards in a way that reports a faithful representation of the company's financial position and operating performance is always the most ethical course of action. A thorough understanding of ethics requires more study than we can accomplish in this book. However, remember that when you are making accounting decisions, you should not check your ethics at the door!

 # DECISION GUIDELINES

DECISION FRAMEWORK FOR MAKING ETHICAL JUDGMENTS

Making tough ethical judgments in business and accounting requires a decision framework. Answering the following four questions will help you to make ethical business decisions:

Decision	Guidelines
1. What is the issue?	1. The issue will usually deal with making a judgment about an accounting measurement or disclosure that results in economic consequences, often to numerous parties.
2. Who are the stakeholders, and what are the consequences of the decision to each of them?	2. Stakeholders include anyone who might be affected by the decision—you, your company, and potential users of the information (investors, creditors, regulatory agencies). Consequences can be economic, legal, or ethical in nature.
3. What are the decision alternatives, and how do they affect each stakeholder?	3. Analyze the impact of the decision on all stakeholders, using economic, legal, and ethical criteria. Ask, "Who will be helped or hurt, whose rights will be exercised or denied, and in what way?"
4. What decision alternative will you choose?	4. Choose the alternative that best balances your economic, legal, and ethical responsibilities to your stakeholders. Also, assess how your decision makes you feel. If it makes you feel uneasy, determine why and consider choosing another alternative.

To simplify, we might ask three questions:

1. Is the action legal? If not, steer clear, unless you want to go to jail or pay monetary damages to injured parties. If the action is legal, go on to questions (2) and (3).
2. Who will be affected by the decision and how? Be as thorough about this analysis as possible, and analyze it from all three standpoints (economic, legal, and ethical).
3. How will this decision make me feel afterward? How would it make me feel if my family reads about it in the newspaper?

In later chapters we will apply this model to different accounting decisions.

Chartered Professional Accountants
Code of Professional Conduct

The decision framework for making ethical judgments provides general guidance for everyone, regardless of one's profession or industry. Many professional organizations, businesses, and other entities adopt their own ethical guidelines or codes of conduct so their members have more-specific guidance.

The Chartered Professional Accountants of Ontario ("CPA Ontario") is one such organization.

The CPA Ontario has a code of professional conduct that applies to all of its members. Excerpts from the basic principles of the CPA Code of Professional Conduct are as follows*:

PROFESSIONAL BEHAVIOUR PRINCIPLE. In carrying out their responsibilities as professionals, members shall conduct themselves at all times in a manner which will maintain the good reputation of the profession and serve the public interest.

In doing so, members and firms are expected to avoid any action that would discredit the profession.

There are business considerations involved in the creation and development of any organization, whether it is a professional practice or an entity that operates outside of that domain. A member's involvement in any organization should be based primarily upon a reputation for professional excellence. In particular, members who occupy positions of senior authority should recognize that such positions include an obligation to influence events, practices and attitudes within that organization. Accordingly, such members should encourage an ethics-based culture in their organizations that emphasizes the importance of ethical behaviour and compliance with generally accepted standards of practice of the profession.

At all times, members and firms are expected to act in relation to other professional colleagues with the courtesy and consideration they would expect to be accorded by their professional colleagues.

INTEGRITY AND DUE CARE PRINCIPLE. To maintain and broaden public confidence, members shall perform professional services with integrity and due care.

Members and firms are expected to be straightforward, honest, and fair dealing in all professional relationships. They are also expected to act diligently and in accordance with applicable technical and professional standards when providing professional services. Diligence includes the responsibility to act, in respect of any professional service, carefully, thoroughly, and on a timely basis. Members are required to ensure that those performing professional services under their authority have adequate training and supervision.

OBJECTIVITY PRINCIPLE. A member shall not allow their professional or business judgment to be compromised by bias, conflict of interest, or the undue influence of others.

Clients, employers and the public generally expect that members and firms will bring objectivity and sound professional judgment to their services. It thus becomes essential that a member or firm will not subordinate professional judgment to external influences or the will of others.

---

*The Fundamental Principles Governing Conduct content (the "Content"), taken from the CPA Code of Professional Conduct is reproduced by permission of Chartered Professional Accountants of Ontario ("CPA Ontario"), and may not be further reproduced without the prior written permission of CPA Ontario. The Content is subject to revision and change at any time. The most current version is available from CPA Ontario at https://www.cpaontario.ca.

The principle of objectivity underlies the rules related to potential conflicts of interest as well as the requirement for independence in relation to the performance of assurance engagements. With respect to both independence and conflicts of interest, the profession employs the criterion of whether a reasonable observer would conclude that a specified situation or circumstance posed an unacceptable threat to a member's or firm's objectivity and professional judgment. Only then can public confidence in the objectivity and integrity of the member or firm be sustained, and it is upon this public confidence that the reputation and usefulness of the profession rest. The reasonable observer should be regarded as a hypothetical individual who has knowledge of the facts which the member or firm knew or ought to have known, and applies judgment objectively with integrity and due care.

PROFESSIONAL COMPETENCE PRINCIPLE. A member shall maintain their professional skills and competence by keeping informed of, and complying with, developments in their area of professional service.

Clients, employers and the public generally expect the accounting profession to maintain a high level of competence. This underscores the need for maintaining individual professional skill and competence by keeping abreast of and complying with developments in the professional standards and pertinent legislation in all functions where a member or firm performs professional services, or where others rely upon a member's or firm's calling.

CONFIDENTIALITY PRINCIPLE. A member shall protect confidential information acquired as a result of professional, employment and business relationships and do not disclose it without proper and specific authority, nor do they exploit such information for their personal advantage or the advantage of a third party.

The principle of confidentiality obliges members to protect and maintain the confidentiality of information both outside of and within a member's firm or employing organization and to properly address a situation that may arise when confidentiality is breached.

The disclosure of confidential information by a member or firm may be required or appropriate where such disclosure is:

- Permitted or authorized by the client or employer;
- Required by law; or
- Permitted or required by a professional right or duty, when not prohibited by law.

Even though you may never be a CPA governed by the Code of Professional Conduct, the basic principles contained in it can be applied to a wide range of professions and organizations. In addition, you may interact with CPAs in the future, so it is helpful to understand the principles to which they must adhere.

STOP + THINK (1-5)

Suppose you are the chief accountant for a public company listed on the Toronto Stock Exchange. You are finalizing the company's financial statements for the 2020 year and it appears that net income will come in about $1 million below what financial analysts predicted. Your boss, the company's CEO, asks you to record $1.2 million in fictitious sales to bring net income above the analysts' target. Use the Decision Framework for Making Ethical Judgments to decide how you would respond to the CEO's request.

Summary of IFRS-ASPE Differences

Concepts	IFRS	ASPE
The income statement (p. 8)	This financial statement is called the statement of profit or loss.	This financial statement is called the income statement.
Changes in retained earnings during an accounting period (p. 10)	These changes are reported in the statement of changes in owners' equity.	These changes are reported in the statement of retained earnings.
The balance sheet (p. 11)	This financial statement is called the statement of financial position.	This financial statement is called the balance sheet.
The cash flow statement (p. 15)	This financial statement is called the statement of cash flows.	This financial statement is called the cash flow statement.
Application of IFRS and ASPE (p. 20)	Publicly accountable enterprises or those enterprises planning to become one must apply IFRS.	Private enterprises have the option of applying IFRS, but almost all apply ASPE, which is simpler and less costly for these smaller enterprises.
Historical-cost assumption (p. 23)	Certain assets and liabilities are permitted to be recorded at their fair values rather than being kept on the books at their historical costs.	Assets and liabilities are typically carried at their historical costs.

SUMMARY

SUMMARY OF LEARNING OBJECTIVES

LEARNING OBJECTIVE	SUMMARY
❶ **Explain** why accounting is the language of business	Accounting is an information system that measures and records business activities, processes data into reports, and reports results to decision makers. The better you understand the language used to prepare and report accounting information, the better you can make decisions using this information.
❷ **Describe** the purpose and **explain** the elements of each financial statement	The income statement (or statement of operations) measures a company's operating performance for a specified period of time. The income statement has two main elements, income and expenses, and also reports a company's net income for the period (Total Income – Total Expenses).
	The statement of retained earnings reports the changes in a company's retained earnings during the same period covered by the income statement. Under ASPE, this statement is often added to the bottom of the income statement, whereas under IFRS, information on the changes in retained earnings is included in the statement of changes in owners' equity. In its basic form, this statement adds net income to and deducts dividends from the opening retained earnings balance for the period to arrive at the ending retained earnings balance.
	The balance sheet (or statement of financial position) reports a company's financial position as at a specific date, which almost always falls on the last day of a monthly, quarterly, or annual reporting period. A company's financial position consists of three elements: the assets it controls, the liabilities it is obligated to pay, and the equity its owners have accumulated in the business. The balance sheet takes its name from the fact that the assets it reports must always equal—or be in balance with—the sum of the liabilities and equity it reports. This relationship is known as the accounting equation, and it provides the foundation for the double-entry method of accounting you will begin to learn in Chapter 2.

The statement of cash flows reports the specific business activities that generated cash receipts or resulted in cash payments during the same period covered by the income statement. These business activities are classified into three categories: operating, investing, and financing activities.

❸ Prepare financial statements and **analyze** the relationships among them

Certain key financial statement items serve as links among the financial statements:
1. Net income from the income statement is included in the calculation of retained earnings on the statement of retained earnings (which is included as part of the statement of changes in owners' equity under IFRS).
2. The closing retained earnings balance from the statement of retained earnings is included in the calculation of owners' equity on the balance sheet.
3. The closing cash balance from the statement of cash flows appears as an asset on the balance sheet.

❹ Explain and **apply** underlying accounting concepts, assumptions, and principles

In Canada there are two main sets of GAAP. Publicly accountable enterprises (or those planning to become one) must use International Financial Reporting Standards (IFRS), whereas private enterprises have the option of applying IFRS or Accounting Standards for Private Enterprises (ASPE). Most private enterprises choose the ASPE because it is simpler and less costly to apply.

Both IFRS and ASPE rest on a conceptual framework, which helps ensure that accounting information is useful for decision-making purposes. This framework includes the fundamental qualitative characteristics of relevance and faithful representation, as well as four enhancing qualitative characteristics: comparability, verifiability, timeliness, and understandability. The cost of obtaining certain types of accounting information is sometimes a constraint on what is reported to the users of financial statements.

Underlying the conceptual framework are four assumptions: the going-concern, separate-entity, historical-cost, and stable-monetary-unit assumptions.

❺ Ethically evaluate business decisions

Accountants must often use professional judgment when applying IFRS and ASPE because many accounting standards do not have clear-cut rules that specify how transactions or events should be accounted for. When using professional judgment, the accountant's goal is to make a decision that fulfills their ethical responsibilities to every party with a stake in the decision. Professional accountants are governed by rules of professional conduct, which provide guidance meant to ensure that ethical standards are upheld when applying professional judgment.

MyLab Accounting

END-OF-CHAPTER SUMMARY PROBLEM

J. J. Booth and Marie Savard incorporated Tara Inc., a consulting engineering company, and began operations on April 1, 2020. During April, the business provided engineering services for clients. It is now April 30, and J. J. and Marie wonder how well Tara Inc. performed during its first month. They also want to know the business's financial position as at April 30 and cash flows during the month.

The following data are listed in alphabetical order:

Accounts payable..................................	$ 1,800	Land...	$ 18,000
Accounts receivable............................	2,000	Office supplies.................................	3,700
Adjustments to reconcile net income to net cash provided by operating activities.....................	(3,900)	Payments of cash: Acquisition of land .... Dividends...................................	40,000 2,100
Cash balance at beginning of April	0	Rent expense	1,100
Cash balance at end of April...............	33,300	Retained earnings at beginning of April...	0
Cash receipts:			
Issuance (sale) of shares..................	50,000	Retained earnings at end of April....	?
Sale of land.......................................	22,000	Salary expense.................................	1,200
Common shares	50,000	Service revenue	10,000
		Utilities expense	400

Requirements

1. Prepare the income statement, the statement of retained earnings, and the statement of cash flows for the month ended April 30, 2020, and the balance sheet as at April 30, 2020. Draw arrows linking the pertinent items in the statements.
2. Answer the investors' underlying questions.
   a. How well did Tara Inc. perform during its first month of operations?
   b. Where does Tara Inc. stand financially at the end of the first month?

ANSWERS

Requirement 1

Financial Statements of Tara Inc.

	A	B	C	D
1	**Tara Inc.** Income Statement For the Month Ended April 30, 2020			
2	Income:			
3	Service revenue		$ 10,000	
4	Expenses:			
5	Salary expense	$ 1,200		
6	Rent expense	1,100		
7	Utilities expense	400		
8	Total expenses		2,700	
9	Net income		$ 7,300	
10				

The title must include the name of the company, "Income Statement," and the specific period of time covered. It is critical that the time period be defined.

Gather all the income and expense accounts from the account listing. List the income accounts first. List the expense accounts next.

The title must include the name of the company, "Statement of Retained Earnings," and the specific period of time covered. It is critical that the time period be defined.

The net income amount (or net loss amount) is transferred from the income statement. Retained earnings at the end of the period is the result of a calculation, and is an accumulation of the corporation's performance since it began.

①

	A	B	C
1	**Tara Inc.** **Statement of Retained Earnings** **For the Month Ended April 30, 2020**		
2	Retained earnings, April 1, 2020		$ 0
3	Add: Net income for the month		7,300
4			7,300
5	Less: Dividends		(2,100)
6	Retained earnings, April 30, 2020		$ 5,200
7			

The title must include the name of the company, "Balance Sheet," and the date of the balance sheet. It shows the financial position at the end of the day.

Gather all the asset, liability, and equity accounts from the account listing. List assets first, then liabilities, then equity accounts. The retained earnings amount is transferred from the statement of retained earnings.

It is imperative that total assets = total liabilities + shareholders' equity.

②

	A	B	C	D
1	**Tara Inc.** **Balance Sheet** **As at April 30, 2020**			
2	**Assets**		**Liabilities**	
3	Cash	$ 33,300	Accounts payable	$ 1,800
4	Accounts receivable	2,000	**Shareholders' Equity**	
5	Office supplies	3,700	Common shares	50,000
6	Land	18,000	Retained earnings	5,200
7			Total shareholders' equity	55,200
8	Total assets	$ 57,000	Total liabilities and shareholders' equity	$ 57,000
9				

The title must include the name of the company, "Statement of Cash Flows," and the specific period of time covered. It is critical that the time period be defined.

Net income comes from the income statement. The adjustments amount was provided. In later chapters, you will learn how to calculate this amount.

Include all transactions that involve investing the company's cash, which involve any changes in the property, plant, and equipment.

Include all cash transactions relating to shares and long-term debt obligations.

③

	A	B	C
1	**Tara Inc.** **Statement of Cash Flows** **For the Month Ended April 30, 2020**		
2	Cash flows from operating activities:		
3	Net income		$ 7,300
4	Adjustments to reconcile net income to net cash provided by operating activities		(3,900)
5	Net cash provided by operating activities		3,400
6	Cash flows from investing activities:		
7	Acquisition of land	$(40,000)	
8	Sale of land	22,000	
9	Net cash used for investing activities		(18,000)
10	Cash flows from financing activities:		
11	Issuance (sale) of shares	$ 50,000	
12	Payment of dividends	(2,100)	
13	Net cash provided by financing activities		47,900
14	Net increase in cash		$ 33,300
15	Cash balance, April 1, 2020		0
16	Cash balance, April 30, 2020		$ 33,300
17			

Requirement 2

Consider the net income from the income statement.

Consider net worth, which is total assets minus total liabilities.

2. a. The company performed rather well in April. Net income was $7,300—very good in relation to service revenue of $10,000. Tara was able to pay cash dividends of $2,100.

b. The business ended April with cash of $33,300. Total assets of $57,000 far exceed total liabilities of $1,800. Shareholders' equity of $55,200 provides a good cushion for borrowing. The business's financial position at April 30, 2020, is strong. The company has plenty of cash, and assets far exceed liabilities. Operating activities generated positive cash flow in the first month of operations. Lenders like to see these features before making a loan.

TRY IT *in* EXCEL ® ▶▶▶

If you've had a basic course in Excel, you can prepare financial statements easily using an Excel spreadsheet. In this chapter, you learned the accounting equation (see Exhibit 1-7 on page 12). In Exhibit 1-3 you learned the formulas for computing net income and the ending balance of retained earnings. Using the balance sheet for Tara Inc. in the End-of-Chapter Summary Problem, it is easy to prepare an Excel template for a balance sheet by programming cells for total assets (cell B8) and total liabilities and shareholders' equity (cell D8). Then, as long as you know what accounts belong in each category, you can use the insert function to insert individual assets, liabilities, and shareholders' equity accounts from a list into various cells of the spreadsheet (don't forget to include both description and amounts). You can insert subtotals for current assets, non-current assets, current liabilities, non-current liabilities, and shareholders' equity. You can also build a basic Excel template for the income statement for Tara Inc. by listing and totaling revenues and listing and totaling expenses, then subtracting total expenses from total revenues to compute net income (cell C9). You can build an Excel template for the statement of retained earnings by programming a cell for the ending balance of retained earnings (beginning balance + net income (loss) − dividends) (cell C6). Then simply insert the individual amounts and your spreadsheet does all the math for you.

Don't forget the proper order of financial statement preparation: (1) income statement, (2) statement of retained earnings, (3) balance sheet, and (4) statement of cash flows. If you have to prepare all four statements, it's best to follow that order so that you can link the income statement cell containing net income to the corresponding cell in the statement of retained earnings; link the value of the ending balance of retained earnings to the cell containing the retained earnings amount in the balance sheet; and link the ending balance of cash on the statement of cash flows to the balance of cash on the balance sheet as of the year end. These links correspond to the amounts connected by arrows (1, 2, and 3) on pages 31–32.

The beauty of this approach is that once you build a set of basic templates, you can save and use them over and over again as you progress through the course.

REVIEW

MyLab Accounting

Make the grade with MyLab Accounting: The Quick Quiz questions, Short Exercises, Exercises, and Problems (Group A) marked with a ⊕ can be found on MyLab Accounting. You can practise them as often as you want, and most feature step-by-step guided instructions to help you find the right answer.

QUICK QUIZ (ANSWERS APPEAR ON THE LAST PAGE OF THIS CHAPTER.)

1. The *primary* objective of financial reporting is to provide ⊕ information
   a. useful for making investment and credit decisions.
   b. about the profitability of the enterprise.
   c. on the cash flows of the company.
   d. to the federal government.

2. For a business of a certain size, which type of business ⊕ organization provides the least amount of protection for bankers and other creditors of the company?
   a. Proprietorship
   b. Partnership
   c. Both a and b
   d. Corporation

3. International Financial Reporting Standards (IFRS) were developed because
   a. Canadian GAAP were outdated.
   b. corporations wanted to change their reporting.
   c. different GAAP in countries of the world made global comparisons difficult.
   d. new assumptions were defined.

4. During January, assets increased by $20,000, and liabilities increased by $4,000. Shareholders' equity must have
   a. increased by $16,000.
   b. increased by $24,000.
   c. decreased by $16,000.
   d. decreased by $24,000.

5. The amount a company expects to collect from customers appears on the
   a. income statement in the expenses section.
   b. balance sheet in the current assets section.
   c. balance sheet in the shareholders' equity section.
   d. statement of cash flows.

6. All of the following are current assets except
   a. cash.
   b. accounts receivable.
   c. inventory.
   d. sales revenue.

7. Revenues are
   a. increases in share capital resulting from the owners investing in the business.
   b. increases in income resulting from selling products or performing services.
   c. decreases in liabilities resulting from paying off loans.
   d. All of the above.

8. The financial statement that reports revenues and expenses is called the
   a. statement of retained earnings.
   b. income statement.
   c. statement of cash flows.
   d. balance sheet.

9. Another name for the balance sheet is the
   a. statement of operations.
   b. statement of earnings.
   c. statement of profit and loss.
   d. statement of financial position.

10. Baldwin Corporation began the year with cash of $35,000 and a computer that cost $20,000. During the year, Baldwin earned sales revenue of $140,000 and had the following expenses: salaries, $59,000; rent, $8,000; and utilities, $3,000. At year-end, Baldwin's cash balance was down to $16,000. How much net income (or net loss) did Baldwin experience for the year?

   a. ($19,000)
   b. $70,000
   c. $107,000
   d. $140,000

11. Quartz Instruments had retained earnings of $145,000 at December 31, 2019. Net income for 2020 totalled $90,000, and dividends for 2020 were $30,000. How much retained earnings should Quartz report at December 31, 2020?
    a. $205,000
    b. $235,000
    c. $140,000
    d. $175,000

12. Net income appears on which financial statement(s)?
    a. Income statement
    b. Statement of retained earnings
    c. Both a and b
    d. Balance sheet

13. Cash paid to purchase a building appears on the statement of cash flows among the
    a. operating activities.
    b. financing activities.
    c. investing activities.
    d. shareholders' equity.

14. The shareholders' equity of Chernasky Company at the beginning and end of 2020 totalled $15,000 and $18,000, respectively. Assets at the beginning of 2020 were $25,000. If the liabilities of Chernasky Company increased by $8,000 in 2020, how much were total assets at the end of 2020? Use the accounting equation.
    a. $36,000
    b. $16,000
    c. $2,000
    d. Some other amount (fill in the blank)

15. Drexler Company had the following on the dates indicated:

	12/31/20	12/31/19
Total assets	$750,000	$520,000
Total liabilities	300,000	200,000

    Drexler had no share transactions in 2020, and thus, the change in shareholders' equity for 2020 was due to net income and dividends. If dividends were $50,000, how much was Drexler's net income for 2020? Use the accounting equation and the statements of retained earnings.
    a. $100,000
    b. $130,000
    c. $180,000
    d. Some other amount (fill in the blank)

ACCOUNTING VOCABULARY

accounting An information system that measures and records business activities, processes data into reports, and reports results to decision makers. (p. 3)

accounting equation Assets = Liabilities + Owners' Equity. Provides the foundation for the double-entry method of accounting. (p. 11)

Accounting Standards for Private Enterprises (ASPE) Canadian accounting standards that specify the *generally accepted accounting principles* applicable to *private enterprises* that are required to follow *GAAP* and choose not to apply *IFRS*. (p. 8)

asset A resource owned or controlled by a company as a result of past events and from which the company expects to receive future economic benefits. (p. 11)

auditor An accountant who provides an independent opinion on whether an entity's financial statements have been prepared in accordance with generally accepted accounting principles. (p. 17)

balance sheet Reports a company's financial position as at a specific date. In particular, it reports a company's assets, liabilities, and owners' equity. Also called the *statement of financial position*. (p. 11)

board of directors Group elected by the shareholders to set policy for a corporation and to appoint its officers. (p. 6)

carrying amount The historical cost of an asset net of its accumulated depreciation. (p. 13)

comparability Investors like to compare a company's financial statements from one year to the next. Therefore, a company must consistently use the same accounting method each year. (p. 21)

corporation An incorporated business owned by one or more *shareholders*, which according to the law is a legal "person" separate from its owners. (p. 6)

current asset An asset that is expected to be converted to cash, sold, or consumed during the next 12 months, or within the business's normal operating cycle if longer than a year. (p. 11)

current liability A debt due to be paid within one year or within the entity's operating cycle if the cycle is longer than a year. (p. 14)

deficit The term used when *retained earnings* is a negative balance. (p. 10)

ethical standards Standards that govern the way we treat others and the way we restrain our selfish desires. They are shaped by our cultural, socioeconomic, and religious backgrounds. (p. 25)

expense A cost incurred to purchase the goods and services a company needs to run its business on a day-to-day basis. The opposite of revenue. (p. 9)

fair value The amount that a business could sell an asset for, or the amount that a business could pay to settle a liability. (p. 24)

faithful representation A fundamental qualitative characteristic of accounting information. Information is a faithful representation if it is complete, neutral, accurate, and reflects the economic substance of the underlying transaction or event. (p. 20)

financial accounting The branch of accounting that provides information for managers inside a business and for decision makers outside the business. (p. 5)

financial statements The reports that companies use to convey the financial results of their business activities to various user groups, which can include managers, investors, creditors, and regulatory agencies. (p. 2)

financing activities Activities that result in changes in the size and composition of a company's contributed equity and borrowings. (p. 15)

gain A type of income other than revenue that results in an increase in economic benefits to a company, and usually occurs outside the course of the company's ordinary business activities. (p. 8)

generally accepted accounting principles (GAAP) The guidelines of financial accounting, which specify the standards for how accountants must record, measure, and report financial information. (p. 7)

going-concern assumption The assumption that an entity will continue operating normally for the foreseeable future. (p. 22)

historical-cost assumption Holds that assets should be recorded at their actual cost, measured on the date of purchase as the amount of cash paid plus the dollar value of all non-cash consideration (other assets, privileges, or rights) also given in exchange. (p. 22)

income Consists of a company's *revenues* and *gains*. (p. 8)

income statement The financial statement that measures a company's operating performance for a specified period of time. In particular, it reports income, expenses, and net income. Also called the *statement of profit or loss*. (p. 8)

International Financial Reporting Standards (IFRS) International accounting standards that specify the *generally accepted accounting principles* which must be applied by *publicly accountable enterprises* in Canada and over 100 other countries. (p. 7)

investing activities Activities that include the purchase and sale of long-term assets and other investments that result in cash inflows or outflows related to resources used for generating future income and cash flows. (p. 15)

liability An obligation (or debt) owed by a company, which it expects to pay off in the future using some of its assets. (p. 13)

liquidity A measure of how quickly an asset can be converted to cash. The higher an asset's liquidity, the more quickly it can be converted to cash. (p. 11)

long-term asset Another term for *non-current asset*. (p. 13)

long-term liability Another term for *non-current liability*. (p. 14)

loss A type of expense that results in a decrease in economic benefits to a company, and usually occurs outside the course of the company's ordinary business activities. The opposite of a gain. (p. 9)

management accounting The branch of accounting that generates information for the internal decision makers of a business, such as top executives. (p. 5)

material Accounting information is material if it is significant enough in nature or magnitude that omitting or misstating it could affect the decisions of an informed user. (p. 21)

net assets Another name for *owners' equity*. (p. 14)

net earnings Another name for *net income*. (p. 10)

net income The excess of a company's total income over its total expenses. (p. 10)

net loss Occurs when a company's total expenses exceed its total income. (p. 10)

net profit Another term for *net income*. (p. 10)

non-current asset Any asset that is not classified as a current asset. (p. 11)

non-current liability A liability a company expects to pay off beyond one year from the balance sheet date. (p. 14)

operating activities Activities that comprise the main revenue-producing activities of a company, and generally result from the transactions and other events that determine net income. (p. 15)

owners' equity The company owners' remaining interest in the assets of the company after deducting all its liabilities.   (p. 14)

partnership An unincorporated business with two or more parties as co-owners, with each owner being a partner in the business. (p. 5)

private enterprise An entity that has not issued and does not plan to issue shares or debt on public markets.   (p. 7)

proprietorship An unincorporated business with a single owner, called the proprietor.   (p. 5)

publicly accountable enterprises (PAEs) Corporations that have issued or plan to issue shares or debt in a public market. (p. 7)

relevance A fundamental qualitative characteristic of accounting information. Information is relevant if it has predictive value, confirmatory value, or both, and is *material*.   (p. 20)

retained earnings Represent the accumulated net income of a company since the day it started business, less any net losses and dividends declared during this time.   (p. 10)

revenue Consists of amounts earned by a company in the course of its ordinary, day-to-day business activities. The vast majority of a company's revenue is earned through the sale of its primary goods and services.   (p. 8)

separate-entity assumption Holds that the business activities of the reporting entity are separate from the activities of its owners.   (p. 22)

shareholder A party who owns shares of a corporation.   (p. 6)

shareholders' equity Another term for *owners' equity*.   (p. 14)

shares Legal units of ownership in a corporation.   (p. 6)

stable-monetary-unit assumption Holds that regardless of the reporting currency used, financial information is always reported under the assumption that the value of the currency is stable, despite the fact that its value does change due to economic factors such as inflation.   (p. 22)

statement of cash flows Reports cash receipts and cash payments classified according to the entity's major activities: operating, investing, and financing.   (p. 15)

statement of financial position Another name for the *balance sheet*.   (p. 11)

statement of retained earnings Summary of the changes in the retained earnings of a corporation during a specific period.   (p. 10)

Timeliness The need to report accounting information to users in time for it to influence their decisions.   (p. 21)

understandability The need to clearly and concisely classify and present financial information so that reasonably knowledgeable and diligent users of the the information can understand it. (p. 21)

verifiability The ability to check financial information for accuracy, completeness, and reliability.   (p. 21)

ASSESS YOUR PROGRESS

SHORT EXERCISES

LEARNING OBJECTIVE ❷

Distinguish between assets, liabilities, and equity

S1-1 Accounting definitions are precise, and you must understand the vocabulary to properly use accounting. Sharpen your understanding of key terms by answering the following questions:

1. How do the *assets* and *shareholders' equity* of Dollarama differ from each other? Which one (assets or shareholders' equity) must be at least as large as the other? Which one can be smaller than the other?
2. How are Dollarama's *liabilities* and *shareholders' equity* similar? How are they different?

LEARNING OBJECTIVE ❷

Apply the accounting equation

S1-2 Use the accounting equation to show how to determine the amount of the missing term in each of the following situations.

Total Assets	=	Total Liabilities	+	Shareholders' Equity
a. $?		$150,000		$150,000
b. 290,000		90,000		?
c. 220,000		?		120,000

LEARNING OBJECTIVE ❷

Apply the accounting equation

S1-3 Review the accounting equation on page 12.

1. Use the accounting equation to show how to determine the amount of a company's shareholders' equity. How would your answer change if you were analyzing your own household or a single Dairy Queen restaurant?
2. If you know assets and shareholders' equity, how can you measure liabilities? Give the equation.

S1-4 Consider Walmart, the world's largest bricks-and-mortar retailer. Classify the following items as an asset (A), a liability (L), or an shareholders' equity (E) item for Walmart:

_____ **a.** Accounts payable   _____ **g.** Accounts receivable
_____ **b.** Common shares   _____ **h.** Long-term debt
_____ **c.** Cash   _____ **i.** Merchandise inventories
_____ **d.** Retained earnings   _____ **j.** Notes payable
_____ **e.** Land   _____ **k.** Accrued expenses payable
_____ **f.** Prepaid expenses   _____ **l.** Equipment

LEARNING OBJECTIVE ❷
Classify assets, liabilities, and owners' equity

S1-5
1. Identify the two basic categories of items on an income statement.
2. What do we call the bottom line of the income statement?

LEARNING OBJECTIVE ❷
Explain the elements of the income statement

S1-6 Split Second Wireless Inc. began 2020 with total assets of $110 million and ended 2020 with assets of $160 million. During 2020, Split Second earned revenues of $90 million and had expenses of $20 million. Split Second paid dividends of $10 million in 2020. Prepare the company's income statement for the year ended December 31, 2020, complete with the appropriate heading.

LEARNING OBJECTIVE ❸
Prepare an income statement

S1-7 Mondala Ltd. began 2020 with retained earnings of $200 million. Revenues during the year were $400 million and expenses totalled $300 million. Mondala declared dividends of $40 million. What was the company's ending balance of retained earnings? To answer this question, prepare Mondala's statement of retained earnings for the year ended December 31, 2020, complete with its appropriate heading.

LEARNING OBJECTIVE ❸
Prepare a statement of retained earnings

S1-8 At December 31, 2020, Skate Sharp Limited has cash of $13,000, receivables of $2,000, and inventory of $40,000. The company's equipment totals $75,000, and other assets amount to $10,000. Skate Sharp owes accounts payable of $10,000 and short-term notes payable of $5,000, and also has long-term debt of $70,000. Share capital is $15,000. Prepare Skate Sharp Limited's balance sheet at December 31, 2020, complete with its appropriate heading.

LEARNING OBJECTIVE ❸
Prepare a balance sheet

S1-9 Brazos Medical, Inc., ended 2019 with cash of $24,000. During 2020, Brazos earned net income of $120,000 and had adjustments to reconcile net income to net cash provided by operations totalling $20,000 (this is a negative amount).

Brazos paid $300,000 for equipment during 2020 and had to borrow half of this amount on a long-term note. During the year, the company paid dividends of $15,000 and sold old equipment, receiving cash of $60,000.

Prepare Brazos's statement of cash flows with its appropriate heading for the year ended December 31, 2020. Follow the format in the summary problem on pages 31–32.

LEARNING OBJECTIVE ❸
Prepare a statement of cash flows

S1-10 John Grant is chairman of the board of The Grant Group Ltd. Suppose John has just founded this company, and assume that he treats his home and other personal assets as part of The Grant Group. Answer these questions about the evaluation of The Grant Group.

1. Which accounting assumption governs this situation?
2. How can the proper application of this accounting assumption give John Grant a realistic view of The Grant Group? Explain in detail.

LEARNING OBJECTIVE ❹
Apply accounting assumptions

S1-11 Accountants follow ethical guidelines in the conduct of their work. What are these standards of professional conduct designed to produce? Why is this goal important?

LEARNING OBJECTIVE ❺
Make ethical judgments

S1-12 Suppose you are analyzing the financial statements of a Canadian company. Identify each item with its appropriate financial statement, using the following abbreviations: income statement (IS), statement of retained earnings (SRE), balance sheet (BS), and statement of cash flows (SCF).

LEARNING OBJECTIVE ❷
Classify items on the financial statements

Three items appear on two financial statements, and one item shows up on three statements.

a. Dividends _____
b. Salary expense _____
c. Inventory _____
d. Sales revenue _____
e. Retained earnings _____
f. Net cash provided by operating
   activities _____
g. Net income _____

h. Cash _____
i. Net cash provided by financing
   activities _____
j. Accounts payable _____
k. Common shares _____
l. Interest revenue _____
m. Long-term debt _____
n. Net increase or decrease in cash _____

EXERCISES

LEARNING OBJECTIVE ❶

Organize a business

E1-13 Mary Wu, the proprietor of Quality Environmental Services, is wondering how she should organize her new business. Answer the following questions about the different ways in which Mary might organize the business. Explain each answer.

a. What form of organization will enable Mary to limit her risk of loss to the amount she has invested in the business?
b. What form of business organization will give Mary the most freedom to manage the business as she wishes?
c. What form of organization will give creditors the maximum protection in the event that Quality Environmental fails and cannot pay its liabilities?
d. If you were Mary and could organize the business as you wish, what form of organization would you choose for Quality Environmental?

LEARNING OBJECTIVES ❷❸❺

Describe the purpose of the financial statements; use the financial statements to make decisions; make ethical business decisions

E1-14 Ed Eisler wants to open a café in Digby, Nova Scotia. In need of cash, he asks a bank for a loan. The bank requests financial statements showing the likely results of operations for the year and the expected financial position at year-end. With little knowledge of accounting, Ed doesn't understand the request.

Requirements

1. Explain to Ed the information provided by the income statement and the balance sheet.
2. Explain to Ed how items on the income statement are relevant to making a lending decision.
3. Explain to Ed how items on the balance sheet are relevant to making a lending decision.
4. Given how the bank will use the income statement and balance sheet to make a lending decision, how might Ed be biased to present key items on each of these statements? Would it be ethical for Ed to do this and why?

LEARNING OBJECTIVE ❹

Apply accounting assumptions

E1-15 Identify the accounting assumption that best applies to each of the following situations.

a. Wendy's, the restaurant chain, sold a store location to Burger King. How can Wendy's determine the sale price of the store: by a professional appraisal, Wendy's cost, or the amount actually received from the sale?
b. If Trammel Crow Realtors had to liquidate its assets, their value would be less than the carrying amounts of the assets.
c. Toyota Canada wants to determine which division of the company—Toyota or Lexus—is more profitable.
d. You get an especially good buy on a laptop, paying only $399 for a computer that normally costs $799. What is your accounting value for this computer?

LEARNING OBJECTIVE ❷

Apply the accounting equation

E1-16 Compute the missing amount in the accounting equation for each company (amounts in millions):

	Assets	Liabilities	Shareholders' Equity
TELUS	$?	$10,061	$ 6,926
Scotiabank	411,510	?	18,804
Shoppers Drug Mart	5,644	2,434	?

E1-17 Assume Maple Leaf Foods Inc. has current assets of $633.6 million, capital assets of $1,126.7 million, and other assets totalling $1,237.5 million. Current liabilities are $591.2 million and long-term liabilities total $1,245.2 million.

LEARNING OBJECTIVES ❷❸

Apply the accounting equation; analyze financial statements

Requirements

1. Use these data to write Maple Leaf Foods's accounting equation.
2. How much in resources does Maple Leaf Foods have to work with?
3. How much does Maple Leaf Foods owe creditors?
4. How much of the company's assets do the Maple Leaf Foods shareholders actually own?

E1-18 We Store For You Ltd.'s comparative balance sheets at December 31, 2020, and December 31, 2019, report the following (in millions):

LEARNING OBJECTIVES ❷❸

Apply the accounting equation; analyze relationships among financial statements

	2020	2019
Total assets	$40	$30
Total liabilities	10	8

Requirements

Below are three situations about We Store For You's issuance of shares and payment of dividends during the year ended December 31, 2020. For each situation, use the accounting equation and statement of retained earnings to compute the amount of We Store For You's net income or loss during the year ended December 31, 2020.

1. We Store For You issued shares for $2 million and paid no dividends.
2. We Store For You issued no shares and paid dividends of $3 million.
3. We Store For You issued shares for $11 million and paid dividends of $2 million.

E1-19 Answer these questions about two companies:

LEARNING OBJECTIVES ❷❸

Apply the accounting equation; analyze relationships among financial statements

1. Mortimer Limited began the year with total liabilities of $400,000 and total shareholders' equity of $300,000. During the year, total assets increased by 20%. How much are total assets at the end of the year?
2. Aztec Associates began a year with total assets of $500,000 and total liabilities of $200,000. Net income for the year was $100,000 and no dividends were paid. How much is shareholders' equity at the end of the year?

E1-20 Assume Dollarama is expanding into the United States. The company must decide where to locate, and how to finance the expansion. Identify the financial statement in which decision makers can find the following information about Dollarama. In some cases, more than one statement will report the needed data.

LEARNING OBJECTIVE ❷

Identify financial statement information

a. Common shares
b. Income tax payable
c. Dividends
d. Income tax expense
e. Ending balance of retained earnings
f. Total assets
g. Long-term debt
h. Revenue

i. Cash spent to acquire equipment
j. Selling, general, and administrative expenses
k. Adjustments to reconcile net income to net cash provided by operations
l. Ending cash balance
m. Current liabilities
n. Net income
o. Cost of goods sold

E1-21 Amounts of the assets and liabilities of Torrance Associates Inc., as of December 31, 2020, are given as follows. Also included are revenue and expense figures for the year ended on that date (amounts in millions):

LEARNING OBJECTIVES ❷❸

Apply the accounting equation; prepare a balance sheet

Property and equipment, net	$ 4	Total revenue	$ 35
Investment	72	Receivables	253
Long-term liabilities	73	Current liabilities	290
Other expenses	14	Common shares	12
Cash	28	Interest expense	3
Retained earnings, beginning	19	Salary and other employee expense	9
Retained earnings, ending	?	Other assets	43

Requirement

Prepare the balance sheet of Torrance Associates Inc. at December 31, 2020.

LEARNING OBJECTIVE ❸

Prepare an income statement and statement of retained earnings

⊕ **E1-22** Refer to the data of Torrance Associates Inc. in exercise E1-21.

Requirements

1. Prepare the income statement of Torrance Associates Inc. for the year ended December 31, 2020.
2. What amount of dividends did Torrance declare during the year ended December 31, 2020?

LEARNING OBJECTIVES ❷❸

Prepare a statement of cash flows; identify elements of financial statements; identify activities that affect financial statements

⊕ **E1-23** Groovy Limited is a recording studio used by musicians to record music. It began 2020 with $95,000 in cash. During 2020, Groovy earned net income of $300,000, and adjustments to reconcile net income to net cash provided by operations totalled $60,000, a positive amount. Investing activities used cash of $400,000, and financing activities provided cash of $70,000. Groovy ended 2020 with total assets of $250,000 and total liabilities of $110,000.

Requirements

1. Identify the items that are not relevant to preparing the statement of cash flows for Groovy Limited and indicate which financial statement reports these items.
2. Prepare Groovy Limited's statement of cash flows for the year ended December 31, 2020.
3. Identify specific types of investing activities that could have used some of Groovy Limited's cash during the year.
4. Identify specific types of financing activities that could have provided Groovy Limited with cash during the year.

LEARNING OBJECTIVE ❸

Prepare an income statement and a statement of retained earnings

⊕ **E1-24** Assume Cober Printing Inc. ended the month of July 2020 with these data:

Payments of cash:		Cash receipts:	
Acquisition of equipment	$36,000	Issuance (sale) of shares to	
Dividends	2,000	owners	$35,000
Retained earnings at July 1, 2020	0	Rent expense	700
Retained earnings at July 31, 2020	?	Common shares	35,000
Utilities expense	200	Equipment	36,000
Adjustments to reconcile net income		Office supplies expense	1,200
to cash provided by operations	3,200	Accounts payable	3,200
Salary expense	4,000	Service revenue	14,000
Cash balance July 1, 2020	0		
Cash balance July 31, 2020	8,100		

Requirement

Prepare the income statement and the statement of retained earnings of the company for the month ended July 31, 2020.

LEARNING OBJECTIVE ❸

Prepare a balance sheet

⊕ **E1-25** Refer to the data in the preceding exercise. Prepare the balance sheet of the company at July 31, 2020.

LEARNING OBJECTIVE ❸

Prepare a statement of cash flows

⊕ **E1-26** Refer to the data in exercise E1-24. Prepare the statement of cash flows of the company for the month ended July 31, 2020. Draw arrows linking the pertinent items in the statements you prepared for exercises E1-24 through E1-26.

LEARNING OBJECTIVE ❸

Use financial statements for decision making

⊕ **E1-27** This exercise should be used in conjunction with exercises E1-24 through E1-26. The owner of Cober Printing Inc. now seeks your advice as to whether the company should cease operations or continue operating. Write a report giving the owner your opinion of operating results, dividends, financial position, and cash flows during the company's first month of operations. Cite specifics from the financial statements to support your opinion. Conclude your report with advice on whether to stay in business or cease operations.

E1-28 Apply your understanding of the relationships among the financial statements to answer these questions:

LEARNING OBJECTIVE ❸

Explain relationships among financial statements

a. How can a business earn large profits but have a small balance of retained earnings?
b. Give two reasons why a business can have a steady stream of net income over a five-year period and still experience a cash shortage.
c. If you could pick a single source of cash for your business, what would it be? Why?
d. How can a business suffer net losses for several years in a row and still have plenty of cash?

PROBLEMS (GROUP A)

P1-29A Assume that the Special Contract Division of Staples experienced the following transactions during the year ended December 31, 2020:

LEARNING OBJECTIVES ❷❸❹

Prepare an income statement; apply underlying accounting concepts and assumptions

a. Suppose the division provided copy services to a customer for the discounted price of $250,000. Under normal conditions, Staples would have provided these services for $280,000. Other revenues totalled $50,000.
b. Salaries cost the division $20,000 to provide these services. The division had to pay employees overtime. Ordinarily, the salary cost for these services would have been $18,000.
c. Other expenses totalled $240,000. Income tax expense was 30% of income before tax.
d. Staples has two operating divisions. Each division is accounted for separately to indicate how well each is performing. At year-end, Staples combines the statements of divisions to show results for Staples as a whole.
e. Inflation affects the amounts that Staples must pay for copy machines. To show the effects of inflation, net income would drop by $3,000.
f. If Staples were to go out of business, the sale of its assets would bring in $150,000 in cash.

Requirements

1. Prepare the Special Contracts Division's income statement for the year ended December 31, 2020.
2. Identify the accounting concepts, assumptions, or principles used in accounting for the items described in a through f. State how you have applied the concept, assumption, or principle in preparing the Division's income statement.

P1-30A Below are selected financial data (in millions) for three fencing companies.

LEARNING OBJECTIVES ❷❸

Apply the accounting equation; analyze the relationships among financial statements

	Link Ltd.	Chain Inc.	Fence Corp.
Beginning			
Assets	$ 78	$ 30	?
Liabilities	47	19	$ 2
Common shares	6	1	2
Retained earnings	?	10	3
Ending			
Assets	?	$ 48	$ 9
Liabilities	$ 48	30	?
Common shares	6	1	2
Retained earnings	27	?	4
Dividends	$ 3	$ 2	$ 0
Income statement			
Revenues	$216	?	$20
Expenses	211	$144	19
Net income	?	9	1

Requirements

1. Compute the missing amounts (indicated by a ?) for each company.
2. What two line items above would be most relevant to determining which company is the largest? Why?
3. Which company reported the highest net income for the year? The highest net income as a percentage of revenues? Which of these two amounts is better for comparing the operating performance of the companies for the year? Why?

LEARNING OBJECTIVES ❷❸

Prepare and analyze a balance sheet; identify on which financial statement to include an account

P1-31A Dan Shoe, the manager of STRIDES Inc., prepared the company's balance sheet while the accountant was ill. The balance sheet contains numerous errors. In particular, Shoe knew that the balance sheet should balance, so he plugged in the shareholders' equity amount needed to achieve this balance. The shareholders' equity amount is *not* correct. All other amounts are accurate.

	A	B	C	D
1	**STRIDES Inc.** Balance Sheet For the Month Ended July 31, 2020			
2	**Assets**		**Liabilities**	
3	Cash	$ 25,000	Accounts receivable	$ 20,000
4	Store fixtures	10,000	Sales revenue	80,000
5	Accounts payable	16,000	Interest expense	800
6	Rent expense	4,000	Note payable	9,000
7	Salaries expense	15,000	Total	109,800
8	Land	44,000		
9	Advertising expense	3,000	**Shareholders' Equity**	
10			Shareholders' equity	7,200
11	Total assets	$ 117,000	Total liabilities and shareholders' equity	$ 117,000
12				

Requirements

1. Identify the accounts listed on the incorrect balance sheet that should not be reported on the balance sheet. On which financial statement should these accounts appear?
2. Prepare the correct balance sheet and date it properly.
3. Is STRIDES Inc. actually in better or worse financial position than the erroneous balance sheet reports? Give the reason for your answer.

LEARNING OBJECTIVES ❷❸❹

Understand and prepare a balance sheet; apply underlying accounting assumptions

P1-32A Alexa Markowitz is a realtor. She buys and sells properties on her own, and she also earns commission as an agent for buyers and sellers. She organized her business as a corporation on March 16, 2020. The business received $60,000 cash from Markowitz and issued common shares in return. Consider the following facts as of March 31, 2020:

a. Markowitz has $5,000 in her personal bank account and $14,000 in the business bank account.
b. Office supplies on hand at the real estate office total $1,000.
c. Markowitz's business spent $25,000 for a ReMax franchise, which entitles her to represent herself as an agent. ReMax is a national affiliation of independent real estate agents. This franchise is a business asset.
d. The business owes $60,000 on a note payable for some undeveloped land acquired for a total price of $110,000.
e. Markowitz owes $100,000 on a personal mortgage on her personal residence, which she acquired in 2005 for a total price of $350,000.
f. Markowitz owes $1,800 on a personal charge account with Holt Renfrew.
g. Markowitz acquired business furniture for $10,000 on March 25. Of this amount, the business owes $6,000 on accounts payable at March 31.

Requirements

1. Identify and explain why some of the data included in items *a-g* above are not relevant to preparing the company's balance sheet as at March 31, 2020.
2. Prepare the company's balance sheet as at March 31, 2020.
3. Identify the items on the balance sheet that are relevant to assessing whether the company can pay its short-term debts.
4. Does it appear the company can pay its short-term debts? Why?

🌐 **P1-33A** The assets and liabilities of Web Services Inc. as of December 31, 2020 and revenues and expenses for the year ended on that date are listed here.

LEARNING OBJECTIVES ❷❸

Prepare and use the income statement, statement of retained earnings, and balance sheet

Land	$ 8,000	Equipment	$ 11,000
Note payable	32,000	Interest expense	4,000
Property tax expense	2,000	Interest payable	2,000
Rent expense	15,000	Accounts payable	15,000
Accounts receivable	25,000	Salary expense	40,000
Service revenue	150,000	Building	126,000
Supplies	2,000	Cash	8,000
Utilities expense	3,000	Common shares	15,000

Beginning retained earnings were $60,000, and dividends totalled $30,000 for the year.

Requirement

1. The CEO of Web Services Inc., would like you to answer the following questions and then tell her if she should be pleased with Web Services's overall performance in 2020. Be sure to prepare and cite all the accounting information needed to answer these questions.

    a. Was Web Services profitable during 2020? By how much?
    b. Did retained earnings increase or decrease? By how much?
    c. Who has a larger claim on Web Services's assets, its creditors or its shareholders?

🌐 **P1-34A** The following data are from financial statements of Stuart Inc. for the fiscal year ended March 1, 2020 (in millions):

LEARNING OBJECTIVE ❸

Prepare analyze a statement of cash flows

Purchases of capital assets and other assets	$ 144	Accounts receivable	$168
Issuance of long-term debt	164	Repurchase of common shares	177
Net loss	(251)	Payment of dividends	31
Adjustments to reconcile net income (loss) to cash provided by operations	397	Common shares	715
		Issuance of common shares	1
		Sales of capital assets and other assets	1
Revenues	1,676	Retained earnings	752
Cash, beginning of year	41	Repayment of long-term debt	1
Cash, end of year	0		
Cost of goods sold	1,370		

Requirements

1. Prepare a statement of cash flows for the fiscal year ended March 1, 2020. Follow the format of the summary problem on pages 31–32. Not all items given are reported in the statement of cash flows.
2. What was the largest source of cash? Is this a sign of financial strength or weakness?

LEARNING OBJECTIVES ❷❸

Analyze a company's financial statements; explain relationships among the financial statements

P1-35A Summarized versions of the Gonzales Corporation's financial statements are given below for two years.

	(in thousands)	
	2020	**2019**
Statement of Income		
Revenues	$ k	$16,000
Cost of goods sold	11,500	a
Other expenses	1,300	1,200
Earnings before income taxes	4,000	3,700
Income taxes (35% tax rate)	l	1,300
Net earnings	$ m	$ b
Statement of Retained Earnings		
Beginning balance	$ n	$ 3,500
Net earnings	o	c
Dividends	(300)	(200)
Ending balance	$ p	$ d
Balance Sheet		
Assets:		
Cash	$ q	$ e
Capital assets	3,000	1,800
Other assets	r	11,200
Total assets	$ s	$15,000
Liabilities:		
Current liabilities	$ t	$ 5,600
Notes payable and long-term debt	4,500	3,200
Other liabilities	80	200
Total liabilities	$ 9,100	$ f
Shareholders' Equity:		
Common shares	$ 300	$ 300
Retained earnings	u	g
Total shareholders' equity	v	6,000
Total liabilities and shareholders' equity	$ w	$ h
Statement of Cash Flows		
Net cash provided by operating activities	$ x	$ 1,900
Net cash used for investing activities	(1,000)	(900)
Net cash used for financing activities	(700)	(1.010)
Increase (decrease) in cash	400	i
Cash at beginning of year	y	2,010
Cash at end of year	$ z	$ j

Requirements

1. Determine the missing amounts denoted by the letters.
2. As Gonzales Corporation's CEO, use the financial statements to answer these questions about the company. Explain each of your answers, and identify the financial statement where you found the information.
   a. Did operations improve or deteriorate during 2020?
   b. What is the company doing with most of its income?
   c. How much in total resources does the company have to work with as it moves into the year 2021?

d. At the end of 2019, how much did the company owe creditors? At the end of 2020, how much did the company owe? Is this trend good or bad in comparison to the trend in assets?

e. What is the company's major source of cash? Is cash increasing or decreasing? What is your opinion of the company's ability to generate cash?

P1-36A Blackwell Services, Inc., has current assets of $240 million; property, plant, and equipment of $350 million; and other assets totaling $170 million. Current liabilities are $150 million, and long-term liabilities total $360 million.

LEARNING OBJECTIVE ❷

Apply the accounting equation; understand elements of the balance sheet

Requirements

1. Use these data to write Blackwell Services, Inc.'s accounting equation.
2. How much in resources does Blackwell Services have to work with?
3. How much does Blackwell Services owe creditors?
4. How much of the company's assets do the Blackwell Services shareholders actually own?

PROBLEMS (GROUP B)

P1-37B Snap Fasteners Inc. experienced the following transactions during the year ended December 31, 2020:

LEARNING OBJECTIVES ❷❸❹

Prepare an income statement; apply underlying accounting concepts and assumptions

a. All other expenses, excluding income taxes, totalled $14.9 million for the year. Income tax expense was 35% of income before tax.

b. Snap has several operating divisions. Each division is accounted for separately to show how well each division is performing. However, Snap's financial statements combine the statements of all the divisions to report on the company as a whole.

c. Inflation affects Snap's cost to manufacture goods. If Snap's financial statements were to show the effects of inflation, assume the company's reported net income would drop by $0.250 million.

d. If Snap were to go out of business, the sale of its assets might bring in over $5 million in cash.

e. Snap sold products for $56.2 million. Company management believes that the value of these products is approximately $60.5 million.

f. It cost Snap $40.0 million to manufacture the products it sold. If Snap had purchased the products instead of manufacturing them, Snap's cost would have been $43.0 million.

Requirements

1. Prepare Snap's income statement for the year ended December 31, 2020.
2. For items a through f, identify the accounting concepts, assumptions, or principles that determined how you accounted for the item described. State how you have applied the concept, assumption, or principle in preparing Snap's income statement.

P1-38B Below are selected financial data (in millions) for three utility companies.

LEARNING OBJECTIVES ❷❸

Apply the accounting equation; analyze the relationships among financial statements

	Gas Limited	Electric Inc.	Water Corp.
Beginning			
Assets	$11,200	$ 3,256	$ 909
Liabilities	4,075	1,756	564
Ending			
Assets	$12,400	$?	$1,025
Liabilities	4,400	1,699	565
Owners' Equity			
Issuance (Repurchase) of shares	$ (36)	$ (0)	$?
Dividends	341	30	0
Income Statement			
Revenues	$11,288	$11,099	$1,663
Expenses	?	10,879	1,568

Requirements

1. Compute the missing amounts (indicated by a ?) for each company.
2. What two line items above would be most relevant to determining which company is the largest? Why?
3. Which company reported the highest net income for the year? The highest net income as a percentage of revenues? Which of these two amounts is better for comparing the operating performance of the companies for the year? Why?

Prepare and analyze a balance sheet; identify on which financial statement to include an account

P1-39B Ned Robinson, the manager of Lunenberg Times Inc., prepared the balance sheet of the company while the accountant was ill. The balance sheet contains numerous errors. In particular, the manager knew that the balance sheet should balance, so he plugged in the shareholders' equity amount needed to achieve this balance. The shareholders' equity amount, however, is *not* correct. All other amounts are accurate.

	A	B	C	D
1	**Lunenberg Times Inc.** Balance Sheet For the Month Ended October 31, 2020			
2	**Assets**		**Liabilities**	
3	Cash	$ 25,000	Accounts receivable	$ 10,000
4	Office furniture	15,000	Sales revenue	70,000
5	Note payable	16,000	Salary expense	20,000
6	Rent expense	4,000	Accounts payable	8,000
7	Inventory	30,000	Total	108,000
8	Land	34,000	**Shareholders' Equity**	
9	Advertising expense	2,500	Shareholders' equity	18,500
10	Total assets	$ 126,000	Total liabilities	$ 126,500
11				

Requirements

1. Identify the accounts listed in the incorrect balance sheet that should not be reported on the balance sheet. Which financial statement should these accounts appear on?
2. Prepare the correct balance sheet, and date it properly.
3. Is Lunenberg Times Inc. actually in better or worse financial position than the erroneous balance sheet reports? Give the reason for your answer.

LEARNING OBJECTIVES ❷❸❹

Understand and prepare a balance sheet; apply underlying accounting assumptions

P1-40B Luis Fantano is a realtor. He buys and sells properties on his own and also earns commission as an agent for buyers and sellers. Fantano organized his business as a corporation on July 10, 2020. The business received $75,000 from Fantano and issued common shares in return. Consider these facts as of July 31, 2020:

a. Fantano owes $5,000 on a personal charge account with Visa.
b. Fantano's business owes $80,000 on a note payable for some undeveloped land acquired for a total price of $135,000.
c. Fantano has $5,000 in his personal bank account and $10,000 in the business bank account.
d. Office supplies on hand at the real estate office total $1,000.
e. Fantano's business spent $35,000 for a Century 21 real estate franchise, which entitles him to represent himself as a Century 21 agent. Century 21 is a national affiliation of independent real estate agents. This franchise is a business asset.
f. Fantano owes $125,000 on a personal mortgage on his personal residence, which he acquired in 2007 for a total price of $300,000.
g. Fantano acquired business furniture for $18,000 on July 15. Of this amount, his business owes $10,000 on open account at July 31.

Requirements

1. Identify and explain why some of the data included in items *a-g* above are not relevant to preparing the company's balance sheet as at July 31, 2020.
2. Prepare the company's balance sheet as at July 31, 2020.
3. Identify the items on the balance sheet that are relevant to assessing whether the company can pay its short-term debts.
4. Does it appear the company can pay its debts? Why?

P1-41B The assets and liabilities of Beckwith Garden Supply, Inc., as of December 31, 2020, and revenues and expenses for the year ended on that date follow:

LEARNING OBJECTIVES ❷❸

Prepare and use the income statement, statement of retained earnings, and balance sheet

Equipment	$119,000
Interest expense	10,200
Interest payable	2,500
Accounts payable	24,000
Salary expense	108,500
Building	401,000
Cash	41,000
Common shares	12,700
Land	27,000
Note payable	99,500
Property tax expense	7,300
Rent expense	40,600
Accounts receivable	84,600
Service revenue	457,600
Supplies	6,800
Utilities expense	8,500

Beginning retained earnings was $364,200, and dividends declared totalled $106,000 for the year.

Requirement

1. As Chief Financial Officer of Beckwith Garden Supply, answer the following questions and then decide if you are pleased with the company's overall performance in 2020. Be sure to prepare and cite all the accounting information needed to answer these questions.
   a. Was Beckwith Garden Supply profitable during 2020? By how much?
   b. Did retained earnings increase or decrease? By how much?
   c. Who has a greater claim to Beckwith Garden Supply's assets, creditors of the company or the Beckwith Garden Supply shareholders?

P1-42B The data below are adapted from the financial statements of Long Boat Ltd. at the end of a recent year (in thousands).

LEARNING OBJECTIVE ❷

Prepare and analyze a statement of cash flows

Adjustments to reconcile net income		Sales of capital assets	$ 2
to cash provided by operations	$ 65	Payment of long-term debt	26
Revenues	3,870	Cost of goods sold	3,182
Bank overdraft, beginning of year	(11)	Common shares	212
Cash, end of year	23	Accounts receivable	271
Purchases of capital assets	123	Issuance of common shares	4
Long-term debt	234	Change in bank loan	(44)
Net income	180	Payment of dividends	24
Retained earnings	1,000		

Requirements

1. Prepare Long Boat's statement of cash flows for the year. Follow the solution to the summary problem starting on page 31. Not all the items given appear on the statement of cash flows.
2. Which activities provided the bulk of Long Boat's cash? Is this a sign of financial strength or weakness?

LEARNING OBJECTIVES ❷❸

Analyze a company's financial statements; explain relationships among the financial statements

P1-43B Condensed versions of Your Phone Ltd.'s financial statements, with certain amounts omitted, are given for two years.

	(thousands)	
	2020	2019
Statement of Income		
Revenues	$94,500	$ a
Cost of goods sold	k	65,400
Other expenses	15,660	13,550
Income before income taxes	5,645	9,300
Income taxes	1,975	3,450
Net income	$ l	$ b
Statement of Retained Earnings		
Beginning balance	$ m	$10,000
Net income	n	c
Dividends	(480)	(450)
Ending balance	$ o	$ d
Balance Sheet		
Assets:		
Cash	$ p	$ 400
Capital assets	23,790	e
Other assets	q	17,900
Total assets	$ r	$38,500
Liabilities:		
Current liabilities	$11,100	$10,000
Long-term debt and other liabilities	s	12,500
Total liabilities	24,500	f
Shareholders' Equity:		
Common shares	$ 400	$ 600
Retained earnings	t	g
Total shareholders' equity	u	16,000
Total liabilities and shareholders' equity	$ v	$ h
Statement of Cash Flows		
Net cash provided by operating activities	$ w	$ 3,600
Net cash used for investing activities	(2,700)	(4,150)
Net cash provided by financing activities	250	900
Increase (decrease) in cash	50	i
Cash at beginning of year	x	50
Cash at end of year	$ y	$ j

Requirements

1. Determine the missing amounts denoted by the letters.
2. Use Your Phone's financial statements to answer these questions about the company. Explain each of your answers.
   a. Did operations improve or deteriorate during 2020?
   b. What is the company doing with most of its income—retaining it for use in the business or using it for dividends?
   c. How much in total resources does the company have to work with as it moves into 2021? How much in total resources did the company have at the end of 2019?

d. At the end of 2019, how much did the company owe outsiders? At the end of 2020, how much did the company owe?

e. What is the company's major source of cash? What is your opinion of the company's ability to generate cash? How is the company using most of its cash? Is the company growing or shrinking?

P1-44B Whiteboard Services Inc. has current assets of $320 million; property, plant, and equipment of $250 million; and other assets totaling $140 million. Current liabilities are $190 million, and long-term liabilities total $410 million.

LEARNING OBJECTIVE ❷

Apply the accounting equation; understand elements of the balance sheet

Requirements
1. Use these data to write Whiteboard Services Inc.'s accounting equation.
2. How much in resources does Whiteboard Services have to work with?
3. How much does Whiteboard Services owe creditors?
4. How much of the company's assets do the Whiteboard Services shareholders actually own?

APPLY YOUR KNOWLEDGE

DECISION CASES

Case 1. Two businesses, Web Services and PC Providers, have sought business loans from you. To decide whether to make the loans, you have requested their balance sheets.

This section's material reflects CPA enabling competencies, including:

I   Professional and ethical behaviour

II   Problem-solving and decision-making

III   Communication

IV   Self-management

V   Teamwork and leadership

Based on Chartered Professional Accountant standards

	A	B	C	D
1	**Web Services** Balance Sheet As at October 31, 2020			
2	**Assets**		**Liabilities**	
3	Cash	$ 11,000	Accounts payable	$ 13,000
4	Accounts receivable	4,000	Notes payable	377,000
5	Furniture	36,000	Total liabilities	390,000
6	Software	79,000	**Shareholders' Equity**	
7	Computers	300,000	Shareholders' equity	40,000
8	Total assets	$ 430,000	Total liabilities and shareholders' equity	$430,000
9				

LEARNING OBJECTIVE ❷

Evaluate business operations; use financial statements

	A	B	C	D
1	**PC Providers Inc.** Balance Sheet As at October 31, 2020			
2	**Assets**		**Liabilities**	
3	Cash	$ 9,000	Accounts payable	$ 12,000
4	Accounts receivable	24,000	Note payable	28,000
5	Merchandise inventory	85,000	Total liabilities	40,000
6	Furniture and fixtures	9,000		
7	Building	82,000	**Shareholders' Equity**	
8	Land	14,000	Shareholders' equity	183,000
9	Total assets	$ 223,000	Total liabilities and shareholders' equity	$ 223,000
10				

Requirements

1. Using only these balance sheets, to which entity would you be more comfortable lending money? Explain fully, citing specific items and amounts from the respective balance sheets.
2. Is there other financial information you would consider before making your decision? Be specific.

LEARNING OBJECTIVE ❷

Analyze a company's financial statements

Case 2. After you have been out of college for a year, you have $5,000 to invest. A friend has started My Dream Inc., and she asks you to invest in her company. You obtain My Dream Inc.'s financial statements, which are summarized at the end of the first year as follows:

	A	B	C
1	**My Dream Inc.** Income Statement For the Year Ended December 31, 2020		
2	Revenues	$ 80,000	
3	Expenses	60,000	
4	Net income	$ 20,000	
5			

	A	B	C	D	E
1	**My Dream Inc.** Balance Sheet As at December 31, 2020				
2	Cash	$ 13,000	Liabilities	$ 35,000	
3	Other assets	67,000	Equity	45,000	
4	Total assets	$ 80,000	Total liabilities and equity	$ 80,000	
5					

Visits with your friend turn up the following facts:

a. The company owes an additional $10,000 for TV ads that was incurred in December but not recorded in the books.
b. Software costs of $20,000 were recorded as assets. These costs should have been expensed. My Dream paid cash for these expenses and recorded the cash payment correctly.
c. Revenues and receivables of $10,000 were overlooked and omitted.

Requirement

Will you invest in My Dream? Explain to your friend why you reached this decision, being sure to incorporate the most accurate financial statement data available given the information provided above.

LEARNING OBJECTIVES ❷❸

Prepare and analyze financial statements; make business decisions using financial statements

Case 3. Island Coffee Roasters Corporation ended the month of August 2020 with these data:

Payments of cash:			
Acquisition of equipment	$200,000	Cash balance, August 1, 2020	$ 0
Dividends.................................	2,700	Cash balance, August 31, 2020	6,000
Retained earnings		Cash receipts:	
August 1, 2020..........................	0	Issuance (sale) of shares	
Retained earnings		to owners	13,700
August 31, 2020........................	?	Rent expense	1,800
Utilities expense	5,800	Common shares	13,700
Adjustments to reconcile		Equipment	200,000
net income to net cash		Office supplies	7,500
provided by operations..............	1,400	Accounts payable	8,900
Salary expense...............................	78,100	Service revenue	279,300

Requirement

The owner of Island Coffee Roasters Corporation wants your advice as to whether she should cease operations or continue the business. Prepare a report giving her your opinion of the company's net income, dividends, financial position, and cash flows during its first month of operations. Be sure to prepare and include all the information underlying your opinions in the report. Conclude your report with advice on whether to stay in business or cease operations.

ETHICAL DECISIONS

LEARNING OBJECTIVE 5

Make ethical business decisions

Decision 1: You are studying frantically for an accounting exam tomorrow. You are having difficulty in this course, and the grade you make on this exam can make the difference between receiving a final grade of B or C. If you receive a C, it will lower your grade point average to the point that you could lose your academic scholarship. An hour ago, a friend, also enrolled in the course but in a different section under the same professor, called you with some unexpected news. In her sorority test files, she has just found a copy of an old exam from the previous year. In looking at the exam, it appears to contain questions that come right from the class notes you have taken, even the very same numbers. She offers to make a copy for you and bring it over.

You glance at your course syllabus and find the following: "You are expected to do your own work in this class. Although you may study with others, giving, receiving, or obtaining information pertaining to an examination is considered an act of academic dishonesty, unless such action is authorized by the instructor giving the examination. Also, divulging the contents of an essay or objective examination designated by the instructor as an examination is considered an act of academic dishonesty. Academic dishonesty is considered a violation of the student honour code and will subject the student to disciplinary procedures, which can include suspension from the university." Although you have heard a rumour that fraternities and sororities have cleared their exam files with professors, you are not sure.

Requirements

1. What is the ethical issue in this situation?
2. Who are the stakeholders? What are the possible consequences to each?
3. Analyze the alternatives from the following standpoints: (a) economic, (b) legal, and (c) ethical.
4. What would you do? How would you justify your decision? How would your decision make you feel afterward?
5. How is this similar to a business situation?

Decision 2: Jane Hill, an accountant for Stainton Hardware Inc., discovers that her supervisor, Drew Armor, made several errors last year. Overall, the errors overstated Stainton Hardware's net income by 20%. It is not clear whether the errors were deliberate or accidental. What should Jane Hill do?

Decision 3: For each of the situations listed, identify which principles (professional behaviour, integrity and due care, objectivity, professional competence, confidentiality) from the CPA Code of Professional Conduct have been violated. Assume all persons listed in the situations are CPAs. (Note: Refer to the CPA Code of Professional Conduct contained on pages 27–28 for descriptions of the principles.)

a. Erica is eager to please her supervisor and wants to earn a promotion at the CPA firm. When Erica puts together her firm's financial statements and related information for the past year, she buries unfavourable results deep in the report and presents the good news prominently. She figures that by making the firm look good, it will make her case for promotion stronger.

b. Evan is in charge of putting together his company's financial statements, but does not understand the newest financial reporting standard that went into effect last year. He decides to do the best he can with interpreting and applying the new standard because he does not have time right now to learn about the new standard in depth.

     c. Jay receives a large year-end bonus if his company's sales grow by 8% this year. Sales only grew by 7.5%, so Jay created false sales documentation to make it appear that the sales growth goal was met.

     d. This year, Gabby's company incurred higher cost of goods sold than expected, which resulted in an overall net loss for the company. Gabby does not want the company to lose investors due to the net loss, so she adjusts cost of goods sold so that the company has a positive net income.

FOCUS ON FINANCIAL STATEMENT ANALYSIS

LEARNING OBJECTIVE ❷

Evaluate a company using financial statements

Dollarama Inc.

This case is based on the financial statements of Dollarama, which you can find in Appendix A at the back of the book and on MyLab Accounting. As you work with Dollarama's financial statements throughout this book, you will develop the ability to use actual financial statements.

MyLab Accounting

Requirements

1. Suppose you own shares in Dollarama. If you could pick one item on the company's income statement to increase year after year, what would it be? Why is this item so important? Did this item increase or decrease during the year ended January 28, 2018? Is this good news or bad news for the company?

2. What was Dollarama's largest expense each year? In your own words, explain the meaning of this item. Give specific examples of items that make up this expense. Why is this expense less than sales revenue?

3. Use the balance sheet as at January 28, 2018, to answer these questions. How much in total resources did Dollarama have to work with? How much did the company owe? How much of its assets did the company's shareholders actually own? Use these amounts to write Dollarama's accounting equation at January 28, 2018 (express all items in millions of dollars).

4. How much cash did Dollarama have at January 29, 2017? How much cash did it have at January 28, 2018? What type of activities generated the most cash during 2018? What type of activities used the most cash?

5. Does Dollarama's financial condition look strong or weak? How can you tell?

CHECK YOUR WORK

STOP + THINK ANSWERS

STOP + THINK (1-1)

1. The business is incorporated with two shareholders, so it is a corporation.

2. The business is unincorporated and the owners share the workload and profits, so it is a partnership.

3. The business is unincorporated and run by Agata alone, so it is a proprietorship.

STOP + THINK (1-2)

1. $160,000 ($240,000 − $80,000)

2. $290,000 ($160,000 + $130,000)

3. Net income of $44,000 ($129,000 − $85,000); income minus expenses.

4. $115,000 [$100,000 beginning balance + net income of $25,000 ($75,000 − $50,000) − dividends of $10,000]

STOP + THINK (1-3)

After correcting for the missing $1,000 cash sale of services on December 31, 2020, Huron Ltd.'s financial statements would change as follows:

Income Statement

- Income will increase to $701,000 due to the extra $1,000 in sales revenue.
- Net income will increase to $31,000 because of the $1,000 increase in income.

Statement of Retained Earnings

- Ending retained earnings will increase to $141,000 due to the $1,000 increase in net income.

Balance Sheet

- Cash will increase to $26,000 because of the $1,000 in cash received from the customer.
- Total assets will increase to $301,000 after the $1,000 increase in cash.
- Retained earnings will increase to $141,000 (see above).
- Total liabilities and shareholders' equity will increase to $301,000 due to the $1,000 increase in retained earnings.

Statement of Cash Flows

- Net cash provided by operating activities will increase to $91,000 as a result of the $1,000 increase in net income.
- The Net increase in cash will now be $21,000 as a result of the added $1,000 in cash from operating activities.
- The ending cash balance will now be $26,000, which agrees to the new cash balance on the balance sheet noted above.

STOP + THINK (1-4)

1. According to the historical-cost assumption, the land would be recorded at a value of $46,000, its initial actual cost.
2. According to the historical-cost and going-concern assumptions, no adjustment would be made to the value of the land despite its increase in value to $60,000. IFRS do permit companies to adjust assets such as land to their fair values, but it is rare for companies to actually make these adjustments. Even under IFRS, assets are almost always left on the books at their historical costs.

STOP + THINK (1-5)

What Is the Issue?

Your boss has asked you to engage in fraudulent financial reporting by intentionally recording $1.2 million in fictitious sales to increase net income to a level that exceeds analysts' predicted amount.

Who Are the Stakeholders, and What Are the Consequences of the Decision to Each of Them?

You: If you do what the CEO wants, the CEO will be pleased and you may be rewarded with a bonus or promotion, but you will also have committed fraud and if it is ever discovered, you will be subject to criminal charges. If you have a CPA designation, you would also lose that if the fraud is discovered. If you do not do what the CEO wants, you may be fired or demoted, the company's share price may decline as a result of missing the analysts' forecast, and the CEO's reputation as a good manager could be tarnished, but you will not have committed fraud and therefore will not have to worry about losing your designation or being criminally charged.

CEO: If you do what the CEO wants, net income will come in above analysts' predictions, so the CEO will look like a good manager of the company's affairs and may be rewarded with a bonus and stock options. The value of any shares he owns may also increase, or at least will be less likely to decrease, so his wealth will benefit, but they would also be subject to criminal charges if the fraud is uncovered. If you do not do what the CEO wants, the company's share price may decline as a result of missing the analysts' forecast, and the CEO's reputation as a good manager could be tarnished, but they will not have committed fraud and therefore will not have to worry about being criminally charged.

Shareholders: If you do what the CEO wants, the value of the company's shares may increase, or at least will be less likely to decrease, so the shareholders' wealth will benefit in the short term, but if the fraud is eventually uncovered, the share price will likely drop drastically, perhaps all the way to zero, and all the shareholders will suffer significant financial losses. If you do not do what the CEO wants, the company's share price may decline in the short term as a result of missing the analysts' forecast, but if the CEO and other company managers can improve performance in future years, the share price may turn around, so in the long run, shareholders may end up much better off financially.

What Are the Decision Alternatives and How do they Affect Each Stakeholder?

The main alternatives are to do what the CEO asks and record the fictitious sales or to decline the request and leave the records as is. See above for the impact of each of these alternatives on the key stakeholders.

What Decision Alternative will you Choose?

The best decision from an ethical, legal, and long-term economic perspective is to leave the records as is and report the truthful results for the year. While this is the obvious best response, many accountants in practice have engaged in such fraudulent financial reporting because they viewed some of the other personal and wealth-related consequences above to outweigh the legal, ethical, and economic benefits of not engaging in fraud.

QUICK QUIZ ANSWERS

1. *a*
2. *a*
3. *c*
4. *a* ($20,000 − $4,000 = $16,000)
5. *b*
6. *d*
7. *b*
8. *b*
9. *d*
10. *b* ($140,000 − $59,000 − $8,000 − $3,000 = $70,000)
11. *a* ($145,000 + $90,000 − $30,000 = $205,000)
12. *c*
13. *c*

14. *a*

	Assets	=	Liabilities	+	Shareholders' Equity
beg	$25,000		$10,000		$15,000
change	+11,000		+8,000		+3,000
end	$36,000		$18,000		$18,000

15. *c*

	Assets	=	Liabilities	+	Shareholders' equity
2019	$520,000		$200,000		$320,000
2020	$750,000		$300,000		$450,000

$450,000 + $50,000 − 320,000 = $180,000

Recording Business Transactions

2

SPOTLIGHT

Apple Inc. Records Millions of Transactions a Year! Each time you purchase an app from Apple's App Store, it results in a business transaction.

And that's just the tip of the iceberg. If you go to Apple's online store or its iTunes store, as millions of people do every day, you can buy an iPhone, acquire accessories for your MacBook, download movies, and stream music—all for a price. All of these actions result in business transactions.

Apple earned $229.2 billion in revenues in 2017. The company also incurred $180.9 billion in expenses of various types, resulting in net income of about $48.4 billion that year. Where did those figures come from? From millions and millions of business transactions. In this chapter, we discuss business transactions, how they are recorded, and the role they play in the preparation of financial statements.

Zurijeta/Shutterstock

LEARNING OBJECTIVES

1. **Recognize** a business transaction and **describe** the various types of accounts in which it can be recorded
2. **Determine** the impact of business transactions on the accounting equation
3. **Analyze** business transactions using T-accounts
4. **Record** business transactions in the journal and **post** them to the ledger
5. **Prepare** and **use** a trial balance

CPA COMPETENCIES

Competencies addressed in this chapter:

1.3.1 Prepares financial statements

Based on Chartered Professional Accountant standards

The diagram below shows this chapter's learning objectives, which comprise the first five steps in the accounting cycle:

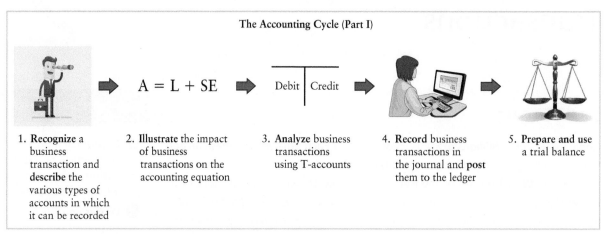

The Accounting Cycle (Part I)

1. **Recognize** a business transaction and **describe** the various types of accounts in which it can be recorded

2. **Illustrate** the impact of business transactions on the accounting equation

   $A = L + SE$

3. **Analyze** business transactions using T-accounts

4. **Record** business transactions in the journal and **post** them to the ledger

5. **Prepare and use** a trial balance

Images: Dim Tik/Shutterstock; Ganna Rassadnikova/123RF; Michelangelus/Shutterstock.

OBJECTIVE

❶ **Recognize** a business transaction and **describe** the various types of accounts in which it can be recorded

RECOGNIZE A BUSINESS TRANSACTION AND DESCRIBE THE VARIOUS TYPES OF ACCOUNTS IN WHICH IT CAN BE RECORDED

Businesses engage in many different activities, and most of these activities result in transactions that must be recorded in the accounting records. A **transaction** is any event that has a financial impact on a business and that can be reliably measured. For example, Apple pays engineers to create new hardware and software. Apple also sells computers, buys other companies, and repays debts. All four of these activities generate transactions that affect Apple's financial statements.

But not all activities qualify as transactions. The iPhone may be featured in TV ads, for example, which motivates some people to *consider* buying one. No transaction occurs, however, until someone *actually buys* an iPhone, which results in a positive financial impact on the company. A transaction must occur before Apple records anything in its accounting records.

Before we can record a transaction, we must also be able to reliably assign a dollar value to it, so that we have a measure of its financial impact on the business. If you were to purchase an iPhone from Apple's online store for $500, then Apple could reliably assign a dollar value to the transaction and it would then be permissible to record this sale in its accounting records.

Recall the accounting equation introduced in Chapter 1:

Assets = Liabilities + Shareholders' Equity

Each asset, liability, and element of shareholders' equity has its own **account**, which is used to record all the transactions affecting the related asset, liability, or element of shareholders' equity during an accounting period. Before we start learning how to record transactions in accounts, let's review some common types of accounts that companies such as Apple have in their accounting records.

Asset Accounts

Assets are economic resources that provide a future benefit for a business. Most companies have the following asset accounts in their accounting records:

CASH. Cash consists of bank account balances, paper currency and coins, and undeposited cheques.

ACCOUNTS RECEIVABLE. Accounts Receivable represent the amounts owing from customers who have purchased goods or services but not yet paid for them. In other words, they have purchased goods or services *on account* or *on credit*. The seller will *receive* payments on these *accounts* at some point in the near future. If Apple sells $1 million worth of iPads to a customer who promises to pay within 30 days, it would record an account receivable of $1 million from this customer.

INVENTORY. Inventory consists of the goods a company sells to its customers. Apple's inventory includes the iPhones, Apple Watches, and other products you see in its stores and advertisements. Companies that make the products they sell also have inventory consisting of the raw materials used to produce the finished products (e.g., the screens used to make iPhones) and any partially finished products (e.g., half-assembled MacBook computers), also known as work-in-progress inventory.

PREPAID EXPENSES. Prepaid Expenses are expenses a company has paid for in advance of actually using the product or service it has purchased. If, for example, on September 15, 2020, Apple paid $2 million for TV advertising time during the Super Bowl at the end of January 2021, this amount would be included in prepaid expenses on September 30, 2020, because Apple will not realize the benefit of this expense until the ads run four months after its September year-end date.

LAND. This account includes any land a company owns.

BUILDINGS. Any office buildings, factories, and other buildings owned by a company are included in the Buildings account.

EQUIPMENT, FURNITURE, AND FIXTURES. These accounts include a variety of office, computer, and manufacturing equipment, as well as any furniture and fixtures owned by a company.

Liability Accounts

Liabilities are obligations that will be repaid in the future using economic resources. You will see the following liability accounts in the accounting records of many companies:

ACCOUNTS PAYABLE. Accounts Payable represent the amounts a company owes to suppliers who have sold the company goods or services on credit. If Apple buys $1 million worth of flash drives from a supplier and promises to pay within 30 days, it would record an account payable of $1 million to this supplier.

ACCRUED LIABILITIES. An accrued liability is a liability for an expense that has been incurred but not yet billed or paid for. Examples include interest owed on bank loans, salaries owed to employees, and amounts owed to suppliers who have not yet sent invoices requesting payment.

LOANS PAYABLE. Loans Payable include funds a company has borrowed from banks and other creditors to finance its business activities.

Shareholders' Equity Accounts

Shareholders' equity represents the owners' claims to the assets of the corporation. The Shareholders' Equity accounts found in a corporation's accounting records include the following:

SHARE CAPITAL. The Share Capital account includes the capital (usually in the form of cash) a company has received from its owners in exchange for shares of the company. This account is sometimes called Common Shares, which is the most basic element of equity.

RETAINED EARNINGS. The Retained Earnings account shows the cumulative net income earned by the company over its lifetime, minus its cumulative net losses and dividends.

DIVIDENDS. The Dividends account includes dividends that have been declared during the current fiscal period. Dividends are payments to shareholders that represent the distribution of some of the company's past earnings. Dividends decrease a company's Retained Earnings.

REVENUES. Revenues are a form of income that companies typically earn through the sale of their primary goods and services. Apple, for instance, would use an iPhone Revenue account to record its sales of that product. Scotiabank loans money to its clients and uses an Interest Revenue account to track the interest it receives on these loans. Revenues increase a company's Retained Earnings.

EXPENSES. Expenses consist mainly of the costs incurred to purchase the goods and services a company needs to run its business. Common types of expenses include Salary Expense, Rent Expense, Advertising Expense, and Utilities Expense. Expenses decrease a company's Retained Earnings.

MyLab Accounting

STOP + THINK (2-1)

You were reading Apple's most recent financial statements and wondered:

1. What are two distinct types of transactions that would increase Apple's shareholders' equity?
2. What are two distinct types of transactions that would decrease Apple's shareholders' equity?

OBJECTIVE

❷ **Determine** the impact of business transactions on the accounting equation

DETERMINE THE IMPACT OF BUSINESS TRANSACTIONS ON THE ACCOUNTING EQUATION

To illustrate accounting for business transactions, let's return to J.J. Booth and Marie Savard. You met them in Chapter 1, when they opened a consulting engineering company on April 1, 2020, and incorporated it as Tara Inc. (Tara for short).

We will consider 11 transactions and use a spreadsheet to illustrate the effects of each one on Tara's accounting equation. In the latter part of the chapter, we will record these same 11 transactions using the formal accounting records of Tara.

TRY IT *in* EXCEL®▶▶▶

As you review the 11 transactions, build an Excel spreadsheet. Use the accounting equation in Chapter 1 on page 12 as a model. Remember that each transaction has either an equal effect on both the left- and right-hand sides of the accounting equation, or an offsetting effect (both positive and negative) on the same side of the equation. Recreate the spreadsheet in Exhibit 2-1, Panel B (page 64), step by step, as you go along. In Excel, open a new blank spreadsheet.

Step 1 Format the worksheet. Label cell A2 "Trans." You will put transaction numbers corresponding to the transactions below in the cells in column A. Row 1 will contain the elements of the accounting equation. Enter "Assets" in cell D1. Enter an "=" sign in cell F1. Enter "Liabilities +Shareholders' equity" in cell G1. Enter "Type of SE (abbreviation for shareholders' equity) Transaction" in cell J1. Highlight cells B1 through E1 and click "merge and center" on the top toolbar. Highlight cells G1 through I1 and click "merge and center." Now you will have a spreadsheet organized around the elements of the accounting equation: "Assets = Liabilities + Shareholders' equity" and, for all transactions impacting shareholders' equity, you will be able to enter the type (common shares, revenue, expense, or dividends). This will be important for later when you construct the financial statements (Exhibit 2-2, page 65).

Step 2 Continue formatting. In cells B2 through E2, enter the asset account titles that transactions 1–11 deal with. B2: Cash; C2: AR (an abbreviation for accounts receivable); D2: Supplies; E2: Land. In cells G2 through I2, enter the liability and shareholders' equity account titles that Tara Inc.'s transactions deal with. G2: AP (an abbreviation for accounts payable); H2: C Shares (an abbreviation for common shares); and I2: RE (abbreviation for retained earnings; this is where all transactions impacting revenue, expenses, and dividends will go for now).

Step 3 In row 15, sum each column from B through E and G through I. For example, the formula in cell B15 should be "=sum(B3:B14)." In cell A15, enter "Bal." This will allow you to keep a running sum of the accounts in the balance sheet as you enter each transaction.

Step 4 In cell A16, enter "Totals." In cell C16, enter "=sum(B15:E15)." In cell H16, enter "=sum(G15:I15)." You can use the short cut symbol "Σ" followed by highlighting the respective cells. Excel allows you to keep a running sum of the column totals on each side of the equation. You should find that the running sum of the column totals on the left-hand side of the equation always equals the running sum of the column totals on the right-hand side, so the accounting equation always stays in balance. As a final formatting step, highlight cells B3 through I16. Using the "number" tab on the toolbar at the top of the spreadsheet, select "Accounting" as for format with no $ sign, and select "decrease decimal" to zero places. Now you're ready to process the transactions.

TRANSACTION 1. Booth, Savard, and several fellow engineers invest $50,000 to begin Tara, and the business issues common shares to the shareholders. The effects of this transaction on the accounting equation are as follows:

	ASSETS Cash	} = {	LIABILITIES	+	SHAREHOLDERS' EQUITY Share Capital	TYPE OF SHAREHOLDERS' EQUITY TRANSACTION
(1)	+50,000				+50,000	Issued common shares

For every transaction, the net amount on the left side of the equation must equal the net amount on the right side so that the equation stays in balance. The first transaction increases both the cash and the share capital of the business by $50,000. If you're following along in Excel, enter 1 in cell A3 of the spreadsheet you are creating. Enter 50000 in cell B3 (under Cash) and 50000 in cell H3 (under C Shares). To the right of the transaction in cell J3 write "Issued common shares" to show the reason for the increase in shareholders' equity. You don't have to enter commas; Excel will do that for you. Notice that the sum of Cash (cell B15) is now $50,000 and the sum of Common Shares (cell H15) is also $50,000. The total of accounts on the left side of the accounting equation is 50,000 (cell C16) and it equals the total of accounts on the right side of the accounting equation (cell H16).

	A	B	C	D	E
1	**Tara Inc.** Balance Sheet As at April 1, 2020				
2	**Assets**		**Liabilities**		
3	Cash	$ 50,000	None		
4			**Shareholders' Equity**		
5			Common shares	$ 50,000	
6			Total shareholders' equity	50,000	
7	Total assets	$ 50,000	Total liabilities and shareholders' equity	$ 50,000	
8					

Every transaction affects the financial statements, and we can prepare the statements after one, two, or any number of transactions. Tara, for example, could prepare the above balance sheet after its first transaction. This balance sheet reports that Tara has $50,000 in cash, no liabilities, and share capital of $50,000 as at April 1, 2020, its first day of operations.

As a practical matter, entities report their financial statements at the end of an accounting period, typically monthly, quarterly, and annually. An accounting system can, however, produce statements whenever managers need to know where the business stands.

TRANSACTION 2. Tara purchases land for an office location and pays cash of $40,000. The effect of this transaction on the accounting equation is:

	ASSETS			LIABILITIES	+	SHAREHOLDERS' EQUITY
	Cash	+	Land			Share Capital
Balance	50,000					50,000
(2)	−40,000		+40,000	=		
Bal.	10,000		40,000			50,000
		50,000				50,000

The purchase increases one asset (Land) and decreases another asset (Cash) by the same amount. If you're following along in Excel, enter a 2 in cell A4. Enter −40000 in cell B4 and 40000 in cell E4. The spreadsheet automatically updates, showing that after the transaction is completed, Tara has cash of $10,000, land of $40,000, total assets of $50,000, and no liabilities. Shareholders' equity is unchanged at $50,000. Note that, as shown in cells C16 and H16, total assets still equal total liabilities plus shareholders' equity.

TRANSACTION 3. Tara buys stationery and other office supplies on account, agreeing to pay $3,700 within 30 days. This transaction increases both the assets and the liabilities of the business. Its effect on the accounting equation is:

	ASSETS				LIABILITIES	+	SHAREHOLDERS' EQUITY
	Cash	+	Office Supplies	+ Land	Accounts Payable	+	Share Capital
Bal.	10,000			40,000			50,000
(3)			+3,700		+3,700		
Bal.	10,000		3,700	40,000	3,700		50,000
			53,700			53,700	

The new asset is Office Supplies (which is a prepaid expense), and the liability is Accounts Payable. If you're following along in Excel, enter 3 in cell A5, 3700 in cell D5 under the account "Supplies" and 3700 in cell G5 under "AP" (accounts payable). Notice that the spreadsheet now reflects 3 assets in row 15: cash with a balance of $10,000 (cell B15), supplies with a balance of $3,700 (cell D15), and land with a balance of $40,000 (cell E15), for total assets of $53,700 (cell C16). On the right-hand side of the accounting equation, Tara now has accounts payable (a liability) of $3,700 (cell G15) and common shares (cell H15) of $50,000, for a total of $53,700 (cell H16).

TRANSACTION 4. Tara earns service revenue by providing engineering services. Assume the business provides $7,000 in such services and collects this amount in cash. The effect on the accounting equation is an increase in the asset Cash and an increase in Retained Earnings, a shareholders' equity account:

	ASSETS					LIABILITIES	+	SHAREHOLDERS' EQUITY			TYPE OF SHAREHOLDERS' EQUITY TRANSACTION
	Cash	+	Office Supplies	+	Land	Accounts Payable	+	Share Capital	+ Retained Earnings		
Bal.	10,000		3,700		40,000	3,700		50,000			
(4)	+7,000								7,000		Service revenue
Bal.	17,000		3,700		40,000	3,700		50,000	7,000		
			60,700					60,700			

To the right we record "Service revenue" to show where the $7,000 increase in Retained Earnings came from. In the Excel spreadsheet on line 6, we enter 7000 under Cash (cell B6) and 7000 under Retained Earnings (cell I6). In cell J6, we enter "Service revenue" to show where the $7,000 increase in Retained Earnings came from. Our grand totals on the bottom of the spreadsheet now show $60,700 for total assets as well as $60,700 for total liabilities and shareholders' equity.

TRANSACTION 5. In this transaction, Tara provides $3,000 in engineering services to King Contracting Ltd., and King promises to pay Tara within one month. This promise represents an asset for Tara in the form of an account receivable. The impact of this transaction on the accounting equation is as follows:

	ASSETS					LIABILITIES +		SHAREHOLDERS' EQUITY			TYPE OF SHAREHOLDERS' EQUITY TRANSACTION
	Cash +	Accounts Receivable +	Office Supplies	+ Land		Accounts Payable	+	Share Capital	+ Retained Earnings		
Bal.	17,000		3,700	40,000		3,700		50,000	7,000		
(5)		+3,000							+3,000		Service revenue
Bal.	17,000	3,000	3,700	40,000		3,700		50,000	10,000		
			63,700					63,700			

Tara records (or recognizes) revenue when it performs the service, regardless of whether it receives the cash now or later. You will learn more about revenue recognition in the next chapter. In your Excel spreadsheet, enter 3000 under Accounts Receivable on the left-hand side (cell C7) and 3000 under Retained Earnings (RE) on the right-hand side (cell I7). Also enter "Service revenue" in cell J7 to keep a record of the type of transaction (revenue) that affects shareholders' equity.

TRANSACTION 6. During the month, Tara pays for the following expenses: office rent, $1,100; employee salary, $1,200; and utilities, $400. The effect on the accounting equation is:

		ASSETS				LIABILITIES	+	SHAREHOLDERS' EQUITY			TYPE OF SHAREHOLDERS' EQUITY TRANSACTION
	Cash +	Accounts Receivable +	Office Supplies +	Land		Accounts Payable	+	Share Capital +	Retained Earnings		
Bal.	17,000	3,000	3,700	40,000		3,700		50,000	10,000		
(6)	−1,100				=				−1,100		Rent expense
	−1,200								−1,200		Salary expense
	− 400								− 400		Utilities expense
Bal.	14,300	3,000	3,700	40,000		3,700		50,000	7,300		
		61,000						61,000			

This transaction will take up lines 8, 9, and 10 of the Excel spreadsheet. Enter −2700 under Cash (cell B8); −1100 under Retained Earnings (cell I8); −1200 under Retained Earnings (cell I9); and −400 under Retained Earnings (cell I10). Enter the type of transaction beside each amount (rent expense, salary expense, utilities expense) to account for the type of transaction impacting shareholders' equity (SE). These expenses decrease Tara's Cash and Retained Earnings. We list each expense separately to keep track of its amount and to facilitate the preparation of the income statement later.

TRANSACTION 7. Tara pays $1,900 of the balance owing to the store from which it purchased Office Supplies in Transaction 3. The transaction decreases Cash (cell B11) and also decreases Accounts Payable (cell G11):

		ASSETS				LIABILITIES	+	SHAREHOLDERS' EQUITY		
	Cash +	Accounts Receivable +	Office Supplies +	Land		Accounts Payable	+	Share Capital +	Retained Earnings	
Bal.	14,300	3,000	3,700	40,000	=	3,700		50,000	7,300	
(7)	−1,900					−1,900				
Bal.	12,400	3,000	3,700	40,000		1,800		50,000	7,300	
		59,100						59,100		

TRANSACTION 8. J.J. Booth paid $30,000 to remodel his home. This event is a personal transaction of J.J. Booth, so according to the separate-entity assumption from Chapter 1, we do not record it in the accounting records of Tara. Business transactions must be kept separate from the personal transactions of the business's owners.

TRANSACTION 9. In Transaction 5, Tara Inc. performed services for King Contracting on account. Tara now collects $1,000 from King Contracting, which means Tara will record an increase in Cash and a decrease in Accounts Receivable. This is not service revenue now because Tara already recorded the revenue in Transaction 5. The effect of this transaction is:

| | ASSETS | | | | | LIABILITIES | + | SHAREHOLDERS' EQUITY | | |
	Cash +	Accounts + Receivable	Office + Supplies	Land		Accounts Payable	+	Share Capital	+	Retained Earnings
Bal.	12,400	3,000	3,700	40,000	=	1,800		50,000		7,300
(9)	+1,000	−1,000								
Bal.	13,400	2,000	3,700	40,000		1,800		50,000		7,300
		59,100						59,100		

This transaction is entered on line 12 of the Excel spreadsheet as an increase in Cash (cell B12) and a decrease in AR (cell C12).

TRANSACTION 10. Tara sells part of the land purchased in Transaction 2 for $22,000, which is the same amount Tara paid for that part of the land. Tara receives $22,000 cash, and the effect on the accounting equation is:

| | ASSETS | | | | | LIABILITIES | + | SHAREHOLDERS' EQUITY | | |
	Cash +	Accounts + Receivable	Office + Supplies	Land		Accounts Payable	+	Share Capital	+	Retained Earnings
Bal.	13,400	2,000	3,700	40,000	=	1,800		50,000		7,300
(10)	+22,000			−22,000						
Bal.	35,400	2,000	3,700	18,000		1,800		50,000		7,300
		59,100						59,100		

Note that the company did not sell all its land; Tara still owns $18,000 worth of land. This transaction is entered in the Excel spreadsheet as an increase in Cash (cell B13) and a decrease in Land (cell E13).

TRANSACTION 11. Tara pays the shareholders a $2,100 cash dividend. The effect on the accounting equation is:

| | ASSETS | | | | | LIABILITIES | + | SHAREHOLDERS' EQUITY | | | TYPE OF SHAREHOLDERS' EQUITY TRANSACTION |
	Cash +	Accounts + Receivable	Office + Supplies	Land		Accounts Payable	+	Share Capital	+	Retained Earnings	
Bal.	35,400	2,000	3,700	18,000	=	1,800		50,000		7,300	
(11)	−2,100									−2,100	Dividends
Bal.	33,300	2,000	3,700	18,000		1,800		50,000		5,200	
		57,000						57,000			

The dividend decreases both Cash (cell B14) and the Retained Earnings (cell I14) of the business. *Dividends, however, are not an expense*; they directly reduce Retained Earnings. Therefore, enter "Dividend" in cell J14. We now have all the transactions affecting shareholders' equity labelled properly, which will facilitate the preparation of the financial statements later.

Transactions and Financial Statements

Exhibit 2-1 summarizes the 11 preceding transactions. Panel A gives the details of the transactions, and Panel B illustrates the impact on the accounting equation for each one that affects the business. As you study the exhibit, note that every transaction in Panel B keeps the accounting equation in balance.

EXHIBIT 2-1
Transaction Analysis: Tara Inc.

MyLab Accounting

Panel A—Transaction Details

(1) Received $50,000 cash and issued shares to the owners
(2) Paid $40,000 cash for land
(3) Bought $3,700 of office supplies on account
(4) Received $7,000 cash from customers for engineering services performed
(5) Performed services for customers on account, $3,000
(6) Paid cash for expenses: rent, $1,100; employee salary, $1,200; utilities, $400

(7) Paid $1,900 on the account payable from Transaction 3
(8) Shareholder uses personal funds to remodel home, which is *not* a transaction of the business
(9) Received $1,000 of the accounts receivable from Transaction 5
(10) Sold land for cash at its cost of $22,000
(11) Declared and paid a dividend of $2,100 to the shareholders

Panel B—Transaction Analysis

	A	B	C	D	E	F	G	H	I	J
1			**Assets**			**=**	**Liabilities +**	**Shareholders' Equity**		**Type of SE transaction**
2	Trans	Cash	AR	Supplies	Land		AP	C Shares	RE	
3	1	50,000						50,000		Issued common shares
4	2	(40,000)			40,000					
5	3			3,700			3,700			
6	4	7,000							7,000	Service revenue
7	5		3,000						3,000	Service revenue
8	6	(2,700)							(1,100)	Rent expense
9									(1,200)	Salary expense
10									(400)	Utilities expense
11	7	(1,900)					(1,900)			
12	9	1,000	(1,000)							
13	10	22,000			(22,000)					
14	11	(2,100)							(2,100)	Dividend
15	Bal	33,300	2,000	3,700	18,000		1,800	50,000	5,200	
16	Totals		57,000					57,000		
17										

Statement of Cash Flows Data (rows 3–14, column A/B)

Income Statement Data (rows 6–10, column I/J)

Statement of Retained Earnings Data (rows 14–15)

Balance Sheet Data

Panel B in Exhibit 2-1 also provides the data needed to prepare Tara's financial statements:

- *Income statement* data appear as revenues and expenses under Retained Earnings. The revenues increase Retained Earnings; the expenses decrease Retained Earnings.

- The *balance sheet* data are composed of the ending balances of the assets, liabilities, and shareholders' equity shown at the bottom of the exhibit. The accounting equation shows that total assets ($57,000) equal total liabilities plus shareholders' equity ($57,000).

- The *statement of retained earnings* reports net income (or net loss) from the income statement. Dividends are subtracted. Ending retained earnings is the final result.

- Data for the *statement of cash flows* are aligned under the Cash account. Cash receipts increase cash, and cash payments decrease cash.

Exhibit 2-2 presents the Tara Inc. financial statements for April, the company's first month of operations. Follow the flow of data to observe the following:

1. The income statement reports revenues, expenses, and either a net income or a net loss for the period. During April, Tara earned net income of $7,300. From the transaction analysis spreadsheet in Exhibit 2-1, Panel B, service revenue

EXHIBIT 2-2
Financial Statements of Tara Inc.

	A	B	C	D
1	**Tara Inc.** Income Statement For the Month Ended April 30, 2020			
2	Revenues			
3	Service revenue ($7,000 + $3,000)		$ 10,000	
4	**Expenses**			
5	Salary expense	$ 1,200		
6	Rent expense	1,100		
7	Utilities expense	400		
8	Total expenses		2,700	
9	Net income		$ 7,300	
10				

	A	B	C	D
1	**Tara Inc.** Statement of Retained Earnings For the Month Ended April 30, 2020			
2	Retained earnings, April 1, 2020		$ 0	
3	Add: Net income for the month		7,300	
4	Subtotal		7,300	
5	Less: Dividends declared		(2,100)	
6	Retained earnings, April 30, 2020		$ 5,200	
7				

	A	B	C	D	E
1	**Tara Inc.** Balance Sheet As at April 30, 2020				
2	**Assets**		**Liabilities**		
3	Cash	$ 33,300	Accounts payable	$ 1,800	
4	Accounts receivable	2,000	**Shareholders' Equity**		
5	Office supplies	3,700	Common shares	50,000	
6	Land	18,000	Retained earnings	5,200	
7			Total shareholders' equity	55,200	
8	Total assets	$ 57,000	Total liabilities and shareholders' equity	$ 57,000	
9					

①

②

consists of the sum of cells I6 and I7 ($7,000 for cash and $3,000 on account). Expenses (salary $1,200 from cell I9, rent $1,100 from cell I8, and utilities $400 from cell I10) are listed separately in the income statement. The sum of these expenses is $2,700. Net income consists of the difference between service revenue and total expenses ($10,000 − $2,700 = $7,300). This is known as a "single-step" income statement because it includes only two types of accounts: revenues and expenses.

2. The statement of retained earnings starts with the beginning balance of retained earnings (zero for a new business). Add net income for the period from the income statement $7,300 (arrow ①), subtract dividends ($2,100 from cell I14 of the transaction analysis spreadsheet in Exhibit 2-1, Panel B), and compute the ending balance of retained earnings ($5,200).

3. The balance sheet lists the assets, liabilities, and shareholders' equity of the business at the end of the period. The assets consist of the totals of cash, accounts receivable, supplies, and land (see cells B15 through E15 in Exhibit 2-1 Panel B). Liabilities consist of only accounts payable (cell G15). Common shares carries over from cell H15. Also included in shareholders' equity is retained earnings, which comes from the statement of retained earnings (arrow ②). It has also been accumulated in cell I15 of Exhibit 2-1, Panel B.

TRY IT *in* EXCEL® ▶▶▶

If you are familiar with Excel, a quick look at Exhibit 2-2 should convince you of how easy it is to prepare the income statement, statement of retained earnings, and balance sheet in Excel. Prepare three simple templates for each of these financial statements for Tara Inc. You may use these templates again, and add to them, in Chapter 3 as you learn the adjusting-entry process. The mid-chapter summary problem will illustrate this using another small company.

STOP + THINK (2-2)

If on May 1, 2020, Tara Inc. receives a $5,000 loan from its bank, what effects would this transaction have on the assets, liabilities, and shareholders' equity of the business as reported in its April 30, 2020, balance sheet shown in Exhibit 2-2?

MyLab Accounting

MID-CHAPTER SUMMARY PROBLEM

Margaret Jarvis opens a research services business near a college campus. She names the corporation Jarvis Research Inc. During the first month of operations, July 2020, Margaret and the business engage in the following activities:

a. Jarvis Research Inc. issues common shares to Margaret Jarvis, who invests $25,000 to open the business.

b. The company purchases, on account, office supplies costing $350.

c. Jarvis Research Inc. pays cash of $20,000 to acquire a lot near the campus. The company intends to use the land as a building site for a business office.

d. Jarvis Research Inc. performs services for clients and receives cash of $1,900.

e. Jarvis Research Inc. pays $100 on the account payable from Transaction (b).

f. Margaret Jarvis pays $2,000 in personal funds for a vacation.

g. Jarvis Research Inc. pays cash expenses for office rent ($400) and utilities ($100).

h. The business sells a small parcel of the land it purchased for its cost of $5,000.

i. The business declares and pays a cash dividend of $1,200.

Requirements

1. Using Excel, build a spreadsheet to analyze the preceding transactions in terms of their effects on the accounting equation of Jarvis Research Inc. Use Exhibit 2-1, Panel B, as a guide.

2. Using Excel, prepare the income statement, statement of retained earnings, and balance sheet of Jarvis Research Inc., after recording the transactions. Draw arrows linking the statements. Use Exhibit 2-2 as a guide.

> **Name:** Jarvis Research Inc.
> **Industry:** Research services
> **Fiscal Period:** Month of July 2020
> **Key Facts:** New business

SOLUTIONS

Requirement 1

> Add all the asset balances and add all the liabilities and shareholders' equity balances. Make sure that Total assets = Total liabilities + Shareholders' equity.

	A	B	C	D	E	F	G	H	I
1			Assets		=	Liabilities +	Shareholders' Equity		Type of SE transaction
2	Trans	Cash	Office Supplies	Land		AP	C Shares	RE	
3	a	25,000					25,000		Issued common shares
4	b		350			350			
5	c	(20,000)		20,000					
6	d	1,900						1,900	Service revenue
7	e	(100)				(100)			
8	f(n/a)								
9	g	(400)						(400)	Rent expense
10		(100)						(100)	Utilities expense
11	h	5,000		(5,000)					
12	i	(1,200)						(1,200)	Dividend
13	Bal	10,100	350	15,000		250	25,000	200	
14	Totals		25,450				25,450		
15									

Requirement 2

The title must include the name of the company, "Income Statement," and the specific period of time covered. It is critical that the time period be defined.

	A	B	C	D
1	**Jarvis Research Inc.** Income Statement For the Month Ended July 31, 2020			
2	**Revenues**			
3	Service revenue		$ 1,900	
4	**Expenses**			
5	Rent expense	$ 400		
6	Utilities expense	100		
7	Total expenses		500	
8	Net income		$ 1,400	
9				

Use the revenue and expense amounts from the Retained Earnings column and names from the Type of Shareholders' Equity Transaction column.

The title must include the name of the company, "Statement of Retained Earnings," and the specific period of time covered. It is critical that the time period be defined.

	A	B	C	D
1	**Jarvis Research Inc.** Statement of Retained Earnings For the Month Ended July 31, 2020			
2	Retained earnings, July 1, 2020		$ 0	
3	Add: Net income for the month		1,400	
4	Subtotal		1,400	
5	Less: Dividends declared		(1,200)	
6	Retained earnings, July 31, 2020		$ 200	
7				

Beginning retained earnings is $0 because this is the first year of operations. The net income amount is transferred from the income statement. The dividends amount is from the Retained Earnings column.

The title must include the name of the company, "Balance Sheet," and the date of the balance sheet. It shows the financial position at the end of business on a specific date.

Gather the asset, liability, and shareholders' equity accounts. Insert the final balances for each account from the Balance row. The retained earnings amount is transferred from the statement of retained earnings. It is imperative that Total assets = Total liabilities + Shareholders' equity.

	A	B	C	D	E
1	**Jarvis Research Inc.** Balance Sheet As at July 31, 2020				
2	**Assets**		**Liabilities**		
3	Cash	$ 10,100	Accounts payable	$ 250	
4	Office supplies	350	**Shareholders' Equity**		
5	Land	15,000	Common shares	25,000	
6			Retained earnings	200	
7			Total shareholders' equity	25,200	
8	Total assets	$ 25,450	Total liabilities and shareholders' equity	$ 25,450	
9					

ANALYZE BUSINESS TRANSACTIONS USING T-ACCOUNTS

We could use the accounting equation to record all of a business's transactions, but it would be very cumbersome, even for a small business with a low volume of transactions. In this section, we introduce the **double-entry system** of accounting, which is the method that all but the smallest of businesses use to record transactions.

It is called the double-entry system because every transaction has two sides and affects two (or more) accounts. When Tara Inc. issued common shares for $50,000 in cash, for example, one side of the transaction was a $50,000 increase in the Cash account and the other side was a $50,000 increase in the Share Capital account. We must record both sides of every transaction to keep the accounting equation in balance. If we record only a single entry for the $50,000 increase in Cash, the accounting equation would be out of balance, so we must make a second entry in Share Capital to account for the $50,000 increase in equity.

Chart of Accounts

An organization uses a **chart of accounts** to keep track of all its accounts. The chart of accounts lists the name of every account and its unique account number, but it does not provide the account balances. If an accountant is unsure about what account to use when recording a transaction, they can consult the chart of accounts to help them choose the most appropriate one. If the chart of accounts does not contain an appropriate account, the accountant can add a new account to the chart and use it to record the transaction.

Exhibit 2-3 presents Tara Inc.'s chart of accounts. The gaps between account numbers leave room to insert new accounts. In the illustrations that follow, we leave out the account numbers to avoid cluttering the presentation.

EXHIBIT 2-3
Chart of Accounts—Tara Inc.

Balance Sheet Accounts		
Assets	**Liabilities**	**Shareholders' Equity**
101 Cash	201 Accounts Payable	301 Share Capital
111 Accounts Receivable	231 Notes Payable	311 Dividends
141 Office Supplies		312 Retained Earnings
151 Office Furniture		
191 Land		

Income Statement Accounts (Part of Shareholders' Equity)	
Revenues	**Expenses**
401 Service Revenue	501 Rent Expense
	502 Salary Expense
	503 Utilities Expense

The T-Account

We can represent an account using the letter T, which we call a *T-account*. The vertical line divides the account into left and right sides, while the account title rests on the horizontal line. The Cash T-account, for example, looks like this:

Cash
(Left side) | (Right side)
Debit | *Credit*

The left side of the account is called the **debit** side, and the right side is called the **credit** side. Students are often confused by the words *debit* and *credit*, so it may help to remember that for every account:

Debit = Left side | Credit = Right side

Using these terms, we can refine our description of a transaction as having two sides: a debit side and a credit side. The double-entry system records both sides and requires that *the debit side equals the credit side* so that the accounting equation stays in balance.

Increases and Decreases in the Accounts: The Rules of Debit and Credit

The way we record increases and decreases to an account under the double-entry system varies by account type. *The rules of debit and credit* are as follows (see Exhibit 2-4 for an illustration):

- *Increases* in assets are recorded on the *left* (*debit*) side of the T-account, whereas *decreases* are recorded on the *right* (*credit*) side. When a business receives cash, the Cash account *increases*, so we *debit* the *left side* of the Cash account to record the increase in this asset. When a business makes a cash payment, we *credit* the *right* side of the Cash account to record the *decrease* in this account.

- Conversely, *increases* in liabilities and shareholders' equity are recorded on the *right* (*credit*) side of the T-account, whereas *decreases* are recorded on the *left* (*debit*) side. When a business receives a loan, the Loan Payable account *increases*, so we *credit* the *right side* of the Loan Payable account to record the increase in this liability. When a business makes a loan payment, we *debit* the *left* side of the Loan Payable account to record the *decrease* in this account.

EXHIBIT 2-4
Accounting Equation and the Rules of Debit and Credit

Let's use Tara Inc.'s first two transactions to apply the rules of debit and credit illustrated in Exhibit 2-4. In Transaction (1), Tara received $50,000 in cash and issued common shares in return. As a result, we debit the left side of the Cash account to record the increase in this asset and credit the right side of the Share Capital account to record the increase in shareholders' equity. These two entries are illustrated in the T-accounts in Exhibit 2-5. After recording both sides of this transaction, the debits equal the credits ($50,000 each), so the accounting equation is in balance.

EXHIBIT 2-5
T-accounts After Tara Inc.'s First Two Transactions

	Cash				Share Capital
(1) Debit for increase	50,000	(2) Credit for decrease	40,000		(1) Credit for increase 50,000
Balance	10,000				Balance 50,000

	Land
(2) Debit for increase	40,000
Balance	40,000

In Transaction (2), Tara purchased land for $40,000 in cash. To record the two sides of this transaction, we debit the left side of the Land account to record the increase in this asset and credit the right side of the Cash account to record the decrease in this asset. Again, the debits equal the credits ($40,000 each) after recording both sides of this transaction.

After both transactions, the Cash account has a $10,000 debit balance, the Land account a $40,000 debit balance, and the Share Capital account a $50,000 credit balance. The total of the debit balances ($50,000) equals the only credit balance, so the accounting equation is in balance after these transactions, as illustrated in Exhibit 2-6.

EXHIBIT 2-6
The Accounting Equation After Tara Inc.'s First Two Transactions

	Assets	=	Liabilities	+	Shareholders' Equity
Cash $10,000					
Land $40,000					Share capital
$50,000					$50,000

The Expanded Accounting Equation

Because several accounts from three separate financial statements affect shareholders' equity, we can expand the accounting equation to explicitly reflect the impact of changes in these accounts on shareholders' equity, as shown in Exhibit 2-7. Revenues and expenses are shown in parentheses to indicate their inclusion in the calculation of net income.

EXHIBIT 2-7
The Expanded Accounting Equation

Based on this expanded equation, we can express the rules of debit and credit in more detail, as shown in Exhibit 2-8. *You should not proceed until you have learned these rules*, and you must remember the following:

- To record an increase in assets, use a debit.
- To record a decrease in assets, use a credit.

For liabilities and shareholders' equity, these rules are reversed:

- To record an increase in liabilities or shareholders' equity, use a credit.
- To record a decrease in liabilities or shareholders' equity, use a debit.

EXHIBIT 2-8
The Expanded Rules of Debit and Credit

ASSETS	=	LIABILITIES	+		SHAREHOLDERS' EQUITY		
Assets		Liabilities		Share Capital	Retained Earnings		Dividends

Debit	Credit		Debit	Credit		Debit	Credit		Debit	Credit		Debit	Credit
+	–		–	+		–	+		–	+		+	–
Normal				Normal			Normal			Normal		Normal	
balance				balance			balance			balance		balance	

	Revenues		Expenses	
	Debit	Credit	Debit	Credit
	–	+	+	–
		Normal	Normal	
		balance	Balance	

Recall that *increases* in Dividends and Expenses result in *decreases* to shareholders' equity, so applying the last rule above means that increases to Dividends and Expenses are recorded using debits, which is the opposite of the "increase = credit" rule for all other shareholders' equity accounts.

Exhibit 2-8 also highlights which side of each account the *normal balance* (debit or credit) falls on, which is the side where increases to the account are recorded (denoted by a "+" sign).

Analyzing Transactions Using Only T-Accounts

We can quickly assess the financial impact of a proposed business transaction by analyzing it informally using T-accounts. Assume, for example, that a manager is considering (a) taking out a $100,000 loan to (b) purchase $100,000 worth of equipment. The manager could record these proposed transactions in T-accounts as follows:

Cash		Equipment		Loan Payable	
(a) 100,000	(b) 100,000	(b) 100,000			(a) 100,000

This informal analysis shows the manager that the net impact of these proposed transactions will be a $100,000 increase in Equipment, with a corresponding increase in the Loan Payable account. Managers who can analyze proposed transactions this way can make business decisions with a clear idea of their impact on the company's financial statements.

STOP + THINK (2-3)

In Stop + Think 2-2, Tara Inc. received a $5,000 loan from its bank. Use debit and credit terminology to explain the effects of this transaction on Tara's accounts.

RECORD BUSINESS TRANSACTIONS IN THE JOURNAL AND POST THEM TO THE LEDGER

OBJECTIVE

❹ **Record** business transactions in the journal and **post** them to the ledger

When recording transactions, accountants use a chronological record called a **journal**. The recording process follows these three steps:

1. Specify each account affected by the transaction.
2. Use the rules of debit and credit to determine whether each account is increased or decreased by the transaction.
3. Record the transaction in the journal, including a brief explanation for the entry and the date of the transaction. The debit side is entered on the left margin, and the credit side is indented slightly to the right.

Step 3 is also called "recording the journal entry" or "journalizing the transaction." Let's apply the steps to record the first transaction of Tara Inc.

Step 1 The business receives cash and issues shares. Cash and Share Capital are affected.

Step 2 Both Cash and Share Capital increase. Debit Cash to record an increase in this asset. Credit Share Capital to record an increase in this equity account.

Step 3 Record the journal entry for the transaction, as illustrated in Panel A of Exhibit 2-9.

EXHIBIT 2-9
Recording a Journal Entry and Posting it to the Ledger

PANEL A—Recording the Journal Entry

	A	B	C	D	E
1	Date	Accounts and Explanation	Debit	Credit	
2	Apr. 1, 2020	Cash	50,000		
3		Share Capital		50,000	
4		Issued common shares.			
5					

PANEL B—Posting it to the Ledger

Cash	Share Capital
50,000	50,000

Posting from the Journal to the Ledger

The journal is a chronological record containing all of a company's transactions. The journal does not, however, indicate the balances in any of the company's accounts. To obtain these balances, we must transfer information from the journal to the **ledger**, which is an accounting process we call **posting**.

The ledger contains all of a company's accounts, along with their balances as of the most recent posting date. Posting is a simple process of directly transferring information from the journal to the ledger: debits in the journal are posted as debits in the ledger accounts, and likewise for credits. Exhibit 2-9 shows the posting of Tara Inc.'s first transaction from the journal to the ledger.

The Flow of Accounting Data

Exhibit 2-10 summarizes the flow of accounting data from the business transaction to the ledger. Let's practise using this process by revisiting Tara Inc.'s transactions for the month of April 2020. We will analyze each transaction, record it in Tara's journal (if necessary), then post it to the ledger.

EXHIBIT 2-10
Flow of Accounting Data

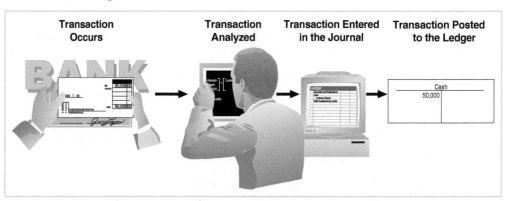

| Transaction Occurs | Transaction Analyzed | Transaction Entered in the Journal | Transaction Posted to the Ledger |

TRANSACTION 1 ANALYSIS. Tara received $50,000 cash from shareholders and in turn issued Share Capital to them. The accounting equation, journal entry, and posting details for this transaction are as follows:

Accounting equation	**ASSETS**	**=**	**LIABILITIES**	**+**	**SHAREHOLDERS' EQUITY**
	+50,000	=	0	+	50,000

	A	B	C	D
1		**Debit**	**Credit**	
2	Cash	50,000		
3	Share Capital		50,000	
4	*Issued common shares.*			
5				

	Cash		Share Capital
The ledger accounts	(1)* 50,000		(1)* 50,000

*The numbers in parentheses indicate the transaction number for purposes of this illustration.

TRANSACTION 2 ANALYSIS. The business paid $40,000 cash for land, resulting in a decrease (credit) to Cash and an increase (debit) in Land.

Accounting equation	**ASSETS**	**=**	**LIABILITIES**	**+**	**SHAREHOLDERS' EQUITY**
	+40,000	=	0	+	0
	−40,000				

	A	B	C	D
1		Debit	Credit	
2	Land	40,000		
3	Cash		40,000	
4	Paid cash for land.			
5				

Cash		Land	
(1) 50,000	(2) 40,000	(2) 40,000	

The ledger accounts

TRANSACTION 3 ANALYSIS. The business purchased $3,700 in office supplies on account. The purchase increased Office Supplies, an asset, and Accounts Payable, a liability.

Accounting equation	**ASSETS**	**=**	**LIABILITIES**	**+**	**SHAREHOLDERS' EQUITY**
	+3,700	=	+3,700	+	0

	A	B	C	D
1		Debit	Credit	
2	Office Supplies	3,700		
3	Accounts Payable		3,700	
4	Purchased office supplies on account.			
5				

Office Supplies		Accounts Payable	
(3) 3,700			(3) 3,700

The ledger accounts

TRANSACTION 4 ANALYSIS. The business performed engineering services for clients and received cash of $7,000. The transaction increased Cash and Service Revenue.

Accounting equation	**ASSETS**	**=**	**LIABILITIES**	**+**	**SHAREHOLDERS' EQUITY**	**+**	**REVENUES**
	+7,000	=	0	+	0	+	7,000

	A	B	C	D
1		Debit	Credit	
2	Cash	7,000		
3	Service Revenue		7,000	
4	Performed services for cash.			
5				

Cash		Service Revenue	
(1) 50,000	(2) 40,000		(4) 7,000
(4) 7,000			

The ledger accounts

TRANSACTION 5 ANALYSIS. Tara performed $3,000 in services for King Contracting on account. The transaction increased Accounts Receivable and Service Revenue.

Accounting equation	**ASSETS**	**=**	**LIABILITIES**	**+**	**SHAREHOLDERS' EQUITY**	**+**	**REVENUES**
	+3,000	=	0			+	3,000

	A	B	C	D
1		Debit	Credit	
2	Accounts Receivable	3,000		
3	Service Revenue		3,000	
4	*Performed services on account.*			
5				

	Accounts Receivable		Service Revenue	
The ledger accounts	(5) 3,000			(4) 7,000
				(5) 3,000

TRANSACTION 6 ANALYSIS. Tara paid cash for the following expenses: office rent, $1,100; employee salary, $1,200; and utilities, $400. Debit each expense account for the amount of the expense and credit Cash for the sum of these expenses.

Accounting equation	ASSETS	=	LIABILITIES	+	SHAREHOLDERS' EQUITY	–	EXPENSES
	−2,700	=	0			–	2,700

	A	B	C	D
1		Debit	Credit	
2	Rent Expense	1,100		
3	Salary Expense	1,200		
4	Utilities Expense	400		
5	Cash		2,700	
6	*Paid expenses.*			
7				

	Cash		Rent Expense	
The ledger accounts	(1) 50,000	(2) 40,000	(6) 1,100	
	(4) 7,000	(6) 2,700		

	Salary Expense		Utilities Expense	
	(6) 1,200		(6) 400	

TRANSACTION 7 ANALYSIS. The business paid $1,900 on the account payable created in Transaction 3. Credit Cash for the payment. The payment decreased a liability, so debit Accounts Payable.

Accounting equation	ASSETS	=	LIABILITIES	+	SHAREHOLDERS' EQUITY
	−1,900	=	−1,900	+	0

	A	B	C	D
1		Debit	Credit	
2	Accounts Payable	1,900		
3	Cash		1,900	
4	*Paid cash on account.*			
5				

	Cash		Accounts Payable	
The ledger accounts	(1) 50,000	(2) 40,000	(7) 1,900	(3) 3,700
	(4) 7,000	(6) 2,700		
		(7) 1,900		

TRANSACTION 8 ANALYSIS. J.J. Booth, a shareholder of Tara Inc., remodelled his personal residence. This is not a transaction of the engineering consultancy, so Tara does not record it.

TRANSACTION 9 ANALYSIS. The business collected $1,000 cash on account from the client in Transaction 5. Debit Cash for the increase in this asset, and credit Accounts Receivable for the decrease in this asset.

Accounting equation	ASSETS	=	LIABILITIES	+	SHAREHOLDERS' EQUITY
	+1,000	=	0	+	0
	−1,000				

	A	B	C	D
1		Debit	Credit	
2	Cash	1,000		
3	Accounts Receivable		1,000	
4	*Collected cash on account.*			
5				

	Cash			Accounts Receivable	
The ledger accounts	(1) 50,000	(2) 40,000		(5) 3,000	(9) 1,000
	(4) 7,000	(6) 2,700			
	(9) 1,000	(7) 1,900			

TRANSACTION 10 ANALYSIS. Tara sold a portion of its land at cost for $22,000, receiving cash in return. This transaction resulted in an increase to Cash and a decrease in Land.

Accounting equation	ASSETS	=	LIABILITIES	+	SHAREHOLDERS' EQUITY
	+22,000	=	0	+	0
	−22,000				

	A	B	C	D
1		Debit	Credit	
2	Cash	22,000		
3	Land		22,000	
4	*Sold land.*			
5				

	Cash			Land	
The ledger accounts	(1) 50,000	(2) 40,000		(2) 40,000	(10) 22,000
	(4) 7,000	(6) 2,700			
	(9) 1,000	(7) 1,900			
	(10) 22,000				

TRANSACTION 11 ANALYSIS. Tara paid its shareholders cash dividends of $2,100. We credit Cash for the decrease in this asset, and debit Dividends to account for the decrease in shareholders' equity.

Accounting equation	ASSETS	=	LIABILITIES	+	SHAREHOLDERS' EQUITY	−	DIVIDENDS
	−2,100	=	0			−	2,100

	A	B	C	D
1		Debit	Credit	
2	Dividends	2,100		
3	Cash		2,100	
4	*Declared and paid dividends.*			
5				

The ledger accounts

Cash

(1) 50,000	(2) 40,000
(4) 7,000	(6) 2,700
(9) 1,000	(7) 1,900
(10) 22,000	(11) 2,100

Dividends

(11) 2,100	

Accounts After Posting to the Ledger

Exhibit 2-11 presents Tara Inc.'s ledger accounts after all transactions have been posted to them. For each account, a horizontal line separates the transaction amounts from the account balance (Bal.) at the end of the month. If the sum of an account's debits exceeds the sum of its credits, then the account will have a debit balance at the end of the period, as illustrated by the Cash debit balance of $33,300. If total credits exceed total debits, a credit balance results, as reflected in the Accounts Payable credit balance of $1,800.

EXHIBIT 2-11
Tara Inc.'s Ledger Accounts After Posting

Assets	=	Liabilities	+	Shareholders' Equity

Cash

(1) 50,000	(2) 40,000
(4) 7,000	(6) 2,700
(9) 1,000	(7) 1,900
(10) 22,000	(11) 2,100
Bal. 33,300	

Accounts Payable

(7) 1,900	(3) 3,700
	Bal. 1,800

Share Capital

	(1) 50,000
	Bal. 50,000

Dividends

(11) 2,100	
Bal. 2,100	

Accounts Receivable

(5) 3,000	(9) 1,000
Bal. 2,000	

REVENUE

Service Revenue

	(4) 7,000
	(5) 3,000
	Bal. 10,000

EXPENSES

Rent Expense

(6) 1,100	
Bal. 1,100	

Office Supplies

(3) 3,700	
Bal. 3,700	

Salary Expense

(6) 1,200	
Bal. 1,200	

Utilities Expense

(6) 400	
Bal. 400	

Land

(2) 40,000	(10) 22,000
Bal. 18,000	

STOP + THINK (2-4)

Describe a transaction that would result in a $10,000 debit to a company's Equipment ledger account and a corresponding credit to the Accounts Payable ledger account.

PREPARE AND USE A TRIAL BALANCE

A **trial balance** lists all of a business's ledger accounts and their balances. Asset accounts are listed first, followed by the liability accounts, and then all the accounts that affect shareholders' equity. We add all the debit balances and all the credit balances and place the totals at the bottom of the trial balance. If the total debits equal the total credits, we can go on to prepare the financial statements using the account balances from the trial balance. Exhibit 2-12 presents Tara Inc.'s trial balance at the end of April 2020.

⑤ Prepare and **use** a trial balance

EXHIBIT 2-12
Tara Inc.'s Trial Balance

	A	B	C	D
1	**Tara Inc.** Trial Balance April 30, 2020			
2		**Balance**		
3	**Account Title**	**Debit**	**Credit**	
4	Cash	$ 33,300		
5	Accounts receivable	2,000		
6	Supplies	3,700		
7	Land	18,000		
8	Accounts payable		$ 1,800	
9	Common shares		50,000	
10	Dividends	2,100		
11	Service revenue		10,000	
12	Rent expense	1,100		
13	Salary expense	1,200		
14	Utilities expense	400		
15	Total	$ 61,800	$ 61,800	
16				

The trial balance facilitates the preparation of the financial statements. We can prepare an income statement, statement of retained earnings, and balance sheet from the data shown in a trial balance such as the one in Exhibit 2-12. For Tara Inc., the financial statements would appear exactly as shown in Exhibit 2-2 on page 65. We do not normally construct the financial statements at this point, however, because the accounts do not yet contain end-of-period adjustments, which are covered in Chapter 3.

TRY IT in EXCEL® ▶ ▶ ▶

Try building Exhibit 2-12 in Excel. Open a new blank worksheet. Format the title (company name, trial balance, and date), and provide column headings (account title, debit, and credit) exactly as shown in Exhibit 2-12. Then on successive lines, enter account titles and amounts from the general ledger accounts, being careful to enter amounts in the proper debit or credit columns. Finally, sum both debit and credit columns. The total amounts of debits and credits should agree.

STOP + THINK (2-5)

If you were to prepare a trial balance for Tara Inc. on May 1, 2020, after it received the $5,000 loan from its bank, describe how it would differ from the April 30, 2020, trial balance presented in Exhibit 2-12.

DECISION GUIDELINES

HOW TO MEASURE RESULTS OF OPERATIONS AND FINANCIAL POSITION

Every manager must assess their company's profitability, financial position, and cash flows, but before they can do this, the company's transactions must be recorded in the accounting records. Here are some guidelines for the manager to follow when making decisions between the transaction stage and the reporting stage of the accounting process.

Decision	Guidelines
Has a transaction occurred?	If the event affects the entity's financial position **and** it can be reliably measured—Yes
	If either condition is absent—No
Where should the transaction be recorded?	In the *journal*, the chronological record of transactions
What accounts should be used to record the transaction in the journal?	Look in the *chart of accounts* for the most appropriate accounts to use
Should the affected accounts be debited or credited?	The rules of *debit* and *credit* state:

	Increase	Decrease
Assets	Debit	Credit
Liabilities	Credit	Debit
Share capital	Credit	Debit
Retained earnings	Credit	Debit
Dividends	Debit	Credit
Revenues	Credit	Debit
Expenses	Debit	Credit

Decision	Guidelines
Where are all the transactions for each account summarized?	In the *ledger*, the book of accounts
Where are all the accounts and their balances listed?	In the *trial balance*
Where are the results of operations reported?	In the *income statement* (Revenues − Expenses = Net income or net loss)
Where is the financial position reported?	In the *balance sheet* (Assets = Liabilities + Shareholders' equity)
Where are the cash flows reported?	In the *statement of cash flows*

Summary of IFRS-ASPE Differences

Concepts	IFRS	ASPE
There are no differences between IFRS and ASPE in this chapter.		

SUMMARY

SUMMARY OF LEARNING OBJECTIVES

LEARNING OBJECTIVE	SUMMARY
❶ **Recognize** a business transaction and **describe** the various types of accounts in which it can be recorded	A business transaction is any event that has a financial impact on a business and that can be reliably measured. Business transactions are recorded in the accounts affected by the transactions. An account is the record of all transactions affecting a particular asset, liability, or element of shareholders' equity. Here are the common accounts of each type:
	Assets: Cash, Accounts Receivable, Inventory, Prepaid Expenses, Land, Buildings, Equipment
	Liabilities: Accounts Payable, Accrued Liabilities, Loans Payable
	Shareholders' equity: Share Capital, Retained Earnings, Dividends, Revenues, Expenses
❷ **Determine** the impact of business transactions on the accounting equation	Recall the accounting equation introduced in Chapter 1:
	$$\text{Assets} = \text{Liabilities} + \text{Shareholders' Equity}$$
	Every business transaction affects at least one element of the accounting equation. When a company issues shares in exchange for $50,000 in cash, for example, the Cash asset increases by $50,000 and so does the Share Capital component of shareholders' equity. After each transaction is recorded in the accounting equation, the equation must remain in balance, as it is in our example, with $50,000 on each side of the equation. If the equation is out of balance, the transaction has been recorded incorrectly and must be revised.
❸ **Analyze** business transactions using T-accounts	We can represent an account using the letter T, which we call a T-account. The vertical line divides the account into left (debit) and right (credit) sides, while the account title rests on the horizontal line. The left side of the account is called the debit side, and the right side is called the credit side. We can use these T-accounts to record transactions instead of using the cumbersome accounting equation approach.
	When using T-accounts to record transactions, we apply the following rules of debit and credit, which help us translate the impacts of transactions on the accounting equation into impacts on specific accounts:
	• To record an increase in assets, use a debit.
	• To record a decrease in assets, use a credit.
	For liabilities and shareholders' equity, these rules are reversed:
	• To record an increase in liabilities or shareholders' equity, use a credit.
	• To record a decrease in liabilities or shareholders' equity, use a debit.
	Recall that increases in Dividends and Expenses result in decreases to shareholders' equity, so applying the last rule above means that increases to Dividends and Expenses are recorded using debits, which is the opposite of the "increase = credit" rule for all other shareholders' equity accounts.
	Every transaction involves at least one debit and one credit, and after recording a transaction, the total debits must equal the total credits. This ensures that the accounting equation remains in balance after each transaction.
	The normal balance of each account falls on the same side as where the increases to the account are recorded. The normal balance of an asset account, for example, falls on the left (debit) side, whereas the normal balance of a liability falls on the right (credit) side of the account.

④ Record business transactions in the journal and **post** them to the ledger

When formally recording transactions in the accounting records, accountants use a journal, a chronological record of all a business's transactions. When making a journal entry to record a transaction, we follow these three steps:

1. Specify each account affected by the transaction.
2. Determine whether the transaction increases or decreases each account affected by the transaction, and apply the rules of debit and credit to determine whether each account should be debited or credited.
3. Record the transaction in the journal, including a brief explanation of the transaction and its date.

Before we can obtain the balance of an account at the end of an accounting period, we must post all of the transactions from the journal to the ledger. The ledger contains all of a business's accounts, and posting is a simple process of directly transferring information from the journal to the ledger. Debits in the journal are posted as debits to the ledger accounts, and likewise for credits.

⑤ Prepare and **use** a trial balance

A trial balance lists all of a business's ledger accounts and their balances. Asset accounts are listed first, followed by the liability accounts, and then all the accounts that affect shareholders' equity. We add all the debit balances and all the credit balances and place the totals at the bottom of the trial balance. If the total debits equal the total credits, we can go on to prepare the financial statements using the account balances from the trial balance.

MyLab Accounting

END-OF-CHAPTER SUMMARY PROBLEM

The trial balance of Bos Personnel Services Inc. on March 1, 2020, lists the entity's assets, liabilities, and shareholders' equity on that date.

Account Title	Balance Debit	Balance Credit
Cash	$26,000	
Accounts receivable	4,500	
Accounts payable		$ 2,000
Share capital		10,000
Retained earnings		18,500
Total	$30,500	$30,500

During March, the business completed the following transactions:

a. Borrowed $70,000 from the bank, with C. Bos signing a note payable in the name of the business.
b. Paid cash of $60,000 to a real estate company to acquire land.
c. Performed service for a customer and received cash of $5,000.
d. Purchased supplies on credit, $300.
e. Performed customer service and earned revenue on account, $4,000.

f. Paid $1,200 on account.

g. Paid the following cash expenses: salary, $3,000; rent, $1,500; and interest, $400.

h. Received $3,100 on account.

i. Received a $200 utility bill that will be paid next month.

j. Declared and paid a dividend of $300.

Name: Bos Personnel Services Inc.
Industry: Human Resources
Fiscal Period: Month of March 2020
Key Fact: An existing, ongoing business

Requirements

1. Open the following accounts, with the balances indicated, in the ledger of Bos Personnel Services Inc. Use the T-account format.
   - Assets—Cash, $26,000; Accounts Receivable, $4,500; Supplies, no balance; Land, no balance
   - Liabilities—Accounts Payable, $2,000; Note Payable, no balance
   - Shareholders' Equity—Share Capital, $10,000; Retained Earnings, $18,500; Dividends, no balance
   - Revenues—Service Revenue, no balance
   - Expenses—Salary Expense, Rent Expense, Interest Expense, Utilities Expense (none have balances)

2. Journalize the transactions listed above. Key the journal entries by transaction letter.

3. Post all transactions to the ledger and show the balance in each account after all the transactions have been posted.

4. Use Excel to prepare the trial balance of Bos Personnel Services Inc. at March 31, 2020.

5. To determine the net income or net loss of the entity during the month of March, use Excel to prepare the income statement for the month ended March 31, 2020. List expenses in order from the largest to the smallest.

> Prepare a T-account for each account name. Place the opening balance in the T-account, remembering that the normal balance in an asset account is a debit, in a liability or equity account is a credit, in a revenue account is a credit, and in an expense account is a debit.
>
> For each transaction, ensure that Debits = Credits.

> Refer to the rules of debit and credit shown in Exhibit 2-8 on page 72.

ANSWERS

Requirement 1

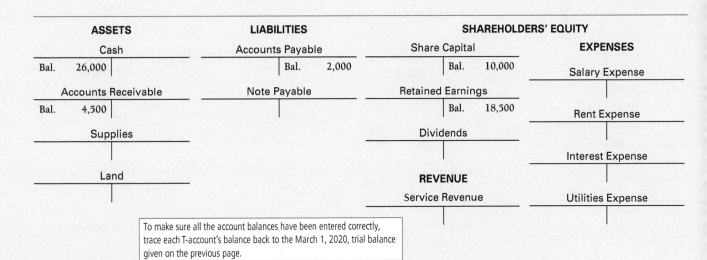

ASSETS	LIABILITIES	SHAREHOLDERS' EQUITY
Cash	Accounts Payable	Share Capital
Bal. 26,000	Bal. 2,000	Bal. 10,000
Accounts Receivable	Note Payable	Retained Earnings
Bal. 4,500		Bal. 18,500
Supplies		Dividends
Land		REVENUE
		Service Revenue

EXPENSES

Salary Expense

Rent Expense

Interest Expense

Utilities Expense

> To make sure all the account balances have been entered correctly, trace each T-account's balance back to the March 1, 2020, trial balance given on the previous page.

Requirement 2

Accounts and Explanation	Debit	Credit		Accounts and Explanation	Debit	Credit
a. Cash	70,000		**g.**	Salary Expense	3,000	
Note Payable		70,000		Rent Expense	1,500	
Borrowed cash on note payable.				Interest Expense	400	
b. Land	60,000			Cash		4,900
Cash		60,000		Paid cash expenses.		
Purchased land for cash.			**h.**	Cash	3,100	
c. Cash	5,000			Accounts Receivable		3,100
Service Revenue		5,000		Received on account.		
Performed service and received cash.			**i.**	Utilities Expense	200	
d. Supplies	300			Accounts Payable		200
Accounts Payable		300		Received utility bill.		
Purchased supplies on account.			**j.**	Dividends	300	
e. Accounts Receivable	4,000			Cash		300
Service Revenue		4,000		Declared and paid dividends.		
Performed service on account.						
f. Accounts Payable	1,200					
Cash		1,200				
Paid on account.						

> Selected transactions explained more fully:
> d. Increase Supplies (asset) and increase Accounts Payable (liability) because supplies were purchased on credit. Cash will be paid for the supplies in the future.
> e. Increase Accounts Receivable (asset) and increase Service Revenue (revenue) because the service was performed on account. Cash will be received for the service in the future.
> g. This transaction could also have been recorded with three journal entries, with a debit to the expense and a credit to Cash for each of the expenses.
> I. Increase Utilities Expense (expense) and increase Accounts Payable (liability) because cash will be paid for the utility bill in the future.

Requirement 3

ASSETS

Cash

Bal.	26,000	(b)	60,000
(a)	70,000	(f)	1,200
(c)	5,000	(g)	4,900
(h)	3,100	(j)	300
Bal.	37,700		

Accounts Receivable

Bal.	4,500	(h)	3,100
(e)	4,000		
Bal.	5,400		

Supplies

(d)	300	
Bal.	300	

Land

(b)	60,000	
Bal.	60,000	

LIABILITIES

Accounts Payable

(f)	1,200	Bal.	2,000
		(d)	300
		(i)	200
		Bal.	1,300

Note Payable

	(a)	70,000
	Bal.	70,000

SHAREHOLDERS' EQUITY

Share Capital

Bal.	10,000

Retained Earnings

Bal.	18,500

Dividends

(j)	300	
Bal.	300	

REVENUE

Service Revenue

	(c)	5,000
	(e)	4,000
	Bal.	9,000

EXPENSES

Salary Expense

(g)	3,000	
Bal.	3,000	

Rent Expense

(g)	1,500	
Bal.	1,500	

Interest Expense

(g)	400	
Bal.	400	

Utilities Expense

(i)	200	
Bal.	200	

> Make sure each transaction is posted to the proper T-account, and make sure no transactions were missed. Make sure that Assets = Liabilities + Shareholders' Equity for each transaction before going to the next transaction.

Requirement 4

	A	B	C	D
1	**Bos Personnel Services Inc.** Trial Balance March 31, 2020			
2		**Balance**		
3	**Account Title**	**Debit**	**Credit**	
4	Cash	$ 37,700		
5	Accounts receivable	5,400		
6	Supplies	300		
7	Land	60,000		
8	Accounts payable		$ 1,300	
9	Notes payable		70,000	
10	Share capital		10,000	
11	Retained earnings		18,500	
12	Dividends	300		
13	Service revenue		9,000	
14	Salary expense	3,000		
15	Rent expense	1,500		
16	Interest expense	400		
17	Utilities expense	200		
18	Total	$ 108,800	$ 108,800	
19				

The title must include the name of the company, "Trial Balance," and the date of the trial balance. It shows the account balances on one specific date. List all the accounts that have a balance in their T-accounts. Write the "Bal." amount for each account from Requirement 3 into the debit or credit column of the trial balance. Make sure that the total of the Debit column equals the total of the Credit column. Double-underline the totals to show that the columns have been added and the totals are final.

Requirement 5

	A	B	C	D
1	**Bos Personnel Services Inc.** Income Statement For the Month Ended March 31, 2020			
2	**Revenues**			
3	Service revenue		$ 9,000	
4				
5	**Expenses**			
6	Salary expense	$ 3,000		
7	Rent expense	1,500		
8	Interest expense	400		
9	Utilities expense	200		
10	Total expenses		5,100	
11	Net income		$ 3,900	
12				

The title must include the name of the company, "Income Statement," and the specific period of time covered. It is critical that the time period be defined. Prepare the income statement by listing the revenue and expense account names from the trial balance. Then transfer the amounts from the trial balance to the income statement.

REVIEW

MyLab Accounting

Make the grade with MyLab Accounting: The Quick Quiz questions, Short Exercises, Exercises, and Problems (Group A) marked with a ⊕ can be found on MyLab Accounting. You can practise them as often as you want, and most feature step-by-step guided instructions to help you find the right answer.

QUICK QUIZ (ANSWERS APPEAR ON THE LAST PAGE OF THIS CHAPTER.)

Test your understanding of business transactions by answering the following questions. Select the best choice from among the possible answers.

1. An investment of cash into the business will
   a. decrease total assets.
   b. decrease total liabilities.
   c. increase shareholders' equity.
   d. have no effect on total assets.

2. Purchasing a computer on account will
   a. increase total assets.
   b. increase total liabilities.
   c. have no effect on shareholders' equity.
   d. All of the above.

3. Performing a service on account will
   a. increase total assets.
   b. increase shareholders' equity.
   c. Both a and b.
   d. increase total liabilities.

4. Receiving cash from a customer on account will
   a. have no effect on total assets.
   b. increase total assets.
   c. decrease liabilities.
   d. increase shareholders' equity.

5. Purchasing computer equipment for cash will
   a. increase both total assets and total liabilities.
   b. decrease both total assets and shareholders' equity.
   c. decrease both total liabilities and shareholders' equity.
   d. have no effect on total assets, total liabilities, or shareholders' equity.

6. Purchasing a building for $100,000 by paying cash of $20,000 and signing a note payable for $80,000 will
   a. increase both total assets and total liabilities by $100,000.
   b. increase both total assets and total liabilities by $80,000.
   c. decrease total assets, and increase total liabilities by $20,000.
   d. decrease both total assets and total liabilities by $20,000.

7. What is the effect on total assets and shareholders' equity of paying the electric bill as soon as it is received each month?

	Total assets	Shareholders' equity
a.	Decrease	No effect
b.	No effect	No effect
c.	Decrease	Decrease
d.	No effect	Decrease

8. Which of the following transactions will increase an asset and increase a liability?
   a. buying equipment on account
   b. purchasing office equipment for cash
   c. issuing shares
   d. making a payment on account

9. Which of the following transactions will increase an asset and increase shareholders' equity?
   a. collecting cash from a customer on an account receivable
   b. performing a service on account for a customer
   c. borrowing money from a bank
   d. purchasing supplies on account

10. Where do we first record a transaction?
    a. ledger
    b. trial balance
    c. account
    d. journal

11. Which of the following is not an asset account?
    a. Share Capital
    b. Salary Expense
    c. Service Revenue
    d. None of the above accounts is an asset

12. Which of the following statements is false?
    a. Revenues are increased by credits.
    b. Assets are increased by debits.
    c. Dividends are increased by credits.
    d. Liabilities are decreased by debits.

13. The journal entry to record the receipt of land and a building and issuance of common shares
    a. debits Land and Building, and credits Share Capital.
    b. debits Land, and credits Share Capital.
    c. debits Share Capital, and credits Land and Building.
    d. credits Land and Building, and debits Share Capital.

14. The journal entry to record the purchase of supplies on account
    a. credits Supplies, and debits Cash.
    b. debits Supplies, and credits Accounts Payable.
    c. debits Supplies Expense, and credits Supplies.
    d. credits Supplies, and debits Accounts Payable.

15. If the credit to record the purchase of supplies on account is not posted,
    a. liabilities will be understated.
    b. expenses will be overstated.
    c. assets will be understated.
    d. shareholders' equity will be understated.

16. The journal entry to record a payment on account to a
🌐 supplier will
    a. debit Accounts Payable, and credit Retained Earnings.
    b. debit Cash, and credit Expenses.
    c. debit Expenses, and credit Cash.
    d. debit Accounts Payable, and credit Cash.

17. If the credit to record the payment of an account payable
🌐 is not posted,
    a. liabilities will be understated.
    b. expenses will be understated.
    c. cash will be overstated.
    d. cash will be understated.

18. Which statement is false?
🌐   **a.** A trial balance lists all the accounts with their current balances.
    b. A trial balance is the same as a balance sheet.
    c. A trial balance can verify the equality of debits and credits.
    d. A trial balance can be taken at any time.

19. A business's purchase of a $100,000 building with an
🌐 $85,000 mortgage payable and issuance of $15,000 of common shares will
    a. increase shareholders' equity by $15,000.
    b. increase assets by $15,000.
    c. increase assets by $85,000.
    d. increase shareholders' equity by $100,000.

20. A new company completed these transactions:
🌐   **1.** Shareholders invested $50,000 cash and inventory worth $25,000.
    2. Sales on account, $12,000.

What will total assets equal?
    a. $75,000
    b. $87,000
    c. $63,000
    d. $62,000

ACCOUNTING VOCABULARY

account The record of the changes that have occurred in a particular asset, liability, or element of shareholders' equity during a period. (p. 56)

chart of accounts List of a company's accounts and their account numbers. (p. 69)

credit The right side of an account. (p. 70)

debit The left side of an account. (p. 70)

double-entry system An accounting system that uses debits and credits to record the dual effects of each business transaction. (p. 69)

journal The chronological accounting record of an entity's transactions. (p. 73)

ledger The book of accounts and their balances. (p. 73)

posting Transferring amounts from the journal to the ledger. (p. 73)

transaction An event that has a financial impact on a business and that can be reliably measured. (p. 56)

trial balance A list of all the ledger accounts with their balances. (p. 79)

ASSESS YOUR PROGRESS

SHORT EXERCISES

🌐 **S2-1** Sue Deliveau opened a software consulting firm that immediately paid $2,000 for a computer. Was this event a transaction for the business?

LEARNING OBJECTIVE ❶
Recognize a business transaction

🌐 **S2-2** Hourglass Software began with cash of $10,000. Hourglass then bought supplies for $2,000 on account. Separately, Hourglass paid $5,000 for a computer. Answer these questions:
    1. How much in total assets does Hourglass have?
    2. How much in liabilities does Hourglass owe?

LEARNING OBJECTIVE ❷
Analyze the effects of transactions on the accounting equation

LEARNING OBJECTIVE ❸

Analyze transactions using
T-accounts

S2-3 Marsha Solomon, a physiotherapist, opened a practice. The business completed the following transactions:

May	1	Solomon invested $25,000 cash to start her practice. The business issued shares to Solomon.
	1	Purchased medical supplies on account totalling $9,000.
	2	Paid monthly office rent of $4,000.
	3	Recorded $8,000 revenue for service rendered to patients, received cash of $2,000, and sent bills to patients for the remainder.

After these transactions, how much cash does the business have to work with? Use T-accounts to show your answer.

LEARNING OBJECTIVES ❶❷❸

Analyze transactions using
T-accounts; determine accounts
affected by transactions; assess
impact of transactions on
accounting equation

S2-4 Refer to exercise S2-3. Which of the transactions of Marsha Solomon, P.T., increased the total assets of the business? For each transaction, identify the asset that was increased or decreased.

S2-5 After operating for several months, artist Paul Marciano completed the following transactions during the latter part of June:

LEARNING OBJECTIVES ❶❹

Determine accounts affected by
transactions; record transactions in
the journal

June	15	Borrowed $25,000 from the bank, signing a note payable.
	22	Painted a portrait for a client on account totalling $9,000.
	28	Received $5,000 cash on account from clients.
	29	Received a utility bill of $600, which will be paid during July.
	30	Paid monthly salary of $2,500 to gallery assistant.

Journalize the transactions of Paul Marciano, Artist. Include an explanation with each journal entry.

LEARNING OBJECTIVES ❸❹

Analyze transactions using
T-accounts; record transactions in
the journal and post them to the
ledger

S2-6 Architect Sonia Biaggi purchased supplies on account for $5,000. Later, Biaggi paid $3,000 on account.

1. Journalize the two transactions on the books of Sonia Biaggi, Architect. Include an explanation for each transaction.
2. Open a T-account for Accounts Payable and post to Accounts Payable. Compute the balance and denote it as Bal.
3. How much does Biaggi's business owe after both transactions? In which account does this amount appear?

LEARNING OBJECTIVES ❷❸❹

Determine the impact of
transactions on the accounting
equation; analyze transactions
using T-accounts; record
transactions in the journal and
post them

S2-7 Family Services Centre (The Centre) performed service for a client who could not pay immediately. The Centre expected to collect the $500 the following month. A month later, The Centre received $100 cash from the client.

1. Record the two transactions on the books of Family Services Centre. Include an explanation for each transaction.
2. Open these T-accounts: Cash, Accounts Receivable, and Service Revenue. Post to all three accounts. Compute each account balance and denote as Bal.
3. Answer these questions based on your analysis:

   a. How much did The Centre earn? Which account shows this amount?
   b. How much in total assets did The Centre acquire as a result of the two transactions? Show the amount of each asset.

LEARNING OBJECTIVE 5

Prepare and use a trial balance

S2-8 Assume that Lululemon Athletica Inc. reported the following summarized data at December 31, 2020. Accounts appear in no particular order; dollar amounts are in millions.

Revenues	$275
Other liabilities	38
Other assets	101
Cash and other current assets	53
Accounts payable	5
Expenses	244
Shareholders' equity	80

Prepare the trial balance of Lululemon at December 31, 2020. List the accounts in their proper order, as on page 79. How much was Lululemon's net income or net loss?

S2-9 Blackburn Inc.'s trial balance follows:

LEARNING OBJECTIVE 5

Use a trial balance

	A	B	C	D
1	**Blackburn Inc.** Trial Balance June 30, 2020			
2		Debit	Credit	
3	Cash	$ 6,000		
4	Accounts receivable	13,000		
5	Supplies	4,000		
6	Equipment	22,000		
7	Land	50,000		
8	Accounts payable		$ 19,000	
9	Note payable		20,000	
10	Share capital		10,000	
11	Retained earnings		8,000	
12	Service revenue		70,000	
13	Salary expense	21,000		
14	Rent expense	10,000		
15	Interest expense	1,000		
16	Total	$ 127,000	$ 127,000	
17				

Compute these amounts for Blackburn:

1. Total assets
2. Total liabilities
3. Net income or loss during June
4. Total shareholders' equity

S2-10 The accounts of Custom Pool Service, Inc., follow with their normal balances at June 30, 2020. The accounts are listed in no particular order.

LEARNING OBJECTIVE 5

Prepare a trial balance

Account	Balance	Account	Balance
Common shares	$ 8,300	Dividends	$ 5,800
Accounts payable	4,100	Utilities expense	1,700
Service revenue	22,300	Accounts receivable	15,200
Land	29,600	Delivery expense	900
Loan payable	11,500	Retained earnings	24,700
Cash	9,200	Salary expense	8,500

Prepare the company's trial balance at June 30, 2020, listing accounts in proper sequence, as illustrated in the chapter. For example, Accounts Receivable comes before Land. List the expense with the largest balance first, the expense with the next largest balance second, and so on.

LEARNING OBJECTIVES ❶❷❹ 🌐 **S2-11** Canada's Wonderland is an amusement park in Vaughan, Ontario. Over 3.5 million

Identify business transactions; determine impact of transactions on accounting equation; record transactions in the journal

people visit Wonderland each year between May and October. It covers 330 acres and has more than 200 rides and attractions, including 16 roller coasters. Wonderland has been the most-visited seasonal amusement park in North America for several years. Millions of transactions occur at Wonderland each year. The following items are possible transactions:

May	1	Sell admission tickets, $100,000, cash
May	3	Purchase merchandise inventory, $5,000, on account
May	6	Rent lockers to guests, $500, cash
May	8	Sign a letter of intent to switch electricity suppliers starting in June
May	15	Pay employees, $75,000, cash
May	18	Make an offer of employment for a new position in the Merchandise and Games office
May	20	Borrow money from bank by signing a six-month note, $200,000

Requirements

1. What criteria does an item have to meet to qualify as a business transaction? Identify which of the listed items are business transactions.
2. Record each of the business transactions in the journal.
3. Indicate how the company's assets, liabilities, and shareholders' equity would be affected by each transaction.

LEARNING OBJECTIVE ❸ 🌐 **S2-12** Canadian Prairies Investments began by issuing common shares for cash of $100,000.

Record transactions using T-accounts

The company immediately purchased computer equipment on account for $60,000.

1. Set up the following T-accounts for the company: Cash, Computer Equipment, Accounts Payable, Share Capital.
2. Record the transactions directly in the T-accounts without using a journal.
3. Show that total debits equal total credits.

EXERCISES

LEARNING OBJECTIVES ❶❷❸ 🌐 **E2-13** The Gap has opened a new store in Ottawa, investing $100,000 in cash in return for

Analyze transactions using T-accounts; Determine accounts affected by transactions; determine the impact of transactions on the accounting equation

common shares of the new company that will operate the store. Susan Harper is the store's manager. During the first week of operations, Harper signed a note payable to purchase land for $40,000 and a building for $130,000. The store also paid $50,000 for store fixtures and $40,000 for inventory to use in the business. All these were paid for in cash.

The Gap's head office requires store managers to provide a weekly report that summarizes and discusses the details of the store's financial position and how it has changed since the previous report. Susan has asked for your help with this request. Prepare the report for head office (assume all events above took place in the first week of operations).

LEARNING OBJECTIVES ❶❷ 🌐 **E2-14** During April, Spokes Ltd., a store that sells bicycles and related accessories, completed a

Create business transactions; determine impact of transactions on the accounting equation

series of transactions. For each of the following items, give an example of a business transaction that has the described effect on the accounting equation of Spokes Ltd.

a. Increase one asset, and decrease another asset.
b. Decrease an asset, and decrease shareholders' equity.
c. Decrease an asset, and decrease a liability.
d. Increase an asset, and increase shareholders' equity.
e. Increase an asset, and increase a liability.

E2-15 Fill out the following chart to show the impact on the accounting equation from each transaction.

LEARNING OBJECTIVE ❷

Analyze transactions using the accounting equation

Date	Description	Assets		Liabilities		Shareholders' equity	
		Increase	Decrease	Increase	Decrease	Increase	Decrease
Jan 2	Purchased office supplies on account for $500						
Jan 4	Issued common shares for cash for $5,000						
Jan 10	Sold services on account for $2,000						
Jan 15	Paid amount owed to vendor for the office supplies purchased on account on January 2						
Jan 18	Sold services for cash $200						
Jan 21	Received cash for payment on account from sale on January 10						
Jan 31	Paid employees for monthly payroll $1,500						

E2-16 The following selected events were experienced by either Problem Solvers Inc., a corporation, or Pierce Laflame, the major shareholder. State whether each event (1) increased, (2) decreased, or (3) had no effect on the total assets of the business. Where applicable, specify the asset(s) affected by a transaction.

LEARNING OBJECTIVES ❶❷

Identify business transactions; analyze transactions using the accounting equation

a. Received $9,000 cash from customers on account.
b. Laflame used personal funds to purchase a swimming pool for his home.
c. Sold land and received cash of $60,000 (the land was carried on the company's books at $60,000).
d. Borrowed $50,000 from the bank.
e. Made cash purchase of land for a building site, $85,000.
f. Received $20,000 cash and issued shares to a shareholder.
g. Paid $60,000 cash on accounts payable.
h. Purchased equipment and signed a $100,000 promissory note in payment.
i. Purchased supplies on account for $15,000.
j. The business paid Laflame a cash dividend of $4,000.

E2-17 Joseph Ohara opens a dental practice. During the first month of operation (March), the practice, titled Joseph Ohara Dental Clinic Ltd., experienced the following events:

LEARNING OBJECTIVES ❶❷❸

Analyze transactions using the accounting equation and T-accounts

March	6	Ohara invested $50,000 in the business, which in turn issued its common shares to him.
	9	The business paid cash for land costing $30,000. Ohara plans to build a professional services building on the land.
	12	The business purchased dental supplies for $3,000 on account.
	15	Joseph Ohara Dental Clinic Ltd. officially opened for business.
	15–31	During the rest of the month, Ohara treated patients and earned service revenue of $10,000, receiving cash for half the revenue earned.
	15–31	The practice paid cash expenses: employee salaries, $1,400; office rent, $1,000; utilities, $300.
	31	The practice used dental supplies with a cost of $250.
	31	The practice borrowed $10,000, signing a note payable to the bank.
	31	The practice paid $2,000 on account to a supplier.

Requirement

Dr. Ohara has the following questions about his practice after the first month of operations. Provide him with the answers.

a. What are the total assets of the practice?
b. How much is owing to the practice from patients?
c. How much does the practice owe in total?
d. How much of the practice's assets does Dr. Ohara have a claim to?
e. How much net income did the practice earn?

LEARNING OBJECTIVE ❹

Journalize transactions

E2-18 Refer to exercise E2-17. Record the transactions in the journal of Joseph Ohara Dental Clinic Ltd. List the transactions by date, and give an explanation for each transaction.

LEARNING OBJECTIVES ❶❹

Determine accounts affected by transactions; record transactions in the journal

E2-19 Perfect Printers Inc. completed the following transactions during October 2020, its first month of operations:

Oct. 1   Received $25,000, and issued common shares.

2   Purchased $800 of office supplies on account.

4   Paid $20,000 cash for land to use as a building site.

6   Performed service for customers, and received cash of $5,000.

9   Paid $100 on accounts payable.

17   Performed service for Waterloo School Board on account totalling $1,500.

23   Collected $1,000 from Waterloo School Board on account.

31   Paid the following expenses: salary, $1,000; rent, $500.

Requirement

1. Record the transactions in the journal of Perfect Printers Inc. Key transactions by date, and include an explanation for each entry, as illustrated in the chapter.

LEARNING OBJECTIVES ❹❺

Post to the ledger and prepare and use a trial balance

E2-20 Refer to exercise E2-19.

Requirements

1. After journalizing the transactions of exercise E2-19, post the entries to the ledger using T-accounts. Key transactions by date. Date the ending balance of each account October 31, 2020.
2. Prepare the trial balance of Perfect Printers Inc., at October 31, 2020.
3. How much are total assets, total liabilities, and total shareholders' equity on October 31, 2020?

LEARNING OBJECTIVE ❹

Journalize transactions

E2-21 The first seven transactions of Splash Water Park Ltd. have been posted to the company's accounts as follows:

Cash			Supplies		Equipment		Land	
(1) 20,000	(3) 8,000	(4) 1,000	(5) 100	(6) 8,000		(3) 31,000	
(2) 7,000	(6) 8,000						
(5) 100	(7) 400						

Accounts Payable		Note Payable		Share Capital	
(7) 400	(4) 1,000		(2) 7,000		(1) 20,000
			(3) 23,000		

Requirement

Prepare the journal entries that served as the sources for the seven transactions. Include an explanation for each entry. As Splash Water Park moves into the next period, how much cash does the business have? How much does Splash Water Park owe its creditors?

LEARNING OBJECTIVE ❺

Prepare and use a trial balance

E2-22 The accounts of Victoria Garden Care Ltd. follow with their normal balances at September 30, 2020. The accounts are listed in no particular order.

Account	Balance	Account	Balance
Dividends..	6,000	Common shares	8,500
Utilities expense	1,400	Accounts payable.................................	4,300
Accounts receivable............................	17,500	Service revenue	24,000
Delivery expense	300	Equipment	29,000
Retained earnings...............................	21,400	Note payable	13,000
Salary expense.....................................	8,000	Cash...	9,000

Requirements

1. Prepare the company's trial balance at September 30, 2020, listing accounts in proper sequence, as illustrated in the chapter. For example, Accounts Receivable comes before Equipment. List the expense with the largest balance first, the expense with the next largest balance second, and so on.
2. Prepare the financial statement for the month ended September 30, 2020, that will tell the company's top managers the results of operations for the month.

E2-23 The trial balance of Sam's Deli Inc. at October 31, 2020, does not balance:

LEARNING OBJECTIVES ❹❺

Record transactions in the journal; correct errors in a trial balance

CT

	A	B	C	D
1	Cash	$ 4,200		
2	Accounts receivable	13,000		
3	Inventory	17,000		
4	Supplies	600		
5	Land	55,000		
6	Accounts payable		$ 12,000	
7	Share capital		47,900	
8	Sales revenue		32,100	
9	Salary expense	1,700		
10	Rent expense	800		
11	Utilities expense	700		
12	Total	$ 93,000	$ 92,000	
13				

The accounting records contain the following errors:

a. Recorded a $1,000 cash revenue transaction by debiting Accounts Receivable. The credit entry was correct.
b. Posted a $1,000 credit to Accounts Payable as $100.
c. Did not record utilities expense or the related account payable in the amount of $200.
d. Understated Share Capital by $1,100.
e. Omitted insurance expense of $1,000 from the trial balance.

Requirements

1. Prepare the correct trial balance at October 31, 2020, complete with a heading. Journal entries are not required but will be helpful in correcting the trial balance.
2. Organize the elements of the trial balance in a way that would assist a bank manager who has to decide whether to loan money to Sam's Deli.

E2-24 Set up the following T-accounts: Cash, Accounts Receivable, Office Supplies, Office Furniture, Accounts Payable, Share Capital, Dividends, Service Revenue, Salary Expense, and Rent Expense.

LEARNING OBJECTIVE ❸

Record transactions in T-accounts

Record the following transactions directly in the T-accounts without using a journal. Use the letters to identify the transactions. Calculate the account balances and denote as Bal.

a. In the month of May 2020, Sonia Rothesay opened an accounting firm by investing $10,000 cash and office furniture valued at $5,000. Organized as a professional corporation, the business issued common shares to Rothesay.
b. Paid monthly rent of $1,600.
c. Purchased office supplies on account, $600.
d. Paid employees' salaries of $2,000.
e. Paid $200 of the account payable created in transaction (c).
f. Performed accounting service on account, $12,100.
g. Declared and paid dividends of $2,000.

LEARNING OBJECTIVE ⑤

Prepare and use a trial balance

E2-25 Refer to exercise E2-24.

Requirements

1. After recording the transactions in exercise E2-24, prepare the trial balance of Sonia Rothesay, Accountant, at May 31, 2020.
2. How well did the business perform during its first month? Give the basis for your answer.

LEARNING OBJECTIVES ②⑤

Analyze transactions using the accounting equation; prepare and use a trial balance

E2-26 The trial balance of 4AC, Inc., at October 31, 2020, does not balance.

Cash	$ 3,900	Common shares	$24,100
Accounts receivable	7,100	Retained earnings	1,700
Land	30,100	Service revenue	9,400
Accounts payable	6,200	Salary expense	2,900
Note payable	5,900	Advertising expense	1,400

Requirements

1. Prepare a trial balance for the ledger accounts of 4AC, Inc., as of October 31, 2020.
2. Determine the out-of-balance amount. The error lies in the Accounts Receivable account.

Add the out-of-balance amount to, or subtract it from, Accounts Receivable to determine the correct balance of Accounts Receivable. After correcting Accounts Receivable, advise the top management of 4AC, Inc., on the company's
a. total assets.
b. total liabilities.
c. net income or net loss for October.

LEARNING OBJECTIVE ②

Analyze transactions using the accounting equation

E2-27 Frontland Advertising creates, plans, and handles advertising campaigns in three provinces. Recently, Frontland had to replace an inexperienced office worker in charge of bookkeeping because of some serious mistakes that had been uncovered in the accounting records. You have been hired to review these transactions to determine any corrections that might be necessary. In all cases, the bookkeeper made an accurate description of the transaction but did not correctly record the transaction in the journal.

	A	B	C	D	E
1	May 1	Accounts receivable	100		
2		Service revenue		100	
3		*Collected an account receivable.*			
4	2	Rent expense	20,000		
5		Cash		20,000	
6		*Paid monthly rent, $2,000.*			
7	5	Cash	2,800		
8		Accounts receivable		2,800	
9		*Collected cash for services provided.*			
10	10	Supplies	3,100		
11		Accounts payable		3,100	
12		*Purchased office equipment on account.*			
13	16	Dividends	5,600		
14		Cash		5,600	
15		*Paid salaries.*			
16	25	Accounts receivable	5,400		
17		Cash		5,400	
18		*Paid for supplies purchased earlier an account.*			
19					

Requirements

1. For each of the preceding entries, indicate the effect of the error on cash, total assets, and net income. The answer for the first transaction has been provided as an example.

Date	Effect on Cash	Effect on Total Assets	Effect on Net Income
May 1	Understated $100	Overstated $100	Overstated $100

2. What is the correct balance of cash if the balance of cash on the books before correcting the preceding transactions was $6,400?
3. What is the correct amount of total assets if the total assets on the books before correcting the preceding transactions was $28,000?
4. What is the correct net income for May if the reported income before correcting the preceding transactions was $8,000?

E2-28 Web Marketing Services Inc. completed these transactions during the first part of January 2020:

Jan.	2	Received $5,000 cash from investors, and issued common shares.
	2	Paid monthly office rent, $500.
	3	Paid cash for a Dell computer, $3,000, with the computer expected to remain in service for five years.
	4	Purchased office furniture on account, $6,000, with the furniture projected to last for five years.
	5	Purchased supplies on account, $900.
	9	Performed marketing service for a client, and received cash for the full amount of $800.
	12	Paid utility expenses, $200.
	18	Performed marketing service for a client on account, $1,700.

LEARNING OBJECTIVES ❸❹❺

Analyze transactions using T-accounts; record transactions in the journal and post them; prepare a trial balance

Requirements

1. Set up T-accounts for Cash, Accounts Receivable, Supplies, Equipment, Furniture, Accounts Payable, Share Capital, Dividends, Service Revenue, Rent Expense, Utilities Expense, and Salary Expense.
2. Journalize the transactions. Explanations are not required.
3. Post to the T-accounts. Key all items by date and denote an account balance on January 18 as Bal.
4. Prepare a trial balance at January 18. In Exercise 3-34 of Chapter 3, we add transactions for the remainder of January and update the trial balance at January 31, 2020.

E2-29 Following is selected financial information for the Canadiana Gallery Ltd. for the month of March:

LEARNING OBJECTIVE ❸

Analyze transactions using T-accounts

	Balance		
			Additional Information
Account	Feb. 28	Mar. 31	for the Month of March
1. Cash	10,000	5,000	Cash receipts, $80,000
2. Accounts Receivable	26,000	24,000	Sales on account, $50,000
3. Notes Payable	13,000	21,000	New borrowing, $25,000

Requirement

Provide the gallery's manager with the following information for March:

a. Total cash disbursements.
b. Cash collections from customers.
c. Cash payments on Notes Payable.

LEARNING OBJECTIVES ❸❹❺ ⊕ **E2-30** The trial balance of You Build Inc. at December 31, 2020, does not balance.

Analyze transactions using
T-accounts; prepare and use a trial
balance; post transactions

Cash	$ 3,900	Common shares	$20,000
Accounts receivable	7,200	Retained earnings	7,300
Land	34,000	Service revenue	9,100
Accounts payable	5,800	Salary expense	3,400
Note payable	5,000	Advertising expense	900

Requirements

1. How much out of balance is the trial balance? Assume the error lies in the Accounts Receivable account. What is the correct balance of Accounts Receivable?
2. You Build Inc. also failed to record the following transactions during December:

   a. Purchased additional land for $60,000 by signing a note payable.
   b. Earned service revenue on account, $10,000.
   c. Paid salary expense of $1,400.
   d. Purchased a TV advertisement for $1,000 on account. This account will be paid during January.

   Add these amounts to, or subtract them from, the appropriate accounts to properly include the effects of these transactions. Then prepare the corrected trial balance of You Build Inc.
3. After correcting the accounts, advise the top management of You Build Inc. on the company's:

   a. Total assets.
   b. Total liabilities.
   c. Net income or loss.

LEARNING OBJECTIVES ❶❷ ⊕ **E2-31** This question concerns the items and the amounts that two entities, City of Regina and Public Health Organization, Inc. (PHO), should report in their financial statements.

Analyze transactions using the
accounting equation; identify
accounts affected by transactions

During August, PHO provided City of Regina with medical checks for new school pupils and sent the City a bill for $30,000. On September 7, Regina sent a cheque to PHO for $25,000. The City began August with a cash balance of $50,000; PHO began with cash of $0.

Requirements

1. Specify everything that both Regina and PHO will report on their August and September income statements and on their balance sheets at August 31 and September 30 in connection with the above transactions between them.
2. Briefly explain how the City of Regina and PHO data relate to each other. Be specific.

PROBLEMS (GROUP A)

P2-32A The trial balance of Amusement Specialties Inc. follows:

LEARNING OBJECTIVE ⑤
Use a trial balance

	A	B	C	D
1	**Amusement Specialties Inc.** Trial Balance December 31, 2020			
2	Cash	$ 14,000		
3	Accounts receivable	11,000		
4	Prepaid expenses	4,000		
5	Equipment	171,000		
6	Building	100,000		
7	Accounts payable		$ 30,000	
8	Note payable		120,000	
9	Share capital		102,000	
10	Retained earnings		40,000	
11	Dividends	22,000		
12	Service revenue		86,000	
13	Rent expense	14,000		
14	Advertising expense	3,000		
15	Wage expense	32,000		
16	Supplies expense	7,000		
17	Total	$ 378,000	$ 378,000	
18				

Sue Sibalius, your best friend, is considering investing in Amusement Specialties Inc. She seeks your advice in interpreting this information. Specifically, she wants to know the company's total assets, total liabilities, and net income or net loss for the year, as well as how to compute these amounts.

Requirement

Write a short note to answer Sue's questions.

P2-33A The following amounts summarize the financial position of Blythe Spirit Consulting, Inc. on May 31, 2020:

LEARNING OBJECTIVE ②
Analyze transactions with the accounting equation and prepare the financial statements

	ASSETS				=	LIABILITIES	+	SHAREHOLDERS' EQUITY	
Cash	+	Accounts Receivable	+ Supplies +	Land	=	Accounts Payable	+	Common Shares	+	Retained Earnings
1,300		1,000		12,000		8,000		4,000		2,300

During June 2020, the business completed these transactions:

a. Received cash of $5,000, and issued common shares.

b. Performed services for a client, and received cash of $7,600.

c. Paid $4,000 on accounts payable.

d. Purchased supplies on account, $1,500.

e. Collected cash from a customer on account, $1,000.

f. Consulted on the design of a business report, and billed the client for services rendered, $2,500.

g. Recorded the following business expenses for the month: paid office rent, $900; paid advertising, $300.

h. Declared and paid a cash dividend of $2,000.

Requirements

1. Prepare the income statement of Blythe Spirit Consulting, Inc. for the month ended June 30, 2020. List expenses in decreasing order by amount.
2. Prepare the entity's statement of retained earnings for the month ended June 30, 2020.
3. Prepare the balance sheet of Blythe Spirit Consulting, Inc. at June 30, 2020.

LEARNING OBJECTIVE ④

Journalize and post transactions

 P2-34A Use this problem in conjunction with problem P2-33A.

Requirements

1. Journalize the transactions of Blythe Spirit Consulting, Inc. Explanations are not required.
2. Set up the following T-accounts: Cash, Accounts Receivable, Supplies, Land, Accounts Payable, Share Capital, Retained Earnings, Dividends, Service Revenue, Rent Expense, and Advertising Expense. Insert in each account its balance as given (example: Cash $1,300). Post the transactions to the accounts.
3. Compute the balance in each account. For each asset account, each liability account, and for Share Capital, compare its balance to the ending balance you obtained in problem P2-33A. Are the amounts the same or different?

LEARNING OBJECTIVES ①②④

Analyze transactions with the accounting equation; journalize transactions

P2-35A Mountain View Estates Ltd. experienced the following events during the organizing phase and its first month of operations. Some of the events were personal and did not affect the business. Others were business transactions.

Sept.	4	Gayland Jet, the major shareholder of the company, received $50,000 cash from an inheritance.
	5	Jet deposited $50,000 cash in a new business bank account titled Mountain View Estates Ltd. The business issued common shares to Jet.
	6	The business paid $300 cash for letterhead stationery for the new office.
	7	The business purchased office furniture. The company paid cash of $20,000 and agreed to pay the account payable for the remainder, $5,000, within three months.
	10	Jet sold Telus shares, which he had owned for several years, receiving $30,000 cash from his stockbroker.
	11	Jet deposited the $30,000 cash from the sale of the Telus shares in his personal bank account.
	12	A representative of a large company telephoned Jet and told him of the company's intention to put a down payment of $10,000 on a lot.
	18	Jet finished a real estate deal on behalf of a client and submitted his bill for services, $10,000. Jet expects to collect from this client within two weeks.
	21	The business paid half its account payable for the furniture purchased on September 7.
	25	The business paid office rent of $4,000.
	30	The business declared and paid a cash dividend of $2,000.

Requirements

1. Classify each of the preceding events as one of the following:

   a. A business-related event but not a transaction to be recorded by Mountain View Estates Ltd.
   b. A personal transaction for a shareholder, not to be recorded by Mountain View Estates Ltd.
   c. A business transaction to be recorded by the business of Mountain View Estates Ltd.

2. Analyze the effects of the preceding events on the accounting equation of Mountain View Estates Ltd. Use a format similar to that in Exhibit 2-1, Panel B.
3. At the end of the first month of operations, Jet has a number of questions about the financial standing of the business. Explain the following to him:

   a. How the business can have more cash than retained earnings.
   b. How much in total resources the business has, how much it owes, and what Jet's ownership interest is in the assets of the business.

4. Record the transactions of the business in its journal. Include an explanation for each entry.

P2-36A During October, All Pets Veterinary Clinic Ltd. completed the following transactions:

LEARNING OBJECTIVE ❹

Journalize and post transactions

Oct.	1	Dr. Squires deposited $8,000 cash in the business bank account. The business issued common shares to her.
	5	Paid monthly rent, $1,000.
	9	Paid $5,000 cash, and signed a $25,000 note payable to purchase land for an office site.
	10	Purchased supplies on account, $1,200.
	19	Paid $600 on account.
	22	Borrowed $10,000 from the bank for business use. Dr. Squires signed a note payable to the bank in the name of the business.
	31	Revenues earned during the month included $7,000 cash and $5,000 on account.
	31	Paid employees' salaries ($2,000), advertising expense ($1,500), and utilities ($1,100).
	31	Declared and paid a cash dividend of $3,000.

The clinic uses the following accounts: Cash, Accounts Receivable, Supplies, Land, Accounts Payable, Notes Payable, Share Capital, Dividends, Service Revenue, Salary Expense, Rent Expense, Utilities Expense, and Advertising Expense.

Requirements

1. Journalize each transaction of All Pets Veterinary Clinic Ltd. Explanations are not required.
2. Prepare T-accounts for Cash, Accounts Payable, and Notes Payable. Post to these three accounts.
3. After these transactions, how much cash does the business have? How much in total does it owe?

P2-37A During the first month of operations, May 2020, New Pane Windows Inc. completed the following transactions:

LEARNING OBJECTIVES ❶❹❺

Journalize and post transactions; prepare and use a trial balance; specify accounts affected by transactions

May	2	New Pane received $30,000 cash and issued common shares to shareholders.
	3	Purchased supplies, $1,000, and equipment, $2,600, on account.
	4	Performed services, and received cash, $1,500.
	7	Paid cash to acquire land for an office site, $22,000.
	11	Repaired a window, and billed the customer $500.
	16	Paid for the equipment purchased May 3 on account.
	17	Paid the telephone bill, $95.
	18	Received partial payment from client on account, $250.
	22	Paid the water and electricity bills, $400.
	29	Received $2,000 cash for installing a new window.
	31	Paid employee salary, $1,300.
	31	Declared and paid dividends of $1,500.

Requirements

1. Record each transaction in the journal using account titles that accurately reflect the nature of the activities being allocated to them. Key each transaction by date. Explanations are not required.
2. Post the transactions to T-accounts, using transaction dates as posting references. Label the ending balance of each account Bal., as shown in the chapter.
3. Prepare the trial balance of New Pane Windows, at May 31, 2020.
4. The manager asks you how much in total resources the business has to work with, how much it owes, and whether May 2020 was profitable (and by how much). Calculate the amounts needed to answer her questions.

P2-38A During the first month of operations (January 2020), Music Services Ltd. completed the following selected transactions:

LEARNING OBJECTIVES ❶❸❺

Record transactions in T-accounts; prepare and use a trial balance; specify accounts affected by transactions

a. The business has cash of $10,000 and a building valued at $50,000. The corporation issued common shares to the shareholders in exchange for these investments.
b. Borrowed $50,000 from the bank, and signed a note payable.

c. Paid $60,000 for music equipment.
d. Purchased supplies on account, $1,000.
e. Paid employees' salaries, $1,500.
f. Received $800 for service performed for customers.
g. Performed service to customers on account, $4,500.
h. Paid $100 of the account payable created in transaction (d).
i. Received a $600 utility bill that will be paid in the near future.
j. Received cash on account, $3,100.
k. Paid the following cash expenses: rent, $1,000; advertising, $800.

Requirement
Prepare the trial balance of Music Services Ltd. at January 31, 2020.

PROBLEMS (GROUP B)

LEARNING OBJECTIVE ❺

Use a trial balance

P2-39B The owners of Opera Tours Inc. are selling the business. They offer the trial balance that appears at the top of the next page to prospective buyers.

Your best friend is considering buying Opera Tours. She seeks your advice in interpreting this information. Specifically, she would like to know how this information gets converted into a balance sheet and income statement and would like to see these statements for Opera Tours Inc. for the 2020 fiscal year.

Requirement
Write a memo to answer your friend's questions.

	A	B	C
1	**Opera Tours Inc.** Trial Balance December 31, 2020		
2	Cash	$ 12,000	
3	Accounts receivable	45,000	
4	Prepaid expenses	4,000	
5	Equipment	231,000	
6	Accounts payable		$ 105,000
7	Note payable		92,000
8	Common shares		30,000
9	Retained earnings		32,000
10	Service revenue		139,000
11	Salary expense	69,000	
12	Tour expenses	26,000	
13	Rent expense	7,000	
14	Advertising expense	4,000	
15	Total	$ 398,000	$ 398,000
16			

LEARNING OBJECTIVE ❷

Analyze transactions with the accounting equation and prepare the financial statements

P2-40B Doug Hanna operates and is the major shareholder of an interior design studio called DH Designers, Inc. The following amounts summarize the financial position of the business on April 30, 2020:

	ASSETS				=	LIABILITIES	+	SHAREHOLDERS' EQUITY	
Cash	+	Accounts Receivable	+ Supplies +	Land	=	Accounts Payable	+	Common Shares	+	Retained Earnings
Bal. 1,700		2,200		24,100		5,400		10,000	12,600

During May 2020, the business completed these transactions:

a. Hanna received $30,000 as a gift and deposited the cash in the business bank account. The business issued common shares to Hanna.

b. Paid $1,000 on accounts payable.

c. Performed services for a client and received cash of $5,100.

d. Collected cash from a customer on account, $700.

e. Purchased supplies on account, $800.

f. Consulted on the interior design of a major office building and billed the client for services rendered, $15,000.

g. Received cash of $1,700 and issued common shares to a shareholder.

h. Recorded the following expenses for the month: paid office rent, $2,100; paid advertising, $1,600.

i. Declared and paid a cash dividend of $2,000.

Requirements

In order to guide Doug Hanna:

1. Prepare the income statement of DH Designers, Inc. for the month ended May 31, 2020. List expenses in decreasing order by amount.

2. Prepare the statement of retained earnings of DH Designers, Inc. for the month ended May 31, 2020.

3. Prepare the balance sheet of DH Designers, Inc. at May 31, 2020.

P2-41B Use this problem in conjunction with problem P2-40B.

LEARNING OBJECTIVE ④

Journalize and post transactions

Requirements

1. Journalize the transactions of DH Designers, Inc. Explanations are not required.

2. Set up the following T-accounts: Cash, Accounts Receivable, Supplies, Land, Accounts Payable, Share Capital, Retained Earnings, Dividends, Service Revenue, Rent Expense, and Advertising Expense. Insert in each account its balance as given (example: Cash $1,700). Post to the accounts.

3. Compute the balance in each account. For each asset account, each liability account, and for Share Capital, compare its balance to the ending balance you obtained in problem P2-40B. Are the amounts the same or different?

P2-42B Lane Kohler opened a consulting practice that he operates as a corporation. The name of the new entity is Lane Kohler, Consultant, Inc. Kohler experienced the following events during the organizing phase of his new business and its first month of operations. Some of the events were personal transactions of the shareholder and did not affect the consulting practice. Others were transactions that should be accounted for by the business.

LEARNING OBJECTIVES ①②④

Record transactions using the accounting equation and journal entries

March	1	Kohler sold 1,000 shares of BlackBerry stock and received $100,000 cash from his stockbroker.
	2	Kohler deposited in his personal bank account the $100,000 cash from sale of the BlackBerry shares.
	3	Kohler received $150,000 cash through an inheritance from his grandfather.
	5	Kohler deposited $50,000 cash in a new business bank account titled Lane Kohler, Consultant, Inc. The business issued common shares to Kohler.
	6	A representative of a large company telephoned Kohler and told him of the company's intention to give $15,000 of consulting business to Kohler.
	7	The business paid $450 cash for letterhead stationery for the consulting office.
	9	The business purchased office furniture. Kohler paid cash of $5,000 and agreed to pay the account payable for the remainder, $10,500, within three months.
	23	Kohler finished an analysis for a client and submitted his bill for services $4,000. He expected to collect from this client within one month.
	29	The business paid $5,000 of its account payable on the furniture purchased on March 9.
	30	The business paid office rent of $2,100.
	31	The business declared and paid a cash dividend of $1,000.

Requirements

1. Classify each of the preceding events as one of the following:

   a. A personal transaction of a shareholder not to be recorded by the business of Lane Kohler, Consultant, Inc.

   b. A business transaction to be recorded by the business of Lane Kohler, Consultant, Inc.

   c. A business-related event but not a transaction to be recorded by the business of Lane Kohler, Consultant, Inc.

2. Analyze the effects of the preceding events on the accounting equation of the business of Lane Kohler, Consultant, Inc. Use a format similar to Exhibit 2-1, Panel B.

3. At the end of the first month of operations, Kohler has a number of questions about the financial standing of the business. Answer the following questions for him:

   a. How can the business have more cash than retained earnings?

   b. How much in total resources does the business have? How much does it owe? What is Kohler's ownership interest in the assets of the business?

4. Record the transactions of the business in its journal. Include an explanation for each entry.

LEARNING OBJECTIVE ❹
Journalize and post transactions

P2-43B Wimberley Glass, Inc. has shops in the shopping malls of a major metropolitan area. The business completed the following transactions:

June	1	Received cash of $25,000, and issued common shares to a shareholder.
	2	Paid $10,000 cash, and signed a $30,000 note payable to purchase land for a new glassworks site.
	7	Received $20,000 cash from sales, and deposited that amount in the bank.
	10	Purchased supplies on account, $1,000.
	15	Paid employees' salaries, $2,800, and rent on a shop, $1,800.
	15	Paid advertising expense, $1,100.
	16	Paid $1,000 on account.
	17	Declared and paid a cash dividend of $2,000.

Wimberley Glass, Inc. uses the following accounts: Cash, Supplies, Land, Accounts Payable, Note Payable, Share Capital, Dividends, Sales Revenue, Salary Expense, Rent Expense, and Advertising Expense.

Requirements

1. Journalize each transaction. Explanations are not required.
2. Prepare T-accounts for Cash, Accounts Payable, and Notes Payable. Post to these three accounts.
3. After these transactions, how much cash does the business have? How much does it owe in total?

LEARNING OBJECTIVES ❶❹❺
Journalize and post transactions; prepare and use a trial balance; specify accounts affected by transactions

P2-44B During the first month of operations, October 2020, Barron Environmental Services Inc. completed the following transactions:

Oct.	3	Received $20,000 cash, and issued common shares.
	4	Performed services for a client, and received $5,000 cash.
	6	Purchased supplies, $300, and furniture, $2,500, on account.
	7	Paid $15,000 cash to acquire land for an office site.
	7	Worked for a client, and billed the client $1,500.
	16	Received partial payment from a client on account, $500.
	24	Paid the telephone bill, $110.
	24	Paid the water and electricity bills, $400.
	28	Received $2,500 cash for helping a client meet environmental standards.
	31	Paid secretary's salary, $1,200.
	31	Paid $2,500 of the account payable created on October 6.
	31	Declared and paid dividends of $2,400.

Requirements

1. Record each transaction in the journal using the account titles that accurately reflect the nature of the activities being allocated to them. Key each transaction by date. Explanations are not required.
2. Post the transactions to T-accounts, using transaction dates as posting references. Label the ending balance of each account Bal., as shown in the chapter.
3. Prepare the trial balance of Barron Environmental Services Inc. at October 31, 2020.
4. Report to the shareholder how much in total resources the business has to work with, how much it owes, and whether October was profitable (and by how much).

P2-45B During the first month of operations (June 2020), Schulich Graphics Service Inc. completed the following selected transactions:

LEARNING OBJECTIVES ❶❸❺

Record transactions directly in T-accounts; prepare and use a trial balance; specify accounts affected by transactions

a. Began the business with an investment of $20,000 cash and a building valued at $60,000. The corporation issued common shares to the shareholders in exchange for these investments.
b. Borrowed $90,000 from the bank, and signed a note payable.
c. Paid $35,000 for computer equipment.
d. Purchased office supplies on account for $1,300.
e. Performed computer graphic service on account for a client, $2,500.
f. Received $1,200 cash on account.
g. Paid $800 of the account payable created in transaction (d).
h. Received a $500 bill for advertising expense that will be paid in the near future.
i. Performed service for clients, and received $1,100 in cash.
j. Paid employees' salaries totalling $2,200.
k. Paid the following cash expenses: rent, $700; utilities, $400.

Requirement

Prepare the trial balance of Schulich Graphics Service Inc. at June 30, 2020.

APPLY YOUR KNOWLEDGE

DECISION CASES

Case 1. A friend named Tom Tipple has asked what effect certain transactions will have on his company. Time is short, so you cannot apply the detailed procedures of journalizing and posting. Instead, you must analyze the transactions without the use of a journal. Tipple will continue the business only if he can expect to earn monthly net income of $10,000. The following transactions occurred this month:

a. Tipple deposited $10,000 cash in a business bank account, and the corporation issued common shares to him.
b. Paid $300 cash for supplies.
c. Purchased office furniture on account, $4,400.
d. Earned revenue on account, $7,000.
e. Borrowed $5,000 cash from the bank, and signed a note payable due within one year.
f. Paid the following cash expenses for one month: employee's salary, $1,700; office rent, $600.
g. Collected cash from customers on account, $1,200.
h. Paid on account, $1,000.
i. Earned revenue, and received $2,500 cash.
j. Purchased advertising in the local newspaper for cash, $800.

This section's material reflects CPA enabling competencies, including:

I. Professional and ethical behaviour

II. Problem-solving and decision-making

III. Communication

IV. Self-management

V. Teamwork and leadership

Based on Chartered Professional Accountant standards

LEARNING OBJECTIVES ❶❸❺

Record transactions directly in T-accounts, prepare a trial balance, and measure net income or loss; determine which accounts to records transactions in

Requirements

1. Prepare a trial balance at the current date. List expenses with the largest amount first, the next largest amount second, and so on. The business name will be Tipple Networks, Inc.

2. Compute the amount of net income or net loss for this first month of operations. Why would you recommend that Tipple continue or not continue in business?

LEARNING OBJECTIVE ⑤

Correct financial statements; decide whether to expand a business

Case 2. Barbara Boland opened a flower shop. Business has been good, and Boland is considering expanding with a second shop. A cousin has produced the following financial statements at December 31, 2020, the end of the first three months of operations:

	A	B	C
1	**Barbara Boland Blossoms Inc.** Income Statement Quarter Ended December 31, 2020		
2	Sales revenue	$ 36,000	
3	Common shares	10,000	
4	Total revenue	46,000	
5	Accounts payable	8,000	
6	Advertising expense	5,000	
7	Rent expense	6,000	
8	Total expenses	19,000	
9	Net income	$ 27,000	
10			

	A	B	C
1	**Barbara Boland Blossoms Inc.** Balance Sheet As at December 31, 2020		
2	Assets		
3	Cash	$ 6,000	
4	Cost of goods sold (expense)	22,000	
5	Flower inventory	5,000	
6	Store fixtures	10,000	
7	Total assets	$ 43,000	
8	Liabilities		
9	None		
10	Shareholders' Equity	$ 43,000	
11			

In these financial statements, all amounts are correct except for Shareholders' Equity. Boland's cousin heard that total assets should equal total liabilities plus shareholders' equity, so he plugged in the amount of shareholders' equity at $43,000 to make the balance sheet come out evenly.

Requirement

Barbara Boland has asked whether she should expand the business. Her banker says Boland may be wise to expand if (a) net income for the first quarter reaches $5,000 and (b) total assets are at least $25,000. It appears that the business has reached these milestones, but Boland doubts her cousin's understanding of accounting. Boland needs your help in making this decision. Prepare a corrected income statement and balance sheet. After preparing the statements, give Boland your recommendation as to whether she should expand the flower shop.

ETHICAL DECISIONS

Decision 1. Scruffy Murphy is the president and principal shareholder of Scruffy's Bar and Grill Limited. To expand, the business is applying for a $250,000 bank loan. The bank requires the company to have shareholders' equity of at least as much as the loan. Currently, shareholders' equity is $150,000. To get the loan, Murphy is considering two options for beefing up the shareholders' equity of the business:

> *Option 1.* Issue $100,000 of common shares for cash. A friend has been wanting to invest in the company. This may be the right time to extend the offer.

> *Option 2.* Transfer $100,000 of Murphy's personal land to the business, and issue common shares to Murphy. Then, after obtaining the loan, Murphy can transfer the land back to himself and cancel the common shares.

Requirements

1. Journalize the transactions required by each option.
2. Use the Framework for Making Ethical Judgments in Chapter 1 (p. 26) to determine which plan would be ethical.

Decision 2. Community Charities has a standing agreement with Royal Bank of Canada (RBC). The agreement allows Community Charities to overdraw its cash balance at the bank when donations are running low. In the past, Community Charities managed funds wisely and rarely used this privilege. Recently, however, Beatrice Grand has been named president of Community Charities. To expand operations, she is acquiring office equipment and spending a lot for fundraising. During Grand's presidency, Community Charities has maintained a negative bank balance of about $3,000.

Requirements

What is the ethical issue in this situation? Do you approve or disapprove of Grand's management of Community Charities's and RBC's funds? Why? Use the Framework for Making Ethical Judgments in Chapter 1 (p. 26) in answering this question.

Decision 3. For each of the situations listed, identify which of three principles (integrity, objectivity and independence, or due care) from the CPA Code of Professional Conduct is violated. Assume all persons listed in the situations are CPAs. (Note: Refer to the CPA Code of Professional Conduct contained on pages 27–28 in Chapter 1 for descriptions of the principles.)

a. Yanjun recently received a promotion and is required to do more complex journal entries than in her previous position. Since Yanjun is embarrassed that she does not know how to do the journal entries, she does not attend a training session at her company. She figures that she can figure it out on her own; after all, the company promoted her.

b. Turja is in charge of entering accounts receivable journal entries. Turja is notorious for transposing the numbers in his journal entries, so his supervisor requires him to review his work at the end of each day. Turja is annoyed by this policy and leaves work without reviewing his journal entries.

c. Hammad, the managing partner of a CPA firm, received two tickets for platinum seats at an upcoming Toronto Maple Leafs game from an accounting software vendor. The CPA firm is currently conducting an audit of that accounting software vendor. These tickets sell for over $500 each.

d. Jackie sets up a fake supplier account and then creates false invoices and bills her company for work done by this fictitious supplier. Once the cheque is prepared for the fake supplier, Jackie deposits it in her own bank account.

FOCUS ON FINANCIAL STATEMENT ANALYSIS

LEARNING OBJECTIVE ❹

Journalize and post transactions

MyLab Accounting

Task 1 Refer to the Dollarama financial statements in Appendix A at the back of the book. Assume that Dollarama completed the following selected transactions during its 2018 fiscal year (all amounts in millions).

a. Sold goods on account, $180.1.
b. Sold goods for cash, $3,086.0.
c. Collected accounts receivable, $180.2.
d. Purchased inventory on account, $1,990.4.
e. Sold inventory that cost $1,965.2. Debit "Cost of sales."
f. Purchased TV advertising for cash, $50.1.
g. Paid accounts payable, $1,960.5.
h. Received cash from new long-term debt, $336.9.
i. Purchased property and equipment for cash, $53.9.

Requirements

1. For the following items, set up T-accounts with the given opening balances (note that the debits do not equal the credits because this is only a subset of Dollarama's accounts):
   - Cash, debit balance of $62.0
   - Accounts Receivable, debit balance of $15.4
   - Inventories, debit balance of $465.7
   - Property, Plant and Equipment, debit balance of $437.1
   - Accounts Payable and Accrued Liabilities, credit balance of $198.5
   - Long-Term Debt, credit balance of $1,328.7
   - Sales, balance of $0
   - Cost of Sales, balance of $0
   - General, Administrative and Store Operating Expenses, balance of $0

2. Record Dollarama's transactions (a) through (i) in the journal. Explanations are not required.

3. Post the transactions in Requirement (2) to the T-accounts (key them by letter) and compute the balance in each account.

4. For each of the following accounts, compare your balance to the actual balance in Dollarama's financial statements in Appendix A. Your balances should agree with the actual balances.
   - Accounts Receivable
   - Inventories
   - Property, Plant and Equipment
   - Accounts Payable and Accrued Liabilities
   - Long-term Debt (Current + Non-Current portions)
   - Sales
   - Cost of Sales

LEARNING OBJECTIVE ❹

Analyze transactions and financial statements

MyLab Accounting

Task 2 Refer to the Dollarama financial statements in Appendix A at the end of the book. Suppose you are an investor considering buying Dollarama's shares. The following questions are important:

1. Explain which of Dollarama's credit sales or collections from customers was the largest amount during the year ended January 3, 2015. Analyze trade receivables to answer this question.

2. A major concern of lenders, such as banks, is the amount of long-term debt a company owes. How much long-term debt does Dollarama owe at January 28, 2018? What must have happened to Dollarama's long-term debt during the 2018 fiscal year?

3. Investors are very interested in a company's sales and earnings, and its trends of sales and earnings over time. Consider Dollarama's Sales and Net Earnings (or Net Income) during the year ended January 28, 2018. Compute the percentage change in Sales and also in Net Earnings during this period. Which item changed more during this period? (For convenience, show dollar amounts in millions.) Which provides a better indicator of business success? Give the reason for your answer.

CHECK YOUR WORK

STOP + THINK (2-1)

1. The issuance of shares and the sale of electronics products

2. The declaration and payment of dividends and the payment of expenses

STOP + THINK (2-2)

Cash would increase by $5,000 to $38,300, causing total assets to increase to $63,000.

A new account, Loan Payable, would increase by $5,000, causing liabilities to increase to $6,800.

Shareholders' equity would not change, so total liabilities and shareholders' equity would increase to $63,000.

STOP + THINK (2-3)

The loan transaction would result in a $5,000 debit (or increase) to the Cash account and a $5,000 credit (or increase) to the Loan Payable account.

STOP + THINK (2-4)

The company purchases $10,000 worth of equipment from a supplier on credit.

STOP + THINK (2-5)

Cash would have a debit balance of $38,300.

A new account, Loan payable, would appear below Accounts payable, with a credit balance of $5,000.

Total Debits and Total Credits would each equal $66,800.

QUICK QUIZ ANSWERS

1. *c.*	6. *b.*	11. *d.*	16. *d.*
2. *d.*	7. *c.*	12. *c.*	17. *c.*
3. *c.*	8. *a.*	13. *a.*	18. *b.*
4. *a.*	9. *b.*	14. *b.*	19. *a.*
5. *d.*	10. *d.*	15. *a.*	20. *b.*

3

Accrual Accounting and the Financial Statements

LEARNING OBJECTIVES

1. **Explain** how accrual accounting differs from cash-basis accounting
2. **Apply** the revenue and expense recognition principles
3. **Record** adjusting journal entries
4. **Prepare** the financial statements
5. **Record** closing journal entries
6. **Analyze** and **evaluate** a company's debt-paying ability

CPA COMPETENCIES

Competencies addressed in this chapter:

1.2.1 Develops or evaluates appropriate accounting policies and procedures

1.2.2 Evaluates treatment for routine transactions

1.3.1 Prepares financial statements

1.4.4 Interprets financial reporting results for stakeholders (external or internal)

Based on Chartered Professional Accountant standards

SPOTLIGHT

Le Château has been selling fashion apparel, footwear, and accessories in Canada for over 50 years. What started as a single, family-owned store in Montreal in 1959 is now one of Canada's longest-running fashion brands, with its merchandise sold in over 150 stores across Canada. As the company's promotional materials state, Le Château's "success is a result of our time-tested business strategies that include the quick identification of and response to fashion trends through our design, product development and vertically integrated operations."

As you can see from Le Château's statement of loss on the next page, the company sold just over $200 million in merchandise in its fiscal 2018 year. Unfortunately, its expenses for the year were higher, so it ended up reporting a net loss of about $24 million. How does Le Château determine when to recognize the revenues and expenses it reports on this statement? Read on and you will find out!

JHVEPhoto/Shutterstock

	A	B	C
1	**Le Château Inc.** Consolidated Statement of Loss (Adapted) For the Year Ended January 27, 2018		
2	*(in thousands of dollars)*		
3	Income		
4	Sales	$ 204,369	
5	**Expenses**		
6	Cost of sales	72,737	
7	Selling	118,694	
8	General and administrative	29,915	
9	Finance and other costs	6,996	
10	**Total expenses**	228,342	
11	**Net loss**	$ (23,973)	
12			

Source: Data From Le Château Inc. Annual Report – 2018.

Chapter 2 focused on measuring and recording transactions up to the trial balance. This chapter completes our coverage of the accounting cycle by discussing the adjustment process, the preparation of financial statements, and the closing of the books at the end of the period. It also includes a discussion of accounting principles that govern the recognition of revenue and expenses. At the end of the chapter, you will learn how to evaluate a company's debt-paying ability.

EXPLAIN HOW ACCRUAL ACCOUNTING DIFFERS FROM CASH-BASIS ACCOUNTING

OBJECTIVE

❶ **Explain** how accrual accounting differs from cash-basis accounting

Managers want to earn a profit. Investors search for companies whose share prices will increase. Banks seek borrowers who will pay their debts. Accounting provides the information these people use for decision making. Accounting information can be prepared using either the cash basis or the accrual basis of accounting.

When using **cash-basis accounting**, we record only business transactions involving the receipt or payment of cash. All other business transactions are ignored. If a business makes a $1,000 sale on account, for example, with the customer taking delivery of the goods but not paying for them until a later date, we would not record the sale transaction until we receive the cash payment from the customer. Similarly, the business would not record the purchase of $2,000 of inventory on account until it actually pays cash for the goods at some future date, despite having already received the inventory items from its supplier.

In contrast, when using **accrual accounting**, *the receipt or payment of cash is irrelevant* to deciding whether a business transaction should be recorded. What matters is whether the business has acquired an asset, earned revenue, taken on a liability, or incurred an expense. If it has, the transaction is recorded in the accounting records.

After the above sale on account, for example, the business has both gained an asset and earned revenue despite receiving no cash. Recall from Chapter 1 that an asset is a resource controlled by a company as a result of a past event and from which it expects to receive future economic benefits. The sale on account creates a $1,000 account receivable, which is an asset because it entitles the company to receive the economic benefit of cash at a future date when the customer pays off its account. The business has also earned $1,000 in revenue by delivering goods to the customer, which is a key activity in its day-to-day business operations. Because this transaction results in both an asset and revenue, we record it under the accrual basis of accounting.

Similarly, after the preceding purchase of inventory on account, the business has acquired $2,000 in assets in the form of goods it can sell to its customers in return for cash at some future date. It also has an obligation—in the form of a $2,000 account payable—that it must settle by paying cash to its supplier at some future date, so the business has also taken on a liability. Since this transaction results in an asset and a liability, we must record it under the accrual basis of accounting.

If the business were using the cash basis of accounting, neither of these initial transactions would have been recorded, leading to the following understatements in the business's financial statements: $3,000 in assets, $2,000 in liabilities, and $1,000 in revenue and net income. As a result, users relying on these cash-basis financial statements would have incomplete information about the company's financial position and results of operations, which would likely lead them to make poor business decisions.

Because the cash basis of accounting is inconsistent with the conceptual framework of accounting introduced in Chapter 1, it is not permitted by IFRS or ASPE, both of which provide extensive guidance on how to apply the accrual basis of accounting to prepare financial statements that present a relevant and faithful representation of a company's business activities.

Let's look at a simple example that illustrates the differences between the two methods of accounting. Suppose Pointz Corporation has the following transactions during July 2020:

1. Provides services to a customer for $500 in cash.

2. Provides services to a customer for $800 on account.

3. Pays employees' salaries of $450 in cash.

4. Receives a $50 hydro bill for electricity used during July.

The income statements for Pointz Corporation under the accrual basis and the cash basis of accounting appear as follows:

	A	B	C
1	**Pointz Corporation** Income Statement Using Accrual Accounting For the Month Ended July 31, 2020		
2	Revenue	$ 1,300	
3	Expenses:		
4	Salaries	450	
5	Hydro	50	
6	Net income	$ 800	
7	**Pointz Corporation** Income Statement Using Cash-Basis Accounting For the Month Ended July 31, 2020		
8	Revenue	$ 500	
9	Expenses:		
10	Salaries	450	
11	Hydro	0	
12	Net income	$ 50	
13			

The accrual-accounting statement reports an additional $800 in revenue because we have recorded the sale on account that is ignored in the cash-basis statement. The accrual statement also includes the $50 cost of hydro consumed during the month, which we have excluded from the cash statement because it remained unpaid at the end of the month. As a result of these differences, we report an additional $750 in net income for the month ($800 in revenue less $50 in expenses) on the accrual basis compared to the cash basis.

Next we discuss the formal principles used to determine when revenues and expenses should be recognized under accrual accounting.

STOP + THINK (3-1)

Death Valley's Little Brother (DVLB), a local independent coffee shop, sells an Americano for $3. Customers can also purchase 10 Americanos for $25 and receive a coffee card, with the card being punched every time the customer orders one of their 10 Americanos on future visits. DVLB uses accrual accounting. Briefly explain when DVLB would record revenue on the sale of a single Americano and on the sale of 10 Americanos via a coffee card.

APPLY THE REVENUE AND EXPENSE RECOGNITION PRINCIPLES

The Revenue Recognition Principle

In Chapter 1 we provided you with a basic definition of revenue, which stated that it consists of amounts earned by a company in the course of its ordinary, day-to-day business activities, primarily through the sale of goods and services. Now that you are more familiar with many fundamental accounting terms and concepts, we will provide the formal IFRS definition of revenue. IFRS define revenue as "the gross inflow of economic benefits during the period arising in the course of the ordinary activities of an entity when those inflows result in increases in equity, other than increases relating to contributions from equity participants" (ASPE has a fundamentally equivalent definition of revenue). Restating this in terms of the accounting equation, revenue is earned when ordinary business activities result in increases to both assets and shareholders' equity, other than when shareholders contribute capital to the business. When a business delivers goods to a customer who pays cash for them, the Cash asset increases and so does Shareholders' Equity (via Retained Earnings), so the business has earned revenue. But when a shareholder purchases additional shares in the business, which also increases Cash and Shareholders' Equity (via Share Capital), no revenue has been earned because the shareholder has simply injected more capital into the business.

Under the ASPE revenue recognition standard, a sales transaction must satisfy *all three* of these criteria before the seller can recognize revenue:

1. The ownership (or control) and benefits of the goods have been transferred to the customer, or the services have been provided to the customer.

2. The amount of revenue to be received can be reliably measured.

3. It is probable that the customer will pay for the goods or services when payment becomes due.

The IFRS revenue recognition standard is based on the idea that all business transactions involve contracts that exchange goods or services for cash or claims to receive cash. When determining how to recognize revenue for a transaction, the business selling the good or service must:

1. Identify the contract with the customer, specify its terms, and evaluate the probability the customer will pay the transaction price when it becomes due.

2. Identify the separate performance obligations in the contract.

3. Determine the transaction price.

4. Allocate the transaction price to the separate performance obligations in the contract.

5. Recognize revenue when (or as) the business satisfies each performance obligation.

These criteria often require significantly more professional judgment to apply than the ASPE criteria, depending on the nature of the sales transaction being evaluated. Contracts in industries such as software development, building construction, motion pictures, or natural resources can be complicated, making it challenging to determine when and how to recognize revenue from them. The examples and problems in this textbook deal mostly with basic retail, wholesale, and service businesses, where companies enter into simple contracts to sell finished goods or to render routine services. For businesses like these, applying the IFRS standard is straightforward and results in recognizing revenue the same way as under the ASPE standard. Let's use two examples to illustrate the application and similarity of these standards for basic retail and service transactions.

Suppose you go shopping at Le Château and purchase a pair of pants for $75, which you pay cash for and take home with you. When would Le Château recognize revenue from the sale of these pants under ASPE and IFRS revenue recognition criteria? Exhibit 3-1 presents the application of each standard's criteria to the terms of this transaction. As it illustrates, under both standards, Le Château would recognize revenue of $75 immediately after it provides you with the pants. However, suppose instead that you find a pair of $75 pants you like but the store does not have your size in stock, so the sales clerk orders a pair in your size from another store, and tells you to come back to pick up and pay for them in three days. At this point, Le Château has not provided you with the pants, so ASPE criterion #1 and IFRS criterion #5 are not met. Only if you return to the store to pick up and pay for the pants will Le Château be able to recognize any revenue under ASPE or IFRS. In general, revenue from goods is recognized when the goods are delivered, assuming the price is reliably measurable and collection is probable.

As an example of service revenue recognition, assume a plumber comes to repair a leaky pipe under your bathroom sink, taking one hour and charging you $75, which you pay for by credit card. As Exhibit 3-1 shows, under both ASPE and IFRS the plumber can recognize $75 in revenue immediately after repairing your pipe. In contrast, assume you simply call the plumber to arrange for him to come to your home in two days to fix the leaky pipe, which he estimates will take one hour and cost $75. In this case, ASPE criterion #1 and IFRS criterion #5 would not be met until the plumber completes the repair in two days, so he cannot recognize any revenue until that point. In general, revenue from services is recognized as the services are performed, assuming the price is reliably measurable and collection is probable.

EXHIBIT 3-1
Application of ASPE and IFRS Revenue Recognition Criteria

Criteria	Sale of Pants by Le Château	Repair of Pipe by Plumber
ASPE		
1. The ownership (or control) and benefits of the goods have been transferred to the customer, or the services have been provided to the customer.	You own the pants and can now benefit from wearing them.	The plumber has repaired the pipe.
2. The amount of revenue to be received can be reliably measured.	The price of the pants is $75.	The price of the repair is $75.
3. It is probable that the customer will pay for the goods or services when payment becomes due.	You paid the full $75 in cash.	You paid the full $75 with your credit card.
	All three criteria are met, so Le Château can recognize revenue of $75 after providing you the pants.	All three criteria are met, so the plumber can recognize revenue of $75 after repairing the pipe.
IFRS		
1. Identify the contract with the customer, specify its terms, and evaluate the probability the customer will pay the transaction price when it becomes due.	You did not sign a formal contract with Le Château, but by purchasing the pants, you implicitly agreed to its terms of sale, which included the sales price and the requirement to pay for the pants before leaving the store with them, which you did.	You did not sign a formal contract with the plumber, but by booking the repair, you implicitly agreed to their terms of service, which included the rate per hour and the requirement to pay for the repair upon completion, which you did.
2. Identify the separate performance obligations in the contract.	Le Château has one performance obligation, which is to provide you with the pants.	The plumber has one performance obligation, which is to repair your pipe.
3. Determine the transaction price.	The price of the pants is $75.	The price of the repair is $75.
4. Allocate the transaction price to the separate performance obligations in the contract.	The full $75 price is allocated to the pants.	The full $75 price is allocated to the repair of the pipe.
5. Recognize revenue when (or as) the business satisfies each performance obligation.	Le Château can recognize revenue of $75 after providing you the pants.	The plumber can recognize revenue of $75 after repairing the pipe.

The Expense Recognition Principle

In Chapter 1 we defined expenses as costs incurred to purchase the goods and services a company needs to run its business on a day-to-day basis. As with revenue recognition, IFRS and ASPE contain formal principles which set out the criteria that must be satisfied before an expense can be recognized:

1. There has been a decrease in future economic benefits caused by a decrease in an asset *or* an increase in a liability.
2. The expense can be reliably measured.

So, for example, once you have left the store with your new pants, Le Château's pants inventory (an asset) decreases by one pair, so the first expense recognition condition has been met. Le Château can check its inventory records to determine the cost of the pants it sold you, so the expense can be reliably measured. Both conditions have now been satisfied, so Le Château can recognize an expense in the form of Cost of Sales. As for the situation where you are waiting for pants to be shipped from another store, Le Château cannot recognize an expense because its pants inventory will not decrease until you have actually purchased the pants.

In the case of the plumber who has fixed your leaky pipe, the plumbing company that employs him is now obligated to pay him for the one hour of work he did for you, which increases the company's Wages Payable liability. The plumber's hourly wage rate can be used to reliably measure the expense, so with both conditions satisfied, the company can recognize the wage expense associated with the plumber's work on your pipe. As for the situation where you have to wait two days for the plumber to come and fix your pipe, the plumbing company is not yet obligated to pay the plumber because he has not done the work for you. Without an increase in the Wages Payable liability, the first condition has not been met, so no expense can be recognized.

STOP + THINK (3-2)

1. A client pays Windsor Group Ltd. $900 on March 15 for consulting service to be performed April 1 to June 30. Assuming the company uses accrual accounting, has Windsor Group Ltd. earned revenue on March 15? When will Windsor Group Ltd. earn the revenue?

2. Windsor Group Ltd. pays $4,500 on July 31 for office rent for the next three months. Has the company incurred an expense on July 31?

OBJECTIVE

❸ **Record** adjusting journal entries

RECORD ADJUSTING JOURNAL ENTRIES

At the end of a period, the business prepares its financial statements. This process begins with the trial balance introduced in Chapter 2. We refer to this trial balance as *unadjusted* because the accounts are not yet ready for the financial statements. In most cases, the simple label "Trial Balance" means "Unadjusted Trial Balance."

Because IFRS and ASPE require accrual accounting, we must record adjusting journal entries to ensure that all assets and liabilities have been recorded at period end, and that all revenues earned and expenses incurred during the period have been included in the accounts. These entries are recorded at the end of the accounting period, just before the financial statements are prepared.

Types of Adjusting Entries

There are three main types of adjusting entries: deferrals, depreciation, and accruals. We will use a variety of transactions and related adjusting entries for the fictional Moreau Ltd. to illustrate each main type of adjustment. Other miscellaneous adjusting entries are usually required at the end of an accounting period. We will address some of these as they arise in later chapters of the book. The table below provides an overview of the main types of adjusting entries.

Main Types of Adjusting Entries	
Type	**Description**
Deferrals	An adjusting entry must be recorded when a company receives (pays) cash in advance of providing (receiving) the related good or service that has been paid for. This type of adjusting entry results in the deferral of the recognition of the related revenue (expense) until the future period in which the economic benefit is actually provided.
Depreciation	An adjusting entry must be recorded to reflect that the future economic benefits of a tangible asset decline with age. This type of adjusting entry, which can be considered a special form of deferral, results in the depreciation (amortization under ASPE) of the value of the asset over its useful life by expensing the portion of the asset's economic benefits that has been used up during an accounting period.
Accruals	An adjusting entry must be recorded when a company delivers (or receives) a good or service in advance of it being billed and paid for. This type of adjusting entry results in the accrual of the related revenue (expense) in the period in which the good or service is actually provided, regardless of the fact that it will not be billed or paid for until a future period.

Deferrals—Prepaid Expenses

A prepaid expense is an expense a company has paid for in advance of actually using the benefit. Because it will provide a future economic benefit to the company, it is recorded as an asset when the cash payment is made. Recording the initial transaction this way results in the **deferral** of the expense to the future period in which the related benefit is realized. Let's look at the initial and adjusting entries for prepaid rent and supplies.

PREPAID RENT. Rent is usually paid in advance of the rented item being used, creating an asset for the renter, who gains the benefit of using the rented item during the future rental period. Suppose Moreau Ltd. prepays three months' office rent ($3,000) on April 1. The journal entry for the prepayment of three months' rent is as follows:

	A	B	C	D	E
1	Apr. 1	Prepaid Rent ($1,000 × 3)	3,000		
2		Cash		3,000	
3		*Paid three months' rent in advance.*			
4					

The accounting equation shows that one asset increases and another decreases. Total assets are unchanged.

ASSETS	=	LIABILITIES	+	SHAREHOLDERS' EQUITY
3,000	=	0	+	0
−3,000				

After posting, the Prepaid Rent account appears as follows:

Prepaid Rent

Apr. 1	3,000

At the end of April, Moreau has only two months of future rental benefits remaining (2/3 of $3,000), so we must adjust the Prepaid Rent account to reflect this and to expense the $1,000 in Prepaid Rent used up during April (1/3 of $3,000).*

	A	B	C	D	E
1	Apr. 30	Rent Expense	1,000		
2	*Adjusting entry a*	Prepaid Rent		1,000	
3		*To record rent expense.*			
4					

Both assets and shareholders' equity decrease.

ASSETS	=	LIABILITIES	+	SHAREHOLDERS' EQUITY	
−1,000	=	0	−	1,000	Rent Expense

After posting, Prepaid Rent and Rent Expense appear as follows:

	Prepaid Rent				Rent Expense	
Apr. 1	3,000	Apr. 30	1,000 →	Apr. 30	1,000	
Bal.	2,000			Bal.	1,000	

SUPPLIES. Businesses often have a stock of unused supplies on hand at the end of an accounting period, which represents an asset that will be used up in future periods. These unused supplies are another type of prepaid expense. On April 2, Moreau paid cash for $700 of office supplies, requiring the following journal entry:

	A	B	C	D	E
1	Apr. 2	Supplies	700		
2		Cash		700	
3		*Paid cash for supplies.*			
4					

ASSETS	=	LIABILITIES	+	SHAREHOLDERS' EQUITY
700	=	0	+	0
−700				

Moreau used some of these supplies during April, so to expense their use and adjust the Supplies asset to reflect the future benefit remaining at April 30, we need an adjusting entry. By counting and valuing the supplies on hand at April 30, we can determine the amount of the adjustment needed. If Moreau's count shows that $400 in supplies remain at April 30, then we know that $300 worth of supplies have been used during April ($700 − $400), and we can record this adjusting entry:

	A	B	C	D	E
1	Apr. 30	Supplies Expense ($700 – $400)	300		
2	*Adjusting entry b*	Supplies		300	
3		*To record supplies expense.*			
4					

---

*See Exhibit 3-4, page 124, for a summary of adjustments a through h.

ASSETS	=	LIABILITIES	+	SHAREHOLDERS' EQUITY	
−300	=	0	−	300	Supplies Expense

After posting, the Supplies and Supplies Expense accounts appear as follows:

Supplies					Supplies Expense		
Apr. 2	700	Apr. 30	300	→	Apr. 30	300	
Bal.	400				Bal.	300	

MyLab Accounting

STOP + THINK (3-3)

At the beginning of the month, supplies were $5,000. During the month, $7,000 of supplies were purchased. At month's end, $3,000 of supplies were still on hand. What adjusting entry is needed to account for the supplies, and what is the ending balance in the Supplies account?

Deferrals—Unearned Revenues

Businesses sometimes receive cash from customers before providing them with the goods or services they have paid for. Because the goods or services have not been delivered, the revenue recognition principle deems this to be **unearned revenue**. In fact, the business now has an obligation to provide the goods or services at some future date, which requires it to record a liability instead of revenue. Recording such transactions in this way results in a deferral of revenue recognition until the liability has been settled by providing the goods or services to the customer.

Suppose a customer engages Moreau Ltd. to provide consulting services over the next year, agreeing to pay Moreau $450 per month for nine hours of services ($50/hour), effective immediately. If Moreau receives the first $450 payment on April 20, it records this entry to reflect the unearned revenue:

	A	B	C	D	E
1	Apr. 20	Cash	450		
2		Unearned Service Revenue		450	
3		*Received cash in advance of providing services.*			
4					

ASSETS	=	LIABILITIES	+	SHAREHOLDERS' EQUITY
450	=	450	+	0

After posting, the liability account appears as follows:

Unearned Service Revenue		
	Apr. 20	450

Unearned Service Revenue is a liability because Moreau Ltd. is obligated to perform nine hours of services for the client. During the last 10 days of April, Moreau performed three hours of services for the client, so by April 30, Moreau has settled one-third of the liability and earned one-third of the revenue ($450 \times 1/3 = $150). The following adjusting entry is needed to reflect these events:

	A	B	C	D	E
1	Apr. 30	Unearned Service Revenue	150		
2	*Adjusting entry c*	Service Revenue		150	
3		*To adjust unearned service revenue that has*			
		been earned ($450 × 1/3).			

ASSETS	=	LIABILITIES	+	SHAREHOLDERS' EQUITY	
0	=	−150	+	150	Service Revenue

This adjusting entry shifts $150 of the total amount received ($450) from liability to revenue. After posting, Unearned Service Revenue is reduced to $300, and Service Revenue is increased by $150, as follows:

Unearned Service Revenue					Service Revenue		
Apr. 30	150	Apr. 20	450				7,000
		Bal.	300			Apr. 30	150
						Bal.	7,150

Any time a business receives cash from a customer in advance of providing the related goods or services, similar initial and adjusting entries are required to properly reflect the obligation and defer the recognition of revenue until the goods or services have been provided.

Also note that one company's unearned revenue is another company's prepaid expense. As at April 30, for example, the $300 in Unearned Service Revenue on Moreau's books would be reflected as $300 in Prepaid Consulting Services on its customer's books. Under accrual accounting, the deferral of revenue by one company will result in the deferral of an expense by another company.

Depreciation of Property, Plant, and Equipment

Property, plant, and equipment, such as buildings, furniture, and machinery, are long-term tangible assets that provide several years of economic benefits to a company. Because the future benefits of a tangible asset decline with age, however, we must reduce its carrying value each year to reflect this decline. To accomplish this, we record adjusting entries for **depreciation** (amortization under ASPE), which gradually reduce the value of the asset over its useful life by expensing the portion of the asset's economic benefits that has been used up during each accounting period. An exception is made for land, which we do not depreciate because it has an unlimited useful life, so its future economic benefits generally do not decline with age.

To illustrate depreciation, suppose that on April 3, Moreau Ltd. purchased $16,500 of office furniture, including desks, chairs, and storage cabinets, on account. The entry to record this purchase is as follows:

	A	B	C	D	E
1	Apr. 3	Furniture	16,500		
2		Accounts Payable		16,500	
3		*Purchased office furniture on account.*			

ASSETS	=	LIABILITIES	+	SHAREHOLDERS' EQUITY
16,500	=	16,500	+	0

After posting, the Furniture account appears as follows:

Furniture

Apr. 3	16,500

Moreau Ltd.'s furniture is expected to remain useful for five years and then be worthless. One way to *estimate* the amount of depreciation for each year is to divide the cost of the asset ($16,500 in our example) by its expected useful life (five years). This procedure—called the straight-line depreciation method—yields annual depreciation of $3,300, or monthly depreciation of $275 ($3,300/12). (Chapter 6 covers depreciation and property, plant, and equipment in more detail.)

The adjusting entry to record depreciation for April is therefore:

	A	B	C	D	E
1	Apr. 30	Depreciation Expense—Furniture	275		
2	*Adjusting entry d*	Accumulated Depreciation—Furniture		275	
3		*To record depreciation.*			

ASSETS	=	LIABILITIES	+	SHAREHOLDERS' EQUITY	
−275	=	0	−	275	Depreciation

Note that the adjusting entry does not decrease Assets by directly crediting the Furniture asset account. Instead, we decrease Assets by crediting an account called Accumulated Depreciation—Furniture, which is known as a contra asset account. A **contra account** has two distinguishing features:

1. It always has a companion account.
2. Its normal balance is opposite that of the companion account.

In this case, the Furniture account is the companion to the Accumulated Depreciation contra account. Since the Furniture account's normal balance is a debit, the normal balance of the Accumulated Depreciation account is a credit.

As its name suggests, the **Accumulated Depreciation** account accumulates all the depreciation recorded on the asset(s) included in the related companion account, so its balance increases over the life of the related assets being depreciated. A business's chart of accounts normally contains a separate Accumulated Depreciation account for each major category of depreciable asset.

After posting, the furniture-related accounts of Moreau Ltd. are as follows:

Furniture			Accumulated Depreciation—Furniture			Depreciation Expense—Furniture		
Apr. 3	16,500			Apr. 30	275	Apr. 30	275	
Bal.	16,500			Bal.	275	Bal.	275	

As at April 30, the **carrying amount** of Moreau's furniture is $16,225, which is obtained by deducting the asset's accumulated depreciation ($275) from its original cost ($16,500). All long-term tangible assets are reported at their carrying amounts on the balance sheet, with the details of their original costs and accumulated depreciation normally disclosed in a note to the financial statements.

STOP + THINK (3-4)

What will the carrying amount of Moreau Ltd.'s furniture be at the end of May 2020?

Accruals—Accrued Expenses

Businesses often incur expenses they have not yet been billed for, let alone paid. Utility bills, for example, usually arrive after the business has consumed the electricity or gas being billed. For some types of expenses, such as salaries or loan interest, no bills will ever be received. At the end of each accounting period, businesses must record adjusting entries called **accruals** to get these unbilled, unpaid expenses, which we call **accrued expenses**, into the books. By recording these accruals, we ensure the related expenses and liabilities are properly reflected in the financial statements for the period.

SALARIES. Let's use Salary Expense to illustrate this concept. Suppose Moreau Ltd. has one employee who receives a monthly salary of $1,900, which is paid in equal $950 amounts on the 15th and last day of each month. If a payday falls on a weekend, the salary is paid on the following Monday. The following calendar illustrates Moreau's pay days for April:

			April			
Sun.	Mon.	Tue.	Wed.	Thur.	Fri.	Sat.
					1	2
3	4	5	6	7	8	9
10	11	12	13	14	(15)	16
17	18	19	20	21	22	23
24	25	26	27	28	29	(30)

On April 15, a Friday, Moreau records this entry to account for the first half-month's salary:

	A	B	C	D	E
1	Apr. 15	Salary Expense	950		
2		Cash		950	
3		*To pay salary.*			

ASSETS	=	LIABILITIES	+	SHAREHOLDERS' EQUITY	
−950	=	0	−	950	Salary Expense

After posting, the Salary Expense account is:

Salary Expense	
10,000	
Apr. 15 950	

Because April 30 falls on a Saturday, the employee will not receive the second half of the salary for April until Monday, May 2, two days after the end of the April accounting period. In this case, the business has incurred a half-month of Salary Expense that it owes the employee as at April 30. To reflect these facts, we record this accrual adjusting entry:

	A	B	C	D	E
1	Apr. 30	Salary Expense	950		
2	*Adjusting entry e*	Salary Payable		950	
3		*To accrue salary expense.*			

The accounting equation shows that an accrued expense increases liabilities and decreases shareholders' equity:

ASSETS	=	LIABILITIES	+	SHAREHOLDERS' EQUITY	
0	=	950	−	950	Salary Expense

After posting, the Salary Payable and Salary Expense accounts appear as follows:

Salary Payable	
Apr. 30	950
Bal.	950

Salary Expense	
	10,000
Apr. 15	950
Apr. 30	950
Bal.	11,900

After the accrual, Moreau's accounts contain accurate salary information for April: it incurred $1,900 in Salary Expense during the month and owed $950 of this amount as at April 30.

INTEREST. Interest on loans and other debts is another common type of expense we must accrue at period ends. Assume on January 31, 2020, Moreau Ltd. obtained a $10,000 bank loan bearing interest at 6% per year, with semi-annual interest payments of $300 due on January 31 and July 31 each year. At the end of April, Moreau therefore owes the bank interest for April, but it will not actually pay this interest until its next payment on July 31. Moreau must therefore accrue $50 of interest expense at April 30 ($300/6 months × 1 month). To reflect these facts, we record this accrual adjusting entry:

	A	B	C	D	E
1	Apr. 30	Interest Expense	50		
2	*Adjusting entry f*	Interest Payable		50	
3		*To accrue interest expense.*			

The impact on the accounting equation is as follows:

ASSETS	=	LIABILITIES	+	SHAREHOLDERS' EQUITY	
0	=	50	−	50	Interest Expense

After posting, the Interest Payable and Interest Expense accounts appear as follows:

Interest Payable			Interest Expense		
		100			100
Apr. 30		50	Apr. 30		50
Bal.		150	Bal.		150

After the accrual, Moreau's accounts contain accurate interest information for April. All accrued-expense adjustments are typically recorded this way—by debiting an expense account and crediting a liability account.

Accruals—Accrued Revenues

At the end of each accounting period, we must also consider the need to record accruals to account for **accrued revenues**, which are the opposite of accrued expenses. Businesses sometimes earn revenues they have not yet billed their customers for, let alone collected cash for. Service businesses such as accounting firms, for example, often provide services to their clients prior to invoicing for the work. Some types of revenues, such as loan interest, will never be invoiced. By recording accruals for these unbilled, uncollected revenues, we ensure that the related assets and revenues are properly reflected in the financial statements for the period.

SERVICES. To illustrate this type of accrual, assume that during the last half of April, Moreau performed $250 worth of services for a client that were not invoiced until early May. The adjusting entry to record this accrual is as follows:

	A	B	C	D	E
1	Apr. 30	Accrued Service Revenue	250		
2	*Adjusting entry g*	Service Revenue		250	
3		*To accrue service revenue.*			

ASSETS	=	LIABILITIES	+	SHAREHOLDERS' EQUITY	
250	=	0	+	250	Service Revenue

This entry increases Assets, in the form of Accrued Service Revenue, because Moreau will receive the economic benefit of cash after it bills and collects the $250 from its client. Note that we have used Accrued Service Revenue instead of Accounts Receivable because the customer has not yet been billed, so no formal account receivable exists. This entry also increases Service Revenue by the same amount to reflect the revenue it has earned by providing the services in April. After posting, these accounts appear as follows:

Accrued Service Revenue			Service Revenue		
		2,250			7,000
Apr. 30		250	Apr. 30		150
			Apr. 30		250
Bal.		2,500	Bal.		7,400

In May, when Moreau invoices the client for the work in April, it will record an entry that debits Accounts Receivable and credits Accrued Service Revenue for $250, since there is now a formal account receivable from this client.

GOODS. Companies sometimes ship goods to customers just before a period ends, but do not bill them for the goods until after the next period has begun. Suppose Moreau shipped $500 worth of goods to a customer on April 29 but did not invoice the customer for this sale until May 3. The adjusting entry to record this sale is as follows:

	A	B	C	D	E
1	Apr. 30	Accrued Sales Revenue	500		
2	*Adjusting entry h*	Sales Revenue		500	
3		*To accrue sales revenue.*			

ASSETS	=	LIABILITIES	+	SHAREHOLDERS' EQUITY	
500	=	0	+	500	Sales Revenue

After posting, the accounts appear as follows:

Accrued Sales Revenue			Sales Revenue		
	1,000				10,000
Apr. 30	500			Apr. 30	500
Bal.	1,500			Bal.	10,500

We record similar accrual entries for other kinds of accrued revenues—an accrued revenue account is debited and a revenue account is credited.

MyLab Accounting

STOP + THINK (3-5)

Suppose Moreau Ltd. holds a loan receivable from a client. At the end of April, $125 of interest revenue has been earned but not received. Prepare the adjusting entry at April 30.

Summary of the Adjusting Process

At the end of every accounting period, we must record adjusting journal entries to ensure that we properly measure income for the period and that we accurately reflect the business's financial position as at the end of the period. Exhibit 3-2 summarizes the main types of adjusting entries, along with the types of accounts they affect.

Exhibit 3-3 details the specific deferral and accrual adjusting entries needed at the end of each accounting period, as well as the journal entries to record the transactions that precede the deferrals and succeed the accruals.

EXHIBIT 3-2
Summary of Adjusting Entries

	Type of Account	
Type of Adjusting Entry	Debit	Credit
Deferral—Prepaid Expense......................................	Expense	Asset
Deferral—Unearned Revenue	Liability	Revenue
Depreciation...	Expense	Contra asset
Accrual—Accrued Expense	Expense	Liability
Accrual—Accrued Revenue	Asset	Revenue

Adapted from material provided by Beverly Terry.

EXHIBIT 3-3
Deferral and Accrual Adjusting Entries

DEFERRALS—Cash First								
	First				**Later**			
Prepaid expenses	*Pay cash and record an asset:*			→	*Record an expense and decrease the asset:*			
	Prepaid Expense.................................	XXX			Expense...	XXX		
	Cash...		XXX		Prepaid Expense		XXX	
Unearned revenues	*Receive cash and record unearned revenue:*			→	*Record a revenue and decrease unearned revenue:*			
	Cash..	XXX			Unearned Revenue	XXX		
	Unearned Revenue		XXX		Revenue..		XXX	

ACCRUALS—Cash Later								
	First				**Later**			
Accrued expenses	*Accrue expense and a payable:*			→	*Pay cash and decrease the payable:*			
	Expense...	XXX			Payable	XXX		
	Payable		XXX		Cash		XXX	
Accrued revenues	*Accrue revenue:*			→	*Invoice customer and record a receivable:*			
	Accrued Revenue................................	XXX			Receivable	XXX		
	Revenue..		XXX		Accrued Revenue.............................		XXX	

COOKING the BOOKS

issues in Accrual Accounting

Accrual accounting provides some ethical challenges that cash accounting avoids. Suppose that on December 1, 2020, for example, Shop Online Inc. (SOI) pays $3 million in cash for an advertising campaign, which will run during December, January, and February. The ads start running immediately. If SOI properly applies the expense recognition principle discussed earlier in the chapter, it should record one-third of the expense ($1 million) during the year ended December 31, 2020, and leave the remaining $2 million as a prepaid expense that will be recognized as an expense in 2021.

But also suppose that 2020 is a great year for SOI, with its net income being much higher than expected. SOI's top managers believe, however, that 2021 will be much less profitable due to increased competition. In this case, company managers have a strong incentive to expense the full $3 million during 2020, an unethical action that would keep $2 million of advertising expense off the 2021 income statement and increase its net income by the same amount (ignoring income taxes).

Unethical managers can also exploit the revenue recognition principle to artificially improve reported liabilities, revenues, and net income. Suppose it is now December 31, 2020, and Highfield Computer Products Ltd., which is having a poor fiscal year, has just received a $1 million advance cash payment for merchandise it will deliver early in January. If top managers are unethical, the company can "manufacture" revenue and net income by recording the $1 million cash payment as revenue in 2020 instead of as unearned revenue (a liability) at the end of the year.

Exhibit 3-4 summarizes the adjusting process we followed for Moreau Ltd. as at April 30, 2020. Panel A contains the information used to record each adjusting entry in Panel B, while Panel C presents all of Moreau's ledger accounts, with each adjusting entry keyed with the corresponding letter from Panel A.

EXHIBIT 3-4
The Adjusting Process of Moreau Ltd.

Panel A—Information for Adjustments at April 30, 2020

(a) Prepaid rent expired, $1,000.
(b) Supplies on hand, $400.
(c) Amount of unearned service revenue that has been earned, $150.
(d) Depreciation on furniture, $275.

(e) Accrued salary expense, $950. This entry assumes the pay period ended April 30 and the employee was paid May 2.
(f) Accrued interest expense, $50.
(g) Accrued service revenue, $250.
(h) Accrued sales revenue, $500.

Panel B—Adjusting Entries

(a) Rent Expense	1,000	
Prepaid Rent		1,000
To record rent expense.		
(b) Supplies Expense	300	
Supplies		300
To record supplies used.		
(c) Unearned Service Revenue	150	
Service Revenue		150
To record unearned revenue that has been earned.		
(d) Depreciation Expense—Furniture	275	
Accumulated Depreciation—Furniture		275
To record depreciation.		
(e) Salary Expense	950	
Salary Payable		950
To accrue salary expense.		
(f) Interest Expense	50	
Interest Payable		50
To accrue interest expense.		
(g) Accrued Service Revenue	250	
Service Revenue		250
To accrue service revenue.		
(h) Accrued Sales Revenue	500	
Sale Revenue		500
To accrue sales revenue.		

Panel C—Ledger Accounts

Assets

Cash

Bal.	34,800	

Accrued Service Revenue

	2,250	
(g)	250	
Bal.	2,500	

Accrued Sales Revenue

	1,000	
(h)	500	
Bal.	1,500	

Supplies

	700	(b)	300
Bal.	400		

Prepaid Rent

	3,000	(a)	1,000
Bal.	2,000		

Furniture

Bal.	16,500	

Accumulated Depreciation—Furniture

		(d)	275
		Bal.	275

Liabilities

Accounts Payable

		Bal.	14,100

Salary Payable

		(e)	950
		Bal.	950

Unearned Service Revenue

(c)	150		450
		Bal.	300

Interest Payable

			100
		(f)	50
		Bal.	150

Loan Payable

		Bal.	10,000

Shareholders' Equity

Share Capital

		Bal.	20,000

Retained Earnings

		Bal.	11,250

Dividends

Bal.	3,200	

Revenue

Service Revenue

			7,000
		(c)	150
		(g)	250
		Bal.	7,400

Sales Revenue

			10,000
		(h)	500
		Bal.	10,500

Expenses

Rent Expense

(a)	1,000	
Bal.	1,000	

Salary Expense

	10,000	
	950	
(e)	950	
Bal.	11,900	

Supplies Expense

(b)	300	
Bal.	300	

Depreciation Expense—Furniture

(d)	275	
Bal.	275	

Utilities Expense

Bal.	400	

Interest Expense

	100	
(f)	50	
Bal.	150	

The Adjusted Trial Balance

Before we prepare the financial statements, it is helpful to compile an **adjusted trial balance** listing all of the ledger accounts and their adjusted balances, which are what we need to report on the financial statements. Exhibit 3-5 contains the adjusted trial balance for Moreau Ltd. Note how clearly the adjusted trial balance presents the adjustments made to the account balances contained in the initial unadjusted trial balance. This presentation format makes it easy for us to see the impacts of all our adjusting entries on the accounts in the ledger. We see, for example, that we adjusted Supplies downward by $300 to arrive at the account's $400 balance as at April 30, 2020.

EXHIBIT 3-5
Worksheet for the Preparation of Adjusted Trial Balance

	A	B	C	D	E	F	G	
1	**Moreau Ltd.** Preparation of Adjusted Trial Balance April 30, 2020							
2		Unadjusted Trial Balance		Adjustments		Adjusted Trial Balance		
3	Account Title	Debit	Credit	Debit	Credit	Debit	Credit	
4	Cash	34,800				34,800		⎫
5	Accrued service revenue	2,250		(g) 250		2,500		
6	Accrued sales revenue	1,000		(h) 500		1,500		
7	Supplies	700			(b) 300	400		
8	Prepaid rent	3,000			(a) 1,000	2,000		
9	Furniture	16,500				16,500		
10	Accumulated depreciation—furniture				(d) 275		275	**Balance Sheet**
11	Accounts payable		14,100				14,100	*(Exhibit 3-8)*
12	Salary payable				(e) 950		950	
13	Unearned service revenue		450	(c) 150			300	
14	Interest payable		100		(f) 50		150	
15	Loan payable		10,000				10,000	
16	Share capital		20,000				20,000	⎭
17	Retained earnings		11,250				11,250	**Statement of Retained Earnings**
18	Dividends	3,200				3,200		
19	Service revenue		7,000		(c) 150		7,400	*(Exhibit 3-7)*
20					(g) 250			
21	Sales revenue		10,000		(h) 500		10,500	
22	Rent expense			1,000		1,000		
23	Salary expense	10,950		(e) 950		11,900		**Income Statement**
24	Supplies expense			(b) 300		300		*(Exhibit 3-6)*
25	Depreciation expense—furniture			(d) 275		275		
26	Utilities expense	400				400		
27	Interest expense	100		(f) 50		150		
28		72,900	72,900	3,475	3,475	74,925	74,925	
29								

TRY IT *in* EXCEL®▶▶▶

The adjusted trial balance in Exhibit 3-5 was prepared using an Excel spreadsheet. You can use it as a template to solve future problems just by changing the initial trial balance data. To prepare the Excel template, follow these steps:

1. Open a blank Excel spreadsheet. Format the spreadsheet header and column headings exactly as you see in Exhibit 3-5.
2. Enter the account titles and account balances from the "Unadjusted Trial Balance" columns.
3. Sum the debits and credits in the "Unadjusted Trial Balance" columns.
4. Enter adjusting journal entries (a) through (g) one at a time in the "Adjustments" columns. For example, for adjusting journal entry (a) enter 1,000 in the debit column on the "Rent expense" line, and 1,000 in the credit column of the "Prepaid rent" line. Do not enter the letters (a) through (g); use only the amounts.
5. In the "Adjusted Trial Balance" debit and credit columns, enter formulas as follows:
   - For asset, dividend, and expense accounts: = + (debit amounts from "Unadjusted Trial Balance" and "Adjustments" columns) − (credit amounts from "Adjustments" columns).
   - For contra asset, liability, share capital, retained earnings, and service revenue accounts: = + (credit amounts from "Unadjusted Trial Balance" and "Adjustments" columns) − (debit amounts from "Adjustments" columns).
6. Sum the "Adjustments" debit and credit columns.
7. Sum the "Adjusted Trial Balance" debit and credit columns.

PREPARE THE FINANCIAL STATEMENTS

OBJECTIVE

❹ **Prepare** the financial statements

The April 2020 financial statements of Moreau Ltd. can be prepared from the adjusted trial balance in Exhibit 3-5. The right side of the exhibit highlights which financial statement(s) the accounts are reported on.

- The income statement (Exhibit 3-6) reports the revenue and expense accounts.
- The statement of retained earnings (Exhibit 3-7) reports the changes in retained earnings.
- The balance sheet (Exhibit 3-8) reports assets, liabilities, and shareholders' equity.
- The arrows in Exhibits 3-6, 3-7, and 3-8 show the flow of data from one statement to the next.

TRY IT *in* EXCEL®▶▶▶

If you have already prepared Excel templates for the income statement, statement of retained earnings, and balance sheet for Tara Inc. in Chapter 2 (see Exhibit 2-2), you may use these to prepare Moreau Ltd.'s April 30, 2020, financial statements. You will have to insert and delete line items as needed because some of Moreau's accounts differ from Tara's. The value of Excel is that once you have prepared the templates for the adjusted trial balance worksheet and financial statements, you can reuse them as needed.

EXHIBIT 3-6
Income Statement

	A	B	C
1	**Moreau Ltd.** Income Statement For the Month Ended April 30, 2020		
2	Revenue:		
3	Sales revenue	$ 10,500	
4	Service revenue	7,400	$ 17,900
5	Expenses:		
6	Salary	11,900	
7	Rent	1,000	
8	Utilities	400	
9	Supplies	300	
10	Depreciation	275	
11	Interest	150	14,025
12	Net income		$ 3,875
13			

①

EXHIBIT 3-7
Statement of Retained Earnings

	A	B	C
1	**Moreau Ltd.** Statement of Retained Earnings For the Month Ended April 30, 2020		
2	Retained earnings, April 1, 2020		$ 11,250
3	Add: Net income		3,875
4			15,125
5	Less: Dividends		(3,200)
6	Retained earnings, April 30, 2020		$ 11,925
7			

②

EXHIBIT 3-8
Balance Sheet

	A	B	C	D	E
1	**Moreau Ltd.** Balance Sheet As at April 30, 2020				
2	**Assets**			**Liabilities**	
3	Cash		$ 34,800	Accounts payable	$ 14,100
4	Accrued service revenue		2,500	Salary payable	950
5	Accrued sales revenue		1,500	Unearned service revenue	300
6	Supplies		400	Interest payable	150
7	Prepaid rent		2,000	Loan payable	10,000
8	Furniture	16,500		Total liabilities	25,500
9	Less accumulated depreciation	(275)	16,225	**Shareholders' Equity**	
10				Share capital	20,000
11				Retained earnings	11,925
12				Total shareholders' equity	31,925
13	Total assets		$ 57,425	Total liabilities and shareholders' equity	$ 57,425
14					

Why is the income statement prepared first and the balance sheet last?

1. The income statement is prepared first because it reports net income (revenues minus expenses), which is needed to prepare the statement of retained earnings. This link is illustrated by arrow 1 between Exhibits 3-6 and 3-7.

2. The balance sheet is prepared last because it relies on the ending balance from the statement of retained earnings to complete the shareholders' equity section of the statement. This link is illustrated by arrow 2 between Exhibits 3-7 and 3-8.

You will note that the statement of cash flows is not included in the list of statements that are prepared from the adjusted trial balance. The reason it is not included, as you will discover in Chapter 9, is that the statement of cash flows is not prepared from the adjusted trial balance, but rather from the comparative balance sheets, the income statement, and other sources.

Formats for the Financial Statements

Companies can format their balance sheets and income statements in various ways. Here we will highlight some of the most common balance sheet and income statement formats.

BALANCE SHEET FORMATS. In Chapter 1 we introduced you to the difference between current and non-current (or long-term) assets. Recall that a current asset is an asset we expect to convert to cash, sell, or consume *within one year* of the balance sheet date, or within the business's normal operating cycle if it is longer than one year. A non-current asset is any asset that does not qualify as a current asset. We make a similar distinction between current and non-current liabilities, with a current liability being one we expect to repay within one year of the balance sheet date, or within the business's normal operating cycle if it is longer than one year; while a non-current liability will be repaid beyond one year or the normal operating cycle. A **classified balance sheet** separates current assets from non-current assets and current liabilities from non-current liabilities, and it also subtotals the current assets and current liabilities. Exhibit 3-9 contains the classified balance sheet of Le Château as at January 27, 2018. An unclassified balance sheet does not separate current and non-current assets or liabilities. Regardless of which of these two formats is used, current assets are always listed in order of decreasing **liquidity**, which is a measure of how quickly they can be converted to cash, the most liquid asset. IFRS and ASPE require the use of classified balance sheets.

A balance sheet prepared in **report format** lists assets at the top, followed by liabilities, and then shareholders' equity. Le Château's balance sheet in Exhibit 3-9 is in report format.

A balance sheet prepared in **account format** uses a T-account as a framework, with assets (debits) listed on the left side and liabilities and shareholders' equity (credits) on the right. The Moreau Ltd. balance sheet in Exhibit 3-8 is in account format. Companies are free to choose the report format or the account format when preparing their balance sheets.

EXHIBIT 3-9
Classified Balance Sheet
of Le Château Inc.

Source: Data From Le Château Inc.
Annual Report – 2018.

	A	B	C
1	**Le Château Inc.** Consolidated Balance Sheet (Adapted) As at January 27, 2018		
2	*(in thousands of dollars)*		
3	ASSETS		
4	**Current assets**		
5	Accounts receivable	$ 957	
6	Income taxes refundable	449	
7	Inventories	89,911	
8	Prepaid expenses	1,747	
9	**Total current assets**	93,064	
10	Deposits	485	
11	Property and equipment	27,052	
12	Intangible assets	2,434	
13	**Total assets**	$ 123,035	
14			
15	**LIABILITIES AND SHAREHOLDERS' EQUITY**		
16	**Current liabilities**		
17	Bank indebtedness	$ 261	
18	Current portion of credit facility	6,322	
19	Trade and other payables	17,342	
20	Deferred revenue	2,842	
21	Current portion of provision for onerous leases	576	
22	**Total current liabilities**	27,343	
23	Credit facility	32,221	
24	Long-term debt	30,518	
25	Provision for onerous leases	924	
26	Deferred lease credits	7,111	
27	First Preferred shares series 1	24,718	
28	**Total liabilities**	122,835	
29			
30	**Shareholders' equity**		
31	Share capital	47,967	
32	Contributed surplus	9,600	
33	Deficit	(57,637)	
34	**Total shareholders' equity**	200	
35	**Total liabilities and shareholders' equity**	$ 123,035	
36			

INCOME STATEMENT FORMATS. A **single-step income statement** lists all the revenues together under a heading such as Revenues or Income. The expenses are also listed together in a single category titled Expenses, or Expenses and Losses. This format contains only a single step: the subtracting of Total Expenses from Total Revenues to arrive at Net Income. Le Château's statement of loss at the opening of the chapter is in single-step format.

A **multi-step income statement** contains a number of subtotals to highlight important relationships among revenues and expenses. Le Château's multi-step statement of loss in Exhibit 3-10 highlights gross profit and, results from operating activities prior to arriving at the net loss reported at the bottom of the tatement. We will discuss the components of the income statement in more detail in Chapter 8.

Companies are free to use either format for their income statements, or they can use a format of their own design if it better suits their reporting needs.

EXHIBIT 3-10
Multi-Step Statement of Loss for Le Château Inc.

Source: Data From Le Château Inc. Annual Report – 2018.

	A	B	C
1	**Le Château Inc.** Consolidated Statement of Loss (Adapted) For the Year Ended January 27, 2018		
2	*(in thousands of dollars)*		
3	**Sales**	$ 204,369	
4	Cost of sales	72,737	
5	**Gross profit**	131,632	
6			
7	**Operating expenses**		
8	Selling	118,694	
9	General and administrative	29,915	
10	**Total operating expenses**	148,609	
11	**Results from operating activities**	(16,977)	
12	Finance costs	5,460	
13	Accretion of First Preferred shares series 1	1,536	
14	**Net loss**	$ (23,973)	
15			

STOP + THINK (3-6)

Refer to Le Château's fiscal 2018 financial statements in Exhibits 3-9 and 3-10. Assume the company suffers a net loss of $20,000,000 in fiscal 2019. What direct impact will this have on the Shareholders' Equity section of its balance sheet at the end of the 2019 fiscal year?

MyLab Accounting

MID-CHAPTER SUMMARY PROBLEM

The trial balance of Goldsmith Inc. shown below pertains to December 31, 2020, which is the end of its fiscal year. Data needed for the adjusting entries include the following (all amounts in thousands):

a. Supplies on hand at year-end, $2.
b. Depreciation on furniture and fixtures, $20.
c. Depreciation on building, $10.
d. Salary owed but not yet paid, $5.
e. Accrued service revenue, $12.
f. Of the $45 balance of unearned service revenue, $32 was earned during the year.
g. Accrued income tax expense, $35.

Requirements

1. Open the ledger accounts with their unadjusted balances. Show dollar amounts in thousands, as shown for Accounts Receivable:

Accounts Receivable	
370	

2. Journalize the Goldsmith Inc. adjusting entries at December 31, 2020. Key entries by letter, as in Exhibit 3-4, page 124. Make entries in thousands of dollars.
3. Post the adjusting entries.
4. Using an Excel spreadsheet, prepare a worksheet for the adjusted trial balance, as shown in Exhibit 3-5.
5. Prepare the income statement, the statement of retained earnings, and the balance sheet. (At this stage, it is not necessary to classify assets or liabilities as current or long term.) Draw arrows linking these three financial statements.

Name: Goldsmith Inc.
Industry: Service corporation
Fiscal Period: Year ended December 31, 2020

	A	B	C	D
1	**Goldsmith Inc.** Trial Balance December 31, 2020			
2	*(in thousands of dollars)*			
3	Cash	$ 198		
4	Accrued service revenue	370		
5	Supplies	6		
6	Furniture and fixtures	100		
7	Accumulated depreciation—furniture and fixtures		$ 40	
8	Building	250		
9	Accumulated depreciation—building		130	
10	Accounts payable		380	
11	Salary payable			
12	Unearned service revenue		45	
13	Income tax payable			
14	Share capital		100	
15	Retained earnings		193	
16	Dividends	65		
17	Service revenue		286	
18	Salary expense	172		
19	Supplies expense			
20	Depreciation expense—furniture and fixtures			
21	Depreciation expense—building			
22	Income tax expense			
23	Miscellaneous expense	13		
24	Total	$ 1,174	$ 1,174	
25				

ANSWERS

Requirements 1 and 3 (amounts in thousands)

Assets

Cash

Bal.	198	

Accrued Service Revenue

	370	
(e)	12	
Bal.	382	

Supplies

	6	(a)	4
Bal.	2		

Furniture and Fixtures

Bal.	100	

Accumulated Depreciation— Furniture and Fixtures

		40
	(b)	20
	Bal.	60

Liabilities

Accounts Payable

	Bal.	380

Salary Payable

	(d)	5
	Bal.	5

Unearned Service Revenue

(f)	32	45
	Bal.	13

Shareholders' Equity

Share capital

	Bal.	100

Retained Earnings

	Bal.	193

Dividends

Bal.	65	

Expenses

Salary Expense

	172	
(d)	5	
Bal.	177	

Supplies Expense

(a)	4	
Bal.	4	

Depreciation Expense— Furniture and Fixtures

(b)	20	
Bal.	20	

Depreciation Expense—Building

(c)	10	
Bal.	10	

Building	
Bal. 250	

Accumulated Depreciation—Building	
	130
	(c) 10
	Bal. 140

Income Tax Payable	
	(g) 35
	Bal. 35

Income Tax Expense	
(g) 35	
Bal. 35	

Miscellaneous Expense	
Bal. 13	

> For Requirement 1, create a T-account for each account name listed in the December 31, 2020, trial balance. Insert the opening balances into the T-accounts from the trial balance, ensuring debit and credit balances in the trial balance are debit and credit balances in the T-accounts. To make sure all the account balances have been entered correctly, trace each T-account's balance back to the December 31, 2020, trial balance.
>
> For Requirement 3, make sure each transaction is posted to the proper T-account, and make sure no transactions were missed.

Revenue

Service Revenue	
	286
(e)	12
(f)	32
Bal.	330

Requirement 2

	A	B	C	D	E
1	2020	*(amounts in thousands of dollars)*			
2	Dec. 31	Supplies Expense	4		
3		Supplies		4	
4		*To record supplies used ($6 − $2).*			
5	Dec. 31	Depreciation Expense—Furniture and Fixtures	20		
6		Accumulated Depreciation—Furniture and Fixtures		20	
7		*To record depreciation expense on furniture and fixtures.*			
8	Dec. 31	Depreciation Expense—Building	10		
9		Accumulated Depreciation—Building		10	
10		*To record depreciation expense on building.*			
11	Dec. 31	Salary Expense	5		
12		Salary Payable		5	
13		*To accrue salary expense.*			
14	Dec. 31	Accrued Service Revenue	12		
15		Service Revenue		12	
16		*To accrue service revenue.*			
17	Dec. 31	Unearned Service Revenue	32		
18		Service Revenue		32	
19		*To record unearned service revenue that has been earned.*			
20	Dec. 31	Income Tax Expense	35		
21		Income Tax Payable		35	
22		*To accrue income tax expense.*			
23					

> Refer to the rules of debit and credit shown in Chapter 2, Exhibit 2-8, on page 72.
>
> Make sure that Assets = Liabilities + Shareholders' Equity for each transaction before going to the next transaction.

Requirement 4

	A	B	C	D	E	F	G
1	**Goldsmith Inc.** Preparation of Adjusted Trial Balance December 31, 2020						
2		Unadjusted Trial Balance		Adjustments		Adjusted Trial Balance	
3	*(amounts in thousands of dollars)*	Debit	Credit	Debit	Credit	Debit	Credit
4	Cash	198				198	
5	Accrued service revenue	370		(e) 12		382	
6	Supplies	6			(a) 4	2	
7	Furniture and fixtures	100				100	
8	Accumulated depreciation—furniture and fixtures		40		(b) 20		60
9	Building	250				250	
10	Accumulated depreciation—building		130		(c) 10		140
11	Accounts payable		380				380
12	Salary payable				(d) 5		5
13	Unearned service revenue		45	(f) 32			13
14	Income tax payable				(g) 35		35
15	Share capital		100				100
16	Retained earnings		193				193
17	Dividends	65				65	
18	Service revenue		286		(e) 12		330
19					(f) 32		
20	Salary expense	172		(d) 5		177	
21	Supplies expense			(a) 4		4	
22	Depreciation expense—furniture and fixtures			(b) 20		20	
23	Depreciation expense—building			(c) 10		10	
24	Income tax expense			(g) 35		35	
25	Miscellaneous expense	13				13	
26		1,174	1,174	118	118	1,256	1,256
27							

Create a worksheet with columns for the unadjusted trial balance, adjustments, and the adjusted trial balance. List all the account names that have a balance in their T-accounts. Write the account balances from the December 31, 2020, trial balance in the first two columns. Write the adjustment amounts in the next two columns. Write the "Bal." amounts from the T-accounts in the Adjusted Trial Balance columns. Ensure total debits equal total credits for each pair of columns. Double-check the Adjusted Trial Balance amounts by adding the Adjustments to the Unadjusted Trial Balance amounts. Double-underline the totals to show that the columns have been added and the totals are final.

Requirement 5

	A	B	C	D
1	**Goldsmith Ltd.** Income Statement For the Year Ended December 31, 2020			
2	*(amounts in thousands of dollars)*			
3	Revenue:			
4	Service revenue		$ 330	
5	Expenses:			
6	Salary	$ 177		
7	Depreciation—furniture and fixtures	20		
8	Depreciation—building	10		
9	Supplies	4		
10	Miscellaneous	13	224	
11	Income before tax		106	
12	Income tax expense		35	
13	Net income		$ 71	
14				

The title must include the name of the company, "Income Statement," and the specific period of time covered. It is critical that the time period is defined.

Gather all the revenue and expense account names and amounts from the Debit and Credit Adjusted Trial Balance columns of the worksheet.

Notice that income tax expense is always reported separately from the other expenses, and it appears as the last item before net income (or net loss).

	A	B	C	D
1	**Goldsmith Inc.** Statement of Retained Earnings For the Year Ended December 31, 2020			
2	*(amounts in thousands of dollars)*			
3	Retained earnings, January 1, 2020		$ 193	
4	Add: Net income		71	
5			264	
6	Less: Dividends		(65)	
7	Retained earnings, December 31, 2020		$ 199	
8				

The title must include the name of the company, "Statement of Retained Earnings," and the specific period of time covered. It is critical that the time period is defined.

Beginning retained earnings and dividends are from the Adjusted Trial Balance columns of the worksheet.

The net income amount is transferred from the income statement.

	A	B	C	D	E	F
1	**Goldsmith Inc.** Balance Sheet As at December 31, 2020					
2	**Assets**			**Liabilities**		
3	*(amounts in thousands of dollars)*					
4	Cash		$ 198	Accounts payable	$ 380	
5	Accounts receivable		382	Salary payable	5	
6	Supplies		2	Unearned service revenue	13	
7	Furniture and fixtures	$ 100		Income tax payable	35	
8	Less accumulated depreciation	(60)	40	Total liabilities	433	
9				**Shareholders' Equity**		
10	Building	$ 250		Share capital	100	
11	Less accumulated depreciation	(140)	110	Retained earnings	199	
12				Total shareholders' equity	299	
13	Total assets		$ 732	Total liabilities and shareholders' equity	$ 732	
14						

The title must include the name of the company, "Balance Sheet," and the date of the balance sheet. It shows the financial position on one specific date.

Gather all the asset, liability, and equity accounts and amounts from the Adjusted Trial Balance columns of the worksheet. The retained earnings amount is transferred from the statement of retained earnings.

It is imperative that Total assets = Total liabilities + Shareholders' equity.

RECORD CLOSING JOURNAL ENTRIES

Recall that a business's Retained Earnings represent the accumulated net income of the business since its inception, less any net losses and dividends declared during this time. To keep track of this balance, at the end of each fiscal year we must record **closing entries**, which are journal entries that transfer the balances in all revenue, expense, and dividend accounts into the Retained Earnings account. After these entries, all the income statement and dividend accounts have zero balances, leaving them ready to begin tracking revenues, expenses, and dividends for the next fiscal year.

Because the revenue, expense, and dividend accounts are closed at the end of each year, we call them **temporary accounts**. In effect, they temporarily contain a business's revenues, expenses, and dividends for a year, and then are returned to zero balances before starting the next fiscal year. In contrast, all the asset, liability, and shareholders' equity accounts we report on the balance sheet are **permanent accounts** because their balances carry forward from year to year. The balances in these accounts at the end of one fiscal year become the beginning balances of the next fiscal year.

To record and post the closing journal entries at the end of a fiscal year, follow this process:

① Debit each revenue account for the amount of its credit balance. Credit Retained Earnings for the sum of the revenues. Now the sum of the revenues has been added to Retained Earnings.

② Credit each expense account for the amount of its debit balance. Debit Retained Earnings for the sum of the expenses. The sum of the expenses has now been deducted from Retained Earnings.

③ Credit the Dividends account for the amount of its debit balance. Debit Retained Earnings for the same amount. The dividends have now been deducted from Retained Earnings.

④ Post all of the closing journal entries to the ledger to close the accounts for the year.

Exhibit 3-11 illustrates the process of journalizing and posting the closing entries for Moreau Ltd. at the end of April. Panel A contains the closing journal entries, which have been prepared using the revenue, expense, and dividend account balances contained in Moreau's adjusted trial balance in Exhibit 3-5. Panel B shows these entries being posted to the ledger accounts. Note that after the closing entries have been posted, the ending credit balance of $11,925 in the Retained Earnings account matches the Retained Earnings balance in the statement of retained earnings in Exhibit 3-7 and the balance sheet in Exhibit 3-8. If the ending balance in the Retained Earnings account does not match the balance reported in these financial statements, then you know you have made an error in the closing process.

EXHIBIT 3-11
Journalizing and Posting Closing Entries

PANEL A—Journalizing the Closing Entries

Closing Entries

Apr. 30	Service Revenue		7,400	
	Sales Revenue		10,500	
①		Retained Earnings		17,900
30	Retained Earnings		14,025	
②		Rent Expense		1,000
		Salary Expense		11,900
		Supplies Expense		300
		Depreciation Expense—Furniture		275
		Utilities Expense		400
		Interest Expense		150
30	Retained Earnings		3,200	
③		Dividends		3,200

PANEL B—Posting to the Accounts

Rent Expense

Adj.	1,000		
Bal.	1,000	Clo.	1,000

Salary Expense

	10,950		
Adj.	950		
Bal.	11,900	Clo.	11,900

Supplies Expense

Adj.	300		
Bal.	300	Clo.	300

Depreciation Expense

Adj.	275		
Bal.	275	Clo.	275

Utilities Expense

	400		
Bal.	400	Clo.	400

Interest Expense

	100		
Adj.	50		
Bal.	150	Clo.	150

Service Revenue

			7,000
		Adj.	250
		Adj.	150
Clo.	7,400	Bal.	7,400

①

Sales Revenue

			10,000
		Adj.	500
Clo.	10,500	Bal.	10,500

Retained Earnings

Clo.	14,025		11,250
Clo.	3,200	Clo.	17,900
		Bal.	11,925

②

Dividends

Bal.	3,200	Clo.	3,200

③

Adj. = Amount posted from an adjusting entry
Clo. = Amount posted from a closing entry
Bal. = Balance

STOP + THINK (3-7)

Refer to Le Château's financial statements in Exhibits 3-9 and 3-10. The company reported $250,210,000 in sales for the year ended January 27, 2018. When the company opened for business on January 28, 2018, how many dollars in sales would have been recorded in the Sales account of their general ledger? Now take a look at their balance sheet. What balance would have been reported in their Bank Indebtedness account when they opened for business on January 28, 2018?

OBJECTIVE

❻ **Analyze** and **evaluate** a company's debt-paying ability

ANALYZE AND EVALUATE A COMPANY'S DEBT-PAYING ABILITY

As we have noted, managers, investors, and creditors use accounting information to make business decisions. A bank considering lending money must predict whether the borrower can repay the loan. If the borrower already has a lot of debt compared to its assets, the probability of repayment may be low. If the borrower owes relatively little, however, the odds of repayment are higher. To evaluate a company's debt-paying ability, decision makers examine data and ratios calculated using information in the financial statements. Let's see how this process works.

Net Working Capital

Net working capital (or simply working capital) is a figure that indicates a company's liquidity. In this context, liquidity refers to the ease with which a company will be able to use its current assets to pay off its current liabilities. The higher a company's liquidity, the easier it will be able to pay off its current liabilities. The calculation for net working capital is:

$$\text{Net working capital} = \text{Total current assets} - \text{Total current liabilities}$$

Generally, a company is considered to be liquid when its current assets sufficiently exceed its current liabilities. The sufficiency of the excess is usually evaluated using the current ratio, which we discuss below, and typically varies by industry.

Using the balance sheet data in Exhibit 3-9, we can calculate Le Château's net working capital at the end of 2018 (all dollar amounts in thousands from here on):

$$\text{Net working capital} = \$93,064 - \$27,343 = \$65,721$$

Le Château's current assets exceed its current liabilities by $65,721, meaning that after the company pays all of its current liabilities, it will still have almost $66,000 in current assets to fund other business activities. For a company of its size, Le Château would be considered highly liquid.

Current Ratio

Another means of evaluating a company's liquidity using its current assets and current liabilities is via the **current ratio**, which is calculated as follows:

$$\text{Current ratio} = \frac{\text{Total current assets}}{\text{Total current liabilities}}$$

The higher the current ratio, the better we consider the company's liquidity. As a rule of thumb, a company's current ratio should be at least 1.50, which indicates the company has $1.50 in current assets for every $1.00 in current liabilities. The threshold does, however, vary by industry, and in some cases can be as low as 1.00 or as high as 2.00. A current ratio of less than 1.00 is considered low by any standard, as it indicates that current liabilities exceed current assets, or that the net working capital is negative.

Le Château's current ratio at January 27, 2018, was:

$$\text{Current ratio} = \frac{\text{Total current assets}}{\text{Total current liabilities}} = \frac{\$93,064}{\$27,343} = 3.4$$

Le Château's current ratio of 3.4 is very strong and indicates to current and potential lenders that the company should have little trouble paying its current liabilities.

Debt Ratio

We can also evaluate a company's debt-paying ability using the **debt ratio**, which is calculated as follows:

$$\text{Debt ratio} = \frac{\text{Total liabilities}}{\text{Total assets}}$$

This ratio indicates the proportion of a company's assets that is financed with debt, which helps evaluate the company's ability to pay both current and long-term debts (total liabilities). In contrast to the current ratio, a low debt ratio is better than a high debt ratio because it indicates a company has not used an excessive amount of debt to finance its assets, which means it should be easier for the company to use its assets to generate the cash needed to pay off its liabilities. Companies with low debt ratios are less likely to encounter financial difficulty.

Le Château's debt ratio at January 27, 2018, was:

$$\text{Debt ratio} = \frac{\text{Total liabilities}}{\text{Total assets}} = \frac{\$122,835}{\$123,035} = 1.0$$

As with the current ratio, the threshold for an acceptable debt ratio varies by industry, but most companies have a ratio between 0.60 and 0.70 (60% and 70%). Le Château's debt ratio of 1.0 (100%) is therefore well above the norm, and indicates the company may have difficulty paying down its debts.

How Do Transactions Affect the Ratios?

Companies such as Le Château are keenly aware of how transactions affect their ratios. Lending agreements often require that a company's current ratio not fall below a certain level, or that its debt ratio not rise above a specified threshold. When a company fails to meet one of these conditions, it is said to default on its lending agreements. The penalty for default can be severe, and in the extreme can require immediate repayment of the loan. As noted, Le Château's debt-paying ability is very low, so it may be in danger of default. Companies that face this danger can pursue a variety of strategies to avoid default, including:

- Increase sales to enhance both net income and current assets.
- Decrease expenses to improve net income and reduce liabilities.
- Sell additional shares to increase cash and shareholders' equity.

Let's use Le Château Inc. to examine the effects of some transactions on the company's current ratio and debt ratio. As shown in the preceding section, Le Château's ratios are as follows:

$$\text{Current ratio} = \frac{\$93,064}{\$27,343} = 3.4 \qquad \text{Debt ratio} = \frac{\$122,835}{\$123,035} = 1.0$$

The managers of any company would be concerned about how inventory purchases, collections on account, expense accruals, and depreciation would affect its ratios. Let's see how Le Château would be affected by some typical transactions. For each transaction, the journal entry helps identify the effects on the ratios. Note that the impact of each transaction is being analyzed in isolation.

a.   Issued shares and received cash of $5 million (all journal entry amounts in thousands of dollars).

	A	B	C	D
1	Cash (Bank Indebtedness)	5,000		
2	Share Capital		5,000	
3				

Le Château reported Bank Indebtedness of $261 million on its balance sheet at the end of 2018 (line 17 of Exhibit 3-9). Bank Indebtedness is the term used when a company has a negative balance in its Cash account. It is reported as a current liability because in effect the company has borrowed this amount from the bank on a short-term basis. The $5 million in Cash received from issuing Share Capital in this transaction would allow Le Château to pay off the $261,000 it owes the Bank, leaving $4,739,000 in its Cash account. This affects both ratios as follows:

$$\text{Current ratio} = \frac{\$93,064 + \$4,739}{\$27,343 - \$261} = 3.61$$

$$\text{Debt ratio} = \frac{\$122,835 - \$261}{\$123,035 + \$4,739} = 0.96$$

The issuance of shares slightly improves both ratios, as current assets increase while liabilities decrease slightly.

b.   Made cash sales of $30 million. The inventory sold had a cost of $20 million.

	A	B	C	D
1	Cash	30,000		
2	Sales Revenue		30,000	
3	Cost of Sales	20,000		
4	Inventory		20,000	

This transaction causes an increase in current and total assets while liabilities decrease slightly:

$$\text{Current ratio} = \frac{\$93,064 + \$30,000 - \$261 - \$20,000}{\$27,343 - \$261} = 3.80$$

$$\text{Debt ratio} = \frac{\$122,835 - \$261}{\$123,035 + \$30,000 - \$261 - \$20,000} = 0.92$$

As a result, both ratios are better after this entry is recorded.

c. Accrued expenses of $3 million.

	A	B	C	D
1	Operating Expenses	3,000		
2	Accrued Expenses Payable		3,000	
3				

$$\text{Current ratio} = \frac{\$93,064}{\$27,343 + \$3,000} = 3.07$$

$$\text{Debt ratio} = \frac{\$122,835 + \$3,000}{\$123,035} = 1.02$$

After this entry, current and total liabilities increase while assets remain unchanged, so both ratios are slightly hurt by this accrual.

STOP + THINK (3-8)

Le Château's income statement in Exhibit 3-10 reports that the company's cost of sales was $72,737,000 in fiscal 2018, which represents the cost of the inventory they sold to customers during the year. According to their balance sheet in Exhibit 3-9, they had inventory worth $89,911,000 on hand at the end of fiscal 2018. This balance represents almost 97% of the company's total current assets at the end of the year. Does this information cause you any concern about Le Château's current ratio going into its 2019 fiscal year?

The following Decision Guidelines summarize the key factors to consider when evaluating a company's debt-paying ability.

 # DECISION GUIDELINES

EVALUATE DEBT-PAYING ABILITY USING NET WORKING CAPITAL, THE CURRENT RATIO, AND THE DEBT RATIO

In general, a *larger* amount of net working capital is preferable to a smaller amount. Similarly, a *high* current ratio is preferable to a low current ratio. *Increases* in net working capital and *increases* in the current ratio improve debt-paying ability. By contrast, a *low* debt ratio is preferable to a high debt ratio. Improvement in debt-paying ability is indicated by a decrease in the debt ratio.

No single ratio gives the whole picture about a company. Therefore, lenders and investors use many ratios to evaluate a company. Let's apply what we have learned. Suppose you are a loan officer at the TD Bank, and Le Château has asked you for a $20 million loan to remodel its stores. How will you make this loan decision? The Decision Guidelines show how bankers and investors use two key ratios.

USING NET WORKING CAPITAL AND THE CURRENT RATIO

Decision	Guidelines
How can you measure a company's ability to pay current liabilities with current assets?	Net working capital = Total current assets − Total current liabilities $$\text{Current ratio} = \frac{\text{Total current assets}}{\text{Total current liabilities}}$$
Who uses net working capital and the current ratio for decision making?	*Lenders and other creditors*, who must predict whether a borrower can pay its current liabilities. *Investors*, who know that a company that cannot pay its debts is not a good investment because it may go bankrupt. *Managers*, who must have enough cash to pay the company's current liabilities.
What are good net working capital and current ratio values?	There is no correct answer for this. It depends on the industry as well as the individual entity's ability to quickly generate cash from operations. An entity with strong operating cash flow can operate successfully with a low amount of net working capital as long as cash comes in through operations at least as fast as accounts payable become due. A current ratio of, say, 1.10–1.20 is sometimes sufficient. An entity with relatively low cash flow from operations needs a higher current ratio of, say, 1.30–1.50. Traditionally, a current ratio of 2.00 was considered ideal. Recently, acceptable values have decreased as companies have been able to operate more efficiently. Today, a current ratio of 1.50 is considered strong. Although not ideal, cash-rich companies can operate with a current ratio below 1.0.

USING THE DEBT RATIO

Decision	Guidelines
How can you measure a company's ability to pay total liabilities?	$$\text{Debt ratio} = \frac{\text{Total liabilities}}{\text{Total assets}}$$
Who uses the debt ratio for decision making?	*Lenders and other creditors,* who must predict whether a borrower can pay its debts. *Investors*, who know that a company that cannot pay its debts is not a good investment because it may go bankrupt. *Managers*, who must have enough assets to pay the company's debts.
What is a good debt ratio value?	Depends on the industry: A company with strong cash flow can operate successfully with a high debt ratio of, say, 0.70–0.80. A company with weak cash flow needs a lower debt ratio of, say, 0.50–0.60. Traditionally, a debt ratio of 0.50 was considered ideal. Recently, values have increased as companies have been able to operate more efficiently. Today, a normal value of the debt ratio is around 0.60–0.70.

Summary of IFRS-ASPE Differences

Concepts	IFRS	ASPE

There are no substantive differences between IFRS and ASPE in this chapter.

SUMMARY

SUMMARY OF LEARNING OBJECTIVES

LEARNING OBJECTIVE	SUMMARY
❶ **Explain** how accrual accounting differs from cash-basis accounting	When using the cash basis of accounting, we record only business transactions involving the receipt or payment of cash. All other business transactions are ignored.
	In contrast, when using accrual accounting, *the receipt or payment of cash is irrelevant* to deciding whether a business transaction should be recorded. What matters is whether the business has acquired an asset, earned revenue, taken on a liability, or incurred an expense. If it has, the transaction is recorded in the accounting records.
❷ **Apply** the revenue and expense recognition principles	According to the revenue recognition principle, a transaction must satisfy *all three* of these conditions before the business can recognize revenue:
	1. The ownership (or control) and benefits of the goods have been transferred to the customer, or the services have been provided to the customer.
	2. The amount of revenue can be reliably measured.
	3. It is probable that the business will receive the economic benefits associated with the transaction, which usually come in the form of cash receipts.
	The expense recognition principle sets out the two criteria that must be satisfied before an expense can be recognized:
	1. There has been a decrease in future economic benefits caused by a decrease in an asset *or* an increase in a liability.
	2. The expense can be reliably measured.
❸ **Record** adjusting journal entries	Under accrual accounting, we must record adjusting journal entries at the end of each accounting period to ensure that all assets and liabilities have been recorded at period end and that all revenues earned and expenses incurred during the period have been included in the accounts.
	There are three main types of adjusting entries: deferrals, depreciation (amortization under ASPE), and accruals. Deferrals include adjustments related to transactions for which a business has received or paid cash in advance of delivering or receiving goods and services. Depreciation adjustments are made to expense the benefits of capital assets that have been used up during the period. Accruals include adjustments related to revenues earned or expenses incurred prior to any cash or invoices changing hands.
❹ **Prepare** the financial statements	The financial statements can be prepared using the account balances from the adjusted trial balance. The income statement is prepared first, followed by the statement of retained earnings, and then the balance sheet.
	A classified balance sheet reports current assets and liabilities separately from their non-current counterparts. A balance sheet prepared using a report format lists assets first, followed by liabilities, and then shareholders' equity. A balance sheet in account format lists assets on the left and liabilities and shareholders' equity on the right.
	A single-step income statement reports all revenue items together, followed by all expense items, whereas a multi-step income statement splits revenues and expenses into two or more categories to highlight important subtotals (e.g., gross profit, income from operations) useful to decision makers.
❺ **Record** closing journal entries	At the end of each fiscal year we must record closing entries, which are journal entries that transfer the balances in all revenue, expense, and dividend accounts into the Retained Earnings account. After these entries, all the income statement and dividend accounts have zero balances, leaving them ready to begin tracking revenues, expenses, and dividends for the next fiscal year.
❻ **Analyze** and **evaluate** a company's debt-paying ability	We can evaluate a company's debt-paying ability using net working capital, the current ratio, and the debt ratio. A business's net working capital equals its total current assets minus its total current liabilities, and this figure should be sufficiently in excess of zero for a company to avoid debt-paying troubles. The current ratio equals total current assets divided by total current liabilities, so a higher current ratio is correlated with a stronger debt-paying ability. The debt ratio is calculated by dividing total liabilities by total assets, so for this ratio, a lower ratio indicates a higher debt-paying ability.

MyLab Accounting

END-OF-CHAPTER SUMMARY PROBLEM

This problem follows on the mid-chapter summary problem that begins on page 131.

Requirements

1. Make Goldsmith Inc.'s closing entries at December 31, 2020. Explain what the closing entries accomplish and why they are necessary.
2. Post the closing entries to Retained Earnings and compare Retained Earnings' ending balance with the amount reported on the balance sheet on page 135. The two amounts should be the same.
3. Prepare Goldsmith Inc.'s classified balance sheet to identify the company's current assets and current liabilities. (Goldsmith Inc. has no long-term liabilities.) Then compute the company's current ratio and debt ratio at December 31, 2020.
4. The top management of Goldsmith Inc. has asked you for a $500,000 loan to expand the business. They propose to pay off the loan over a 10-year period. Recompute Goldsmith Inc.'s debt ratio assuming you make the loan.

Name: Goldsmith Inc.
Industry: Service corporation
Fiscal Period: Year ended December 31, 2020
Key Fact: Existing, ongoing business

ANSWERS

Requirement 1

To close revenue accounts, debit each revenue account for the amounts reported on the income statement, and credit Retained Earnings for the total of the debits.

To close expense accounts, credit each expense account for the amounts reported on the income statement, and debit Retained Earnings for the total of the credits.

To close the dividend accounts, credit each dividend account for the amounts reported on the statement of retained earnings, and debit Retained Earnings for the total of the credits.

2020				(in thousands)	
Dec.	31	Service Revenue...		330	
		Retained Earnings..			330
	31	Retained Earnings..		259	
		Salary Expense			177
		Depreciation Expense—Furniture and Fixtures.................			20
		Depreciation Expense—Building.......................................			10
		Supplies Expense..			4
		Income Tax Expense...			35
		Miscellaneous Expense			13
	31	Retained Earnings..		65	
		Dividends...			65

Explanation of Closing Entries

The closing entries set the balance of each revenue, expense, and Dividends account back to zero for the start of the next accounting period. They also add the year's net income to and deduct any dividends declared from Retained Earnings, so this account accurately reflects the earnings that have been retained by the company.

Requirement 2

The balance in the Retained Earnings T-account should equal the Retained Earnings balance reported on the balance sheet.

Retained Earnings			
Clo.	259		193
Clo.	65	Clo.	330
		Bal.	199

The balance in the Retained Earnings account agrees with the amount reported on the balance sheet, as it should.

Requirement 3

	A	B	C	D	E	F
1	**Goldsmith Inc.** Balance Sheet As at December 31, 2020					
2	**Assets**			**Liabilities**		
3	*(amounts in thousands of dollars)*					
4	Current assets			Current liabilities		
5	Cash		$ 198	Accounts payable	$ 380	
6	Accounts receivable		382	Salary payable	5	
7	Supplies		2	Unearned service revenue	13	
8	Total current assets		582	Income tax payable	35	
9	Capital assets			Total current liabilities	433	
10	Furniture and fixtures	$ 100				
11	Less accumulated			**Shareholders' Equity**		
12	depreciation	(60)	40	Share capital	100	
13	Building	$ 250		Retained earnings	199	
14	Less accumulated depreciation	(140)	110	Total shareholders' equity	299	
15	Total assets		$ 732	Total liabilities and shareholders' equity	$ 732	
16						

$$\text{Current ratio} = \frac{\$582}{\$433} = 1.34 \quad \text{Debt ratio} = \frac{\$433}{\$732} = 0.59$$

The title must include the name of the company, "Balance Sheet," and the date of the balance sheet. It shows the financial position on one specific date.

The classified balance sheet uses the same accounts and balances as those on page 135. However, segregate current assets (assets expected to be converted to cash within one year) from capital assets, and segregate current liabilities (liabilities expected to be paid or settled within one year) from other liabilities.

$$\text{Current ratio} = \frac{\text{Current assets}}{\text{Current liabilities}}$$
$$\text{Debt ratio} = \frac{\text{Total liabilities}}{\text{Total assets}}$$

Requirement 4

$$\text{Debt ratio assuming the loan is made} = \frac{\$433 + \$500}{\$732 + \$500} = \frac{\$933}{\$1,232} = 0.76$$

You must add $500,000 to the current liabilities and total assets to account for the additional $500,000 loan.

REVIEW

MyLab Accounting

Make the grade with MyLab Accounting: The Quick Quiz questions, Short Exercises, Exercises, and Problems (Group A) marked with a ⊕ can be found on MyLab Accounting. You can practise them as often as you want, and most feature step-by-step guided instructions to help you find the right answer.

QUICK QUIZ (ANSWERS APPEAR ON THE LAST PAGE OF THIS CHAPTER.)

Questions 1 through 3 are based on the following facts:

Freddie Handel began a music business in July 2020. Handel prepares monthly financial statements and uses the accrual basis of accounting. The following transactions are Handel Company's only activities during July through October:

July 14 Bought music supplies on account for $10, with payment to the supplier due in 90 days

Aug. 3 Performed a job on account for Joey Bach for $25, collectible from Bach in 30 days. Used up all the music supplies purchased on July 14

Sept. 16 Collected the $25 receivable from Bach

Oct. 22 Paid the $10 owed to the supplier from the July 14 transaction

1. In which month should Handel record the cost of the music supplies as an expense?
  a. July
  b. August
  c. September
  d. October

2. In which month should Handel report the $25 revenue on its income statement?
  a. July
  b. August
  c. September
  d. October

3. If Handel Company uses the *cash* basis of accounting instead of the accrual basis, in what month will Handel report revenue and in what month will it report expense?

	Revenue	Expense
a.	September	October
b.	September	July
c.	August	October
d.	September	August

4. In which month should revenue be recorded?
  a. In the month that goods are ordered by the customer
  b. In the month that goods are shipped to the customer
  c. In the month that the invoice is mailed to the customer
  d. In the month that cash is collected from the customer

5. On January 1 of the current year, Aladdin Company paid $600 rent to cover six months (January through June). Aladdin recorded this transaction as follows:

Prepaid Rent..	600	
Cash		600

Aladdin adjusts the accounts at the end of each month. Based on these facts, the adjusting entry at the end of January should include
  a. a credit to Prepaid Rent for $500.
  b. a debit to Prepaid Rent for $500.
  c. a debit to Prepaid Rent for $100.
  d. a credit to Prepaid Rent for $100.

6. Assume the same facts as in the previous problem. Aladdin's adjusting entry at the end of February should include a debit to Rent Expense in the amount of
  a. $0.
  b. $500.
  c. $200.
  d. $100.

7. What effect does the adjusting entry in Question 3-6 have on Aladdin's net income for February?
  a. increase by $100
  b. increase by $200
  c. decrease by $100
  d. decrease by $200

8. An adjusting entry recorded March salary expense that will be paid in April. Which statement best describes the effect of this adjusting entry on the company's accounting equation at the end of March?
  a. Assets are not affected, liabilities are decreased, and shareholders' equity is decreased.
  b. Assets are decreased, liabilities are increased, and shareholders' equity is decreased.
  c. Assets are not affected, liabilities are increased, and shareholders' equity is decreased.
  d. Assets are decreased, liabilities are not affected, and shareholders' equity is decreased.

9. On April 1, 2020, Metro Insurance Company sold a one-year insurance policy covering the year ended April 1, 2021. Metro collected the full $1,200 on April 1, 2020. Metro made the following journal entry to record the receipt of cash in advance:

Cash..	1,200	
Unearned Revenue		1,200

Nine months have passed, and Metro has made no adjusting entries. Based on these facts, the adjusting entry needed by Metro at December 31, 2020, is

a.	Unearned Revenue	300	
	Insurance Revenue............................		300
b.	Insurance Revenue	300	
	Unearned Revenue............................		300
c.	Unearned Revenue	900	
	Insurance Revenue............................		900
d.	Insurance Revenue	900	
	Unearned Revenue............................		900

10. The Unearned Revenue account of Dean Incorporated began 2020 with a normal balance of $5,000 and ended 2020 with a normal balance of $12,000. During 2020, the Unearned Revenue account was credited for $19,000 that Dean will earn later. Based on these facts, how much revenue did Dean earn in 2020?
  a. $5,000
  b. $19,000
  c. $24,000
  d. $12,000

11. What is the effect on the financial statements of recording depreciation on equipment?
  a. Assets are decreased, but net income and shareholders' equity are not affected.
  b. Net income, assets, and shareholders' equity are all decreased.
  c. Net income and assets are decreased, but shareholders' equity is not affected.
  d. Net income is not affected, but assets and shareholders' equity are decreased.

12. For 2020, Monterrey Company had revenues in excess of expenses. Which statement describes Monterrey's closing entries at the end of 2020?

  a. Revenues will be debited, expenses will be credited, and retained earnings will be debited.

  b. Revenues will be credited, expenses will be debited, and retained earnings will be debited.

  c. Revenues will be debited, expenses will be credited, and retained earnings will be credited.

  d. Revenues will be credited, expenses will be debited, and retained earnings will be credited.

13. Which of the following accounts would *not* be included in the closing entries?

  a. Accumulated Depreciation
  b. Service Revenue
  c. Depreciation Expense
  d. Retained Earnings

14. A major purpose of preparing closing entries is to

  a. zero out the liability accounts.
  b. close out the Supplies account.
  c. adjust the asset accounts to their correct current balances.
  d. update the Retained Earnings account.

15. Selected data for Austin Company follow:

Current assets.....	$50,000	Current liabilities........	$40,000
Capital assets......	70,000	Long-term liabilities ...	35,000
Total revenues	30,000	Total expenses............	20,000

Based on these facts, what are Austin's ratios?

	Current ratio	Debt ratio
a.	2 to 1	0.5 to 1
b.	0.83 to 1	0.5 to 1
c.	1.25 to 1	0.625 to 1
d.	2 to 1	0.633 to 1

ACCOUNTING VOCABULARY

account format A balance sheet format that lists assets on the left side and liabilities above shareholders' equity on the right side. (p. 129)

accrual An adjustment related to revenues earned or expenses incurred prior to any cash or invoice changing hands. (p. 120)

accrual accounting A basis of accounting that records transactions based on whether a business has acquired an asset, earned revenue, taken on a liability, or incurred an expense, regardless of whether cash is involved. (p. 109)

accrued expense An expense that has been incurred but not yet paid or invoiced. (p. 120)

accrued revenue A revenue that has been earned but not yet collected or invoiced. (p. 122)

accumulated depreciation The account showing the sum of all depreciation expense from the date of acquiring a capital asset. (p. 119)

adjusted trial balance A list of all the ledger accounts with their adjusted balances. (p. 126)

carrying amount (of a capital asset) The asset's cost minus accumulated depreciation. (p. 119)

cash-basis accounting Accounting that records only transactions in which cash is received or paid. (p. 109)

classified balance sheet A balance sheet that shows current assets separate from long-term assets, and current liabilities separate from long-term liabilities. (p. 129)

closing entries Entries that transfer the revenue, expense, and dividend balances from these respective accounts to the Retained Earnings account. (p. 136)

contra account An account that always has a companion account and whose normal balance is opposite that of the companion account. (p. 119)

current ratio Current assets divided by current liabilities. Measures a company's ability to pay current liabilities with current assets. (p. 138)

debt ratio Ratio of total liabilities to total assets. States the proportion of a company's assets that is financed with debt. (p. 139)

deferral An adjustment related to a transaction for which a business has received or paid cash in advance of delivering or receiving goods or services. (p. 115)

depreciation An expense to recognize the portion of a capital asset's economic benefits that has been used up during an accounting period. (p. 118)

liquidity A measure of how quickly an asset can be converted to cash. The higher an asset's liquidity, the more quickly it can be converted to cash. (p. 129)

multi-step income statement An income statement that contains subtotals to highlight important relationships between revenues and expenses. (p. 130)

net working capital Current assets – current liabilities. Measures the ease with which a company will be able to use its current assets to pay off its current liabilities. (p. 138)

permanent accounts Assets, liabilities, and shareholders' equity accounts, which all have balances that carry forward to the next fiscal year. (p. 136)

report format A balance sheet format that lists assets at the top, followed by liabilities and then shareholders' equity. (p. 129)

single-step income statement Lists all revenues together and all expenses together; there is only one step in arriving at net income. (p. 130)

temporary accounts Revenue, expense, and dividend accounts, which do not have balances that carry forward to the next fiscal year. (p. 136)

unearned revenue A liability that arises when a business receives cash from a customer prior to providing the related goods or services. (p. 117)

ASSESS YOUR PROGRESS

SHORT EXERCISES

LEARNING OBJECTIVE ❶

Apply accrual accounting

S3-1 Marquis Inc. made sales of $700 million during 2020. Of this amount, Marquis Inc. collected cash for all but $30 million. The company's cost of goods sold was $300 million, and all other expenses for the year totalled $350 million. Also during 2020, Marquis Inc. paid $400 million for its inventory and $280 million for everything else. Beginning cash was $100 million. The company uses accrual accounting. Marquis Inc.'s top management is interviewing you for a job and you are asked two questions:

a. How much was Marquis Inc.'s net income for 2020?
b. How much was Marquis Inc.'s cash balance at the end of 2020?

LEARNING OBJECTIVE ❶

Apply accrual accounting

S3-2 Great Sporting Goods Inc. began 2020 owing notes payable of $4.0 million. During 2020, the company borrowed $2.6 million on notes payable and paid off $2.5 million of notes payable from prior years. Interest expense for the year was $1.0 million, including $0.2 million of interest payable accrued at December 31, 2020. Show what Great Sporting Goods Inc. should report for these facts on the following financial statements:

- Income Statement
  Interest expense
- Balance Sheet
  Notes payable
  Interest payable

LEARNING OBJECTIVE ❷

Apply the revenue recognition principles

S3-3 Ford Canada sells large fleets of vehicles to auto rental companies, such as Budget and Avis. Suppose Budget is negotiating a contract with Ford to purchase 1,000 Explorers by the end of next year. Write a short report to explain to Ford when it can recognize revenue from this potential sale according to IFRS.

LEARNING OBJECTIVE ❸

Record adjusting journal entries

S3-4 Answer the following questions about prepaid expenses:

a. On November 1, World Travel Ltd. prepaid $6,000 for three months' rent. Give the adjusting entry to record rent expense at December 31. Include the date of the entry and an explanation. Then post all amounts to the two accounts involved, and show their balances at December 31. World Travel adjusts the accounts only at December 31.
b. On December 1, World Travel paid $800 for supplies. At December 31, World Travel has $500 of supplies on hand. Make the required journal entry at December 31. Post all accounts to the accounts and show their balances at December 31.

LEARNING OBJECTIVES ❸❹

Record depreciation adjustments and prepare financial statements

S3-5 Suppose that on January 1, Roots Ltd. paid cash of $30,000 for computers that are expected to remain useful for three years. At the end of three years, the computers' values are expected to be zero.

1. Make journal entries to record (a) the purchase of the computers on January 1, and (b) the annual depreciation on December 31. Include dates and explanations, and use the following accounts: Computer Equipment; Accumulated Depreciation—Computer Equipment; and Depreciation Expense—Computer Equipment.
2. Post to the accounts and show their balances at December 31.
3. What is the computers' carrying amount at December 31?
4. Which account(s) will Roots report on the income statement for the year? Which accounts will appear on the balance sheet of December 31? Show the amount to report for each item on both financial statements.

LEARNING OBJECTIVES ❷❹

Apply the revenue and expense recognition principles and prepare financial statements

S3-6 During 2020, Many Miles Trucking paid salary expense of $40 million. At December 31, Many Miles accrued salary expense of $2 million. Many Miles paid $1.9 million to its employees on January 3, 2021, the company's next payday after the end of the 2020 year. For this sequence of transactions, show what Many Miles would include on its 2020 income statement and its balance sheet at the end of 2020.

S3-7 Schwartz & Associates Inc. borrowed $100,000 on October 1 by signing a note payable to Scotiabank. The interest expense for each month is $500. The loan agreement requires Schwartz & Associates Inc. to pay interest on December 31.

1. Make Schwartz & Associates Inc.'s adjusting entry to accrue interest expense and interest payable at October 31, at November 30, and at December 31. Date each entry and include its explanation.
2. Post all three entries to the Interest Payable account. You need not take the balance of the account at the end of each month.
3. Record the payment of three months' interest at December 31.

LEARNING OBJECTIVE ❸
Record adjusting journal entries

S3-8 Return to the situation in exercise S3-7. Here you are accounting for the same transactions on the books of Scotiabank, which lent the money to Schwartz & Associates Inc. Perform all three steps in exercise S3-7 for Scotiabank using the bank's own accounts.

LEARNING OBJECTIVE ❸
Record adjusting journal entries

S3-9 Write a paragraph explaining why unearned revenues are liabilities instead of revenues. In your explanation, use the following actual example: *Maclean's* magazine collects cash from subscribers in advance and later delivers magazines to subscribers over a one-year period. Explain what happens to the unearned subscription revenue over the course of a year as *Maclean's* delivers magazines to subscribers. Into what account does the unearned subscription revenue go as *Maclean's* delivers magazines?

Give the journal entries that *Maclean's* would make to:

a. Collect $40,000 of subscription revenue in advance.
b. Record earning $10,000 of subscription revenue.

LEARNING OBJECTIVES ❷❸
Apply the revenue recognition principle and record adjusting journal entries

S3-10 Birdie Golf Ltd. prepaid three months' rent ($6,000) on January 1. At March 31, Birdie prepared a trial balance and made the necessary adjusting entry at the end of the quarter. Birdie adjusts its accounts every quarter of the fiscal year, which ends December 31.

What amount appears for Prepaid Rent on

a. Birdie's unadjusted trial balance at March 31?
b. Birdie's adjusted trial balance at March 31?

What amount appears for Rent Expense on

a. Birdie's unadjusted trial balance at March 31?
b. Birdie's adjusted trial balance at March 31?

LEARNING OBJECTIVE ❸
Report prepaid expenses

S3-11 Josie Inc. collects cash from customers two ways:

1. Accrued Revenue. Some customers pay Josie after Josie has performed service for the customer. During 2020, Josie made sales of $50,000 on account and later received cash of $40,000 on account from these customers.
2. Unearned Revenue. A few customers pay Josie in advance, and Josie later performs service for the customer. During 2020, Josie collected $7,000 cash in advance and later earned $6,000 of this amount.

Journalize the following for Josie:

a. Earning service revenue of $50,000 on account and then collecting $40,000 on account
b. Receiving $7,000 in advance and then earning $6,000 as service revenue

LEARNING OBJECTIVES ❷❸
Apply revenue recognition principles; Record adjusting journal entries

S3-12 Entertainment Centre Ltd. reported the following data at March 31, 2020, with amounts adapted and in thousands:

LEARNING OBJECTIVE ❹
Prepare the financial statements

Retained earnings, March 31, 2019..	$ 1,300	Cost of goods sold.........................	$126,000
Accounts receivable...........................	27,700	Cash...	900
Net revenues	174,500	Property and equipment, net........	7,200
Total current liabilities......................	53,600	Share capital.................................	26,000
All other expenses	45,000	Inventories	33,000
Other current assets	4,800	Long-term liabilities	13,500
Other assets......................................	24,300	Dividends......................................	0

You are the CFO responsible for reporting Entertainment Centre Ltd. (ECL) results. Use these data to prepare ECL's income statement for the year ended March 31, 2020, the statement of retained earnings for the year ended March 31, 2020, and the classified balance sheet at March 31, 2020. Use the report format for the balance sheet. Draw arrows linking the three statements to explain the information flows between the statements.

LEARNING OBJECTIVE ⑤

Prepare closing entries

S3-13 Use the Entertainment Centre Ltd. data in exercise S3-12 to make the company's closing entries at March 31, 2020. Then set up a T-account for Retained Earnings and post to that account. Compare Retained Earnings' ending balance to the amount reported on ECL's statement of retained earnings and balance sheet. What do you find? Why is this important?

LEARNING OBJECTIVE ⑥

Evaluate a company's debt-paying ability

S3-14 Use the Entertainment Centre Ltd. data in exercise S3-12 to compute ECL's

a. Current ratio

b. Debt ratio

Round to two decimal places. Report to the CEO whether these values look strong, weak, or middle-of-the-road.

LEARNING OBJECTIVE ⑥

Use the financial statements

S3-15 Use the Entertainment Centre Ltd. data in exercise S3-12 to answer the following questions.

1. Was the net revenue high enough to cover all of ECL's costs?

2. What could you do to improve this situation?

EXERCISES

LEARNING OBJECTIVE ①

Apply accrual and cash-basis accounting

E3-16 During 2020, Organic Foods Inc. made sales of $4,000 (assume all on account) and collected cash of $4,100 from customers. Operating expenses totalled $800, all paid in cash. At December 31, 2020, Organic Foods's customers owed the company $400. Organic Foods owed creditors $700 on account. All amounts are in millions.

1. For these facts, show what Organic Foods Inc. would report on the following 2020 financial statements:
  - Income statement
  - Balance sheet

2. Suppose Organic Foods had used cash-basis accounting. What would Organic Foods Ltd. have reported for these facts?

LEARNING OBJECTIVE ①

Apply accrual and cash-basis accounting

E3-17 During 2020, Valley Sales Inc. earned revenues of $500,000 on account. Valley Sales collected $410,000 from customers during the year. Expenses totalled $420,000, and the related cash payments were $400,000. Compute Valley Sales Inc.'s net income using both the cash basis and accrual basis of accounting. If you were thinking of investing in Valley Sales, which basis would you want the company to use to determine its net income and why?

LEARNING OBJECTIVE ①

Apply accrual and cash-basis accounting

E3-18 Riverside Corporation began 2020 owing notes payable of $3.5 million. During 2020, Riverside borrowed $1.7 million on notes payable and paid off $1.6 million of notes payable from prior years. Interest expense for the year was $0.4 million, including $0.2 million of interest payable accrued at December 31, 2020.

Show what Riverside should report for these facts on the following financial statements:

1. Income statement for 2020
  a. Interest expense

2. Balance sheet as of December 31, 2020
  a. Notes payable
  b. Interest payable

E3-19 During 2020, Dish Networks Inc. earned revenues of $700 million. Expenses totalled $540 million. Dish collected all but $20 million of the revenues and paid $530 million on its expenses. Dish's top managers are evaluating the year, and they ask you the following questions:

  a. Under accrual accounting, what amount of revenue should the company report for 2020? Is the $700 million revenue earned, or is it the amount of cash actually collected?
  b. Under accrual accounting, what amount of total expense should Dish report for the year—$540 million or $530 million?
  c. Which financial statement reports revenues and expenses? Which statement reports cash receipts and cash payments?

LEARNING OBJECTIVE ❷

Recognize revenue and record expenses under accrual basis of accounting

E3-20 Write a short paragraph to explain in your own words the concept of depreciation as used in accounting.

LEARNING OBJECTIVE ❷

Apply expense recognition principles

E3-21 Answer each of the following questions.

  a. Employees earned wages of $20,000 during the current month, but were not paid until the following month. Should the employer record any expenses at the end of the current month?
  b. The current year has been a poor one, so the business is planning to delay the recording of some expenses until they are paid early the following year. Is this acceptable?
  c. A dentist performs a surgical operation and bills the patient's insurance company. It may take three months to collect from the insurance company. Should the dentist record revenue now or wait until cash is collected?
  d. A construction company is building a highway system, and construction will take three years. How do you think it should record the revenue it earns—over the year or over three years?
  e. A utility bill is received on December 30 and will be paid next year. When should the company record utility expense?

LEARNING OBJECTIVE ❷

Apply revenue and expense recognition principles

E3-22 An accountant made the following adjustments at December 31, the end of the accounting period:

  a. Prepaid insurance, beginning, $700. Payments for insurance during the period, $2,100. Prepaid insurance, ending, $800.
  b. Interest revenue accrued, $900.
  c. Unearned service revenue, beginning, $800. Unearned service revenue, ending, $300.
  d. Depreciation, $6,200.
  e. Employees' salaries owed for three days of a five-day work week; weekly payroll, $9,000.
  f. Income before income tax expense, $20,000. Income tax rate is 25%.

LEARNING OBJECTIVE ❸

Record adjusting journal entries and analyze their effects on net income

Requirements

1. Journalize the adjusting entries.
2. If the accountant was biased to report a better operating performance for the period than actually occurred, which of the preceding adjustments would he have not made and why? Would it have been ethical for him to do this?

E3-23 On December 1, 2019, Neu Consulting Ltd. signed a contract with Kraftwerk Inc., which obligated Neu to provide Kraftwerk with 10 hours of consulting services per month from January through December of 2020. The contract requires Kraftwerk to pay a total of $36,000 for these services, with payments of $3,000 due at the end of each month. Neu has provided similar services to Kraftwerk in the past and has always collected its fees on a timely basis.

LEARNING OBJECTIVE ❷

Apply revenue recognition principles

Requirement

Use Exhibit 3-1 on page 113 as a guide to determine how Neu Consulting Inc. would recognize revenue from this transaction under both ASPE and IFRS.

LEARNING OBJECTIVE ❸

Record adjusting entries

🌐 **E3-24** Clark Motors Ltd. faced the following situations. Journalize the adjusting entry needed at year-end (December 31, 2020) for each situation. Consider each fact separately.

a. The business paid interest expense of $9,000 early in January 2021 related to a loan received in January 2020.

b. Interest revenue of $3,000 has been earned but not yet received.

c. When the business collected $12,000 in advance three months ago, the accountant debited Cash and credited Unearned Revenue. The client was paying for two cars, one delivered in December, the other to be delivered in February 2021.

d. Salary expense is $1,000 per day—Monday through Friday—and the business pays employees each Friday. For example purposes, assume that this year, December 31 falls on a Tuesday.

e. The unadjusted balance of the Supplies account is $3,100. The total cost of supplies on hand is $800.

f. Equipment was purchased at the beginning of this year at a cost of $60,000. The equipment's useful life is five years. Record the depreciation for this year and then determine the equipment's carrying amount.

LEARNING OBJECTIVE ❸

Record adjusting entries directly in T-accounts

🌐 **E3-25** The accounting records of Lalonde Ltée include the following unadjusted balances at May 31: Accounts Receivable, $1,300; Supplies, $900; Salary Payable, $0; Unearned Sales Revenue, $800; Sales Revenue, $14,400; Salary Expense, $4,200; Supplies Expense, $0. As Lalonde's accountant you have developed the following data for the May 31 adjusting entries:

a. Supplies on hand, $300

b. Salary owed to employees, $2,000

c. Sales revenue accrued, $600

d. Unearned sales revenue that has been earned, $700

Open the foregoing T-accounts with their beginning balances. Then record the adjustments directly in the accounts, keying each adjustment amount by letter. Show each account's adjusted balance. Journal entries are not required.

LEARNING OBJECTIVE ❹

Prepare the financial statements

🌐 **E3-26** The adjusted trial balance of Honeybee Hams Inc. follows.

	A	B	C	D
1	**Honeybee Hams Inc.** Adjusted Trial Balance December 31, 2020			
2		**Adjusted Trial Balance**		
3	(in thousands of dollars)	Debit	Credit	
4	Cash	$ 3,300		
5	Accounts receivable	1,800		
6	Inventories	1,100		
7	Prepaid expenses	1,900		
8	Capital assets	6,600		
9	Accumulated depreciation		$ 2,400	
10	Other assets	9,900		
11	Accounts payable		7,700	
12	Income tax payable		600	
13	Other liabilities		2,200	
14	Share capital		4,900	
15	Retained earnings (December 31, 2019)		4,500	
16	Dividends	1,700		
17	Sales revenue		41,000	
18	Cost of goods sold	25,000		
19	Selling, administrative, and general expense	10,000		
20	Income tax expense	2,000		
21		$ 63,300	$ 63,300	
22				

Requirement

Prepare Honeybee Hams's income statement and statement of retained earnings for the year ended December 31, 2020, and its balance sheet on that date. Draw arrows linking the three statements.

E3-27 The adjusted trial balances of Tower Development Inc. for March 31, 2019, and March 31, 2020, include these amounts (in millions):

LEARNING OBJECTIVE ❹

Determine financial statement amounts

	2020	2019
Receivables	$300	$200
Prepaid insurance	180	110
Accrued liabilities (for other operating expenses)	700	600

Tower Development completed these transactions during the year ended March 31, 2020.

Collections from customers	$20,800
Payment of prepaid insurance	400
Cash payments for other operating expenses	4,100

Compute the amount of sales revenue, insurance expense, and other operating expense to report on the income statement for the year ended March 31, 2020.

E3-28 This question deals with the items and the amounts that two entities, Mountain Services Inc. (Mountain) and City of Squamish (Squamish), should report in their financial statements.

LEARNING OBJECTIVES ❷❹

Apply revenue and expense recognition principles, and report on the financial statements

1. On March 31, 2020, Mountain collected $12,000 in advance from Squamish, a client. Under the contract, Mountain is obligated to provide consulting services for Squamish evenly during the year ended March 31, 2021. Assume you are Mountain.

   Mountain's income statement for the year ended December 31, 2020, will report _____ of $_____.

   Mountain's balance sheet at December 31, 2020, will report _____ of $_____.

2. Assume that you are Squamish. Squamish's income statement for the year ended December 31, 2020, will report _____ of $_____.

   Squamish's balance sheet at December 31, 2020, will report _____ of $_____.

E3-29 You have just signed a contract with Rogers Wireless that provides you with a new iPhone and two years of wireless phone and data service. The terms of the contract specify that the price of the phone is $1,000 and the price for the wireless service is $75 per month, which will be billed to your credit card monthly. After signing the contract, you pay for and receive your iPhone and provide your credit card details for monthly billing purposes.

LEARNING OBJECTIVE ❽

Apply the revenue recognition principle

Requirement

Use Exhibit 3-1 on page 113 as a guide to explain how Rogers will recognize the revenue from your transaction. Rogers is a public company, so it uses IFRS to prepare its financial statements.

E3-30 Prepare the required closing entries for the following selected accounts from the records of SouthWest Transport Inc. at December 31, 2020 (amounts in thousands):

LEARNING OBJECTIVE ❺

Record closing entries

Cost of services sold	$11,600	Service revenue	$23,600
Accumulated depreciation	17,800	Depreciation expense	4,100
Selling, general, and		Other revenue	600
administrative expense	6,900	Income tax expense	400
Retained earnings,		Dividends	400
December 31, 2019	1,900	Income tax payable	300

How much net income did SouthWest Transport Inc. earn during the year ended December 31, 2020? Prepare a T-account for Retained Earnings to show the December 31, 2020, balance of Retained Earnings.

LEARNING OBJECTIVES ❸❺

Identify and record adjusting and
closing entries

E3-31 The unadjusted trial balance and the income statement amounts from the December 31, 2020, adjusted trial balance of Yosaf Portraits Ltd. are given below.

	A	B	C	D	E	F
1	**Yosaf Portraits Ltd.** Trial Balance December 31, 2020					
2	**Account Title**	**Unadjusted Trial Balance**		**From the Adjusted Trial Balance**		
3	Cash	10,200				
4	Prepaid rent	1,100				
5	Equipment	32,100				
6	Accumulated depreciation		3,800			
7	Accounts payable		4,600			
8	Salary payable					
9	Unearned service revenue		8,400			
10	Interest payable					
11	Note payable, long term		10,000			
12	Share capital		8,700			
13	Retained earnings		1,300			
14	Dividends	1,000				
15	Service revenue		12,800		19,500	
16	Salary expense	4,000		4,900		
17	Rent expense	1,200		1,400		
18	Depreciation expense			300		
19	Interest expense			1,600		
20		49,600	49,600	8,200	19,500	
21	Net income			11,300		
22				19,500	19,500	
23						

Requirement

Journalize the adjusting and closing entries of Yosaf Portraits Ltd. at December 31, 2020. There was only one adjustment to Service Revenue.

LEARNING OBJECTIVES ❹❻

Prepare a classified balance sheet
and evaluate a company's debt-
paying ability

E3-32 Refer to exercise E3-31.

Requirements

1. After solving exercise E3-30, use the data in that exercise to prepare Yosaf Portraits Ltd.'s classified balance sheet at December 31, 2020. Use the report format. First you must compute the adjusted balance for several balance sheet accounts.
2. Compute Yosaf Portraits Ltd.'s current ratio and debt ratio at December 31, 2020. A year ago, the current ratio was 1.55 and the debt ratio was 0.45. Indicate whether the company's ability to pay its debts—both current and total—improved or deteriorated during the current year.

LEARNING OBJECTIVE ❻

Evaluate debt-paying ability

E3-33 Le Gasse Inc. reported this information at December 31:

	2020	2019	2018
Current assets	$ 20	$ 15	$ 8
Total assets	50	57	35
Current liabilities	10	8	6
Total liabilities	20	20	10
Sales revenue	204	190	175
Net income	28	20	25

Requirements

1. Using this information, calculate the current ratio and the debt ratio for 2020, 2019, and 2018.
2. Explain whether each ratio improved or deteriorated over the three years. In each case, what does your answer indicate?

E3-34 Refer to exercise E2-28 of Chapter 2. Start from the trial balance and the posted T-accounts prepared at January 18, 2020. Later in January, the business completed these transactions:

LEARNING OBJECTIVES ❸❹❺❻

Adjust the accounts, prepare the financial statements, close the accounts, and use financial statements to evaluate the business

2020

Jan.	21	Received $900 in advance for marketing work to be performed evenly over the next 30 days
	21	Hired a secretary to be paid on the 15th day of each month
	26	Paid $900 on account
	28	Collected $600 on account
	31	Declared and paid dividends of $1,000

Requirements

1. Open these T-accounts: Accumulated Depreciation—Equipment, Accumulated Depreciation—Furniture, Salary Payable, Unearned Service Revenue, Retained Earnings, Depreciation Expense—Equipment, Depreciation Expense—Furniture, and Supplies Expense. Also, use the T-accounts opened for exercise E2-28.
2. Journalize the transactions of January 21 through 31.
3. Post the January 21 to January 31 transactions to the T-accounts, keying all items by date. Denote account balances as Bal.
4. Prepare a trial balance at January 31. Also, set up columns for the adjustments and for the adjusted trial balance, as illustrated in Exhibit 3-5, on page 126.
5. At January 31, the following information is gathered for the adjusting entries:

   a. Accrued service revenue, $1,000
   b. Earned $300 of the service revenue collected in advance on January 21
   c. Supplies on hand, $300
   d. Depreciation expense—equipment, $100; furniture, $200
   e. Accrued expense for secretary's salary, $1,000

   Make these adjustments directly in the adjustments columns and complete the adjusted trial balance at January 31, 2020.
6. Journalize and post the adjusting entries. Denote each adjusting amount as Adj. and an account balance as Bal.
7. Prepare the income statement and statement of retained earnings of Web Marketing Services Inc. for the month ended January 31, 2020, and the classified balance sheet at that date. Draw arrows to link the financial statements.
8. Journalize and post the closing entries at January 31, 2020. Denote each closing amount as Clo. and an account balance as Bal.
9. Using the information you have prepared, compute the current ratio and the debt ratio of Web Marketing Services Inc. (to two decimals) and evaluate these ratio values as indicative of a strong or weak financial position.

E3-35 Valley Bleu Ltée reported the following current accounts at December 31, 2019 (amounts in thousands):

LEARNING OBJECTIVES ❸❹❻

Compute financial statement amounts, analyze debt-paying ability

a. Cash	$1,700
b. Receivables	5,600
c. Inventory	1,800
d. Prepaid expenses	800
e. Accounts payable	2,400
f. Unearned revenue	1,200
g. Accrued expenses payable	1,700

During 2020, Valley Bleu completes these transactions:

- Used inventory of $3,800
- Sold services on account, $6,500
- Depreciation expense, $400
- Paid for accrued expenses, $500
- Collected from customers on account, $7,500
- Accrued expenses, $1,300
- Purchased inventory of $3,500 on account
- Paid on account, $5,000
- Used up prepaid expenses, $600

Compute Valley Bleu's current ratio at December 31, 2019, and again at December 31, 2020. Did the current ratio improve or deteriorate during 2020? Comment on the company's current ratio.

LEARNING OBJECTIVES ❸❹

Compute financial statement amounts

⊕ **E3-36** The accounts of Maritime Specialists Ltd. prior to the year-end adjustments are given below.

Cash	$ 4,000	Share capital	$ 10,000
Accounts receivable	7,000	Retained earnings	43,000
Supplies	4,000	Dividends	16,000
Prepaid insurance	3,000	Sales revenue	155,000
Building	107,000	Salary expense	32,000
Accumulated depreciation—building	14,000	Depreciation expense—building	0
Land	51,000	Supplies expense	0
Accounts payable	6,000	Insurance expense	0
Salary payable	0	Advertising expense	7,000
Unearned sales revenue	5,000	Utilities expense	2,000

Adjusting data at the end of the year include:

a. Unearned sales revenue that has been earned, $1,000
b. Accrued sales revenue, $2,000
c. Supplies used in operations, $3,000
d. Accrued salary expense, $3,000
e. Prepaid insurance expired, $1,000
f. Depreciation expense, building, $2,000

Jon Whale, the principal shareholder, has received an offer to sell Maritime Specialists. He needs to know the following information within one hour:

a. Net income for the year covered by these data
b. Total assets
c. Total liabilities
d. Total shareholders' equity
e. Proof that Total assets = Total liabilities + Total shareholders' equity, after all items are updated

Requirement

Without opening any accounts, making any journal entries, or using a worksheet, provide Whale with the requested information. Ignore income taxes. Show all computations.

LEARNING OBJECTIVES ❶❸❻

Apply accrual accounting, record adjusting entries, and analyze and evaluate a company's debt-paying ability

⊕ **E3-37** Satterfield Corporation reported the following current accounts at December 31, 2019 (amounts in thousands):

Cash	$1,500
Receivables	5,900
Inventory	2,700
Prepaid expenses	1,000
Accounts payable	2,600
Unearned revenue	1,600
Accrued expenses payable	1,900

During January 2020, Satterfield completed these selected transactions:

- Sold services on account, $9,000
- Depreciation expense, $400
- Paid for expenses, $7,300
- Collected from customers on account, $8,100
- Accrued expenses, $500
- Paid on account, $1,400
- Used up prepaid expenses, $700

Compute Satterfield's net working capital and current ratio at December 31, 2019, and again at January 31, 2020. Did the net working capital and current ratio improve or deteriorate during January 2020? Comment on the level of the company's net working capital and current ratio.

E3-38 Tidy Car, Inc., provides mobile detailing to its customers. The Income Statement for the month ended January 31, 2020, the Balance Sheet for December 31, 2019, and details of postings to the Cash account in the general ledger for the month of January 2020 follow:

LEARNING OBJECTIVE ❹
Prepare the financial statements

	A	B	C	D
1	**Tidy Car, Inc.** Income Statement Month ended January 31, 2020			
2	Revenue			
3	Detailing revenue	$ 36,500		
4	Gift certificates redeemed	700	$ 37,200	
5	Expenses:			
6	Salary expense	$ 10,000		
7	Depreciation expense—equipment	6,800		
8	Supplies expense	3,100		
9	Advertising expense	3,000	22,900	
10	Net income		$ 14,300	
11				

	A	B	C	D	E	F
1	**Tidy Car, Inc.** Balance Sheet December 31, 2019					
2	**Assets**			**Liabilities**		
3	Cash		$ 1,900	Accounts payable	$ 3,500	
4	Accounts receivable		2,600	Salary payable	1,700	
5	Supplies		1,800	Unearned service revenue	1,200	
6	Equipment	$34,000		Total liabilities	6,400	
7	Less: Accumulated			**Shareholders' Equity**		
8	depreciation	(6,800)	27,200	Common shares	10,000	
9				Retained earnings	17,100	
10				Total shareholders' equity	27,100	
11				Total liabilities and		
12	Total assets		$ 33,500	shareholders' equity	$ 33,500	
13						

Cash			
Bal 12/31/2019	1,900		
Cash collections from customers	38,700	Salaries paid	11,400
Issuance of common shares	12,000	Dividends paid	1,300
		Purchase of equipment	6,000
		Payments of accounts payable	1,800
		Advertising paid	2,800
Bal 1/31/2020	?		

The following additional information is also available:

1. $1,100 of the cash collected from customers in January 2020 was for gift certificates for detailing services to be performed in the future. As of January 31, 2020, $1,600 of gift certificates were still outstanding.
2. $3,300 of supplies were purchased on account.
3. Employees are paid monthly during the first week after the end of the pay period.

Requirement

Based on these statements, prepare the Balance Sheet for January 31, 2020.

PROBLEMS (GROUP A)

LEARNING OBJECTIVES ❶❹

Apply accrual accounting and prepare financial statements

P3-39A Lewitas Ltd. earned revenues of $35 million during 2020 and ended the year with income of $8 million. During 2020, Lewitas Ltd. collected $33 million from customers and paid cash for all of its expenses plus an additional $1 million for accounts payable. Answer these questions about Lewitas's operating results, financial position, and cash flows during 2020:

Requirements

1. How much were the company's total expenses? Show your work.
2. Identify all the items that Lewitas will report on its 2020 income statement. Show each amount.
3. Lewitas began 2020 with receivables of $4 million. All sales were on account. What was the company's receivables balance at the end of 2020? Identify the appropriate financial statement, and show how Lewitas will report ending receivables in the 2020 annual report.
4. Lewitas began 2020 owing accounts payable totalling $9 million. How much in accounts payable did the company owe at the end of the year? Identify the appropriate financial statement, and show how Lewitas will report these accounts payable in its 2020 annual report.

P3-40A Prairies Consultants Inc. had the following selected transactions in August 2020:

LEARNING OBJECTIVE ❶

Apply accrual and cash-basis accounting

Aug. 1	Prepaid insurance for August through December, $1,000
4	Purchased software for cash, $800
5	Performed service and received cash, $900
8	Paid advertising expense, $300
11	Performed service on account, $3,000
19	Purchased computer on account, $1,600
24	Collected for the August 11 service
26	Paid account payable from August 19
29	Paid salary expense, $900
31	Adjusted for August insurance expense (see Aug. 1)
31	Earned revenue of $800 that was collected in advance in July

Requirements

1. Show how each transaction would be handled using the cash basis and the accrual basis. Under each column, give the amount of revenue or expense for August. Journal entries are not required. Use the following format for your answer, and show your computations. Assume depreciation expense of $30 for software and $30 for the computer.

	A	B	C	D
1	**Prairies Consultants Inc.** Amount of Revenue (Expense) for August 2020			
2	Date	**Cash Basis**	**Accrual Basis**	
3				

2. Compute August income (loss) before tax under each accounting method.
3. Indicate which measure of net income or net loss is preferable. Use the transactions on August 11 and 24 to explain.

P3-41A Write a memo to explain to a new employee the difference between the cash basis of accounting and the accrual basis. Mention the basis on which revenues and expenses are recorded under each method.

LEARNING OBJECTIVE ❶

Explain the difference between accrual and cash accounting

P3-42A Journalize the adjusting entry needed on December 31, 2020, the end of the current accounting period, for each of the following independent cases affecting Callaway Corp. Include an explanation for each entry.

LEARNING OBJECTIVE ❸

Record adjusting journal entries

a. Details of Prepaid Insurance are shown in the account:

Prepaid Insurance		
Jan 1	Bal.	400
Mar. 31		3,600

Callaway prepays insurance on March 31 each year. At December 31, $900 is still prepaid.
b. Callaway pays employees each Friday. The amount of the weekly payroll is $6,000 for a five-day work week. The current accounting period ends on Wednesday.
c. Callaway has a note receivable. During the current year, the company has earned accrued interest revenue of $500 that it will receive next year.
d. The beginning balance of Supplies was $2,600. During the year, Callaway purchased supplies costing $6,100, and at December 31 the cost of supplies on hand is $2,100.

e. Callaway delivered goods to a customer on December 31, 2020. On January 2, it invoiced the customer $5,000 for these goods.

f. Depreciation for the current year includes Office Furniture, $1,000, and Equipment, $2,700. Make a compound entry.

LEARNING OBJECTIVES ❸❹❻

Prepare an adjusted trial balance and the financial statements; Evaluate debt-paying ability

P3-43A The unadjusted trial balance of The Rock Industries Ltd. at January 31, 2020, appears below.

	A	B	C	D
1	**The Rock Industries Ltd.** Trial Balance January 31, 2020			
2	Cash	$ 8,000		
3	Accounts receivable	10,000		
4	Prepaid rent	3,000		
5	Supplies	2,000		
6	Furniture	36,000		
7	Accumulated depreciation		$ 3,000	
8	Accounts payable		10,000	
9	Salary payable			
10	Share capital		26,000	
11	Retained earnings (December 31, 2019)		13,000	
12	Dividends	4,000		
13	Service revenue		14,000	
14	Salary expense	2,000		
15	Rent expense			
16	Utilities expense	1,000		
17	Depreciation expense			
18	Supplies expense			
19	Total	$ 66,000	$ 66,000	
20				

Adjustment data:

a. Accrued service revenue at January 31, $2,000

b. Prepaid rent expired during the month. The unadjusted prepaid balance of $3,000 relates to the period January through March.

c. Supplies used during January, $2,000

d. Depreciation on furniture for the month. The estimated useful life of the furniture is three years.

e. Accrued salary expense at January 31 for Monday, Tuesday, and Wednesday. The five-day weekly payroll of $5,000 will be paid on Friday, February 2.

Requirements

1. Using Exhibit 3-5, page 126, as an example, prepare the adjusted trial balance of The Rock Industries Ltd. at January 31, 2020. Key each adjusting entry by letter.

2. Prepare the income statement, the statement of retained earnings, and the classified balance sheet. Draw arrows linking the three financial statements.

3. **a.** Compare the business's net income for January to the amount of dividends paid to the owners. Suppose this trend continues into February. What will be the effect on the business's financial position, as shown by its accounting equation?

   b. Will the trend make it easier or more difficult for Rock Industries to borrow money if the business gets in a bind and needs cash? Why?

   c. Does either the current ratio or the cash position suggest the need for immediate borrowing? Explain.

P3-44A Sundance Apartments Inc.'s unadjusted and adjusted trial balance at April 30, 2020, follow:

LEARNING OBJECTIVES ❸❹

Record adjusting journal entries and prepare the balance sheet

	A	B	C	D	E	F
1	**Sundance Apartments Inc.** Adjusted Trial Balance April 30, 2020					
2		**Trial Balance**		**Adjusted Trial Balance**		
3	**Account Title**	**Debit**	**Credit**	**Debit**	**Credit**	
4	Cash	$ 8,300		$ 8,300		
5	Accounts receivable	6,300		6,800		
6	Interest receivable			300		
7	Note receivable	4,100		4,100		
8	Supplies	900		200		
9	Prepaid insurance	2,400		700		
10	Building	66,400		66,400		
11	Accumulated depreciation		$ 16,000		$ 18,200	
12	Accounts payable		6,900		6,900	
13	Wages payable				400	
14	Unearned rental revenue		600		100	
15	Share capital		18,000		18,000	
16	Retained earnings		42,700		42,700	
17	Dividends	3,600		3,600		
18	Rental revenue		9,900		10,900	
19	Interest revenue				300	
20	Wages expense	1,600		2,000		
21	Insurance expense			1,700		
22	Depreciation expense			2,200		
23	Property tax expense	300		300		
24	Supplies expense			700		
25	Utilities expense	200		200		
26		$ 94,100	$ 94,100	$ 97,500	$ 97,500	
27						

Requirements

1. Make the adjusting entries that account for the differences between the two trial balances.
2. Compute Sundance Apartments Inc.'s total assets, total liabilities, total equity, and net income. Prove your answer with the accounting equation.

P3-45A The adjusted trial balance of Marshall Ltd. at December 31, 2020, is given on page 162.

LEARNING OBJECTIVES ❹❻

Prepare financial statements and analyze debt-paying ability

Requirements

1. Prepare Marshall Ltd.'s 2020 income statement, statement of retained earnings, and balance sheet. List expenses (except for income tax) in decreasing order on the income statement, and show total liabilities on the balance sheet. Draw arrows linking the three financial statements.
2. Marshall Ltd.'s lenders require that the company maintain a debt ratio no higher than 0.50. Compute Marshall Ltd.'s debt ratio at December 31, 2020, to determine whether the company is in compliance with this debt restriction. If not, suggest a way that Marshall Ltd. could have avoided this difficult situation.

	A	B	C	D
1	**Marshall Ltd.** Adjusted Trial Balance December 31, 2020			
2	Cash	$ 1,400		
3	Accounts receivable	8,900		
4	Supplies	2,300		
5	Prepaid rent	1,600		
6	Equipment	37,100		
7	Accumulated depreciation		$ 4,300	
8	Accounts payable		3,700	
9	Interest payable		800	
10	Unearned service revenue		600	
11	Income tax payable		2,100	
12	Note payable		18,600	
13	Share capital		5,000	
14	Retained earnings		1,000	
15	Dividends	24,000		
16	Service revenue		107,900	
17	Depreciation expense	1,600		
18	Salary expense	39,900		
19	Rent expense	10,300		
20	Interest expense	3,100		
21	Insurance expense	3,800		
22	Supplies expense	2,900		
23	Income tax expense	7,100		
24	Total	$ 144,000	$ 144,000	
25				

P3-46A The accounts of Marciano Services Ltd. at March 31, 2020, are listed in alphabetical order.

Accounts payable	$14,700	Note payable, long term	6,200
Accounts receivable	16,500	Other assets	14,100
Accumulated depreciation—		Prepaid expenses	5,300
equipment	7,100	Retained earnings, March 31, 2019	20,200
Advertising expense	10,900	Salary expense	17,800
Cash	7,500	Salary payable	2,400
Current portion of note payable	800	Service revenue	94,100
Depreciation expense	1,900	Share capital	9,100
Dividends	31,200	Supplies	3,800
Equipment	43,200	Supplies expense	4,600
Insurance expense	600	Unearned service revenue	2,800

Requirements

1. All adjustments have been journalized and posted, but the closing entries have not been made. Journalize Marciano Ltd.'s closing entries at March 31, 2020.
2. Set up a T-account for Retained Earnings and post to that account. Compute Marciano's net income for the year ended March 31, 2020. What is the ending balance of Retained Earnings?
3. Did retained earnings increase or decrease during the year? What caused the increase or the decrease?

P3-47A Refer to problem P3-46A.

1. Use the Marciano Ltd. data in problem P3-46A to prepare the company's classified balance sheet at March 31, 2020. Show captions for total assets, total liabilities, and shareholders' equity.
2. Evaluate Marciano's debt position as strong or weak, giving your reason. Assess whether Marciano's ability to pay both current and total debts improved or deteriorated during 2017. In order to complete your evaluation, compute Marciano's current and debt ratios at March 31, 2020, rounding to two decimal places. At March 31, 2019, the current ratio was 1.30 and the debt ratio was 0.30.

LEARNING OBJECTIVES ❹❻
Prepare a balance sheet and evaluate debt-paying ability

P3-48A The balance sheet at December 31, 2018, 2019, and 2020 and income statement for the years ended December 31, 2018, 2019, and 2020 for Ojibway Inc. include the following data:

LEARNING OBJECTIVE ❻
Evaluate debt-paying ability

Ojibway Inc.
Balance Sheet
As at December 31
(in thousands)

	2020	2019	2018
Assets			
Current assets			
Cash	$ 3.0	$ 1.0	$ 0.5
Accounts receivable	8.0	5.0	3.5
Total current assets	11.0	6.0	4.0
Furniture and equipment, net	16.0	9.5	3.0
Total assets	$ 27.0	$ 15.5	$ 7.0
Liabilities			
Current liabilities			
Accounts payable	$ 5.0	$ 4.5	$ 3.0
Salaries payable	1.5	1.0	0.5
Total current liabilities	6.5	5.5	3.5
Notes payable	9.0	5.0	3.5
Total liabilities	15.5	10.5	7.0
Shareholders' equity			
Shareholders' equity	11.5	5.0	0.0
Total liabilities and shareholders' equity	$ 27.0	$ 15.5	$ 7.0

Ojibway Inc.
Income Statement
For the year ended December 31
(in thousands)

	2020	2019	2018
Revenue			
Service revenue	$100.0	$ 90.0	$ 64.0
Expenses			
Salary	60.0	57.5	46.0
Rent	18.0	16.0	12.0
Supplies	4.0	3.0	2.0
Utilities	4.5	4.0	2.0
Depreciation	5.0	3.0	2.0
Total expenses	91.5	83.5	64.0
Income before taxes	8.5	6.5	0.0
Income tax expense	2.0	1.5	
Net income	$ 6.5	$ 5.0	$ 0.0

Requirements

Use the years of data to answer the following:
1. Calculate the current ratio for 2018, 2019, and 2020.
2. Calculate the debt ratio for 2018, 2019, and 2020.
3. Evaluate each ratio and determine if the ratio has improved or deteriorated over the three years. Explain what the changes mean.

PROBLEMS (GROUP B)

LEARNING OBJECTIVES ❸❹

Apply accrual accounting and prepare financial statements

P3-49B During 2020, Schubert Inc. earned revenues of $19 million from the sale of its products. Schubert ended the year with net income of $4 million. Schubert collected cash of $20 million from customers.

Answer these questions about Schubert's operating results, financial position, and cash flows during 2020:

1. How much were Schubert's total expenses? Show your work.
2. Identify all the items that Schubert will report on its income statement for 2020. Show each amount.
3. Schubert began 2020 with receivables of $6 million. All sales are on account. What was Schubert's receivables balance at the end of 2020? Identify the appropriate financial statement and show how Schubert will report its ending receivables balance in the company's 2020 annual report.
4. Schubert began 2020 owing accounts payable of $9 million. Schubert incurs all expenses on account. During 2020, Schubert paid $18 million on account. How much in accounts payable did Schubert owe at the end of 2020? Identify the appropriate financial statement and show how Schubert will report these accounts payable in its 2020 annual report.

LEARNING OBJECTIVE ❶

Apply accrual and cash-basis accounting

P3-50B Fred's Catering Ltd. had the following selected transactions during May 2020:

May	1	Received $800 in advance for a banquet to be served later
	5	Paid electricity expenses, $700
	9	Received cash for the day's sales, $2,000
	14	Purchased two food warmers, $1,800
	23	Served a banquet, receiving a note receivable, $700
	31	Accrued salary expense, $900
	31	Prepaid $3,000 building rent for June and July

Requirements

1. Show how each transaction would be handled using the cash basis and the accrual basis. Under each column, give the amount of revenue or expense for May. Journal entries are not required. Use the following format for your answer, and show your computations. Ignore depreciation expense.

	A	B	C	D
1	**Fred's Catering Ltd.** Amount of Revenue (Expense) for May 2020			
2	Date	**Cash Basis**	**Accrual Basis**	
3				

2. Compute income (loss) before tax for May under the two accounting methods.
3. Which method better measures income and assets? Use the last transaction to explain.

P3-51B As the controller of Stuart Enterprises Inc. you have hired a new employee, whom you must train. She objects to making an adjusting entry for accrued utilities at the end of the period. She reasons, "We will pay the utilities soon. Why not wait until payment to record the expense? In the end, the result will be the same." Write a reply to explain to the employee why the adjusting entry is needed for accrued utility expense.

LEARNING OBJECTIVES ❶❷

Explain accrual accounting and expense recognition

P3-52B Journalize the adjusting entry needed on December 31, 2020, the end of the current accounting period, for each of the following independent cases affecting Lee Computer Systems Inc. (LCSI). Include explanations for each entry.

LEARNING OBJECTIVE ❸

Record adjusting journal entries

a. Each Friday, LCSI pays employees for the current week's work. The amount of the payroll is $5,000 for a five-day work week. The current accounting period ends on Tuesday.

b. LCSI has received notes receivable from some clients for services. During the current year, LCSI has earned accrued interest revenue of $1,100, which will be received next year.

c. The beginning balance of Supplies was $1,800. During the year, LCSI purchased supplies costing $12,500, and at December 31 the inventory of supplies on hand is $2,900.

d. LCSI is developing software for a client and the client paid LCSI $20,000 at the start of the project. LCSI recorded this amount as Unearned Service Revenue. The software development will take several months to complete. LCSI executives estimate that the company has earned three-quarters of the total fee during the current year.

e. Depreciation for the current year includes Computer Equipment, $6,300, and Building, $3,700. Make a compound entry.

f. Details of Prepaid Insurance are shown in the Prepaid Insurance account. LCSI pays the annual insurance premium (the payment for insurance coverage is called a premium) on September 30 each year. At December 31, nine months of insurance is still prepaid.

Prepaid Insurance		
Jan. 1 Bal.	1,800	
Sept. 30	3,600	

P3-53B Consider the unadjusted trial balance of Creative Advertising Ltd. at October 31, 2020, and the related month-end adjustment data.

LEARNING OBJECTIVES ❸❹❻

Record adjusting entries, prepare financial statements, and evaluate debt-paying ability

	A	B	C	D
1	**Creative Advertising Ltd.** Trial Balance October 31, 2020			
2	Cash	$ 16,300		
3	Accounts receivable	7,000		
4	Prepaid rent	4,000		
5	Supplies	600		
6	Computers	36,000		
7	Accumulated depreciation		$ 3,000	
8	Accounts payable		8,800	
9	Salary payable			
10	Share capital		15,000	
11	Retained earnings (September 30, 2019)		21,000	
12	Dividends	4,600		
13	Advertising revenue		25,400	
14	Salary expense	4,400		
15	Rent expense			
16	Utilities expense	300		
17	Depreciation expense			
18	Supplies expense			
19	Total	$ 73,200	$ 73,200	
20				

Adjustment data:

a. Accrued advertising revenue at October 31, $2,900

b. Prepaid rent expired during the month: The unadjusted prepaid balance of $4,000 relates to the period October 2020 through January 2021.

c. Supplies used during October, $200

d. Depreciation on computers for the month: The computers' expected useful life is three years.

e. Accrued salary expense at October 31 for Monday through Thursday; the five-day weekly payroll is $2,000.

Requirements

1. Using Exhibit 3-5, page 126, as an example, prepare the adjusted trial balance of Creative Advertising Ltd. at October 31, 2020. Key each adjusting entry by letter.

2. Prepare the income statement, the statement of retained earnings, and the classified balance sheet. Draw arrows linking the three financial statements.

3. **a.** Compare the business's net income for October to the amount of dividends paid to the owners. Suppose this trend continues into November. What will be the effect on the business's financial position, as shown by its accounting equation?

   b. Will the trend make it easier or more difficult for Creative Advertising Ltd. to borrow money if the business gets in a bind and needs cash? Why?

   c. Does either the current ratio or the cash position suggest the need for immediate borrowing? Explain.

LEARNING OBJECTIVES ❸❹

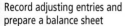

Record adjusting entries and prepare a balance sheet

P3-54B Your Talent Agency Ltd.'s unadjusted and adjusted trial balances at December 31, 2020, are shown below.

	A	B	C	D	E	F
1	**Your Talent Agency Ltd.** Adjusted Trial Balance December 31, 2020					
2		**Trial Balance**		**Adjusted Trial Balance**		
3	**Account Title**	Debit	Credit	Debit	Credit	
4	Cash	$ 4,100		$ 4,100		
5	Accounts receivable	11,200		12,400		
6	Supplies	1,000		700		
7	Prepaid insurance	2,600		900		
8	Office furniture	21,600		21,600		
9	Accumulated depreciation		$ 8,200		$ 9,300	
10	Accounts payable		6,300		6,300	
11	Salary payable				900	
12	Interest payable				400	
13	Note payable		6,000		6,000	
14	Unearned commission revenue		1,500		1,100	
15	Share capital		5,000		5,000	
16	Retained earnings		3,500		3,500	
17	Dividends	18,300		18,300		
18	Commission revenue		72,800		74,400	
19	Depreciation expense			1,100		
20	Supplies expense			300		
21	Utilities expense	4,900		4,900		
22	Salary expense	26,600		27,500		
23	Rent expense	12,200		12,200		
24	Interest expense	800		1,200		
25	Insurance expense			1,700		
26		$ 103,300	$ 103,300	$ 106,900	$ 106,900	
27						

Requirements

1. Make the adjusting entries that account for the difference between the two trial balances.
2. Compute Your Talent Agency Ltd.'s total assets, total liabilities, total equity, and net income.
3. Prove your answer with the accounting equation.

P3-55B The adjusted trial balance of Reid and Campbell Ltd. at December 31, 2020, appears below.

LEARNING OBJECTIVES ❹❻

Prepare financial statements and evaluate debt-paying ability

	A	B	C	D
1	**Reid and Campbell Ltd.** Adjusted Trial Balance December 31, 2020			
2	Cash	$ 11,600		
3	Accounts receivable	41,400		
4	Prepaid rent	1,300		
5	Store furnishings	67,600		
6	Accumulated depreciation		$ 12,900	
7	Accounts payable		3,600	
8	Deposits		4,500	
9	Interest payable		900	
10	Salary payable		2,100	
11	Income tax payable		8,800	
12	Note payable		26,200	
13	Share capital		12,000	
14	Retained earnings, Dec. 31, 2019		20,300	
15	Dividends	48,000		
16	Sales		165,900	
17	Depreciation expense	11,300		
18	Salary expense	44,000		
19	Rent expense	12,000		
20	Interest expense	1,200		
21	Income tax expense	18,800		
22	Total	$ 257,200	$ 257,200	
23				

Requirements

1. Prepare Reid and Campbell Ltd.'s 2020 income statement, statement of retained earnings, and balance sheet. List expenses in decreasing order on the income statement and show total liabilities on the balance sheet. Draw arrows linking the three financial statements.
2. Compute Reid and Campbell Ltd.'s debt ratio at December 31, 2020, rounding to two decimal places. Evaluate the company's debt ratio as strong or weak.

P3-56B The accounts of For You eTravel Inc. at December 31, 2020, are listed in alphabetical order.

LEARNING OBJECTIVE ❺

Record closing journal entries

Accounts payable	$ 5,100	Other assets	3,600
Accounts receivable	6,600	Retained earnings	
Accumulated depreciation—furniture	11,600	December 31, 2019	5,300
Advertising expense	2,200	Salary expense	24,600
Cash	7,300	Salary payable	3,900
Depreciation expense	1,300	Service revenue	93,500
Dividends	47,400	Share capital	15,000
Furniture	41,400	Supplies	7,700
Interest expense	800	Supplies expense	5,700
Note payable, long term	$10,600	Unearned service revenue	3,600

Requirements

1. All adjustments have been journalized and posted, but the closing entries have not been made. Journalize For You eTravel Inc.'s closing entries at December 31, 2020.
2. Set up a T-account for Retained Earnings and post to that account. Compute For You's net income for the year ended December 31, 2020. What is the ending balance of Retained Earnings?
3. Did Retained Earnings increase or decrease during the year? What caused the increase or the decrease?

LEARNING OBJECTIVES ④⑥

Prepare a balance sheet and evaluate debt-paying ability

P3-57B Refer to Problem 3-56B.

1. Use the For You eTravel Inc. data in problem P3-56B to prepare the company's classified balance sheet at December 31, 2020. Show captions for total assets, total liabilities, and total liabilities and shareholders' equity.
2. Evaluate For You's debt position as strong or weak, giving your reason. Assess whether For You's ability to pay both current and total debts improved or deteriorated during 2020. In order to complete your evaluation, compute For You's current and debt ratios at December 31, 2020, rounding to two decimal places. At December 31, 2019, the current ratio was 1.50 and the debt ratio was 0.45.

LEARNING OBJECTIVE ⑥

Evaluate debt-paying ability

P3-58B A company's balance sheet at December 31, 2018, 2019, and 2020 and income statement for the years ended December 31, 2018, 2019, and 2020 include the data on pages 168–169.

Requirements

Use the years of data to answer the following:
1. Calculate the current ratio for 2018, 2019, and 2020.
2. Calculate the debt ratio for 2018, 2019, and 2020.
3. Evaluate each ratio and determine if the ratio has improved or deteriorated over the three years. Explain what the changes mean.

Balance Sheet
As at December 31
(in thousands)

	2020	2019	2018
Assets			
Current assets			
Cash.....................	$ 6.0	$ 4.0	$ 3.5
Accounts receivable......................	11.0	8.0	6.5
Total current assets.....................	17.0	12.0	10.0
Furniture and equipment, net	19.0	12.5	6.0
Total assets	$36.0	$24.5	$16.0
Liabilities			
Current liabilities			
Accounts payable...........	$ 8.0	$ 7.0	$ 6.0
Salaries payable	4.5	4.0	3.5
Total current liabilities...............	12.5	11.0	9.5
Notes payable.......................	12.0	6.0	5.5
Total liabilities	24.5	17.0	15.0
Shareholders' equity			
Shareholders' equity.....................	11.5	7.5	1.0
Total liabilities and shareholders' equity	$36.0	$24.5	$16.0

Income Statement
For the year ended December 31
(in thousands)

	2020	2019	2018
Revenue			
Service revenue	$110.0	$99.0	$75.0
Expenses			
Salary	65.0	59.0	48.0
Rent	20.0	18.0	17.0
Supplies	7.5	6.0	3.0
Utilities	6.0	4.5	3.5
Depreciation	6.0	3.0	2.0
Total expenses	104.5	90.5	73.5
Income before taxes	5.5	8.5	1.5
Income tax expense	1.5	2.0	.5
Net income	$ 4.0	$ 6.5	$ 1.0

APPLY YOUR KNOWLEDGE

DECISION CASES

Case 1. Below is a list of accounts of Patel Consulting Ltd. at January 31, 2020. The unadjusted trial balance of Patel Consulting Ltd. at January 31, 2020, does not balance. In addition, the trial balance needs to be updated before the financial statements at January 31, 2020, can be prepared. The manager needs to know the current ratio of Patel Consulting Ltd.

	A	B	C	D
1	**Patel Consulting Ltd.** List of Accounts January 31, 2020			
2	Cash	$ 6,000		
3	Accounts receivable	2,200		
4	Supplies	800		
5	Prepaid rent	12,000		
6	Land	41,000		
7	Accounts payable		10,000	
8	Salary payable		0	
9	Unearned service revenue		1,500	
10	Note payable, due in three years		25,400	
11	Share capital		15,000	
12	Retained earnings		7,300	
13	Service revenue		9,100	
14	Salary expense	3,400		
15	Rent expense	0		
16	Advertising expense	900		
17	Supplies expense	0		
18		?	?	
19				

This section's material reflects CPA enabling competencies, including:

I Professional and ethical behaviour

II Problem-solving and decision-making

III Communication

IV Self-management

V Teamwork and leadership

Based on Chartered Professional Accountant standards

LEARNING OBJECTIVES

Adjust and correct the accounts, and evaluating debt-paying ability

Requirements

1. How much *out of balance* is the trial balance? The error is in the Land account.
2. Patel Consulting Ltd. needs to make the following adjustments at January 31:
   a. Supplies of $600 were used during January.
   b. The balance of Prepaid Rent was paid on January 1 and covers the rest of 2020. No adjustment was made January 31.
   c. At January 31, Patel Consulting owes employees $400.
   d. Unearned service revenue of $800 was earned during January.

   Prepare a corrected, adjusted trial balance. Give Land its correct balance.
3. After the error is corrected and after these adjustments are made, compute the current ratio of Patel Consulting Ltd. If your business had this current ratio, could you sleep at night?

LEARNING OBJECTIVE ❹

Prepare financial statements and make an expansion decision

Case 2. On October 1, Sue Skate opened a restaurant named Silver Skates Ltd. After the first month of operations, Skate is at a crossroads. The October financial statements paint a glowing picture of the business, and Skate has asked you whether she should expand Silver Skates. To expand the business, Sue Skate wants to be earning net income of $10,000 per month and have total assets of $35,000. Based on the financial information available to her, Skate believes she is meeting both goals.

To start the business, she invested $20,000, not the $10,000 amount reported as "Share capital" on the balance sheet. The bookkeeper plugged the $10,000 "Share capital" amount into the balance sheet to make it come out even. The bookkeeper made other mistakes too. Skate shows you the following financial statements that the bookkeeper prepared.

	A	B	C	D
1	**Silver Skates Ltd.** Income Statement For the Month Ended October 31, 2020			
2	Revenues:			
3	Investments by owner	$ 20,000		
4	Unearned banquet sales revenue	3,000		
5			$ 23,000	
6	**Expenses:**			
7	Wages expense	$ 5,000		
8	Rent expense	4,000		
9	Dividends	3,000		
10	Depreciation expense—fixtures	1,000		
11			13,000	
12	Net income		$ 10,000	
13				

	A	B	C	D	E
1	**Silver Skates Ltd.** Balance Sheet October 31, 2020				
2	Assets:		Liabilities:		
3	Cash	$ 6,000	Accounts payable	$ 5,000	
4	Prepaid insurance	1,000	Sales revenue	32,000	
5	Insurance expense	1,000	Accumulated depreciation—		
6	Food inventory	3,000	fixtures	1,000	
7	Cost of goods sold (expense)	14,000		38,000	
8	Fixtures (tables, chairs, etc.)	19,000	Shareholders' equity:		
9	Dishes and silverware	4,000	Share capital	10,000	
10		$ 48,000		$ 48,000	
11					

Requirement

Prepare a corrected income statement, statement of retained earnings, and balance sheet for Silver Skates Ltd. Then, based on your corrected statements, recommend to Sue Skate whether she should expand her business.

Case 3. Walter Liu has owned and operated LW Media Inc. since its beginning 10 years ago. Recently, Liu mentioned that he would consider selling the company for the right price.

LEARNING OBJECTIVE ④

Prepare financial statements and compute a purchase price

Assume that you are interested in buying this business. You obtain its most recent monthly trial balance, which follows. Revenues and expenses vary little from month to month, and June is a typical month. Your investigation reveals that the trial balance does not include the effects of monthly revenues of $5,000 and expenses totalling $1,100. If you were to buy LW Media Inc., you would hire a manager so you could devote your time to other duties. Assume that your manager would require a monthly salary of $6,000.

Requirements

1. Assume that the most you would pay for the business is 20 times the monthly net income *you could expect to earn* from it. Compute this possible price.
2. Walter Liu states that the least he will take for the business is 1.5 times shareholders' equity on June 30, 2020. Compute this amount.
3. Under these conditions, how much should you offer Liu? Give your reason.

	A	B	C	D
1	**LW Media Inc.** Trial Balance June 30, 2020			
2	Cash	$ 10,000		
3	Accounts receivable	4,900		
4	Prepaid expenses	3,200		
5	Equipment	115,000		
6	Accumulated depreciation		$ 76,500	
7	Land	158,000		
8	Accounts payable		13,800	
9	Salary payable			
10	Unearned revenue		56,700	
11	Share capital		50,000	
12	Retained earnings		88,000	
13	Dividends	9,000		
14	Revenue		20,000	
15	Rent expense			
16	Salary expense	4,000		
17	Utilities expense	900		
18	Depreciation expense			
19	Supplies expense			
20	Total	$ 305,000	$ 305,000	
21				

ETHICAL DECISIONS

Decision 1. ARAS Inc. is in its third year of operations and the company has grown. To expand the business, ARAS borrowed $1 million from Royal Bank of Canada. As a condition for making this loan, the bank required that ARAS maintain a current ratio of at least 1.50 and a debt ratio of no more than 0.50.

Business recently has been worse than expected. Expenses have brought the current ratio down to 1.47 and the debt ratio up to 0.51 at December 15. Shane Rollins, the general manager, is considering the implication of reporting this current ratio to the bank. Rollins is considering recording this year some revenue on account that ARAS will earn next year. The contract for this job has been signed, and ARAS will perform the service during January.

Requirements

1. Journalize the revenue transaction, omitting amounts, and indicate how recording this revenue in December would affect the current ratio and the debt ratio.
2. State whether it is ethical to record the revenue transaction in December. Identify the accounting principle relevant to this situation.
3. Propose to ARAS a course of action that is ethical.

Decision 2. The net income of Accent Photography Company Ltd. decreased sharply during 2020. Mark Smith, owner of the company, anticipates the need for a bank loan in 2021. Late in 2020, he instructed the accountant to record a $20,000 sale of portraits to the Smith family, even though the photos will not be shot until January 2021. Smith also told the accountant *not* to make the following December 31, 2020, adjusting entries:

Salaries owed to employees	$5,000
Prepaid insurance that has expired	1,000

Requirements

1. Compute the overall effect of these transactions on the company's reported income for 2020. Is income overstated or understated?
2. Why did Smith take these actions? Are they ethical? Give your reason, identifying the parties helped and the parties harmed by Smith's action.
3. As a personal friend, what advice would you give the accountant?

Decision 3. For each of the situations listed, identify which of the principles (professional behaviour, integrity and due care, objectivity, professional competence, confidentiality) from the CPA Code of Professional Conduct is violated. Assume all persons listed in the situations are CPAs. (Note: Refer to the CPA Code of Professional Conduct contained on pages 27–28 in Chapter 1 for descriptions of the principles.)

a. Drew purposely excludes a large amount of accrued salaries payable from this year's financial statements so his company's debt ratio appears lower to investors.
b. Abbey's company determines year-end bonuses based on revenue growth. Abbey records the sales of gift cards during this month as revenue rather than as unearned revenue. None of these gift cards have been used by customers as of the end of the current month. By recording the gift card sales as revenue in the current period, revenue will be higher and Abbey's bonus will, as a result, be higher as well.
c. Debbie, a CPA, is an associate at a regional public accounting firm. Debbie's firm is auditing a local payroll company. Debbie does not disclose that her husband is a manager at the payroll company.
d. A new revenue recognition standard has been issued by the Canadian Accounting Standards Board. John does not attend training on the new revenue recognition standard because he is busy dealing with the accounting impact of a merger.

FOCUS ON FINANCIAL STATEMENT ANALYSIS

LEARNING OBJECTIVES ③⑥

Record journal entries and evaluate debt-paying ability

Dollarama Inc.

Task 1. Like all other businesses, Dollarama adjusts accounts prior to year-end to measure assets, liabilities, revenues, and expenses for the financial statements. Examine Dollarama's balance sheet in Appendix A, and pay particular attention to (a) Prepaid Expenses and (b) Accounts Payable and Accrued Liabilities.

Requirements

1. Why aren't Prepaid Expenses "true" expenses?

2. Open T-accounts for the Prepaid Expenses account and the Accounts Payable and Accrued Liabilities account. Insert Dollarama's balances (in millions) at January 29, 2017.

3. Journalize the following for the year ended January 28, 2018. Key entries by letter, and show amounts in millions. Explanations are not required.

   a. Paid the beginning balance of Accounts Payable and Accrued Liabilities.

   b. Adjusted Prepaid Expenses of $7.2 to General, Administrative and Store Operating Expenses.

   c. Recorded Accounts Payable and Accrued Liabilities in the amount of $228.4. Assume this relates to General, Administrative and Store Operating Expenses.

   d. Recorded a prepayment of $8.6 in services to Prepaid Expenses.

4. Post these entries and show that the balances in Prepaid Expenses and in Accounts Payable and Accrued Liabilities agree with the corresponding amounts reported in the January 28, 2018, balance sheet.

5. Compute the current ratios and debt ratios for Dollarama at January 29, 2017, and at January 28, 2018. Did the ratio values improve, deteriorate, or hold steady during the year ended January 28, 2018? Do the ratio values indicate financial strength or weakness?

Task 2. During the fiscal year ended January 28, 2018, Dollarama had numerous accruals and deferrals. As a new member of Dollarama's accounting and financial staff, it is your job to explain the effects of accruals and deferrals on Dollarama's net earnings for this year. The accrual and deferral data follow, along with questions that Dollarama's shareholders have raised (all amounts in millions):

1. Beginning Accounts Receivable for 2018 were $15.4. Ending Receivables for 2018 are $15.3. Which of these amounts did Dollarama collect in 2017? Which amount did Dollarama earn in 2018? Which amount is included in Dollarama's Sales for 2018?

2. Accumulated Depreciation on Property, Plant, and Equipment stood at $306.3 at January 29, 2017, and at $361.8 as at January 28, 2018. Accumulated Depreciation was reduced by $2.4 for assets sold during the year. Calculate the Depreciation Expense for the year, and compare to the Depreciation Expense reported in Note 17 of the 2018 financial statements in Appendix A.

Task 3. Go to the Investor Relations section of Dollarama's website and open the financial statements for its most recent annual reporting period. Go to the Notes section and find the note in which Dollarama describes its Significant Accounting Policies. Use the relevant information from this note to describe how Dollarama recognizes revenue from its sales.

CHECK YOUR WORK

STOP + THINK ANSWERS

STOP + THINK (3-1)

When a customer purchases a single Americano, DVLB would record $3 in revenue immediately upon the sale because it has both acquired an asset ($3 in cash) and earned revenue by delivering the Americano to the customer. When a customer purchases 10 Americanos via a coffee card, however, DVLB has acquired an asset ($25 in cash), but they haven't yet earned any revenue because no Americanos have been delivered to the customer. In fact, upon the sale of a coffee card, DVLB has taken on a liability because it now owes the customer 10 Americanos, which it will deliver to the customer in the future. Each time the customer orders an Americano in the future using the coffee card, DVLB will record $2.50 in revenue ($25/10 Americanos) because only then will they have delivered the Americano to the customer. DVLB's liability to this customer will go down by the same amount.

STOP + THINK (3-2)

1. No, Windsor Group has yet to perform any services, so it cannot recognize revenue. It can begin to recognize revenue as it performs the services the customer has paid for.

2. No, Windsor group has not experienced a decrease in future economic benefits, so it has not incurred an expense. This transaction results in prepaid rent, an asset that will benefit the company over the next three months.

STOP + THINK (3-3)

Supplies Expense ($5,000 + $7,000 − $3,000)	9,000	
Supplies...		9,000

To adjust supplies at period end.
The ending balance in the Supplies account is $3,000, the value of supplies on hand at the end of the month.

STOP + THINK (3-4)

$16,500 − $275 − $275 = $15,950.

STOP + THINK (3-5)

Interest Receivable..	125	
Interest Revenue		125

To accrue interest revenue.

STOP + THINK (3-6)

Because of the $20,000,000 net loss in fiscal 2019, Le Château's Deficit in the Shareholders' Equity section of its balance sheet would be reduced by this amount, bringing it to a balance of $(77,367,000) (opening balance of $(57,367,000) − net loss of $20,000,000). Assuming no other changes to the components of Shareholders' Equity, this increase in the deficit would also push Total Shareholders' Equity into a negative position of $(20,999,800), in which case the section and corresponding total would be renamed Shareholders' Deficit.

STOP + THINK (3-7)

The amount of sales in Le Château's Sales account at the open of business on January 28, 2018, would have been nil because the sales from the prior year would have been closed out to the Deficit account at the end of fiscal 2018. Le Château would have a credit balance of $261,000 in its Bank Indebtedness account at the open of business on January 28, 2018, the same amount it reported at the close of business on January 27, because balance sheet balances carry forward to the next fiscal year.

STOP + THINK (3-8)

In all of fiscal 2018, Le Château sold inventory with a total cost of $72,737,000 and at the end of that year they had total inventory on hand of $89,911,000, meaning they had almost $20M more inventory in stock at the beginning of fiscal 2019 than they sold in the entire preceding year. In addition, the company sells fashion apparel, which goes out of style quickly. Therefore, given the amount and nature of their inventory, they may be unable to sell much of the inventory they have on hand at the beginning of fiscal 2019. If they are unable to sell a significant amount of this inventory, then they won't get any cash for it, which will reduce the amount of money they have available to pay off current liabilities. So, even though the current ratio of 3.4 looks healthy at the end of fiscal 2018, the fact that so much of the company's current assets are tied up in potentially slow-moving inventory means that they may still have trouble paying their current liabilities in fiscal 2019.

QUICK QUIZ ANSWERS

1. b	5. d	9. c	13. a
2. b	6. d	10. d	14. d
3. a	7. c	11. b	15. c
4. b	8. c	12. c	

COMPREHENSIVE CASE

CHAPTERS 1–3

This comprehensive case requires you to apply concepts learned throughout Chapters 1-3. You may find it helpful to review these chapters before responding to the case requirements.

Agata Polanska opened her first Pierogi Factory restaurant in Kitchener, Ontario in 2015. Customers love her authentic Polish pierogi, so Agata has steadily expanded her business to include four restaurants and a central kitchen facility. Pierogi Factory Ltd.'s most recent fiscal year ended on December 31, 2020.

Requirements

1. What form of business organization is the Pierogi Factory? How do you know? Why might have Agata decided to use this form of organization?
2. Information regarding Pierogi Factory's assets, liabilities, shareholder's equity, sales, expenses, and cash flows for its 2020 fiscal year is given below.

Accounts payable	$ 41,564		Income tax expense	$ 52,274
Accounts receivable	15,632		Interest and other expense, net	9,225
Accrued liabilities	334,962		Inventories	49,518
Cash flows provided by operating activities	352,520		Long-term liabilities	313,586
Cash flows used by financing activities	133,074		Other operating expenses	700,090
Cash flows used in investing activities	159,461		Prepaid expenses	52,438
Cash, beginning of year	43,854		Property and equipment, net	1,071,892
Cash, end of year	?		Retained earnings, beginning of year	495,983
Common shares	10,000		Retained earnings, end of year	?
Cost of goods sold	526,628		Salaries and wages	759,998
Depreciation expense	88,010		Sales	2,275,719
Dividends paid	42,270			

Use this information and Excel to prepare a trial balance at December 31, 2020.

3. Use the information from Requirement 2 and Excel to prepare all four of the company's financial statements for 2020.

Before proceeding to the next Requirements, you should compare your response to Requirement #2 to the solution and correct any errors you made.

4. Did the Pierogi Factory have net income or net loss for its fiscal year 2020? Over what period of time was this amount earned?
5. How much in total resources does the Pierogi Factory have to work with at December 31, 2020? How much does the Pierogi Factory owe to creditors at December 31, 2020? How much of the company's assets does Agata have a claim to?
6. Pierogi Factory Ltd. owns the land on which the kitchen facility is located. Its original cost was $250,000 back in 2017. In late December, Agata had the property appraised in anticipation of financing she may seek in the near future. The appraiser assessed its market value at around $500,000. Does the property's increased market value affect anything reported in the company's 2020 financial statements? Explain your answer.
7. Pierogi Factory sells gift cards to customers. When it sells a gift card, it debits Cash and credits Unredeemed Gift Cards, a current liability. Why does Pierogi Factory record the initial sale of a Gift Cards as a liability instead of as revenue?
8. What is the company's primary source of cash? Is this a sign of financial strength or weakness?

9. Prepare the company's closing entries for 2020 to get the company's records ready for fiscal 2021.

10. Listed below are some of the transactions that occurred during January 2021:

January 1	Received $15,000, cash, from restaurant sales. The inventory sold had a cost of $5,000.
2	Purchased flour (inventory), $11,000, on account.
8	Paid for January advertising in local media, $2,000, cheque.
11	Paid employees, $7,500, bank transfers, for the one-week pay period ending January 10.
12	Borrowed money from bank by signing a six-month note payable, $80,000.
15	Received and paid the electricity bills for all restaurants, $1,500, cheque.
19	Paid $11,000 on account for the purchase of flour on January 2, cheque.
20	Sold Pierogi Factory gift cards, $1,000, cash.
27	Paid January rent for one of the restaurant locations, $3,500, cheque.
30	Agata made the monthly payment on her personal house mortgage, $1,200, cash.

What would be the journal entry for each of the transactions?

11. Assign each journal entry from Requirement 10 a number and post the entry to T-accounts in the ledger, using its number as a reference (ignore opening balances).

12. How would each transaction from Requirement 10 affect Pierogi Factory's assets, liabilities, and shareholder's equity?

13. At each year end, Pierogi Factory makes several adjusting entries so that its assets, liabilities, income and expenses are recorded properly and in the correct time period. Here is a partial list of some accounts that require adjusting entries at the end of 2021:

Prepaid Expenses: This current asset includes the cost of napkins, straws, tablecloths, dishes, flatware, and a variety of other supplies needed to stock its restaurants. The balance of these prepaid expense items at December 31, 2020, was $13,378. A physical count of these items performed on December 31, 2021, revealed that $12,580 of prepaid expense items were on hand. Assume that purchases of napkins, straws, tablecloths, dishes, flatware, and other items during 2021 totalled $63,500.

Equipment Depreciation: Pierogi Factory uses a variety of equipment in its restaurants and kitchen. At the end of 2020, the company's equipment had a total original cost of $425,000 and accumulated depreciation of $123,500. The fixed asset ledger shows that depreciation on this equipment should be $71,250 for 2021, but it has not yet been recorded. Also, early in 2021, the company acquired new equipment for $75,000. The company depreciates its equipment on a straight-line basis over five years.

Gift Cards: As noted in Requirement 7, Pierogi Factory sells gift cards to its customers. As at December 31, 2020, it had $15,629 in outstanding, unredeemed gift cards. Assume that during 2021, it sold $37,000 in gift cards. As at December 31, 2021, there were $12,619 in unredeemed gift cards outstanding.

Salaries and Wages Payable: The balance of Salaries and Wages Payable at December 31, 2020, was $31,570, which represented salaries and wages earned by Pierogi Factory employees in 2020 that were then paid in January 2021. When Pierogi Factory paid the $31,570 in January 2021, it reduced Salaries and Wages Payable and credited Cash. As at December 31, 2021, Pierogi Factory employees had earned salaries and wages of $39,401 that would be paid in early January 2022.

Prepare adjusting journal entries at December 31, 2021, to account for the items above.

14. If these adjusting journal entries had not been made for 2021, what would have been the impact on Pierogi Factory's operating income?

Cash and Receivables

4

SPOTLIGHT

CGI Group Inc. is one of the largest independent information technology and business process services firms in the world. Based in Montreal, QC, it provides IT services to clients in Canada, the United States, Europe, and the Asia Pacific region.

Take a look at CGI's comparative balance sheets (excerpt) for 2017 and 2016 on the following page. Notice how cash and cash equivalents are the first item reported under CGI's current assets. Cash equivalents are highly liquid short-term investments that can be converted into cash immediately. As you can see, CGI had about $165 million of cash and cash equivalents at the end of 2017.

Another category of current assets is accounts receivable. On CGI's balance sheet, accounts receivable is the largest component of their current assets. This balance represents the amount of money customers owe CGI at the end of the year. Let's see why.

BalkansCat/Shutterstock

LEARNING OBJECTIVES

1. **Report** cash on the balance sheet
2. **Prepare** a bank reconciliation
3. **Account for** accounts receivable
4. **Evaluate** collectibility using the allowance for uncollectible accounts
5. **Account** for notes receivable and interest revenue
6. **Explain** how to improve cash flows from sales and receivables
7. **Evaluate** liquidity using ratios

CPA COMPETENCIES

Competencies addressed in this chapter:

1.2.2 Evaluates treatment for routine transactions

1.3.1 Prepares financial statements

1.4.4 Interprets financial reporting results for stakeholders (external or internal)

Based on Chartered Professional Accountant standards

	A	B	C	D
1	**CGI Group Inc.** Consolidated Balance Sheets (Excerpt, Adapted) As at September 30, 2017 and 2016			
2	*(in thousands, Canadian dollars)*	**2017**	**2016**	
3	**Assets**			
4	Current Assets			
5	Cash and cash equivalents	$ 165,872	$ 596,529	
6	Accounts receivable	1,285,880	1,101,606	
7	Work in progress	922,620	935,496	
8	Current financial instruments	8,152	22,226	
9	Prepaid expenses and other	160,402	170,393	
10	Income taxes	6,541	7,876	
11	Total current assets before funds held for clients	2,549,467	2,834,126	
12	Funds held for clients	313,552	369,530	
13	Total current assets	$ 2,863,019	$ 3,203,656	
14				

Source: Data from CGI – 2017 Annual Review.

This chapter shows how to account for cash and receivables. We also examine liquidity, which measures how quickly an item can be converted to cash. We begin our discussion with cash.

OBJECTIVE

❶ **Report** cash on the balance sheet

REPORT CASH ON THE BALANCE SHEET

Most companies have cash on hand. They use it for such things as paying bills and employees' salaries, repaying loans, and buying equipment. Most companies have numerous bank accounts, but they usually combine all cash amounts into a single total on the balance sheet called "Cash and cash equivalents," as in the CGI balance sheet above. Cash is the most liquid asset because it is the medium of exchange. Companies keep their cash in a bank for safekeeping. **Cash equivalents** include liquid assets such as treasury bills, commercial paper, and money market funds, which are interest-bearing accounts that are very close to maturity (three months or less at the time of purchase). Slightly less liquid than cash, cash equivalents are sufficiently similar to be reported along with cash.

Most public companies include additional information about cash and cash equivalents in the footnotes to their financial statements. For example, Note 3 (Summary of Significant Accounting Policies) of CGI's 2017 financial statements contains the following brief comment about cash and cash equivalents:

Cash and cash equivalents
Cash and cash equivalents consist of unrestricted cash and short-term investments having an initial maturity of three months or less.

When a company sells their goods or services, they either receive the cash right away or through **electronic funds transfer** (EFT) or receive cheques by mail from the customer. The company deposits the cash and cheques into their bank account. Electronic funds transfer moves cash by electronic communication through debit and credit card transactions and if the customer pays their account through online banking.

To pay cash, the company can write a cheque, which tells the bank to pay the designated party a specified amount or pay through electronic funds transfer. It is cheaper for a company to pay employees by EFT (direct deposit) than by issuing payroll cheques. Many people pay their regular bills, such as mortgage, rent, and utilities, by EFT.

PREPARE A BANK RECONCILIATION

Cash is the most liquid asset because it is the medium of exchange, but it is easy to conceal and relatively easy to steal. As a result, most businesses have specific controls for cash.

Keeping cash in a bank account helps control cash. This is an important option because banks have established procedures for safeguarding customers' money. Following are the documents used to control bank accounts.

OBJECTIVE

❷ **Prepare** a bank reconciliation

Signature Card

Banks require each person authorized to sign on an account to provide a *signature card*. This protects against forgery.

Deposit Slip

Banks supply standard account forms such as *deposit slips*. The customer fills in the amount of each deposit. As proof of the transaction, the customer keeps a deposit receipt.

Cheque

To pay cash, the depositor can write a **cheque**, which tells the bank to pay the designated party a specified amount. There are three parties to a cheque:

- the maker, who signs the cheque,
- the payee, to whom the cheque is paid, and
- the bank on which the cheque is drawn.

Exhibit 4-1 shows a cheque drawn by Nixon Partners Inc., the maker. The cheque has two parts, the cheque itself and the **remittance advice** below it. This optional attachment, which may often be scanned electronically, tells the payee the reason for the payment and is used as a source document for posting the proper accounts.

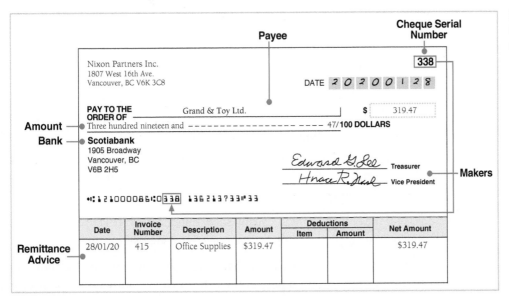

EXHIBIT 4-1
Cheque With Remittance Advice

EXHIBIT 4-2
Bank Statement

ACCOUNT STATEMENT

Scotiabank
1905 Broadway Vancouver, BC V6B 2H5

Nixon Partners Inc.
1807 West 16th Avenue
Vancouver, BC V6K 3C8

BUSINESS CHEQUING ACCOUNT 136–213733

CHEQUING ACCOUNT SUMMARY AS OF 01/31/20

BEGINNING BALANCE	TOTAL DEPOSITS	TOTAL WITHDRAWALS	SERVICE CHARGES	ENDING BALANCE
6,556.12	4,352.64	4,963.00	14.25	5,931.51

BUSINESS CHEQUING ACCOUNT TRANSACTIONS

DEPOSITS	DATE	AMOUNT
Deposit	Jan04	1,000.00
Deposit	Jan04	112.00
Deposit	Jan06	194.60
EFT—Collection of rent	Jan10	904.03
Bank Collection	Jan16	2,114.00
Interest	Jan20	28.01

CHARGES	DATE	AMOUNT
Service Charge	Jan31	14.25
Cheques:		

CHEQUES				BALANCES			
Number	Date	Amount	Date	Balance	Date	Balance
332	Jan06	3,000.00	Dec31	6,556.12	Jan16	7,378.75
656	Jan06	100.00	Jan04	7,616.12	Jan20	7,045.76
333	Jan10	150.00	Jan06	4,710.72	Jan25	5,945.76
334	Jan12	100.00	Jan10	5,464.75	Jan31	5,931.51
335	Jan12	100.00	Jan12	5,264.75		
336	Jan25	1,100.00				

OTHER CHARGES	DATE	AMOUNT
NSF	Jan04	52.00
EFT—Insurance	Jan20	361.00

MONTHLY SUMMARY

Withdrawals: 8	Minimum Balance: 4,710.72	Average Balance: 6,215.00

Bank Statement

Banks send monthly statements to customers in paper form or the statements may be available on the bank's website. A **bank statement** reports the activity in a bank account. The statement shows the account's beginning and ending balances, cash receipts, payments, and electronic funds transfers. Exhibit 4-2 is the January 2020 bank statement of Nixon Partners Inc.

Bank Reconciliation

There are two records of a business's cash:

1. The Cash account in the company's general ledger. Exhibit 4-3 shows that Nixon Partners Inc.'s ending cash balance is $3,294.21.

2. The bank statement, which shows the cash receipts and payments transacted through the bank. In Exhibit 4-2, the bank shows an ending balance of $5,931.51 for Nixon Partners.

The books and the bank statement usually show different cash balances. Differences arise because of a time lag in recording transactions. Here are two examples:

- When you write a cheque, you immediately record it in your chequebook as a deduction. But the bank does not subtract the cheque from your account until

ACCOUNT Cash

EXHIBIT 4-3
Cash Records of Nixon Partners Inc.

Date	Item	Debit	Credit	Balance
2020				
Jan. 1	Balance			6,556.12
2	Cash receipt	1,112.00		7,668.12
5	Cash receipt	194.60		7,862.72
31	Cash payments		6,160.14	1,702.58
31	Cash receipt	1,591.63		3,294.21

Cash Payments

	A	B	C	D	E
1	**Cheque No.**	**Amount**	**Cheque No.**	**Amount**	
2	332	$ 3,000.00	338	$ 319.47	
3	333	510.00	339	83.00	
4	334	100.00	340	203.14	
5	335	100.00	341	458.53	
6	336	1,100.00			
7	337	286.00	Total	$ 6,160.14	
8					

the payee cashes it at a later date. Likewise, you immediately record the cash receipts for all your deposits as additions. But it may take a day or two for the bank to add deposits to your balance.

- Your EFT payments and cash receipts are recorded by the bank before you learn of them.

To ensure accurate cash records, you need to update your cash record—either online or after you receive your bank statement. The result of this updating process allows you to prepare a **bank reconciliation**. The bank reconciliation explains all differences between your cash records and your bank statement balance.

The person who prepares a company's bank reconciliation should have no other cash duties and be independent of cash activities. Otherwise, he or she can steal cash and manipulate the reconciliation to conceal the theft.

Preparing the Bank Reconciliation

Here are the items that appear on a bank reconciliation. They all cause differences between the bank balance and the book balance to occur. We call your cash record (also known as a "chequebook") the "books."

BANK SIDE OF THE RECONCILIATION.

1. Items to show on the *Bank* side of the bank reconciliation include the following:
   a. *Deposits in transit* (outstanding deposits). You have recorded these deposits, but the bank has not. Add **deposits in transit** on the bank reconciliation.
   b. *Outstanding cheques.* You have recorded these cheques, but the payees have not yet cashed them. Subtract **outstanding cheques**.
   c. *Bank errors.* Correct all bank errors on the Bank side of the reconciliation. For example, the bank may erroneously subtract from your account a cheque written by someone else. These items are recorded in the company's books but not by the bank.

   These items are recorded on the company's books but not by the bank.

BOOK SIDE OF THE RECONCILIATION.

1. Items to show on the *Book* side of the bank reconciliation include the following:

   a. *Bank collections.* **Bank collections** are cash receipts that the bank has recorded for your account. But you haven't recorded the cash receipt yet. Many businesses have their customers pay directly to their bank. This is called a *lockbox system* and reduces theft. An example is a bank collecting an account receivable for you. Add bank collections on the bank reconciliation.

   b. *Electronic funds transfers.* The bank may receive or pay cash on your behalf. An electronic funds transfer (EFT) may be a cash receipt or a cash payment. EFTs are set up with a bank using a code and bank account number for the company. It allows electronic cheques to be sent (or received) digitally to (or from) the bank, who then disburses the money from (or deposits the money to) the company account. Add EFT receipts and subtract EFT payments.

   c. *Service charge.* This cash payment is the bank's fee for processing your transactions. Subtract service charges.

   d. *Interest income.* On certain types of bank accounts, you earn interest if you keep enough cash in your account. The bank statement tells you of this cash receipt. Add interest income.

   e. *Nonsufficient funds (NSF) cheques.* **Nonsufficient funds (NSF) cheques** are cash receipts from customers who do not have sufficient funds in their bank account to cover the amount. NSF cheques (sometimes called bad cheques) are treated as cash payments on your bank reconciliation. Subtract NSF cheques.

   f. *The cost of printed cheques.* This cash payment is handled like a service charge. Subtract this cost.

   g. *Book errors.* Correct all book errors on the Book side of the reconciliation. For example, you may have recorded a $120 cheque that you wrote as $210. These items are recorded by the bank but not by the company; therefore, journal entries must be prepared.

   These items are recorded by the bank but not by the company, therefore, journal entries must be prepared.

In a business, the bank reconciliation can be a part of internal control if it is done on a regular basis and if someone independent of the person preparing the bank reconciliation (for example, someone from another department) reviews the reconciliation.

BANK RECONCILIATION ILLUSTRATED. The bank statement in Exhibit 4-2 indicates that the January 31 bank balance of Nixon Partners Inc. is $5,931.51. However, Exhibit 4-3 shows that the company's Cash account on the books has a balance of $3,294.21. This situation calls for a bank reconciliation. Exhibit 4-4, Panel A, lists the reconciling items for easy reference, and Panel B shows the completed reconciliation.

After the reconciliation in Exhibit 4-4, the adjusted bank balance equals the adjusted book balance. This equality checks the accuracy of both the bank and the books.

RECORDING TRANSACTIONS FROM THE BANK RECONCILIATION. The bank reconciliation is an accountant's tool separate from the journals and ledgers. It does *not* account for transactions in the journal. To get the transactions into the accounts, we must record journal entries and post them to the ledger. All items on the *Book* side of the bank reconciliation require journal entries.

EXHIBIT 4-4
Bank Reconciliation

PANEL A—Reconciling Items

Bank side:
1. Deposit in transit, $1,591.63
2. Bank error: The bank deducted $100.00 on January 6 for a cheque written by another company. Add $100.00 to the bank balance.
3. Outstanding cheques—total of $1,350.14

	A	B	C
1	**Cheque No.**	**Amount**	
2	337	$ 286.00	
3	338	319.47	
4	339	83.00	
5	340	203.14	
6	341	458.53	
7			

Book side:
4. EFT receipt of your interest revenue earned on an investment, $904.03.
5. Bank collection of your note receivable, including interest of $214.00, $2,114.00.
6. Interest revenue earned on your bank balance, $28.01.
7. Book error: You recorded cheque no. 333 for $510.00. The amount you actually paid on account was $150.00. Add $360.00 to your book balance.
8. Bank service charge, $14.25.
9. NSF cheque from a customer, $52.00. Subtract $52.00 from your book balance.
10. EFT payment of insurance expense, $361.00.

PANEL B—Bank Reconciliation

	A	B	C	D	E	F
1			**Nixon Partners Inc.** Bank Reconciliation January 31, 2020			
2	**Bank**			**Books**		
3	Balance, January 31		$ 5,931.51	Balance, January 31		$3,294.21
4	Add:			Add:		
5	**1.** Deposit in transit		1,591.63	**4.** EFT receipt of interest revenue		904.03
6	**2.** Correction of bank error		100.00	**5.** Bank collection of note		
7			7,623.14	receivable		2,114.00
8				**6.** Interest revenue earned on		
9				bank balance		28.01
10				**7.** Correction of book error—		
11	Less:			overstated our cheque no. 333		360.00
12	**3.** Outstanding cheques					6,700.25
13	No. 337	$ 286.00				
14	No. 338	319.47		Less:		
15	No. 339	83.00		**8.** Service charge	$ 14.25	
16	No. 340	203.14		**9.** NSF cheque	52.00	
17	No. 341	458.53	(1,350.14)	**10.** EFT payment of insurance expense	361.00	(427.25)
18	Adjusted bank balance		$ 6,273.00	Adjusted book balance		$6,273.00
19						

These amounts should agree.

Summary of the Various Reconciling Items:

Bank Balance—Always:
- *Add* deposits in transit.
- *Subtract* outstanding cheques.
- *Add* or *subtract* corrections of bank errors.

Book Balance—Always:
- *Add* bank collections, interest revenue, and EFT receipts.
- *Subtract* service charges, NSF cheques, and EFT payments.
- *Add* or *subtract* corrections of book errors.

The bank reconciliation in Exhibit 4-4 requires Nixon Partners to make journal entries to bring the Cash account up to date. These journal entries are detailed below. Numbers in parentheses correspond to the reconciling items listed in Exhibit 4-4, Panel A.

	A	B	C	D	E	F
1	(4)	Jan. 31	Cash	904.03		
2			Interest revenue		904.03	
3			*Receipt of interest revenue.*			
4	(5)	Jan. 31	Cash	2,114.00		
5			Note receivable		1,900.00	
6			Interest revenue		214.00	
7			*Note receivable collected by bank.*			
8	(6)	Jan. 31	Cash	28.01		
9			Interest revenue		28.01	
10			*Interest earned on bank balance.*			
11	(7)	Jan. 31	Cash	360.00		
12			Accounts payable—Brown Co. Ltd.		360.00	
13			*Correction of cheque no. 333.*			
14	(8)	Jan. 31	Bank service charge expense	14.25		
15			Cash		14.25	
16			*Bank service charge.*			
17	(9)	Jan. 31	Accounts receivable—L. Ross	52.00		
18			Cash		52.00	
19			*NSF customer cheque returned by bank.*			
20	(10)	Jan. 31	Insurance expense	361.00		
21			Cash		361.00	
22			*Payment of monthly insurance.*			
23						

The entry for the NSF cheque (entry 9) needs explanation. Upon learning that a customer's $52.00 cheque to us was not good, we must credit Cash to update the Cash account. Unfortunately, we still have a receivable from the customer, so we must debit Accounts Receivable to reinstate our receivable.

Online Banking

Online banking allows you to pay bills and view your account electronically—you don't have to wait until the end of the month to get a bank statement. With online banking you can reconcile transactions at any time and keep your account current whenever you wish.

MyLab Accounting

STOP + THINK (4-1)

You have been asked to prepare a bank reconciliation and are given the following information. The bank statement balance is $4,500 and shows a service charge of $15, interest earned of $5, and an NSF cheque for $300. Deposits in transit total $1,200; outstanding cheques are $575. You recorded as $152 a cheque of $125 in payment of an account payable.

1. What is the adjusted bank balance?

2. What was the book balance of cash before the reconciliation?

MyLab Accounting

MID-CHAPTER SUMMARY PROBLEM

The Cash account of Chima Inc. at February 29, 2020, is as follows:

		Cash				
Feb.	1	Balance	3,995	Feb.	5	400
	6		800		12	3,100
	15		1,800		19	1,100
	22		1,100		26	500
	28		2,400		27	900
Feb.	29	Balance	4,095			

Aneil Chima deposits all cash receipts in the bank and makes all cash payments by cheque. Chima Inc. receives this bank statement on February 29, 2020 (as always, negative amounts are in parentheses):

	A	B	C	D
1	**Bank Statement for February 2020**			
2	Beginning balance		$ 3,995	
3	Deposits:			
4	Feb. 7	$ 800		
5	15	1,800		
6	23	1,100	3,700	
7	Cheques (total per day):			
8	Feb. 8	$ 400		
9	16	3,100		
10	23	1,100	(4,600)	
11	Other items:			
12	Service charge		(10)	
13	NSF cheque from M. E. Crown		(700)	
14	Bank collection of note receivable		1,000*	
15	EFT—monthly rent expense		(330)	
16	Interest on account balance		15	
17	Ending balance		$ 3,070	
18	*Includes interest of $119			

Name: Chima Inc.
Accounting Period: Month of February 2020

Requirements

1. Prepare the bank reconciliation of Chima Inc. at February 29, 2020.
2. Record the journal entries based on the bank reconciliation.

ANSWERS

Requirement 1

Before creating the bank reconciliation, compare the Cash account and the bank statement. Cross out all items that appear in both places. The items that remain are the reconciling items.

	A	B	C	D
1	**Chima Inc.** Bank Reconciliation February 29, 2020			
2	**Bank:**			
3	Balance, February 29, 2020		$ 3,070	
4	Add: Deposit of February 28 in transit		2,400	
5			5,470	
6	Less: Outstanding cheques issued on			
7	Feb. 26 ($500) and Feb. 27 ($900)		(1,400)	
8	Adjusted bank balance, February 29, 2020		$ 4,070	
9	**Books:**			
10	Balance, February 29, 2020		$ 4,095	
11	Add: Bank collection of note receivable, including interest of $119		1,000	
12	Interest earned on bank balance		15	
13			5,110	
14	Less: Service charge	$ 10		
15	NSF cheque	700		
16	EFT—Rent expense	330	(1,040)	
17	Adjusted book balance, February 29, 2020		$ 4,070	
18				

Begin with the ending balance on the bank statement.
- Add deposits (debits) from the Cash account not on the bank statement.
- Deduct cheques (credits) from the Cash account not on the bank statement.

Begin with the ending balance in the Cash general ledger account.
- Add money received by the bank on behalf of the company (increases to the bank statement balance).
- Deduct bank charges, NSF cheques, or pre-authorized payments (decreases to the bank statement balance).

Requirement 2

	A	B	C	D	E
1	Feb. 29	Cash	1,000		
2		Note receivable ($1,000 – $119)		881	
3		Interest revenue		119	
4		*Note receivable collected by bank.*			
5	29	Cash	15		
6		Interest revenue		15	
7		*Interest earned on bank balance.*			
8	29	Bank service charge expense	10		
9		Cash		10	
10		*Bank service charge.*			
11	29	Accounts receivable—M. E. Crown	700		
12		Cash		700	
13		*NSF cheque returned by bank.*			
14	29	Rent expense	330		
15		Cash		330	
16		*Monthly rent expense.*			
17					

Prepare journal entries for all reconciling items from the "Books" section of the bank reconciliation.

ACCOUNT FOR ACCOUNTS RECEIVABLE

Receivables are the third most-liquid asset after cash and short-term investments. Most of the remainder of this chapter shows how to account for receivables.

Types of Receivables

Receivables are monetary claims against others. They are acquired mainly by selling goods and services on account (accounts receivable) and by lending money (notes receivable). Journal entries to record receivables can be shown as follows:

Performing a Service on Account		Lending Money on a Note Receivable	
Accounts Receivable...............	XXX	Note Receivable.................................	XXX
Service Revenue....................	XXX	Cash..	XXX
Performed a service on account.		*Loaned money to another company.*	

The two major types of receivables are accounts receivable and notes receivable. A business's *accounts receivable* are the amounts collectible from customers from the sale of goods and services. Accounts receivable, which are *current assets*, are sometimes called *trade receivables* or merely *receivables*.

The Accounts Receivable account in the general ledger serves as a *control account* that summarizes the total amount receivable from all customers. Companies also keep a *subsidiary ledger* of accounts receivable with a separate account for each customer, illustrated as follows:

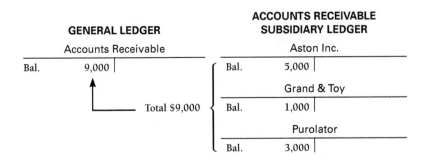

Notes receivable are more formal contracts than accounts receivable. The borrower signs a written promise to pay the creditor a definite sum at the *maturity* date, plus interest. This is why notes receivable are also called promissory notes. The note may require the borrower to pledge *security* for the loan. This means that the borrower gives the lender permission to claim certain assets, called *collateral*, if the borrower fails to pay the amount due.

Other Receivables is a miscellaneous category for all receivables other than accounts receivable and notes receivable. Examples include interest receivable and advance to employees.

By selling on credit, companies run the risk of not collecting some receivables, and unfortunately, some customers don't pay their debts. The prospect that we may fail to collect from a customer provides the biggest challenge in accounting for receivables. How do we minimize this risk? The Decision Guidelines below provide some advice.

DECISION GUIDELINES

MANAGING AND ACCOUNTING FOR ACCOUNTS RECEIVABLE

Here are the management and accounting issues a company faces when it extends credit to customers. Let's look at a business situation: Suppose you and a friend open a health club near your school. Assume you will let customers use the club and charge bills to their accounts. What challenges will you encounter by extending credit to customers?

The main issues in *managing* receivables, along with a plan of action, are the following:

Decision	Guidelines
1. What are the benefits and the costs of extending credit to customers?	**1.** Benefit—increase in sales. Cost—risk of not collecting.
2. Extend credit only to creditworthy customers.	**2.** Run a credit check on prospective customers.
3. Pursue collection from customers to maximize cash flow.	**3.** Keep a close eye on customer paying habits. Offer a sales discount for early payment. Send second, and third, statements to slow-paying customers, if necessary. Charge interest on overdue accounts. Do not extend credit to overdue accounts. Better solution: Have customers sign agreements for automatic payment by electronic fund transfers (EFTs) from their bank accounts each month.

The main issues in accounting for receivables and the related plans of action are as follows (amounts are assumed):

Decision	Guidelines
How should receivables be reported?	Report receivables at net realizable value:
	Balance sheet
	Receivables $1,000 Less: Allowance for uncollectibles (80) Receivables, net $ 920
	Managers This is the amount the company expects to collect and the appropriate amount to report for receivables.
	Investors and Creditors They are interested in seeing the net receivables because this is the amount the company actually expects to collect. They understand that legally the company is owed $1,000, but in reality, $920 is the amount expected to be collected.
How should the bad debt expense be reported?	This expense of not collecting from customers is called *bad debt expense* and is reported on the income statement.
	Income statement
	Sales (or service) revenue $8,000 Expenses: Bad debt expense 60
	Managers The company measures and reports the expense associated with the failure to collect receivables.
	Investors and Creditors Because investors and creditors are interested in the profitability of the company, the bad debt expense on the income statement reflects the cost associated with selling goods on credit.

These guidelines lead to our next topic, accounting for uncollectible receivables.

MyLab Accounting

STOP + THINK (4-2)

You are considering an investment in Black Corporation and are looking at Black's June 30, 2020, financial statements, which are stated in thousands of dollars. In particular, you are focusing on Black's accounts receivable. The balance sheet includes the following:

	June 30	
	2020	2019
Accounts receivable, net of Allowance for uncollectible accounts of $3,974 as of June 30, 2020, and $2,089 as of June 30, 2019..	$134,396	$128,781

At June 30, 2020, how much did customers owe Black Corporation? How much did Black expect *not* to collect? How much of the receivables did Black expect to collect?

EVALUATE COLLECTIBILITY USING THE ALLOWANCE FOR UNCOLLECTIBLE ACCOUNTS

OBJECTIVE

❹ **Evaluate** collectibility using the allowance for uncollectible accounts

A company gets an account receivable only when it sells its product or service on credit. You'll recall that the entry to record the earning of revenue on account is (amount assumed):

	A	B	C	D	E
1		Accounts Receivable	1,000		
2		Sales Revenue (or Service Revenue)		1,000	
3		*Earned revenue on account.*			
4					

Companies rarely collect all of their accounts receivable, so they must account for what they do not collect.

As stated above, selling on credit creates both a benefit and a cost:

- *Benefit*: Customers who cannot pay cash immediately can buy on credit, so company profits rise as sales increase.

- *Cost*: When a customer doesn't pay, the debt has gone bad, so this cost is commonly called an **uncollectible account expense**, a **doubtful account expense**, or a **bad debt expense**.

Accounts receivable are reported in the financial statements at cost minus an appropriate allowance for uncollectible accounts (that is, net realizable value). This is the amount a company expects to collect.

A company may present the allowance for uncollectible accounts in the notes to the financial statements, or disclose the information on the balance sheet as follows:

Accounts Receivable (net of allowance for
uncollectible accounts of $120,000)....................................... $2,005,234

From this information we can determine several things about the company's receivables. From the amount of its allowance for uncollectible accounts, we can see that *it does not expect to collect* $120,000 of its accounts receivable at year-end. The *net realizable value* of its receivables is $2,005,234, which is the amount it *expects to collect* from its customers. If we add the uncollectible account to the net realizable value, we get the company's *total accounts receivable* at year-end: $2,125,234.

Bad debt expense is an expense associated with the failure to collect receivables. It is usually reported as an operating expense on the income statement. To measure bad debt expense, accountants use the *allowance method.*

Allowance Method

The best way to measure bad debts is by the **allowance method**. This method records losses from failure to collect receivables. Management does not wait to see which customers will not pay. Managers estimate bad debt expense on the basis of the company's history of collections from customers and their professional judgment. The company records the estimated amount as Bad Debt Expense and sets up an **Allowance for Uncollectible Accounts**. Other titles for this account are **Allowance for Doubtful Accounts** and **Allowance for Bad Debts**. This is a contra account to Accounts Receivable, which means that it is deducted from Accounts Receivable. The allowance shows the amount of the receivables that the business *does not expect* to collect. Management does not know yet which customer will not pay. The use of a contra account eliminates the problem of having to reduce an accounts receivable of a specific customer. To estimate uncollectibles, the company uses the **aging-of-receivables method**.

AGING-OF-RECEIVABLES METHOD. This method is a *balance-sheet approach* because it focuses on what should be the most relevant and faithful representation of accounts receivable as of the balance sheet date. In the aging method, individual receivables from specific customers are analyzed based on how long they have been outstanding.

Accounting software packages are designed to age the company's accounts receivable. Exhibit 4-5 shows an assumed aging of receivables for Black at June 30, 2020. Black's receivables total $138,370 (in thousands of dollars). Of this amount, the aging schedule shows that the company will *not* collect $6,156, but the allowance for uncollectible accounts is not yet up to date. Suppose Black's accounts are as follows *before the year-end adjustment* (in thousands):

Accounts Receivable		Allowance for Uncollectible Accounts	
138,370			346

EXHIBIT 4-5
Aging the Accounts Receivable of Black Corporation

		Dollar Amounts (in thousands) Number of Days Outstanding			
Customer	Total	0–30	31–60	61–90	over 90
City of Regina	$ 500	$ 500			
IBM Canada	1,000	1,000			
Keady Pipe Corp.	2,100		$ 1,000	$ 1,100	
TorBar Inc.	200			200	
Others	134,570	66,070	57,000	9,000	$2,500
	$138,370	$67,570	$58,000	$10,300	$2,500
Estimated % Uncollectible		2%	5%	10%	35%
Total Estimated Uncollectible Accounts	$ 6,156	$ 1,351	$ 2,900	$ 1,030	$ 875

Using the aging method, the accounts are listed in categories based on the number of days they have been outstanding. For example, in Exhibit 4-5, the total accounts receivable is $138,370. This amount is further divided into days outstanding: 0–30 days, 31–60 days, 61–90 days, and over 90 days.

If you look under the 0–30 days category, you will see that credit sales of $67,570 were made within the last 30 days and the company is still waiting to collect cash from the customers. Management estimated that 2% or $1,351 ($67,570 × 2%) would not be collected. The estimated percentages are based on management's professional judgment and past experience with collections. The percentages could change from year to year based on industry, general economic conditions, and customer circumstances. Under the 31–60 days category, $58,000 was sold on account more than 30 days ago but less than 60 days. Management estimates that 5% of the $58,000 will not be collected. Each of the other categories has its estimated percentage of uncollectible accounts indicated as well. Adding up the total estimated uncollectible accounts for each column ($1,351 + $2,900 + $1,030 + $875), it totals $6,156. This means that Black expects *not* to collect $6,156, but the allowance for bad debts is not yet up to date. The aging method will bring the balance of the allowance account ($346) to the needed amount ($6,156) as determined by the aging schedule in Exhibit 4-5. To update the allowance, Black Corporation would make this entry:

	A	B	C	D	E
1	2020				
2	June 30	Bad Debt Expense ($6,156 – $346)	5,810		
3		Allowance for Uncollectible Accounts		5,810	
4		*Recorded expense for the year.*			
5					

Both assets and shareholders' equity decrease, as shown by the accounting equation:

ASSETS	=	LIABILITIES	+	SHAREHOLDERS' EQUITY
−5,810	=	0		−5,810 Expense

When the company uses the allowance method, expenses are properly recognized in the period they were incurred, which is the same period in which the related sales took place.

Now the balance sheet can report the amount that Black Corporation actually expects to collect from customers: $132,214 ($138,370 − $6,156). This is the net realizable value of Black's trade receivables. Black's accounts are now ready for the balance sheet, as follows:

Accounts Receivable	Allowance for Uncollectible Accounts		Bad Debt Expense
138,370		346	5,810
	Adj.	5,810	
	End. Bal.	6,156	

Net accounts receivable, $132,214

Exhibit 4-6 summarizes the aging-of-receivables method.

EXHIBIT 4-6
Summary of the Aging-of-Receivables Method for Estimating Uncollectible Accounts

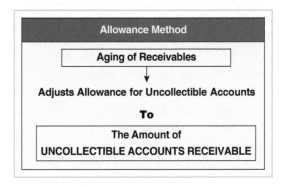

WRITING OFF UNCOLLECTIBLE ACCOUNTS. Suppose that early in July 2020, Black's credit department determines that Black cannot collect from customers Keady Pipe Corporation and TorBar Inc. (see Exhibit 4-5). Black Corporation then writes off the receivables from these two delinquent customers with the following entry (in thousands of dollars):

	A	B	C	D	E
1	2020				
2	July 12	Allowance for Uncollectible Accounts	2,300		
3		Accounts Receivable—Keady Pipe Corporation		2,100	
4		Accounts Receivable—TorBar Inc.		200	
5		*Wrote off uncollectible receivables.*			
6					

After the write-off, Black's accounts show these amounts:

Accounts Receivable—Keady Pipe Corp.		Accounts Receivable—TorBar Inc.		Allowance for Uncollectible Accounts	
2,100	2,100	200	200	2,300	6,156
				End Bal.	3,856

Accounts Receivable Others	
134,570	

Accounts Receivable—City of Regina	
500	

Accounts Receivable—IBM Canada	
1,000	

Total Accounts Receivable = $136,070   Allowance = $3,856

Accounts Receivable, Net = $132,214

If the write-offs are greater than the balance in the Allowance for Uncollectible Accounts, it will result in a debit balance in the Allowance account. This means that management's estimate of bad debts was too low and needs to be higher. The accounting equation shows that the write-off of uncollectibles has no effect on total assets; the net realizable value of accounts receivable is still $132,214. There is no effect on net income either, because no expense account is affected.

ASSETS	=	LIABILITIES	+	SHAREHOLDERS' EQUITY
+2,300				
−2,300	=	0	+	0

Recovery of an Uncollectible Account

Even though an account has been written off as uncollectible, the customer still owes the money and will sometimes pay off the account, at least in part.

Some companies turn delinquent receivables over to a collection agency to help recover some of their cash. This is called the *recovery of an uncollectible account*. Recall that on July 12, 2020, Black Corporation wrote off the $200 account receivable from TorBar. Suppose it is now September 1, 2020, and the company unexpectedly receives the $200 from TorBar. To account for this recovery, the company makes two journal entries to (1) reverse the earlier write-off and (2) record the cash collection, as follows:

	A	B	C	D	E
1	2020				
2	Sept. 1	Accounts Receivable—TorBar Inc.	200		
3		Allowance for Uncollectible Accounts		200	
4		*Reinstated TorBar's account receivable.*			
5		Cash	200		
6		Accounts Receivable—TorBar Inc.		200	
7		*Collected on account.*			
8					

Summary of Transactions for Accounts Receivable

Exhibit 4-7 summarizes the journal entries to record the transactions affecting accounts receivable.

During the accounting period:

Record sales on account:
Accounts receivable
    Sales revenue

Record collections from customers:
Cash
    Accounts receivable

Record write-off of uncollectible accounts:
Allowance for uncollectible accounts
    Accounts receivable

Record recovery of an uncollectible account:
Accounts receivable
    Allowance for uncollectible accounts
Cash
    Accounts receivable

At the end of the accounting period:

Estimate bad debt expense:
Bad debt expense
    Allowance for uncollectible accounts

EXHIBIT 4-7
Summary of Accounts Receivable Transactions

Computing Cash Collections from Customers

A company earns revenue and then collects the cash from customers. For Black Corporation (and most other companies), there is a time lag between earning the revenue and collecting the cash. Collections from customers are the single most important source of cash for any business. You can compute a company's collections from customers by analyzing its Accounts Receivable account. Receivables typically hold only five different items, as follows (amounts assumed):

Accounts Receivable

Beg. balance (left from last period)	200	Write-offs of uncollectible accounts	100**
		Collections from customers	$X = 1,500†$
Sales (or service) revenue	1,800*		
End. balance (carries over to next period)	400		

*The journal entry that places revenue into the receivable account is:

	A	B	C	D
1	Accounts Receivable	1,800		
2	Sales (or Service) Revenue		1,800	
3				

**The journal entry for write-offs is:

	A	B	C	D
1	Allowance for Uncollectible Accounts	100		
2	Accounts Receivable		100	
3				

†The journal entry that places collections into the receivable account is:

	A	B	C	D
1	Cash	1,500		
2	Accounts Receivable		1,500	
3				

Suppose you know all these amounts except collections from customers. You can compute collections by solving for X in the T-account.***

Often write-offs are not known and must be omitted. Then the computation of collections becomes an approximation.

COOKING the BOOKS

shifting sales Into the Current Period

Suppose it is December 26. Late in the year a company's business dried up: Its profits are running below what everyone predicted. The company needs a loan and its banker requires financial statements to support the loan request. Unless the company acts quickly, it won't get the loan.

Fortunately, next year looks better. The company has standing orders for sales of $50,000. As soon as the company gets the merchandise, it can ship it to customers and record the sales. An old accounting trick can solve the problem. Book the $50,000 of sales in December. After all, the company will be shipping the goods on January 2 of next year. What difference does two days make?

It makes all the difference in the world. Shifting the sales into the current year will make the company look better immediately. Reported profits will rise, the current ratio will improve, and the company can then get the loan needed. Also, this false information could lead to investors making decisions that would not otherwise have been made if the information had been recorded in the proper time period. But what are the consequences? If caught, the company could be prosecuted for fraud, and lenders and investors will lose confidence in the company. Remember that the company shifted next year's sales into the current year. Next year's sales will be lower than the true amount, and profits will suffer. If next year turns out to be like this year, the company will be facing the same shortage again. Also, something may come up to keep the company from shipping the goods on January 2.

***An equation may help you solve for X. The equation is $200 + 1,800 - X - 100 = 400$. $X = 1,500$.

STOP + THINK (4-3)

Neal Company had the following information relating to credit sales in 2020:

Accounts receivable, December 31, 2020	$9,500
Allowance for uncollectible accounts, credit balance, December 31, 2020	900
(before adjustment)	
Sales during 2020	46,000
Collections from customers on account during 2020	49,500

The aging-of-receivables method determined the uncollectible accounts to be $1,350. How much should Neal Company record as the bad debt expense for 2020?

ACCOUNT FOR NOTES RECEIVABLE AND INTEREST REVENUE

OBJECTIVE

❺ **Account** for notes receivable and interest revenue

As stated earlier, notes receivable are more formal than accounts receivable. Notes receivable due within one year or less are current assets. Notes due beyond one year are *long-term receivables* and are reported as non-current. Some notes receivable are collected in instalments. The portion due within one year is a current asset and the remainder is a long-term asset. Assume, for example, that a company issues a $20,000 note receivable to a customer, with quarterly instalments of $2,500 due over the next two years. If six instalments are still owing at year-end, then $10,000 of the note would be a current asset (four quarterly payments of $2,500), and the remaining $5,000 would be reported as a long-term asset.

Before launching into the accounting for notes receivable, let's define some key terms:

Creditor	The party to whom money is owed. The creditor is also called the *lender*. The debt is a *note receivable* from the *borrower*.
Debtor	The party that borrowed and owes money on the note. The debtor is also called the *maker* of the note or the *borrower*. The debt is a *note payable* to the *lender*.
Interest	Interest is the cost of borrowing money. The interest is stated as an annual percentage rate.
Maturity date	The date on which the debtor must pay the note.
Principal	The amount of money borrowed by the debtor.
Term	The length of time the debtor has to repay the note.

The debtor signs the note and thereby creates a contract with the creditor. Exhibit 4-8 shows a typical promissory note.

The *principal* amount of the note ($1,000) is the amount borrowed by the debtor and lent by the creditor. This six-month note runs from July 1, 2020, to December 31, 2020, when Lauren Holland (the maker) promises to pay Canadian Western Bank (the creditor) the principal of $1,000 plus 9% interest per year. *Interest* is revenue to the creditor and an expense to the debtor.

EXHIBIT 4-8
A Promissory Note

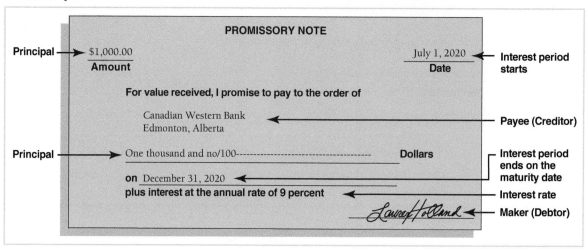

Accounting for Notes Receivable

Consider the promissory note shown in Exhibit 4-8. After Lauren Holland (the maker) signs the note, Canadian Western Bank gives her $1,000 cash. The bank would record the following journal entry:

	A	B	C	D	E
1	2020				
2	July 1	Note Receivable—L. Holland	1,000		
3		Cash		1,000	
4		*Made a loan.*			
5					

Note Receivable—L. Holland	
1,000	

The bank gave one asset, cash, in return for another asset, a note receivable, so the total assets did not change:

ASSETS	=	LIABILITIES	+	SHAREHOLDERS' EQUITY
+1,000				
−1,000	=	0	+	0

Assume Canadian Western Bank has an October 31 year-end. The bank earns interest revenue during July, August, September, and October. At October 31, 2020, the bank accrues interest revenue for four months as follows:

	A	B	C	D	E
1	2020				
2	Oct. 31	Interest Receivable ($1,000 × 0.09 × 4/12*)	30		
3		Interest Revenue		30	
4		*Accrued interest revenue.*			
5					

*For ease of calculations, 12 months is used instead of 365 days.

The bank's assets and its revenue increase.

The bank reports these amounts in its financial statements at October 31, 2020:

Balance sheet

Current assets:

Note receivable $1,000

Interest receivable 30

Income statement

Interest revenue .... $ 30

The bank collects the note on December 31, 2020, and records:

	A	B	C	D	E
1	2020				
2	Dec. 31	Cash	1,045		
3		Note Receivable—L. Holland		1,000	
4		Interest Receivable		30	
5		Interest Revenue ($1,000 × 0.09 × 2/12)		15	
6		Collected note at maturity.			
7					

This entry eliminates the Note Receivable and Interest Receivable and also records the interest revenue earned from November 1 to December 31, 2020.

Note Receivable—L. Holland
1,000	1,000

In its 2021 financial statements, the only item that Canadian Western Bank will report is the interest revenue of $15 that was earned in November and December 2020, part of its 2021 fiscal period. There's no note receivable or interest receivable on the balance sheet because those items were zeroed out when the bank collected the note at maturity.

Three aspects of these entries deserve mention:

1. Interest rates are always for an annual period unless stated otherwise. In this example, the annual interest rate is 9%. At October 31, 2020, Canadian Western Bank accrues interest revenue for the four months the bank has held the note. The interest computation is:

$$\textbf{Principal} \times \textbf{Interest rate} \times \textbf{Time} = \textbf{Amount of Interest}$$
$$\$1,000 \times \quad 0.09 \quad \times 4/12 = \quad \$30$$

2. The time element (4/12) is the fraction of the year that the note has been in force during the year ended October 31, 2020.

3. Interest is often completed for a number of days. For example, suppose you loaned out $10,000 on April 10. The note receivable runs for 90 days and specifies interest at 8%.

   a. Interest starts accruing on April 10, the day the money is borrowed, and continues to accrue until the note comes due 90 days later (July 8):

Month	Number of Days That Interest Accrues
April	21
May	31
June	30
July	8
Total	90

   b. The interest computation is: $\$10,000 \times 0.08 \times 90/365 = \$197$

Some companies sell goods and services on notes receivable (versus selling on accounts receivable). This often occurs when the payment term extends beyond the customary accounts receivable period of 30 to 60 days.

Suppose that on March 20, 2020, West Fraser Timber Co. Ltd. sells lumber for $15,000 to Darmal Const. Inc. West Fraser receives Darmal's 90-day promissory note at 10% annual interest. The entries to record the sale and collection from Darmal follow the pattern illustrated previously for Canadian Western Bank and Lauren Holland, with one exception. At the outset, West Fraser would credit Sales Revenue (instead of Cash) because West Fraser is making a sale (and not lending money to Darmal). Short-term notes receivable are valued the same way as regular accounts receivable, so we must set up an appropriate allowance for any uncollectible short-term notes. Any notes with a maturity date beyond 365 days of year-end, however, must be valued at their amortized cost by discounting them to reflect the time value of money.

A company may also accept a note receivable from a trade customer whose account receivable is past due. The customer signs a note, and the company then credits the account receivable and debits a note receivable. We would say the company "received a note receivable from a customer on account."

For example, assume that on February 1, 2020, Power Ltd. purchased $5,000 of building supplies from Piercy's Building Supplies with 60-day credit terms. Piercy's records the sale as follows:

	A	B	C	D	E
1	2020				
2	Feb. 1	Accounts Receivable—Power Ltd.	5,000		
3		Sales		5,000	
4		To record sale to Power Ltd.			
5					

If on April 1, 2020, Power Ltd. agrees to sign a 30-day note receivable to replace the account receivable due on that date, then Piercy's would record the following journal entry:

	A	B	C	D	E
1	2020				
2	Apr. 1	Notes Receivable	5,000		
3		Accounts Receivable—Power Ltd.		5,000	
4		To record conversion of account receivable to note receivable			
5					

Now let's examine some strategies to speed up cash flow.

STOP + THINK (4-4)

Saturn Company received a four-month, 5%, $4,800 note receivable on December 1. How much interest revenue should they accrue on December 31?

EXPLAIN HOW TO IMPROVE CASH FLOWS FROM SALES AND RECEIVABLES

All companies want speedy cash receipts. Rapid cash flow means companies have the ability to pay off their current liabilities faster, as well as to finance new products, research, and development. Consequently, companies develop strategies to shorten the credit cycle and collect cash more quickly. For example, they might offer sales discounts for early payment (discussed in Chapter 5). They might also charge interest on customer accounts that exceed a certain age. They adopt more effective credit and collection procedures. As electronic banking has become more popular, a common strategy has been to emphasize credit card or bank card sales. Let's look at some of these ways that companies can hasten their cash receipts from sales.

CREDIT CARD SALES. The merchant sells merchandise and lets the customer pay with a credit card, such as VISA, MasterCard, or a company credit card such as HBC (Hudson's Bay Company). This strategy may dramatically increase sales, but the added revenue comes at a cost. Let's see how credit cards work from the seller's perspective.

Suppose you purchase an iPhone from TELUS in Fredericton, New Brunswick, for $500 and you pay with a MasterCard. TELUS would record the sale as follows:

	A	B	C	D	E
1		Cash	485		
2		Credit Card Fee	15		
3		Sales Revenue		500	
4		*Record credit card sale.*			
5					

ASSETS	=	LIABILITIES	+	SHAREHOLDERS' EQUITY
+485	=	0	+	+500 Revenue
				−15 Expense

TELUS enters the transaction in the credit-card machine. The machine, linked to a MasterCard server, automatically credits TELUS's account for a discounted portion—say, $485—of the $500 sales amount. MasterCard gets 3%, or $15 ($500 × 0.03 = $15). To the merchant, the credit card fee is an operating expense similar to interest expense.

DEBIT CARD SALES. The merchant sells merchandise, and the customer pays by swiping a bank card such as a Scotiabank ScotiaCard or a TD Canada Trust Green Card using the Interac System. In this case, the bank card is being used as a debit card. To a merchant or service provider, a debit card is just like cash; when the card is swiped and the personal identification number (PIN) is entered, the merchant receives payment immediately as the Interac System takes money directly from the cardholder's bank account and transfers the money to the merchant's bank account less a processing fee. As with credit cards, the merchant is charged a fee. To record a sale of groceries for $65.48, Sobeys would record this entry:

	A	B	C	D	E
1		Cash	64.48		
2		Interac Fee (assumed rate)	1.00		
3		Sales Revenue		65.48	
4		*Record sale paid using Interac.*			
5					

ASSETS	=	LIABILITIES	+	SHAREHOLDERS' EQUITY
+64.48	=	0	+	+65.48 Revenue
				−1.00 Expense

One advantage for the merchant is that the payment is just like cash without the task of having to deposit the money. One advantage to the customer is that there is no need to carry cash. A second advantage to the cardholder is the cash-back feature (some merchants offer this service to their customers); the cardholder can ask for cash back, and the merchant will record an entry that includes the purchase plus the requested cash. Using the above date and assuming the cardholder requested $40.00 cash back, the entry would be:

	A	B	C	D	E
1		Cash	104.48		
2		Interac Fee (assumed rate)	1.00		
3		Sales Revenue		65.48	
4		Cash (to cardholder)		40.00	
5		*Record sale paid using Interac and cash back of $40.00.*			
6					

SELLING (FACTORING) RECEIVABLES. Suppose Black Corporation makes normal sales on account, debiting Accounts Receivable and crediting Sales Revenue. Black can then sell its accounts receivable to another business, called a *factor*. The factor earns revenue by paying a discounted price for the receivables and then collecting the full amount from the customers. The benefit to the company is the immediate receipt of cash.

To illustrate, suppose Black wishes to speed up cash flow and therefore sells $100,000 of accounts receivable, receiving cash of $95,000. Black would record the sale of the receivables as follows:

	A	B	C	D	E
1		Cash	95,000		
2		Financing Expense	5,000		
3		Accounts Receivable		100,000	
4		*Sold accounts receivable.*			
5					

The Financing Expense is typically reported as an operating expense, although some companies report it as a non-operating loss. Factoring a note receivable is similar to selling an account receivable; however, the credit is to Notes Receivable (instead of Accounts Receivable).

Reporting on the Statement of Cash Flows

Receivables appear on the balance sheet as current assets. We saw these in CGI Group Inc.'s balance sheet at the beginning of the chapter. We've also seen how to report the related revenue and expense on the income statement. Because receivables affect cash, their effects must also be reported on the statement of cash flows.

Receivables bring in cash when the business collects from customers. These transactions are reported as *operating* activities on the statement of cash flows because they result from sales. Chapter 9 shows how companies report their cash flows on the statement of cash flows. In that chapter, we will see exactly how to report cash flows related to receivables.

STOP + THINK (4-5)

Why is it so important for companies to convert their sales to cash receipts as quickly as possible?

EVALUATE LIQUIDITY USING RATIOS

OBJECTIVE

❼ **Evaluate** liquidity using ratios

Managers, investors, and creditors use ratios to evaluate the financial health of a company. They care about the liquidity of assets. Liquidity is a measure of how quickly an item can be converted to cash. Remember, a balance sheet lists current assets in order of relative liquidity:

- *Cash and cash equivalents* come first because they are the most liquid assets.
- *Short-term investments* come next because they are almost as liquid as cash. They can be sold for cash whenever the owner wishes.
- *Current receivables* are less liquid than short-term investments because the company must collect the receivables.
- *Merchandise inventory* is less liquid than receivables because the goods must be sold first.
- *Prepaid expenses* are listed after inventories because they are expenses where cash has already been paid in advance.

We introduced the current ratio in Chapter 3. Recall that the current ratio is computed as follows:

$$\text{Current ratio} = \frac{\text{Total current assets}}{\text{Total current liabilities}}$$

The current ratio measures the company's ability to pay current liabilities with current assets.

Lending agreements often require the borrower to maintain a current ratio at some specified level, say 1.50 or greater. What happens when the borrower's current ratio falls below 1.50? The consequences can be severe:

- The lender can call the loan for immediate payment.
- If the borrower cannot pay, then the lender may pursue legal action to enforce collections.

Suppose it's December 10 and it looks like Black Corporation's current ratio will end the year at a value of 1.48. That would put Black in default on the lending agreement of maintaining a 1.50 or greater current ratio and create a bad situation. With three weeks remaining in the year, how can Black improve its current ratio?

There are several strategies for increasing the current ratio, such as the following:

1. Launch a major sales effort. The increase in cash and receivables will more than offset the decrease in inventory, total current assets will increase, and the current ratio will improve.

2. Pay off some current liabilities before year-end. Both current assets in the numerator and current liabilities in the denominator will decrease by the same amount. The proportionate impact on current liabilities in the denominator will be greater than the impact on current assets in the numerator, and the current ratio will increase. This strategy increases the current ratio when the current ratio is already above 1.0.

3. A third strategy, although questionable, reveals one of the accounting games that unethical companies sometimes play. Suppose Black has some long-term investments (investments that Black plans to hold for longer than a year—these are long-term assets). Before year-end, Black might choose to reclassify these long-term investments as current assets. The reclassification of these investments increases Black's current assets, and that increases the current ratio. This strategy would be acceptable if Black does in fact plan to sell the investments within the next year. But the strategy would be unethical and dishonest if Black in fact plans to keep the investments for longer than a year.

From this example you can see that accounting is not cut-and-dried or all black-and-white. It takes good judgment—which includes ethics—to become a successful accountant.

Other ratios, including the *acid-test* (or *quick ratio*) and the number of *days' sales in receivables*, also help investors measure liquidity.

Acid-Test (or Quick) Ratio

The **acid-test ratio** (or **quick ratio**) is a more stringent measure of a company's ability to pay current liabilities. The acid-test ratio is similar to the current ratio but it excludes inventory and prepaid expenses.

Inventory takes time to sell before the company is able to collect its cash. A company with lots of inventory may have an acceptable current ratio but find it hard to pay its bills. Prepaid expenses are also excluded from the acid-test ratio because the cash has already been paid for these assets that will be expensed as they are used up. The formula is:

$$\text{Acid-test ratio} = \frac{\text{Cash} + \text{Short-term investments} + \text{Net receivables}}{\text{Total current liabilities}}$$

Using CGI Group Inc.'s balance sheet in the chapter-opening story, the acid-test ratio is:

$$\text{2017 CGI} = \frac{\$166 + \$1,285}{\$2,701^*} = 0.54$$

The higher the acid-test ratio, the easier it is to pay current liabilities. CGI's acid-test ratio of 0.54 means that CGI has $0.54 of quick assets to pay each $1.00 of current liabilities. Does this mean that CGI is in trouble? No, although CGI's quick ratio is relatively low, when analyzing ratios you might find it useful to consider other information found in the annual report. In CGI's case, over the past several years they have been busy expanding their business.

What is an acceptable acid-test ratio? The answer depends on the industry. Auto dealers can operate smoothly with an acid-test ratio of 0.20. How can auto dealers

---

*Amount taken from 2017 balance sheet in annual report.

survive with so low an acid-test ratio? GM, Toyota, and the other auto manufacturers help finance their dealers' inventory. Most dealers, therefore, have a financial safety net. In general, a quick ratio of 1.0 is considered healthy for this industry.

Days' Sales in Receivables

After a business makes a credit sale, the *next* step is collecting the receivable. **Days' sales in receivables**, also called the *collection period*, tells how long it takes to collect the average level of receivables. Shorter is better because cash is coming in quickly. The longer the collection period, the less cash is available to pay bills and expand.

Days' sales in receivables can be computed in two logical steps, as follows. First, compute accounts receivable turnover. Ideally, only credit sales should be used. Then divide 365 days by the accounts receivable turnover. We show days' sales in receivables for CGI Group Inc. as follows:

For CGI Group Inc. (in thousands)*

1. $\text{Accounts receivable turnover} = \dfrac{\text{Net sales}}{\text{Average net accounts receivable**}}$

$$\dfrac{\$10{,}845^*}{(\$1{,}285 + \$1{,}101)/2^*} = 9.09 \text{ times}$$

2. $\text{Days sales in receivables} = \dfrac{365 \text{ days}}{\text{Accounts receivable turnover}}$

$$= \dfrac{365}{9.09} = 40 \text{ days}$$

*Data taken from 2017 income statement and balance sheet.
**Average net accounts receivable = (Beginning net receivables + Ending net receivables)/2

Net sales come from the income statement and the receivables amounts are taken from the balance sheet. Average receivables is the simple average of the beginning and ending balances. Another approach would be to simply take Average net receivables in the numerator divided by Net sales/365 days in the denominator.

The length of the collection period depends on the credit terms of the company's sales. For example, sales on "net 30" terms should be collected within approximately 30 days. CGI's days' sales in receivables was 40 days in the 2017 financial statements, compared to an industry average of 42 days. While CGI's collections were longer than 30 days, this was shorter than other companies operating in the same industry.

Companies watch their collection periods closely. Whenever the collections get slow, the business must find other sources of financing, such as borrowing cash or factoring receivables. During recessions, customers pay more slowly, and a longer collection period may be unavoidable.

STOP + THINK (4-6)

Why are inventory and prepaid expenses excluded from the computation of the quick ratio?

DECISION GUIDELINES

USING LIQUIDITY RATIOS IN DECISION MAKING

A company needs cash to pay their bills, buy more inventory, and finance new products and services. Two new ratios that measure liquidity were introduced in the chapter. Let's see how they are used in decision making.

Decision	Guidelines
How do you measure a company's ability to pay all current liabilities if they come due immediately?	$$\text{Quick ratio} = \frac{\text{Cash + Short-term investments + Net receivables}}{\text{Current liabilities}}$$
How do you determine if a company is collecting cash from their customers in a timely manner?	$$\text{Days' sales in receivables} = \frac{\text{Average net receivables}}{\text{Net sales/365}}$$
Who uses the quick ratio and days' sales in receivables for decision making and why?	*Managers* need to ensure that cash is available to pay current liabilities if they come due immediately. They know that some of this cash is tied up in accounts receivables waiting for customers to pay them. This is why companies set up policies and procedures to ensure they can receive their cash from customers quickly so it is available to pay their current debt.
	Investors know that it is important for a company to have enough cash on hand to pay back liabilities, particularly if they are due immediately. Using these ratios helps them to determine how quickly the company is able to collect what is owed them and if this cash is enough to meet current obligations.
	Creditors are expecting to be repaid and look to see how much cash the company has on hand as well as any cash the company expects to receive in the near future. They look to see if the company is able to collect from their customers quickly and if this cash is enough to pay back current liabilities if they are due immediately.

Summary of IFRS-ASPE Differences

Concepts	IFRS	ASPE

There are no differences between IFRS and ASPE in this chapter

SUMMARY

SUMMARY OF LEARNING OBJECTIVES

LEARNING OBJECTIVE	SUMMARY
1 Report cash on the balance sheet	Cash and cash equivalents are the most liquid asset and are reported as the first item under current assets on the balance sheet. Cash equivalents includes items such as treasury bills and money market funds where they will mature within three months from the date of purchase.
2 Prepare a bank reconciliation	To ensure accurate cash records, a bank reconciliation is prepared. It explains all differences between cash records and the bank statement.
3 Account for accounts receivables	Accounts receivable result from a company selling its products or services on credit. They are classified as a current asset because the company expects to collect cash from the customer within a short period of time.
4 Evaluate collectibility using the allowance for uncollectible accounts	Managers use the allowance method (aging of receivables method) to estimate the uncollectible accounts. An accounts receivable is written off when a company is not able to collect from a customer. Sometimes, though, an account receivable may be recovered after it has been written off.
5 Account for notes receivable and interest revenue	Notes receivable are formal arrangements in which the debtor signs a promissory note, agreeing to pay back both the principal borrowed plus a stated percentage of interest on a certain date. The creditor has a note receivable and the debtor has a note payable.
6 Explain how to improve cash flows from sales and receivables	Rather than wait to collect cash from customers, a company can allow the customer to pay with a credit card or debit card, or the company can sell their receivables to another business. Collections from customers are reported as operating activities on the statement of cash flows. They could also offer sales discounts to encourage customers to pay early, and adopt more effective credit and collection procedures.
7 Evaluate liquidity using ratios	Key ratios used in decision making include the acid-test (quick ratio) and the days' sales in receivables. These ratios help managers, investors, and creditors measure the liquidity of the company. Liquidity relates to how quickly a company can obtain and pay cash.

MyLab Accounting

END-OF-CHAPTER SUMMARY PROBLEM

CHC Helicopter Corporation is Vancouver-based and is the world's largest provider of helicopter services to the global offshore oil and gas industry. Assume the company's balance sheet at April 30, 2019, adapted, reported the following:

	(in millions)
Accounts receivable	$240.6
Allowance for uncollectible accounts	(8.4)

Requirements

1. How much of the April 30, 2019, balance of accounts receivable did CHC Helicopter Corporation expect to collect? Stated differently, what was the expected net realizable value of these receivables?

2. Journalize, without explanations, 2020 entries for CHC Helicopter, assuming the following:
   a. The write-offs of uncollectible accounts receivable total $8.0 million. Prepare a T-account for Allowance for Uncollectible Accounts and post to this account.
   b. The April 30, 2020, aging of receivables indicates that $3.1 million of the total receivables of $303.4 million is uncollectible at year-end. Post to Allowance for Uncollectible Accounts as well, and show its adjusted balance at April 30, 2020.
3. Show how CHC Helicopter's receivables and related allowance will appear on the April 30, 2020, balance sheet.
4. Show what CHC Helicopter's income statement will report for the foregoing transactions.

Name: CHC Helicopter Corporation
Industry: Helicopter services
Accounting Period: Years ended April 30, 2019, and April 30, 2020

The expected net realizable value of receivables is the full value less the Allowance for Uncollectible Accounts.

ANSWERS

Requirement 1

	(in millions)
Expected net realizable value of receivables ($240.6 − $8.4)	$232.2

The estimate increases both the Expense and the Allowance for Uncollectible Accounts.

Requirement 2

Write-offs reduce the Allowance for Uncollectible Accounts and Accounts Receivable. They do *not* affect the bad-debt expense.

	A	B	C	D	E
1	a.	Allowance for Uncollectible Accounts	8.0		
2		Accounts Receivable		8.0	
3					

First, determine the balance in Allowance for Uncollectible Accounts by filling in its T-account using the opening balance (given), and deducting the write-offs from 2a.

Allowance for Uncollectible Accounts

2020 Write-offs	8.0	April 30, 2019	8.4
		2020 Balance	0.4

The final balance in the Allowance for Uncollectible Accounts must be $3.1 (estimated in 2b). The balance in the T-account is already $0.4 (given in the T-account above). Therefore, Bad Debt Expense and Allowance for Uncollectible Accounts must be increased by the difference of $2.7.

	A	B	C	D	E
1	b.	Bad Debt Expense ($3.1 − $0.4)	2.7		
2		Allowance for Uncollectible Accounts		2.7	
3					

Allowance for Uncollectible Accounts

	0.4
	2.7
	3.1

Requirement 3

Accounts receivable are always shown at net realizable value, the amount actually expected to be collected.

	(in millions)
Accounts receivable (net of allowance for uncollectibe accounts of $3.1)	$300.3

Requirement 4

Add the Bad Debt Expense amount from Requirement 2b. The $2.7 is the estimate from the aging of the receivables.

	(in millions)
Expenses: Bad Debt expense for 2020	$2.7

REVIEW

MyLab Accounting

Make the grade with MyLab Accounting: The Quick Quiz questions, Short Exercises, Exercises, and Problems (Group A) marked with a ⊕ can be found on MyLab Accounting. You can practise them as often as you want, and most feature step-by-step guided instructions to help you find the right answer.

QUICK QUIZ (ANSWERS APPEAR ON THE LAST PAGE OF THIS CHAPTER.)

1. In a bank reconciliation, an EFT cash payment is
   a. added to the book balance.
   b. deducted from the book balance.
   c. added to the bank balance.
   d. deducted from the bank balance.

2. If a bookkeeper mistakenly recorded a $58 deposit as $85, the error would be shown on the bank reconciliation as a(n)
   a. $27 addition to the book balance.
   b. $85 deduction from the book balance.
   c. $27 deduction from the book balance.
   d. $85 addition to the book balance.

3. Under the allowance method for uncollectible receivables, the entry to record bad debt expense has what effect on the financial statements?
   a. Increases expenses and increases owners' equity
   b. Decreases assets and has no effect on net income
   c. Decreases owners' equity and increases liabilities
   d. Decreases net income and decreases assets

4. Snead Company uses the aging method to adjust the allowance for uncollectible accounts at the end of the period. At December 31, 2020, the balance of accounts receivable is $210,000 and the allowance for uncollectible accounts has a credit balance of $3,000 (before adjustment). An analysis of accounts receivable produced the following age groups:

Current	$150,000
60 days past due...	50,000
Over 60 days past due	10,000
	$210,000

   Based on past experience, Snead estimates that the percentages of accounts that will prove to be uncollectible within the three groups are 2%, 8%, and 20%, respectively. Based on these facts, the adjusting entry for bad debt expense should be made in the amount of
   a. $3,000.   c. $9,000.
   b. $6,000.   d. $13,000.

5. Refer to question 4. The net receivables on the balance sheet are ___.

6. Accounts Receivable has a debit balance of $3,200, and the Allowance for Uncollectible Accounts has a credit balance of $300. A $100 accounts receivable is written off. What is the amount of net receivables (net realizable value) after the write off?
   a. $2,800
   b. $2,900
   c. $3,000
   d. $3,100

7. Refer to question 6. The balance of Allowance for Uncollectible Accounts, after adjustment, will be
   a. $100.
   b. $200.
   c. $300.
   d. impossible to determine from the information given.

8. Refer to questions 6 and 7. Early the following year, Harper wrote off $150 of old receivables as uncollectible. The balance in the Allowance account is now ___.

   The next four questions use the following data:

   On August 1, 2019, Maritimes Ltd. sold equipment and accepted a six-month, 9%, $10,000 note receivable. Maritimes's year-end is December 31.

9. How much interest revenue should Maritimes Ltd. accrue on December 31, 2019?
   a. $225
   b. $450
   c. $375
   d. Some other amount ___

10. If Maritimes Ltd. fails to make an adjusting entry for the accrued interest, which of the following will happen?
    a. Net income will be understated, and liabilities will be overstated.
    b. Net income will be understated, and assets will be understated.
    c. Net income will be overstated, and liabilities will be understated.
    d. Net income will be overstated, and assets will be overstated.

11. How much interest does Maritimes Ltd. expect to collect on the maturity date (February 1, 2020)?
  a. $450
  b. $280
  c. $75
  d. Some other amount ___

12. Which of the following accounts will Maritimes Ltd. credit in the journal entry at maturity on February 1, 2020, assuming collection in full?
  a. Interest Receivable
  b. Note Payable
  c. Interest Payable
  d. Cash

13. Write the journal entry for question 12.

14. Which of the following is included in the calculation of the acid-test ratio?
  a. Cash and accounts receivable
  b. Prepaid expenses and cash

  c. Inventory and short-term investment
  d. Inventory and prepaid expenses

15. A company with net sales of $1,217,000, beginning net receivables of $90,000, and ending net receivables of $110,000, has a days' sales in accounts receivable value of
  a. 50 days.
  b. 55 days.
  c. 30 days.
  d. 33 days.

16. The company in question 15 sells on credit terms of "net 30 days." Its days' sales in receivables figure is
  a. too high.
  b. too low.
  c. about right.
  d. impossible to evaluate from the data given.

ACCOUNTING VOCABULARY

acid-test ratio Ratio of the sum of cash plus short-term investments plus net current receivables to total current liabilities. Tells whether the entity can pay all its current liabilities if they come due immediately. Also called the *quick ratio*. (p. 202)

aging-of-receivables method A way to estimate bad debts by analyzing accounts receivable according to the length of time they have been receivable from the customer. Also called the *balance-sheet approach* because it focuses on accounts receivable. (p. 190)

allowance for bad debts Another name for *allowance for uncollectible accounts*. (p. 190)

allowance for doubtful accounts Another name for *allowance for uncollectible accounts*. (p. 190)

allowance for uncollectible accounts A contra account, related to accounts receivable, that holds the estimated amount of collection losses. (p. 190)

allowance method A method of recording collection losses based on estimates of how much money the business will not collect from its customers. (p. 190)

bad debt expense A cost to the seller of extending credit to customers. Arises from a failure to collect an account receivable in full. (p. 189)

bank collections Collections of money by the bank on behalf of a depositor. (p. 182)

bank reconciliation A document explaining the reasons for the difference between a depositor's records and the bank's records about the depositor's cash. (p. 181)

bank statement Document showing the beginning and ending balances of a particular bank account and listing the month's transactions that affected the account. (p. 180)

cash equivalents Investments such as term deposits, guaranteed investment certificates, or high-grade government securities that are considered so similar to cash that they are combined with cash for financial disclosure on the balance sheet. (p. 178)

cheque Document instructing a bank to pay the designated person or business the specified amount of money. (p. 179)

creditor The party to whom money is owed. (p. 195)

days' sales in receivables Ratio of average net accounts receivable to one day's sales. Indicates how many days' sales remain in Accounts Receivable awaiting collection. Also called the *collection period* and *days sales outstanding*. (p. 203)

debtor The party who owes money. (p. 195)

deposits in transit A deposit recorded by the company but not yet recorded by its bank. (p. 181)

doubtful account expense Another name for *bad debt expense*. (p. 189)

electronic funds transfer System that transfers cash by electronic communication rather than by paper documents. (p. 178)

interest The borrower's cost of renting money from a lender. Interest is revenue for the lender and expense for the borrower. (p. 195)

maturity date The date on which a debt instrument must be paid. (p. 195)

nonsufficient funds (NSF) cheque A cheque for which the payer's bank account has insufficient money to pay the cheque. NSF cheques are cash receipts that turn out to be worthless. (p. 182)

outstanding cheques Cheques issued by the company and recorded on its books but not yet paid by its bank. (p. 181)

principal The amount borrowed by a debtor and lent by a creditor. (p. 195)

quick ratio Another name for *acid-test ratio*. (p. 202)

receivables Monetary claims against a business or an individual, acquired mainly by selling goods or services and by lending money. (p. 187)

remittance advice An optional attachment to a cheque (sometimes a perforated tear-off document and sometimes capable of being electronically scanned) that indicates the payer, date, and purpose of the cash payment. The remittance advice is often used as the source document for posting cash receipts or payments. (p. 179)

term The length of time from inception to maturity. (p. 195)

uncollectible account expense Another name for bad debt expense. (p. 189)

ASSESS YOUR PROGRESS

SHORT EXERCISES

S4-1 Describe the types of assets that are typically included under the heading "cash and cash equivalents" on the balance sheet. What is a "cash equivalent"?

LEARNING OBJECTIVE ❶
Report cash on the balance sheet

S4-2 At December 31, 2020, before any year-end adjustments are made, White Corporation had a $50 balance in Accounts Receivable and a $0.6 debit balance in the Allowance for Uncollectible Accounts.

LEARNING OBJECTIVE ❹
Apply the allowance method

Requirements
1. What is the normal balance in the Allowance for Uncollectible Accounts? What would cause this account to have a debit balance?
2. How does management determine the amount of uncollectible accounts?
3. The aging of receivables indicates that White Corporation will not collect $1.5 million of its accounts receivables. Prepare the journal entry to record the bad debt expense for 2020.

S4-3 Collins Woodworking accepts VISA and MasterCard at its store. Collins is charged a processing fee of 3% of the total amount of any credit card sale. Assume that Russell Knight purchases $8,000 of custom furniture and pays with a VISA card. Make the entry to record the sale to Knight. (You do not need to make the cost of goods sold entry.)

LEARNING OBJECTIVE ❻
Record a credit card sale

S4-4 The Cash account of SWITZER Ltd. reported a balance of $2,500 at August 31, 2020. Included were outstanding cheques totalling $900 and an August 31 deposit of $500 that did not appear on the bank statement. The bank statement, which came from HSBC Bank, listed an August 31, 2020, balance of $3,405. Included in the bank balance was an August 30 collection of $550 on account from a customer who pays the bank directly. The bank statement also shows a $20 service charge, $10 of interest revenue that SWITZER earned on its bank balance, and an NSF cheque for $35.

Prepare a bank reconciliation to determine how much cash SWITZER actually has at August 31, 2020.

LEARNING OBJECTIVE ❷
Prepare a bank reconciliation

S4-5 After preparing the SWITZER Ltd. bank reconciliation in Exercise S4-4, make the company's journal entries for transactions that arise from the bank reconciliation. Include an explanation with each entry.

LEARNING OBJECTIVE ❷
Record transactions from a bank reconciliation

S4-6 Jordan Quinn manages the local homeless shelter. He fears that a trusted employee has been stealing from the shelter. This employee receives cash from supporters and also prepares the monthly bank reconciliation. To check on the employee, Quinn prepares his own bank reconciliation as in Exhibit 4-4 on page 183.

LEARNING OBJECTIVE ❷
Use a bank reconciliation to detect fraud

Homeless Shelter
Bank Reconciliation
August 31, 2020

Bank		Books	
Balance, August 31	$ 3,300	Balance, August 31	$2,820
Add		Add	
Deposits in transit	400	Bank collections	800
		Interest revenue	10
Less		Less	
Outstanding cheques	(1,100)	Service charge	(30)
Adjusted bank balance	$ 2,600	Adjusted book balance	$3,600

Does it appear that the employee stole from the shelter? If so, how much? Explain your answer. Which side of the bank reconciliation shows the shelter's true cash balance?

LEARNING OBJECTIVE ❹

Apply the allowance method to account for uncollectibles

S4-7 During its first year of operations, Environmental Products Inc. had sales of $875,000, all on account. Industry experience suggests that Environmental Products's bad debt expense will be $17,500. At December 31, 2019, Environmental Products's accounts receivable total $80,000. The company uses the allowance method to account for uncollectibles.

1. Make Environmental Products's journal entry for bad debt expense.
2. Show how Environmental Products could report accounts receivable on its balance sheet at December 31, 2019, by disclosing the allowance for uncollectible accounts.

LEARNING OBJECTIVES ❸❹

Account for accounts receivable and uncollectible accounts

S4-8 This exercise continues the situation of exercise S4-7, in which Environmental Products ended the year 2019 with accounts receivable of $80,000 and an allowance for uncollectible accounts of $17,500. During 2020, Environmental Products completed the following transactions:

1. Credit sales, $1,000,000
2. Collections on account, $880,000
3. Write-offs of uncollectibles, $16,000
4. Bad debt expense, $15,000

Journalize the 2020 transactions for Environmental Products. Explanations are not required.

LEARNING OBJECTIVES ❸❹

Account for accounts receivable and uncollectible accounts

S4-9 Use the solution to exercise S4-8 to answer these questions about Environmental Products Inc. for 2020.

1. Start with Accounts Receivable's beginning balance ($80,000) and then post to the Accounts Receivable T-account. How much do Environmental Products's customers owe the company at December 31, 2020?
2. Start with the Allowance account's beginning credit balance ($17,500) and then post to the Allowance for Uncollectible Accounts T-account. How much of the receivables at December 31, 2020, does the company expect *not* to collect?
3. At December 31, 2020, what is the net realizable value of the company's accounts receivable?

LEARNING OBJECTIVES ❸❹

Account for accounts receivable and uncollectible accounts

S4-10 Gulig and Durham, a law firm, started 2020 with accounts receivable of $60,000 and an allowance for uncollectible accounts of $5,000. The 2020 service revenue on account was $400,000, and cash collections on account totalled $410,000. During 2020, Gulig and Durham wrote off uncollectible accounts receivable of $7,000. At December 31, 2020, the aging-of-receivables method indicated that Gulig and Durham will *not* collect $10,000 of its accounts receivable.

Journalize Gulig and Durham's (a) service revenue, (b) cash collections on account, (c) write-offs of uncollectible receivables, and (d) bad debt expense for the year. Explanations are not required. Prepare a T-account for Allowance for Uncollectible Accounts to show your computation of bad debt expense for the year.

LEARNING OBJECTIVES ❸❹

Account for accounts receivable and uncollectible accounts

S4-11 Perform the following accounting for the receivables of Benoit, Brown & Hill, an accounting firm, at December 31, 2020.

1. Start with the beginning balances for these T-accounts:
   • Accounts Receivable, $80,000
   • Allowance for Uncollectible Accounts, $9,000

   Post the following 2020 transactions to the T-accounts:

   a. Service revenue of $850,000, all on account
   b. Collections on account, $790,000
   c. Write-offs of uncollectible accounts, $7,000
   d. Bad debt expense (allowance method), $8,000

2. What are the ending balances of Accounts Receivable and Allowance for Uncollectible Accounts?
3. Show two ways Benoit, Brown & Hill could report accounts receivable on its balance sheet at December 31, 2020.

S4-12 Metro Credit Union in Charlottetown, Prince Edward Island, loaned $90,000 to David Mann on a six-month, 8% note. Record the following for Metro Credit Union:
a. Lending the money on March 6.
b. Collecting the principal and interest at maturity. Specify the date. Explanations are not required.

LEARNING OBJECTIVE ❺
Account for a note receivable

S4-13
1. Compute the amount of interest during 2018, 2019, and 2020 for the following note receivable: On June 30, 2018, Scotiabank loaned $100,000 to Heather Hutchison on a two-year, 8% note.
2. Which party has a (an)
   a. note receivable?
   b. note payable?
   c. interest revenue?
   d. interest expense?
3. How much in total would Scotiabank collect if Hutchison paid off the note early—say, on October 31, 2018?

LEARNING OBJECTIVE ❺
Account for a note receivable and interest revenue

S4-14 On May 31, 2019, Nancy Thomas borrowed $6,000 from Assiniboine Credit Union. Thomas signed a note payable, promising to pay the credit union principal plus interest on May 31, 2020. The interest rate on the note is 8%. The accounting year of Assiniboine Credit Union ends on December 31, 2019. Journalize Assiniboine Credit Union's (a) lending money on the note receivable at May 31, 2019, (b) accruing interest at December 31, 2019, and (c) collecting the principal and interest at May 31, 2020, the maturity date of the note.

LEARNING OBJECTIVE ❺
Account for a note receivable and interest thereon

S4-15 Using your answers to exercise S4-14, show how the Assiniboine Credit Union will report the following:
a. Whatever needs to be reported on the bank's classified balance sheet at December 31, 2019. (Ignore Cash).
b. Whatever needs to be reported on the bank's income statement for the year ended December 31, 2019.
c. Whatever needs to be reported on the bank's classified balance sheet at December 31, 2020. (Ignore Cash).
d. Whatever needs to be reported on the bank's income statement for the year ended December 31, 2020.

LEARNING OBJECTIVE ❺
Report notes receivable and interest revenue

S4-16 Botany Clothiers reported the following amounts in its 2020 financial statements. The 2019 figures are given for comparison.

LEARNING OBJECTIVE ❼
Evaluate the acid-test ratio and days' sales in receivables

	A	B	C	D	E	F
1			2020		2019	
2	Current assets:					
3	Cash		$ 9,000		$ 7,000	
4	Short-term investments		12,000		10,000	
5	Accounts receivable	$ 60,000		$ 54,000		
6	Less allowance for uncollectibles	(5,000)	55,000	(5,000)	49,000	
7	Inventory		170,000		172,000	
8	Prepaid insurance		1,000		1,000	
9	Total current assets		$ 247,000		$ 239,000	
10	Total current liabilities		$ 80,000		$ 70,000	
11	Net sales		$ 803,000		$ 750,000	
12						

Requirements

1. Compute Botany's acid-test ratio at the end of 2020. Round to two decimal places. How does the acid-test ratio compare with the industry average of 0.95?
2. Compare Botany's days' sales in receivables measure for 2020 with the company's credit terms of net 30 days. Assume all sales are on account.
3. Recommend two ways that Botany Clothiers can speed up cash flow from its accounts receivable.

LEARNING OBJECTIVES ❸❼

Report receivables and other accounts in the financial statements and evaluate liquidity

S4-17 Victoria Medical Service reported the following selected items (amounts in thousands):

Unearned revenues (current)	$ 207	Service revenue	$8,613
Allowance for		Other assets	767
doubtful accounts	109	Property, plant, and equipment	3,316
Other expenses	2,569	Operating expense	1,620
Accounts receivable	817	Cash	239
Accounts payable	385	Notes payable (long-term)	719

1. Classify each item as (a) income statement or balance sheet and as (b) debit balance or credit balance.
2. How much net income (or net loss) did Victoria report for the year?
3. Compute Victoria's current ratio. Round to two decimal places. Evaluate the company's liquidity position.

EXERCISES

LEARNING OBJECTIVE ❷

Use the bank reconciliation

E4-18 Green Construction Inc. has poor internal control. Recently, Jean Ouimet, the owner, has suspected the bookkeeper of stealing. Here are some details of the business's cash position at June 30, 2020:

a. The Cash account shows a balance of $10,402. This amount includes a June 30 deposit of $3,794 that does not appear on the June 30 bank statement.

b. The June 30 bank statement shows a balance of $8,224. The bank statement lists a $200 bank collection, an $8 service charge, and a $36 NSF cheque. The bookkeeper has not recorded any of these items.

c. At June 30, the following cheques are outstanding:

Cheque No.	Amount
154	$116
256	150
278	853
291	990
292	206
293	145

d. The bookkeeper records all incoming cash and makes bank deposits. He also reconciles the monthly bank statement. Here is his June 30 reconciliation:

Balance per books, June 30		$10,402
Add: Outstanding cheques		1,460
Bank collection		200
Subtotal		12,062
Less: Deposits in transit	$3,794	
Service charge	8	
NSF cheque	36	(3,838)
Balance per bank, June 30		$ 8,224

Requirements

1. Prepare the bank reconciliation. There are no bank or book errors.
2. Using the facts provided, identify the information that would be relevant to determining whether or not the bookkeeper has stolen cash from the business.
3. Recommend to Ouimet any changes needed to prevent this from happening again.

E4-19 The following items appear on a bank reconciliation:

_____ **1.** Outstanding cheques

_____ **2.** Bank error: The bank credited our account for a deposit made by another bank customer.

_____ **3.** Service charge

_____ **4.** Deposits in transit

_____ **5.** NSF cheque

_____ **6.** Bank collection of a note receivable on our behalf

_____ **7.** Book error: We debited Cash for $100. The correct debit was $1,000.

Classify each item as (a) an addition to the bank balance, (b) a subtraction from the bank balance, (c) an addition to the book balance, or (d) a subtraction from the book balance.

E4-20 LeAnn Bryant's chequebook lists the following:

Date	Cheque No.	Item	Cheque	Deposit	Balance
Nov. 1					$ 705
4	622	Direct Energy	$ 19		686
9		Dividends		$116	802
13	623	Canadian Tire	43		759
14	624	Petro-Canada	58		701
18	625	Cash	50		651
26	626	St. Mark's Church	25		626
28	627	Bent Tree Apartments	275		351
30		Paycheque		846	1,197

The November bank statement shows:

Balance..				$ 705
Add deposits				116
Deduct cheques	No.		Amount	
	622		$19	
	623		43	
	624		85*	
	625		50	(197)
Other charges:				
NSF cheque...			$ 8	
Service charge			12	(20)
Balance..				$ 604

*This is the correct amount for cheque number 624.

Requirement

Prepare Bryant's bank reconciliation at November 30.

E4-21 Tim Wong operates a FedEx Kinko's store. He has just received the monthly bank statement at May 31, 2020, from Royal Bank of Canada, and the statement shows an ending balance of $595. Listed on the statement are an EFT customer collection of $300, a service charge of $12, two NSF cheques totalling $120, and a $9 charge for printed cheques. In reviewing his cash records, Wong identifies outstanding cheques totalling $603 and a May 31 deposit in transit of $1,788. During May, he recorded a $290 cheque for the salary of a part-time employee as $29. Wong's Cash account shows a May 31 cash balance of $1,882. How much cash does Wong actually have at May 31?

LEARNING OBJECTIVE ②

Prepare and use a bank
reconciliation

E4-22 Use the data from exercise E4-21 to make the journal entries that Wong should record on May 31 to update his Cash account. Include an explanation for each entry.

LEARNING OBJECTIVES ③④

Report uncollectible accounts by the
allowance method

E4-23 At December 31, 2020, Credit Valley Nissan has an Accounts Receivable balance of $101,000. Allowance for Uncollectible Accounts has a credit balance of $2,000 before the year-end adjustment. Service revenue for 2020 was $800,000. Credit Valley estimates that bad debt expense for the year is $8,000. Make the December 31 entry to record bad debt expense. Show how the accounts receivable and the allowance for uncollectible accounts are reported on the balance sheet. Use the reporting format "Accounts receivable, net of allowance for uncollectible accounts $—" in 2020. Insert the value you've calculated for the allowance.

LEARNING OBJECTIVES ③④

Use the allowance method for
uncollectible accounts

E4-24 On June 30, 2020, Perfect Party Planners (PPP) had a $40,000 balance in Accounts Receivable and a $3,000 credit balance in Allowance for Uncollectible Accounts. During July, PPP made credit sales of $75,000. July collections on account were $60,000, write-offs of uncollectible receivables totalled $2,200, and an account of $1,000 was recovered. Bad debt expense is estimated to be $1,500.

Requirements

1. Journalize sales, collections, write-offs of uncollectibles, recovery of accounts receivable, and bad debt expense by the allowance method during July. Explanations are not required.
2. Show the ending balances in Accounts Receivable, Allowance for Uncollectible Accounts, and *Net* Accounts Receivable at July 31. How much does PPP expect to collect?
3. Show how PPP will report Accounts Receivable on its July 31 balance sheet. Use the format "Accounts Receivable, net of allowance for uncollectible accounts of $—" at July 31, 2020. Insert the value you've calculated for the allowance.

LEARNING OBJECTIVE ④

Using the allowance method for
uncollectible account

E4-25 Refer to exercise E4-24.

Requirements

1. Determining bad debt expense by using the allowance method is management's estimate of uncollectible accounts and not an accurate measurement. Why not wait until a company finds out which customers can't pay and write the accounts receivable off as they occur?
2. If the allowance method is not used to estimate uncollectible accounts, what effect would this have on accounts receivable (balance sheet) and bad debt expense (income statement)?

LEARNING OBJECTIVE ④

Use the aging method to estimate
uncollectible accounts

E4-26 At December 31, 2020, before any year-end adjustments, the Accounts Receivable balance of Sunset Hills Clinic is $235,000. Allowance for Uncollectible Accounts has a $6,500 credit balance. Sunset Hills prepares the following aging schedule for accounts receivable:

	Age of Accounts			
Total Balance	0–30 Days	31–60 Days	61–90 Days	Over 90 Days
$235,000	$110,000	$60,000	$50,000	$15,000
Estimated uncollectible	0.5%	1.0%	6.0%	40%

Requirements

1. Based on the aging-of-receivables method, is the unadjusted balance of the allowance account adequate? Is it too high or too low? How does management determine what percentages to use for estimating uncollectible accounts?
2. Make the entry required by the aging schedule. Prepare a T-account for the allowance.
3. Show how Sunset Hills Clinic will report Accounts Receivable on its December 31 balance sheet.

E4-27 University Travel experienced the following revenue and accounts receivable write-offs:

LEARNING OBJECTIVE ❹

Measure and account for uncollectibles

Month	Service Revenue	Accounts Receivable Write-Offs			
		January	February	March	Total
January	$ 6,800	$53	$ 86		$139
February	7,000		105	$ 33	138
March	7,500	___	___	115	115
	$21,300	$53	$191	$148	$392

University Travel estimates bad debt expense to be $150.

Journalize service revenue (all on account), bad debt expense, and write-offs during March. Include explanations. Is the estimate of bad debts of $150 being uncollectible reasonable?

E4-28 Record the following note receivable transactions in the journal of Town & Country Realty. How much interest revenue did Town & Country earn this year? Use a 365-day year for interest computations, and round interest amounts to the nearest dollar.

LEARNING OBJECTIVE ❺

Record notes receivable and accrue interest revenue

Oct.	1	Loaned $50,000 cash to Springfield Co. on a one-year, 9% note.
Nov.	3	Performed service for Joplin Corporation, receiving a 90-day, 12% note for $10,000.
Dec.	16	Received a $2,000, six-month, 12% note on account from Afton, Inc.
	31	Accrued interest revenue for the year.

E4-29 Mattson Loan Company completed these transactions:

LEARNING OBJECTIVE ❺

Report the effects of note receivable transactions on the balance sheet and income statement

2019		
Apr.	1	Loaned $20,000 to Charlene Baker on a one-year, 5% note.
Dec.	31	Accrued interest revenue on the Baker note.
2020		
Apr.	1	Collected the maturity value of the note from Baker (principal plus interest).

Show what Mattson would report for these transactions on its 2019 and 2020 balance sheets and income statements. Mattson's accounting year ends on December 31.

E4-30 Answer these questions about receivables and uncollectibles. For the true-false questions, explain any answers that are false.

LEARNING OBJECTIVES ❸❺

Understand receivables

1. True or false? Credit sales increase receivables. Collections and write-offs decrease receivables.
2. Which receivables figure, the *total* amount that customers *owe* the company or the *net* amount the company expects to collect, is more interesting to investors as they consider buying the company's shares? Give your reason.
3. Show how to determine net accounts receivable.
4. Caisse Desjardins lent $100,000 to Chicoutimi Ltée on a six-month, 6% note. Which party has interest receivable? Which party has interest payable? Which party has interest expense, and which has interest revenue? How much interest will these organizations record one month after Chicoutimi Ltée signs the note?
5. When Caisse Desjardins accrues interest on the Chicoutimi Ltée note, show the directional effects on the bank's assets, liabilities, and equity (increase, decrease, or no effect).

⊕ **E4-31** Assume Black Corporation reported the following items at year-ends 2020 and 2019.

A	B	C	D	E	F	G
Black Corporation Consolidated Balance Sheets (Summarized)	**March 1, 2020**	**March 3, 2019**		**March 1, 2020**	**March 3, 2019**	
(*amounts in millions*)						
Current assets:			**Current liabilities:**			
Cash	$ 1,184.4	$ 677.1	Accounts payable	$ 271.1	$ 130.3	
Short-term investments	420.7	310.1	Other current liabilities	1,203.3	416.3	
Accounts receivable, net	1,174.7	572.6	Long-term liabilities	103.2	58.8	
Inventories	396.3	255.9				
Other current assets	301.3	103.6	Shareholders' equity	3,933.6	2,483.5	
Capital assets	2,033.8	1,169.6				
Total assets	$ 5,511.2	$ 3,088.9	Total liabilities and equity	$ 5,511.2	$ 3,088.9	
Income Statement (partial): 2020						
Revenue		$ 6,009.4				

Requirements

1. Using the facts provided, calculate the information that is relevant in measuring the liquidity of the company for 2020. Assume Black sells on terms of net 30 days.
2. Recommend two ways the company can speed up its cash flow.

⊕ **E4-32** Assume Loblaw Companies Limited reported these figures in millions of dollars:

	2020	2019
Net sales	$29,384	$28,640
Receivables at end of year	885	728

Requirements

1. Compute Loblaw's average collection period during 2020.
2. Was Loblaw's collection period long or short? Potash Corporation of Saskatchewan takes 36 days to collect its average level of receivables. FedEx, the overnight shipper, takes 40 days. What causes Loblaw's collection period to be so different?

⊕ **E4-33** Ripley Shirt Company sells on credit and manages its own receivables. Average experience for the past three years has been as follows:

	Cash	Credit	Total
Sales	$300,000	$300,000	$600,000
Cost of goods sold	165,000	165,000	330,000
Bad debt expense	—	10,000	10,000
Other expenses	84,000	84,000	168,000

John Ripley, the owner, is considering whether to accept credit cards (VISA, MasterCard). Ripley expects total sales to increase by 10% but cash sales to remain unchanged. If Ripley switches to credit cards, the business can save $8,000 on other expenses, but VISA and MasterCard charge 2% on credit card sales. Ripley figures that the increase in sales will be due to the increased volume of credit card sales.

Requirement

Should Ripley Shirt Company start accepting credit cards? Show the computations of net income under the present plan and under the credit card plan.

E4-34 Nixtel Inc. reported net receivables of $2,583 million and $2,785 million at December 31, 2020, and 2019, after subtracting allowances of $62 million and $88 million at these respective dates. Nixtel earned total revenue of $10,948 million (all on accounts) and recorded bad debt expense of $2 million for the year ended December 31, 2020.

LEARNING OBJECTIVES ❸❹

Reconstruct receivables and uncollectible-account amounts

Requirements

Use this information to measure the following amounts for the year ended December 31, 2020:

a. Write-offs of uncollectible receivables
b. Collections from customers

PROBLEMS (GROUP A)

P4-35A The cash data of Alta Vista Toyota for June 2020 follow:

LEARNING OBJECTIVE ❷

Prepare the bank reconciliation

Cash

Date	Item	Jrnl. Ref.	Debit	Credit	Balance
June 1	Balance				5,011
30		CR6	10,578		15,589
30		CP11		10,924	4,665

Cash Receipts (CR)		Cash Payments (CP)	
Date	Cash Debit	Cheque No.	Cash Credit
June 2	$ 4,174	3113	$ 891
8	407	3114	147
10	559	3115	1,930
16	2,187	3116	664
22	1,854	3117	1,472
29	1,060	3118	1,000
30	337	3119	632
Total	$10,578	3120	1,675
		3121	100
		3122	2,413
		Total	$10,924

Alta Vista received the following bank statement on June 30, 2020:

Bank Statement for June 2020			
Beginning balance			$ 5,011
Deposits and other additions			
June 4...	$ 326 EFT		
4...	4,174		
9...	407		
12...	559		
17...	2,187		
22...	1,701 BC		
23...	1,854	11,208	
Cheques and other deductions			
June 7...	$ 891		
13...	1,390		
14...	903 US		
15...	147		
18...	664		
21...	219 EFT		
26...	1,472		
30...	1,000		
30...	20 SC	(6,706)	
Ending balance			$ 9,513

Explanation: EFT—electronic funds transfer, BC—bank collection, US—unauthorized signature, SC—service charge

Additional data for the bank reconciliation include the following:

a. The EFT deposit was a receipt of a monthly car lease. The EFT debit was a monthly insurance payment.
b. The bank collection was of a note receivable.
c. The unauthorized signature cheque was received from a customer.
d. The correct amount of cheque number 3115, a payment on account, is $1,390. (Alta Vista's accountant mistakenly recorded the cheque for $1,930.)

Requirement
Prepare the Alta Vista Toyota bank reconciliation at June 30, 2020.

LEARNING OBJECTIVE ❷

Prepare a bank reconciliation and the related journal entries

⊕ **P4-36A** The May 31 bank statement of Family Services Association (FSA) has just arrived from Scotiabank. To prepare the FSA bank reconciliation, you gather the following data:

a. FSA's Cash account shows a balance of $2,256.14 on May 31.
b. The May 31 bank balance is $4,023.05.
c. The bank statement shows that FSA earned $38.19 of interest on its bank balance during May. This amount was added to FSA's bank balance.
d. FSA pays utilities ($250) and insurance ($100) by EFT.
e. The following FSA cheques did not clear the bank by May 31:

Cheque No.	Amount
237	$ 46.10
288	141.00
291	578.05
293	11.87
294	609.51
295	8.88
296	101.63

f. The bank statement includes a donation of $850, electronically deposited to the bank for FSA.

g. The bank statement lists a $10.50 bank service charge.

h. On May 31, the FSA treasurer deposited $16.15, which will appear on the June bank statement.

i. The bank statement includes a $300 deposit that FSA did not make. The bank added $300 to FSA's account for another company's deposit.

j. The bank statement includes two charges for returned cheques from donors. One is a $395 cheque received from a donor with the imprint "Unauthorized Signature." The other is a nonsufficient funds cheque in the amount of $146.67 received from a client.

Requirements

1. Prepare the bank reconciliation for FSA.

2. Journalize the May 31 transactions needed to update FSA's Cash account. Include an explanation for each entry.

P4-37A FedEx Corporation sells its services for cash and on account. By selling on credit, FedEx cannot expect to collect 100% of its accounts receivable. Assume that at May 31, 2020 and 2019, respectively, FedEx reported the following on its balance sheet (adapted and in millions of U.S. dollars):

LEARNING OBJECTIVES ❸❹
Account for receivables, collections, and uncollectibles

	May 31	
	2020	**2019**
Accounts receivable	$4,517	$4,078
Less: Allowance for uncollectibles	(318)	(136)
Accounts receivable, net	$4,199	$3,942

During the year ended May 31, 2020, FedEx earned service revenue and collected cash from customers. Assume bad debt expense for the year was $380 million and that FedEx wrote off uncollectible receivables.

Requirements

1. Prepare T-accounts for Accounts Receivable and Allowance for Uncollectibles, and insert the May 31, 2019, balances as given.

2. Journalize the following assumed transactions of FedEx for the year ended May 31, 2020. Explanations are not required.

   a. Service revenue on account, $37,953 million

   b. Collections on account, $37,314 million

   c. Bad debt expense, $380 million

   d. Write-offs of uncollectible accounts receivable, $200 million

   e. Recovered an account receivable, $2 million

   f. On May 1, FedEx received a two-month, 8%, $50 million note receivable from one of its large customers in exchange for the customer's past due account. FedEx made the proper year-end adjusting entry for the interest on this note.

3. Post your entries to the Accounts Receivable and the Allowance for Uncollectibles T-accounts.

4. Compute the ending balances for the two T-accounts, and compare your balances to the actual May 31, 2020 amounts. They should be the same.

5. Show what FedEx would report on its income statement for the year ended May 31, 2020.

6. Recommend several ways for FedEx to improve cash collections from receivables.

P4-38A The October 1, 2020, records of First Data Communications include these accounts:

LEARNING OBJECTIVES ❹❺
Use the aging approach for uncollectibles and account for notes receivable

Accounts Receivable	$225,000
Allowance for Uncollectible Accounts	(8,500)

At year-end, the company ages its receivables and adjusts the balance in Allowance for Uncollectible Accounts to correspond to the aging schedule. During the last quarter of 2020, the company completed the following selected transactions:

2020
Nov. 30 Wrote off as uncollectible the $1,100 account receivable from Rainbow Carpets and the $600 account receivable from Show-N-Tell Antiques.
Dec. 31 One of its customers, Peplar Ltd., agreed to sign a 60-day note receivable to replace the $1,500 accounts receivable due on that day.
Dec. 31 Adjusted the Allowance for Uncollectible Accounts, and recorded Bad Debt Expense at year-end, based on the aging of receivables, which follows.

| | Age of Accounts | | | |
Total Balance	0–30 Days	31–60 Days	61–90 Days	Over 90 Days
$230,000	$150,000	$40,000	$14,000	$26,000
Estimated uncollectible	0.2%	0.5%	5.0%	30.0%

Requirements

1. Record the transactions in the journal. Explanations are not required.
2. Prepare a T-account for Accounts Receivable and the Allowance for Uncollectible Accounts, and post to those accounts.
3. Show how First Data would report its accounts receivable on a comparative balance sheet for 2019 and 2020. At December 31, 2019, the company's Accounts Receivable balance was $212,000 and the Allowance for Uncollectible Accounts stood at $4,200.

LEARNING OBJECTIVES    **P4-39A** Assume Deloitte & Touche, the accounting firm, advises Pappadeaux Seafood that Pappadeaux's financial statements must be changed to conform to IFRS. At December 31, 2020, Pappadeaux's accounts include the following:

Account for uncollectibles, and use ratios to evaluate a business

Cash	$ 51,000
Short-term trading investments	17,000
Accounts receivable	37,000
Inventory	61,000
Prepaid expenses	14,000
Total current assets	$180,000
Accounts payable	$ 62,000
Other current liabilities	41,000
Total current liabilities	$103,000

Deloitte & Touche advised Pappadeaux that:
- Cash includes $20,000 that is deposited in a restricted account that is tied up until 2022.
- Pappadeaux did not estimate their uncollectible accounts but rather wrote them off when they found out that the customer could not pay them. During 2020, Pappadeaux wrote off bad receivables of $7,000. Deloitte & Touche determines that bad debt expense for the year should be for 2020 should be $15,000 based on the allowance method.
- Pappadeaux reported net income of $92,000 in 2020.

Requirements

1. Restate Pappadeaux's current accounts to conform to IFRS.
2. Using the facts provided, calculate the information that is relevant to determining the liquidity of the company before and after the corrections.
3. Determine Pappadeaux's correct net income for 2020.
4. How does using the allowance method to estimate uncollectible accounts benefit the investors and creditors?

P4-40A Assume that General Mills Canada, famous for Cheerios, Chex snacks, and Yoplait yogurt, completed the following selected transactions:

LEARNING OBJECTIVE ⑤

Account for notes receivable and accrued interest revenue

2019		
Nov.	30	Sold goods to Sobeys Inc., receiving a $50,000, three-month, 5% note.
Dec.	31	Made an adjusting entry to accrue interest on the Sobeys note.
2020		
Feb.	28	Collected the Sobeys note.
Mar.	1	Received a 90-day, 5%, $6,000 note from Louis Joli Goût on account.
	1	Sold the Louis note to Caisse Populaire, receiving cash of $5,900.
Dec.	16	Loaned $25,000 cash to Betty Crocker Brands, receiving a 90-day, 8% note.
	31	Accrued the interest on the Betty Crocker Brands note.

Requirements

1. Record the transactions in General Mills's journal. Round interest amounts to the nearest dollar. Explanations are not required.
2. Show what General Mills will report on its comparative classified balance sheet at December 31, 2019, and December 31, 2020.

P4-41A The comparative financial statements of Sunset Pools Inc. for 2020, 2019, and 2018 included the following selected data:

LEARNING OBJECTIVES ⑥⑦

Use ratio data to evaluate a company's financial position

	(in millions)		
	2020	**2019**	**2018**
Balance sheet:			
Current assets:			
Cash	$ 86	$ 60	$ 70
Short-term investments	130	174	112
Receivables, net of allowance for uncollectible accounts of $27, $21, and $15, respectively	243	245	278
Inventories	330	375	362
Prepaid expenses	10	25	26
Total current assets	$ 799	$ 879	$ 848
Total current liabilities	$ 403	$ 498	$ 413
Income statement:			
Net sales	$2,898	$2,727	$2,206

Requirements

1. As a financial advisor to an investor of Sunset Pools, identify or calculate the information for 2020 and 2019 that would be relevant in determining the company's liquidity position, and specify how each item of information is relevant to your decision.
2. Write a memo explaining to your client the results of your evaluation including recommendations that will help Sunset Pools improve its liquidity.

PROBLEMS (GROUP B)

LEARNING OBJECTIVE ❷

Prepare a bank reconciliation

P4-42B The cash data of Navajo Products for September 2020 follow:

Cash

Date	Item	Jrnl. Ref.	Debit	Credit	Balance
Sept. 1	Balance				7,078
30		CR 10	9,106		16,184
30		CP 16		11,353	4,831

Cash Receipts (CR)		Cash Payments (CP)	
Date	**Cash Debit**	**Cheque No.**	**Cash Credit**
Sept. 1	$ 2,716	1413	$ 1,465
9	544	1414	1,004
11	1,655	1415	450
14	896	1416	8
17	367	1417	775
25	890	1418	88
30	2,038	1419	4,126
Total	$ 9,106	1420	970
		1421	200
		1422	2,267
		Total	$11,353

On September 30, 2020, Navajo received this bank statement:

Bank Statement for September 2020

Beginning balance		$ 7,078
Deposits and other additions		
Sept. 1..	$ 625 EFT	
5..	2,716	
10..	544	
12..	1,655	
15..	896	
18..	367	
25..	890	
30..	1,400 BC	9,093
Cheques and other deductions		
Sept. 8..	$ 441 NSF	
9..	1,465	
13..	1,004	
14..	450	
15..	8	
19..	340 EFT	
22..	775	
29..	88	
30..	4,216	
30..	25 SC	(8,812)
Ending balance...		$ 7,359

Explanation: BC—bank collection, EFT—electronic funds transfer, NSF—nonsufficient funds cheque, SC—service charge

Additional data for the bank reconciliation:

a. The EFT deposit was for monthly rent revenue. The EFT deduction was for monthly insurance expense.
b. The bank collection was of a note receivable.
c. The NSF cheque was received from a customer.
d. The correct amount of cheque number 1419, a payment on account, is $4,216. (The Navajo accountant mistakenly recorded the cheque for $4,126.)

Requirement

Prepare the bank reconciliation of Navajo Products at September 30, 2020.

P4-43B The January 31 bank statement of Bed & Bath Accessories has just arrived from Royal Bank of Canada. To prepare the Bed & Bath bank reconciliation, you gather the following data:

a. The January 31 bank balance is $8,400.82.
b. Bed & Bath's Cash account shows a balance of $7,391.55 on January 31.
c. The following Bed & Bath cheques are outstanding at January 31:

Cheque No.	Amount
616	$403.00
802	74.02
806	36.60
809	161.38
810	229.05
811	48.91

d. The bank statement includes two special deposits: $899.14, which is the amount of dividend revenue the bank collected from IBM on behalf of Bed & Bath; and $16.86, the interest revenue Bed & Bath earned on its bank balance during January.
e. The bank statement lists a $6.25 bank service charge.
f. On January 31 the Bed & Bath treasurer deposited $381.14, which will appear on the February bank statement.
g. The bank statement includes a $410.00 deduction for a cheque drawn by Bonjovi Music Company.
h. The bank statement includes two charges for returned cheques from customers. One is a nonsufficient funds cheque in the amount of $67.50 received from a customer. The other is a $195.03 cheque received from another customer. It was returned by the customer's bank with the imprint "Unauthorized Signature."
i. A few customers pay monthly bills by EFT. The January bank statement lists an EFT deposit for sales revenue of $200.23.

Requirements

1. Prepare the bank reconciliation for Bed & Bath Accessories at January 31.
2. Journalize the transactions needed to update the Cash account. Include an explanation for each entry.

P4-44B Brubacher Service Company sells for cash and on account. By selling on credit, Brubacher cannot expect to collect 100% of its accounts receivable. At December 31, 2020, and 2019, respectively, Brubacher reported the following on its balance sheet (in thousands of dollars):

	December 31	
	2020	2019
Accounts receivable	$500	$400
Less: Allowance for uncollectibles	(100)	(60)
Accounts receivable, net	$400	$340

LEARNING OBJECTIVE ❷
Prepare a bank reconciliation and the related journal entries

LEARNING OBJECTIVES ❸❹
Account for receivables, collections, and uncollectibles

During the year ended December 31, 2020, Brubacher earned service revenue and collected cash from customers. Bad debt expense for the year was $335 thousand and Brubacher wrote off uncollectible accounts receivable.

Requirements

1. Prepare T-accounts for Accounts Receivable and Allowance for Uncollectibles, and insert the December 31, 2019, balances as given.
2. Journalize the following transactions of Brubacher for the year ended December 31, 2020. Explanations are not required.

   a. Service revenue on account, $6,700 thousand
   b. Collections from customers on account, $6,300 thousand
   c. Bad debt expense, $335 thousand
   d. Write-offs of uncollectible accounts receivable, $300 thousand
   e. Recovered an account receivable, $5 thousand
   f. On December 1, Brubacher received a 2 month, 7%, $45 thousand note receivable from one of its large customers in exchange for the customer's past due account. Brubacher made the proper year-end adjusting entry for the interest on this note.

3. Post to the Accounts Receivable and Allowance for Uncollectibles T-accounts.
4. Compute the ending balances for the two T-accounts, and compare to the Brubacher Service amounts at December 31, 2020. They should be the same.
5. Show what Brubacher should report on its income statement for the year ended December 31, 2020.
6. Recommend several ways for Brubacher to improve cash collections from receivables.

P4-45B The September 30, 2020, records of Synetics Computers show:

Accounts Receivable	$110,000
Allowance for Uncollectible Accounts	(4,100)

At year-end, Synetics ages its receivables and adjusts the balance in Allowance for Uncollectible Accounts to correspond to the aging schedule. During the last quarter of 2020, Synetics completed the following selected transactions:

2020
Oct. 31 Wrote off the following accounts receivable as uncollectible: Cisco Foods, $300; Tindall Storage, $400; and Tiffany Energy, $1,100.
Dec. 31 One of its customers, Canlon Company, agreed to sign a 60-day notes receivable to replace a $1,200 accounts receivable due on that day.
Dec. 31 Adjusted the Allowance for Uncollectible Accounts and recorded bad debt expense at year-end, based on the aging of receivables, which follows.

	Age of Accounts			
Total Balance	0–30 Days	31–60 Days	61–90 Days	Over 90 Days
$114,000	$80,000	$20,000	$4,000	$10,000
Estimated uncollectible	0.5%	1.0%	5.0%	40.0%

Requirements

1. Record the transactions in the journal. Explanations are not required.
2. Prepare a T-account for Accounts Receivable and the Allowance for Uncollectible Accounts, and post to those accounts.
3. Show how Synetics Computers would report its accounts receivable in a comparative balance sheet for 2019 and 2020. At December 31, 2019, the company's Accounts Receivable balance was $111,000 and the Allowance for Uncollectible Accounts stood at $3,700.

P4-46B The top managers of Whelan Gift Stores seek the counsel of Ernst & Young, the accounting firm, and learn that Whelan must make some changes to bring its financial statements into conformity with IFRS. At December 31, 2020, Whelan Gift Stores accounts include the following:

Cash	$ 23,000
Short-term trading investments	24,000
Accounts receivable	54,000
Inventory	45,000
Prepaid expenses	17,000
Total current assets	$163,000
Accounts payable	46,000
Other current liabilities	69,000
Total current liabilities	$115,000

As the accountant from Ernst & Young, you draw the following conclusions:

- Cash includes $6,000 that is deposited in a restricted account that will be tied up until 2022.
- Whelan Gift Stores did not estimate their uncollectible accounts but rather wrote them off when they found out that the customer could not pay them. During 2020, the company wrote off bad receivables of $4,000. Ernst & Young determines that bad debt expense for 2020 should be $9,000 based on the allowance method.
- Whelan Gift Stores reported net income of $81,000 for 2020.

Requirements

1. Restate all current accounts to conform to IFRS.
2. Using the facts provided, calculate the information that is relevant in determining the liquidity of the company before and after the corrections.
3. Determine Whelan Gift Stores' correct net income for 2020.
4. How does using the allowance method to estimate uncollectible accounts benefit the investors and creditors?

P4-47B Lilley & Taylor, partners in an accounting practice, completed the following selected transactions:

2019		
Oct.	31	Performed service for Berger Manufacturing Inc., receiving a $30,000, three-month, 5% note.
Dec.	31	Made an adjusting entry to accrue interest on the Berger note.
2020		
Jan.	31	Collected the Berger note.
Feb.	18	Received a 90-day, 8%, $10,000 note from Emerson Ltd., on account.
	19	Sold the Emerson note to a financial institution, receiving cash of $9,700.
Nov.	11	Loaned $20,000 cash to Diaz Insurance Agency, receiving a 90-day, 9% note.
Dec.	31	Accrued the interest on the Diaz note.

Requirements

1. Record the transactions in Lilley & Taylor's journal. Round all amounts to the nearest dollar. Explanations are not required.
2. Show what Lilley & Taylor will report on its comparative classified balance sheet at December 31, 2020, and December 31, 2019.

LEARNING OBJECTIVES ❻❼

Use ratio data to evaluate a
company's financial position

CT

P4-48B The comparative financial statements of New World Piano Company for 2020, 2019, and 2018 included the following selected data:

	2020	2019	2018
	(in millions)		
Balance sheet:			
Current assets:			
Cash	$ 67	$ 66	$ 62
Short-term investments	73	81	70
Receivables, net of allowance for uncollectible accounts of $7, $6, and $4, respectively	226	174	195
Inventories	398	375	349
Prepaid expenses	22	19	16
Total current assets	$ 786	$ 715	$ 692
Total current liabilities	$ 420	$ 405	$ 388
Income statement:			
Net sales	$2,071	$2,005	$1,965

Requirements

1. As a financial advisor to an investor in New World Piano Company, identify or calculate the information for 2020 and 2019 that would be relevant in determining the company's liquidity position, and specify how each piece of information is relevant to your decision.
2. Write a memo explaining to your client the results of your evaluation including recommendations that will help New World Piano Company improve its liquidity.

APPLY YOUR KNOWLEDGE

DECISION CASES

This section's material reflects CPA enabling competencies, including:

I   Professional and ethical behaviour

II   Problem-solving and decision-making

III Communication

IV   Teamwork and leadership

Based on Chartered Professional Accountant standards

Case 1. A fire during 2020 destroyed most of the accounting records of Morris Financial Services Inc. The only accounting data for 2020 that Morris can come up with are the following balances at December 31, 2020. The general manager also knows that bad debt expense should be $47,000.

Accounts receivable	$180,000
Less: Allowance for uncollectibles	(22,000)
Total expenses, excluding bad debt expense	670,000
Collections from customers	840,000
Write-offs of bad receivables	30,000
Accounts receivable, December 31, 2019	110,000

LEARNING OBJECTIVES ❸❹

Account for receivables, collections, and uncollectible accounts on receivables

As the insurance claims officer, prepare a summary income statement for Morris Financial Services Inc. for the year ended December 31, 2020. The insurance claim will be affected by whether the company was profitable in 2020. Use a T-account for Accounts Receivable to compute service revenue.

LEARNING OBJECTIVES ❹❼

Estimate the collectibility of accounts receivable and evaluate liquidity

Case 2. Suppose you work in the loan department of CIBC. Dean Young, owner of Dean Young Sports Equipment, has come to you seeking a loan for $500,000 to expand operations. Young proposes to use accounts receivable as collateral for the loan and has provided you with the following information from the company's most recent financial statements:

	(in thousands)		
	2020	**2019**	**2018**
Sales...	$1,475	$1,001	$902
Cost of goods sold...	876	647	605
Gross profit	599	354	297
Other expenses...	518	287	253
Net profit or (loss) before taxes......................	$ 81	$ 67	$ 44
Accounts receivable...	$ 128	$ 107	$ 94
Allowance for uncollectible accounts..............	13	11	9

Requirement

Analyze the trends of sales, days' sales in receivables, and cash collections from customers for 2020 and 2019. Would you make the loan to Young? Support your decision with facts and figures.

ETHICAL DECISIONS

Decision 1 Eric Thorman owns shoe stores in Halifax and Lunenburg. Each store has a manager who is responsible for sales and store expenses, and runs advertisements in the local newspaper. The managers transfer cash to Thorman monthly and prepare their own bank reconciliations. The manager in Lunenburg has been stealing large sums of money. To cover the theft, he understates the amount of the outstanding cheques on the monthly bank reconciliation. As a result, each monthly bank reconciliation appears to balance. However, the balance sheet reports more cash than Thorman actually has in the bank. While negotiating the sale of the shoe stores, Thorman shows the balance sheet to prospective investors.

Requirements

1. Identify two parties other than Thorman who can be harmed by this theft. In what ways can they be harmed?
2. Discuss the role accounting plays in this situation.

Decision 2 Sunnyvale Loan Company is in the consumer loan business. Sunnyvale borrows from banks and loans out the money at higher interest rates. Sunnyvale's bank requires Sunnyvale to submit quarterly financial statements to keep its line of credit. Sunnyvale's main asset is Notes Receivable. Therefore, Bad Debt Expense and Allowance for Uncollectible Accounts are important accounts for the company. Kimberly Burnham, the company's owner, prefers for net income to reflect a steady increase in a smooth pattern, rather than increase in some periods and decrease in other periods. To report smoothly increasing net income, Burnham underestimates Bad Debt Expense in some periods. In other periods, Burnham overestimates the expense. She reasons that the income overstatements roughly offset the income understatements over time.

Requirement

Is Sunnyvale Loan's practice of smoothing income ethical? Why or why not?

FOCUS ON FINANCIAL STATEMENT ANALYSIS

Dollarama Inc.

LEARNING OBJECTIVES ❶❷❸❹

Account for cash and cash equivalents and accounts receivable

MyLab Accounting

Refer to Dollarama's financial statements in Appendix A at the end of the book. Suppose Dollarama's bank statement has just arrived at company headquarters. Further assume the bank statement shows Dollarama's cash balance at $664.2 thousand and also assume that cash and cash equivalents has a balance of $658.2 thousand on the books.

1. You must determine how much to report for cash and cash equivalents on the January 28, 2018 balance sheet. Suppose you uncover these reconciling items (all amounts in thousands): (thousands)

   a. Interest earned on bank balance, $2.2
   b. Outstanding cheques, $6.4
   c. Bank collections of various items, $4
   d. Deposits in transit, $4.3
   e. Transposition error—Dollarama overstated cash by $1.3
   f. Bank charges of $1

   Prepare a bank reconciliation to show how Dollarama arrived at the correct amount of cash and cash equivalents to report on its January 28, 2018, balance sheet. Journal entries are not required.

2. How much were Dollarama's receivables at Janaury 28, 2018, and January 29, 2017? What can you assume from this information?

3. Assume that Dollarama wrote off $125 thousand as uncollectible. How much did Dollarama collect from customers during fiscal year 2018?

LEARNING OBJECTIVES ❹❼

Analyze accounts receivable and liquidity

MyLab Accounting

4. Does Dollarama disclose the Allowance for Uncollectible Accounts in its financial statements? How can you determine what Dollarama expects to collect from its reported Accounts Receivable?*

5. Evaluate Dollarama's liquidity for fiscal 2018, and compare it with fiscal 2017. What other information might be helpful in your evaluation?

CHECK YOUR WORK

STOP + THINK ANSWERS

STOP + THINK (4-1)

1. $5,125 ($4,500 + $1,200 − $575).
2. $5,408 ($5,125 + $15 − $5 + $300 − $27)

The adjusted book and bank balances are the same. The answer can be determined by working backward from the adjusted balance.

STOP + THINK (4-2)

	(in thousands)
Customers owed Black Corporation	$138,370
Black expected not to collect	3,974
Receivables, net (or the amount Black expected to collect)	$134,396

STOP + THINK (4-3)

Aging-of-receivables: bad debt expense = $1,350 − $900 = $450

STOP + THINK (4-4)

They should accrue interest revenue on the note receivable in the amount of $20.
($4,800 × 5% × 1/12)

STOP + THINK (4-5)

Companies need cash as quickly as possible so they can use it to pay liabilities and invest in new products, new technology, and research and development.

STOP + THINK (4-6)

Inventory is excluded from the quick ratio because it takes time to sell and collect the cash. Prepaid expenses are also excluded because the cash has already been paid for these assets that will be expensed as they are used up.

QUICK QUIZ ANSWERS

1. *b*
2. *c*
3. *d*
4. *b*
5. $201,000 ($210,000 − $9,000 = $201,000)
6. *b* ($3,200 − $100) − ($300 − $100)
7. *b* $200 (300 − 100)
8. $50 ($300 − $100 − 150)
9. *c* ($10,000 × 0.09 × 5/12 = $375)
10. *b*

11. *a* ($10,000 × 0.09 × 6/12 = $450)
12. *a*
13. Cash 10,450

Note Receivable	10,000
Interest Receivable	375
Interest Revenue	75

14. *a*
15. *c* ($1,217,000 / ([$90,000 + $110,000]/2)) = 12.17 *times*
    365/12.17 = 30 days)
16. *c*

5

Inventory and Cost of Goods Sold

LEARNING OBJECTIVES

1. **Show** how to account for inventory
2. **Apply** and **compare** various inventory costing methods
3. **Explain** how accounting standards apply to inventory
4. **Compute** and **evaluate** gross profit percentage, inventory turnover, and days' inventory outstanding
5. **Analyze** the effects of inventory errors

CPA COMPETENCIES

Competencies addressed in this chapter:

1.2.2 Evaluates treatment for routine transactions

1.4.4 Interprets financial reporting results for stakeholders (external or internal)

Based on Chartered Professional Accountant standards

SPOTLIGHT

Leon's Furniture Limited is Canada's largest retailer of furniture, appliances, and electronics. The company began operations over 100 years ago and today has 303 retail stores coast to coast. Since its acquisition of The Brick in 2013, Leon's has opened up 10 new retail stores.

Leon's Furniture Limited's balance sheet (partial) is summarized on the next page. You can see that merchandise inventory (labelled simply as inventories) is one of Leon's Furniture's biggest assets. Inventories composed about 54% of its current assets ($317.9 million/$588.5 million on December 31, 2017). That's not surprising since Leon's like other retail stores attracts customers with goods they can purchase and take home immediately.

Leon's Income Statement for the year ending December 31, 2017, shows sales of $2,212.2 million, an increase of 3.2% over the previous year ($2,143.7 million). Cost of goods sold, the largest expense on the Income Statement, was $1,261.1 million, an increase of 2.7% over the previous year ($1,228.5 million). Gross profit (Sales minus Cost of goods sold) of $951.1 million also increased by 3.9% over 2016 ($915.2 million). This means that the company was more profitable on sales of its product in 2017 than it was in 2016.

Vince Talotta/Toronto Star/Getty Images

	A	B	C	D
1	**Leon's Furniture Limited** Consolidated Balance Sheets (partial, adapted) As at December 31			
2	*(millions)*	**2017**	**2016**	
3	**Assets**			
4	Current			
5	Cash and cash equivalents	$ 36.2	$ 43.9	
6	Marketable securities	13.8	16.6	
7	Trade receivables	138.5	128.1	
8	Inventories	317.9	308.8	
9	Other current assets	82.1	57.9	
10	**Total current assets**	588.5	555.3	
11	Other assets	736.3	740.9	
12	Property, plant, and equipment	336.7	315.5	
13	**Total Assets**	$ 1,661.5	$ 1,611.7	
14				

Source: Data taken from Leon's Furniture Limited Annual Report 2014.

We also present Leon's Furniture Limited's income statement. While sales increased in 2017, gross profit, as a percentage of sales, remained steady at 43% from 2016 to 2017.

	A	B	C	D
1	**Leon's Furniture Limited** Consolidated Income Statements (adapted) Years ending December 31			
2	*(millions)*	**2017**	**2016**	
3	Sales	$ 2,212.2	$ 2,143.7	
4	Cost of sales	1,261.1	1,228.5	
5	Gross profit	951.1	915.2	
6	General and administrative expenses	809.2	786.6	
7	Operating profit	141.9	128.6	
8	Finance costs (net)	10.5	14.5	
9	Profit before income tax	131.4	114.1	
10	Income tax expense	34.8	30.6	
11	Net income	$ 96.6	$ 83.5	
12				

Source: Data taken from Leon's Furniture Limited Annual Report 2014.

You can see that the *cost of sales* (another name for **cost of goods sold**) is by far Leon's Furniture's largest expense. The account titled Cost of Sales perfectly describes that expense. In short,

- Leon's buys inventory, an asset carried on the books at cost.
- the goods that Leon's sells are no longer Leon's assets. The cost of inventory that's sold gets shifted into the expense account, Cost of Sales.

Merchandise inventory is the heart of a merchandising business, and cost of goods sold is the most important expense for a company that sells goods rather than services. This chapter explains how inventory and cost of goods sold are accounted for and how they affect a business's profit measures. This chapter also discusses inventory turnover measures, which indicate how fast products are sold. All of these are important measures of success for a merchandising company.

SHOW HOW TO ACCOUNT FOR INVENTORY

We begin by showing how the financial statements of a merchandiser such as Leon's Furniture Limited differ from those of service entities such as Royal LePage Real Estate. Merchandisers have two accounts that service entities don't need: Inventory on the balance sheet and Cost of Goods Sold on the income statement. The financial statements in Exhibit 5-1 highlight these differences.

EXHIBIT 5-1
Contrasting a Service Company With a Merchandiser

	A	B
1	**Service Company** **Royal LePage Real Estate** Income Statement For the Year Ended December 31, 2017	
2		
3	Service revenue	$ XXX
4	Expenses	
5	Operating and administrative	X
6	Depreciation	X
7	Income tax	X
8	Net income	$ X
9		
10		
11		

	A	B
1	**Merchandising Company** **Leon's Furniture Ltd.** Income Statement For the Year Ended December 31, 2017	
2	(amounts in millions)	
3	Sales revenue	$ 2,212.2
4	Cost of goods sold	1,261.1
5	Gross profit	$ 951.1
6	Operating expenses	
7	Operating and administrative	X
8	Depreciation	X
9	Income tax	X
10	Net income	$ 96.6
11		

	A	B
1	**Royal LePage Real Estate** Balance Sheet As at December 31, 2017	
2	Assets	
3		
4	Current assets	
5	Cash	$ X
6	Temporary investments	X
7	Accounts receivable, net	X
8	Prepaid expenses	X
9		
10		

	A	B
1	**Leon's Furniture Ltd.** Balance Sheet As at December 31, 2017	
2	Assets	
3	(amounts in millions)	
4	Current assets	
5	Cash	$ X
6	Temporary investments	X
7	Accounts receivable, net	X
8	Inventory	317.9
9	Prepaid expenses	X
10		

Accounting for Inventory

The value of inventory affects two financial statement accounts: inventory, reported as a current asset on the balance sheet; and cost of goods sold, shown as an expense on the income statement. This basic concept of accounting for merchandise inventory can be illustrated with an example. Suppose Leon's Furniture has in stock three chairs that cost $300 each. Leon's Furniture marks the chairs up by $200 and sells two of the chairs for $500 each.

- Leon's Furniture's balance sheet reports the one chair that the company still holds in inventory.
- The income statement reports the cost of the two chairs sold, as shown in Exhibit 5-2.

EXHIBIT 5-2
Inventory and Costs of Goods Sold When Inventory Cost Is Constant

Balance Sheet (Partial)		Income Statement (Partial)	
Current assets		Sales revenue	
Cash..	$XXX	(2 chairs @ sales price of $500)....	$1,000
Short-term investments.......................	XXX	Cost of goods sold	
Accounts receivable	XXX	(2 chairs @ cost of $300)..............	600
Inventory (1 chair @ cost of $300)	300	Gross profit	$ 400
Prepaid expenses	XXX		

Here is the basic concept of how we identify inventory, the asset, from cost of goods sold, the expense.

Inventory's cost shifts from asset to expense when the seller delivers the goods to the buyer.

Sales Price Versus Cost of Inventory

Note the difference between the sale price of inventory and the cost of inventory. In our Leon's Furniture example:

- Sales revenue is based on the *sale price* of the inventory sold ($500 per chair).
- Cost of goods sold is based on the *cost* of the inventory sold ($300 per chair).
- Inventory on the balance sheet is based on the *cost* of the inventory still on hand ($300 per chair).

Exhibit 5-2 shows these items.

Gross profit, also called **gross margin**, is the excess of sales revenue over cost of goods sold. It is called *gross profit* because operating expenses have not yet been subtracted. The actual inventory and cost of goods sold data (cost of sales) from the financial statements of Leon's Furniture Limited are:

Leon's inventory of $317.9 million represents:

$$\frac{\text{Inventory}}{\text{(balance sheet)}} = \frac{\text{Number of units of}}{\text{inventory } on \, hand} \times \frac{\text{Cost per unit}}{\text{of inventory}}$$

Leon's cost of goods sold ($1,261.1) represents:

$$\frac{\text{Cost of goods sold}}{\text{(income statement)}} = \frac{\text{Number of units of}}{\text{inventory } sold} \times \frac{\text{Cost per unit}}{\text{of inventory}}$$

Let's see what "units of inventory" and "cost per unit" mean.

NUMBER OF UNITS OF INVENTORY. This figure simply represents the number of units of inventory a business has on hand at a certain point in time. At each year-end, the business normally conducts a physical count of its inventory so it has an accurate record of the number of units on hand at that time. Leon's, for example, would conduct a physical inventory count on December 31 each year to determine the number of chairs, beds, tables, and other types of furniture it has on hand at year-end. Leon's needs an accurate count of inventory so it can properly determine the total cost of inventory to report on its year-end balance sheet.

The manager must also take into account inventory that has been shipped. Who owns it? Determining the ownership of inventory at the time of shipment depends on who has legal title. If inventory is shipped **FOB (free on board) shipping point**, it should be included on the books of the buyer, who has legal title, as soon as it leaves the shipper's dock. If the goods are shipped **FOB (free on board) destination**, the inventory in transit still belongs on the books of the seller until it is delivered to the buyer.

COST PER UNIT OF INVENTORY. Determining the cost per unit of inventory poses a challenge because companies purchase goods at different prices throughout the year. Which unit costs go into the ending inventory for the balance sheet? Which unit costs go to cost of goods sold?

What Goes into Inventory Cost?

The cost of merchandise in Leon's Furniture Limited's balance sheet represents all the costs that Leon's Furniture incurred to bring the inventory to the point of sale. Both IFRS and ASPE state the following:

> *The cost of inventories shall comprise all costs of purchase, costs of conversion and other costs incurred in bringing the inventories to their present location and condition.*

Inventory's cost includes its basic purchase price, plus freight-in, insurance while in transit, and any costs paid to get the inventory ready to sell, less returns, allowances, and discounts.

Once a product is sitting in a Leon's Furniture showroom, other costs incurred, such as advertising and delivery costs, are not included as the cost of inventory. Advertising, sales commissions, and delivery costs are expenses.

The next section shows how the different accounting methods determine the cost of ending inventory on the balance sheet and cost of goods sold for the income statement. First, however, you need to understand how inventory accounting systems work.

Accounting for Inventory in the Perpetual System

There are two main types of inventory accounting systems: the periodic system and the perpetual system. The **periodic inventory system** is used for inexpensive goods. A fabric store or a small hardware store won't keep a running record of every bolt of fabric or every nail. Instead, at the end of the period, the business counts inventory to determine the quantities on hand.

A **perpetual inventory system** uses computer software to keep a running record of inventory on hand. This system achieves control over goods such as parts at a Ford dealer, lumber at Home Depot, furniture at Leon's, and all the various groceries and other items that a Loblaws store sells. Today, most businesses use the perpetual inventory system.

Even with a perpetual system, the business still counts the inventory on hand annually. The physical count serves as a check on the accuracy of the perpetual records and establishes the correct amount of ending inventory for preparing the financial statements. The chart below compares the perpetual and periodic systems.

Perpetual Inventory System

- Used for all types of goods
- Keeps a running record of all goods bought, sold, and on hand
- Inventory counted at least once a year

Periodic Inventory System

- Used for inexpensive goods
- Does not keep a running record of all goods bought, sold, and on hand
- Inventory counted at least once a year

HOW THE PERPETUAL SYSTEM WORKS. Let's use an everyday situation to show how a perpetual inventory system works. Suppose you are buying a pair of Nike cross-trainer shoes from Sport Chek. The clerk scans the bar code on the product label of your purchase. Exhibit 5-3 illustrates a typical bar code. The bar code on the product or product label holds lots of information. The optical scanner reads the bar code, and the computer records the sale and updates the inventory records.

David R. Frazier Photolibrary, Inc./Science Source

EXHIBIT 5-3
Bar Code for Electronic Scanner

By keeping a running record of all items purchased as well as sold, in addition to beginning and ending inventories, a company always has a record of how much inventory should be on hand.

RECORDING TRANSACTIONS IN THE PERPETUAL SYSTEM. Each purchase of inventory is recorded as a debit to Inventory and a credit to Cash or Accounts Payable.

When Leon's Furniture makes a sale, two entries are needed in the perpetual system:

	A	B	C	D	E
1		The company records the sale:			
2		Dr Cash or Accounts Receivable			
3		Cr Sales Revenue			
4					
5		Leon's Furniture also records the cost of inventory sold:			
6		Dr Cost of Goods Sold			
7		Cr Inventory			
8					

RECORDING TRANSACTIONS IN THE PERIODIC SYSTEM. In the periodic inventory system, the business keeps no running record of the merchandise. Instead, at the end of the period, the business counts inventory on hand and applies the unit costs to determine the cost of ending inventory. This inventory figure appears on the balance sheet and is used to compute cost of goods sold.

In the periodic system, throughout the period the Inventory account carries the beginning balance left over from the preceding period. The business records purchases of inventory in the Purchases account (an expense). Then, at the end of the period, the Inventory account must be updated for the financial statements. A journal entry removes the beginning balance by crediting Inventory and debiting Cost of Goods Sold. A second journal entry sets up the ending Inventory balance, based on the physical count. The final entry in this sequence transfers the amount of Purchase related accounts to Cost of Goods Sold. These end-of-period entries can be made during the closing process and are shown in Exhibit 5-4, Panel A. When Leon's Furniture records a sale, the only journal entry needed in the periodic system is:

	A	B	C	D	E
1		Dr Cash or Accounts Receivable			
2		Cr Sales Revenue			
3					

Exhibit 5-4 shows the accounting for inventory in a perpetual system and a periodic system. Panel A gives the journal entries and Panel B presents the income statement and the balance sheet. All amounts are assumed.

The cost of the inventory, $560,000,* is the net amount of the purchases, determined as follows (using assumed amounts):

Purchase price of the inventory from the seller	$600,000
+Freight-in (transportation cost to move the goods from the seller to the buyer)	4,000
−Purchase returns for unsuitable goods returned to the seller	(25,000)
−Purchase allowances granted by the seller	(5,000)
−Purchase discounts for early payment	(14,000)
=Net purchases of inventory	$560,000

Freight-in is the transportation cost paid by the buyer under terms FOB shipping point to move goods from the seller to the buyer. Freight-in is accounted for as part of the cost of inventory. Freight-out paid by the seller is not part of the cost of inventory. Instead, freight-out is a delivery expense. It is the seller's expense of delivering merchandise to customers. A **purchase return** is a decrease in the cost of inventory because the buyer returned the goods to the seller. A **purchase allowance** also decreases the cost of inventory because the buyer got an allowance (a deduction) from the amount owed—often because of a merchandise defect. Throughout this book, we often refer to net purchases simply as purchases.

A **purchase discount** is a decrease in the buyer's cost of inventory that is earned by paying quickly. A common arrangement states payment terms of 2/10, n/30. This means the buyer can take a 2% discount for payment within 10 days, or pay the full amount within 30 days. Another common credit term is "net 30," which directs the customer to pay the full amount within 30 days.

In summary,

```
NET PURCHASES =  PURCHASES
                −PURCHASE RETURNS AND ALLOWANCES
                −PURCHASE DISCOUNTS
                +FREIGHT-IN
```

Now study Exhibit 5-4 on the next page.

*The price shown does *not* include Canada's goods and services tax (GST)/harmonized sales tax (HST).

EXHIBIT 5-4
Recording and Reporting Inventory—Perpetual System and Periodic System (Amounts Assumed)

	A	B	C	D
1		Perpetual System		
2		PANEL A—Recording Transactions		
3	Jan. 2	Inventory	600,000	
4		Accounts payable		600,000
5		*Purchased 1,000 units on account.*		
6	3	Inventory	4,000	
7		Accounts payable		4,000
8		*Record freight fee on purchases.*		
9	9	Accounts payable	25,000	
10		Inventory		25,000
11		*Returned goods to supplier for credit.*		
12	11	Accounts payable	5,000	
13		Inventory		5,000
14		*Record purchase allowance.*		
15	16	Accounts payable	14,000	
16		Inventory		14,000
17		*Record purchase discount.*		
18	16	Accounts payable	560,000	
19		Cash		560,000
20		*Record payment.*		
21	31	Accounts receivable	900,000	
22		Sales revenue		900,000
23		*Record sales on account.*		
24	31	Cost of goods sold	540,000	
25		Inventory		540,000
26		*Update inventory and COGS.*		
27	31	No adjustments required.		
28				
29				
30				
31				
32				
33				
34				
35				
36				

	A	B	C	D
1		Periodic System		
2		PANEL A—Recording Transactions (all amounts are assumed)		
3	Jan. 2	Purchases	600,000	
4		Accounts payable		600,000
5		*Purchased 1,000 units on account.*		
6	3	Freight-in	4,000	
7		Accounts payable		4,000
8		*Record freight fee on purchases.*		
9	9	Accounts payable	25,000	
10		Purchase returns		25,000
11		*Returned goods to supplier for credit.*		
12	11	Accounts payable	5,000	
13		Purchase allowance		5,000
14		*Record purchase allowance.*		
15	16	Accounts payable	14,000	
16		Purchase discount		14,000
17		*Record purchase discount.*		
18	16	Accounts payable	560,000	
19		Cash		560,000
20		*Record payment.*		
21	31	Accounts receivable	900,000	
22		Sales revenue		900,000
23		*Record sales on account.*		
24	31	No entry.		
25				
26				
27	31	Cost of goods sold	540,000	
28		Inventory, * ending balance	120,000	
29		Purchase allowance	5,000	
30		Purchase returns	25,000	
31		Purchase discount	14,000	
32		Purchases		600,000
33		Freight-in		4,000
34		Inventory, beginning		100,000
35		Update the inventory records by closing out the beginning inventory, set up ending inventory and close all Purchase-related accounts including Freight-in. After the process is complete, Inventory has its correct balance of $120,000 and Cost of Goods Sold shows $540,000.		
36		*Determined by physical count.		

PANEL B—Reporting in the Financial Statements (Perpetual)

Income Statement (Partial)
Sales revenue, net $900,000
Cost of goods sold   540,000
Gross profit $360,000

Ending Balance Sheet (Partial)
Current assets:
Cash .... $ XXX
Temporary investments..... XXX
Accounts receivable XXX
Inventory........................ 120,000
Prepaid expenses XXX

PANEL B—Reporting in the Financial Statements (Periodic)

Income Statement (Partial)
Sales revenue, net $900,000
Cost of goods sold:
Beginning inventory..... $100,000
Net Purchases.............   560,000
Goods available for sale 660,000
Ending inventory .... (120,000)
Cost of goods sold   540,000
Gross profit................. $360,000

Ending Balance Sheet (Partial)
Current Assets:
Cash .... $ XXX
Temporary investments.... XXX
Accounts receivable XXX
Inventory........................ 120,000
Prepaid expenses XXX

Since the various transactions that make up the $560,000 may occur on different dates, it is instructive to now view each entry separately for both the perpetual and the periodic inventory systems with assumed dates in Exhibit 5-4.

Net sales are computed as follows:

NET SALES = SALES REVENUE
− SALES RETURNS AND ALLOWANCES
− SALES DISCOUNTS

SALES RETURNS AND ALLOWANCES. Retailers and consumers have a right to return unsatisfactory or damaged merchandise for a refund or exchange. This is called **sales returns and allowances**. In these cases, the seller is obligated to accept the returned product if the customer chooses to return it. Returned merchandise means lost profits. For example, suppose that of the goods Black Corporation sold to a customer, $9 worth of goods are returned (or Black grants them an allowance). The cost of the merchandise sold is $5. Assuming a perpetual inventory system, Black Corporation would record the following entries:

	A	B	C	D	E
1		Sales Returns and Allowances	9		
2		Accounts Receivable		9	
3					

	A	B	C	D	E
1		Dr Inventory	5		
2		Cr Cost of goods sold		5	
3					

Retailers, wholesalers, and manufacturers typically disclose sales revenue at the *net* amount, which means after the sales discounts and sales returns and allowances have been subtracted. Using hypothetical data for discounts and returns, Black Corporation's net sales (revenue) for 2020, compared with the last two years, is as follows:

Black Corporation
(2020, Adapted)

Gross revenue	$59,000
−Sales discounts	(900)
−Sales returns and allowances	(262)
=Net revenue	$57,838

	2020	2019	2018
Net revenue (in millions)	$57,838	$43,232	$43,251

SALES DISCOUNTS. Sometimes businesses offer customers **sales discounts** for early payment in order to speed up cash flow. A typical sales discount incentive might be stated as follows:

2/10, n/30

This expression means that the seller is willing to discount the order by 2% if the buyer pays the invoice within 10 days. After that time, the seller withdraws the discount offer, and the buyer is supposed to pay in full within 30 days. Assume Black Corporation sells goods to a customer and invoices them for $1,500, 2/10, n/30.

If the customer pays the invoice within 10 days, it is entitled to a $30 discount, making the full amount due to settle Black Corporation's invoice $1,470 rather than $1,500. The entry to record the collection of this sale would be as follows:

	A	B	C	D	E
1		Cash	1,470		
2		Sales Discount	30		
3		Accounts Receivable		1,500	
4					

If for some reason, the customer does not pay its discounted invoice within the prescribed time period of 10 days, it forfeits its contractual right to the sales discount and would be obligated to pay Black Corporation the full amount. In that event, collection of the accounts receivable would be recorded as follows:

	A	B	C	D	E
1		Cash	1,500		
2		Accounts Receivable		1,500	
3					

STOP + THINK (5-1)

Suppose you are planning to open up a small pet food and accessories store in your neighbourhood. Would you use the perpetual inventory system or the periodic inventory system to account for inventory? Why?

APPLY AND COMPARE VARIOUS INVENTORY COSTING METHODS

OBJECTIVE

❷ **Apply** and **compare** various inventory costing methods

A manager must choose one of three costing methods to apply when valuing inventory for reporting purposes. The costing method selected affects the profits to be reported, the amount of income taxes to be paid, and the values of the inventory turnover, days' inventory outstanding, and gross profit percentage ratios derived from the financial statements.

Inventory Costing Methods

Determining the cost of inventory is easy when the unit cost remains constant, as in Exhibit 5-2, but unit cost usually changes. For example, the prices of products sometimes rise, and fuel prices can also rise, which increases the transportation costs to ship merchandise. Salomon snowboards that cost The Source Board Shop $150 in October may cost $160 in November and $180 in December. The Source Board Shop sells 50 snowboards in November. How many of the Salomon snowboards sold cost $150, how many cost $160, and how many cost $180?

To compute cost of goods sold and the cost of ending inventory still on hand, we must assign a unit cost to the items. Three generally accepted inventory methods are the following:

1. Specific identification cost
2. Weighted-average cost
3. First-in, first-out (FIFO) cost

As we shall see, these methods can have very different effects on reported inventory balances, profits, income taxes, and cash flows. Therefore, companies select their inventory method with great care.

SPECIFIC IDENTIFICATION COST METHOD. Some businesses deal in unique inventory items, such as antique furniture, jewels, and real estate. These businesses cost their inventories at the specific cost of the particular unit. For instance, a Toyota dealer may have two vehicles in the showroom—a "stripped-down" model that cost $22,000 and a "loaded" model that cost $29,000. If the dealer sells the loaded model, cost of goods sold is $29,000. The stripped-down auto will be the only unit left in inventory, so ending inventory is $22,000.

The **specific identification cost method** is too expensive to use for inventory items that have common characteristics, such as metres of lumber, litres of paint, or number of automobile tires.

The other acceptable inventory accounting methods—weighted-average and FIFO—do not use the specific cost of a particular unit. Instead, they assign different costs to units sold and units remaining in inventory based on an assumed flow of inventory.

ILLUSTRATION OF WEIGHTED-AVERAGE AND FIFO COSTING METHODS. To illustrate weighted-average and FIFO costing, we will use a common set of data, given in Exhibit 5-5.

EXHIBIT 5-5
Inventory Data Used to Illustrate Inventory Costing Methods

		Inventory		
Begin. bal.	(10 units @ $11)	110		
Purchases:				
No. 1	(20 units @ $14)	280	Cost of goods sold	
No. 2	(15 units @ $16)	240	(40 units @ $?)	?
No. 3	(15 units @ $18)	270		
Ending bal.	(20 units @ $?)	?		

In Exhibit 5-5, Leon's began the period with 10 lamps that cost $11 each; the beginning inventory was therefore $110. During the period, Leon's bought 50 more lamps, sold 40 lamps, and ended the period with 20 lamps, summarized in the T-account in Exhibit 5-5 and as follows:

	Number of Units	Total Cost
Goods available for sale	= 10 + 20 + 15 + 15 = 60 units	$110 + $280 + $240 + $270 = $900
Cost of goods sold	= 40 units	?
Ending inventory	= 20 units	?

The big accounting questions are:

1. What is the cost of goods sold for the income statement?
2. What is the cost of the ending inventory for the balance sheet?

The answers to these questions depend on which inventory method Leon's uses. Leon's actually uses FIFO, but we will look at weighted-average costing first.

WEIGHTED-AVERAGE COST–PERPETUAL. The **weighted-average-cost method**, sometimes called the average cost method, is based on the average cost of inventory during the period. Since the inventory records are updated each time merchandise is bought and sold, *a new average cost per unit* is computed every time a purchase is made. To illustrate, we will use the data in Exhibit 5-5:

Item	COGS	Balance
Beginning Inventory: 10 units × $11		$110
Purchase #1: 20 units × $14 = $280		390
New unit cost: $390/(10 + 20) = $13		($110 + $280)
Purchase #2: 15 units × $16 = $240		630
New unit cost: $630/(10 + 20 + 15) = $14		($390 + $240)
Sold 40 units × $14	$560	70
		($630 − $560)
Purchase #3: 15 units × $18 = $270		340
New unit cost: $340/20* = $17		($70 + $270)
*(20 units = 10 + 20 + 15 − 40 + 15)		
Cost of goods sold	$560	
Ending inventory		$340

The steps to calculate the weighted-average cost per unit after each purchase are:

1. Calculate the weighted-average cost per unit:

$$\frac{\text{Weighted-average}}{\text{cost per unit}} = \frac{\text{Cost of goods available}}{\text{Number of units available}}$$

$$\text{Purchase \#1} = \frac{\overset{\text{(Beg. inv. + Purch.1)}}{\$110 + \$280}}{10 + 20} = \frac{\$390}{30} = \$13$$

$$\text{Purchase \#2} = \frac{\overset{\text{(Beg. inv. + Purch.1 + Purch.2)}}{\$110 + \$280 + \$240}}{10 + 20 \quad + 15} = \frac{\$630}{45} = \$14$$

2. Determine the value for cost of goods sold:

$$\frac{\text{Cost of}}{\text{goods sold}} = \frac{\text{Number of}}{\text{units sold}} \times \frac{\text{weighted-average}}{\text{cost per unit}}$$

$$40 \text{ units sold} \times \$14 = \$560$$

3. Calculate the cost of ending inventory:

The cost of ending inventory is determined by taking the 5 units left over from Purchase No. 2 plus the 15 units bought from Purchase No. 3. The balance in ending inventory is:

$$\begin{aligned} \text{Ending inventory} &= 5 \text{ units left after sale of goods @14} = \$\ 70 \\ &+ \underline{15} \text{ units from Purchase No. 3 @18} = \underline{\ 270} \\ &\ \ \underline{20} \text{ units} \qquad\qquad\qquad\qquad\qquad \$340 \end{aligned}$$

Notice how the weighted-average cost per unit only changes after a purchase is made.

WEIGHTED-AVERAGE COST–PERIODIC. Under the periodic inventory system, the cost of inventory is based on the average cost of the inventory for the **entire period**.

Using the data from Exhibit 5-5, the values for cost of goods sold and ending inventory are determined as follows:

1. Calculate the weighted-average cost per unit:

$$\frac{\text{Weighted-average}}{\text{cost per unit}} = \frac{\text{Cost of goods available*}}{\text{Number of units available}} = \frac{\$110 + \$280 + \$240 + \$270}{10 + 20 + 15 + 15}$$

$$= \frac{\$900}{60} = \$15$$

*Cost of goods available = Beginning inventory + Purchases (for the *entire period*)

2. Determine the value for cost of goods sold:

Cost of goods sold	=	Number of units sold	×	weighted-average cost per unit	
		40 units sold	×	$15	= $600

3. Calculate the cost of ending inventory:

Ending inventory	=	Number of units on hand	×	weighted-average cost per unit	
		20 units on hand	×	$15	= $300

These amounts are different from the values given under the perpetual inventory method. Why? For the perpetual inventory method, a new unit cost is computed each time a purchase is made while for the periodic inventory method; the unit cost is based on the cost of goods (and units) available for the entire period.

The following T-account shows the effects of weighted-average costing:

Inventory (at weighted-average cost–periodic)

Begin. bal.	(10 units @ $11)	110		
Purchases:				
No. 1	(20 units @ $14)	280		
No. 2	(15 units @ $16)	240	Cost of goods sold (40 units	
No. 3	(15 units @ $18)	270	@ average cost of $15 per unit)	600
Ending bal.	(20 units @ average cost of $15 per unit)	300		

FIFO COST–PERPETUAL. Under the **first-in, first-out (FIFO) cost method**, the first costs into inventory are the first costs assigned to cost of goods sold—hence, the name *first-in, first-out*. The following T-account shows how to compute FIFO cost of goods sold and ending inventory for Leon's lamps (data from Exhibit 5-5):

Inventory (at FIFO cost–perpetual)

Begin. bal.	(10 units @ $11)	110		
Purchases:				
No. 1	(20 units @ $14)	280		
No. 2	(15 units @ $16)	240	Cost of goods sold (40 units):	
			(10 units @ $11) 110 ⎫	
			(20 units @ $14) 280 ⎬ 550	
			(10 units @ $16) 160 ⎭	
No. 3	(15 units @ $18)	270		
Ending bal.	(5 units @ $16) = 80 ⎫ (15 units @ $18) = 270 ⎭	350		

Looking at the Cost of goods sold, FIFO assumes that all of the 10 units in beginning inventory were sold along with the 20 units from Purchase No. 1 but only 10 of the 15 units from Purchase No. 2 were sold. The ending inventory contains the 5 units left from Purchase No. 2 and all of the 15 units from Purchases No. 3.

FIFO COST–PERIODIC. Just like the perpetual inventory system, the first costs into inventory are assigned to the first units sold. Using the data from Exhibit 5-5:

Inventory (at FIFO cost–periodic)

Begin. bal.	(10 units @ $11)	110	
Purchases:			Cost of goods sold (40 units):
No. 1	(20 units @ $14)	280	(10 units @ $11) 110 ⎫
No. 2	(15 units @ $16)	240	(20 units @ $14) 280 ⎬ 550
No. 3	(15 units @ $18)	270	(10 units @ $16) 160 ⎭
Ending bal.	(5 units @ $16) = 80 ⎫ (15 units @ $18) = 270 ⎭	350	

Under the periodic inventory system, all of the information for the entire period is taken into account. This means that FIFO assumes that all of the 10 units in beginning inventory were sold, along with the 20 units from the No. 1 purchase and 10 of the 15 units of the No. 2 purchase. The cost of ending inventory is based on the units remaining: 5 units from the No. 2 purchase and all of the 15 units from the No. 3 purchase. Notice how the amounts for cost of goods sold and ending inventory are the *same* under both the *perpetual and periodic inventory methods.*

The Effects of FIFO and Weighted-Average Cost on Cost of Goods Sold, Gross Profit, and Ending Inventory

In our Leon's example, the cost of inventory rose from $11 to $14 and up to $18. When inventory unit costs change this way, the various inventory methods produce different cost-of-goods-sold figures. Exhibit 5-6 summarizes the income effects of the two inventory methods (remember that prices are rising). Study the exhibit carefully, focusing on cost of goods sold and gross profit assuming the periodic system.

Exhibit 5-6 compares both perpetual and periodic methods. Notice how gross profit is highest under FIFO when inventory costs are increasing.

EXHIBIT 5-6
Effects of the FIFO and Weighted-Average Inventory Methods

	Perpetual FIFO	Periodic FIFO	Perpetual Weighted-average	Periodic Weighted-average
Sales revenue (assumed)	$1,000	$1,000	$1,000	$1,000
Cost of goods sold	550	550	560	600
Gross profit	$ 450	$ 450	$ 440	$ 400

Let's use the gross profit data from Exhibit 5-6 to illustrate the potential tax effects of the two methods in a period of rising prices:

	Perpetual FIFO	Periodic FIFO	Perpetual Weighted-average	Periodic Weighted-average
Gross profit	$450	$450	$440	$400
Operating expenses (assumed)	260	260	260	260
Income before income tax	$190	$190	$180	$140
Income tax expense (35%)	$ 67*	$ 67*	$ 63	$ 49

*rounded

Income tax expense is lower under weighted-average and higher under FIFO.

Exhibit 5-7 demonstrates the effect of increasing and decreasing costs of inventory on cost of goods sold and ending inventory. Study this exhibit carefully; it will help you really understand the FIFO and weighted-average inventory methods.

In a period of rising prices, FIFO will generally lead to higher profits and higher taxes than weighted-average, while the opposite is true in a period of falling prices. The difference between the two methods on profit and income taxes may be small, and each of the two methods is appropriate for certain types of inventory.

EXHIBIT 5-7
Cost of Goods Sold and Ending Inventory—FIFO and Weighted-Average; Increasing Costs and Decreasing Costs

When inventory costs are decreasing:

	Income Statement Effects Cost of Goods Sold (COGS)	Balance Sheet Effects Ending Inventory (EI)	Cash Flow Effects Income Taxes
FIFO	FIFO COGS is highest because it's based on the oldest costs, which are high. Gross profit is, therefore, the lowest.	FIFO EI is lowest because it's based on the most recent costs, which are low.	Less cash is paid for taxes, so FIFO could be used by firms seeking to minimize taxes.
Weighted-Average	Weighted-average COGS is lowest because it's based on an average of the costs for the period, which is lower than the oldest costs. Gross profit is, therefore, the highest.	Weighted-average EI is highest because the average cost for the period is higher than the most recent costs.	More cash is paid for taxes, but weighted-average may still be popular with firms seeking to maximize reported income.

When inventory costs are increasing:

	Income Statement Effects Cost of Goods Sold (COGS)	Balance Sheet Effects Ending Inventory (EI)	Cash Flow Effects Income Taxes
FIFO	FIFO COGS is lowest because it's based on oldest costs, which are low. Gross profit is, therefore, the highest.	FIFO EI is highest because it's based on the most recent costs, which are high.	More cash is paid for taxes, but FIFO may still be popular with firms seeking to maximize reported income.
Weighted-Average	Weighted-average COGS is highest because it's based on an average of the costs for the period, which is higher than the oldest costs. Gross profit is, therefore the lowest.	Weighted-average EI is lowest because the average cost for the period is lower than the most recent costs.	Less cash is paid for taxes, so weighted-average could be used by firms seeking to minimize taxes.

Comparison of the Inventory Methods

Let's compare the weighted-average and FIFO inventory methods.

1. How well does each method measure income by allocating inventory expense—cost of goods sold—against revenue? Weighted-average results in the most

realistic net income figure, it is an average that combines all costs (old costs and recent costs). In contrast, FIFO uses old inventory costs against revenue. FIFO income is therefore less realistic than weighted-average income.

2. Which method reports the most up-to-date inventory cost on the balance sheet? FIFO reports the most current inventory cost on the balance sheet. Weighted-average can value inventory at very old costs because weighted-average leaves the oldest prices in ending inventory.

3. What effects do the methods have on income taxes? As we have seen in Exhibit 5-7, in a period of rising costs, FIFO uses old inventory costs against revenue, resulting in higher income taxes. Weighted-average is an average that combines all costs (old costs and recent costs), which leads to lower profits and lower income taxes.

STOP + THINK (5-2)

King Company had 25 units @$5 in beginning inventory; bought 30 units @$6 and then sold 50 units. Assume King Company uses the FIFO perpetual inventory system. Compute the (a) cost of goods sold and the (b) cost of ending inventory.

▶ DECISION GUIDELINES

MANAGING INVENTORY

Suppose Leon's Furniture stocks two basic categories of merchandise:

- Furniture pieces, such as tables and chairs
- Small items of low value, near the checkout stations, such as flower vases and other small accent pieces

Jacob Stiles, the store manager, is considering how accounting will affect the business. Let's examine several decisions that Stiles must make to achieve his goals for his company.

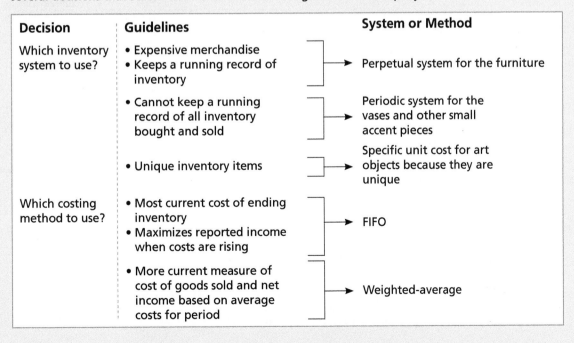

Decision	Guidelines	System or Method
Which inventory system to use?	• Expensive merchandise • Keeps a running record of inventory	Perpetual system for the furniture
	• Cannot keep a running record of all inventory bought and sold	Periodic system for the vases and other small accent pieces
	• Unique inventory items	Specific unit cost for art objects because they are unique
Which costing method to use?	• Most current cost of ending inventory • Maximizes reported income when costs are rising	FIFO
	• More current measure of cost of goods sold and net income based on average costs for period	Weighted-average

MyLab Accounting

MID-CHAPTER SUMMARY PROBLEM

Suppose a division of DIY Building Products Inc. has these inventory records for January 2020:

Date		Item	Quantity	Unit Cost
Jan.	1	Beginning inventory	100 units	$ 8
	6	Purchase	60 units	9
	21	Purchase	150 units	9
	24	Sales	300 units	
	27	Purchase	90 units	10

Name: DIY Building Products Inc.
Industry: Building products
Fiscal Period: Month of January 2020
Key Fact: Perpetual inventory system and periodic inventory system

Operating expense for January was $1,900, and the 300 units sold on January 24 generated sales revenue of $6,770.

Requirements

1. Prepare the January income statement, showing amounts for FIFO and weighted-average cost assuming that (a) a periodic inventory system is used, and (b) a perpetual inventory system is used. Label the bottom line "Operating income." (Round figures to whole-dollar amounts.) Show your computations, and compute cost of goods sold.
2. Explain which inventory method would result in:
   a. Reporting the highest operating income
   b. Reporting inventory on the balance sheet at the most recent cost
   c. Attaining the best measure of net income for the income statement

ANSWERS

Requirement 1(a) Periodic Inventory System

		A	B	C	D	E	F
	1	**DIY Building Products Inc.** Income Statement for Division For the Month Ended January 31, 2020					
Sales revenue is given.	2			FIFO		Weighted-Average	
Beginning inventory is given.	3	Sales revenue		$ 6,770		$ 6,770	
See the Computations section.	4	Cost of goods sold:					
Beginning inventory + Purchases	5	Beginning inventory	$ 800		$ 800		
See the Computations section.	6	Purchases	2,790		2,790		
Cost of goods available for sale − Ending inventory	7	Cost of goods available for sale	3,590		3,590		
	8	Ending inventory	(990)		(898)		
Sales revenue − Cost of goods sold	9	Cost of goods sold		2,600		2,692	
	10	Gross profit		4,170		4,078	
Operating expenses are given.	11	Operating expenses		1,900		1,900	
Gross profit − Operating expenses	12	Operating income		$ 2,270		$ 2,178	
	13						

Computations:

Beginning inventory:	100 × $8 = $800
Purchases:	(60 × $9) + (150 × $9) + (90 × $10) = $2,790
*Ending inventory—FIFO:	(10 × $9) + (90 × $10) = $990
Weighted-average:	100 × $8.975** = $898 (rounded from $897.50)

---

*Number of units in ending inventory = 100 + 60 + 150 + 90 − 300 = 100
**$3,590/400 units† = $8.975 per unit
†Number of units available = 100 + 60 + 150 + 90 = 400

Requirement 1(b) Perpetual Inventory System

	A	B	C	D
1	**DIY Building Products Inc.** Income Statement for Division For the Month Ended January 31, 2020			
2		FIFO	Weighted- Average	
3	Sales revenue	$ 6,770	$ 6,770	
4	Cost of goods sold	2,600	2,603	
5	Gross profit	4,170	4,167	
6	Operating expenses	1,900	1,900	
7	Operating income	$ 2,270	$ 2,267	
8				

Computations:

FIFO:
Cost of goods sold = $(100 \times \$8) + (60 \times \$9) + (140 \times \$9) = \$2,600$
Ending inventory = $(10 \times \$9) + (90 \times \$10) = \$990$

Weighted-average:
Cost of goods sold = $(100 \times \$8) + (60 \times \$9) + (150 \times \$9) = \$2,690$
$2,690/310 units = $8.677 per unit
300 units sold × $8.677/unit = $2,603 (rounded)
Ending inventory = 10 units left after sale (310 available − 300 units sold)
× $8.677 = $87 (rounded)
90 units bought × $10 = 900
Ending inventory   = $987 ($87 + $900)

> Use the quantities and unit costs given in the question to calculate beginning inventory and purchases. Recall that FIFO ending inventory calculations use the most current purchase prices. Weighted-average ending inventory calculations use the average purchase prices.

Requirement 2

a. Use FIFO to report the highest operating income. Income under FIFO is highest when inventory unit costs are increasing, as in this situation.

b. Use FIFO to report inventory on the balance sheet at the most current cost. The oldest inventory costs are expensed as cost of goods sold, leaving the most recent (most current) costs of the period in ending inventory.

c. Use weighted-average to attain the best measure of net income. Weighted-average inventory costs, which are expensed as part of goods sold, are closer to the most recent (most current) inventory costs than FIFO costs are.

> Because beginning inventory, purchases, and operating expense are the same for both inventory methods, use the ending inventory and operating income amounts you calculated in Requirement 1 to help you answer these questions.

EXPLAIN HOW ACCOUNTING STANDARDS APPLY TO INVENTORY

OBJECTIVE

❸ **Explain** how accounting standards apply to inventory

At this point, we need to consider how accounting standards apply to inventory.

Investors like to compare a company's financial statements from one period to the next so they can use this information to make a decision. In order to do this, the company must use the same accounting method for inventory *consistently* from one accounting period to another.

Suppose you are analyzing Leon's Furniture's net income pattern over a two-year period. Now, suppose Leon's switched from one inventory method to another during that time and its net income increased dramatically, but only because of the change in inventory method. If you did not know about the change, you might believe that Leon's Furniture's income increased due to improved operations, which is not the case.

Recall from Chapter 1 that one of the enhancing qualitative characteristics of accounting information is **comparability**. For accounting information to be comparable, it must be reported in a way that makes it possible to compare it to similar information being reported by other companies and by comparing it with its own financial statements from one period to the next. It must also be reported in a way that is *consistent* with how it was reported in previous periods. This does not mean that a company is not permitted to change its accounting methods. Both IFRS and ASPE allow such a change, indicating that it is acceptable if it "results in the financial statements providing reliable and more relevant information." Companies are required to **disclose** the inventory accounting methods in the notes as well as the substance of all material transactions that affect the proper valuation of the inventory. This allows creditors and investors to make informed decisions.

Lower of Cost and Net Realizable Value

The **lower-of-cost-and-net-realizable-value (LCNRV) rule** is based on the premise that inventory can become obsolete or damaged or its selling price can decline. Both IFRS and ASPE require that inventory be reported in the financial statements at whichever is lower—the inventory's cost or its **net realizable value (NRV)**, that is, the amount the business could get if it sold the inventory, less any costs incurred to sell it. If the net realizable value of inventory falls below its historical cost, the business must write down the value of its goods to net realizable value because it is the most relevant and representationally faithful measure of the inventory's true worth to the business. On the balance sheet, the business reports ending inventory at its LCNRV. How is the write-down accomplished?

Suppose Klassen Furniture Inc. paid $3,000 for inventory on September 26. By December 31, Klassen determines that it will be able to sell this inventory for only $2,000, net of selling costs. Because the inventory's net realizable value is less than its original cost, Klassen's December 31 balance sheet must report the inventory at $2,000. Exhibit 5-8 presents the effects of LCNRV on the balance sheet and the income statement. Before any LCNRV effect, cost of goods sold is $9,000.

An LCNRV write-down decreases Inventory and increases Cost of Goods Sold, as follows:

Inventory	
Sept. 26 $3,000	
	$1,000 Dec. 31
Balance $2,000	

	A	B	C	D	E
1	Dec. 31	Cost of Goods Sold	1,000		
2		Inventory		1,000	
3		*Write inventory down to net realizable value.*			
4					

Inventory that has been written down to net realizable value should be reassessed each period. If the net realizable value has increased, the previous write-down should be reversed up to the new net realizable value. Of course, the inventory cannot be written up to a value that exceeds its original cost.

Balance Sheet

Current assets:	$	XXX
Cash		XXX
Short-term investments		XXX
Accounts receivable		XXX
Inventories, at net realizable value (which is lower than $3,000 cost)		2,000
Prepaid expenses		XXX
Total current assets		$X,XXX

Income Statement

Sales revenue	$21,000
Cost of goods sold ($9,000 + $1,000)	10,000
Gross profit	$11,000

Assume that Klassen's inventory described above was still on hand at the end of the next period and that the net realizable value had increased to $2,400. The journal entry to reverse a previous write-down would be as follows:

	A	B	C	D	E
1		Inventory	400		
2		Cost of Goods Sold		400	
3		*Write inventory up to the net realizable value.*			
4					

Companies disclose how they apply LCNRV in a note to their financial statements as shown in the following excerpt from Leon's 2017 audited annual report.

Summary of Significant Accounting Policies

Inventories

Inventories are valued at the lower of cost determined on a first-in, first-out basis, and net realizable value. . . .

STOP + THINK (5-3)

Do you think it is a problem for investors trying to interpret the financial statements of companies using different methods?

COMPUTE AND EVALUATE GROSS PROFIT PERCENTAGE, INVENTORY TURNOVER, AND DAYS' INVENTORY OUTSTANDING

Managers, investors, and creditors use ratios to evaluate a business. The ratios that relate directly to inventory are the gross profit percentage, inventory turnover, and days' inventory outstanding.

Gross Profit Percentage

Gross profit—sales minus cost of goods sold—is a key indicator of a company's ability to sell inventory at a profit. Merchandisers strive to increase **gross profit percentage**, also called the *gross margin percentage*. Gross profit percentage is stated as a percentage of a merchandiser's net sales. Gross profit percentage is computed as follows for Leon's Furniture. Data (in millions) for 2017 are taken from the financial statements, page 231.

$$\text{Gross profit percentage} = \frac{\text{Gross profit}}{\text{Net sales revenue}} = \frac{\$951.1}{\$2,212.2} = 0.4299 = 43.0\%$$

Managers and investors watch the gross profit percentage carefully. A 43.0% gross profit means that each dollar of sales generates 43.0 cents of gross profit. On average, cost of goods sold consumes 57.0 cents of each sales dollar for Leon's. For most firms, the gross profit percentage changes little from year to year, so a small downturn may signal trouble.

Leon's gross profit was 43.8%, 42.7%, and 43.0% for the years 2015 through 2017, respectively. Even though the company faces stiff competition from other retailers and specialty stores, the gross profit remained relatively similar over the three-year period. Since its acquisition of The Brick in 2013, Leon's has opened up 10 new stores. Leon's gross profit of 43.0% in 2017 was higher than Walmart (24.7%), and Pier 1 (36.6%). Both Pier 1 and Leon's handle higher-priced merchandise than Walmart, which may explain their higher gross profit. Exhibit 5-9 graphs the gross profit for these three companies.

EXHIBIT 5-9
Gross Profit Percentages of Three Leading Retailers

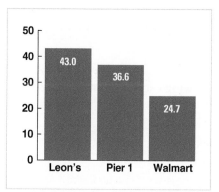

Inventory Turnover and Days' Inventory Outstanding

Leon's strives to sell its inventory as quickly as possible because furniture and fixtures generate no profit until they are sold. The faster the sales, the higher the company's income; the slower the sales, the lower the company's income. **Inventory turnover**, the ratio of cost of goods sold to average inventory, indicates how rapidly inventory is sold. The 2017 computation for Leon's follows (data in millions from the financial statements, page 231):

$$\begin{array}{c}\text{Inventory} \\ \text{(balance sheet)}\end{array} = \frac{\text{Cost of goods sold}}{\text{Average inventory}} = \frac{\text{Cost of goods sold}}{\left(\dfrac{\text{Beginning}}{\text{inventory}} + \dfrac{\text{Ending}}{\text{inventory}}\right) \div 2}$$

$$= \frac{\$1,261.1}{(\$317.9 + \$308.8)/2} = 4.02 \text{ or } 4.0 \text{ times per year}$$

The inventory turnover statistic shows how many times the company sold (or turned over) its average level of inventory during the year. Inventory turnover varies from industry to industry. To calculate **days' inventory outstanding**, which indicates how long it takes to sell inventory, take 365 days and divide by the inventory turnover. For Leon's, it would be 365/4.02 = 90.8 days.

Leon's and other specialty retailers turn their inventory over slowly. Retailers must keep lots of inventory on hand because visual appeal is critical in retailing. Department stores such as The Bay and discounters such as Walmart also keep a lot of inventory on hand. Exhibit 5-10 shows the inventory turnover rates for three leading retailers.

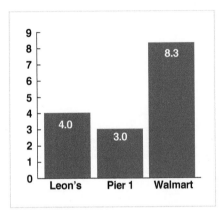

EXHIBIT 5-10
Inventory Turnover Rates of
Three Leading Retailers

STOP + THINK (5-4)

You have received a gift of cash from your grandparents and are considering investing in the stock market. You have carefully researched the market and have decided that you will invest in one of three companies: Leon's Furniture, Pier 1, or Walmart. Assume your analysis has resulted in Exhibits 5-9 and 5-10. What do the ratio values in the two exhibits say about the merchandising (pricing) strategies of Leon's, Pier 1, and Walmart?

 # DECISION GUIDELINES

Companies buy and sell inventory to generate revenue. Ratios that relate directly to inventory are the inventory turnover, days' inventory outstanding, and the gross profit percentage. Let's see how they are used in decision making.

Decision	Guidelines
Who uses the inventory turnover, days' inventory outstanding, and the gross profit percentage ratios for decision making and why?	*Managers* keep their eye on inventory to make sure it is selling quickly. Slow-moving inventory could be a sign that it is outdated or no longer in demand. Also, determining the selling price for inventory affects gross profit and, ultimately, net income. If the gross profit is too low, it may indicate that the inventory is costing too much or the selling price is not high enough.
	Investors want to know if inventory is selling quickly because it affects revenue and, ultimately, net income. They examine gross profit to see if it is high enough to cover all the other expenses and still provide for a reasonable profit.
	Creditors are interested in how inventory is selling because the faster inventory is sold, the sooner the cash flows in and the company can pay its debts.

OBJECTIVE

⑤ **Analyze** the effects of
inventory errors

ANALYZE THE EFFECTS OF INVENTORY ERRORS

Inventory errors sometimes occur. In Exhibit 5-11, start with period 1, in which ending inventory is *overstated* by $5,000 and cost of goods sold is therefore *understated* by $5,000. Then compare period 1 with period 3, which is correct. *Period 1 should look exactly like period 3.*

Inventory errors counterbalance in two consecutive periods. Why? Recall that period 1's ending inventory becomes period 2's beginning inventory amount. Thus, the error in period 1 carries over into period 2. Trace the ending inventory of $15,000 from period 1 to period 2. Then compare periods 2 and 3. *All periods should look exactly like period 3.* The amounts **in bold type** in Exhibit 5-11 are incorrect.

EXHIBIT 5-11
Inventory Errors: An Example

	A	B	C	D	E	F	G	H
1		Period 1		Period 2		Period 3		
2		Ending Inventory Overstated by $5,000		Beginning Inventory Overstated by $5,000		Correct		
3	Sales revenue		$ 100,000		$ 100,000		$ 100,000	
4	Cost of goods sold:							
5	Beginning inventory	$ 10,000		**$ 15,000**		$ 10,000		
6	Purchases	50,000		50,000		50,000		
7	Cost of goods available for sale	60,000		**65,000**		60,000		
8	**Ending inventory**	**(15,000)**		(10,000)		(10,000)		
9	Cost of goods sold		**45,000**		**55,000**		50,000	
10	**Gross profit**		**$ 55,000**		**$ 45,000**		$ 50,000	
11								

Source: The authors thank Professor Carl High for this example.

$ 100,000

Beginning inventory and ending inventory have opposite effects on cost of goods sold (beginning inventory is added; ending inventory is subtracted); therefore, after two periods, an inventory accounting error "washes out" (counterbalances) as illustrated in Exhibit 5-11. Notice that total gross profit for periods 1 and 2 combined is correct ($100,000), even though each period's gross profit is wrong by $5,000. The correct gross profit is $50,000 for each period as shown in period 3.

Note that there is a direct relationship between ending inventory (EI) and gross profit (GP), but an inverse relationship between beginning inventory (BI) and gross profit. That is, an understatement of ending inventory results in an understatement of gross profit, but an understatement of beginning inventory results in an overstatement of gross profit. (COGS = cost of goods sold)

EI↓ results in COGS↑ results in GP↓ (Direct relationship between EI and GP)

BI↓ results in COGS↓ results in GP↑ (Inverse relationship between BI and GP)

Inventory Errors

Inventory errors cannot be ignored simply because they counterbalance. Suppose you are analyzing trends in the operations of the company presented above.

Exhibit 5-11 shows a drop in gross profit from period 1 to period 2, followed by an increase in period 3. Did the company really get worse and then better again? No, that picture of operations is inaccurate because of the accounting error. The correct gross profit is $50,000 for each period. We must have accurate information for all periods. Exhibit 5-12 summarizes the effects of inventory accounting errors.

EXHIBIT 5-12
Effects of Inventory Errors

	A	B	C	D	E	F
		Period 1		Period 2		
		Cost of	Gross Profit	Cost of	Gross Profit	
2	Inventory Error	Goods Sold	and Net Income	Goods Sold	and Net Income	
3	Period 1	Understated	Overstated	Overstated	Understated	
4	Ending inventory overstated					
5	Period 1					
6	Ending inventory understated	Overstated	Understated	Understated	Overstated	
7						

Reporting on the Statement of Cash Flows

Inventories appear on the balance sheet as current assets. Since inventory transactions affect cash, their effects are reported on the statement of cash flows.

Inventory transactions are *operating activities* because the purchase and sale of merchandise drives a company's operations. The purchase of inventory requires a cash payment and the sale of inventory requires a cash receipt. We will see in Chapter 9 how to report inventory transactions on the statement of cash flows.

COOKING *the* BOOKS

with Inventory

No area of accounting has a deeper ethical dimension than inventory. Managers of companies whose profits do not meet shareholder expectations are sometimes tempted to "cook the books" to increase reported income. The increase in reported income may lead investors and creditors into thinking the business is more successful than it really is.

What do managers hope to gain from fraudulent accounting? In some cases, they are trying to keep their jobs. In other cases, their bonuses are tied to reported income: the higher the company's net income, the higher the managers' bonuses.

The easiest is simply to overstate ending inventory. The two most common ways to "cook the books" with inventory are (1) inserting fictitious inventory, thus overstating quantities; and (2) deliberately overstating unit prices used in the computation of ending inventory amounts. The upward-pointing arrows in the accounting equation indicate an overstatement: reporting more assets and equity than are actually present.

ASSETS	=	LIABILITIES	+	SHAREHOLDERS' EQUITY
↑	=	0	+	↑

STOP + THINK (5-5)

It's year-end and a physical count revealed $1,500 on hand, while the accounting records indicated there should be $1,600. If this error is not corrected, what effect would this have on the year-end's (a) Cost of goods sold, (b) Net income, and (c) Shareholders' equity?

Summary of IFRS-ASPE Differences

Concepts	IFRS	ASPE
There are no differences between IFRS and ASPE in this chapter.		

SUMMARY

SUMMARY OF LEARNING OBJECTIVES

LEARNING OBJECTIVE	SUMMARY
1 Show how to account for inventory	When inventory is bought, it is a current asset on the balance sheet, and when it is sold, it is an expense on the income statement. A company can use either the perpetual inventory system or the periodic inventory system to account for its inventory. A perpetual inventory system keeps a continuous record of inventory bought and sold. A periodic inventory system does not keep a continuous record of inventory; a physical count is performed to determine ending inventory. Cost of goods sold is a computation.
2 Apply and **compare** various inventory costing methods	The inventory methods are the specific identification; first-in, first-out (FIFO); and the weighted-average-cost method. Specific identification is used for unique inventory items where the company identifies the specific cost of the inventory item. Under the FIFO method, the first costs into inventory are the first costs assigned to cost of goods sold. The weighted-average-cost method assigns an average cost to inventory based on the cost of the inventory for the period.
3 Explain how accounting standards apply to inventory	Comparability (including consistency) says that businesses should use the same accounting methods and procedures from period to period so users can compare information. The lower-of-cost-and-net-realizable-value (LCNRV) rule requires that inventory be reported in the financial statements at the lower of its cost and net realizable value. Net realizable value is the amount the business could get if it sold the inventory less any costs of selling it.
4 Compute and **evaluate** gross profit, inventory turnover, and days' inventory outstanding	Ratios that are used to evaluate inventory: Gross profit percentage = Gross profit/Net sales revenue (the gross profit percentage indicates the company's ability to sell inventory at a profit) Inventory turnover = Cost of goods sold/Average inventory (inventory turnover shows how rapidly inventory is sold) Days' inventory outstanding = 365 days/Inventory turnover (shows how many days it takes the company to sell inventory)
5 Analyze the effects of inventory errors	Inventory errors, if not corrected, can affect the values of inventory on the balance sheet, and cost of goods sold, gross profit, and net income on the income statement.

END-OF-CHAPTER SUMMARY PROBLEM

During February 2020—its first month of operations–Blanc Company reported the following transactions:

Feb.	1	Purchased 20,000 units on account for $2.50 each
Feb.	15	Purchased 25,000 units on account for $2.75 each
Feb.	20	Sold on account 35,000 units for $3.25 each
Feb.	23	Purchased 10,000 units on account for $2.70 each
Feb.	25	Paid for the purchases made on Feb. 1
Feb.	27	Collected $75,000 from customers on account
Feb.	28	Incurred on account $11,000 in operating expenses

The company uses the perpetual inventory method and pays 35% income tax.

Requirements

1. Prepare journal entries to record the transactions for the month of February assuming the company uses the FIFO inventory method. Explanations are not required.
2. Determine the ending inventory assuming the company uses the FIFO inventory method. (Hint: You might find it helpful to use a T-account.)
3. Prepare the company's multi-step income statement for the month of February.
4. Compute the company's gross profit percentage and the inventory turnover for the month. How does this company compare with the industry average of 17% for the gross profit and an inventory turnover of three times? Round to one decimal place.
5. Assume instead that the company uses the weighted-average method to value inventory; calculate the cost of goods sold and the ending inventory value.

Name: Blanc Company
Industry: Retail corporation
Fiscal Period: Month ended February 29, 2020
Key Fact: Perpetual inventory system

Because the company uses the perpetual inventory system, record inventory purchases and sales as they occur.

All merchandise is purchased on account.

ANSWERS

Requirement 1

All sales are made on account.

	A	B	C	D	E
1	Feb. 1	Inventory (20,000 units × $2.50)	50,000		
2		Accounts payable		50,000	
3	Feb. 15	Inventory (25,000 units × $2.75)	68,750		
4		Accounts payable		68,750	
5	Feb. 20	Accounts receivable (35,000 × $3.25)	113,750		
6		Sales Revenue		113,750	
7		Cost of goods sold (20,000 × $2.50 + 15,000 × $2.75)	91,250		
8		Inventory		91,250	
9	Feb. 23	Inventory (10,000 units × $2.70)	27,000		
10		Accounts payable		27,000	
11	Feb. 25	Accounts payable	50,000		
12		Cash		50,000	
13	Feb. 27	Cash	75,000		
14		Accounts receivable		75,000	
15	Feb. 28	Operating expenses	11,000		
16		Accounts payable		11,000	
17	Feb. 29	Income tax expense (from Requirement 3)	4,025		
18		Tax payable		4,025	
19					

Use FIFO (oldest costs) to calculate cost of the 35,000 units sold:
Opening inventory: $0 (company just started)
From Feb. 1 purchase: $50,000 (20,000 units)
From Feb. 15 purchase: $68,750 (25,000 units)

Operating expenses were incurred ($11,000).

Income tax expense is 35% of net income before taxes (Sales revenue − Cost of goods sold − Operating expenses).

Requirement 2

FIFO − Ending inventory = $50,000 + $68,750 − $91,250 + $27,000 = $54,500

Inventory			
Feb. 1	50,000		
Feb. 15	68,750	91,250	Feb. 20
Feb. 23	27,000		
Balance			
Feb. 29	54,500		

FIFO ending inventory:
Beginning inventory + Purchases − Cost of goods sold

Beginning inventory must be the same amount as the inventory on the previous year's balance sheet.

Blanc Company just started, so there is no previous year's balance.

Ending inventory must be the same amount as the inventory on this year's balance sheet.

Sales revenue − Cost of goods sold

Gross profit − Operating expenses

IFRS require that income tax expense be presented separately from all other expenses.

Gross profit ÷ Sales revenue

Cost of goods sold ÷ Average inventory, where Average inventory = (Beginning inventory + Ending inventory) ÷ 2

Net income ÷ Sales revenue

Requirement 3

	A	B	C	D
1	**Blanc Company** Income Statement For the Month Ended February 29, 2020			
2	Sales revenue	$ 113,750		
3	Cost of goods sold	91,250		
4	Gross profit	$ 22,500		
5	Operating expenses	11,000		
6	Income before tax	$ 11,500		
7	Income tax expense (35%)	4,025		
8	Net income	$ 7,475		
9				

Requirement 4

Gross profit percentage = $22,500/$113,750 = 19.8%
Inventory turnover = $91,250/$54,500* = 1.7 times
Compared to the industry averages, Blanc Company's gross profit percentage is higher, which suggests that the company is able to sell its inventory at a profit. However, the inventory turnover is low, which means that the company has too much inventory on hand.

Requirement 5

$$\text{Weighted average—calculate the unit cost} = \frac{\text{Cost of goods available for sale}}{\text{Number of units available for sale}}$$

A new unit cost must be calculated after a purchase is made.

$$\text{Feb. 15—New unit cost} = \frac{\$50,000 \ (\text{Feb. 1}) + \$68,750 \ (\text{Feb. 15})}{20,000 + 25,000} = \$2.64 \text{ each}$$

Feb. 20—Cost of goods sold = 35,000 units sold × $2.64 = $92,400
Feb. 23—New unit cost is calculated as follows:
Units left after the sale on Feb. 20 (45,000 available − 35,000 sold) = 10,000 × $2.64 = $26,400
Units bought on Feb. 23 = 10,000 × $2.70 = $27,000
Total cost = $53,400 ($26,400 + $27,000) divided by 20,000 (number of units on hand) = $2.67

Therefore, ending inventory = $2.67 × 20,000 units = $53,400

_____

*Since the company just started, there is no beginning inventory and, therefore, an average is not used.

REVIEW

MyLab Accounting

Make the grade with MyLab Accounting: The Quick Quiz questions, Short Exercises, Exercises, and Problems (Group A) marked with a ⊕ can be found on MyLab Accounting. You can practise them as often as you want, and most feature step-by-step guided instructions to help you find the right answer.

QUICK QUIZ (ANSWERS APPEAR ON THE LAST PAGE OF THIS CHAPTER.)

Test your understanding of accounting for inventory by answering the following questions. Select the best choice from among the possible answers given.

1. Riverside Software began January with $3,500 of merchandise inventory. During January, Riverside made the following entries for its inventory transactions:

	A	B	C	D
1	Inventory	6,000		
2	Accounts Payable		6,000	
3	Accounts Receivable	7,200		
4	Sales Revenue		7,200	
5	Cost of Goods Sold	5,500		
6	Inventory		5,500	
7				

   What was the value of Riverside's inventory at the end of January?
   a. $0   c. $4,500
   b. $4,000   d. $5,500

2. Use the data in question 1. What is Riverside's gross profit for January?
   a. $0   c. $5,500
   b. $1,700   d. $7,200

3. When does the cost of inventory become an expense?
   a. When cash is collected from the customer
   b. When inventory is purchased from the supplier
   c. When payment is made to the supplier
   d. When inventory is delivered to a customer

   Questions 4 and 5 use the following facts. Leading Edge Frame Shop wants to know the effect of different inventory costing methods on its financial statements. The company uses the periodic inventory system. Inventory and purchases data for April follow.

		Units	Unit Cost	Total Cost
April 1	Beginning inventory	2,000	$10.00	$20,000
4	Purchase	1,000	10.60	10,600
9	Sale	(1,500)		

4. If Leading Edge uses the FIFO method, the cost of the ending inventory will be
   a. $10,600.   c. $15,300.
   b. $15,000.   d. $15,600.

5. If Leading Edge uses the weighted-average-cost method, cost of goods sold will be
   a. $10,600.   c. $15,300.
   b. $15,000.   d. $15,600.

6. In a period of rising prices
   a. gross profit under FIFO will be higher than under weighted-average cost.
   b. weighted-average-cost inventory will be greater than FIFO inventory.
   c. cost of goods sold under weighted-average cost will be less than under FIFO.
   d. net income under weighted-average cost will be higher than under FIFO.

7. The income statement for Heritage Health Foods shows gross profit of $144,000, operating expenses of $130,000, and cost of goods sold of $216,000. What is the amount of net sales revenue?
   a. $274,000
   b. $246,000
   c. $360,000
   d. $490,000

8. The phrase "net realizable value" as used in "the lower of cost and net realizable value" generally means
   a. original cost.
   b. market value.
   c. retail market price.
   d. liquidation price.

9. The sum of ending inventory and cost of goods sold is
   a. goods available for sale.
   b. net purchases.
   c. gross profit.
   d. beginning inventory.

10. The following data come from the inventory records of Dodge Company:

Net sales revenue	$620,000
Beginning inventory	60,000
Ending inventory	40,000
Net purchases	400,000

Based on these facts, the gross profit for Dodge Company is
a. $150,000.
b. $220,000.
c. $190,000.
d. some other amount ($_____).

11. Elizabeth Baker Cosmetics ended May with inventory of $20,000. Elizabeth Baker expects to end June with inventory of $15,000 after cost of goods sold of $90,000. How much inventory must Elizabeth Baker purchase during June to accomplish these results?
a. $85,000
b. $95,000
c. $105,000
d. Cannot be determined from the data given

12. Two financial ratios that clearly distinguish a discount chain such as Walmart from a high-end retailer such as Tiffany & Co. are the gross profit percentage and the rate of inventory turnover. Which set of relationships is most likely for Tiffany?

	Gross Profit Percentage	Inventory Turnover
a.	High	High
b.	Low	Low
c.	Low	High
d.	High	Low

13. Sales are $500,000, and cost of goods sold is $300,000. Beginning and ending inventories are $25,000 and $35,000, respectively. How many times did the company turn its inventory over during this period?
a. 16.7 times
b. 6.7 times
c. 8 times
d. 10 times

14. Tulsa Inc. reported the following data:

Freight-in	$ 20,000	Sales returns.........	$ 10,000
Purchases	205,000	Purchase returns.........	6,000
Beginning inventory	50,000	Sales revenue........	490,000
Purchase discounts........	4,000	Ending inventory	40,000

Tulsa's gross profit percentage is
a. 47.9%.
b. 52.1%.
c. 53.1%.
d. 54.0%.

15. Sales discounts should appear in the financial statements
a. as an addition to inventory.
b. as an addition to sales.
c. as an operating expense.
d. as a deduction from sales.

16. An error understated Rice Corporation's December 31, 2020, ending inventory by $40,000. What effect will this error have on total assets and net income for 2020?

	Assets	Net Income
a.	No effect	No effect
b.	No effect	Overstate
c.	Understate	Understate
d.	Understate	No effect

17. What is the effect of Rice Corporation's 2020 inventory error on net income for 2021?
a. No effect
b. Understate
c. Overstate

ACCOUNTING VOCABULARY

comparability Investors like to compare a company's financial statements from one year to the next. Therefore, a company must consistently use the same accounting method each year. (p. 248)

cost of goods sold Cost of the inventory the business has sold to customers. Also called *cost of sales*. (p. 231)

days' inventory outstanding Calculated as 365 days divided by inventory turnover. Indicates how many days it takes to sell inventory. (p. 251)

disclosure A company's financial statements should report enough information for users to make informed decisions about the company. (p. 248)

entire period Length of time during which beginning inventory and purchases are taken into account when calculating unit cost. (p. 241)

first-in, first-out (FIFO) cost method Inventory costing method by which the first costs into inventory are the first costs out to cost of goods sold. Ending inventory is based on the costs of the most recent purchases. (p. 242)

FOB (free on board) destination The inventory is included in the books of the seller. (p. 234)

FOB (free on board) shipping point The inventory is included in the books of the buyer. (p. 234)

gross margin Another name for *gross profit*. (p. 233)

gross profit Sales revenue minus cost of goods sold. Also called *gross margin*. (p. 233)

gross profit percentage Gross profit divided by net sales revenue. Also called the *gross margin percentage*. (p. 250)

inventory turnover Ratio of cost of goods sold to average inventory. Indicates how rapidly inventory is sold. (p. 250)

lower-of-cost-and-net-realizable-value (LCNRV) rule Requires that an asset be reported in the financial statements at whichever is lower—its historical cost or its net realizable value. (p. 248)

net realizable value (NRV) The amount a business could get if it sold the inventory less the costs of selling it. (p. 248)

periodic inventory system An inventory system in which the business does not keep a continuous record of the inventory on hand. Instead, at the end of the period, the business makes a physical count of the inventory on hand and applies the appropriate unit costs to determine the cost of the ending inventory.   (p. 234)

perpetual inventory system An inventory system in which the business keeps a continuous record for each inventory item to show the inventory on hand at all times.   (p. 234)

purchase allowance A decrease in the cost of purchases because the seller has granted the buyer a discount (an allowance) from the amount owed.   (p. 236)

purchase discount A decrease in the cost of purchases earned by making an early payment to the vendor.   (p. 236)

purchase return A decrease in the cost of purchases because the buyer returned the goods to the seller.   (p. 236)

sales discount Percentage reduction of sale price by the seller as an incentive for early payment before the due date. A typical way to express a sales discount is "2/10, n/30." This means the seller will grant a 2% discount if the invoice is paid within 10 days, or the full amount is due within 30 days.   (p. 238)

sales returns and allowances Merchandise returned for credit or refunds for services provided.   (p. 238)

specific identification cost method Inventory costing method based on the specific cost of particular units of inventory.   (p. 240)

weighted-average-cost method Inventory costing method based on the average cost of inventory for the period. Weighted-average-cost is determined by dividing the cost of goods available by the number of units available. Also called the *average cost method*.   (p. 240)

ASSESS YOUR PROGRESS

SHORT EXERCISES

S5-1 Journalize the following assumed transactions for Shoppers Drug Mart Corporation. Show amounts in millions.

- Cash purchases of inventory, $3,900 million
- Sales on account (including credit cards), $19,400 million
- Cost of goods sold (perpetual inventory system), $4,200 million
- Collections on account, $18,900 million

LEARNING OBJECTIVE ❶
Account for inventory transactions

S5-2 Riley Kilgo Inc. purchased inventory costing $100,000 and sold 80% of the goods for $240,000. All purchases and sales were on account. Kilgo later collected 20% of the accounts receivable.

1. Journalize these transactions for Kilgo, which uses the perpetual inventory system.
2. For these transactions, show what Kilgo will report for inventory, revenues, and expenses on its financial statements. Report gross profit on the appropriate statement.

LEARNING OBJECTIVE ❶
Account for inventory transactions

S5-3 Allstate Sporting Goods started April with an inventory of 10 sets of golf clubs that cost a total of $1,500. During April, Allstate purchased 20 sets of clubs for $3,200. At the end of the month, Allstate had six sets of golf clubs on hand. The store manager must select an inventory costing method, and he asks you to tell him both cost of goods sold and ending inventory under these two accounting methods, assuming the periodic system is used.

1. a. Weighted-average cost
   b. FIFO
2. If the store manager wants the most current cost for ending inventory, which method should he choose?

LEARNING OBJECTIVE ❷
Apply the weighted-average-cost and FIFO methods

S5-4 University Copy Centre Ltd. uses laser printers. The company started the year with 100 containers of ink (weighted-average cost of $9.20 each, FIFO cost of $9 each). During the year, University Copy Centre purchased 700 containers of ink at $10 each and sold 600 units for $20 each. The company paid operating expenses throughout the year, to a total of $3,000. University Copy Centre is not subject to income tax. Prepare University Copy Centre Ltd.'s income statement for the year ended December 31, 2020, under the weighted-average and FIFO inventory costing methods assuming periodic system is used. Include a complete statement heading.

LEARNING OBJECTIVE ❷
Apply the weighted-average-cost and FIFO methods

S5-5 This exercise should be used in conjunction with exercise S5-4. Now assume that University Copy Centre in exercise S5-4 is a corporation subject to an 18% income tax. Compute University Copy Centre's income tax expense under the weighted-average cost and FIFO inventory costing methods. Which method would you select to (a) maximize income before tax and (b) minimize income tax expense?

LEARNING OBJECTIVE ❷
Understand income tax effects of the inventory costing methods

LEARNING OBJECTIVE ❸

Understand accounting standards related to inventory

S5-6 You are opening a new bookstore catering to the students at Queen's University. Once you have established this operation, you plan to approach investors to support an expansion to locations in other Canadian university communities. Explain to your accountant what accounting standards you expect him to maintain in accounting for inventory and the reasons for your expectations.

LEARNING OBJECTIVE ❸

Apply the lower-of-cost-and-net-realizable-value rule to inventory

S5-7 It is December 31, 2020, end of year, and the controller of Garcia Corporation is applying the lower-of-cost-and-net-realizable-value (LCNRV) rule to inventories. Before any year-end adjustments Garcia has these data:

Cost of goods sold	$410,000
Historical cost of ending inventory, as determined by a physical count	60,000

Garcia determines that the net realizable value of ending inventory is $49,000. Show what Garcia should report for ending inventory and for cost of goods sold. Identify the financial statement where each item appears. How would investors and creditors know about the change in inventory value?

LEARNING OBJECTIVE ❹

Use ratio data to evaluate operations

S5-8 Assume Gildan Activewear Inc. made sales of $964.4 million during 2020. Cost of goods sold for the year totalled $655.3 million. At the end of 2019, Gildan's inventory stood at $200.7 million, and Gildan ended 2020 with inventory of $240 million. Compute Gildan's gross profit percentage and rate of inventory turnover for 2020. Assume the industry average is 35% for the gross profit percentage and 2.9 times for the inventory turnover. How do the company's ratios compare to the industry averages?

LEARNING OBJECTIVE ❺

Assess the effect of an inventory error—one year only

S5-9 CWD Inc. reported these figures for its fiscal year (amounts in millions):

Net sales	$1,700
Cost of goods sold	1,180
Ending inventory	360

Suppose CWD later learns that ending inventory was overstated by $10 million. What are CWD's correct amounts for (a) net sales, (b) ending inventory, (c) cost of goods sold, and (d) gross profit?

LEARNING OBJECTIVE ❺

Assess the effect of an inventory error on two years

S5-10 Suppose Staples Inc.'s $1.9 million cost of inventory at its fiscal year-end on January 31, 2019, was understated by $0.5 million.

1. Would 2019 reported gross profit of $5.2 million be overstated, understated, or correct? What would be the correct amount of gross profit for 2019?
2. Will 2020's gross profit of $5.6 million be overstated, understated, or correct? What would be the correct amount of gross profit for 2020?

LEARNING OBJECTIVE ❶

Record inventory transactions in the periodic system

S5-11 Capital Technologies Inc. began 2020 with inventory of $20,000. During the year, Capital purchased inventory costing $100,000 and sold goods for $140,000, with all transactions on account. Capital ended the year with inventory of $30,000. Journalize all the necessary transactions under the periodic inventory system.

LEARNING OBJECTIVE ❶

Compute cost of goods sold and prepare the income statement— periodic system

S5-12 Use the data in exercise S5-11 to do the following for Capital Technologies Inc.:

1. Post to the Inventory and Cost of Goods Sold accounts.
2. Compute cost of goods sold using the example given in Exhibit 5-4, Panel B.
3. Prepare the December 2020 income statement of Capital Technologies Inc. through gross profit.

EXERCISES

E5-13 Accounting records for Red Deer Tire Ltd. yield the following data for the year ended December 31, 2020 (amounts in thousands):

LEARNING OBJECTIVE ❶

Account for inventory transactions—perpetual and periodic systems

Inventory, December 31, 2019	$ 550
Purchases of inventory (on account)..	1,200
Sales of inventory—80% on account; 20% for cash (cost $900)	2,000
Inventory at FIFO cost, December 31, 2020..	850

Requirements

1. Journalize Red Deer Tire's inventory transactions for the year under (a) the perpetual system and (b) the periodic system. Show all amounts in thousands. Use Exhibit 5-4 as a model, on page 237.
2. What differences do you notice in the journal entries between the perpetual system and the periodic system?
3. Report ending inventory, sales, cost of goods sold, and gross profit on the appropriate financial statement (amounts in thousands), assuming the perpetual inventory system is used.

E5-14 Langley Inc. inventory records for a particular development program show the following at October 31, 2020:

LEARNING OBJECTIVES ❶❷

Analyze inventory transactions—perpetual system

Oct.	1	Beginning inventory	5 units @	$150 =	$ 750
	15	Purchase..................................	11 units @	160 =	1,760
	26	Purchase..................................	5 units @	170 =	850

At October 31, ten of these programs are on hand. Langley uses the perpetual inventory system.

Requirements

1. Journalize for Langley:
   a. Total October purchases in one summary entry. All purchases were on credit.
   b. Total October sales and cost of goods sold in two summary entries. The selling price was $500 per unit, and all sales were on credit. Langley uses the FIFO inventory method.
2. Under FIFO, how much gross profit would Langley earn on these transactions? What is the FIFO cost of Langley's ending inventory?

E5-15 Use the data for Langley Inc. in exercise E5-14 to answer the following.

LEARNING OBJECTIVES ❶❷

Determine inventory amounts by three methods—perpetual system—and compare net income

Requirements

1. Compute cost of goods sold and ending inventory, using each of the following methods:
   a. Specific unit cost, with two $150 units, three $160 units, and five $170 units still on hand at the end
   b. Weighted-average cost
   c. First-in, first-out cost
2. Which method would be most relevant to producing the highest net income? Why?

E5-16 Use the data in exercise E5-14 to illustrate Langley's income tax advantage from using weighted-average cost over FIFO cost. Sales revenue is $6,000, operating expenses are $1,100, and the income tax rate is 25%. How much in taxes would Langley save by using the weighted-average-cost method versus FIFO?

LEARNING OBJECTIVE ❷

Compute the tax advantage of weighted-average cost over FIFO

LEARNING OBJECTIVES ❶❷❸

Determine inventory values—FIFO versus weighted-average cost–perpetual—and apply accounting standards

E5-17 MusicBiz.net Ltd. specializes in sound equipment. Because each inventory item is expensive, MusicBiz uses a perpetual inventory system. Company records indicate the following data for a line of speakers:

Date	Item	Quantity	Unit Cost	Sale Price
June 1	Balance	6	$ 95	
8	Sale	3		$155
10	Purchase	11	100	
30	Sale	5		160

Requirements

1. Determine the amounts that MusicBiz should report for cost of goods sold and ending inventory in the following two ways:

   a. FIFO

   b. Weighted-average cost

2. MusicBiz uses the FIFO method. Prepare MusicBiz's income statement for the month ended June 30, 2020, reporting gross profit. Operating expenses totalled $319, and the income tax rate was 25%.

3. Music Biz is thinking of changing inventory costing methods from FIFO to weighted-average cost. Are they allowed to make this change? Briefly explain.

LEARNING OBJECTIVES ❶❷

Measure gross profit—FIFO versus weighted-average cost, falling prices–periodic system

E5-18 Suppose a Johnson store in Ottawa, Ontario, ended November 2020 with 800,000 units of merchandise that cost an average of $8 each. Suppose the store then sold 600,000 units for $5.0 million during December. Further, assume the store made two large purchases during December as follows:

December 6	100,000 units @ $7 =	$ 700,000
26	400,000 units @ 6 =	2,400,000

1. At December 31, the store manager needs to know the store's gross profit under both FIFO and weighted-average cost. Supply this information. Johnson uses the periodic inventory system.

2. What caused the FIFO and weighted-average cost gross profit figures to differ?

LEARNING OBJECTIVE ❷

Manage income under the weighted-average-cost method

E5-19 Deitrick Guitar Company is nearing the end of its worst year ever. With three weeks until year-end, it appears that net income for the year will have decreased by 20% from the previous year. Jim Deitrick, the president and principal shareholder, is distressed with the year's results.

Deitrick asks you, the financial vice-president, to come up with a way to increase the business's net income. Inventory quantities are a little higher than normal because sales have been slow during the last few months. Deitrick uses the weighted-average-cost inventory method, and inventory costs have risen dramatically during the latter part of the year.

Requirement

Write a memorandum to Jim Deitrick to explain how the company can increase its net income for the year. Explain your reasoning in detail. Deitrick is a man of integrity, so your plan must be completely ethical.

LEARNING OBJECTIVES ❶❷❸

Identify effects of the inventory methods and evaluate operations

E5-20 This exercise tests your understanding of accounting for inventory. Provide a word or phrase that best fits the description. Assume that the cost of inventory is rising.

_____ 1. Generally associated with saving income taxes.

_____ 2. Results in a cost of ending inventory that is close to the current cost of replacing the inventory.

_____ 3. Used to account for automobiles, jewellery, and art objects.

_____ 4. Maximizes reported income.

_____ 5. Inventory system that keeps a running record of all goods bought, sold, and on hand.

_____ **6.** Characteristic that enables investors to compare a company's financial statements from one period to the next.

_____ **7.** Writes inventory down when net realizable value drops below historical cost.

_____ **8.** Key indicator of a company's ability to sell inventory at a profit.

_____ **9.** A decrease in the buyer's cost of inventory earned by paying quickly.

E5-21 Tavistock Inc. uses a perpetual inventory system. Tavistock has these account balances at December 31, 2020, prior to making the year-end adjustments:

LEARNING OBJECTIVE ❸

Apply the lower-of-cost-and-net-realizable-value rule to inventories

Inventory		Cost of Goods Sold		Sales Revenue	
Beg. bal. 12,400					
End bal. 14,000		Bal. 78,000		Bal. 125,000	

A year ago, the net realizable value of Tavistock's ending inventory was $13,000, which exceeded cost of $12,400. Tavistock has determined that the net realizable value of the December 31, 2020, ending inventory is $12,000.

Requirement

Prepare Tavistock Inc.'s 2020 income statement through gross profit to show how the company would apply the lower-of-cost-and-net-realizable-value rule to its inventories.

E5-22 Supply the missing income statement amounts for each of the following companies (amounts in millions, at January 31, 2020):

LEARNING OBJECTIVE ❶

Determine amounts for the income statement

Company	Net Sales	Beginning Inventory	Purchases	Ending Inventory	Cost of Goods Sold	Gross Profit
Myers Confectionary	$543	$29	$470	$24	(a)	(b)
Canada Computers	74	7	(c)	8	(d)	19
Best Taste Beverages	(e)	(f)	16	2	16	19
Value for $	31	2	24	(g)	23	(h)

Prepare the income statement for Myers Confectionary Ltd., in millions of dollars, for the year ended January 31, 2020. Compute cost of goods sold using the example given in Exhibit 5-4, Panel B. Myers's operating and other expenses for the year were $204. Ignore income tax.

E5-23 Refer to the data in Exercise E5-22. Compute all ratio values to answer the following questions:
- Which company has the highest gross profit percentage? Which company has the lowest?
- Which company has the highest rate of inventory turnover? Which company has the lowest?

LEARNING OBJECTIVE ❹

Evaluate profitability and inventory turnover

Based on your figures, which company appears to be the most profitable?

E5-24 Suppose a company you are considering as an investment made sales of $54.8 billion in the year ended December 31, 2020. Collections from customers totalled $55 billion. The company began the year with $6.6 billion in inventories and ended with $7.9 billion. During the year, purchases of inventory added up to $39.8 billion. Of the purchases, the company paid $37.9 billion to suppliers.

As an investor searching for a good investment, you would identify several critical pieces of information about the company's operations during the year.

Using the facts provided, identify or calculate the information that is relevant to deciding whether to invest in this company, and specify how each piece is relevant to your decision.

LEARNING OBJECTIVE ❹

Measure and evaluate gross profit and inventory turnover—periodic

LEARNING OBJECTIVES ④⑤

Correct an inventory error and measure profitability

E5-25 Dijon Mustard Ltée. reported the following comparative income statement for the years ended September 30, 2019 and 2020:

	A	B	C	D	E	F
1	**Dijon Mustard Ltée.** Income Statement For the Years Ended September 30					
2			2020		2019	
3	Sales revenue		$ 194,000		$ 158,000	
4	Cost of goods sold					
5	Beginning inventory	$ 23,000		$ 16,000		
6	Purchases	97,000		86,000		
7	Goods available for sale	120,000		102,000		
8	Ending inventory	(21,000)		(23,000)		
9	Cost of goods sold		99,000		79,000	
10	Gross profit		95,000		79,000	
11	Operating expenses		20,000		20,000	
12	Net income		$ 75,000		$ 59,000	
13						

Dijon's shareholders are thrilled by the company's boost in sales and net income during 2020. Then they discover that the 2019 ending inventory was understated by $10,000. How well did Dijon really perform in 2020, as compared with 2019?

LEARNING OBJECTIVES ①②

Compare ending inventory and cost of goods sold for all three inventory costing methods—periodic system

E5-26 Suppose a technology company's inventory records for a particular computer chip indicate the following at October 31:

Oct.	1	Beginning inventory	5 units @ $160 =	$ 800
	8	Purchase...	4 units @ 160 =	640
	15	Purchase...	11 units @ 170 =	1,870
	26	Purchase...	5 units @ 180 =	900

The physical count of inventory at October 31 indicates that 8 units of inventory are on hand.

Requirements

Compute ending inventory and cost of goods sold using each of the following methods, using the periodic inventory system. Round all amounts to the nearest dollar.
1. Specific unit cost, assuming four $160 units and four $170 units are on hand
2. Weighted-average cost
3. First-in, first-out cost
4. Which inventory costing method resulted in the highest cost of ending inventory? Explain your answer.

LEARNING OBJECTIVES ①②

Journalize inventory transactions in the periodic system; compute cost of goods sold

E5-27 Use the data in exercise E5-26 to journalize the following for the periodic system:

1. Total October purchases in one summary entry. All purchases were on credit.
2. Total October sales in a summary entry. Assume that the selling price was $300 per unit and that all sales were on credit.
3. October 31 entries for inventory. The company uses weighted-average cost. Post to the Cost of Goods Sold T-account to show how this amount is determined. Label each item in the account.
4. Show the computation of cost of goods sold using the example given in Exhibit 5-4, Panel B.
5. Assume it is year end. Prepare the journal entries to update the inventory records.

E5-28 Assume a Roots outlet store began August 2020 with 40 units of inventory that cost $30 each. The sale price of these units was $60. During August, the store completed the following inventory transactions.

LEARNING OBJECTIVES ❶❷❹

Compute cost of goods sold and gross profit on sales—periodic system—and evaluate gross profit

		Units	Unit Cost	Unit Sale Price
Aug. 3	Sale	16	$30	$60
8	Purchase	70	31	62
11	Sale	24	30	60
19	Sale	8	31	62
24	Sale	30	31	62
30	Purchase	28	32	73
31	Sale	15	31	62

Requirements

1. Determine the store's cost of goods sold for August under the periodic inventory system. Assume the FIFO method.
2. Compute gross profit for August.
3. Last year, gross profit was $3,150. What could management do to improve gross profit?

E5-29 Accounting records for Cookies for You Ltd. yield the following data for the year ended December 31, 2020 (amounts in thousands):

LEARNING OBJECTIVE ❶

Record transactions in the periodic system; report inventory items in the financial statements

Inventory, December 31, 2019	$ 410
Purchases of inventory (on account)	3,200
Sales of inventory—80% on account; 20% for cash	4,830
Inventory at the lower of FIFO cost and net realizable value, December 31, 2020	600

Requirements

1. Journalize Cookies for You's inventory transactions for the year under the periodic system. Show all amounts in thousands.
2. Report ending inventory, sales, cost of goods sold, and gross profit on the appropriate financial statement (amounts in thousands). Show the computation of cost of goods sold.
3. Why would Cookies for You choose the periodic inventory system instead of the perpetual inventory system?

E5-30 On April 3, Parker Company sold $5,000 of merchandise to Wheeler Corporation, terms 2/10, n/30, FOB shipping point. Parker Company's cost of sales for this merchandise was $4,000. The merchandise left Parker Company's facility on April 4 and arrived at Wheeler Corporation on April 10. Wheeler Corporation paid the invoice for the merchandise on April 11.

LEARNING OBJECTIVE ❶

Account for inventory

Requirements

1. Prepare the journal entries for Parker Company for the sale of the merchandise, the cost of the sale, and the related receipt of payment from Wheeler Corporation. Assume that Wheeler Corporation takes the discount if payment is within the discount period. (You do not need to record any estimated returns/refunds for this exercise.)
2. Indicate which company (Parker Company or Wheeler Corporation) owns the merchandise at the end of each of the following dates:
   a. April 3
   b. April 4
   c. April 10

LEARNING OBJECTIVE ❷

Make inventory policy decisions

🌐 **E5-31** For each of the following situations, identify the inventory method that you would use or, given the use of a particular method, state the strategy that you would follow to accomplish your goal:

a. Inventory costs are increasing. Your company uses weighted-average cost and is having an unexpectedly good year. It is near year-end, and you need to keep net income from increasing too much in order to save on income tax.

b. Suppliers of your inventory are threatening a labour strike, and it may be difficult for your company to obtain inventory. This situation could increase your income taxes.

c. Inventory costs are decreasing, and your company's board of directors wants to minimize income taxes.

d. Inventory costs are increasing, and the company prefers to report high income.

e. Inventory costs have been stable for several years, and you expect costs to remain stable for the indefinite future. (Give the reason for your choice of method.)

LEARNING OBJECTIVES ❶❷

Assess the impact of a year-end
purchase of inventory—periodic

🌐 **E5-32** Suppose Holt Renfrew, the specialty retailer, had these records for ladies' evening gowns during 2020.

Beginning inventory (30 @ $1,000)..	$ 30,000
Purchase in February (25 @ $1,100)...	27,500
Purchase in June (60 @ $1,200)...	72,000
Purchase in December (25 @ $1,300)	32,500
Goods available	$162,000

Assume sales of evening gowns totalled 130 units during 2020 and that Holt uses the weighted-average-cost method under the periodic inventory system to account for inventory. The income tax rate is 30%.

Requirements

1. Compute Holt's cost of goods sold for evening gowns in 2020.

2. Compute what cost of goods sold would have been if Holt had purchased enough inventory in December—at $1,300 per evening gown—to keep year-end inventory at the same level it was at the beginning of the year, 30 units.

LEARNING OBJECTIVE ❹

Evaluate a company's profitability

🌐 **E5-33** Cheri's Beauty Products Ltd. reported the figures below at December 31, 2020, 2019 and 2018. The business has declared bankruptcy. You have been asked to review the business and explain why it failed.

	A	B	C	D	E
1	**Cheri's Beauty Products Ltd.** Statement of Income For the Years Ended December 31, 2020, 2019, and 2018				
2	*(Thousands)*	**2020**	**2019**	**2018**	
3	Sales	$ 41.0	$ 39.5	$ 37.1	
4	Cost of sales	32.7	30.9	28.9	
5	Selling expenses	8.0	7.2	6.8	
6	Other expenses	0.4	1.0	0.8	
7	Net income (net loss)	$ (0.1)	$ 0.4	$ 0.6	
8	Additional data:				
9	Ending inventory	9.2	8.6	7.7	
10					

Requirement

Evaluate the trend of Cheri's Beauty Products's results of operations during 2018 through 2020. Consider the trends of sales, gross profit, and net income. Track the gross profit percentage (to three decimal places) and the rate of inventory turnover (to one decimal place) in each year—2018, 2019, and 2020. The ending inventory value for 2017 is $7.0. Also, discuss the role that selling expenses must have played in Cheri's Beauty Products's difficulties.

PROBLEMS (GROUP A)

P5-34A Assume a Watercrest Sports outlet store began October 2020 with 47 pairs of water skis that cost the store $38 each. The sale price of these water skis was $67. During October, the store completed these inventory transactions:

		Units	Unit Cost	Unit Sale Price
Oct. 2	Sale	19	$38	$67
9	Purchase	83	40	
13	Sale	28	38	67
18	Sale	10	40	68
22	Sale	34	40	68
29	Purchase	24	42	

LEARNING OBJECTIVES ❶❷❸
Determine inventory method, cost of goods sold—perpetual system—and apply accounting standards to inventory

Requirements
1. The preceding data are taken from the store's perpetual inventory records. Which cost method does the store use? Explain how you arrived at your answer.
2. Determine the store's cost of goods sold for October. Also compute gross profit for October.
3. What is the cost of the store's October 31 inventory of water skis?
4. Assume that ending inventory declined by $200. What value would the company report as inventory on the balance sheet? Include in your answer why it chose that value. How would it account for this difference?

P5-35A Best Buy purchases merchandise inventory by the crate; each crate of inventory is a unit. The fiscal year of Best Buy ends each February 28.

Assume you are dealing with a single Best Buy store in Toronto, Ontario, and that the store experienced the following: The store began fiscal year 2020 with an inventory of 20,000 units that cost a total of $1,000,000. During the year, the store purchased merchandise on account as follows:

LEARNING OBJECTIVES ❶❷❹
Account for inventory in a perpetual system and compute gross profit percentage

April (30,000 units @ cost of $60)	$1,800,000
August (50,000 units @ cost of $64)	3,200,000
November (60,000 units @ cost of $70)	4,200,000
Total purchases	$9,200,000

Cash payments on account totalled $8,800,000.

During fiscal year 2020, the store sold 150,000 units of merchandise for $14,400,000. Cash accounted for $5,000,000 of this, and the balance was on account. Best Buy uses the FIFO method for inventories.

Operating expenses for the year were $4,000,000. The store paid 80% in cash and accrued the rest as accrued liabilities. The store accrued income tax at the rate of 33%.

Requirements
1. Make summary journal entries to record the store's transactions for the year ended February 28, 2020. Best Buy uses a perpetual inventory system.
2. Prepare a T-account to show the activity in the Inventory account.
3. Prepare the store's income statement for the year ended February 28, 2020. Show totals for gross profit, income before tax, and net income.
4. Compute the gross profit percentage. How does this compare with last year's gross profit percentage of 36%? What are some possible reasons for the change?

LEARNING OBJECTIVES ❶❷

Measure cost of goods sold and ending inventory—perpetual system—and determine which method to use

P5-36A Assume an outlet of The Runner's Store began August 2020 with 40 pairs of running shoes that cost the store $40 each. The sale price of these shoes was $70. During August, the store completed these inventory transactions:

		Units	Unit Cost	Unit Sale Price
Aug. 3	Sale	16		$70
8	Purchase	80	41	
11	Sale	24		70
19	Sale	9		72
24	Sale	30		72
30	Purchase	18	42	

Requirements

1. Determine the store's cost of goods sold, gross profit, and ending inventory using (a) FIFO and (b) weighted-average assuming the perpetual system is used.
2. How would your answer change under (a) FIFO and (b) weighted-average cost if the periodic system was used?
3. Using the facts provided, identify the information that is relevant in determining which inventory system to use to keep track of the store's inventory. Specify how each information item is relevant to your decision.

LEARNING OBJECTIVES ❶❷

Compute and compare inventory by two methods—perpetual system—and prepare an income statement

P5-37A Army-Navy Surplus Ltd. began March 2020 with 70 tents that cost $20 each. During the month, Army-Navy Surplus made the following purchases at cost:

March	4	100 tents @ $22 = $2,200
	19	160 tents @ 24 = 3,840
	25	40 tents @ 25 = 1,000

Army-Navy Surplus sold 320 tents (150 tents on March 22 and 170 tents on March 30), and at March 31 the ending inventory consists of 50 tents. The sale price of each tent was $45.

Requirements

1. Determine the cost of goods sold and ending inventory amounts for March under (a) weighted-average cost and (b) FIFO cost assuming the perpetual system is used. Round weighted-average cost per unit to four decimal places, and round all other amounts to the nearest dollar.
2. Explain why cost of goods sold is highest under weighted-average cost. Be specific.
3. Prepare Army-Navy Surplus's income statement for March 2020. Report gross profit. Operating expenses totalled $4,000. Army-Navy Surplus uses weighted-average costing for inventory. The income tax rate is 21%.

LEARNING OBJECTIVES ❶❷

Prepare a partial income statement using different inventory costing methods

P5-38A The records of Armstrong Aviation Supply Inc. include the following accounts for inventory of aviation fuel at December 31, 2020:

			Inventory	
Jan.	1	Balance	700 units @ $7.00	4,900
Mar.	6	Purchase	300 units @ 7.05	2,115
June	22	Purchase	8,400 units @ 7.50	63,000
Oct.	4	Purchase	500 units @ 8.50	4,250

		Sales Revenue	
	Dec. 31	9,000 units	127,800

Requirements

1. Prepare a partial income statement through gross profit under the weighted-average-cost and FIFO methods assuming the periodic system is used. Round weighted-average cost per unit to four decimal places and all other amounts to the nearest dollar.
2. Which inventory method would you use to minimize income tax? Explain why this method causes income tax to be the lowest.

P5-39A AMC Trade Mart has recently had lacklustre sales. The rate of inventory turnover has dropped, and the merchandise is gathering dust. At the same time, competition has forced AMC's suppliers to lower the prices that AMC will pay when it replaces its inventory. It is now December 31, 2020, and the current net realizable value of AMC's ending inventory is $80,000 below what AMC actually paid for the goods, which was $190,000. Before any adjustments at the end of the period, the Cost of Goods Sold account has a balance of $780,000.

Identify and explain how accounting standards apply to inventory. Include in your answer how the information that is relevant to inventory is reported in AMC's financial statements.

LEARNING OBJECTIVE ❸

Apply the lower-cost-and-net-realizable-value rule to inventories—perpetual system

P5-40A Chocolate Treats Ltd. and Coffee Bars Inc. are both specialty food chains. The two companies reported these figures, in thousands:

LEARNING OBJECTIVE ❹

Use gross profit percentage and inventory turnover to evaluate two companies

	A	B	C	D
1	**Chocolate Treats Ltd.** Statement of Operations			
2		**Fiscal Year**		
3	*(Thousands)*	**2020**	**2019**	
4	**Revenues:**			
5	Net sales	$ 543	$ 708	
6	Costs and Expenses:			
7	Cost of goods sold	475	598	
8	General and administrative expenses	68	55	
9				

	A	B	C	D
1	**Chocolate Treats Ltd.** Balance Sheet			
2		**January 31,**		
3	*(Thousands)*	**2020**	**2019**	
4	**Assets**			
5	Current assets:			
6	Cash and cash equivalents	$ 17	$ 28	
7	Receivables	27	30	
8	Inventories	24	29	
9				

	A	B	C	D
1	**Coffee Bars Inc.** Statement of Earnings			
2		**Fiscal Year**		
3	*(Thousands)*	**2020**	**2019**	
4	**Net sales**	$ 7,787	$ 6,369	
5	Cost of goods sold	3,179	2,605	
6	Selling, general, and administrative expenses	2,948	2,363	
7				

	A	B	C	D
1	**Coffee Bars Inc.** Balance Sheet			
2		**Year End**		
3	*(Thousands)*	**2020**	**2019**	
4	**Assets**			
5	Current assets:			
6	Cash and temporary investments	$ 313	$ 174	
7	Receivables, net	224	191	
8	Inventories	636	546	
9				

Requirements

1. Compute the gross profit percentage and the rate of inventory turnover for Chocolate Treats and for Coffee Bars for 2020.
2. Based on these statistics, which company looks more profitable? Why? What other expense category should we consider in evaluating these two companies?

LEARNING OBJECTIVES ❹❺

Correct inventory errors over a three-year period and analyze net income

P5-41A Columbia Video Sales Ltd. reported the following data. The shareholders are very happy with Columbia's steady increase in net income.

Auditors discovered that the ending inventory for 2018 was understated by $1 million and that the ending inventory for 2019 was also understated by $1 million. The ending inventory for 2020 was correct.

	A	B	C	D	E	F	G	H
1	**Columbia Video Sales Ltd.** Income Statements for the Years Ended							
2	*(Amounts in millions)*		**2020**		**2019**		**2018**	
3	Net sales revenue		$ 36		$ 33		$ 30	
4	Cost of goods sold:							
5	Beginning inventory	$ 6		$ 5		$ 4		
6	Purchases	26		24		22		
7	Goods available for sale	32		29		26		
8	Less: Ending inventory	(7)		(6)		(5)		
9	Cost of goods sold		25		23		21	
10	Gross profit		11		10		9	
11	Total operating expenses		8		8		8	
12	Net income		$ 3		$ 2		$ 1	
13								

Requirements

1. Show corrected income statements for each of the three years.
2. How much did these assumed corrections add to or take away from Columbia's total net income over the three-year period? How did the corrections affect the trend of net income?
3. Will Columbia's shareholders still be happy with the company's trend of net income? Give a reason for your answer.

LEARNING OBJECTIVES ❶❹

Account for sales, sales discounts, and sales returns, and compute gross profit percentage

P5-42A Chic Interiors reported the following transactions in November 2020:

Nov 3 Sold merchandise on account to Ella Barron, $1,500, terms 1/10, n/30.
5 Sold merchandise on account to Amanda O'Connor, $2,500, terms 2/10, n30.
8 Bought $1,600 of merchandise inventory on account. Paid $150 for the freight fee on the inventory.
10 Collected payment from Ella Barron for the November 3 sale.
13 Amanda O'Connor returned $500 of the merchandise bought on November 5.
14 Collected payment from Amanda O'Connor for the balance of the November 5 sale.
15 Returned $50 of inventory that was defective from the November 8 purchase.
26 Paid the account payable from the November 8 purchase.
30 Physical count indicated that Chic Interiors had $250 in ending inventory. The balance in beginning inventory is $400.

Requirements

1. Record the transactions for the month of November assuming the *periodic* inventory system is used.
2. Prepare a partial income statement through gross profit for the month ending November 30, 2020.
3. Assume it is the company's year-end. Prepare the end-of-period entries to update inventory and record cost of goods sold.
4. Assume last month's gross profit percentage was 48%. Has this improved or declined in November? What likely accounts for this change?

PROBLEMS (GROUP B)

P5-43B Assume a Cross Country Sports outlet store began March 2020 with 49 pairs of running shoes that cost the store $35 each. The sale price of these shoes was $70. During March, the store completed these inventory transactions:

LEARNING OBJECTIVES ❶❷❸

Determine inventory method, cost of goods sold–perpetual system– and apply accounting standards to inventory

		Units	Unit Cost	Unit Sale Price
Mar. 2	Sale	17	$35	$70
9	Purchase	83	37	
13	Sale	32	35	70
18	Sale	12	37	71
22	Sale	34	37	71
29	Purchase	18	39	

Requirements

1. The preceding data are taken from the store's perpetual inventory records. Which cost method does the store use? Explain how you arrived at your answer.
2. Determine the store's cost of goods sold for March. Also compute gross profit for March.
3. What is the cost of the store's March 31 inventory of running shoes?
4. Assume that ending inventory declined by $150. What value would the company report as inventory on the balance sheet? How would it account for this difference?

P5-44B Italian Leather Goods Inc. began 2020 with an inventory of 50,000 units that cost $1,500,000. During the year, the store purchased merchandise on account as follows:

LEARNING OBJECTIVES ❶❷❹

Account for inventory in a perpetual system and compute gross profit percentage

March (40,000 units @ cost of $32)	$1,280,000
August (40,000 units @ cost of $34)	1,360,000
October (180,000 units @ cost of $35)	6,300,000
Total purchases	$8,940,000

Cash payments on account totalled $8,610,000.

During 2020, the company sold 260,000 units of merchandise for $12,900,000. Cash accounted for $4,700,000 of this, and the balance was on account. Italian Leather Goods uses the FIFO method for inventories.

Operating expenses for the year were $2,080,000. Italian Leather Goods paid 60% in cash and accrued the rest as accrued liabilities. The company accrued income tax at the rate of 32%.

Requirements

1. Make summary journal entries to record the Italian Leather Goods transactions for the year ended December 31, 2020. The company uses a perpetual inventory system.
2. Prepare a T-account to show the activity in the Inventory account.
3. Prepare the Italian Leather Goods Inc. income statement for the year ended December 31, 2020. Show totals for gross profit, income before tax, and net income.
4. Compute the gross profit percentage. How does this compare with last year's gross profit percentage of 35%? What are some possible reasons for the change?

LEARNING OBJECTIVES ❶❷

Measure cost of goods sold and ending inventory—perpetual system—and determine which inventory method to use

P5-45B Whitewater Sports Ltd. began July 2020 with 50 backpacks that cost $19 each. The sale price of each backpack was $36. During July, Whitewater completed these inventory transactions:

			Units	Unit Cost	Unit Sale Price
July	2	Purchase...	12	$20	
	8	Sale	37		$36
	13	Sale	13		36
		Sale	4		37
	17	Purchase...	24	20	
	22	Sale	15		37

Requirements

1. Determine the store's cost of goods sold, gross profit, and ending inventory using (a) FIFO and (b) weighted-average assuming the perpetual system is used.
2. How would your answer change under (a) FIFO and (b) weighted-average cost if the periodic system was used?
3. Using the facts provided, identify the information that is relevant in determining which inventory system to use to keep track of the store's inventory. Specify how each information item is relevant to your decision.

LEARNING OBJECTIVES ❶❷

Compute and compare inventory by two methods—perpetual system— and prepare an income statement

P5-46B Spice Inc. began October 2020 with 100 shirts that cost $76 each. During October, the store made the following purchases at cost:

Oct.	3		200 @ $81 = $16,200
	12		90 @ 82 = 7,380
	24		240 @ 85 = 20,400

Spice sold 500 shirts (320 shirts on October 18 and 180 shirts on October 28) and ended October with 130 shirts. The sale price of each shirt was $130.

Requirements

1. Determine the cost of goods sold and ending inventory amounts by the weighted-average-cost and FIFO cost methods assuming the perpetual system is used. Round weighted-average cost per unit to three decimal places, and round all other amounts to the nearest dollar.
2. Explain why cost of goods sold is highest under weighted-average cost. Be specific.
3. Prepare Spice's income statement for October 2020. Report gross profit. Operating expenses totalled $10,000. Spice uses the weighted-average-cost method for inventory. The income tax rate is 23%.

LEARNING OBJECTIVES ❶❷

Prepare a partial income statement using different inventory costing methods

P5-47B The records of Sonic Sound Systems Inc. include the following for cases of CDs at December 31, 2020:

Inventory			
Jan.	1 Balance	300 cases @ $300	121,500
		100 cases @ 315	
May 19 Purchase		600 cases @ 335	201,000
Aug. 12 Purchase		400 cases @ 350	140,000
Oct. 4 Purchase		700 cases @ 370	259,000

Sales Revenue			
	Dec. 31	1,800 cases	910,000

Requirements

1. Prepare a partial income statement through gross profit under the weighted-average-cost and FIFO cost methods assuming the periodic system is used. Round weighted-average cost per unit to four decimal places and all other amounts to the nearest dollar.
2. Which inventory method would you use to report the highest net income? Explain why this method produces the highest reported income.

P5-48B Westside Copiers Ltd. has recently been plagued with lacklustre sales. The rate of inventory turnover has dropped, and some of the company's merchandise is gathering dust. At the same time, competition has forced some of Westside's suppliers to lower the prices that Westside will pay when it replaces its inventory. It is now December 31, 2020. The current net realizable value of Westside's ending inventory is $6,800,000, which is far less than the amount Westside paid for the goods, $8,900,000. Before any adjustments at the end of the period, Westside's Cost of Goods Sold account has a balance of $36,400,000.

Identify and explain how accounting standards apply to inventory. Include in your answer how the information that is relevant to inventory is reported in Westside's financial statements.

P5-49B Trans Canada Motors Ltd. and X Country Trucks Inc. are competitors. The companies reported the following amounts, in millions. In January 2020, you wish to make an investment in one of these companies. Results for 2019 are not yet available.

LEARNING OBJECTIVE ❸

Apply the lower-of-cost-and-net-realizable-value rule to inventories—perpetual system

LEARNING OBJECTIVE ❹

Use gross profit percentage and inventory turnover to evaluate two leading companies

	A	B	C	D	E
1	**Trans Canada Motors Ltd.** Statement of Earnings				
2			Fiscal Years		
3	*(Amounts in millions)*	2020	2019	2018	
4	Net sales	$ 84.2	$ 73.6	$ 68.9	
5	Cost of sales	63.4	55.2	52.6	
6	Selling, general, and administrative expenses	12.2	11.3	11.2	
7					

	A	B	C	D	E
1	**Trans Canada Motors Ltd.** Balance Sheet				
2			Year-End		
3	*(Amounts in millions)*	2020	2019	2018	
4	Assets				
5	Cash and cash equivalents	$ 11.3	$ 16.4	$ 13.9	
6	Accounts receivable	13.4	10.9	9.9	
7	Inventories	8.0	7.8	6.9	
8					

	A	B	C	D	E
1	**X Country Trucks Inc.** Statement of Operations				
2			Fiscal Years		
3	*(Amounts in millions)*	2020	2019	2018	
4	Net sales	$ 24.0	$ 19.3	$ 13.9	
5	Cost of sales	15.9	13.7	9.9	
6	Selling, general, and administrative expenses	3.0	2.4	1.9	
7					

	A	B	C	D	E
1	**X Country Trucks Inc.** Balance Sheet				
2			Year-End		
3	*(Amounts in millions)*	2020	2019	2018	
4	Assets				
5	Cash and cash equivalents	$ 9.4	$ 6.4	$ 3.5	
6	Accounts receivable	6.0	1.3	0.9	
7	Inventories	0.4	0.3	0.2	
8					

Requirements

1. Compute both companies' gross profit percentage and their rates of inventory turnover during 2020 and 2019.
2. Can you tell from these statistics which company should be more profitable in percentage terms? Why? What other important category of expenses do the gross profit percentage and the inventory turnover ratio fail to consider?

LEARNING OBJECTIVES ④⑤

Correct inventory errors over a three-year period and analyze net income

P5-50B The accounting records of Oriental Rugs show these data (in thousands).

As the auditor, you discovered that the ending inventory for 2018 was overstated by $100,000 and that the ending inventory for 2019 was understated by $50,000. The ending inventory at December 31, 2020, was correct.

	A	B	C	D	E	F	G	H
1	**Oriental Rugs** Income Statements for the Years Ended							
2	*(Amounts in thousands)*		2020		2019		2018	
3	Net sales revenue		$ 1,400		$ 1,200		$ 1,100	
4	Cost of goods sold:							
5	Beginning inventory	$ 400		$ 300		$ 200		
6	Purchases	800		700		600		
7	Goods available for sale	1,200		1,000		800		
8	Less ending inventory	(500)		(400)		(300)		
9	Cost of goods sold		700		600		500	
10	Gross profit		700		600		600	
11	Total operating expenses		500		430		450	
12	Net income		$ 200		$ 170		$ 150	
13								

Requirements

1. Show correct income statements for each of the three years.
2. How much did these corrections add to, or take away from, Oriental Rugs's total net income over the three-year period? How did the corrections affect the trend of net income?
3. Will Oriental Rugs's shareholders still be happy with the company's trend of net income? Give a reason for your answer.

LEARNING OBJECTIVES ①④

Account for sales, sales discounts, and sales returns, and compute gross profit percentage

P5-51B Wolford Interiors reported the following transactions in June:

June 3   Sold merchandise on account to Maxine Holder, $1,000, terms 2/10, n/30. The cost of goods sold is $550.

5   Sold merchandise on account to Alexis Pinney, $2,600, terms 2/10, n/30. Cost of goods sold is $1,352.

8   Bought $1,800 of merchandise inventory on account. Paid $100 for the freight fee on the inventory.

10   Collected payment from Maxine Holder for the June 3 sale.

13   Alexis Pinney returned $500 of the merchandise bought on June 5.

14   Collected payment from Alexis Pinney for the balance of the June 5 sale.

16   Returned $100 of inventory that was defective from the June 8 purchase.

24   Paid the account payable from the June 8 purchase.

30   A physical count indicated that Wolford Interiors had $300 in ending inventory. The balance in beginning inventory was $350.

Requirements

1. Record the transactions for the month of June assuming the *periodic* inventory system is used.
2. Prepare a partial income statement through gross profit for the month ending June 30, 2020.
3. Assume it is the company's year-end. Prepare the end-of-period entries to update inventory and record cost of goods sold.
4. Assume last month's gross profit percentage was 35%. Calculate the gross profit percentage for the month of June. Has this improved or declined in June? What likely accounts for this change?

APPLY YOUR KNOWLEDGE

DECISION CASES

This section's material reflects CPA enabling competencies, including:

I   Professional and ethical behaviour

II Problem-solving and decision-making

III Communication

IV Self-management

V   Teamwork and leadership

Based on Chartered Professional Accountant standards

Case 1. Duracraft Corporation is nearing the end of its first year of operations. Duracraft made inventory purchases of $926,000 during the year, as follows:

January	1,500 units	@	$120.00	=	$180,000
July	3,000		142.00		426,000
November	2,000		160.00		320,000
Totals	6,500				$926,000

Sales for the year are 6,000 units for $1,800,000 of revenue. Expenses other than cost of goods sold and income taxes total $425,000. The president of the company is undecided about whether to adopt the FIFO method or the weighted-average-cost method for inventories. The company uses the periodic inventory system. The income tax rate is 30%.

Requirements

1. To aid company decision making, prepare income statements under FIFO and under weighted-average cost.
2. Compare the net income under FIFO with net income under weighted-average cost. Which method produces the higher net income? What causes this difference? Be specific.

LEARNING OBJECTIVES

Prepare and compare an income statement under different inventory methods—periodic system

Case 2. The inventory costing method a company chooses can affect the financial statements and, thus, the decisions of the people who use those statements.

Requirements

1. Company A uses the weighted-average-cost inventory method and discloses this in notes to the financial statements. Company B uses the FIFO method to account for its inventory, but does not disclose which inventory method it uses. Company B reports a higher net income than Company A. In which company would you prefer to invest? Give your reason. Assume rising inventory costs.
2. The lower-of-cost-and-net-realizable-value rule is an accepted accounting concept. Would you want management to follow this rule in accounting for inventory if you were a shareholder or a creditor of a company? Give your reason.
3. Super Sports Company follows the lower-of-cost-and-net-realizable-value rule (LCNRV) and writes the value of its inventory of tents down to net realizable value, which has declined below cost. The following year, an unexpected camping craze results in a demand for tents that far exceeds supply, and the net realizable value increases above the previous cost. What effect will the LCNRV rule have on the income of Super Sports over the two years?

LEARNING OBJECTIVES

Assess the impact of the inventory costing method on the financial statements

ETHICAL DECISIONS

Decision 1 During 2019, Vanguard Inc. changed to the weighted-average-cost method of accounting for inventory. Suppose that during 2020, Vanguard changes back to the FIFO method, and the following year Vanguard switches back to weighted-average cost again.

Requirements

1. What would you think of a company's ethics if it changed accounting methods every year?
2. What accounting characteristic would changing methods every year violate?
3. Who can be harmed when a company changes its accounting methods too often? How?

Decision 2 Determine whether each of the following actions in buying, selling, and accounting for inventories is ethical or unethical. Give your reason for each answer.

1. In applying the lower-of-cost-and-net-realizable-value rule to inventories, Terre Haute Industries recorded an excessively low net realizable value for ending inventory. This allowed the company to pay less income tax for the year.

2. Laminated Photo Film purchased lots of inventory shortly before year-end to increase the weighted-average cost of goods sold and decrease reported income for the year.

3. Madison Inc. delayed the purchase of inventory until after December 31, 2020, to keep 2020's cost of goods sold from growing too large. The delay in purchasing inventory helped net income in 2020 to reach the level of profit demanded by the company's investors.

4. Dover Sales Company deliberately overstated ending inventory in order to report higher profits (net income).

5. Roberto Corporation deliberately overstated purchases to produce a high figure for cost of goods sold (low amount of net income). The real reason was to decrease the company's income tax payments to the government.

FOCUS ON FINANCIAL STATEMENT ANALYSIS

LEARNING OBJECTIVES ❶❸❹

Analyze inventories

MyLab Accounting

Dollarama

The notes are part of the financial statements. They give details that would clutter the statements. This case will help you learn to use a company's inventory notes. Refer to Dollarama's statements and related notes in Appendix A at the end of the book and answer the following questions:

1. How much was Dollarama's inventory at January 28, 2018? What about at January 29, 2017?

2. How does Dollarama value its inventories? Which cost method does the company use?

3. Using the cost-of-goods-sold as shown in Exhibit 5-4, Panel B, compute Dollarama's purchase of inventory during the year ended January 28, 2018.

4. Did Dollarama's gross profit percentage and rate of inventory turnover improve or deteriorate in 2018 (versus 2017)? Ending inventory for 2016 was $470,195. Considering the overall effect of these two ratios, did Dollarama improve during 2018? How did these factors affect the net income for 2018?

MyLab Accounting

Dollarama

Refer to Dollarama's financial statements in Appendix A at the end of the book to answer the following questions. Show amounts in millions.

1. Three important pieces of inventory information are (a) the cost of inventory on hand, (b) the cost of goods sold, and (c) the cost of inventory purchases. Identify or compute each of these items for Dollarama at January 28, 2018.

2. Which item in Requirement 1 is most directly related to cash flow? Why?

3. Assume that all inventory purchases were made on account, and that only inventory purchases increased Accounts Payable. Compute Dollarama's cash payment for inventory during 2018.

CHECK YOUR WORK

STOP + THINK ANSWERS

STOP + THINK (5-1)
The periodic inventory system would work best in this situation because of all of the small items available for sale. It would be almost impossible to keep track of inventory using the perpetual inventory system.

STOP + THINK (5-2)
a. Cost of goods sold = (25 units × $5) + (25 units × $6) = $275

b. Ending inventory = 5 units × $6 = 30

STOP + THINK (5-3)
Investors must always consider differences in methods of companies, but as long as the companies maintain a consistent method of accounting for inventory, and an investor understands the implications to cost of goods sold and inventory when prices are rising/falling, they should be able to compare and analyze different companies.

STOP + THINK (5-4)
It's obvious that both Leon's and Pier 1 sell higher-end merchandise. Leon's has a higher gross profit than Pier 1 and a much higher gross profit than Walmart. At the same time, Leon's turnover rate is higher than Pier 1 but lower than Walmart. Generally, the lower the price, the faster the turnover, and the higher the price, the slower the turnover.

STOP + THINK (5-5)
The overstatement of ending inventory in the accounting records would cause (a) Cost of goods sold to be understated, (b) Net income to be overstated, and (c) Shareholders' equity to be overstated.

QUICK QUIZ ANSWERS

1. b ($3,500 + $6,000 − $5,500 = $4,000)
2. b ($7,200 − $5,500 = $1,700)
3. d
4. d (1,000 @ $10.60 + 500 @ $10 = $15,600)

5. c $\dfrac{(\$20,000 + \$10,600)}{2,000 + 1,000} \times 1,500$
   $= \$10.20 \times 1,500 = \$15,300$

6. a
7. c ($144,000 + $216,000 = $360,000)
8. b
9. a
10. d [$620,000 − ($60,000 + $400,000 − $40,000) = $200,000]

11. a ($20,000 + X − $15,000 = $90,000; X = $85,000)
12. d
13. d [$300,000 ÷ (($25,000 + $35,000) / 2)] = 10 times
14. c

   Net sales = $480,000($490,000 − $10,000)
   COGS = $50,000 + ($205,000 + $20,000 − $4,000 − $6,000) − $40,000
   $= \$225,000$
   GP% = ($480,000 − $225,000) / $480,000
   $= 0.531 = 53.1\%$

15. d
16. c
17. c

6

Property, Plant, and Equipment, and Intangible Assets

CPA COMPETENCIES

Competencies addressed in this chapter:

1.2.2 Evaluates treatment for routine transactions

1.4.4 Interprets financial reporting results for stakeholders (external or internal)

Based on Chartered Professional Accountant standards

SPOTLIGHT

Many years ago, two brothers got their start in business by buying a tire and garage shop. Several years later, they incorporated what we know today as Canadian Tire. With more than 1,500 operations, they sell more than just tires. In some locations, you can even fill up your car with gas. Over the years, they expanded their business by offering financial services, clothing, and hardware.

Included in Canadian Tire's total assets are property and equipment as well as goodwill and intangible assets. A partial balance sheet along with the accompanying notes are presented on the following page. The company owns $4,193.3 million of property as of December 30, 2017. Notice that over the estimated useful lives of these assets, the company has built up accumulated depreciation of about $3,408.3 million (Note 13) indicating that the assets are almost half used up as of that date ($3,408.3 million/$7,601.6 million). The carrying amount of Canadian Tire's property and equipment is $4,193.3 million (Note 13). The company also owns about $1,292.9 million (Note 11) in goodwill and other intangible assets. When you complete this chapter, you will understand better what these terms and concepts are.

David Cooper/Toronto Star/Getty Images

	A	B	C	D
1	**Canadian Tire Corporation, Limited** Partial Balance Sheet (adapted) Long-Lived Assets			
2	*($ in millions)*	**As at Dec. 30, 2017**	**As at Dec. 31, 2016**	
3	**Non-Current Assets**			
4	Long-term receivables and other assets	$ 717.8	$ 763.7	
5	Long-term investments	165.0	175.2	
6	Goodwill and intangible assets (Note 11)	1,292.9	1,280.3	
7	Investment property	344.7	266.4	
8	Property and equipment (Note 13)	4,193.3	4,097.2	
9	Deferred income taxes	114.4	82.3	
10				

Note 11—Goodwill and Intangible Assets:

Cost	$ 2,453.2
Less: Accumulated amortization and impairment	(1,160.3)
Carrying amount	$ 1,292.9

Note 13—Property and Equipment:

Cost	$ 7,601.6
Less: Accumulated depreciation	(3,408.3)
Carrying amount	$ 4,193.3

Source: Management's Discussion and Analysis Canadian Tire Corporation, Limited Fourth Quarter and Full Year 2017.

Businesses use several types of assets that are classified as long-lived, such as property, plant, and equipment, and intangible assets. These assets are used in the business and are not held for sale.

Tangible long-lived assets are also called property, plant, and equipment. For example, buildings, airplanes, and equipment are tangible long-lived assets that do not last forever. Therefore, the cost of these assets must be expensed over their useful lives, and the expense associated with this is called depreciation. Of these assets, land is unique. Land is not expensed over time because its usefulness does not decrease. Many companies report tangible long-lived assets as property, plant, and equipment on the balance sheet. Canadian Tire calls them property and equipment. Looking at the partial balance sheet above, Canadian Tire owns $4,193.3 (million) in property and equipment. To find out what is included under this category, you need to read the notes that accompany the financial statements. These notes are used to explain the numbers reported. Reading Canadian Tire's Note 13 found in their annual report reveals that these assets include land, buildings, fixtures, equipment, and leasehold improvements.

Intangible assets are useful because of the special rights they carry. They have no physical form. Patents, copyrights, and trademarks are intangible assets, as is goodwill. Accounting for intangibles, except goodwill, is similar to accounting for tangible long-lived assets. Canadian Tire has several intangible assets on its balance sheet, including goodwill. Reading Note 11 found in their annual report indicates that Canadian Tire's intangible assets include items such as their store banners, trademarks, and franchise agreements.

Not all companies have both types of assets. For example, U-Haul, a subsidiary of Amerco, is a moving and storage company that owns land, buildings, equipment, rental trucks, and trailers, but does not own any intangible assets.

Accounting for long-lived tangible assets and intangibles has its own terminology. Different names apply to the individual assets and their corresponding expense accounts, as shown in Exhibit 6-1.

EXHIBIT 6-1
Long-Lived Asset and Related Expense Accounts

Asset Account (Balance Sheet)	Related Expense Account (Income Statement)
Tangible Long-Lived Assets	
Land	None
Buildings, machinery, and equipment	Depreciation
Furniture and fixtures	Depreciation
Computers	Depreciation
Intangible Assets	
Copyrights	Amortization
Patents	Amortization
Goodwill	Impairment losses

OBJECTIVE

❶ **Explain** how to account for the cost of property, plant, and equipment

EXPLAIN HOW TO ACCOUNT FOR THE COST OF PROPERTY, PLANT, AND EQUIPMENT

Here is a basic working rule for determining the cost of an asset:

The cost of any asset is the sum of all the costs incurred to bring the asset to its location and intended use. The cost of property, plant, and equipment includes its purchase price plus any taxes, commissions, and other amounts paid to make the asset ready for use. Because the specific costs differ for the various categories of property, plant, and equipment, we discuss the major groups individually.

Land

The cost of land includes its purchase price, real estate commission, survey fees, legal fees, and any back property taxes that the purchaser pays. Land cost also includes expenditures for grading and clearing the land and demolishing or removing unwanted buildings.

The cost of land does *not* include the cost of fencing, paving, sprinkler systems, and lighting. These are recorded in a separate account—called *land improvements*—and they are subject to depreciation.

Suppose Canadian Tire signs a $300,000 note payable to purchase 20 hectares of land for a new retail store. Canadian Tire also pays $10,000 for real estate commission, $8,000 of back taxes, $5,000 for removal of an old building, a $1,000 survey fee, and $260,000 to pave the parking lot—all in cash. What is Canadian Tire's cost of this land?

Purchase price of land		$300,000
Add related costs:		
Real estate commission	$10,000	
Back property tax	8,000	
Removal of building	5,000	
Survey fee	1,000	
Total related costs		24,000
Total cost of land		$324,000

Note that the cost to pave the parking lot, $260,000, is *not* included in the land's cost, because the pavement is a land improvement and wears out over time. Canadian Tire would record the purchase of this land as follows:

	A	B	C	D	E
1		Land	324,000		
2		Note Payable		300,000	
3		Cash		24,000	
4		*To record the purchase of land.*			
5					

ASSETS	=	LIABILITIES	+	SHAREHOLDERS' EQUITY
+324,000	=	+300,000	+	0
−24,000				

The purchase increases both assets and liabilities. There is no effect on equity.

Buildings, Machinery, and Equipment

The cost of constructing a building includes architectural fees, building permits, contractors' charges, and payments for material, labour, and overhead. If a company borrows money to finance the construction, the cost of the building will also include the interest on the loan until the point in time when the asset is ready for its intended use.

When an existing building (new or old) is purchased, its cost includes the purchase price, brokerage commission, sales and other taxes paid, and all expenditures to repair and renovate the building for its intended purpose.

The cost of machinery and equipment includes its purchase price less any discounts, plus transportation, insurance while in transit, non-refundable sales and other taxes, purchase commission, installation costs, and any expenditures to test the asset before it is placed in service. The equipment cost will also include the cost of any special platforms used to support the equipment. After the asset is up and running, insurance, taxes, and maintenance costs are recorded as expenses, not as part of the asset's cost.

Land Improvements and Leasehold Improvements

For the Canadian Tire building, the cost to pave a parking lot ($260,000) would be recorded in a separate account titled Land Improvements. This account includes costs for other items such as driveways, signs, fences, and sprinkler systems. Although these assets are located on the land, they are subject to decay, and their cost should therefore be depreciated.

An airline such as WestJet leases some of its airplanes and other assets. The company customizes these assets to meet its special needs. For example, WestJet paints its logo on airplanes. These improvements are assets of WestJet Airlines Ltd., even though the company does not own the airplane. The cost of improvements to leased assets may appear under Property, Plant, and Equipment, or Other Long-Term Assets. The cost of leasehold improvements should be depreciated over the term of the lease or the life of the asset, whichever is shorter.

Lump-Sum (or Basket) Purchases of Assets

Businesses often purchase several assets as a group, or in a "basket," for a single lump-sum amount. For example, Great-West Lifeco Inc. may pay one price for land and a building. The company must identify the cost of each asset because buildings are depreciated and land is not, so the two assets have to be accounted for separately. The total cost is divided among the assets according to their relative fair values.

Suppose Great-West purchases land and a building in St. John's, Newfoundland, for a sales office. The building sits on two hectares of land, and the combined purchase price of land and building is $2,800,000. An appraisal indicates that the land's fair value is $300,000 and that the building's fair value is $2,700,000.

Great-West first calculates the ratio of each asset's fair value to the total fair value. Total appraised value is $2,700,000 + $300,000 = $3,000,000. Thus, the land, valued at $300,000, is 10% of the total fair value. The building's appraised value is 90% of the total. These percentages are then used to determine the cost of each asset, as follows:

Asset	Fair Value		Total Fair Value		Percentage of Total Fair Value		Total Cost		Cost of Each Asset
Land	$ 300,000	÷	$3,000,000	=	10%	×	$2,800,000	=	$ 280,000
Building	2,700,000	÷	3,000,000	=	90	×	2,800,000	=	2,520,000
Total	$3,000,000				100%				$2,800,000

If Great-West pays cash, the entry to record the purchase of the land and building is:

	A	B	C	D	E
1		Land	280,000		
2		Building	2,520,000		
3		Cash		2,800,000	
4					

ASSETS	=	LIABILITIES	+	SHAREHOLDERS' EQUITY
+280,000				
+2,520,000	=	0	+	0
−2,800,000				

Total assets don't change—the transaction is merely an exchange of cash for two tangible long-lived assets.

Capital Expenditure Versus an Immediate Expense

When a company spends money on property, plant, and equipment, it must decide whether to record an asset or an expense. Examples of these expenditures range from WestJet Airlines's purchase of a flight simulator from CAE Electronics to replacing a tire on a plane.

Expenditures that increase the asset's productivity or extend its useful life are called **capital expenditures** (also called *betterments*). For example, the cost of a major overhaul that extends the useful life of a Canadian Tire truck is a capital expenditure. Capital expenditures are said to be *capitalized,* which means the cost is added to an asset account and not expensed immediately. A major decision in accounting for property, plant, and equipment is whether to capitalize or expense a certain cost.

Costs that do not extend the asset's productivity or its useful life, but merely maintain the asset or restore it to working order, are considered repairs and are recorded as expenses. The costs of repainting a Canadian Tire truck, repairing a dented fender, and replacing tires are also expensed immediately. Exhibit 6-2 illustrates the distinction between capital expenditures and immediate expenses for van expenditures.

Record an Asset for Capital Expenditures/Betterments	Record Repair and Maintenance Expense for an Expense
Extraordinary repairs:	*Ordinary repairs:*
Major engine overhaul	Repair of transmission or other mechanism
Modification of body for new use of van	Oil change, lubrication, and so on
Addition to storage capacity of van	Replacement tires, windshield, or a paint job

The distinction between a capital expenditure (long-lived asset) and an immediate expense requires judgment: Does the cost extend the asset's productivity or its useful life? If so, record an asset. If the cost merely repairs or maintains the asset or returns it to its prior condition, then record an expense.

Most companies expense all small (immaterial) costs, say, below $1,000. For higher (material) costs, they follow the rule we gave above: they capitalize costs that extend the asset's usefulness or its useful life, and they expense all other costs. A conservative policy is one that avoids overstating assets and profits. A company that overstates its assets may get into trouble and have to defend itself in court. Whenever investors lose money because a company overstated its profits or its assets, the investors might file a lawsuit. The courts tend to be sympathetic to investor losses caused by shoddy accounting.

Accounting misstatements sometimes occur for asset costs. For example, a company may:

- Expense a cost that should have been capitalized. This error overstates expenses and understates net income in the year of the error.

- Capitalize a cost that should have been expensed. This error understates expenses and overstates net income in the year of the error.

STOP + THINK (6-1)

Why are land improvements and leasehold improvements depreciated?

EXPLAIN HOW TO ACCOUNT FOR DEPRECIATION ON PROPERTY, PLANT, AND EQUIPMENT

❷ **Explain** how to **account** for depreciation on property, plant, and equipment

As we've seen in previous chapters, property, plant, and equipment are reported on the balance sheet at carrying amount, which is:

$$\text{Carrying amount of property, plant, and equipment} = \text{Cost} - \text{Accumulated depreciation}$$

Property, plant, and equipment wears out, grows obsolete, and loses value over time. To account for this process, we allocate an asset's cost to expense over its life—a process called **depreciation**. The depreciation process begins when an asset is available for use and continues until the asset is removed. It follows the expense recognition principle discussed in Chapter 3. Depreciation apportions the cost of using property, plant, and equipment over time by allocating a portion of that cost against the revenue the asset helps earn each period. Recall that depreciation expense (not accumulated depreciation) is reported on the income statement. In the private enterprise sector, it is referred to as amortization.

Only land has an unlimited life and is not depreciated for accounting purposes. For most property, plant, and equipment, depreciation is caused by one of the following:

- **Physical wear and tear**. For example, physical deterioration takes its toll on the usefulness of WestJet's airplanes, vehicles, and buildings.
- **Obsolescence**. Computers and other electronic equipment may be *obsolete* before they deteriorate. An asset is obsolete when another asset can do the job more efficiently. An asset's useful life may be shorter than its physical life. WestJet and other companies depreciate their computers over a short period of time—perhaps four years—even though the computers will remain in working condition much longer.

Suppose WestJet buys a computer for use in scheduling flight crews. WestJet believes it will get four years of service from the computer, which will then be worthless. Under straight-line depreciation, WestJet expenses one-quarter of the asset's cost in each of its four years of use.

You've just seen what depreciation accounting is. Let's see what it is *not*.

1. **Depreciation is not a process of valuation.** Businesses do not record depreciation based on changes in the fair value of their property, plant, and equipment. Instead, businesses allocate the asset's cost to the periods of its useful life based on a specific depreciation method.

2. **Depreciation does not mean setting aside cash to replace assets as they wear out.** Any cash fund is entirely separate from depreciation.

How to Measure Depreciation

To measure depreciation for property, plant, and equipment, we must know its:

1. Cost
2. Estimated useful life
3. Estimated residual value

We have already discussed cost, which is a known amount. The other two factors must be estimated.

Estimated useful life is the length of service expected from using the asset, which can be expressed in years, units of output, kilometres, or some other measure. For example, the useful life of a building is stated in years. The useful life of a WestJet airplane or van may be expressed as the total number of kilometres the aircraft or vehicle is expected to travel. Companies base such estimates on past experience and information from industry and government publications.

Estimated residual value—also called *scrap value* or *salvage value*—is the expected cash value of an asset at the end of its useful life. For example, WestJet may believe that a baggage-handling machine will be useful for seven years. After that time, WestJet may expect to sell the machine as scrap metal. The amount WestJet believes it can get for the machine is the estimated residual value. In computing depreciation, the asset's estimated residual value is *not* depreciated because WestJet expects to receive this amount from selling the asset. If there's no expected residual value, the full cost of the asset is depreciated. An asset's **depreciable cost** is measured as follows:

Depreciable cost = Asset's cost − Estimated residual value

Depreciation Methods

There are three main depreciation methods that will be discussed in this text:

- Straight-line
- Units-of-production
- Diminishing-balance—an accelerated depreciation method

These methods allocate different amounts of depreciation to each period. However, they all result in the same total amount of depreciation, which is the asset's depreciable cost. Exhibit 6-3 presents assumed data, which we will use to illustrate depreciation computations for a Canadian Tire van.

Data Item	Amount
Cost of van, January 1, 2018	$41,000
Less estimated residual value	(1,000)
Depreciable cost	$40,000
Estimated useful life:	
Years	5 years
Units of production	100,000 units [kilometres]

EXHIBIT 6-3
Data for Depreciation Computations—A Canadian Tire Van

STRAIGHT-LINE METHOD. In the **straight-line (SL) method**, an equal amount of depreciation is assigned to each year (or period) of asset use. Depreciable cost is divided by useful life in years to determine the annual depreciation expense. Applied to the Canadian Tire van data from Exhibit 6-3, straight-line depreciation is:

$$\text{Straight} - \text{line depreciation per year} = \frac{\text{Cost} - \text{Residual value}}{\text{Useful life, in years}}$$

$$= \frac{\$41,000 - \$1,000}{5}$$

$$= \$8,000$$

The entry to record depreciation is:

	A	B	C	D	E
1		Depreciation Expense	8,000		
2		Accumulated Depreciation		8,000	
3					

ASSETS	=	LIABILITIES	+	SHAREHOLDERS' EQUITY
−8,000	=	0		−8,000 Expenses

Observe that depreciation decreases the asset (through Accumulated Depreciation) and also decreases equity (through Depreciation Expense). Let's assume that Canadian Tire purchased this van on January 1, 2018; Canadian Tire's fiscal year ends on

EXHIBIT 6-4
Straight-Line Depreciation Schedule for a Canadian Tire Van

	A	B	C	D	E	F	G
1	Date	Asset Cost	Depreciation Rate	Depreciable Cost	Depreciation Expense	Accumulated Depreciation	Asset Carrying Amount
2	01-01-2018	$ 41,000					$ 41,000
3	31-12-2018		0.20*	$ 40,000	$ 8,000	$ 8,000	33,000
4	31-12-2019		0.20	40,000	8,000	16,000	25,000
5	31-12-2020		0.20	40,000	8,000	24,000	17,000
6	31-12-2021		0.20	40,000	8,000	32,000	9,000
7	31-12-2022		0.20	40,000	8,000	40,000	1,000
8							

$* \dfrac{1}{5 \text{ Years}} = 0.20$ per year.

December 31. Exhibit 6-4 gives a *straight-line depreciation schedule* for the van. The final column of the exhibit shows the *asset's carrying amount*, which is its cost less accumulated depreciation.

As an asset is used in operations, accumulated depreciation increases, and the carrying amount of the asset decreases. An asset's final carrying amount is its *residual value* ($1,000 in Exhibit 6-4). At the end of its useful life, the asset is said to be *fully depreciated*.

TRY IT *in* EXCEL® ▶▶▶

Building depreciation schedules such as the one in Exhibit 6-4 is easy with Excel. Use the information in Exhibit 6-3, the exhibit on the preceding page, and the formula on page 285 to help you program the cells. To construct Exhibit 6-4 depreciation schedule in Excel:

1. Open a new workbook. In cells A1 through G1, insert column headings to correspond to those of Exhibit 6-4, the preceding exhibit. You will have to adjust the column width of your spreadsheet to accommodate the headings.
2. In cells B2 and G2 (asset cost and carrying amount), type in the original gross cost (41,000). The remainder of the cells in column B should be blank.
3. In cell A2, type in the original purchase date (1/1/2018). In cells A3 through A7, type in the year-end dates of 12/31/2018 through 12/31/2022, respectively. Change the formatting of these cells to "date."
4. In cells C3 through C7, enter the depreciation rate for each year, which is the reciprocal of the asset's useful life (1/5, or 20%). Enter .2 in cell C3 and copy this value down through cell C7.
5. In cell D2, calculate the depreciable cost of $40,000. Enter =B2 − 1000. Copy this value down through cell D7.
6. In cell E3, enter the formula =C3*D3. The value $8,000 should appear. Copy this formula to cells E4 through E7.
7. Column F keeps a running sum of accumulated depreciation. Start with cell F3. Enter the formula =F2+E3. $8,000 (accumulated depreciation at the end of year 1) should appear. Copy cell F3 down to cells F4 through F7. You should get the same values as you see in Exhibit 6-4.
8. Column G keeps a running calculation of the declining net book value of the asset. Start with cell G3. Freeze the value of the original cost of the asset ($41,000) in cell G2 by entering "$" before both the column and row. Then subtract the value of accumulated depreciation (cell F3). The formula in cell G3 becomes =$G$2 − F3. The result should be $33,000 ($41,000 − $8,000). Copy cell G3 down through cell G7.

UNITS-OF-PRODUCTION METHOD. In the **units-of-production (UOP) method**, a fixed amount of depreciation is assigned to each *unit of output*, or service, produced by the asset. Depreciable cost is divided by useful life—in units of production—to determine this amount. This per-unit depreciation expense is then multiplied by the number of units produced each period to compute depreciation. The units-of-production depreciation for the Canadian Tire van data in Exhibit 6-3 is:

$$\frac{\text{Units-of-production}}{\text{depreciation per unit of output}} = \frac{\text{Cost} - \text{Residual value}}{\text{Useful life, in units of production}}$$

$$= \frac{\$41,000 - \$1,000}{100,000 \text{ km}} = \$0.40/\text{km}$$

Assume that the van is driven 20,000 km during the first year, 30,000 km during the second, 25,000 km during the third, 15,000 km during the fourth, and 10,000 km during the fifth. Exhibit 6-5 shows the UOP depreciation schedule.

The amount of UOP depreciation varies with the number of units the asset produces. In our example, the total number of units produced is 100,000 km. UOP depreciation does not depend directly on time, as do the other methods.

EXHIBIT 6-5
Units-of-Production Depreciation Schedule for a Canadian Tire Van

	A	B	C	D	E	F	G
1	Date	Asset Cost	Depreciation Rate	Number of Units	Depreciation Expense	Accumulated Depreciation	Asset Carrying Amount
2	01-01-2018	$ 41,000					$ 41,000
3	31-12-2018		$ 0.40*	20,000	$ 8,000	$ 8,000	33,000
4	31-12-2019		0.40	30,000	12,000	20,000	21,000
5	31-12-2020		0.40	25,000	10,000	30,000	11,000
6	31-12-2021		0.40	15,000	6,000	36,000	5,000
7	31-12-2022		0.40	10,000	4,000	40,000	1,000
8							

*($41,000 – $1,000)/100,000 km = $0.40/km.

TRY IT *in* EXCEL® ▶▶▶ —————————————————

If you built the straight-line depreciation schedule in Exhibit 6-4 with Excel, changing the spreadsheet for units-of-production depreciation is a snap. Steps 1–3 and 6–8 are identical. Only steps 4 and 5, dealing with columns C and D, change. You might want to start by opening the straight-line schedule you prepared and saving it under another name: "units-of-production depreciation." Next, change the column headings for column C and column D. Column C should be labeled "Rate per unit." Column D should be labeled "Number Units." Assuming you do this, here are the modified steps 4 and 5 of the process we used before:

4. In column C, calculate a per-unit (rather than per-year as we did with straight-line) depreciation rate by dividing the depreciable cost ($41,000 − $1,000 in Exhibit 6-3) by the number of units (100,000 miles) to get a fixed depreciation rate per mile ($0.40). Enter .4 in cell C3 and copy down through cell C7.
5. In cells D3 through D7, respectively, enter the number of miles driven in years 1 through 5 of the asset's useful life. These are 20,000, 30,000, 25,000, 15,000, and 10,000, respectively.

All of the other amounts in the table will automatically recalculate to reflect units-of-production depreciation, exactly as shown in Exhibit 6-5.

DIMINISHING-BALANCE METHOD. An **accelerated depreciation method** writes off a larger amount of the asset's cost near the start of its useful life than the straight-line method does. Double-diminishing-balance is the main accelerated depreciation method. The **double-diminishing-balance (DDB) method** computes annual depreciation by multiplying the asset's declining carrying amount by a constant percentage, which is two times the straight-line depreciation rate. Double-diminishing-balance amounts are computed as follows:

- *First,* compute the straight-line depreciation rate per year. A 5-year asset has a straight-line depreciation rate of 1/5, or 20% each year. A 10-year asset has a straight-line rate of 1/10, or 10%, and so on.

- *Second,* multiply the straight-line rate by 2 to compute the DDB rate. For a 5-year asset, the DDB rate is 40% (20% × 2). A 10-year asset has a DDB rate of 20% (10% × 2).

- *Third,* multiply the DDB rate by the period's beginning asset carrying amount (cost less accumulated depreciation). Under the DDB method, the residual value of the asset is ignored in computing depreciation, except during the final year. The DDB rate for the Canadian Tire van in Exhibit 6-3 (page 285) is:

$$
\text{DDB depreciation rate per year} = \frac{1}{\text{Useful life, in years}} \times 2
$$

$$
= \frac{1}{5 \text{ years}} \times 2
$$

$$
= 20\% \times 2
$$

$$
= 40\%
$$

- *Fourth,* determine the final year's depreciation amount by adjusting the depreciation expense so that the remaining carrying amount of the asset is equal to the residual value. In Exhibit 6-6, the fifth and final year's DDB depreciation is $4,314: the carrying amount of $5,314 less the $1,000 residual value. Notice how the carrying amount, $1,000, is now equal to the residual value, $1,000. *The residual value should not be depreciated since because it is the amount you expect to receive when you sell the asset.* It should remain on the books until the asset is disposed of even if the asset is still being used.

EXHIBIT 6-6
Double-Diminishing-Balance Depreciation Schedule for a Canadian Tire Van

	A	B	C	D	E	F	G
1	Date	Asset Cost	DDB Rate	Asset Carrying Amount	Depreciation Expense	Accumulated Depreciation	Asset Carrying Amount
2	01-01-2018	$ 41,000					$ 41,000
3	31-12-2018		0.40	$ 41,000	$ 16,400	$ 16,400	24,600
4	31-12-2019		0.40	24,600	9,840	26,240	14,760
5	31-12-2020		0.40	14,760	5,904	32,144	8,856
6	31-12-2021		0.40	8,856	3,542	35,686	5,314
7	31-12-2022				4,314*	40,000	1,000
8							

*Last-year depreciation is the amount needed to reduce the asset's carrying amount to the residual value ($5,314 − $1,000 = $4,314).

The DDB method differs from the other methods in two ways:

1. Residual value is ignored when calculating depreciation expense because that is the amount the company expects to receive from selling the asset; depreciation is computed on the asset's full cost.

2. Depreciation expense in the final year is whatever amount is needed to reduce the asset's carrying amount to its residual value.

TRY IT *in* EXCEL® ▶▶▶

If you built the straight-line and UOP depreciation schedules in Exhibits 6-4 and 6-5 with Excel, changing the spreadsheet for DDB depreciation is easy. Steps 1–3 and 7–8 are identical. The other steps differ only slightly. You might want to start by opening the straight-line schedule you prepared and saving it under another name: "DDB depreciation." Next, change the column heading for column C to "DDB Rate." Right-click on column D (labeled "depreciable cost" in Exhibit 6-4) and delete the entire column. This moves the "yearly expense" over to column D. Here are modified steps 4 and 5 of the process we used for the straight-line rate:

4. In column C, calculate a new depreciation rate, which is double the straight-line rate. In our example, the straight-line rate is 20% per year. The DDB rate is 40% (2 × 20%). Enter .4 in cell C3 and copy down through cell C7.

5. Column D now contains a calculated amount for yearly depreciation expense. The yearly depreciation expense is the product of the previous carrying amount of the asset (in column F) times the DDB rate (in column C). For 2016, depreciation expense is $16,400, which is calculated in Excel as =F2*C3. Enter this formula in cell D3. Your result should be $16,400. Copy this formula down through cell D6 (not cell D7, for reasons explained below).

All of the other amounts in the table through line 6 will automatically recalculate to reflect DDB depreciation, exactly as shown in Exhibit 6-6.

Comparing Depreciation Methods

Let's compare the three methods in terms of the yearly amount of depreciation. The yearly amount of depreciation varies by method, but the total $40,000 depreciable cost is the same under all methods.

	Amount of Depreciation Per Year		
Year	Straight-Line	Units-of-Production	Accelerated Method Double-Diminishing-Balance
1	$ 8,000	$ 8,000	$16,400
2	8,000	12,000	9,840
3	8,000	10,000	5,904
4	8,000	6,000	3,542
5	8,000	4,000	4,314
Total	$40,000	$40,000	$40,000

IFRS directs a business to choose a depreciation method that reflects the pattern in which the asset will be used. For an asset that generates revenue evenly over time, the straight-line method best meets this criterion. The units-of-production method best fits those assets that wear out because of physical use rather than obsolescence. The accelerated method (DDB) applies best to assets that generate greater amounts of revenue earlier in their useful lives and less in later years.

Exhibit 6-7 graphs annual depreciation amounts for the straight-line, units-of-production, and accelerated (DDB) methods. The graph of straight-line depreciation is flat through time because annual depreciation is the same in all periods. Units-of-production depreciation follows no particular pattern because annual depreciation depends on the use of the asset. Accelerated depreciation is greatest in the first year and less in the later years.

Recent surveys of companies in Canada and the United States indicate that straight-line depreciation is used by more than 80% of them. Around 10% of companies use some form of accelerated depreciation, and the rest use units of production and other methods. Many companies use more than one method.

EXHIBIT 6-7
Depreciation Patterns
Through Time

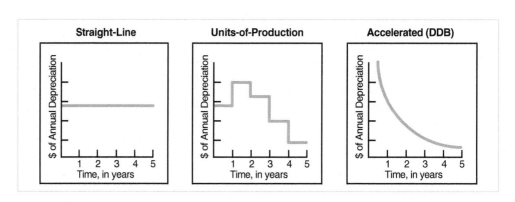

COOKING *the* BOOKS

through Depreciation

Waste Management

Since property, plant, and equipment usually involve relatively large amounts and relatively large number of assets, sometimes a seemingly subtle change in the way they are accounted for can have a tremendous impact on the financial statements. When these changes are made in order to cook the books, the results can be devastating.

Waste Management, Inc., is North America's largest integrated waste service company providing collection, transfer, recycling, disposal, and waste-to-energy services for commercial, industrial, municipal, and residential customers from coast to coast. Starting in 1992, six top executives decided that the company's profits weren't growing fast enough to meet "earnings targets," which were tied to their executive bonuses. Among several fraudulent financial tactics these top executives employed to cook the books were (1) assigning unsupported and inflated residual values to garbage trucks, (2) unjustifiably extending the estimated useful lives of their garbage trucks, and (3) assigning arbitrary residual values to other assets that previously had no residual value. All of these tactics had the effect of decreasing the amount of depreciation expense in the income statements resulting in an increase in net income of $1.7 billion. When the fraud was disclosed, Waste Management shareholders lost over $6 billion in the market value of their investments as the stock price plummeted by more than 33%. The company and these officers eventually settled civil lawsuits for approximately $700 million because of the fraud.

STOP + THINK (6-2)

Imagine a company purchased a machine for $13,000 that had a useful life of five years and residual value of $3,000. If the asset's carrying amount was $7,000, how many more years of use would the machine have assuming the company uses the straight-line method of depreciation?

MyLab Accounting

MID-CHAPTER SUMMARY PROBLEM

Suppose you are a manager at Canadian Tire. The company purchased equipment on January 1, 2020, for $44,000. The expected useful life of the equipment is 10 years or 100,000 units of production, and its residual value is $4,000. Under three depreciation methods, the annual depreciation expense and the balance of accumulated depreciation at the end of 2020 and 2021 are as follows:

	Method A		Method B		Method C	
Year	Annual Depreciation Expense	Accumulated Depreciation	Annual Depreciation Expense	Accumulated Depreciation	Annual Depreciation Expense	Accumulated Depreciation
2020	$4,000	$4,000	$8,800	$ 8,800	$1,200	$1,200
2021	4,000	8,000	7,040	15,840	5,600	6,800

Requirements

1. Your assistant has provided you with the above information. Identify the depreciation method used in each instance, and show the equation and computation for each. (Round to the nearest dollar.)
2. Assume continued use of the same method through the year 2022. Determine the annual depreciation expense, accumulated depreciation, and carrying amount of the equipment for 2020 through 2022 under each method, assuming 12,000 units of production in 2022.
3. How does a manager decide which method to use to depreciate their property, plant, and equipment?

> **Name:** Canadian Tire
> **Industry:** Retailer
> **Accounting Period:** The years 2020, 2021, 2022

ANSWERS

Requirement 1

Method A: Straight-Line

> The straight-line method assigns the same depreciation expense to each year.

Depreciable cost = $40,000 ($44,000 − $4,000)

Each year: $40,000/10 years = $4,000

Method B: Double-Diminishing-Balance

> The double-diminishing-balance method assigns an expense amount that gets smaller every year. Do not include the residual value when using this method.

$$\text{Rate} = \frac{1}{10 \text{ years}} \times 2 = 10\% \times 2 = 20\%$$

2020: 0.20 × $44,000 = $8,800

2021: 0.20 × ($44,000 − $8,800) = $7,040

With the units-of-production method, there is a direct correlation to the number of units produced.

Subtract the residual value from the original cost. Calculate the depreciation per unit. Then divide the annual depreciation expense by the unit cost to determine the number of units produced each year.

Method C: Units-of-Production

$$\text{Depreciation per unit} = \frac{\$44,000 - \$4,000}{100,000 \text{ units}} = \$0.40/\text{unit}$$

2020: $1,200 ÷ $0.40 = 3,000 units

2021: $5,600 ÷ $0.40 = 14,000 units

Requirement 2

Use the same $4,000 annual depreciation expense used for the prior years.

Method A: Straight-Line

Year	Annual Depreciation Expense	Accumulated Depreciation	Carrying Amount
Start			$44,000
2020	$4,000	$ 4,000	40,000
2021	4,000	8,000	36,000
2022	4,000	12,000	32,000

The depreciation expense is calculated as 20% of the prior year's carrying amount.

Method B: Double-Diminishing-Balance

Year	Annual Depreciation Expense	Accumulated Depreciation	Carrying Amount
Start			$44,000
2020	$8,800	$ 8,800	35,200
2021	7,040	15,840	28,160
2022	5,632	21,472	22,528

Use the same $0.40 per unit amount used for the prior years. Multiply by the number of units produced during 2022.

Method C: Units-of-Production

Year	Annual Depreciation Expense	Accumulated Depreciation	Carrying Amount
Start			$44,000
2020	$1,200	$ 1,200	42,800
2021	5,600	6,800	37,200
2022	4,800	11,600	32,400

Computations for 2022

Straight-line	$40,000/10 years = $4,000
Double-diminishing-balance	0.20 × $28,160 = $5,632
Units-of-production	$0.40 × 12,000 units = $4,800

Requirement 3

Managers choose the method that best reflects the way in which the asset is used up. For example, buildings normally wear out over time, so the straight-line depreciation method might be used. Equipment that produces units would wear out after continued use, so the units of production might be the best method. Diminishing balance might be used for computer equipment because of new technology advancements.

EXPLAIN ADDITIONAL TOPICS IN ACCOUNTING FOR LONG-LIVED TANGIBLE ASSETS

OBJECTIVE

❸ **Explain** additional topics in accounting for long-lived tangible assets

Depreciation for Partial Years

Companies purchase property, plant, and equipment whenever they need them. They do not wait until the beginning of a year or a month. Therefore, companies must compute *depreciation for partial years*. Suppose the County Line Bar-B-Q restaurant in Edmonton purchases a building on April 1 for $500,000. The building's estimated life is 20 years, and its estimated residual value is $80,000. The restaurant's fiscal year ends on December 31. Let's consider how the company computes depreciation for April through December:

- First compute depreciation for a full year.
- Then multiply the full year's depreciation by the fraction of the year that the company held the asset.

Assuming the straight-line method, the year's depreciation for County Line's building is $15,750, as follows:

$$\text{Full-year depreciation} = \frac{\$500,000 - \$80,000}{20} = \$21,000$$

Partial-year depreciation: $\$21,000 \times 9/12 = \$15,750$

What if County Line bought the asset on April 18? Many businesses record no monthly depreciation on assets purchased after the 15th of the month, and they record a full month's depreciation on an asset bought on or before the 15th.

Most companies use computerized systems to account for property, plant, and equipment. Each asset has a unique identification number that links to the asset's cost, estimated life, residual value, and depreciation method. The system will automatically calculate the depreciation expense for each period. Accumulated Depreciation is automatically updated.

Changing the Useful Life of a Depreciable Asset

Managers must decide on an asset's useful life to compute its depreciation. After an asset is put into use, managers may change its useful life on the basis of experience and new information. Such a change in accounting estimate is very rare in Canada.

An example from the United States is illustrative. Disney Enterprises, Inc., made such a change, called a *change in accounting estimate*, several years ago. The company recalculated depreciation on the basis of revised useful lives of several of its theme park assets. The following note in company's financial statements reported this change in accounting estimate:

> **Note 5**
> … [T]he Company extended the estimated useful lives of certain theme park ride and attraction assets based upon historical data and engineering studies. The effect of this change was to decrease [depreciation] by approximately $8 million (an increase in net income of approximately $4.2 million …).
>
> *Source*: From Disney Enterprises, Inc.'s Financial Statements, 2014.

Assume that a Disney hot-dog stand cost $40,000 and that the company originally believed the asset had an eight-year useful life with no residual value. Using the straight-line method, the company would record $5,000 depreciation each year ($40,000/8 years = $5,000). Suppose Disney used the asset for two years. Accumulated depreciation reached $10,000, leaving a remaining depreciable carrying amount (cost *less* accumulated depreciation *less* residual value) of $30,000 ($40,000 − $10,000). From its experience, management believes the asset will remain useful for ten more years. The company would spread the remaining depreciable carrying amount over the asset's remaining life as follows:

$$\begin{array}{ccc} \text{Asset's remaining} & & (\text{New}) \text{ Estimated} & & (\text{New}) \text{ Annual} \\ \text{depreciable carrying amount} & \div & \text{useful life remaining} & = & \text{depreciation} \\ \$30,000 & \div & 10 \text{ years} & = & \$3,000 \end{array}$$

The yearly depreciation entry based on the new estimated useful life is:

	A	B	C	D	E
1		Depreciation Expense—Hot-Dog Stand	3,000		
2		Accumulated Depreciation—Hot-Dog Stand		3,000	
3					

ASSETS	=	LIABILITIES	+	SHAREHOLDERS' EQUITY
−3,000	=	0		−3,000 Expenses

Fully Depreciated Assets

A *fully depreciated asset* is an asset that has reached the end of its estimated useful life. Suppose Canadian Tire has fully depreciated equipment with zero residual value (cost was $40,000). Canadian Tire's accounts will appear as follows:

Equipment		Accumulated Depreciation		Carrying amount
40,000	−	40,000	=	$0

The equipment's carrying amount is zero, but that doesn't mean the equipment is worthless. Canadian Tire may continue using the equipment for a few more years but will not take any more depreciation.

When Canadian Tire disposes of the equipment, it will remove both the asset's cost ($40,000) and its accumulated depreciation ($40,000) from the books. The next section shows how to account for disposals of property, plant, and equipment.

Derecognition of Property, Plant, and Equipment

Derecognition is a term IFRS uses to refer to property, plant, and equipment that is either no longer useful or has been sold. When this occurs, the related accounts are removed from the company's books and a gain or loss is recorded.

Eventually, property, plant, and equipment cease to serve a company's needs. The asset may wear out, become obsolete, or for some other reason cease to be useful. Before accounting for the disposal of the asset, the business should bring depreciation up to date to:

- Record the expense up to the date of sale
- Measure the asset's final carrying amount

To account for disposal, the asset and its related accumulated depreciation are removed from the books. Suppose the final year's depreciation expense has just been recorded to fully depreciate a machine that cost $50,000 and is estimated to have zero residual value. The machine's accumulated depreciation thus totals $50,000. Assuming that this asset is disposed of, not sold, the entry to record its disposal is:

	A	B	C	D	E
1		Accumulated Depreciation—Machinery	50,000		
2		Machinery		50,000	
3		*To dispose of a fully depreciated machine.*			
4					

ASSETS	=	LIABILITIES	+	SHAREHOLDERS' EQUITY
+50,000	=	0	+	0
−50,000				

There is no gain or loss on this disposal, so there is no effect on equity.

If assets are "junked" before being fully depreciated, the company incurs a loss on the disposal. Suppose M&M Meat Shops disposes of store fixtures that cost $4,000. Accumulated depreciation is $3,000, and the carrying amount is, therefore, $1,000. Junking these store fixtures results in a loss as follows:

	A	B	C	D	E
1		Accumulated Depreciation—Store Fixtures	3,000		
2		Loss on Disposal of Store Fixtures	1,000		
3		Store Fixtures		4,000	
4		*To dispose of store fixtures.*			
5					

ASSETS	=	LIABILITIES	+	SHAREHOLDERS' EQUITY
+3,000	=	0	+	−1,000 Loss
−4,000				

M&M Meat Shops got rid of an asset with a $1,000 carrying amount and received nothing. The result is a $1,000 loss, which decreases both total assets and equity.

The Loss on Disposal of Store Fixtures is reported as Other Income (Expense) on the income statement. Losses decrease net income exactly as expenses do. Gains increase net income in the same manner as revenues.

SELLING PROPERTY, PLANT, AND EQUIPMENT. Suppose M&M Meat Shops sells fixtures on September 30, 2020, that cost $10,000 when purchased on January 1, 2017, and have been depreciated on a straight-line basis. M&M Meat Shops originally estimated a 10-year useful life and no residual value. Prior to recording the sale, the M&M Meat Shops accountants must update the asset's depreciation. Suppose the business uses the calendar year as its accounting period. Partial-year depreciation must be recorded for the asset's expense from January 1, 2020, to the sale date. The straight-line depreciation entry at September 30, 2020, is:

	A	B	C	D	E
1	Sept. 30	Depreciation Expense ($10,000/10 years × 9/12)	750		
2		Accumulated Depreciation—Fixtures		750	
3		*To update depreciation.*			
4					

The Fixtures account and the Accumulated Depreciation—Fixtures account appear as follows. Observe that the fixtures' carrying amount is $6,250 ($10,000 − $3,750).

Fixtures			Accumulated Depreciation—Fixtures		
Jan. 1, 2017	10,000		Dec. 31, 2017	1,000	
			Dec. 31, 2018	1,000	
			Dec. 31, 2019	1,000	= Carrying amount $6,250
			Sep. 30, 2020	750	
			Balance	3,750	

Suppose M&M Meat Shops sells the fixtures for $7,000 cash. The gain on the sale is $750, determined as follows:

Cash received from sale of the asset		$7,000
Carrying amount of asset sold:		
Cost	$10,000	
Less accumulated depreciation	(3,750)	6,250
Gain on sale of the asset		$ 750

The entry to record the sale of the fixtures for $7,000 cash is:

	A	B	C	D	E
1	Sept. 30	Cash	7,000		
2		Accumulated Depreciation—Fixtures	3,750		
3		Gain on Sale of Fixtures		750	
4		Fixtures		10,000	
5		*To sell fixtures.*			
6					

ASSETS	=	LIABILITIES	+	SHAREHOLDERS' EQUITY
+7,000				
+3,750	=	0	+	750 Gain
−10,000				

Gains are recorded as credits, in the same manner as revenues; losses are recorded as debits, in the same manner as expenses. Gains and losses on asset disposals appear on the income statement as Other income (expense) or Other gains (losses).

T-Accounts for Analyzing Property, Plant, and Equipment Transactions

You can perform quite a bit of analysis if you know how transactions affect the property, plant, and equipment accounts. The following are some of these accounts with descriptions of the activity in each.

Building (or Equipment)	
Beginning balance	
Cost of assets purchased	Cost of assets disposed of
Ending balance	

Accumulated Depreciation	
Accum. depreciation of assets disposed of	Beginning balance
	Depreciation expense for the current period
	Ending balance

Cash	
Cash proceeds for assets disposed of	Cash paid for assets purchased

Long-Term Debt	
	New Debt incurred for assets purchased

Depreciation Expense	
Depreciation expense for the current period	

Gain on Sale of Building (or Equipment)	
	Gain on sale

Loss on Sale of Building (or Equipment)	
Loss on sale	

You can analyze transactions as they flow through these accounts to answer very useful questions such as the amount of cash paid to purchase new property, plant, and equipment, the cost of assets purchased, and the cost as well as the carrying amount of the assets sold. Example: Suppose you started the year with buildings that cost $100,000. During the year you bought another building for $150,000 and ended the year with buildings that cost $180,000. What was the cost of the building you sold?

Building			
Beginning balance	100,000		
Cost of assets purchased	150,000	Cost of assets sold	? = $70,000
Ending balance	180,000		

Special Issues in Accounting for Property, Plant, and Equipment

Long-lived assets such as property, plant, and equipment are complex because:

- Depreciation affects income taxes
- Significant components of property, plant, and equipment should be depreciated separately
- Assets should be tested regularly for impairment
- The revaluation method could be used to measure property, plant, and equipment assets

Depreciation for Tax Purposes

Many businesses use the straight-line method for reporting property, plant, and equipment on the balance sheet and depreciation expense on the income statement.

However, for income tax purposes, they also keep a separate set of depreciation records. The *Income Tax Act* requires taxpayers to use accelerated and sometimes straight-line depreciation (up to specified capital cost allowance [CCA] maximums) for tax purposes. In other words, a taxpayer may use one method of depreciation for accounting purposes and another method for tax purposes.

Depreciating Significant Components

IFRS require that significant components of an item of property, plant, and equipment be depreciated separately. What does this mean? Take, for example, Air Canada or WestJet, which buy aircraft for use in their operations. Air Canada depreciates their aircraft and engines over 20–25 years, while the cabin and interior equipment are depreciated over the lesser of 5 years or the remaining useful life of the aircraft. Under ASPE, depreciating separate components is done only when practicable.

Impairment

At each reporting date, a company should review its property, plant, and equipment to see if an asset is impaired. Impairment occurs when the carrying amount exceeds its recoverable amount. Recoverable amount is determined to be the higher of an asset's fair value (less costs to sell) and its value in use. Value in use is the present value of estimated future cash flows expected to be earned from the continuing use of an asset and from its disposal at the end of its useful life.

Impairment may be caused by many factors, including obsolescence, physical damage, and loss in market value. For example, let's assume that FedEx has a long-term asset with the following information at year-end:

Carrying amount $100 million

Recoverable amount = higher of:

a. Value in use $60 million

b. Fair value $70 million

A two-stage impairment process is:

Step   1   Impairment test: Is Carrying amount > Recoverable amount? (Answer: Yes, so the asset is impaired)

Step   2   Impairment loss = Carrying amount − Higher of (a) Value in use and (b) Fair value
= $100 million − $70 million (higher of the two amounts)
= $30 million

The journal entry to record impairment is:

	A	B	C	D	E
1		Loss on Impairment	$30,000,000		
2		Accumulated Depreciation		$30,000,000	
3					

If the situation changes, IFRS do permit a company to reverse the impairment loss by writing the asset up to its carrying amount. The accounting standards for private enterprises require a company to review its property, plant, and equipment only when impairment is suspected. No reversal of the write-off is allowed under ASPE.

In a note to its financial statements, Air Canada states that for its property, plant, and equipment,

> Assets that are subject to depreciation are reviewed for impairment whenever events or changes in circumstances indicate that the carrying amount may not be recoverable. An impairment test is performed by comparing the carrying amount of the asset or group of assets to their recoverable amount.

Revaluation Model

Throughout this chapter, we have shown you what IFRS refers to as the cost model. This means that a company measures property, plant, and equipment at cost less any accumulated depreciation less any accumulated impairment losses.

Another method a company could choose to measure property, plant, and equipment is called the revaluation model. Under this method, an asset would be recorded at cost when purchased but subsequently measured at its fair value less any accumulated depreciation less any accumulated impairment losses. It may be revalued at year-end or when the company believes a change in the asset value has taken place. With every new change in the asset account, depreciation has to be revised accordingly based on the new carrying amount. This topic is discussed in greater detail in an intermediate accounting course.

Example: A company chooses to use the revaluation method for a building that was bought for $1.8 million and is being depreciated over 25 years, with no residual value. Subsequently, if the appraised value is $2 million, the increase of $200,000 will be recognized through equity by the following journal entry:

	A	B	C	D	E
1		Building	200,000		
2		Revaluation surplus		200,000	
3					

Revaluation Surplus is an equity account that is reported as other comprehensive income. Only the cost model is used under ASPE.

STOP + THINK (6-3)

1. Suppose a company was having a bad year—net income was well below expectations and lower than last year's income. For depreciation purposes, the company extended the estimated useful lives of its depreciable assets. How would this accounting change affect the company's (a) depreciation expense, (b) net income, and (c) owners' equity?

2. Suppose that the company's accounting change turned a loss year into a profitable year. Without the accounting change, the company would have reported a net loss for the year. The accounting change enabled the company to report net income. Under IFRS, the company's annual report must disclose the accounting change and its effect on net income. Would investors evaluate the company as better or worse for having made this accounting change?

DECISION GUIDELINES

USING PROPERTY, PLANT, AND EQUIPMENT AND RELATED EXPENSES IN DECISION MAKING

Companies must make decisions about how to account for property, plant, and equipment. Let's look at some ways property, plant, and equipment are used in decision making.

Decision	Guidelines
Capitalize or expense a cost?	*Managers*
(a) New asset	Capitalize all costs that bring the asset to its intended use, including asset purchase price, transportation charges, and taxes paid to acquire the asset.
(b) Existing asset	Capitalize only those costs that add to the asset's productivity or to its useful life.
	Expense all other costs as maintenance or repairs.
Which depreciation method to use?	*Managers*
	Use the method that best allocates the cost of an asset through depreciation expense against the revenues produced by the asset. As discussed earlier, each method will produce varying amounts of depreciation expense each year, but overall, they will result in the same total amount of depreciation. If the asset generates revenue evenly over time, the straight-line method is best; if it wears out through physical use, the units-of-production method should be used; if greater revenue is generated earlier in the asset's useful life, then diminishing-balance is the method to use.
	Investors and Creditors
	Both investors and creditors read the notes to the financial statements to see which depreciation methods management used. Why do they do this? As we have already seen, the depreciation method chosen affects both the income statement and the balance sheet. Remember, if management chooses to use the straight-line method, then depreciation expense will be the same amount each year. However, if the double-diminishing balance is used, then depreciation expense is highest in the early years of the asset's life, causing net income to be lower. This information is useful when comparing companies using different depreciation methods.

EXPLAIN HOW TO ACCOUNT FOR INTANGIBLE ASSETS

As we saw earlier, *intangible assets* are long-lived assets with no physical form. Intangibles are valuable because they carry special rights from patents, copyrights, trademarks, franchises, and goodwill. Like buildings and equipment, an intangible asset is recorded at its acquisition cost. Intangibles are often the most valuable assets of high-tech companies and other companies that depend on research and development. The residual value of most intangibles is zero.

Intangible assets fall into two categories:

- Intangibles with *finite lives* that can be measured. We record **amortization** for these intangibles. Amortization works like depreciation and is usually computed on a straight-line basis, but one of the other methods could be used.

- Intangibles with *indefinite lives*. No amortization for these intangibles is recorded. Instead, check them annually for any loss in value (impairment), and record a loss when it occurs. Goodwill is the most prominent example of an intangible asset with an indefinite life.

The table below summarizes these categories:

	Goodwill	Indefinite life intangible	Definite life intangible
Amortized?	No	No	Yes
Annual assessment of impairment required?	Yes	Yes	No*
Reversal of impairment loss allowed in subsequent periods?	No	Yes	Yes

*Not required unless there are signs to suggest that impairment has occurred.

In the following discussions, we illustrate the accounting for both categories of intangibles.

Accounting for Specific Intangibles

Each type of intangible asset is unique, and the accounting can vary from one intangible to another.

PATENTS. **Patents** are federal government grants giving the holder the exclusive right for 20 years to produce and sell an invention. The invention may be a product or a process—for example, IMAX's projection process. Like any other asset, a patent may be purchased. Suppose Bombardier pays $170,000 to acquire a patent on January 1, and the business believes the expected useful life of the patent is five years. Amortization expense is $34,000 per year ($170,000/5 years). Bombardier records the acquisition and amortization for this patent as follows:

	A	B	C	D	E
1	Jan. 1	Patents	170,000		
2		Cash		170,000	
3		To acquire a patent.			
4	Dec. 31	Amortization Expense—Patents ($170,000/5)	34,000		
5		Accumulated Amortization		34,000	
6		To amortize the cost of a patent.			
7					

ASSETS	=	LIABILITIES	+	SHAREHOLDERS' EQUITY
−34,000	=	0		−34,000 Expense

Amortization for an intangible decreases both assets and equity exactly as it does for equipment.

COPYRIGHTS. **Copyrights** are exclusive rights to reproduce and sell a book, musical composition, film, or other work of art. Copyrights also protect computer software programs, such as Microsoft Word. Issued by the federal government, copyrights extend 50 years beyond the author's (composer's, artist's, or programmer's) death. The cost of obtaining a copyright from the government is low, but a company may pay a large sum to purchase an existing copyright from the owner. For example, a publisher may pay the author of a popular novel $1 million or more for the book copyright. A copyright is usually amortized over its useful life.

TRADEMARKS AND TRADE NAMES. Trademarks and trade names (or **brand names**) are distinctive identifications of products or services. You are probably familiar with McDonald's golden arches or Apple Inc.'s famous apple. Tim Hortons and Roots are names we all recognize. Advertising slogans, such as "Red Bull gives you wings," are also protected.

The cost of a trademark or trade name may be amortized over its useful life, but if the trademark is expected to generate cash flow for the indefinite future, the business should not amortize the trademark's cost.

FRANCHISES AND LICENCES. Franchises and licences are privileges granted by a private business or a government to sell a product or service in accordance with specified conditions. The Edmonton Oilers hockey organization is a franchise granted to its owner by the National Hockey League. Swiss Chalet restaurants and Canadian Tire are popular franchises. Companies purchase licences for the right to use computer software. Coca-Cola sells licences to companies around the world, which allow the companies to produce and distribute Coca-Cola beverages in specified markets. The useful lives of many franchises and licences are indefinite and, therefore, are not amortized.

GOODWILL. In accounting, **goodwill** has a very specific meaning. It is defined as the excess of the cost of purchasing another company over the sum of the market values of its net assets (assets minus liabilities). A purchaser is willing to pay for goodwill when it buys another company with abnormal earning power.

Canadian Tire expanded into another line of business when it acquired The Forzani Group in August 2011. The purchase price was $800.6 million. The fair value of the assets was $1,149.9 million, and the fair value of the liabilities was $657.7 million, so Canadian Tire paid $308.4 million for goodwill, computed as follows:

Purchase paid for The Forzani Group (FGL).....................		$ 800.6 million
Sum of the fair values of FGL's assets	$1,149.9 million	
Less: Fair value of FGL's liabilities	657.7 million	
Value of FGL's net assets..		492.2 million
Excess is called *goodwill*		$ 308.4 million

Canadian Tire would consolidate The Forzani Group's financial statements, but if Canadian Tire were to combine FGL's records with its own, the entry, including goodwill, would be:

	A	B	C	D	E
1		Assets (Cash, Receivables, Inventories, Property,			
2		Plant, and Equipment, Other Assets, all at fair value)	1,149,900,000		
3		Goodwill	308,400,000		
4		Liabilities		657,700,000	
5		Cash		800,600,000	
6					

ASSETS	=	LIABILITIES	+	SHAREHOLDERS' EQUITY
+1,149,900,000				
+308,400,000	=	+657,700,000	+	0
−800,600,000				

Note that Canadian Tire has acquired both The Forzani Group's assets and its liabilities.

Goodwill has special features, as follows:

1. Goodwill is recorded *only* when it is purchased in the acquisition of another company. A purchase transaction provides objective evidence of the value of goodwill. Companies never record goodwill that they have created for their own business.

2. Goodwill is not amortized because it has an indefinite life. As you will see below, if the value of goodwill is impaired, it must be written down.

Accounting for the Impairment of an Intangible Asset

Some intangibles—such as goodwill, licences, and some trademarks—have indefinite lives and, therefore, are not subject to amortization. But all intangibles are subject to a write-down when the carrying amount exceeds its recoverable amount. Go back and reexamine the two step process for determining impairment of an asset on page 298. The 2016 annual report of Canadian Tire reported that

> The impairment on goodwill pertains to the Company's Retail operating segment and is reported in other income in the consolidated statement of income.

As a result of the impairment test, Canadian Tire recognized a goodwill impairment loss of $0.6 million. This impairment loss is recorded as an expense on the income statement.

Canadian Tire would record the write-down of goodwill as follows:

	A	B	C	D	E
1	2016				
2	Dec. 31	Loss on Goodwill Impairment	$0.6		
3		Goodwill		$0.6	
4					

ASSETS	=	LIABILITIES	+	SHAREHOLDERS' EQUITY
−0.6	=	0		−0.6 Expense

Under ASPE, impairment of intangible assets is tested only when there is an indication of impairment.

Accounting for Research and Development Costs

Accounting for research and development (R&D) costs is one of the most difficult issues the accounting profession has faced. R&D is the lifeblood of companies such as BlackBerry, Open Text, TELUS, and Bombardier because it is vital to the development of new products and processes. The cost of R&D activities is one of these companies' most valuable (intangible) assets.

Both IFRS and ASPE require *development costs* meeting certain criteria to be capitalized and then expensed over the life of the product, while *research costs* are to be expensed as incurred.

STOP + THINK (6-4)

Suppose the *Globe and Mail* paid $1 million for a rural newspaper in Ontario three years ago. The newspaper's assets were valued at $1,000,000 and its liabilities at $150,000. The company recorded $150,000 as goodwill at the time of purchase. What amortization expense will be recorded for the current year?

OBJECTIVE

5 **Analyze** a company's return on assets

ANALYZE A COMPANY'S RETURN ON ASSETS

Evaluating company performance is a key goal of financial statement analysis. Shareholders and creditors entrust managers to develop business strategies that utilize a company's assets in a way that both effectively and efficiently generates a profit. One way to evaluate how well managers have performed in this regard is to examine the company's **return on assets (ROA)**.

ROA, also known as *rate* of return on assets, measures how profitably management has used the assets that shareholders and creditors have provided the company. The basic formula for the ROA ratio is as follows:

$$ROA = \frac{\text{Net income} + \text{Interest Expense}}{\text{Average total assets}}$$

where Average total assets = (Beginning total assets + Ending total assets)/2

ROA measures how much the entity earned for each dollar of assets invested by both shareholders and creditors. Companies with high ROA have both selected assets and managed them more successfully than companies with low ROA. ROA is often computed on a divisional or product-line basis to help identify less profitable segments and improve their performance.

To illustrate, let's consider Masimo Corporation, a company that produces electronic instruments used in the health-care industry. The following table contains approximate financial data adapted from Masimo's income statements and balance sheets for 2020 and 2021:

Masimo Corporation Selected (Adapted) Financial Data		
	(Amounts in thousands)	
	2021	**2020**
Net sales..	$439,000	$493,000
Net income..	60,000	61,000
Interest expense..	$ 4,000	$ 4,000
Average total assets	338,000	371,000

Masimo Corporation
Return on Assets

ROA

Net income + Interest expense/Average total assets

2021 = $60,000 + $4,000/$338,000 = 18.9 or 19%

2020 = $61,000 + $4,000/$371,000 = 17.5 or 18%

Overall, despite the decrease in net income from $61,000 to $60,000, the company was still able to increase the ROA from 18% to 19%. In addition, Massimo sold unproductive plant assets, reducing total average assets from $371,000 to $338,000.

STOP + THINK (6-5)

Why is interest expense added to net income in the numerator of the Return on Assets ratio?

 DECISION GUIDELINES

USING THE RETURN ON ASSETS IN DECISION MAKING

The fundamental goal of a company is to earn a profit. The return on asset (ROA) measures how profitably a company uses its assets. Let's see how the ROA is used in making decisions.

Decision	Guidelines
How profitable was the company?	*Managers*
	Managers try to increase the profitability of the company, whether it is through increasing sales, reducing expenses, or a combination of both. They know that investors and creditors expect them to use the assets of the company to generate a profit.
	Investors and Creditors
	Since investors and creditors provide the financing for the assets that a company owns, they are looking to see if managers were able to use these assets to generate a profit. For the investor, share prices generally react favourably when the company is profitable—and the company will be able to pay them dividends. For the creditor, profitability means the company will be able to pay back their debt.

ANALYZE THE CASH FLOW IMPACT OF LONG-LIVED ASSET TRANSACTIONS

OBJECTIVE

❻ **Analyze** the cash flow impact of long-lived asset transactions

Three main types of long-lived asset transactions appear on the statement of cash flows:

- Acquisitions
- Sales
- Depreciation and amortization

Acquisitions and sales of long-lived assets are *investing* activities. For example, a company invests in property, plant, and equipment by paying cash or incurring a liability. The purchase of buildings and equipment are investing activities that appear on the statement of cash flows. The sale of property, plant, and equipment results in a cash receipt, as illustrated in Exhibit 6-8, which excerpts data from the statement of cash flows of Canadian Tire. The acquisitions, sales, and depreciation of property, plant, and equipment and intangible assets are denoted in lines 7, 8, 12, 13, and 14.

Let's examine the investing activities first. During the year-end December 30, 2017 Canadian Tire paid $471 million for property and equipment and $161.6 million for intangible assets. Canadian Tire received $13.6 million from the disposal of these assets during the year. A gain or loss on the sale of these assets is not reported as an investing activity on the statement of cash flows.

Canadian Tire's statement of cash flows reports Depreciation (Amortization) in the operating activities section (line 7). You may be wondering why depreciation appears on the statement of cash flows—after all, depreciation does not affect cash. Depreciation (Amortization) decreases net income in the same way that all other expenses do, but it does not affect cash. Depreciation (Amortization) is therefore added back to net income to measure cash flows from operations under the indirect method.

Canadian Tire's cash flows are strong—cash provided by operating activities was $972.8 million. With this amount and with some financing, the company has bought property and equipment as well as other intangible assets needed to expand and run its business.

EXHIBIT 6-8
Reporting Long-lived Asset Transactions on Statement of Cash Flows

	A	B	C	D
1	**Canadian Tire Corporation, Limited** Consolidated Statement of Cash Flows (partial, adapted) For the Year Ended December 30, 2017			
2	*(amounts in millions)*			
3	**Operating Activities:**			
4	Net earnings	$818.8		
5	**Adjustments to reconcile net income**			
6	**to cash provided by operating activities:**			
7	**Depreciation**	335.0		
8	**Amortization of intangible assets**	133.7		
9	Other items (summarized)	(314.7)		
10	Cash generated from operating activities	$972.8		
11	**Investing Activities:**			
12	**Purchases of property and equipment**	(471.0)		
13	**Additions to intangible assets**	(161.6)		
14	**Proceeds from disposals of assets**	13.6		
15	Other items (summarized)	(20.9)		
16	Cash used for investing activities	(639.9)		
17	**Financing Activities:**			
18	Cash used in financing activities (summarized)	(719.7)		
19	Cash used in the year	(386.8)		
20	Cash and cash equivalents at beginning of year	823.8		
21	Cash and cash equivalents at end of year	$437.0		
22				

STOP + THINK (6-6)

Test your ability to understand the statement of cash flows.

1. How much cash did Canadian Tire spend on purchases of property, plant, and equipment and intangibles during the year?

2. Suppose the carrying amount of the property, plant and equipment that Canadian Tire sold for $13.6 million was

$14.6 million (a cost of $808.1 million minus accumulated depreciation of $793.5 million). Write a sentence to explain why the sale transaction resulted in a loss for Canadian Tire.

3. Where would Canadian Tire report any gain or loss on the sale of the capital assets—on which financial statement, under which heading?

Summary of IFRS-ASPE Differences

Concepts	IFRS	ASPE
Depreciation (p. 283)	This concept is called depreciation.	This concept is called amortization.
Significant components of an item of property, plant, or equipment (p. 298)	Significant components shall be depreciated separately.	Significant components are amortized separately only when it is practical to do so.
Impairment (p. 298)	A company shall assess at the end of each reporting period whether there are any signs that an asset may be impaired. Irrespective of any signs of impairment, a company must annually review goodwill and intangible assets with indefinite useful lives for impairment.	A company shall test an asset for impairment whenever events or circumstances indicate its carrying amount may not be recoverable.
	If an impaired asset subsequently increases in value, a company may reverse all or part of any previous write-down but not on goodwill.	A company may not reverse any write-downs, even if an impaired asset subsequently increases in value.
Revaluation (p. 299)	A company may choose to use the revaluation model to measure its property, plant, and equipment.	A company must use the cost method; no revaluation is permitted.

SUMMARY

SUMMARY OF LEARNING OBJECTIVES

LEARNING OBJECTIVE	SUMMARY
❶ **Explain** how to **account** for the cost of property, plant, and equipment	The cost of property, plant, and equipment is the sum of all the costs incurred to bring the asset to its location and intended use. Costs incurred after the asset has been placed in use are either capitalized (if it increases the asset's productivity or extends its useful life) or expensed (if it maintains the asset and keeps it in good working order).
❷ **Explain** how to **account** for depreciation on property, plant, and equipment	Because assets decline in value either from wearing out, becoming obsolete, or losing value, depreciation is used to allocate their cost to the periods of their useful life. Three depreciation methods discussed include the straight-line method, the units-of-production method, and the diminishing or double-diminishing-balance method. If an asset is bought during the year, depreciation is computed for the partial year. Managers may revise their estimate of an asset's useful life and recalculate depreciation. If a fully depreciated asset is still being used, it is left on the company's records.

❸ **Explain** additional topics in accounting for long-lived tangible assets	Depreciation affects income taxes because the depreciation method used for accounting purposes may be different than the depreciation method required for tax purposes. Subsequent to the acquisition of property, plant, and equipment, a company can choose to measure these assets using either the cost method or the revaluation method. The cost method uses cost as its measurement, while the revaluation method uses fair value. Significant components of property, plant, and equipment shall be depreciated separately. Property, plant, and equipment are checked annually for any impairment.
❹ **Explain** how to **account** for intangible assets	Intangible assets are long-lived assets with no physical form and include patents, copyrights, trademarks, franchises, and licences, and goodwill. Two categories of intangibles are those with finite lives (record amortization) and those with indefinite lives (no amortization is recorded). All intangible assets are checked each year for impairment, and a loss is recorded when it occurs.
❺ **Analyze** a company's return on assets	The return on assets ratio measures how profitably management has used the assets that shareholders and creditors have provided the company.
❻ **Analyze** the cash flow impact of long-lived asset transactions	On the statement of cash flows, acquisitions and sales of property, plant, and equipment and intangibles are recorded under investing activities, while the depreciation and amortization expenses are added to net income under operating activities.

MyLab Accounting

END-OF-CHAPTER SUMMARY PROBLEM

The figures that follow appear in the *Answers to the Mid-Chapter Summary Problem*, Requirement 2, on page 292, for Canadian Tire.

	Method A: Straight-Line			Method B: Double-Diminishing-Balance		
Year	Annual Depreciation Expense	Accumulated Depreciation	Carrying amount	Annual Depreciation Expense	Accumulated Depreciation	Carrying Amount
Start			$44,000			$44,000
2020	$4,000	$ 4,000	40,000	$8,800	$ 8,800	35,200
2021	4,000	8,000	36,000	7,040	15,840	28,160
2022	4,000	12,000	32,000	5,632	21,472	22,528

Name: Canadian Tire
Industry: Retailer
Accounting Period: The years 2020, 2021, 2022

Problem

Suppose Canadian Tire purchased the equipment described in the table on January 1, 2020. Management has depreciated the equipment by using the double-diminishing-balance method. On July 1, 2022, Canadian Tire sold the equipment for $27,000 cash.

Requirement

Record depreciation for 2022 and the sale of the equipment on July 1, 2022.

ANSWERS

Problem

To record depreciation to date of sale, and then the sale of the equipment:

	A	B	C	D	E
1	2022				
2	July 1	Depreciation Expense—Equipment ($5,632 × 1/2 year)	2,816		
3		Accumulated Depreciation—Equipment		2,816	
4		*To update depreciation.*			
5					
6	July 1	Cash	27,000		
7		Accumulated Depreciation—Equipment ($15,840 + $2,816)	18,656		
8		Equipment		44,000	
9		Gain on Sale of Equipment		1,656	
10		*To record sale of equipment.*			
11					

> Depreciation expense must first be recorded for the portion of the year that the asset was used before it was sold.

> The gain on the sale is the excess of the cash received over the carrying amount of the asset.

REVIEW

MyLab Accounting

Make the grade with MyLab Accounting: The Quick Quiz questions, Short Exercises, Exercises, and Problems (Group A) marked with a ⊕ can be found on MyLab Accounting. You can practise them as often as you want, and most feature step-by-step guided instructions to help you find the right answer.

QUICK QUIZ (ANSWERS APPEAR ON THE LAST PAGE OF THIS CHAPTER.)

1. Argyle Corp. purchased a tract of land, a small office ⊕ building, and some equipment for $1,500,000. The appraised value of the land was $850,000; the building, $675,000; and the equipment, $475,000. What is the cost of the land?
   a. $850,000
   b. $637,500
   c. $482,776
   d. None of the above

2. Which of the following statements about depreciation is ⊕ false?
   a. Recording depreciation creates a fund to replace the asset at the end of its useful life.
   b. The cost of a building minus accumulated depreciation equals the building's carrying amount.
   c. Depreciation is a process of allocating the cost of property, plant, and equipment over its useful life.
   d. Depreciation is caused by physical wear and tear or obsolescence.

Use the following data for Questions 3 through 6.

On August 1, 2020, Major Link Inc. purchased a new piece of equipment that cost $25,000. The estimated useful life is five years, and estimated residual value is $2,500.

3. Assume Major Link purchased the equipment on ⊕ August 1, 2020. If Major Link uses the straight-line method for depreciation, what is the depreciation expense for the year ended December 31, 2020?
   a. $1,875
   b. $1,500
   c. $2,083
   d. $4,500

4. Assume Major Link purchased the equipment on ⊕ January 1, 2020. If Major Link uses the straight-line method for depreciation, what is the asset's carrying amount at the end of 2021?
   a. $13,500   c. $18,625
   b. $15,000   d. $16,000

5. Assume Major Link purchased the equipment on January 1, 2020. If Major Link uses the double-diminishing-balance method of depreciation, what is the depreciation expense for the year ended December 31, 2021?

    a. $5,400
    b. $6,000
    c. $8,333
    d. $15,000

6. Return to Major Link's original purchase date of August 1, 2020. Assume that Major Link uses the straight-line method of depreciation and sells the equipment for $11,500 on August 1, 2024. Based on the result of the sale of the equipment, what gain (or loss) will Major Link realize?

    a. $4,500
    b. $13,500
    c. $(9,000)
    d. $0

7. A company bought a new machine for $17,000 on January 1. The machine is expected to last four years and to have a residual value of $2,000. If the company uses the double-diminishing-balance method, what is the accumulated depreciation at the end of year 2?

    a. $10,880
    b. $11,250
    c. $12,750
    d. $15,000

8. Which of the following is *not* a capital expenditure?

    a. The addition of a building wing
    b. A complete overhaul of an air-conditioning system
    c. A tune-up of a company vehicle
    d. Replacement of an old motor with a new one in a piece of equipment
    e. The cost of installing a piece of equipment

9. Which of the following assets is *not* subject to a decreasing carrying amount through amortization /depreciation?

    a. Goodwill
    b. Patents
    c. Land improvements
    d. Copyrights

10. Why would a business select an accelerated method of depreciation for reporting purposes?

    a. Accelerated depreciation results in a constant amount of depreciation.
    b. Accelerated depreciation generates a greater amount of depreciation over the life of the asset than does straight-line depreciation.
    c. Accelerated depreciation is easier to calculate because residual value is ignored.
    d. Accelerated depreciation generates higher depreciation expense immediately, and therefore lower net income in the early years of the asset's life.

11. A company sells an asset that originally cost $300,000 for $100,000 on December 31, 2020. The accumulated depreciation account had a balance of $120,000 after the current year's depreciation of $30,000 had been recorded. The company should recognize a(n)

    a. $200,000 loss on disposal.
    b. $80,000 loss on disposal.
    c. $80,000 gain on disposal.
    d. $50,000 loss on disposal.

12. Which item among the following is *not* an intangible asset?

    a. A trademark
    b. A copyright
    c. A patent
    d. All of the above are intangible assets

13. An important measure of profitability is

    a. inventory turnover.
    b. quick (acid test) ratio.
    c. return on assets (ROA).
    d. net sales.

14. In 2020, return on assets for JBC Company has increased. This means that the

    a. company has become more effective.
    b. company has become more efficient.
    c. company has become more effective and more efficient.
    d. company has neither become more effective nor more efficient.

ACCOUNTING VOCABULARY

accelerated depreciation method A depreciation method that writes off a relatively larger amount of the asset's cost nearer the start of its useful life than the straight-line method does. (p. 288)

amortization Allocation of the cost of an intangible asset with a finite life over its useful life. (p. 301)

brand name A distinctive identification of a product or service. Also called a *trademark* or *trade name*. (p. 302)

capital expenditure Expenditure that increases an asset's capacity or efficiency, or extends its useful life. Capital expenditures are debited to an asset account. Also called *betterments*. (p. 282)

copyright Exclusive right to reproduce and sell a book, musical composition, film, other work of art, or computer program. Issued by the federal government, copyrights extend 50 years beyond the author's life. (p. 301)

depreciable cost The cost of a tangible asset minus its estimated residual value.   (p. 285)

depreciation An expense to recognize the portion of a capital asset's economic benefits that has been used up during an accounting period.   (p. 283)

double-diminishing-balance (DDB) method An accelerated depreciation method that computes annual depreciation by multiplying the asset's decreasing carrying amount by a constant percentage, which is two times the straight-line rate.   (p. 288)

estimated residual value Expected cash value of an asset at the end of its useful life. Also called *scrap value* or *salvage value*.   (p. 284)

estimated useful life Length of service that a business expects to get from an asset. May be expressed in years, units of output, kilometres, or other measures.   (p. 284)

franchises and licences Privileges granted by a private business or a government to sell a product or service in accordance with specified conditions.   (p. 302)

goodwill Excess of the cost of an acquired company over the sum of the market values of its net assets (assets minus liabilities).   (p. 302)

intangible assets Long-lived assets with no physical form that convey a special right to current and expected future benefits.   (p. 279)

obsolescence Occurs when an asset becomes outdated or no longer produces revenue for the company.   (p. 284)

patent A federal government grant giving the holder the exclusive right for 20 years to produce and sell an invention.   (p. 301)

physical wear and tear Occurs when the usefulness of the asset deteriorates.   (p. 284)

return on assets (ROA) Measures how profitably management has used the assets that shareholders and creditors have provided the company.   (p. 304)

straight-line (SL) method Depreciation method in which an equal amount of depreciation expense is assigned to each year of asset use.   (p. 285)

tangible long-lived assets Also called property, plant, and equipment.   (p. 279)

trademark, trade name A distinctive identification of a product or service. Also called a *brand name*.   (p. 302)

units-of-production (UOP) method Depreciation method by which a fixed amount of depreciation is assigned to each unit of output produced by the plant asset.   (p. 287)

ASSESS YOUR PROGRESS

SHORT EXERCISES

🌐 **S6-1** Examine Riverside's assets as follows:

LEARNING OBJECTIVE ❶

Measure the cost and carrying amount of a company's property, plant, and equipment

	A	B	C	D
1	**Riverside Corporation** Consolidated Balance Sheets (Partial, Adapted)			
2		May 31		
3	*(in millions)*	2020	2019	
4	**Assets**			
5	Current assets			
6	Cash and cash equivalents	$ 2,088	$ 257	
7	Receivables, less allowances of $144 and $125	2,770	2,623	
8	Spare parts, supplies, and fuel	4,653	4,509	
9	Prepaid expenses and other	467	423	
10	Total current assets	9,978	7,812	
11	Property and equipment, at cost			
12	Aircraft	2,392	2,392	
13	Package handling and ground support equipment	12,229	12,132	
14	Computer and electronic equipment	28,159	26,102	
15	Vehicles	581	452	
16	Facilities and other	1,432	1,589	
17	Total cost	44,793	42,667	
18	Less: Accumulated depreciation	(14,900)	(12,944)	
19	Net property and equipment	29,893	29,723	
20	Other long-term assets			
21	Goodwill	722	722	
22	Prepaid pension cost	1,340	1,271	
23	Intangible and other assets	329	333	
24	Total other long-term assets	2,391	2,326	
25	Total assets	$ 42,262	$ 39,861	
26				

1. What is Riverside's largest category of assets? List all 2020 assets in the largest category and their amounts as reported by Riverside.

2. What was Riverside's cost of property and equipment at May 31, 2020? What was the carrying amount of property and equipment on this date? Why is carrying amount less than cost?

LEARNING OBJECTIVE ❶

Measure the cost of property

S6-2 Page 280 of this chapter lists the costs included for the acquisition of land. First is the purchase price of the land, which is obviously included in the cost of the land. The reasons for including the related costs are not so obvious. For example, property tax is ordinarily an expense, not part of the cost of an asset. State why the related costs listed on page 280 are included as part of the cost of the land. After the land is ready for use, will these related costs be capitalized or expensed?

LEARNING OBJECTIVE ❶

Measure and record the lump-sum purchase of assets

S6-3 Suppose you have purchased land, a building, and some equipment. At the time of the acquisition, the land has a current fair value of $75,000, the building's fair value is $60,000, and the equipment's fair value is $15,000. Journalize the lump-sum purchase of the three assets for a total cost of $140,000. Assume you sign a note payable for this amount.

LEARNING OBJECTIVE ❶

Measure and account for equipment

S6-4 Assume WestJet repaired one of its Boeing 737 aircraft at a cost of $0.8 million, which WestJet paid in cash. Further, assume that the WestJet accountant erroneously capitalized this cost as part of the cost of the plane.

Show the effects of the accounting error on WestJet's income statement and balance sheet.

LEARNING OBJECTIVE ❷

Compute depreciation by three methods—first year only

S6-5 Assume that at the beginning of 2020, Porter Airlines purchased a Bombardier Q400 aircraft at a cost of $25,000,000. Porter expects the plane to remain useful for five years (5,000,000 km) and to have a residual value of $5,000,000. Porter expects the plane to be flown 750,000 km the first year and 1,250,000 km each year during years 2 through 4, and 500,000 km the last year.

1. Compute Porter's first-year depreciation on the plane using the following methods:

    a. Straight-line
    b. Units-of-production
    c. Double-diminishing-balance

2. Show the airplane's carrying amount at the end of the first year under each depreciation method. Which method results in the highest carrying amount? Which method produces the lowest carrying amount? Briefly explain why.

LEARNING OBJECTIVE ❷

Compute depreciation by three methods—final year only

S6-6 Use the assumed Porter Airlines data in exercise S6-5 to compute Porter's fifth-year depreciation on the plane using the following methods:

    a. Straight-line
    b. Units-of-production
    c. Double-diminishing-balance

LEARNING OBJECTIVES ❷❸

Compute partial-year depreciation

S6-7 Assume that on September 30, 2020, Swiss, the national airline of Switzerland, purchased an Airbus aircraft at a cost of €40,000,000 (€ is the symbol for the euro). Swiss expects the plane to remain useful for seven years (5,000,000 km) and to have a residual value of €5,000,000. Swiss expects the plane to be flown 500,000 km during the remainder of the first year ended December 31, 2020. Compute Swiss's depreciation on the plane for the year ended December 31, 2020, using the following methods:

    a. Straight-line
    b. Units-of-production
    c. Double-diminishing-balance

Which method would produce the highest net income for 2020? Which method produces the lowest net income? How does management choose which depreciation method to use?

S6-8 Canada's Wonderland paid $60,000 for a concession stand. Depreciation was recorded by the straight-line method over 10 years with zero residual value. Suppose that after using the concession stand for four years, Canada's Wonderland determines that the asset will remain useful for only three more years. How will this affect depreciation on the concession stand for year 5 by the straight-line method?

LEARNING OBJECTIVE ❸

Compute and record depreciation after a change in useful life of the asset

S6-9 On January 1, 2017, Big Rock Brewery purchased a van for $45,000. Big Rock expects the van to have a useful life of five years and a residual value of $5,000. The depreciation method used was straight-line. On December 31, 2020, the van was sold for $15,000 cash.

1. What was the carrying amount of the van on the date of sale?
2. Record the sale of the van on December 31, 2020.

LEARNING OBJECTIVE ❸

Record a gain or loss on derecognition under two depreciation methods

S6-10 Define patents and goodwill, which are both intangible assets. Explain how the accounting differs between a patent and goodwill.

LEARNING OBJECTIVE ❹

Account for intangible assets

S6-11 Consider the purchase of a supplier by Canadian Tire.

1. Suppose the fair value of the net assets at the date of purchase (February 1, 2020) had been $180.3 million. What would the goodwill cost have been if Canadian Tire had paid $200 million?
2. Explain how Canadian Tire will have been accounting for this goodwill up to February 1, 2022.

LEARNING OBJECTIVE ❹

Analyze a company's goodwill

S6-12 Suppose Jaguar Automobiles Ltd. paid $500,000 to research a new global positioning system. Jaguar also paid $1,200,000 to acquire a patent on a new motor. After readying the motor for production, Jaguar's sales revenue for the first year totalled $6,500,000. Cost of goods sold was $3,200,000, and selling expenses were $300,000. All these transactions occurred during fiscal 2020. Jaguar expects the patent to have a useful life of three years.

Prepare Jaguar's income statement for the fiscal year ended December 31, 2020.

LEARNING OBJECTIVE ❹

Account for patents and research cost

S6-13 You are reviewing the financial statements of Rising Yeast Co. During 2020, Rising Yeast purchased two other companies for $17 million. Also during fiscal 2020, Rising Yeast made capital expenditures of $2 million to expand its market share. During the year, the company sold operations, receiving cash of $25 million, and experienced a gain of $6 million on the disposal. Overall, Rising Yeast reported net income of $1 million during 2020. What would you expect the section for cash flows from investing activities on its statement of cash flows for 2020 to report? What total amount for net cash provided by (used in) investing activities do you anticipate?

LEARNING OBJECTIVE ❻

Report investing activities on the statement of cash flows

S6-14 In 2020, Artesia, Inc., reported $300 million in sales, $17 million in net income, $1 million in interest expense, and average total assets of $120 million. What is Artesia's return on assets in 2020? Assume an industry average of 16%. Did the company's return on assets improve or deteriorate? What could be some reasons for the change?

LEARNING OBJECTIVE ❺

Calculate return on assets

S6-15 Ochoa Optical, Inc., provides a full line of designer eyewear to optical dispensaries. Ochoa reported the following information for 2019 and 2020:

LEARNING OBJECTIVE ❺

Calculate return on assets

	2020	2019
Sales revenue	$500,000	$450,000
Net income	$ 44,500	$ 42,000
Interest expense	$ 500	$ 500
Average total assets	$250,000	$240,000

Compute return on assets for 2019 and 2020. Did the return on assets improve in 2020? What would cause this ratio to change?

LEARNING OBJECTIVE ❶

Distinguish a capital expenditure
from an immediate expense

S6-16 Identify each of the following items as either a capital expenditure (C), expense on the income statement (E), or neither (N):

Type of Expenditure (C, E, or N)	Transaction
	1. Paid property taxes of $75,000 for the first year the new building is occupied.
	2. Paid interest on a note payable during construction of a new plant building, $550,000.
	3. Repaired plumbing in main plant, paying $270,000 cash.
	4. Purchased equipment for new manufacturing plant, $6,000,000; financed with long-term note.
	5. Paid dividends of $40,000.
	6. Purchased a computer and peripheral equipment for $29,000 cash.
	7. Paved a parking lot on leased property for $300,000.
	8. Paid $90,000 in cash for installation of equipment in (4).
	9. Paid $148,000 to tear down old building on new plant site.
	10. Paid $31,000 maintenance on equipment in (4) during its first year of use.

LEARNING OBJECTIVE ❹

Measure and record goodwill

S6-17 Crunchies, Inc., dominates the snack-food industry with its Salty Chip brand. Assume that Crunchies, Inc., purchased Healthy Snacks, Inc., for $5.8 million cash. The market value of Healthy Snacks's assets is $7 million, and Healthy Snacks has liabilities with a market value of $6.0 million.

Requirements
1. Compute the cost of the goodwill purchased by Crunchies.
2. Explain how Crunchies will account for goodwill in future years.

LEARNING OBJECTIVES ❸❹

Record the effect of asset
impairment on financial statements

S6-18 For each of the following scenarios, indicate whether a long-term asset has been impaired (Y for yes and N for no) and, if so, the amount of the loss that should be recorded. Prepare any necessary journal entry.

Asset	Carrying Amount	Value in Use	Fair Value	Impaired? (Y or N)	Amount of Loss
a. Equipment	$ 180,000	$ 140,000	$ 100,000		
b. Trademark	$ 320,000	$ 460,000	$ 375,000		
c. Land	$ 52,000	$ 24,000	$ 21,000		
d. Factory building	$9 million	$9 million	$7 million		

EXERCISES

LEARNING OBJECTIVES ❶❷

Determine the cost and depreciation
of property

E6-19 Moody Inc. purchased land, paying $150,000 cash as a down payment and signing a $100,000 note payable for the balance. Moody also had to pay delinquent property tax of $5,000, title insurance costing $3,000, and $25,000 to level the land and to remove an unwanted building. The company paid $70,000 to remove earth for the foundation and then constructed an office building at a cost of $3,750,000. It also paid $100,000 for a fence around the property, $10,500 for the company sign near the property entrance, and $18,000 for lighting of the grounds. Determine the cost and prepare the journal entry for the company's land, land improvements, and building. How does management determine the cost of an asset?

 E6-20 Assume Trois Cuisines Manufacturing bought three machines in a $100,000 lump-sum purchase. An independent appraiser valued the machines as follows:

Machine No.	Appraised Value
1	$27,000
2	45,000
3	36,000

LEARNING OBJECTIVES ❶❸

Allocate costs to assets acquired in a lump-sum purchase; derecognize equipment

Trois Cuisines paid one-third in cash and signed a note payable for the remainder. What is each machine's individual cost? Immediately after making this purchase, Trois Cuisines sold machine 2 for its appraised value. What is the result of the sale? Round to three decimal places. Prepare the journal entry to record the sale.

 E6-21 Assume Hershey Chocolate Ltd. purchased a piece of manufacturing machinery. Classify each of the following expenditures as an asset expenditure or an immediate expense related to machinery: (a) sales tax paid on the purchase price, (b) transportation and insurance while machinery is in transit from seller to buyer, (c) purchase price, (d) installation, (e) training of personnel for initial operation of the machinery, (f) special reinforcement to the machinery platform, (g) income tax paid on income earned from the sale of products manufactured by the machinery, (h) major overhaul to extend useful life by three years, (i) ordinary repairs to keep the machinery in good working order, (j) lubrication of the machinery before it is placed in service, and (k) periodic lubrication after the machinery is placed in service. What criteria differentiated an asset expenditure from an immediate expense?

LEARNING OBJECTIVE ❶

Distinguish asset expenditures from expenses

 E6-22 During 2020, Roberts Inc. paid $200,000 for land and built a restaurant in Collingwood, Ontario. Prior to construction, the City of Collingwood charged Roberts Inc. $2,250 for a building permit, which Roberts Inc. paid. Roberts Inc. also paid $20,000 for architect's fees. The construction cost of $700,000 was financed by a long-term note payable issued on January 1, 2020, with interest cost of $29,000 paid at December 31, 2020. The building was completed September 30, 2020. Roberts Inc. will depreciate the building by the straight-line method over 25 years, with an estimated residual value of $60,000.

LEARNING OBJECTIVES ❶❷❸

Measure, depreciate, and report property and plant, determine effect on financial statements

1. Journalize transactions for the following (explanations are not required):

   a. Purchase of the land
   b. All the costs chargeable to the building, in a single entry
   c. Depreciation on the building

2. Report this transaction in the Property, Plant, and Equipment on the company's balance sheet at December 31, 2020.
3. What will Roberts Inc.'s income statement for the year ended December 31, 2020, report for the building?
4. Suppose in 2021, Roberts Inc. changed the useful life of the building from 25 years to 30 years. How will this affect the income statement and balance sheet?

E6-23 Assume you have a flower shop and you bought a delivery van for $30,000. You expect the van to remain in service for three years (150,000 km). At the end of its useful life, you estimate that the van's residual value will be $3,000. You estimate the van will travel 40,000 km the first year, 60,000 km the second year, and 50,000 km the third year. Prepare an estimate of the *depreciation expense* per year for the van under the three depreciation methods. Show your computations.

LEARNING OBJECTIVE ❷

Determine depreciation amounts by three methods

Which method do you think tracks the useful life cost on the van most closely? How does management determine which depreciation method to use?

LEARNING OBJECTIVES ❶❷❻

Report property, plant, and equipment depreciation and invest cash flow

E6-24 In January 2020, suppose a Starbucks franchise in Regina purchased a building, paying $50,000 cash and signing a $100,000 note payable. The franchise paid another $50,000 to remodel the facility. Equipment and store fixtures cost $50,000; dishes and supplies—a current asset—were obtained for $10,000.

The franchise is depreciating the building over 25 years by the straight-line method, with estimated residual value of $50,000. The equipment and store fixtures will be replaced at the end of five years; these assets are being depreciated by the double-diminishing-balance method, with zero residual value. At the end of the first year, the franchise has dishes and supplies worth $2,000.

Show what the franchise will report for supplies, property, plant, and equipment and cash flows at the end of the first year on its:

- Income statement
- Balance sheet
- Statement of cash flows (investing section only)

LEARNING OBJECTIVE ❺

Calculate return on assets

E6-25 Suppose Loblaws, one of the nation's largest grocery retailers, reported the following information (adapted) for its fiscal year ended January 31, 2020.

	January 31, 2020	January 31, 2019
Net sales	$48,815	$47,220
Net earnings	$ 2,000	$ 1,773
Interest expense	$ 10	$ 10
Average total assets	$33,699	$33,005

Requirements

1. Compute return on assets for the years ended January 31, 2019 and 2020.
2. Did return on assets improve or deteriorate? What are some possible causes for this change?

LEARNING OBJECTIVES ❷❸

Change a building's useful life and analyze the effects of a change in its useful life

E6-26 Assume The Salvation Army purchased a building for $900,000 and depreciated it on a straight-line basis over 30 years. The estimated residual value was $100,000. After using the building for 10 years, the Salvation Army realized that the building will remain useful for only 10 more years. Starting with the 11th year, the Salvation Army began depreciating the building over the newly revised total life of 20 years and decreased the estimated residual value to $75,000. Compute the depreciation expense for years 11 and 12. What effect will this have on the Income statement and balance sheet?

LEARNING OBJECTIVES ❷❸

Record depreciation and the sale of equipment

E6-27 Assume that on January 2, 2019, a Pizza Hut franchise purchased fixtures for $15,000 cash, expecting the fixtures to remain in service five years. The restaurant has depreciated the fixtures on a double-diminishing-balance basis, with $1,000 estimated residual value. On June 30, 2020, Pizza Hut sold the fixtures for $5,000 cash.

Requirements

1. Record the sale of the fixtures.
2. Management is thinking of switching to the straight-line method of depreciation. Do you agree? Why or why not?

LEARNING OBJECTIVES ❷❸

Measure equipment's cost, use UOP depreciation, and derecognize a used asset

E6-28 Bison Transport is a large trucking company that operates from Ontario to British Columbia in Canada and in the United States. Bison uses the units-of-production (UOP) method to depreciate its trucks because its managers believe UOP depreciation best measures wear and tear.

Bison Transport trades in its trucks often to keep driver morale high and maximize fuel efficiency. Assume that in 2017, the company acquired a tractor-trailer rig costing $280,000 and expected it to remain in service for five years or 1,000,000 km. Estimated residual value would be $40,000. During 2017, the truck was driven 130,000 km; during 2018, 180,000 km;

and during 2019, 180,000 km. After 90,000 km in 2020, the company wishes to trade in the tractor-trailer rig for a new rig. Assume the trade-in value of the old rig is $0.

Requirements

1. Prepare the journal entry to derecognize the rig.
2. What effect does this have on the financial statements?

E6-29 Following is an excerpt from the balance sheet of On the Edge Technologies Inc.:

LEARNING OBJECTIVE ❹

Analyze intangible assets

	(in thousands)	
	2020	2019
Goodwill (Note 4)	$60.7	$51.8
Intangible assets (Note 4)	48.4	42.4

A potential investor in On the Edge has asked you for advice. Identify the information that you would look for in the accompanying notes to the financial statements that would be relevant to providing advice about the investment decision.

E6-30 Holze Music Company purchased for $600,000 a patent for a new sound system. Although it gives legal protection for 20 years, the patent is expected to provide the company with a competitive advantage for only six years. Make journal entries to record (a) the purchase of the patent and (b) amortization for year 1.

LEARNING OBJECTIVES ❸❹

Record intangibles, amortization, and a change in the asset's useful life

After using the patent for two years, Holze Music Company's research director learns at a professional meeting that BOSE is designing a more powerful system. On the basis of this new information, Holze Music Company determines that the patent's total useful life is only four years. Record amortization for year 3.

E6-31 BlackBerry, who sells BlackBerry smartphones, recently reported in the statement of cash flows and notes to the financial statements in its annual report that it had made acquisitions of USD $6.2 million. Assume the balance sheet reported an increase in goodwill for the year in the amount of USD $4.5 million.

LEARNING OBJECTIVES ❹❻

Understand goodwill and statement of cash flows

Requirements

1. What is the definition of goodwill?
2. Explain the meaning of (a) the $6.2 million that BlackBerry reported on the statement of cash flows and (b) the $4.5 million increase in goodwill on the balance sheet.
3. BlackBerry's income statement and statement of cash flows do not show any charges for amortization of goodwill during the year. Explain the reason for the lack of charges.

E6-32 Assume that Google paid $18 million to purchase MySpace.com. Assume further that MySpace had the following summarized data at the time of the Google acquisition (amounts in millions of U.S. dollars).

LEARNING OBJECTIVE ❹

Measure and record goodwill

Assets		Liabilities and Equity	
Current assets..	$10	Total liabilities...	$24
Long-term assets.....................................	20	Shareholders' equity..............................	6
	$30		$30

MySpace's long-term assets had a fair value of only $15 million.

Requirements

1. Compute the cost of the goodwill purchased by Google.
2. Record the purchase of MySpace.
3. Explain how Google will account for goodwill in the future.

LEARNING OBJECTIVE ❻

Interpret a statement of cash flows

E6-33 The following items are excerpted from an annual report of a large retailer.

	A	B	C	D
1	Consolidated Statement of Cash Flows (Partial, Adapted) For the Year Ended December 30, 2020			
2	*(amounts in millions)*			
3	**Cash flow from operating activities:**			
4	Net income	$ 185.1		
5	Noncash items:			
6	Depreciation	90.9		
7	**Cash flow from investing activities:**			
8	Property, plant, and equipment	$ (233.6)		
9	Other investments	(0.6)		
10	Disposal of assets	17.0		
11				

Requirements
1. Why is depreciation listed on the statement of cash flows?
2. Explain in detail each investing activity.

LEARNING OBJECTIVE ❻

Report cash flows for property and equipment

E6-34 Assume Flowers to Go Ltd., a chain of flower shops, completed the following transactions. For each transaction, show what the company would report for investing activities on its statement of cash flows. Show negative amounts in parentheses.

a. Sold a building for $600,000. The building had cost $1,000,000, and at the time of the sale its accumulated depreciation totalled $400,000.

b. Lost a store building in a fire. The warehouse cost $300,000 and had accumulated depreciation of $180,000. The insurance proceeds received were $120,000.

c. Renovated a store at a cost of $400,000, paying cash.

d. Purchased store fixtures for $60,000. The fixtures are expected to remain in service for five years and then be sold for $10,000. Flowers to Go uses the straight-line depreciation method.

LEARNING OBJECTIVE ❺

Calculate return on assets

E6-35 Lowe's Companies, Inc. reported the following information (adapted) for its fiscal year ended January 31, 2020:

	January 31, 2020	January 31, 2019
Net sales	$82,189	$76,733
Net earnings	$ 1,111	$ 65
Interest expense	$ 5	$ 5
Average total assets	$23,505	$23,126

Using the facts provided, identify or calculate the information that is relevant to deciding whether or not the company was profitable and specify how each piece is relevant to your decision.

LEARNING OBJECTIVE ❶

Distinguish capital expenditures from expenses

E6-36 Assume Akro Products, Inc., purchased conveyor-belt machinery. Classify each of the following expenditures as a capital expenditure or an immediate expense related to machinery:

a. Major overhaul to extend the machinery's useful life by five years

b. Periodic lubrication after the machinery is placed in service

c. Purchase price

d. Training of personnel for initial operation of the machinery

e. Special reinforcement to the machinery platform

f. Transportation and insurance while machinery is in transit from seller to buyer

g. Ordinary repairs to keep the machinery in good working order

h. Lubrication of the machinery before it is placed in service

i. Sales tax paid on the purchase price

j. Installation of the conveyor-belt machinery

k. Income tax paid on income earned from the sale of products manufactured by the machinery

What criteria differentiated a capital expenditure from an immediate expense?

 E6-37 Good Life Clubs purchased exercise equipment at a cost of $100,000 each. In addition, Good Life paid $2,000 for a special platform on which to stabilize the equipment for use. Freight costs of $2,500 to ship the equipment were paid by the equipment supplier. Good Life will depreciate the equipment by the units-of-production method, based on an expected useful life of 50,000 hours of exercise. The estimated residual value of the equipment is $10,000. How many hours of usage can Good Life expect from the equipment if budgeted depreciation expense is $10,304 for the year? Why would management choose the units-of-production method and not one of the other methods?

> **LEARNING OBJECTIVES ❶❷**
>
> Understand units-of-production depreciation

 E6-38 Collicutt Energy Services Ltd. of Calgary, Alberta, reported the following for land, buildings, and equipment (in millions):

> **LEARNING OBJECTIVE ❸**
>
> Determine the gain or loss on sale of property and equipment

	December 31	
	2020	2019
Land, buildings, and equipment	$ 544.1	$ 575.1
Accumulated depreciation	(195.1)	(209.4)

During 2020, Collicutt Energy paid $74.2 million for new property and equipment. Depreciation for the year totalled $38.1 million. During 2020, Collicutt sold property and equipment for $20.2 million. How much was Collicutt's gain or loss on the sale of the property and equipment? How would this gain or loss be reported on the income statement? Record the sale of the property and equipment.

 E6-39 Rindy Inc. has a popular line of beaded jewellery. Rindy reported net earnings of $21,000 for 2020. Rindy depreciates furniture, fixtures, equipment and automotive assets on a straight-line basis over five years and assumes no residual value. Depreciation expense for the year totaled $1,000 and the assets are four years old.

What would net income be for 2020 if Rindy used the double-diminishing balance (DDB) instead? The company's income tax rate is 25%. How does management choose which depreciation method to use?

> **LEARNING OBJECTIVE ❷**
>
> Determine net income after a change in depreciation method

 E6-40 Air New Zealand (ANZ) is a Star Alliance member airline. Assume that early in 2020, ANZ purchased equipment at a cost of $200,000 (NZ). Management expects the equipment to remain in service for four years and the estimated residual value to be negligible. ANZ uses the straight-line depreciation method. Through an accounting error, ANZ expensed the entire cost of the equipment at the time of purchase.

> **LEARNING OBJECTIVE ❶**
>
> Determine equipment capitalizing versus expensing; measure the effect of an error

Requirements

Prepare a schedule to show the overstatement or understatement in the following items at the end of each year over the four-year life of the equipment. Ignore income taxes.

1. Total current assets

2. Equipment, net

3. Net income

4. Shareholders' equity

PROBLEMS (GROUP A)

LEARNING OBJECTIVES ❶❷

Measure and account for assets; distinguish a capital asset from an expense and record depreciation

P6-41A Assume Milne's Moving & Storage Ltd. (MMS) of Regina, Saskatchewan, incurred the following costs in acquiring land, making land improvements, and constructing and furnishing its own storage warehouse:

a.	Purchase price of 4 acres of land, including an old building that will be used for an office (land fair value is $320,000, building fair value is $80,000)	$350,000
b.	Landscaping (additional dirt and earth moving)...	8,100
c.	Fence around the land..	31,600
d.	Lawyer fee for title search on the land	1,000
e.	Delinquent real estate taxes on the land to be paid by MMS	7,500
f.	Company signs at front of the company property..	3,400
g.	Building permit for the warehouse	1,500
h.	Architect fee for the design of the warehouse..	24,500
i.	Masonry, carpentry, roofing, and other labour to construct the warehouse	920,000
j.	Renovation of the office building..	50,200
k.	Interest cost on construction loan for warehouse...	9,700
l.	Landscaping (trees and shrubs)...	8,200
m.	Parking lot, concrete walks, and lights on the property	57,600
n.	Concrete, wood, and other materials used in the construction of the warehouse	234,300
o.	Supervisory salary of construction supervisor (85% to warehouse, 5% to land improvements, 10% to office building)..	60,000
p.	Office furniture	115,700
q.	Transportation and installation of furniture	2,300

Assume MMS depreciates buildings over 40 years, land improvements over 20 years, and furniture over 8 years, all on a straight-line basis with zero residual value.

Requirements

1. Set up columns for Land, Land Improvements, Warehouse, Office Building, and Furniture. Show how to account for each of MMS's costs by listing the cost under the correct account. Determine the total cost of each asset.
2. Assuming that all construction was complete and the assets were placed in service on September 1, 2020, record depreciation for the year ended December 31, 2020. Round to the nearest dollar.
3. Identify the management issues included in this problem and what effect they have on business operations.

LEARNING OBJECTIVES ❶❷

Record property, plant, and equipment transactions; report on the balance sheet

P6-42A Lifestyle Lighting Ltd. reported the following on its balance sheet at December 31, 2019:

Property, plant and equipment, at cost:	
Land...	$ 150,000
Buildings	400,000
Less Accumulated depreciation..	(87,500)
Equipment	600,000
Less Accumulated depreciation..	(260,000)

In early July 2020, Lifestyle Lighting Ltd. expanded operations and purchased additional equipment at a cost of $100,000. The company depreciates buildings by the straight-line method over 20 years with residual value of $50,000. Due to obsolescence, the equipment has a useful life of only 10 years and is being depreciated by the double-diminishing-balance method with zero residual value.

Requirements

1. Journalize Lifestyle Lighting Ltd.'s property, plant, and equipment purchase and depreciation transactions for 2020. Why is land not depreciated?
2. Report property, plant, and equipment on the December 31, 2020, balance sheet.

P6-43A Assume that Inter-Provincial Transport Ltd.'s balance sheet includes the following assets under Property, Plant, and Equipment: Land, Buildings, and Motor-Carrier Equipment. Inter-Provincial has a separate accumulated depreciation account for each of these assets except land. Further, assume that Inter-Provincial completed the following transactions:

LEARNING OBJECTIVES ❶❷❸

Record property, plant, and equipment transactions, derecognition

2020

Jan. 2 Sold motor-carrier equipment with accumulated depreciation of $67,000 (cost of $130,000) for $70,000 cash. Purchased similar new equipment with a cash price of $176,000.

July 3 Sold a building that had cost $650,000 and had accumulated depreciation of $145,000 through December 31 of the preceding year. Depreciation is computed on a straight-line basis. The building had a 40-year useful life and a residual value of $250,000. Inter-Provincial received $100,000 cash and a $400,000 note receivable.

Oct. 29 Purchased land and a building for a single price of $420,000. An independent appraisal valued the land at $150,000 and the building at $300,000.

Dec. 31 Recorded depreciation as follows:

New motor-carrier equipment has an expected useful life of six years and an estimated residual value of 5% of cost. Depreciation is computed on the double-diminishing-balance method.

Depreciation on buildings is computed by the straight-line method. The new building carries a 40-year useful life and a residual value equal to 10% of its cost.

Requirements

1. Record the transactions in Inter-Provincial Transport Ltd.'s journal.
2. How does management choose which depreciation method to use?

P6-44A The board of directors of Special Services is reviewing its 2020 annual report. A new board member—a nurse with little business experience—questions the accountant about the depreciation amounts. The nurse wonders why depreciation expense has decreased from $200,000 in 2018 to $184,000 in 2019 to $172,000 in 2020. She states that she could understand the decreasing annual amounts if the company had been disposing of buildings each year, but that has not occurred. Further, she notes that growth in the city is increasing the values of company buildings and wonders why the company is recording depreciation when the property values are increasing.

LEARNING OBJECTIVE ❷

Explain the concept of depreciation

Requirement

Explain to the new board member how recording depreciation is relevant to preparing financial statements.

P6-45A On January 3, 2020, B.W. Soffer Inc. paid $224,000 for a computer system. In addition to the basic purchase price, the company paid a setup fee of $6,200, $6,700 sales tax, and $3,100 for special installation. Management estimates that the computer will remain in service for five years and have a residual value of $20,000. The computer will process 50,000 documents the first year, decreasing annually by 5,000 during each of the next four years (that is, 45,000 documents in 2021, 40,000 documents in 2022, and so on). In trying to decide which depreciation method to use, the company president has requested a depreciation schedule for each of three depreciation methods (straight-line, units-of-production, and double-diminishing-balance).

LEARNING OBJECTIVES ❶❷

Compute depreciation by three methods

Requirements

1. Prepare a depreciation schedule for each of the three depreciation methods listed, showing asset cost, depreciation expense, accumulated depreciation, and asset carrying amount.
2. B.W. Soffer Inc. reports to shareholders and creditors in the financial statements using the depreciation method that maximizes reported income in the early years of asset use. Consider the first year B.W. Soffer Inc. uses the computer system. Identify the depreciation method that meets the company's objectives. Discuss the advantages of each depreciation method.

LEARNING OBJECTIVES
1 2 3 6

Analyze property, plant, and equipment transactions from a company's financial statements

P6-46A The excerpts that follow are adapted from financial statements of a Canadian not-for-profit organization.

(amounts in thousands)	March 31	
Balance Sheet	2020	2019
Assets		
Total current assets	$277,631	$261,015
Property, plant, and equipment	68,406	61,225
Less accumulated depreciation	(26,909)	(22,725)
Long-term investments	108,302	147,165

	For the Year Ended March 31	
Consolidated Statement of Cash Flows	2020	2019
Operating excess of revenues over expense	$13,068	$ 15,321
Noncash items affecting net income:		
Depreciation	4,184	3,748
Cash flows from investing activities:		
Additions to property, plant, and equipment	(7,181)	(8,623)
Reduction of (addition to) long-term investments	38,863	(96,316)

Requirements

1. How much was the entity's cost of property, plant, and equipment at March 31, 2020? How much was the carrying amount of property, plant, and equipment? Show computations.
2. The financial statements give four pieces of evidence that the entity purchased property, plant, and equipment and sold long-term investments during 2020. What is the evidence?
3. Prepare T-accounts for Property, Plant and Equipment, Accumulated Depreciation, and Long-Term Investments. Then show all the activity in these accounts during 2020. Label each increase or decrease and give its dollar amount.
4. Why is depreciation added to net income on the statement of cash flows?

LEARNING OBJECTIVE 4

Account for intangibles and the related expenses

P6-47A Part 1. Sobeys Inc.'s balance sheet reports the asset Cost in Excess of Net Assets of Purchased Businesses. Assume that Sobeys acquired another company, which carried these figures:

Carrying amount of net assets	$3.8 million
Fair value of assets	4.1 million

Requirements

1. What is the term used in Canadian financial reporting for the asset Cost in Excess of Net Assets of Purchased Businesses?
2. Record Sobeys Inc.'s purchase of the other company for $5.3 million cash.
3. Assume that Sobeys determined that the asset Cost in Excess of Net Assets of Purchased Businesses increased in value by $800,000. How would this transaction be recorded?

Then, suppose Cost in Excess of Net Assets of Purchased Businesses decreased in value by $800,000. How would this transaction be recorded? Discuss the basis for your decision in each case.

Part 2. Suppose Ford paid $2.6 million for a patent related to an integrated system, including hands-free cell phone, GPS, and iPod connectivity. The company expects to install this system in its automobiles for four years. Ford will sell this as an "extra" for $1,500. In the first year, 10,000 units were sold. All costs per unit totalled $835.

Requirements

1. As the CFO, how would you record transactions relating to the patent in the first year?
2. Prepare the income statement for the integrated system's operations for the first year. Evaluate the profitability of the integrated system's operations. Use an income tax rate of 38%.
3. Explain what items were recorded as assets and why.

P6-48A At the end of 2019, Geothermal Heating Ltd. had total assets of $17.4 million and total liabilities of $9.2 million. Included among the assets were property, plant, and equipment with a cost of $4.8 million and accumulated depreciation of $3.4 million.

LEARNING OBJECTIVES ❶❸❻

Report property, plant, and equipment transactions on the financial statements

Assume that Geothermal Heating completed the following selected transactions during 2020. The company earned total revenues of $26.5 million and incurred total expenses of $21.3 million, which included depreciation of $1.7 million. During the year, Geothermal Heating paid $1.4 million for new equipment and sold old equipment for $0.3 million. The cost of the assets sold was $0.8 million, and their accumulated depreciation was $0.4 million.

Requirements

1. Explain how to determine whether Geothermal Heating had a gain or loss on the sale of old equipment during the year. What was the amount of the gain or loss, if any?
2. How will Geothermal Heating report property, plant, and equipment on the balance sheet at December 31, 2020, after all the year's activity?
3. How will Geothermal Heating report operating activities and investing activities on its statement of cash flows for 2020? The company's statement of cash flows starts with net income.

P6-49A Black Corporation operates general merchandise and food discount stores in the United States. The company reported the following information for the three years ending January 31, 2020:

LEARNING OBJECTIVE ❺

Calculate return on assets

	A	B	C	D	E
1	**Black Corporation** Income Statement (Adapted) For the years ended				
2	*(in millions)*	Jan. 31, 2020	Jan. 31, 2019	Jan. 31, 2018	
3	Total net revenue	$ 67,390	$ 65,357	$ 64,948	
4	Cost of revenue	45,725	44,062	44,157	
5	Selling, general, and administrative	16,413	16,622	16,389	
6	Operating income or loss	5,252	4,673	4,402	
7	Other revenue (expense)	(757)	(801)	(866)	
8	Income before tax	4,495	3,872	3,536	
9	Income tax expense	(1,575)	(1,384)	(1,322)	
10	Net income	$ 2,920	$ 2,488	$ 2,214	
11					

	A	B	C	D	E
1	**Black Corporation** Partial Balance Sheet (Condensed)				
2	(in millions)	Jan. 31, 2020	Jan. 31, 2019	Jan. 31, 2018	
3	Total current assets	$ 17,213	$ 18,424	$ 17,488	
4	Property, plant, and equipment	25,493	25,280	25,756	
5	Other assets	999	829	862	
6	Total assets	$ 43,705	$ 44,533	$ 44,106	
7					

Requirement

Using the facts provided, identify or calculate the information that is relevant to deciding whether or not the company was profitable and specify how each piece is relevant to your decision.

LEARNING OBJECTIVES ❸❻

Analyze the effect of a plant asset disposal and the cash flow impact of long-lived asset transactions

P6-50A Cook Corporation reported the following related to property and equipment (all in millions):

From the balance sheets:

	12/31/20	12/31/19
Property and equipment	$ 26,430	$ 24,220
Accumulated depreciation	(16,045)	(15,210)

From the investing activities section of the 2020 cash flow statement:

Cash used to purchase property and equipment	($2,820)
Proceeds from sale of property and equipment	43

From the 2020 income statement:

Depreciation expense	$1,145
Gain or loss on the sale of equipment	??

Requirements

1. Draw T-accounts for Property and Equipment and Accumulated Depreciation. Enter information as presented and solve for the unknown in each account.
2. Based on your calculations in requirement 1, calculate the carrying amount of assets sold during 2020. What is the difference between the sales price and the carrying amount?
3. Prepare the journal entry for the sale of property and equipment during 2020. Describe the effect of this transaction on the financial statements. Compare the sales price and the carrying amount in the journal entry, and compare this to the difference you calculated in requirement 2. Describe briefly.
4. Prepare a T-account for Property and Equipment, Net. Repeat requirement 1.

PROBLEMS (GROUP B)

P6-51B McMillan Tire Inc. operates in several provinces. The head office incurred the following costs in acquiring land and a building, making land improvements, and constructing and furnishing a garage showroom:

LEARNING OBJECTIVES ❶❷

Measure and account for assets; distinguish a capital asset from expense and record depreciation

a.	Purchase price of land, including a building that will be enlarged to be a warehouse (land fair value is $150,000; building fair value is $50,000)..............	$180,000
b.	Fence around the land..	26,000
c.	Company signs near front and rear approaches to the company property................	25,000
d.	Title insurance on the land acquisition...	1,200
e.	Renovation of the warehouse...	21,300
f.	Landscaping (additional dirt and earth moving).......................................	3,550
g.	Architect fee for the design of the garage/showroom................................	45,000
h.	Building permit for the building..	200
i.	Delinquent real estate taxes on the land to be paid by McMillan..............................	3,700
j.	Concrete, wood, and other materials used in the construction of the garage/showroom..	322,000
k.	Supervisory salary of construction supervisor (90% to garage/showroom 6% to land improvements, and 4% to building renovation).......................................	55,000
l.	Landscaping (trees and shrubs)..	5,350
m.	Masonry, carpentry, roofing, and other labour to construct the garage/showroom......	234,000
n.	Lights for the parking lot, walkways, and company signs............................	8,900
o.	Parking lots and concrete walks on the property	17,450
p.	Interest cost on construction loan for garage/showroom.............................	3,300
q.	Installation of equipment	8,000
r.	Equipment for the garage/showroom..	80,000

McMillan Tire depreciates buildings over 40 years, land improvements over 10 years, and equipment over 8 years, all on a straight-line basis with zero residual value.

Requirements

1. Determine the total cost of each asset. Set up columns for Land, Land Improvements, Garage/Showroom, Warehouse, and Equipment. Decide how to account for each of McMillan's costs by listing the cost under the correct account.
2. All construction was complete and the assets were placed in service on March 29. Record depreciation for the year ended December 31. Round figures to the nearest dollar.
3. Identify the issues of this problem, and discuss how your decisions would affect the results of McMillan Tire Inc.

P6-52B Moreau Lock & Key Ltd. has a hefty investment in security equipment, as reported in the company's balance sheet at December 31, 2019:

LEARNING OBJECTIVES ❶❷

Record property, plant, and equipment transactions; report on the balance sheet

Property, plant, and equipment, at cost:	
Land..	$ 200,000
Buildings	310,000
Less Accumulated depreciation...	(40,000)
Security equipment	620,000
Less Accumulated depreciation...	(370,000)

In early October 2020, Moreau Lock & Key purchased additional security equipment at a cost of $80,000. The company depreciates buildings by the straight-line method over

20 years with a residual value of $70,000. Due to obsolescence, security equipment has a useful life of only eight years and is being depreciated by the double-diminishing-balance method with zero residual value.

Requirements

1. How will Moreau Lock & Key's equipment purchase be recorded? What will the 2020 depreciation expense be? Why is land not depreciated?
2. Report property, plant, and equipment on the company's December 31, 2020, balance sheet.

LEARNING OBJECTIVES ❶❷❸

Record property, plant, and equipment transactions, derecognition

P6-53B Schmaltz Cable Company's balance sheet reports the following assets under Property, Plant, and Equipment: Land, Buildings, Office Furniture, Communication Equipment, and Televideo Equipment. The company has a separate accumulated depreciation account for each of these assets except land. Assume that Schmaltz Cable completed the following transactions:

2020

Jan. 4 Sold communication equipment with accumulated depreciation of $85,000 (cost of $96,000) for $18,000. Purchased new equipment for $118,000.

June 30 Sold a building that had cost $495,000 and had accumulated depreciation of $255,000 through December 31 of the preceding year. Depreciation is computed on a straight-line basis. The building has a 40-year useful life and a residual value of $95,000. The company received $50,000 cash and a $250,000 note receivable.

Nov. 4 Purchased used communication and televideo equipment from Rogers Cable Company. Total cost was $80,000 paid in cash. An independent appraisal valued the communication equipment at $75,000 and the televideo equipment at $25,000.

Dec. 31 Depreciation is recorded as follows:

   Equipment is depreciated by the double-diminishing-balance method over a five-year life with zero residual value. Depreciation is recorded separately on the equipment purchased on January 4 and on November 4.

Requirements

1. Record the transactions in Schmaltz Cable's journal.
2. How does management choose which depreciation method to use?

LEARNING OBJECTIVE ❷

Explain the concept of depreciation

P6-54B The board of directors of the Canadian Red Cross is having its regular quarterly meeting. Accounting policies are on the agenda, and depreciation is being discussed. A new board member, a social worker, has some strong opinions about two aspects of depreciation policy. The new board member argues that depreciation must be coupled with a fund to replace company assets. Otherwise, there is no substance to depreciation, he argues. He also challenges the three-year estimated life over which the Canadian Red Cross is depreciating association computers. He notes that the computers will last much longer and should be depreciated over at least 10 years.

Requirement

Explain to the new board member how recording depreciation is relevant to preparing financial statements.

LEARNING OBJECTIVES ❶❷

Compute depreciation by three methods

P6-55B On January 2, 2018, Yuki Sporting Goods Ltd. purchased branding equipment at a cost of $63,000. Before placing the equipment in service, the company spent $2,200 for delivery, $4,000 to customize the equipment, and $800 for installation. Management estimates that the equipment will remain in service for six years and have a residual value of $16,000. The equipment can be expected to brand 18,000 pieces in each of the first four years and 14,000 pieces in each of the next two years. In trying to decide which depreciation method to use, George Yuki requests a depreciation schedule for each method (straight-line, units-of-production, and double-diminishing-balance).

Requirements

1. Prepare a depreciation schedule for each of the depreciation methods listed, showing asset cost, depreciation expense, accumulated depreciation, and asset carrying amount.
2. Yuki Sporting Goods reports to its banker in the financial statements using the depreciation method that maximizes reported income in the early years of asset use. Consider the first year that Yuki Sporting Goods uses the equipment. Identify the depreciation method that meets the company's objectives. Explain your choice.

P6-56B CrossCanada Transport Inc. (CC) provides warehouse and distribution services. The excerpts that follow are adapted from CC's financial statements for fiscal year 2020.

LEARNING OBJECTIVES
❶❷❸❹❻

Analyze property, plant, and equipment transactions from a company's financial statements

(amounts in thousands)	October 31	
Balance Sheet	2020	2019
Assets		
Total current assets	$237,936	$208,530
Premises and equipment	5,941	5,246
Less Accumulated depreciation	(3,810)	(3,428)
Goodwill	4,752	4,304

	For the Year Ended October 31	
Statement of Cash Flows (in millions)	2020	2019
Cash provided from operating activities:		
Net income from continuing operations	$5,492	$4,757
Noncash items affecting net income:		
Depreciation	434	405
Cash used in investing activities:		
Acquisition of premises and equipment	(706)	(511)
Cash used in acquisitions (including $41 of premises and equipment)	(373)	(256)

Requirements

1. How much was CC's cost of property and equipment at October 31, 2020? How much was the carrying amount of premises and equipment? Show computations.
2. The financial statements give three pieces of evidence that CC purchased premises and equipment during 2020. What are they?
3. Prepare T-accounts for Premises and Equipment and Accumulated Depreciation. Then show all the activity in these accounts during 2020. Did CC dispose of any assets and, if so, what was the carrying amount?
4. Why has goodwill not been amortized?

P6-57B Part 1. The Coca-Cola Company's (CCC) balance sheet reports the asset Goodwill. Assume that CCC purchased an asset to be included in Goodwill as part of the acquisition of another company, which carried these figures (thousands of dollars):

LEARNING OBJECTIVE ❹

Account for intangibles and the related expenses

Carrying amount of long-term assets	$34,550
Fair value of assets	49,000
Liabilities	4,500

Requirements

1. Explain the terms *carrying amount of assets*, *fair value of assets*, and *goodwill*. On what would you base the purchase price of the acquisition?
2. Make the journal entry to record CCC's purchase of the other company for $50,000 cash.

Part 2. Joshua Thomas has written a new dance song which Luv Sound Inc. would like to record. Joshua is negotiating the rights to the new song. It is estimated that Luv Sound will sell about 500,000 recordings either on CD, to radio station airings, or to iPod sales. Joshua would like to receive $2,000,000 for the copyright to this song.

Requirements

1. As the CFO of Luv Sound, decide whether $2,000,000 is an appropriate amount to pay for the copyright for Joshua Thomas's song.
2. If you chose to purchase the copyright, show how you would record the transaction.
3. What would be the accumulated amortization after 300,000 copies of the song had been sold by Luv Sound Inc.?

LEARNING OBJECTIVES ❶❸❻

Report property, plant, and equipment transactions on the financial statements

P6-58B At the end of 2019, a telecommunications company had total assets of $15.3 billion and total liabilities of $10.7 billion. Included among the assets were property, plant, and equipment with a cost of $16.4 billion and accumulated depreciation of $9.1 billion.

Suppose that the company completed the following selected transactions during 2020. The company earned total revenues of $11.6 billion and incurred total expenses of $9.89 billion, which included depreciation of $1.84 billion. During the year, the company paid $1.8 billion for new property, plant, and equipment, and sold old property, plant, and equipment for $0.2 billion. The cost of the assets sold was $0.29 billion and their accumulated depreciation was $0.29 billion.

Requirements

1. Explain how to determine whether the company had a gain or a loss on the sale of the old property, plant, and equipment. What was the amount of the gain or loss, if any?
2. Show how the company would report property, plant, and equipment on the balance sheet at December 31, 2020.
3. Show how the company would report operating activities and investing activities on its statement of cash flows for 2020. The company's statement of cash flows starts with net income.

LEARNING OBJECTIVE ❺

Calculate return on assets

P6-59B Kohl's Corporation operates family oriented department stores that sell moderately priced apparel and housewares. The company reported the following information (adapted) for the three years ending January 31, 2020:

	A	B	C	D	E
1	**Kohl's Corporation** Income Statement (Adapted)				
2		Jan. 31, 2020	Jan. 31, 2019	Jan. 31, 2018	
3	Net sales	$ 18,391	$ 17,178	$ 16,389	
4	Cost of merchandise sold	11,359	10,680	10,334	
5	Selling, general, and administrative	5,118	4,786	4,519	
6	Operating income	1,914	1,712	1,536	
7	Other revenue (expense)	(132)	(124)	(111)	
8	Income before tax	1,782	1,588	1,425	
9	Provision for income tax	(668)	(597)	(540)	
10	Net income	$ 1,114	$ 991	$ 885	
11					

Source: Based on the data from Kohl's Corporation Annual Report.

	A	B	C	D	E
1	**Kohl's Corporation** Partial Balance Sheet				
2		Jan. 31, 2020	Jan. 31, 2019	Jan. 31, 2018	
3	Total current assets	$ 5,645	$ 5,485	$ 3,728	
4	Long-term investments	386	336	333	
5	Property, plant, and equipment	7,256	7,018	6,984	
6	Other assets	277	321	318	
7	Total assets	$ 13,564	$ 13,160	$ 11,363	
8					

Requirement

Using the facts provided, identify or calculate the information that is relevant to deciding whether or not the company was profitable and specify how each piece is relevant to your decision.

P6-60B Morgan Corporation reported the following related to property and equipment (all in millions):

From the balance sheets:

LEARNING OBJECTIVES ❸❻

Analyze the effect of a plant asset disposal and the cash flow impact of long-lived asset transactions

	12/31/20	12/31/19
Property and equipment	$23,530	$21,350
Accumulated depreciation	(18,395)	(17,530)

From the investing activities section of the 2020 cash flow statement:

Cash used to purchase property and equipment	($2,820)
Proceeds from sale of property and equipment	56

From the 2020 income statement:

Depreciation expense	$1,145
Gain or loss on the sale of equipment	??

Requirements

1. Draw T-accounts for Property and Equipment and Accumulated Depreciation. Enter information as presented and solve for the unknown in each account.
2. Based on your calculations in requirement 1, calculate the carrying amount of assets sold during 2020. What is the difference between the sales price and the carrying amount?
3. Prepare the journal entry for the sale of property and equipment during 2020. Describe the effect of this transaction on the financial statements. Compare the sales price and the carrying amount in the journal entry, and compare this to the difference you calculated in requirement 2. Describe briefly.
4. Prepare a T-account for Property and Equipment, Net. Repeat requirement 1.

APPLY YOUR KNOWLEDGE

DECISION CASE

LEARNING OBJECTIVE ❷

Measure profitability based on different depreciation methods

Suppose you are considering investing in two businesses, La Petite France Bakery and Burgers Ahoy Inc. The two companies are virtually identical, and both began operations at the beginning of the current year.

In early January, both companies purchased equipment costing $175,000 that had a 10-year estimated useful life and a $10,000 residual value. La Petite France uses the depreciation method that maximizes income for reporting purposes. In contrast, Burgers Ahoy uses the double-diminishing-balance method for depreciation purposes. Assume that both companies' trial balances at December 31 included the following:

Sales revenue	$350,000
Cost of goods sold	94,000
Operating expenses before depreciation	50,000

The income tax rate is 25%.

Requirements

1. Prepare both companies' income statements.
2. Write an investment newsletter to address the following questions for your clients. Which company appears to be more profitable? If prices continue rising over the long term, in which company would you prefer to invest? Why?

ETHICAL DECISIONS

Decision 1 Vitner's Ltd. purchased land and a building for the lump sum of $6.0 million. To report a higher net income, Mary Drink allocated 60% of the purchase price to the building and only 40% to the land. A more realistic allocation would have been 80% to the building and 20% to the land.

Requirements

1. Explain the advantage of allocating too little to the building and too much to the land.
2. Was Vitner's allocation ethical? If so, state why. If not, why not? Identify who was harmed.

Decision 2 The following questions are unrelated except that they all apply to property, plant, and equipment and intangible assets:

1. The manager of Fashion Forward Ltd. regularly buys property, plant, and equipment and debits the cost to Repairs and Maintenance Expense. Why would she do that, since she knows this action violates IFRS?
2. The manager of Greytown Express Inc. regularly debits the cost of repairs and maintenance of property, plant, and equipment to Plant and Equipment. Why would he do that, since he knows he is violating IFRS?
3. It has been suggested that because many intangible assets have no value except to the company that owns them, they should be valued at $1.00 or zero on the balance sheet. Many accountants disagree with this view. Which view do you support? Why?

FOCUS ON FINANCIAL STATEMENT ANALYSIS

Dollarama Inc.

Refer to Dollarama's financial statements in Appendix A at the end of this book, and answer the following questions.

1. Which depreciation method does Dollarama use for reporting to shareholders and creditors in the financial statements?

2. During 2017, Dollarama sold building, fixtures, and equipment (assets). What were the proceeds? What was the cost of the building, fixtures, and equipment disposed of?

3. How much did Dollarama pay for land, building, and fixtures during 2017? What about in 2016? Evaluate the trend in these expenditures as to whether it conveys good news for Dollarama.

4. During 2017, Dollarama added new property, plant, and equipment. Therefore, it is possible that the company's property and equipment at the end of 2017 were proportionately newer than the assets the company held at the end of 2016. Were property and equipment proportionately newer or older at the end of 2017 (versus 2016)?

5. How much was Dollarama's depreciation and amortization expense during fiscal year 2017? How much was Dollarama's accumulated depreciation and amortization at the end of year 2016? Explain why accumulated depreciation and amortization exceeds depreciation and amortization expense for the year 2017.

6. Explain why Dollarama adds depreciation and amortization expenses back to net income in the computation of net cash from operating activities.

7. Does Dollarama have any goodwill? In 2017, was amortization on goodwill charged? Dollarama describes intangible assets. What are they? How much amortization of intangible assets did Dollarama record in 2017?

CHECK YOUR WORK

STOP + THINK ANSWERS

STOP + THINK (6-1)

These improvements wear out over time, and in the case of leasehold improvements, they expire once the terms of the lease are up.

STOP + THINK (6-2)

The yearly depreciation would be $2,000 [($13,000 − $3,000)/5]. Therefore, 2 years of use would be left [($7,000 − $3,000)/($2,000)].

STOP + THINK (6-3)

1. An accounting change that lengthens the estimated useful lives of depreciable assets

   (a) decreases depreciation expense, and

   (b, c) increases net income and owners' equity.

2. Investor reactions are not always predictable. There is research to indicate that companies cannot fool investors.

In this case, investment advisors would *probably* subtract from the company's reported net income the amount added by the accounting change. Investors could then use the remaining net *loss* figure to evaluate the company's lack of progress during the year. Investors would probably view the company as worse for having made this accounting change. It is probably for this reason that such changes in accounting estimates are so rare in Canada.

STOP + THINK (6-4)

Goodwill is not amortized because it has an indefinite life. If the value of goodwill is impaired, it must be written down.

STOP + THINK (6-5)

The ROA ratio measures how profitably management has used the assets that both the shareholders and creditors have provided the company. Net income belongs to the shareholders, and the creditors earn the interest.

STOP + THINK (6-6)

1. Canadian Tire spent $471.0 million on property, plant, and equipment, and $161.6 million on intangible assets.

2. The company sold assets for $13.6 million that had a carrying amount of $14.6 million. The result of the sale was a loss of $1 million ($13.6 million received and $14.6 million carrying amount).

3. Report the loss on the *income statement* under the heading *Non-operating income (expense)*. The gain or loss from disposal also appears on the statement of cash flows under the indirect method in the operating activities section.

QUICK QUIZ ANSWERS

1. *b* [($850,000/[$850,000 + $675,000 + $475,000]) × $1,500,000 = $637,500]
2. *a*
3. *a* [($25,000 − $2,500)/5 × 5/12 = $1,875]
4. *d* [($25,000 − $2,500)/5 × 2 = $9,000; $25,000 − $9,000 = $16,000]
5. *b* [$25,000 × 2/5 = $10,000; ($25,000 − $10,000) × 2/5 = $6,000]

6. *a* [($25,000 − $2,500)/5 × 4 = $18,000; $25,000 − $18,000 = $7,000; $11,500 − $7,000 = *gain of $4,500, therefore, a gain will be realized*]
7. *c* [$17,000 × 2/4 = $8,500; ($17,000 − $8,500) × 2/4 = $4,250; $8,500 + $4,250 = $12,750]
8. *c*
9. *a*
10. *d*

11. *b*
12. *e*
13. *c*
14. *c*

COMPREHENSIVE CASE

CHAPTERS 4–6

This comprehensive case requires you to apply concepts learned throughout Chapters 4-6. You may find it helpful to review these chapters before responding to case requirements.

Marshall Corporation is a small private corporation that sells desktop printers to local businesses and schools. On May 1, 2020, the following were the account balances of Marshall Corporation:

	Debits		Credits
Cash	$32,790	Allowance for doubtful accounts	$ 1,403
Accounts receivable	19,932	Accumulated dep.-delivery van	43,000
Inventory (100 units)	20,200	Accumulated dep.-furniture & fix.	2,000
Delivery van	45,000	Accounts payable	8,445
Furniture & fixtures	10,000	Common shares	10,000
		Retained earnings	63,074
Total debits	$127,922	Total credits	$127,922

The selling price for each of the printers is $508. The company uses the FIFO method under the perpetual inventory system to account for inventory. During May, the following transactions took place:

May 1   Bought 200 desktop printers for $210 each on account.

Bought a delivery van, paying $10,000 cash as a down payment and signed a six-month $40,000, 6% note payable for the balance. The company paid $750 to have its company logo painted on the side of the van. The residual value is $5,000. The old delivery van was sold for $5,000; it cost $45,000 and accumulated depreciation up to the date of disposal is $43,000.

10   Sold 160 printers to Rose Company on account.

12   One of the company's customers agreed to sign a 60-day notes receivable to replace a $1,500 accounts receivable due on that day. The interest rate on the note is 10%.

20   Sold 5 printers to a school using a VISA card to pay for the transaction. A 3% service fee is charged by VISA.

22   Sold 80 printers to Dellrose Public School on account.

24   Returned for credit 2 damaged printers from Rose Company, costing $202 each.

28   Received payment in full from Rose Company for the balance owing.

28   Wrote off as uncollectible $1,000 of accounts receivable.

29   Paid accounts payable, $20,000.

30   Recovered an accounts receivable that was written off in April, $500.

31   Paid operating expenses totalling $59,048.

31   Recorded depreciation on the delivery van, and the furniture and fixtures. The company uses the straight-line method of depreciation for the delivery van.

The furniture and fixtures are depreciated using the straight-line method over 5 years. There is no residual value on the furniture and fixtures.

31   Recorded interest on the note payable.

31   Recorded interest on the notes receivable.

31   The company records the bad debt expense based on the aging of accounts receivables, which follows:

		Number of	Days	Outstanding	
	Total	0–30 days	31–60 days	61–90 days	Over 90 days
Accounts receivable	$58,056	43,180	$10,876	$3,000	$1,000
Estimated percentage uncollectible		2%	5%	10%	20%

Requirements

1. Prepare the journal entries for the transactions including any adjusting journal entries for the month of May 31, 2020. Round all final numbers to the nearest dollar. Do not round during calculations.
2. Post the journal entries to T-accounts and prepare an adjusted trial balance.
3. Prepare the income statement for the month of May 2020 (ignore income taxes) and the asset section of the balance sheet as at May 31, 2020.
4. The company uses the FIFO method to value inventory. Why is it important for a company to use the same inventory costing method year after year? Are companies allowed to change the method?
5. The company is looking for ways to improve cash collections as quickly as possible from sales and accounts receivable. What steps could it take?

6. Assume that Marshall overstated its ending inventory by $1,696. How does this affect cost of goods sold, gross profit, and net income in the year it is discovered? If the error is undetected, what is the impact on cost of goods sold, gross profit, and net income for the following year?

7. Assume that Marshall uses the LCNRV to report inventory on the balance sheet. The NRV of $1,200 is less than the FIFO cost. Prepare the journal entry. How would readers of the financial statements know about this change in inventory value?

8. Management chose to use the straight-line method to depreciate the delivery van, and the furniture and fixtures because it is simple and easy to use. Management has always stayed away from the diminishing balance and units of production method. Is this reasoning in accordance with IFRS?

Liabilities

7

SPOTLIGHT

WestJet Airlines: A Success Story WestJet began operations in 1996 by serving five cities in Western Canada and now flies across Canada and to many destinations in the United States, Mexico, and the Caribbean. The airline decided at its start to operate with a single type of plane, the Boeing 737, in order to reduce operating costs. WestJet also decided to encourage share ownership by employees, so the front-desk staff, pilots, and flight attendants also own part of the company. This has led to a high level of service, which encourages passengers to "fly WestJet."

Airlines have some interesting liabilities. WestJet collects fares in advance and recognizes the revenue when the passenger actually takes the trip. Thus, WestJet had a liability called "advance ticket sales" of about $740 million on its balance sheet at June 30, 2018. When passengers change or cancel flights, they may receive credits that they can apply toward future WestJet flights. This "nonrefundable guest credits" liability was $65 million at June 30, 2018. In this chapter, you will learn more about these and other types of liabilities commonly found on financial statements.

LEARNING OBJECTIVES

1. **Explain** and **account** for current liabilities
2. **Explain** the types, features, and pricing of bonds payable
3. **Account** for bonds payable
4. **Calculate** and **account** for interest expense on bonds payable
5. **Explain** the advantages and disadvantages of financing with debt versus equity
6. **Analyze** and **evaluate** a company's debt-paying ability
7. **Describe** other types of long-term liabilities
8. **Report** liabilities on the balance sheet

CPA COMPETENCIES

Competencies addressed in this chapter:

1.2.2 Evaluates treatment for routine transactions

1.4.4 Interprets financial reporting results for stakeholders (external or internal)

Based on Chartered Professional Accountant standards

Heather Dunbar/Shutterstock

	A	B	C	D
1	**WestJet Airlines Ltd.** Liabilities As at June 30, 2018 (in thousands)			
2	**Liabilities**			
3	Current liabilities:			
4	Accounts payable and accrued liabilities	$ 434,295		
5	Advance ticket sales	739,858		
6	Deferred Rewards program	205,691		
7	Non-refundable guest credits	64,897		
8	Current portion of maintenance provisions	106,082		
9	Current portion of long-term debt	153,718		
10		1,704,541		
11	Non-current liabilities:			
12	Maintenance provisions	261,116		
13	Long-term debt	1,883,372		
14	Other liabilities	16,528		
15	Deferred income tax	401,856		
16	Total liabilities	$ 4,267,413		
17				

Source: Excerpted from WestJet Airlines Ltd. Consolidated Balance Sheet as at June 30, 2018.

OBJECTIVE

❶ **Explain** and **account** for current liabilities

EXPLAIN AND ACCOUNT FOR CURRENT LIABILITIES

Current liabilities are obligations due within one year, or within the company's normal operating cycle if it is longer than one year. Obligations due beyond that are classified as *long-term liabilities* or *non-current liabilities*, as in WestJet's Liabilities section above.

Current liabilities are of two kinds:

- Known amounts
- Estimated amounts

We look first at current liabilities of known amounts.

Current Liabilities of Known Amount

SHORT-TERM BORROWINGS. Companies sometimes need to borrow money on a short-term basis to cover temporary shortfalls in cash needed to run their businesses. For example, a ski resort that earns most of its revenues during the winter months may need to temporarily borrow money to supplement the minimal cash flows it generates from operations during the summer. A **line of credit** allows a company to access credit on an as-needed basis up to a maximum amount set by the lender. The ski resort, for example, could arrange with its bank to borrow up to $250,000 to help run its business over the slow summer months.

ACCOUNTS PAYABLE. Amounts owed for products or services purchased on credit are **accounts payable**. For example, WestJet purchases on account the food and beverages it serves its passengers. We have seen many other examples of accounts payable in previous chapters. One of a merchandiser's most common transactions is the credit purchase of inventory. Dollarama and Sobeys, for example, buy their inventory on account.

ACCRUED LIABILITIES (OR ACCRUED EXPENSES). An *accrued liability* results from an expense the business has incurred but has not yet been billed for or paid. Because accrued liabilities often arise from expenses, they are sometimes called *accrued expenses*.

For example, WestJet's salaries and wages payable accrue as employees work for the company. Interest expense accrues with the passage of time. Common types of accrued liabilities are:

- Salaries and Wages Payable
- Interest Payable
- Income Taxes Payable

Salaries and Wages Payable is the liability for salaries, wages, and related payroll expenses not yet paid at the end of the period (see the Payroll Liabilities section on page 339 for more details on this accrual). This category also includes payroll deductions withheld from employee paycheques. *Interest Payable* is the company's interest payable on notes, loans, and bonds payable. *Income Taxes Payable* is the amount of income tax the company still owes at year-end.

SHORT-TERM NOTES PAYABLE. In Chapter 4 we introduced you to promissory notes from a lender's perspective, so we called them notes *receivable*. When we record these same notes in the borrower's books, they are notes *payable*. **Short-term notes payable** are notes payable due within one year. Robertson Construction Inc. may issue short-term notes payable to borrow cash or to purchase assets. For its notes payable, Robertson must accrue interest expense at the end of each reporting period. The following sequence of entries covers the purchase of inventory, accrual of interest expense, and payment of a short-term note payable:

	A	B	C	D	E
1	2020				
2	Oct. 1	Inventory	8,000		
3		Note Payable, Short-Term		8,000	
4		*Purchase of inventory by issuing a six-month 10% note payable.*			

This transaction increases both an asset and a liability:

ASSETS	=	LIABILITIES	+	SHAREHOLDERS' EQUITY
+8,000	=	+8,000		

Assume Robertson Construction's year-end is December 31. At year-end, Robertson must accrue interest expense at 10% per year for October through December. (For ease of exposition, accrued interest has been calculated based on months rather than days. In practice, days are typically used.)

	A	B	C	D	E
1	2020				
2	Dec. 31	Interest Expense ($8,000 × 0.10 × 3/12)	200		
3		Interest Payable		200	
4		*Adjusting entry to accrue interest expense at year-end.*			

Liabilities increase, and equity decreases because of the expense:

ASSETS	=	LIABILITIES	+	SHAREHOLDERS' EQUITY
0	=	+200		−200 Interest Expense

The balance sheet at year-end will report the note payable of $8,000 and the related interest payable of $200 as current liabilities. The income statement will report interest expense of $200.

The following entry records the note's payment at March 31, 2021:

	A	B	C	D	E
1	2021				
2	Mar. 31	Note Payable, Short-Term	8,000		
3		Interest Payable	200		
4		Interest Expense ($8,000 × 0.10 × 3/12)	200		
5		Cash [$8,000 + ($8,000 × 0.10 × 6/12)]		8,400	
6		*Payment of a note payable and interest at maturity.*			
7					

ASSETS	=	LIABILITIES	+	SHAREHOLDERS' EQUITY
−8,400	=	−8,000		−200 Interest Expense
		−200		

The debits eliminate the two payables and also record Robertson's interest expense for January, February, and March.

SALES TAX PAYABLE. The federal government and most provinces levy taxes on the sale of goods and services. Sellers collect these taxes from customers, creating **sales tax payable** to the government levying the tax. Canada has three types of sales taxes:

- Goods and services tax (GST) is a value-added tax levied by the federal government. At the time of writing, the tax is 5%. It applies to most goods and services.

- Provincial or regional sales tax (PST) is a retail tax applied to goods and services purchased by individuals or businesses *for their own use,* not for resale, with the rates varying by province or region. At the time of writing, Alberta, the Northwest Territories, Nunavut, and Yukon do not levy a provincial or regional sales tax.

- Harmonized sales tax (HST), which combines PST and GST, is also a value-added tax. Prince Edward Island, New Brunswick, Newfoundland and Labrador, Nova Scotia, and Ontario, together with the federal government, levy an HST.

The final consumer of a GST- or HST-taxable product or service bears the tax, while entities further down the supply chain from the end consumer do pay GST or HST, but receive an input tax credit (ITC) equal to the tax they have paid. These ITCs are deducted from any GST or HST collected to arrive at the net GST or HST payable to the government. For example, if a company collected $10,000 in HST on its sales and paid $8,000 in HST on goods and services it purchased, then it would end the period with HST payable of $2,000 ($10,000 in HST collected less $8,000 in ITCs).

GST or HST payable is always a current liability, as it is payable annually, quarterly, or monthly, depending on the collector's volume of business. GST and HST are remitted to the Canada Revenue Agency (CRA), which in turn remits the provincial portion of the HST to the respective provinces, with all GST and the federal portion of the HST being remitted to the federal government.

GST and HST are accounted for in the same way, so the following illustration using GST is applicable for HST as well, except for the difference in tax rates. Assume Kitchen Hardware Ltd., of Brandon, Manitoba, purchases lawn rakes for $3,000 plus 5% GST for a total of $3,150. Subsequently, Kitchen sells the rakes for $6,000 plus GST of $300 (provincial sales tax is ignored for this example but is covered below). The entries to record the purchase of the rakes, the sale of the rakes, and the remittance of the GST payable by Kitchen are as follows:

	A	B	C	D
1	Inventory	3,000		
2	GST Recoverable	150		
3	Accounts Payable		3,150	
4	To record purchase of inventory.			
5	Accounts Receivable	6,300		
6	Cost of Goods Sold	3,000		
7	Sales		6,000	
8	Inventory		3,000	
9	GST Payable		300	
10	To record sale of inventory.			
11	GST Payable	300		
12	GST Recoverable		150	
13	Cash		150	
14	To record payment of GST collected less GST paid.			

PST is levied at the point of sale to the final consumer, unlike GST and HST. It would apply to Kitchen Hardware when it purchases a cash register and to Mary Fortin, a customer of Kitchen, when she purchases light bulbs. Because only the final consumer pays PST, there are no ITCs for provincial taxes (except for Quebec's QST). PST payable is always a current liability as it is payable quarterly or monthly, depending on the payer's volume of business.

With respect to Kitchen Hardware's sale of rakes for $6,000, the GST would be $300 and the PST would be $420, as Manitoba's tax rate is 7%. So the total price to the consumer would be $6,720. The entries to record the sale of the rakes (including GST and PST payable) and the remittance of the PST payable by Kitchen are as follows:

	A	B	C	D
1	Accounts Receivable	6,720		
2	Cost of Goods Sold	3,000		
3	Sales		6,000	
4	Inventory		3,000	
5	GST Payable		300	
6	PST Payable		420	
7	To record sale of inventory.			
8	PST Payable	420		
9	Cash		420	
10	To record payment of PST collected.			
11				

PAYROLL LIABILITIES. Payroll, also called *employee compensation*, is a major expense for most companies. For service organizations—such as law firms, real estate brokers, and accounting firms—compensation is *the* major expense, just as cost of goods sold is the major expense for a merchandising company.

Employee compensation takes different forms. A *salary* is employee pay stated at a yearly or monthly rate. A *wage* is employee pay stated at an hourly rate. Sales employees often earn a *commission*, which is a percentage of the sales the employee has made. A *bonus* is an amount over and above regular compensation.

Exhibit 7-1 illustrates the typical journal entries used to record payroll expenses and liabilities each pay period. *Salary Expense* represents the total (or gross) pay earned by employees during the pay period. The gross pay in Exhibit 7-1 is $10,000. Employees rarely get to take home their full gross pay, however, because the government requires employers to withhold and remit several amounts from employees' pay:

- *Employee Income Taxes Payable* is the amount of federal and provincial income taxes that have been withheld from employees' gross pay so they can be remitted to the government on the employees' behalf. The percentage of income tax withheld depends mostly on the employee's gross pay for the period, so the higher their gross pay, the higher the percentage of income tax that must be withheld. As of 2019, the federal income tax withholding rates ranged from 0% to 33% (provincial rates vary by province). In Exhibit 7-1, $1,500 in incomes taxes have been withheld for remittance to the government.

- *Canada Pension Plan Payable* is the amount of CPP contributions withheld from employees. The CPP is a government pension plan that provides workers with pension income upon their retirement at age 60 or beyond. In Quebec, the Quebec Pension Plan supplants the CPP but operates in similar fashion. As of 2019, an employee is required to contribute 5.1% of their gross pay to the CPP, to a maximum of about $2,750 per year. Applying this rate results in CPP Payable of $510 on Line 3 of Exhibit 7-1.

- *Employment Insurance Payable* is the amount of EI premiums withheld from employees pay. The EI plan is a government insurance plan that provides workers with income for a limited period of time if they lose their job at some future date. In Quebec, the EI plan operates in conjunction with the Quebec Parental Insurance Plan. As of 2019, an employee is required to pay a premium of 1.62% of their gross pay, to a maximum of about $860 per year. Applying this rate results in EI Payable of $162 on Line 4 of Exhibit 7-1.

Salary Payable represents the employees' gross pay for the period *net* of the income taxes, CPP contributions, and EI premiums withheld from their pay. This amount is commonly called "take-home pay" because it is the amount of pay the employees actually get to take home with them at the end of each pay period. After deducting the above withholdings, the Salary Payable in Exhibit 7-1 is $7,828.

In addition to withholding and remitting CPP contributions and EI premiums from their employees' pay, employers must also make CPP contributions and pay EI premiums for each employee. The employer must match the employee's CPP contribution dollar for dollar, which on Line 8 of Exhibit 7-1 results in *Canada Pension Plan Expense* of $510. For EI, the employer must pay a premium of $1.40 for every dollar in premiums paid by the employee, so we see *Employment Insurance Expense* of $227 ($162 × 1.4) on Line 9 of Exhibit 7-1. Lines 10 and 11 report the corresponding payables related to these two expenses.

EXHIBIT 7-1
**Accounting for Payroll
Expenses and Liabilities**

	A	B	C	D
1	Salary Expense	10,000		
2	Employee Income Taxes Payable		1,500	
3	Canada Pension Plan Payable		510	
4	Employment Insurance Payable		162	
5	Salary Payable		7,828	
6	*To record salary expense and employee withholdings.*			
7				
8	Canada Pension Plan Expense	510		
9	Employment Insurance Expense	227		
10	Canada Pension Plan Payable		510	
11	Employment Insurance Payable		227	
12	*To record employer's share of Canada Pension Plan and Employment Insurance.*			

ASSETS	=	LIABILITIES	+	SHAREHOLDERS' EQUITY
		+1,500		
		+ 510		
0	=	+ 162		−10,000 Salary Expense
		+7,828		
0	=	+ 510		−510 CPP Expense
		+ 227		−227 EI Expense

INCOME TAXES PAYABLE. Corporations, like individuals, must pay taxes on their incomes. Personal and corporate tax rates differ, and corporate tax rates also vary by type of company and by province.

The accounting for corporate income taxes is complicated by the fact that income for accounting purposes (or **pretax accounting income**) usually differs from income for tax purposes. We determine income for accounting purposes by applying IFRS or ASPE, whereas we determine income for tax purposes by applying the rules in federal and provincial Income Tax Acts. The differences between accounting standards and tax rules result in differences between accounting income, which is used to determine a corporation's *income tax expense*, and **taxable income**, which is the income figure used to determine a corporation's *income tax payable*.

In general, income tax expense and income tax payable can be computed as follows:*

Income tax *expense*	=	Income before income tax (from the *income statement*)	×	Income tax rate
Income tax *payable*	=	Taxable income (from the *income tax return filed with tax authorities*)	×	Income tax rate

Income tax expense commonly differs from income tax payable because certain revenues and expenses are treated differently for accounting purposes than they are for tax purposes. The depreciation of capital assets is one area where such differences occur. Under IFRS and ASPE, companies have some leeway to choose the methods and rates they use to depreciate their assets, whereas tax rules specify the method and rate to be used for each asset type. We will use a simple example to illustrate the accounting impact of this kind of difference.

---

*The authors thank Jean Marie Hudson for suggesting this presentation.

Suppose a company reports $10 million in pretax accounting income for the year ended December 31, 2020. Its operating expenses for 2020 include $2 million of depreciation, which was calculated using the straight-line method. The tax rules, however, require the use of an accelerated depreciation method, which results in depreciation for tax purposes of $2.8 million. If we assume there are no other accounting versus tax differences, then the company's taxable income for 2020 is $9.2 million, which is lower than its pretax accounting income due to the extra $800,000 ($2.8 million − $2 million) in depreciation for tax purposes. Assuming an income tax rate of 30%, the following journal entry is needed to account for the company's 2020 income taxes (dollar amounts in millions):

	A	B	C	D	E
1	2020				
2	Dec. 31	Income Tax Expense ($10 × 0.30)	3.00		
3		Income Tax Payable ($9.2 × 0.30)		2.76	
4		Deferred Income Tax Liability		0.24	
5		*Recorded income tax for the year.*			
6					

ASSETS	=	LIABILITIES	+	SHAREHOLDERS' EQUITY
0	=	$2.76 + $0.24		−$3.00 Income Tax Expense

The Income Tax Payable liability of $2.76 million (30% of taxable income of $9.2 million) represents the amount of income tax the company will actually have to remit to the government in 2021, so it would be reported as a current liability. The **Deferred Income Tax Liability** of $240,000, which is the difference between the company's income tax expense of $3 million and its income tax payable of $2.76 million, represents the amount of income taxes payable in future periods as a result of differences between accounting income and taxable income in the current and prior periods. Deferred income taxes are typically reported as long-term liabilities, as in WestJet's partial balance sheet at the beginning of the chapter. When income tax payable exceeds income tax expense, the difference is debited to a Deferred Income Tax Asset account. Under ASPE, deferred income taxes are referred to as future income taxes. Deferred and future income taxes are covered in greater depth in intermediate accounting courses.

UNEARNED REVENUES. A business sometimes collects cash from its customers before it provides the goods or services the customer has paid for. This creates a liability called **unearned revenues** because the business owes goods or services to the customer.

WestJet, for example, sells tickets and collects cash in advance of passengers actually taking their flights. WestJet therefore reports Advance Ticket Sales for airline tickets sold in advance. At June 30, 2018, WestJet owed customers $740 million of air travel (see page 367). Let's see how WestJet accounts for unearned ticket revenue.

Assume that on September 1 WestJet collects $800 for a round-trip ticket from Vancouver to Montreal, departing September 26 and returning October 10. WestJet's entries would be as follows:

	A	B	C	D	E
1	Sept. 1	Cash	800		
2		Advance Ticket Sales		800	
3		*To record cash received for future return airfare from Vancouver to Montreal.*			
4					

Advance Ticket Sales
800

WestJet's assets and liabilities increase equally. There is no revenue yet.

ASSETS	=	LIABILITIES	+	SHAREHOLDERS' EQUITY
+800	=	+800	+	0

When the passenger flies from Vancouver to Montreal on September 26, WestJet can record $400 of revenue because it has provided half of the air travel it owes the customer:

	A	B	C	D	E
1	Sept. 26	Advance Ticket Sales	400		
2		Ticket Revenue ($800/2)		400	
3		*To record revenue earned that was collected in advance.*			
4					

The liability decreases and revenue increases:

Advance Ticket Sales		Ticket Revenue	
400	800		400

At September 30, WestJet reports:

- $400 of advance ticket sales (a liability) on the balance sheet for the return flight it still owes the customer
- $400 of ticket revenue on the income statement

When the customer returns to Vancouver on October 10, WestJet has earned the remaining $400 of revenue:

	A	B	C	D	E
1	Oct. 10	Advance Ticket Sales	400		
2		Ticket Revenue ($800/2)		400	
3		*Earned revenue that was collected in advance.*			
4					

Now the liability balance is zero because WestJet has provided both of the flights it owed the customer.

CURRENT PORTION OF LONG-TERM DEBT. The **current portion of long-term debt** is the amount of long-term debt that is payable within the next year. At the end of each year, a company reclassifies (from long-term debt to a current liability) the amount of its long-term debt that must be paid during the upcoming year. We will cover the accounting for long-term debt in the second half of this chapter.

STOP + THINK (7-1)

You are thinking of purchasing WestJet shares and are concerned about WestJet's debt. You examine WestJet's partial balance sheet on page 367 to answer the following questions about the company's current and long-term debt:

1. At June 30, 2018, how much in total did WestJet owe on current and long-term debt?

2. How much of the long-term debt did WestJet expect to pay by June 30, 2019? How much was the company scheduled to pay after this date?

Current Liabilities That Must Be Estimated

A business may know that it has a present obligation and that it is *probable* it will have to settle this obligation in the future, but it may be uncertain of the timing or amount of the liability. Despite this uncertainty, IFRS require the business to estimate and record a **provision** for this obligation in its financial statements. A provision is a specific type of contingent liability (see page 335 for further information on contingent liabilities).

Estimated liabilities vary among companies and include such things as warranties, vacation pay, and income taxes. Warranty liabilities are quite common, so we will use them to illustrate the accounting for estimated liabilities.

ESTIMATED WARRANTY PAYABLE. Many companies guarantee their products under *warranty* agreements that cover some period of time after their customers purchase them. Automobile companies accrue liabilities for vehicle warranties, which usually extend for several years. The sale of a product with a warranty attached is a past event that creates a present obligation, which will require company resources (repair or replacement) to settle at some future date. At the time of the sale, however, the company does not know which products will be defective or how much it will cost to fix or replace them. The exact amount of warranty expense cannot be known with certainty, so the business must estimate warranty expense and the related warranty liability.

Assume that Black & Decker Canada Inc., which manufactures power tools, sold 4,000 tools subject to one-year warranties. If, in past years, between 2% and 4% of products proved defective and it cost an average of $50 to replace each tool, Black & Decker could estimate that 3% of the products it sells this year will require repair or replacement. In that case, Black & Decker would estimate warranty expense of $6,000 (4,000 × 0.03 × $50) for the period and make the following entry:

	A	B	C	D	E
1		Warranty Expense	6,000		
2		Estimated Warranty Payable		6,000	
3		*To accrue warranty expense.*			
4					

Estimated Warranty Payable
	6,000

If Black & Decker actually ends up replacing 100 defective tools with new tools costing $4,800, it would record the following:

	A	B	C	D	E
1		Estimated Warranty Payable	4,800		
2		Inventory		4,800	
3		*To replace defective products sold under warranty.*			
4					

Estimated Warranty Payable
4,800		6,000	
	Bal.	1,200	

At the end of the year, Black & Decker will report Estimated Warranty Payable of $1,200 as a current liability. The income statement reports Warranty Expense of $6,000 for the year. Then, next year Black & Decker will repeat this process. The Estimated Warranty Payable account probably won't ever zero out.

Contingent Liabilities

Contingent liabilities are *possible* obligations that will become *actual* obligations only if some uncertain future event occurs. They also include present obligations for which there is doubt about the need for the eventual outflow of resources to settle the obligation, or for which the amount of the obligation cannot be reliably estimated. Lawsuits in progress, debt guarantees, and audits by the Canada Revenue Agency are examples of contingent liabilities.

Under ASPE, contingent liabilities that are *likely* to occur and can be *reasonably estimated* are accrued as liabilities, similar to the above treatment for provisions under IFRS. Other less-certain contingent liabilities, under both IFRS and ASPE, are simply disclosed in the notes. Even note disclosure is not required if there is only a remote chance the contingent liability will occur. Determining the proper accounting treatment of contingent liabilities is beyond the scope of this text.

Are All Liabilities Reported on the Balance Sheet or Disclosed in the Notes?

The big danger with liabilities is that a company may fail to report a debt on its balance sheet. What is the consequence of not reporting a liability? The company would definitely understate its liabilities and would probably overstate its net income. In short, its financial statements would make the company look stronger than it really is. Any such misstatement, if significant, hurts a company's credibility.

Contingent liabilities are very easy to overlook because they aren't actual debts. How would you feel if you owned shares in a company that failed to report a contingency that put the company out of business? In this case, you would hire a lawyer to file suit against the company for negligent financial reporting. If you had known of the contingency, you could have sold the shares and avoided the loss.

COOKING *the* BOOKS

with Liabilities

Crazy Eddie, Inc.

Accidentally understating liabilities is one thing, but doing it intentionally is quite another. When unethical management decides to cook the books in the area of liabilities, its strategy is to *deliberately understate recorded liabilities*. This can be done by intentionally under-recording the amount of existing liabilities or by omitting certain liabilities altogether.

Crazy Eddie, Inc., was a large electronics retailer, like Best Buy, that used multiple tactics to overstate its financial position over a period of four consecutive years from 1984 to 1987. In addition to overstating inventory (thus understating cost of goods sold and overstating income), the management of the company deliberately understated accounts payable by issuing fictitious debit memos from suppliers. A debit memo is issued for goods returned to a supplier, such as Sony. When a debit memo is issued, accounts payable are debited (reduced), thus reducing current liabilities and increasing the current ratio. Eventually, expenses are also decreased, and profits are correspondingly increased through reduction of expenses. Crazy Eddie, Inc., issued $3 million of fictitious debit memos in one year, making the company's current ratio and working capital look better than they actually were, as well as overstating profits.

Summary of Current Liabilities

Let's summarize what we've covered thus far. A company can report its current liabilities on the balance sheet as follows:

	A	B	C	D	E
1	**Hudson Ltd.** Balance Sheet December 31, 2020				
2	Assets		Liabilities		
3	**Current assets**		**Current liabilities**		
4	Cash		Accounts payable		
5	Short-term investments		Salary payable*		
6	Etc.		Interest payable*		
7			HST/GST payable**		
8			PST payable*		
9			CPP payable*		
10			EI payable*		
11			Income tax payable		
12	Property, plant, and equipment:		Unearned revenue		
13	Land		Estimated warranty payable		
14	Etc.		Notes payable, short-term		
15			Current portion of long-term debt		
16			**Total current liabilities**		
17	Other assets:		**Long-term liabilities**		
18			**Shareholders' Equity**		
19			Share capital		
20			Retained earnings		
21	Total assets	$ XXX	Total liabilities and shareholders' equity	$ XXX	
22					

*These items are often combined and reported in a single total as "Accrued Liabilities" or "Accrued Expenses Payable."
**ASPE requires separate disclosure of the amount payable with respect to government remittances (other than income taxes), either on the face of the balance sheet or in the notes.

MyLab Accounting

MID-CHAPTER SUMMARY PROBLEM

Assume that Korvar Plastics Inc., a manufacturer of plastic pipe for the construction industry and located in Red Deer, Alberta, faced the following liability situations at June 30, 2020, the end of the company's fiscal year:

a. Long-term debt totals $10 million and is payable in annual instalments of $1 million each. The interest rate on the debt is 7%, and interest is paid each December 31.

b. Salary expense for the last payroll period of the year was $90,000. Of this amount, employees' income tax of $12,000 was withheld, and other withholdings and employee benefits were $6,000. These payroll amounts will be paid early in July.

c. Since the last reporting period, GST of $200,000 had been collected and ITCs of $76,000 had been earned.

d. On fiscal-year 2020 sales of $40 million, management estimates warranty expense of 2%. One year ago, at June 30, 2019, Estimated Warranty Liability stood at $100,000. Warranty payments were $300,000 during the year ended June 30, 2020.

Show how Korvar Plastics Inc. would report these liabilities on its balance sheet at June 30, 2020.

Name: Korvar Plastics Inc.
Industry: Manufacturing
Accounting Period: June 30, 2020

ANSWERS

a. Current liabilities:

Current portion of long-term debt...	$1,000,000
Interest payable ($10,000,000 × 0.07 × 6/12)	350,000
Long-term debt ($10,000,000 − $1,000,000)..	9,000,000

> Current liabilities include the amount due to be paid within one year:
> • Principal repayment
> • Interest payment

b. Current liabilities:

Salary payable ($90,000 − $12,000 − $6,000)...	$ 72,000
Employee withheld income tax payable	12,000
Other employee withholdings and benefits payable	6,000

> Salaries payable to employees are net of all withholdings

c. Current liabilities:

GST payable ($200,000 − $76,000)	$ 124,000

> GST payable is net of applicable ITC credits.

d. Current liabilities:

Estimated warranty payable..	$ 600,000
[$100,000 + ($40,000,000 × 0.02) − $300,000]	

> Estimated warranty liability must be reduced by any warranty payments made during the year.

EXPLAIN THE TYPES, FEATURES, AND PRICING OF BONDS PAYABLE

Large companies, such as Bombardier, Canadian Tire, and TransCanada, cannot borrow billions of dollars from a single lender. So how do large corporations borrow huge amounts? They issue (sell) bonds to the public. **Bonds payable** are groups of notes issued to multiple lenders, called *bondholders*. Bombardier can borrow large amounts by issuing bonds to thousands of investors, who each lend a modest amount to Bombardier. Here, we treat bonds and long-term notes payable together because their accounting is similar.

Bonds: An Introduction

Each bond that is issued is, in effect, a long-term note payable. Bonds payable are debts of the issuing company.

Each bond has a *principal* amount which is typically stated in units of $1,000; principal is also called the bond's **face value** or *maturity value*. The bond obligates the issuing company to pay the debt at a specific future time called the *maturity date*.

Interest is the rental fee on money borrowed. The bond states the interest rate that the issuer will pay the holder and the dates that the interest payments are due (generally twice a year).

Issuing bonds usually requires the services of a securities firm (for example, RBC Dominion Securities) to act as the underwriter of the bond issue. The **underwriter** purchases the bonds from the issuing company and resells them to its clients, or it may hold some of the bonds for its own account and sell them at a later time.

TYPES OF BONDS. All the bonds in a particular issue may mature at a specified time (**term bonds**) or in instalments over a period of time (**serial bonds**). Serial bonds are like instalment notes payable. Some of TransCanada Corporation's long-term debts are serial in nature because they come due in instalments.

Secured, or *mortgage*, *bonds* give the bondholder the right to take specified assets of the issuer if the company *defaults*, that is, fails to pay interest or principal. *Unsecured bonds*, called **debentures**, are backed only by the good faith of the borrower. Debentures carry a higher rate of interest than secured bonds because debentures are riskier investments.

BOND PRICES. Investors buy and sell bonds through bond markets. Bond prices are quoted at a percentage of their maturity value. For example:

- A $1,000 bond quoted at 100 is bought or sold for $1,000, which is 100% of its face value.

- The same bond quoted at 101.5 has a market price of $1,015 (101.5% of face value = $1,000 × 1.015). Any excess of the bond's price over its face value is called a **bond premium**.

- A $1,000 bond quoted at 88.375 is priced at $883.75 ($1,000 × 0.88375). When the price of a bond is below its face value, the difference is called a **bond discount**.

As with stocks, bond prices are reported in a wide variety of online sources. For example, on October 23, 2018, the *Globe and Mail* website reported price information for Province of Alberta bonds. On that day, Province of Alberta $1,000 face value bonds with an interest rate of 4.50% and maturity date of December 1, 2040, were quoted at a price of 124.19, so it would have cost you $1,241.90 to purchase one of these bonds ($1,000 face value + bond premium of $241.90). Bond prices change regularly due to changes in market demand and supply.

BOND INTEREST RATES DETERMINE BOND PRICES. Bonds are always sold at their **market price**, which is the amount investors are willing to pay. A bond's market price is determined by its present value, which equals the present value of the future principal payment plus the present value of the future interest payments. Interest is usually paid semi-annually. Some issuers pay annually or quarterly.

Two interest rates determine the price of a bond:

- The **stated interest rate** (or *coupon rate*) is the actual interest rate of the bond. The stated interest rate determines the amount of interest the borrower pays—and the investor receives—each year. For example, the Province of Alberta's 4.5% bonds have a stated interest rate of 4.5%. Thus, Alberta pays $45 of interest annually on each $1,000 bond. Each semi-annual interest payment is $22.50 ($1,000 × 0.045 × 6/12).

- The **market interest rate**, or *effective interest rate*, is the rate that investors demand for loaning their money. The market rate varies by the minute.

An entity may issue bonds with a stated interest rate that differs from the prevailing market interest rate. In fact, the two interest rates often differ because the issuer often has to finalize details of the bond weeks or months before the bonds are actually issued.

Exhibit 7-2 shows how the stated interest rate and the market interest rate interact to determine the price of a bond payable for three separate cases. If the stated interest rate does happen to equal the market rate, the bond will be issued at face value (Case A).

Alberta may, however, issue 6% bonds when the market rate has risen to 7%. Will the Alberta bonds attract investors in this market? No, because investors can earn 7% on other bonds of similar risk. Therefore, investors will purchase Alberta bonds only at a *discount* (Case B). Conversely, if the market interest rate is 5%, Alberta's 6% bonds will be so attractive that investors will pay a *premium* for them (Case C). It is useful to remember that there is an inverse relationship between the market rate and bond prices—a market rate higher than the stated rate results in a discounted bond price, whereas a market rate lower than the stated rate results in a premium price.

EXHIBIT 7-2
How the Stated Interest Rate and the Market Interest Rate Interact to Determine the Price of a Bond

				Issuance Price of Bonds Payable
Case A:				
Stated interest rate on a bond payable	equals	Market interest rate	implies	Face price
Example: 6%	=	6%	→	*Face: $1,000 bond issued for $1,000*
Case B:				
Stated interest rate on a bond payable	less than	Market interest rate	implies	Discount price (price *below* face value)
Example: 6%	<	7%	→	*Discount: $1,000 bond issued for a price below $1,000*
Case C:				
Stated interest rate on a bond payable	greater than	Market interest rate	implies	Premium price (price *above* face value)
Example: 6%	>	5%	→	*Premium: $1,000 bond issued for a price above $1,000*

STOP + THINK (7-2)

Answer the following questions about various bonds:

1. The stated interest rate on a bond is 8% and the market rate at the time the bond was issued as issued was 9%. Would the bond have been issued at a discount or a premium?

2. The stated interest rate on a bond is 9.5% and the market rate at the time the bond was issued as issued was 7.75%. Would the bond have been issued at a discount or a premium?

3. How much would you pay for $250,000 in bonds with a market price of 89.75?

4. How much would you pay for $175,000 in bonds with a market price of 101.25?

ACCOUNT FOR BONDS PAYABLE

Issuing Bonds at Face Value

Suppose Great-West Lifeco Inc. plans to issue $50,000 in 6% bonds that mature in five years. Assume that Great-West issues these bonds at face value on January 1, 2020. The issuance entry is as follows:

	A	B	C	D	E
1	2020				
2	Jan. 1	Cash	50,000		
3		Bonds Payable		50,000	
4		*To issue 6%, five-year bonds at face value.*			
5					

Bonds Payable

| 50,000

ASSETS	**=**	**LIABILITIES**	**+**	**SHAREHOLDERS' EQUITY**
+50,000	=	+50,000		

Great-West, the borrower, makes a one-time entry to record the receipt of cash and the issuance of bonds. Afterward, investors buy and sell the bonds through the bond markets. These buy-and-sell transactions between outside investors do *not* involve Great-West at all.

Interest payments occur each January 1 and July 1. Great-West's entry to record the first semi-annual interest payment is as follows:

	A	B	C	D	E
1	2020				
2	July 1	Interest Expense	1,500		
3		Cash		1,500	
4		*To pay semi-annual interest. ($50,000 × 0.06 × 6/12)*			
5					

ASSETS	**=**	**LIABILITIES**	**+**	**SHAREHOLDERS' EQUITY**
−1,500	=			−1,500 Interest Expense

At year-end, Great-West must accrue interest expense and interest payable for six months (July through December), as follows:

	A	B	C	D	E
1	2020				
2	Dec. 31	Interest Expense ($50,000 × 0.06 × 6/12)	1,500		
3		Interest Payable		1,500	
4		*To accrue interest.*			
5					

ASSETS	**=**	**LIABILITIES**	**+**	**SHAREHOLDERS' EQUITY**
0	=	+1,500		−1,500 Interest Expense

At maturity, Great-West will pay off the bonds as follows (any interest owing will be paid separately):

	A	B	C	D	E
1	2025				
2	Jan. 1	Bonds Payable	50,000		
3		Cash		50,000	
4		To pay bonds payable at maturity.			
5					

Bonds Payable

50,000	50,000
	Bal. 0

ASSETS	=	LIABILITIES	+	SHAREHOLDERS' EQUITY
−50,000	=	−50,000		

Issuing Bonds at a Discount

Market conditions may force a company to issue bonds at a discount. Suppose Canadian Tire issues $100,000 of 9% five-year bonds when the market interest rate is 10%. The market price of the bonds drops, and Canadian Tire receives $96,149 at issuance. The transaction is recorded as follows:

	A	B	C	D	E
1	2020				
2	Jan. 1	Cash	96,149		
3		Discount on Bonds Payable	3,851		
4		Bonds Payable		100,000	
5		To issue 9%, five-year bonds at a discount.			
6					

ASSETS	=	LIABILITIES	+	SHAREHOLDERS' EQUITY
+96,149	=	−3,851		
		+100,000		

Now the bond accounts have a net balance of $96,149 as follows:

Bonds Payable + **Discount on Bonds Payable** = Net carrying amount of bonds payable

| 100,000 | 3,851 | = $96,149 |

Canadian Tire's balance sheet immediately after issuance of the bonds would report the following:

Total current liabilities		$ XXX
Long-term liabilities		
Bonds payable, 9%, due 2025	$100,000	
Less: Discount on bonds payable	(3,851)	96,149

Discount on Bonds Payable is a contra account to Bonds Payable, which decreases the company's liabilities. Subtracting the discount from Bonds Payable yields the *carrying amount* of the bonds. Thus, Canadian Tire's liability is $96,149, which is the amount the company borrowed.

STOP + THINK (7-3)

Suppose TD Bank issued a five-year $10,000 bond with stated interest rate of 7.25% when the market interest rate was 7.25%. TD's fiscal year ends on October 31. Journalize the following transactions (no explanations are needed):

a. Issuance of the bond, payable on May 1, 2020
b. Accrual of interest expense on October 31, 2020 (rounded to the nearest dollar)
c. Payment of cash interest on November 1, 2020
d. Payment of the bonds at maturity, including any interest owing (give the date)

OBJECTIVE

❹ **Calculate** and **account** for interest expense on bonds payable

CALCULATE AND ACCOUNT FOR INTEREST EXPENSE ON BONDS PAYABLE

Canadian Tire pays interest on its bonds semi-annually, which is common practice. Each semi-annual interest *payment* remains the same over the life of the bonds:

$$\text{Semi-annual interest payment} = \$100{,}000 \times 0.09 \times 6/12$$
$$= \$4{,}500$$

This payment amount is fixed by the bond contract. But Canadian Tire's interest *expense* increases from period to period as the bonds march toward maturity. Remember, these bonds were issued at a discount.

Panel A of Exhibit 7-3 summarizes the Canadian Tire bond data used above. Panel B provides an amortization table that:

- determines the periodic interest expense (column C)
- shows the bond carrying amount at each semi-annual interest date (column F)

Study the exhibit carefully because the amounts we will be using come directly from the amortization table. This exhibit shows the *effective-interest method of amortization*, which is the required way of amortizing bond premiums and discounts under IFRS. ASPE permit this method, as well as the *straight-line method*, which is discussed briefly later in this section.

TRY IT *in* EXCEL® ▶▶▶ ————————————

Bond amortization tables are a snap when you prepare them in Excel. Open a blank Excel spreadsheet.

- In line 1, label the columns as shown in Panel B of Exhibit 7-3.
- Column A. Starting in line 2, enter the issue date (1/1/2020) followed by each of the semiannual interest payment dates. This will continue through line 12 with the last interest payment on January 1, 2025. Highlight all cell values in rows 2 through 12 of column A, and click on the drop down box in the "number" field on the ruler at the top of the spreadsheet. Choose the "date" category and click OK to change all cell values in Column A to the date format.
- Line 2, column E. Enter 3851 in cell E2. Enter the formula = 100000 − E2 in cell F2. The calculated value of 96149 should appear in cell F2, representing the initial carrying value of the bond.
- Line 3, column B. Enter formula =.045*100000 in cell B3. A calculated value of 4500 should appear, representing the amount of the first cash interest payment.
- Line 3, column C. In cell C3, enter formula =.05*F2. A calculated value of 4807 should appear, representing the calculated amount of interest expense, based on the carrying amount of the bond. If the cell shows a decimal fraction, use the "decrease decimal" command in the

- "number" field of the toolbar to reduce the decimals to none. This will round the value to the nearest dollar.
- Line 3, column D. In cell D3, enter formula = C3−B3. A value of 307 should appear, representing the amount of discount amortization included in interest expense on the first interest payment date.
- Line 3, column E. In cell E3, enter formula = E2−D3. A value of 3544 should appear, representing the unamortized discount remaining after the first interest payment.
- Line 3, column F. In cell F3, enter formula =100000−E3. A value of 96456 should appear, representing the adjusted carrying value of the bond after the first interest payment.
- For columns B through F, copy line 3 down through line 12. All of the numbers in the table should fill in. Line 12 will have to be adjusted for rounding by taking the remaining unamortized discount from cell E11 (461) and substituting that value in cell D12 (discount amortization). Also, substitute 4961 for interest expense in cell C12. This will adjust the final bond carrying amount to the maturity value of $100,000 and the unamortized discount to 0.
- Highlight cells B2 through F12, and insert commas to make the table easier to read. When you insert the commas, Excel automatically inserts two decimals and zeros, so use the "decrease decimal" key to format the table to whole dollars.

EXHIBIT 7-3
Debt Amortization for a Bond Discount
PANEL A—Bond Data

	A	B	C
1	Issue date—January 1, 2020	Market interest rate at time of issue—10% annually, 5% semi-annually	
2	Maturity (face) value—$100,000	Issue price—$96,149	
3	Stated interest rate—9%	Maturity date—January 1, 2025	
4	Interest paid—4½% semi-annually, $4,500 = $100,000 × 0.09 × 6/12		
5			

PANEL B—Amortization Table

	A	B	C	D	E	F	G
1	Semi-Annual Interest Date	Interest Payment (4½% of Maturity Value)	Interest Expense (5% of Preceding Bond Carrying Amount)	Bond Discount Amortization (C − B)	Bond Discount Account Balance (Preceding E − D)	Bond Carrying Amount ($100,000 − E)	
2	Jan. 1, 2020				$3,851	$ 96,149	
3	July 1	$4,500	$4,807	$307	3,544	96,456	
4	Jan. 1, 2021	4,500	4,823	323	3,221	96,779	
5	July 1	4,500	4,839	339	2,882	97,118	
6	Jan. 1, 2022	4,500	4,856	356	2,526	97,474	
7	July 1	4,500	4,874	374	2,152	97,848	
8	Jan. 1, 2023	4,500	4,892	392	1,760	98,240	
9	July 1	4,500	4,912	412	1,348	98,652	
10	Jan. 1, 2024	4,500	4,933	433	951	99,085	
11	July 1	4,500	4,954	454	461	99,539	
12	Jan. 1, 2025	4,500	4,961*	461	0	100,000	
13							

*Adjusted for the effect of rounding.

Notes

*Column B   The semi-annual interest payments are constant (fixed by the bond contract).
*Column C   The interest expense each period = Preceding bond carrying amount × Market interest rate.
             Interest expense increases as the bond carrying amount (F) increases.
*Column D   The excess of interest expense (C) over interest payment (B) is the discount amortization (D) for the period.
*Column E   The discount balance (E) decreases when amortized.
*Column F   The bond carrying amount (F) increases from $96,149 at issuance to $100,000 at maturity.

Interest Expense on Bonds Issued at a Discount

In Exhibit 7-3, Canadian Tire borrowed $96,149 cash but must pay $100,000 when the bonds mature. What happens to the $3,851 balance of the discount account over the life of the bond issue?

The $3,851 is additional interest expense to Canadian Tire over and above the stated interest that Canadian Tire pays each six months. Exhibit 7-4 graphs the interest expense and the interest payment on the Canadian Tire bonds over their lifetime. Observe that the semi-annual interest payment is fixed—by contract—at $4,500 (column B in Exhibit 7-3), but the amount of interest expense (column C) increases each period as the bond carrying amount moves upward toward maturity.

EXHIBIT 7-4
Interest Expense on Bonds Payable Issued at a Discount

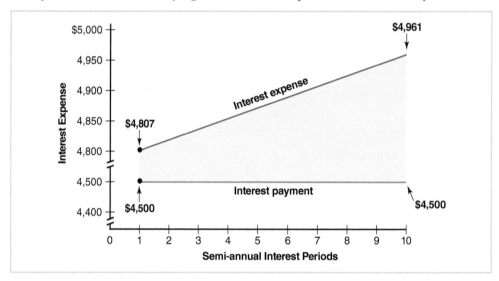

The discount is allocated to interest expense through amortization each period over the term of the bonds. Exhibit 7-5 illustrates the amortization of the bonds' carrying value from $96,149 at the start to $100,000 at maturity using the effective interest method. These amounts come from Exhibit 7-3, column F.

Now let's see how to account for the Canadian Tire bonds issued at a discount. In our example, Canadian Tire issued its bonds on January 1, 2020. On July 1, Canadian Tire made the first $4,500 semi-annual interest payment. But Canadian Tire's interest expense is greater than $4,500. Canadian Tire's journal entry to record interest expense and the interest payment for the first six months follows (with all amounts taken from Exhibit 7-3):

	A	B	C	D	E
1	2020				
2	July 1	Interest Expense	4,807		
3		Discount on Bonds Payable		307	
4		Cash		4,500	
5		*To pay semi-annual interest and amortize bond discount.*			
6					

The credit to Discount on Bonds Payable serves two purposes:

- It adjusts the bonds' carrying amount as the bonds approach maturity value.
- It amortizes the discount to interest expense.

ASSETS	=	LIABILITIES	+	SHAREHOLDERS' EQUITY
−4,500	=	+307		−4,807 Interest Expense

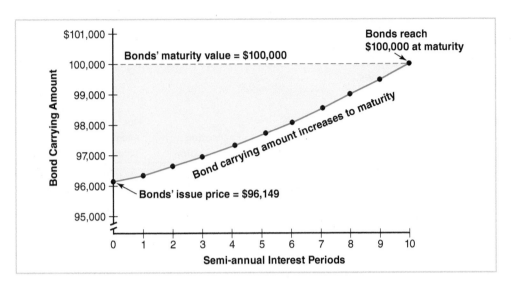

EXHIBIT 7-5
Amortizing Bonds Payable
Issued at a Discount

At December 31, 2020, Canadian Tire accrues interest and amortizes the bond discount for July through December with this entry (amounts from Exhibit 7-3):

	A	B	C	D	E
1	2020				
2	Dec. 31	Interest Expense	4,823		
3		Discount on Bonds Payable		323	
4		Interest Payable		4,500	
5		To accrue semi-annual interest and amortize bond discount.			
6					

ASSETS	=	LIABILITIES	+	SHAREHOLDERS' EQUITY
0	=	+323		−4,823 Interest Expense
		+4,500		

At December 31, 2020, Canadian Tire's bond accounts appear as follows:

Bonds Payable		Discount on Bonds Payable	
	100,000	3,851	307
			323
		Bal. 3,221	

Bond carrying amount, $96,779 = $100,000 − $3,221 from Exhibit 7-3

STOP + THINK (7-4)

What would you expect Canadian Tire's 2020 income statement and year-end balance sheet to report for these bonds?

Partial-Period Interest Amounts

Companies don't always issue bonds at the beginning or the end of their accounting year. They issue bonds when market conditions are most favourable, and that may be on May 16, August 1, or any other date. To illustrate partial-period interest, assume Goldcorp Inc. issues $100,000 of 8% bonds payable at 96 on August 31, 2020. The market rate of interest was 9%, and these bonds pay semi-annual interest on February 28 and August 31 each year. The first few lines of Goldcorp's amortization table are as follows:

Semi-Annual Interest Date	4% Interest Payment	4½% Interest Expense	Discount Amortization	Discount Account Balance	Bond Carrying Amount
Aug. 31, 2020				$4,000	$96,000
Feb. 28, 2021	$4,000	$4,320	$320	3,680	96,320
Aug. 31, 2021	4,000	4,334	334	3,346	96,654

Goldcorp's accounting year ends on December 31, so at year-end Goldcorp must accrue interest and amortize the bond discount for four months (September through December). At December 31, 2020, Goldcorp will make this entry:

	A	B	C	D	E
1	2020				
2	Dec. 31	Interest Expense ($4,320 × 4/6)	2,880		
3		Discount on Bonds Payable ($320 × 4/6)		213	
4		Interest Payable ($4,000 × 4/6)		2,667	
5		To accrue interest and amortize discount at year-end.			
6					

The year-end entry at December 31, 2020, uses 4/6 of the upcoming semi-annual amounts at February 28, 2021 because the September–December period covers four of the six months of interest to be paid on that date. This example clearly illustrates the benefit of an amortization schedule.

Issuing Bonds at a Premium

Let's modify the Canadian Tire bond example to illustrate issuance of the bonds at a premium. Assume that on January 1, 2020, Canadian Tire issues $100,000 of five-year, 9% bonds that pay interest semi-annually. If the bonds are issued when the market interest rate is 8%, their issue price is $104,100. The premium on these bonds is $4,100, and Exhibit 7-6 shows how to amortize the bonds by the effective-interest method.

Canadian Tire's entries to record issuance of the bonds on January 1, 2020, and to make the first interest payment and amortize the bonds on July 1, are as follows:

	A	B	C	D	E
1	2020				
2	Jan. 1	Cash	104,100		
3		Bonds Payable		100,000	
4		Premium on Bonds Payable		4,100	
5		To issue 9%, five-year bonds at a premium.			
6					

At the beginning, Canadian Tire's liability is $104,100—not $100,000. The accounting equation makes this clear.

EXHIBIT 7-6
Debt Amortization for a Bond Premium
PANEL A—Bond Data

	A	B	C
1	Issue date—January 1, 2020	Market interest rate at time of issue—8% annually, 4% semi-annually	
2	Maturity (face) value—$100,000	Issue price—$104,100	
3	Contract interest rate—9%	Maturity date—January 1, 2025	
4	Interest paid—4½% semi-annually, $4,500 = $100,000 × 0.09 × 6/12		
5			

PANEL B—Amortization Table

	A	B	C	D	E	F	G
1	Semi-Annual Interest Date	Interest Payment (4½% of Maturity Value)	Interest Expense (4% of Preceding Bond Carrying Amount)	Bond Premium Amortization (B – C)	Bond Premium Account Balance (Preceding E – D)	Bond Carrying Amount ($100,000 + E)	
2	Jan. 1, 2020				$4,100	$104,100	
3	July 1	$4,500	$4,164	$336	3,764	103,764	
4	Jan. 1, 2021	4,500	4,151	349	3,415	103,415	
5	July 1	4,500	4,137	363	3,052	103,052	
6	Jan. 1, 2022	4,500	4,122	378	2,674	102,674	
7	July 1	4,500	4,107	393	2,281	102,281	
8	Jan. 1, 2023	4,500	4,091	409	1,872	101,872	
9	July 1	4,500	4,075	425	1,447	101,447	
10	Jan. 1, 2024	4,500	4,058	442	1,005	101,005	
11	July 1	4,500	4,040	460	545	100,545	
12	Jan. 1, 2025	4,500	3,955*	545	0	100,000	
13							

*Adjusted for the effect of rounding.

Notes
- Column B   The semi-annual interest payments are constant (fixed by the bond contract).
- Column C   The interest expense each period = Preceding bond carrying amount × Market interest rate.
  Interest expense decreases as the bond carrying amount (F) decreases.
- Column D   The excess of each interest payment (B) over interest expense (C) is the premium amortization (D) for the period.
- Column E   The premium balance (E) decreases when amortized.
- Column F   The bond carrying amount (F) decreases from $104,100 at issuance to $100,000 at maturity.

ASSETS	=	LIABILITIES	+	SHAREHOLDERS' EQUITY
+104,100	=	+100,000		
		+4,100		

	A	B	C	D	E
1	2020				
2	July 1	Interest Expense	4,164		
3		Premium on Bonds Payable	336		
4		Cash		4,500	
5		To pay semi-annual interest and amortize bond premium.			

ASSETS	=	LIABILITIES	+	SHAREHOLDERS' EQUITY
−4,500	=	−336		−4,164 Interest Expense

Immediately after issuing the bonds at a premium on January 1, 2020, Canadian Tire would report the bonds payable on the balance sheet as follows:

Total current liabilities...		$ XXX
Long-term liabilities:		
Bonds payable	$100,000	
Add: Premium on bonds payable..	4,100	104,100

The premium is *added* to the balance of bonds payable to determine the carrying amount.

In Exhibit 7-6, Canadian Tire borrowed $104,100 cash but must pay only $100,000 at maturity. The $4,100 premium on the bonds results in a reduction in Canadian Tire's interest expense over the term of the bonds. Exhibit 7-7 graphs Canadian Tire's interest payments (column B from Exhibit 7-6) and interest expense (column C).

TRY IT *in* EXCEL® ▶▶▶

If you prepared a debt amortization table for bond discount with Excel (Exhibit 7-3), it's easy to prepare an amortization table for bond premium. Open a blank Excel spreadsheet.

- In line 1, label the columns as shown in Panel B of Exhibit 7-6.
- Column A. Starting in line 2, enter the issue date (1/1/2020) followed by each of the semi-annual interest payment dates. This will continue through line 12 with the last interest payment on January 1, 2025. Highlight all cell values in rows 2 through 12 of column A, and click on the drop down box in the "number" field on the ruler at the top of the spreadsheet. Choose the "date" category and click OK to change all cell values in Column A to the date format.
- Line 2, column E. Enter 4100 in cell E2. Enter the formula =100000+E2 in cell F2. The calculated value of 104100 should appear in cell F2, representing the initial carrying value of the bond.
- Line 3, column B. In cell B3, enter formula =.045*100000. A calculated value of 4500 should appear, representing the first cash interest payment.
- Line 3, column C. In cell C3, enter formula =.04*F2. A calculated value of 4164 should appear, representing interest expense recognized on the first interest payment date. If the cell shows a decimal fraction, use the "decrease decimal" command in the "number" field of the toolbar to reduce the decimals to none. This will round the value to the nearest dollar.
- Line 3, column D. In cell D3, enter formula = B3−C3. A value of 336 should appear, representing the amount of premium amortization deducted from interest expense on the first interest payment date.
- Line 3, column E. In cell E3, enter formula = E2−D3. A value of 3764 should appear, representing the remaining unamortized premium after the first interest payment.
- Line 3, column F. In cell F3, enter formula =100000+E3. A value of 103764 should appear, representing the adjusted carrying value of the bond after the first interest payment.
- For columns B to F, copy line 3 down through line 12. All of the numbers in the table should fill in. Line 12 will have to be adjusted for rounding by taking the remaining unamortized premium from cell E11 (544) and substituting that value in cell D12 (premium amortization). Also, substitute 3955 for interest expense in cell C12. This will adjust the final bond carrying amount to the maturity value of $100,000 and the unamortized premium to 0. Your Excel table may be $1 off in some places because of rounding.
- Highlight cells B2 through F12 and format them for commas but no decimals, as you did for Exhibit 7-3.

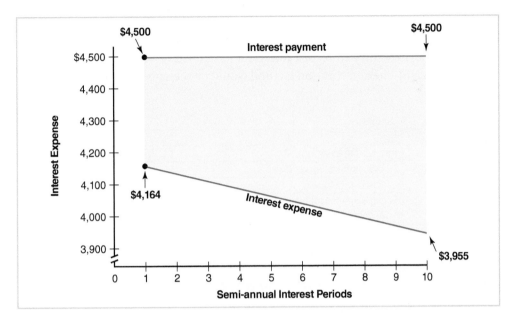

EXHIBIT 7-7
Interest Expense on Bonds
Payable Issued at a Premium

EXHIBIT 7-7
Interest Expense on Bonds
Payable Issued at a Premium

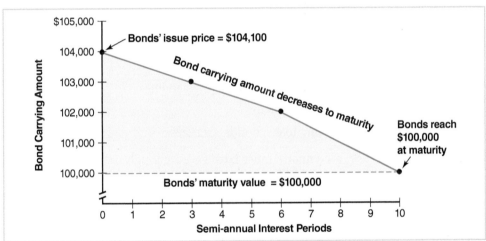

EXHIBIT 7-8
Amortizing Bonds Payable
Issued at a Premium

Through amortization, the premium decreases interest expense each period over the term of the bonds. Exhibit 7-8 diagrams the amortization of the bond carrying amount from the issue price of $104,100 to the maturity value of $100,000. All amounts are taken from Exhibit 7-6.

The Straight-Line Amortization Method

ASPE permit a simpler method of amortizing discounts and premiums. The *straight-line amortization method* divides a bond discount (or premium) into equal periodic amounts over the bond's term. The amount of interest expense is the same for each interest period.

Let's apply the straight-line method to the Canadian Tire bonds issued at a discount and illustrated in Exhibit 7-3. The amortization for each semi-annual period is calculated by dividing the total bond discount of $3,851 by 10, which is the number of semi-annual interest periods over the life of the bond. This method results in the following semi-annual interest expense:

Semi-annual cash interest payment ($100,000 × 0.09 × 6/12)...	$4,500
+Semi-annual amortization of discount ($3,851 ÷ 10)...	385
=Semi-annual interest expense	$4,885

The straight-line amortization method uses these same amounts every period over the term of the bonds.

Canadian Tire's entry to record interest and amortization of the bond discount under the straight-line amortization method would be the same for every semi-annual interest period:

	A	B	C	D	E
1		Interest Expense	4,885		
2		Discount on Bonds Payable		385	
3		Cash		4,500	
4		To pay semi-annual interest and amortize bond discount.			

EXPLAIN THE ADVANTAGES AND DISADVANTAGES OF FINANCING WITH DEBT VERSUS EQUITY

Managers must decide where to get the money needed to fund acquisitions, expansion, and other operational activities. There are three main ways to finance business activities:

- By using excess cash not needed for operating activities
- By raising capital from issuing shares
- By borrowing money using loans, bonds, or notes

1. To use *excess cash*, a company must have saved enough cash and short-term investments from past profitable operations so that it can self-finance its desired business activities. This is a low-risk and low-cost option because it does not require taking on more debt or issuing more shares.

2. *Raising capital by issuing new shares* creates no new liabilities and requires no interest payments, so it does not increase a company's credit risk. Dividend payments on shares are usually optional, so they can be avoided if cash flows are poor or the company has other needs for its cash. Issuing shares, however, can cost a lot in legal and other financing fees, and can also dilute the control and earnings per share of existing shareholders.

3. *Borrowing money* does not dilute control of the company because no shares are being issued, but it can still be somewhat costly in terms of financing fees paid to arrange the debt. Taking on more debt can also increase a company's credit risk, and it requires the company to make regular principal and interest payments, which cannot be postponed when cash flows are poor. The leverage gained by borrowing money can often increase the company's earnings per share, which is beneficial to shareholders.

Earnings per share (EPS) represents the amount of net income (or loss) earned by each of a company's outstanding common shares. It is useful for evaluating the earnings performance of a company and also assessing the impact of various financing options on earnings.

Suppose Athens Corporation needs $500,000 for expansion. Assume Athens has net income of $300,000 and 100,000 common shares outstanding. Management is considering two financing plans. Plan 1 is to issue $500,000 of 6% bonds, and plan 2 is to issue 50,000 common shares for $500,000. Management believes the new cash can be invested in operations to earn income of $200,000 before interest and taxes.

Exhibit 7-9 shows the earnings-per-share advantage of borrowing. As you can see, Athens Corporation's EPS amount is higher if the company borrows by issuing bonds (compare lines 11 and 12). Athens earns more on the investment ($102,000) than the interest it pays on the bonds ($30,000).

In this case, borrowing results in higher earnings per share than issuing shares. Borrowing has its disadvantages, however. Interest expense may be high enough to eliminate net income and lead to losses. Also, borrowing creates liabilities that must be paid during bad years as well as good years. In contrast, a company that issues shares can omit its dividends during a bad year.

 # DECISION GUIDELINES

FINANCING WITH DEBT OR WITH SHARES

Suppose you are the owner of El Taco, a regional chain of Tex-Mex restaurants in western Canada. You are planning to expand into central Canada, so you must make some key decisions about how to finance the expansion.

Decision	Guidelines
How will you finance El Taco's expansion?	Your financing plan depends on El Taco's ability to generate cash flow, your willingness to give up some control of the business, the amount of financing risk you are willing to take, and El Taco's credit rating.
Do El Taco's operations generate enough cash to meet all its financing needs?	If yes, the business needs little outside financing. There is no need to borrow.
	If no, the business will need to issue additional shares or borrow the money.
Are you willing to give up some of your control of the business?	If yes, then issue shares to other shareholders, who can vote their shares to elect the company's directors.
	If no, then borrow from bondholders, who have no vote in the management of the company.
How much leverage (financing risk) are you willing or able to take?	If much, then borrow as much as you can, and you may increase El Taco's earnings per share. But this will increase the business's debt ratio and the risk of being unable to pay its debts.
	If little, then borrow sparingly. This will hold the debt ratio down and reduce the risk of default on borrowing agreements, but El Taco's earnings per share may be lower than if you were to borrow.
How good is the business's credit rating?	The better the credit rating, the easier it is to borrow on favourable terms. A good credit rating also makes it easier to issue shares. Neither shareholders nor creditors will entrust their money to a company with a bad credit rating.

EXHIBIT 7-9
Earnings-per-Share Advantage of Borrowing

	A	B	C	D	E	F
1		Plan 1		Plan 2		
2		Borrow $500,000 at 6%		Issue 50,000 Common Shares for $500,000		
3	Net income before expansion		$ 300,000		$ 300,000	
4	Expected project income before interest and income tax	$ 200,000		$ 200,000		
5	Less interest expense ($500,000 × 0.06)	(30,000)		0		
6	Expected project income before income tax	170,000		200,000		
7	Less income tax expense (40%)	(68,000)		(80,000)		
8	Expected project net income		102,000		120,000	
9	Total company net income		$ 402,000		$ 420,000	
10	Earnings per share after expansion:					
11	Plan 1 Borrow ($402,000/100,000 shares)		$ 4.02			
12	Plan 2 ($420,000/150,000 shares)				$ 2.80	
13						

ANALYZE AND EVALUATE A COMPANY'S DEBT-PAYING ABILITY

ACCOUNTS PAYABLE TURNOVER. In Chapter 3 we used working capital and the current ratio to analyze a company's liquidity. Another important measure of liquidity for a business is **accounts payable turnover (T/O)**, which measures the number of times a year a company is able to pay its accounts payable. The ratio is computed as follows:

> Accounts payable turnover (T/O) = Cost of goods sold ÷ Average accounts payable
> Turnover expressed in days = 365 ÷ T/O (computed above)

The average accounts payable amount is calculated using the year's opening and closing balances. Once the turnover is computed, it is usually expressed in number of days, or **days payable outstanding (DPO)**, by dividing the turnover into 365. Here are recent comparative ratios for accounts payable turnover for Best Buy and The Source, two large consumer electronics retailers:

(In millions)	Best Buy	The Source
Cost of goods sold..	$37,611	$2,462
Average accounts payable	5,085	268
Accounts payable turnover (T/O)	7.40	9.19
Turnover in days (365 ÷ T/O), or days payable outstanding (DPO)........	49 days	40 days

Because different industries have different business models and standard business practices, it is important to compare companies with competitors in the same industry. Since Best Buy and The Source are both in the consumer electronics industry, purchasing many of their products from the same vendors, it is reasonable to compare them on the basis of accounts payable turnover. The Source pays its accounts payable in about 40 days, whereas Best Buy takes 49 days to pay its accounts payable. If you were a supplier of these two giant companies, which would you rather do business with, on the basis of this ratio? If cash collections are important to you in order to pay your own bills, the obvious answer is The Source, based strictly on this ratio.

What makes an accounts payable turnover ratio strong or weak in the eyes of creditors and investors? Generally, a high turnover ratio (short period in days) is better than a low turnover ratio. Companies with shorter payment periods are generally better credit risks than those with longer payment periods. However, some companies with strong credit ratings strategically follow shrewd cash management policies, withholding payment to suppliers as long as possible, while speeding up collections, in order to conserve cash. For example, Walmart's accounts payable turnover is about 37 days, which is longer than a typical 30-day credit period. The company strategically stretches its payment period, which is tough on suppliers, but because of Walmart's size, market share, and buying power, few suppliers can afford not to do business with the company.

To be sure, credit and sales decisions are based on far more information than accounts payable turnover, so it's wise not to oversimplify. However, combined with inventory turnover (discussed in Chapter 5) and accounts receivable turnover (discussed in Chapter 4), all expressed in days, accounts payable turnover is an important ingredient in computing the *cash conversion cycle*, which is an overall measure of liquidity. Combined with the current ratio (discussed in Chapter 3) and the quick ratio (discussed in Chapter 4), studying the cash conversion cycle helps users of financial statements determine the overall liquidity of a company. We will discuss the cash conversion cycle in more depth in Chapter 10.

The Leverage Ratio

As discussed and illustrated above, financing with debt can be advantageous, but management of a company must be careful not to incur too much debt. Chapter 3 discussed the debt ratio, which measures the proportion of total liabilities to total assets, two elements of the fundamental accounting equation:

$$\text{Debt ratio} = \frac{\text{Total debt (liabilities)}}{\text{Total assets}}$$

We can rearrange this relationship between total assets, total liabilities, and shareholders' equity in a different manner to illustrate the impact that leverage can have on profitability. The **leverage ratio** is commonly calculated as follows, although other methods are sometimes used:

$$\text{Leverage ratio} = \frac{\text{Total assets}}{\text{Total shareholders' equity}}$$

This ratio shows a company's total assets per dollar of shareholders' equity. A leverage ratio of exactly 1.0 would mean a company has no debt, because total assets would exactly equal total shareholders' equity. This condition is almost nonexistent, because virtually all companies have liabilities, and, therefore, have leverage ratios in excess of 1.0. In fact, as we have shown previously, having a healthy amount of debt can actually enhance a company's profitability, in terms of the shareholders' investment. The higher the leverage ratio, the more it magnifies return on shareholders' equity (Net Income/Average Shareholders' Equity, or ROE). If net income is positive, return on assets (ROA) is positive. The leverage ratio magnifies this positive return to make return on equity (ROE) even more positive. This is because the company is using borrowed money to earn a profit (a concept known as *trading on the equity*). However, if earnings are negative (losses), ROA is negative, and the leverage ratio makes ROE even more negative. We will analyze ROE in more detail when we discuss shareholders' equity in Chapter 8. For now, let's just focus on understanding the meaning of the leverage ratio by looking at two fictional airlines, Northeast and Provincial. Here are the leverage ratios and debt ratios for the two companies:

(In millions)	Northeast	Provincial
1. Total assets	$15,463	$40,552
2. Shareholders' equity	$ 6,237	$ 1,912
3. Leverage ratio (1 ÷ 2)	2.48	21.2
4. Total debt (1 − 2)	$ 9,226	$38,640
5. Debt ratio (4 ÷ 1)	59.7%	95.3%

These figures show that Northeast has $2.48 of total assets for each dollar of shareholders' equity. This translates to a debt ratio of 59.7%, which we learned in Chapter 3 is about normal for many companies. However, Provincial has a leverage ratio of 21.2, meaning there are $21.20 of assets for each dollar of shareholders' equity. Rearranging the elements to show debt to total assets, Provincial has an astonishing ratio of 95.3%. This company is drowning in debt!

The Times-Interest-Earned Ratio

The debt ratio measures the effect of debt on the company's *financial position* but says nothing about the ability to pay interest expense. Analysts use a second ratio—the **times-interest-earned ratio**—to relate income to interest expense. To compute this ratio, we divide *income from operations* (also called *operating income* or *earnings before interest and taxes*) by interest expense. This ratio measures the number of times that operating income can *cover* interest expense. The ratio is also called the **interest-coverage ratio**. A high times-interest-earned ratio indicates ease in paying interest expense; a low value suggests difficulty. Let's see how Sobeys Inc. and Loblaw Companies Limited, two leading grocery chains, compare on the times-interest-earned ratio.

			Sobeys Inc.	Loblaw Companies Limited
Times-interest-earned ratio	$=$	$\dfrac{\text{Operating income}}{\text{Interest expense}} =$	$\dfrac{\$406 \text{ million}}{\$60 \text{ million}}$	$\dfrac{\$1,205 \text{ million}}{\$269 \text{ million}}$
			$= 6.8 \text{ times}$	$= 4.5 \text{ times}$

Sobeys's income from operations covers its interest expense 6.8 times. Loblaw's interest-coverage ratio is 4.5 times. Both companies have healthy ratios, but Sobeys's higher ratio indicates less risk relative to Loblaw's ratio.

STOP + THINK (7-5)

Suppose you are a loan officer at a bank and you must decide which of the two companies below would present a lower risk to the bank if you were to loan it money. Which company would you prefer to loan money to?

	Company A	Company B
Total assets	$4,858	$14,991
Total liabilities	$4,178	$ 8,718
Total Shareholders' equity	680	6,273
Total liabilities and Shareholders' equity	$4,858	$14,991
Operating income	$ 241	$ 1,068
Interest expense	$ 101	$ 211

DESCRIBE OTHER TYPES OF LONG-TERM LIABILITIES

Term Loans

Companies can often satisfy their long-term financing needs without resorting to the issuance of bonds in a public market. **Term loans** are a common form of long-term financing, which, like bonds, allow a company to borrow a fixed amount of money up front and repay it over a specified number of years at a stated interest rate. Unlike bonds, however, a term loan is typically arranged with a single lender, such as a bank or other financial institution. A term loan is usually secured by certain assets of the borrower, often the assets acquired using the proceeds of the loan. WestJet, for example, had $838 million in term loans payable at June 30, 2018. Each of the loans comprising this balance was secured by the airplane WestJet purchased with the original loan proceeds. Term loans secured by real property, such as land and buildings, are called **mortgages**. As with other forms of long-term debt, term loans are split between their current and long-term portions on the balance sheet, and the terms of the loans, including principal repayments over the next five years, are disclosed in the notes.

Leases

A **lease** is a rental agreement in which the renter (**lessee**) agrees to make rent payments to the property owner (**lessor**) in exchange for the use of the asset for an agreed period of time. Leasing allows the lessee to acquire the use of a needed asset without having to make the large upfront payment that purchase agreements require. WestJet, for example, may lease some of its planes instead of buying them outright. Accountants distinguish between two types of leases: finance leases and operating leases. ASPE uses the term capital leases instead of finance leases. For simplicity, this section uses the term finance leases.

IFRS and ASPE are consistent in their definitions of **finance leases**: they are leases that transfer to the lessee substantially all the risks and rewards incidental to the ownership of an asset, even though formal legal title of the asset may remain with the lessor. For an **operating lease**, substantially all the risks and rewards of ownership remain with the lessor. Under IFRS, lessees must treat all leases as finance leases, whereas ASPE allows lessees to treat some leases as operating leases. Both IFRS and

ASPE allow lessors to treat leases as finance or operating leases, depending on the lease terms and conditions. Determining whether a lease should be treated as a finance lease or an operating lease is beyond the scope of this text, so the decision criteria are not presented here.

Because a finance lease transfers to the lessee substantially all the risks and rewards incidental to the ownership of an asset, the lessee records the leased property as an asset on its financial statements, following all of the relevant accounting standards presented for property, plant, and equipment in Chapter 6. The finance lease contract also creates a formal legal obligation for the lessee, so the lessee must record a liability that reflects the future payments to be made according to the terms of the lease. Finance lease obligations are split into their current and long-term portions for balance sheet presentation purposes, just as with other forms of long-term debt. The lessor treats a finance lease as if they had sold the asset being leased, recording a sale on the income statement and a corresponding receivable on the balance sheet in respect of the future lease payments they will receive from the lessee. The detailed accounting for finance leases is beyond the scope of this text.

Under an operating lease, the risks and rewards of ownership do not transfer to the lessee, so they record neither an asset nor a liability; they simply expense the lease payments as they come due, and also disclose at least the next five years of operating-lease commitments in the notes to the financial statements. Lessors record the lease payments as revenue as they come due.

Post-Employment Benefits

Employee benefits are forms of consideration given by a company in exchange for services rendered by employees. **Post-employment benefits** are a special type of employee benefits that do not become payable until after a person has completed employment with the company. They include such things as pension benefits, medical and dental insurance, and prescription drug benefits. A company's obligations for these future benefits must be recorded as liabilities on its balance sheet, split into current and long-term portions where applicable. The formal accounting for these benefits is complex and beyond the scope of this text.

OBJECTIVE

❽ **Report** liabilities on the balance sheet

REPORT LIABILITIES ON THE BALANCE SHEET

Exhibit 7-10 again presents the liabilities of WestJet as at June 30, 2018.

Investors and creditors need the information illustrated in Exhibit 7-10 and discussed below in order to evaluate WestJet's balance sheet and the company.

Exhibit 7-10 includes Note 9 (adapted) from WestJet's financial statements, which gives additional information about the company's long-term debt. This note shows that WestJet's long-term debt consists of three tranches of term loans that have been used to finance the purchase of aircraft, as well as some unsecured notes payable and another loan. The current portion of this debt, about $154 million, can be traced to the partial balance sheet presented above the note.

Note 15 in Exhibit 7-10 presents the details of WestJet's operating leases and other commitments. We can see that they leased a variety of items, including aircraft, computer hardware, and inflight entertainment. Their total commitment under operating leases and other contracts was about $872 million at June 30, 2018.

Working back and forth between the financial statements and the notes to the financial statements is an important part of financial analysis. You now have the tools to understand the liabilities on an actual balance sheet.

	A	B	C	D
1	**WestJet Airlines Ltd.** Liabilities As at June 30, 2018 (in thousands)			
2	**Liabilities**			
3	Current liabilities:			
4	Accounts payable and accrued liabilities	$ 434,295		
5	Advance ticket sales	739,858		
6	Deferred rewards program	205,691		
7	Non-refundable guest credits	64,897		
8	Current portion of maintenance provisions	106,082		
9	Current portion of long-term debt	153,718		
10		1,704,541		
11	Non-current liabilities:			
12	Maintenance provisions	261,116		
13	Long-term debt	1,883,372		
14	Other liabilities	16,528		
15	Deferred income tax	401,856		
16	Total liabilities	$ 4,267,413		
17				
18	**8. LONG-TERM DEBT (Partial, Adapted)**			
19	Term loans—purchased aircraft	$ 35,038		
20	Term loan—purchased aircraft	146,504		
21	Term loan—purchased aircraft	656,648		
22	Senior unsecured notes	921,715		
23	Non-revolving loan	277,185		
24		2,037,090		
25	Current portion	(153,718)		
26		$ 1,883,372		
27				
28	**14. COMMITMENTS (Partial, Adapted)**			
29	(b) Leases and contractual commitments The Corporation has entered into operating leases and commitments for aircraft, land, buildings, equipment, computer hardware, software licences and inflight entertainment. As at June 30, 2018, the future payments under these commitments are as follows:			
30	Within 1 year	$ 259,008		
31	1–5 years	505,926		
32	Over 5 years	106,857		
33		$ 871,791		
34				

EXHIBIT 7-10
Reporting Liabilities of WestJet

Source: Based on WestJet Airlines Ltd. Consolidated Balance Sheet as at June 30, 2018.

STOP + THINK (7-6)

Assume that Discount Tennis Equipment completed these selected transactions during December 2020:

a. Sales of $4,000,000 are subject to estimated warranty cost of 4%. The estimated warranty payable at the beginning of the year was $40,000, and warranty payments for the year totalled $80,000.

b. On December 1, 2020, Discount signed a $200,000 note that requires annual payments of $40,000 plus 6% interest on the unpaid balance each December 1.

c. Tennis Hut, a chain of tennis stores, ordered $150,000 of tennis equipment. With its order, Tennis Hut sent a cheque for $150,000, and Discount shipped $100,000 of the goods. Discount will ship the remainder of the goods on January 3, 2021.

d. The December payroll of $120,000 is subject to employee-withheld income tax, Canada Pension Plan and Employment Insurance, and the company's share of Canada Pension Plan and Employment Insurance totalling $35,000 and benefits of $11,000. On December 31, Discount pays employees their take-home pay and accrues all tax amounts.

Requirements

1. For each liability, classify it as current or long-term and state the amount that would appear on Discount's balance sheet at December 31, 2020.

2. Calculate the total current liabilities as at December 31, 2020.

Summary of IFRS-ASPE Differences

Concepts	IFRS	ASPE
Differences between income tax expense and income tax payable (p. 342)	Accounted for as deferred income taxes.	Accounted for as future income taxes.
Provisions and contingent liabilities (p. 344)	A contingent liability is recorded as a provision when it is probable that an outflow of economic benefits will be required to settle the liability. *Probable* is generally considered to mean that an outflow is *more likely than not* to occur.	A contingent liability is recorded as a liability when it is likely that an outflow of economic benefits will be required to settle the liability. *Likely* is generally considered to be a higher threshold to meet than *probable*, so fewer contingent liabilities will be recorded under ASPE than under IFRS.
Government remittances (p. 346)	No separate disclosure of these liabilities is required.	Government remittances (other than income taxes) such as sales taxes, Employment Insurance, and Canada Pension Plan payable must be disclosed separately, either on the balance sheet or in the notes.
Amortization of discounts and premiums (p. 352)	The effective-interest method must be used to amortize discounts and premiums.	The straight-line method is available as an amortization option.
Finance leases (p. 365)	Leases that transfer substantially all the risks and rewards incidental to the ownership of assets to the lessee are called finance leases.	The equivalent term is capital leases. There are no differences in accounting for these leases.

SUMMARY

SUMMARY OF LEARNING OBJECTIVES

LEARNING OBJECTIVE	SUMMARY
❶ **Explain** and **account** for current liabilities	Current liabilities are obligations due within one year of the balance sheet date, or within the company's operating cycle if it is longer than one year. Obligations due beyond that time period are long-term liabilities.
	Current liabilities are of two kinds: (1) known amounts, such as short-term borrowings, accounts payable, short-term notes payable, sales taxes, accrued liabilities, payroll liabilities, unearned revenues, and the current portion of long-term debts; and (2) estimated amounts, such as warranties payable and contingent liabilities.
❷ **Explain** the types, features, and pricing of bonds payable	Bonds payable are groups of notes issued to multiple lenders. Bonds may be term bonds, which have a fixed maturity date, or serial bonds, which mature in instalments over a certain period of time. Some bonds are secured by specific assets of the issuing company, whereas others are debentures, which are unsecured bonds.
	Bonds are bought and sold through bond markets. The price of a bond is dependent on the relationship between the stated interest rate on the bond and the current market interest rate. When the stated rate exceeds the market rate, the bond is issued at a premium above face value; when the opposite is true, the bond is issued at a discount below face value.

❸ **Account** for bonds payable

Bonds payable are initially recorded as long-term liabilities at their face value less (plus) any bond discount (premium). Bond discounts and premiums are amortized to interest expense over the life of the bonds, so that by the time the bonds mature, any related discounts or premiums have been eliminated. Any bonds maturing within one year of the balance sheet date are classified as current liabilities.

❹ **Calculate** and **account** for interest expense on bonds payable

Bonds pay interest semi-annually at their stated interest rate times the face value of the bonds. The interest expense is equal to the interest payment plus (minus) the amortization of any discount (premium). IFRS require interest expense to be calculated using the effective-interest method, whereas ASPE also permit use of the simpler straight-line method.

❺ **Explain** the advantages and disadvantages of financing with debt versus equity

A company that wishes to fund expansion, acquisitions, or other operational activities has three main options: using excess cash, issuing new shares, or borrowing money. Each of these methods has advantages and disadvantages related to the dilution of control, the flexibility of cash payments, and impact on earnings per share.

❻ **Analyze** and **evaluate** a company's debt-paying ability

Accounts payable turnover (Cost of goods sold/Average accounts payable) measures the number of times during the year a company is able to fully pay off its accounts payable. It is an important indicator of a company's liquidity, or its ability to pay off its short-term debts.

The leverage ratio (Total assets/Total shareholders' equity) shows how many dollars of assets a company has per dollar of shareholders' equity. A leverage ratio above 1.0 can enhance returns to shareholders because it means the company is using debt to invest in additional assets, which will presumably generate additional net income to be shared among the owners. An excessive leverage ratio can be dangerous, however, as it often leads to a company's inability to meet its debt payments.

The times-interest-earned ratio (Operating income/Interest expense) measures the number of times a company's operating income can cover its interest payments. The higher the ratio, the easier it is for a company to make its payments.

❼ **Describe** other types of long-term liabilities

A term loan is a long-term loan at a stated interest rate, typically from a single lender such as a bank, which must be repaid over a specified number of years. It is usually secured by specific assets of the borrower, often the ones acquired using the loan proceeds. A mortgage is a term loan secured by real property such as land and buildings.

A lease is a rental agreement in which the lessee agrees to make rent payments to the lessor (property owner) in exchange for the use of property. There are two types of leases: a finance (or capital) lease that transfers to the lessee substantially all the risks and rewards incidental to the ownership of the property; and an operating lease, in which the lessor retains the risks and rewards of ownership. Finance leases are recorded as liabilities and accounted for in the same way as other long-term debts, whereas operating lease payments are expensed as they come due.

Post-employment benefits are a special type of employee benefits that do not become payable until after a person has completed employment with the company. They include such things as pension benefits, medical and dental insurance, and prescription drug benefits.

❽ **Report** liabilities on the balance sheet

Financial statement users should review all of the current and long-term liabilities reported on a company's balance sheet. In order to properly interpret this information, users should also consult related information in the statement of cash flows and the notes to the financial statements.

MyLab Accounting

END-OF-CHAPTER SUMMARY PROBLEM

TransCanada Corporation has a number of bond issues outstanding in various amounts with various interest rates and maturities. Assume TransCanada has outstanding an issue of 8% bonds that mature in 2030. Suppose the bonds are dated October 1, 2020, and pay interest each April 1 and October 1.

Requirements

1. Use Excel to complete the following effective-interest amortization table through October 1, 2022:

   Bond Data
   Maturity value—$100,000
   Contract interest rate—8%
   Interest paid—4% semi-annually, $4,000 ($100,000 × 0.08 × 6/12)
   Market interest rate at the time of issue—9% annually, 4½% semi-annually
   Issue price—93.80

	A	B	C	D	E	F	G
1	Amortization Table						
2	Semi-Annual Interest Date	Interest Payment (4% of Maturity Amount)	Interest Expense (4½% of Preceding Bond Carrying Amount)	Bond Discount Amortization (C – B)	Bond Discount Account Balance (Preceding E – D)	Bond Carrying Amount ($100,000 – E)	
3	01-10-20						
4	01-04-21						
5	01-10-21						
6	01-04-22						
7	01-10-22						
8							

Name: TransCanada Corporation
Industry: Pipeline provider
Accounting Period: The years 2020, 2021, 2022

2. Using the amortization table, record the following transactions:
   a. Issuance of the bonds on October 1, 2020.
   b. Accrual of interest and amortization of the bonds on December 31, 2020.
   c. Payment of interest and amortization of the bonds on April 1, 2021.

ANSWERS
Requirement 1

The semi-annual interest payment is constant ($4,000). The interest expense is calculated as 4.5% of the previous period's carrying value. The discount account balance reflects that the issue price of $93.80 is less than $100.00.

	A	B	C	D	E	F	G
1	Semi-Annual Interest Date	Interest Payment (4% of Maturity Amount)	Interest Expense (4½% of Preceding Bond Carrying Amount)	Bond Discount Amortization (C – B)	Bond Discount Account Balance (Preceding E – D)	Bond Carrying Amount ($100,000 – E)	
2	01-10-20				$6,200	$93,800	
3	01-04-21	$4,000	$4,221	$221	5,979	94,021	
4	01-10-21	4,000	4,231	231	5,748	94,252	
5	01-04-22	4,000	4,241	241	5,507	94,493	
6	01-10-22	4,000	4,252	252	5,255	94,745	
7							

Requirement 2

	A	B	C	D	E
1	a. 2020				
2	Oct. 1	Cash	93,800		
3		Discount on Bonds Payable	6,200		
4		Bonds Payable		100,000	
5		To issue 8%, ten-year bonds at a discount.			
6	b. Dec. 31	Interest Expense ($4,221 × 3/6)	2,111		
7		Discount on Bonds Payable ($221 × 3/6)		111	
8		Interest Payable ($4,000 × 3/6)		2,000	
9		To accrue interest and amortize the bonds.			
10	c. 2021				
11	Apr. 1	Interest Expense	2,110		
12		Interest Payable	2,000		
13		Discount on Bonds Payable ($221 × 3/6)		110*	
14		Cash		4,000	
15		To pay semi-annual interest, part of which was accrued, and amortize the bonds.			
16					

*The total amortization was $221, of which $111 was recognized at December 31, 2020.

The bonds were issued for less than $100,000, reflecting a discount. Use the amounts from columns D and E for 01-10-20 from the amortization table.

The accrued interest is calculated, and the bond discount is amortized. Use 3/6 of the amounts from columns A, B, and C for 01-04-21 from the amortization table.

The semi-annual interest payment is made ($4,000 from column A). Only the January-to-March 2021 interest expense is recorded, because the October-to-December interest expense was already recorded in Requirement 2(b). The same is true for the discount on bonds payable. Reverse Interest Payable from Requirement 2(b), because cash is paid now.

REVIEW

MyLab Accounting

Make the grade with MyLab Accounting: The Quick Quiz questions, Short Exercises, Exercises, and Problems (Group A) marked with a ⊕ can be found on MyLab Accounting. You can practise them as often as you want, and most feature step-by-step guided instructions to help you find the right answer.

QUICK QUIZ (ANSWERS APPEAR ON THE LAST PAGE OF THIS CHAPTER.)

1. For the purpose of classifying liabilities as current or non-current, the term *operating cycle* refers to which of the following?
   a. A period of one year
   b. The time period between date of sale and the date the related revenue is collected
   c. The time period between purchase of merchandise and the conversion of this merchandise back to cash
   d. The average time period between business recessions

2. Failure to accrue interest expense results in which of the following?
   a. An overstatement of net income and an overstatement of liabilities
   b. An understatement of net income and an overstatement of liabilities
   c. An understatement of net income and an understatement of liabilities
   d. An overstatement of net income and an understatement of liabilities

3. Sportscar Warehouse operates in a province with a 6% sales tax. For convenience, Sportscar Warehouse credits Sales Revenue for the total amount (selling price plus sales tax) collected from each customer. If Sportscar Warehouse fails to make an adjustment for sales taxes, which of the following will be true?
   a. Net income will be overstated, and liabilities will be overstated.
   b. Net income will be overstated, and liabilities will be understated.
   c. Net income will be understated, and liabilities will be overstated.
   d. Net income will be understated, and liabilities will be understated.

4. What kind of account is *Unearned Revenue*?
  a. Asset account
  b. Liability account
  c. Revenue account
  d. Expense account

5. An end-of-period adjusting entry that debits Unearned Revenue will most likely credit which of the following?
  a. A revenue
  b. An asset
  c. An expense
  d. A liability

6. Adrian Inc. manufactures and sells computer monitors with a three-year warranty. Warranty costs are expected to average 8% of sales during the warranty period. The following table shows the sales and actual warranty payments during the first two years of operations:

Year	Sales	Warranty Payments
2019	$500,000	$ 4,000
2020	700,000	32,000

    Based on these facts, what amount of warranty liability should Adrian Inc. report on its balance sheet at December 31, 2020?
  a. $32,000
  b. $36,000
  c. $60,000
  d. $96,000

7. Today's Fashions has a debt that has been properly reported as a long-term liability up to the present year (2020). Some of this debt comes due in 2020. If Today's Fashions continues to report the current position as a long-term liability, the effect will be to do which of the following?
  a. Overstate the current ratio
  b. Overstate net income
  c. Understate total liabilities
  d. Understate the debt ratio

8. A bond with a face amount of $10,000 has a current price quote of 102.875. What is the bond's price?
  a. $1,028,750
  b. $10,200.88
  c. $10,028.75
  d. $10,287.50

9. Bond carrying value equals Bonds Payable
  a. minus Premium on Bonds Payable.
  b. plus Discount on Bonds Payable.
  c. plus Premium on Bonds Payable.
  d. minus Discount on Bonds Payable.
  e. Both a and b
  f. Both c and d

10. What type of account is *Discount on Bonds Payable*, and what is its normal balance?

Type of account	Normal balance
a. Contra liability	Debit
b. Reversing account	Debit
c. Adjusting amount	Credit
d. Contra liability	Credit

Questions 11 through 14 use the following data:

11. Sweetwater Company sells $100,000 of 10%, 15-year bonds for 97 on April 1, 2020. The market rate of interest on that day is 10½%. Interest is paid each year on April 1. The entry to record the sale of the bonds on April 1 would be which of the following?

a. Cash	97,000	
Bonds Payable		97,000
b. Cash	100,000	
Bonds Payable		100,000
c. Cash	97,000	
Discount on Bonds Payable	3,000	
Bonds Payable		100,000
d. Cash	100,000	
Discount on Bonds Payable		3,000
Bonds Payable		97,000

12. Sweetwater Company uses the straight-line amortization method. The sale price of the bonds was $97,000. The amount of interest expense on April 1 of each year will be which of the following?
  a. $4,080
  b. $4,000
  c. $4,200
  d. $10,200
  e. None of these. The interest expense is ___.

13. Write the adjusting entry required at December 31, 2020.

14. Write the journal entry required at April 1, 2021.

15. McPherson Corporation issued $100,000 of 10%, five-year bonds on January 1, 2020, for $92,280. The market interest rate when the bonds were issued was 12%. Interest is paid semi-annually on January 1 and July 1. The first interest payment is July 1, 2020. Using the effective-interest amortization method, how much interest expense will McPherson record on July 1, 2020?
  a. $6,000
  b. $5,228
  c. $6,772
  d. $5,000
  e. Some other amount ($___)

16. Using the facts in the preceding question, McPherson's journal entry to record the interest expense on July 1, 2020, will include a
    a. debit to Bonds Payable.
    b. credit to Interest Expense.
    c. debit to Premium on Bonds Payable.
    d. credit to Discount on Bonds Payable.

17. Amortizing the discount on bonds payable does which of the following?
    a. Increases the recorded amount of interest expense
    b. Is necessary only if the bonds were issued at more than face value
    c. Reduces the semi-annual cash payment for interest
    d. Reduces the carrying value of the bond liability

18. The journal entry on the maturity date to record the payment of $1,000,000 of bonds payable that were issued at a $70,000 discount includes
    a. a debit to Discount on Bonds Payable for $70,000.
    b. a credit to Cash for $1,070,000.
    c. a debit to Bonds Payable for $1,000,000.
    d. All of the above.

19. The payment of the face amount of a bond on its maturity date is regarded as which of the following?
    a. An operating activity
    b. An investing activity
    c. A financing activity

ACCOUNTING VOCABULARY

account payable A liability for goods or services purchased on credit and backed by the general reputation and credit standing of the debtor. (p. 336)

accounts payable turnover (T/O) A liquidity ratio that measures the number of times per year a company was able to repay its accounts payable in full. Calculated by dividing the cost of goods sold by the average accounts payable balance for the year. (p. 362)

bond discount Excess of a bond's face (par) value over its issue price. (p. 348)

bonds payable Groups of notes payable issued to multiple lenders called *bondholders*. (p. 347)

bond premium Excess of a bond's issue price over its face value. (p. 348)

contingent liability A possible obligation that arises from past events and whose existence will be confirmed only by the occurrence or non-occurrence of one or more uncertain future events not wholly within the control of the company. (p. 345)

current portion of long-term debt The amount of the principal that is payable within one year. Also called *current instalment of long-term debt*. (p. 343)

days payable outstanding (DPO) Another way of expressing the accounts payable turnover ratio, this measure indicates how many days it will take to pay off the accounts payable balance in full. Calculated by dividing the *accounts payable turnover* into 365. (p. 362)

debentures Unsecured bonds—bonds backed only by the good faith of the borrower. (p. 348)

deferred income tax liability The amount of income taxes payable in future periods as a result of differences between accounting income and taxable income in current and prior periods. Under ASPE, this is known as a *future income tax liability*. (p. 342)

earnings per share (EPS) Amount of a company's net income per outstanding common share. (p. 360)

face value of bond The principal amount payable by the issuer. Also called *maturity value*. (p. 347)

finance lease Under IFRS, a lease that transfers substantially all the risks and rewards incidental to ownership of assets to the lessee. (p. 365)

interest-coverage ratio Another name for the *times-interest-earned ratio*. (p. 364)

lease Rental agreement in which the tenant (lessee) agrees to make rent payments to the property owner (lessor) in exchange for the use of the asset. (p. 365)

lessee Tenant in a lease agreement. (p. 365)

lessor Property owner in a lease agreement. (p. 365)

leverage ratio Shows the ratio of a company's total assets to total shareholders' equity. It is an alternative way of expressing how much debt a company has used to fund its assets, or in other words, how much leverage it has used. (p. 363)

line of credit A method of short-term borrowing that provides a company with as-needed access to credit up to a maximum amount specified by its lender. (p. 336)

market interest rate Interest rate that investors demand for loaning their money. Also called *effective interest rate*. (p. 349)

market price The price an investor is willing to pay of a bond. (p. 348)

mortgage A *term loan* secured by real property, such as land and buildings. (p. 365)

operating lease A lease in which the risks and rewards of asset ownership are not transferred to the lessee. (p. 365)

payroll Employee compensation, a major expense of many businesses. (p. 339)

post-employment benefits A special type of employee benefits that do not become payable until after a person has completed employment with the company. They include such things as pension benefits, medical and dental insurance, and prescription drug benefits. (p. 366)

pretax accounting income Income before tax on the income statement; the basis for computing income tax expense. (p. 341)

provision Under IFRS, a present obligation of uncertain timing or amount that is recorded as a liability because it is probable that economic resources will be required to settle it. (p. 344)

sales tax payable The amount of HST, GST, and provincial sales tax owing to government bodies. (p. 338)

serial bonds Bonds that mature in instalments over a period of time. (p. 348)

short-term notes payable Notes payable due within one year. (p. 337)

stated interest rate Interest rate printed on the bond certificate that determines the amount of cash interest the borrower pays and the investor receives each year. Also called the *coupon rate* or *contract interest rate*. (p. 348)

taxable income The basis for computing the amount of tax to pay the government. (p. 341)

term bonds Bonds that all mature at the same time for a particular issue. (p. 348)

term loan A long-term loan at a stated interest rate, typically from a single lender such as a bank, which must be repaid over a specified number of years. Usually secured by specific assets of the borrower, often the ones acquired using the loan proceeds. (p. 365)

times-interest-earned ratio Ratio of income from operations to interest expense. Measures the number of times that operating income can cover interest expense. Also called the *interest-coverage ratio*. (p. 364)

underwriter Organization that purchases the bonds from an issuing company and resells them to its clients or sells the bonds for a commission, agreeing to buy all unsold bonds. (p. 348)

unearned revenue A liability that arises when a business receives cash from a customer prior to providing the related goods or services. (p. 342)

ASSESS YOUR PROGRESS

SHORT EXERCISES

LEARNING OBJECTIVE ❶

Account for payroll expenses and liabilities

S7-1 Encore Records has two employees who are paid on the 1st and 15th of each month for the work they performed in the preceding half-month. At February 28, each employee is owed gross pay of $1,000, but each one must have 10% of their pay withheld for income taxes. Each must also make Canada Pension Plan contributions of 5.1% of their gross pay and pay Employment Insurance premiums of 1.62% of their gross pay. Prepare the payroll journal entries required to reflect these amounts, along with Encore's share of CPP contributions and EI premiums, in Encore's February 28 financial statements.

LEARNING OBJECTIVE ❽

Report payroll expenses and liabilities in the financial statements

S7-2 Refer to the data in exercise S7-1. Show what Encore would report on its balance sheet at February 28, and on its income statement for the month ended on that date.

LEARNING OBJECTIVE ❶

Account for warranty expense and estimated warranty payable

S7-3 General Motors of Canada Limited guarantees automobiles against defects for five years or 160,000 km, whichever comes first. Suppose GM Canada can expect warranty costs during the five-year period to add up to 3% of sales.

Assume that Forbes Motors in Waterloo, Ontario, made sales of $2,000,000 on their Buick line during 2020. Forbes received cash for 10% of the sales and took notes receivable for the remainder. Payments to satisfy customer warranty claims totalled $50,000 during 2020.

1. Record the sales, warranty expense, and warranty payments for Forbes. Ignore any reimbursement that Forbes may receive from GM Canada.
2. Post to the Estimated Warranty Payable T-account. The beginning balance was $40,000. At the end of 2020, how much in estimated warranty payable does Forbes owe its customers?

LEARNING OBJECTIVES ❶❽

Report warranties in the financial statements

S7-4 Refer to the data given in exercise S7-3. What amount of warranty expense will Forbes report during 2020? Does the warranty expense for the year equal the year's cash payments for warranties? Explain the relevant accounting principle as it applies to measuring warranty expense.

LEARNING OBJECTIVE ❻

Analyze accounts payable turnover

S7-5 Wardlow Sales, Inc.'s comparative income statements and balance sheets show the following selected information for 2019 and 2020:

	2020	2019
Cost of goods sold	$2,700,000	$2,500,000
Average accounts payable	$ 300,000	$ 250,000

Requirements

1. Calculate the company's accounts payable turnover and days payable outstanding (DPO) for 2019 and 2020.
2. On the basis of this computation alone, has the company's liquidity position improved or deteriorated during 2020?

S7-6 Compute the price of the following bonds:

a. $1,000,000 quoted at 89.75
b. $500,000 quoted at 110.375
c. $100,000 quoted at 97.50
d. $400,000 quoted at 102.625

LEARNING OBJECTIVES ❷❸

Price bonds

S7-7 Determine whether the following bonds will be issued at face value, a premium, or a discount:

a. The market interest rate is 9%. Star Inc. issues bonds with a stated rate of 8½%.
b. Charger Corporation issued 7½% bonds when the market rate was 7½%.
c. Explorer Corporation issued 8% bonds when the market interest rate was 6⅞%.
d. Tundra Company issued bonds that pay cash interest at the stated interest rate of 7%. At the date of issuance, the market interest rate was 8¼%.

LEARNING OBJECTIVES ❷❸

Determine bond prices at face value, a discount, or a premium

S7-8 Suppose Scotiabank issued a six-year $10,000 bond with stated interest rate of 6.25% when the market interest rate was 6¼%. Assume that the accounting year of Scotiabank ends on October 31. Journalize the following transactions, including an explanation for each entry.

a. Issuance of the bond payable on May 1, 2020
b. Accrual of interest expense on October 31, 2020 (rounded to the nearest dollar)
c. Payment of cash interest on November 1, 2020
d. Payment of the bonds at maturity (give the date)

LEARNING OBJECTIVES ❷❸❹

Journalize basic bond payable transactions

S7-9 Standard Autoparts Inc. issued $100,000 of 7%, 10-year bonds at a price of 87 on January 31, 2020. The market interest rate at the date of issuance was 9%, and the standard bonds pay interest semi-annually.

1. Prepare an effective-interest amortization table for the bonds through the first three interest payments. Use Exhibit 7-3, page 353, as a guide, and round amounts to the nearest dollar.
2. Record Standard's issuance of the bonds on January 31, 2020, and payment of the first semi-annual interest amount and amortization of the bonds on July 31, 2020. Explanations are not required.

LEARNING OBJECTIVES ❷❸❹

Record bond transactions and calculate interest using the effective-interest method

S7-10 Use the amortization table that you prepared for Standard Autoparts in exercise S7-9 to answer these questions about the company's long-term debt:

1. How much cash did Standard Autoparts borrow on January 31, 2020? How much cash will Standard Autoparts pay back at maturity on January 31, 2030?
2. How much cash interest will Standard Autoparts pay each six months?
3. How much interest expense will Standard Autoparts report on July 31, 2020, and on January 31, 2021? Why does the amount of interest expense increase each period? Explain in detail.

LEARNING OBJECTIVE ❹

Analyze interest on long-term debt

S7-11 Max Industries Ltd. borrowed money by issuing a $10,000 6.5%, 10-year bond. Assume the issue price was 94 on July 1, 2020.

1. How much cash did Max Industries receive when it issued the bond?
2. How much must Max Industries pay back at maturity? When is the maturity date?
3. How much cash interest will Max Industries pay each six months? Carry the interest amount to the nearest cent.
4. How much interest expense will Max Industries report each six months? Assume the straight-line amortization method, and carry the interest amount to the nearest cent.

LEARNING OBJECTIVES ❷❸❹

Determine bonds payable amounts; amortize bonds by the straight-line method

LEARNING OBJECTIVES ❸❹

Record bond transactions and calculate interest using the straight-line method

S7-12 Return to the Max Industries bond in exercise S7-11. Assume that Max Industries issued the bond on July 1, 2020, at a price of 90. Also assume that Max Industries's accounting year ends on December 31. Journalize the following transactions for Max Industries, including an explanation for each entry:

a. Issuance of the bonds on July 1, 2020.

b. Accrual of interest expense and amortization of bonds on December 31, 2020. (Use the straight-line amortization method, and round amounts to the nearest dollar.)

c. Payment of the first semi-annual interest amount on January 1, 2021.

LEARNING OBJECTIVE ❻

Calculate the leverage ratio, debt ratio, and times-interest-earned, and evaluate debt-paying ability

S7-13 Examine the following selected financial information for Best Buy Co., Inc., and Walmart Stores, Inc.:

(in millions)	Best Buy Co., Inc.	Walmart Stores, Inc.
1. Total assets	$17,849	$180,663
2. Shareholders' equity	$ 7,292	$ 71,247
3. Operating income	$ 2,114	$ 25,542
4. Interest expense	$ 87	$ 1,928
5. Leverage ratio		
6. Total debt		
7. Debt ratio		
8. Times interest earned		

1. Complete the table, calculating all the requested information for the two companies.
2. Evaluate each company's long-term debt-paying ability (strong, medium, weak).

LEARNING OBJECTIVE ❻

Compute and evaluate three ratios

S7-14 Evensen Plumbing Products Ltd. reported the following data in 2020 (in millions):

	2020
Net operating revenues	$ 29.1
Operating expenses	25.0
Operating income	4.1
Nonoperating items:	
Interest expense	(1.1)
Other	(0.2)
Net income	$ 2.8
Total assets	$100.0
Total shareholders' equity	40.0

Compute Evensen's leverage ratio, debt ratio, and times-interest-earned ratio, and write a sentence to explain what those ratio values mean. Would you be willing to lend Evensen $1 million? State your reason.

LEARNING OBJECTIVE ❽

Report liabilities

S7-15 Trinidad Industries Inc. has the following selected accounts at December 31, 2020:

GST Payable (net of ITC)	$ 17,000
Bonds payable	300,000
Equipment	120,000
Current portion of bonds payable	40,000
Notes payable, long-term	100,000
Interest payable (due March 1, 2021)	10,000
Accounts payable	44,000
Discount on bonds payable (all long-term)	10,000
Accounts receivable	34,000

Prepare the liabilities section of Trinidad's balance sheet at December 31, 2020, to show how Trinidad would report these items. Report total current liabilities and total liabilities.

EXERCISES

E7-16 The accounting records of Audio-Video Inc. included the following balances before the year-end adjustments:

LEARNING OBJECTIVES **1** **6** **8**

Account for and report warranty expense and the related liability; assess debt-paying ability

Estimated Warranty Payable	Sales Revenue	Warranty Expense
Beg. bal. 8,000	150,000	

In the past, Audio-Video's warranty expense has been 6% of sales. During the current period, the business paid $9,400 to satisfy the warranty claims of customers.

Requirements

1. Record Audio-Video's warranty expense for the period and the company's cash payments to satisfy warranty claims. Explanations are not required.
2. Show everything Audio-Video will report on its income statement and balance sheet for this situation.
3. Which data item from Requirement 2 will affect Audio-Video's current ratio? Will Audio-Video's current ratio increase or decrease as a result of this item?

E7-17 *Ontario Traveller Magazine* completed the following transactions during 2020:

LEARNING OBJECTIVES **1** **8**

Record and report current liabilities

Aug.	31	Sold one-year subscriptions, collecting cash of $1,500, plus HST of 13%.
Dec.	31	Remitted (paid) HST to Canada Revenue Agency (CRA).
	31	Made the necessary adjustment at year-end.

Journalize these transactions (explanations are not required). Then report any liability on the company's balance sheet at December 31.

E7-18 At January 31, Penske Talent Search owes its employees gross salaries totalling $20,000 for work they performed in the last half of January. The income taxes to be withheld from these earnings total $5,000. Employees' required Canada Pension Plan contributions are 5.1% of their gross pay, while Employment Insurance premiums are 1.62% of their gross pay. Penske will pay all related amounts owing, including the employer portions of CPP and EI payable, in early February. Prepare the payroll journal entries required to reflect these amounts in Penske's January 31 financial statements.

LEARNING OBJECTIVES **1** **8**

Account for payroll expenses and liabilities

E7-19 Joy's Bar and Grill completed the following note-payable transactions:

LEARNING OBJECTIVE **1**

Record note-payable transactions

2020		
Aug.	1	Purchased kitchen equipment costing $60,000 by issuing a one-year, 5% note.
Dec.	31	Accrued interest on the note payable.
2021		
Aug.	1	Paid the note payable at maturity.

Answer these questions for Joy's Bar and Grill:

1. How much interest expense must be accrued at December 31, 2020?
2. Determine the amount of Joy's final payment on July 31, 2021.
3. How much interest expense will Joy's report for 2020 and for 2021?

E7-20 Geodesic Domes, Inc., builds environmentally sensitive structures. The company's 2020 revenues totalled $2,800 million. At December 31, 2020, and 2019, the company had $661 million and $600 million in current assets, respectively. Accounts payable at the end of 2018 was $190 million. The December 31, 2020, and 2019, balance sheets and income statements reported the following amounts:

LEARNING OBJECTIVES **1** **6** **8**

Analyze current and long-term liabilities; evaluate debt-paying ability

At Year-End (in millions)	2020	2019
Liabilities and shareholders' equity		
Current liabilities		
Accounts payable	$ 110	$ 182
Accrued expenses	97	177
Employee compensation and benefits	45	15
Current portion of long-term debt	7	20
Total current liabilities	259	394
Long-term debt	1,394	1,315
Post-retirement benefits payable	102	154
Other liabilities	8	20
Shareholders' equity	1,951	1,492
Total liabilities and shareholders' equity	$3,714	$3,375
Year-end (in millions)		
Cost of goods sold	$1,656	$1,790

Requirements

1. Describe each of Geodesic Domes, Inc.'s liabilities and state how the liability arose.
2. Evaluate whether the company's ability to pay its long-term debts improved, deteriorated, or remained about the same over the year.
3. Evaluate whether the company's ability to pay its short-term debts improved, deteriorated, or remained about the same over the year.

LEARNING OBJECTIVES ❶❻❽ ⊕ **E7-21** Mills Geothermal Ltd. installs environmental heating/cooling systems. The company's 2020 revenues totalled $360 million, and at December 31, 2020, the company had $65 million in current assets. The December 31, 2020, balance sheet reported the liabilities and shareholders' equity as follows:

Analyze liabilities and debt-paying ability

At Year-End (in millions)	2020	2019
Liabilities and shareholders' equity		
Current liabilities		
Accounts payable	$ 29	$ 26
Accrued expenses	16	20
Employee compensation and benefits	9	11
Current portion of long-term debt	5	—
Total current liabilities	59	57
Long-term debt	115	115
Post-retirement benefits payable	31	27
Other liabilities	21	17
Shareholders' equity	73	70
Total liabilities and shareholders' equity	$299	$286

Requirements

1. Describe each of Mills Geothermal Ltd.'s liabilities, and state how the liability arose.
2. What were the company's total assets at December 31, 2020? Was the company's debt ratio at the end of 2020 high, low, or in a middle range?

LEARNING OBJECTIVE ❻ ⊕ **E7-22** Companies that operate in different industries may have very different financial ratio values. These differences may grow even wider when we compare companies located in different countries.

Evaluate debt-paying ability

Compare three companies on their current ratio, debt ratio, leverage ratio, and times-interest-earned ratio. Compute the ratios for Company B, Company N, and Company V.

(amounts in millions or billions)	Company B	Company N	Company V
Income data			
Total revenues	$9,732	¥7,320	€136,146
Operating income...	295	230	5,646
Interest expense..	41	27	655
Net income..	22	7	450
Balance sheet data			
(amounts in millions or billions)			
Total current assets	429	5,321	144,720
Long-term assets...	81	592	65,828
Total current liabilities.....................................	227	2,217	72,000
Long-term liabilities	77	2,277	111,177
Shareholders' equity	206	1,419	27,371

Note: ¥ is the symbol for a Japanese yen; € for a euro.

Based on your computed ratio values, which company looks the least risky?

🌐 **E7-23** Assume that Premium Golf Equipment completed these selected transactions during December 2020:

a. Sales of $3,000,000 are subject to estimated warranty cost of 3%. The estimated warranty payable at the beginning of the year was $30,000, and warranty payments for the year totalled $60,000.

b. On December 1, 2020, Premium signed a $150,000 note that requires annual payments of $30,000 plus 5% interest on the unpaid balance each December 1.

c. Golf Town, a chain of golf stores, ordered $125,000 of golf equipment. With its order, Golf Town sent a cheque for $125,000, and Premium shipped $100,000 of the goods. Premium will ship the remainder of the goods on January 3, 2021.

d. The December gross payroll of $100,000 is subject to employee income tax withholdings of $25,000, Canada Pension Plan contributions of 5.1%, and Employment Insurance premiums of 1.62%, along with the company's share of Canada Pension Plan contributions and Employment Insurance premiums. On December 31, Premium pays employees their take-home pay and accrues all tax amounts owing for the December payroll.

Requirement

For each transaction, determine the types and amounts of liabilities to be reported on the December 31, 2020 balance sheet and classify them as current or long-term. Show a total for current liabilities.

🌐 **E7-24** On January 31, 2020, Triumph Sports Cars issued 10-year, 6% bonds with a face value of $100,000. The bonds were issued at 97 and pay interest on January 31 and July 31. Triumph amortizes bonds by the straight-line method. Record (a) issuance of the bonds on January 31, (b) the semi-annual interest payment and discount amortization on July 31, and (c) the interest accrual and discount amortization on December 31.

🌐 **E7-25** Moreau Manufacturing Inc. has $200,000 of 8% debenture bonds outstanding. The bonds were issued at 102 in 2020 and mature in 2040.

Requirements

1. How much cash did Moreau receive when it issued these bonds?
2. How much cash *in total* will Moreau pay the bondholders through the maturity date of the bonds?

LEARNING OBJECTIVES ❶❽

Account for and report current and long-term liabilities

LEARNING OBJECTIVES ❷❸❹

Record bond transactions and calculate interest using the straight-line method

LEARNING OBJECTIVES ❷❸❹

Measure cash amounts for a bond; amortize the bonds by the straight-line method

3. Take the difference between your answers to Requirements 1 and 2. This difference represents Moreau's total interest expense over the life of the bonds.

4. Compute Moreau's annual interest expense by the straight-line amortization method. Multiply this amount by 20. Your 20-year total should be the same as your answer to Requirement 3.

LEARNING OBJECTIVES ❷❸❹

Record bond transactions and calculate interest using the effective-interest method

E7-26 Family General Stores Inc. is authorized to issue $500,000 of 7%, 10-year bonds. On December 31, 2020, when the market interest rate is 8%, the company issues $400,000 of the bonds and receives cash of $372,660. Family General amortizes bonds by the effective-interest method. The semi-annual interest dates are January 31 and July 31.

Requirements

1. Prepare a bond amortization table for the first four semi-annual interest periods.

2. Record issuance of the bonds on December 31, 2020, and the semi-annual interest payments on January 31, 2021, and on July 31, 2021.

LEARNING OBJECTIVES ❷❸❹

Record bond transactions and calculate interest using the effective-interest method

E7-27 On June 30, 2020, the market interest rate is 7%. Dellaca Enterprises issues $500,000 of 8%, 20-year bonds at 110.625. The bonds pay interest on June 30 and December 31. Dellaca amortizes bonds by the effective-interest method.

Requirements

1. Prepare a bond amortization table for the first four semi-annual interest periods.

2. Record issuance of the bonds on June 30, 2020, the payment of interest at December 31, 2020, and the semi-annual interest payment on June 30, 2021.

LEARNING OBJECTIVES ❸❹

Create a debt payment and bond amortization schedule

E7-28 Carlson Candies issued $300,000 of 83/8%, five-year bonds on January 1, 2020, when the market interest rate was 9½%. The company pays interest annually at year-end. The issue price of the bonds was $287,041.

Requirement

Create a spreadsheet model to prepare a schedule to amortize the bonds. Use the effective-interest method of amortization. Round to the nearest dollar, and format your answer as shown here.

	A	B	C	D	E	F
1						
2						Bond
3		Interest	Interest	Bond Discount	Bond Discount	Carrying
4	Date	Payment	Expense	Amortization	Balance	Amount
5	1-1-2020					287,041
6	12-31-2020	$⬚	$⬚	$⬚	$⬚	$⬚
7	12-31-2021					
8	12-31-2022					
9	12-31-2023					
10	12-31-2024					

$$300{,}000 \times 0.08375 \quad + \text{F5} \times 0.095 \quad + \text{C6} - \text{B6} \qquad\qquad 300{,}000 - \text{F5} \quad + \text{F5} + \text{D6}$$

LEARNING OBJECTIVES ❶❻❽

Analyze current and long-term liabilities; evaluate debt-paying ability

E7-29 Green Earth Homes, Inc., builds environmentally sensitive structures. The company's 2020 revenues totalled $2,785 million. At December 31, 2020 and 2019, the company had $643 million and $610 million in current assets, respectively. Accounts payable at the end of 2018 was $195. The December 31, 2020 and 2019 balance sheets and income statements reported the following amounts:

At Year-End (in millions)	2020	2019
Liabilities and shareholders' equity		
Current liabilities		
Accounts payable	$ 137	$ 181
Accrued expenses	163	169
Employee compensation and benefits	51	16
Current portion of long-term debt	17	10
Total current liabilities	368	376
Long-term debt	1,497	1,326
Post-retirement benefits payable	138	112
Other liabilities	20	22
Shareholders' equity	2,027	1,492
Total liabilities and shareholders' equity	$4,050	3,328
Year-end (in millions)		
Cost of goods sold	$1,885	$2,196

Requirements

1. Describe each of Green Earth Homes, Inc.'s liabilities and state how the liability arose.

2. Evaluate whether the company's ability to pay its long-term debts improved, deteriorated, or remained about the same over the year.

3. Evaluate whether the company's ability to pay its short-term debts improved, deteriorated, or remained about the same over the year.

🌐 **E7-30** Companies that operate in different industries may have very different financial ratio values. These differences may grow even wider when we compare companies located in different countries.

    Compare three leading companies on their current ratio, debt ratio, and times-interest-earned ratio. Compute three ratios for Sobeys (the Canadian grocery chain), Sony (the Japanese electronics manufacturer), and Daimler (the German auto company).

LEARNING OBJECTIVE ❻

Use ratios to compare companies

	(amounts in millions or billions)		
Income data	**Sobeys**	**Sony**	**Daimler**
Total revenues	$12,853	¥7,475	€151,589
Operating income	332	191	2,072
Interest expense	35	29	913
Net income	197	124	3,227
Asset and liability data			
Total current assets	$ 1,235	¥3,770	€ 93,131
Long-term assets	2,504	6,838	96,891
Total current liabilities	1,230	3,200	59,977
Long-term liabilities	674	4,204	95,890
Shareholders' equity	1,835	3,204	34,155

    Based on your computed ratio values, which company looks the least risky?

🌐 **E7-31** Companies that operate in different industries may have very different financial ratio values. These differences may grow even wider when we compare companies located in different countries.

    Compare three companies on their current ratio, debt ratio, leverage ratio, and times-interest-earned ratio. Compute the ratios for Company F, Company K, and Company R.

LEARNING OBJECTIVE ❻

Evaluate debt-paying ability

	(amounts in millions or billions)		
Income data	Company F	Company K	Company R
Total revenues	$9,724	¥7,307	€136,492
Operating income...	292	224	5,592
Interest expense...	46	33	736
Net income...	23	15	448
Assets and liability data			
Total current assets...	434	5,383	148,526
Long-term assets...	96	405	49,525
Total current liabilities...	207	2,197	72,100
Long-term liabilities	107	2,318	110,107
Shareholders' equity...	216	1,273	15,844

Based on your computed ratio values, which company looks the least risky?

LEARNING OBJECTIVES ❶❻❽
Assess the impact of transactions on key ratios

E7-32 The top management of Marquis Manufacturing Services examines the following company accounting records at August 29, immediately before the end of the year, August 31:

Total current assets...	$ 324,500
Non-current assets	1,098,500
	$1,423,000
Total current liabilities...	$ 173,800
Non-current liabilities	247,500
Shareholders' equity...	1,001,700
	$1,423,000

1. Suppose Marquis's management wants to achieve a current ratio of 2. How much in current liabilities should Marquis pay off within the next two days in order to achieve its goal?
2. If Marquis were to take out a bank loan of $400,000 and use the full proceeds to buy equipment on August 30, what effects would this have on the company's leverage and debt ratios at year-end?

LEARNING OBJECTIVES ❺❻
Understand how structuring debt transactions can affect a company

E7-33 The Cola Company reported the following comparative information at December 31, 2020, and December 31, 2019 (amounts in millions and adapted):

	2020	2019
Current assets...	$21,579	$17,551
Total assets	72,921	48,671
Current liabilities...	18,508	13,721
Total shareholders' equity...	31,317	25,346
Net sales...	35,119	30,990
Net income...	11,809	6,824

Requirements

1. Calculate the following ratios for 2020 and 2019:
   a. Current ratio
   b. Debt ratio
2. At the end of 2020, The Cola Company issued $1,590 million of long-term debt that was used to retire short-term debt. What would the current ratio and debt ratio have been if this transaction had not been made?

3. The Cola Company reports that its lease payments under operating leases will total $965 million in the future and $205 million will occur in the next year (2021). What would the current ratio and debt ratio have been if these leases had been capitalized?

E7-34 Mark IV Industries Inc. issued $100 million 13% debentures due March 15, 2025, with interest payable March 15 and September 15; the price was 96.5.

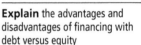
LEARNING OBJECTIVES ❷❸❹
Analyze bond transactions

Requirements

Answer these questions:

1. Journalize Mark IV Industries Inc.'s issuance of these bonds on March 15, 2020. No explanation is required, but describe the transaction in detail, indicating who received cash, who paid cash, and how much.
2. Why is the stated interest rate on these bonds so high?
3. Compute the semi-annual cash interest payment on the bonds.
4. Compute the semi-annual interest expense under the straight-line amortization method.
5. Compute both the first-year (from March 15, 2020, to March 15, 2021) and the second-year interest expense (March 15, 2021, to March 15, 2022) under the effective-interest amortization method. The market rate of interest at the date of issuance was 14%. Why is interest expense greater in the second year?

E7-35 Nautical Marina needs to raise $1.0 million to expand the company. Nautical Marina is considering the issuance of either

LEARNING OBJECTIVE ❺
Explain the advantages and disadvantages of financing with debt versus equity

- $1,000,000 of 8% bonds payable, or
- 100,000 common shares at $10 per share.

Before any new financing, Nautical Marina expects to earn net income of $400,000, and the company already has 100,000 shares of common shares outstanding. Nautical Marina believes the expansion will increase income before interest and income tax by $100,000. The income tax rate is 40%.

Prepare an analysis to determine which plan is likely to result in the higher earnings per share. Based solely on the earnings-per-share comparison, which financing plan would you recommend for Nautical Marina?

PROBLEMS (GROUP A)

P7-36A Sea Spray Marina experienced these events during 2020.

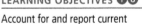
LEARNING OBJECTIVES ❶❽
Account for and report current liabilities

a. December revenue totalled $110,000 and, in addition, Sea Spray collected sales tax of 7%. The sales tax amount will be remitted to the province of British Columbia early in January.
b. On October 31, Sea Spray signed a six-month, 7% note to purchase a boat costing $90,000. The note requires payment of principal and interest at maturity.
c. On August 31, Sea Spray received cash of $1,800 in advance for service revenue. This revenue will be earned evenly over six months.
d. Revenues of $900,000 were covered by Sea Spray's service warranty. At January 1, estimated warranty payable was $11,300. During the year, Sea Spray recorded warranty expense of $31,000 and paid warranty claims of $34,700.
e. Sea Spray owes $100,000 on a long-term note payable. At December 31, 6% interest for the year plus $20,000 of this principal are payable within one year.

Requirement

For each item, indicate the account and the related amount to be reported as a *current* liability on the Sea Spray Marina balance sheet at December 31, 2020.

LEARNING OBJECTIVE ❶

Record liability-related transactions

P7-37A The following transactions of Smooth Sounds Music Company occurred during 2020 and 2021:

2020

Mar. 3   Purchased a Steinway piano (inventory) for $40,000, signing a six-month, 5% note.

Apr. 30 Borrowed $50,000 on a 9% note payable that calls for annual instalment payments of $25,000 principal plus interest. Record the short-term note payable in a separate account from the long-term note payable.

Sept. 3 Paid the six-month, 5% note at maturity.

Dec. 31 Accrued warranty expense, which is estimated at 2% of sales of $190,000.

31   Accrued interest on the outstanding note payable.

2021

Apr. 30 Paid the first instalment plus interest for one year on the outstanding note payable.

Requirement

Record the transactions in Smooth Sounds's journal. Explanations are not required.

LEARNING OBJECTIVES ❷❸❹❽

Issue bonds at face value, record accrual and payment of interest, and report bonds payable on the balance sheet

P7-38A The board of directors of Circuits Plus authorizes the issue of $9,000,000 of 8%, 25-year bonds payable. The semiannual interest dates are May 31 and November 30. The bonds are issued on May 31, 2019, at face value.

Requirements

1. Journalize the following transactions:
   a. Issuance of half of the bonds on May 31, 2019
   b. Payment of interest on November 30, 2019
   c. Accrual of interest on December 31, 2019
   d. Payment of interest on May 31, 2020
2. Report interest payable and bonds payable as they would appear on the Circuits Plus Balance sheet at December 31, 2019.

LEARNING OBJECTIVES ❷❸❹❽

Issue bonds at a discount, amortize by the straight-line method, and report bonds payable on the balance sheet

P7-39A On February 28, 2020, ETrade Inc. issues 8½%, 20-year bonds with a face value of $200,000. The bonds pay interest on February 28 and August 31. ETrade amortizes bonds by the straight-line method.

Requirements

1. If the market interest rate is 7⅝% when ETrade issues its bonds, will the bonds be priced at face value, a premium, or a discount? Explain.
2. If the market interest rate is 9% when ETrade issues its bonds, will the bonds be priced at face value, a premium, or a discount? Explain.
3. Assume that the issue price of the bonds is 97. Journalize the following bond transactions:
   a. Issuance of the bonds on February 28, 2020
   b. Payment of interest and amortization of the bonds on August 31, 2020
   c. Accrual of interest and amortization of the bonds on December 31, 2020
   d. Payment of interest and amortization of the bonds on February 28, 2021
4. Report interest payable and bonds payable as they would appear on the ETrade balance sheet at December 31, 2020.

LEARNING OBJECTIVES ❷❸❹

Account for bonds payable at a discount and amortize by the straight-line method

P7-40A

1. Journalize the following transactions of Trekker Boot Company:

2020

Jan. 1   Issued $600,000 of 8%, 10-year bonds at 97.

July 1   Paid semi-annual interest and amortized bonds by the straight-line method on the 8% bonds payable.

Dec. 31   Accrued semi-annual interest expense and amortized bonds by the straight-line method on the 8% bonds payable.

2021

Jan. 1   Paid semi-annual interest.

2030

Jan. 1   Paid the 8% bonds at maturity.

2. At December 31, 2020, after all year-end adjustments, determine the carrying amount of Trekker's bonds payable, net.
3. For the six months ended July 1, 2020, determine the following for Trekker:
   a. Interest expense
   b. Cash interest paid
   What causes interest expense on the bonds to exceed cash interest paid?

⊕ P7-41A Summit Medical Goods is embarking on a massive expansion. Assume the plans call for opening 20 new stores during the next two years. Each store is scheduled to be 30% larger than the company's existing locations, offering more items of inventory and with more elaborate displays. Management estimates that company operations will provide $1.0 million of the cash needed for expansion. Summit Medical must raise the remaining $4.75 million from outsiders.

LEARNING OBJECTIVE ⑤

Explain the advantages and disadvantages of financing with debt versus equity

The board of directors is considering obtaining the $4.75 million either through borrowing at 3% or by issuing an additional 100,000 shares of common shares. This year the company has earned $1.5 million before interest and taxes and has 100,000 common shares outstanding. The market price of the company's common shares is $47.50 per share. Assume that income before interest and taxes is expected to grow by 10% each year for the next two years. The company's marginal income tax rate is 20%.

Requirements
1. Use Excel to evaluate the effect of the above projected alternatives on net income and earnings per share two years from now.
2. Write a memo to Summit's management discussing the advantages and disadvantages of borrowing and of issuing common shares to raise the needed cash. Which method of raising the funds would you recommend?

⊕ P7-42A Notes to the Maritime Industries Ltd. financial statements reported the following data on December 31, 2020 (the end of the fiscal year):

LEARNING OBJECTIVES ②③④⑧

Analyze a company's long-term debt and report long-term debt on the balance sheet (effective-interest method)

Note 6, Indebtedness		
Bonds payable 5% due in 2025	$600,000	
Less Discount	(25,274)	$574,726
Notes payable 8.3% payable in $50,000 annual instalments starting in Year 2024		250,000

Maritime Industries amortizes bonds by the effective-interest method.

Requirements
1. Answer the following questions about Maritime's long-term liabilities:
   a. What is the maturity value of the 5% bonds?
   b. What are Maritime's annual cash interest payments on the 5% bonds?
   c. What is the carrying amount of the 5% bonds at December 31, 2020?
2. Prepare an amortization table through December 31, 2023, for the 5% bonds. The market interest rate for these bonds was 6%. Maritime pays interest annually on December 31. How much is Maritime's interest expense on the 5% bonds for the year ended December 31, 2023?
3. Show how Maritime Industries would report the bonds payable and notes payable at December 31, 2023.

⊕ P7-43A On December 31, 2020, Digital Connections issued 8%, 10-year bonds payable with a maturity value of $500,000. The semi-annual interest dates are June 30 and December 31. The market interest rate is 9%, and the issue price of the bonds is 94. Digital Connections amortizes bonds by the effective-interest method.

LEARNING OBJECTIVES ②③④⑧

Issuing bonds at a discount, amortizing by the effective-interest method, and reporting the bonds payable on the balance sheet

Requirements
1. Prepare an effective-interest-method amortization table for the first four semi-annual interest periods.

2. Journalize the following transactions:
   a. Issuance of the bonds on December 31, 2020. Credit Bonds Payable.
   b. Payment of interest and amortization of the bonds on June 30, 2021
   c. Payment of interest and amortization of the bonds on December 31, 2021
3. Show how Digital Connections would report the remaining bonds payable on its balance sheet at December 31, 2021.

LEARNING OBJECTIVE ⑤

Finance operations with debt or with shares

P7-44A Outback Sporting Goods is embarking on a massive expansion. Assume plans call for opening 20 new stores during the next two years. Each store is scheduled to be 50% larger than the company's existing locations, offering more items of inventory, and with more elaborate displays. Management estimates that company operations will provide $1 million of the cash needed for expansion. Outback must raise the remaining $6 million from outsiders. The board of directors is considering obtaining the $6 million either through borrowing or by issuing common shares.

Requirement

Write a memo to Outback's management discussing the advantages and disadvantages of borrowing and of issuing common shares to raise the needed cash. Which method of raising the funds would you recommend?

LEARNING OBJECTIVES ①⑥⑧

Assess key ratios and the impact of transactions on them

P7-45A The accounting records of Brighton Foods, Inc., include the following items at December 31, 2020:

Mortgage note payable,		Total assets	$4,500,000
current portion............................	$ 92,000	Accumulated depreciation	
Accumulated pension		equipment................................	166,000
benefit obligation..........................	450,000	Discount on bonds payable	
Bonds payable, long-term.................	200,000	(all long-term)	25,000
Mortgage note payable,		Operating income.......................	370,000
long-term	318,000	Equipment	744,000
Bonds payable, current portion	500,000	Pension plan assets	
Interest expense.............................	229,000	(market value).........................	420,000
		Interest payable	75,000

Requirements

1. Why is the interest-payable amount so much less than the amount of interest expense?
2. Assume that all of the existing liabilities are included in the information provided. Calculate the leverage ratio and debt ratio of the company. Evaluate the health of the company from a leverage point of view. What other information would be helpful in making your evaluation?
3. Independent of your answer to (2), assume that Footnote 8 of the financial statements discloses commitments for operating leases over the next 15 years in the amount of $3,000,000. If the company had to capitalize these leases in 2020, how would it change the leverage ratio and the debt ratio? How would this change impact your assessment of the company's health from a leverage point of view?

LEARNING OBJECTIVES ⑥⑧

Report liabilities on the balance sheet; calculate times-interest-earned ratio

P7-46A The accounting records of Pacer Foods Inc. include the following items at December 31, 2020.

Mortgage note payable		Accumulated depreciation	
current	$ 50,000	equipment................................	$219,000
Bonds payable, long-term.................	490,000	Discount on bonds payable	
Mortgage note payable		(all long-term)	7,000
long-term	150,000	Operating income.......................	291,000
Bonds payable, current portion	70,000	Equipment	487,000
Interest expense.............................	67,000	Interest payable	9,000

Requirements

1. Show how each relevant item would be reported on the Pacer Foods Inc. classified balance sheet, including headings and totals for current liabilities and long-term liabilities.
2. Answer the following questions about Pacer's financial position at December 31, 2020:
   a. What is the carrying amount of the bonds payable? (Combine the current and long-term amounts.)
   b. Why is the interest-payable amount so much less than the amount of interest expense?
3. How many times did Pacer cover its interest expense during 2020?

P7-47A The board of directors of Harmony Electronics authorizes the issue of $8,000,000 of 10%, 25-year bonds payable. The semiannual interest dates are May 31 and November 30. The bonds are issued on May 31, 2019, at par.

LEARNING OBJECTIVES ❶❷

Record bond transactions [at par]; report bonds payable on the balance sheet

Requirements

1. Journalize the following transactions:
   a. Issuance of the bonds on May 31, 2019
   b. Payment of interest on November 30, 2019
   c. Accrual of interest on December 31, 2019
   d. Payment of interest on May 31, 2020
2. Report interest payable and bonds payable as they would appear on the Harmony Electronics balance sheet at December 31, 2019

PROBLEMS (GROUP B)

P7-48B Goldwater Corporation experienced these five events during 2020:

a. December sales totalled $50,000, and Goldwater collected harmonized sales tax (HST) of 13%. The HST will be remitted to CRA in January 2021. Reporting requirements are the segregation of the provincial portion (8%) and federal portion (5%).
b. On November 30, Goldwater received rent of $6,000 in advance for a lease on unused store space. This rent will be earned evenly over three months.
c. On September 30, Goldwater signed a six-month, 9% note to purchase store fixtures costing $12,000. The note requires payment of principal and interest at maturity.
d. Sales of $400,000 were covered by Goldwater's product warranty. At January 1, estimated warranty payable was $12,400. During the year, Goldwater recorded warranty expense of $22,300 and paid warranty claims of $24,600.
e. Goldwater owes $100,000 on a long-term note. At December 31, 5% interest since July 31 and $20,000 of this principal are payable within one year.

LEARNING OBJECTIVES ❶❽

Account for and report current liabilities

Requirement

For each item, indicate the account and the related amount to be reported as a *current* liability on the Goldwater Corporation balance sheet at December 31, 2020.

P7-49B Assume that the following transactions of Sleuth Book Store occurred during 2020 and 2021:

LEARNING OBJECTIVE ❶

Record liability-related transactions

2020		
Jan. 9	Purchased store fixtures at a cost of $50,000, signing an 8%, six-month note for that amount.
June 30	Borrowed $200,000 on a 9% note that calls for annual instalment payments of $50,000 principal plus interest. Record the short-term note payable in a separate account from the long-term note payable.
July 9	Paid the six-month, 8% note at maturity.
Dec. 31	Accrued warranty expense, which is estimated at 3% of sales of $600,000.
31	Accrued interest on the outstanding note payable.
2021		
June 30	Paid the first instalment and interest for one year on the outstanding note payable.

Requirement

Record the transactions in the company's journal. Explanations are not required.

P7-50B Assume the board of directors of The Saddledome Foundation authorizes the issue of $1 million of 8%, 20-year bonds. The semi-annual interest dates are March 31 and September 30. The bonds are issued on March 31, 2020, at face value.

Requirements

1. Journalize the following transactions:
   a. Issuance of the bonds on March 31, 2020
   b. Payment of interest on September 30, 2020
   c. Accrual of interest on December 31, 2020
   d. Payment of interest on March 31, 2021
2. Report interest payable and bonds payable as they would appear on the Saddledome Foundation balance sheet at December 31, 2020.

P7-51B On February 28, 2020, Panorama Ltd. issues 7%, 10-year notes with a face value of $300,000. The notes pay interest on February 28 and August 31, and Panorama amortizes notes by the straight-line method.

Requirements

1. If the market interest rate is 6% when Panorama issues its notes, will the notes be priced at face value, a premium, or a discount? Explain.
2. If the market interest rate is 8% when Panorama issues its notes, will the notes be priced at face value, a premium, or a discount? Explain.
3. Assume that the issue price of the notes is 96. Journalize the following note payable transactions:
   a. Issuance of the notes on February 28, 2020
   b. Payment of interest and amortization of the bonds on August 31, 2020
   c. Accrual of interest and amortization of the bonds on December 31, 2020
   d. Payment of interest and amortization of the bonds on February 28, 2021
4. Report interest payable and notes payable as they would appear on Panorama's balance sheet at December 31, 2020.

P7-52B

1. Journalize the following transactions of Farm Equipment Limited:

2020		
Jan.	1	Issued $100,000 of 8%, five-year bonds at 94.
July	1	Paid semi-annual interest and amortized the bonds by the straight-line method on our 8% bonds payable.
Dec. 31		Accrued semi-annual interest expense and amortized the bonds by the straight-line method on our 8% bonds payable.
2021		
Jan.	1	Paid semi-annual interest.
2025		
Jan.	1	Paid the 8% bonds at maturity.

2. At December 31, 2020, after all year-end adjustments, determine the carrying amount of Farm Equipment Limited's bonds payable, net.
3. For the six months ended July 1, 2020, determine the following for Farm Equipment Limited:
   a. Interest expense
   b. Cash interest paid
   What causes interest expense on the bonds to exceed cash interest paid?

P7-53B The notes to the Community Charities financial statements reported the following data on December 31, 2020 (end of the fiscal year):

LEARNING OBJECTIVES ❷❸❹❽

Analyze a company's long-term debt and report the long-term debt on the balance sheet (effective-interest method)

Note D—Long-Term Debt

7% bonds payable, due in 2026	$500,000	
Less: Discount	(26,032)	$473,968
6½% notes payable; principal due in annual amounts of		
$50,000 in 2024 through 2029		300,000

Community Charities amortizes bonds by the effective-interest method and pays all interest amounts at December 31.

Requirements

1. Answer the following questions about Community Charities's long-term liabilities:
   a. What is the maturity value of the 7% bonds?
   b. What is Community Charities's annual cash interest payment on the 7% bonds?
   c. What is the carrying amount of the 7% bonds at December 31, 2020?
2. Prepare an amortization table through December 31, 2023, for the 7% bonds. The market interest rate on the bonds was 8%. Round all amounts to the nearest dollar. How much is Community Charities's interest expense on the 7% bonds for the year ended December 31, 2023?
3. Show how Community Charities would report the 7% bonds payable and the 6½% notes payable at December 31, 2023.

P7-54B Two businesses in very different circumstances are pondering how to raise $2 million.

LEARNING OBJECTIVE ❺

Finance operations with debt or shares

HighTech.com has fallen on hard times. Net income has been low for the last three years, even falling by 10% from last year's level of profits, and cash flow also took a nose dive. Top management has experienced some turnover and has stabilized only recently. To become competitive again, High Tech needs $2 million to invest in new technology.

Decorator Services is in the midst of its most successful period since it began operations three years ago. Net income has increased by 25%. The outlook for the future is bright with new markets opening up and competitors unable to compete with Decorator. As a result, Decorator is planning a large-scale expansion.

Requirement

Propose a plan for each company to raise the needed cash. Which company should borrow? Which company should issue shares? Consider the advantages and disadvantages of raising money by borrowing and by issuing shares, and discuss them in your answer.

P7-55B The accounting records of Braintree Foods, Inc., include the following items at December 31, 2020:

LEARNING OBJECTIVES ❶❻❽

Assess key ratios and the impact of transactions on them

Mortgage note payable			Total assets	$4,200,000
current portion............................	$ 97,000		Accumulated depreciation	
Accumulated pension			equipment.................................	162,000
benefit obligation.........................	470,000		Discount on bonds payable	
Bonds payable, long-term................	1,680,000		(all long-term)..........................	22,000
Mortgage note payable			Operating income........................	390,000
long-term	314,000		Equipment	745,000
Bonds payable, current portion	420,000		Pension plan assets	
Interest expense.............................	227,000		(market value)..........................	425,000
			Interest payable	74,000

Requirements

1. Why is the interest-payable amount so much less than the amount of interest expense?
2. Assume that all of the existing liabilities are included in the information provided. Calculate the leverage ratio and debt ratio of the company. Evaluate the health of the company from a leverage point of view. What other information would be helpful in making your evaluation?
3. Independent of your answer to (2), assume that Footnote 8 of the financial statements discloses commitments for operating leases over the next 15 years in the amount of $3,000,000. If the company had to capitalize these leases in 2020, how would it change the leverage ratio and the debt ratio? How would this change impact your assessment of the company's health from a leverage point of view?

LEARNING OBJECTIVES ❻❽

Report liabilities on the balance sheet; calculate times-interest-earned ratio

P7-56B The accounting records of Toronto Financial Services include the following items at December 31, 2020:

Premium on bonds payable (all long-term)	$ 13,000
Interest payable	3,900
Operating income	104,000
Interest expense	39,000
Bonds payable, current portion	50,000
Accumulated depreciation, building	70,000
Mortgage note payable, long-term	215,000
Bonds payable, long-term	250,000
Building	160,000

Requirements

1. Show how each relevant item would be reported on Toronto Financial Services's classified balance sheet. Include headings and totals for current liabilities and long-term liabilities.
2. Answer the following questions about the financial position of Toronto Financial Services at December 31, 2020:
   a. What is the carrying amount of the bonds payable? (Combine the current and long-term amounts.)
   b. Why is the interest payable amount so much less than the amount of interest expense? (Challenge)
3. How many times did Toronto cover its interest expense during 2020?

LEARNING OBJECTIVES ❶❷

Record bond transactions [at par]; report bonds payable on the balance sheet)

P7-57B The board of directors of Laptops Plus authorizes the issue of $9,000,000 of 7%, 15-year bonds payable. The semiannual interest dates are May 31 and November 30. The bonds are issued on May 31, 2019, at face value.

Requirements

1. Journalize the following transactions:
   a. Issuance of half of the bonds on May 31, 2019
   b. Payment of interest on November 30, 2019
   c. Accrual of interest on December 31, 2019
   d. Payment of interest on May 31, 2020
2. Report interest payable and bonds payable as they would appear on the Laptops Plus balance sheet at December 31, 2019.

APPLY YOUR KNOWLEDGE

DECISION CASES

Case 1. In 2001, Enron Corporation filed for Chapter 11 bankruptcy protection, shocking the business community: How could a company this large and this successful go bankrupt? This case explores the causes and the effects of Enron's bankruptcy.

At December 31, 2000, and for the four years ended on that date, Enron reported the following (amounts in millions):

Balance Sheet (summarized)

Total assets	$65,503
Total liabilities	54,033
Total shareholders' equity	11,470

Income Statements (excerpts)

	2000	1999	1998	1997
Net income	$ 979*	$893	$703	$105
Revenues	100,789			

*Operating Income = $1,953
Interest expense = $838

This section's material reflects CPA enabling competencies, including:

I Professional and ethical behaviour

II Problem-solving and decision-making

III Self-management

IV Teamwork and leadership

Based on Chartered Professional Accountant standards

LEARNING OBJECTIVE

Explore an actual bankruptcy; calculate leverage ratio, ROA debt ratio, and times-interest-earned ratio

Unknown to investors and lenders, Enron also controlled hundreds of partnerships that owed vast amounts of money. These special-purpose entities (SPEs) did not appear on the Enron financial statements. Assume that the SPEs' assets totalled $7,000 million and their liabilities stood at $6,900 million; assume a 10% interest rate on these liabilities.

During the four-year period up to December 31, 2000, Enron's stock price shot up from $17.50 to $90.56. Enron used its escalating stock price to finance the purchase of the SPEs by guaranteeing lenders that Enron would give them Enron stock if the SPEs could not pay their loans.

In 2002, the SEC launched an investigation into Enron's accounting practices. It was alleged that Enron should have been including the SPEs in its financial statements all along. Enron then restated net income for years up to 2000, wiping out nearly $600 million of total net income (and total assets) for this four-year period. Assume that $300 million of this loss applied to 2000. Enron's stock price tumbled, and the guarantees to the SPEs' lenders added millions to Enron's liabilities (assume the full amount of the SPEs' debt). To make matters worse, the assets of the SPEs lost much of their value; assume that their market value is only $500 million.

Requirements

1. Compute the debt ratio that Enron reported at the end of 2000. Compute Enron's return on total assets (ROA) for 2000. For this purpose, use only total assets at the end of 2000, rather than the average of 1999 and 2000.
2. Compute Enron's leverage ratio. Now compute Enron's return on equity (ROE) by multiplying the ROA computed in part 1 by the leverage ratio. Can you see anything unusual in these ratios that might have caused you to question them? Why or why not?
3. Add the asset and liability information about the SPEs to the reported amounts provided in the table. Recompute all ratios after including the SPEs in Enron's financial statements. Also, compute Enron's times-interest-earned ratio both ways for 2000. Assume that the changes to Enron's financial position occurred during 2000.
4. Why does it appear that Enron failed to include the SPEs in its financial statements? How do you view Enron after including the SPEs in the company's financial statements?

LEARNING OBJECTIVE ❺

Analyze alternative ways of raising $5 million

Case 2. Business is going well for Park'N Fly, the company that operates remote parking lots near major airports. The board of directors of this family-owned company believes that Park'N Fly could earn an additional $2 million income before interest and taxes by expanding into new markets. However, the $5 million that the business needs for growth cannot be raised within the family. The directors, who strongly wish to retain family control of the company, must consider issuing securities to outsiders. The directors are considering three financing plans.

Plan A is to borrow at 6%. Plan B is to issue 100,000 common shares. Plan C is to issue 100,000 non-voting, $3.75 preferred shares ($3.75 is the annual dividend paid on each preferred share).* Park'N Fly currently has net income of $3.5 million and 1 million common shares outstanding. The company's income tax rate is 25%.

Requirements

1. Prepare an analysis to determine which plan will result in the highest earnings per common share.
2. Recommend one plan to the board of directors. Give your reasons.

ETHICAL DECISIONS

Decision 1: Microsoft Corporation is the defendant in numerous lawsuits claiming unfair trade practices. Microsoft has strong incentives not to disclose these contingent liabilities; however, IFRS and ASPE generally require that companies disclose their contingent liabilities in the notes to their financial statements.

Requirements

1. Why would a company prefer not to disclose its contingent liabilities?
2. Describe how a bank could be harmed if a company seeking a loan did not disclose its contingent liabilities.
3. What is the ethical tightrope that companies must walk when they report their contingent liabilities?

Decision 2: The top managers of Medtech.com borrowed heavily to develop a prescription-medicine distribution system. Medtech's outlook was bright, and investors poured millions into the company. Sadly, Medtech never lived up to its potential, and the company is in bankruptcy. It can't pay about half of its liabilities.

Requirement

Is it unethical for managers to saddle a company with a high level of debt? Or, is it just risky? Who could be hurt by a company's taking on too much debt? Discuss.

Decision 3: For each of the situations listed, identify which principles (professional behaviour, integrity and due care, objectivity, professional competence, confidentiality) from the CPA Code of Professional Conduct are violated. Assume all persons listed in the situations are CPAs. (Note: Refer to the CPA Code of Professional Conduct contained on pages 27–28 in Chapter 1 for descriptions of the principles.)

a. Lance recently graduated with an accounting degree and found a job in the payables department of Sawyer Sneaker Company. Lance is in charge of adjusting entries for accrued liabilities that have been paid, but he does not remember how to treat these entries because he has not seen them since one of his courses from his junior year in college. Lance assumes the accrued liabilities for this month are the same amounts as last month, so he does not enter in the new accrual entries for this month and does not reverse last month's entries.

---

*For a discussion of preferred shares, see Chapter 8.

b. Frankie Candle Co. is a small, family-owned company that only employs one accountant, Jenny. Since Jenny is in charge of all areas of accounting and knows she will not get caught, she decides to create fictitious accounts payable entries at Frankie Candle Co. for the company she owns, Candle Supply Inc.

c. April is a newly hired auditor for Penny & Blake, a CPA firm. Her father owns E&E Veterinary Supply. April is excited to be assigned to work on the account of E&E since she understands the business well from working part-time during summers there when she was growing up. April does not disclose that her father owns E&E because she knows she will not have any bias.

d. Anne works in the payables department of Yellow Steel, Inc. She noticed that her company's current ratio is a little lower than the industry average. In an attempt to improve the current ratio, she decides not to accrue wages payable for this month.

FOCUS ON FINANCIAL STATEMENT ANALYSIS

Dollarama Inc.

Refer to Dollarama's financial statements in Appendix A at the end of this book.

Task 1. How much did Dollarama report as the current portion of long-term debt at the end of 2018? Why is this portion of long-term debt reported as a current liability?

Task 2. Dollarama's Notes to the Financial Statements include note 10, "Leases and commitments." What information does this note provide to the user of these financial statements?

Task 3. How would you rate Dollarama's debt-paying ability at the end of 2018: excellent, neutral, or poor? Support your conclusion with relevant ratios.

LEARNING OBJECTIVES ❶❻❽

Report current and long-term liabilities

MyLab Accounting

CHECK YOUR WORK

STOP + THINK ANSWERS

STOP + THINK (7-1)

1. $2,037 million ($154 current portion + $1,883 long-term portion)

2. Pay by June 30, 2019: $154 million; pay thereafter: $1,883 million

STOP + THINK (7-2)

1. The bond would be issued at a discount because the market rate is less than the stated rate.

2. The bond would be issued at a premium because the market rate is greater than the stated rate.

3. You would pay $224,375 ($250,000 * .8975).

4. You would pay $177,187.50 ($175,000 * 1.0125).

STOP + THINK (7-3)

Date	Account Titles and Explanation	Debit	Credit
2020			
a. May 1	Cash..................................	10,000	
	Bonds Payable................		10,000
	To issue bond at face value.		
2020			
b. Oct. 31	Interest Expense ($10,000 × 0.0725 × 6/12)..................	363	
	Interest Payable..............		363
	To accrue interest expense.		

Date	Account Titles and Explanation	Debit	Credit
2020			
c. Nov. 1	Interest Payable...............	363	
	Cash..........................		363
	To pay semiannual interest on bonds.		
2025			
d. May 1	Bonds Payable	10,000	
	Interest Expense	363	
	Cash..........................		10,363
	To pay bonds at maturity.		

STOP + THINK (7-4)

Income Statement for 2020

Interest expense ($4,807 + $4,823)	$9,630

Balance Sheet at December 31, 2020

Current liabilities:		
Interest payable		$4,500
Long-term liabilities:		
Bonds payable	$100,000	
Less: Discount on bonds payable	(3,221)	96,779

STOP + THINK (7-5)

	Company A	Company B
Debt ratio	86.0%	58.2%
Leverage ratio	7.14	2.39
Times-interest-earned ratio	2.39	5.06

Based on the ratios above, Company B shows a higher debt-paying ability, so it would present a lower risk to the bank than Company A. B's debt ratio is within the comfort range of 60%–70%, whereas A's is well above this range at 86%. A is also more highly leveraged than B (7.14 vs. 2.39) and has a much lower interest-coverage ratio, at only 2.39 compared to B's much more comfortable ratio of 5.06. I would therefore prefer to loan money to the less-risky Company B.

STOP + THINK (7-6)

1. a. Current liability: Estimated warranty payable [$40,000 + ($4,000,000 × 0.04) − $80,000].................................		120,000
b. Current liability: Current portion of long-term note payable.		40,000
Current liability: Interest payable ($200,000 × 0.06 × 1/12).................		1,000
Long-term liability: Note payable ($200,000 − $40,000).......................		160,000
c. Current liability: Unearned sales revenue ($150,000 − $100,000).......................		50,000
d. Current liability: Employee withholdings and company CPP & EI.......................		35,000
Current liability: Employee Benefits Payable		11,000
2. Total current liabilities: $257,000		

QUICK QUIZ ANSWERS

1. *a*

2. *d*

3. *b*

4. *b*

5. *a*

6. *c* [($500,000 + $700,000) × 0.08] − $4,000 − $32,000 = $60,000

7. *a*

8. *d*

9. *f*

10. *a*

11. *c*

12. *d* ($100,000 × 0.10 + [($100,000 − $97,000) / 15] = $10,200

13. *Interest Expense* 7,650
Discount on Bonds Payable ($3,000/15 × 9/12).................................... 150
Interest Payable ($100,000 × 0.10 × 9/12)... 7,500

14. *Interest Payable* 7,500
Interest Expense 2,550
Discount on Bonds Payable ($3,000/15 × 3/12) 50
Cash ($100,000 × 0.10)........................ 10,000

15. *e* ($92,280 × 0.12 × 6/12 = $5,537)

16. *d*

17. *a*

18. *c*

19. *c*

Shareholders' Equity

8

SPOTLIGHT

Dollarama Inc. was founded in Matane, Quebec in 1992 by Larry Rossy, a third-generation family retailer. In its early days, the members of the Rossy family were the company's main shareholders. Since its initial public offering of shares in 2009, Dollarama has been a widely held public company with tens of thousands of shareholders. During 2018, there were several changes in Dollarama's shareholders' equity accounts. By the end of this chapter, you should be able to explain and account for many of these changes.

In this chapter, we'll show you how companies like Dollarama account for the issuance of shares to investors. We'll also discuss other major components of shareholders' equity, such as Contributed Surplus and Retained Earnings, plus dividends and stock splits. In addition, you will learn how to interpret information about a company's share price and performance to decide if you'd want to buy shares in a company like Dollarama. On the next page, you'll find details on the company's shareholders' equity as at January 28, 2018.

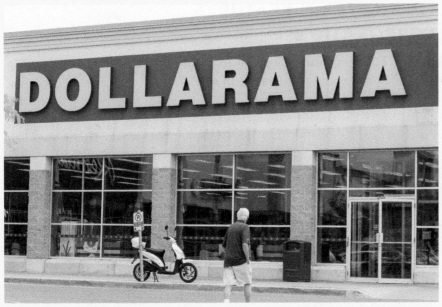

Jill Morgan/Alamy Stock Photo

LEARNING OBJECTIVES

1. **Explain** the main features of a corporation
2. **Account** for the issuance of shares
3. **Explain** why a company repurchases shares
4. **Account** for retained earnings, dividends, and stock splits
5. **Distinguish** between fair value and book value per share
6. **Evaluate** a company's return on assets and return on equity
7. **Report** equity transactions and events in the financial statements

CPA COMPETENCIES

Competencies addressed in this chapter:

1.1.1 Evaluates financial reporting needs

1.2.2 Evaluates treatment for routine transactions

1.4.4 Interprets financial reporting results for stakeholders (external or internal)

Based on Chartered Professional Accountant standards

	A	B	C	D
1	**Dollarama Inc.** Shareholders' Equity (Deficit) [Adapted]			
2	*(in thousands)*	**January 28, 2018**	**January 29, 2017**	

3	Common share capital
	  Authorized: Unlimited number of common shares
	  without par value; issued and outstanding: 109,325,859
	  shares at January 28, 2018 and 115,051,349 at
	  January 29, 2017
		415,787	420,266	

4	Contributed surplus	27,699	24,321	
5	Accumulated other comprehensive loss	(32,423)	(1,346)	
6	Deficit	(663,421)	(342,957)	
7		(252,358)	100,284	
8				

Source: Data's from Dollarama Inc.

Chapters 4 to 7 discussed accounting for assets and liabilities. By this time, you should be familiar with most of the assets and liabilities listed on Dollarama's balance sheet, so we will now focus on the major components of shareholders' equity. In this chapter, we discuss some of the issues a company faces when issuing shares and paying dividends.

Let's begin by looking at the key features of a corporation.

OBJECTIVE

❶ **Explain** the main features of a corporation

EXPLAIN THE MAIN FEATURES OF A CORPORATION

Anyone starting a business must decide how to organize the company. Corporations differ from proprietorships and partnerships in several ways.

SEPARATE LEGAL ENTITY. A corporation is a business entity formed under federal or provincial law. The federal or provincial government grants *articles of incorporation*, which consist of documents giving the governing body permission to form a corporation. A corporation is a distinct entity, an artificial person that exists apart from its owners, the shareholders. The corporation has many of the same rights as a person. For example, a corporation may buy, own, and sell property. Assets and liabilities in the business belong to the corporation, not to its owners. The corporation may also enter into contracts, sue, and be sued.

Nearly all well-known companies, including Dollarama, WestJet, and Loblaws, are corporations. Their legal names include *Limited*, *Corporation*, or *Incorporated* at the end (abbreviated *Ltd.*, *Corp.*, and *Inc.*) to indicate that they are corporations.

CONTINUOUS LIFE AND TRANSFERABILITY OF OWNERSHIP. Corporations have *continuous lives* regardless of changes in their ownership. The shareholders of a corporation may transfer shares as they wish. They may sell or trade the shares to another person, give them away, bequeath them in a will, or dispose of them in any other way. The transfer of the shares from one person to another does not affect the continuity of the corporation. In contrast, proprietorships and partnerships terminate when ownership changes.

LIMITED LIABILITY. Shareholders have **limited liability** for the corporation's debts, so they have no personal obligation to repay the company's liabilities. The most that a shareholder can lose on an investment in a corporation's shares is the cost of the investment. Limited liability is one of the most attractive features of the corporate form of organization. It enables corporations to raise more capital from a wider group of investors than proprietorships and partnerships. In contrast, proprietors and partners are personally liable for all the debts of their businesses (unless the business is organized as a limited liability partnership [LLP] or a limited liability company [LLC]).

SEPARATION OF OWNERSHIP AND MANAGEMENT. Shareholders own the corporation, but a *board of directors*—elected by the shareholders—appoints officers to manage the business. Thus, shareholders may invest $1,000 or $1 million in the corporation without having to manage it.

Company managers should run the business in the best interests of its shareholders, who rightfully own the company, but the separation between owners and managers may create problems. Corporate officers may run the business for their own benefit and not for the shareholders'. For example, the chief financial officer of Enron Corporation set up deals between Enron and several partnerships that he personally owned, enriching himself in the process, but harming the company and shareholders he worked for.

Some managers believe that their goal is to maximize the firm's value. Other managers believe that they should consider some or all of the other stakeholders of the corporation, such as employees, customers, the community where the company is located, and the environment.

CORPORATE TAXATION. Because corporations are separate legal entities, they must pay income taxes separate from those borne by their individual shareholders. Sole proprietors and partners pay individual income taxes based on their share of the business's income.

GOVERNMENT REGULATION. Because shareholders have only limited liability for corporation debts, outsiders doing business with the corporation can look no further than the corporation if it fails to pay. To protect a corporation's creditors and the shareholders, both federal and provincial governments monitor corporations. This regulation consists mainly of ensuring that corporations disclose the information in financial statements that investors and creditors need to make informed decisions.

Exhibit 8-1 summarizes the advantages and disadvantages of the corporate form of business organization.

EXHIBIT 8-1
Advantages and Disadvantages of a Corporation

Advantages	Disadvantages
1. Can raise more capital than a proprietorship or partnership 2. Continuous life 3. Ease of transferring ownership 4. Limited liability of shareholders	1. Separation of ownership and management 2. Corporate taxation 3. Government regulation

Controlling and Managing a Corporation

The ultimate control of a corporation rests with the shareholders. The shareholders elect a *board of directors*, which sets the company policy and appoints officers. The board elects a **chairperson**, who usually is the most powerful person in the organization. The board also appoints the chief executive officer (CEO), who often also acts as the **president** in charge of day-to-day operations. Large corporations may also have vice-presidents in charge of sales, manufacturing, accounting and finance (the chief financial officer, or CFO), and other key areas. Exhibit 8-2 shows the authority structure in a large corporation.

EXHIBIT 8-2
Authority Structure in a Large Corporation

Shareholders

elect the

Board of Directors*

which appoints the

President/Chief Executive Officer

who leads the

| Vice-President, Sales | Vice-President, Manufacturing | Chief Financial Officer | Vice-President, Personnel | Secretary |

who manage day-to-day-operations

| Controller (Accounting Officer) | Treasurer (Finance Officer) |

*The Board elects one of its members to be chairperson.

Shareholders' Rights

Ownership of shares entitles shareholders to four basic rights, unless specific rights are withheld by agreement with the shareholders:

1. *The right to sell the shares.* Shareholders have the right to sell their shares to other parties when they no longer wish to own them.

2. *The right to vote.* Shareholders have the right to participate in management by voting on matters that come before them. This is the shareholder's sole voice in the management of the corporation. A shareholder is normally entitled to one vote for each common share owned. There are some classes of common shares that give the holder multiple votes or no vote.

3. *The right to receive dividends.* Shareholders have the right to receive a proportionate share of any distributions from the company's retained earnings. Each share in a particular class receives an equal dividend.

4. *The right to receive a residual interest upon liquidation.* Shareholders have the right to receive a proportionate share of any assets remaining after the corporation pays all liabilities upon liquidation. When a company goes out of business, it sells its assets, pays its liabilities, and distributes any residual (or remaining) assets to shareholders.

Shareholders' Equity

As we saw in Chapter 1, *shareholders' equity* represents the shareholders' ownership interest in the assets of a corporation. Shareholders' equity has four common and separate components:

1. *Share capital*—amounts contributed by shareholders in exchange for shares in the corporation.
2. *Contributed surplus*—any amounts contributed by shareholders in excess of amounts allocated to share capital.
3. *Accumulated other comprehensive income*—IFRS require companies to report Accumulated Other Comprehensive Income, which is an accumulation of past earnings not included in retained earnings. This equity item requires an advanced understanding of accounting concepts, so it will not be covered in this textbook. ASPE do not require companies to account for this item.
4. *Retained earnings*—the accumulated balance of a corporation's net income since inception, less any net losses and dividends declared during this time. When the accumulation is a negative number, as it is for Dollarama, the term *deficit* is used to describe it.

A corporation issues *share certificates* to its owners in exchange for their investment in the business—usually cash. The basic unit of share capital is called a *share*. A corporation may issue a share certificate for any number of shares it wishes—one share, 100 shares, or any other number—but the total number of *authorized* shares is limited by charter. Shares are sometimes referred to as *stock*, particularly in the United States, but owning stock in a company means the same thing as owning shares in that company.

The terms *authorized*, *issued*, and *outstanding* are frequently used to describe a corporation's shares. *Authorized* refers to the maximum number of shares a corporation is allowed to distribute to shareholders. Companies incorporated under the *Canada Business Corporations Act* are permitted to issue an unlimited number of shares. *Issued* refers to the number of shares sold or transferred to shareholders. *Outstanding shares* are those actually in the hands of shareholders. Sometimes a company repurchases shares it has previously issued so that the number of shares outstanding will be less than the number of shares issued. For example, if a corporation issued 100,000 shares and later repurchased 20,000 shares, then the number of shares outstanding would be 80,000. The total number of shares outstanding at any time represents 100% ownership of the corporation.

Classes of Shares

Corporations issue different types of shares to appeal to a variety of investors. Every corporation issues *common shares*, which IFRS also refer to as *ordinary shares*, meaning they are subordinate to all other classes of shares a company is authorized to issue. Unless designated otherwise, the word *share* is understood to mean "common share."

Common shareholders have the four basic rights of share ownership, unless a right is specifically withheld. For example, some companies, such as Canadian Tire and Magna, issue voting and non-voting common shares. In describing a corporation, we would say the common shareholders are the owners of the business. They stand to benefit the most if the corporation succeeds because they take the most risk by investing in common shares. The shares of a corporation may be either common shares or preferred shares.

Preferred shares give their owners certain advantages over common shareholders. Preferred shareholders receive dividends before the common shareholders and receive assets before the common shareholders if the corporation liquidates. Preferred shares are typically non-voting shares, but they have the other three basic shareholder rights. Companies may issue different classes of preferred shares (Class A and Class B or Series A and Series B, for example). Each class is recorded in a separate account.

Preferred shares are a hybrid of common shares and long-term debt. Like debt, preferred shares pay a fixed amount to the investor in the form of a dividend. Like common shares, the dividend does not have to be paid unless the board of directors has declared the dividend. Also, companies have no obligation to pay back true preferred shares. Preferred shares that must be redeemed (paid back) by the corporation are a liability masquerading as a stock and must be accounted for as such.

Preferred shares are much less frequently issued than common shares. A recent survey of over 600 companies found that fewer than 10% of them had issued preferred shares. TELUS, for example, is authorized to issue 2 billion preferred shares, but as at the end of 2018, none of them had actually been issued.

PAR VALUE AND STATED VALUE. Par value shares are shares of stock that have a value assigned to them by the articles of incorporation, which specify the legal details associated with a company's incorporation. *The Canada Business Corporations Act* and most provincial incorporating acts now require common and preferred shares to be issued without par value. Dollarama's common shares do not have a par value. Instead, the shares are assigned a value when they are issued; this value is known as the **stated value**.

STOP + THINK (8-1)

At the end of its 2017 fiscal year, Canadian Tire had 3.4 million voting regular common shares outstanding and 63 million non-voting Class A common shares outstanding. Why would so many investors be interested in owning Canadian Tire's Class A shares, given they do not get to vote on how the company is governed and managed?

OBJECTIVE

❷ **Account** for the issuance of shares

ACCOUNT FOR THE ISSUANCE OF SHARES

Large corporations, such as Hudson's Bay Company and EnCana Corp., need huge amounts of money to operate. Such corporations usually sell their newly issued shares though an *underwriter*, such as the brokerage firms ScotiaMcLeod and BMO Nesbitt Burns.

ISSUING SHARES FOR CASH. Suppose that on January 8, 2020, George Weston Ltd. issued 100,000 common shares for cash for $50 each. The entry to record the issuance of these shares is:

	A	B	C	D	E
1	2020				
2	Jan. 8	Cash	5,000,000		
3		Common Share Capital		5,000,000	
4		To issue common shares at $50.00 per share (100,000 × $50.00).			
5					

ASSETS	=	LIABILITIES	+	SHAREHOLDERS' EQUITY
+5,000,000	=		+	5,000,000 Share Capital

After this transaction, the number of common shares outstanding would increase by 100,000, and the company's common share capital would increase by $5,000,000.

It is important to note that when one shareholder of a company sells some of their shares to another shareholder, there is no impact on the accounts of the company due to the separate-entity concept, which was introduced in Chapter 1. Only when a company is party to a share transaction are its accounts affected.

STOP + THINK (8-2)

Examine the details of Dollarama's Shareholders' Equity (Deficit) on page 413, then answer these questions:

1. If Dollarama wanted to eliminate its shareholders' deficit at the end of 2018 by issuing common shares at $40 per share, how many shares would it have to issue?
2. What is the average issue price of Dollarama's common shares outstanding?

ISSUING SHARES FOR ASSETS OTHER THAN CASH. Companies sometimes issue shares in return for assets other than cash. When a transaction like this occurs, the company is required to measure the transaction based on the fair value of the assets received. If that fair value cannot be determined, the fair value of the shares given up will be the value assigned to the transaction.

For example, if on November 12, 2020, Kahn Corporation issued 15,000 common shares in return for equipment worth $4,000 and a building worth $120,000, it would record this entry:

	A	B	C	D	E
1	2020				
2	Nov. 12	Equipment	4,000		
3		Building	120,000		
4		Common Share Capital		124,000	
5		To issue common shares in exchange for equipment and a building.			
6					

ASSETS	=	LIABILITIES	=	SHAREHOLDERS' EQUITY
+4,000 +120,000	=			+124,000 Share capital

Accounting for the issuance of preferred shares (or other kinds of non-voting shares) for cash or other assets is the same as that for common shares, except for the name of the share capital account used, which will match the type of shares being issued.

COOKING *the* BOOKS

with Share Capital

The issuance of shares for *cash* poses no ethical challenge. There is no difficulty in valuing shares issued for cash because the value of the cash—and therefore the shares—is obvious.

Issuing shares for *assets other than cash*, however, can pose an ethical challenge. The company issuing the shares often wishes to record a large amount for the non-cash asset received (such as land or a building) and for the shares that it is issuing. Why? Because large asset and shareholders' equity amounts on the balance sheet make the business look more prosperous and more creditworthy.

A company is supposed to record an asset received at its current fair value. But one person's perception of a particular asset's fair value can differ from another person's opinion. One person may appraise land at a fair value of $400,000. Another may honestly believe the land is worth only $300,000. A company receiving land in exchange for its shares must decide whether to record the land received and the shares issued at $300,000, at $400,000, or at some amount in between.

The ethical course of action is to record the asset at its current fair value, as determined by a good-faith estimate of fair value from independent appraisers. It is rare for a corporation to be found guilty of *understating* the asset values on its balance sheet, but companies have been embarrassed by *overstating* these values. Investors who rely on the financial statements may be able to prove in court that an overstatement of asset values caused them to pay too much for the company's shares. Creditors who rely on financial statements may also be able to prove in court that an overstatement of asset values caused them to loan the corporation more than if the asset values were correctly stated. In both cases, the court may render a judgment against the company. For this reason, companies often value assets conservatively.

MyLab Accounting

MID-CHAPTER SUMMARY PROBLEM

1. Test your understanding of the first half of this chapter by deciding whether each of the following statements is true or false.
   a. The policy-making body in a corporation is called the board of directors.
   b. The owner of 100 preferred shares has greater voting rights than the owner of 100 common shares.
   c. Issuance of 1,000 common shares at $12 per share increases share capital by $12,000.
   d. A corporation issues its preferred shares in exchange for land and a building with a combined fair value of $200,000. This transaction increases the corporation's owners' equity by $200,000 regardless of the assets' prior book values.
   e. Preferred shares are a riskier investment than common shares.

2. Adolfo Inc., an auto parts manufacturer, has two classes of common shares. Class A shares are entitled to one vote, whereas Class B shares are entitled to 100 votes. The two classes rank equally for dividends. The following is extracted from a recent annual report:

Shareholders' Equity	
Share capital	
Class A common shares, no stated value (authorized and issued 1,260 shares)..........	$ 1,260
Class B common shares, no stated value (authorized and issued 46,200 shares)........	11,000
	12,260
Retained earnings	872,403
	$884,663

Requirements

a. Record the issuance of the Class A common shares. Use the Adolfo Inc. account titles.

b. Record the issuance of the Class B common shares. Use the Adolfo Inc. account titles.

c. How much of Adolfo Inc.'s shareholders' equity was contributed by the shareholders? How much was provided by profitable operations? Does this division of equity suggest that the company has been successful? Why or why not?

d. Write a sentence to describe what Adolfo Inc.'s shareholders' equity balance means.

ANSWERS

1. a. True   **b.** False (preferred shares typically do not have voting rights)   **c.** True

   d. True   **e.** False (preferred shares typically have a fixed dividend right and first claim to residual assets upon dissolution or liquidation of the company)

2. a. Cash 1,260

    Class A Common Shares 1,260

    To record issuance of Class A common shares.

> a. and b. Share issuances increase assets (cash) and shareholders' equity.

b. Cash 11,000

    Class B Common Shares.. 11,000

    To record issuance of Class B common shares.

> Compare the fraction of shareholders' equity contributed by shareholders to the fraction contributed by retained earnings. A greater retained earnings fraction is positive.

c. Contributed by the shareholders: $12,260 ($1,260 + $11,000).

    Provided by profitable operations: $872,403.

    This division suggests that the company has been successful because almost all of its shareholders' equity has come from profitable operations.

d. The total of Adolfo's shareholders' equity indicates that the shareholders have a claim to $884,663 of the company's assets.

> Shareholders' equity is the net worth of the company (Assets − Liabilities).

EXPLAIN WHY A COMPANY REPURCHASES SHARES

OBJECTIVE

❸ **Explain** why a company repurchases shares

Corporations may repurchase their own shares for several reasons:

1. The company needs the **repurchased shares** to fulfill future share issuance commitments, such as those related to share option plans and conversions of bonds and preferred shares into common shares.

2. The purchase may help support the share's current **market price** by decreasing the supply of shares available to the public, which will usually result in an increase in the market price per share.

3. Management wants to avoid a takeover by an outside party, so it repurchases a significant proportion of its own shares to prevent the other party from acquiring them.

In basic terms, when a company repurchases shares, share capital and total shareholders' equity decrease, but the actual IFRS guidance on accounting for share repurchases is vague and sometimes difficult to interpret. In addition, ASPE offer two choices for how to account for repurchases, both of which differ from IFRS guidance. Given the complex and differing treatments of share repurchases, accounting for them will be left for those students who take intermediate financial accounting.

STOP + THINK (8-3)

During the fiscal years 2017 through 2019, Dollarama repurchased millions of its common shares. Search the Web to find out why Dollarama regularly repurchased these shares. Is the reason consistent with any of the reasons cited above?

OBJECTIVE

❹ **Account** for retained earnings, dividends, and stock splits

ACCOUNT FOR RETAINED EARNINGS, DIVIDENDS, AND STOCK SPLITS

The Retained Earnings account carries the accumulated balance of the corporation's net income less its net losses and any dividends declared over its lifetime. *The Retained Earnings account is not a reservoir of cash available for paying dividends or investing in other business activities.* In fact, the corporation may have a large balance in Retained Earnings, but not have any cash for dividends or investing. *Cash and Retained Earnings are two entirely separate accounts with no relationship to each other.* A $500,000 balance in Retained Earnings says nothing about the company's Cash balance.

A *credit* balance in Retained Earnings is normal, indicating that the corporation's lifetime earnings exceed its lifetime losses and dividends. A *debit* balance in Retained Earnings arises when a corporation's lifetime losses and dividends exceed its lifetime earnings. Called a **deficit**, this amount is subtracted from the sum of the other equity accounts to determine total shareholders' equity. Deficits are not uncommon.

Declaring and Paying Dividends

Corporations distribute past earnings to shareholders by declaring and then paying *dividends*. The majority of dividends are paid in cash, but companies sometimes pay stock dividends as well. In this section, we first present the accounting for cash dividends and then show you how to account for stock dividends.

Cash Dividends

Before a company can pay a cash dividend, it must have:

1. retained Earnings in excess of the desired dividend and
2. enough Cash to pay the dividend.

A corporation *declares* a dividend before paying it, and only the board of directors has the authority to declare a dividend. The corporation has no obligation to pay a dividend until the board declares one, but once declared, the dividend becomes a legal liability of the corporation. There are three relevant dates for dividends: the *date of declaration*, the *date of record*, and the *date of payment*. The following example illustrates the distinction between these dates.

1. The **date of declaration** is the date on which the board of directors officially declares the payment of a dividend, creating a liability for the amount declared. If the board declares a dividend of $50,000 on June 19, 2020, the entry to account for it is:

	A	B	C	D	E
1	June 19	Retained Earnings*	50,000		
2		Dividends Payable		50,000	
3		*Declared a cash dividend.*			
4					

*In Chapter 2, we debited a Dividends account to clearly identify the purpose of the payment. From here on, we follow the more common practice of debiting the Retained Earnings account for dividend declarations.

ASSETS   =   LIABILITIES   +   SHAREHOLDERS' EQUITY

$$0 \quad = \quad +50{,}000 \quad\quad -50{,}000 \text{ Retained Earnings}$$

2. The **date of record** follows the declaration date. In order to receive the declared dividend, one must be officially registered as a shareholder of the company on this date. Let's assume the date of record in our illustration is July 1. This date has no accounting implications, so no entry is needed.

3. The **date of payment** is the date on which the dividend is actually paid to shareholders. If the $50,000 dividend declared on June 19 to shareholders of record on July 1 is paid on July 10, the entry would be:

	A	B	C	D	E
1	July 10	Dividends Payable	50,000		
2		Cash		50,000	
3		*Paid cash dividend.*			
4					

ASSETS   =   LIABILITIES   +   SHAREHOLDERS' EQUITY

$$-50{,}000 \quad = \quad -50{,}000$$

The preceding illustration applies to cash dividends declared and paid on any type of shares.

Stock Dividends

When a company declares a **stock dividend**, it eventually pays the dividend by issuing additional shares of the company instead of by distributing cash. The total dollar value of a stock dividend is determined by multiplying the number of shares to be issued by the market price of the shares on the date of declaration. For example, if a stock dividend totalling 100,000 shares is declared on a day when the shares are valued at $10 each, then the amount of the dividend would be $1,000,000.

The relevant dates for stock dividends are the same as those for cash dividends, but the journal entries differ. On the date of declaration, we debit Retained Earnings and credit Stock Dividends Distributable (a contra-equity account). On the date of payment, we debit Stock Dividends Distributable and credit the relevant Share Capital account. A stock dividend, therefore, has no impact on the total shareholders' equity balance because Share Capital increases and Retained Earnings decreases by the same amount.

The corporation distributes stock dividends to shareholders in proportion to the number of shares they already own. If you own 300 common shares of TELUS, for example, and TELUS distributes a 10% common shares dividend, you will receive 30 (300 × 0.10) additional shares. You would then own 330 common shares.

All other TELUS shareholders would also receive additional shares equal to 10% of their prior holdings.

Why would a company issue a stock dividend instead of a cash dividend? A corporation may choose to distribute stock dividends for the following reasons:

1. **To continue dividends but conserve cash.** A company may wish to conserve cash to fund its business activities while still distributing dividends to its shareholders. It can achieve these goals by issuing a stock dividend. Shareholders pay tax on stock dividends the same way they pay tax on cash dividends.

2. **To reduce the per-share market price of its shares.** When a company issues a stock dividend, the number of shares issued and outstanding increases, but the market value of the company does not change. As a result, the market value of each outstanding share will be lower after the distribution of a stock dividend. This makes the company's shares less expensive, and therefore more affordable to some investors. Assume, for example, that a company with 100,000 common shares outstanding and a market value of $1,000,000 declares and pays a 10% stock dividend. Before the dividend, the market value per share is $10 ($1,000,000/100,000 shares), but after the dividend it is only $9.09 ($1,000,000/110,000 shares).

STOP + THINK (8-4)

Company A and Company B both have 200,000 common shares outstanding. On June 30, Company A declares a 10% stock dividend and Company B declares a 20% stock dividend.

The common shares of both companies have a $10 market value per share on this date.

1. Which company's shareholders' equity will decrease the most after distributing these stock dividends?

2. Which company will have a lower market value per share after distributing these dividends?

Dividends on Preferred Shares

EXPRESSING THE DIVIDEND ON PREFERRED SHARES. Dividends on preferred shares are expressed as an annual dollar figure or as a percentage of the share's stated value. Scotiabank, for example, issued a new series of preferred shares in October 2018 at a price of $25 per share. Each share pays a dividend of 4.85% per year, entitling the shareholder to $1.2125 in dividends per year ($25 × 4.85).

DIVIDENDS ON PREFERRED AND COMMON SHARES. When a company has issued both preferred and common shares, the preferred shareholders receive their dividends first. The common shareholders receive dividends only if the total declared dividend is large enough to pay the preferred shareholders in full.

Pinecraft Industries Inc. has 100,000 shares of $1.50 cumulative preferred shares outstanding in addition to its common shares. Assume that in 2020, Pinecraft declares an annual dividend of $1,000,000. The allocation to preferred and common shareholders is as follows:

Preferred dividend (100,000 shares × $1.50 per share)	$ 150,000
Common dividend (remainder: $1,000,000 − $150,000)	850,000
Total dividend	$1,000,000

If Pinecraft declares only a $200,000 dividend, preferred shareholders receive $150,000, and the common shareholders receive the remaining, $50,000 ($200,000 − $150,000). A dividend of $150,000 or less would result in the common shareholders receiving no dividend.

DIVIDENDS ON CUMULATIVE AND NON-CUMULATIVE PREFERRED SHARES. The allocation of dividends may be complex if the preferred shares are *cumulative*. Corporations sometimes fail to pay a dividend to preferred shareholders. This is called *passing the dividend*, and any passed dividends on cumulative preferred shares are said to be *in arrears*. The owners of **cumulative preferred shares** must receive all dividends in arrears plus the current year's dividend before the corporation can pay dividends to the common shareholders. Preferred shares are assumed to be non-cumulative, unless otherwise stated.

The preferred shares of Pinecraft Industries Inc. are cumulative. Suppose the company passed the 2019 preferred dividend of $150,000. Before paying dividends to its common shareholders in 2020, the company must first pay preferred dividends of $150,000 for both 2019 and 2020, a total of $300,000. Assume that Pinecraft declared a dividend of $500,000 on September 6, 2020. The entry to record this declaration is:

	A	B	C	D	E
1	2020				
2	Sep. 6	Retained Earnings	500,000		
3		Dividends Payable, Preferred ($150,000 × 2)		300,000	
4		Dividends Payable, Common ($500,000 − $300,000)		200,000	
5		*To declare a cash dividend.*			
6					

Note that even though dividends of $150,000 were in arrears at the end of 2019, no liability for these dividends is recorded until the board declares a dividend. If the preferred shares are *non-cumulative*, the corporation is not obligated to pay preferred dividends in arrears.

Stock Splits

When a company wishes to increase or decrease its market value per share without altering its assets, liabilities, or shareholders' equity, it can declare a **stock split**, which results in an increase or decrease in the number of issued and outstanding shares of the company, but does not affect any financial statement balances. On June 14, 2018, for example, Dollarama executed a 3-for-1 stock split, which resulted in its common shareholders receiving three company shares in exchange for each one they already owned. As a result of this split, the number of Dollarama shares issued and outstanding tripled from 109,242,359 to 327,727,077. Just prior to the split, SKX shares were trading at around $150. With three times as many shares outstanding after the split, the price per share immediately declined to about $50 because neither the total market value nor the book value of Dollarama changed as a result of the stock split.

Companies typically split their stock when they think their share price has become too expensive or if the stock price is trading too far above similar companies' stock. If a company wishes to alter its share price by something other than the 66% decrease seen for Dollarama, it merely has to change the split ratio. If, for example, a company wanted to decrease its share price from $400 to $200, it would execute a

2-for-1 stock split, which would result in there being twice times as many shares issued and outstanding after the split.

Sometimes, companies want to *increase* their share price because a very low share price often deters investors from buying the stock. Assume, for instance, that a company wants to increase its share price from $0.50 to $1.50 so it is no longer considered a penny stock (an unflattering term for a stock trading below $1 per share). It could do this by executing a 1-for-3 stock split, which means the company would issue one share in exchange for every three shares owned by a shareholder. After this split, there would be one-third as many shares issued and outstanding, resulting in a tripling of the share price. Splits like this, where the number of shares issued and outstanding decreases, are often called *reverse stock splits*.

Regardless of whether a company executes a normal stock split or a reverse split, there is no impact *on the accounts of the company,* so no journal entries are needed in the event of a stock split. From a record-keeping perspective, the only change is the number of shares issued and outstanding, and this change, along with a description of the stock split, would be disclosed in the statement of owners' equity and the notes to the financial statements.

Summary of the Effects on Assets, Liabilities, and Shareholders' Equity

We've seen how to account for the basic shareholders' equity transactions and events:

- Issuance of shares (pp. 400–402)
- Repurchase of shares (pp. 422)
- Cash dividends (pp. 404–405)
- Stock dividends (pp. 405–406)
- Stock splits (pp. 407–408)

How do these transactions and events affect assets, liabilities, and equity? Exhibit 8-3 provides a helpful summary.

EXHIBIT 8-3

Effects of Share-Related Transactions and Events on Assets, Liabilities, and Equity

Transaction	Assets	=	Liabilities	+	Shareholders' Equity
Issuance of shares—common and preferred	Increase		No effect		Increase
Repurchase of shares	Decrease		No effect		Decrease
Declaration of cash dividend	No effect		Increase		Decrease
Payment of cash dividend	Decrease		Decrease		No effect
Declaration and distribution of stock dividend	No effect		No effect		No effect
Stock split	No effect		No effect		No effect

OBJECTIVE

❺ **Distinguish** between fair value and book value per share

DISTINGUISH BETWEEN FAIR VALUE AND BOOK VALUE PER SHARE

Investors commonly use two share values to assist with investment decisions—*fair value* and *book value*. It is important to understand the distinction between these two share values and how they can affect investing decisions.

Fair Value

The **fair value** (or market price) of a share of a company's stock is the price that a willing buyer would pay a willing seller to acquire the share. The fair values of the shares of companies that are traded on public stock exchanges, such as the Toronto Stock Exchange (TSX), are easily determined by examining the prices at which the shares trade on these exchanges. On November 5, 2018, for example, one common share of Dollarama had a fair value of $37.33 based on the closing price of the stock on the TSX that day. Shares of private companies do not trade on public exchanges, so their fair values must generally be determined with the assistance of professional business valuators.

Book Value

The **book value** of a share of a company's common stock indicates the dollar value of net assets a common shareholder would receive for each share *after* any preferred shareholders have received their share of the company's net assets. If the company has only common shares outstanding, its book value is computed by dividing the total shareholders' equity by the number of common shares *outstanding*. For example, a company with shareholders' equity of $180,000 and 5,000 common shares outstanding has a book value of $36 per share ($180,000 ÷ 5,000 shares).

If the company has both preferred shares and common shares outstanding, the preferred shareholders have the first claim to the company's net assets, so their equity in the net assets, *including any cumulative dividends in arrears*, must be deducted from shareholders' equity before computing the book value per common share. In general, the formula for calculating book value per common share is:

$$\text{Book value per common share} = \frac{\text{Total shareholders equity} - \text{Preferred shareholders' equity}}{\text{Number of common shares outstanding}}$$

To illustrate the use of this formula, assume a company's shareholders' equity consists of the following:

	A	B	C
1	**Shareholders' Equity**		
2	Preferred shares, 400 shares issued	$ 40,000	
3	Common shares, 5,000 shares issued	131,000	
4	Retained earnings	70,000	
5	Total shareholders' equity	$ 241,000	
6			

Its book value per common share would then be $40.20 [($241,000 − $40,000)/ 5,000 shares].

STOP + THINK (8-5)

Using the information in the following Shareholders' Equity section of the balance sheet (as at December 31, 2020), respond to the questions below. If the information you need to answer a question is not provided, answer "unknown." Consider each question to be independent of the others, unless otherwise stated.

Shareholders' Equity	2020
Authorized shares	
1,000,000 non-voting preferred shares, no par value, non-cumulative dividend of $1.00 per share	
Unlimited number of common shares, no par value	
Issued and outstanding shares	
50,000 preferred shares	$ 500,000
500,000 common shares	6,750,000
Retained earnings	3,250,000
Total Shareholders' Equity	$10,500,000

1. How much equity financing has the company received from shareholders since it was incorporated?
2. Assuming the company has paid $1,650,000 in dividends over its life to date, what is its total net income since inception?
3. At the end of 2020, how much cash does the company have available to pay dividends or otherwise fund its operations?
4. What is the book value of the assets owned by the company's common shareholders?
5. If the company paid dividends totalling $310,000 in 2020, how much of this total did the common shareholders receive (in dollars)?
6. If on January 1, 2021, the company implemented a 3-for-2 stock split of its common shares, how many common shares would be issued and outstanding after the split? If the shares had a market price of $20 on that date, what impact would the split have on shareholders' equity (in dollars)?

OBJECTIVE

6 **Evaluate** a company's return on assets and return on equity

EVALUATE A COMPANY'S RETURN ON ASSETS AND RETURN ON EQUITY

Investors search for companies whose stocks are likely to increase in value. They're constantly comparing companies, but a comparison of Dollarama with a start-up company is not meaningful. Dollarama's revenues run into the billions, far exceeding a new company's revenues. In addition, management of the company has spent years investing in assets and managing both borrowed resources and shareholders' invested capital. Does this automatically make Dollarama a better investment? Not necessarily. To compare profitability of companies of different size, investors use standard profitability measures, including return on assets and return on equity.

Return on Assets

The rate of return on total assets, or simply **return on assets (ROA)**, measures a company's success in using its assets to earn income for the two groups who finance the business:

- Creditors to whom the corporation owes money (creditors want interest)
- Shareholders who own the corporation's shares (shareholders want net income)

The sum of net income and interest expense is the return to the two groups who finance a corporation. This sum is the numerator of the return-on-assets ratio. The denominator of the ratio is average total assets, which is computed by taking the average of the company's total assets at each of the last two fiscal year-ends. Return on assets is computed as follows, using data from Dollarama's 2018 financial statements (dollar amounts in millions):

$$\text{Return on assets} = \frac{\text{Net income} + \text{Interest expense}}{\text{Average total assets}}$$

$$= \frac{519.4 + 37.9}{(1,934.3 + 1,863.5)/2} = 29.3\%$$

What is a good rate of return on total assets? Ten percent is considered a strong benchmark in most industries. Rates of return on assets vary by industry, however, because the components of ROA are different across industries. Some high-technology companies earn much higher returns than do utility companies, retailers, and manufacturers of consumer goods such as toothpaste and paper towels. Companies that are efficient, generating a large amount of sales per dollar of assets invested, or companies that can differentiate their products and earn higher margins on them, have higher ROA than companies that do not have these attributes.

Return on Equity

The rate of return on common shareholders' equity, usually called simply **return on equity (ROE)**, shows the relationship between net income and common shareholders' equity. Return on equity is computed only on common share capital because the return to preferred shareholders is usually limited to a specified dividend (for example, 5%).

The numerator of ROE is net income minus preferred dividends, if any. The denominator is *average common shareholders' equity*—total shareholders' equity minus preferred shareholders' equity, if any. Since most companies do not have preferred shares, adjustments for preferred dividends and preferred equity are usually not necessary. Dollarama's ROE for 2018 is computed as follows (dollar amounts in millions):

$$\text{Return on equity} = \frac{\text{Net income} - \text{Preferred dividends}}{\text{Average common shareholders' equity}}$$

$$= \frac{519.4 - 0.0}{(-252.3 + 100.3)/2} = (683.4)\%$$

Because Dollarama has no preferred shares, preferred dividends are zero. With no preferred shares outstanding, average common shareholders' equity is the same as average total equity—the average of the beginning and ending amounts. While Dollarama's negative ROE of almost 700% seems very bad, this result is due to its sizable net income combined with its small average deficit in the denominator of the ratio. Viewed in this way, the ratio is actually very positive for Dollarama's shareholders because the company was able to earn a large profit despite having a negative equity position.

ROE is typically higher than ROA for a successful company. This difference results from the interest-expense component of return on assets. Companies borrow money at one rate (say, 6%) and invest the funds to earn a higher rate (say, 12%). Borrowing at a lower rate than the company's return on investments is called using leverage. Leverage increases net income as long as operating income exceeds the interest expense from borrowing. This also makes sense from an economic standpoint. Shareholders take a lot more investment risk than creditors, so the shareholders demand that ROE exceed ROA. They expect the return on their investment to exceed the amount they have to pay their creditors for borrowed funds. Investors and creditors use ROE in much the same way they use ROA—to compare companies. The higher the rate of return, the more successful the company is. In many industries, 15% is considered a good ROE.

Are Dollarama's ROA and ROE strong, weak, or somewhere in between? To answer these questions, it is necessary to have other information, such as:

- comparative returns for Dollarama from prior years and
- comparative returns for other companies in the same industry.

The Decision Guidelines that follow offer suggestions for what to consider when investing in stock. You will also use all of these ratios more in Chapter 10.

STOP + THINK (8-6)

Suppose you recently sold some shares in your Tax-Free Savings Account for proceeds of $5,000. You plan to reinvest these proceeds and have narrowed your choice down to the common shares of two companies in the same industry that have a history of paying steadily increasing dividends and rising share prices. Company A had a return on assets of 10.1% and a return on equity of 18.3% in its most recent fiscal year, while Company B had an ROA of 6.7% and an ROE of 13.4%. If you were to invest all $5,000 in only one of these companies, which one would you choose and why?

 # DECISION GUIDELINES

INVESTING IN STOCK

Suppose you've saved $5,000 to invest. You visit a nearby Edward Jones office, where the broker probes for your risk tolerance. Are you investing mainly for dividends or for growth in the stock price? You must make some key decisions.

Investor Decision	Guidelines
Which category of stock to buy for:	
• A safe investment?	Preferred shares are safer than common shares, but for even more safety, invest in high-grade corporate bonds or government securities.
• Steady dividends?	Consider cumulative preferred shares. But remember, the company is not obligated to declare preferred dividends, and the dividends are unlikely to increase.
• Increasing dividends?	Consider common shares, as long as the company's net income is increasing and the company has adequate cash flow to pay a dividend after meeting all obligations and other cash demands.
• Increasing stock price?	Consider common shares, but again only if the company's net income and cash flow are increasing.
How to identify a good stock to buy?	There are many ways to pick stock investments. One strategy that works reasonably well is to invest in companies that consistently earn higher rates of return on assets and on equity than competing firms in the same industry. Also, select industries that are expected to grow.

REPORT EQUITY TRANSACTIONS AND EVENTS IN THE FINANCIAL STATEMENTS

Reporting Changes in Shareholders' Equity

OBJECTIVE

❼ **Report** equity transactions and events in the financial statements

The **statement of changes in shareholders' equity** reports the details of all the changes in the shareholders' equity section of the balance sheet during the period. Exhibit 8-4 presents Dollarama's statement for the year ended January 28, 2018. The statement contains a column for each major element of equity, starting with Share Capital on the left and ending with a column summarizing the total changes for the period. The top row (line 3) reports the beginning balance for each element as at January 29, 2017, while the next eight rows (lines 4–10) detail the causes of the changes in each element during the 2018 fiscal year.

	A	B	C	D	E	F
1	**Dollarama Inc.** Consolidated Statement of Changes in Shareholders' Equity (Deficit) For the Year Ended January 28, 2018					
2	*(in millions)*	Share Capital	Contri- buted Surplus	Accumu- lated Compre- hensive Loss	Deficit	Total
3	**Balance as at January 29, 2017**	$ 420.3	$ 24.3	$ (1.3)	$ (343.0)	$ 100.3
4	Net earnings				519.4	519.4
5	Other comprehensive loss			(31.1)		(31.1)
6	Issuance of common shares	14.6				14.6
7	Repurchase and cancellation of common shares	(22.3)			(790.4)	(812.7)
8	Share-based compensation		6.6			6.6
9	Dividends				(49.5)	(49.5)
10	Reclassification for the exercise of share options	3.2	(3.2)			-
11	**Balance as at January 28, 2018**	$ 415.8	$ 27.7	$ (32.4)	$ (663.5)	$ (252.4)
12						

EXHIBIT 8-4
Dollarama Inc. – Statement of Changes in Shareholders' Equity (Adapted)
Source: Data's from Dollarama Inc.

Let's briefly examine some of the changes in Dollarama's shareholders' equity during 2018. On line 4, we see the year's net earnings of $519.4 million being added to the opening Deficit, just as it would be in a stand-alone statement of retained earnings (deficit). Line 5 reports the components of comprehensive income that affect the Deficit and Accumulated Other Comprehensive Loss. Line 6 reports that an additional $14.6 million in common share capital was issued during 2018, while line 7 shows that the company repurchased some common shares for a total cost that was $790.4 million higher than the $22.3 million they were originally issued for. On line 9, we see dividends of $49.5 million being deducted from the Deficit—again, just like they would be in a separate statement of retained earnings (deficit).

The statement ends with the closing balances for each element as at January 28, 2018 (line 11). All of the closing balances are carried forward to the shareholders' deficit section of the balance sheet, which is reported in Exhibit 8-5.

	A	B	C
1	**Dollarama Inc.** Consolidated Balance Sheet (Partial) As at January 28, 2018		
2	*(in millions)*		
3	**Shareholders' deficit**		
4	Share capital	$ 415.8	
5	Contributed surplus	27.7	
6	Accumulated other comprehensive loss	(32.4)	
7	Deficit	(663.4)	
8	**Total shareholders' deficit**	$ (252.3)	
9			

ASPE require only a statement of retained earnings, which you have seen in previous chapters. Such a statement for Dollarama would contain only the information in the Deficit column of Exhibit 8-4.

Reporting in the Balance Sheet and Notes

Businesses often use terminology and formats in reporting shareholders' equity that differ from our examples. We use a more detailed format in this book to help you learn the main components of shareholders' equity.

One of the most important skills you will take from this textbook is the ability to understand the financial statements of real companies. Exhibit 8-6 presents a side-by-side comparison of our general textbook format for reporting shareholders' equity and a format you will commonly encounter in the real world.

EXHIBIT 8-6
Formats for Reporting Shareholders' Equity

	A	B	C	D	E
1	**General Textbook Format**		**Common Real-World Format**		
2	Shareholders' equity		Shareholders' equity		
3	Share capital:				
4	Preferred shares, $0.80, cumulative, 30,000 shares authorized and outstanding	$ 300,000	Contributed capital Share capital (Note 9)	$ 2,500,000	
5	Common shares, 100,000 shares authorized, 60,000 shares outstanding	2,200,000	Contributed surplus	11,000	
6			Retained earnings	1,542,000	
6			Accumulated other comprehensive income	15,000	
7	Contributed surplus from retirement of preferred shares	8,000	Total shareholders' equity	$ 4,068,000	
8	Contributed surplus from repurchase of common shares	3,000	**Notes to the Financial Statements** 1.		
9	Total capital stock	2,511,000	.		
10	Retained earnings	1,542,000	.		
11	Accumulated other comprehensive income	15,000	.		
12	Total shareholders' equity	$ 4,068,000	**9. Share capital**		
13			Preferred shares, $0.80 cumulative 30,000 shares authorized and outstanding	$ 300,000	
14			Common shares, 100,000 shares authorized, 60,000 outstanding	2,200,000	
15			Total share capital	$ 2,500,000	
16					

In general, the following are a few of the key pieces of equity information that must be disclosed in the balance sheet, statement of changes in owners' equity, or the notes:

- Number of authorized, issued, and outstanding shares, and changes in these amounts during the year, for each class of share capital; their par value, if any; dividend rights and preferences; and other restrictions and features.
- Contributed surplus.
- Accumulated other comprehensive income (IFRS only).
- Retained earnings.

STOP + THINK (8-7)

Using the information in Dollarama's Statement of Changes in Shareholders' Equity in Exhibit 8-4, determine the total original cost of the common shares that Dollarama repurchased during 2018.

Summary of IFRS-ASPE Differences

Concepts	IFRS	ASPE
Accumulated other comprehensive income (p. 399)	Included as a component of shareholders' equity.	No accounting or reporting of this component is required.
Statement of changes in shareholders' (or owners') equity (p. 413)	Companies must report this statement.	Companies must report only a statement of retained earnings, which contains only a subset of the information reported in the statement of changes in shareholders' equity.

SUMMARY

SUMMARY OF LEARNING OBJECTIVES

LEARNING OBJECTIVE	SUMMARY
❶ **Explain** the main features of a corporation	1. A corporation is a separate legal entity that exists apart from its shareholders.
	2. A corporation has a continuous life regardless of changes in ownership, and its shareholders may buy and sell their shares as they wish.
	3. A corporation's shareholders have limited liability for the company's debts. The most they can lose is the amount of their initial investment.
	4. Shareholders own the corporation, but company policy is set by the board of directors and implemented by company management.
	5. Corporations pay income taxes separate from those borne by their shareholders.
	6. Corporations are regulated by the government to ensure they report and disclose the information in their financial statements that investors and creditors need to make informed decisions.

❷ Account for the issuance of shares

Shares are normally issued for cash, but they can also be issued in exchange for other assets, such as land or equipment. When shares are issued, the relevant Asset account is debited and the relevant Share Capital account is credited.

❸ Explain why a company repurchases shares

Corporations repurchase their shares for several reasons:
1. To fulfill future share issuance commitments, such as those related to stock option plans.
2. To help support the corporation's market price per share by reducing the number of shares outstanding.
3. To avoid a takeover by an outside party.

❹ Account for retained earnings, dividends, and stock splits

Retained earnings are the accumulation of a corporation's net income since inception less any net losses and dividends distributed.

Dividends are commonly paid in cash, but they can also be distributed in the form of additional stock in the corporation, which is known as a stock dividend. On the date of declaration, Retained Earnings is debited and Dividends Payable is credited for the amount of the cash dividend declared. Parties officially registered as shareholders of the corporation on the date of record will receive the dividend when it is paid (no journal entry is needed in connection with the date of record). On the date of payment of a cash dividend, Dividends Payable is debited and Cash is credited. For a stock dividend, on the date of declaration, we debit Retained Earnings and credit Stock Dividends Distributable (a contra-equity account). On the date of payment, we debit Stock Dividends Distributable and credit the relevant Share Capital account.

Stock splits are executed to increase or decrease the number of shares issued and outstanding, thereby decreasing or increasing the market price per share. An X-for-Y stock split, when X is greater than Y, increases the number of shares issued and outstanding and reduces the market price per share. If X is less than Y, the number of shares issued and outstanding decreases, and the market price per share increases. Stock splits have no effect on the corporation's shareholders' equity balances.

❺ Distinguish between fair value and book value per share

The fair value (or market price) of a share of a company's stock is the price that a willing buyer would pay a willing seller to acquire the share.

The book value of a share of a company's common stock indicates the dollar value of net assets a common shareholder would receive for each share *after* the preferred shareholders (if any) have received their share of the net assets.

❻ Evaluate a company's return on assets and return on equity

A company's return on assets (ROA) indicates how well it has used its assets to earn money for its creditors and shareholders. It is calculated as follows:

$$\text{ROA} = \frac{\text{Net income} + \text{Interest expense}}{\text{Average total assets}}$$

A company's return on equity (ROE) indicates how much profit it has generated for each dollar of common shareholders' equity it has. It is calculated as follows:

$$\text{ROE} = \frac{\text{Net income} - \text{Preferred dividends}}{\text{Average common shareholders' equity}}$$

Generally, the higher a company's ROA and ROE, the better its profitability. A company's ROA and ROE are best evaluated by comparing them to prior years' returns and to the returns of major competitors.

❼ Report equity transactions and events in the financial statements

The statement of changes in shareholders' equity reports the details of all the changes in the shareholders' equity section of the balance sheet during the period. It typically reports changes in the following equity items:

- Share capital
- Contributed surplus
- Retained earnings
- Accumulated other comprehensive income

A corporation must also disclose the following equity information in its balance sheet, statement of changes in owners' equity, or the notes:

- Number of authorized, issued, and outstanding shares and changes in these amounts during the year for each class of share capital; their par value, if any; dividend rights and preferences; and other restrictions and features
- Contributed surplus
- Accumulated other comprehensive income (IFRS only)
- Retained earnings

MyLab Accounting

END-OF-CHAPTER SUMMARY PROBLEM

1. The balance sheet of Quetico Inc. reported the following at December 31, 2020:

	A	B	C
1	**Shareholders' Equity**		
2	Preferred shares, $0.40, 10,000 shares authorized and issued	$ 100,000	
3	Common shares, 100,000 shares authorized*	400,000	
4	Accumulated other comprehensive income	224,000	
5	Retained earnings	476,500	
6	Total shareholders' equity	$ 1,200,500	
7			

*The common shares were issued at a stated value of $8.00 per share.

Requirements

a. Are the preferred shares cumulative or non-cumulative? How can you tell?
b. What is the total amount of the annual preferred dividend?
c. How many common shares are outstanding?
d. Compute the book value per share of the common shares. No preferred dividends are in arrears, and Quetico Inc. has not yet declared the 2020 dividend.

2. Use the following accounts and related balances to prepare the classified balance sheet of Gandhi Ltd. at September 30, 2020. Use the account format of the balance sheet.

Common shares, 50,000 shares authorized, 20,000 shares issued	$100,000	Property, plant, and equipment, net	$266,000
		Accounts receivable, net	23,000
Dividends payable	4,000	Preferred shares, $3.75,	
Cash	9,000	10,000 shares authorized,	
Accounts payable	28,000	2,000 shares issued	24,000
Long-term note payable	80,000	Accrued liabilities	3,000
Inventory	85,000	Retained earnings	104,000
Accumulated other comprehensive income	40,000		

All features must be specified in the financial statements.	

ANSWERS

1. a. The preferred shares are not cumulative because they are not specifically labelled cumulative.

Details should be given on the balance sheet.	

  b. Total annual preferred dividend: $4,000 (10,000 × $0.40).

Each common share was sold for the $8 stated value.	

  c. Common shares outstanding: 50,000 shares ($400,000 ÷ $8 stated value).

  d. Book value per common share:

Book value per common share must exclude any amounts pertaining to preferred shares.	

Common:

Total shareholders' equity	$ 1,200,500
Less shareholders' equity allocated to preferred	(100,000)
Shareholders' equity allocated to common...	$1,100,500
Book value per share ($1,100,500 ÷ 50,000 shares)	$ 22.01

The classified balance sheet must specify current assets and current liabilities. Make sure that Total assets = Total liabilities + Shareholders' equity.	

2.

	A	B	C	D	E	F
1			**Gandhi Ltd.** Balance Sheet As at September 30, 2020			
2	**Assets**		**Liabilities**			
3	Current		Current			
4	Cash	$ 9,000	Accounts payable	$ 28,000		
5	Accounts receivable, net	23,000	Dividends payable	4,000		
6	Inventory	85,000	Accrued liabilities	3,000		
7	Total current assets	117,000	Total current liabilities	35,000		
8	Property, plant, and equipment, net	266,000	Long-term note payable	80,000		
9			Total liabilities		$115,000	
10						
11			**Shareholders' Equity**			
12			Preferred shares, $3.75,			
13			10,000 shares authorized,			
14			2,000 shares issued	$ 24,000		
15			Common shares,			
16			50,000 shares authorized,			
17			20,000 shares issued	100,000		
18			Retained earnings	104,000		
19			Accumulated other			
20			comprehensive income	40,000		
21			Total shareholders' equity		268,000	
22			Total liabilities and			
23	Total assets	$ 383,000	shareholders' equity		$383,000	
24						

REVIEW

MyLab Accounting

Make the grade with MyLab Accounting: The Quick Quiz questions, Short Exercises, Exercises, and Problems (Group A) marked with a ⊕ can be found on MyLab Accounting. You can practise them as often as you want, and most feature step-by-step guided instructions to help you find the right answer.

QUICK QUIZ (ANSWERS APPEAR ON THE LAST PAGE OF THIS CHAPTER.)

1. Which of the following is a characteristic of a corporation?
   a. Mutual agency
   b. No income tax
   c. Limited liability of shareholders
   d. Both a and b

2. Team Spirit Inc. issues 240,000 common shares for $5 per share. The journal entry is:

   a. Cash................................... 240,000
      Common Shares   240,000
   b. Cash................................. 1,200,000
      Common Shares   240,000
      Gain on the Sale of Shares...   960,000
   c. Cash 1,200,000
      Common Shares   1,200,000
   d. Cash.................................. 1,200,000
      Common Shares   480,000
      Contributed Surplus on
         Common Shares   720,000

3. Which of the following is true about stated value?
   a. It represents what a share is worth.
   b. It represents the original selling price for a share.
   c. It is established for a share after it is issued.
   d. It is an arbitrary amount assigned by a company to a share at the time of issue.
   e. It may exist for common shares but not for preferred shares.

4. The contributed capital portion of shareholders' equity does not include
   a. preferred shares.
   b. contributed surplus.
   c. retained earnings.
   d. common shares.

5. Preferred shares are *least* likely to have which of the following characteristics?
   a. Preference as to assets on liquidation of the corporation
   b. Extra liability for the preferred shareholders
   c. The right of the holder to convert to common shares
   d. Preference as to dividends

6. Which of the following classifications represents the largest quantity of common shares?
   a. Issued shares
   b. Outstanding shares
   c. Unissued shares
   d. Authorized shares

Use the following information for questions 7 through 12:

These account balances at December 31 relate to Sportaid Inc.:

Accounts Payable........	$ 51,700	Preferred shares,	
Accounts		$0.01, 890,000	
Receivable..............	81,350	shares issued	89,000
Common Shares.........	593,000	Retained Earnings...	71,800
Bonds Payable	3,400	Notes Receivable.....	12,500

7. What is total share capital for Sportaid Inc.?
   a. $682,000
   b. $701,345
   c. $694,445
   d. $753,800
   e. None of the above

8. What is total shareholders' equity for Sportaid Inc.?
   a. $766,300
   b. $758,800
   c. $753,800
   d. $764,735
   e. None of the above

9. Sportaid's net income for the period is $119,600, and beginning common shareholders' equity is $681,400 and it declared the full amount of annual dividends on the preferred shares. What is Sportaid's return on common shareholders' equity?
   a. 15.7%
   b. 16.4%
   c. 17.5%
   d. 18.6%

10. If the average issue price of Sportaid's outstanding common shares is $11.86, how many common shares are issued and outstanding?
   a. 50,000
   b. 100,000
   c. 593,000
   d. Unknown

11. If Sportaid's board of directors decided to declare a dividend on December 31, what is the largest dividend it could declare?
   a. $753,800
   b. $71,800
   c. $8,900
   d. $593,000

12. If the board of directors declares a dividend of $20,000 on December 31, how much of this total would the common shareholders receive? No other dividends have been declared during the year.
   a. $8,900
   b. $0
   c. $20,000
   d. $11,100

13. Shareholders are eligible for a dividend if they own the shares on the date of
   a. declaration.
   b. record.
   c. payment.
   d. issuance.

14. Mario's Foods has outstanding 500 $7.00 preferred shares and 1,200 common shares. Mario's declares dividends of $14,300. The correct entry is:

   a. Retained Earnings......................... 14,300
         Dividends Payable, Preferred......   3,500
         Dividends Payable, Common....   10,800
   b. Dividends Expense....................... 14,300
         Cash   14,300
   c. Retained Earnings......................... 14,300
         Dividends Payable, Preferred......   7,150
         Dividends Payable, Common....   7,150
   d. Dividends Payable, Preferred........ 3,500
      Dividends Payable, Common....... 10,800
         Cash   14,300

15. A corporation has 20,000 $8.00 preferred shares outstanding with a stated value of $2,000,000. Also, there are 20,000 common shares outstanding. If a $350,000 dividend is paid, how much goes to the preferred shareholders?
   a. $0
   b. $350,000

   c. $160,000
   d. $120,000
   e. $320,000

16. Assume the same facts as in question 15. What is the amount of dividends per share on common shares?
   a. $9.50
   b. $8.00
   c. $17.50
   d. $1.50
   e. None of the above

17. Which of the following is *not* true about a 10% stock dividend?
   a. Shareholders do not receive additional shares.
   b. No assets are affected.
   c. Retained Earnings decreases.
   d. The market price of the share is needed to record the stock dividend.
   e. Total shareholders' equity remains the same.

18. A company declares a 5% stock dividend. The debit to Retained Earnings is an amount equal to the
   a. stated value of original shares.
   b. excess of the market price over the original issue price of the shares to be issued.
   c. book value of the shares to be issued.
   d. fair value of the shares to be issued.

19. Which of the following statements is *not* true about a 3-for-1 stock split?
   a. Stated value is reduced to one-third of what it was before the split.
   b. Total shareholders' equity increases.
   c. The market price of each share will decrease.
   d. A shareholder with 10 shares before the split owns 30 shares after the split.
   e. Retained Earnings remains the same.

20. Franco Company's net income and preferred dividends are $44,000 and $4,000, respectively, and average total common shareholders' equity is $384,000. How much is Franco's return on equity?
   a. 10.4%
   b. 11.5%
   c. 12.5%
   d. 13.1%

ACCOUNTING VOCABULARY

book value (of a share) Amount of owners' equity on the company's books for each share of its stock. (p. 409)

chairperson Elected by a corporation's board of directors, usually the most powerful person in the corporation. (p. 398)

cumulative preferred shares Preferred shares whose owners must receive all dividends in arrears plus the current year's

dividend before the corporation can pay dividends to the common shareholders. (p. 407)

date of declaration The date on which the Board of Directors declares a dividend to shareholders. (p. 404)

date of payment The date on which a dividend is actually paid to shareholders. (p. 405)

date of record The date on which a person must be recorded as a shareholder in order to receive a dividend. (p. 405)

deficit The term used when *retained earnings* is a negative balance. (p. 404)

fair value (of a share) The price that a willing buyer would pay a willing seller to acquire a share. (p. 409)

limited liability No personal obligation of a shareholder for corporation debts. A shareholder can lose no more on an investment in a corporation's shares than the cost of the investment. (p. 397)

market price (of a share) The price that a willing buyer would pay a willing seller to acquire a share. (p. 403)

par value shares Shares of stock that have a value assigned to them by articles of the corporation. (p. 400)

preferred shares Shares that give their owners certain advantages, such as the priority to receive dividends before the common shareholders and the priority to receive assets before the common shareholders if the corporation liquidates. (p. 400)

president Chief executive officer in charge of managing the day-to-day operations of a corporation. (p. 398)

repurchased shares A corporation's own shares that it has issued and later reacquired. (p. 403)

return on assets (ROA) Measures how profitably management has used the assets that shareholders and creditors have provided the company. (p. 410)

return on equity (ROE) Net income divided by average total assets. This ratio measures how profitably management has used the assets that shareholders and creditors have provided the company. (p. 411)

stated value An arbitrary amount assigned by a company to a share of its stock at the time of issue. (p. 400)

statement of changes in shareholders' equity Reports the changes in all categories of shareholders' equity during the period. (p. 413)

stock dividend A proportional distribution by a corporation of its own shares to its shareholders. (p. 405)

stock split An increase in the number of authorized, issued, and outstanding shares of stock coupled with a proportionate reduction in the share's book value. (p. 407)

ASSESS YOUR PROGRESS

SHORT EXERCISES

S8-1 What are two main advantages that a corporation has over a proprietorship and a partnership? What are two main disadvantages of a corporation?

LEARNING OBJECTIVE ❶
Understand the advantages and disadvantages of a corporation

S8-2 Consider The Authority Structure in a Corporation, as Diagrammed in Exhibit 8-2, Page 398.

1. What group holds the ultimate power in a corporation?
2. Who is the most powerful person in the corporation? What's the abbreviation of this person's title?
3. Who is in charge of day-to-day operations? What's the abbreviation of this person's title?
4. Who is in charge of accounting and finance? What's the abbreviation of this person's title?

LEARNING OBJECTIVE ❶
Summarize the characteristics of authority structure in a corporation

S8-3 Answer the following questions about the characteristics of a corporation's shares:

1. Who are the real owners of a corporation?
2. What privileges do preferred shareholders have over common shareholders?
3. Which class of shareholders reaps greater benefits from a highly profitable corporation? Explain.

LEARNING OBJECTIVE ❶
Identify the characteristics of preferred and common shares

S8-4 Study George Weston Ltd.'s January 8, 2020, share issuance entry given on pages 400–401, and answer these questions about the nature of the transaction:

1. If George Weston had sold the shares for $80, would the $30 ($80 − $50) be profit for George Weston?
2. Suppose the shares had been issued at different times and different prices. Will shares issued at higher prices have more rights than those issued at lower prices? Give the reason for your answer.

LEARNING OBJECTIVES ❶❷❼
Assess the rights of shareholders; Understand the effect of a share issuance on net income

S8-5 On December 31, 2020, shareholders' equity accounts of Green Products Inc. (GPI) had the balances shown below. GPI paid dividends of $4,096 on December 1, 2020.

	2020	2019
Common shares	$ 82,968	$ 64,968
Retained earnings	80,435	78,881
Total shareholders' equity	$163,403	$143,849

LEARNING OBJECTIVES ❷❹
Issue shares and analyze retained earnings

1. GPI sold 10,000 common shares on June 30, 2020. What was the average selling price of these shares if this was the only common-shares transaction during 2020?

2. Journalize GPI's sale of the common shares on June 30, 2020.

3. Based only on the above information, did GPI earn a profit or suffer a loss during 2020? Calculate the profit or loss.

LEARNING OBJECTIVES ❷❼

Account for and assess impact of share issuances on the financial statements

S8-6 This Short Exercise demonstrates the similarity and the difference between two ways to acquire capital assets.

Case A—Issue shares and buy the assets in separate transactions:	Case B—Issue shares to acquire the assets in a single transaction:
Longview Corporation issued 10,000 common shares for cash of $200,000. In a separate transaction, Longview used the cash to purchase a warehouse building for $160,000 and equipment for $40,000. Journalize the two transactions.	Tyler Corporation issued 10,000 common shares to acquire a warehouse valued at $160,000 and equipment worth $40,000. Journalize this transaction.

Compare the balances in all the accounts after making both sets of entries. Are the account balances the same or different?

LEARNING OBJECTIVE ❼

Prepare the shareholders' equity section of a balance sheet

S8-7 The financial statements of Eppley Employment Services Inc. reported the following accounts (adapted, with dollar amounts in thousands):

Common shares:			Total revenues	$1,390
600 shares issued	$600		Accounts payable..............................	420
Long-term debt	25		Retained earnings.............................	646
			Other current liabilities	2,566
			Total expenses	805

Prepare the shareholders' equity section of Eppley's balance sheet. Net income has already been closed to Retained Earnings.

LEARNING OBJECTIVES ❹❼

Account for and report shareholders' equity data

S8-8 Use the Eppley Employment Services data in exercise S8-7 to compute Eppley's:

a. Net income

b. Total liabilities

c. Total assets

LEARNING OBJECTIVES ❶❸

Explain how a repurchase of shares could help fight off a takeover of a corporation

S8-9 Karen Knox Exports, Inc., is a public company located in Clancy, New Mexico. The Knox family still owns a third of the outstanding voting shares. Knox is the only company with reliable sources for its imported gifts. The company does a brisk business with specialty stores such as Neiman Marcus. Knox's recent success has made the company a prime target for a takeover. An investment group is attempting to buy 52% of Knox's outstanding shares against the wishes of Knox's board of directors. Board members are convinced that the investors would sell the most desirable pieces of the business and leave little of value.

At the most recent board meeting, several suggestions were advanced to fight off the hostile takeover bid. The suggestion with the most promise is to repurchase a significant quantity of outstanding shares. Knox has the cash to carry out this plan.

Requirement

Suppose you are a significant shareholder of Karen Knox Exports, Inc. Write a memorandum to explain to the board how the repurchase of shares would make it difficult for the investor group to take over Knox. Include in your memo a discussion of the effect that repurchasing shares would have on shares outstanding and on the size of the corporation.

LEARNING OBJECTIVE ❹

Account for cash dividends

S8-10 Gleneagles Corporation earned net income of $70,000 during the year ended December 31, 2020. On December 15, Gleneagles had declared the annual cash dividend on its $0.50 preferred shares (10,000 shares issued for $100,000) and a $0.60 per share cash dividend on its common shares (25,000 shares issued for $50,000). Gleneagles then paid the dividends on January 4, 2021.

Journalize the following for Gleneagles Corporation:

a. Declaring the cash dividends on December 15, 2020
b. Paying the cash dividends on January 4, 2021

Did Retained Earnings increase or decrease during 2020? If so, by how much?

S8-11 Refer to the allocation of dividends for Pinecraft Industries Inc. on page 406. Answer these questions about Pinecraft's cash dividends:

1. How much in dividends must Pinecraft declare each year before the common shareholders receive any cash dividends for the year?
2. Suppose Pinecraft declares cash dividends of $300,000 for 2020. How much of the dividends go to preferred? How much go to common?
3. Are Pinecraft's preferred shares cumulative or non-cumulative? How can you tell?
4. Pinecraft passed the preferred dividend in 2018 and 2019. Then in 2020, Pinecraft declares cash dividends of $800,000. How much of the dividends go to preferred? How much go to common?

LEARNING OBJECTIVE ❹

Divide cash dividends between preferred and common shares

S8-12 On May 1, Fidelity Software Ltd. has 80,000 common shares issued and outstanding. Suppose Fidelity distributes a 10% stock dividend on May 11 when the market price (fair value) of its shares is $10.50 per share.

1. Journalize Fidelity's declaration of the shares dividend. An explanation is not required.
2. What was the overall effect of the stock dividend on Fidelity's total assets? What about on its total liabilities and its total shareholders' equity?

LEARNING OBJECTIVES ❹❼

Account for and report the impact of stock dividends on the financial statements

S8-13 Refer to the real-world format of shareholders' equity in Exhibit 8-6, page 414. That company has passed its preferred dividends for three years including the current year. Compute the book value of one of the company's common shares.

LEARNING OBJECTIVE ❺

Compute book value per share

S8-14 Use the statement of changes in shareholders' equity in Exhibit 8-4 (p. 413) to answer the following questions:

1. How much additional share capital did the issuance of shares raise during 2018?
2. What effect did the payment of dividends have on shareholders' equity during 2018?

LEARNING OBJECTIVE ❼

Use the statement of changes in shareholders' equity

S8-15 POLA Corporation's 2021 financial statements reported the following items, with 2020 figures given for comparison (in millions; ¥ is the symbol for the Japanese yen):

LEARNING OBJECTIVE ❻

Evaluate returns on assets and return on equity

	2021	2020
Balance sheet		
Total assets	¥10,632	¥9,523
Total liabilities	¥ 7,414	¥6,639
Total shareholders' equity (all common)	3,218	2,884
Total liabilities and shareholders' equity	¥10,632	¥9,523
Income statement		
Revenues and other income	¥ 7,632	
Operating expense	7,289	
Interest expense	31	
Other expense	194	
Net income	¥ 118	

Evaluate POLA's return on assets and return on equity for 2021. What additional information would be helpful in making this evaluation?

LEARNING OBJECTIVES ②④⑦

Account for issuance of shares and dividends; Prepare a statement of changes in shareholders' equity

S8-16 At December 31, 2019, Lake Air Mall Inc. reported shareholders' equity as follows:

Common shares, 500,000 shares authorized, 300,000 shares issued	$ 870,000
Retained earnings	680,000
	$1,550,000

During 2020, Lake Air Mall completed these transactions (listed in chronological order):

a. Declared and issued a 5% stock dividend on the outstanding shares. At the time, Lake Air Mall shares were quoted at a market price of $10 per share.

b. Issued 20,000 common shares at the price of $12 per share.

c. Net income for the year, $320,000.

d. Declared cash dividends of $100,000.

Requirement

Prepare Lake Air Mall's statement of changes in shareholders' equity for 2020, using the format of Exhibit 8-4 (p. 413) as a model.

EXERCISES

LEARNING OBJECTIVE ⑥

Evaluate returns on assets and equity

E8-17 Lofty Inns reported these figures for 2020 and 2019 (in millions):

	2020	2019
Balance sheet		
Total assets	$27,000	$18,400
Common share capital..	43	389
Retained earnings	11,525	16,523
Other shareholders' equity...	(3,008)	(9,300)
Income statement		
Net sales..	$30,500	$28,200
Operating income..	4,022	3,819
Net income..	2,100	1,546

Evaluate Lofty's return on assets and return on equity for 2020. What additional information would help you make this evaluation?

LEARNING OBJECTIVES ②⑦

Account for the issuance of shares and report shareholders' equity

E8-18 Burgers & Fries, Inc., is authorized to issue an unlimited number of common shares and 10,000 preferred shares. During its first year, the business completed the following share issuance transactions:

July	19	Issued 10,000 common shares for cash of $6.50 per share.
Oct.	3	Issued 500 $1.50 preferred shares for $50,000 cash.
	11	Received inventory valued at $11,000 and equipment with fair value of $8,500 for 3,300 common shares.

Requirements

1. Journalize the transactions. Explanations are not required.

2. Prepare the shareholders' equity section of Burgers & Fries's balance sheet. The ending balance of Retained Earnings is a deficit of $42,000.

E8-19 Citadel Sporting Goods is authorized to issue 5,000 preferred shares and 10,000 common shares. During a two-month period, Citadel completed these share-issuance transactions:

Sept.	23	Issued 1,000 common shares for cash of $16 per share.
Oct.	2	Issued 300 $4.50 preferred shares for $20,000 cash.
	12	Received inventory valued at $15,000 and equipment with fair value of $43,000 for 4,000 common shares.

Prepare the shareholders' equity section of the Citadel Sporting Goods balance sheet for the transactions given in this exercise. Retained Earnings has a balance of $49,000. Journal entries are not required.

LEARNING OBJECTIVES ❷❹

Assess the impact of share issuances on shareholders' equity; Prepare the shareholders' equity section of a balance sheet

E8-20 Trans World Publishing Inc. was recently organized. The company issued common shares to a lawyer who provided legal services of $15,000 to help organize the corporation. Trans World also issued common shares to an inventor in exchange for his patent with a fair value of $80,000. In addition, Trans World received cash both for the issuance of 5,000 of its preferred shares at $110 per share and for the issuance of 20,000 common shares at $20 per share. During the first year of operations, Trans World earned net income of $55,000 and declared a cash dividend of $20,000. Without making journal entries, determine the total share capital created by these transactions.

LEARNING OBJECTIVES ❷❹

Measure the share capital of a corporation

E8-21 Sagebrush Software Ltd. had the following selected account balances at December 31, 2020 (in thousands).

Inventory	$ 653	Class A common shares,		
Property, plant, and equipment, net	857	unlimited number authorized,		
Contributed surplus	901	3,600 shares issued	$	90
Class B common shares,		Deficit		2,400
unlimited number authorized,		Accounts receivable, net		600
5,000 shares issued	1,380	Notes payable		1,122

Prepare the shareholders' equity section of Sagebrush Software's balance sheet (in thousands). Explain what is meant by "Deficit."

LEARNING OBJECTIVES ❷❹

Prepare shareholders' equity section of a balance sheet

E8-22 Journalize the following transactions of Concilio Video Productions Inc.:

April	19	Issued 2,000 common shares at $10 per share.
July	22	Declared and paid a cash dividend of $0.50 per common share (21,000 common shares outstanding).
Nov.	11	Issued 800 common shares at $12 per share.

What was the overall effect of these transactions on Concilio's shareholders' equity?

LEARNING OBJECTIVES ❷❹❼

Record share transactions and measure their effects on shareholders' equity

E8-23 At December 31, 2019, Blumenthall Corporation reported the shareholders' equity accounts shown here (as adapted, with dollar amounts in millions):

Common shares	
1,800 million shares issued	$2,700
Retained earnings	1,200
Total shareholders' equity	$3,900

Blumenthall's 2020 transactions included the following:

a. Issuance of 6 million common shares for $12.50 per share
b. Declared cash dividends of $25 million.
c. Paid the dividends declared in (b).

Journalize Blumenthall's transactions. Explanations are not required.

LEARNING OBJECTIVES ❷❹

Record share issuance and dividend transactions

LEARNING OBJECTIVE ❼

Report shareholders' equity after a sequence of transactions

E8-24 Blumenthall Corporation earned $350 million in net income in 2020. Use this and the data in exercise E8-23 to prepare the shareholders' equity section of the company's balance sheet at December 31, 2020.

LEARNING OBJECTIVES
❷❸❹❼

Infer transactions based on changes in a company's shareholders' equity

E8-25 Optical Products Company reported the following shareholders' equity on its balance sheet:

Shareholders' Equity (dollars and shares in millions)	December 31,	
	2020	2019
Preferred shares; authorized 20 shares; Convertible Preferred shares; issued and outstanding: 2020 and 2019—0 and 2 shares, respectively..	$ 0	$ 12
Common shares; authorized unlimited shares; issued: 2020 and 2019—564 and 364 shares, respectively.................................	3,270	1,900
Retained earnings	6,280	5,006
Total shareholders' equity..	$ 9,550	$ 6,918
Total liabilities and shareholders' equity	$48,918	$45,549

Requirements

1. What could have caused Optical Products's preferred shares to decrease during 2020? Cite all the possible causes.
2. What could have caused Optical Products's common shares to increase during 2020? Identify all the possible causes.
3. How many shares of Optical Products were outstanding at December 31, 2020?
4. Optical Products's net income during 2020 was $1,410 million. How much were Optical Products's dividends during the year?

LEARNING OBJECTIVE ❹

Compute dividends on preferred and common shares

E8-26 Great Lakes Manufacturing Inc. reported the following:

Shareholders' Equity	
Preferred shares, cumulative, $0.10, 80,000 shares issued......................	$ 80,000
Common shares, 8,130,000 shares issued	813,000

Great Lakes Manufacturing has paid all preferred dividends through 2016.

Requirement

Compute the total amounts of dividends to both preferred and common shareholders for 2019 and 2020 if total dividends are $50,000 in 2019 and $100,000 in 2020.

LEARNING OBJECTIVES ❹❼

Record a stock dividend and report shareholders' equity

E8-27 The shareholders' equity for Best in Show Cinemas Ltd. (BSC) (adapted) at December 31, 2019, appears as follows:

Shareholders' Equity	
Common shares, 2,000,000 shares authorized, 500,000 shares issued	$1,012,000
Retained earnings	7,122,000
Total shareholders' equity..	$8,134,000

On April 15, 2020, the market price of BSC common shares was $17 per share. Assume BSC declared a 10% stock dividend on this date and distributed the stock dividend on April 30.

Requirements

1. Journalize the declaration and distribution of the stock dividend.
2. Prepare the shareholders' equity section of the balance sheet after the stock dividend.
3. Why is total shareholders' equity unchanged by the stock dividend?
4. Suppose BSC had a cash balance of $540,000 on April 16, 2020. What is the maximum amount of cash dividends BSC can declare?

E8-28 Identify the effects—both the direction and the dollar amount—of the following assumed transactions on the total shareholders' equity of a large corporation. Each transaction is independent.

a. Declaration of cash dividends of $80 million
b. Payment of the cash dividend declared
c. 10% stock dividend. Before the dividend, 69 million common shares were outstanding; the market price was $7.625 at the time of the dividend.
d. A 50% stock dividend. Before the dividend, 69 million common shares were outstanding; the market price was $13.75 at the time of the dividend.
e. Sale of 600 common shares for $5.00 per share
f. A 3-for-1 stock split. Prior to the split, 69 million common shares were outstanding.

LEARNING OBJECTIVES ❷❹
Measure the effects of share issuance, dividends, and share split transactions

E8-29 Solartech Inc. had the following shareholders' equity at January 31 (dollars in millions):

LEARNING OBJECTIVES ❹❼
Report shareholders' equity after a stock split

Common shares, 500 million shares authorized,	
440 million shares issued	$ 318
Contributed surplus	44
Retained earnings	2,393
Total shareholders' equity	$2,755

Assume that on March 7, Solartech split its common shares 2 for 1. Prepare the shareholders' equity section of the balance sheet immediately after the split.

E8-30 The balance sheet of Oriental Rug Company reported the following:

LEARNING OBJECTIVE ❺
Measure the book value per share of common shares

Cumulative preferred shares, $0.06,	
outstanding 6,000 shares	$10,000
Common shareholders' equity:	
8,000 shares issued and outstanding	87,200
Total shareholders' equity	$97,200

Requirements
1. Compute the book value per share for the common shares, assuming all preferred dividends are fully paid up (none in arrears).
2. Compute the book value per share of the common shares, assuming that three years' preferred dividends, including the current year, are in arrears.
3. Oriental Rug's common shares recently traded at a market price of $7.75 per share. Does this mean that Oriental Rug's shares are a good buy at $7.75?

E8-31 Lexington Inns reported these figures for 2020 and 2019 (in millions):

LEARNING OBJECTIVE ❻
Evaluate returns on assets and equity

	2020	2019
Balance sheet		
Total assets	$15,702	$13,728
Common share capital	80	680
Retained earnings	11,519	16,499
Other shareholders' equity	(3,005)	(9,095)
Income statement		
Net sales	$25,500	$27,500
Operating income	4,025	3,813
Net income	1,500	1,550

Requirement

Evaluate Lexington's return on assets and return on equity for 2020. What additional information would help you make this evaluation?

LEARNING OBJECTIVE ⑥

Evaluate returns on assets and equity

E8-32 Easton Company included the following items in its financial statements for 2020, the current year (amounts in millions):

Payment of long-term debt	$17,200	Dividends paid	$	195
Proceeds from issuance of		Net sales:		
common shares	8,405	Current year		65,000
Total liabilities:		Preceding year		62,000
Current year-end	32,309	Net income:		
Preceding year-end	38,033	Current year		2,200
Total shareholders' equity:		Preceding year		1,995
Current year-end	23,471	Operating income:		
Preceding year-end	14,037	Current year		9,125
Borrowings	6,585	Preceding year		4,002

Evaluate Easton's return on assets and return on equity for 2020.

LEARNING OBJECTIVES ❷❹

Reconstruct transactions from the financial statements

E8-33 A-1 Networking Solutions Inc. began operations on January 1, 2020. A-1's balance sheet at December 31, 2020, reported the following shareholders' equity:

Common shares	$253,500
Retained earnings	38,000
Total shareholders' equity	$291,500

During 2020, A-1:
a. Issued 50,000 common shares for $5 per share.
b. Issued additional common shares for $7 per share.
c. Earned Revenues of $171,000 and incurred Expenses totalling $115,000.
d. Declared and paid cash dividends.

Requirement

Record all of the journal entries that yield the reported shareholders' equity balances at December 31, 2020.

LEARNING OBJECTIVES ❷❹❼

Explain the changes in shareholders' equity

CT

E8-34 Startech Limited reported the following shareholders' equity data (all dollars in millions):

	December 31,	
	2020	**2019**
Preferred shares	$ 604	$ 740
Common shares	2,390	2,130
Retained earnings	20,661	19,108

Startech earned net income of $2,960 during 2020. Common shares were issued for $20.00 each. For each account except Retained Earnings, one transaction explains the change from the December 31, 2019, balance to the December 31, 2020, balance. Two transactions affected Retained Earnings. Give a full explanation, including the dollar amount, for the change in each account.

E8-35 Fun City Inc. ended 2019 with 8 million common shares issued and outstanding. The average issue price was $1.50. Beginning retained earnings totalled $40 million.

- In March 2020, Fun City issued 2 million common shares at a price of $2 per share.
- In May, the company declared and distributed a 10% stock dividend at a time when Fun City's common shares had a fair value of $3 per share.
- Then in October, Fun City's stock price dropped to $1 per share and the company executed a 1-for-2 stock split.
- For the year, Fun City earned net income of $26 million and declared cash dividends of $17 million.

Determine what Fun City should report for shareholders' equity at December 31, 2020. Journal entries are not required.

LEARNING OBJECTIVES ❷❹❼

Account for changes in shareholders' equity

PROBLEMS (GROUP A)

P8-36A The board of directors of Freestroke Swim Centres Inc. is meeting to address the concerns of shareholders. Shareholders have submitted the following questions for discussion at the board meeting. Answer each question.

1. Why did Freestroke organize as a corporation if a corporation must pay an additional layer of income tax?
2. How are preferred shares similar to common shares? How are preferred shares similar to debt?
3. Would Freestroke investors prefer to receive cash dividends or stock dividends? Explain your reasoning.

LEARNING OBJECTIVES ❶❷❹

Explain the advantages and disadvantages associated with being a corporation

P8-37A The articles of incorporation from the province of Ontario authorize Challenger Canoes Inc. to issue 10,000 shares of $6 preferred shares and 100,000 common shares. In its first month, Challenger completed the following transactions:

LEARNING OBJECTIVES ❷❹❼

Record corporate transactions and prepare the shareholders' equity section of the balance sheet

2020		
Oct.	6	Issued 300 common shares to the lawyer for assistance with chartering the corporation. The lawyer's fee was $1,500. Debit Organization Expense.
	9	Issued 9,000 common shares to Jerry Spence and 12,000 shares to Sheila Markle in return for cash equal to the shares, market price of $5 per share. Spence and Markle are executives of the company.
	10	Issued 400 preferred shares to acquire a patent with a fair value of $40,000.
	26	Issued 2,000 common shares for cash of $12,000.

Requirements
1. Record the transactions in the journal.
2. Prepare the shareholders' equity section of the Challenger balance sheet at October 31, 2020. The ending balance of Retained Earnings is $49,000.

P8-38A Samuells' Sportswear's articles of incorporation authorize the company to issue 5,000 $5 preferred shares and 500,000 common shares. Samuells' issued 1,000 preferred shares at $100 per share. It issued 100,000 common shares for $427,000. The company's Retained Earnings balance at the beginning of 2020 was $61,000. Net income for 2020 was $80,000, and the company declared a $5 cash dividend on preferred shares for 2020.

LEARNING OBJECTIVES ❷❹❼

Assess the impact of shareholders' equity transactions; Prepare the shareholders' equity section of the balance sheet

Requirement
Prepare the shareholders' equity section of Samuells' Sportswear Inc.'s balance sheet at December 31, 2020. Show the computation of all amounts. Journal entries are not required.

LEARNING OBJECTIVE ❸

Explain how to fight off a takeover of a corporation

P8-39A Calpak Winter Sports Ltd. is positioned ideally in the winter business. Located in Whistler, B.C., Calpak is the only company with a distribution network for its imported goods. Calpak's recent success has made the company a prime target for a takeover. Against the wishes of Calpak's board of directors, an investment group from Vancouver is attempting to buy 51% of Calpak's outstanding shares. Board members are convinced that the Vancouver investors would sell off the most desirable pieces of the business and leave little of value. At the most recent board meeting, several suggestions were advanced to fight off the hostile takeover bid.

Requirement

Suppose you are a significant shareholder of Calpak Winter Sports. Write a short memo to the board to propose an action that would make it difficult for the investor group to take over Calpak. Include in your memo a discussion of the effect your proposed action would have on the company's assets, liabilities, and total shareholders' equity.

LEARNING OBJECTIVES ❷❹❼

Measure the effects of share issuance and dividend transactions on shareholders' equity

P8-40A Wholegrain Health Foods Inc. is authorized to issue 5,000,000 common shares. In its initial public offering during 2016, Wholegrain issued 500,000 common shares for $7.00 per share. Over the next year, Wholegrain's share price increased and the company issued 400,000 more shares at an average price of $8.50.

During the five years from 2016 through 2020, Wholegrain earned net income of $920,000 and declared and paid cash dividends of $140,000. A 10% stock dividend was declared and distributed to the shareholders in 2020 on the shares outstanding. The market price was $8.00 per share when the stock dividend was distributed. At December 31, 2020, the company has total assets of $14,500,000 and total liabilities of $6,820,000.

Requirement

Show the computation of Wholegrain's total shareholders' equity at December 31, 2020. Present a detailed computation of each element of shareholders' equity.

LEARNING OBJECTIVES ❷❹

Analyze the shareholders' equity and dividends of a corporation

P8-41A Steeltrap Security Inc. included the following shareholders' equity on its balance sheet at December 31, 2020:

Shareholders' Equity	($ millions)
Preferred Shares:	
Authorized 20,000 shares in each class:	
$5.00 Cumulative Preferred Shares, 2,500 shares issued	$ 125,000
$2.50 Cumulative Preferred Shares, 4,000 shares issued	100,000
Common Shares:	
Authorized 80,000 shares, issued 48,000 shares..............................	384,000
Retained earnings...	529,000
	$1,138,000

Requirements

1. Identify the different issues of shares Steeltrap Security has outstanding.
2. What was the value at which the $2.50 Cumulative Preferred Shares were issued?
3. Suppose Steeltrap decided not to pay its preferred dividends for one year. Would the company have to pay these dividends in arrears before paying dividends to the common shareholders? Why?
4. What amount of preferred dividends must Steeltrap declare and pay each year to avoid having preferred dividends in arrears?

5. Assume preferred dividends are in arrears for 2019. Journalize the declaration of a $50,000 cash dividend for 2020. No explanation is needed.

P8-42A Exquisite Jewellery Limited reported the following summarized balance sheet at December 31, 2019:

LEARNING OBJECTIVES ❷❹❼

Account for share issuance and dividends; Report shareholders' equity on the balance sheet

Assets	
Current assets..	$33,400
Property and equipment, net	51,800
Total assets	$85,200
Liabilities and Equity	
Liabilities..	$37,800
Shareholders' equity:	
$0.50 cumulative preferred shares, 400 shares issued................	2,000
Common shares, 6,000 shares issued	23,400
Retained earnings	22,000
Total liabilities and equity..	$85,200

During 2020, Exquisite completed these transactions that affected shareholders' equity:

Feb.	13	Issued 5,000 common shares for $4 per share.
June	7	Declared the regular cash dividend on the preferred shares.
July	24	Paid the cash dividend.
Aug.	9	Declared a 10% stock dividend on the common shares. Market price of the common shares was $5 per share.
Aug.	23	Distributed the stock dividend.
Nov.	20	Issued 200 common shares for $8 per share.

Requirements
1. Journalize Exquisite's transactions. Explanations are not required.
2. Report Exquisite Jewellery Limited's shareholders' equity at December 31, 2020. Net income for 2020 was $27,000.

P8-43A Niles Corporation completed the following selected transactions during the current year:

LEARNING OBJECTIVES ❷❹

Measure the effects of dividend and share transactions on a company

Mar.	3	Declared and distributed a 10% stock dividend on the 90,000 common shares outstanding. The market price of the common shares was $25 per share.
May	16	Declared a cash dividend on the $5 preferred shares (5,000 shares outstanding).
	30	Paid the cash dividends.
Dec.	8	Issued 1,500 common shares for $27 per share.
	19	Issued 10,000 common shares for $28 per share.

Requirement
Analyze each transaction in terms of its effect (in dollars) on the accounting equation of Niles Corporation.

LEARNING OBJECTIVES ❷❹❻ **P8-44A** The following accounts and related balances of Bluebird Designers, Inc., as of December 31, 2020, are arranged in no particular order.

Prepare a corporation's balance sheet; assess returns on assets and equity

Cash...	$ 45,000	Interest expense............................	$ 16,300
Accounts receivable, net..............	25,000	Property, plant, and	
Contributed surplus.....................	53,800	equipment, net..........................	359,000
Accrued liabilities.........................	22,000	Common shares	
Long-term note payable................	97,000	500,000 shares authorized,	
Inventory......................................	89,000	110,000 shares issued	197,000
Dividends payable	9,000	Prepaid expenses.........................	14,000
Retained earnings.........................	?	Common shareholders'	
Accounts payable..........................	135,000	equity, December 31, 2019.......	220,000
Trademarks, net............................	9,000	Net income..................................	90,000
Goodwill	18,000	Total assets,	
		December 31, 2019..................	500,000
		Net sales.....................................	750,000

Requirements

1. Prepare Bluebird's classified balance sheet in the account format at December 31, 2020.
2. Compute Bluebird's return on total assets and return on equity for the year ended December 31, 2020.
3. Do these rates of return suggest strength or weakness? Give your reason.

LEARNING OBJECTIVE ❼

Use a statement of changes in shareholders' equity

CT

P8-45A Asian Food Specialties Inc. reported the following statement of changes in shareholders' equity for the year ended June 30, 2020. The company was founded in 2017 and issued 455 million common shares. There had been no further share transactions until 2020.

Asian Food Specialties Inc.
Statement of Changes in Shareholders' Equity
For the Year Ended June 30, 2020

(in millions)	Common Shares	Retained Earnings	Total
Balance, June 30, 2019			
455 shares outstanding.........................	$2,275	$1,702	$3,977
Net income...		540	540
Cash dividends...		(117)	(117)
Issuance of shares (5 shares).....................	50		50
Stock dividend (36 shares)	186	(186)	–
Issuance of shares (2 shares).....................	20		20
Balance, June 30, 2020.............................	$2,531	$1,939	$4,470

Requirements

Answer these questions about Asian Food Specialties's shareholders' equity transactions:

1. If the company's income tax rate is 33%, how much income before income tax did Asian Food Specialties report on the income statement?
2. What is the stated value of a common share at June 30, 2019?
3. At what price per share did Asian Food Specialties issue its common shares during the year?
4. Asian Food Specialties's statement of changes in shareholders' equity lists the share transactions in the order in which they occurred. What was the percentage of the stock dividend?

PROBLEMS (GROUP B)

P8-46B Reinhart Industries Limited is conducting a special meeting of its board of directors to address some concerns raised by the shareholders. Shareholders have submitted the following questions. Answer each question.

1. Why are common shares and retained earnings shown separately in the shareholders' equity section of the balance sheet?
2. Lou Harris, a Reinhart shareholder, proposes to give some land she owns to the company in exchange for company shares. How should Reinhart Industries Limited determine the number of shares to issue for the land?
3. Preferred shares generally are preferred with respect to dividends and in the event of a liquidation. Why would investors buy *common* shares when *preferred* shares are available?
4. One of the Reinhart shareholders owns 100 shares of Reinhart, and someone has offered to buy her shares for their book value. What formula should be used to compute the book value of her shares?

LEARNING OBJECTIVES ❶❷❹❺

Explain the features of elements of shareholders' equity; explain how to calculate book value per share

P8-47B The partners who own Bassett Furniture Co. wished to avoid the unlimited personal liability of the partnership form of business, so they incorporated as BFC Inc. The articles of incorporation from the province of Manitoba authorize the corporation to issue 10,000 $6 preferred shares and 250,000 common shares. In its first month, BFC completed the following transactions:

LEARNING OBJECTIVES ❷❹❼

Record corporate transactions and prepare the shareholders' equity section of the balance sheet

2020		
Jan.	3	Issued 1,000 common shares to the promoter for assistance with issuance of the common shares. The promotional fee was $10,000. Debit Organization Expense.
	6	Issued 5,000 common shares to Jo Bassett, and 3,800 shares to Mel Bassett in return for cash equal to the market price of $11 per share. (The Bassetts were partners in Bassett Furniture Co.)
	12	Issued 1,000 preferred shares to acquire a patent with a fair value of $110,000.
	22	Issued 1,500 common shares for $12 cash per share.

Requirements

1. Record the transactions in the journal.
2. Prepare the shareholders' equity section of the BFC Inc. balance sheet at January 31. The ending balance of Retained Earnings is $89,000.

P8-48B Northwest Territories Inc. has the following shareholders' equity information:

Northwest's incorporation authorizes the company to issue 10,000 $5 cumulative preferred shares and 400,000 common shares. The company issued 1,000 preferred shares at $100 per share. It issued 100,000 common shares for a total of $370,000. The company's Retained Earnings balance at the beginning of 2020 was $40,000, and net income for the year was $90,000. During 2020, Northwest declared the specified dividend on preferred shares and a $0.50 per-share dividend on common shares. Preferred dividends for 2019 were in arrears.

LEARNING OBJECTIVES ❷❹❼

Assess the impact of shareholders' equity transactions; Prepare the shareholders' equity section of the balance sheet

Requirement

Prepare the shareholders' equity section of Northwest Territories Inc.'s balance sheet at December 31, 2020. Show the computation of all amounts. Journal entries are not required.

P8-49B Gary Swan Imports Inc. is located in Stratford, Ontario. Swan is the only company with reliable sources for its imported gifts. The company does a brisk business with specialty stores such as Bowring. Swan's recent success has made the company a prime target for a takeover. An investment group from Toronto is attempting to buy 51% of Swan's

LEARNING OBJECTIVE ❸

Explain how to fight off a takeover of the corporation

outstanding shares against the wishes of Swan's board of directors. Board members are convinced that the Toronto investors would sell the most desirable pieces of the business and leave little of value.

At the most recent board meeting, several suggestions were made to fight off the hostile takeover bid. The suggestion with the most promise is to repurchase a huge quantity of common shares. Swan has the cash to carry out this plan.

Requirement

Suppose you are a significant shareholder of Gary Swan Imports Inc. Write a memorandum to explain to the board how the repurchase of common shares would make it difficult for the Toronto group to take over Swan. Include in your memo a discussion of the effect that repurchasing common shares would have on shares outstanding and on the size of the corporation.

LEARNING OBJECTIVES ❷❹❼

Measure the effects of share issuance, net income and dividend transactions on shareholders' equity

P8-50B Western Agriculture Industries Ltd. is authorized by the province of Saskatchewan to issue 500,000 common shares.

In its initial public offering during 2016, Western Agriculture issued 200,000 of its common shares for $12 per share. Over the next year, Western Agriculture's common share price increased, and the company issued 100,000 more shares at an average price of $14.50.

During the five years from 2016 to 2020, Western Agriculture earned net income of $395,000 and declared and paid cash dividends of $119,000. Stock dividends of $135,000 were declared and distributed to the shareholders in 2019 when the share market price was $10. At December 31, 2020, total assets of the company are $7,030,000, and liabilities add up to $2,904,000.

Requirement

Show the computation of Western Agriculture Industries Ltd.'s total shareholders' equity at December 31, 2020. Present a detailed computation of each element of shareholders' equity.

LEARNING OBJECTIVES ❷❹

Analyze the shareholders' equity and dividends of a corporation

P8-51B Teak Outdoor Furniture Limited included the following shareholders' equity on its year-end balance sheet at February 28, 2020:

Shareholders' Equity	
Preferred shares, $1.10 cumulative; authorized 100,000 shares in each class	
Class A—issued 75,000 shares	$ 1,500,000
Class B—issued 92,000 shares	1,840,000
Common shares; authorized 1,000,000 shares, issued 280,000 shares	6,940,000
Retained earnings	8,330,000
	$18,610,000

Requirements

1. Identify the different issues of shares that Teak Outdoor Furniture Limited has outstanding.
2. Give the summary entries to record issuance of all the Teak shares. Assume that all the shares were issued for cash. Explanations are not required.
3. Suppose Teak did not pay its preferred dividends for three years. Would the company have to pay those dividends in arrears before paying dividends to the common shareholders? Give your reason.

4. What amount of preferred dividends must Teak declare and pay each year to avoid having preferred dividends in arrears?

5. Assume that preferred dividends are in arrears for 2019. Record the declaration of an $800,000 dividend on February 28, 2020. An explanation is not required.

P8-52B Winnipeg Enterprises Inc. reported the following summarized balance sheet at December 31, 2019:

LEARNING OBJECTIVES ❷❹❼

Account for share issuance and dividends; report shareholders' equity on the balance sheet

Assets	
Current assets..	$18,200
Property and equipment, net	34,700
Total assets	$52,900
Liabilities and Equity	
Liabilities..	$ 6,200
Shareholders' equity:	
$5 cumulative preferred shares, 180 shares issued....................	1,800
Common shares, 2,400 shares issued	25,900
Retained earnings	19,000
Total liabilities and equity..	$52,900

During 2020, Winnipeg Enterprise completed these transactions that affected shareholders' equity:

Feb.	22	Issued 1,000 common shares for $16 per share.
May	4	Declared the regular cash dividend on the preferred shares.
	24	Paid the cash dividend.
July	9	Declared 10% stock dividend on the common shares. Market price of the common shares was $18 per share.
July	23	Distributed the stock dividend.
Dec.	8	Issued 600 common shares for $15 per share.

Requirements

1. Journalize Winnipeg Enterprise's transactions. Explanations are not required.
2. Report Winnipeg Enterprise's shareholders' equity at December 31, 2020. Net income for 2020 was $62,000.

P8-53B Cones Inc. of Baie-Comeau completed the following transactions during 2020, the company's tenth year of operations:

LEARNING OBJECTIVES ❷❹

Measure the effects of dividend and share transactions on a company

Feb.	2	Issued 10,000 common shares for cash of $250,000.
Apr.	22	Sold 700 common shares for $26 per share.
Aug.	6	Declared a cash dividend on the 10,000 $0.60 preferred shares.
Sept.	1	Paid the cash dividends.
Nov.	18	Declared and distributed a 10% stock dividend on the 30,000 common shares outstanding. The market value of the common shares was $25 per share.

Requirement

Analyze each transaction in terms of its effect (in dollars) on the accounting equation of Cones Inc.

LEARNING OBJECTIVES ❷❹❻

Prepare a corporation's balance sheet; assess returns on assets and equity

P8-54B The following accounts and related balances of Dove Designers, Inc., as of December 31, 2020, are arranged in no particular order.

Cash	$ 53,000	Interest expense	$ 16,200
Accounts receivable, net	27,000	Property, plant, and	
Contributed surplus	75,600	equipment, net	355,000
Accrued liabilities	25,000	Common shares,	
Long-term note payable	95,000	1,250,000 shares authorized,	
Inventory	98,000	118,000 shares issued	211,000
Dividends payable	6,000	Prepaid expenses	14,000
Retained earnings	?	Common shareholders'	
Accounts payable	130,000	equity, December 31, 2019	233,000
Trademark net	3,000	Net income	71,000
Goodwill	18,000	Total assets,	
		December 31, 2019	495,000
		Net sales	800,000

Requirements

1. Prepare Dove's classified balance sheet in the account format at December 31, 2020.
2. Compute Dove's return on total assets and return on equity for the year ended December 31, 2020.
3. Do these rates of return suggest strength or weakness? Give your reason.

LEARNING OBJECTIVE ❼

Use a statement of shareholders' equity

P8-55B Datacom Services Inc. reported the following statement of changes in shareholders' equity for the year ended October 31, 2020.

Datacom Services Inc.			
Statement of Changes in Shareholders' Equity			
For the Year Ended October 31, 2020			
(in millions)	**Common Shares**	**Retained Earnings**	**Total**
Balance, Oct. 31, 2019,			
675 shares outstanding	$2,025	$904	$2,929
Net income		360	360
Cash dividends		(194)	(194)
Issuance of shares (13 shares)	49		49
Stock dividend (55 shares)	166	(166)	–
Balance, Oct. 31, 2020	$2,240	$904	$3,144

Requirements

Answer these questions about Datacom Services's shareholders' equity transactions:

1. If Datacom's income tax rate is 33%, much income before income tax did Datacom report on the income statement?
2. What is the stated value of a common share at October 31, 2020?
3. At what price per share did Datacom Services issue its common shares during the year?
4. Datacom Services's statement lists the share transactions in the order they occurred. What was the percentage of the stock dividend?

APPLY YOUR KNOWLEDGE

DECISION CASES

This section's material reflects CPA enabling competencies, including:

I   Professional and ethical behaviour

II Problem-solving and decision-making

III Self-management

IV Teamwork and leadership

Based on Chartered Professional Accountant standards

Case 1. Nate Smith and Darla Jones have written a smartphone app. They need additional capital to market the app, so they plan to incorporate their business. Smith and Jones are considering alternative capital structures for the corporation. Their primary goal is to raise as much capital as possible without giving up control of the business. Smith and Jones plan to receive 50,000 common shares of the corporation in return for the net assets of their old business. After the old company's books are closed and the assets adjusted to current fair value, Smith's and Jones's capital balances will each be $25,000.

The company's incorporation plans include an authorization to issue 10,000 preferred shares and 500,000 common shares. Smith and Jones are uncertain about the most desirable features for the preferred shares. Prior to incorporating, Smith and Jones are discussing their plans with two investment groups. The corporation can obtain capital from outside investors under either of the following plans:

- **Plan 1.** Group 1 will invest $80,000 to acquire 800 $6, non-voting preferred shares.
- **Plan 2.** Group 2 will invest $55,000 to acquire 500 $5 preferred shares and $35,000 to acquire 35,000 common shares. Each preferred share receives 50 votes on matters that come before the shareholders.

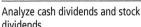

LEARNING OBJECTIVES ❶❷❹❼

Account for share transactions; Prepare the shareholders' equity section of the balance sheet; Evaluate alternative ways of raising capital

Requirements

Assume that the company is incorporated.

1. Journalize the issuance of common shares to Smith and Jones. Debit each person's capital account for its balance.
2. Journalize the issuance of shares to the outsiders under both plans.
3. Assume that net income for the first year is $120,000 and total dividends are $30,000. Prepare the shareholders' equity section of the corporation's balance sheet under both plans.
4. Recommend one of the plans to Smith and Jones. Give your reasons.

Case 2. Suppose the balance sheet of the financial statements you are analyzing had the following shareholders' equity amounts on December 31, 2020 (adapted, in millions):

LEARNING OBJECTIVE ❹

Analyze cash dividends and stock dividends

Common Shares; 1,135 shares issued	$ 278
Retained earnings	$9,457
Total shareholders' equity	$9,735

During 2020, the corporation paid a cash dividend of $0.715 per share. Assume that, after paying the cash dividends, the corporation distributed a 10% dividend. Assume further that the following year, the corporation declared and paid a cash dividend of $0.65 per share. Suppose you own 10,000 of this corporation's common shares acquired three years ago, prior to the 10% stock dividend. The market price of the shares was $61.02 per share before the stock dividend.

Requirements

1. How does the stock dividend affect your proportionate ownership in the corporation? Explain.
2. What amount of cash dividends did you receive last year? What amount of cash dividends will you receive after the above dividend action?
3. Assume that immediately after the stock dividend was declared and distributed, the market price of the corporation's shares decreased from $61.02 per share to $55.473 per share. Does this decrease represent a loss to you? Explain.

4. Suppose the corporation announces at the time of the stock dividend that the company will continue to pay the annual $0.715 cash dividend per share, even after distributing the stock dividend. Would you expect the market price of the common shares to decrease to $55.473 per share as in Requirement 3? Explain.

ETHICAL DECISIONS

Ethical Decisions 1. *Note:* This case is based on a real situation.

George Campbell paid $50,000 for a franchise that entitled him to market Success Associates software programs in the countries of the European Union. Campbell intended to sell individual franchises for the major language groups of Western Europe: German, French, English, Spanish, and Italian. Naturally, investors considering buying a franchise from Campbell asked to see the financial statements of his business.

Believing the value of the franchise to be greater than $50,000, Campbell sought to capitalize his own franchise at $500,000. The law firm of McDonald & LaDue helped Campbell form a corporation chartered to issue 500,000 common shares. Attorneys suggested the following chain of transactions:

a. A third party borrows $500,000 and purchases the franchise from Campbell.
b. Campbell pays the corporation $500,000 to acquire all its shares.
c. The corporation buys the franchise from the third party, who repays the loan.

In the final analysis, the third party is debt-free and out of the picture. Campbell owns all the corporation's shares, and the corporation owns the franchise. The corporation's balance sheet lists a franchise acquired at a cost of $500,000. This balance sheet is Campbell's most valuable marketing tool.

Requirements

1. What is unethical about this situation?
2. Who can be harmed in this situation? How can they be harmed? What role does accounting play here?

Ethical Decision 2. St. Genevieve Petroleum Corp. is a public, independent oil producer. St. Genevieve's year-end is June 30. In February 2020, company geologists discovered a pool of oil that tripled the company's proven reserves. The March 31, 2020, interim financial statements did not disclose the new pool of oil. During February and March 2020, St. Genevieve's managers quietly purchased most of its shares. The June 30, 2020, annual financial statements did disclose the new pool of oil, and the company's share price increased from $6 to $48.

Requirements

1. Did St. Genevieve's managers behave ethically? Explain your answer.
2. Identify the fundamental qualitative characteristic of financial statements relevant to this situation (see the Conceptual Framework in Chapter 1).
3. Who was helped and who was harmed by management's actions?

Ethical Decision 3. For each of the situations listed, identify which of which of the principles (professional behaviour, integrity, due care, objectivity, professional competence, confidentiality) from the CPA Code of Professional Conduct is violated. Assume all persons listed in the situations are CPAs. (Note: Refer to the CPA Code of Professional Conduct contained on pages 27–28 in Chapter 1 for descriptions of the principles.)

a. Shontelle's company, Hollow Technologies, recently decided to repurchase shares from its shareholders. Shontelle is in charge of booking the entries for these repurchases; however, she does not know how to record share repurchase transactions, so she just deducts the amount repurchased from Common Share Capital.

b. Haylee is a senior auditor for Leonarda & Calloway and has worked on its client, Blue Iron Inc., for the past few years. A few months ago, Blue Iron offered Haylee a position in its internal audit department. Haylee accepted the position and works very closely with the external auditors. In fact, she often prepares the work papers for the external auditor, since she knows the systems better than the new auditors.

c. Andrew is a senior manager at Ford & Hill, a regional public accounting firm. Ford & Hill recently obtained a new client, Vista, Inc. Andrew's sister is the CEO of Vista, a fact that he did not disclose to the board.

d. Connor is the CFO for Tree Street Coffee Corporation and is going to take the company public within the next six months. In an effort to make the stock look more appealing and therefore sell at a higher price, Connor overrides the system controls and records fictitious sales entries.

FOCUS ON FINANCIAL STATEMENT ANALYSIS

Dollarama Inc.'s financial statements appear in Appendix A at the end of this book. Use information in these financial statements and the notes to the financial statements to answer the following (Note: Dollarama's total assets were $1,813.9 and its common shareholders' equity was $466.9 at the end of 2016.):

LEARNING OBJECTIVES ②④⑥⑦

Analyze common shares and retained earnings; Evaluate return on assets and return on equity

Task 1 Describe the classes of shares that Dollarama has authorized? How many of each class are issued and outstanding at the end of 2018?

Task 2 Did Dollarama issue any new shares during 2018? If so, how many did it issue and what was the average issue price?

MyLab Accounting

Task 3 What was the total dollar value of dividends that Dollarama declared in 2018? How much cash did it use to pay dividends in 2018? Why are these figures different?

Task 4 Compute Dollarama's return on assets and return on equity for 2018 and 2017. Based on this information, what is your assessment of Dollarama's performance in 2018 compared to 2017?

CHECK YOUR WORK

STOP + THINK ANSWERS

STOP + THINK (8-1)

Despite being unable to vote, the Class A shareholders of Canadian Tire still have the other three main rights of shareholders: the right to sell the shares (hopefully for a gain), the right to receive dividends (which they currently receive each quarter), and the right to receive a residual interest in the company if it is ever liquidated. These benefits are more than enough to entice investors in the absence of the right to vote.

STOP + THINK (8-2)

1. It would have to issue at least 6,308,950 shares to eliminate the deficit ($252,358,000 / $40).

2. Average issue price per common share = $3.80 ($415,787,000 of common share capital/109,325,859 shares outstanding).

STOP + THINK (8-3)

Dollarama press releases during 2017–2019 indicate that it regularly repurchased common shares to "increase shareholder value." This is consistent with reason #2 on page 403.

STOP + THINK (8-4)

1. There will be no decrease in shareholders' equity for either company because stock dividends have no net impact on this total. Share capital increases and retained earnings decrease by the same amount, regardless of the size of the stock dividend.

2. Company A's market value per share after stock dividend = $9.09 ($2,000,000 total market value/220,000 shares issued and outstanding).

Company B's market value per share after stock dividend = $8.33 ($2,000,000 total market value/240,000 shares issued and outstanding).

Company B will have a lower market value per share after the stock dividends are distributed.

STOP + THINK (8-5)

1. $7,250,000 ($500,000 from preferred shareholders + $6,750,000 from common shareholders)

2. $4,900,000 (Retained Earnings of $3,250,000 + Dividends Paid of $1,650,000)

3. Unknown (Cash balance not provided; *Retained Earnings does not equal cash*)

4. $10,000,000 or $20/share (Total shareholders' equity of $10,500,000 − Preferred shareholders' equity of $500,000 = Common shareholders' equity of $10,000,000/500,000 shares = $20/share)

5. $260,000 ($310,000 total − $50,000 to preferred shareholders)

6. 750,000 (500,000 common shares outstanding divided by 2, then multiplied by 3). The split would have no effect on shareholders' equity, as only the number of shares issued and outstanding changes.

STOP + THINK (8-6)

Given that the two companies are comparable in terms of their industry, dividend history, and share price increases, it would make sense to focus on their relative ROA and ROE ratios. Because Company A has the healthier ROA and ROE compared to Company B (both ratios are higher than Company B's and both are higher than their benchmarks of 10% and 15%, respectively), it would make sense to invest in Company A.

STOP + THINK (8-7)

On Line 7 of the statement in Exhibit 8-4 we see that the company deducted a total of $22.3 million from its share capital in connection with the repurchase of the common shares in 2018, so this was the total original cost the repurchased shares.

QUICK QUIZ ANSWERS

1. c
2. c
3. d
4. c
5. b
6. d
7. a ($593,000 + $89,000 = $682,000)
8. c ($682,000 + $71,800 = $753,800)
9. b {($119,600 − $8,900) / [($681,400 + $664,800*) / 2] = .164}
    *($593,000 + $71,800 = $664,800)

10. a (593,000 / $11.86 = 50,000)
11. b (providing that sufficient cash was available)
12. d
13. b
14. a
15. c (20,000 × $8.00 = $160,000)
16. a ($350,000 − $160,000) / 20,000 = $9.50
17. a
18. d
19. b
20. a [($44,000 − $4,000) / $384,000 = .104]

COMPREHENSIVE CASE

CHAPTERS 7–8

This comprehensive case requires you to apply concepts learned throughout Chapters 7 and 8. You may find it helpful to review these chapters before responding to the case requirements.

In this case, we return to the Pierogi Factory Ltd., the company from the comprehensive case for Chapters 1–3. Agata Polanska's small chain of restaurants in Kitchener, Ontario has expanded to include eight restaurants and a central kitchen facility. Pierogi Factory Ltd.'s most recent fiscal year ended on December 31, 2022.

Requirements

1. Pierogi Factory's general ledger contains the following liabilities accounts:

> Accounts payable
> CPP and EI payable
> Current portion of notes payable
> Employee income taxes payable
> Gift cards
> HST payable (net of ITC)
> Income taxes payable
> Interest payable on notes
> Line of credit
> Notes payable (due dates range from March 31, 2024 to December 31, 2024)
> Salaries and wages payable

Describe each of the company's liabilities, state how it arose, and specify whether it's a current or long-term liability.

2. Listed below is information regarding some of Pierogi Factory's liabilities at December 31, 2022.

a. The company has a $50,000 operating line of credit from its bank to assist with covering short-term needs for additional operating funds. As at the end of 2022, the company had drawn $20,000 of this credit.

b. Pierogi Factory's employees are paid on the 1st and 15th of each month for the work they performed in the preceding half-month. At December 31, 2022, employees were owed gross pay of $62,500, but in total, 20% of this gross must be withheld and remitted for income taxes. Each must also make Canada Pension Plan contributions of 5.7% of their gross pay and pay Employment Insurance premiums of 1.62% of their gross pay. Employers are required to match their employees' CPP contributions and pay EI premiums at 1.4 times the employees' rate.

c. The company remits HST on a quarterly basis. Since the last reporting period, GST of $146,250 has been collected and ITCs of $78,100 have been earned.

d. As at December 31, 2021, Pierogi Factory had $12,619 in outstanding, unredeemed gift cards. During 2022, it sold $69,000 in gift cards and customers redeemed $55,831 in gift cards.

e. On March 31, 2022, the company issued a two-year, 5% note payable in the amount of $250,000 to finance one of its new restaurants. Interest is payable semi-annually and equal annual principal payments are due each March 31 until the note is repaid.

f. The company pays corporate income tax at the rate of 11.5% of taxable income, which the company's tax advisor estimates will be about $400,000 in 2022.

For each of the above items, determine what liabilities must be reported on Pierogi Factory's December 31, 2022 balance sheet.

3. Agata has never paid herself much of a salary because she wanted to retain as much money in the company as possible to fund its operations and growth. The company has been doing very well lately, however, so she feels it's time to reward herself by taking $40,000 out of the company to pay for some renovations to her house. Pierogi Factory's tax advisor has suggested to Agata that she take this $40,000 out in the form of dividends rather than salary because dividends are taxed at a lower rate than the marginal rate she would pay on the additional salary, and her personal savings would exceed the additional tax the company would have to pay as a result of paying her a dividend rather than additional salary. Agata likes the idea of paying less tax, but she wants to understand the financial reporting implications of paying dividends versus paying additional salary. Given the company's corporate income tax rate of 11.5%, explain to Agata how the company's financial statements would be affected by a $40,000 dividend compared to how they would be affected by an additional $40,000 in salary (Agata has already made the maximum annual CPP contributions and paid the maximum EI premiums, so no CPP or EI would be due on the additional salary).

4. It is now June 2023 and the continuing popularity of Agata's Polish pierogi has her thinking about significantly increasing the number of restaurants and expanding the main kitchen to accommodate the higher demand. Her advisor has suggested she consider financing this major expansion by issuing common shares to a small number of local investors rather than borrowing funds to finance it, as she has always done in the past. She has never considered this option and would like to know what factors to consider before deciding how to finance the expansion. Explain to Agata the advantages and disadvantages of financing with debt versus equity.

5. To further assist Agata with her decision about using debt or equity to finance the expansion, explain what impacts each of the following options would have on the December 31, 2023 income statement and balance sheet of Pierogi Factory.

    Debt option: The company has been offered a five-year term loan from its bank, which bears interest at 6% per annum. The $500,000 loan would be issued on July 1 and would be repayable in five equal annual instalments, with interest payable quarterly.

    Equity option: Five local investors would each invest $100,000 in the company, with each one receiving 100 common shares in return.

The Statement of Cash Flows

9

SPOTLIGHT

Dollarama Inc.'s statement of cash flows on the next page shows how much cash the company generated from and used in its operating, investing, and financing activities during 2018. The company generated about $637 million in cash from its operating activities, which include such things as the purchase and sale of store merchandise, the payment of salaries and wages, and the rental of store premises. During 2018, Dollarama also used about $131 million in cash to perform investing activities, such as purchasing property and equipment. Dollarama's financing activities, including the issuance of long-term debt and repurchase of shares, resulted in net cash outflows of over $513 million. Combined, these cash flow activities yielded a $7.2 million decrease in cash during 2018, leaving Dollarama with $54.8 million in cash at the end of the year.

SPOTLIGHT

Studio Specialty/Shutterstock

LEARNING OBJECTIVES

1. **Explain** the uses of the statement of cash flows
2. **Explain** and **classify** cash flows from operating, investing, and financing activities
3. **Prepare** a statement of cash flows using the indirect method of determining cash flows from operating activities
A-1 **Prepare** a statement of cash flows using the direct method of determining cash flows from operating activities

CPA COMPETENCIES

Competencies addressed in this chapter:

1.2.2 Evaluates treatment for routine transactions

1.3.1 Prepares financial statements

Based on Chartered Professional Accountant standards

	A	B	C
1	**Dollarama Inc.** Consolidated Statements of Cash Flows (Adapted) For the Years Ended January 28, 2018 and January 29, 2017		
2	*(in millions of dollars)*		
3		**2018**	**2017**
4	**Operating activities**		
5	Net earnings	$ 519.4	$ 445.6
6	Adjustments to reconcile net earnings to net cash generated from operating activities:		
7	Depreciation and amortization	67.9	55.0
8	Financing costs on long-term debt	1.5	0.3
9	Loss on disposal of assets	0.2	0.0
10	Other reconciling items	22.4	7.9
11		611.4	508.8
12	Changes in non-cash working capital components	25.9	(3.6)
13	**Net cash generated from operating activities**	637.3	505.2
14			
15	**Investing activities**		
16	Additions to property, plant and equipment	(112.8)	(153.7)
17	Additions to intangible assets	(19.1)	(12.6)
18	Proceeds from disposal of property, plant and equipment	0.7	0.5
19	**Net cash used in investing activities**	(131.2)	(165.8)
20			
21	**Financing activities**		
22	Proceeds from long-term debt issued	550.0	525.0
23	Repayments of other credit facilities	(214.0)	(120.0)
24	Issuance of common shares	14.6	4.9
25	Dividends paid	(48.9)	(46.9)
26	Repurchase of common shares	(812.3)	(696.7)
27	Other financing activities	(2.7)	(2.9)
28	**Net cash used in financing activities**	(513.3)	(336.6)
29			
30	**Increase (decrease) in cash**	(7.2)	2.8
31	**Cash – beginning of year**	62.0	59.2
32	**Cash – end of year**	$ 54.8	$ 62.0
33			

Source: Data's from Dollarama Inc.

In Chapter 1 we introduced you to the statement of cash flows, and in later chapters we briefly discussed cash flows from a variety of operating, investing, and financing activities, such as accounts receivable, long-lived assets, and long-term debt. In this chapter, we provide you with more detailed guidance on how to prepare and use the statement of cash flows. We begin by discussing how managers, investors, and creditors use the statement of cash flows to make business decisions. Following this introduction, we provide additional guidance on how to classify many of the common operating, investing, and financing activities performed by a company. We end the chapter by offering detailed instruction on how to prepare the statement of cash flows using *the indirect method* of determining cash flows from operating activities, which is the method used by the vast majority of companies to prepare their statements of cash flows. The chapter's Appendix provides details on how to prepare the statement of cash flows using *the direct method* of determining cash flows from operating activities, which is actually the method preferred (but not required) by IFRS and ASPE.

This method is rarely used in practice, however, because the indirect method gained prominence in the past and now continues to be used for reasons of comparability and user familiarity. After working through this chapter, you will be able to prepare, analyze, and interpret a company's statement of cash flows.

EXPLAIN THE USES OF THE STATEMENT OF CASH FLOWS

OBJECTIVE

❶ **Explain** the uses of the statement of cash flows

A company's balance sheet reports its cash position at a specific date, and its balance sheets from consecutive financial periods show whether its cash balance increased or decreased over the interim period. But the balance sheet doesn't tell us *what caused the cash balance to change*. The income statement reports a company's revenues, expenses, and net income, but because it is prepared on an accrual basis, it provides limited information about *how cash flows were affected by the company's business activities* during the reporting period. To gain insight into how a company's cash flows affected its cash position during a reporting period, we need another financial statement: the statement of cash flows.

IFRS and ASPE, which provide similar guidance on the statement of cash flows, explain that the information disclosed by a company about its cash flows provides decision-relevant information to users of the company's financial statements. This statement includes details about a company's cash receipts and cash disbursements from operating, investing, and financing activities and permits a user to determine exactly what caused the company's cash balance to increase or decrease during the period. Because the statement describes cash flow activities *during a particular fiscal period* and not at a specific point in time, it is dated the same way as the income statement and the statement of changes in shareholders' equity. The Dollarama statement of cash flows at the beginning of the chapter, for example, is dated "For the year ended January 28, 2018." Exhibit 9-1 illustrates the relative timing of the four basic financial statements.

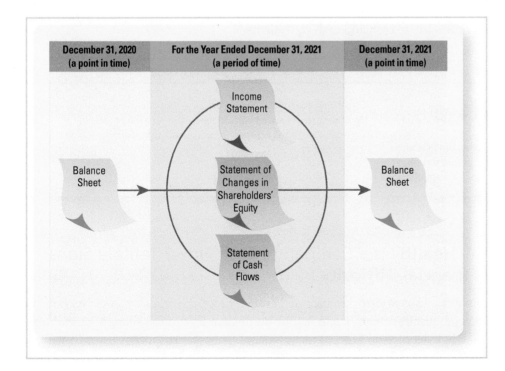

EXHIBIT 9-1
Timing of the Financial Statements

The statement of cash flows helps managers, investors, and creditors perform the following functions:

1. **Predict future cash flows.**   Past cash receipts and payments are reasonably good predictors of future cash flows.

2. **Evaluate management decisions.**   Businesses that make wise investment decisions prosper, and those that make unwise decisions suffer losses. The statement of cash flows reports how managers got cash and how they used cash to run the business.

3. **Determine ability to pay dividends and interest.**   Shareholders want dividends on their investments. Creditors collect interest and principal on their loans. The statement of cash flows reports on the ability to make these payments.

4. **Assess the relationship of net income to cash flows.**   Usually, cash and net income move together. High levels of income tend to lead to increases in cash, and low levels of income tend to lead to decreases in cash. A company's cash flow can, however, suffer even when net income is high, or improve when it suffers a net loss.

5. **Compare the operating performance of different companies.**   Because it eliminates the effects of using different accounting treatments for the same types of transactions and events, the statement of cash flows allows users to better compare the operating performance of multiple companies.

On a statement of cash flows, *cash* means more than just cash in the bank. It includes **cash equivalents**, which are short-term investments that are readily convertible to known amounts of cash, and which are very unlikely to change in value. Generally, only investments with maturities of three months or less meet these criteria. Examples include money-market investment accounts and three-month government Treasury bills. *Bank overdraft* balances should also be netted against the cash and cash equivalents total, as you can see on the last line of the Dollarama statement of cash flows presented at the beginning of this chapter. Throughout this chapter, the term *cash* refers to cash and cash equivalents.

STOP + THINK (9-1)

Examine the "Operating Activities" section of Dollarama's Statement of Cash Flows on page 444. In that section, you can see various types of depreciation and amortization being added back to net earnings. Why are these two types of expenses added back to net earnings in the process of calculating the company's cash flows from operating activities?

How Healthy Is a Company's Cash Flow? Telltale Signs of Financial Difficulty

Companies want to earn net income because profit measures success. Without net income, a business sinks. There will be no dividends, and the share price will likely suffer. High net income helps attract investors, but companies can't pay bills with net income—that requires cash.

A company needs both net income and strong cash flow. Income and cash flow usually move together because net income generates cash. Sometimes, however, net income and cash flow follow different patterns. To illustrate, consider Fastech Company Ltd.:

	A	B	C	D	E	F	G
1	**Fastech Company Ltd.** Income Statement For the Year Ended December 31, 2020		**Fastech Company Ltd.** Balance Sheet As at December 31, 2020				
2	Sales revenue	$ 100,000	Cash	$ 3,000	Total current liabilities	$ 50,000	
3	Cost of goods sold	30,000	Receivables	37,000	Long-term liabilities	20,000	
4	Operating expenses	10,000	Inventory	40,000			
5			PPE, net	60,000	Shareholders' equity	70,000	
6	Net income	$ 60,000	Total assets	$ 140,000	Total liabilities and equity	$ 140,000	
7							

What can we glean from Fastech's income statement and balance sheet?

- Fastech is profitable. Net income is 60% of revenue. Fastech's profitability looks outstanding.
- The current ratio is 1.6, and the debt ratio is only 50%. These measures suggest little trouble in paying bills.
- But Fastech is on the verge of bankruptcy. Can you spot the problems? Three trouble spots leap out to a financial analyst:
  1. The cash balance is very low. Three thousand dollars isn't enough cash to pay the bills of a company with sales of $100,000.
  2. Fastech isn't selling inventory fast enough. Fastech turned over its inventory only 0.75 times during the year. As we saw in Chapter 5, many companies have inventory turnover rates of 3 to 8 times a year. A turnover ratio of 0.75 times means it takes a very long time to sell inventory, and that delays cash collections.
  3. Fastech's days' sales in receivables ratio is 135 days. Very few companies can wait that long to collect from customers. With standard credit terms of net 30 days, Fastech should collect cash within around 45 days. Fastech cannot survive with a collection period of 135 days.

The take-away lesson from this discussion is this: A company needs both net income and strong cash flow to succeed in business.

Let's now examine the three types of cash flow activities.

EXPLAIN AND CLASSIFY CASH FLOWS FROM OPERATING, INVESTING, AND FINANCING ACTIVITIES

OBJECTIVE

❷ **Explain** and **classify** cash flows from operating, investing, and financing activities

A business engages in three types of business activities:

- Operating activities
- Investing activities
- Financing activities

Operating activities comprise the main revenue-producing activities of a company and generally result from the transactions and other events that determine net income. Other activities that are not *investing* or *financing* activities are also classified as operating activities.[1] Common operating activities include cash receipts from a company's sales of its primary goods and services and cash payments to suppliers and employees for the goods and services they provide to generate these sales. When Dollarama pays suppliers for the goods it sells to its customers, for example, the payment is an operating activity that results in a cash outflow. Similarly, when a customer pays Dollarama for something they have purchased, a cash inflow from operating activities results.

In Dollarama's statement of cash flows on page 444, we see that the company generated $637 million in cash flows from operating activities in 2018, and earned $519 million in net earnings on an accrual basis. The fact that Dollarama generated more cash from operating activities than it earned in net earnings is a sign of excellent financial health because it indicates Dollarama has generated more than enough cash from its operating activities to fund capital expenditures, pay dividends, and finance its day-to-day operations without the aid of outside financing. A company that does not regularly generate sufficient cash flows from operating activities will eventually suffer liquidity and solvency problems.

Investing activities include the purchase and sale of long-term assets and other investments that do not qualify as cash equivalents. They generally consist of transactions that result in cash inflows or outflows related to resources used for generating future income and cash flows. IFRS and ASPE state that only expenditures related to assets that are recognized on the balance sheet qualify as investing activities. Cash payments to acquire tangible and intangible long-lived assets, and the cash received on the sale of these assets, are common investing activities. Investing activities also include cash flows from the purchase and sale of equity and debt instruments of other companies, and those related to both short-term and long-term advances and loans made to other entities. Any short-term investments that qualify as cash equivalents are excluded from investing activities.

In 2018, Dollarama spent over $130 million on tangible and intangible assets. It also received $700,000 in cash proceeds from the sale of property, plant, and equipment. Like its operating activities, Dollarama's 2018 investing activities indicate excellent future prospects for the company because they show that the company invested $131 million in net new long-term assets that will help it earn additional revenues in coming years.

Financing activities result in changes in the size and composition of a company's contributed equity and borrowings. Common financing activities include the issuance and repurchase of the company's shares; the payment of cash dividends; the cash proceeds from loans, bonds, and notes; and the repayment of amounts borrowed. With the exception of bank overdrafts, which are included in cash and cash equivalents, both short-term and long-term borrowings are included in financing activities.

---

[1] A simplifying assumption is made throughout Chapter 9 that all current asset accounts and all current liability accounts and their related cash flows should be classified as operating activities on the statement of cash flows.

There are, in fact, a number of current asset and current liability accounts that reflect investing and financing activities, respectively. For example, current assets may include short-term investments and short-term notes receivable. The cash flows from these accounts should be classified as investing activities on the statement of cash flows. Current liabilities may include short-term loans payable, and their related cash flows should be classified as financing activities on the statement of cash flows.

The Financing Activities section of Dollarama's 2018 statement of cash flows contains more good news for the company's investors: it was able to pay them $141 million in cash dividends without having to issue any new shares (there are no proceeds from the issuance of share capital) or take on sizable amounts of new debt (net cash inflows from short-term borrowings, loans, and long-term debt were only $160 million).

In sum, Dollarama's 2018 statement of cash flows portrays a company with very high cash flows from operating activities, which it used to invest in assets that will hopefully produce more income and cash in the future, while also having enough cash left over to pay dividends to shareholders and repurchase a sizable amount of shares. Overall, Dollarama ended 2018 with roughly the same amount of cash as it had at the end of 2017.

Classifying Interest and Dividends

IFRS and ASPE offer different guidance on classifying cash flows related to interest and dividends. IFRS note that there is no consensus on the classification of interest paid or interest and dividends received. Under IFRS, interest paid and interest and dividends received may be classified as operating cash flows because they enter into the determination of net income. Alternatively, interest paid may be classified as a financing cash flow because it is a cost of obtaining financial resources, while interest and dividends received may be classified as investing cash flows because they represent returns on investments. Under IFRS, a company is free to choose either classification scheme but must use it consistently from then onward. ASPE require that all interest paid and all interest and dividends received and included in the determination of net income be classified as operating activities.

IFRS also offers a choice when classifying dividends paid: they may either be classified as a financing cash flow because they are a cost of obtaining financial resources, or they may be classified as cash flows from operating activities so that users may determine the company's ability to pay dividends out of operating cash flows. ASPE, however, require that any dividends paid and charged against retained earnings be classified as a financing activity.

For the sake of simplicity and consistency, this text classifies all interest paid and interest and dividends received as operating activities, while classifying dividends paid as a financing activity. All questions and problems in this chapter should be answered using this convention.

MyLab Accounting

STOP + THINK (9-2)

Classify each of the following as an operating activity, an investing activity, or a financing activity on the statement of cash flows prepared by the *indirect* method.

a. Issuance of shares

b. Borrowing

c. Sales revenue

d. Payment of dividends

e. Purchase of land

f. Repurchase of shares

g. Paying bonds payable

h. Interest expense

i. Sale of equipment

j. Cost of goods sold

k. Purchase of another company

l. Making a loan

Two Methods of Determining Cash Flows from Operating Activities

There are two methods of determining cash flows from operating activities on the statement of cash flows:

- **Indirect method**, in which net income is adjusted for non-cash transactions, for any deferrals or accruals of past or future operating cash receipts or payments, and for items of income or expense associated with investing or financing cash flows. (pp. 451 to 458)
- **Direct method**, which reports all cash receipts and cash payments from operating activities. (pp. 490 to 497)

The two methods use different computations, but they produce the same figure for cash from *operating activities*. IFRS and ASPE suggest that the direct method provides the most useful information to users, but this method is rarely used in practice because of the historical prominence of the indirect method. We present the indirect method below and detail the direct method in the Appendix to this chapter. The two methods do not affect *investing* or *financing* activities.

OBJECTIVE

❸ **Prepare** a statement of cash flows using the indirect method of determining cash flows from operating activities

PREPARE A STATEMENT OF CASH FLOWS USING THE INDIRECT METHOD OF DETERMINING CASH FLOWS FROM OPERATING ACTIVITIES

To illustrate the statement of cash flows we use Bradshaw Corporation, a dealer in playground equipment. Proceed as shown in the following steps to prepare the statement of cash flows by the indirect method.

Step 1 Lay out the template as shown in Exhibit 9-2. The exhibit is comprehensive. The diagram in Exhibit 9-3 (p. 452) gives a visual picture of the statement.

Step 2 Use the comparative balance sheet to determine the increase or decrease in cash during the period. The change in cash is the "check figure" for the statement of cash flows. Exhibit 9-4 (p. 453) gives Bradshaw Corporation's comparative balance sheet with cash highlighted. Bradshaw's cash decreased by $20,000 during 2020. *Why* did cash decrease? The statement of cash flows provides the answer.

Step 3 From the income statement, take net income, depreciation and amortization expense, and any gains or losses on the sale of long-term assets. Print these items on the statement of cash flows. Exhibit 9-5 (p. 453) gives Bradshaw Corporation's income statement, with relevant items highlighted.

Step 4 Use the income statement and the balance sheet data to prepare the statement of cash flows. The statement of cash flows is complete only after you have explained the year-to-year changes in all the balance sheet accounts.

EXHIBIT 9-2
Template of the Statement of Cash Flows: Indirect Method

	A	B
1	**Bradshaw Corporation** Statement of Cash Flows For the Year Ended December 31, 2020	
2	**Cash flows from operating activities:**	
3	Net income	
4	Adjustments to reconcile net income to net cash provided by (used for) operating activities:	
5	+ Depreciation and amortization expense	
6	+ Loss on sale of investing assets	
7	– Gain on sale of investing assets	
8	– Increases in operating current assets other than cash	
9	+ Decreases in operating current assets other than cash	
10	+ Increases in operating current liabilities	
11	– Decreases in operating current liabilities	
12	Net cash provided by (used for) operating activities	
13	**Cash flows from investing activities:**	
14	+ Proceeds from sales of tangible and intangible assets	
15	– Purchase of tangible and intangible assets	
16	+ Sales of investments that are not cash equivalents	
17	– Purchase of investments that are not cash equivalents	
18	+ Collecting on loans and advances to others	
19	– New loans and advances to others	
20	Net cash provided by (user for) investing activities	
21	**Cash flows from financing activities:**	
22	+ Proceeds from issuance of shares	
23	– Repurchase of shares	
24	+ Borrowing money (loans, bonds, notes)	
25	– Repaying debts (loans, bonds, notes)	
26	– Payment of dividends	
27	Net cash provided by (used for) financing activities	
28	**Net increase (decrease) in cash and cash equivalents during the year**	
29	+ Cash and cash equivalents at December 31, 2019	
30	= Cash and cash equivalents at December 31, 2020	
31		

Cash Flows from Operating Activities

Operating activities comprise the main revenue-producing activities of a company, and generally result from the transactions and other events that determine net income.

The operating section of the statement of cash flows begins with net income, taken from the income statement (Exhibit 9-5), and is followed by "Adjustments to reconcile net income to net cash provided by (used for) operating activities" (Exhibit 9-6). Let's discuss these adjustments.

Ⓐ **DEPRECIATION AND AMORTIZATION EXPENSES.** When we record these expenses, we debit depreciation/amortization expense and credit accumulated depreciation/amortization. As a result, net income decreases, but there is no corresponding outflow of cash. To reverse these non-cash expenses, we add them back to net income when determining operating cash flows.

EXHIBIT 9-3
Positive and Negative Items on the Statement of Cash Flows: Indirect Method

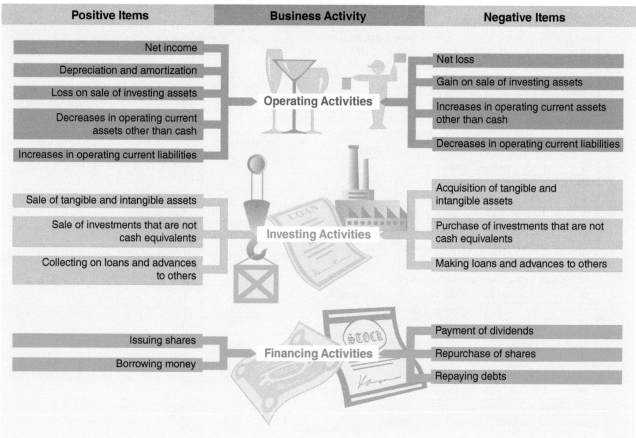

Example: Suppose you had only two transactions during the period, a $1,000 cash sale and depreciation expense of $300. Net income is $700 ($1,000 − $300). Cash flow from operations is $1,000. To go from net income ($700) to cash flow ($1,000), we must add back the depreciation ($300).

Ⓑ **GAINS AND LOSSES ON THE SALE OF INVESTING ASSETS.** Sales of tangible and intangible assets and investments other than cash equivalents are *investing* activities, and there is often a gain or loss on these sales. On the statement of cash flows, a gain or loss on the sale is an adjustment to net income. Exhibit 9-6 includes an adjustment for a gain. During 2020, Bradshaw sold equipment for $62,000. The carrying amount was $54,000 (see calculation of carrying amount on page 459), so there was a gain of $8,000.

The $62,000 of cash received from the sale, which includes the $8,000 gain, is an investing activity. Net income also includes the gain, so we must subtract the gain from net cash provided from operations, as shown in Bradshaw Corporation's statement of cash flows (Exhibit 9-6). (We explain investing activities in the next section.)

A loss on the sale of investing assets also creates an adjustment in the operating section. Losses are *added back* to net income to compute cash flow from operations, because the amount of the loss does not represent an actual outflow of cash. Assume, for example, that the asset with the $54,000 carrying amount was sold for $50,000 instead of $62,000, yielding a loss of $4,000. The only cash involved in

EXHIBIT 9-4
Comparative Balance Sheet for Bradshaw Corporation

	A	B	C	D	
1	**Bradshaw Corporation** Comparative Balance Sheet As at December 31, 2020 and 2019				
2	*(in thousands)*	**2020**	**2019**	**Increase (Decrease)**	
3	**Assets**				
4	Current:				
5	Cash	$ 22	$ 42	$ (20)	⎫
6	Accounts receivable	93	80	13	⎪
7	Interest receivable	3	1	2	⎬ *Changes in current assets—Operating*
8	Inventory	135	138	(3)	⎪
9	Prepaid expenses	8	7	1	⎭
10	Long-term note receivable from another company	11	—	11	⎫
11	Property, plant, and equipment assets, net of depreciation	353	219	134	⎬ *Changes in non-current assets—Investing*
12	Total	$ 625	$ 487	$ 138	⎭
13	**Liabilities**				
14	Current:				⎫
15	Accounts payable	$ 91	$ 57	$ 34	⎪
16	Salary and wages payable	4	6	(2)	⎬ *Changes in current liabilities—Operating*
17	Accrued liabilities	1	3	(2)	⎭
18	Long-term debt	160	77	83	⎱ *Change in long-term liabilities and*
19	**Shareholders' Equity**				*contributed capital accounts—Financing*
20	Share capital	259	258	1	⎰ *Change due to net income—Operating*
21	Retained earnings	110	86	24	*Change due to dividends—Financing*
22	Total	$ 625	$ 487	$ 138	
23					

EXHIBIT 9-5
Income Statement for Bradshaw Corporation

	A	B	C	D
1	**Bradshaw Corporation** Income Statement For the Year Ended December 31, 2020			
2	*(in thousands)*			
3	Revenues and gains:			
4	Sales revenue	$ 284		
5	Interest revenue	12		
6	Dividend revenue	9		
7	Gain on sale of property, plant, and equipment	8		
8	Total revenues and gains		$ 313	
9	Expenses:			
10	Cost of goods sold	150		
11	Salary and wages expense	56		
12	Depreciation expense	18		
13	Other operating expense	17		
14	Interest expense	16		
15	Income tax expense	15		
16	Total expenses		272	
17	Net income		$ 41	
18				

EXHIBIT 9-6
Statement of Cash Flows—Operating Activities by the Indirect Method

	A	B	C	D
1	**Bradshaw Corporation** Statement of Cash Flows For the Year Ended December 31, 2020			
2	*(in thousands)*			
3	**Cash flows from operating activities:**			
4	Net income		$ 41	
5	Adjustments to reconcile net income to net cash provided by operating activities:			
6	(A) Depreciation	$ 18		
7	(B) Gain on sale of property, plant, and equipment	(8)		
8	Increase in accounts receivable	(13)		
9	Increase in interest receivable	(2)		
10	Decrease in inventory	3		
11	(C) Increase in prepaid expenses	(1)		
12	Increase in accounts payable	34		
13	Decrease in salary and wages payable	(2)		
14	Decrease in accrued liabilities	(2)	27	
15	Net cash provided by operating activities		$ 68	
16				

this transaction is the receipt of the $50,000 proceeds, which is recorded as an inflow in the investing section, just like the $62,000 above. The $4,000 loss is added back to net income in the operating section, because there is no corresponding outflow of cash.

© **CHANGES IN NON-CASH OPERATING WORKING CAPITAL ACCOUNTS.** A company's operating activities affect many of its non-cash current asset and liability accounts. When a company sells goods on credit, for example, accounts receivable increase and inventory decreases. Similarly, when a company incurs an expense but doesn't pay for it until later, accounts payable increase. As in Dollarama's statement of cash flows at the beginning of the chapter, these accounts are commonly referred to as **non-cash operating working capital accounts**. In this case, *non-cash* does not necessarily mean the underlying activity did not involve cash, because it often does. Instead, it simply means that the *account* itself (e.g., accounts receivable, unearned revenue) is not one that is included in the *cash and cash equivalents* balance on the statement of cash flows. These accounts are described as *operating* accounts because they derive from *operating activities*, and they are all components of a company's *working capital* balance (current assets – current liabilities). Let's examine how transactions and events in some of the common non-cash operating working capital accounts affect the operating section of the statement of cash flows.

Accounts receivable When a company makes a sale on credit, net income increases via the increase in revenue, but there is no corresponding increase in cash. So, to reconcile net income to cash flows from operations (CFO), we must *deduct* any *increase* in accounts receivable during the year. When a customer pays down its account, however, cash increases but net income is not affected. In this case, any *decrease* in accounts receivable during the year must be *added* to net income to reconcile it with CFO. Changes in other types of *non-investing* receivables (e.g., income taxes receivable) are treated the same way.

Inventory When a company purchases inventory, cash decreases but there is no impact on net income. So, to reconcile net income to CFO, we must *deduct* an *increase* in inventory from net income. Adjustments to CFO for inventory purchased on account are made via the change in *accounts payable and accrued liabilities*, which is discussed below. When inventory is sold, net income decreases via an increase in cost of goods sold, but there is no corresponding decrease in cash. Any *decrease* in inventory is therefore *added* to net income to arrive at CFO.

Prepaid expenses If a company prepays an expense, there is a cash outflow with no consequent decrease in net income, so an *increase* in prepaid expenses must be *deducted* from net income to get CFO. When we adjust prepaid expenses at the end of a reporting period to recognize the expenses related to the period, expenses increase and net income decreases, but cash is not affected. We must therefore *add* a *decrease* in prepaids to net income to reconcile it with CFO.

Accounts payable and accrued liabilities When a company incurs an expense but does not pay for it until later, net income decreases via an increase in the affected expense account, but cash does not decrease. So we must *add* any *increases* in accounts payable and accrued liabilities to net income to get CFO. When the company eventually pays the debt, cash decreases but net income is not affected, so *decreases* in accounts payable and accrued liabilities are *deducted* from net income to reconcile it with CFO. Changes in similar types of *non-financing* liabilities (e.g., provisions) are treated the same way.

Unearned revenue If a customer pays a company before receiving the related goods or services, then cash increases, but there is no impact on net income. Any *increases* in unearned revenue must therefore be *added* to net income when reconciling it with CFO. When the company eventually provides the related goods or services, net income increases via the increase in revenue, but cash is not affected. So we must *deduct* any *decrease* in unearned revenue from net income to get CFO.

As a rule, increases (decreases) in non-cash operating current asset accounts result in decreases (increases) to net income when determining CFO—*the account impact is the opposite of the CFO impact*. In contrast, increases (decreases) in non-cash operating current liability accounts result in increases (decreases) to net income when reconciling to CFO—*the account impact is consistent with the CFO impact*. Exhibit 9-7 summarizes the impacts of these changes in non-cash operating working capital accounts on cash and net income, as well as the adjustments needed to reconcile net income to CFO. We can apply these rules to Bradshaw's balance sheet data in Exhibit 9-4, which results in the CFO impacts disclosed in the Operating Activities section of its statement of cash flows in Exhibit 9-6.

EVALUATING CASH FLOWS FROM OPERATING ACTIVITIES. Let's step back and evaluate Bradshaw's operating cash flows during 2020. Bradshaw generated $68,000 in cash flows from operating activities, which is $27,000 more than it reported in net income. This is a sign that Bradshaw has a high quality of earnings and is not using accruals and other estimates to inflate its net income. Now let's examine Bradshaw's investing and financing activities, as reported in Exhibit 9-8.

EXHIBIT 9-7
Impacts of Changes in Non-cash Operating Working Capital Accounts on Cash Flows from Operations

Account	Transaction or Event	Account Impact	Cash Impact	Non-cash Net Income Impact	Cash Flows From Operations Impact
Current assets					
Accounts receivable	Sale on account	**Increase**	None	Increase	**Decrease**
Accounts receivable	Collection of account	**Decrease**	Increase	None	**Increase**
Inventory	Purchase	**Increase**	Decrease	None	**Decrease**
Inventory	Sale	**Decrease**	Increase	Decrease	**Increase**
Prepaid expenses	Prepayment of expense	**Increase**	Decrease	None	**Decrease**
Prepaid expenses	Recognition of expense	**Decrease**	None	Decrease	**Increase**
Current liabilities					
Payables and accruals	Purchase on account or accrual of expense	**Increase**	None	Decrease	**Increase**
Payables and accruals	Payment	**Decrease**	Decrease	None	**Decrease**
Unearned revenue	Cash received in advance of sale	**Increase**	Increase	None	**Increase**
Unearned revenue	Goods or services delivered	**Decrease**	None	Increase	**Decrease**

EXHIBIT 9-8
Statement of Cash Flows—Indirect Method

	A	B	C	D
1	**Bradshaw Corporation** Statement of Cash Flows For the Year Ended December 31, 2020			
2	*(in thousands)*			
3	**Cash flows from operating activities:**			
4	Net income		$ 41	
5	Adjustments to reconcile net income to net cash provided by operating activities:			
6	Ⓐ Depreciation	$ 18		
7	Ⓑ Gain on sale of property, plant, and equipment	(8)		
8	Increase in accounts receivable	(13)		
9	Increase in interest receivable	(2)		
10	Decrease in inventory	3		
11	Ⓒ Increase in prepaid expenses	(1)		
12	Increase in accounts payable	34		
13	Decrease in salary and wages payable	(2)		
14	Decrease in accrued liabilities	(2)	27	
15	Net cash provided by operating activities		68	
16	**Cash flows from investing activities:**			
17	Acquisition of property, plant, and equipment	(206)		
18	Loan to another company	(11)		
19	Proceeds from sale of property, plant, and equipment	62		
20	Net cash used for investing activities		(155)	
21	**Cash flows from financing activities:**			
22	Proceeds from issuance of common shares	1		
23	Proceeds from issuance of long-term debt	94		
24	Repayment of long-term debt	(11)		
25	Payment of dividends	(17)		
26	Net cash provided by financing activities		67	
27	**Net decrease in cash**		(20)	
28	Cash balance, December 31, 2019		42	
29	Cash balance, December 31, 2020		$ 22	
30				

MyLab Accounting

MID-CHAPTER SUMMARY PROBLEM

Lucas Corporation reported the following income statement and comparative balance sheets, along with transaction data for 2020:

	A	B	C	D
1	**Lucas Corporation** Income Statement Year Ended December 31, 2020			
2	Sales revenue		$ 662,000	
3	Cost of goods sold		560,000	
4	Gross profit		102,000	
5	Operating expenses			
6	Salary expenses	$ 46,000		
7	Depreciation expense—equipment	7,000		
8	Amortization expense—patent	3,000		
9	Rent expense	2,000		
10	Total operating expenses		58,000	
11	Income from operations		44,000	
12	Other items:			
13	Loss on sale of equipment		(2,000)	
14	Income before income tax		42,000	
15	Income tax expense		16,000	
16	Net income		$ 26,000	
17				

	A	B	C	D	E	F	G
1	**Lucas Corporation** Comparative Balance Sheets December 31, 2020 and 2019						
2	**Assets**	**2020**	**2019**	**Liabilities and Shareholders' Equity**	**2020**	**2019**	
3	Current:			Current:			
4	Cash and equivalents	$ 19,000	$ 3,000	Accounts payable	$ 35,000	$ 26,000	
5	Accounts receivable	22,000	23,000	Accrued liabilities	7,000	9,000	
6	Inventories	34,000	31,000	Income tax payable	10,000	10,000	
7	Prepaid expenses	1,000	3,000	Total current liabilities	52,000	45,000	
8	Total current assets	76,000	60,000	Long-term note payable	44,000	—	
9	Long-term investments	18,000	10,000	Bonds payable	40,000	53,000	
10	Equipment, net	67,000	52,000	Shareholders' equity:			
11	Patent, net	44,000	10,000	Share capital	42,000	15,000	
12				Retained earnings	27,000	19,000	
13	Total assets	$ 205,000	$ 132,000	Total liabilities and equity	$ 205,000	$ 132,000	
14							

Requirement

Use the indirect method to prepare the Operating Activities section of Lucas Corporation's 2020 statement of cash flows.

ANSWER

	A	B	C	D
1	**Lucas Corporation** Statement of Cash Flows Year Ended December 31, 2020			
2	**Cash flows from operating activities:**			
3	Net income		$ 26,000	
4	Adjustments to reconcile net income to net cash provided by operating activities:			
5	Depreciation	$ 7,000		
6	Amortization	3,000		
7	Loss on sale of equipment	2,000		
8	Changes in non-cash operating working capital			
9	Decrease in accounts receivable	1,000		
10	Increase in inventories	(3,000)		
11	Decrease in prepaid expenses	2,000		
12	Increase in accounts payable	9,000		
13	Decrease in accrued liabilities	(2,000)	19,000	
14	Net cash provided by operating activities		45,000	
15				

Cash Flows from Investing Activities

Investing activities include the purchase and sale of long-term assets and other investments that do not qualify as cash equivalents. Purchases result in cash outflows from investing activities, whereas sales yield cash inflows. Cash inflows and outflows related to the same type of investing activity must be reported separately in the statement of cash flows.

ACQUISITIONS AND SALES OF TANGIBLE AND INTANGIBLE ASSETS. Companies with significant quantities of tangible assets typically keep track of them in a subledger, which details the cost, accumulated depreciation, and carrying amount of each item of property, plant, and equipment. When an asset is sold, its carrying amount can be deducted from the cash sale proceeds to determine the gain or loss on the sale of the asset. These details on individual asset sales can be accumulated to arrive at the total cash sale proceeds and net gain or loss on sales to be reported on the statement of cash flows for a given fiscal period. Without the detailed information from a company's asset subledger, we can use an alternative method to calculate this information.

To illustrate, we will use information from Bradshaw's balance sheet and income statement in Exhibits 9-4 and 9-5.

- At the beginning of 2020, Bradshaw's balance sheet shows that its carrying amount of property, plant, and equipment was $219,000. By the end of the year, it had increased to $353,000 (Exhibit 9-4).
- Bradshaw's income statement discloses depreciation expense of $18,000 and a gain on sale of property, plant, and equipment of $8,000 for 2020 (Exhibit 9-5).

Bradshaw's purchases of property, plant, and equipment total $206,000 (take this amount as given; see Exhibit 9-8). How much, then, are the proceeds from the sale of property, plant, and equipment? First, we must determine the carrying amount of property, plant, and equipment sold, as follows:

Property, plant, and equipment (net)

Beginning balance	+	Acquisitions	−	Depreciation	−	Carrying amount of assets sold	=	Ending balance
$219,000	+	$206,000	−	$18,000		−X	=	$353,000
						−X	=	$353,000 − $219,000 − $206,000 + $18,000
						X	=	$54,000

The sale proceeds are $62,000, determined as follows:

Sale proceeds	=	Carrying amount of assets sold	+	Gain	−	Loss
	=	$54,000	+	$8,000	−	$0
	=	$62,000				

Trace the sale proceeds of $62,000 to the statement of cash flows in Exhibit 9-8. The Property, Plant, and Equipment T-account provides another look at the computation of the carrying amount of the assets sold.

Property, Plant, and Equipment, Net

Beginning balance	219,000	Depreciation	18,000
Acquisitions	206,000	Carrying amount of assets sold	54,000
Ending balance	353,000		

If the sale had resulted in a loss of $3,000, the sale proceeds would have been $51,000 ($54,000 − $3,000), and the statement would report $51,000 as a cash receipt from this investing activity.

The same process can be used to determine cash proceeds from the sale of intangible assets, although there would be no amortization to deal with in the case of intangibles with indefinite useful lives.

ACQUISITIONS AND SALES OF INVESTMENTS OTHER THAN CASH EQUIVALENTS. The carrying amount of investments sold can be computed in the manner illustrated for property, plant, and equipment. Investment carrying amounts are easier to calculate because there is no depreciation to account for, as shown in the following equation (Bradshaw has no investments, so the information below is for illustration only):

Investments						
Beginning balance	+	Purchases	−	Carrying amount of investments sold	=	Ending balance
$100,000	+	$50,000		−X	=	$140,000
				−X	=	$140,000 − $100,000 − $50,000
				X	=	$10,000

The Investments T-account provides another look:

Investments			
Beginning balance	100		
Purchases	50	Carrying amount of investments sold	10
Ending balance	140		

If Bradshaw had realized a $15,000 gain on the sale of these investments, then the cash sale proceeds would have been $25,000 ($10,000 carrying amount + $15,000 gain), which we would report as a cash inflow in the Investing Activities section. The investment purchases of $50,000 in the illustration above would be reported as a cash outflow in the Investing section.

MAKING AND COLLECTING LOANS AND ADVANCES TO OTHERS. The beginning and ending balances of (short-term and long-term) Loans or Notes Receivable can be found on the balance sheet. If the amount of either the new loans/advances or the collections of loans/advances is known, the other amount can be computed. Bradshaw has a long-term note receivable of $11,000 at the end of 2020; this balance was zero at the end of 2019 (Exhibit 9-4; assume there were no collections during 2020). Using this information, we can determine the amount of loans/advances made during 2020 as follows:

Notes Receivable						
Beginning balance	+	New loans made	−	Collections	=	Ending balance
$0	+	$X		−0	=	$11,000
		X			=	$11,000

Notes Receivable			
Beginning balance	0		
New loans made	11	Collections	0
Ending balance	11		

This $11,000 loan to another company can be seen as a cash outflow in the Investing Activities section of Bradshaw's statement of cash flows in Exhibit 9-8.

Cash Flows from Financing Activities

Financing activities result in changes in the size and composition of a company's contributed equity and borrowings. The issuance of equity or borrowings results in a cash inflow; the repurchase of equity and repayment of borrowings are cash out-flows. Cash inflows and outflows related to the same type of financing activity must be reported separately in the statement of cash flows.

BORROWING MONEY AND REPAYING DEBTS. The beginning and ending balances of (short-term and long-term) borrowings, such as Loans, Bonds, and Notes Payable, can be found on the balance sheet. If the amount of either the new borrowings or the repayment of debts is known, the other amount can be computed. Bradshaw's long-term debt increased from $77,000 at the end of 2019 to $160,000 by the end of 2020 (Exhibit 9-4; assume new borrowings of long-term debt were $94,000 in 2020). Using this information, we can determine the amount of long-term debt repayments made during 2020 as follows:

Long-Term Debt

Beginning balance	+	Borrowing of new debt	−	Repayments of debt	=	Ending balance
$77,000	+	$94,000		−X	=	$160,000
				−X	=	$160,000 − $77,000 − $94,000
				X	=	$11,000

This same information can be determined using a T-account as follows:

Long-Term Debt

		Beginning balance	77,000
Payments	11,000	Issuance of new debt	94,000
		Ending balance	160,000

The $94,000 cash inflow from new borrowing and the $11,000 cash outflow from the repayment of debts can be seen in the Financing Activities section in Exhibit 9-8.

Common Shares

Beginning balance	+	Issuance of new shares	−	Repurchase of shares	=	Ending balance
$258,000	+	$X	−	$0	=	$259,000
					=	$1,000

Here is the same information presented in a T-account:

Common Shares

		Beginning balance	258,000
		Issuance of new shares	1,000
		Ending balance	259,000

The $1,000 cash inflow from issuing new shares can also be seen in the Financing Activities section of Exhibit 9-8.

PAYMENT OF DIVIDENDS. Dividend payments can usually be found in the Statement of Retained Earnings (or Statement of Changes in Owners' Equity), but they can also be determined as follows, using information from Bradshaw's balance sheet (Exhibit 9-4) and income statement (Exhibit 9-5):

Retained Earnings							
Beginning balance	+	Net income	−	Dividends declared	=	Ending balance	
$86,000	+	$41,000		−X	=	$110,000	
				−X	=	$110,000 − $86,000 − $41,000	
				X	=	$17,000	

The T-account provides another view of the dividend payment computation:

Retained Earnings			
Dividend declarations	17,000	Beginning balance	86,000
		Net income	41,000
		Ending balance	110,000

The $17,000 dividend payment can be seen as a cash outflow in the Financing Activities section in Exhibit 9-8. Any increase or decrease in a Dividend Payable account is treated the same way as a change in a non-cash operating current liability account, except that the adjustment to cash flows is included in the Financing Activities section. If, for example, Bradshaw had a Dividends Payable account that had increased by $5,000 during 2020, then we would add this increase as a *Change in non-cash financing working capital* to the Financing Activities section of its statement of cash flows.

STOP + THINK (9-3)

Midwest Airlines
Statement of Cash Flows

(in millions)	2021	2020	2019
Cash Flows from Operating Activities			
Net income	548	313	442
Items not affecting cash:			
Depreciation and amortization	502	467	417
Loss (gain) on disposal of equipment	(25)	101	-
Changes in non-cash operating working capital items:			
(Increase) decrease in accounts receivable	(9)	(75)	43
(Increase) decrease in inventory	(13)	6	(19)
Increase (decrease) in accounts payable	855	231	129
Net Cash Inflow (Outflow) from Operating Activities	1,858	1,043	1,012

Midwest Airlines
Statement of Cash Flows

(in millions)	2021	2020	2019
Cash Flows from Investing Activities			
Business acquisitions	-	(400)	-
Proceeds from sale of investments	6	-	23
Purchase of property, plant, and equipment	(1,316)	(1,505)	(1,261)
Proceeds from disposal of equipment	100	55	-
Net Cash Inflow (Outflow) from Investing Activities	(1,210)	(1,850)	(1,238)
Cash Flows from Financing Activities			
Payment of dividends	(14)	(14)	(14)
Proceeds from sale of shares	132	88	93
Repurchase of shares	(55)	(246)	-
Proceeds from long-term debt	300	520	-
Repayment of long-term debt	(150)	(215)	(127)
Net Cash Inflow (Outflow) from Financing Activities	213	133	(48)
Increase (Decrease) in Cash and Cash Equivalents	861	(674)	(274)
Cash and Cash Equivalents, Beginning of Year	3	677	951
Cash and Cash Equivalents, End of Year	864	3	677

Based on the information in Midwest Airlines' statements of cash flows for 2019–2021, answer the following questions:

1. Has Midwest been expanding or down-sizing its business?
2. What was the carrying amount of the equipment Midwest sold in 2020?
3. If you were a financial analyst following Midwest, would you be pleased with its operating cash flows?
4. Has Midwest been relying more on debt or equity financing in recent years? Cite information about both debt and equity to support your conclusion.
5. Overall, does Midwest have a strong or poor cash position? Cite two pieces of information to support your conclusion.

Non-Cash Investing and Financing Activities

Companies sometimes engage in financing and investing activities that do not involve cash flows. An example of a non-cash transaction that involves both investing and financing is the acquisition of a subsidiary company in exchange for shares of the acquiring company. In this transaction, the acquiring company has *invested* in a new asset, the subsidiary company, and *financed* it with its own shares, but because the transaction does not involve cash, these activities are not included in the statement of cash flows. IFRS and ASPE do, however, require note disclosure of non-cash investing and financing activities. A sample disclosure of the above transaction and two other non-cash transactions is included in Exhibit 9-9.

	A	B	C
1	*(amounts in thousands)*		
2	**Note 22: Non-Cash Investing and Financing Activities**		
3	Acquisition of subsidiary by issuing common shares	$ 320	
4	Acquisition of equipment by finance lease	70	
5	Conversion of bonds payable to common shares	150	
6	Total non-cash investing and financing activities	$ 540	
7			

EXHIBIT 9-9
Sample Disclosure on Non-cash Investing and Financing Activities

Measuring Cash Adequacy: Free Cash Flow

Throughout this chapter, we have focused on cash flows from operating, investing, and financing activities. Some investors, creditors, and managers want to know how much cash a company can "free up" for new opportunities. The business world changes so quickly that new possibilities arise almost daily. A company with a significant free cash flow is better able to respond to new opportunities. **Free cash flow** is the amount of cash available from operations after paying for property, plant, and equipment. Free cash flow can be computed as follows:

$$\text{Free cash flow} = \frac{\text{Net cash flow provided by}}{\text{operating activites}} - \frac{\text{Capital expenditures on}}{\text{property, plant,}} \text{ and equipment}$$

Using information from Dollarama's statement of cash flows on page 444, we can calculate its free cash flow for 2018. It generated cash from operating activities of $637.3 million and spent $112.8 million on capital expenditures, leaving $524.5 million in free cash flow for 2018. This information suggests that Dollarama is well poised to take advantage of new business opportunities—even after spending over $100 million on property and equipment in 2018, it still had over $500 million of free cash flow to spend on other things.

It is important to note, however, that a negative free cash flow is not necessarily a bad sign for investors. It could mean that the company has made a significant investment in property, plant, and equipment that will pay off in the form of increased future revenues and profits.

 # DECISION GUIDELINES

INVESTORS' AND CREDITORS' USE OF CASH-FLOW AND RELATED INFORMATION

Jan Childres is a private investor. Through years of experience she has devised some guidelines for evaluating both share investments and bond investments. Childres uses a combination of accrual-accounting data and cash-flow information. Here are her decision guidelines for both investors and creditors.

INVESTORS

Questions	Factors to Consider	Financial Statement Predictor*
1. How much in dividends can I expect to receive from an investment in shares?	Expected future net income	Income from continuing operations
	Expected future cash balance	Net cash flows from (in order): • operating activities • investing activities • financing activities
	Future dividend policy	Current and past dividend policy
2. Is the share price likely to increase or decrease?	Expected future income from continuing operations	Income from continuing operations
	Expected future cash flows from operating activities	Income from continuing operations Net cash flow from operating activities

CREDITORS

Question	Factors to Consider	Financial Statement Predictor*
Can the company pay the interest and principal at the maturity of a loan?	Expected future net cash flow from operating activities	Income from continuing operations Net cash flow from operating activities

*There are many other factors to consider in making these decisions. These are some of the more common ones.

Summary of IFRS-ASPE Differences

Concepts	IFRS	ASPE
Classification of interest paid and interest and dividends received (p. 449)	Interest paid may be classified as either an operating activity or a financing activity.	Interest paid must be classified as an operating activity.
Classification of interest and dividends received (p. 449)	Interest and dividends received may be classified as either operating activities or investing activities.	Interest and dividends received must be classified as operating activities.
Classification of dividends paid (p. 449)	Dividends paid may be classified as either an operating activity or a financing activity. *Note: Once a classification scheme has been chosen for each of the above items, it must be used consistently thereafter.*	Dividends paid must be classified as a financing activity.

SUMMARY

SUMMARY OF LEARNING OBJECTIVES

LEARNING OBJECTIVE	SUMMARY
❶ **Explain** the uses of the statement of cash flows	The information disclosed by a company in its statement of cash flows provides decision-relevant information to users of the company's financial statements. This statement includes details about a company's cash receipts and cash disbursements from operating, investing, and financing activities, and permits a user to determine exactly what caused the company's cash balance to increase or decrease during the period.

Specifically, the statement of cash flows helps users do the following:

1. Predict future cash flows.
2. Evaluate management decisions.
3. Determine ability to pay interest and dividends.
4. Assess the relationship of net income to cash flows.
5. Compare the operating performance of different companies.

Cash includes cash equivalents, which are short-term investments that are readily convertible to known amounts of cash, and which are very unlikely to change in value.

❷ **Explain** and **classify** cash flows from operating, investing, and financing activities

Operating activities comprise the main revenue-producing activities of a company, and generally result from the transactions and other events that determine net income. Other activities that are not *investing* or *financing* activities are also classified as operating activities.

There are two methods of determining cash flows from operating activities, both resulting in the same net cash flows from operating activities:

- Indirect method, in which net income is adjusted for non-cash transactions, any deferrals or accruals of past or future operating cash receipts or payments, and items of income or expense associated with investing or financing cash flows
- Direct method, which explicitly reports all cash receipts and cash payments from operating activities

Investing activities include the purchase and sale of long-term assets and other investments that do not qualify as cash equivalents. They generally consist of transactions that result in cash inflows or outflows related to resources used for generating future income and cash flows. Only expenditures related to assets that are recognized on the balance sheet qualify as investing activities.

Financing activities result in changes in the size and composition of a company's contributed equity and borrowings.

❸ **Prepare** a statement of cash flows using the indirect method of determining cash flows from operating activities

To determine cash flows from operating activities using the indirect method, begin with net income and adjust it as follows:

- Add non-cash expenses, such as depreciation and amortization
- Add losses (deduct gains) on sales of tangible and intangible assets and investments
- Add decreases (deduct increases) in non-cash operating current asset accounts
- Add increases (deduct decreases) in non-cash operating current liability accounts

To determine cash flows from investing activities:

- Add sales (deduct purchases) of tangible and intangible assets and investments other than cash equivalents
- Add collection (deduct issuance) of loans and advances to others

To determine cash flows from financing activities:

- Add issuance (deduct repurchase) of shares
- Add borrowing (deduct repayment) of short-term and long-term debts
- (Deduct payment) of dividends

Non-cash investing and financing activities, such as the acquisition of a business using common shares, are excluded from the statement of cash flows, but must be disclosed in the notes to the financial statements.

MyLab Accounting

END-OF-CHAPTER SUMMARY PROBLEM

Lucas Corporation, a private company, reported the following income statement and comparative balance sheet, along with transaction data for 2020:

	A	B	C	D
1	**Lucas Corporation** Income Statement For the Year Ended December 31, 2020			
2	Sales revenue		$ 662,000	
3	Cost of goods sold		560,00	
4	Gross margin		102,00	
5	Operating expenses:			
6	Salary expenses	$ 46,000		
7	Depreciation expense, equipment	7,000		
8	Amortization expense, patent	3,000		
9	Rent expense	2,000		
10	Total operating expenses		58,000	
11	Income from operations		44,000	
12	Other items:			
13	Loss on sale of equipment		(2,000)	
14	Income before income tax		42,000	
15	Income tax expense		16,000	
16	Net income		$ 26,000	
17				

	A	B	C	D	E	F	G
1		**Lucas Corporation** Balance Sheet As at December 31, 2020 and 2019					
2	**Assets**	**2020**	**2019**	**Liabilities and Shareholders' Equity**	**2020**	**2019**	
3	Current:			Current:			
4	Cash and equivalents	$ 19,000	$ 3,000	Accounts payable	$ 35,000	$ 26,000	
5	Accounts receivable	22,000	23,000	Accrued liabilities	7,000	9,000	
6	Inventories	34,000	31,000	Income tax payable	10,000	10,000	
7	Prepaid expenses	1,000	3,000	Total current liabilities	52,000	45,000	
8	Total current assets	76,000	60,000	Long-term note payable	44,000	—	
9	Long-term investments	18,000	10,000	Bonds payable	40,000	53,000	
10	Equipment, net	67,000	52,000	Shareholders' equity:			
11	Patent, net	44,000	10,000	Share capital	42,000	15,000	
12				Retained earnings	27,000	19,000	
13				Total liabilities and			
14	Total assets	$ 205,000	$ 132,000	shareholders' equity	$ 205,000	$ 132,000	
15							

	A	B	C
1	**Transaction Data for 2020:**		
2	Purchase of equipment	$ 98,000	
3	Payment of cash dividends	18,000	
4	Issuance of common shares to repay bonds payable	13,000	
5	Purchase of long-term investment	8,000	
6	Issuance of long-term note payable to purchase patent	37,000	
7	Issuance of long-term note payable to borrow cash	7,000	
8	Issuance of common shares for cash	19,000	
9	Proceeds on sale of equipment (carrying amount, $76,000)	74,000	
10	Repurchase of common shares	5,000	
11			

Requirements

Prepare Lucas Corporation's statement of cash flows for the year ended December 31, 2020. Determine operating cash flows by the indirect method. Follow the four steps outlined below. For Step 4, prepare a T-account to show the transaction activity in each long-term balance sheet account. For each capital asset, use a single account, net of accumulated depreciation or amortization (for example: Equipment, net).

Name: Lucas Corporation
Fiscal Period: Year ended December 31, 2020

Step 1 Lay out the template of the statement of cash flows.

Step 2 From the comparative balance sheet, determine the increase in cash during the year.

Step 3 From the income statement, take net income, depreciation and amortization, and the loss on sale of equipment, to the statement of cash flows.

Step 4 Complete the statement of cash flows. Account for the year-to-year change in each balance sheet account.

ANSWER

The title must include the name of the company, "Statement of Cash Flows," and the specific period of time covered. There are three sections: Cash flows from operating, investing, and financing activities.

Add back non-cash items: depreciation, amortization; and deduct gains/add loss from sales of long-term assets.

$2,000 = $76,000 − $74,000

Any changes in current assets and current liabilities are included in the operating activities section. Calculate as 2020 balance − 2019 balance from the balance sheets.

Any cash changes in the long-term assets are included in the investing activities section. Check "Transaction Data for 2020."

	A	B	C
1	**Lucas Corporation** Statement of Cash Flows For the Year Ended December 31, 2020		
2	**Cash flows from operating activities:**		
3	Net income		$ 26,000
4	Adjustments to reconcile net income to net cash provided by operating activities:		
5	Depreciation	$ 7,000	
6	Amortization	3,000	
7	Loss on sale of equipment	2,000	
8	Changes in non-cash operating working capital accounts:		
9	Decrease in accounts receivable	1,000	
10	Increase in inventories	(3,000)	
11	Decrease in prepaid expenses	2,000	
12	Increase in accounts payable	9,000	
13	Decrease in accrued liabilities	(2,000)	19,000
14	Net cash provided by operating activities		45,000
15			
16	**Cash flows from investing activities:**		
17	Purchase of equipment	(98,000)	
18	Sale of equipment	74,000	
19	Purchase of long-term investment	(8,000)	
20	Net cash used for investing activities		(32,000)
21			

	A	B	C
22	**Cash flows from financing activities:**		
23	Issuance of common shares	19,000	
24	Payment of cash dividends	(18,000)	
25	Issuance of long-term note payable	7,000	
26	Repurchase of common shares	(5,000)	
27	Net cash provided by financing activities		3,000
28			
29	**Net increase in cash**		16,000
30	**Cash balance, December 31, 2019**		3,000
31	**Cash balance, December 31, 2020**		$ 19,000
32			
33	**Non-cash investing and financing activities:**		
34	Issuance of long-term note payable to purchase patent		$ 37,000
35	Issuance of common shares to repay bonds payable		13,000
36	Total non-cash investing and financing activities		$ 50,000

Any cash changes in the long-term liabilities and contributed capital accounts are included in the financing activities section. Check "Transaction Data for 2020."

This result should equal the Dec. 31, 2020, balance sheet Cash amount.

Check "Transaction Data for 2020."

Long-Term Investments

Bal.	10,000	
	8,000	
Bal.	18,000	

Equipment, Net

Bal.	52,000	
	98,000	76,000
		7,000
Bal.	67,000	

Patent, Net

Bal.	10,000	
	37,000	3,000
Bal.	44,000	

Long-Term Note Payable

		Bal.	0
			37,000
			7,000
		Bal.	44,000

Bonds Payable

		Bal.	53,000
	13,000		
		Bal.	40,000

Share Capital

		Bal.	15,000
			13,000
	5,000		19,000
		Bal.	42,000

Retained Earnings

		Bal.	19,000
	18,000		26,000
		Bal.	27,000

Use the 2019 and 2020 balance sheet amounts and the transaction data for 2020 to complete these T-accounts.

REVIEW

QUICK QUIZ (ANSWERS APPEAR ON THE LAST PAGE OF THIS CHAPTER.)

Test your understanding of the statement of cash flows by answering the following questions.

1. Paying off bonds payable is reported on the statement of cash flows under
   a. operating activities.
   b. investing activities.
   c. financing activities.
   d. non-cash investing and financing activities.

2. The sale of inventory for cash is reported on the statement of cash flows under
   a. operating activities.
   b. investing activities.
   c. financing activities.
   d. non-cash investing and financing activities.

3. Selling equipment is reported on the statement of cash flows under
   a. operating activities.
   b. investing activities.
   c. financing activities.
   d. non-cash investing and financing activities.

4. Which of the following terms appears on a statement of cash flows—indirect method?
   a. Payments to suppliers
   b. Amortization expense
   c. Collections from customers
   d. Cash receipt of interest revenue

5. On an indirect-method statement of cash flows, an increase in prepaid insurance would be
   a. included in payments to suppliers.
   b. added to net income.
   c. added to increases in current assets.
   d. deducted from net income.

6. On an indirect-method statement of cash flows, an increase in accounts payable would be
   a. reported in the investing activities section.
   b. reported in the financing activities section.
   c. added to net income in the operating activities section.
   d. deducted from net income in the operating activities section.

7. On an indirect-method statement of cash flows, a gain on the sale of plant assets would be
   a. ignored, because the gain did not generate any cash.
   b. reported in the investing activities section.
   c. deducted from net income in the operating activities section.
   d. added to net income in the operating activities section.

8. Paying cash dividends is a/an _____ activity.
   Receiving cash dividends is a/an _____ activity.

9. Matlock Camera Co. sold equipment with a cost of $20,000 and accumulated depreciation of $8,000 for an amount that resulted in a gain of $3,000. What amount should Matlock report on the statement of cash flows as "proceeds from sale of plant and equipment"?
   a. $9,000
   b. $17,000
   c. $15,000
   d. Some other amount ($ _____)

Questions 10 through 18 use the following data. Trudeau Corporation determines operating cash flows by the indirect method.

	A	B	C	D
1	**Trudeau Corporation** Income Statement For the Year Ended December 31, 2020			
2	Sales revenue	$ 180,000		
3	Gain on sale of equipment	8,000	$ 188,000	
4	Cost of goods sold	110,000		
5	Depreciation	6,000		
6	Other operating expenses	25,000	141,000	
7	Net income		$ 47,000	
8				

	A	B	C	D	E	F	G
1				**Trudeau Corporation** Comparative Balance Sheet As at December 31, 2020 and 2019			
2	**Assets**	**2020**	**2019**	**Liabilities and Shareholders' Equity**	**2020**	**2019**	
3	Cash	$ 4,000	$ 1,000	Accounts payable	$ 6,000	$ 7,000	
4	Accounts receivable	7,000	11,000	Accrued liabilities	7,000	3,000	
5	Inventories	10,000	9,000	Common shares	20,000	10,000	
6	Plant and equipment, net	93,000	69,000	Retained earnings	81,000	70,000	
7		$ 114,000	$ 90,000		$ 114,000	$ 90,000	

10. How many items enter into the computation of Trudeau's net cash provided by operating activities?
 a. 2
 b. 3
 c. 5
 d. 7

11. How do Trudeau's accrued liabilities affect the company's statement of cash flows for 2020?
 a. They don't because the accrued liabilities are not yet paid
 b. Increase in cash provided by operating activities
 c. Increase in cash used by investing activities
 d. Increase in cash used by financing activities

12. How do accounts receivable affect Trudeau's cash flows from operating activities for 2020?
 a. Increase in cash provided by operating activities
 b. Decrease in cash provided by operating activities
 c. They don't because accounts receivable result from investing activities
 d. Decrease in cash used by investing activities

13. Trudeau's net cash provided by operating activities during 2020 was
 a. $3,000.
 b. $47,000.
 c. $51,000.
 d. $58,000.

14. How many items enter into the computation of Trudeau's net cash flow from investing activities for 2020?
 a. 2
 b. 3
 c. 5
 d. 7

15. The carrying amount of equipment sold during 2020 was $20,000. Trudeau's net cash flow from investing activities for 2020 was
 a. net cash used of $22,000.
 b. net cash used of $28,000.

 c. net cash used of $50,000.
 d. net cash provided of $28,000.

16. How many items enter into the computation of Trudeau's net cash flow from financing activities for 2020?
 a. 2
 b. 3
 c. 5
 d. 7

17. Trudeau's largest financing cash flow for 2020 resulted from the
 a. sale of equipment.
 b. purchase of equipment.
 c. issuance of common shares.
 d. payment of dividends.

18. Trudeau's net cash flow from financing activities for 2020 was
 a. net cash used of $25,000.
 b. net cash used of $20,000.
 c. net cash provided of $10,000.
 d. net cash used of $26,000.

19. Sales totalled $800,000, accounts receivable increased by $40,000, and accounts payable decreased by $35,000. How much cash did this company collect from customers?
 a. $760,000
 b. $795,000
 c. $800,000
 d. $840,000

20. Income Tax Payable was $5,000 at the end of the year and $2,800 at the beginning. Income tax expense for the year totalled $59,100. What amount of cash did this company pay for income tax during the year?
 a. $56,900
 b. $59,100
 c. $61,300
 d. $61,900

ACCOUNTING VOCABULARY

cash equivalents Investments such as term deposits, guaranteed investment certificates, or high-grade government securities that are considered so similar to cash that they are combined with cash for financial disclosure on the balance sheet.   (p. 446)

direct method A method of determining cash flows from operating activities in which all cash receipts and cash payments from operating activities are directly reported on the statement of cash flows.   (p. 450)

financing activities Activities that result in changes in the size and composition of a company's contributed equity and borrowings.   (p. 448)

free cash flow A measure of how much cash a company has available to pursue new business opportunities. Calculated by deducting capital expenditures from cash flow from operating activities.   (p. 464)

indirect method A method of determining cash flows from operating activities in which net income is adjusted for non-cash

transactions, any deferrals or accruals of past or future operating cash receipts or payments, and items of income or expense associated with investing or financing cash flows.   (p. 450)

investing activities Activities that include the purchase and sale of long-term assets and other investments that result in cash inflows or outflows related to resources used for generating future income and cash flows.   (p. 448)

non-cash operating working capital account A current asset or current liability account that derives from an operating activity and is not included in cash and cash equivalents.   (p. 454)

operating activities Activities that comprise the main revenue-producing activities of a company, and generally result from the transactions and other events that determine net income.   (p. 448)

ASSESS YOUR PROGRESS

Recall that for the sake of simplicity and consistency, this text classifies all interest paid and interest and dividends received as operating activities, and classifies dividends paid as a financing activity. All questions and problems in this chapter should be answered using this convention.

SHORT EXERCISES

LEARNING OBJECTIVE ❶

Understand purposes of the statement of cash flows

S9-1 State how the statement of cash flows helps investors and creditors perform each of the following functions:

a. Predict future cash flows.

b. Evaluate management decisions.

LEARNING OBJECTIVE ❷

Evaluate operating cash flows—indirect method

S9-2 Examine the Dollarama statement of cash flows on page 444. Suppose Dollarama's operating activities *used*, rather than *provided*, cash. Identify three things under the indirect method that could cause operating cash flows to be negative.

LEARNING OBJECTIVE ❸

Report cash flows from operating activities—indirect method

S9-3 Canada Wide Transportation (CWT) began 2020 with accounts receivable, inventory, and prepaid expenses totalling $65,000. At the end of the year, CWT had a total of $78,000 for these current assets. At the beginning of 2020, CWT owed current liabilities of $42,000, and at year-end, current liabilities totalled $40,000.

Net income for the year was $80,000. Included in net income were a $4,000 gain on the sale of land and depreciation expense of $9,000.

Show how CWT should report cash flows from operating activities for 2020. CWT uses the *indirect* method. Use Exhibit 9-6 (p. 454) as a guide.

LEARNING OBJECTIVE ❷

Identify items for reporting cash flows from operations—indirect method

S9-4 Bewell Clinic Inc. is preparing its statement of cash flows (indirect method) for the year ended November 30, 2020. Consider the following items in preparing the company's statement of cash flows. Identify each item as an operating activity—addition to net income (O+), or subtraction from net income (O–); an investing activity (I); a financing activity (F); or an activity that is not used to prepare the statement of cash flows by the indirect method (N). Place the appropriate symbol in the blank space.

_____ **a.** Loss on sale of land	_____ **h.** Increase in accounts payable
_____ **b.** Depreciation expense	_____ **i.** Net income
_____ **c.** Increase in inventory	_____ **j.** Payment of dividends
_____ **d.** Decrease in prepaid expense	_____ **k.** Decrease in accrued liabilities
_____ **e.** Decrease in accounts receivable	_____ **l.** Issuance of common shares
_____ **f.** Purchase of equipment	_____ **m.** Gain on sale of building
_____ **g.** Collection of cash from customers	_____ **n.** Retained earnings

🌐 **S9-5** (Exercise S9-6 is an alternative exercise.) Edwards Corporation Inc. accountants have assembled the following data for the year ended June 30, 2020:

LEARNING OBJECTIVES ❷❸

Compute operating cash flows—indirect method

Payment of dividends.........................	$ 6,000	Other operating expenses..................	$35,000
Proceeds from issuance		Purchase of equipment......................	40,000
of common shares	20,000	Decrease in operating current	
Sales revenue......................................	224,000	liabilities..	5,000
Increase in operating current		Payment of note payable...................	30,000
assets other than cash....................	30,000	Proceeds from sale of land.................	60,000
Repurchase of common shares...........	5,000	Depreciation expense	8,000
Cost of goods sold.............................	100,000		

Prepare the *operating activities section* of Edwards's statement of cash flows for the year ended June 30, 2020. Edwards uses the *indirect* method for operating cash flows.

🌐 **S9-6** Use the data in exercise S9-5 to prepare Edwards Corporation's statement of cash flows for the year ended June 30, 2020. Edwards uses the *indirect* method for operating activities. Use Exhibit 9-8, page 456, as a guide, but you may stop after determining the net increase (or decrease) in cash.

LEARNING OBJECTIVES ❷❸

Prepare a statement of cash flows—indirect method

🌐 **S9-7** Williams Corporation accountants have assembled the following data for the year ended June 30, 2020:

LEARNING OBJECTIVES ❷❸

Prepare a statement of cash flows using the indirect method

Net income...	$?
Cost of goods sold...	$116,000
Payment of dividends..	6,100
Other operating expenses...	34,000
Proceeds from the issuance of common shares	18,000
Purchase of equipment with cash	42,000
Sales revenue...	225,000
Increase in current liabilities..	10,000
Increase in current assets other than cash..	29,000
Payment of note payable...	30,000
Proceeds from sale of land..	27,000
Repurchase of common shares..	7,000
Depreciation expense	5,000

Prepare Williams Corporation's statement of cash flows for the year ended June 30, 2020. Williams uses the indirect method for operating activities.

LEARNING OBJECTIVE ❸

Compute investing cash flows

S9-8 Autos of Red Deer Inc. reported the following financial statements for 2020:

	A	B	C
1	**Autos of Red Deer Inc.** Income Statement For the Year Ended December 31, 2020		
2	*(in thousands)*		
3	Sales revenue	$ 710	
4	Cost of goods sold	340	
5	Salary expense	70	
6	Depreciation expense	20	
7	Other expenses	130	
8	Total expenses	560	
9	Net income	$ 150	
10			

	A	B	C	D	E	F	G
1	**Autos of Red Deer Inc.** Comparative Balance Sheet As at December 31, 2020 and 2019						
2	*(in thousands)*						
3	**Assets**	**2020**	**2019**	**Liabilities**	**2020**	**2019**	
4	Current:			Current:			
5	Cash	$ 19	$ 16	Accounts payable	$ 47	$ 42	
6	Accounts receivable	59	48	Salary payable	23	21	
7	Inventories	75	84	Accrued liabilities	8	11	
8	Prepaid expenses	3	2	Long-term notes payable	68	58	
9	Long-term investments	55	75	**Shareholders' Equity**			
10	Property, plant, and equipment	225	185	Common shares Retained earnings	40 250	32 246	
11	Total	$ 436	$ 410	Total	$ 436	$ 410	
12							

Compute the following investing cash flows:

a. Acquisitions of plant and equipment (all were for cash). Autos of Red Deer sold no plant and equipment.

b. Proceeds from the sale of investments. Autos of Red Deer purchased no investments.

LEARNING OBJECTIVE ❸

Compute financing cash flows

S9-9 Use the Autos of Red Deer data in exercise S9-8 to compute:

a. New borrowing or payment of long-term notes payable. Autos of Red Deer had only one long-term note payable transaction during the year.

b. Issuance of common shares or repurchase of common shares. Autos of Red Deer had only one common share transaction during the year.

c. Payment of cash dividends (same as dividends declared).

EXERCISES

LEARNING OBJECTIVE ❶

Identify the purposes of the statement of cash flows

E9-10 B.C. Plating Inc. has experienced an unbroken string of 10 years of growth in net income. Nevertheless, the company is facing bankruptcy. Creditors are calling all B.C. Plating's loans for immediate payment, and the cash is simply not available. It is clear that the company's top managers overemphasized profits and gave too little attention to cash flow.

Requirement

Write a brief memo, in your own words, to explain to the managers of B.C. Plating the purposes of the statement of cash flows.

E9-11 Carter-Pierce Investments specializes in low-risk government bonds. Identify each of Carter-Pierce's transactions as operating (O), investing (I), financing (F), non-cash investing and financing (NIF), or a transaction that is not reported on the statement of cash flows (N). Indicate whether each item increases (+) or decreases (−) cash. The *indirect* method is used for operating activities.

LEARNING OBJECTIVE ❷

Identify activities for the statement of cash flows—indirect method

_____ a. Acquisition of building by cash payment

_____ b. Decrease in merchandise inventory

_____ c. Depreciation of equipment

_____ d. Decrease in accrued liabilities

_____ e. Payment of cash dividend

_____ f. Purchase of long-term investment

_____ g. Issuance of long-term note payable to borrow cash

_____ h. Increase in prepaid expenses

_____ i. Accrual of salary expense

_____ j. Acquisition of equipment by issuance of note payable

_____ k. Sale of long-term investment

_____ l. Issuance of common shares for cash

_____ m. Increase in accounts payable

_____ n. Amortization of intangible assets

_____ o. Loss on sale of equipment

_____ p. Payment of long-term debt

_____ q. Cash sale of land

_____ r. Repurchase of common shares

_____ s. Net income

E9-12 Indicate whether each of the following transactions affects an operating activity, an investing activity, a financing activity, or a non-cash investing and financing activity:

LEARNING OBJECTIVE ❷

Classify transactions for the statement of cash flows—indirect method

a.	Cash	61,000	g.	Equipment	11,000
	Common Shares	61,000		Cash	11,000
b.	Furniture and Fixtures	18,000	h.	Dividends Payable	13,000
	Cash	18,000		Cash	13,000
c.	Cash	52,000	i.	Salary Expense	14,000
	Accounts Receivable	11,000		Cash	14,000
	Service Revenue	63,000	j.	Building	105,000
d.	Cash	7,000		Note Payable—Long-Term	105,000
	Long-Term Investment	7,000	k.	Common Shares	12,000
e.	Loss on Disposal of Equipment	1,000		Cash	12,000
	Equipment, Net	1,000	l.	Depreciation Expense	5,000
f.	Land	15,000		Accumulated Depreciation	5,000
	Cash	15,000	m.	Bonds Payable	35,000
				Cash	35,000

E9-13 The accounting records of South Central Distributors, Inc., reveal the following:

LEARNING OBJECTIVES ❷❸

Compute cash flows from operating activities—indirect method

Net income	$ 42,000	Depreciation	$ 6,000
Collection of dividend revenue	7,100	Decrease in current liabilities	25,000
Payment of interest	12,000	Increase in current assets other	
Sales revenue	307,000	than cash	29,000
Gain on sale of land	26,000	Payment of dividends	7,700
Acquisition of land	35,000	Payment of income tax	14,000

Requirement

Compute cash flows from operating activities by the *indirect* method. Use the format of the operating activities section of Exhibit 9-6. Also evaluate the operating cash flow of South Central Distributors. Give the reason for your evaluation.

LEARNING OBJECTIVE ❸

Compute cash flows from operating activities—indirect method

🌐 **E9-14** The accounting records of Ashby Fur Traders include these accounts:

Cash				Accounts Receivable			
Aug. 1	80,000			Aug. 1	8,000		
Receipts	418,000	Payments	450,000	Receipts	522,000	Collections	418,000
Aug. 31	48,000			Aug. 31	112,000		

Inventory				Equipment			
Aug. 1	6,000			Aug. 1	181,000		
Purchases	433,000	Cost of Sales	333,000	Acquisition	4,000		
Aug. 31	106,000			Aug. 31	185,000		

Accumulated Depreciation—Equipment				Accounts Payable			
		Aug. 1	45,000			Aug. 1	15,000
		Depreciation	5,000	Payments	334,000	Purchases	433,000
		Aug. 31	50,000			Aug. 31	114,000

Accrued Liabilities				Retained Earnings			
		Aug. 1	14,000	Quarterly		Aug. 1	63,000
Payments	35,000	Receipts	30,000	Dividend	20,000	Net Income	25,000
		Aug. 31	9,000			Aug. 31	68,000

Requirement

Compute Ashby's net cash provided by (used for) operating activities during August. Use the *indirect* method. Do you see any potential problems in Ashby's cash flows from operations? How can you tell?

LEARNING OBJECTIVES ❷❸

Prepare the statement of cash flows—indirect method

🌐 **E9-15** The income statement and additional data of Breen Travel Products, Inc., follow:

	A	B	C	D
1	**Breen Travel Products, Inc.** Income Statement For the Year Ended December 31, 2020			
2	Revenues:			
3	Sales revenue	$ 283,000		
4	Dividend revenue	8,700	$ 291,700	
5	Expenses:			
6	Cost of goods sold	96,000		
7	Salary expense	54,000		
8	Depreciation expense	27,000		
9	Advertising expense	4,300		
10	Interest expense	2,100		
11	Income tax expense	6,000	189,400	
12	Net income		$ 102,300	
13				

Additional data:

a. Acquisition of plant assets was $200,000. Of this amount, $160,000 was paid in cash and $40,000 by signing a note payable.

b. Proceeds from sale of land totalled $23,000.

c. Proceeds from issuance of common share totalled $60,000.

d. Payment of long-term note payable was $13,000.

e. Payment of dividends was $10,000.

f. From the balance sheet:

	December 31,	
	2020	**2019**
Current assets:		
Cash..	$150,000	$138,900
Accounts receivable...	44,000	57,000
Inventory..	104,000	72,000
Prepaid expenses..	9,500	8,300
Current liabilities:		
Accounts payable..	$ 38,000	$ 23,000
Accrued liabilities..	11,000	24,000

Requirements

1. Prepare Breen's statement of cash flows for the year ended December 31, 2020, using the *indirect* method.
2. Evaluate Breen's cash flows for the year. In your evaluation, mention all three categories of cash flows and give the reason for your evaluation.

E9-16 Consider three independent cases for the cash flows of Texas Tires Corp. For each case, identify from the statement of cash flows how Texas Tires Corp. generated the cash to acquire new plant assets. Rank the three cases from the most healthy financially to the least healthy.

LEARNING OBJECTIVE ❸
Interpret a statement of cash flows—indirect method

	Case A	Case B	Case C
Cash flows from operating activities:			
Net income...	$ 14,000	$ 14,000	$ 14,000
Depreciation and amortization..	17,000	17,000	17,000
Increase in operating current assets	(1,000)	(7,000)	(3,000)
Decrease in operating current liabilities........................	(3,000)	(27,000)	(4,000)
	27,000	(3,000)	24,000
Cash flows from investing activities:			
Acquisition of plant assets	(141,000)	(141,000)	(141,000)
Sales of plant assets	148,000	28,000	47,000
	7,000	(113,000)	(94,000)
Cash flows from financing activities:			
Issuance of share	26,000	149,000	104,000
Payment of debt...	(38,000)	(28,000)	(45,000)
	(12,000)	121,000	59,000
Net increase (decrease) in cash	$ 22,000	$ 5,000	$ (11,000)

E9-17 Compute the following items for the statement of cash flows:

a. Beginning and ending Plant Assets, Net, are $125,000 and $115,000, respectively. Depreciation for the period was $9,000, and purchases of new plant assets were $45,000. Plant assets were sold at a $10,000 gain. What were the cash proceeds of the sale?

b. Beginning and ending Retained Earnings are $44,000 and $69,000, respectively. Net income for the period was $61,000, and stock dividends were $10,000. How much were cash dividends?

LEARNING OBJECTIVE ❸
Compute investing and financing amounts for the statement of cash flows

LEARNING OBJECTIVE ③

Use the balance sheet and the
statement of cash flows together

E9-18 Crown Specialties Ltd. reported the following at December 31, 2020 (in thousands):

	2020	2019
From the comparative balance sheet:		
Property and equipment, net	$11,150	$9,590
Long-term notes payable	4,400	3,080
From the statement of cash flows:		
Depreciation	$ 1,920	
Capital expenditures	(4,130)	
Proceeds from sale of property and equipment	770	
Proceeds from issuance of long-term note payable	1,190	
Payment of long-term note payable	(110)	
Issuance of common shares	383	

Determine the following items for Crown Specialties during 2020:

1. Gain or loss on the sale of property and equipment
2. Amount of long-term debt issued for something other than cash

LEARNING OBJECTIVES ② ③

Infer information about cash flows
using the income statement and
balance sheet

E9-19 Top Notch, Inc., reported the following in its financial statements for the year ended May 31, 2020 (in thousands):

	A	B	C	D
1		**2020**	**2019**	
2	Income Statement			
3	Net sales	$ 23,984	$ 21,115	
4	Cost of sales	18,088	15,333	
5	Depreciation	259	234	
6	Other operating expenses	3,880	4,248	
7	Income tax expense	536	485	
8	Net income	$ 1,221	$ 815	
9	Balance Sheet			
10	Cash and cash equivalents	$ 15	$ 14	
11	Accounts receivable	597	609	
12	Inventory	3,060	2,790	
13	Property and equipment, net	4,345	3,425	
14	Accounts payable	1,549	1,366	
15	Accrued liabilities	942	639	
16	Income tax payable	201	190	
17	Long-term liabilities	476	463	
18	Common shares	520	446	
19	Retained earnings	4,329	3,734	
20				

Requirement

Determine the following cash receipts and payments for Top Notch, Inc., during 2020 (enter all amounts in thousands):

a. Collections from customers
b. Payments for inventory
c. Payments for other operating expenses
d. Payment of income tax
e. Proceeds from issuance of common shares
f. Payment of cash dividends

E9-20 The December 31, 2019, balance sheet and the 2020 statement of cash flows for McFarland Corporation follow:

LEARNING OBJECTIVES ❷❸

Interpret information in the statement of cash flows for use in preparing the balance sheet

	A	B	C
1	**McFarland Corporation** Balance Sheet As at December 31, 2019		
2	**Assets:**		
3	Cash	$ 17,000	
4	Accounts receivable (net)	78,400	
5	Inventory	50,700	
6	Prepaid expenses	2,200	
7	Land	95,600	
8	Machinery and equipment (net)	73,500	
9	Total assets	$ 317,400	
10	**Liabilities:**		
11	Accounts payable	$ 40,600	
12	Unearned revenue	8,600	
13	Income taxes payable	5,500	
14	Long-term debt	86,000	
15	**Total liabilities**	140,700	
16	**Shareholders' equity:**		
17	Common shares	51,200	
18	Retained earnings	125,500	
19	Total shareholders' equity	176,700	
20	Total liabilities and shareholders' equity	$ 317,400	
21			

	A	B	C
1	**McFarland Corporation** Statement of Cash Flows For the Year Ended December 31, 2020		
2	**Cash flows from operating activities:**		
3	Net income		$ 18,400
4	Adjustments to reconcile net income to net cash provided by operating activities:		
5	Depreciation	$ 13,900	
6	Loss on sale of equipment	18,000	
7	Gain on sale of land	(7,100)	
8	Change in assets and liabilities:		
9	Decrease in Accounts receivable	50,100	
10	Increase in Inventory	(17,600)	
11	Decrease in Prepaid expenses	1,300	
12	Increase in Accounts payable	1,200	
13	Decrease in Income Taxes payable	(4,100)	
14	Increase in Unearned revenue	11,400	67,100
15	Net cash provided by operating activities		$ 85,500
16	**Cash flows from investing activities:**		
17	Purchase of equipment	(15,000)	
18	Sale of equipment	14,000	
19	Sale of land	61,000	
20	Net cash provided by investing activities		60,000

(Continued)

	A	B	C
21	**Cash flows from financing activities:**		
22	Repayment of long-term debt	(21,000)	
23	Issuance of common shares	17,700	
24	Dividends paid (dividends declared, $6,000)	(5,000)	
25	Net cash used for financing activities		(8,300)
26	Increase (decrease) in cash		137,200
27	Cash balance, December 31, 2019		17,000
28	Cash balance, December 31, 2020		$ 154,200
29			

Requirement

1. Prepare the December 31, 2020, balance sheet for McFarland.

PROBLEMS (GROUP A)

LEARNING OBJECTIVES ❶❷

Use cash-flow data to evaluate performance

P9-21A Top managers of Relax Inns are reviewing company performance for 2020. The income statement reports a 20% increase in net income over 2019. However, most of the increase resulted from a gain on insurance proceeds from fire damage to a building. The balance sheet shows a large increase in receivables. The statement of cash flows, in summarized form, reports the following:

Net cash used for operating activities	$(80,000)
Net cash provided by investing activities	40,000
Net cash provided by financing activities	50,000
Increase in cash during 2020	$ 10,000

Requirement

Write a memo giving Relax Inns' managers your assessment of 2020 operations and your outlook for the future. Focus on the information content of the cash-flow data.

LEARNING OBJECTIVES ❷❸

Prepare an income statement, balance sheet, and statement of cash flows—indirect method

P9-22A Vintage Automobiles of Orangeville Ltd. was formed on January 1, 2020, when Vintage issued common shares for $300,000. Early in January 2020, Vintage made the following cash payments:

a. $150,000 for equipment
b. $120,000 for inventory (four cars at $30,000 each)
c. $20,000 for 2020 rent on a store building

In February 2020, Vintage purchased six cars for inventory on account. Cost of this inventory was $260,000 ($43,333.33 each). Before year-end, Vintage paid $208,000 of this debt. Vintage uses the FIFO method to account for inventory.

During 2020, Vintage sold eight vintage autos for a total of $500,000. Before year-end, Vintage collected 80% of this amount.

The business employs three people. The combined annual payroll is $95,000, of which Vintage owes $4,000 at year-end. At the end of the year, Vintage paid income tax of $10,000.

Late in 2020, Vintage declared and paid cash dividends of $11,000.

For equipment, Vintage uses the straight-line depreciation method over five years with zero residual value.

Requirements

1. Prepare Vintage Automobiles of Orangeville Ltd.'s income statement for the year ended December 31, 2020. Use the single-step format, with all revenues listed together and all expenses listed together.
2. Prepare Vintage's balance sheet at December 31, 2020.
3. Prepare Vintage's statement of cash flows for the year ended December 31, 2020. Format cash flows from operating activities by using the *indirect* method.
4. Comment on the business performance based on the statement of cash flows.

P9-23A Primrose Software Inc. has assembled the following data for the year ended December 31, 2020.

LEARNING OBJECTIVES ❷❸

Prepare the statement of cash flows—indirect method

	December 31	
	2020	2019
Current Accounts:		
Current assets:		
Cash and cash equivalents	$38,700	$22,700
Accounts receivable	69,700	64,200
Inventories	88,600	83,000
Prepaid expenses	5,300	4,100
Current liabilities:		
Accounts payable	57,200	55,800
Income tax payable	18,600	16,700
Accrued liabilities	15,500	27,200

Transaction Data for 2020:

Acquisition of land by issuing		Repurchase of common shares	$14,300
long-term note payable	$ 95,000	Loss on sale of equipment	11,700
Stock dividends	31,800	Payment of cash dividends	18,300
Collection of loan	8,700	Issuance of long-term note	
Depreciation expense	27,100	payable to borrow cash	34,400
Purchase of building	125,300	Net income	45,100
Repayment of bonds payable by		Issuance of common shares	
issuing common shares	65,000	for cash	41,200
Purchase of long-term investment	31,600	Proceeds from sale of equipment	58,000

Requirement

Prepare Primrose Software Inc.'s statement of cash flows using the *indirect* method to report operating activities. Include an accompanying schedule of non-cash investing and financing activities. How much of the cash used for investing activities was provided by operations?

P9-24A The comparative balance sheet of Northern Movie Theatre Company at March 31, 2020, reported the following:

LEARNING OBJECTIVES ❷❸

Prepare the statement of cash flows—indirect method

	March 31,	
	2020	2019
Current assets:		
Cash and cash equivalents	$ 9,900	$14,000
Accounts receivable	14,900	21,700
Inventories	63,200	60,600
Prepaid expenses	1,900	1,700
Current liabilities:		
Accounts payable	30,300	27,600
Accrued liabilities	10,700	11,100
Income tax payable	8,000	4,700

Northern's transactions during the year ended March 31, 2020, included the following:

Acquisition of land by		Sale of long-term investment	$13,700
issuing note payable	$101,000	Depreciation expense	17,300
Payment of cash dividend	30,000	Cash purchase of building	47,000
Cash purchase of equipment	78,700	Net income	50,000
Issuance of long-term note		Issuance of common shares for cash	11,000
payable to borrow cash	50,000	Stock dividend	18,000

Requirements

1. Prepare Northern Movie Theatre Company's statement of cash flows for the year ended March 31, 2020, using the *indirect* method to report cash flows from operating activities. Report non-cash investing and financing activities in an accompanying schedule.
2. Evaluate Northern's cash flows for the year. Mention all three categories of cash flows and give the reason for your evaluation.

LEARNING OBJECTIVES ②③

Prepare the statement of cash flows—indirect method

CT

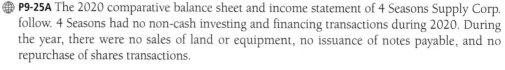

P9-25A The 2020 comparative balance sheet and income statement of 4 Seasons Supply Corp. follow. 4 Seasons had no non-cash investing and financing transactions during 2020. During the year, there were no sales of land or equipment, no issuance of notes payable, and no repurchase of shares transactions.

	A	B	C	D
1	**4 Seasons Supply Corp.** Comparative Balance Sheet As at December 31, 2020 and 2019			
2		**December 31**		
3		**2020**	**2019**	**Increase (Decrease)**
4	Current assets:			
5	Cash and cash equivalents	$ 17,600	$ 5,300	$ 12,300
6	Accounts receivable	27,200	27,600	(400)
7	Inventories	83,600	87,200	(3,600)
8	Prepaid expenses	2,500	1,900	600
9	Property, plant, and equipment:			
10	Land	89,000	60,000	29,000
11	Equipment, net	53,500	49,400	4,100
12	Total assets	$ 273,400	$ 231,400	$ 42,000
13	Current liabilities:			
14	Accounts payable	$ 35,800	$ 33,700	$ 2,100
15	Salary payable	3,100	6,600	(3,500)
16	Other accrued liabilities	22,600	23,700	(1,100)
17	Long-term liabilities:			
18	Notes payable	75,000	100,000	(25,000)
19	Shareholders' equity:			
20	Common shares	88,300	64,700	23,600
21	Retained earnings	48,600	2,700	45,900
22	Total liabilities and shareholders' equity	$ 273,400	$ 231,400	$ 42,000
23				

	A	B	C	D
1	**4 Seasons Supply Corp.** Income Statement For the Year Ended December 31, 2020			
2	Revenues:			
3	Sales revenue		$ 228,700	
4	Expenses:			
5	Cost of goods sold	$ 70,600		
6	Salary expense	27,800		
7	Depreciation expense	4,000		
8	Other operating expense	10,500		
9	Interest expense	11,600		
10	Income tax expense	29,100		
11	Total expenses		153,600	
12	Net income		$ 75,100	
13				

Requirements

1. Prepare the 2020 statement of cash flows, formatting operating activities by using the *indirect* method.
2. How will what you learned in this problem help you evaluate an investment?

PROBLEMS (GROUP B)

P9-26B Top managers of Culinary Imports Limited are reviewing company performance for 2020. The income statement reports a 15% increase in net income, the fourth consecutive year showing an income increase above 10%. The income statement includes a non-recurring loss without which net income would have increased by 16%. The balance sheet shows modest increases in assets, liabilities, and shareholders' equity. The assets posting the largest increases are plant and equipment because the company is halfway through a five-year expansion program. No other asset and no liabilities are increasing dramatically. A summarized version of the statement of cash flows reports the following:

LEARNING OBJECTIVES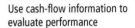

Use cash-flow information to evaluate performance

Net cash provided by operating activities	$ 310,000
Net cash used for investing activities	(290,000)
Net cash provided by financing activities..	50,000
Increase in cash during 2020..	$ 70,000

Requirement

Write a memo giving top managers of Culinary Imports Limited your assessment of 2020 operations and your outlook for the future. Focus on the net income and the cash-flow data.

P9-27B Cruise Canada Motorhomes Inc. (CCM) was formed on January 1, 2020, when the company issued its common shares for $200,000. Early in January, CCM made the following cash payments:

LEARNING OBJECTIVES ❷❸

Prepare an income statement, balance sheet, and statement of cash flows—indirect method

a. For showroom fixtures, $50,000
b. For inventory, two motorhomes at $60,000 each, a total of $120,000
c. For rent on a store building, $12,000

In February, CCM purchased three motorhomes on account. Cost of this inventory was $160,000 ($53,333.33 each). Before year-end, CCM paid $140,000 of this debt. CCM uses the FIFO method to account for inventory.

During 2020, CCM sold four motorhomes for a total of $560,000. Before year-end, CCM collected 90% of this amount.

The store employs three people. The combined annual payroll is $90,000, of which CCM owes $3,000 at year-end. At the end of the year, CCM paid income tax of $64,000.

Late in 2020, CCM declared and paid cash dividends of $40,000.

For showroom fixtures, CCM uses the straight-line depreciation method over five years with zero residual value.

Requirements

1. Prepare CCM's income statement for the year ended December 31, 2020. Use the single-step format, with all revenues listed together and all expenses listed together.
2. Prepare CCM's balance sheet at December 31, 2020.
3. Prepare CCM's statement of cash flows for the year ended December 31, 2020. Format cash flows from operating activities by the indirect method.
4. Comment on the business performance based on the statement of cash flows.

LEARNING OBJECTIVES ❷❸

Prepare the statement of cash flows—indirect method

P9-28B Accountants for Crowne Plaza Products Inc. have assembled the following data for the year ended December 31, 2020:

	December 31	
	2020	**2019**
Current Accounts:		
Current assets:		
Cash and cash equivalents	$29,100	$34,800
Accounts receivable	70,100	73,700
Inventories	90,600	96,500
Prepaid expenses	3,200	2,100
Current liabilities:		
Accounts payable	71,600	67,500
Income tax payable	5,900	6,800
Accrued liabilities	28,300	23,200

Transaction Data for 2020:

Payment of cash dividends	$48,300	Stock dividends	$12,600
Issuance of long-term note		Collection of loan	10,300
payable to borrow cash	71,000	Purchase of equipment	69,000
Net income	31,000	Payment of note payable by	
Issuance of preferred shares for cash	36,200	issuing common shares	89,400
Sale of long-term investment	12,200	Purchase of long-term investment	44,800
Depreciation expense	30,300	Acquisition of building by issuing	
Payment of long-term note payable	47,800	long-term note payable	201,000
Gain on sale of investment	3,500		

Requirement

Prepare Crowne Plaza Products's statement of cash flows using the *indirect* method to report operating activities. Include an accompanying schedule of non-cash investing and financing activities. How much of the cash used for investing activities was provided by operations?

LEARNING OBJECTIVES ❷❸

Prepare the statement of cash flows—indirect method

P9-29B The comparative balance sheet of Crossbow Novelties Corp. at December 31, 2020, reported the following:

	December 31	
	2020	**2019**
Current Assets:		
Cash and cash equivalents	$28,800	$12,500
Accounts receivable	28,600	29,300
Inventories	51,600	53,000
Prepaid expenses	4,200	3,700
Current Liabilities:		
Accounts payable	31,100	28,000
Accrued liabilities	14,300	16,800
Income tax payable	11,000	14,300

Crossbow's transactions during 2020 included the following:

Cash purchase of building	$124,000	Depreciation expense	$17,800
Net income	52,000	Payment of cash dividends	17,000
Issuance of common shares		Cash purchase of equipment	55,000
for cash	105,600	Issuance of long-term note	
Stock dividend	13,000	payable to borrow cash	32,000
Sale of long-term investment	6,000	Repayment of note payable by	
		issuing common shares	30,000

Requirements

1. Prepare the statement of cash flows of Crossbow Novelties Corp. for the year ended December 31, 2020. Use the *indirect* method to report cash flows from operating activities. Report non-cash investing and financing activities in an accompanying schedule.
2. Evaluate Crossbow's cash flows for the year. Mention all three categories of cash flows, and give the reason for your evaluation.

P9-30B The 2020 comparative balance sheet and income statement of Riverbend Pools Inc. follow. Riverbend had no non-cash investing and financing transactions during 2020. During the year, there were no sales of land or equipment, no issuances of notes payable, and no share repurchase transactions.

LEARNING OBJECTIVES ❷❸
Prepare the statement of cash flows—indirect method

	A	B	C	D	E
1	**Riverbend Pools Inc.** Comparative Balance Sheet As at December 31, 2020 and 2019				
2		**2020**	**2019**	**Increase (Decrease)**	
3	Current assets:				
4	Cash and cash equivalents	$ 28,700	$ 15,600	$ 13,100	
5	Accounts receivable	47,100	44,000	3,100	
6	Inventories	94,300	89,900	4,400	
7	Prepaid expenses	1,700	2,200	(500)	
8	Property, plant, and equipment:				
9	Land	35,100	10,000	25,100	
10	Equipment, net	100,900	93,700	7,200	
11	Total assets	$ 307,800	$ 255,400	$ 52,400	
12	Current liabilities:				
13	Accounts payable	$ 22,700	$ 24,600	$ (1,900)	
14	Salary payable	2,100	1,400	700	
15	Other accrued liabilities	24,400	22,500	1,900	
16	Long-term liabilities:				
17	Notes payable	55,000	65,000	(10,000)	
18	Shareholders' equity:				
19	Common shares	131,100	122,300	8,800	
20	Retained earnings	72,500	19,600	52,900	
21	Total liabilities and shareholder's equity	$ 307,800	$ 255,400	$ 52,400	
22					

	A	B	C	D
1	**Riverbend Pool Inc.** Income Statement For the Year Ended December 31, 2020			
2	Revenues:			
3	Sales revenue		$ 438,000	
4	Interest revenue		$ 11,700	
5	Total revenues		449,700	
6	Expenses:			
7	Cost of goods sold	$ 185,200		
8	Salary expense	76,400		
9	Depreciation expense	15,300		
10	Other operating expense	49,700		
11	Interest expense	24,600		
12	Income tax expense	16,900		
13	Total expenses		368,100	
14	Net income		$ 81,600	
15				

Requirements

1. Prepare the statement of cash flows of Riverbend Pools Inc. for the year ended December 31, 2020. Determine cash flows from operating activities by the indirect method.
2. How will what you learned in this problem help you evaluate an investment?

APPLY YOUR KNOWLEDGE

DECISION CASES

This section's material reflects CPA enabling competencies, including:

II Problem-solving and decision-making

Based on Chartered Professional Accountant standards

LEARNING OBJECTIVE ❸

Prepare and use the statement of cash flows to evaluate operations

Case 1. The 2020 income statement and the 2020 comparative balance sheet of T-Bar-M Camp Inc. have just been distributed at a meeting of the camp's board of directors. The directors raise a fundamental question: Why is the cash balance so low? This question is especially troublesome because 2020 showed record profits. As the controller of the company, you must answer the question.

	A	B	C
1	**T-Bar-M Camp Inc.** Income Statement For the Year Ended December 31, 2020		
2	*(in thousands)*		
3	Revenue:		
4	Sales revenue	$ 436	
5	Expenses:		
6	Cost of goods sold	$ 221	
7	Salary expense	48	
8	Depreciation expense	57	
9	Interest expenses	13	
10	Total expenses	339	
11	Net income	$ 97	
12			

	A	B	C	D
1	**T-Bar-M Camp Inc.** Comparative Balance Sheet As at December 31, 2020 and 2019			
2	*(in thousands)*	**2020**	**2019**	
3	**Assets**			
4	Cash	$ 17	$ 63	
5	Accounts receivable, net	72	61	
6	Inventories	194	181	
7	Long-term investments	31	0	
8	Property, plant, and equipment	369	259	
9	Accumulated depreciation	(244)	(198)	
10	Patents, net	177	188	
11	Totals	$ 616	$ 554	
12	**Liabilities and Shareholders' Equity**			
13	Accounts payable	$ 63	$ 56	
14	Accrued liabilities	12	17	
15	Notes payable, long-term	179	264	
16	Common shares	149	61	
17	Retained earnings	213	156	
18	Totals	$ 616	$ 554	
19				

Requirements

1. Prepare a statement of cash flows for 2020 in the format that best shows the relationship between net income and operating cash flow. The company sold no plant and equipment or long-term investments and issued no notes payable during 2020. There were *no* non-cash investing and financing transactions during the year. Show all amounts in thousands.

2. Answer the board members' question: Why is the cash balance so low? Point out the two largest cash payments during 2020.

3. Considering net income and the company's cash flows during 2020, was it a good year or a bad year? Give your reasons. Explain the format you chose for the statement of cash flows.

Case 2. Applied Technology Inc. and Four-Star Catering Ltd. are asking you to recommend their shares to your clients. Because Applied and Four-Star earn about the same net income and have similar financial positions, your decision depends on their statements of cash flows, which are summarized as follows:

LEARNING OBJECTIVES **❶❷**

Use cash-flow data to evaluate an investment

	Applied Technology Inc.		Four-Star Catering Ltd.	
Net cash provided by operating activities		$30,000		$70,000
Cash provided by (used for) investing activities:				
Purchase of property, plant, and equipment	$(20,000)		$(100,000)	
Sale of property, plant, and equipment	40,000	20,000	10,000	(90,000)
Cash provided by (used for) financing activities:				
Issuance of common shares		—		30,000
Paying off long-term debt		(40,000)		—
Net increase in cash...		$10,000		$10,000

Based on their cash flows, which company looks better? Give your reasons.

ETHICAL DECISIONS

Decision 1. Columbia Industries is having a bad year. Net income is only $37,000. Also, two important overseas customers are falling behind in their payments to Columbia, and Columbia's accounts receivable are ballooning. The company desperately needs a loan. The Columbia board of directors is considering ways to put the best face on the company's financial statements. Columbia's bank closely examines cash flow from operations. Daniel Peavey, Columbia's controller, suggests reclassifying the receivables from the slow-paying clients as long-term. He explains to the board that removing the $80,000 rise in accounts receivable from current assets will increase net cash provided by operations. This approach may help Columbia get the loan.

Requirements

1. Identify the ethical issue(s) in this situation.
2. Who are the stakeholders in this situation?
3. What is the potential impact of this reporting issue on each stakeholder?
4. What should the board do?
5. Under what conditions would the reclassification of the receivables be considered ethical?

Decision 2. For each of the situations listed, identify which of the principles (professional behaviour, integrity, due care, objectivity, or professional competence) from the CPA Code of Professional Conduct is violated. Assume all persons listed in the situations are CPAs. (Note: Refer to the CPA Code of Professional Conduct contained on pages 27–28 in Chapter 1 for descriptions of the principles.)

a. Eleanor has been the CFO of Solaris Technologies for 15 years, and has never uncovered any material mistakes or fraud on its financial statements. Eleanor is sure this year that nothing has changed, so she signs off on the financial statements without reviewing them first because she has more urgent matters demanding her attention.

b. Patty is a newly hired accountant at Trucking Systems. Her responsibilities include preparing all of the company's financial statements including its statement of cash flows. Trucking Systems uses the direct method to prepare its statement of cash flows. Patty has not prepared a statement of cash flows in many years and cannot remember how to prepare it using the direct method. Patty prepares the statement of cash flows using the indirect method and hopes that no one will notice.

c. Reagan is the accounting manager of Velocity, Inc., and has approved the acquisition of expensive, new equipment without approval from her boss. She knows her boss will find out when looking at the financial statements so Reagan asks one of the staff accountants to hide the cash flow in another category where it will not be noticed.

d. Albert is an accountant who is close to retirement at Image Industries. Since he does not have much time left with the company, he has been a little careless with the preparation of the company's statement of cash flows. The ending cash balance does not match the cash balance on the balance sheet, but Albert forces it to balance with a plug figure.

FOCUS ON FINANCIAL STATEMENT ANALYSIS

LEARNING OBJECTIVES ❶❷❸
Use the statement of cash flows

MyLab Accounting

Use Dollarama's statement of cash flows along with the company's other financial statements, all in Appendix A at the end of the book, to answer the following questions.

Requirements

Task 1. By which method does Dollarama report cash flows from operating activities? Explain your answer.

Task 2. Evaluate Dollarama's change in cash in fiscal year 2018 compared with 2017.

Task 3. What was Dollarama's main source of cash? Is this a positive result? What was its main use of cash?

Task 4. Explain in detail the two main reasons why net cash from operating activities differs from net earnings.

Task 5. Which of Dollarama's financial statements report dividend-related information? How does the dividend information reported differ across these statements?

CHECK YOUR WORK

STOP + THINK ANSWERS

STOP + THINK (9-1)

Depreciation and amortization are non-cash expenses that reduce net income, so to determine Dollarama's cash flows from operating activities, they must be added back to net income. Essentially, the Operating Activities section of the statement of cash flows converts accrual-based net income to a figure approximate to what net income would have been had it been determined using the cash basis of accounting.

STOP + THINK (9-2)

a. Financing	e. Investing	i. Investing
b. Financing	f. Financing	j. Operating
c. Operating	g. Financing	k. Investing
d. Financing	h. Operating	l. Investing

STOP + THINK (9-3)

1. Midwest has been expanding. It has acquired new business(es) for $400, with no significant disposals over three years. It also has total property, plant, and equipment purchases of $4,082 over the three years, with no significant disposals.

2. $156 (Proceeds of $55 − Carrying amount = loss of $101)

3. Yes, I would be pleased with Midwest's operating cash flows, as they are consistently higher than net income, which indicates a high quality of earnings. The company also has net cash inflows from operations of over $1,000 in each year, with a significant increase in 2021.

4. Midwest has been relying more on debt, as its net proceeds from equity issuances are only $12 over the three years, whereas its net proceeds from borrowing are $328 during this period.

5. Midwest has a strong cash position. It has over $850 in cash at the end of 2021, which is almost $200 more than it had at the end of 2019. Also, its cash flows from operations are its most significant source of cash in all three years.

QUICK QUIZ ANSWERS

1. *c*
2. *a*
3. *b*
4. *b*
5. *d*
6. *c*
7. *c*
8. Paying dividends *financing*
   Earning dividends *operating*
9. *c [Carrying value = $12,000 ($20,000 − $8,000; Gain = $3,000; Proceeds = $15,000 ($12,000 + $3,000)]*
10. *d*
11. *b*
12. *a*
13. *c*   *Gain   Depr.   A/Rec.*
    [$47,000 − $8,000 + $6,000 + ($11,000 − $7,000)
         Invy.   A/Pay.
    − ($10,000 − $9,000) − ($7,000 − $6,000)
        Accr. Liab.
    + ($7,000 − $3,000) = $51,000]

14. *a*
15. *a Cash received = $28,000 ($20,000 + $8,000)*
    Cash paid = $50,000 ($69,000 − $20,000 − $6,000 + $X = $93,000; X = $50,000)
    Net cash used = $22,000 ($50,000 − $28,000)
16. *a*
17. *d*
18. *d Cash received from issuance of shares = $10,000 ($20,000 − $10,000)*
    Cash paid for dividends (X) = $36,000 ($70,000 + net income $47,000 − $X = $81,000; Dividends = $36,000)
    Net cash used = $26,000 ($36,000 − $10,000)
19. *a ($800,000 − $40,000 = $760,000)*
20. *a [$59,100 − ($5,000 − $2,800) = $56,900]*

Appendix 9A

Preparing the Statement of Cash Flows: Direct Method

PREPARE A STATEMENT OF CASH FLOWS USING THE DIRECT METHOD OF DETERMINING CASH FLOWS FROM OPERATING ACTIVITIES

IFRS and ASPE encourage companies to prepare the statement of cash flows using the direct method because it provides clearer information about the sources and uses of cash. Very few companies use this method, however, because the indirect method gained prominence in the past and now continues to be used for reasons of comparability and user familiarity. Investing and financing cash flows are unaffected by the chosen method of reporting operating cash flows.

To illustrate the statement of cash flows, we use Bradshaw Corporation, a dealer in playground equipment. To prepare the statement of cash flows by the direct method, proceed as follows:

Step 1 Lay out the template of the *operating activities* section of the statement of cash flows by the direct method, as shown in Exhibit 9A-1.

Step 2 Use the comparative balance sheet to determine the increase or decrease in cash during the period. The change in cash is the "check figure" for the statement of cash flows. Bradshaw Corporation's comparative balance sheet indicates that Bradshaw's cash decreased by $20,000 during 2020 (Exhibit 9-4, p. 453). *Why* did Bradshaw's cash fall during 2020? The statement of cash flows explains.

Step 3 Use the available data to prepare the statement of cash flows. Bradshaw's transaction data appear in Exhibit 9A-2. These transactions affected both the income statement (Exhibit 9-5, p. 453) and the statement of cash flows. Some transactions affect one statement and some, the other.

EXHIBIT 9A-1
Template of the Operating Activities Section of the Statement of Cash Flows: Direct Method

	A
1	**Bradshaw Corporation** Statement of Cash Flows For the Year Ended December 31, 2020
2	**Cash flows from operating activities:**
3	Receipts:
4	Collections from customers
5	Interest received on notes receivable
6	Dividends received on investments in shares
7	Other operating receipts
8	Total cash receipts
9	Payments:
10	To suppliers
11	To employees
12	For interest
13	For income tax
14	Other operating payments
15	Total cash payments
16	Net cash provided by (used for) operating activities
17	

EXHIBIT 9A-2
Summary of Bradshaw
Corporation's 2020 Operating
Activities Transactions

	A
1	**Operating Activities**
2	1. Sales on credit, $284,000
3	*2. Collections from customers, $271,000
4	3. Interest revenue on notes receivable, $12,000
5	*4. Collection of interest receivable, $10,000
6	*5. Cash receipt of dividend revenue on investments in shares, $9,000
7	6. Cost of goods sold, $150,000
8	7. Purchases of inventory on credit, $147,000
9	*8. Payments to suppliers, $133,000
10	9. Salary and wages expense, $56,000
11	*10. Payments of salary and wages, $58,000
12	11. Depreciation expense, $18,000
13	12. Other operating expense, $17,000
14	*13. Interest expense and payments, $16,000
15	*14. Income tax expense and payments, $15,000
16	

*Indicates a cash flow to be reported on the statement of cash flows.
Note: Income statement data are taken from Exhibit 9-A6, page 494.

For example, sales (item 1) are reported on the income statement. Cash collections (item 2) go on the statement of cash flows. Other transactions, such as the cash receipt of dividend revenue (item 5), affect both statements. *The statement of cash flows reports only those transactions with cash effects* (those with an asterisk in Exhibit 9A-2). Exhibit 9A-3 gives Bradshaw Corporation's statement of cash flows for 2020.

EXHIBIT 9A-3
Statement of Cash Flows—
Direct Method

	A	B	C	D
1	**Bradshaw Corporation** Statement of Cash Flows For the Year Ended December 31, 2020			
2	*(in thousands)*			
3	**Cash flows from operating activities:**			
4	Receipts:			
5	Collections from customers	$ 271		
6	Interest received on notes receivable	10		
7	Dividends received on investments in shares	9		
8	Total cash receipts		$ 290	
9	Payments:			
10	To suppliers	(133)		
11	To employees	(58)		
12	For interest	(16)		
13	For income tax	(15)		
14	Total cash payments		(222)	
15	Net cash provided by operating activities		(68)	
16				

Cash Flows from Operating Activities

Operating cash flows are listed first because they are the most important. Exhibit 9A-3 shows that Bradshaw is sound; operating activities were the largest source of cash.

CASH COLLECTIONS FROM CUSTOMERS. Both cash sales and collections of accounts receivable are reported on the statement of cash flows as "Collections from customers . . . $271,000" in Exhibit 9A-3.

CASH RECEIPTS OF INTEREST. The income statement reports interest revenue. Only the cash receipts of interest appear on the statement of cash flows—$10,000 in Exhibit 9A-3.

CASH RECEIPTS OF DIVIDENDS. Dividends are earned on investments in shares. Dividend revenue is reported on the income statement, and only cash receipts are reported on the statement of cash flows—$9,000 in Exhibit 9A-3. (Dividends *received* are operating activities, but dividends *paid* are financing activities.)

PAYMENTS TO SUPPLIERS. Payments to suppliers include all payments for inventory and operating expenses except employee compensation, interest, and income taxes. *Suppliers* are those entities that provide the business with its inventory and essential services. For example, a clothing store's suppliers may include Arrow Shirts, Gildan Activewear, and Levi Strauss. Other suppliers provide advertising, utilities, and various services that are operating expenses. Exhibit 9A-3 shows that Bradshaw Corporation paid suppliers $133,000.

PAYMENTS TO EMPLOYEES. This category includes payments for salaries, wages, commissions, and other forms of employee compensation. Accrued amounts are excluded because they have not yet been paid. The statement of cash flows in Exhibit 9A-3 reports only the cash payments ($58,000).

PAYMENTS FOR INTEREST EXPENSE AND INCOME TAX EXPENSE. Interest and income tax payments are reported separately. Bradshaw Corporation paid all its interest and income tax expenses in cash. Therefore, the same amount appears on the income statement and the statement of cash flows. Interest payments are operating cash flows because the interest is an expense.

DEPRECIATION EXPENSE. This expense is *not* listed on the statement of cash flows in Exhibit 9A-3 because it does not affect cash.

GAIN ON SALE OF PROPERTY, PLANT, AND EQUIPMENT. This gain is not listed on the statement of cash flows in Exhibit 9A-3 because it does not affect cash. The proceeds from selling the property, plant, and equipment will be included as a cash inflow under investing activities.

MyLab Accounting

STOP + THINK (9A-1)

Classify each of the following as an operating activity, an investing activity, or a financing activity. Also identify those items that are not reported on the statement of cash flows prepared by the *direct* method.

a. Net income
b. Payment of dividends
c. Borrowing
d. Payment of cash to suppliers
e. Making a loan
f. Receipt of cash dividends
g. Depreciation expense
h. Purchase of equipment
i. Issuance of shares
j. Purchase of another company
k. Payment of a note payable
l. Payment of income taxes
m. Collections from customers
n. Accrual of interest revenue
o. Expiration of prepaid expense

Now let's see how to compute the amounts of the operating cash flows by the direct method.

Computing Operating Cash Flows by the Direct Method

To compute operating cash flows by the direct method, we use the income statement and the *changes* in the related balance sheet accounts. Exhibit 9A-4 diagrams the process. Exhibit 9A-5 is Bradshaw Corporation's income statement and Exhibit 9A-6 (page 494) is the comparative balance sheet.

EXHIBIT 9A-4
Direct Method of Computing Cash Flows From Operating Activities

RECEIPTS/PAYMENTS	From Income Statement Account	Change in Related Balance Sheet Account
RECEIPTS:		
From customers	Sales Revenue	+ Decrease in Accounts Receivable − Increase in Accounts Receivable
Of interest	Interest Revenue	+ Decrease in Interest Receivable − Increase in Interest Receivable
PAYMENTS:		
To suppliers	Cost of Goods Sold	+ Increase in Inventory / − Decrease in Inventory → + Decrease in Accounts Payable / − Increase in Accounts Payable
	Operating Expense	+ Increase in Prepaids / − Decrease in Prepaids → + Decrease in Accrued Liabilities / − Increase in Accrued Liabilities
To employees	Salary (Wages) Expense	+ Decrease in Salary (Wages) Payable − Increase in Salary (Wages) Payable
For interest	Interest Expense	+ Decrease in Interest Payable − Increase in Interest Payable
For income tax	Income Tax Expense	+ Decrease in Income Tax Payable − Increase in Income Tax Payable

We thank Barbara Gerrity for suggesting this exhibit.

EXHIBIT 9A-5
Income Statement for the Bradshaw Corporation

	A	B	C	D
1	**Bradshaw Corporation** Income Statement For the Year Ended December 31, 2020			
2	*(in thousands)*			
3	Revenues and gains:			
4	Sales revenue	$ 284		
5	Interest revenue	12		
6	Dividend revenue	9		
7	Gain on sale of property, plant, and equipment	8		
8	Total revenues and gains		$ 313	
9	Expenses:			
10	Cost of goods sold	150		
11	Salary and wages expense	56		
12	Depreciation expense	18		
13	Other operating expense	17		
14	Interest expense	16		
15	Income tax expense	15		
16	Total expenses		272	
17	Net income		$ 41	
18				

EXHIBIT 9A-6
Comparative Balance Sheet for Bradshaw Corporation

	A	B	C	D	
1	**Bradshaw Corporation** Comparative Balance Sheet As at December 31, 2020 and 2019				
2	*(amounts in thousands)*	**2020**	**2019**	**Increase (Decrease)**	
3	**Assets**				
4	Current:				
5	Cash	$ 22	$ 42	$ (20)	⎫
6	Accounts receivable	93	80	13	⎪
7	Interest receivable	3	1	2	⎬ *Changes in current assets—Operating*
8	Inventory	135	138	(3)	⎪
9	Prepaid expenses	8	7	1	⎭
10	Long-term note receivable from another company	11	—	11	⎫
11	Property, plant, and equipment assets, net of depreciation	353	219	134	⎬ *Changes in non-current assets—Investing*
12	Total	$ 625	$ 487	$ 138	⎭
13	**Liabilities**				
14	Current:				⎫
15	Accounts payable	$ 91	$ 57	$ 34	⎪
16	Salary and wages payable	4	6	(2)	⎬ *Changes in current liabilities—Operating*
17	Accrued liabilities	1	3	(2)	⎭
18	Long-term debt	160	77	83	⎫
19	**Shareholders' Equity**				⎬ *Change in long-term liabilities and* *contributed capital accounts—Financing*
20	Share capital	259	258	1	⎭ *Change due to net income—Operating*
21	Retained earnings	110	86	24	*Change due to dividends—Financing*
22	Total	$ 625	$ 487	$ 138	
23					

COMPUTING CASH COLLECTIONS FROM CUSTOMERS. Collections start with sales revenue (an accrual-basis amount). Bradshaw Corporation's income statement (Exhibit 9A-5) reports sales of $284,000. Accounts Receivable increased from $80,000 at the beginning of the year to $93,000 at year-end, a $13,000 increase (Exhibit 9A-6). Based on those amounts, Cash Collections equal $271,000. We must solve for cash collections (X).

Accounts Receivable					
Beginning balance	+	Sales	− Collections	=	Ending balance
$80,000	+	$284,000	−X	=	$93,000
			−X	=	$93,000 − $80,000 − $284,000
			−X	=	$271,000

The T-account for Accounts Receivable provides another view of the same computation:

Accounts Receivable			
Beginning balance	80,000		
Sales	284,000	Collections	271,000
Ending balance	93,000		

Accounts Receivable increased, so collections must be less than sales.

All collections of receivables are computed in this way. Let's turn now to other cash receipts. In our example, Bradshaw Corporation earned interest revenue. Interest Receivable's balance increased by $2,000 (Exhibit 9A-6). Cash receipts of interest were $10,000 (Interest Revenue of $12,000 minus the $2,000 increase in Interest Receivable). Exhibit 9A-4 shows how to make this computation.

COMPUTING PAYMENTS TO SUPPLIERS. This computation includes two parts:

- Payments for inventory
- Payments for operating expenses (other than interest and income tax)

Payments for inventory are computed by converting cost of goods sold to the cash basis. We use Cost of Goods Sold, Inventory, and Accounts Payable. First, we must solve for purchases. All amounts come from Exhibits 9A-5 and 9A-6.

Cost of Goods Sold

Beginning inventory	+	Purchases	−	Ending inventory	=	Cost of goods sold
$138,000	+	X		$135,000	=	$150,000
		X			=	$150,000 − $138,000 + $135,000
		X			=	$147,000

Now we can compute cash payments for inventory (Y), as follows:

Accounts Payable

Beginning balance	+	Purchases	−	Payments for inventory	=	Ending balance
$57,000	+	$147,000		−Y	=	$91,000
				−Y	=	$91,000 − $57,000 − $147,000
				−Y	=	$113,000

The T-accounts show where the data come from:

Inventory					Accounts Payable			
Beg. Inventory	138,000	Cost of goods sold	150,000		Payments for		Beg. bal.	57,000
Purchases	147,000				inventory	113,000	Purchases	147,000
End. Inventory	$135,000						End bal.	91,000

Accounts Payable increased, so payments are less than purchases.

COMPUTING PAYMENTS FOR OPERATING EXPENSES. Payments for operating expenses other than interest and income tax can be computed from three accounts: Prepaid Expenses, Accrued Liabilities, and Other Operating Expenses. All Bradshaw Corporation data come from Exhibits 9A-5 and 9A-6.[2]

Prepaid Expenses							
Beginning balance	+	Payments	−	Expiration of prepaid expense	=	Ending balance
$7,000	+	X		$7,000	=	$8,000
		X			=	$8,000 − $7,000 + $7,000
		X			=	$8,000

Accrued Liabilities							
Beginning balance	+	Accrual of expense at year-end	−	Payments	=	Ending balance
$3,000	+	$1,000		−X	=	$1,000
				−X	=	$1,000 − $3,000 − $1,000
				−X	=	$3,000

Other Operating Expenses							
Accrual of expense at year-end	+	Expiration of prepaid expense	+	Payments	=	Ending balance
$1,000	+	$7,000	+	X	=	$17,000
				X	=	$17,000 − $1,000 − $7,000
				X	=	$9,000
		Total payments for operating expenses			=	$8,000 + $3,000 + $9,000
					=	$20,000

The T-accounts give another picture of the same data:

Prepaid Expenses					Accrued Liabilities				Operating Expenses		
Beg. bal.	7,000	Expiration of prepaid expense	7,000	Payment	3,000	Beg. bal.	3,000	Accrual of expense at year-end	1,000		
Payments	8,000					Accrual of expense at year-end	1,000	Expiration of prepaid expense	7,000		
End. bal.	8,000					End. bal.	1,000	Payments	9,000		
								End. bal.	17,000		

---

[2]A simplifying assumption has been made in this example that the entire opening prepaid expenses will expire during the year and that all opening accrued liabilities will be paid during the year.

COMPUTING PAYMENTS TO EMPLOYEES. It is convenient to combine all payments to employees into one account, Salary and Wages Expense. We then adjust the expense for the change in Salary and Wages Payable, as shown here:

Salary and Wages Payable

Beginning balance	+	Salary and wages expense	–	Payments	=	Ending balance
$6,000	+	$56,000		–X	=	$4,000
				–X	=	$4,000 – $6,000 – $56,000
				–X	=	$58,000

The T-account gives another picture of the same data:

Salary and Wages Payable

		Beginning balance	6,000
Payments to employees	58,000	Salary and wages expense	56,000
		Ending balance	4,000

COMPUTING PAYMENTS OF INTEREST AND INCOME TAXES. Bradshaw Corporation's expense and payment amounts are the same for interest and income tax, so no analysis is required. If the expense and the payment differ, the payment can be computed as shown in Exhibit 9A-4.

Cash Flows from Investing and Financing Activities

Investing and financing cash flows are explained on pages 448–449. These computations are the same for both the direct and indirect methods.

MyLab Accounting

STOP + THINK (9A-2)

Fidelity Company reported the following for 2020 and 2019 (in millions):

As at December 31,	2020	2019
Receivables, net	$ 3,500	$3,900
Inventory	5,200	5,000
Accounts payable	900	1,200
Income taxes payable	600	700

Year Ended December 31,	2020
Revenues	$23,000
Cost of goods sold	14,100
Income tax expense	900

Based on these figures, how much cash did

- Fidelity collect from customers during 2020?
- Fidelity pay for inventory during 2020?
- Fidelity pay for income taxes during 2020?

SUMMARY

SUMMARY OF LEARNING OBJECTIVES

LEARNING OBJECTIVE	SUMMARY
A-1 **Prepare** a statement of cash flows using the direct method of determining cash flows from operating activities	To determine cash flows from operating activities using the direct method, sum cash receipts from operating activities and deduct cash payments for operating activities.

Cash receipts from operating activities include:

- Collections from customers
- Interest received from loans and advances to others and from investments
- Dividends received

Cash payments for operating activities include:

- Payments to suppliers
- Payments to employees
- Payments of interest
- Payment of income taxes

The net cash flows from operating activities determined using the direct method will always equal the net cash flows from operating activities determined using the indirect method.

Cash flows from investing and financing activities are not affected by the method used to determine cash flows from operating activities.

MyLab Accounting

END-OF-APPENDIX SUMMARY PROBLEM

Kapoor Products Inc. reported the following comparative balance sheet and income statement for 2020:

	A	B	C	D
1	**Kapoor Products Inc.** Balance Sheet As at December 31, 2020 and 2019			
2		**2020**	**2019**	
3	Cash	$ 19,000	$ 3,000	
4	Accounts receivable	22,000	23,000	
5	Inventories	34,000	31,000	
6	Prepaid expenses	1,000	3,000	
7	Equipment (net)	90,000	79,000	
8	Intangible assets	9,000	9,000	
9		$ 175,000	$ 148,000	
10	Accounts payable	$ 14,000	$ 9,000	
11	Accrued liabilities	16,000	19,000	
12	Income tax payable	14,000	12,000	
13	Long-term debt	45,000	50,000	
14	Share capital	22,000	18,000	
15	Retained earnings	64,000	40,000	
16		$ 175,000	$ 148,000	
17				

	A	B	C	D
1	**Kapoor Products Inc.** Income Statement For the Years Ended December 31, 2020 and 2019			
2		**2020**	**2019**	
3	Sales revenue	$ 190,000	$ 165,000	
4	Gain on sale of equipment	6,000	—	
5	Total revenue and gains	196,000	165,000	
6	Cost of goods sold	85,000	70,000	
7	Depreciation expense	19,000	17,000	
8	Other operating expenses	36,000	33,000	
9	Total expenses	140,000	120,000	
10	Income before income tax	56,000	45,000	
11	Income tax expense	18,000	15,000	
12	Net income	$ 38,000	$ 30,000	
13				

Assume that you are an investment analyst for Canmore Investments Ltd. and have been tasked with analyzing Kapoor Products Inc. as Canmore is considering purchasing it. You determine that you need the following Kapoor cash-flow data for 2020. There were no non-cash investing and financing activities.

a. Collections from customers
b. Cash payments for inventory
c. Cash payments for operating expenses
d. Cash payment for income tax
e. Cash received from the sale of equipment, with Kapoor Products Inc. paying $40,000 for new equipment during the year
f. Issuance of common shares
g. Issuance of long-term debt, with Kapoor Products Inc. paying off $20,000 of long-term debt during the year
h. Cash dividends, with no stock dividends

Provide your colleagues with the needed data. Show your work.

Name: Kapoor Products Inc.
Fiscal Period: Year ended December 31, 2020

ANSWERS

a. Analyze Accounts Receivable (let X = Collections from customers):

The change in Accounts Receivable of $1,000 ($22,000 − $23,000) is a result of sales and collections from customers.

Beginning	+	Sales	−	Collections	=	Ending
$23,000	+	$190,000	−	X	=	$22,000
				X	=	$191,000

b. Analyze Inventory and Accounts Payable (let X = Purchases, and let Y = Payments for inventory):

First calculate the amount of purchases. Then calculate the change in Accounts Payable that relates to cash payments.

Beginning Inventory	+	Purchases	−	Ending Inventory	=	Cost of Goods Sold
$31,000	+	X	−	$34,000	=	$85,000
		X			=	$88,000

Beginning Accounts Payable	+	Purchases	−	Payments	=	Ending Accounts Payable
$9,000	+	$88,000	−	Y	=	$14,000
				Y	=	$83,000

Cash payments for operating expenses must account for the changes that relate to prepaid expenses and accrued liabilities.

c. Start with Other Operating Expenses, and adjust for the changes in Prepaid Expenses and Accrued Liabilities:

Other Operating Expenses		+ Increase, or − Decrease in Prepaid Expenses		− Increase, or + Decrease in Accrued Liabilities	=	Payments for Operating Expenses
$36,000	−	$2,000	+	3,000	=	$37,000

The change in Income Tax Payable of $2,000 ($14,000 − $12,000) is a result of income tax expense and income tax payments made.

d. Analyze Income Tax Payable (let X = Payments of income tax):

	Beginning	+	Income Tax Expense	−	Payments	=	Ending
	$12,000	+	$18,000	−	X	=	$14,000
					X	=	$16,000

Cash received from the sale of equipment is the carrying amount of the equipment plus the gain or minus the loss on the sale. First determine the carrying amount of the equipment sold.

e. Analyze Equipment (Net) (Let X = Carrying amount of equipment sold. Then combine with gain or loss on sale to compute cash received from sale.)

Beginning	+	Acquisitions	−	Depreciation	−	Carrying Amount Sold	=	Ending
$79,000	+	$40,000	−	$19,000	−	X	=	$90,000
						X	=	$10,000

Cash received from sale	=	Carrying Amount Sold	+	Gain, or − Loss on Sale
$16,000	=	$10,000	+	$6,000

The change in Common Shares of $4,000 ($22,000 − $18,000) is a result of issuing shares.

f. Analyze Common Shares (let X = issuance):

	Beginning	+	Issuance	=	Ending
	$18,000	+	X	=	$22,000
			X	=	$ 4,000

Long-Term Debt declined by $5,000 ($45,000 − $50,000). However, because a $20,000 payment was made during the year, $15,000 of long-term debt must have been issued.

g. Analyze Long-Term Debt (let X = issuance):

	Beginning	+	Issuance	−	Payment	=	Ending
	$50,000	+	X	−	$20,000	=	$45,000
			X			=	$15,000

The change in Retained Earnings of $24,000 ($64,000 − $40,000) is a result of net income ($38,000 from the 2020 income statement) and the payment of cash dividends. The same information is shown on the statement of retained earnings.

h. Analyze Retained Earnings (let X = dividends):

	Beginning	+	Net Income	−	Dividends	=	Ending
	$40,000	+	$38,000	−	X	=	$64,000
					X	=	$14,000

ASSESS YOUR PROGRESS

Recall that for the sake of simplicity and consistency, this text classifies all interest paid and interest and dividends received as operating activities, and classifies dividends paid as a financing activity. All questions and problems in this chapter should be answered using this convention.

SHORT EXERCISES

S9A-1 Tally-Ho Horse Farm Inc. began 2020 with cash of $44,000. During the year, Tally-Ho earned service revenue of $500,000 and collected $510,000 from customers. Expenses for the year totalled $420,000, with $400,000 paid in cash to suppliers and employees. Tally-Ho also paid $100,000 to purchase equipment and a cash dividend of $50,000 to shareholders. During 2020, Tally-Ho borrowed $20,000 by issuing a note payable.

Prepare the company's statement of cash flows for the year. Format operating activities by the direct method.

LEARNING OBJECTIVES ❷Ⓐ-❶
Prepare a statement of cash flows—direct method

S9A-2 (Exercise S9A-3 is an alternative exercise.) Maritime Fisheries Ltd. provides the following data for the year ended June 30, 2020:

LEARNING OBJECTIVES ❷Ⓐ-❶
Compute operating cash flows—direct method

Cost of goods sold	$100,000	Payment of dividends	$ 6,000
Payments to suppliers	87,000	Proceeds from issuance of	
Purchase of equipment	40,000	common shares	20,000
Payments to employees	70,000	Sales revenue	210,000
Payment of note payable	30,000	Collections from customers	180,000
Proceeds from sale of land	60,000	Payment of income tax	10,000
Depreciation expense	8,000	Repurchase of common shares	5,000

Prepare the *operating activities section* of Maritime Fisheries Ltd.'s statement of cash flows for the year ended June 30, 2020. Maritime Fisheries uses the *direct* method for operating cash flows. Use Exhibit 9A-3 on page 491 as a guide.

S9A-3 Use your response and other data from exercise S9A-2 to prepare the rest of Maritime Fisheries Ltd.'s statement of cash flows for the year ended June 30, 2020. Maritime Fisheries uses the *direct* method for operating activities.

LEARNING OBJECTIVES ❷Ⓐ-❶
Prepare a statement of cash flows—direct method

S9A-4 Autos of Red Deer Inc. reported the following financial statements for 2020:

LEARNING OBJECTIVE Ⓐ-❶
Compute operating cash flows—direct method

	A	B	C
1	**Autos of Red Deer Inc.** Income Statement For the Year Ended December 31, 2020		
2	*(in thousands)*		
3	Sales revenue	$ 710	
4	Cost of goods sold	340	
5	Salary expense	70	
6	Depreciation expense	20	
7	Other expenses	130	
8	Total expenses	560	
9	Net income	$ 150	
10			

	A	B	C	D	E	F	G
1	Autos of Red Deer Inc. Comparative Balance Sheet As at December 31, 2020 and 2019						
2	*(in thousands)*						
3	**Assets**	**2020**	**2019**	**Liabilities**	**2020**	**2019**	
4	Current:			Current:			
5	Cash	$ 19	$ 16	Accounts payable	$ 47	$ 42	
6	Accounts receivable	59	48	Salary payable	23	21	
7	Inventories	75	84	Accrued liabilities	8	11	
8	Prepaid expenses	3	2	Long-term notes payable	68	58	
9	Long-term investments	55	75	**Shareholders' Equity**			
10	Property, plant, and equipment	225	185	Share capital Retained earnings	40 250	32 246	
11	Totals	$ 436	$ 410	Total	$ 436	$ 410	
12							

Compute the following:

a. Collections from customers

b. Payments for inventory

LEARNING OBJECTIVE A-1

Compute operating cash flows—direct method

S9A-5 Use the Autos of Red Deer data in exercise S9A-4 to compute the following:

a. Payments to employees

b. Payments of other expenses

EXERCISES

LEARNING OBJECTIVES 2 A-1

Identify activities for the statement of cash flows—direct method

E9A-6 Identify each of the following transactions as operating (O), investing (I), financing (F), non-cash investing and financing (NIF), or not reported on the statement of cash flows (N). Indicate whether each transaction increases (+) or decreases (−) cash. The *direct* method is used for operating activities.

_____ a. Repurchase of common shares

_____ b. Issuance of common shares for cash

_____ c. Payment of accounts payable

_____ d. Issuance of preferred shares for cash

_____ e. Payment of cash dividend

_____ f. Sale of long-term investment

_____ g. Amortization of patent

_____ h. Collection of accounts receivable

_____ i. Issuance of long-term note payable to borrow cash

_____ j. Depreciation of equipment

_____ k. Acquisition of equipment by issuance of note payable

_____ l. Payment of long-term debt

_____ m. Acquisition of building by payment of cash

_____ n. Accrual of salary expense

_____ o. Purchase of long-term investment

_____ p. Payment of wages to employees

_____ q. Collection of cash interest

_____ r. Cash sale of land

_____ s. Distribution of stock dividend

LEARNING OBJECTIVES 2 A-1

Classify transactions for the statement of cash flows—direct method

E9A-7 Indicate where, if at all, each of the following transactions would be reported on a statement of cash flows prepared by the *direct* method and the accompanying schedule of non-cash investing and financing activities.

a.	Equipment	18,000		d.	Building	164,000	
	Cash...		18,000		Cash.......................................		164,000
b.	Cash...	7,200		e.	Cash.......................................	1,400	
	Long-Term Investment		7,200		Accounts Receivable		1,400
c.	Bonds Payable	45,000		f.	Dividends Payable	16,500	
	Cash...		45,000		Cash.......................................		16,500

g.	Furniture and Fixtures	22,100			k.	Accounts Payable............................	8,300	
	Note Payable, Short-Term		22,100			Cash...		8,300
h.	Retained Earnings	36,000			l.	Salary Expense	4,300	
	Common Shares.........................		36,000			Cash..		4,300
i.	Cash...	2,000			m.	Cash.......................................	81,000	
	Interest Revenue.......................		2,000			Common Shares........................		81,000
j.	Land..	87,700			n.	Common Shares............................	13,000	
	Cash..		87,700			Cash..		13,000

E9A-8 The accounting records of Jasmine Pharmaceuticals Inc. reveal the following:

LEARNING OBJECTIVES ❷ A-1

Compute cash flows from operating activities—direct method

Payment of salaries and wages	$34,000	Net income...	$34,000
Depreciation.......................................	22,000	Payment of income tax	13,000
Decrease in current liabilities..............	20,000	Collection of dividend revenue...........	7,000
Increase in current assets		Payment of interest	16,000
other than cash..............................	27,000	Cash sales..	38,000
Payment of dividends	12,000	Loss on sale of land	5,000
Collection of		Acquisition of land	37,000
accounts receivable.........................	93,000	Payment of accounts payable	54,000

Requirement

Compute cash flows from operating activities by the *direct* method. Use the format of the operating activities section of Exhibit 9A-3. Also, evaluate Jasmine's operating cash flow. Give the reason for your evaluation.

E9A-9 Selected accounts of Fishbowl Antiques Inc. show the following:

LEARNING OBJECTIVES ❷ A-1

Identify items for the statement of cash flows—direct method

Salary Payable

		Beginning balance	9,000
Payments	40,000	Salary expense	38,000
		Ending balance	7,000

Buildings

Beginning balance	90,000	Depreciation	18,000
Acquisitions	145,000	Carrying amount of	
		building sold	109,000*
Ending balance	108,000		

*Sale price was 140,000

Notes Payable

		Beginning balance	273,000
Payments	69,000	Issuance of note payable	
		for cash	83,000
		Ending balance	287,000

Requirement

For each account, identify the item or items that should appear on a statement of cash flows prepared by the *direct* method. State where to report the item.

LEARNING OBJECTIVES ❷Ⓐ①

Prepare the statement of cash
flows—direct method

 E9A-10 The income statement and additional data of Floral World Ltd. follow:

	A	B	C	D
1	**Floral World Ltd.** Income Statement For the Year Ended December 31, 2020			
2	Revenues:			
3	Sales revenue	$ 229,000		
4	Dividend revenue	15,000	$ 244,000	
5	Expenses:			
6	Cost of goods sold	103,000		
7	Salary expense	45,000		
8	Depreciation expense	29,000		
9	Advertising expense	11,000		
10	Interest expense	2,000		
11	Income tax expense	9,000	199,000	
12	Net income		$ 45,000	
13				

Additional data:

a. Collections from customers are $30,000 more than sales.

b. Payments to suppliers are $1,000 more than the sum of cost of goods sold plus advertising expense.

c. Payments to employees are $1,000 more than salary expense.

d. Dividend revenue, interest expense, and income tax expense equal their cash amounts.

e. Acquisition of plant and equipment is $150,000. Of this amount, $101,000 is paid in cash and $49,000 by signing a note payable.

f. Proceeds from sale of land total $24,000.

g. Proceeds from issuance of common shares total $30,000.

h. Payment of long-term note payable is $15,000.

i. Payment of dividends is $11,000.

j. Cash balance, December 31, 2019, was $20,000.

Requirements

1. Prepare Floral World Ltd.'s statement of cash flows and accompanying schedule of non-cash investing and financing activities. Report operating activities by the *direct* method.

2. Evaluate Floral World's cash flows for the year. In your evaluation, mention all three categories of cash flows and give the reason for your evaluation.

LEARNING OBJECTIVE Ⓐ①

Compute amounts for the statement
of cash flows—direct method

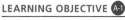 **E9A-11** Compute the following items for the statement of cash flows:

a. Beginning and ending Accounts Receivable are $22,000 and $32,000, respectively. Credit sales for the period total $60,000. How much are cash collections from customers?

b. Cost of goods sold is $111,000. Beginning Inventory was $25,000, and ending Inventory is $21,000. Beginning and ending Accounts Payable are $14,000 and $8,000, respectively. How much are cash payments for inventory?

LEARNING OBJECTIVE Ⓐ①

Compute cash-flow amounts

E9A-12 Morgan Industries Inc. reported the following in its financial statements for the year ended August 31, 2020 (in thousands):

	2020	2019
Income Statement		
Net sales...	$24,623	$21,207
Cost of sales..	18,048	15,466
Depreciation..	269	230
Other operating expenses...	3,883	4,248
Income tax expense..	537	486
Net income..	$ 1,886	$ 777
Balance Sheet		
Cash and cash equivalents...	$ 17	$ 13
Accounts receivable..	601	615
Inventory...	3,100	2,831
Property and equipment, net...	4,345	3,428
Accounts payable..	1,547	1,364
Accrued liabilities...	938	631
Income tax payable...	201	194
Long-term liabilities..	478	464
Common shares...	519	446
Retained earnings...	4,380	3,788

Determine the following cash receipts and payments for Morgan Industries Inc. during 2020:

a. Collections from customers
b. Payments for inventory
c. Payments for other operating expenses

d. Payment of income tax
e. Proceeds from issuance of common shares
f. Payment of cash dividends

PROBLEMS (GROUP A)

🌐 **P9A-13A** World Mosaic Furniture Gallery Inc. provided the following data from the company's records for the year ended April 30, 2020:

a. Credit sales, $583,900
b. Loan to another company, $12,500
c. Cash payments to purchase property, plant, and equipment, $59,400
d. Cost of goods sold, $382,600
e. Proceeds from issuance of common shares, $8,000
f. Payment of cash dividends, $48,400
g. Collection of interest, $4,400
h. Acquisition of equipment by issuing short-term note payable, $16,400
i. Payments of salaries, $93,600
j. Proceeds from sale of property, plant, and equipment, $22,400, including $6,800 loss
k. Collections on accounts receivable, $428,600
l. Interest revenue, $3,800
m. Cash receipt of dividend revenue, $4,100

n. Payments to suppliers, $368,500
o. Cash sales, $171,900
p. Depreciation expense, $59,900
q. Proceeds from issuance of note payable, $19,600
r. Payments of long-term notes payable, $50,000
s. Interest expense and payments, $13,300
t. Salary expense, $95,300
u. Loan collections, $12,800
v. Proceeds from sale of investments, $9,100, including $2,000 gain
w. Payment of short-term note payable by issuing long-term note payable, $63,000
x. Depreciation expense, $2,900
y. Income tax expense and payments, $37,900
z. Cash balance: April 30, 2019, $39,300; April 30, 2020, $36,600

LEARNING OBJECTIVES ❷ A-1
Prepare the statement of cash flows—direct method

Requirements

1. Prepare World Mosaic Furniture Gallery Inc.'s statement of cash flows for the year ended April 30, 2020. Use the *direct* method for cash flows from operating activities. Follow the format of Exhibit 9A-3 (p. 491), but do *not* show amounts in thousands. Include an accompanying schedule of non-cash investing and financing activities.
2. Evaluate 2020 from a cash-flow standpoint. Give your reasons.

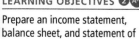
P9A-14A Vintage Automobiles of Orangeville Ltd. was formed on January 1, 2020, when Vintage issued common shares for $300,000. Early in January 2020, Vintage made the following cash payments:

a. $150,000 for equipment

b. $120,000 for inventory (four cars at $30,000 each)

c. $20,000 for 2020 rent on a store building

In February 2020, Vintage purchased six cars for inventory on account. Cost of this inventory was $260,000 ($43,333.33 each). Before year-end, Vintage paid $208,000 of this debt. Vintage uses the FIFO method to account for inventory.

During 2020, Vintage sold eight vintage autos for a total of $500,000. Before year-end, Vintage collected 80% of this amount.

The business employs three people. The combined annual payroll is $95,000, of which Vintage owes $4,000 at year-end. At the end of the year, Vintage paid income tax of $10,000.

Late in 2020, Vintage declared and paid cash dividends of $11,000.

For equipment, Vintage uses the straight-line depreciation method over five years with zero residual value.

Requirements

1. Prepare Vintage's income statement for the year ended December 31, 2020. Use the single-step format, with all revenues listed together and all expenses listed together.
2. Prepare Vintage's balance sheet at December 31, 2020.
3. Prepare Vintage's statement of cash flows for the year ended December 31, 2020. Format cash flows from operating activities by using the *direct* method.

 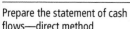
P9A-15A The 2020 comparative balance sheet and income statement of 4 Seasons Supply Corp. follow. 4 Seasons had no non-cash investing and financing transactions during 2020. During the year, there were no sales of land or equipment, no issuance of notes payable, and no repurchase of shares transactions.

	A	B	C	D
1	**4 Seasons Supply Corp.** Comparative Balance Sheet As at December 31, 2020 and 2019			
2			**December 31**	
3		**2020**	**2019**	**Increase (Decrease)**
4	Current assets:			
5	Cash and cash equivalents	$ 17,600	$ 5,300	$ 12,300
6	Accounts receivable	27,200	27,600	(400)
7	Inventories	83,600	87,200	(3,600)
8	Prepaid expenses	2,500	1,900	600
9	Property, plant, and equipment:			
10	Land	89,000	60,000	29,000
11	Equipment, net	53,500	49,400	4,100
12	Total assets	$ 273,400	$ 231,400	$ 42,000
13	Current liabilities:			
14	Accounts payable	$ 35,800	$ 33,700	$ 2,100
15	Salary payable	3,100	6,600	(3,500)
16	Other accrued liabilities	22,600	23,700	(1,100)
17	Long-term liabilities:			
18	Notes payable	75,000	100,000	(25,000)
19	Shareholders' equity:			
20	Common shares	88,300	64,700	23,600
21	Retained earnings	48,600	2,700	45,900
22	Total liabilities and shareholders' equity	$ 273,400	$ 231,400	$ 42,000
23				

	A	B	C	D
1	**4 Seasons Supply Corp.** Income Statement For the Year Ended December 31, 2020			
2	Revenues:			
3	Sales revenue		$ 228,700	
4	Expenses:			
5	Cost of goods sold	$ 70,600		
6	Salary expense	27,800		
7	Depreciation expense	4,000		
8	Other operating expense	10,500		
9	Interest expense	11,600		
10	Income tax expense	29,100		
11	Total expenses		153,600	
12	Net income		$ 75,100	
13				

Requirements

1. Prepare the 2020 statement of cash flows using the *direct* method.
2. How will what you learned in this problem help you evaluate an investment?

P9A-16A To prepare the statement of cash flows, accountants for Franklin Electric Limited have summarized 2020 activity in two accounts as follows:

LEARNING OBJECTIVES ❷ A-1

Prepare the statement of cash flows—direct method

Cash

Beginning balance	53,600	Payments on accounts payable	399,100
Sale of long-term investment	21,200	Payments of dividends	27,200
Collections from customers	661,700	Payments of salaries and wages	143,800
Issuance of common shares	47,300	Payments of interest	26,900
Receipts of dividends	17,100	Purchase of equipment	31,400
		Payments of operating expenses	34,300
		Payment of long-term note payable	41,300
		Repurchase of common shares	26,400
		Payment of income tax	18,900
Ending balance	51,600		

Common Shares

Repurchase of common shares for cancellation	26,400	Beginning balance	110,800
		Issuance for cash	47,300
		Issuance to acquire land	80,100
		Issuance to retire note payable	19,000
		Ending balance	230,800

Requirement

Prepare the statement of cash flows of Franklin Electric Limited for the year ended December 31, 2020, using the *direct* method to report operating activities. Also prepare the accompanying schedule of non-cash investing and financing activities.

	A	B	C	D
1	**Franklin Electric Limited** Income Statement For the Year Ended December 31, 2020			
2	Revenues:			
3	Sales revenue		$ 689,300	
4	Dividend revenue		17,100	
5	Total revenue		706,400	

(Continued)

	A	B	C	D
6	Expenses and losses:			
7	Cost of goods sold	$ 402,600		
8	Salary and wage expense	150,800		
9	Depreciation expense	19,300		
10	Other operating expense	44,100		
11	Interest expense	28,800		
12	Income tax expense	16,200		
13	Loss on sale of investments	1,100		
14	Total expenses and losses		662,900	
15	Net income		$ 43,500	
16				

	A	B	C
1	**Franklin Electric Limited** Selected Balance Sheet Data		
2		**2020** **Increase** **(Decrease)**	
3	Current assets:		
4	Cash and cash equivalents	$ (2,000)	
5	Accounts receivable	27,600	
6	Inventories	(11,800)	
7	Prepaid expenses	600	
8	Long-term investments	(22,300)	
9	Equipment, net	12,100	
10	Land	80,100	
11	Current liabilities:		
12	Accounts payable	(8,300)	
13	Interest payable	1,900	
14	Salary payable	7,000	
15	Other accrued liabilities	10,400	
16	Income tax payable	(2,700)	
17	Long-term note payable	(60,300)	
18	Share capital	120,000	
19	Retained earnings	16,300	
20			

LEARNING OBJECTIVES ② A-1

Prepare the statement of cash flows—direct method

P9A-17A The comparative balance sheet of Graphic Design Studio Inc. at June 30, 2020, included these amounts:

	A	B	C	D	E
1	**Graphic Design Studio Inc.** Balance Sheet As at June 30, 2020 and 2019				
2		**2020**	**2019**	**Increase** **(Decrease)**	
3	Current assets:				
4	Cash	$ 28,600	$ 8,600	$ 20,000	
5	Accounts receivable	48,800	51,900	(3,100)	
6	Inventories	68,600	60,200	8,400	
7	Prepaid expenses	3,700	2,800	900	
8	Long-term investment	10,100	5,200	4,900	
9	Equipment, net	74,500	73,600	900	
10	Land	42,400	96,000	(53,600)	
11		$ 276,700	$ 298,300	$ (21,600)	

	A	B	C	D	E
12	Current liabilities:				
13	Notes payable, short-term	$ 13,400	$ 18,100	$ (4,700)	
14	Accounts payable	42,400	40,300	2,100	
15	Income tax payable	13,800	14,500	(700)	
16	Accrued liabilities	8,200	9,700	(1,500)	
17	Interest payable	3,700	2,900	800	
18	Salary payable	900	2,600	(1,700)	
19	Long-term note payable	47,400	94,100	(46,700)	
20	Share capital	59,800	51,200	8,600	
21	Retained earnings	87,100	64,900	22,200	
22		$ 276,700	$ 298,300	$ (21,600)	
23					

Transaction data for the year ended June 30, 2020, were:

a. Net income, $60,300
b. Depreciation expense on equipment, $13,400
c. Purchased long-term investment, $4,900
d. Sold land for $46,900, including $6,700 loss
e. Acquired equipment by issuing long-term note payable, $14,300
f. Paid long-term note payable, $61,000
g. Received cash for issuance of common shares, $3,900
h. Paid cash dividends, $38,100
i. Paid short-term note payable by issuing common shares, $4,700

Requirement

Prepare the statement of cash flows of Graphic Design Studio Inc. for the year ended June 30, 2020, using the *direct* method to report operating activities. Also, prepare the accompanying schedule of non-cash investing and financing activities. All current accounts except short-term notes payable result from operating transactions. The accounting records provide the following: collections from customers, $261,800; interest received, $1,300; payments to suppliers, $133,500; payments to employees, $40,500; payments for income tax, $10,600; payment of interest, $5,300.

PROBLEMS (GROUP B)

P9A-18B Rocco's Gourmet Foods Inc. provides the following data from the company's records for the year ended July 31, 2020:

LEARNING OBJECTIVES ❷ A-1
Prepare the statement of cash flows—direct method

a. Salary expense, $105,300
b. Cash payments to purchase property, plant, and equipment, $181,000
c. Proceeds from issuance of note payable, $44,100
d. Payments of long-term note payable, $18,800
e. Proceeds from sale of property, plant, and equipment, $59,700, including $10,600 gain
f. Interest revenue, $12,100
g. Cash receipt of dividend revenue on investments, $2,700
h. Payments to suppliers, $673,300
i. Interest expense and payments, $37,800
j. Cost of goods sold, $481,100

k. Collection of interest revenue, $11,700
l. Acquisition of equipment by issuing short-term note payable, $35,500
m. Payments of salaries, $104,000
n. Credit sales, $768,100
o. Loan to another company, $35,000
p. Income tax expense and payments, $56,400
q. Advertising expense, $27,700
r. Collections on accounts receivable, $741,100
s. Loan collections, $74,400
t. Proceeds from sale of investments, $34,700, including $3,800 loss
u. Payment of long-term note payable by issuing preferred shares, $107,300

v. Depreciation expense, $23,900

w. Cash sales, $146,000

x. Proceeds from issuance of common shares, $50,000

y. Payment of cash dividends, $50,500

z. Cash balance: July 31, 2019—$23,800; July 31, 2020—$31,400

Requirements

1. Prepare Rocco's Gourmet Foods Inc.'s statement of cash flows for the year ended July 31, 2020. Use the *direct* method for cash flows from operating activities. Follow the format of Exhibit 9A-3, but do *not* show amounts in thousands. Include an accompanying schedule of non-cash investing and financing activities.
2. Evaluate 2020 in terms of cash flow. Give reasons for your evaluation.

LEARNING OBJECTIVES ❷ A-1

Prepare an income statement, balance sheet, and statement of cash flows—direct method

P9A-19B Cruise Canada Motorhomes Inc. (CCM) was formed on January 1, 2020, when the company issued its common shares for $200,000. Early in January, CCM made the following cash payments:

a. For showroom fixtures, $50,000

b. For inventory, two motorhomes at $60,000 each, a total of $120,000

c. For rent on a store building, $12,000

In February, CCM purchased three motorhomes on account. Cost of this inventory was $160,000 ($53,333.33 each). Before year-end, CCM paid $140,000 of this debt. CCM uses the FIFO method to account for inventory.

During 2020, CCM sold four motorhomes for a total of $560,000. Before year-end, CCM collected 90% of this amount.

The store employs three people. The combined annual payroll is $90,000, of which CCM owes $3,000 at year-end. At the end of the year, CCM paid income tax of $64,000.

Late in 2020, CCM declared and paid cash dividends of $40,000.

For showroom fixtures, CCM uses the straight-line depreciation method over five years with zero residual value.

Requirements

1. Prepare CCM's income statement for the year ended December 31, 2020. Use the single-step format, with all the revenues listed together and all expenses listed together.
2. Prepare CCM's balance sheet at December 31, 2020.
3. Prepare CCM's statement of cash flows for the year ended December 31, 2020. Format cash flows from operating activities by using the *direct* method.

LEARNING OBJECTIVES ❷ A-1

Prepare the statement of cash flows—direct method

P9A-20B The 2020 comparative balance sheet and income statement of Riverbend Pools Inc. follow. Riverbend had no non-cash investing and financing transactions during 2020. During the year, there were no sales of land or equipment, no issuances of notes payable, and no share repurchase transactions.

	A	B	C	D	E
1	**Riverbend Pools Inc.** Comparative Balance Sheet As at December 31, 2020 and 2019				
2		**2020**	**2019**	**Increase (Decrease)**	
3	Current assets:				
4	Cash and cash equivalents	$ 28,700	$ 15,600	$ 13,100	
5	Accounts receivable	47,100	44,000	3,100	
6	Inventories	94,300	89,900	4,400	
7	Prepaid expenses	1,700	2,200	(500)	

	A	B	C	D	E
8	Property, plant, and equipment:				
9	Land	35,100	10,000	25,100	
10	Equipment, net	100,900	93,700	7,200	
11	Total assets	$ 307,800	$ 255,400	$ 52,400	
12	Current liabilities:				
13	Accounts payable	$ 22,700	$ 24,600	$ (1,900)	
14	Salary payable	2,100	1,400	700	
15	Other accrued liabilities	24,400	22,500	1,900	
16	Long-term liabilities:				
17	Notes payable	55,000	65,000	(10,000)	
18	Shareholder's equity:				
19	Common shares	131,100	122,300	8,800	
20	Retained earnnings	72,500	19,600	52,900	
21	Total liabilities and shareholders' equity	$ 307,800	$ 255,400	$ 52,400	
22					

	A	B	C	D
1	**Riverbend Pools Inc.** Income Statement For the Year Ended December 31, 2020			
2	Revenues:			
3	Sales revenue		$ 438,000	
4	Interest revenue		11,700	
5	Total revenues		449,700	
6	Expenses:			
7	Cost of goods sold	$ 185,200		
8	Salary expense	76,400		
9	Depreciation expense	15,300		
10	Other operating expense	49,700		
11	Interest expense	24,600		
12	Income tax expense	16,900		
13	Total expenses		368,100	
14	Net income		$ 81,600	
15				

Requirements

1. Prepare the 2020 statement of cash flows by using the *direct* method.
2. How will what you learned in this problem help you evaluate an investment?

P9A-21B To prepare the statement of cash flows, accountants for Powers Art Gallery Inc. have summarized 2020 activity in two accounts as follows:

LEARNING OBJECTIVES ❷ A-1

Prepare the statement of cash flows—direct method

Cash

Beginning balance	87,100	Payments of operating expenses	46,100
Issuance of common shares	60,800	Payment of long-term note payable	78,900
Receipts of dividends	1,900	Repurchase of common shares	10,400
Collection of loan	18,500	Payment of income tax	8,000
Sale of long-term investments	9,900	Payments on accounts payable	101,600
Receipts of interest	12,200	Payments of dividends	1,800
Collections from customers	308,100	Payments of salaries and wages	67,500
		Payments of interest	21,800
		Purchase of equipment	79,900
Ending balance	82,500		

Common Shares	
Beginning balance	103,500
Issuance for cash	60,800
Issuance to acquire land	62,100
Issuance to retire long-term note payable	21,100
Ending balance	247,500

Requirement

Prepare Powers's statement of cash flows for the year ended December 31, 2020, using the *direct* method to report operating activities. Also, prepare the accompanying schedule of non-cash investing and financing activities. Powers's 2020 income statement and selected balance sheet data follow.

	A	B	C	D
1	**Power Art Gallery Inc.** Income Statement For the Year Ended December 31, 2020			
2	Revenues and gains:			
3	Sales revenue		$ 291,800	
4	Interest revenue		12,200	
5	Dividend revenue		1,900	
6	Gain on sale of investments		700	
7	Total revenues and gains		306,600	
8	Expenses:			
9	Cost of goods sold	$ 103,600		
10	Salary and wage expense	66,800		
11	Depreciation expense	20,900		
12	Other operating expense	44,700		
13	Interest expense	24,100		
14	Income tax expense	2,600		
15	Total expenses		262,700	
16	Net income		$ 43,900	
17				

	A	B	C
1	**Power Art Gallery Inc.** Selected Balance Sheet Data		
2		**2020 Increase (Decrease)**	
3	Current assets:		
4	Cash and cash equivalents	$ (4,600)	
5	Accounts receivable	(16,300)	
6	Inventories	5,700	
7	Prepaid expenses	(1,900)	
8	Loan receivable	(18,500)	
9	Long-term investments	(9,200)	
10	Equipment, net	59,000	
11	Land	62,100	

	A	B	C
12	Current liabilities:		
13	Accounts payable	$ 7,700	
14	Interest payable	2,300	
15	Salary payable	(700)	
16	Other accrued liabilities	(3,300)	
17	Income tax payable	(5,400)	
18	Long-term note payable	(100,000)	
19	Share capital	133,600	
20	Retained earnings	42,100	
21			

P9A-22B Arts de France Ltée's comparative balance sheet at September 30, 2020, included the following balances:

LEARNING OBJECTIVES ❷ Ⓐ-❶

Prepare the statement of cash flows—direct method

	A	B	C	D	E
1	**Arts de France Ltée** Balance Sheet As at September 30, 2020 and 2019				
2		**2020**	**2019**	**Increase (Decrease)**	
3	Current assets:				
4	Cash	$ 21,700	$ 17,600	$ 4,100	
5	Accounts receivable	46,000	46,800	(800)	
6	Inventories	121,700	116,900	4,800	
7	Prepaid expenses	8,600	9,300	(700)	
8	Long-term investment	51,100	13,800	37,300	
9	Equipment, net	131,900	92,100	39,800	
10	Land	47,100	74,300	(27,200)	
11		$ 428,100	$ 370,800	$ 57,300	
12	Current liabilities:				
13	Notes payable, short-term	$ 22,000	$ 0	$ 22,000	
14	Accounts payable	88,100	98,100	(10,000)	
15	Accrued liabilities	17,900	29,100	(11,200)	
16	Salary payable	1,500	1,100	400	
17	Long-term note payable	123,000	121,400	1,600	
18	Common shares	113,900	62,000	51,900	
19	Retained earnings	61,700	59,100	2,600	
20		$ 428,100	$ 370,800	$ 57,300	
21					

Transaction data for the year ended September 30, 2020, were:

a. Net income, $66,900
b. Depreciation expense on equipment, $8,500
c. Purchased long-term investments, $37,300
d. Sold land for $38,100, including $10,900 gain
e. Acquired equipment by issuing long-term note payable, $26,300
f. Paid long-term note payable, $24,700

g. Received cash of $51,900 for issuance of common shares

h. Paid cash dividends, $64,300

i. Acquired equipment by issuing short-term note payable, $22,000

Requirement

Prepare Arts de France's statement of cash flows for the year ended September 30, 2020, using the *direct* method to report operating activities. Also, prepare the accompanying schedule of non-cash investing and financing activities. All current accounts except short-term notes payable result from operating transactions. Prepare a supplementary schedule showing cash flows from operations by using the *direct* method. The accounting records provide the following: collections from customers, $343,100; interest received, $8,600; payments to suppliers, $216,400; payments to employees, $63,000; payment of income tax, $21,200; payment of interest, $10,700.

CHECK YOUR WORK

STOP + THINK ANSWERS

STOP + THINK (9A-1)

a. Not reported	d. Operating	g. Not reported	j. Investing	m. Operating
b. Financing	e. Investing	h. Investing	k. Financing	n. Not reported
c. Financing	f. Operating	i. Financing	l. Operating	o. Not reported

STOP + THINK (9A-2)

		Beginning receivables	+	Revenues	−	Collections	=	Ending receivable
Collections from customers	=	$3,900	+	$23,000	−		=	$3,500

		Cost of goods sold	+	Increase in inventory	+	Decrease in accounts payable	=	
Payments for inventory	=	$14,100	+	($5,200 − $5,000)	+	($1,200 − $900)	=	

		Beginning income taxes payable	+	Income tax expense	−		=	Ending income taxes payable
Payment of income taxes	=	$700	+	$900	−		=	$600

COMPREHENSIVE CASE

CHAPTER 9

This comprehensive case requires you to apply concepts learned throughout Chapter 9 and its Appendix. You may find it helpful to review these materials before responding to the case requirements.

Hollis Enterprises Inc. is an independently owned manufacturer of vinyl records. The company is run by Mark Hollis and has been thriving in recent years due to the resurgent interest in vinyl among young music buyers. The company's most recent fiscal year ended December 31, 2022. Its income statement and balance sheet for this year, along with selected transaction data, is presented below.

Hollis Enterprises Inc.
Income Statement
For the Year Ended December 31, 2022

Sales revenue	$7,282,000
Cost of goods sold	6,160,000
Gross margin	1,122,000
Operating expenses:	
General and administrative expenses	445,000
Depreciation expense, equipment	77,000
Amortization expense, intangibles	33,000
Interest expense	61,000
Rent expense	22,000
	638,000
Income from operations	484,000
Other items:	
Loss on sale of equipment	(22,000)
Income before income tax	462,000
Income tax expense	176,000
Net income	$ 286,000

Transaction data for 2022:

Purchase of equipment	$ 342,000
Payment of cash dividends	198,000
Issuance of common shares to repay bonds payable	143,000
Purchase of long-term investment	88,000
Issuance of long-term note payable to purchase patent	407,000

Hollis Enterprises Inc.
Balance Sheet
As at December 31, 2022

Assets	2022	2021
Current:		
Cash and equivalents	$ 209,000	$ 33,000
Accounts receivable	242,000	253,000
Inventories	374,000	341,000
Prepaid expenses	11,000	33,000
Total current assets	836,000	660,000
Long-term investments	198,000	110,000
Equipment, net	737,000	572,000
Intangible assets, net	484,000	110,000
Total Assets	$ 2,255,000	$ 1,452,000
Liabilities and Shareholders' Equity		
Current:		
Accounts payable	$ 385,000	$ 286,000
Accrued liabilities	77,000	99,000
Income tax payable	110,000	110,000
Total current liabilities	572,000	495,000
Long-term note payable	484,000	-
Bonds payable	440,000	583,000
Total Liabilities	1,496,000	1,078,000
Shareholders' Equity		
Common shares	462,000	165,000
Retained earnings	297,000	209,000
Total Shareholders' Equity	759,000	374,000
Total Liabilities and Shareholders' Equity	$ 2,255,000	$ 1,452,000

Transaction data for 2022:

Purchase of equipment	$ 342,000
Payment of cash dividends	198,000
Issuance of common shares to repay bonds payable	143,000
Purchase of long-term investment	88,000
Issuance of long-term note payable to purchase patent	407,000
Issuance of long-term note payable to borrow cash	77,000
Issuance of common shares for cash	154,000
Proceeds on sale of equipment (carrying amount, $100,000)	78,000

Requirements

1. Prepare Hollis Enterprises Inc.'s statement of cash flows for the year ended December 31, 2022. Prepare the operating activities section using the indirect method.
2. Prepare the operating activities section of Hollis's statement of cash flows using the direct method.

   Before proceeding to the next Requirements, you should compare your responses to Requirements #1 and #2 to the solution and correct any errors you made.

3. Which type of activity generated the most cash for Hollis in 2022? Is this a good sign or a bad sign of financial health? Explain your answer.
4. What specific investing or financing activity used the most cash in 2022? Is this a good sign or a bad sign of financial health? Explain your answer.
5. Using only the statement of cash flows as evidence, does Hollis Enterprises Inc. appear to be a healthy company? Explain your answer.

Financial Statement Analysis

10

SPOTLIGHT

Throughout this book we have shown you how to account for the financial position, results of operations, and cash flows of a variety of companies, such as Dollarama, CGI, Le Chateau, Leon's, WestJet, and Canadian Tire. Only one aspect of the course remains: financial statement analysis.

Empire Company Limited, which owns Sobeys, is one of Canada's leading grocery chains. Empire's revenues and net earnings look good, but how good *are* they? The analytical tools you learn in this chapter will help you answer this question.

How does a firm stack up to its competitors overall? By analyzing various aspects of their financial statements, you will be able to tell.

The first part of the chapter shows how to evaluate Empire Company Limited from year to year and also how to compare Empire to its competitor, Metro, another of Canada's leading grocery chains. The second part of the chapter discusses the most widely used financial ratios. You have seen many of these ratios in earlier chapters; however, we have yet to use all of them in a comprehensive analysis of a company. We will use the financial statements of Apple, Inc. to perform this analysis.

LEARNING OBJECTIVES

1. **Perform** a horizontal analysis
2. **Perform** a vertical analysis
3. **Prepare** common-size financial statements
4. **Analyze** the statement of cash flows
5. **Use** ratios to make business decisions

CPA COMPETENCIES

Competencies addressed in this chapter:

1.3.1 Prepares financial statements
1.4.4 Interprets financial reporting results for stakeholders (external or internal)

Based on Chartered Professional Accountant standards

Kevin Brine - Editorial/Alamy Stock Photo

	A	B	C	D
1	**Empire Company Limited** Consolidated Statements of Earnings (Adapted) For the Years Ended May 5, 2018 and May 6, 2017			
2	*(in millions of dollars)*	**2018**	**2017**	
3	**Sales**	$ 24,214.6	$ 23,806.2	
4	Other income	135.5	125.7	
5	Operating expenses			
6	Cost of sales	18,314.1	18,099.0	
7	Selling & administrative expenses	5,689.5	5,499.9	
8	**Operating income**	346.5	333.0	
9	Finance costs, net	110.5	118.0	
10	**Earnings before income taxes**	236.0	215.0	
11	Tax expense	56.2	42.5	
12	**Net earnings**	$ 179.8	$ 172.5	
13				

Source: Data from Empire Company Limited - 2018 Annual Report.

How Is a Company Evaluated?

Investors and creditors for both public and private corporations cannot evaluate a company by examining only one year's numerical data. That is why most financial statements cover at least two periods, like Empire's statement of earnings that begins this chapter. In fact, most financial analysis covers periods of three to five years. The goal of financial analysis is to predict the future by examining the past.

Financial analysis involves more than just looking at financial reports and doing some math. Thorough analysis of the financial position and results of operations of a company begins with understanding the business and industry of the company—the big picture. This usually entails quite a bit of reading and research, using all kinds of media—the business press, trade journals and other publications. You can often gain free access to this information on websites such as www.google.ca/finance. There are also some excellent paid sources, such as Hoovers Inc. (www.hoovers.com), where you can purchase industry and company analyses. Learning about what's happening in the industry, the markets, and the economy, along with trends in product development and specific company strategies help you put the accounting numbers in context and understand why they turned out as they did. After all, accounting data should paint a picture of the results of implementing a particular business strategy.

For example, Empire's Consolidated Statement of Earnings on page 554 reveals that operating income increased from $333 million in 2017 to $346.5 million in 2018. Net earnings also increased from $172.5 million in 2017 to $179.8 million in 2018. Looking at these trends in isolation, without knowing some additional facts, the company appears to be operating very profitably in the food retail sector. We can, however, gain additional insight into these numbers by reading industry and company analyses. After reading Empire's annual report, for example, we learn that the company is undertaking initiatives some of which include bolstering their brand, improving the customer's experience and launching online grocery shopping.

Reading the Management's Discussion and Analysis (MD&A) in a company's annual report gives management's perspectives on its operations and lends insight into why they made certain strategic decisions. For example, in the MD&A section of Empire's annual report, you will read that Empire is in the first year of a three year project which will result in reduced costs, while at the same time increased sales. It also discusses the company's expectations of the impact that minimum wage increase in Ontario and Alberta will have on the company's expenses, as well as the implementation of its online grocery shopping business.

Once we have an understanding of the big picture, we can dig more deeply into the numbers and they begin to make sense. Public companies' financial statements are comparative, that is, they cover at least two periods. Since one of the goals of financial analysis is to predict the future, it makes sense to start by mapping the trends of the past. This is particularly true of income statement data such as net sales and the various expenses that make up reported net income.

The graphs in Exhibit 10-1 show Empire's three-year trends in sales and operating income. How would you predict Empire's sales and operating income for 2019 and beyond? Based on the recent past, you would probably extend the sales line and the operating income line upward.

Let's examine some of the tools of financial analysis. We begin with horizontal analysis.

EXHIBIT 10-1
Sales and Operating Income of Empire Company Limited (Adapted)

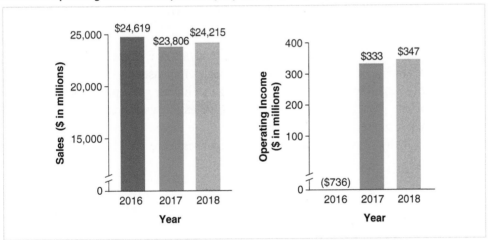

PERFORM A HORIZONTAL ANALYSIS

OBJECTIVE

Many decisions hinge on the trends of a company's sales, expenses, operating income, net income, and other key financial statement figures. Has the sales figure risen from last year? If so, by how much? Suppose that sales have increased by $200,000. Considered alone, this fact is not very informative, but the *percentage change* in sales over time helps a lot. It is better to know that sales have increased by 20% than to know only that the increase is $200,000.

❶ **Perform** a horizontal analysis

The study of percentage changes from year to year is called **horizontal analysis**. Computing a percentage change requires two steps:

1. Compute the dollar amount of the change from one period (the base period) to the next.

2. Divide the dollar amount of change by the base-period amount.

Illustration: Empire Company Limited

Horizontal analysis is illustrated for Empire as follows (dollars in millions):

	2018	2017	Increase (Decrease)	
			Amount	Percentage
Sales	$24,214.6	$23,806.2	$408.4	1.7%

Empire's sales increased by 1.7% during 2018, computed as follows:

Step 1   Compute the dollar amount of change in sales from 2017 to 2018:

$$2018 - 2017 = \text{Increase}$$

$$\$24,215 - \$23,806 = \$409$$

Step 2   Divide the dollar amount of change by the base-period amount. This computes the percentage change for the period:

$$\text{Percentage change} = \frac{\text{Dollar amount of change}}{\text{Base-year amount}} \times 100$$

$$= \frac{\$409}{\$23,806} \times 100 = 0.0172 \times 100 = 1.7\%$$

Exhibits 10-2 and 10-3 present horizontal analyses of Empire Company Ltd. The comparative statement of earnings shows that sales increased by 1.7% during 2018, while cost of sales grew by only 1.2%, resulting in a higher gross profit (Sales less cost of sales) for the year. Selling and administrative expenses increased by 3.4% and finance costs decreased by 6.4%. Operating income increased by 4.1% even though sales increased by only 1.7% and various expenses were also higher for the year.

EXHIBIT 10-2
Comparative Income Statement—Horizontal Analysis

Source: Data from Empire Company Limited - 2018 Annual Report.

	A	B	C	D	E	F
1	**Empire Company Limited** Consolidated Statements of Earnings (Adapted) For the Years Ended May 5, 2018 and May 6, 2017					
2				Increase (Decrease)		
3	*(in millions of dollars)*	2018	2017	Amount	Percentage	
4	Sales	$ 24,214.6	$ 23,806.2	$ 408.4	1.7	
5	Other income	135.5	125.7	9.8	7.8	
6	Operating expenses					
7	Cost of sales	18,314.1	18,099.0	215.1	1.2	
8	Selling & administrative expenses	5,689.5	5,499.9	189.6	3.4	
9	**Operating income**	346.5	333.0	13.5	4.1	
10	Finance costs, net	110.5	118.0	(7.5)	(6.4)	
11	**Earnings before income taxes**	236.0	215.0	21	9.8	
12	Tax expense	56.2	42.5	13.7	32.2	
13	**Net earnings**	$ 179.8	$ 172.5	$ 7.3	4.2	
14						

Note: Any increase from zero to a positive number is treated as an increase of 100%; any decrease to zero is treated as a decrease of 100%. Any decrease in a negative number is treated as an increase; any increase in a negative number is treated as a decrease.

	A	B	C	D	E	F
1	**Empire Company Limited** Consolidated Balance Sheets (Adapted) As at May 5, 2018 and May 6, 2017			**Increase (Decrease)**		
2	*(in millions of dollars)*	**2018**	**2017**	**Amount**	**Percentage**	
3	**Assets**					
4	**Current assets**					
5	Cash and cash equivalents	$ 627.9	$ 207.3	$ 420.6	203	
6	Receivables	433.2	413.6	19.6	4.7	
7	Inventories	1,251.6	1,322.2	(70.6)	(5.3)	
8	Prepaid expenses	126.8	117.5	9.3	7.9	
9	Loans and other receivables	20.9	25.5	(4.6)	(18)	
10	Income taxes receivable	15.2	31.9	(16.7)	(52.4)	
11	Assets held for sale	20.4	48.5	(28.1)	(57.9)	
12		$ 2,496.0	$ 2,166.5	329.5	15.2	
13	Loans and other receivables	80.6	82.1	(1.5)	(1.8)	
14	Investments	—	25.1	(25.1)	100	
15	Investments, at equity	571.8	648.4	(76.6)	(11.8)	
16	Other assets	34.1	43.3	(9.2)	(21.2)	
17	Property and equipment	2,787.3	3,033.3	(246.0)	(8.1)	
18	Investment property	93.9	103.0	(9.1)	(8.8)	
19	Intangibles	842.0	880.5	(38.5)	(4.4)	
20	Goodwill	1,001.9	1,003.4	(1.5)	(0.1)	
21	Deferred tax assets	754.4	709.9	(44.5)	6.3	
22		$ 8,662.0	$ 8,695.5	(33.5)	(0.4)	
23	**Liabilities and Shareholders' Equity**					
24	**Current liabilities**					
25	Accounts payable and accrued liabilities	2,253.8	2,230.2	23.6	1.1	
26	Income taxes payable	53.5	38.4	15.1	39.3	
27	Current portion of long-term debt	527.4	134.0	393.4	293.6	
28	Provisions	127.6	88.1	39.5	44.8	
29		2,962.3	2,490.7	471.6	18.9	
30	Long-term debt	1,139.5	1,736.8	(597.3)	(34.4)	
31	Deferred tax liabilities	141.3	143.8	(2.5)	(1.7)	
32	Other long-term liabilities	158.6	141.7	16.9	11.9	
33	Provisions	129.3	105.8	23.5	22.2	
34	Employee future benefits	361.2	374.0	(12.8)	(3.4)	
35		4,892.2	4,992.8	(100.6)	(2.0)	
36	**Shareholders' Equity**					
37	Common shares	2,039.5	2,034.4	5.1	0.3	
38	Contributed surplus	22.9	25.3	(2.4)	(9.4)	
39	Retained earnings	1,627.9	1,572.8	55.1	3.5	
40	Accumulated other comprehensive income	12.5	11.7	0.8	6.8	
41		3,702.8	3,644.2	58.6	1.6	
42	Non-controlling interest	67.0	58.5	8.5	14.5	
43		3,769.8	3,702.7	67.1	1.8	
44	**Total Liabilities and Shareholders' Equity**	$ 8,662.0	$ 8,695.5	(33.5)	(0.4)	
45						

EXHIBIT 10-3
Comparative Balance Sheet—Horizontal Analysis

Source: Data from Empire Company Limited - 2018 Annual Report.

Other income increased by 7.8%. In Note 19 of Empire's financial statements, we are told that most of the other income came from the sale of assets and lease revenue. Because of this increase in other income, net earnings increased by 4.2%. Also, you will note very little difference between operating income and net earnings. Overall, management was able to increase the company's revenues slightly in 2018 while limiting expenses to a lower rate of increase, resulting in the business operating more efficiently and more profitably for the year.

Studying changes in the balance sheet accounts can enhance our understanding of the current and long-term financial position of the entity. Let's look at a few of the balance sheet changes in Exhibit 10-3. First, cash increased by 203%. While the statement of cash flow would show why cash increased, we are reserving that discussion for later. Reviewing the balance sheet, we can see that cash was used to prepay expenses (increase of 7.9%) and pay back long-term debt (decrease of 34.4%). Current Loans and other receivables decreased by 18%, while long-term Loans and other receivables decreased by 1.8%. Income taxes receivable decreased by 52.4%, meaning that the company is expecting to receive a smaller refund compared to 2017, from the Canada Revenue Agency.

Accounts receivable increased by 4.7% more than sales (1.7%). This means that accounts receivable is growing faster than sales, collections may be too slow and a cash shortage may result. In this case, it's only 1.7% so it is not a concern. Accounts payable also increased less than sales (1.1%), indicating that the company's payments of short-term debt are keeping pace with its overall rate of growth in sales. On the whole, current assets increased by 15.2%, while current liabilities increased by 18.9%, resulting in negative working capital for 2018.

Property, plant, and equipment decreased by 8.1%, meaning the company either disposed of some assets and/or wrote them down due to impairment. Other assets decreased by 21.2%, but there is no indication what they are without reading the notes. Note 8 provides a schedule of the components of this category: the major items include deferred lease assets and restricted cash, which the company is reserving for future use. While long-term debt decreased by 34.4% (the company has paid back some debt), other long-term liabilities increased by 11.9%, indicating the company borrowed more money. There was a slight increase in share capital of 0.3% because the company bought back some non-voting Class A shares (Note 18); this may have resulted in a decrease in contributed surplus. Net earnings of $179.8 contributed to the increase in retained earnings.

TRY IT *in* EXCEL® ▶▶▶

Formatting comparative financial statements for horizontal analysis when the financial statements are in Excel format is quite easy. Try reconstructing Exhibit 10-2 in Excel.

1. Start with the Consolidated Statements of Operations in the opening figure of the chapter.
2. Change the labels to correspond with Exhibit 10-2. Your spreadsheet might be slightly different from Exhibit 10-2, so the cells in which you start to enter formulas might have to be modified accordingly.
3. Insert one column between the 2018 and 2017 columns. Label this "% change".
4. Compute the percentage change as follows. We start in cell E4 (blank). Change the format of the data in the cell to % by clicking on the % box in the number field in the top toolbar. In cell E4, type the following:=(B4-C4)/C4. The result of 1.7% should appear in the cell. Copy this cell formula through line 15 of the sheet to perform this computation for all other income and expenses.

Trend Percentages

Trend percentages are a form of horizontal analysis. Trends indicate the direction a business is taking. How have sales changed over a five-year period? What trend does operating income show? These questions can be answered by trend percentages over a representative period, such as the most recent five years.

Trend percentages are computed by selecting a base year whose amounts are set equal to 100%. The amount for each following year is expressed as a percentage of the base amount. To compute a trend percentage, divide an item for a later year by the base-year amount:

$$\text{Trend \%} = \frac{\text{Any-year \$}}{\text{Base-year \$}}$$

Operating income represents a company's best predictor of the future net inflows from its core business units. Empire showed operating income from continuing operations for the past five years as follows:

(in millions)	2018	2017	2016	2015	2014
Operating income	$346.5	$333.0	($2,418.5)	$743.6	$328.5

We would like to calculate trend percentages for the four-year period 2015 to 2018. The base year is 2014. Trend percentages are computed by dividing each year's amount by the 2014 amount. The trend percentages for the past five years are:

	2018	2017	2016	2015	2014
Operating income	105%	101%	(736%)	226%	100%

Looking at the trend percentages for Empire, we can see that operating income increased dramatically in 2015 but dropped quite a bit in 2016 before rising significantly in 2017, then remaining steady in 2018. According to the Management Discussion and Analysis from the Annual Report in 2015 and 2016, operating income dropped in 2016 due to costs relating to the acquisition and integration of Canada Safeway, as well as an impairment charge relating to long-lived assets and goodwill. In 2015, operating income grew from factors which included food inflation and store closures mandated by the Government of Canada in order for Empire to purchase Safeway Canada.

You can perform a trend analysis on any item you consider important. Trend analysis is widely used for predicting the future.

Horizontal analysis highlights changes in an item over time. However, no single technique gives a complete picture of a business.

② Perform a vertical analysis

PERFORM A VERTICAL ANALYSIS

Vertical analysis shows the relationship of a financial statement item to its base, which is the 100% figure. All items on the particular financial statement are reported as a percentage of that base. For the income statement, total revenue (sales) is usually the base while total assets is the base for the balance sheet. One use of vertical analysis is to reveal items that need to be investigated further. For example, if cost of goods sold as a percentage of sales is 50% in the previous year and 55% in the current year, management is now aware that expenses have increased in a particular area and can take measures to reduce these costs. You can also use a form of vertical analysis by preparing common-size financial statements and using them to compare one company with another. This will be discussed further in the next section.

To perform a vertical analysis using the income statement, total revenue is usually the base. Suppose that investors have come to expect a company's net income to be greater than 8% of net sales revenue. A drop to 4% over a period of two years while general economic conditions are improving may cause investors to become disappointed in the performance of company management. Thus, they might sell the company's shares in favour of companies with more attractive earnings potential.

Illustration: Empire Company Limited

Exhibit 10-4 shows the vertical analysis of Empire's statement of earnings as a percentage of sales. In this case,

$$\text{Vertical analysis } \% = \frac{\text{Each income statement item}}{\text{Sales}}$$

For Empire, the vertical-analysis percentage for cost of sales is 75.2% ($18,314.1/$24,350.1) in 2018, which is only a slight decrease from 75.6% in 2017. Even though it is only a slight decrease, this is a good sign as it indicates that management was able to keep costs down while sales and other income increased. Operating income, as a percentage of sales, remained steady at 1.4, and net earnings

EXHIBIT 10-4
Comparative Statement of Earnings—Vertical Analysis

Source: Data from Empire Company Limited - 2018 Annual Report.

	A	B	C	D	E	F
1	**Empire Company Limited** Consolidated Statements of Earnings (Adapted) For the Years Ended May 5, 2018 and May 6, 2017					
2	*(in millions of dollars)*	2018		2017		
3		Amount	Percentage of Sales	Amount	Percentage of Sales	
4	Sales and other income	$ 24,350.1	100.0%	$ 23,931.9	100.0%	
5	Operating expenses					
6	Cost of sales	18,314.1	75.2	18,099.0	75.6	
7	Selling & administrative expenses	5,689.5	23.4	5,499.9	23.0	
8	**Operating income**	346.5	1.4	333.0	1.4	
9	Finance costs, net	110.5	0.5	118.0	0.5	
10	**Earnings before income taxes**	236.0	0.9	215.0	0.9	
11	Tax expense	56.2	0.2	42.5	0.2	
12	**Net earnings**	$ 179.8	0.7	$ 172.5	0.7	
13						

*differences due to rounding.

as a percentage of sales also remained steady at 0.7. This indicates to management that overall net earnings remained steady because they were able to control their expenses.

TRY IT *in* EXCEL®▶▶▶

Formatting comparative financial statements for vertical analysis when the financial statements are in Excel format is just as easy as it was for horizontal analysis. Try reconstructing Exhibit 10-4 in Excel.

1. Start with the Consolidated Statements of Earnings in the opening figure of the chapter. You will be ahead of the game if you have already prepared this in Excel.
2. Change the labels to correspond with Exhibit 10-4. Your spreadsheet might be slightly different than Exhibit 10-4, so the cells in which you start to enter formulas might have to be modified accordingly.
3. We are preparing two years of comparative data, so insert columns after each of the 2018 and 2017 financial columns. In our example, these become columns C and E with blank cells; label these "% of total."
4. Common-sized income statements set net sales at 100% and express all other income and expenses as percentages of net sales. To set net sales at 100%, we start in cell C3 (blank). In the cell, type the following: =B3/$B$3. It is very important to insert the $ signs in the denominator both before and after the letter B. This "freezes" cell B3 to make it a constant denominator for the values in all other cells in the column. You may also use the F4 function key to freeze the cell value. The result of 100% should appear in the cell. To increase precision, use the "increase decimal" tab in the "number" field in the toolbar. We have adjusted to a precision of two decimal places. Copy this cell formula through line 14 of the sheet to perform this computation for all other income and expenses.
5. Repeat the process in (4) for the 2017 figures columns by entering corresponding formulas in column E. Copy these formulas through line 14. Use the "borders" tab (under "font" in the toolbar) to format the cells to extend the proper underscoring as shown in Exhibit 10-4.
6. Pat yourself on the back. You're learning to use Excel for the very valuable function of vertical analysis! Now let's dig into the numbers to interpret and what they mean.

Exhibit 10-5 shows the vertical analysis of Empire's consolidated balance sheets. The base amount is total assets. The vertical analysis of Empire's balance sheet reveals several things about Empire's financial position at May 5, 2018 relative to 2017:

- While cash increased by 203% from 2017, it also increased as a percentage of total assets from 2.4% to 7.2%. At the same time, receivables increased slightly from 4.8% to 5.0%.

- Inventories as a percentage of total assets decreased from 15.2% to 14.5%.

- The company's debt to total assets of 56.5% in 2018 decreased from 57.4% in 2017. Of the total debt, current liabilities increased from 28.6% in 2017 to 34.2% in 2018, and total long-term liabilities decreased from 28.8% to 22.3%. These debt ratios are still comfortably within reasonable limits for a retail concern.

STOP + THINK (10-2)

Using Empire's data in Exhibit 10-4, did cost of sales increase or decrease from the previous year? Is this a good sign or a bad sign?

EXHIBIT 10-5
Comparative Balance Sheet—Vertical Analysis

Source: Data from Empire Company Limited - 2018 Annual Report.

	A	B	C	D	E	F
1	**Empire Company Limited** Consolidated Balance Sheets (Adapted) As at May 5, 2018 and May 6, 2017					
2	*(in millions of dollars)*	2018		2017		
3		Amount	Percentage of Total	Amount	Percentage of Total	
4	**Assets**					
5	**Current assets**					
6	Cash and cash equivalents	$ 627.9	7.2	$ 207.3	2.4	
7	Receivables	433.2	5.0	413.6	4.8	
8	Inventories	1,251.6	14.5	1,322.2	15.2	
9	Prepaid expenses	126.8	1.5	117.5	1.4	
10	Loans and other receivables	20.9	0.2	25.5	0.3	
11	Income taxes receivable	15.2	0.2	31.9	0.3	
12	Assets held for sale	20.4	0.2	48.5	0.5	
13		$ 2,496.0	28.8	$ 2,166.5	24.9	
14	Loans and other receivables	80.6	0.9	82.1	0.9	
15	Investments	—	0.0	25.1	0.3	
16	Investments, at equity	571.8	6.6	648.4	7.5	
17	Other assets	34.1	0.4	43.3	0.5	
18	Property and equipment	2,787.3	32.2	3,033.3	34.9	
19	Investment property	93.9	1.1	103.0	1.2	
20	Intangibles	842.0	9.7	880.5	10.1	
21	Goodwill	1,001.9	11.6	1,003.4	11.5	
22	Deferred tax assets	754.4	8.7	709.9	8.2	
23		$ 8,662.0	100.0	$ 8,695.5	100.0	
24	**Liabilities and Shareholders' Equity**					
25	**Current liabilities**					
26	Accounts payable and accrued liabilities	2,253.8	26.0	2,230.2	25.6	
27	Income taxes payable	53.5	0.6	38.4	0.4	
28	Current portion of long-term debt	527.4	6.1	134.0	1.5	
29	Other liabilities	127.6	1.5	88.1	1.0	
30		2,962.3	34.2	2,490.7	28.6	
31	Long-term debt	1,139.5	13.2	1,736.8	20.0	
32	Deferred tax liabilities	141.3	1.6	143.8	1.7	
33	Other long-term liabilities	158.6	1.8	141.7	1.6	
34	Provisions	129.3	1.5	105.8	1.2	
35	Employee future benefits	361.2	4.2	374.0	4.3	
36		4,892.2	56.5	4,992.8	57.4	
37	**Shareholders' Equity**					
38	Capital Stock	2,039.5	23.5	2,034.4	23.4	
39	Contributed surplus	22.9	0.3	25.3	0.3	
40	Retained earnings	1,627.9	18.8	1,572.8	18.1	
41	Accumulated other comprehensive income	12.5	0.1	11.7	0.1	
42		3,702.8	42.7	3,644.2	41.9	
43	Non-controlling interest	67.0	0.8	58.5	0.7	
44		3,769.8	43.5	3,702.7	42.6	
45	**Total Liabilities & Shareholders' Equity**	$ 8,662.0	100.0	$ 8,695.5	100.0	
46						

PREPARE COMMON-SIZE FINANCIAL STATEMENTS

OBJECTIVE

❸ **Prepare** common-size financial statements

The percentages in Exhibits 10-4 and 10-5 can be presented as separate statements that report only percentages (no dollar amounts). These statements are called **common-size financial statements**.

On a common-size income statement, each item is expressed as a percentage of the net sales amount. Net sales is the *common size* to which we relate the other amounts. In the balance sheet, the common size is total assets. A common-size statement aids the comparison of different companies because their amounts are stated in percentages, thus expressing the financial results of each comparative company in terms of a common denominator.

Benchmarking

Benchmarking is the comparison of a company to a standard set by others. The goal of benchmarking is improvement. Suppose you are a financial analyst for ScotiaMcLeod. You are considering an investment in the shares of a grocery chain, and you are choosing between Empire Company Limited and Metro Inc. A direct comparison of their financial statements in dollar amounts is not meaningful because the companies differ greatly in size. We can, however, convert the income statements to common size and compare the percentages. The comparison is meaningful, as we shall see.

Benchmarking Against a Key Competitor

Exhibit 10-6 presents the common-size income statements of Empire Company Limited and Metro Inc. Metro serves as an excellent benchmark because it and Empire are both large, successful Canadian grocery chains. Empire's cost of goods sold, operating and other expenses as a percentage of sales are 5.1% (99.1% − 85.6%) higher than Metro's. Metro's net income as a percentage of sales is 11.2% (11.9% − 0.7%) higher than Empire's. When compared to Empire, it would appear that Metro is able to keep their costs down resulting in a higher percentage of net income to sales.

	A	B	C	D
1	**Empire Company Limited** Common-Size Income Statement (Adapted) for Comparison With a Key Competitor For the Years Ended as Indicated			
2		**Empire Company Limited (Adapted) May 5, 2018**	**Metro Inc. (Adapted) September 29, 2018**	
3	Sales	100.0%	100.0%	
4				
5	Cost of goods sold, operating and other expenses	99.1	85.6	
6	Income before income tax	0.9	14.4	
7	Income tax expense	0.2	2.5	
8	Net earnings	0.7%	11.9%	
9				

EXHIBIT 10-6
Common-Size Income Statement Compared With a Key Competitor
Source: Data from Empire Company Limited - 2018 Annual Report.

MyLab Accounting

STOP + THINK (10-3)

Assume you are a financial analyst for an investment bank and have been charged with gathering information about K-M Inc. for a client. You have been provided with the following 2020 income statement by K-M and have decided to calculate the common-size percentages. What does this tell you about the company? Show your calculations.

Net sales	$150,000
Cost of goods sold	60,000
Gross profit	90,000
Operating expense	40,000
Operating income	50,000
Income tax expense	15,000
Net income	$ 35,000

OBJECTIVE

④ **Analyze** the statement of cash flows

ANALYZE THE STATEMENT OF CASH FLOWS

So far, this chapter has focused on the income statement and balance sheet. Let's now move on to examine the consolidated statements of cash flows for Empire, which are presented in Exhibit 10-7. While the operating income is a key figure to use when analyzing a company's performance, it is also critical to examine its cash flow from operating activities, which gives us a different view of the company's operating performance. Because we record operating revenues and expenses using the accrual method, operating income may differ from operating cash flows, which are based solely on cash receipts and cash payments. A company may report significant operating income, for example, but have poor operating cash flows because it cannot sell its inventory or collect cash from its customers on a timely basis. The reverse may also be true: a company may generate significant operating cash flows but report little or no operating income. Generally, the higher the ratio of a company's cash flow from operations to its operating income, the better its quality of earnings.

The income statement and the statement of cash flows can therefore paint different pictures of the same company, so we must analyze both of them, along with the balance sheet, to gain an overall picture of a company's operating performance and financial position.

For 2018, net cash provided by operating activities was the largest source of cash for the company. Net cash provided by operations increased by 24.2% ([$879.7 − 708.5]/708.5). Also, for both 2018 and 2017, net cash provided by operating activities exceeded net income. Both of these relationships are signs of a healthy company. For both 2018 and 2017, net cash used by financing activities was the company's largest use of cash. They paid back debt and also paid dividends on the common shares.

The next thing to look at is how the company used the cash generated from operations. Under investing activities, it shows that in 2018 and 2017, they bought and sold property and equipment. As mentioned above, in 2018, the company paid back debt and still continued to pay dividends to the shareholders.

	A	B	C	D
1	**Empire Company Limited** Consolidated Statements of Cash Flows (Adapted) For the Years Ended May 5, 2018 and May 6, 2017			
2	*(in millions of dollars)*	**2018**	**2017**	
3	**Operating Activities**			
4	Net earnings	179.8	172.5	
5	Adjustments for:			
6	Depreciation	351.8	355.5	
7	Income tax expense	56.2	42.5	
8	Finance costs, net	110.5	118.0	
9	Amortization of intangibles	87.4	88.7	
10	Net gain on disposal of assets	(37.3)	(21.3)	
11	Impairment of non-financial assets	9.2	27.5	
12	Amortization of deferred items	7.2	12.8	
13	Equity in earnings of other entities	69.1	19.9	
14	Employee future benefits	1.5	8.5	
15	Increase in long-term lease obligation	11.2	13.9	
16	Equity based compensation, net	6.9	3.3	
17	Increase (decrease) in long-term provisions	15.8	(35.4)	
18	Net change in non-cash working capital	88.1	0.5	
19	Income taxes, paid, net	(77.7)	(98.4)	
20	Cash flows from operating activities	879.7	708.5	
21	*Operating cash as a % of net income*	489%	411%	
22	**Investing Activities**			
23	Increase in investments	0.0	(0.4)	
24	Property, equipment and investment property	(239.8)	(460.7)	
25	Proceeds on disposal of assets	217.2	425.7	
26	Additions to intangibles	(48.2)	(53.8)	
27	Loans and other receivables	6.1	12.3	
28	Other assets and long-term liabilities	2.9	2.7	
29	Tenant inducements	0.0	58.8	
30	Business acquisitions	(3.8)	(21.9)	
31	Interest received	1.9	1.6	
32	Proceeds on redemption of investment	24.3	0.0	
33	Cash flows from (used) in investing activities	(39.4)	(35.7)	
34	**Financing Activities**			
35	Issue of long-term debt	63.7	55.6	
36	Net repayment of credit facilities	(81.9)	(165.0)	
37	Repayment of long-term debt	(188.2)	(397.2)	
38	Interest paid	(87.4)	(87.0)	
39	Acquisition of shares held in trust	(0.1)	(10.7)	
40	Non-controlling interest	(11.8)	(14.6)	
41	Dividends paid, common shares	(114.0)	(111.3)	
42	Cash flows from (used) in financing activities	(419.7)	(730.2)	
43	Increase (decrease) in cash and cash equivalents	420.6	(57.4)	
44	Cash and cash equivalents, beginning of year	207.3	264.7	
45	Cash and cash equivalents, end of year	$ 627.9	$ 207.3	
46				

EXHIBIT 10-7
Consolidated Statements of Cash Flows—Empire Company Limited

Source: Data from Empire Company Limited - 2018 Annual Report.

Analysts find that the statement of cash flows is more helpful for spotting weakness than for gauging success. Why? Because a *shortage* of cash can throw a company into bankruptcy, but lots of cash doesn't ensure success. Let's now take a look at the cash flow statement for SK Corporation—see if you can find signals of cash flow weakness.

	A	B	C	D
1	**SK Corporation** Statements of Cash Flows For the Year Ended June 30, 2020			
2	*(in millions)*			
3	**Operating activities:**			
4	Net income		$ 35,000	
5	Adjustments for non-cash items:			
6	Depreciation	$ 14,000		
7	Net increase in current assets other than cash	(24,000)		
8	Net increase in current liabilities	8,000	(2,000)	
9	Net cash provided by operating activities		33,000	
10	**Investing activities:**			
11	Sale of property, plant, and equipment	91,000		
12	Net cash provided by investing activities		91,000	
13	**Financing activities:**			
14	Borrowing	22,000		
15	Payment of long-term debt	(90,000)		
16	Repurchase of shares	(9,000)		
17	Payment of dividends	(23,000)		
18	Net cash used for financing activities		(100,000)	
19	Increase in cash		$ 24,000	
20				

- SK Corporation's net cash provided by operations is less than net income. Ordinarily, cash provided by operations exceeds net income because of the add-back of depreciation and amortization. The increases in current assets and current liabilities should cancel out over time. For SK, current assets increased far more than current liabilities during the year. This may be harmless, or it may signal difficulty in collecting receivables or selling inventory. Either event may cause trouble.

- The sale of property, plant, and equipment is SK's major source of cash. This is okay if it is a one-time situation. SK may be shifting from one line of business to another, and it may be selling off old assets. But, if the sale of property, plant, and equipment is the major source of cash for several periods, SK will face a cash shortage. A company cannot continue to sell off its property, plant, and equipment forever. Soon, it will go out of business.

- The only strength shown by the statement of cash flows is that SK paid off more long-term debt than it took on in new borrowing. This will improve the debt ratio and SK's credit standing.

Here are some cash flow signs of a healthy company:

- Operations are a major *source* of cash (not a *use* of cash).
- Investing activities include more purchases than sales of long-term assets.
- Financing activities are not dominated by borrowing.

STOP + THINK (10-4)

Simpson Company's net income for the year was $40,000 yet the overall increase in cash was only $3,000. The statement of cash flow revealed the following:

Net cash flow used for operating activities	($ 7,000)
Net cash flow provided by investing activities	$15,000
Net cash flow used for financing activities	($ 5,000)

Is this a sign of a healthy company? How can you tell?

MyLab Accounting

MID-CHAPTER SUMMARY PROBLEM

You, an employee at a bank lending office, are deciding whether to grant Jamate Corporation, which makes metal detectors, a large loan. You decide to perform a horizontal analysis and a vertical analysis of the comparative income statement of Jamate Corporation. State whether 2020 was a good year or a bad year and give your reasons. We encourage you to use Excel as a tool to perform your analysis.

	A	B	C	D
1	**Jamate Corporation** Comparative Income Statement For the Years Ended December 31, 2020 and 2019			
2		**2020**	**2019**	
3	Total revenues	$ 275,000	$ 225,000	
4	Expenses:			
5	Cost of products sold	194,000	165,000	
6	Engineering, selling, and administrative expenses	54,000	48,000	
7	Interest expense	5,000	5,000	
8	Income tax expense	9,000	3,000	
9	Other expense (income)	1,000	(1,000)	
10	Total expenses	263,000	220,000	
11	Net earnings	$ 12,000	$ 5,000	
12				

Name: Jamate Corporation
Fiscal Period: Years ended December 31, 2020 and 2019

ANSWER

The horizontal analysis shows that total revenues increased 22.2%. This was greater than the 19.5% increase in total expenses, resulting in a 140% increase in net earnings.

	A	B	C	D	E	F
1	**Jamate Corporation** Horizontal Analysis of Comparative Income Statement For the Years Ended December 31, 2020 and 2019				Increase (Decrease)	
2		2020	2019	Amount	Percent	
3	Total revenues	$ 275,000	$ 225,000	$ 50,000	22.2%	
4	Expenses:					
5	Cost of products sold	194,000	165,000	29,000	17.6	
6	Engineering, selling, and administrative expenses	54,000	48,000	6,000	12.5	
7	Interest expense	5,000	5,000	—	—	
8	Income tax expense	9,000	3,000	6,000	200.0	
9	Other expense (income)	1,000	(1,000)	2,000	—*	
10	Total expenses	263,000	220,000	43,000	19.5	
11	Net earnings	$ 12,000	$ 5,000	$ 7,000	140.0%	
12						

*Percentage changes are typically not computed for shifts from a negative to a positive amount, and vice versa.

The vertical analysis shows decreases in the percentages of net sales consumed by the cost of products sold (from 73.3% to 70.5%) and by the engineering, selling, and administrative expenses (from 21.3% to 19.6%). Because these two items are Jamate's largest dollar expenses, their percentage decreases are quite important. The relative reduction in expenses raised 2020's net earnings to 4.4% of sales, compared with 2.2% the preceding year. The overall analysis indicates that 2020 was significantly better than 2019.

	A	B	C	D	E	F
1	**Jamate Corporation** Vertical Analysis of Comparative Income Statement For the Years Ended December 31, 2020 and 2019					
2		2020		2019		
3		Amount	Percent	Amount	Percent	
4	Total revenues	$ 275,000	100.0%	$ 225,000	100.0%	
5	Expenses:					
6	Cost of products sold	194,000	70.5	165,000	73.3	
7	Engineering, selling, and administrative expenses	54,000	19.6	48,000	21.3	
8	Interest expense	5,000	1.8	5,000	2.2	
9	Income tax expense	9,000	3.3	3,000	1.4*	
10	Other expense (income)	1,000	0.4	(1,000)	(0.4)	
11	Total expenses	263,000	95.6	220,000	97.8	
12	Net earnings	$ 12,000	4.4%	$ 5,000	2.2%	
13						

*Number rounded up.

Horizontal analysis compares 2020 with 2019 to determine the changes in each income statement item in dollar amounts and percent ($ and %). Large or unusual changes in $ or % should be investigated.

The net earnings increase of 140% occurred because the dollar amounts are quite small. Income tax expense increased 200%; this would be investigated.

Vertical analysis expresses net earnings and expenses as a percentage of total revenues. The percentages for 2020 are compared with those of 2019. Any large or unexpected differences would be reviewed.

USE RATIOS TO MAKE BUSINESS DECISIONS

Ratios are a major tool of financial analysis. We have discussed the use of many ratios in financial analysis in various chapters throughout the book. A ratio expresses the relationship between various types of financial information. In this section, we review how ratios are computed and used to make business decisions, using Apple Inc.

❺ **Use** ratios to make business decisions

Many companies include ratios in a special section of their annual reports. Exhibit 10-8 shows a summary of selected data from previous Apple Inc. annual reports.

The ratios we discuss in this chapter are classified as follows:

1. Measuring the ability to pay current liabilities
2. Measuring turnover and cash conversion cycle
3. Measuring leverage: overall ability to pay debts
4. Measuring profitability
5. Analyzing stock as an investment

	A	B	C	D	E
1	**Apple Inc.** Results of operations				
2	*(dollar amounts in millions):*	FY2018	FY2017	FY2016	
3	Net sales	$ 265,595	$ 229,234	$ 215,639	
4	Gross profit	$ 101,839	$ 88,186	$ 84,263	
5	Gross profit as percent of net sales	38.3%	38.5%	39.1%	
6	Operating income	$ 70,898	$ 61,344	$ 60,024	
7	Operating income as percent of net sales	26.7%	26.8%	27.8%	
8	Net income after provision for income taxes	$ 59,531	$ 48,351	$ 45,687	
9	Net income as percent of sales	22.4%	21.1%	21.2%	
10	Earnings per weighted-average common share, basic	$ 12.01	$ 9.27	$ 8.35	
11	Return on average shareholders' equity	49.0%	38.0%	36.9%	
12	Cash dividends	$ 13,735	$ 12,803	$ 12,188	
13	**Financial position (dollar amounts in millions):**				
14	Current assets	$ 131,339	$ 128,645	$ 106,869	
15	Current liabilities	116,866	100,814	79,006	
16	Working capital	14,473	27,831	27,863	
17	Current ratio	1.12	1.28	1.35	
18	Quick ratio	0.76	0.91	1.05	
19	Total assets	365,725	375,319	321,686	
20	Total liabilities	258,578	241,272	193,437	
21	Debt ratio	0.70	0.64	0.60	
22					

EXHIBIT 10-8
Financial Summary—Apple Inc.

Source: Based on the content taken from Apple Annual Report - For the Fiscal Year Ended September 29, 2018 and for the Fiscal Year Ended September 24, 2016.

Remember to Start at the Beginning: Company and Industry Information

As stated at the beginning of the chapter, financial analysis is just massaging numbers unless we give the numbers a context. That comes from understanding the company and the industry and from knowing not only its history but where it appears to be headed in the future. Apple is known as perhaps the world's most innovative company. The company was founded in 1976 and went public in 1977. For more than two decades, Apple was predominately a manufacturer of personal computers. It faced intense competition and low market share during the 1990s.

Apple began developing innovative products including the iPhone, iPod Touch, iPad, and Apple TV and sales skyrocketed, establishing itself as a leader in the consumer electronics and media sales industris.

As of April 2017, Apple was the largest publicly traded corporation in the world, with a total market capitalization of over $730 billion, larger than Facebook and Exxon-Mobil combined. As of the end of 2016 fiscal year, the company had generated an enormous stockpile in cash and marketable securities. During this period of rapid growth, Apple increased its dividend per share by 10% and kept its debt levels respectfully low.

Under pressure from the shareholders, the company's board of directors voted to pay Apple's first dividend at the end of fiscal 2012, as well as to engage in an aggressive share repurchase program over a period of several years. Looking for ways to reduce taxes, Apple decided to borrow the money to pay shareholder dividends and to repurchase their shares. In spite of the stockpile of cash, Apple took on a combination of short-term and long-term debt. In addition, the company declared a 7-for-1 stock split in 2014, distributing 7 shares for each share owned by its existing shareholders. This reduced the market price of the share from over $700 per share to less than $100 per share. The impact of these decisions on the company's liquidity and profitability ratios over the past two years has been significant, as you will see in the discussion that follows.

NOW LET'S DO THE NUMBERS Once you gain knowledge about a company and its industry, how do you determine whether the company's performance has been strong or weak, based on its current-period ratios? You can only make that decision if you have the following ratios to compare the current period against: (1) prior-year ratios; and (2) industry comparables, either in the form of an industry average or the ratios of a strong competitor. In the case of all the ratios in the following sections, we compare Apple's current-year ratios with (1) its prior years' ratios and (2) ratios for the industry (if available) or ratios of one of Apple Inc.'s competitors. We have selected Alphabet, Inc., the parent of Google, because its Apple's main competitor in its primary market—smartphones.

Measuring the Ability to Pay Current Liabilities

Working capital is defined as follows:

$$\text{Working capital} = \text{Current assets} - \text{Current liabilities}$$

Working capital measures the ability to pay current liabilities with current assets. In general, the larger the working capital, the better the ability to pay debts. Recall that capital is total assets minus total liabilities. Working capital is like a "current" version of total capital. Consider two companies with equal working capital:

	Company	
	Jones	Smith
Current assets..	$100,000	$200,000
Current liabilities....................................	50,000	150,000
Working capital.......................................	$ 50,000	$ 50,000

Both companies have working capital of $50,000, but Jones's working capital is as large as its current liabilities. Smith's working capital is only one-third as large as current liabilities. Jones is in a better position because its working capital is a higher percentage of current liabilities. As shown in Exhibit 10-8, Apple's working capital as of September 29, 2018 (the end of its 2018 fiscal year), was $14,473 million. This compares with $27,831 million and $27,863 million at the end of its 2017 and 2016 fiscal years, respectively. Why the dramatic change in working capital? The company's reduction in working capital reflects its strategic decision to return cash to its shareholders starting in 2018. The company returned $13.7 billion more cash to shareholders in the form of cash dividends in 2018. Also, in their annual report, Apple stated that they spent $73.1 billion to buy back shares in fiscal 2018. This left Apple Inc.'s working capital substantially lower, but still not depleted to a critical level, because the company continues to generate billions of dollars in sales monthly, mostly for cash. Let's look at two key ratios that help tell the rest of the story.

CURRENT RATIO. The most common ratio for evaluating current assets and current liabilities is the **current ratio**, which is current assets divided by current liabilities. As discussed in Chapter 3, the current ratio measures the ability to pay current liabilities with current assets. Exhibit 10-9 and Exhibit 10-10 show the consolidated statements of operations and the consolidated balance sheets of Apple Inc.

Using figures from Exhibit 10-10, the following are current ratios of Apple at September 29, 2018 and September 30, 2017.

		Apple Inc.'s Current Ratio	
Formula		**2018**	**2017**
Current ratio = $\dfrac{\text{Current assets}}{\text{Current liabilities}}$		$\dfrac{\$131,339}{\$116,866} = 1.12$	$\dfrac{\$128,645}{\$100,814} = 1.27$

	A	B	C	D	E
1	**Apple Inc.** Consolidated Statements of Operations (USD $) For the Years Ended 2018, 2017, 2016				
2	*(in millions, except share data in thousands, and per share amounts)*	Sept. 29 2018	Sept. 30 2017	Sept. 24 2016	
3	Net sales	$ 265,595	$ 229,234	$ 215,639	
4	Cost of Sales	163,756	141,048	131,376	
5	Gross profit	101,839	88,186	84,263	
6	**Operating expenses:**				
7	Research and development	14,236	11,581	10,045	
8	Selling, general, and administrative	16,705	15,261	14,194	
9	Total operating expenses	30,941	26,842	24,239	
10	Operating income	70,898	61,344	60,024	
11	Other income/(expense), net	2,005	2,745	1,348	
12	Income before provision for income taxes	72,903	64,089	61,372	
13	Provision for income taxes	13,372	15,738	15,685	
14	Net income	$ 59,531	$ 48,351	$ 45,687	
15	**Earning per common share:**				
16	Basic	$ 12.01	$ 9.27	$ 8.35	
17	Diluted	$ 11.91	$ 9.21	$ 8.31	
18	**Shares used in computing earnings per share:**				
19	Basic	4,955,377	5,217,242	5,470,820	
20	Diluted	5,000,109	5,251,692	5,500,281	
21					

EXHIBIT 10-9
Comparative Consolidated Statements of Operations— Apple Inc.

Source: Apple Annual Report - for the Fiscal Year Ended September 29, 2018.

EXHIBIT 10-10
Comparative Consolidated
Balance Sheets—Apple Inc.

Source: Apple Annual Report - for the
Fiscal Year Ended September 29, 2018.

	A	B	C	D
1	**Apple Inc.** Consolidated Balance Sheets (USD $) As at September 29, 2018 and September 30, 2017			
2	*(in millions)*	**Sept. 29, 2018**	**Sept. 30, 2017**	
3	**Current assets:**			
4	Cash and cash equivalents	$ 25,913	$ 20,289	
5	Short-term marketable securities	40,388	53,892	
6	Accounts receivable, net	23,186	17,874	
7	Inventories	3,956	4,855	
8	Vendor non-trade receivables	25,809	17,799	
9	Other current assets	12,087	13,936	
10	Total current assets	131,339	128,645	
11	Long-term marketable securities	170,799	194,714	
12	Property, plant, and equipment, net	41,304	33,783	
13	Other non-current assets	22,283	18,177	
14	**Total assets**	365,725	375,319	
15	**Current liabilities:**			
16	Accounts payable	55,888	44,242	
17	Other current liabilities	32,687	30,551	
18	Deferred revenue	7,543	7,548	
19	Commercial paper	11,964	11,977	
20	Term debt	8,784	6,496	
21	Total current liabilities	116,866	100,814	
22	Deferred revenue-non-current	2,797	2,836	
23	Term debt	93,735	97,207	
24	Other non-current liabilities	45,180	40,415	
25	Total liabilities	258,578	241,272	
26	Commitments and contingencies			
27	**Shareholders' equity:**			
28	Share Capital	40,201	35,867	
29	Retained earnings	70,400	98,330	
30	Accumulated other comprehensive income/(loss)	(3,454)	(150)	
31	Total shareholders' equity	107,147	134,047	
32	**Total liabilities and shareholders' equity**	$ 365,725	$ 375,319	
33				

Apple's current ratio decreased during 2017, from 1.27 to 1.12, for the same reason that its working capital decreased: use of excess cash to pay dividends and repurchase shares from shareholders. Further examination of current assets and current liabilities in Exhibit 10-10 shows that current liabilities increased by 15.9% (($116,866 − $100,814)/$100,814) during 2018, while current assets increased by 2.1% (($131,339 − $128,645)/$128,645). Accounts payable increased by 26.3% (($55,888 − $44,242)/$44,242) in 2018 over 2017. This is a natural consequence of the growth the company has experienced. It is hardly a sign of trouble, especially since the current ratio is within the bounds of what is considered healthy from the standpoint of the ability to pay current liabilities. In general, a higher current ratio indicates a stronger financial position. Apple certainly has more than sufficient current assets to maintain its operations. Apple's current ratio of 1.12 is much lower than the current ratio of its competitor, Alphabet, Inc. partly because Alphabet, Inc. is a newer company and hasn't yet paid a dividend. Paying a dividend would have reduced Alphabet, Inc's current ratio.

What is an acceptable current ratio? The answer depends on the industry. The norm for companies in most industries is around 1.50. Apple Inc.'s current ratio of 1.12 is less than average.

QUICK (ACID-TEST) RATIO. As discussed in Chapter 4, the **quick (acid-test) ratio** tells us whether the entity could pass the acid test of paying all its current liabilities if they came due immediately (quickly). The quick ratio uses a narrower base to measure liquidity than the current ratio does.

To compute the quick ratio, we add cash, short-term investments, and accounts receivable (net of allowances), and divide by current liabilities. Inventory and prepaid expenses are excluded because they are less liquid. A business may be unable to convert inventory to cash immediately.

Using the information in Exhibit 10-10, Apple's quick ratios for 2018 and 2017 follow:

		Apple Inc.'s Quick Ratio	
Formula		2018	2017
Quick ratio = $\dfrac{\text{Cash and cash equivalents} + \text{Short-term investments} + \text{Net current receivables}}{\text{Current liabilities}}$		$\dfrac{\$25{,}913 + \$40{,}388 + \$23{,}186}{\$116{,}866} = 0.76$	$\dfrac{\$20{,}289 + \$53{,}892 + \$17{,}874}{\$100{,}814} = 0.91$

Like the current ratio, the company's quick ratio declined during 2018. However, because of Apple's ability to generate cash quickly, a low quick ratio doesn't spell liquidity problems. In addition, Apple is still competitive with other major companies in its industry. Compare Apple Inc.'s quick ratio with the quick ratio of its competitor, Alphabet, Inc., which is 6.0. Alphabet, Inc's quick ratio is higher for the same reasons as the current ratio. It is a younger company that has yet to pay dividends.

A quick ratio of 0.90 to 1.00 is acceptable in most industries. How can many retail companies function with low quick ratios? Because they price their inventories to turn over (sell) quickly and because they collect most of the revenues in cash. This points us to the next group of ratios, which measure turnover.

Measuring Turnover and the Cash Conversion Cycle

The ability to sell inventory and collect receivables, as well as pay accounts payable, is the lifeblood of any retail, wholesale, or manufacturing concern. In this section, we discuss three ratios that measure this ability—inventory turnover, accounts receivable turnover, and accounts payable turnover—as well as the relationship between them, called the *cash conversion cycle*.

INVENTORY TURNOVER. Companies generally strive to sell their inventory as quickly as possible. The faster inventory sells, the sooner cash comes in.

Inventory turnover, discussed in Chapter 5, measures the number of times a company sells its average level of inventory during a year. A fast turnover indicates ease in selling inventory; a low turnover indicates difficulty. A value of 6 means that the company's average level of inventory has been sold six times during the year, and that's usually better than a turnover of three times. But too high a value can mean that the business is not keeping enough inventory on hand, which can lead to lost sales if the company can't fill orders. Therefore, a business strives for the most *profitable* rate of turnover, not necessarily the *highest* rate.

To compute inventory turnover, divide cost of goods sold by the average inventory for the period. We use the cost of goods sold—*not sales*—in the computation because both cost of goods sold and inventory are stated *at cost*. Apple Inc.'s inventory turnover for 2018 is as follows:

	Formula		Apple Inc.'s Inventory Turnover	Competitor (Alphabet, Inc.)
Inventory turnover $=$	$\dfrac{\text{Cost of goods sold}}{\text{Average inventory}}$	$\dfrac{\$163,756}{\$4,405.5}$ $= 37.2$		89.6
Days' inventory outstanding $(\text{DIO}) =$	$\dfrac{365}{\text{Turnover}}$	$\dfrac{365}{37.2}$ $= 9.8$ days		4 days

Cost of goods sold comes from the consolidated statement of operations (Exhibit 10-9). Average inventory is the average of beginning ($4,855) and ending inventory ($3,956). (See the balance sheet, Exhibit 10-10.) If inventory levels vary greatly from month to month, you should compute the average by adding the 12 monthly balances and dividing the sum by 12.

Inventory turnover varies widely with the nature of the business. For example, Apple's inventory turned over 37.2 times in 2018. On a daily basis (**days' inventory outstanding**), that means once every 9.8 or 10 days (365/37.2)! In 2017, Apple's inventory turned over 40.4 times. Alphabet, Inc.'s inventory turnover for 2017 was 89.6 times (once every 4.1 days). Computer and electronics manufacturers purposely keep very low inventory levels because of their ability to manufacture inventory quickly and because technology is subject to rapid obsolescence.

To evaluate inventory turnover, compare the ratio over time as well as with industry averages or competitors. Steadily increasing inventory turnover is a positive sign particularly if gross profits are also increasing. A sharp decline in inventory turnover suggests the need to take action to increase sales, usually by lowering prices. Unfortunately, this will reduce gross profits until excess inventory can be disposed of.

ACCOUNTS RECEIVABLE TURNOVER. **Accounts receivable turnover** measures the ability to collect cash from customers. In general, the higher the ratio, the better. However, a receivable turnover that is too high may indicate that credit is too tight, and that may cause a company to lose sales to good customers.

To compute accounts receivable turnover, divide net sales by average net accounts receivable. Ideally, net credit sales should be used but it cannot always be obtained. The ratio tells how many times during the year average receivables were turned into cash. Apple's accounts receivable turnover ratio for 2018 was as follows:

	Formula		Apple Inc.'s Accounts Receivable Turnover	Competitor (Alphabet, Inc.)
Accounts receivable turnover	$=$	$\dfrac{\text{Net sales}}{\substack{\text{Average net} \\ \text{accounts receivable}}}$	$\dfrac{\$265,595}{\$20,530}$ $= 12.9$	6.8
Days' sales outstanding (DSO) (or days'-sales-in-receivables)	$=$	$\dfrac{365}{\text{Turnover}}$	$\dfrac{365}{12.9}$ $= 28$ days	54 days

Net sales comes from Exhibit 10-9. Average net accounts receivable (Exhibit 10-10) is figured by adding beginning ($17,874) and ending receivables ($23,186), then dividing by 2. If accounts receivable vary widely during the year, compute the average by using the 12 monthly balances. Apple collected its average accounts receivable 12.9 times during 2018. Alphabet, Inc.'s accounts receivable turnover for 2017 was 6.8.

Apple's accounts receivable turnover of 12.9 times per year is faster than the industry average. Apple owns and operates a large number of retail stores, and much of its sales are for cash, which makes the receivables balance very low relative to the sales balance.

DAYS' SALES IN RECEIVABLES. Businesses must convert accounts receivable to cash. All else being equal, the lower the receivable balance, the better the cash flow.

The *days' sales outstanding (DSO)* or **days' sales in receivables ratio**, discussed in Chapter 4, shows how many days' sales remain in accounts receivable. First, if you have already calculated receivables turnover (see the previous section), simply divide the turnover into 365. For Apple, days' sales in receivables works out to 28.3 (rounded to 28) days (365/12.9).

In comparison, Alphabet, Inc.'s DSO in 2017 was 54 days (365/6.8 turnover). Apple owns and operates a large number of retail stores, and much of its sales are for cash, which makes the company's accounts receivables balance very low relative to its sales.

ACCOUNTS PAYABLE TURNOVER. Discussed in Chapter 7, *accounts payable turnover* measures the number of times per year that the entity pays off its accounts payable. To compute **accounts payable turnover**, divide cost of goods sold by average accounts payable. For Apple, this ratio is as follows:

	Formula	Apple Inc.'s Accounts Payable Turnover	Competitor (Alphabet, Inc.)
Accounts payable turnover $=$	$\dfrac{\text{Cost of goods sold}}{\text{Average accounts payable}}$	$\dfrac{\$163,756}{\$50,065} = 3.27$	17.6
Days payable outstanding $=$ (DPO)	$\dfrac{365}{\text{Turnover}}$	$\dfrac{365}{3.27} = 111.6$ days	21 days

On average, Apple pays off its accounts payable 3.27 times per year, which is about every 112 days. To convert accounts payable turnover to **days' payable outstanding (DPO)**, divide the turnover into 365 ($365 \div 3.27 = 111.6$ days). In comparison, Alphabet, Inc.'s accounts payable turnover is 17.6 times per year, or about every 21 days.

CASH CONVERSION CYCLE. By expressing the three turnover ratios in days, we can compute a company's **cash conversion cycle** as follows:

	Formula	Apple Inc.'s Cash Conversion Cycle	Competitor (Alphabet, Inc.)
Cash conversion cycle $=$	DIO + DSO − DPO	$10 + 28 - 112 = -74$ days	79 days
where DIO	$=$ Days' inventory outstanding		
DSO	$=$ Days' sales outstanding		
DPO	$=$ Days' payable outstanding		

At first glance, a negative amount for the cash conversion cycle looks odd. What does it mean? Apple is in the enviable position of being able to sell inventory and collect from its customers 74 days before it has to pay its suppliers who provided the parts and materials to produce those inventories. This means that Apple can stock less inventory and hold on to cash longer than other companies. It also helps explain why the company could afford to keep over $40 billion in short-term marketable securities (Exhibit 10-10)—to "sop up" its excess cash—and using it to make still more money while waiting to pay off suppliers. Apple's competitor Alphabet, Inc. has a positive cash conversion cycle of 79 days in 2017. Retail companies that have a more "normal" inventory turnover (about four times per year, or about every 90 days) have cash conversion cycles in the range of 30 to 60 days, depending on how long it takes to collect from customers. The cash conversion cycle for service-oriented businesses consists only of (DSO − DPO) because service businesses typically do not carry inventory.

Measuring Leverage: Overall Ability to Pay Debts

The ratios discussed so far relate to current assets and current liabilities. They measure the ability to sell inventory, collect receivables, and pay current bills. Two indicators of the ability to pay total liabilities are the *debt ratio* and the *times-interest-earned ratio*.

DEBT RATIO. Suppose you are a bank loan officer and you have received loan applications for $500,000 from two similar companies. The first company already owes $600,000, and the second owes only $250,000. Which company gets the loan? Company 2 may look like the stronger candidate, because it owes less.

This relationship between total liabilities and total assets is called the **debt ratio**. Discussed in Chapters 3 and 7, the debt ratio tells us the proportion of assets financed with debt. A debt ratio of 1 reveals that debt has financed all the assets. A debt ratio of 0.50 means that debt finances half the assets. The higher the debt ratio, the greater the pressure to pay interest and principal. The lower the debt ratio, the lower the company's credit risk.

The debt ratios for Apple in 2018 and 2017 follow:

| | | Apple Inc.'s Debt Ratio | | Competitor |
Formula		2018	2017	(Alphabet, Inc.)
Debt ratio = $\dfrac{\text{Total liabilities}}{\text{Total assets}}$		$\dfrac{\$258,578}{\$365,725} = 0.71$	$\dfrac{\$241,272}{\$375,319} = 0.64$	0.23

Although Apple's debt ratio increased during 2018, it is still comparable to its competitors and compared with many other public companies. In order to understand why the debt level for Apple is so high, it helps to read the business news to gain insight from an analyst's point of view. Some articles suggest that one reason Apple does not bring a lot of the cash generated from overseas operations back to the U.S. is to avoid paying taxes in the U.S. The debt ratio is related to the leverage ratio discussed in the next section.

TIMES-INTEREST-EARNED RATIO. Analysts use a second ratio—the **times-interest-earned ratio** (introduced in Chapter 7)—to relate income to interest expense. To compute the times interest-earned ratio, divide income from operations (operating income) by interest expense. This ratio measures the number of times operating income can *cover* interest expense, and is also called the **interest-coverage ratio**. A high ratio indicates ease in paying interest; a low value suggests difficulty.

| | | Apple Inc.'s Times-Interest-Earned Ratio | | Competitor |
Formula		2018	2017	(Alphabet, Inc.)
Times-interest-earned ratio $=$	$\dfrac{\text{Income from operations}}{\text{Interest expense}}$	$\dfrac{\$70{,}898}{\$3{,}240^*} = 21.9$	$\dfrac{\$61{,}344}{\$2{,}323^*} = 26.4$	240

*Interest expense is given in Note 3.

Apple's interest expense for fiscal 2018 was $3,240 million, up from $2,323 million in 2017. Income from operations covered these amounts by 21.9 times and 26.4 times, respectively. Apple has more than enough operating income to cover the costs of interest on its debt. Although Apple's competitor Alphabet, Inc. has a relatively low debt ratio (0.23), its times-interest-earned ratio is quite a bit higher (240), meaning that Alphabet, Inc. is quite capable of servicing its interest payments. In summary, the judgment about the adequacy of interest coverage, like so many other factors of financial statement analysis, is very much dependent on the industry, as well as the company being studied.

Measuring Profitability

The fundamental goal of business is to earn a profit, and so the ratios that measure profitability are reported widely in the media.

GROSS PROFIT PERCENTAGE. In Chapter 5, we defined gross profit as net sales – cost of goods sold. That is, gross profit is the amount of profit that the entity makes from merely selling a product before other operating costs are subtracted. Let's look at Apple's gross profit percentages:

| | | Apple Inc.'s Gross Profit % | | Competitor |
Formula		2018	2017	(Alphabet, Inc.)
Gross profit % $=$	$\dfrac{\text{Gross profit}}{\text{Net sales}}$	38.3%	38.5%	41.1%

Apple is known as *the* innovator in the technology field. The company is constantly inventing new technology that everyone literally stands in line to purchase! Do you remember the last time you visited an Apple store (perhaps when a new version of the iPhone was introduced)? How much were you willing to pay for your new iPhone, iPad, or iMac? Do you remember how crowded the store was? As we discussed in Chapter 6, because of the creative talents of their people, some companies have been able to adopt a "product differentiation" business strategy, which allows them to sell their products for more than their competitors. When everyone wants the product, they are usually willing to pay more for it. As shown in Exhibit 10-8, Apple's gross profit percentage of 38.3% in 2018 declined slightly than what it was in 2017. Although Apple is the recognized industry leader, it does not have a monopoly on smart computing devices. Alphabet, Inc., which is largely a service business with very little inventory, has a higher gross profit (41.1%).

OPERATING INCOME (PROFIT) PERCENTAGE. Operating income (profit) percentage is net income from operations as a percentage of net sales. It is a function of all of its individual elements: sales revenue, cost of goods sold, gross profit, and operating expenses. It is an important statistic because it measures the percentage of profit earned from each sales dollar in a company's core business operations. The first component of high operating earnings is a high gross profit percentage. After that, maximizing operating income depends on keeping operating costs as low as possible, given the level of desired product quality and customer service. Apple's operating income percentages, compared with Alphabet, Inc., follow:

		Apple Inc.'s Operating Income %		Competitor
Formula		2018	2017	(Alphabet, Inc.)
Operating income % = $\dfrac{\text{Operating income}}{\text{Net sales}}$		26.7%	26.8%	23.6%

Apple is slightly ahead of the competition on earnings from its core operations. However according to Exhibit 10-8, because of a slight decline in gross profit percentage in recent years, the company's operating income percentage has also slightly declined.

RETURN (NET PROFIT MARGIN) ON SALES. In business, *return* refers to profitability. Consider the **return on net sales**, or simply *return on sales* (ROS). (The word *net* is usually omitted for convenience.) It measures how much each sales dollar generates net income. Recall that net income can be increased in one of three ways: (1) increasing sales volume, or the amount of goods or services sold or performed; (2) increasing sales prices; or (3) decreasing cost of goods sold and operating expenses. The return-on-sales ratios for Apple are as follows:

		Apple Inc.'s Return on Sales		Competitor
Formula		2018	2017	(Alphabet, Inc.)
$\dfrac{\text{Return on sales}}{(\text{Net profit margin})}$ = $\dfrac{\text{Net income}}{\text{Net sales}}$		$\dfrac{\$59,531}{\$265,595}$ = 22.4%	$\dfrac{\$48,351}{\$229,234}$ = 21.1%	11.4%

Companies strive for a high return on sales. The higher the percentage, the more profit is being generated by sales dollars. Apple's return on sales in 2018 has increased slightly from where it was in 2017. Compare Apple's return on sales with Alphabet, Inc.'s (11.4%).

ASSET TURNOVER. **Asset turnover** measures the amount of net sales generated for each dollar invested in assets. This is a measure of how effectively and efficiently the company manages its assets. Asset turnover can be increased by (1) increasing sales in the ways just described above; (2) keeping less inventory on hand; or (3) closing unproductive facilities, selling idle assets, and consolidating operations to fewer places to reduce the amount of plant assets needed. Companies with high asset turnover tend to be more productive than companies with low asset turnover. Let's examine Apple's asset turnover for 2018 compared with 2017, and then compare it to competitor Alphabet, Inc's asset turnover:

		Apple Inc.'s Asset Turnover		Competitor
Formula		2018	2017	(Alphabet, Inc.)
Asset turnover = $\dfrac{\text{Net sales}}{\text{Average total assets}}$		$\dfrac{\$265,595}{\$370,522}$ = 0.72	$\dfrac{\$229,234}{\$348,502}$ = 0.66	0.61

Both Apple and Alphabet, Inc. have invested more in assets per dollar of sales. This is often the case with innovative companies, as opposed to companies that sell products at a low cost. To make major product innovations requires a significant investment in both tangible and intangible assets. That being said, Apple was slightly more efficiently run than Alphabet, Inc.

RETURN ON TOTAL ASSETS (ROA). **Return on assets (ROA)** measures how much the entity earned for each dollar of assets invested by both shareholders and creditors. Companies with high ROA have both selected assets and managed them more successfully than companies with low ROA.

Return on assets (ROA)	Apple Inc.'s ROA		Competitor (Alphabet, Inc.)
	2018	2017	
$\dfrac{\text{Net income + Interest expense}}{\text{Average total assets}}$	$\dfrac{\$59,531 + \$3,240}{\$370,522} = 16.9\%$	$\dfrac{\$48,351 + \$2,323}{\$348,503} = 14.5\%$	7%

Successful manufacturing firms often choose between a mixture of two different strategies: product differentiation or low-cost. We see from these computations that for Apple, ROA is driven principally by its high profitability due to their product innovation strategies. In contrast, Alphabet, Inc.'s ROA is based more on efficiency than profitability.

LEVERAGE (EQUITY MULTIPLIER) RATIO. **Leverage** measures the impact of debt financing on profitability. You learned in Chapters 7 and 8 that it can be advantageous to use borrowed capital to finance a business. Earlier, we expressed the debt ratio as the ratio of total liabilities to total assets. The **leverage ratio**, or equity multiplier, measures the proportion of each dollar of assets financed with shareholders' equity. Because total assets − shareholders' equity = total liabilities, the leverage ratio is a way of inversely expressing the debt ratio—it merely looks at financing from the other side of the fundamental accounting equation. Let's examine Apple's leverage ratios for 2018 and 2017, compared with those of its competitor, Alphabet, Inc.

Formula	Apple Inc.'s Leverage Ratios		Competitor (Alphabet, Inc.)
	2018	2017	
Leverage ratio $= \dfrac{\text{Average total assets}}{\text{Average common shareholders' equity}}$	$\dfrac{\$370,522}{\$120,597} = 3.07$	$\dfrac{\$348,503}{\$131,148} = 2.66$	1.25

As we pointed out in a previous section, Apple has built up a high debt ratio (71% and 64% for 2018 and 2017, respectively). This translates to leverage ratios for Apple (3.07 and 2.65 for 2018 and 2017, respectively). In comparison, Alphabet, Inc. has a comparatively low debt ratio (23% for 2017). Therefore, Apple uses much more borrowed capital than equity capital to finance its operations, and its leverage ratio is much higher (3.07).

RETURN ON COMMON SHAREHOLDERS' EQUITY (ROE). A popular measure of profitability is **return on common shareholders' equity**, often shortened to *return on equity* (ROE). Also discussed in Chapter 8, this ratio shows the relationship between net income and common shareholders' investment in the company—how much income is earned for every $1 invested.

To compute this ratio, first subtract preferred dividends, if any, from net income to measure income available to the common shareholders. Then divide income available to common shareholders' by average common equity during the year. Common equity is total equity minus preferred equity. The 2018 return on common shareholders' equity for Apple is as follows:

	Formula		Apple Inc.'s 2018 Return on Common Shareholders' Equity	Competitor (Alphabet, Inc.)
Rate of return on common shareholders' equity	$=$	$\dfrac{\text{Net income} - \text{Preferred dividends}}{\text{Average common shareholders' equity}}$	$\dfrac{\$59{,}531 - \$0}{\$120{,}597} = 49.4\%$	8.7%

Here we see that Apple's ROE (49.4%) is higher than Alphabet, Inc.'s ROE (8.7%). Now, let's consider the impact of leverage by analyzing the components of ROE:

Rate of Return on Shareholders' Equity (ROE)	Apple Inc.'s ROE		Competitor (Alphabet, Inc.)
	2018	2017	
ROA	16.1%*	14.5%	7%
×	×	×	×
Leverage ratio	3.07	2.65	1.25
=	=	=	=
ROE	(rounded) 49%	(rounded) 38%	8.7

*Effect of interest has been removed from ROA

Apple's ROA is much higher than Alphabet, Inc.'s ROA. In addition, Apple used quite a bit more debt, or leverage, to finance its operations than Alphabet, Inc.

To be sure, the use of leverage by a company is often a good thing, as long as it is kept within reasonable limits. The practice of using leverage is called **trading on the equity**. Companies like Apple that finance operations with debt are said to *leverage* their positions.

As we pointed out in Chapter 8, leverage can hurt ROE as well as help. If profits and cash flows drop, debts still must be paid. Therefore, leverage is a double-edged sword. It increases profits during good times but also compounds losses during bad times.

EARNINGS PER COMMON SHARES. Discussed in Chapters 7 and 8, *earnings per share of common stock,* or simply **earnings per share (EPS)**, is the amount of net income earned for each share of outstanding *common* stock. EPS is the most widely quoted of all financial statistics. It's the only ratio that appears on the income statement of a publicly traded company. For private companies that follow ASPE, EPS is not required to be reported.

Earnings per share is computed by dividing net income available to common shareholders by the average number of common shares outstanding during the year. Preferred dividends are subtracted from net income because the preferred shareholders have a prior claim to their dividends. Apple Inc. has no preferred stock and thus has no preferred dividends. The firm's EPS for 2018 and 2017 follows (based on Exhibit 10-9):

	Formula	Apple Inc.'s Earnings Per Share (Basic)	
		2018	2017
Earnings per share of common stock	$= \dfrac{\text{Net income} - \text{Preferred dividends (in thousands)}}{\text{Average number of common shares outstanding (in thousands)}}$	$\dfrac{\$59,531,000 - \$0}{4,955,377} = \$12.01$	$\dfrac{\$48,351,000 - \$0}{5,217,242} = \$9.27$

Apple's EPS increased 29.5% (($12.01 − $9.27)/$9.27) during 2018, and that's good news. Such moderate increases in earnings have certainly had an impact on the company's stock price. But is it still a good buy at this price? That's the relevant question a prospective shareholder wants to know. The next section gives you some information on how analysts make this decision.

Analyzing Shares as an Investment

Investors buy shares to earn a return on their investment. This return consists of two parts: (1) gains (or losses) from selling the shares, and (2) dividends.

PRICE/EARNINGS RATIO (MULTIPLE). The **price/earnings ratio (multiple)** is the ratio of common share price to earnings per share. This ratio, abbreviated P/E, appears in stock listings of many newspapers and online. It shows the market price of $1 of earnings.

Calculations for the P/E ratios of Apple follow. The market price of Apple's common shares was $225.74 at the close on Sept. 28, 2018 (the end of its 2018 fiscal year), and $154.12 at the close on Sept. 29, 2017 (the end of its 2017 fiscal year). Share prices can be obtained from a company's website or various other financial websites.

	Formula	Apple Inc.'s Price/Earnings Ratio	
		2018	2017
P/E ratio $=$	$\dfrac{\text{Market price per share of common stock}}{\text{Earnings per share}}$	$\dfrac{\$225.74}{\$12.01} = 18.8$	$\dfrac{\$154.12}{\$9.27} = 16.6$

Given Apple's 2018 P/E ratio of 18.8, we would say that the company's common shares are selling at about 18.8 times earnings. Each $1 of Apple's earnings is worth 18.8 to the stock market. Shares trade in ranges, and public companies report updated EPS quarterly. These earnings are annualized and projected for the upcoming year (quarterly earnings multiplied by 4). Because Apple's yearly earnings were reported in 2018, its shares have traded in the range of $165 to $228 per share. New competitors, like Samsung and Alphabet, Inc., are threatening Apple with smart devices that perform comparably for a lower price. Market prices of shares are based on consensus estimations of what may happen in the future—business cycles, government policies, new product announcements, foreign trade deals, currency fluctuations—even the health of key company executives may significantly impact the estimates. Markets run on sentiment and are very difficult to predict. Some analysts study past trends in P/E multiples and try to estimate future trading ranges. If the P/E multiple of a particular share drifts toward the low end of a range, and if its projected earnings are increasing, it means that the price of the shares is becoming more attractive, which may be a signal to buy. As P/E multiples drift higher given projected earnings, the shares becomes too expensive, and the analyst would recommend a "hold" or "sell." Would you buy it?

DIVIDEND YIELD. Dividend yield is the ratio of dividends per share to the share's market price. This ratio measures the percentage of a share's market value returned annually to the shareholders as dividends. Although dividends are never guaranteed, some well-established companies have continued to pay dividends even through turbulent economic times. *Preferred* shareholders pay special attention to this ratio because they invest primarily to receive dividends. However, certain companies, such as TELUS, Bank of Montreal, or Rogers Communications, also pay attractive dividends on their common shares. In periods of low interest rates on certificates of deposit or money-market funds, dividend-paying shares become more attractive alternatives for conservative investors.

Since paying its first quarterly dividend in 2012, Apple has paid regular dividends. For the year ended September 29, 2018, Apple's common shares paid $2.72 per share in dividends. So, Apple's dividend yield on its common shares was as follows:

		Dividend Yield on Apple Common Shares
	Formula	2018
Dividend yield on common stock*	$= \dfrac{\text{Dividend per common share}}{\text{Market price per common share}}$	$\dfrac{\$2.72}{\$225.74} = 0.012$

*Dividend yields may also be calculated for preferred stock.

An investor who buys Apple common shares for $225.74 can expect to receive around 1.2% of the investment annually in the form of cash dividends. You might think that's a very low rate, but compared to current yields on certificates of deposit or bonds, it's pretty attractive. Dividend yields vary widely among companies. They are generally higher for older, established firms and lower to nonexistent for young, growth-oriented companies.

BOOK VALUE PER COMMON SHARE. Book value per common share is simply common shareholders' equity divided by the number of common shares outstanding. Common equity equals total equity less preferred equity. Apple has no preferred shares outstanding. Calculations of its book value per common share follow. Numbers are based on Exhibits 10-9 and 10-10, using weighted-average number of shares outstanding.

		Book Value Per Share of Apple Inc.	
Formula (figures in thousands)		2018	2017
Book value per common share	$= \dfrac{\text{Total shareholders' equity} - \text{Preferred equity}}{\text{Weighted-average number of common shares outstanding (basic)}}$	$\dfrac{\$107,147,000 - \$0}{4,955,377} = \$21.62$	$\dfrac{\$134,047,000 - \$0}{5,217,242} = \$25.69$

Book value per share indicates the recorded accounting amount for each common share outstanding. Many experts believe book value is not useful for investment analysis because it bears no relationship to market value and provides little information beyond what's reported on the balance sheet. But some investors base their investment decisions on book value. For example, some investors rank common shares by the ratio of market price per share to book value per share. The lower the ratio, the more attractive the common share. These investors are called "value" investors, as contrasted with "growth" investors, who focus more on trends in net income.

What does the outlook for the future look like for Apple? If the company can stay on the same path it has followed for the past several years, it looks bright. Its earnings per share are solid, and from the standpoint of liquidity and leverage, the company is in great shape. It has a negative cash conversion cycle, meaning that it sells out inventory and collects cash weeks before accounts payable are due. It has no interest-bearing debt and virtually no long-term debt. The company's recent P/E ratio of 18.8 is relatively low. Beyond that, Apple is one of the most innovative companies in the world, continually putting out personal electronics products that everyone wants. All of these factors make Apple Inc. common shares look like a good investment.

STOP + THINK (10-5)

Ratios can be a useful tool when analyzing a company but it doesn't tell you everything you need to know. What other kinds of information can you gather to aid you in your analysis?

The Limitations of Ratio Analysis

Business decisions are made in a world of uncertainty. As useful as ratios are, they aren't a cure-all. Consider a physician's use of a thermometer. A reading of 38.9° Celsius tells a doctor that something is wrong with the patient but doesn't indicate what the problem is or how to cure it.

In financial analysis, a sudden drop in the current ratio signals that *something* is wrong, but it doesn't identify the problem. A manager must analyze the figures to learn what caused the ratio to fall. A drop in current assets may mean a cash shortage or that sales are slow. The manager must evaluate all the ratios in the light of factors such as increased competition or a slowdown in the economy.

Legislation, international affairs, scandals, and other factors can turn profits into losses. To be useful, ratios should be analyzed over a period of years to consider all relevant factors. Any one year, or even any two years, may not represent the company's performance over the long term. The investment decision, whether in equity investments (shares), bonds, real estate, cash, or more exotic instruments, depends on one's tolerance for risk, and risk is the one factor that is always a certainty!

Red Flags in Financial Statement Analysis

Recent accounting scandals have highlighted the importance of being alert when analyzing financial statements. Signs of trouble that may raise red flags include:

- **Earnings Problems.** Has income from continuing operations and net income decreased significantly for several years in a row? Has income turned into a loss? This may be okay for a company in a cyclical industry, such as an airline or a home builder, but most companies cannot survive consecutive loss years.

- **Decreased Cash Flow.** Cash flow validates earnings. Is cash flow from operations consistently lower than net income? Are the sales of property, plant, and equipment a major source of cash? If so, the company may be facing a cash shortage.

- **Too Much Debt.** How does the company's debt ratio compare to that of major competitors and to the industry average? If the debt ratio is much higher than average, the company may be unable to pay debts during tough times.

- **Inability to Collect Receivables.** Are days' sales in receivables growing faster than for other companies in the industry? A cash shortage may be looming.

- **Buildup of Inventories.** Is inventory turnover slowing down? If so, the company may be unable to move products, or it may be overstating inventory. Recall that one of the easiest ways to overstate net income is to overstate ending inventory.

- **Trends of Sales, Inventory, and Receivables.** Sales, receivables, and inventory generally move together. Increased sales lead to higher receivables and require more inventory to meet demand. Strange movements among these items may spell trouble.

The Decision Guidelines summarize the most widely used ratios.

 # DECISION GUIDELINES

USING RATIOS IN FINANCIAL STATEMENT ANALYSIS

As we have seen in this chapter, ratio analysis is one tool that managers, investors, and creditors use when analyzing a company. How do they determine if a company is able to pay its bills, sell inventory, collect receivables, and so on? They use the standard ratios discussed in this book.

Ratio	Computation	Information Provided
Measuring ability to pay current liabilities:		
Managers must make sure there is enough cash on hand to pay the company's current liabilities.		
Investors know that a company that cannot pay its debts is not a good investment because it could go bankrupt.		
Creditors want to make sure they will be repaid if they loan the company money.		
1. Current ratio	$\dfrac{\text{Current assets}}{\text{Current liabilities}}$	Measures ability to pay current liabilities with current assets
2. Quick (acid-test) ratio	$\dfrac{\text{Cash} + \dfrac{\text{Short-term}}{\text{investments}} + \dfrac{\text{Net current}}{\text{receivables}}}{\text{Current liabilities}}$	Shows ability to pay all current liabilities if they come due immediately

Ratio	Computation	Information Provided
Measuring turnover and cash conversion:		
Managers need to know if there is too much or too little inventory on hand. This helps them decide how much inventory to buy. They also need to monitor their accounts receivable and accounts payable to ensure that cash is being received soon after sales and bills are being paid in a timely fashion.		
Investors like to see inventory being sold quickly because unsold inventory generates no profit. The time it takes to turn accounts receivable into cash and then use it to pay bills can be used to evaluate the company's liquidity.		
Creditors know that collecting cash soon after the sale enables the company to pay its bills and loans on time.		
3. Inventory turnover and days' inventory outstanding (DIO)	$$\text{Inventory turnover} = \frac{\text{Cost of goods sold}}{\text{Average inventory}}$$ $$\text{Days' inventory outstanding (DIO)} = \frac{365}{\text{Inventory turnover}}$$	Indicates saleability of inventory—the number of times a company sells its average level of inventory during a year
4. Accounts receivable turnover	$$\frac{\text{Net credit sales}}{\text{Average net accounts receivable}}$$	Measures ability to collect cash from credit customers
5. Days' sales in receivables or days' sales outstanding (DSO)	$$\frac{365}{\text{Accounts receivable turnover}}$$	Shows how many days' sales remain in Accounts Receivable— how many days it takes to collect the average level of receivables
6. Payables turnover and days' payable outstanding (DPO)	$$\text{Accounts payable turnover} = \frac{\text{Cost of goods sold}}{\text{Average accounts payable}}$$ $$\text{Days' payable outstanding (DPO)} = \frac{365}{\text{Accounts payable turnover}}$$	Shows how many times a year accounts payable turn over, and how many days it takes the company to pay off accounts payable

Ratio	Computation	Information Provided
7. Cash conversion cycle	Cash conversion cycle = DIO + DSO − DPO where DIO = Days' inventory outstanding DSO = Days' sales outstanding DPO = Days' payable outstanding	Shows overall liquidity by computing the total days it takes to convert inventory to receivables and back to cash, less the days to pay off creditors

Measuring ability to pay *long-term debt:*

Managers must make sure they have enough assets on hand to pay the company's debts.

Investors know that a business may be generating a profit but still be low on cash. They want to be sure they are investing in a company that can pay back its debts.

Creditors loan the company money with the anticipation of being paid back. If a company is not able to pay its debts as they come due, they could face serious financial difficulty, and even be forced into bankruptcy.

Ratio	Computation	Information Provided
8. Debt ratio	$$\frac{\text{Total liabilities}}{\text{Total assets}}$$	Indicates percentage of assets financed with debt
9. Times-interest-earned ratio	$$\frac{\text{Income from operations}}{\text{Interest expense}}$$	Measures the number of times operating income can cover interest expense

Measuring profitability:

Managers are evaluated based on how well a company has performed financially.

Investors look to see if a company is able to generate a profit, which could mean an increase in the price of their shares.

Creditors know that a profitable company is able to pay back their debt.

Ratio	Computation	Information Provided
10. Gross profit %	$$\frac{\text{Gross profit}}{\text{Net sales}}$$	Shows the percentage of profit that a company makes from merely selling the product, before any other operating costs are subtracted
11. Operating income %	$$\frac{\text{Income from operations}}{\text{Net sales}}$$	Shows the percentage of profit earned from each dollar in the company's core business, after operating costs have been subtracted
12. Return on net sales	$$\frac{\text{Net income}}{\text{Net sales}}$$	Shows the percentage of each sales dollar earned as net income
13. Asset turnover	$$\frac{\text{Net sales}}{\text{Average total assets}}$$	Measures the amount of net sales generated for each dollar invested in assets
14. Return on total assets (ROA)	$$\frac{\text{Net income} + \text{Interest expense}}{\text{Average total assets}}$$	Measures how profitably a company uses its assets
15. Leverage ratio	$$\frac{\text{Average total assets}}{\text{Average common shareholders' equity}}$$	Otherwise known as the *equity multiplier*, measures the ratio of average total assets to average common shareholders' equity
16. Return on common shareholders' equity (ROE)	$$\frac{\text{Net income} - \text{Preferred dividends}}{\text{Average common shareholders' equity}}$$	Measures how much income is earned for every dollar invested by the company's common shareholders
17. Earnings per common share	$$\frac{\text{Net income} - \text{Preferred dividends}}{\text{Average number of common shares outstanding}}$$	Measures the amount of net income earned for each common share outstanding

Analyzing shares as an investment:

Investors purchase shares to earn a return on their investment. This return consists of two parts: (1) gains (or losses) from selling their shares, and (2) dividends (if any). They want to know if the shares are a worthwhile investment.

Ratio	Computation	Information Provided
18. Price/earnings ratio	$$\dfrac{\text{Market price per common share}}{\text{Earnings per share}}$$	Indicates the market price of $1 of earnings
19. Dividend yield	$$\dfrac{\text{Dividend per common (or preferred) share}}{\text{Market price per common (or preferred) share}}$$	Shows the percentage of a share's market value returned as dividends to shareholders each period
20. Book value per common share	$$\dfrac{\text{Total shareholders' equity} - \text{Preferred equity}}{\text{Number of common shares outstanding}}$$	Indicates the recorded accounting amount for each common share outstanding

Summary of IFRS-ASPE Differences

Concepts	IFRS	ASPE

There are no differences between IFRS and ASPE in this chapter.

SUMMARY

SUMMARY OF LEARNING OBJECTIVES

LEARNING OBJECTIVE	SUMMARY
❶ **Perform** a horizontal analysis	A horizontal analysis is used to study percentage changes in financial statement items, such as sales or net income, from year to year. The dollar amount of the change from one period to the next is divided by the base-year amount. A form of horizontal analysis is a trend percentage that shows how something (such as sales or net income, for example) has changed over a period of time.
❷ **Perform** a vertical analysis	Vertical analysis reveals the relationship of a financial statement item to a specified base. For example, using the income statement, total revenue is usually the base when analyzing income statement relationships.
❸ **Prepare** common-size financial statements	A common-size statement reports only percentages (no dollar amounts). For example, on a common-size balance sheet, each item is expressed as a percentage of total assets. A common-size statement eases the comparison of different companies because their amounts are stated as percentages.
❹ **Analyze** the statement of cash flows	Analyzing a cash flow statement helps to reveal whether or not the company is experiencing cash problems. Generally speaking, a company's main source of cash should come from its operations. If the major source of cash over several periods is from investing (for example, selling property, plant, and equipment), it may signal a cash shortage.
❺ **Use** ratios to make business decisions	Ratios discussed in this chapter to measure the "well being" of a business include: ability to pay current liabilities, ability to sell inventory and collect receivables, ability to pay long-term debt, profitability, and analysis of shares as an investment. Ratios are an important tool of financial analysis, but should be considered as only one source of information when analyzing a company.

MyLab Accounting

END-OF-CHAPTER SUMMARY PROBLEM

The following financial data are adapted from the annual reports of Lampeer Corporation:

	A	B	C	D	E	F
1	**Lampeer Corporation** Four-Year Select Financial Data Years Ended January 31, 2020, 2019, 2018, 2017					
2	**Operating Results***	2020	2019	2018	2017	
3	Net Sales	$ 13,848	$ 13,673	$ 11,635	$ 9,054	
4	Cost of goods sold and occupancy expenses, excluding depreciation and amortization	9,704	8,599	6,775	5,318	
5	Interest expense	109	75	45	46	
6	Income from operations	338	1,445	1,817	1,333	
7	Net earnings (net loss)	(8)	877	1,127	824	
8	Cash dividends	76	75	76	77	
9	**Financial Position:**					
10	Merchandise inventory	1,677	1,904	1,462	1,056	
11	Total assets	7,591	7,012	5,189	3,963	
12	Current ratio	1.48:1	0.95:1	1.25:1	1.20:1	
13	Shareholders' equity	3,010	2,928	2,630	1,574	
14	Average number of common shares outstanding (in thousands)	860	879	895	576	
15						

*Dollar amounts are in thousands.

Requirement
_____

1. Compute the following ratios for 2018 through 2020, and evaluate Lampeer's operating results. Are operating results strong or weak? Did they improve or deteriorate during the three-year period? Your analysis will reveal a clear trend.
   a. Inventory turnover (assume occupancy expenses are included in cost of goods sold)
   b. Gross profit percentage
   c. Operating income (profit) percentage
   d. Return on sales
   e. Asset turnover
   f. Return on assets
   g. Leverage ratio
   h. Return on shareholders' equity
   i. Times-interest-earned ratio
   j. Earnings per share

ANSWERS

	2020	2019	2018
a. Inventory turnover	$\dfrac{\$9{,}704}{(\$1{,}677 + \$1{,}904)/2} = 5.4$ times	$\dfrac{\$8{,}599}{(\$1{,}904 + \$1{,}462)/2} = 5.1$ times	$\dfrac{\$6{,}775}{(\$1{,}462 + \$1{,}056)/2} = 5.4$ times
b. Gross profit percentage	$\dfrac{\$13{,}848 - \$9{,}704}{\$13{,}848} = 29.9\%$	$\dfrac{\$13{,}673 - \$8{,}599}{\$13{,}673} = 37.1\%$	$\dfrac{\$11{,}635 - \$6{,}775}{\$11{,}635} = 41.8\%$
c. Operating income percentage	$\dfrac{\$338}{\$13{,}848} = 2.4\%$	$\dfrac{\$1{,}445}{\$13{,}673} = 10.6\%$	$\dfrac{\$1{,}817}{\$11{,}635} = 15.6\%$
d. Return on sales	$\dfrac{\$(8)}{\$13{,}848} = (0.06)\%$	$\dfrac{\$877}{\$13{,}673} = 6.4\%$	$\dfrac{\$1{,}127}{\$11{,}635} = 9.7\%$
e. Asset turnover	$\dfrac{\$13{,}848}{(\$7{,}591 + \$7{,}012)/2} = 1.897$	$\dfrac{\$13{,}673}{(\$7{,}012 + \$5{,}189)/2} = 2.241$	$\dfrac{\$11{,}635}{(\$5{,}189 + \$3{,}963)/2} = 2.543$
f. Return on assets	$[\$(8) + \$109]/[(\$7{,}591 + \$7{,}012)/2]$ $= 1.38$	$(\$877 + \$75)/[(\$7{,}012 + \$5{,}189)/2]$ $= 15.6\%$	$\$1{,}127 + \$45/[(\$5{,}189 + \$3{,}963)/2]$ $= 25.6\%$
g. Leverage ratio	$\dfrac{(\$7{,}591 + \$7{,}012)/2}{(\$3{,}010 + \$2{,}928)/2} = 2.459$	$\dfrac{(\$7{,}012 + \$5{,}189)/2}{(\$2{,}928 + \$2{,}630)/2} = 2.195$	$\dfrac{(\$5{,}189 + \$3{,}963)/2}{(\$2{,}630 + \$1{,}574)/2} = 2.176$
h. Return on shareholders' equity	$\dfrac{\$(8)}{(\$3{,}010 + \$2{,}928)/2} = (0.27)$	$\dfrac{\$877}{(\$2{,}928 + \$2{,}630)/2} = 31.6\%$	$\dfrac{\$1{,}127}{(\$2{,}630 + \$1{,}574)/2} = 53.6\%$
i. Times-interest-earned ratio	$\dfrac{\$338}{\$109} = 3.1$ times	$\dfrac{\$1{,}445}{\$75} = 19.3$ times	$\dfrac{\$1{,}817}{\$45} = 40.4$ times
j. Earnings per share	$\dfrac{\$(8)}{860} = \$(0.01)$	$\dfrac{\$877}{879} = \$1.00$	$\dfrac{\$1{,}127}{895} = \$1.26$

Evaluation:

During this period, Lampeer's operating results deteriorated on all these measures except inventory turnover. The gross profit percentage is down sharply, as are the times-interest-earned ratio and all the return measures. From these data it is clear that Lampeer could sell its merchandise, but not at the markups the company enjoyed in the past. The final result, in 2020, was a net loss for the year. This yielded a low ROA, and because of leverage, a negative ROE.

REVIEW

MyLab Accounting	Make the grade with MyLab Accounting: The Quick Quiz questions, Short Exercises, Exercises, and Problems (Group A) marked with a ⊕ can be found on MyLab Accounting. You can practise them as often as you want, and most feature step-by-step guided instructions to help you find the right answer.

QUICK QUIZ (ANSWERS APPEAR ON THE LAST PAGE OF THIS CHAPTER.)

Test your understanding of financial statement analysis by answering the following questions. Select the best choice from among the possible answers given. Use the Canada Technology Corporation (CTC) financial statements to answer the questions that follow.

	A	B	C	D
1	**Canada Technology Corporation** Consolidated Statements of Financial Position	**December 31,**		
2	*(in millions)*	2020	2019	
3	**Assets**			
4	Current assets:			
5	Cash and cash equivalents	$ 4,317	$ 4,232	
6	Short-term investments	835	406	
7	Accounts receivable, net	3,635	2,586	
8	Inventories	327	306	
9	Other	1,519	1,394	
10	Total current assets	10,633	8,924	
11	**Property, plant, and equipment, net**	1,517	913	
12	Investments	6,770	5,267	
13	Other non-current assets	391	366	
14	Total assets	$ 19,311	$ 15,470	
15	**Liabilities and Shareholders' Equity**			
16	Current liabilities:			
17	Accounts payable	$ 7,316	$ 5,989	
18	Accrued and other	3,580	2,944	
19	Total current liabilities	10,896	8,933	
20	Long-term debt	505	506	
21	Other non-current liabilities	1,630	1,158	
22	Commitments and contingent liabilities	—	—	
23	Total liabilities	13,031	10,597	
24	**Shareholders' equity:**			
25	Preferred shares; shares issued: 0	—	—	
26	Common share; shares authorized: 7,000; shares issued: 2,556 and 2,579, respectively	284	1,479	
27	Retained earnings	6,131	3,486	
28	Other comprehensive loss	(83)	(33)	
29	Other	(52)	(59)	
30	Total shareholders' equity	6,280	4,873	
31	Total liabilities and shareholders' equity	$ 19,311	$ 15,470	
32				

	A	B	C	D	E
1	**Canada Technology Corporation** Consolidated Statements of Income (in millions, except per share amounts)	**Years Ended December 31,**			
2		**2020**	**2019**	**2018**	
3	Net revenue	$ 41,444	$ 35,404	$ 31,168	
4	Cost of goods sold	33,892	29,055	25,661	
5	Gross profit	7,552	6,349	5,507	
6	**Operating expenses:**				
7	Selling, general, and administrative	3,544	3,050	2,784	
8	Research, development, and engineering	464	455	452	
9	Special charges	—	—	482	
10	Total operating expenses	4,008	3,505	3,718	
11	Operating income	3,544	2,844	1,789	
12	Investment and other income (loss), net	180	183	(58)	
13	Income before income taxes	3,724	3,027	1,731	
14	Income tax expense	1,079	905	485	
15	Net income	$ 2,645	$ 2,122	$ 1,246	
16	**Earnings per common share:**				
17	Basic	$ 1.03	$ 0.82	$ 0.48	
18					

1. During 2020, CTC's total assets
  a. increased by $8,341 million.
  b. increased by 24.8%.
  c. Both a and b.
  d. increased by 19.9%.

2. CTC's current ratio at year-end 2020 is closest to
  a. 1.2.
  b. 1.1.
  c. 1.0.
  d. 0.8.

3. CTC's quick (acid-test) ratio at year-end 2020 is closest to
  a. 0.80.
  b. 0.65.
  c. 0.47.
  d. $8,787 million.

4. What is the largest single item included in CTC's debt ratio at December 31, 2020?
  a. Cash and cash equivalents
  b. Accounts payable
  c. Investments
  d. Common shares

5. Using the earliest year available as the base year, the trend percentage for CTC's net revenue during 2020 was
  a. 117%.
  b. up by $10,276 million.
  c. up by 17.1%.
  d. 133%.

6. CTC's common-size income statement for 2020 would report cost of goods sold as
  a. $33,892 million.
  b. up by 16.6%.
  c. 81.8%.
  d. 132.1%.

7. CTC's days' sales in receivables during 2020 was
  a. 22 days.
  b. 27 days.
  c. 32 days.
  d. 114 days.

8. CTC's inventory turnover during fiscal year 2020 was
  a. very slow.
  b. 54 times.
  c. 107 times.
  d. 129 times.

9. CTC's long-term debt bears interest at 6%. During the year ended December 31, 2020, CTC's times-interest-earned ratio was
  a. 117 times.
  b. 110 times.
  c. 100 times.
  d. 125 times.

10. CTC's trend of return on sales is
  a. improving.
  b. declining.
  c. stuck at 6%.
  d. worrisome.

11. How many common shares did CTC have outstanding, on average, during 2020? Hint: Use the earnings per share formula.
   a. 2,721 million
   b. 2,701 million
   c. 2,645 million
   d. 2,568 million

12. Book value per common share of CTC outstanding at December 31, 2020, was
   a. $2.72.
   b. $4.37.
   c. $6,280.
   d. $2.46.

ACCOUNTING VOCABULARY

accounts payable turnover A liquidity ratio that measures the number of times per year a company was able to repay its accounts payable in full. Calculated by dividing the cost of goods sold by the average accounts payable balance for the year. (p. 539)

accounts receivable turnover Measures a company's ability to collect cash from credit customers. To compute accounts receivable turnover, divide net credit sales by average net accounts receivable. (p. 538)

acid-test ratio Ratio of the sum of cash plus short-term investments plus net current receivables to total current liabilities. Tells whether the entity can pay all its current liabilities if they come due immediately. Also called the *quick ratio*. (p. 537)

asset turnover The dollars of sales generated per dollar of assets invested. Net sales divided by Average total assets. (p. 542)

benchmarking The comparison of a company to a standard set by other companies, with a view toward improvement. (p. 527)

book value per common share Common shareholders' equity divided by the number of common shares outstanding. The recorded amount for each common share outstanding. (p. 546)

cash conversion cycle The number of days it takes to convert cash into inventory, inventory to receivables, and receivables back into cash, after paying off payables. Days inventory outstanding + days sales outstanding − days payables outstanding. (p. 539)

common-size financial statements A financial statement that reports only percentages (no dollar amounts). (p. 527)

current ratio Current assets divided by current liabilities. Measures a company's ability to pay current liabilities with current assets. (p. 535)

days payable outstanding (DPO) Another way of expressing the accounts payable turnover ratio, this measure indicates how many days it will take to pay off the accounts payable balance in full. Calculated by dividing the *accounts payable turnover* into 365. (p. 539)

days' inventory outstanding Calculated as 365 days divided by inventory turnover. Indicates how many days it takes to sell inventory. (p. 538)

days' sales in receivables Ratio of average net accounts receivable to one day's sales. Indicates how many days' sales remain in Accounts Receivable awaiting collection. Also called the *collection period* and *days sales outstanding*. (p. 539)

debt ratio Ratio of total liabilities to total assets. States the proportion of a company's assets that is financed with debt. (p. 540)

dividend yield Ratio of dividends per share to the share's market price per share. Tells the percentage of a share's market value that the company returns to shareholders as dividends. (p. 546)

earnings per share (EPS) Amount of a company's net income per outstanding common share. (p. 544)

horizontal analysis Study of percentage changes over time through comparative financial statements. (p. 519)

interest-coverage ratio Another name for the *times-interest-earned ratio*. (p. 540)

inventory turnover Ratio of cost of goods sold to average inventory. Indicates how rapidly inventory is sold. (p. 537)

leverage Earning more income on borrowed money than the related interest expense, thereby increasing the earnings for the owners of the business. Also called *trading on the equity*. (p. 543)

leverage ratio Ratio of average total assets to average common shareholders' equity. Measures the proportion of average total assets actually owned by the shareholders. (p. 543)

price/earnings ratio (multiple) Ratio of the market price of a common to the company's earnings per share. Measures the value that the stock market places on $1 of a company's earnings. (p. 545)

quick ratio Another name for *acid-test ratio*. (p. 537)

return on assets Net income divided by average total assets. This ratio measures how profitably management has used the assets that shareholders and creditors have provided the company. (p. 543)

return on common shareholders' equity Net income minus preferred dividends, divided by average common shareholders' equity. A measure of profitability. Also called *return on equity (ROE)*. (p. 543)

return on net sales Ratio of net income to net sales. A measure of profitability. Also called *return on sales*. (p. 542)

times-interest-earned ratio Ratio of income from operations to interest expense. Measures the number of times that operating income can cover interest expense. Also called the *interest-coverage ratio*. (p. 540)

trading on the equity Another name for *leverage*. (p. 544)

trend percentages A form of horizontal analysis that indicates the direction a business is taking. (p. 523)

vertical analysis Analysis of a financial statement that reveals the relationship of each statement item to a specified base, which is the 100% figure. (p. 524)

working capital Current assets minus current liabilities; measures a business's ability to meet its short-term obligations with its current assets. Also called *net working capital*. (p. 534)

ASSESS YOUR PROGRESS

SHORT EXERCISES

LEARNING OBJECTIVE ❶

Perform a horizontal analysis of revenues and net income

🌐 **S10-1** Cannes Corporation reported the following amounts on its 2020 comparative income statement:

(in thousands)	2020	2019	2018
Revenues	$10,889	$10,095	$9,777
Total expenses	5,985	5,604	5,194

Perform a horizontal analysis of revenues and net income—both in dollar amounts and in percentages—for 2020 and 2019.

LEARNING OBJECTIVE ❶

Perform a trend analysis of sales and net income

🌐 **S10-2** Zoobilee Inc. reported the following sales and net income amounts:

(in thousands)	2020	2019	2018	2017
Sales	$9,180	$8,990	$8,770	$8,550
Net income	520	500	460	400

Show Zoobilee's trend percentages for sales and net income. Use 2017 as the base year.

LEARNING OBJECTIVE ❷

Perform a vertical analysis to understand a cash shortage

🌐 **S10-3** Vision Software Limited reported the following amounts on its balance sheets at December 31, 2020, 2019, and 2018:

	2020	2019	2018
Cash	$ 6,000	$ 6,000	$ 5,000
Receivables, net	30,000	22,000	19,000
Inventory	148,000	106,000	74,000
Prepaid expenses	2,000	2,000	1,000
Property, plant, and equipment, net	96,000	88,000	87,000
Total assets	$282,000	$224,000	$186,000

Sales and profits are high. Nevertheless, Vision is experiencing a cash shortage. Perform a vertical analysis of Vision Software's assets at the end of years 2020, 2019, and 2018. Use the analysis to explain the reason for the cash shortage.

LEARNING OBJECTIVE ❸

Compare common-size income statements of two companies

🌐 **S10-4** Porterfield Inc. and Beasley Ltd. are competitors. Compare the two companies by converting their condensed income statements to common size.

(in millions)	Porterfield	Beasley
Net sales	$9,489	$19,536
Cost of goods sold	5,785	14,101
Selling and administrative expenses	2,690	3,846
Interest expense	59	16
Other expense	34	38
Income tax expense	331	597
Net income	$ 590	$ 938

Which company earned more net income? Which company's net income was a higher percentage of its net sales? Which company is more profitable? Explain your answer.

S10-5 Examine the financial data of Black Corporation. Show how to compute Black's current ratio from 2018 to 2020. Is the company's ability to pay its current liabilities improving or deteriorating?

LEARNING OBJECTIVE ❺

Evaluate the trend in a company's current ratio

	A	B	C	D	E
1	**Black Corporation**				
2		**Years Ended December 31**			
3	*(dollar amounts in millions)*	**2020**	**2019**	**2018**	
4	Consolidated Financial Measures and Ratios				
5	**Operating results**				
6	Net earnings	$ 769	$ 675	$ 656	
7	Per common share	$ 2.73	$ 2.43	$ 2.39	
8	Operating income	1,312	$ 1,239	$ 1,205	
9	Operating margin	4.4%	4.4%	3.9%	
10	Gross profit percentage	22.2%	22.4%	23.4%	
11	Return on net assets	12%	12%	12%	
12	Return on shareholders' equity	13.2%	12.6%	10.9%	
13	Interest coverage	4.2 times	4.2 times	4.2 times	
14	**Financial position**				
15	Working capital	$ 1,744	$ 1,061	$ 972	
16	Current assets	$ 6,462	$ 6,092	$ 5,995	
17	Current liabilities	$ 4,718	$ 5,031	$ 5,023	
18					

S10-6 Use the Allstott, Inc., balance sheet data below.

1. Compute Allstott, Inc.'s quick (acid-test) ratio at December 31, 2020 and 2019.
2. Use the comparative information from the table on page 597 for Baker, Inc., Calvin Company, and Dunn Companies Limited. Is Allstott's quick (acid-test) ratio for 2020 and 2019 strong, average, or weak in comparison?

LEARNING OBJECTIVE ❺

Evaluate a company's quick (acid-test) ratio

	A	B	C	D	E	F
1	**Allstott, Inc.** **Balance Sheets (Adapted)** **As at December 31, 2020 and 2019**					
2				**Increase (Decrease)**		
3	*(dollar amounts in millions)*	**2020**	**2019**	**Amount**	**Percentage**	
4	**Assets**					
5	Current assets:					
6	Cash and cash equivalents	$ 1,200	$ 900	$ 300	33.3%	
7	Short-term investments	6	70	(64)	(91.4)	
8	Receivables, net	240	250	(10)	(4.0)	
9	Inventories	96	81	15	18.5	
10	Prepaid expenses and other assets	243	363	(120)	(33.1)	
11	Total current assets	1,785	1,664	121	7.3	
12	Property, plant, and equipment, net	3,611	3,376	235	7.0	
13	Intangible assets	1,011	878	133	15.1	
14	Other assets	828	722	106	14.7	
15	Total assets	$ 7,235	$ 6,640	$ 595	9.0%	
16	**Liabilities and Shareholders' Equity**					
17	Current liabilities:					
18	Accounts payable	$ 1,000	$ 900	$ 100	11.1%	
19	Income tax payable	39	61	(22)	(36.1)	
20	Short-term debt	118	111	7	6.3	
21	Other	70	73	(3)	(4.1)	
22	Total current liabilities	1,227	1,145	82	7.2	
23	Long-term debt	3,500	2,944	556	18.9	
24	Other liabilities	1,117	1,036	81	7.8	
25	Total liabilities	5,844	5,125	719	14.0	

(Continued)

	A	B	C	D	E	F
26	Shareholders' equity:					
27	Common shares	2	2	—	—	
28	Retained earnings	1,543	1,689	(146)	(8.6)	
29	Accumulated other comprehensive (loss)	(154)	(176)	22	12.5	
30	Total shareholders' equity	1,391	1,515	(124)	(8.2)	
31	Total liabilities and shareholders' equity	$ 7,235	$ 6,640	$ 595	9.0%	
32						

Company	Quick (Acid-Test) Ratio
Baker, Inc. (Utility)..	0.71
Calvin Company (Department store)...................................	1.01
Dunn Companies Limited (Grocery store)	1.05

LEARNING OBJECTIVE ⑤

Compute and evaluate turnover and the cash conversion cycle

🌐 **S10-7** Use the Allstott 2020 income statement that follows and the balance sheet from exercise S10-6 to compute the following:

	A	B	C	D
1	**Allstott, Inc.** Statements of Income (Adapted) Year Ended December 31, 2020 and 2019			
2	(dollar amounts in millions)	2020	2019	
3	Revenues	$ 9,500	$ 9,309	
4	Expenses:			
5	Food and paper (Cost of goods sold)	2,509	2,644	
6	Payroll and employee benefits	2,138	2,211	
7	Occupancy and other operating expenses	2,413	2,375	
8	General and administrative expenses	1,217	1,148	
9	Interest expense	184	117	
10	Other expense (income), net	19	(34)	
11	Income before income taxes	1,020	848	
12	Income tax expense	285	267	
13	Net income	$ 735	$ 581	
14				

a. Allstott's rate of inventory turnover and days inventory outstanding for 2020
b. Days' sales in average receivables (days sales outstanding) during 2020 (round dollar amounts to one decimal place)
c. Accounts payable turnover and days' payables outstanding
d. Length of cash conversion cycle in days

Do these measures look strong or weak? Give the reason for your answer.

LEARNING OBJECTIVE ⑤

Measure ability to pay long-term debt

🌐 **S10-8** Use the financial statements of Allstott, Inc., in exercises S10-6 and S10-7.

1. Compute the company's debt ratio at December 31, 2020.
2. Compute the company's times-interest-earned ratio for 2020. For operating income, use income before both interest expense and income taxes. You can simply add interest expense back to income before taxes.
3. Is Allstott's ability to pay liabilities and interest expense strong or weak? Comment on the value of each ratio computed for questions 1 and 2.

LEARNING OBJECTIVE ⑤

Measure profitability

🌐 **S10-9** Use the financial statements of Allstott, Inc., in exercises S10-6 and S10-7 to compute the following profitability measures for 2020. Show each computation.

a. Return on sales
b. Asset turnover
c. Return on assets

d. Leverage (equity multiplier) ratio

e. Return on common shareholders' equity

f. Is Allstott, Inc.'s profitability strong, medium, or weak?

S10-10 The annual report of Classic Cars Inc. for the year ended December 31, 2020, included the following items (in thousands):

LEARNING OBJECTIVE ⑤

Compute EPS and the price/earnings ratio

Preferred shares outstanding, $4; 5,000 issued...................................	$500
Net income..	$990
Number of common shares outstanding...	200

1. Compute earnings per share (EPS) and the price/earnings ratio for Classic Cars's common shares. Round to the nearest cent. The price of a common share of Classic Cars is $77.60.
2. How much does the stock market say $1 of Classic Cars's net income is worth?

S10-11 A skeleton of Hill Country Florist Limited's income statement appears as follows (amounts in thousands):

LEARNING OBJECTIVE ⑤

Use ratio data to reconstruct an income statement

	A	B	C	D
1	**Income Statement**			
2	Net sales	$ 7,278		
3	Cost of goods sold	(a)		
4	Selling expenses	1,510		
5	Administrative expenses	351		
6	Interest expense	(b)		
7	Other expenses	126		
8	Income before taxes	1,042		
9	Income tax expense	(c)		
10	Net income	$ (d)		
11				

Use the following ratio data to complete Hill Country Florist's income statement:

a. Inventory turnover was 5 (beginning inventory was $775, ending inventory was $767).

b. Return on sales is 0.12.

S10-12 A skeleton of Hill Country Florist Limited's balance sheet appears as follows (amounts in thousands):

LEARNING OBJECTIVE ⑤

Use ratio data to reconstruct a balance sheet

	A	B	C	D
1	**Balance Sheet**			
2	Cash	$ 253	Total current liabilities	$ 1,164
3	Receivables	(a)	Long-term debt	(e)
4	Inventories	555	Other long-term liabilities	826
5	Prepaid expenses	(b)		
6	Total current assets	(c)		
7	Property, plant, and equipment, net	(d)	Common shares	185
			Retained earnings	2,846
8	Other assets	1,150	Total liabilities and	
9	Total assets	$ 6,315	shareholders' equity	$ (f)
10				

Use the following ratio data to complete Hill Country Florist's balance sheet:

a. Debt ratio is 0.52.

b. Current ratio is 1.20.

c. Acid-test ratio is 0.70.

EXERCISES

LEARNING OBJECTIVE ❶

Compute year-to-year changes in working capital

E10-13 Using the given balance sheet data, what were the dollar amount of change and the percentage of each change in Rocky Mountain Lodge Limited's working capital during 2020 and 2019? Is this trend favourable or unfavourable?

Rocky Mountain Lodge Limited	2020	2019	2018
Total current assets	$326,000	$290,000	$280,000
Total current liabilities	170,000	167,000	150,000

LEARNING OBJECTIVE ❶

Prepare a horizontal analysis of an income statement

E10-14 Prepare a horizontal analysis of the comparative income statement of Stamps Music Ltd. Round percentage changes to the nearest one-tenth percent (three decimal places).

	A	B	C	D
1	**Stamps Music Ltd.** Comparative Income Statement For the Years Ended December 31, 2020 and 2019			
2		2020	2019	
3	Total revenue	$ 403,000	$ 430,000	
4	Expenses:			
5	Cost of goods sold	$ 188,000	$ 202,000	
6	Selling and general expenses	93,000	90,000	
7	Interest expense	4,000	10,000	
8	Income tax expense	37,000	42,000	
9	Total expenses	322,000	344,000	
10	Net income	$ 81,000	$ 86,000	
11				

LEARNING OBJECTIVE ❶

Compute trend percentages

E10-15 Compute trend percentages for Carmel Valley Sales & Service Ltd.'s total revenue and net income for the following five-year period, using year 0 as the base year. Round to the nearest full percent.

(in thousands)	Year 4	Year 3	Year 2	Year 1	Year 0
Total revenue	$1,418	$1,287	$1,106	$1,009	$1,043
Net income	125	104	93	81	85

Which grew faster during the period, total revenue or net income?

LEARNING OBJECTIVE ❷

Perform a vertical analysis of a balance sheet

E10-16 Cobra Golf Limited has requested that you perform a vertical analysis of its balance sheet to determine the component percentages of its assets, liabilities, and shareholders' equity.

	A	B	C	D
1	**Cobra Golf Limited** Balance Sheet As at December 31, 2020			
2	**Assets**			
3	Total current assets			
4	Property, plant, and equipment, net	$ 92,000		
5	Other assets	247,000		
6	Total assets	35,000		
7		$ 374,000		
8	**Liabilities**			
9	Total current liabilities	$ 48,000		
10	Long-term debt	108,000		
11	Total liabilities	156,000		

	A	B	C	D
12	**Shareholders' Equity**			
13	Total shareholders' equity	218,000		
14	Total liabilities and shareholders' equity	$ 374,000		
15				

 E10-17 Prepare a comparative common-size income statement for Stamps Music Ltd. using the 2020 and 2019 data of exercise E10-14 and rounding percentages to one-tenth percent (three decimal places).

LEARNING OBJECTIVE ❸

Prepare a common-size income statement

 E10-18 Identify any weaknesses revealed by the following statement of cash flows of Holland Marsh Farms Limited.

LEARNING OBJECTIVE ❹

Analyze the statement of cash flows

	A	B	C	D
1	**Holland Marsh Farms Limited** Statement of Cash Flows For the Current Year			
2	**Operating activities:**			
3	Income from operations		$ 42,000	
4	Add (subtract) non-cash items:			
5	Depreciation	$ 23,000		
6	Net increase in current assets other than cash	(45,000)		
7	Net decrease in current liabilities exclusive of short-term debt	(7,000)	(29,000)	
8	Net cash provided by operating activities		13,000	
9	**Investing activities:**			
10	Sale of property, plant, and equipment		101,000	
11	**Financing activities:**			
12	Issuance of bonds payable	$ 102,000		
13	Payment of short-term debt	(159,000)		
14	Payment of long-term debt	(79,000)		
15	Payment of dividends	(42,000)		
16	Net cash used for financing activities		(178,000)	
17	Increase (decrease) in cash		$ (64,000)	
18				

 E10-19 The financial statements of National News Inc. include the following items:

LEARNING OBJECTIVE ❺

Compute five ratios

	Current Year	Preceding Year
Balance Sheet:		
Cash	$ 17,000	$ 22,000
Short-term investments	11,000	26,000
Net receivables	64,000	73,000
Inventory	77,000	71,000
Prepaid expenses	16,000	8,000
Total current assets	$185,000	$200,000
Total current liabilities	$111,000	$ 91,000
Income Statement:		
Net credit sales	$654,000	
Cost of goods sold	327,000	

Requirement

Compute the following ratios for the current year:

a. Current ratio

b. Quick (acid-test) ratio

c. Inventory turnover

d. Accounts receivable turnover

e. Days' sales in receivables

LEARNING OBJECTIVE ❺

Analyze the ability to pay current liabilities

E10-20 Using the information provided, calculate the ratios that would be relevant in determining whether or not Patio Furniture Inc. can pay both its current and long-term debt. Comment on whether the company's position has improved during 2020.

	2020	2019
Cash	$ 61,000	$ 47,000
Short-term investments	28,000	—
Net receivables	142,000	116,000
Inventory	286,000	263,000
Prepaid expenses	11,000	9,000
Total assets	643,000	489,000
Total current liabilities	255,000	221,000
Long-term debt	46,000	52,000
Income from operations	165,000	158,000
Interest expense	40,000	39,000

LEARNING OBJECTIVE ❺

Analyze profitability

E10-21 Compute four ratios that measure ability to earn profits for PGI Decor Inc., whose comparative income statement follows:

	A	B	C	D
1	**PGI Decor Inc.** Comparative Income Statement For the Years Ended December 31, 2020 and 2019			
2	*(in thousands)*	2020	2019	
3	Net sales	$ 174,000	$ 158,000	
4	Cost of goods sold	93,000	86,000	
5	Gross profit	81,000	72,000	
6	Selling and general expenses	46,000	41,000	
7	Income from operations	35,000	31,000	
8	Interest expense	9,000	10,000	
9	Income before income tax	26,000	21,000	
10	Income tax expense	9,000	8,000	
11	Net income	$ 17,000	$ 13,000	
12				

Additional data:

	2020	2019	2018
Total assets	$204,000	$191,000	$171,000
Common shareholders' equity	$ 96,000	$ 89,000	$ 79,000
Preferred dividends	$ 3,000	$ 3,000	$ 0
Average common shares outstanding during the year	21,000	20,000	18,000

Using the information provided, calculate the information that would be relevant in deciding whether the company's operating performance improved or deteriorated during 2020.

LEARNING OBJECTIVE ❺

Evaluate shares as an investment

E10-22 Evaluate the common shares of Phillips Distributing Limited as an investment. Specifically, use the three share ratios to determine whether the common shares increased or decreased in attractiveness during the past year.

	2020	2019
Net income...	$112,000	$ 96,000
Common share dividends.......................................	25,000	20,000
Total shareholders' equity at year-end (includes 80,000 common shares)................................	580,000	500,000
Preferred shares, $8; 1,000 shares issued...	100,000	100,000
Market price per common share at year-end......................................	$ 22.50	$ 16.75

E10-23 The following data (dollar amounts in millions) are taken from the financial statements of Phase 1 Industries Inc.:

LEARNING OBJECTIVE ❺

Use ratio data to reconstruct a company's balance sheet

Total liabilities...	$11,800
Preferred shares..	$ 0
Total current assets...	$10,200
Accumulated depreciation.............................	$ 1,400
Debt ratio...	59%
Current ratio	1.50

Requirement

Complete the following condensed balance sheet. Report amounts to the nearest million dollars.

Current assets...		$?
Property, plant, and equipment	$?	
Less accumulated depreciation	(?)	?
Total assets		$?
Current liabilities..		$?
Long-term liabilities		?
Shareholders' equity		?
Total liabilities and shareholders' equity		$?

E10-24 The following data (dollar amounts in millions) are from the financial statements of Provincial Industry Limited:

LEARNING OBJECTIVE ❺

Use ratio data to reconstruct a company's income statement

Average shareholders' equity...	$3,600
Interest expense..	$ 400
Preferred shares..	$ 0
Operating income as a percent of sales	25%
Return on equity	20%
Income tax rate..	40%

Requirement

Complete the following condensed income statement. Report amounts to the nearest million dollars.

Sales...	$?
Operating expense..	?
Operating income..	?
Interest expense..	?
Pretax income...	?
Income tax expense..	?
Net income..	$?

LEARNING OBJECTIVES ❶❸❺
Use trend percentages, common-size percentages, and ratios to reconstruct financial statements

🌐 **E10-25** An incomplete comparative income statement and balance sheet for Emore Corporation follow:

	A	B	C	D
1	**Emore Corporation** Comparative Income Statements Years Ended December 31, 2020 and 2019			
2		**2020**	**2019**	
3	Sales revenue	$ 2,100,000	$ 2,000,000	
4	Cost of goods sold	?	1,100,000	
5	Gross profit	?	900,000	
6	Operating expense	?	700,000	
7	Operating income	?	200,000	
8	Interest expense	20,000	20,000	
9	Income before income tax	?	180,000	
10	Income tax expense (30%)	?	54,000	
11	Net income	?	$ 126,000	
12				

	A	B	C	D
1	**Emore Corporation** Balance Sheet December 31, 2020 and 2019			
2		**2020**	**2019**	
3	**Assets**			
4	Current:			
5	Cash	$?	$ 28,000	
6	Accounts receivable, net	?	145,000	
7	Inventory	?	180,000	
8	Total current assets	?	353,000	
9	Plant and equipment, net	?	447,000	
10	Total assets	$?	$ 800,000	
11	**Liabilities**			
12	Current liabilities	$ 160,000	$ 160,000	
13	10% Bonds payable	?	240,000	
14	Total liabilities	?	400,000	
15	**Shareholders' Equity**			
16	Common shares	?	203,200	
17	Retained earnings	?	196,800	
18	Total shareholders' equity	?	400,000	
19	Total liabilities and shareholders' equity	$?	$ 800,000	
20				

Requirement

Using the ratios, common-size percentages, and trend percentages given, complete the income statement and balance sheet for Emore for 2020. Additional information:

	A	B	C	D
1	**Additional information:**	**2020**	**2019**	
2	Common size cost of goods sold %:	75%	55%	
3	Common size common share %:	27%	25.4%	
4	Trend percentage, Operating income	130%	100%	
5	Asset turnover	2		
6	Accounts receivable turnover	15		
7	Quick (acid-test) ratio	1.30		
8	Current ratio	2.25		
9	Return on equity	35%		
10				

PROBLEMS (GROUP A)

P10-26A Net sales, net income, and total assets for Aaron Shipping, Inc., for a five-year period follow:

LEARNING OBJECTIVES ❶❺

Compute trend percentages, return on sales, asset turnover, and ROA, and compare with industry

(in thousands)	2020	2019	2018	2017	2016
Net sales..	$900	$400	$352	$314	$296
Net income..	50	39	46	37	24
Total assets	308	269	252	231	209

Requirements

1. Compute trend percentages for each item for 2017 through 2020. Use 2016 as the base year and round to the nearest percent.
2. Compute the return on net sales for 2018 through 2020, rounding to three decimal places. Explain what this means.
3. Compute asset turnover for 2018 through 2020. Explain what this means.
4. Compute the return on average total assets (ROA) for 2018 through 2020.
5. How does Aaron Shipping's return on net sales for 2020 compare with previous years? How does it compare with that of the industry? In the shipping industry, rates above 5% are considered good, and rates above 7% are outstanding.
6. Evaluate Aaron Shipping, Inc.'s ROA for 2020, compared with previous years, and against a 15% benchmark for the industry.

P10-27A Top managers of Medical Products Inc. have asked for your help in comparing the company's profit performance and financial position with the average for the industry. The accountant has given you the company's income statement and balance sheet and also the following data for the industry:

LEARNING OBJECTIVES ❸❺

Prepare common size financial statements and analyze ratios

	A	B	C	D
1	**Medical Products Inc.** Income Statement Compared With Industry Average For the Year Ended December 31, 2020			
2		Medical Products	Industry Average	
3	Net sales	$ 957,000	100.0%	
4	Cost of goods sold	652,000	55.9	
5	Gross profit	305,000	44.1	
6	Operating expenses	200,000	28.1	
7	Operating income	105,000	16.0	
8	Other expenses	3,000	2.4	
9	Net income	$ 102,000	13.6%	
10				

	A	B	C	D
1	**Medical Products Inc.** Balance Sheet Compared With Industry Average As at December 31, 2020			
2		Medical Products	Industry Average	
3	Current assets	$ 486,000	74.4%	
4	Property and equipment, net	117,000	20.0	
5	Intangible assets, net	24,000	0.6	
6	Other assets	3,000	5.0	
7	Total	$ 630,000	100.0%	

(Continued)

	A	B	C	D
8	Current liabilities	$ 245,000	45.6%	
9	Long-term liabilities	114,000	19.0	
10	Shareholders' equity	271,000	35.4	
11	Total	$ 630,000	100.0%	
12				

Requirements

1. Prepare a common-size income statement and balance sheet for Medical Products. The first column of each statement should present Medical Products's common-size statement, and the second column should show the industry averages.

2. For the profitability analysis, compute Medical Products's (a) ratio of gross profit to net sales, (b) ratio of operating income to net sales, and (c) ratio of net income to net sales. Compare these figures with the industry average. Is Medical Products's profit performance better or worse than the average for the industry?

3. For the analysis of financial position, compute Medical Products's (a) ratios of current assets and current liabilities to total assets and (b) ratio of shareholders' equity to total assets. Compare these ratios with the industry averages. Is Medical Products's financial position better or worse than the average for the industry?

LEARNING OBJECTIVE ❹
Use the statement of cash flows for decision making

 P10-28A You are evaluating two companies as possible investments. The two companies, similar in size, are commuter airlines that fly passengers up and down the West Coast. All other available information has been analyzed and your investment decision depends on the statement of cash flows.

CT

	A	B	C	D	E	F
1	**Commonwealth Airlines (Comair) Limited** Statement of Cash Flows For the Years Ended November 30, 2020 and 2019					
2			2020		2019	
3	**Operating activities:**					
4	Net income (net loss)		$ (67,000)		$154,000	
5	Adjustments for non-cash items:					
6	Total		84,000		(23,000)	
7	Net cash provided by operating activities		17,000		131,000	
8	**Investing activities:**					
9	Purchase of property, plant, and equipment	$ (50,000)		$ (91,000)		
10	Sale of long-term investments	52,000		4,000		
11	Net cash provided by (used for) investing activities		2,000		(87,000)	
12	**Financing activities:**					
13	Issuance of short-term notes payable	122,000		143,000		
14	Payment of short-term notes payable	(179,000)		(134,000)		
15	Payment of cash dividends	(45,000)		(64,000)		
16	Net cash used for financing activities		(102,000)		(55,000)	
17	Increase (decrease) in cash		(83,000)		(11,000)	
18	Cash balance at beginning of year		92,000		103,000	
19	Cash balance at end of year		$ 9,000		$ 92,000	
20						

	A	B	C	D	E	F
1	**Jetway Inc.** Statement of Cash Flows For the Years Ended November 30, 2020 and 2019					
2			**2020**		**2019**	
3	**Operating activities:**					
4	Net income		$ 184,000		$ 131,000	
5	Adjustments for non-cash items:					
6	Total		64,000		62,000	
7	Net cash provided by operating activities		248,000		193,000	
8	**Investing activities:**					
9	Purchase of property, plant, and equipment	$ (303,000)		$ (453,000)		
10	Sale of property, plant, and equipment	46,000		72,000		
11	Net cash used for investing activities		(257,000)		(381,000)	
12	**Financing activities:**					
13	Issuance of long-term notes payable	174,000		118,000		
14	Payment of short-term notes payable	(66,000)		(18,000)		
15	Net cash provided by financing activities		108,000		100,000	
16	Increase (decrease) in cash		99,000		(88,000)	
17	Cash balance at beginning of year		116,000		204,000	
18	Cash balance at end of year		$ 215,000		$ 116,000	
19						

Requirement

Using the information provided, identify and discuss the strengths and weaknesses for these companies that are relevant to the decision of which company to invest in. Conclude your discussion by recommending one company's shares as an investment.

🌐 **P10-29A** Financial statement data of Metro Engineering Limited include the following items:

LEARNING OBJECTIVE ❺

Understand the effects of business transactions on selected ratios

Cash	$ 47,000	Accounts payable	$142,000
Short-term investments	21,000	Accrued liabilities	50,000
Accounts receivable, net	102,000	Long-term notes payable	146,000
Inventories	274,000	Other long-term liabilities	78,000
Prepaid expenses	15,000	Net income	104,000
Total assets	933,000	Number of common shares	22,000
Short-term notes payable	72,000	outstanding	

Requirements

1. Compute Metro's current ratio, debt ratio, and earnings per share. Use the following format for your answer (use dollar and share amounts in thousands except for EPS):

Requirement 1		
Current ratio	**Debt ratio**	**Earnings per share**

2. Compute the three ratios after evaluating the effect of each transaction that follows. Consider each transaction *separately*.

   a. Borrowed $27,000 on a long-term note payable

   b. Issued 10,000 common shares, receiving cash of $108,000

c. Paid short-term notes payable, $51,000

d. Purchased merchandise of $48,000 on account, debiting Inventory

e. Received cash on account, $6,000

Format your answer as follows:

Requirement 2

| Transaction (letter) | Current ratio | Debt ratio | Earnings per share |

LEARNING OBJECTIVE ❺

Use ratios to evaluate a share investment

⊕ **P10-30A** Comparative financial statement data of Hamden Optical Mart follow:

	A	B	C	D
1	**Hamden Optical Mart** Comparative Income Statement Years Ended December 31, 2020 and 2019			
2		**2020**	**2019**	
3	Net sales	$ 687,000	$ 595,000	
4	Cost of goods sold	375,000	276,000	
5	Gross profit	312,000	319,000	
6	Operating expenses	129,000	142,000	
7	Income from operations	183,000	177,000	
8	Interest expense	37,000	45,000	
9	Income before income tax	146,000	132,000	
10	Income tax expense	36,000	51,000	
11	Net income	$ 110,000	$ 81,000	
12				

	A	B	C	D	E
1	**Hamden Optical Mart** Comparative Balance Sheet December 31, 2020 and 2019				
2		**2020**	**2019**	**2018***	
3	Current assets:				
4	Cash	$ 45,000	$ 49,000		
5	Current receivables, net	212,000	158,000	$ 200,000	
6	Inventories	297,000	281,000	181,000	
7	Prepaid expenses	4,000	29,000		
8	Total current assets	558,000	517,000		
9	Property, plant, and equipment, net	285,000	277,000		
10	Total assets	$ 843,000	$ 794,000	700,000	
11	Accounts payable	150,000	105,000	112,000	
12	Other current liabilities	135,000	188,000		
13	Total current liabilities	$ 285,000	$ 293,000		
14	Long-term liabilities	243,000	231,000		
15	Total liabilities	528,000	524,000		
16	Common shareholders' equity, no par	315,000	270,000	199,000	
17	Total liabilities and shareholders' equity	$ 843,000	$ 794,000		
18					

*Selected 2018 amounts.

Other information:

1. Market price of Hamden common shares: $102.17 at December 31, 2020; and $77.01 at December 31, 2019
2. Average common shares outstanding: 18,000 during 2020 and 17,500 during 2019
3. All sales on credit

Requirements

1. Compute the following ratios for 2020 and 2019:
   a. Current ratio
   b. Quick (acid-test) ratio
   c. Receivables turnover and days' sales outstanding (DSO) (round to the nearest whole day)
   d. Inventory turnover and days' inventory outstanding (DIO) (round to the nearest whole day)
   e. Accounts payable turnover and days' payable outstanding (DPO) (round to the nearest whole day)
   f. Cash conversion cycle (in days)
   g. Times-interest-earned ratio
   h. Return on assets
   i. Return on common shareholders' equity
   j. Earnings per share of common shares
   k. Price/earnings ratio
2. Decide whether (a) Hamden's financial position improved or deteriorated during 2020 and (b) the investment attractiveness of Hamden's common shares appears to have increased or decreased.
3. How will what you learned in this problem help you evaluate an investment?

🌐 **P10-31A** Assume that you are considering purchasing shares as an investment. You have narrowed the choice to two Internet firms, Video.com Inc. and On-Line Express Ltd., and have assembled the following data.

LEARNING OBJECTIVE ❺

Use ratios to decide between two share investments

Selected income statement data for current year:

	Video	Express
Net sales (all on credit)	$603,000	$519,000
Cost of goods sold	454,000	387,000
Income from operations	93,000	72,000
Interest expense	—	12,000
Net income	56,000	38,000

Selected balance sheet and market price data at *end* of current year:

	Video	Express
Current assets:		
Cash	$ 25,000	$ 39,000
Short-term investments	6,000	13,000
Current receivables, net	189,000	164,000
Inventories	211,000	183,000
Prepaid expenses	19,000	15,000
Total current assets	$450,000	$414,000
Total assets	$974,000	$938,000

	Video	Express
Total current liabilities..	366,000	338,000
Total liabilities...	667,000*	691,000 *
Preferred shares $4.00 (250 shares)...		25,000
Common shares (150,000 shares)	150,000	
(20,000 shares)		100,000
Total shareholders' equity..	307,000	247,000
Market price per common share...	$ 9.00	$ 47.50

*Includes long-term debt; Video, $-0-; and Express, $350,000

Selected balance sheet data at *beginning* of current year:

	Video	Express
Current receivables, net..	$142,000	$193,000
Inventories	209,000	197,000
Total assets	842,000	909,000
Long-term debt	—	303,000
Preferred shares, $4.00 (250 shares)...		25,000
Common shares (150,000 shares)	150,000	
(20,000 shares)		100,000
Total shareholders' equity..	263,000	215,000

Your strategy is to invest in companies that have low price/earnings ratios but appear to be in good shape financially. Assume that you have analyzed all other factors and that your decision depends on the results of ratio analysis.

Requirement

Compute the following ratios for both companies for the current year and decide which company's shares better fit your investment strategy:

a. Quick (acid-test) ratio
b. Inventory turnover
c. Days' sales in receivables
d. Debt ratio
e. Times-interest-earned ratio
f. Return on equity
g. Earnings per share
h. Price/earnings ratio

LEARNING OBJECTIVE ❺

Analyze a company based on its ratios

P10-32A Take the role of an investment analyst at Merill Lynch and use the information provided to determine which company to invest in. Based on your findings, write a report to the Merill Lynch Investment Committee including your recommendation and why you picked one company over the other.

Ratio	Fast Mail Ltd.	Message Direct Inc.
Days' sales in receivables	51	43
Inventory turnover	9	7
Gross profit percentage...	62%	71%
Net income as a percent of sales	16%	14%
Times interest earned	12	18
Return on equity	29%	36%
Return on assets	19%	14%

P10-33A The financial statements of Adventure News, Inc., include the following items:

LEARNING OBJECTIVE **5**

Compute ratios; evaluate turnover, liquidity, and current debt-paying ability

	2020	2019	2018
Balance sheet:			
Cash	$ 24,000	$ 30,000	
Short-term investments	12,000	21,000	
Net receivables	58,000	71,000	40,000
Inventory	90,000	73,000	59,000
Prepaid expenses	10,000	10,000	
Total current assets	194,000	205,000	
Accounts payable	40,000	70,000	30,000
Total current liabilities	133,000	95,000	
Income statement:			
Net credit sales	$491,000	$506,000	
Cost of goods sold	277,000	288,000	

Requirements

1. Compute the following ratios for 2020 and 2019.
   a. Current ratio
   b. Quick (acid-test) ratio
   c. Inventory turnover and days' inventory outstanding (DIO)
   d. Accounts receivable turnover
   e. Days' sales in average receivables or days' sales outstanding (DSO)
   f. Accounts payable turnover and days' payable outstanding (DPO). Use cost of goods sold in the formula for accounts payable turnover
   g. Cash conversion cycle (in days)

   When computing days, round your answer to the nearest whole number.
2. Evaluate the company's liquidity and current debt-paying ability for 2020. Has it improved or deteriorated from 2019?
3. As a manager of this company, what would you try to improve next year?

PROBLEMS (GROUP B)

P10-34B Net sales, net income, and total assets for Azbell Shipping, Inc., for a five-year period follow:

LEARNING OBJECTIVES **1 5**

Compute trend percentages, return on sales, asset turnover, and ROA, and compare with industry

(in thousands)	2020	2019	2018	2017	2016
Net sales	$700	$618	$325	$309	$299
Net income	41	39	41	34	27
Total assets	300	262	253	223	201

Requirements

1. Compute trend percentages for each item for 2017 through 2020. Use 2016 as the base year and round to the nearest percent.
2. Compute the return on net sales for 2018 through 2020, rounding to three decimal places. Explain what this means.

3. Compute asset turnover for 2018 through 2020. Explain what this means.
4. Compute the return on average total assets (ROA) for 2018 through 2020.
5. How does Azbell Shipping's return on net sales compare with previous years? How does it compare with that of the industry? In the shipping industry, rates above 5% are considered good, and rates above 7% are outstanding.
6. Evaluate Azbell Shipping, Inc.'s ROA for 2020, compared with previous years, and against a 15% benchmark for the industry.

LEARNING OBJECTIVES ❸❺

Prepare and evaluate common-size financial statements

P10-35B Pathfinder Inc. has asked you to compare the company's profit performance and financial position with the industry average. The proprietor has given you the company's income statement and balance sheet as well as the industry average data for retailers.

	A	B	C	D
1	**Pathfinder Inc.** Income Statement Compared with Industry Average For the Year Ended December 31, 2020			
2		**Pathfinder**	**Industry Average**	
3	Net sales	$ 700,000	100.0%	
4	Cost of goods sold	497,000	65.8	
5	Gross profit	203,000	34.2	
6	Operating expenses	163,000	19.7	
7	Operating income	40,000	14.5	
8	Other expenses	3,000	0.4	
9	Net income	$ 37,000	14.1%	
10				

	A	B	C	D
1	**Pathfinder Inc.** Balance Sheet Compared with Industry Average As at December 31, 2020			
2		**Pathfinder**	**Industry Average**	
3	Current assets	$ 300,000	70.9%	
4	Property and equipment, net	74,000	23.6	
5	Intangible assets, net	4,000	0.8	
6	Other assets	22,000	4.7	
7	Total	$ 400,000	100.0%	
8	Current liabilities	$ 206,000	48.1%	
9	Long-term liabilities	64,000	16.6	
10	Shareholders' equity	130,000	35.3	
11	Total	$ 400,000	100.0%	
12				

Requirements

1. Prepare a common-size income statement and a balance sheet for Pathfinder. The first column of each statement should present Pathfinder's common-size statement, and the second column, the industry averages.
2. For the profitability analysis, compute Pathfinder's (a) ratio of gross profit to net sales, (b) ratio of operating income to net sales, and (c) ratio of net income to net sales. Compare these figures with the industry averages. Is Pathfinder's profit performance better or worse than the industry average?
3. For the analysis of financial position, compute Pathfinder's (a) ratio of current assets to total assets, and (b) ratio of shareholders' equity to total assets. Compare these ratios with the industry averages. Is Pathfinder's financial position better or worse than the industry averages?

P10-36B You have been asked to evaluate two companies as possible investments. The two companies, Norfolk Industries Inc. and Strafford Crystal Limited, are similar in size. Assume that all other available information has been analyzed, and the decision concerning which company's shares to purchase depends on their cash flow data.

LEARNING OBJECTIVE ❹
Use the statement of cash flows for decision making

	A	B	C	D	E	F
1	**Norfolk Industries Inc.** Statement of Cash Flows For the Years Ended September 30, 2020 and 2019					
2			2020		2019	
3	**Operating activities:**					
4	Net income		$ 17,000		$ 44,000	
5	Adjustments for non-cash items:					
6	Total		(14,000)		(4,000)	
7	Net cash provided by operating activities		3,000		40,000	
8	**Investing activities:**					
9	Purchase of property, plant, and equipment	$ (13,000)		$ (3,000)		
10	Sale of property, plant, and equipment	86,000		79,000		
11	Net cash provided by investing activities		73,000		76,000	
12	**Financing activities:**					
13	Issuance of short-term notes payable	43,000		19,000		
14	Payment of short-term notes payable	(101,000)		(108,000)		
15	Net cash used for financing activities		(58,000)		(89,000)	
16	Increase in cash		18,000		27,000	
17	Cash balance at beginning of year		31,000		4,000	
18	Cash balance at end of year		$ 49,000		$ 31,000	
19						

	A	B	C	D	E	F
1	**Strafford Crystal Limited** Statement of Cash Flows For the Years Ended September 30, 2020 and 2019					
2			2020		2019	
3	**Operating activities:**					
4	Net income		$ 89,000		$ 71,000	
5	Adjustments for non-cash items:					
6	Total		19,000		—	
7	Net cash provided by operating activities		108,000		71,000	
8	**Investing activities:**					
9	Purchase of property, plant, and equipment	$ (121,000)		$ (91,000)		
10	Net cash used for investing activities		(121,000)		(91,000)	
11	**Financing activities:**					
12	Issuance of long-term notes payable	46,000		43,000		
13	Payment of short-term notes payable	(15,000)		(40,000)		
14	Payment of cash dividends	(12,000)		(9,000)		
15	Net cash provided by (used for) financing activities		19,000		(6,000)	
16	Increase (decrease) in cash		6,000		(26,000)	
17	Cash balance at beginning of year		54,000		80,000	
18	Cash balance at end of year		$ 60,000		$ 54,000	
19						

Requirement

Using the information provided, identify and discuss the strengths and weaknesses for these companies that are relevant to the decision of which company to invest in. Conclude your discussion by recommending one company's shares as an investment.

LEARNING OBJECTIVE ⑤

Understand the effects of business transactions on selected ratios

P10-37B Financial statement data of HiFlite Electronics Limited include the following items (dollars in thousands):

Cash	$ 22,000
Short-term investments	39,000
Accounts receivable, net	83,000
Inventories	141,000
Prepaid expenses	8,000
Total assets	677,000
Short-term notes payable	49,000
Accounts payable	103,000
Accrued liabilities	38,000
Long-term notes payable	160,000
Other long-term liabilities	31,000
Net income	91,000
Number of common shares outstanding	40,000

Requirements

1. Compute HiFlite's current ratio, debt ratio, and earnings per share. Use the following format for your answer:

Requirement 1		
Current ratio	Debt ratio	Earnings per share

2. Compute the three ratios after evaluating the effect of each transaction that follows. Consider each transaction *separately*.
   a. Purchased store supplies of $46,000 on account
   b. Borrowed $125,000 on a long-term note payable
   c. Issued 5,000 common shares, receiving cash of $120,000
   d. Paid short-term notes payable, $32,000
   e. Received cash on account, $19,000

   Format your answer as follows:

Requirement 2			
Transaction (letter)	Current ratio	Debt ratio	Earnings per share

LEARNING OBJECTIVE ⑤

Use ratios to evaluate a share investment

P10-38B Comparative financial statement data of Panfield Optical Mart follow:

	A	B	C	D
1	**Panfield Optical Mart** Comparative Income Statement For the Years Ended December 31, 2020 and 2019			
2		2020	2019	
3	Net sales	$ 686,000	$ 592,000	
4	Cost of goods sold	380,000	281,000	
5	Gross profit	306,000	311,000	
6	Operating expenses	127,000	148,000	
7	Income from operations	179,000	163,000	
8	Interest expense	30,000	50,000	
9	Income before income tax	149,000	113,000	
10	Income tax expense	38,000	45,000	
11	Net income	$ 111,000	$ 68,000	
12				

	A	B	C	D	E
1	**Panfield Optical Mart** Comparative Balance Sheet As at December 31, 2020 and 2019				
2		**2020**	**2019**	**2018***	
3	**Current assets:**				
4	Cash	$ 32,000	$ 82,000		
5	Current receivables, net	217,000	157,000	$ 200,000	
6	Inventories	297,000	284,000	188,000	
7	Prepaid expenses	7,000	29,000		
8	Total current assets	553,000	552,000		
9	Property, plant, and equipment, net	283,000	271,000		
10	Total assets	$ 836,000	$ 823,000	701,000	
11	Accounts payable	150,000	105,000	112,000	
12	Other current liabilities	135,000	187,000		
13	Total current liabilities	$ 285,000	$ 292,000		
14	Long-term liabilities	240,000	233,000		
15	Total liabilities	525,000	525,000		
16	Common shareholders' equity, no par	311,000	298,000	199,000	
17	Total liabilities and shareholders' equity	$ 836,000	$ 823,000		
18					

*Selected 2018 amounts.

Other information:

1. Market price of Panfield common stock: $94.38 at December 31, 2020; and $85.67 at December 31, 2019
2. Common shares outstanding: 15,000 during 2020 and 10,000 during 2019
3. All sales on credit

Requirements

1. Compute the following ratios for 2020 and 2019.
   a. Current ratio
   b. Quick (acid-test) ratio
   c. Receivables turnover and days' sales outstanding (DSO) (round to nearest whole day)
   d. Inventory turnover and days' inventory outstanding (DIO) (round to nearest whole day)
   e. Accounts payable turnover and days' payable outstanding (DPO) (round to nearest whole day).
   f. Cash conversion cycle (in days)
   g. Times-interest-earned ratio
   h. Return on assets
   i. Return on common shareholders' equity
   j. Earnings per share of common stock
   k. Price/earnings ratio
2. Decide whether (a) Panfield's financial position improved or deteriorated during 2020, and (b) the investment attractiveness of Panfield's common stock appears to have increased or decreased.
3. How will what you learned in this problem help you evaluate an investment?

P10-39B Assume that you are purchasing an investment and have decided to invest in a company in the publishing business. You have narrowed the choice to Thrifty Nickel Corp. and The Village Cryer Limited and have assembled the following data.

LEARNING OBJECTIVE ❺

Use ratios to decide between two share investments

Selected income statement data for the current year:

	Thrifty Nickel	Village Cryer
Net sales (all on credit)...	$371,000	$497,000
Cost of goods sold	209,000	258,000
Income from operations	79,000	138,000
Interest expense..	—	19,000
Net income...	48,000	72,000

Selected balance sheet data at *beginning* of the current year:

	Thrifty Nickel	Village Cryer
Current receivables, net...	$ 40,000	$ 48,000
Inventories	93,000	88,000
Total assets	259,000	270,000
Long-term debt	—	86,000
Preferred shares: $5.00 (200 shares) issued	—	20,000
Common shares: (10,000 shares)	10,000	
(5,000 shares)		12,500
Total shareholders' equity.......................................	118,000	126,000

Selected balance sheet and market price data at *end* of the current year:

	Thrifty Nickel	Village Cryer
Current assets:		
Cash...	$ 22,000	$ 19,000
Short-term investments..	20,000	18,000
Current receivables, net.......................................	42,000	46,000
Inventories...	87,000	100,000
Prepaid expenses	2,000	3,000
Total current assets	$ 173,000	$ 186,000
Total assets	265,000	328,000
Total current liabilities...	108,000	98,000
Total liabilities..	108,000*	131,000*
Preferred shares: $5.00 (200 shares)...........................		20,000
Common shares: (10,000 shares)	10,000	
(5,000 shares)		12,500
Total shareholders' equity.......................................	157,000	197,000
Market price per share of common share...........................	$ 51	$ 112

*Includes long-term debt: Thrifty Nickel, $-0-; and Village Cryer, $86,000

Your strategy is to invest in companies that have low price/earnings ratios but appear to be in good shape financially. Assume that you have analyzed all other factors and your decision depends on the results of ratio analysis.

Requirement

Compute the following ratios for both companies for the current year, and decide which company's shares better fit your investment strategy:

a. Quick (acid-test) ratio
b. Inventory turnover
c. Days' sales in average receivables

d. Debt ratio

e. Times-interest-earned ratio

f. Return on equity

g. Earnings per share

h. Price/earnings ratio

P10-40B Take the role of an investment analyst at RBC Dominion Securities and use the information provided to determine which company to invest in. Based your findings, write a report to the Merill Lynch Investment Committee including your recommendation and why you picked one company over the other.

LEARNING OBJECTIVE ❺

Analyze a company based on its ratios

Ratio	Pain Free Ltd.	Remedy Inc.
Days' sales in receivables	36	42
Inventory turnover	6	8
Gross profit percentage	49%	51%
Net income as a percent of sales	7.2%	8.3%
Times interest earned	16	9
Return on equity	32.3%	21.5%
Return on assets	12.1%	16.4%

P10-41B The financial statements of Carver News, Inc., include the following items:

LEARNING OBJECTIVE ❺

Compute ratios; evaluate turnover, liquidity, and current debt-paying ability

	2020	2019	2018
Balance sheet:			
Cash	$ 77,000	$103,000	
Short-term investments	13,000	27,000	
Net receivables	81,000	84,000	30,000
Inventory	88,000	75,000	60,000
Prepaid expenses	12,000	6,000	
Total current assets	271,000	295,000	
Accounts payable	85,000	70,000	50,000
Total current liabilities	138,000	96,000	
Income statement:			
Net credit sales	$491,000	$505,000	
Cost of goods sold	271,000	279,000	

Requirements

1. Compute the following ratios for 2020 and 2019.

    a. Current ratio

    b. Quick (acid-test) ratio

    c. Inventory turnover and days' inventory outstanding (DIO)

    d. Accounts receivable turnover

    e. Days' sales in average receivables or days' sales outstanding (DSO)

    f. Accounts payable turnover and days' payable outstanding (DPO). Use cost of goods sold in the formula for accounts payable turnover

    g. Cash conversion cycle (in days)

    When computing days, round your answer to the nearest whole number.

2. Evaluate the company's liquidity and current debt-paying ability for 2020. Has it improved or deteriorated from 2019?

3. As a manager of this company, what would you try to improve next year?

APPLY YOUR KNOWLEDGE

DECISION CASES

LEARNING OBJECTIVE ❺

Assess the effects of transactions on a company

Case 1. Assume a major Canadian company had a bad year in 2020, when it suffered a $4.9 billion net loss. The loss pushed most of the return measures into the negative column and the current ratio dropped below 1.0. The company's debt ratio is still only 0.27. Assume top management is pondering ways to improve the company's ratios. In particular, management is considering the following transactions:

1. Sell off a segment of the business for $30 million (receiving half in cash and half in the form of a long-term note receivable). Book value of the segment business is $27 million.
2. Borrow $100 million on long-term debt.
3. Repurchase common shares for $500 million cash.
4. Write off one-fourth of goodwill carried on the books at $128 million.
5. Sell advertising at the normal gross profit of 60%. The advertisements run immediately.
6. Purchase trademarks from a competitor, paying $20 million cash and signing a one-year note payable for $80 million.

Requirements

1. Top management wants to know the effects of these transactions (increase, decrease, or no effect) on the following ratios of the company:
   a. Current ratio
   b. Debt ratio
   c. Times-interest-earned ratio
   d. Return on equity
   e. Book value per common share
2. Some of these transactions have an immediately positive effect on the company's financial condition. Some are definitely negative. Others have an effect that cannot be judged as clearly positive or negative. Evaluate each transaction's effect as positive, negative, or unclear.

LEARNING OBJECTIVE ❺

Analyze the effects of an accounting difference on the ratios

Case 2. Company A uses the first-in, first-out (FIFO) method to account for its inventory, and Company B uses weighted-average cost. Analyze the effect of this difference in accounting methods on the two companies' ratio values. For each ratio discussed in this chapter, indicate which company will have the higher (and the lower) ratio value. Also, identify those ratios that are unaffected by the inventory valuation difference. Ignore the effects of income taxes, and assume inventory costs are increasing. Then, based on your analysis of the ratios, summarize your conclusions as to which company looks better overall.

LEARNING OBJECTIVES ❷❺

Identify action to cut losses and establish profitability

Case 3. Suppose you manage The Runner's Store Inc., a sporting goods store that lost money during the past year. To turn the business around, you must analyze the company and industry data for the current year to learn what is wrong. The company's and industry average data follow:

	A	B	C	D
1	**The Runner's Store Inc.** Common-Size Balance Sheet Data			
2		**Runner's Store**	**Industry Average**	
3	Cash and short-term investments	3.0%	6.8%	
4	Trade receivables, net	15.2	11.0	
5	Inventory	64.2	60.5	
6	Prepaid expenses	1.0	0.0	
7	Total current assets	83.4	78.3	
8	Property and equipment, net	12.6	15.2	
9	Other assets	4.0	6.5	
10	Total assets	100.0%	100.0%	

	A	B	C	D
11				
12	Notes payable, short-term 12%	17.1%	14.0%	
13	Accounts payable	21.1	25.1	
14	Accrued liabilities	7.8	7.9	
15	Total current liabilities	46.0	47.0	
16	Long-term debt, 11%	19.7	16.4	
17	Total liabilities	65.7	63.4	
18	Common shareholders' equity	34.3	36.6	
19	Total liabilities and shareholders' equity	100.0%	100.0%	
20				

	A	B	C	D
1	**The Runner's Store Inc.** Common-Size Income Statement Data			
2		**Runner's Store**	**Industry Average**	
3	Net sales	100.0%	100.0%	
4	Cost of sales	(68.2)	(64.8)	
5	Gross profit	31.8	35.2	
6	Operating expense	(37.1)	(32.3)	
7	Operating income (loss)	(5.3)	2.9	
8	Interest expense	(5.8)	(1.3)	
9	Other revenue	1.1	0.3	
10	Income (loss) before income tax	(10.0)	1.9	
11	Income tax (expense) saving	4.4	(0.8)	
12	Net income (loss)	(5.6)%	1.1%	
13				

Requirement

On the basis of your analysis of these figures, suggest four courses of action The Runner's Store might take to reduce its losses and establish profitable operations. Give your reason for each suggestion.

ETHICAL DECISIONS

Ethical Decision 1. Turnberry Golf Corporation's long-term debt agreements make certain demands on the business. For example, Turnberry may not repurchase common shares in excess of the balance of retained earnings. Also, long-term debt may not exceed shareholders' equity, and the current ratio may not fall below 1.50. If Turnberry fails to meet any of these requirements, the company's lenders have the authority to take over management of the company.

Changes in consumer demand have made it hard for Turnberry to attract customers. Current liabilities have mounted faster than current assets, causing the current ratio to fall to 1.47. Before releasing financial statements, Turnberry management is scrambling to improve the current ratio. The controller points out that an investment can be classified as either long-term or short-term, depending on management's intention. By deciding to convert an investment to cash within one year, Turnberry can classify the investment as short-term: a current asset. On the controller's recommendation, Turnberry's board of directors votes to reclassify long-term investments as short-term.

Requirements

1. What effect will reclassifying the investments have on the current ratio? Is Turnberry's financial position stronger as a result of reclassifying the investments?

2. Shortly after the financial statements are released, sales improve; so, too, does the current ratio. As a result, Turnberry management decides not to sell the investments it had reclassified as short-term. Accordingly, the company reclassifies the investments as long-term. Has management behaved unethically? Give the reasoning underlying your answer.

Ethical Decision 2. Deneen is the senior accounting manager for Kent Co. and is in charge of preparing quarterly reports for the CEO and CFO. These reports compare a variety of Kent's financial ratios to industry averages. This quarter, Kent has done poorly compared to its competitors, so some of its ratios were not favourable. Because of their legendary tempers, Deneen does not want to upset the CEO and CFO. She decides to include only favourable ratios in her report.

Requirements

1. What is the issue?
2. Who might be affected by Deneen's actions?
3. What might be the consequences if Deneen does nothing?
4. What should she do?

FOCUS ON FINANCIAL STATEMENT ANALYSIS

LEARNING OBJECTIVE ⑤

Measure profitability and analyze shares as an investment

MyLab Accounting

Dollarama Inc.

Use the five-year summary of selected financial data (rounded, in thousands) for Dollarama to answer the following questions.

	2018	2017	2016	2015	2014
Revenue....................................	$3,266,090	$2,963,219	$2,650,327	$2,330,805	$2,064,676
Net income.............................	519,410	445,636	385,146	295,410	250,094
Cash from operations	637,334	505,168	449,237	355,872	308,378
Total assets	1,934,339	1,863,451	1,813,874	1,700,838	1,566,780
Total long-term debt................	1,465,752	1,249,765	1,119,996	744,866	538,815

Requirements

1. Using 2014 as the base year, perform trend analysis of Dollarama's selected Financial Highlights for revenue, net income, cash from operations, total assets, and total long-term debt for each year 2014 through 2018.
2. Evaluate Dollarama's operating performance and financial position during 2014 through 2018. Comment on each item computed.
3. During fiscal 2018, Dollarama's net income increased over 2017. Prepare a common-size income statement for 2018 and 2017.
4. Discuss Dollarama's results based on the common-size income statement. What is the company's outlook for the future?

CHECK YOUR WORK

STOP + THINK ANSWERS

STOP + THINK (10-1)

The most important information in the analysis is the fact that net earnings increased by 4.2%. A further examination of the statements will help to determine what might have contributed to this increase.

STOP + THINK (10-2)

Cost of sales increased from the previous year. This is a good thing if the sales increased at a faster pace than the cost of sales.

STOP + THINK (10-3)

Net sales....................	100%	(= $150,000 ÷ $150,000)
Cost of goods sold......	40	(= $60,000 ÷ $150,000)
Gross profit	60	(= $90,000 ÷ $150,000)
Operating expense......	27	(= $40,000 ÷ $150,000)
Operating income.......	33	(= $50,000 ÷ $150,000)
Income tax expense....	10	(= $15,000 ÷ $150,000)
Net income................	23%	(= $35,000 ÷ $150,000)

The company's expenses comprise 77% of net sales (40% + 27% + 10%), leaving 23% net income as a percentage of sales. The lower the expenses, the higher the net income. To determine if this percentage is reasonable, it should be compared with other companies in the same industry.

STOP + THINK (10-4)

No, this is not a good sign. Operations should be a major source of cash. Most of the company's cash is coming from investing activities.

STOP + THINK (10-5)

Understanding the business and industry through reading and researching websites, media, journals, and other publications would be helpful in analyzing a company.

QUICK QUIZ ANSWERS

1. *b* ($19,311 − $15,470 = $3,841 increase; $3,841 / $15,470 = 0.248)
2. *c* ($10,633 / $10,896 = 0.976 ≈ 1.0)
3. *a* [($4,317 + $835 + $3,635) / $10,896 = 0.806 ≈ 0.80]
4. *b*
5. *d* ($41,444 / $31,168 = 1.330)
6. *c* ($33,892 / $41,444 = 0.818)

7. *b* $\left[\dfrac{(\$3,635 + \$2,586)/2}{\$41,444/365} = 27 \text{ days} \right]$

8. *c* $\left[\dfrac{\$33,892}{(\$327 + \$306)/2} = 107 \text{ times} \right]$

9. *a* ($3,544 / (long-term debt of $505 × 0.06) = 116.96 ≈ 117 times)

10. *a* $\left[\begin{array}{l} 2020: \$2,645 / \$41,444 = 0.064 \\ 2019: \$2,122 / \$35,404 = 0.060 \\ 2018: \$1,246 / \$31,168 = 0.040 \end{array} \right]$

11. *d* $\left[EPS\ \$1.03 = \dfrac{\text{Net income } \$2,645}{\text{Shares outstanding } 2,568} \right]$

12. *d* [$6,280/2,568 = $2.45]

COMPREHENSIVE CASE

FINANCIAL STATEMENT ANALYSIS

The objective of this exercise is to develop your ability to perform a comprehensive analysis on a set of financial statements. Use the copy of the 2018 annual report of Dollarama Inc. (year end January 28, 2018) from Appendix A. You may need to go to Dollarama's website to get the full annual report including the annual information return.

Requirement 1

Basic information (provide sources):

a. Using a site such as D&B Hoovers, Google Finance, or Yahoo Finance, look up discount stores. List two competitors of Dollarama.
b. Describe Dollarama's risks related to business operations.
c. Does Dollarama own any other companies?
d. What is Dollarama's largest asset? Largest liability?
e. How many common shares are they authorized to issue? How many are issued? Outstanding?
f. Did Dollarama repurchase any common shares during the year? If so, how many?
g. When does Dollarama record revenue?
h. What inventory method does Dollarama use?
i. Does Dollarama have any business interests in foreign countries? Explain your answer.

Requirement 2

Using information you have learned in the text and elsewhere, evaluate Dollarama's profitability for 2018 compared with 2017. In your analysis, you should compute the following ratios and then comment on what those ratios indicate. NOTE: You will have to look up the annual report for 2017 to obtain total assets and shareholders' equity for 2016. See www.sedar.com or use Dollarama's website.

a. Return on sales
b. Asset turnover
c. Return on assets
d. Leverage ratio
e. Return on equity
f. Gross profit percentage
g. Earnings per share (show computation)
h. Book value per share

Requirement 3

Evaluate the company's ability to sell inventory and pay debts during 2018 and 2017. In your analysis, you should compute the following ratios, and then comment on what those ratios indicate. Since the 2018 annual report only includes the balance sheets for 2018 and 2017, you will need to look up the annual report for 2017 for information about 2016 accounts receivable, inventory, and accounts payable.

a. Accounts receivable turnover and days' sales outstanding
b. Inventory turnover and days' inventory outstanding
c. Accounts payable turnover and days' payable outstanding
d. Cash conversion cycle
e. Current ratio
f. Quick (acid-test) ratio
g. Debt ratio
h. Times interest earned

Requirement 4

Evaluate Dollarama's cash flow.

a. For 2018, what are Dollarama's two main sources of cash?
b. For 2018, is Dollarama's net cash flow from operations greater than or less than net income? What is the primary cause of the difference?
c. For 2017 and 2018, what is the primary source of cash from investing activities? What is the primary use of cash from investing activities for 2017 and 2018?
d. For 2017 and 2018, what is the primary source of cash from financing activities? What is the primary use of cash from financing activities for 2017 and 2018?
e. What trend(s) do you detect from this analysis?

Requirement 5

Other financial analysis.

a. Compute common-size percentages for sales, gross profit, operating income, and net income for 2015–2018. Comment on your results.
b. Compute trend percentages, using 2015 as the base year, for total revenues and net earnings. Comment on your results.

Requirement 6

Evaluate Dollarama's shares as an investment.

a. What was the closing market price of Dollarama's shares on January 29, 2018, the next trading day after the balance-sheet date of January 28, 2018?
b. Compute the price-earnings ratio using your EPS calculation and the market price you just determined. Google Dollarama's stock price on Yahoo Finance; Dollarama's ticker symbol is DOL.TO.
c. Based on Management's Discussion and Analysis (annual report) as well as any business news (Google Finance is an example), would you evaluate the company's shares as a "buy," "hold," or "sell"? State your reasons.

Dollarama Inc.

Consolidated Financial Statements

January 28, 2018 and January 29, 2017

(Expressed in thousands of Canadian dollars, unless otherwise noted)

March 29, 2018

Independent Auditor's Report

**To the Shareholders of
Dollarama Inc.**

We have audited the accompanying consolidated financial statements of Dollarama Inc. and its subsidiaries, which comprise the consolidated statements of financial position as at January 28, 2018 and January 29, 2017 and the consolidated statements of changes in shareholder's equity (deficit), net earnings and comprehensive income (loss) and cash flows for the years then ended, and the related notes, which comprise a summary of significant accounting policies and other explanatory information.

Management's responsibility for the consolidated financial statements

Management is responsible for the preparation and fair presentation of these consolidated financial statements in accordance with International Financial Reporting Standards, and for such internal control as management determines is necessary to enable the preparation of consolidated financial statements that are free from material misstatement, whether due to fraud or error.

Auditor's responsibility

Our responsibility is to express an opinion on these consolidated financial statements based on our audits. We conducted our audits in accordance with Canadian generally accepted auditing standards. Those standards require that we comply with ethical requirements and plan and perform the audit to obtain reasonable assurance about whether the consolidated financial statements are free from material misstatement.

An audit involves performing procedures to obtain audit evidence about the amounts and disclosures in the consolidated financial statements. The procedures selected depend on the auditor's judgment, including the assessment of the risks of material misstatement of the consolidated financial statements, whether due to fraud or error. In making those risk assessments, the auditor considers internal control relevant to the entity's preparation and fair presentation of the consolidated financial statements in order to design audit procedures that are appropriate in the circumstances, but not for the purpose of expressing an opinion on the effectiveness of the entity's internal control. An audit also includes evaluating the appropriateness of accounting policies used and the reasonableness of accounting estimates made by management, as well as evaluating the overall presentation of the consolidated financial statements.

PricewaterhouseCoopers LLP/s.r.l./s.e.n.c.r.l.
1250 René-Lévesque Boulevard West, Montréal, Quebec, Canada H3B 4Y1
T: +1 514 205 5000, F: +1 514 876 1502

"PwC" refers to PricewaterhouseCoopers LLP/s.r.l./s.e.n.c.r.l., an Ontario limited liability partnership.

We believe that the audit evidence we have obtained in our audits is sufficient and appropriate to provide a basis for our audit opinion.

Opinion

In our opinion, the consolidated financial statements present fairly, in all material respects, the financial position of Dollarama Inc. and its subsidiaries as at January 28, 2018 and January 29, 2017 and their financial performance and their cash flows for the years then ended in accordance with International Financial Reporting Standards.

PricewaterhouseCoopers LLP[1]

---

[1] CPA auditor, CA, public accountancy permit No. A117693

Dollarama Inc.
Consolidated Statement of Financial Position as at
(Expressed in thousands of Canadian dollars)

	Note	January 28, 2018 $	January 29, 2017 $
Assets			
Current assets			
Cash		54,844	62,015
Accounts receivable		15,263	15,386
Prepaid expenses		8,649	7,162
Inventories	3	490,927	465,715
Derivative financial instruments	14	286	8,787
		569,969	559,065
Non-current assets			
Property, plant and equipment	6	490,988	437,089
Intangible assets	7	145,600	139,515
Goodwill	7	727,782	727,782
Total assets		1,934,339	1,863,451
Liabilities and shareholders' equity (deficit)			
Current liabilities			
Accounts payable and accrued liabilities	8	228,362	198,486
Dividend payable		12,180	11,591
Income taxes payable		39,491	16,597
Derivative financial instruments	14	35,720	8,085
Current portion of long-term debt	9	405,192	278,643
		720,945	513,402
Non-current liabilities			
Long-term debt	9	1,260,459	1,050,101
Deferred rent and lease inducements	11	92,633	81,827
Deferred income taxes	13	112,660	117,837
Total liabilities		2,186,697	1,763,167
Commitments	10		
Shareholders' equity (deficit)			
Share capital	12	415,787	420,266
Contributed surplus		27,699	24,321
Deficit	12	(663,421)	(342,957)
Accumulated other comprehensive loss	12	(32,423)	(1,346)
Total shareholders' equity (deficit)		(252,358)	100,284
Total liabilities and shareholders' equity (deficit)		1,934,339	1,863,451

Approved by the Board of Directors

(signed) "Stephen Gunn"   *(signed) "Richard Roy"*
Stephen Gunn, Director   Richard Roy, Director

The accompanying notes are an integral part of these consolidated financial statements.

Dollarama Inc.

Consolidated Statement of Changes in Shareholders' Equity (Deficit) for the years ended
(Expressed in thousands of Canadian dollars, except share amounts)

	Note	Number of common shares	Share capital $	Contributed surplus $	Deficit $	Accumulated other comprehensive income (loss) $	Total $
Balance – January 31, 2016	12	122,225,104	439,296	20,136	(62,375)	69,795	466,852
Net earnings		-	-	-	445,636	-	445,636
Other comprehensive loss Unrealized loss on derivative financial instruments, net of reclassification adjustment and income tax recovery of $25,860	12	-	-	-	-	(71,141)	(71,141)
Dividends declared		-	-	-	(47,440)	-	(47,440)
Repurchase and cancellation of common shares	12	(7,420,168)	(26,669)	-	(678,778)	-	(705,447)
Share-based compensation	12	-	-	6,932	-	-	6,932
Issuance of common shares	12	246,413	4,892	-	-	-	4,892
Reclassification for the exercise of share options	12	-	2,747	(2,747)	-	-	-
Balance – January 29, 2017		115,051,349	420,266	24,321	(342,957)	(1,346)	100,284
Balance – January 29, 2017	12	115,051,349	420,266	24,321	(342,957)	(1,346)	100,284
Net earnings		-	-	-	519,410	-	519,410
Other comprehensive loss Unrealized loss on derivative financial instruments, net of reclassification adjustment and income tax recovery of $11,564	12	-	-	-	-	(31,077)	(31,077)
Dividends declared		-	-	-	(49,520)	-	(49,520)
Repurchase and cancellation of common shares	12	(6,104,540)	(22,305)	-	(790,354)	-	(812,659)
Share-based compensation	12	-	-	6,559	-	-	6,559
Issuance of common shares	12	379,050	14,645	-	-	-	14,645
Reclassification for the exercise of share options	12	-	3,181	(3,181)	-	-	-
Balance – January 28, 2018		109,325,859	415,787	27,699	(663,421)	(32,423)	(252,358)

The accompanying notes are an integral part of these consolidated financial statements

Dollarama Inc.

Consolidated Statement of Net Earnings and Comprehensive Income (Loss) for the years ended
(Expressed in thousands of Canadian dollars, except share and per share amounts)

	Note	January 28, 2018 $	January 29, 2017 $
Sales		3,266,090	2,963,219
Cost of sales	17	1,965,171	1,801,935
Gross profit		1,300,919	1,161,284
General, administrative and store operating expenses		474,807	458,026
Depreciation and amortization	17	70,550	57,748
Operating income		755,562	645,510
Financing costs	17	39,877	33,083
Earnings before income taxes		715,685	612,427
Income taxes	13	196,275	166,791
Net earnings		519,410	445,636
Other comprehensive loss			
Items to be reclassified subsequently to net earnings			
Unrealized loss on derivative financial instruments, net of reclassification adjustment		(42,641)	(97,001)
Income tax recovery relating to components of other comprehensive loss		11,564	25,860
Total other comprehensive loss, net of income tax recovery		(31,077)	(71,141)
Total comprehensive income		488,333	374,495
Earnings per common share			
Basic net earnings per common share	16	$4.61	$3.75
Diluted net earnings per common share	16	$4.55	$3.71
Weighted average number of common shares outstanding (*thousands*)	16	112,751	118,998
Weighted average number of diluted common shares outstanding (*thousands*)	16	114,173	120,243

The accompanying notes are an integral part of these consolidated financial statements

Dollarama Inc.

Consolidated Statement of Cash Flows for the years ended
(Expressed in thousands of Canadian dollars)

	Note	January 28, 2018 $	January 29, 2017 $
Operating activities			
Net earnings		519,410	445,636
Adjustments to reconcile net earnings to net cash generated from operating activities:			
Depreciation of property, plant and equipment and amortization of intangible assets	17	70,550	57,748
Amortization of deferred tenant allowances	11	(5,149)	(4,795)
Amortization of deferred leasing costs	7	483	519
Amortization of debt issue costs	17	2,017	1,481
Recognition of realized losses (gains) on foreign exchange contracts	14	3,851	(46,269)
Cash settlement of gains (losses) on foreign exchange contracts		(10,266)	16,108
Deferred lease inducements	11	5,348	6,020
Deferred tenant allowances	11	10,607	8,970
Share-based compensation	12	6,559	6,932
Financing costs on long-term debt		1,548	268
Deferred income taxes	13	6,297	16,105
Loss on disposal of assets		207	40
		611,462	508,763
Changes in non-cash working capital components	18	25,872	(3,595)
Net cash generated from operating activities		637,334	505,168
Investing activities			
Additions to property, plant and equipment	6	(112,786)	(153,574)
Additions to intangible assets	7	(19,134)	(12,640)
Proceeds from disposal of property, plant and equipment		696	462
Net cash used in investing activities		(131,224)	(165,752)
Financing activities			
Proceeds from long-term debt issued (Series 2 Floating Rate Notes)	9	300,000	-
Proceeds from long-term debt issued (2.203% Fixed Rate Notes)	9	250,000	-
Proceeds from long-term debt issued (2.337% Fixed Rate Notes)	9	-	525,000
Proceeds (Repayments) of Credit Facility	9	61,000	(120,000)
Repayment of Series 1 Floating Rate Notes	9	(275,000)	-
Payment of debt issue costs		(2,658)	(2,319)
Repayment of finance lease		-	(588)
Issuance of common shares		14,645	4,892
Dividends paid		(48,932)	(46,936)
Repurchase and cancellation of common shares	12	(812,336)	(696,628)
Net cash used in financing activities		(513,281)	(336,579)
Increase (decrease) in cash		(7,171)	2,837
Cash – beginning of year		62,015	59,178
Cash – end of year		54,844	62,015

The accompanying notes are an integral part of these consolidated financial statements.

Dollarama Inc.
Notes to Consolidated Financial Statements
January 28, 2018 and January 29, 2017
(Expressed in thousands of Canadian dollars, unless otherwise noted)

1   General information

Dollarama Inc. (the "Corporation") was formed on October 20, 2004 under the Canada Business Corporations Act. The Corporation operates dollar stores in Canada that sell all items for $4.00 or less. As at January 28, 2018, the Corporation maintains retail operations in every Canadian province. The Corporation's corporate headquarters, distribution centre and warehouses are located in the Montreal area. The Corporation is listed on the Toronto Stock Exchange ("TSX") under the symbol "DOL" and is incorporated and domiciled in Canada.

The Corporation's fiscal year ends on the Sunday closest to January 31 of each year and usually has 52 weeks. However, as is traditional with the retail calendar, every five to six years, a week is added to the fiscal year. The fiscal years ended January 28, 2018 and January 29, 2017 were comprised of 52 weeks.

The Corporation's head and registered office is located at 5805 Royalmount Avenue, Montreal, Quebec, H4P 0A1.

As at January 28, 2018, the significant entities within the legal structure of the Corporation are as follows:

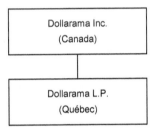

Dollarama L.P. operates the chain of stores and performs related logistical and administrative support activities.

2   Basis of preparation

The Corporation prepares its consolidated financial statements in accordance with generally accepted accounting principles in Canada ("GAAP") as set out in the CPA Canada Handbook – Accounting under Part I, which incorporates International Financial Reporting Standards ("IFRS") as issued by the International Accounting Standards Board ("IASB").

These consolidated financial statements have been prepared on a historical cost basis except for derivative financial instruments, which are measured at fair value. The accounting policies of the Corporation have been applied consistently to all periods in these consolidated financial statements.

These consolidated financial statements were approved by the board of directors of the Corporation for issue on March 29, 2018.

Dollarama Inc.
Notes to Consolidated Financial Statements
January 28, 2018 and January 29, 2017
(Expressed in thousands of Canadian dollars, unless otherwise noted)

3   Summary of significant accounting policies

Subsidiaries

Subsidiaries are all entities over which the Corporation has control. The Corporation determines control based on its ability to exercise power that significantly affects the entities relevant day-to-day activities. Control is also determined by the Corporation's exposure to the variability in returns on investment in the entity, whether favorable or unfavourable. Furthermore, control is defined by the Corporation's ability to direct the decisions made by the entity which ultimately impact return on investment. The existence and effect of substantive voting rights are considered when assessing whether the Corporation controls another entity. Subsidiaries are fully consolidated from the date on which control is determined and they are deconsolidated from the date on which control is deemed to have ceased.

Intercompany transactions, balances and unrealized gains on transactions between group companies are eliminated. Unrealized losses are also eliminated unless the transaction provides evidence of an impairment of the asset transferred. Subsidiaries' accounting policies have been changed where necessary to ensure consistency with the policies adopted by the Corporation. All subsidiaries of the Corporation are wholly-owned subsidiaries.

Foreign currency translation

Functional and presentation currency

Items included in the financial statements of each of the Corporation's entities are measured using the currency of the primary economic environment in which the entity operates (the "functional currency"). The consolidated financial statements are presented in Canadian dollars, which is also the Corporation's functional currency.

Foreign currency transactions and balances

Foreign currency transactions are translated into the functional currency using the exchange rate prevailing at the date of the transactions. Foreign exchange gains and losses resulting from the settlement of foreign currency transactions and from the translation at the year-end exchange rate of monetary assets and liabilities denominated in foreign currencies are recognized in earnings, except where hedge accounting is applied as described below under "Derivative financial instruments".

Segment information

The Corporation manages its business on the basis of one operating segment, which is also the Corporation's only reportable segment, which is consistent with the internal reporting provided to the chief operating decision-maker. The Corporation operates in Canada, which is its country of domicile.

Dollarama Inc.
Notes to Consolidated Financial Statements
January 28, 2018 and January 29, 2017
(Expressed in thousands of Canadian dollars, unless otherwise noted)

3   Summary of significant accounting policies (cont'd)

Financial assets

The Corporation classifies its financial assets in the following categories: financial assets at fair value through profit or loss, and loans and receivables. The classification depends on the purpose for which the financial assets were acquired. Management determines the classification of its financial assets at initial recognition.

a)   Financial assets at fair value through profit or loss

Financial assets at fair value through profit or loss are financial assets held for trading. A financial asset is classified in this category if acquired principally for the purpose of selling in the short term. Derivatives are also categorized as held for trading unless they are designated as hedges.

Financial assets at fair value through profit or loss are initially and subsequently recognized at fair value; transaction costs are expensed in earnings.

b)   Loans and receivables

Loans and receivables comprise cash and accounts receivable. Loans and receivables are non-derivative financial assets with fixed or determinable payments that are neither quoted on an active market nor intended for trading. They are included in current assets, except for maturities greater than 12 months after the statement of financial position date. These are classified as non-current assets. Loans and receivables are subsequently carried at amortized cost using the effective interest method.

Financial liabilities

Financial liabilities comprise accounts payable and accrued liabilities, dividend payable, derivative financial instruments, and long-term debt.

Long-term debt is recognized initially at fair value, net of recognized transaction costs, and is subsequently measured at amortized cost, being the carrying value. Any difference between the carrying value and the redemption value is recognized in the consolidated statement of net earnings and comprehensive income (loss) using the effective interest rate method.

Fees paid on the establishment of revolving credit facilities and on debt issuances are capitalized as a prepayment for liquidity services and amortized over the term of the facility or the notes to which they relate.

Financial liabilities are classified as current liabilities unless the Corporation has an unconditional right to defer settlement of the financial liabilities for at least 12 months after the statement of financial position date.

Offsetting financial instruments

Financial assets and financial liabilities are offset and the net amount is reported in the consolidated statement of financial position when there is a legally enforceable right to offset the recognized amounts and there is an intention to settle on a net basis or to realize the asset and settle the liability simultaneously.

Dollarama Inc.
Notes to Consolidated Financial Statements
January 28, 2018 and January 29, 2017
(Expressed in thousands of Canadian dollars, unless otherwise noted)

3   Summary of significant accounting policies (cont'd)

Derivative financial instruments

The Corporation may use derivative financial instruments in the management of its foreign currency risk on purchases. The Corporation may also use derivative financial instruments in the management of its interest rate exposure. The Corporation designates certain derivatives as hedges of a particular risk associated with a highly probable forecast transaction (cash flow hedge).

When hedge accounting is applied, the Corporation documents at inception the relationships between the hedging instruments and the hedged items, as well as its risk management objective and strategy for undertaking various hedge transactions. This process includes linking derivatives to specific assets and liabilities on the consolidated statement of financial position or to specific firm commitments or forecasted transactions. The Corporation also assesses whether the derivatives that are used in hedging transactions are highly effective in offsetting changes in cash flows of hedged items.

Movements on the hedging reserve in shareholders' equity (deficit) are shown in the consolidated statement of changes in shareholders' equity (deficit). The fair value of a hedging derivative is classified as a non-current asset or liability when the remaining maturity of the hedged item is more than 12 months and as a current asset or liability when the remaining maturity of the hedged item is less than 12 months.

Cash flow hedges

The effective portion of changes in the fair value of derivatives that are designated and qualify as cash flow hedges is recognized in other comprehensive income (loss). The gain or loss relating to the ineffective portion is recognized immediately in earnings. Amounts accumulated in shareholders' equity (deficit) are reclassified to earnings in the periods when the hedged item affects earnings (the vast majority of the reclassification occurs in the first 12 months following the settlement of the derivative financial instrument). The gain or loss relating to the effective portion of the derivatives is recognized as part of cost of sales in the consolidated statement of net earnings and comprehensive income (loss).

When a hedging instrument expires or is sold, or when a hedge no longer meets the criteria for hedge accounting, any cumulative gain or loss existing in shareholders' equity (deficit) at that time remains in shareholders' equity (deficit) and is recognized when the forecast transaction is ultimately recognized in earnings. When a forecast transaction is no longer expected to occur, the cumulative gain or loss that was reported in shareholders' equity (deficit) is immediately transferred to earnings.

Foreign exchange forward contracts are designated as cash flow hedges of specific anticipated transactions.

For cash flow hedges associated with interest rate risk such as a bond forward sale, the derivative is recorded on the consolidated statement of financial position at fair value. The effective portion of changes in the fair value of the derivative is recorded to other comprehensive income (loss), and reclassified to earnings over the same period as the hedged interest payments are recorded in earnings.

Derivatives where hedge accounting is not applied

Derivative financial instruments which are not designated as hedges or have ceased to be effective prior to maturity are recorded at their estimated fair values under assets or liabilities, with changes in their estimated fair values recorded in earnings.

Dollarama Inc.
Notes to Consolidated Financial Statements
January 28, 2018 and January 29, 2017
(Expressed in thousands of Canadian dollars, unless otherwise noted)

3 Summary of significant accounting policies (cont'd)

Property, plant and equipment

Property, plant and equipment are carried at cost and depreciated on a straight-line basis over the estimated useful lives of the assets as follows:

Store and warehouse equipment	10 to 15 years
Vehicles	5 years
Building and roof	20 - 50 years
Leasehold improvements	Lease term
Computer equipment	5 years

The Corporation recognizes in the carrying amount of property, plant and equipment the full purchase price of assets acquired or constructed as well as the costs incurred that are directly incremental as a result of the construction of a specific asset, when they relate to bringing the asset into working condition.

Borrowing costs that are directly attributable to the acquisition or construction of a qualifying asset are capitalized. The rate for calculating the capitalized financing cost is based on the Corporation's weighted average cost of borrowing experienced during the reporting period.

The Corporation also capitalizes the cost of replacing parts of an item when that cost is incurred, if it is probable that the future economic benefits embodied within the item will flow to the Corporation and the cost of the item can be measured reliably. The carrying amount of the replaced part is derecognized.

Estimates of useful lives, residual values and methods of depreciation are reviewed annually. Any changes are accounted for prospectively as a change in accounting estimate. If the expected residual value of an asset is equal to or greater than its carrying value, depreciation on that asset is ceased. Depreciation is resumed when the expected residual value falls below the asset's carrying value. Gains and losses on disposal of an item of property, plant and equipment are determined by comparing the proceeds from disposal with the carrying amount of the item and are recognized directly in the consolidated statement of net earnings and comprehensive income (loss).

Goodwill and intangible assets

The Corporation classifies intangible assets into three categories: (1) intangible assets with finite lives subject to amortization, (2) intangible assets with indefinite lives not subject to amortization and (3) goodwill.

Intangible assets with finite lives subject to amortization

The Corporation determines the useful lives of identifiable intangible assets based on the specific facts and circumstances related to each intangible asset. Finite life intangibles are carried at cost and depreciated on a straight-line basis over the estimated useful lives of the assets as follows:

Computer software	5 years
Deferred leasing costs	Lease term

Dollarama Inc.
Notes to Consolidated Financial Statements
January 28, 2018 and January 29, 2017
(Expressed in thousands of Canadian dollars, unless otherwise noted)

3   Summary of significant accounting policies (cont'd)

The Corporation recognizes in the carrying amount of intangible assets with finite lives subject to amortization the full purchase price of the intangible assets developed or acquired as well as other costs incurred that are directly incremental as a result of the development of a specific intangible asset, when they relate to bringing the asset into working condition.

Intangible assets with indefinite lives not subject to amortization

The trade name is the Corporation's only intangible asset with indefinite life not subject to amortization. The trade name is recorded at cost and is not subject to amortization, having an indefinite life. It is tested for impairment annually, as of the statement of financial position date, or more frequently if events or circumstances indicate that it may be impaired. An impairment loss is recognized for the amount by which the asset's carrying amount exceeds its recoverable amount. The recoverable amount is the higher of an asset's fair value less costs of disposal and value in use. As the trade name does not generate cash flows that are independent from other assets or individual cash-generating units ("CGUs" or "CGU"), trade name is allocated to one group of CGUs that is expected to benefit from the business combination, and which represents the lowest level within the Corporation at which trade name is monitored for internal management purposes.

Goodwill

Goodwill arises on the acquisition of subsidiaries and represents the excess of the consideration transferred over the share of the net identifiable assets acquired of the acquiree and the fair value of the non-controlling interest in the acquiree.

Goodwill is subsequently measured at cost less any accumulated impairment losses. Goodwill is tested for impairment annually, as at the statement of financial position date, or more frequently if events or circumstances indicate that it may be impaired. For the purposes of annual impairment testing, goodwill is allocated to one group of CGUs that is expected to benefit from the business combination, and which represents the lowest level within the Corporation at which goodwill is monitored for internal management purposes.

Impairment of non-financial assets

Assets that are subject to amortization are periodically reviewed for indicators of impairment. Whenever events or changes in circumstances indicate that the carrying amount may not be recoverable, the asset or CGU is tested for impairment. To the extent that the asset or CGU's carrying amount exceeds its recoverable amount, an impairment loss is recognized in the consolidated statement of net earnings and comprehensive income (loss). The recoverable amount of an asset or a CGU is the higher of its fair value less costs of disposal and its value in use. Value in use is the present value of the future cash flows expected to be derived from an asset or CGU. The fair value is the price that could be received for an asset or CGU in an orderly transaction between market participants at the measurement date, less costs of disposal. For the purposes of assessing impairment, assets are grouped at the lowest levels for which there are separately identifiable cash flows (CGUs – these are individual stores). Management undertakes an assessment of relevant market data, which includes the current publicly quoted market capitalization of the Corporation.

Dollarama Inc.
Notes to Consolidated Financial Statements
January 28, 2018 and January 29, 2017
(Expressed in thousands of Canadian dollars, unless otherwise noted)

3   Summary of significant accounting policies (cont'd)

Cash and cash equivalents

Cash and cash equivalents include highly liquid investments with original maturities from the date of purchase of three months or less. The majority of payments due from financial institutions for the settlement of credit card and debit card transactions are processed within one business day, and are therefore classified as cash and cash equivalents.

Inventories

The Corporation's inventories at the distribution centre, warehouses and stores consist primarily of merchandise purchased and held for resale and are valued at the lower of cost and net realizable value.

Cost is determined at the distribution centre and warehouses on a weighted average cost basis and is then assigned to store inventories using the retail inventory method. Costs of inventories include amounts paid to suppliers, duties and freight into the warehouses as well as costs directly associated with warehousing and distribution to stores.

Net realizable value is the estimated selling price in the ordinary course of business, less applicable variable selling expenses.

Accounts payable and accrued liabilities

Accounts payable and accrued liabilities are obligations to pay for goods acquired from suppliers or services rendered by employees and service providers in the ordinary course of business. Accounts payable and accrued liabilities are classified as current liabilities if payment is due or expected within one year or less. Otherwise, they are presented as non-current liabilities.

Accounts payable and accrued liabilities are recognized initially at fair value and subsequently measured at amortized cost.

Provisions

A provision is recognized if, as a result of a past event, the Corporation has a present legal or constructive obligation that can be estimated reliably, and if it is probable that an outflow of economic benefits will be required to settle the obligation. Provisions are not recognized for future operating losses.

If the effect of time value of money is material, provisions are measured at the present value of cash flows expected to be required to settle the obligation using a pre-tax rate that reflects current market assessments of the time value of money and the risks specific to the obligation. The increase in the provision due to the passage of time is recognized as accretion expense under financing costs in the consolidated statement of net earnings and comprehensive income (loss).

Dollarama Inc.
Notes to Consolidated Financial Statements
January 28, 2018 and January 29, 2017
(Expressed in thousands of Canadian dollars, unless otherwise noted)

3   Summary of significant accounting policies (cont'd)

Share capital

Common shares are classified as shareholders' equity (deficit). Incremental costs directly attributable to the issuance of shares or options are shown in shareholders' equity (deficit) as a deduction, net of tax, from the proceeds of issuance.

When the Corporation repurchases common shares under its normal course issuer bid, the portion of the price paid for the common shares that corresponds to the book value of those shares is recognized as a reduction of share capital. The portion of the price paid that is in excess of the book value is recognized as a reduction of retained earnings. As a direct result of the fact that the price paid for each common share significantly exceeds its book value, the Corporation's shareholders' equity is now in a deficit position.

Dividends declared

Dividend distributions to the Corporation's shareholders are recognized as a liability in the Corporation's consolidated financial statements in the period in which the dividends are declared by the board of directors.

Employee future benefits

A defined contribution pension plan is a post-employment benefit plan under which the Corporation pays fixed contributions into a separate legal entity as well as state plans administered by the provincial and federal governments and will have no legal or constructive obligation to pay further amounts. Obligations for contributions to defined contribution retirement plans are recognized as an expense in earnings when they are due.

The Corporation offers a defined contribution pension plan to eligible employees whereby it matches an employee's contributions up to 5% of the employee's salary, subject to a maximum of 50% of the RRSP annual contribution limit.

Short-term employee benefits

Liabilities for bonus plans are recognized based on a formula that takes into consideration individual performance and contributions to the profitability of the Corporation.

Termination benefits

Termination benefits are generally payable when employment is terminated before the normal retirement date or whenever an employee accepts voluntary redundancy in exchange for these benefits. The Corporation recognizes termination benefits when it is demonstrably committed to providing termination benefits as a result of an offer made.

Income taxes

The income tax expense for the year comprises current and deferred tax. Tax is recognized in earnings, except to the extent that it relates to items recognized in other comprehensive income (loss) or directly in shareholders' equity (deficit). In this case, tax is recognized in other comprehensive income (loss) or directly in shareholders' equity (deficit).

Dollarama Inc.
Notes to Consolidated Financial Statements
January 28, 2018 and January 29, 2017
(Expressed in thousands of Canadian dollars, unless otherwise noted)

3 Summary of significant accounting policies (cont'd)

The current income tax charge is calculated on the basis of the tax laws enacted or substantively enacted at the statement of financial position date and any adjustment to tax payable in respect of previous years.

Deferred income tax is recognized using the liability method on temporary differences arising between the tax bases of assets and liabilities and their carrying amounts in the consolidated financial statements. However, deferred income tax liabilities are not recognized if they arise from initial recognition of goodwill or if they arise from initial recognition of an asset or liability in a transaction other than a business combination that at the time of the transaction affects neither accounting nor taxable profit or loss. Deferred income tax is determined using tax rates and laws that have been enacted or substantively enacted by the statement of financial position date and are expected to apply when the related deferred income tax asset is realized or the deferred income tax liability is settled.

Deferred income tax assets are recognized only to the extent that it is probable that future taxable profits will be available against which the temporary differences can be utilized.

Deferred income tax assets and liabilities are offset when there is a legally enforceable right to offset current tax assets against current tax liabilities and when the deferred income tax assets and liabilities relate to income tax levied by the same taxation authority on either the same taxable entity or different taxable entities where there is an intention to settle the balances on a net basis.

Revenue recognition

The Corporation recognizes revenue from the sale of products or the rendering of services when they are earned, specifically when all the following conditions are met: (1) the significant risks and rewards of ownership are transferred to customers and the Corporation retains neither continuing managerial involvement nor effective control; (2) there is clear evidence that an arrangement exists; (3) the amount of revenue and related costs can be measured reliably; and (4) it is probable that the economic benefits associated with the transaction will flow to the Corporation. The recognition of revenue at the store occurs at the time a customer tenders payment for and takes possession of the merchandise.

All sales are final. Revenue is shown net of sales tax and discounts. Gift cards sold are recorded as a liability, and revenue is recognized when gift cards are redeemed.

Gross versus net

The Corporation may enter into arrangements with third parties for the sale of products to customers. When the Corporation acts as the principal in these arrangements, it recognizes revenue based on the amounts billed to customers. Otherwise, the Corporation recognizes the net amount that it retains as revenue.

Cost of sales

Cost of sales includes the cost of inventories, outbound transportation costs, warehousing and distribution costs, store, warehouse and distribution centre occupancy costs, as well as the transfer from accumulated other comprehensive income (loss) (AOCI) of any gains (losses) on qualifying cash flow hedges related to the purchase of inventories.

Dollarama Inc.
Notes to Consolidated Financial Statements
January 28, 2018 and January 29, 2017
(Expressed in thousands of Canadian dollars, unless otherwise noted)

3 Summary of significant accounting policies (cont'd)

Vendor rebates

The Corporation records vendor rebates, consisting of volume purchase rebates, when it is probable that they will be received and the amounts are reasonably estimable. The rebates are recorded as a reduction of inventory purchases and are reflected as a reduction of cost of sales in the consolidated statement of net earnings and comprehensive income (loss).

General, administrative and store operating expenses

The Corporation includes store and head office salaries and benefits, repairs and maintenance, professional fees, store supplies and other related expenses in general, administrative and store operating expenses.

Earnings per common share

Earnings per common share is determined using the weighted average number of common shares outstanding during the year. Diluted earnings per common share is determined using the treasury share method to evaluate the dilutive effect of share options. Under this method, instruments with a dilutive effect are considered to have been exercised at the beginning of the year, or at the time of issuance, if later, and the proceeds received are considered to have been used to redeem common shares at the average market price during the year.

Leases

Finance leases

Assets held under leases which result in the Corporation receiving substantially all the risks and rewards of ownership of the asset ("finance leases") are capitalized at the lower of the fair value of the property and equipment or the estimated present value of the minimum lease payments. The corresponding finance lease obligation is included within interest bearing liabilities. The interest element is amortized using the effective interest rate method.

Operating leases

The Corporation leases stores, five warehouses, a distribution centre and corporate headquarters. Leases in which a significant portion of the risks and rewards of ownership are retained by the lessor are classified as operating leases. The Corporation recognizes rental expense incurred and inducements received from landlords on a straight-line basis over the term of the lease. Any difference between the calculated expense and the amounts actually paid is reflected as deferred lease inducements in the Corporation's consolidated statement of financial position. Contingent rental expense is recognized when the achievement of specified sales targets is considered probable.

Deferred leasing costs and deferred tenant allowances are recorded on the consolidated statement of financial position and amortized using the straight-line method over the term of the respective lease.

Dollarama Inc.
Notes to Consolidated Financial Statements
January 28, 2018 and January 29, 2017
(Expressed in thousands of Canadian dollars, unless otherwise noted)

3   Summary of significant accounting policies (cont'd)

Share-based compensation

The Corporation recognizes a compensation expense for share options granted based on the fair value of those options at the grant date, using the Black-Scholes option pricing model. The options granted by the Corporation vest in tranches (graded vesting); accordingly, the expense is recognized in vesting tranches.

The total amount to be expensed is determined by reference to the fair value of the options granted.

The impact of any service and non-market performance vesting conditions (for example, profitability, sales growth targets and retaining an employee of the entity over a specified time period) are excluded from the fair value calculation. Non-market performance vesting conditions are included in assumptions about the number of options that are expected to vest. The total expense is recognized over the vesting period, which is the period over which all of the specified vesting conditions are to be satisfied. At the end of each reporting period, the Corporation revises its estimates of the number of options that are expected to vest based on the non-market performance vesting conditions. The Corporation recognizes the impact of the revision to original estimates, if any, in the consolidated statement of net earnings and comprehensive income (loss), with a corresponding adjustment to contributed surplus.

When option holders exercise their options, the cash paid for the shares issued is credited, together with the related compensation costs, to share capital (nominal value).

4   Significant new accounting standards not yet adopted

IFRS 16

In January 2016, the IASB issued IFRS 16, "Leases", which will replace IAS 17, "Leases". The new standard will be effective for fiscal years beginning on or after January 1, 2019, with early adoption permitted provided the Corporation has adopted IFRS 15, "Revenue from Contracts with Customers". The new standard requires lessees to recognize a lease liability reflecting future lease payments and a "right-of-use asset" for virtually all lease contracts, and record it on the statement of financial position, except with respect to lease contracts that meet limited exception criteria. Given that the Corporation has significant contractual obligations in the form of operating leases (Note 10) under IAS 17, there will be a material increase to both assets and liabilities upon adoption of IFRS 16, and material changes to the timing of recognition of expenses associated with lease arrangements.

Dollarama Inc.
Notes to Consolidated Financial Statements
January 28, 2018 and January 29, 2017
(Expressed in thousands of Canadian dollars, unless otherwise noted)

4   Significant new accounting standards not yet adopted (cont'd)

The following table outlines the key areas that will be impacted by the adoption of IFRS 16.

Impacted areas of the business	Analysis	Impact
Financial reporting	The analysis includes which contracts will be in scope as well as the options available under the new standard such as whether to early adopt, the two recognition and measurement exemptions and whether to apply the new standard on a full retrospective application in accordance with IAS 8 or choose the "modified retrospective approach".	The Corporation is in the process of analyzing the full impact of the adoption of IFRS 16 on the Corporation's consolidated statement of financial position and consolidated statement of net earnings and comprehensive income (loss). In addition, the Corporation is working with a third party provider of advisory services. As at January 28, 2018, the operating leases disclosed in Note 10 to the audited consolidated financial statements for the year ended January 28, 2018 are in scope with IFRS 16.
Information systems	The Corporation is analyzing the need to make changes within its information systems environment to optimize the management of more than 1,000 leases that will fall within the scope of the new standard.	The Corporation has chosen an IT solution for the eventual recognition and measurement of leases in scope. Integration testing began in the 13-week period ended October 29, 2017 and was ongoing as at January 28, 2018.
Internal controls	The Corporation will be performing an analysis of the changes to the control environment as a result of the adoption of IFRS 16.	Concurrently with integration testing, the Corporation is evaluating the impact of IFRS 16 on its control environment.
Stakeholders	The Corporation will be performing an analysis of the impact on the disclosure to its stakeholders as a result of the adoption of IFRS 16.	The Corporation has begun communicating the impact of IFRS 16 to internal stakeholders.

IFRS 9

In July 2014, the IASB issued the final version of IFRS 9, "Financial Instruments" concerning classification and measurement, impairment and hedge accounting, to supersede IAS 39, "Financial Instruments: Recognition and Measurement". IFRS 9 is effective for years beginning on or after January 1, 2018 with early adoption permitted. On transition to IFRS 9, the Corporation will apply the new hedge accounting requirements to all qualifying hedge relationships existing on the date of transition. IFRS 9 introduces changes to the cash flow hedge accounting model and eliminates the accounting policy choice provided by IAS 39 for the hedge of a forecasted transaction that results in the recognition of a non-financial asset or liability.

Classification under IFRS 9 is based on the concept that financial assets should be classified and measured at fair value, with changes in fair value recognized through profit or loss (FVPL), unless restrictive criteria are met for classifying and measuring the asset at either amortized cost or fair value through other comprehensive income (loss) (FVOCI).

The following table compares the different categories of classification under IAS 39 and IFRS 9:

Current IAS 39 accounting standard		IFRS 9
Classifications	Measurement models	Classifications and measurement models
Loans and receivables	Amortized cost	Amortized cost
FVPL	FVPL	FVPL
Available for sale	FVOCI	FVOCI
Held to maturity	Amortized cost	FVOCI

Dollarama Inc.
Notes to Consolidated Financial Statements
January 28, 2018 and January 29, 2017
(Expressed in thousands of Canadian dollars, unless otherwise noted)

4 Significant new accounting standards not yet adopted (cont'd)

As a result of the adoption of IFRS 9, the Corporation will remove the gains or losses previously recognized in accumulated other comprehensive income (loss) and include them directly in the carrying amount of the asset or the liability (referred to as 'basis adjustment'). This is done in order to better match the settlement of the hedged transaction that has occurred with the carrying amount of the hedged asset, being the portion of the Corporation's inventory that was purchased with a foreign currency. This basis adjustment is not a reclassification adjustment and will not affect the Corporation's consolidated statement of net earnings and comprehensive income (loss).

IFRS 15

In May 2014, the IASB issued IFRS 15, "Revenue from Contracts with Customers". IFRS 15 replaces all previous revenue recognition standards, including IAS 18, "Revenue". In September 2015, the IASB deferred the effective date of IFRS 15 from January 1, 2017 to annual periods beginning on or after January 1, 2018, with early adoption permitted. IFRS 15 is based on the principle that revenue is recognized when control of a good or service is transferred to a customer. A five-step recognition model is used to apply the standard as follows:

1. Identify the contract(s) with the customer;
2. Identify the separate performance obligations in the contract;
3. Determine the transaction price;
4. Allocate the transaction price to separate performance obligations; and
5. Recognize revenue when (or as) each performance obligation is satisfied.

The Corporation is in the final stages of analyzing the impact of the adoption of IFRS 15 on the Corporation's consolidated statement of financial position and consolidated statement of net earnings and comprehensive income (loss). The impact is not expected to be significant.

5 Critical accounting estimates and judgments

The preparation of financial statements requires management to make estimates and assumptions using judgment that affect the application of accounting policies and the reported amounts of assets and liabilities, income and expenses during the reporting period. Estimates and other judgments are continually evaluated and are based on management's experience and other factors, including expectations about future events that are believed to be reasonable under the circumstances. Actual results may differ from those estimates.

The following discusses the most significant accounting judgments and estimates that the Corporation made in the preparation of the consolidated financial statements.

Income taxes

Judgment - Judgment is required in determining income taxes. There are transactions and calculations for which the ultimate tax determination is uncertain. The Corporation recognizes liabilities for anticipated tax audit issues based on estimates of whether additional taxes will be due. Where the final tax outcome of these matters differs from the amounts that were initially recorded, such differences impact the current and deferred income tax assets and liabilities in the period in which such determination is made.

Dollarama Inc.
Notes to Consolidated Financial Statements
January 28, 2018 and January 29, 2017
(Expressed in thousands of Canadian dollars, unless otherwise noted)

5 Critical accounting estimates and judgments (cont'd)

Property, plant and equipment

Estimate - Estimates of useful lives, residual values and methods of depreciation are reviewed annually. Any changes, based on additional available information, are accounted for prospectively as a change in accounting estimate.

Valuation of inventories

Estimate - Store inventories are valued at the lower of cost and net realizable value, with cost being determined by the retail inventory method. Under the retail inventory method, inventories are converted to a cost basis by applying an average cost-to-sell ratio. Inventories that are at the distribution centre or warehouses and inventories that are in transit from suppliers are measured at the lower of cost and net realizable value, with cost determined on a weighted average cost basis.

Inventories include items that have been marked down to management's best estimate of their net realizable value and are included in cost of sales in the period in which the markdown is determined. The Corporation estimates its inventory provisions based on the consideration of a variety of factors, including quantities of slow-moving or carryover seasonal merchandise on hand, historical markdown statistics, future merchandising plans and inventory shrinkage. The accuracy of the Corporation's estimates can be affected by many factors, some of which are beyond its control, including changes in economic conditions and consumer buying trends.

Historically, the Corporation has not experienced significant differences in its estimates of markdowns compared with actual results. Changes to the inventory provisions can have a material impact on the results of the Corporation.

Impairment of goodwill and trade name

Estimate - Goodwill and trade name are not subject to amortization and are tested for impairment annually or more frequently if events or circumstances indicate that the assets might be impaired. Impairment is identified by comparing the recoverable amount of the CGU to its carrying value. To the extent the CGU's carrying amount exceeds its recoverable amount, an impairment loss is recognized in the consolidated statement of net earnings and comprehensive income (loss).

The recoverable amount of the CGU is based on the fair value less costs of disposal. The fair value is the price that could be received for an asset or CGU in an orderly transaction between market participants at the measurement date, less costs of disposal. Management undertakes an assessment of relevant market data, which includes the current publicly quoted market capitalization of the Corporation.

As at January 28, 2018 and January 29, 2017, impairment reviews were performed by comparing the carrying value of goodwill and the trade name with the recoverable amount of the CGU to which goodwill and the trade name have been allocated. Management determined that there has been no impairment.

Dollarama Inc.
Notes to Consolidated Financial Statements
January 28, 2018 and January 29, 2017
(Expressed in thousands of Canadian dollars, unless otherwise noted)

5 Critical accounting estimates and judgments (cont'd)

Fair value of financial instruments and hedging

Estimate - The fair value of financial instruments is based on current interest rates, foreign exchange rates, credit risk, market value and current pricing of financial instruments with similar terms. The carrying value of financial instruments, especially those with current maturities such as cash, accounts receivable, accounts payable and accrued liabilities, and dividend payable, approximates their fair value.

When hedge accounting is used, formal documentation is set up about relationships between hedging instruments and hedged items, as well as the risk management objective and strategy for undertaking various hedge transactions.

This process includes linking derivatives to specific firm commitments or forecasted transactions. As part of the Corporation's hedge accounting, an assessment is made to determine whether the derivatives that arose as hedging instruments are effective in offsetting changes in cash flows of hedged items.

Dollarama Inc.
Notes to Consolidated Financial Statements
January 28, 2018 and January 29, 2017
(Expressed in thousands of Canadian dollars, unless otherwise noted)

6   Property, plant and equipment

	Land $	Buildings $	Store and warehouse equipment $	Computer equipment $	Vehicles $	Leasehold improvements $	Total $
Cost							
Balance January 29, 2017	22,144	45,779	350,325	33,892	4,565	286,695	743,400
Additions	23,222	3,213	39,599	4,766	2,001	39,985	112,786
Transfers [1]	-	(12,484)	12,152	266	-	-	(66)
Dispositions	-	-	(640)	(103)	(1,724)	(861)	(3,328)
Balance January 28, 2018	45,366	36,508	401,436	38,821	4,842	325,819	852,792
Accumulated depreciation							
Balance January 29, 2017	-	-	192,620	9,593	1,669	102,429	306,311
Depreciation	-	851	27,970	7,766	1,115	20,216	57,918
Dispositions	-	-	(640)	(100)	(1,068)	(617)	(2,425)
Balance January 28, 2018	-	851	219,950	17,259	1,716	122,028	361,804
Net book value							
Balance January 28, 2018	45,366	35,657	181,486	21,562	3,126	203,791	490,988
Cost							
Balance January 31, 2016	-	-	316,349	24,596	4,349	249,887	595,181
Additions	22,144	45,779	34,012	13,346	1,163	37,130	153,574
Dispositions	-	-	(36)	(4,050)	(947)	(322)	(5,355)
Balance January 29, 2017	22,144	45,779	350,325	33,892	4,565	286,695	743,400
Accumulated depreciation							
Balance January 31, 2016	-	-	168,517	7,648	1,316	85,475	262,956
Depreciation	-	-	24,111	5,995	927	17,175	48,208
Dispositions	-	-	(8)	(4,050)	(574)	(221)	(4,853)
Balance January 29, 2017	-	-	192,620	9,593	1,669	102,429	306,311
Net book value							
Balance January 29, 2017	22,144	45,779	157,705	24,299	2,896	184,266	437,089

[1]   Racking, fixtures and other equipment (including hardware and software) totalling $12,418 were reclassified from building to store and warehouse equipment and computer equipment on January 30, 2017. The balance of $66 was reclassified from building to computer software on January 30, 2017 (refer to Note 7).

Dollarama Inc.
Notes to Consolidated Financial Statements
January 28, 2018 and January 29, 2017
(Expressed in thousands of Canadian dollars, unless otherwise noted)

7 Intangible assets and goodwill

	Deferred leasing costs $	Computer software $	Trade name [2] $	Total intangible assets $	Goodwill $
Cost					
Balance January 29, 2017	7,046	63,660	108,200	178,906	727,782
Additions	-	19,134	-	19,134	-
Transfers [1]	-	66	-	66	-
Balance January 28, 2018	7,046	82,860	108,200	198,106	727,782
Accumulated amortization					
Balance January 29, 2017	4,009	35,382	-	39,391	-
Amortization	483	12,632	-	13,115	-
Balance January 28, 2018	4,492	48,014	-	52,506	-
Net book value					
Balance January 28, 2018	2,554	34,846	108,200	145,600	727,782
Cost					
Balance January 31, 2016	7,046	55,078	108,200	170,324	727,782
Additions	-	12,640	-	12,640	-
Dispositions	-	(4,058)	-	(4,058)	-
Balance January 29, 2017	7,046	63,660	108,200	178,906	727,782
Accumulated amortization					
Balance January 31, 2016	3,490	29,900	-	33,390	-
Amortization	519	9,540	-	10,059	-
Dispositions	-	(4,058)	-	(4,058)	-
Balance January 29, 2017	4,009	35,382	-	39,391	-
Net book value					
Balance January 29, 2017	3,037	28,278	108,200	139,515	727,782

[1]   Other equipment totalling $66 was reclassified from building to computer software on January 30, 2017.

[2]   Intangible assets with indefinite lives are not subject to amortization.

Dollarama Inc.
Notes to Consolidated Financial Statements
January 28, 2018 and January 29, 2017
(Expressed in thousands of Canadian dollars, unless otherwise noted)

8   Accounts payable and accrued liabilities

	January 28, 2018	January 29, 2017
	$	$
Trade accounts payable	59,674	56,775
Employee benefits payable	57,081	49,686
Inventories in transit	33,782	28,613
Sales tax payable	41,301	32,542
Accrued share repurchases	9,142	8,819
Rent and other expenses	27,382	22,051
	228,362	198,486

9   Long-term debt

Long-term debt issued and outstanding consists of the following as at:

	January 28, 2018	January 29, 2017
	$	$
Senior unsecured notes bearing interest at:		
Fixed annual rate of 2.203% payable in equal semi-annual instalments, maturing November 10, 2022 (the "2.203% Fixed Rate Notes")	250,000	-
Fixed annual rate of 2.337% payable in equal semi-annual instalments, maturing July 22, 2021 (the "2.337% Fixed Rate Notes")	525,000	525,000
Fixed annual rate of 3.095% payable in equal semi-annual instalments, maturing November 5, 2018 (the "3.095% Fixed Rate Notes" and collectively with the 2.203% Fixed Rate Notes and the 2.337% Fixed Rate Notes, the "Fixed Rate Notes")	400,000	400,000
Variable rate equal to 3-month bankers' acceptance rate (CDOR) plus 59 basis points payable quarterly, maturing March 16, 2020 (the "Series 2 Floating Rate Notes")	300,000	-
Variable rate equal to 3-month bankers' acceptance rate (CDOR) plus 54 basis points payable quarterly, matured May 16, 2017 (the "Series 1 Floating Rate Notes", and collectively with the Series 2 Floating Rate Notes, the "Floating Rate Notes")	-	274,834
Unsecured revolving credit facility maturing September 29, 2022 (the "Credit Facility")	191,000	130,000
Less: Unamortized debt issue costs	(5,541)	(4,899)
Accrued interest on the Floating Rate Notes and Fixed Rate Notes	5,192	3,809
	1,665,651	1,328,744
Current portion (includes accrued interest on the Floating Rate Notes and Fixed Rate Notes)	(405,192)	(278,643)
	1,260,459	1,050,101

Dollarama Inc.
Notes to Consolidated Financial Statements
January 28, 2018 and January 29, 2017
(Expressed in thousands of Canadian dollars, unless otherwise noted)

9 Long-term debt (cont'd)

Fixed Rate Notes

On May 10, 2017, the Corporation issued the 2.203% Fixed Rate Notes by way of private placement in reliance upon exemptions from the prospectus requirements under applicable securities legislation. The 2.203% Fixed Rate Notes were issued at par, for aggregate gross proceeds of $250,000, and bear interest at a rate of 2.203% per annum, payable in equal semi-annual instalments, in arrears, on the 10th day of May and November of each year until maturity on November 10, 2022.

As at January 28, 2018, the carrying value of the 2.203% Fixed Rate Notes was $250,186 (January 29, 2017 – n/a). The fair value of the 2.203% Fixed Rate Notes as at January 28, 2018 was determined to be $242,410 valued as a level 2 in the fair value hierarchy (January 29, 2017 – n/a).

As at January 28, 2018, the carrying value of the 2.337% Fixed Rate Notes was $523,597 (January 29, 2017 – $523,192). The fair value of the 2.337% Fixed Rate Notes as at January 28, 2018 was determined to be $519,246 valued as a level 2 in the fair value hierarchy (January 29, 2017 – $526,628). The 2.337% Fixed Rate Notes are due on July 22, 2021.

As at January 28, 2018, the carrying value of the 3.095% Fixed Rate Notes was $402,452 (January 29, 2017 – $401,994). The fair value of the 3.095% Fixed Rate Notes as at January 28, 2018 was determined to be $403,452 valued as a level 2 in the fair value hierarchy (January 29, 2017 – $410,100). The 3.095% Fixed Rate Notes are due on November 5, 2018 and therefore presented as a current liability on the consolidated statement of financial position as at January 28, 2018.

Floating Rate Notes

On May 10, 2017, the Corporation issued additional Series 2 Floating Rate Notes due March 16, 2020 (the "Additional Series 2 Floating Rates Notes"). The Additional Series 2 Floating Rate Notes constitute an increase to the $225,000 principal amount of original Series 2 Floating Rate Notes issued by the Corporation on March 16, 2017. The Additional Series 2 Floating Rate Notes were issued at a premium of 0.284% of the $75,000 principal amount thereof, for aggregate gross proceeds of $75,213. As at the date of issuance, the effective spread over the 3-month bankers' acceptance rate (CDOR) for the Additional Series 2 Floating Rate Notes was 49 basis points (or 0.49%). Once issued, they bear interest at the same rate as the original Series 2 Floating Rate Notes, such rate being equal to the 3-month bankers' acceptance rate (CDOR) plus 59 basis points (or 0.59%), to be set quarterly on the 16th day of March, June, September and December of each year. All other terms and conditions applicable to the original Series 2 Floating Rate Notes also apply to the Additional Series 2 Floating Rate Notes, and those are treated as a single series with the original Series 2 Floating Rate Notes (collectively, the "Series 2 Floating Rate Notes"). As at January 28, 2018, the carrying value of the Series 2 Floating Rate Notes was $300,066 (January 29, 2017 – n/a). The fair value of the Series 2 Floating Rate Notes as at January 28, 2018 was determined to be $302,502 valued as a level 2 in the fair value hierarchy (January 29, 2017 – n/a).

On May 16, 2017, the Corporation repaid the principal and all accrued and unpaid interest on the Series 1 Floating Rate Notes.

Dollarama Inc.
Notes to Consolidated Financial Statements
January 28, 2018 and January 29, 2017
(Expressed in thousands of Canadian dollars, unless otherwise noted)

9　Long-term debt (cont'd)

Credit Facility

The Corporation has access to a $500,000 unsecured revolving credit facility (the "Credit Facility") made available under the Second Amended and Restated Credit Agreement (the "Credit Agreement"), originally dated as of October 25, 2013, amended successively on December 3, 2013, June 10, 2014, November 3, 2014, October 30, 2015, January 29, 2016, November 21, 2016 and June 29, 2017, and finally amended and restated pursuant to an amending agreement dated November 28, 2017.

The Credit Agreement expires on September 29, 2022. Commitments in the amount of $250,000 initially made in 2013 are available until September 29, 2022, and commitments in the amount of $250,000 made in 2016 are available until September 29, 2019.

Under the Credit Agreement, as amended, the Corporation may, under certain circumstances and subject to receipt of additional commitments from existing lenders or other eligible institutions, request increases to the credit facility up to an aggregate amount, together with all then-existing commitments, of $1,500,000.

As at January 28, 2018, an amount of $191,000 was outstanding under the Credit Facility (January 29, 2017 – $130,000), and letters of credit issued for the purchase of inventories amounted to $1,059 (January 29, 2017 – $831). As at January 28, 2018, the Corporation was in compliance with all of its financial covenants.

Dollarama Inc.
Notes to Consolidated Financial Statements
January 28, 2018 and January 29, 2017
(Expressed in thousands of Canadian dollars, unless otherwise noted)

10 Leases and commitments

a) Operating leases

The basic rent and contingent rent expense of operating leases for stores, warehouses, distribution centre and corporate headquarters included in the consolidated statement of net earnings and comprehensive income (loss) are as follows:

	January 28, 2018	January 29, 2017
	$	$
Basic rent	177,862	163,784
Contingent rent	5,178	4,624
	183,040	168,408

b) Commitments

As at January 28, 2018, contractual obligations for operating leases amounted to $1,070,929 (January 29, 2017 – $1,055,938). The leases extend, depending on the renewal option, over various years up to the year 2039.

Non-cancellable operating lease rentals are payable as follows:

	January 28, 2018	January 29, 2017
	$	$
Less than 1 year	177,806	166,859
Between 1 and 5 years	589,116	566,421
More than 5 years	304,007	322,658
Total	1,070,929	1,055,938

Dollarama Inc.
Notes to Consolidated Financial Statements
January 28, 2018 and January 29, 2017
(Expressed in thousands of Canadian dollars, unless otherwise noted)

11   Deferred rent and lease inducements

The following table shows the continuity of other liabilities, which consisted of deferred tenant allowances and deferred lease inducements:

	January 28, 2018	January 29, 2017
	$	$
Deferred tenant allowances, beginning of year	38,555	34,380
Additions	10,607	8,970
Amortization	(5,149)	(4,795)
Deferred tenant allowances, end of year	44,013	38,555
Deferred lease inducements, beginning of year	43,272	37,252
Additions, net of straight-line rent	5,348	6,020
Deferred lease inducements, end of year	48,620	43,272
	92,633	81,827

12   Shareholders' equity (deficit)

a)   Share capital

Normal course issuer bid

During the 12-month period ended June 16, 2017, the Corporation was authorized to repurchase for cancellation up to 5,975,854 common shares, representing 5% of the common shares issued and outstanding as at the close of markets on June 7, 2016 (the "2016-2017 NCIB"). At the expiry of the 2016-2017 NCIB, the Corporation had repurchased for cancellation a total of 5,975,162 common shares.

On June 7, 2017, the Corporation announced the renewal of its normal course issuer bid to repurchase for cancellation up to 5,680,390 common shares, representing 5% of the common shares issued and outstanding as at the close of markets on June 6, 2017, during the 12-month period from June 19, 2017 to June 18, 2018 (the "2017-2018 NCIB").

The total number of common shares repurchased for cancellation under the 2017-2018 NCIB and the 2016-2017 NCIB during the year ended January 28, 2018 amounted to 6,104,540 common shares (January 29, 2017 – 7,420,168 common shares under the 2016-2017 NCIB and the NCIB in effect before that), at a weighted average price of $133.12 per common share, for a total cash consideration of $812,659 (January 29, 2017 - $705,447). For the year ended January 28, 2018, the Corporation's share capital was reduced by $22,305 (January 29, 2017 - $26,669) and the remaining $790,354 (January 29, 2017 - $678,778) was accounted for as an increase in deficit.

On December 21, 2017, as part of the 2017-2018 NCIB, the Corporation announced the completion of a specific share repurchase program with an arm's length third party pursuant to which the Corporation repurchased 437,000 common shares through daily purchases, subject to the conditions of an issuer bid exemption order issued by the Ontario Securities Commission on December 6, 2017.

Dollarama Inc.
Notes to Consolidated Financial Statements
January 28, 2018 and January 29, 2017
(Expressed in thousands of Canadian dollars, unless otherwise noted)

12 Shareholders' equity (deficit) (cont'd)

b) Common shares authorized

The Corporation is authorized to issue an unlimited number of common shares. All common shares are issued as fully paid and without par value.

Movements in the Corporation's share capital are as follows:

| | January 28, 2018 | | January 29, 2017 | |
	Number of common shares	Amount $	Number of common shares	Amount $
Balance, beginning of year	115,051,349	420,266	122,225,104	439,296
Cancellation under NCIB	(6,104,540)	(22,305)	(7,420,168)	(26,669)
Exercise of share options	379,050	17,826	246,413	7,639
Balance, end of year	109,325,859	415,787	115,051,349	420,266

c) Contributed surplus

Share-based compensation

The Corporation established a management option plan whereby its directors, officers and employees may be granted share options to acquire its shares. Under the plan, the number and characteristics of share options granted are determined by the board of directors of the Corporation, and share options have a life not exceeding 10 years.

Outstanding share options under the plan are granted with service requirements (or service conditions). These share options were granted to purchase an equivalent number of common shares. The share options vest at a rate of 20% annually on the anniversary of the grant date.

Outstanding and exercisable share options for the years ended on the dates provided below are as follows:

| | January 28, 2018 | | January 29, 2017 | |
	Number of share options	Weighted average exercise price ($)	Number of share options	Weighted average exercise price ($)
Outstanding – beginning of year	2,572,000	50.68	2,478,200	42.29
Granted	252,000	112.36	420,000	90.59
Exercised	(379,050)	38.63	(326,200)	38.38
Forfeited	(15,400)	81.26	-	-
Outstanding – end of year	2,429,550	58.76	2,572,000	50.68
Exercisable – end of year	1,113,350	42.39	946,400	35.35

Dollarama Inc.
Notes to Consolidated Financial Statements
January 28, 2018 and January 29, 2017
(Expressed in thousands of Canadian dollars, unless otherwise noted)

12 Shareholders' equity (deficit) (cont'd)

During the year ended January 28, 2018, the Corporation recognized a share-based compensation expense of $6,559 (January 29, 2017 - $6,932).

Information relating to share options outstanding and exercisable as at January 28, 2018 is as follows:

Range of exercise prices	Share options outstanding			Share options exercisable		
	Weighted average remaining life (in months)	Number of share options	Weighted average exercise price ($)	Weighted average remaining life (in months)	Number of share options	Weighted average exercise price ($)
$8.75 - $18.89	33	24,000	13.64	33	24,000	13.64
$18.90 - $27.01	48	169,200	21.79	48	169,200	21.79
$27.02 - $40.97	63	666,750	36.32	62	449,150	36.15
$40.98 - $56.17	75	572,600	44.67	74	295,000	44.39
$56.18 - $71.03	86	347,000	71.03	86	107,000	71.03
$71.04 - $90.59	98	401,000	90.59	98	69,000	90.59
$90.60 - $112.07	110	246,000	112.07	-	-	-
$112.08 - $136.81	115	3,000	136.81	-	-	-
	78	2,429,550	58.76	67	1,113,350	42.39

The weighted average fair value of the share options granted during the years ended on the dates indicated below was estimated at the grant date based on the Black-Scholes option pricing model using the following assumptions:

	January 28, 2018	January 29, 2017
Exercise price per share	$112.36	$90.59
Dividend yield	0.4%	0.4%
Risk-free interest rate	1.2%	0.8%
Expected life	6.2 years	6.3 years
Expected volatility	20.4%	20.7%
Weighted average fair value of share options estimated at the grant date	$24.20	$18.91

The expected life is estimated using the average of the vesting period and the contractual life of the share options. Expected volatility is estimated based on weekly observations of the Corporation's publicly traded share price.

Dollarama Inc.
Notes to Consolidated Financial Statements
January 28, 2018 and January 29, 2017
(Expressed in thousands of Canadian dollars, unless otherwise noted)

12 Shareholders' equity (deficit) (cont'd)

d) Accumulated other comprehensive income (loss)

Components of accumulated other comprehensive income (loss) include unrealized gains (losses) on derivative financial instruments designated as hedging instruments, net of reclassification adjustments and income tax:

	January 28, 2018	January 29, 2017
	$	$
Accumulated other comprehensive income (loss) – beginning of year	(1,346)	69,795
Net change in fair value of foreign exchange forward contracts	(36,226)	(66,840)
Realized gains (losses) on foreign exchange forward contracts	(10,266)	16,108
Foreign exchange losses (gains) transferred to earnings	3,851	(46,269)
Income tax thereon	11,564	25,860
Total other comprehensive income (loss), net of income tax recovery	(31,077)	(71,141)
Accumulated other comprehensive income (loss) – end of year	(32,423)	(1,346)

e) Dividends

On March 30, 2017, the Corporation announced that its board of directors had approved a 10% increase of the quarterly dividend for holders of its common shares, from $0.10 per common share to $0.11 per common share.

f) Deficit

As at January 28, 2018, the deficit was $663,421 as a result of: 1) an opening deficit, as at January 30, 2017, of $342,957; 2) net earnings of $519,410; 3) dividends declared of $49,520; and 4) cash paid for the repurchase of common shares under the Corporation's normal course issuer bid of $790,354. The portion of the price paid by the Corporation to repurchase common shares that is in excess of their book value is recognized as a reduction in retained earnings or an increase in deficit, as applicable, whereas the portion of the price paid for the common shares that corresponds to the book value of those shares is recognized as a reduction of share capital. As a result, the Corporation's shareholders' equity (deficit) for accounting purposes was in a deficit position at $252,358 as at January 28, 2018.

Dollarama Inc.
Notes to Consolidated Financial Statements
January 28, 2018 and January 29, 2017
(Expressed in thousands of Canadian dollars, unless otherwise noted)

13 Income taxes

a) Deferred income taxes

The analysis of deferred tax assets and deferred tax liabilities is as follows:

	January 28, 2018 $	January 29, 2017 $
Deferred tax assets		
To be recovered after 12 months	25,204	21,977
To be recovered within 12 months	18,943	5,152
Deferred tax liabilities		
To be settled after 12 months	(154,481)	(144,777)
To be settled within 12 months	(2,326)	(189)
	(112,660)	(117,837)

Gross movement on the deferred income tax liability is as follows:

	January 28, 2018 $	January 29, 2017 $
Deferred income tax liability - beginning of year	117,837	127,592
Credited to consolidated statement of net earnings and comprehensive income (loss)	6,387	16,105
Tax recovery relating to components of other comprehensive income (loss)	(11,564)	(25,860)
Deferred income tax liability - end of year	112,660	117,837

Dollarama Inc.
Notes to Consolidated Financial Statements
January 28, 2018 and January 29, 2017
(Expressed in thousands of Canadian dollars, unless otherwise noted)

13 Income taxes (cont'd)

The significant movements in deferred income tax liabilities during the year, taking into consideration the offsetting of balances within the same tax jurisdiction, are as follows:

	Property, plant and equipment $	Intangible assets and goodwill $	Derivative financial instruments $	Total $
As at January 31, 2016	(27,554)	(104,351)	(18,060)	(149,965)
Charged to consolidated statement of net earnings and comprehensive income (loss)	(7,449)	(5,423)	(7,989)	(20,861)
Credited to components of other comprehensive income (loss)	-	-	25,860	25,860
As at January 29, 2017	(35,003)	(109,774)	(189)	(144,966)
Charged to consolidated statement of net earnings and comprehensive income (loss)	(4,884)	(4,820)	(1,751)	(11,455)
Credited to components of other comprehensive income (loss)	-	-	11,564	11,564
As at January 28, 2018	(39,887)	(114,594)	9,624	(144,857)

The significant movements in deferred income tax assets during the year, taking into consideration the offsetting of balances within the same tax jurisdiction, are as follows:

	Non deductible reserves $	Other liabilities $	Total $
As at January 31, 2016	3,063	19,310	22,373
Charged to consolidated statement of net earnings and comprehensive income (loss)	2,089	2,667	4,756
As at January 29, 2017	5,152	21,977	27,129
Charged to consolidated statement of net earnings and comprehensive income (loss)	1,841	3,227	5,068
As at January 28, 2018	6,993	25,204	32,197

Dollarama Inc.
Notes to Consolidated Financial Statements
January 28, 2018 and January 29, 2017
(Expressed in thousands of Canadian dollars, unless otherwise noted)

13 Income taxes (cont'd)

b) Income taxes

	January 28, 2018 $	January 29, 2017 $
Current tax expense in respect of the current year	189,978	150,686
Deferred tax expense relating to the origination and reversal of temporary differences	6,297	16,105
Income taxes	196,275	166,791

Tax on the Corporation's earnings before income taxes differs from the theoretical amount that would arise using the weighted average tax rate applicable to earnings of the consolidated entities as follows:

	January 28, 2018 $	January 29, 2017 $
Earnings before income taxes	715,685	612,427
Tax calculated at domestic rates applicable to income in Canada and the Canadian provinces	192,721	165,243
Tax effects of:		
Permanent differences	1,913	1,994
Settlement of previous year's tax assessments	(40)	(1,436)
Other	1,681	990
Tax expense	196,275	166,791

The income tax expense is recognized based on management's best estimate of the weighted average annual income tax rate expected for the full fiscal year. The statutory income tax rate for the year ended January 28, 2018 was 26.9% (January 29, 2017 – 27.0%). The Corporation's effective income tax rate for the year ended January 28, 2018 was 27.4% (January 29, 2017 – 27.2%).

Dollarama Inc.
Notes to Consolidated Financial Statements
January 28, 2018 and January 29, 2017
(Expressed in thousands of Canadian dollars, unless otherwise noted)

14   Financial instruments

Exposure and management of risk

The Corporation's activities expose it to a variety of financial risks: market risk (including currency risk, fair value interest rate risk and cash flow interest rate risk), credit risk and liquidity risk. The Corporation's overall risk management program focuses on the unpredictability of the financial market and seeks to minimize potential adverse effects on the Corporation's financial performance. The Corporation uses derivative financial instruments to hedge certain risk exposures.

Risk management is carried out by the finance department under practices approved by the board of directors of the Corporation. This department identifies, evaluates and hedges financial risks based on the requirements of the organization. The board of directors provides guidance for overall risk management, covering many areas of risk including but not limited to foreign exchange risk, interest rate risk, credit risk and the use of derivative financial instruments.

a)   Measurement categories

Financial assets and liabilities have been classified into categories that determine their basis of measurement and, for items measured at fair value, whether changes in fair value are recorded in the consolidated statement of net earnings and comprehensive income (loss). Those categories are, for assets, loans and receivables, as well as fair value through the consolidated statement of net earnings and comprehensive income (loss) and, for liabilities, amortized cost, as well as fair value through the consolidated statement of net earnings and comprehensive income (loss). The following table shows the carrying values of assets and liabilities for each of these categories as at:

	January 28, 2018	January 29, 2017
	$	$
Assets		
Loans and receivables		
Cash	54,844	62,015
Accounts receivable	15,263	15,386
Total loans and receivables	70,107	77,401
Fair value through profit or loss		
Total derivative financial instruments	286	8,787
Liabilities		
Amortized cost		
Trade payables and accrued liabilities	178,298	158,986
Dividend payable	12,180	11,591
Long-term debt	1,665,651	1,328,744
Total amortized cost	1,856,129	1,499,321
Fair value through profit or loss		
Total derivative financial instruments	35,720	8,085

Dollarama Inc.
Notes to Consolidated Financial Statements
January 28, 2018 and January 29, 2017
(Expressed in thousands of Canadian dollars, unless otherwise noted)

14 Financial instruments (cont'd)

b) Market risk

i. *Fair value*

The carrying amounts of financial instruments are presented in the consolidated statement of financial position at fair value or amortized cost according to the Corporation's accounting policies. Current financial assets and liabilities, which include cash, accounts receivable, and accounts payable and accrued liabilities, approximate fair values due to the immediate or short-term maturities of these financial instruments.

ii. *Hierarchy of assessments at fair value*

The three levels of fair value hierarchy under which the Corporation's financial instruments are valued are the following:

Level 1 – Quoted market prices in active markets for identical assets or liabilities;

Level 2 – Inputs other than quoted market prices included in Level 1 that are observable for the asset or liability, either directly (as prices) or indirectly (derived from prices); and

Level 3 – Inputs for the asset or liability that are not based on observable market data.

A summary of the aggregate contractual nominal value, average contract rate (or interest rate), statement of financial position location and estimated fair values of the Corporation's derivative financial instruments as at January 28, 2018 and January 29, 2017 follows:

	Contractual nominal value USD or CAD $	Average contract/ interest rate USD/CAD /interest rate	Statement of financial position Location	Fair value - Asset (Liability) Significant other observable inputs (Level 2) $	Nature of hedging relationship Recurring
As at January 28, 2018					
Hedging instruments					
CAD Bond forward sale contract	110,000	2.186%	Current assets	286	Cash flow hedge
USD Foreign exchange forward contracts	514,000	1.30	Current liabilities	(35,720)	Cash flow hedge
As at January 29, 2017					
Hedging instruments					
USD Foreign exchange forward contracts	215,000	1.28	Current assets	8,787	Cash flow hedge
USD Foreign exchange forward contracts	335,000	1.34	Current liabilities	(8,085)	Cash flow hedge
	550,000	1.31		702	

Dollarama Inc.
Notes to Consolidated Financial Statements
January 28, 2018 and January 29, 2017
(Expressed in thousands of Canadian dollars, unless otherwise noted)

14 Financial instruments (cont'd)

The Corporation formally documents the relationship between hedging instruments and hedged items, as well as its risk management objectives and strategies for undertaking hedging transactions.

Foreign exchange forward contracts are designated as hedging instruments and recorded at fair value, determined using market prices and other observable inputs. The Corporation designates its foreign exchange forward contracts as hedges of the variability in highly probable future cash flows attributable to a recognized forecasted transaction (cash flow hedges). The fair value of the foreign exchange forward contracts is determined using the forward exchange rates at the measurement date, with the resulting value discounted back to present values.

The bond forward sale contract is also designated as a hedging instrument and is recorded on the consolidated statement of financial position at fair value. The effective portion of the change in fair value of the derivative is recorded to other comprehensive income (loss), and will be reclassified to net earnings over the same period as the hedged interest payments are recorded in earnings. The hedged risk is defined as the variability in cash flows associated with coupons paid on the debt to be issued attributable to movements in the CAD benchmark rate. The CAD benchmark rate consists of the interpolated yield of Government of Canada bond curve with a term corresponding to the expected debt. Cash flows related to the expected bond's credit spread over the CAD benchmark rate are not designated as part of the hedging relationship. The debt is anticipated to be issued during the second, third or fourth quarter of the next fiscal year and have a term of between 2 and 7 years.

During the year ended January 28, 2018, a loss of $3,851 (January 29, 2017 - gain of $46,269) was reclassified from AOCI to net earnings. The Corporation has master netting agreements for the vast majority of derivative contracts but no amounts have been netted as at January 28, 2018 or January 29, 2017.

iii. _Interest rate risk_

The Corporation's interest rate risk arises from long-term debt. Long-term debt issued at variable rates exposes the Corporation to cash flow interest rate risk. Long-term debt issued at fixed rates exposes the Corporation to fair value interest rate risk.

When appropriate, the Corporation analyzes its interest rate risk exposure. Various scenarios are simulated, taking into consideration refinancing, renewal of existing positions, alternative financing and hedging. Based on these scenarios, the Corporation calculates the impact on earnings of a defined interest rate shift. The Corporation often uses variable-rate debt to finance a portion of its operations and capital expenditures. These obligations expose the Corporation to variability in interest payments due to changes in interest rates.

The Corporation's 3.095% Fixed Rate Notes, in the aggregate principal amount of $400,000, will mature on November 5, 2018. Assuming market conditions are favorable, the principal amount is expected to be refinanced at maturity by way of a new issuance of fixed rate senior unsecured notes. As such, the Corporation is exposed to the fluctuations of the Government of Canada benchmark yield until the issuance of the new notes. In order to manage its exposure to interest rate risk, the Corporation executed a bond forward sale of $110,000 in connection with the planned debt issuance.

Dollarama Inc.
Notes to Consolidated Financial Statements
January 28, 2018 and January 29, 2017
(Expressed in thousands of Canadian dollars, unless otherwise noted)

14 Financial instruments (cont'd)

As at January 28, 2018, the carrying value of the 2.203% Fixed Rate Notes was $250,186. The carrying value of the 2.203% Fixed Rate Notes was recognized initially at its fair value being $250,000 plus transaction costs, the total of which is referred to as the amortized cost

As at January 28, 2018, the carrying value of the 2.337% Fixed Rate Notes was $523,597. The carrying value of the 2.337% Fixed Rate Notes was recognized initially at its fair value being $525,000 plus transaction costs, the total of which is referred to as the amortized cost.

As at January 28, 2018, the carrying value of the 3.095% Fixed Rate Notes was $402,452. The carrying value of the 3.095% Fixed Rate Notes was recognized initially at its fair value being $400,000 plus transaction costs, the total of which is referred to as the amortized cost.

As at January 28, 2018, the carrying value of the Series 2 Floating Rate Notes was $300,066. The carrying value of the Series 2 Floating Rate Notes was recognized initially at its fair value being $300,000 plus transaction costs, the total of which is referred to as the amortized cost.

The fair value of the 2.203% Fixed Rate Notes, the 2.337% Fixed Rate Notes, the 3.095% Fixed Rate Notes and the Series 2 Floating Rate Notes (collectively, the "Senior Unsecured Notes") as at January 28, 2018 were determined to be $242,410, $519,246, $403,452 and $302,502, respectively. All are valued as a level 2 in the fair value hierarchy. The amortized cost of all Senior Unsecured Notes is measured using the effective interest rate method, which is the rate that exactly discounts estimated future cash payments of the Senior Unsecured Notes through the expected life until maturity.

As at January 28, 2018, a variation of 1% of the 3-month CDOR rate would, all other variables constant, have a favorable/unfavorable impact of approximately $3,600 on net earnings.

iv. *Foreign exchange risk*

The functional currency of the Corporation is the Canadian dollar ("CAD"). Because cash inflows are primarily denominated in Canadian dollars, the Corporation is exposed to the variability in the CAD/U.S. dollars ("USD") exchange rate when paying expenses with USD that relate to imported merchandise.

Foreign exchange forward contracts are entered into in order to manage the currency fluctuation risk associated with forecasted US dollar merchandise purchases sold in stores. These forward contracts are purchased for cash flow hedging as part of the Corporation's risk management process and are designated as the hedging item of highly probable future purchases of merchandise (the "hedged item").

At each reporting date, the Corporation performs an assessment of effectiveness of its cash flow hedges to ensure that the hedging relationship, between the hedging instrument and the hedged item, remains highly effective.

As at January 28, 2018, a variation in the CAD of 10% against the USD on monetary accounts in USD would, all other variables constant, have an approximate favorable/unfavorable impact of approximately $1,000 on net earnings.

Dollarama Inc.
Notes to Consolidated Financial Statements
January 28, 2018 and January 29, 2017
(Expressed in thousands of Canadian dollars, unless otherwise noted)

14 Financial instruments (cont'd)

c)   Credit risk

Credit risk is the risk of an unexpected loss if a third party fails to meet its contractual obligations. Financial instruments that potentially subject the Corporation to credit risk consist of cash, accounts receivable and derivative contracts.

The Corporation offsets the credit risk by depositing its cash, including restricted cash, with major financial institutions whom have been assigned high credit ratings by internationally recognized credit rating agencies.

The Corporation is exposed to credit risk on accounts receivable from landlords for tenant allowances and trade receivables from a third party. In order to mitigate this risk, the Corporation monitors credit risk and may retain offsetting payments until accounts receivable are fully satisfied.

Finally, the Corporation only enters into derivative contracts with major financial institutions for the purchase of USD forward contracts, as described above, and has master netting agreements in place for the vast majority of those derivative contracts.

d)   Liquidity risk

Liquidity risk is the risk that the Corporation will not be able to meet its obligations as they fall due.

The Corporation's funded debts are guaranteed by Dollarama L.P. and Dollarama GP Inc.

The Corporation's objective is to maintain sufficient liquidity to meet its financial liabilities as they become due and remain compliant with financial covenants under the Credit Facility and under the trust indenture governing the Senior Unsecured Notes. The Corporation manages liquidity risk through various means including, monitoring cash balances and planned cash flows generated from operations and used for investing in capital assets.

As at January 28, 2018, the Corporation had issued the 3.095% Fixed Rate Notes in the amount of $400,000 maturing November 5, 2018, the 2.337% Fixed Rate Notes in the amount of $525,000 maturing July 22, 2021, the 2.203% Fixed Rate Notes in the amount of $250,000 maturing November 10, 2022 and the Series 2 Floating Rate Notes in the amount of $300,000 maturing March 16, 2020. In addition, the Corporation had authorized and available credit in the amount of $307,941 under its Credit Facility (refer to Note 9).

Dollarama Inc.
Notes to Consolidated Financial Statements
January 28, 2018 and January 29, 2017
(Expressed in thousands of Canadian dollars, unless otherwise noted)

14 Financial instruments (cont'd)

The table below analyses the Corporation's non-derivative financial liabilities into relevant maturity groupings based on the remaining period from the statement of financial position date to the contractual maturity date. The amounts disclosed in the table are the contractual undiscounted cash flows as at January 28, 2018. Trade payables and accrued liabilities exclude liabilities that are not contractual (such as income tax liabilities that are created as a result of statutory requirements imposed by governments).

(dollars in thousands)	Less than 3 months $	3 months to 1 year $	1-5 years $	Total $
Trade payables and accrued liabilities	178,298	-	-	178,298
Dividend payable	12,180	-	-	12,180
Principal repayment on:				
2.203% Fixed Rate Notes	-	-	250,000	250,000
2.337% Fixed Rate Notes	-	-	525,000	525,000
3.095% Fixed Rate Notes	-	400,000	-	400,000
Series 2 Floating Rate Notes	-	-	300,000	300,000
Credit Facility	-	-	191,000	191,000
Interest payments on:				
2.203% Fixed Rate Notes	-	5,508	22,030	27,538
2.337% Fixed Rate Notes	-	12,269	30,673	42,942
3.095% Fixed Rate Notes	-	12,380	-	12,380
Credit Facility and Series 2 Floating Rate Notes [1]	3,188	9,564	30,379	43,131
	193,666	439,721	1,349,082	1,982,469

[1] Based on interest rates in effect as at January 28, 2018.

The following table summarizes the Corporation's off-balance sheet arrangements and commitments as at January 28, 2018.

(dollars in thousands)	Less than 3 months $	3 months to 1 year $	1-5 years $	Over 5 years $	Total $
Obligations under operating leases [2]	44,452	133,354	589,116	304,007	1,070,929
Letters of credit	1,059	-	-	-	1,059
	45,511	133,354	589,116	304,007	1,071,988

[2] Represent the basic annual rent, exclusive of the contingent rentals, common area maintenance, real estate taxes and other charges paid to landlords that, all together, represent approximately 40% of total lease expenses.

Dollarama Inc.
Notes to Consolidated Financial Statements
January 28, 2018 and January 29, 2017
(Expressed in thousands of Canadian dollars, unless otherwise noted)

14 Financial instruments (cont'd)

Other than operating leases obligations and letters of credit described above, the Corporation has no off-balance sheet arrangements or commitments.

e)   Capital management

The Corporation's capital structure consists of common shares, funded debt, share options to employees and directors, deficit and AOCI. The Corporation manages its capital structure and makes changes pursuant to economic conditions and conditions related to its assets.

	January 28, 2018 $	January 29, 2017 $
Total long-term debt (Note 9)	1,665,651	1,328,744
6x[1] operating leases (Note 10)	1,098,240	1,010,448
Adjusted total debt	2,763,891	2,339,192
EBITDA	826,112	703,258
Operating leases (Note 10)	183,040	168,408
EBITDAR	1,009,152	871,666
Adjusted total debt / EBITDAR	**2.74x**	**2.68x**

[1] The 6x factor is used by DBRS Limited in its rating methodology to account for the Corporation's operating leases in the calculation of adjusted total debt.

The Corporation monitors capital using a number of financial metrics, including but not limited to:

- the leverage ratio, defined as adjusted total debt (sum of (i) total long-term debt and (ii) 6x operating leases) over consolidated EBITDAR (sum of (i) earnings before interest, taxes, depreciation and amortization and (ii) operating leases).

The Corporation's objectives when managing capital are to:

- provide a strong capital base so as to maintain investor, creditor and market confidence and to sustain future development of the business;

- maintain a flexible capital structure that optimizes the cost of capital at acceptable risk and preserves the ability to meet financial obligations; and

- ensure sufficient liquidity to pursue its organic growth strategy.

Dollarama Inc.
Notes to Consolidated Financial Statements
January 28, 2018 and January 29, 2017
(Expressed in thousands of Canadian dollars, unless otherwise noted)

14 Financial instruments (cont'd)

In managing its capital structure, the Corporation monitors performance throughout the year to ensure working capital requirements are funded from operations, available cash on deposit and, where applicable, bank borrowings. The Corporation manages its capital structure and may make adjustments to it in order to support the broader corporate strategy or in response to changes in economic conditions and risk. In order to maintain or adjust its capital structure, the Corporation may: issue shares or new debt; issue new debt to replace existing debt (with different characteristics); reduce the amount of existing debt; purchase shares for cancellation under a normal course issuer bid; and adjust the amount of dividends paid to shareholders.

The Corporation is subject to financial covenants under the Credit Facility and the trust indenture governing the Senior Unsecured Notes, which are measured on a quarterly basis. These covenants include a leverage ratio and an interest coverage ratio. As at January 28, 2018, the Corporation was in compliance with all such covenants.

15 Related party transactions

Rent

Rental expenses charged by entities controlled by a director totalled $18,361 for the year ended January 28, 2018 (January 29, 2017- $18,055).

These transactions were measured at cost, which equals fair value, being the amount of consideration established at market terms.

Compensation of key management and directors

Key management includes the Corporation's Executive Chairman, President and Chief Executive Officer, Chief Financial Officer, Chief Operating Officer, and Senior Vice-President, Import Division.

The remuneration paid to directors and members of key management personnel as well as share-based payments during the years ended on the dates indicated below were as follows:

	January 28, 2018 $	January 29, 2017 $
Short-term benefits	10,087	12,862
Defined contribution plan	53	64
Share-based payments	4,027	4,089
	14,167	17,015

Dollarama Inc.
Notes to Consolidated Financial Statements
January 28, 2018 and January 29, 2017
(Expressed in thousands of Canadian dollars, unless otherwise noted)

15 Related party transactions (cont'd)

Members of key management may have employment agreements with clauses providing for payment in the event of termination without cause or constructive termination. Please refer to Dollarama's 2017 Management Proxy Circular for details applicable to the Corporation's five most highly compensated executive officers.

16 Earnings per share

a) Basic

Basic earnings per common share is calculated by dividing the profit attributable to shareholders of the Corporation by the weighted average number of common shares outstanding during the year.

	January 28, 2018	January 29, 2017
Net earnings attributable to shareholders of the Corporation	$519,410	$445,636
Weighted average number of common shares outstanding during the year (*thousands*)	112,751	118,998
Basic net earnings per common share	$4.61	$3.75

b) Diluted

Diluted earnings per share is calculated by adjusting the weighted average number of common shares outstanding to assume conversion of all dilutive potential common shares. For the share options, the Corporation's only category of dilutive potential common shares, a calculation is performed to determine the number of shares that could have been acquired at fair value (determined as the average annual market share price of the Corporation's shares) based on the exercise price of outstanding share options. The number of shares as calculated above is then compared with the number of shares that would have been issued assuming the exercise of the share options, plus any unrecognized compensation costs.

	January 28, 2018	January 29, 2017
Net earnings attributable to shareholders of the Corporation and used to determine basic and diluted net earnings per common share	$519,410	$445,636
Weighted average number of common shares outstanding during the year (*thousands*)	112,751	118,998
Assumed share options exercised (*thousands*)	1,422	1,245
Weighted average number of common shares for diluted net earnings per common share (*thousands*)	114,173	120,243
Diluted net earnings per common share	$4.55	$3.71

Dollarama Inc.
Notes to Consolidated Financial Statements
January 28, 2018 and January 29, 2017
(Expressed in thousands of Canadian dollars, unless otherwise noted)

17 Expenses by nature included in the consolidated statement of net earnings and comprehensive income (loss)

	January 28, 2018 $	January 29, 2017 $
Cost of sales		
Cost of goods sold, labour, transport and other costs	1,665,771	1,523,272
Occupancy costs	299,400	278,663
Total cost of sales	1,965,171	1,801,935
Depreciation and amortization		
Depreciation of property, plant and equipment (Note 6)	57,918	48,208
Amortization of intangible assets (Note 7)	12,632	9,540
Total depreciation and amortization	70,550	57,748
Employee benefits		
Remuneration for services rendered	345,824	330,338
Share options granted to directors and employees (Note 12)	6,559	6,932
Defined contribution plan	4,830	4,426
Total employee benefit expense	357,213	341,696
Financing costs		
Interest expense and banking fees	37,860	31,602
Amortization of debt issue costs	2,017	1,481
Total financing costs	39,877	33,083

Dollarama Inc.
Notes to Consolidated Financial Statements
January 28, 2018 and January 29, 2017
(Expressed in thousands of Canadian dollars, unless otherwise noted)

18 Consolidated statement of cash flows information

The changes in non-cash working capital components on the dates indicated below are as follows:

	January 28, 2018	January 29, 2017
	$	$
Accounts receivable	124	(4,268)
Prepaid expenses	(1,487)	1,738
Inventories	(25,212)	4,480
Accounts payable and accrued liabilities	29,553	23,496
Income taxes payable	22,894	(29,041)
	25,872	(3,595)
Cash paid for taxes	166,970	179,019
Cash paid for interest	34,907	28,133

Cash paid for taxes and interest are cash flows used in operating activities.

19 Events after the reporting period

Increase of quarterly dividend

On March 29, 2018, the Corporation announced that its board of directors had approved a 9% increase of the quarterly dividend for holders of common shares, from $0.11 per common share to $0.12 per common share. This increased quarterly dividend will be paid on May 2, 2018 to shareholders of record at the close of business on April 20, 2018 and is designated as an "eligible dividend" for Canadian tax purposes.

Proposed three-for-one share split

On March 29, 2018, the Corporation announced that its board of directors had approved a proposed three-for-one share split, subject to approval by shareholders at the annual and special meeting to be held on June 7, 2018 and to requirements of the TSX. Assuming the split is approved by shareholders and pre-cleared by the TSX, shareholders of record at the close of business on June 14, 2018 will be entitled to receive, on or about June 19, 2018, two additional common shares for each common share held.

Expansion of distribution capacity

The Corporation has launched a project to expand its existing distribution centre located in the Town of Mount Royal, Quebec. As part of this expansion, the Corporation has incurred costs to date of $23,222 (see Note 6) for the purchase of two adjacent properties and $39,372, paid subsequent to January 28, 2018, for the purchase of its existing distribution centre, which was previously leased from an entity controlled by the Rossy family. This last purchase was a related-party transaction at fair value, being the amount of consideration established at market terms, based on an independent appraisal.

Dollarama Inc.
Notes to Consolidated Financial Statements
January 28, 2018 and January 29, 2017
(Expressed in thousands of Canadian dollars, unless otherwise noted)

19 Events after the reporting period (cont'd)

Offering of senior unsecured notes

On February 1, 2018, the Corporation issued series 3 floating rate senior unsecured notes due February 1, 2021 (the "Series 3 Floating Rate Notes") at par, for aggregate gross proceeds of $300,000, by way of private placement in reliance upon exemptions from the prospectus requirements under applicable securities legislation. Proceeds were used by the Corporation to repay indebtedness outstanding under the Credit Facility and for general corporate purposes. The Series 3 Floating Rate Notes were assigned a rating of BBB, with a stable trend, by DBRS Limited. The Series 3 Floating Rate Notes bear interest at a rate equal to the 3-month bankers' acceptance rate (CDOR) plus 27 basis points (or 0.27%), set quarterly on the 1st day of February, May, August and November of each year. Interest is payable in cash quarterly, in arrears, over the 3-year term on the 1st day of February, May, August and November of each year.

Investments and the Time Value of Money

SPOTLIGHT

ONEX Corporation holds several different types of investments. Have you ever wondered what you will do with all the money you will be earning once you graduate? Maybe you will start investing through a retirement or savings plan at work, and you may make some investments on your own. The reasons people invest are for current income (interest and dividends) and for appreciation of the investment's value (stocks and real estate, for example). Some very wealthy individuals invest in a wide variety of traditional and non-traditional investments in order to obtain significant influence over, or even to control, corporate entities and to maximize their wealth.

Businesses like ONEX, Dollarama, and TELUS invest their money for the same reasons. If you look at ONEX's balance sheet on the next page, you will see that of the $44,679 million of total assets they own, they have $12,114 million in long-term investments. This increased from the 2016 balance of $8,672 million. In 2016, they held $154 million in short-term investments but in 2017, the balance is $258 million. This means they bought some of their short-term investments and some of their long-term investments. In this chapter you'll learn how to account for investments of all types.

LEARNING OBJECTIVES

1. **Analyze** and **report** non-strategic investments
2. **Analyze** and **report** strategic investments
3. **Analyze** and **report** long-term investments in bonds
4. **Report** investing activities on the statement of cash flows
5. **Explain** the impact of the time value of money on certain types of investments

CPA COMPETENCIES

Competencies addressed in this chapter:

1.2.2 Evaluates treatment for routine transactions

5.1.1 Evaluates the entity's financial state

Based on Chartered Professional Accountant standards

	A	B	C	D
1	**ONEX Corporation** Consolidated Balance Sheet (Partial, Adapted) As at December 31, 2017 and 2016			
2	*(in millions of U.S. dollars)*			
3	**Assets**	**2017**	**2016**	
4	**Current assets**			
5	Cash and cash equivalents	$ 3,376	$ 2,371	
6	Short-term investments	258	154	
7	Accounts receivable	3,306	3,868	
8	Inventories	2,506	2,731	
9	Other current assets	862	1,190	
10	Total current assets	$ 10,308	$ 10,314	
11				
12	Property, plant, and equipment	5,326	4,275	
13	Long-term investments	12,114	8,672	
14	Other non-current assets	821	1,192	
15	Intangible assets	7,887	9,286	
16	Goodwill	8,223	9,174	
17	**Total Assets**	$ 44,679	$ 42,913	
18				

Source: ONEX Management's Discussion and Analysis and Financial Statements.

Founded in 1983, ONEX is an investment firm that buys significant interests in companies with the intention of controlling their operations. Once a company is acquired, they work with the company's management to help them become a leader in their industry. The many companies ONEX has acquired significant control of include Celestica and Cineplex. These investments are reflected in various asset accounts, such as inventory; property, plant, and equipment; and goodwill. In addition, ONEX has long-term investments.

Throughout this course, you have become increasingly familiar with the financial statements of companies such as Dollarama Inc., Leon's Furniture, and CGI Group. You have seen most of the items that appear in a set of financial statements. One of your learning goals should be to develop the ability to interpret whatever you encounter in real-company statements. This Appendix will help you advance toward that goal.

The first part of this Appendix shows how to account for non-strategic and strategic investments, including a brief overview of consolidated financial statements. The second half of this Appendix covers accounting for the time value of money.

Share Investments: A Review

Investments come in all sizes and shapes—ranging from a few shares to the acquisition of an entire company, to interests in other types of investments, such as corporate bonds. In this chapter, we will introduce you to the accounting for various types of investments from the perspective of the purchaser, or investor.

To consider investments, we need to define two key terms. The entity that owns shares in a corporation is the *investor*. The corporation that issued the shares is the *investee*. If you own ONEX common shares, you are an investor and ONEX is the investee.

Share Prices

Investors buy more shares in transactions among themselves than directly from large companies, such as ONEX. Each share is issued only once, but it may be traded

EXHIBIT B-1
Share Price Information for ONEX Corporation

Source: Based on the data taken from ONEX Corporation Annual Information Form.

52-Week		Stock	
Hi	Lo	Symbol	Div
$99.82	$80.80	ONEX	0.30

among investors many times thereafter. You may log onto the Internet or consult a newspaper to learn ONEX's current share price.

Exhibit B-1 presents information on ONEX common shares from a popular financial website for November 27, 2018. During the previous 52 weeks, ONEX shares reached a high price of $99.82 and a low price of $80.80 per share. The annual cash dividend is $0.30 per share.

Reporting Investments on the Balance Sheet

An investment is an asset to the investor. The investment may be short term or long term. *Short-term investments* are current assets and are sometimes called *temporary investments* or *marketable securities*. To be listed as short term on the balance sheet,

- the investment must be *liquid* (readily convertible to cash).
- the investor must intend either to convert the investment to cash within one year or to use it to pay a current liability.

Investments that are not short term are classified as **long-term investments**, a category of non-current assets. Long-term investments include shares and bonds that the investor expects to hold for longer than one year. Exhibit B-2 shows the positions of short-term and long-term investments on the balance sheet.

	A	B	C	D
1	**Current assets:**			
2	Cash	$ X		
3	**Short-term investments**	X		
4	Accounts receivable	X		
5	Inventories	X		
6	Prepaid expenses	X		
7	Total current assets		$ X	
8	**Long-term investments [or simply Investments]**		X	
9	Property, plant, and equipment (net)		X	
10	Intangible assets (net)		X	
11	Other assets		X	
12				

EXHIBIT B-2
Reporting Investments on the Balance Sheet

Accounting for Investments in Shares

This topic is normally covered in an intermediate or advanced accounting course. Accordingly, the following discussion is intended to provide you with a basic understanding of investments. There are two categories of share investments: non-strategic and strategic investments.

1. *Non-strategic investments.* **Non-strategic investments** may be short-term or long-term depending on how long the company intends to hold them. For the long-term investment, if the investor owns less than but up to 20% of the voting shares of the investee, usually the investor has little or no influence on the investee, in which case the strategy would be to hold the investment in periods

beyond the end of the fiscal year. For these investments, the investor records the investment at the price paid and adjusts the investment account for changes in fair value either through net income (current assets) or through other comprehensive income (current or long-term assets).

2. *Strategic investments.*

   a. *Investments subject to significant influence.* An investor owning between 20% and 50% of the investee's voting shares or other ownership interests may significantly influence the business activities of the investee. Significant influence allows the investor to direct the affairs of the investee. Such an investor can probably affect dividend policies, product lines, and other important matters. The investor accounts for the investment using the *equity method* by which the investor's proportionate share of the investee's profits and losses are treated as income or loss by the investor. The investor's share of dividends paid by the investee are treated as a return of investment and are credited to the investment account.

   b. *Investments in subsidiaries.* A subsidiary is a company controlled by another company (the parent), which is entitled to the rewards and bears the risks of the subsidiary. Generally a parent will own more than 50% of the voting shares of the subsidiary. Such an investment allows the investor to elect a majority of the members of the investee's board of directors and thus control the investee's policies, such as its production, distribution (supply chain), financing, and investing decisions. The financial statements of the investee are consolidated with those of the investor.

OBJECTIVE

❶ **Analyze** and **report** non-strategic investments

ANALYZE AND REPORT NON-STRATEGIC INVESTMENTS

As mentioned previously, a non-strategic investment may be short-term or long-term; the investor will hold the investment to earn dividend revenue and/or capital appreciation but has no interest in directing the affairs of the investee. In the case of a long-term investment, the investor usually holds less than 20% of the voting shares and would normally play no important role in the investee's operations.

Non-strategic investments are accounted for at fair value because the company expects to sell the investment at its current market price. The investment is recorded at the price paid and reported on the balance sheet at *fair value*.

Suppose ONEX purchases 1,000 Agrium Inc. common shares at the market price of $50.00 on July 10, 2020 and has no significant influence over Agrium. The company intends to hold this investment for longer than a year. This type of investment is classified as a non-strategic investment. ONEX's entry to record the investment is:

	A	B	C	D	E
1	2020				
2	July 10	Investment in Agrium (1,000 × $50.00)	50,000		
3		Cash		50,000	
4		*Purchased investment.*			
5					

ASSETS	=	LIABILITIES	+	SHAREHOLDERS' EQUITY
+50,000 −50,000	=	0	+	0

Assume on October 5, 2020 that ONEX receives a $0.14 per share cash dividend on the Agrium Inc. shares. ONEX's entry to record receipt of the dividend is:

	A	B	C	D	E
1	2020				
2	Oct. 5	Cash (1,000 × $0.14)	140		
3		Dividend Revenue		140	
4		*Received cash dividend.*			
5					

ASSETS	=	LIABILITIES	+	SHAREHOLDERS' EQUITY
140	=	0	+	+ 140 Revenue

The journal entries given in the example above would be the same for a short-term investment.

What Value of an Investment Is Most Relevant?

Fair value is the amount for which you can buy or sell an investment. Because of the relevance of fair values for decision making, non-strategic investments in shares are reported on the balance sheet at their fair value. On the balance sheet date we therefore adjust non-strategic investments from their last carrying amount to current fair value. Assume that the fair value of the Agrium common shares is $53,000 on December 31, 2020. At initial recognition the investor can choose to report the changes in fair value in non-strategic investments either through net income or through other comprehensive income. For held for trading investments, the changes in fair value are reported through net income. Shown below are the journal entries to report changes in fair value under both approaches.

Changes in fair value in the investment are reported through net income:		Changes in fair value in the investment are reported through other comprehensive income:	
Investment in Agrium	3,000	Investment in Agrium	3,000
Unrealized gain	3,000	Other Comprehensive Income	3,000
Adjusted investment to fair value.		Adjusted investment to fair value.	
Unrealized gains are reported under "Other Income" on the Income statement.		Other Comprehensive Income is reported below net income on the statement of comprehensive income.	

The increase in the investment's fair value creates additional equity for the investor.

ASSETS	=	LIABILITIES	+	SHAREHOLDERS' EQUITY
+3,000	=	0	+	+3,000 Unrealized gain

The Investment in Agrium account and the Other Comprehensive Income or Unrealized Gain account would appear as follows:

Investment in Agrium	Other Comprehensive Income or Unrealized Gain
50,000	
3,000	3,000

If the investment's fair value declines, the Investment in Agrium account is credited. The corresponding debit is to Other Comprehensive Income or Unrealized Loss. *Unrealized* gains and losses result from changes in fair value, not from sales of investments.

Unrealized gains and unrealized losses on non-strategic investments (not held for short-term trading) that occur in a fiscal year are reported in two places in the financial statements:

- *Other Comprehensive Income* is reported in a separate section below net income on the *statement of comprehensive income*. For example, assume the Consolidated Statement of Comprehensive Income section of Leon's Furniture Limited's 2017 annual report states:

  Other Comprehensive Income, Net of Tax
    Unrealized Gain on Financial Assets Arising
      During the Year (Net of Tax of $45).. $223

- *Accumulated Other Comprehensive Income*, which is a separate section of shareholders' equity below retained earnings on the *balance sheet*. The Shareholders' Equity section of the Leon's Furniture Limited's 2017 balance sheet reports:

  Accumulated Other Comprehensive Income .... $(142)

At December 31, 2020, ONEX would close the Other Comprehensive Income account to the shareholders' equity account Accumulated Other Comprehensive Income as follows:

	A	B	C	D	E
1	2020				
2	Dec. 31	Other Comprehensive Income	3,000		
3		Accumulated Other Comprehensive Income		3,000	
4		*To close out the unrealized gain on the investment to accumulated other comprehensive income.*			
5					

If the company chooses to recognize the changes in fair value in the investment through income (called profit or loss), unrealized gains or unrealized losses would be used instead of other comprehensive income. These unrealized gains and losses are reported under Other Income on the income statement.

Selling a Non-Strategic Investment

The sale of a non-strategic investment can result in a *realized* gain or loss. Realized gains and losses measure the difference between the amount received from the sale of the investment and the carrying amount of the investment.

Suppose ONEX sells its investment in Agrium Inc. shares for $57,000 during 2018. ONEX would record the sale as follows:

Changes in fair value in the investment are reported through net income:		Changes in fair value in the investment are reported through other comprehensive income:	
Cash	57,000	Cash	57,000
Investment in Agrium		Investment in Agrium	53,000
Investment	53,000	Other Comprehensive Income	4,000
Gain on Sale of Investment	4,000		
Realized gains and losses are reported under "Other Income" on the income statement.		Realized gains are reported under Other Comprehensive Income on the statement of comprehensive income.	

ANALYZE AND REPORT STRATEGIC INVESTMENTS

An investor who holds less than 20% of the investee's voting shares usually plays no important role in the investee's operations. But an investor with a larger share holding—between 20% and 50% of the investee's voting shares—may significantly influence how the investee operates the business. Such an investor can probably affect the investee's decisions on dividend policy, product lines, and other important matters. The investor will also likely hold one or more seats on the board of directors of the investee company. We use the **equity method** to account for these types of investments.

Accounting for Investments Using the Equity Method

Investments accounted for by the equity method are recorded initially at cost. Suppose NPC Corporation paid $611 million for 32% of the common shares of Bruce Power. NPC's entry to record the purchase of this investment is (in millions):

	A	B	C	D	E
1	2020				
2	Jan. 2	Investment in Bruce Power	611		
3		Cash		611	
4		*To purchase equity investment.*			
5					

$$
\begin{array}{ccccc}
\textbf{ASSETS} & = & \textbf{LIABILITIES} & + & \textbf{SHAREHOLDERS' EQUITY} \\
\begin{array}{c} +611 \\ -611 \end{array} & = & 0 & + & 0
\end{array}
$$

THE INVESTOR'S PERCENTAGE OF INVESTEE INCOME. Under the equity method, NPC, as the investor, applies its percentage of ownership (32% in our example) in recording its share of the investee's net income. Suppose Bruce reports net income of $100 million for 2020; NPC would record 32% of this amount as follows (in millions):

	A	B	C	D	E
1	2020				
2	Dec. 31	Investment in Bruce Power ($100 × 0.32)	32		
3		Investment Revenue		32	
4		*To record investment revenue.*			
5					

$$
\begin{array}{ccccc}
\textbf{ASSETS} & = & \textbf{LIABILITIES} & + & \textbf{SHAREHOLDERS' EQUITY} \\
32 & = & 0 & + & +\,32\ \text{Revenue}
\end{array}
$$

Because of the close relationship between NPC and Bruce, the investor increases the Investment in Bruce Power account and records Investment Revenue when the investee reports income. As Bruce's equity increases, so does the Investment account on NPC's books.

RECEIVING DIVIDENDS UNDER THE EQUITY METHOD. NPC Corporation records its proportionate part of cash dividends received from Bruce. Assume Bruce declares and pays a cash dividend of $9,375,000. NPC receives 32% of this dividend and records this entry (in millions):

	A	B	C	D	E
1	Dec. 31	Cash ($9,375,000 × 0.32)	3		
2		Investment in Bruce Power		3	
3		*To receive cash dividend on equity investment.*			
4					

ASSETS	=	LIABILITIES	+	SHAREHOLDERS' EQUITY
3	=	0	+	0
−3				

The Investment in Bruce Power account is *decreased* for the receipt of a dividend on an equity method investment. Why? Because the dividend decreases the investee's equity and thus the investor's investment.

After the preceding entries are posted, NPC's Investment in Bruce Power account would include its equity in the net assets of Bruce as follows (in millions):

Investment in Bruce Power

2020	Jan. 2	Purchase	611	Dec. 31	Dividends	3
	Dec. 31	Net income	32			
	Dec. 31	Balance	640			

NPC reports Investment in Bruce Power as a long-term investment on the balance sheet and the investment revenue on the income statement as follows:

	(in millions)
Balance sheet (partial):	
Assets	
Total current assets	$XXX
Long-term investments	640
Property, plant, and equipment, net	XXX
Income statement (partial):	
Income from operations	$XXX
Other revenue:	
Revenue from equity investments	32
Net income	$XXX

The gain or loss on the sale of an equity-method investment is measured as the difference between the sale proceeds and the carrying amount of the investment. For example, NPC Corporation's financial statements show that the investment in Bruce Power at December 31, 2020, was $640 million. Suppose NPC sold 10% of its interest in Bruce Power on January 10, 2021, for $62 million. The entry to record the sale would be:

	A	B	C	D	E
1	2021				
2	Jan. 10	Cash	62		
3		Loss on Sale of Investment	2		
4		Investment in Bruce Power ($640 million × 0.10)		64	
5		*Sold 10% of investment.*			
6					

ASSETS	=	LIABILITIES	+	SHAREHOLDERS' EQUITY
62	=	0	+	− 2 Loss
−64				

When there has been a loss in value in an equity investment other than a temporary decline, the investment is written down to reflect the loss. This is different than adjusting the value to fair value, which is done whether the decline is temporary or not.

SUMMARY OF THE EQUITY METHOD. The following T-account illustrates the accounting for equity-method investments.

Equity-Method Investment	
Original cost	Share of losses
Share of income	Share of dividends
Balance	

Analyze and Report Controlling Interests in other Corporations Using Consolidated Financial Statements

Companies buy a significant stake in another company to *influence* the other company's operations. In this section, we cover the situation in which a corporation buys enough of another company to actually *control* that company.

Why Buy Another Company?

Most large corporations own controlling interests in other companies. A **controlling (or majority) interest** is the ownership of usually more than 50% of the investee's voting shares. Such an investment enables the investor to elect a majority of the members of the investee's board of directors and thus control the investee. The investor is called the **parent company**, and the investee company is called the **subsidiary company**. For example, ONEX Partners is a subsidiary of ONEX, the parent. Therefore, the shareholders of ONEX control ONEX Partners, as shown in Exhibit B-3.

EXHIBIT B-3
Ownership Structure of ONEX Partners and ONEX

Consolidation Accounting

Consolidation accounting is a method of combining the financial statements of all the companies controlled by the same parent company. This method reports a single set of financial statements for the consolidated entity, which carries the name of the parent company. Exhibit B-4 summarizes the accounting methods used for long-term share investments.

Percentage of Ownership	Accounting Method
Less than 20% (no influence)	Fair Value
20% to 50% (significant influence)	Equity
Greater than 50% (control)	Consolidation

EXHIBIT B-4
Accounting Methods for Long-Term Investments

Consolidated statements combine the balance sheets, income statements, and other financial statements of the parent company with those of its subsidiaries. The result is as if the parent and its subsidiaries were one company. Users can gain a better perspective on total operations than they could by examining the reports of the parent and each individual subsidiary separately.

In consolidated financial statements, the assets, liabilities, revenues, and expenses of each subsidiary are added to the parent's accounts. For example, the balance in the Cash account of ONEX Partners is added to the balance in the ONEX Cash account, and the sum of the two amounts is presented as a single amount in the ONEX consolidated balance sheet at the beginning of the chapter. Each account balance of a subsidiary loses its identity in the consolidated statements, which bear the name of the parent company, ONEX.

The Consolidated Balance Sheet and the Related Work Sheet

Suppose ONEX purchased 52% of the outstanding common shares of another Canadian company. Both ONEX and that Canadian company keep separate sets of books. ONEX, the parent company, uses a work sheet to prepare the consolidated statements of ONEX and its consolidated subsidiaries. Then ONEX's consolidated balance sheet shows the combined assets and liabilities of ONEX and all its subsidiaries.

Exhibit B-5 shows the work sheet for consolidating the balance sheets of Parent Corporation and Subsidiary Corporation. We use these hypothetical entities to illustrate the consolidation process. Consider elimination entry (a) for the parent-subsidiary ownership accounts. Entry (a) credits the parent's Investment account to eliminate its debit balance. Entry (a) also eliminates the subsidiary's shareholders' equity accounts by debiting the subsidiary's Common Shares and Retained Earnings for their full balances. Without this elimination, the consolidated financial statements would include both the parent company's investment in the subsidiary and the subsidiary company's equity. But these accounts represent the same thing—Subsidiary's equity—and so they must be eliminated from the consolidated totals. If they weren't, the same resources would be counted twice.

EXHIBIT B-5
Work Sheet for a Consolidated Balance Sheet

	A	B	C	D	E	F	G
1		Parent Corporation	Subsidiary Corporation	Eliminations		Parent and Subsidiary Consolidated Amounts	
1				Debit	Credit		
2	**Assets**						
3	Cash	12,000	18,000			30,000	
4	Note receivable from Subsidiary	80,000			(b) 80,000		
5	Inventory	104,000	91,000			195,000	
6	Investment in Subsidiary	150,000			(a) 150,000		
7	Other assets	218,000	138,000			356,000	
8	Total	564,000	247,000			581,000	
9	**Liabilities and Shareholders' Equity**						
10	Accounts payable	43,000	17,000			60,000	
11	Notes payable	190,000	80,000	(b) 80,000		190,000	
12	Common shares	176,000	100,000	(a) 100,000		176,000	
13	Retained earnings	155,000	50,000	(a) 50,000		155,000	
14	Total	564,000	247,000	230,000	230,000	581,000	
15							

The resulting Parent and Subsidiary consolidated balance sheet (far-right column) reports no Investment in Subsidiary account. Moreover, the consolidated totals for Common Shares and Retained Earnings are those of Parent Corporation only. Study the final column of the consolidation work sheet.

In this example, Parent Corporation has an $80,000 note receivable from Subsidiary, and Subsidiary has a note payable to Parent. The parent's receivable and the subsidiary's payable represent the same resources—all entirely within the consolidated entity. Both, therefore, must be eliminated, and entry (b) accomplishes this.

- The $80,000 credit in the Elimination column of the work sheet zeros out Parent's Note Receivable from Subsidiary.
- The $80,000 debit in the Elimination column zeros out the Subsidiary's Note Payable to Parent.
- The resulting consolidated amount for notes payable is the amount owed to creditors outside the consolidated entity, which is appropriate.

After the work sheet is complete, the consolidated amount for each account represents the total asset, liability, and equity amounts controlled by Parent Corporation.

Goodwill and Non-Controlling Interests

Goodwill and Non-Controlling Interests are two accounts that only a consolidated entity can have. *Goodwill*, which we studied in Chapter 6 (see p. 302), arises when a parent company pays more to acquire a subsidiary company than the fair value of the subsidiary's net assets. As we saw in Chapter 6, goodwill is the intangible asset that represents the parent company's excess payment to acquire the subsidiary. ONEX reports goodwill of $8,223 million on its December 31, 2017, balance sheet.

Non-controlling interest arises when a parent company purchases less than 100% of the shares of a subsidiary company. For example, ONEX owns less than 100% of some of the companies it controls. The remainder of the subsidiaries' shares is a non-controlling interest to ONEX. Non-controlling interest is included within shareholders' equity on the balance sheet of the parent company. ONEX reports non-controlling interest on its balance sheet in the amount of $2,128 (millions).

Income of a Consolidated Entity

The income of the parent company is combined with the income of each subsidiary beginning with sales revenue. All intercompany sales and expenses are eliminated, but that is a subject for an advanced accounting text. The following example is a very simplified version of a complex topic. Suppose Parent Company owns all the shares of Subsidiary S-1 and 60% of the shares of Subsidiary S-2. During the year just ended, Parent earned net income of $330,000, S-1 earned $150,000, and S-2 had a net loss of $100,000. Parent Company would report net income of $420,000, computed as follows:

	Net Income (Loss) of Each Company		Parent's Ownership of Each Company		Parent's Consolidated Net Income
Parent Company.............................	$ 330,000	×	100%	=	$ 330,000
Subsidiary S-1	150,000	×	100%	=	150,000
Subsidiary S-2	(100,000)	×	60%	=	(60,000)
Consolidated net income.................					$ 420,000

OBJECTIVE

❸ **Analyze** and report long-term investments in bonds

ANALYZE AND REPORT LONG-TERM INVESTMENTS IN BONDS

Another type of non-strategic investment is when a company buys bonds. The major investors in bonds are financial institutions, pension plans, mutual funds, and insurance companies, such as Manulife Financial Corporation. The relationship between the issuing corporation and the investor (bondholder) may be diagrammed as follows:

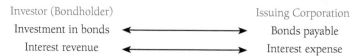

An investment in bonds is classified either as short term (a current asset) or as long term. Short-term investments in bonds are rare. Here, we focus on long-term investments in bonds.

Bonds of public companies are traded on the open market, just as shares are. Bonds are usually issued in $1,000 face (par) denominations, but they typically do not sell at par value. Market prices of bonds fluctuate with market interest rates. If market rates on competing instruments are higher than the interest the company is paying on a particular bond, the bond sells at a discount (below 100% of par, or face value). For example, a quoted bond price of 96.5 means that the $1,000 bond is selling for 96.5% of par, or $965. If market rates are lower, the bond sells at a premium (above 100% of par)—a quoted bond price of 102.5 means that the bond is selling for 102.5% of par, or $1,025 (a premium over par). Bondholders receive interest, usually semi-annually.

IFRS require bond investments that are held to maturity and whose objective is to collect payments and interest to be valued at amortized cost, which determines the carrying amount. **Bond investments** are initially recorded at cost (market price as a percentage × par value of bonds issued). At each semi-annual interest payment date, the investor records interest revenue. In addition, whenever there is a premium or discount on the bond, it is amortized by adjusting the carrying amount of the bond upward or downward toward its par or face value. The amortization of the discount or premium is calculated using the effective interest method (see Chapter 7).

Suppose an investor purchases $100,000 of 5% Government of Canada bonds at a price of $95,735 on June 1, 2020. The bonds pay interest on June 1 and December 1. The investor intends to hold the bonds until their maturity on June 2, 2025. The bonds will be outstanding for five years (10 interest periods). The investor paid a discounted price for the bonds of $95,735 (an effective interest rate of 6%). The investor must amortize the bonds' carrying amount from cost of $95,735 up to $100,000 over their term to maturity. The following are the entries for this long-term investment:

	A	B	C	D	E
1	2020				
2	June 1	Long-Term Investment in Bonds ($100,000 × 95.735)	95,735		
3		Cash		95,735	
4		*To purchase bond investment.*			
5	Dec. 1	Cash ($100,000 × 0.05 × 1/2)	2,500		
6		Interest Revenue		2,500	
7		*To receive semi-annual interest.*			
8		Long-Term Investment in Bonds ([$95,735 × 0.06 × 1/2] − $2,500)	372*		
9		Interest Revenue		372*	
10		*To amortize bond investment.*			
11					

*Rounded

At December 31, the year-end adjustments are:

	A	B	C	D	E
1	Dec. 31	Interest Receivable ($100,000 × 0.05 × 1/12)	417*		
2		Interest Revenue		417*	
3		*To accrue interest revenue.*			
4	Dec. 31	Long-Term Investment in Bonds ([$96,108 × 0.06 × 1/12] − $417)	64*		
5		Interest Revenue		64*	
6		*To amortize bond investment.*			
7					

*Rounded

This amortization entry has two effects:

1. It increases the Long-Term Investment account on its march toward maturity value.
2. It increases the interest by the amount of the increase in the carrying amount of the investment.

The financial statements at December 31, 2020, report the following for this investment in bonds:

Balance sheet at December 31, 2020:

Current assets:

Interest receivable .... $ 417

Long-term investments in bonds ($95,735 + $373 + $64) 96,172

Property, plant, and equipment.. X, XXX

Income statement for the year ended December 31, 2020:

Other revenues:

Interest revenue ($2,500 + $372 + $417 + $64)... $ 3,353

STOP + THINK (B-1)

Suppose that on January 1, 2020, Microsport, Inc. purchased $120,000 face value of the 9% bonds of Service Express, Inc. at 104. The bonds mature on January 1, 2025. How much cash interest would Microsport receive on December 31, 2023?

 # DECISION GUIDELINES

ACCOUNTING METHODS FOR INVESTMENTS

These guidelines show which accounting method to use for each type of investment. A company can have all types of investments—shares, bonds, 25% interests, and controlling interests. How should a company account for its various investments?

Type of Investment	Accounting Method
Non-strategic investments	Fair value
Significantly influenced investments	Equity method
Controlled investments	Consolidation
Investment in bonds	Amortized cost

As we have seen in this chapter, investments may be bought in order to earn either dividend revenue and/or capital appreciation (called *non-strategic*), or they are bought with the intent to significantly influence or control the company's operations (referred to as *strategic*). Let's see how investments are used in decision making.

Decision	Guidelines
Who uses investments in decision making, and why?	*Managers* buy investments with one or more of these intentions in mind. If the company has excess cash on hand, they may decide to invest this cash in a non-strategic investment rather than have it sit in a bank account where it earns little interest. On the other hand, the company may decide to buy another company's shares with a plan to be involved in the company's operations.
	Investors might consider the type of investment. If the investment was non-strategic, they would look at the statements and notes to see whether or not the investment increased or decreased in value and the amount of dividend revenue the company received. If it was a strategic investment, the investor would look to see whether or not this investment generated a reasonable profit for the company.
	Creditors are always looking to see if a company would be a good candidate for a loan and whether there was sufficient profit from operations or investment income to cover current and potentially increased interest costs.

MyLab Accounting

MID-CHAPTER SUMMARY PROBLEM

1. Identify the appropriate accounting method for each of the following long-term investment situations:
   a. Investment in 25% of investee's shares
   b. 10% investment in shares
   c. Investment in more than 50% of investee's shares
2. At what amount should the following long-term investment portfolio be reported on the June 30, 2020, balance sheet? All the investments are less than 5% of the investee's shares and are classified as non-strategic. The investor chooses to record any changes in fair value through other comprehensive income.

Shares	Investment Cost	Fair Value
Bank of Montreal	$75,000	$52,000
Canadian Tire Corp.	24,000	31,000
Jean Coutu Group	32,000	36,000

Journalize any adjusting entry required by these data.
3. Investor Corporation paid $67,900 to acquire a 40% equity-method investment in the common shares of Investee Corporation. At the end of the first year, Investee's net income was $80,000, and Investee declared and paid cash dividends of $55,000. What is Investor's ending balance in its Equity-Method Investment account? Use a T-account to answer.

ANSWERS

For investments:
Less than 20%→Fair value;
20% to 50%→Equity;
Greater than 50%→Consolidation

1. a. Equity
   b. Fair value
   c. Consolidation

2. Report the investments at fair value ($119,000) as follows:

Shares	Investment Cost	Fair Value
Bank of Montreal	$ 75,000	$ 52,000
Canadian Tire	24,000	31,000
Jean Coutu Group	32,000	36,000
Totals	$131,000	$119,000

> Determine the fair value for each investment in the portfolio. Then create the journal entry for any change from investment cost to current fair value.

Adjusting entry:

Other Comprehensive Income ($131,000 − $119,000)....................................	12,000	
Long-Term Investments		12,000
To adjust investments to current fair value.		

3. Equity-Method Investment

Equity-Method Investment			
Cost	67,900	Dividends	22,000**
Income	32,000*		
Balance	77,900		

*$80,000 × 0.40 = $32,000
**$55,000 × 0.40 = $22,000

> The Equity-Method Investment T-account includes:
> 100% of the cost of the investment
> +40% of the investee's net income
> −40% of the investee's cash dividends

REPORT INVESTING ACTIVITIES ON THE STATEMENT OF CASH FLOWS

Investing activities include many types of transactions. In Chapter 6, we covered investing transactions in which companies purchase and sell long-lived assets, such as property, plant, and equipment. In this appendix, we examined long-term investments in shares and bonds. These are also investing activities reported on the statement of cash flows.

Investing activities are usually reported on the statement of cash flows as the second category, after operating activities and before financing activities. Exhibit B-6

OBJECTIVE

4 **Report** investing activities on the statement of cash flows

	A	B	C	D
1	**ONEX Corporation** Consolidated Statement of Cash Flows (Partial, Adapted) For the Year Ended December 31, 2017			
2	*(in millions of U.S. dollars)*			
3	**Investing Activities**			
4	Acquisition of operating companies	$ (974)		
5	Purchase of property, plant, and equipment	(722)		
6	Cash interest received	367		
7	Increase due to other investing activities	2,252		
8	Cash flows used in investing activities of discontinued operations	(240)		
9		$ 683		
10				

EXHIBIT B-6
ONEX Corporation Consolidated Statement of Cash Flows

Source: ONEX Management's Discussion and Analysis and Financial Statements.

provides excerpts from ONEX's statement of cash flows. During 2017, ONEX spent $722 million on new property, plant, and equipment and $974 million to acquire other companies. They also received $367 million in interest from their investments. Alternatively, ONEX could also have reported the interest and dividends as an operating activity. Overall, cash flows provided from investing activities was $683 million.

STOP + THINK (B-2)

Examine Exhibit B-6. Where did the company spend most of its cash?

OBJECTIVE

⑤ Explain the impact of the time value of money on certain types of investments

EXPLAIN THE IMPACT OF THE TIME VALUE OF MONEY ON CERTAIN TYPES OF INVESTMENTS

Future Value

Which would you rather receive: $1,000 today, or $1,000 a year from today? A logical person would answer: "I'd rather have the cash now, because if I get it now, I can invest it so that a year from now I'll have more." The term **future value** means the amount of money that a given current investment will be worth at a specified time in the future, assuming a certain interest rate. The term *time value of money* refers to the fact that money earns interest over time. *Interest* is the cost of using money. To borrowers, interest is the fee paid to the lender for the period of the loan. To lenders, interest is the revenue earned from allowing someone else to use our money for a period of time.

Whether making investments or borrowing money, we must always recognize the interest we receive or pay. Otherwise, we overlook an important part of the transaction. Suppose you invest $4,545 in corporate bonds that pay 10% interest each year. After one year, the value of your investment has grown to $5,000, as shown in the following diagram:

End of Year	Interest	Future Value
0	—	$4,545
1	$4,545 × 0.10 = $455	5,000
2	5,000 × 0.10 = 500	5,500
3	5,500 × 0.10 = 550	6,050
4	6,050 × 0.10 = 605	6,655
5	6,655 × 0.10 = 666	7,321

The difference between your original investment (present value of $4,545) and the future value of the investment ($5,000) is the amount of interest revenue you will earn during the year ($455). Interest becomes more important as the time period lengthens because the amount of interest depends on the span of time the money is invested. The time value of money plays a key role in measuring the value of certain long-term investments, as well as long-term debt.

If the money were invested for five years, you would have to perform five calculations like the one described above. You would also have to consider the compound interest that your investment is earning. *Compound interest* is not only the interest you earn on your principal amount, but also the interest you receive on the interest you have already earned. Most business applications include compound interest.

To calculate the future value of an investment, we need three inputs: (1) the *amount of initial payment (or receipt)*, (2) the length of *time* between investment and future receipt (or *payment*), and (3) the *interest rate*. The table above shows the interest revenue earned on the original $4,545 investment each year for five years at 10%. At the end of five years, your initial $4,545 investment will be worth $7,321.

Present Value

Often a person knows or is able to estimate a future amount and needs to determine the related present value (PV). The term **present value** means the value on a given date of a future payment or series of future payments, discounted to reflect the time value of money. In Exhibit B-7, present value and future value are on opposite ends of the same timeline. Suppose an investment promises to pay you $5,000 at the *end* of one year. How much would you pay *now* to acquire this investment? You would be willing to pay the present value of the $5,000 future amount, which, at 10% interest, is $4,545.

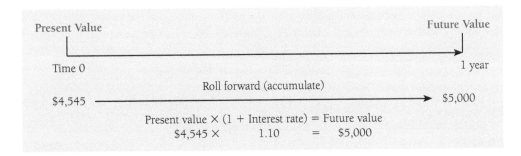

EXHIBIT B-7
Future Value of an Investment

Like future value, present value depends on three factors: (1) the *amount of payment (or receipt)*, (2) the length of *time* between investment and future receipt (or *payment*), and (3) the *interest rate*. The process of computing a present value is called *discounting* because the present value is *less* than the future value.

In our investment example, the future receipt is $5,000. The investment period is one year. Assume that you demand an annual interest rate of 10% on your investment. With all three factors specified, you can compute the present value of $5,000 at 10% for one year:

$$\text{Present value} = \frac{\text{Future value}}{1 + \text{Interest rate}} = \frac{\$5,000}{1.10} = \$4,545$$

By turning the data around into a future-value problem, we can verify the present-value computation:

Amount invested (present value)	$4,545
Expected earnings ($4,545 × 0.10)..	455
Amount to be received one year from now (future value)	$5,000

This example illustrates that present value and future value are based on variations of the same equation:

$$\text{Future value} = \text{Present value} \times (1 + \text{Interest rate})^n$$

$$\text{Present value} = \frac{\text{Future value}}{(1 + \text{Interest rate})^n}$$

$$\text{where } n = \text{number of periods}$$

If the $5,000 is to be received two years from now, you will pay only $4,132 for the investment, as shown in Exhibit B-8. By turning the data around, we verify that $4,132 accumulates to $5,000 at 10% for two years:

Amount invested (present value)	$4,132
Expected earnings for first year ($4,132 × 0.10)	413
Value of investment after one year	4,545
Expected earnings for second year ($4,545 × 0.10)	455
Amount to be received two years from now (future value)	$5,000

$$\text{Formula: Present value} = \frac{\text{Future value}}{(1 + \text{Interest rate})^n}$$

$$4,132 = \frac{5,000}{(1 + 0.10)^2}$$

$$\text{Future value} = \text{Present value} \times (1 + \text{Interest rate})^n$$

$$5,000 = \$4,132 \times (1 + 0.10)^2$$

EXHIBIT B-8
Present Value: An Example

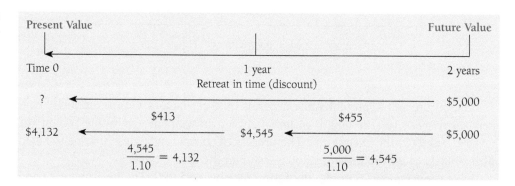

You would pay $4,132—the present value of $5,000—to receive the $5,000 future amount at the end of two years at 10% per year. The $868 difference between the amount invested ($4,132) and the amount to be received ($5,000) is the return on the investment, the sum of the two interest receipts: $413 + $455 = $868.

Present-Value Tables

We have shown the simple formula for computing present value. However, figuring present value "by hand" for investments spanning many years is time-consuming and presents too many opportunities for arithmetic errors. Present-value tables simplify our work. Let's re-examine our examples of present value by using Exhibit B-9, Present Value of $1.

For the 10% investment for one year, we find the junction of the 10% column and row 3 in Exhibit B-9. The figure 0.909 is computed as follows: 1/1.10 = 0.909. This work has been done for us, and only the present values are given in the table. To figure the present value for $5,000, we multiply 0.909 by $5,000. The result is $4,545, which matches the result we obtained by hand.

	A	B	C	D	E	F	G	H	I	J	K
1					Present Value of $1						
2	Period	4%	5%	6%	7%	8%	10%	12%	14%	16%	
3	1	0.962	0.952	0.943	0.935	0.926	0.909	0.893	0.877	0.862	
4	2	0.925	0.907	0.890	0.873	0.857	0.826	0.797	0.769	0.743	
5	3	0.889	0.864	0.840	0.816	0.794	0.751	0.712	0.675	0.641	
6	4	0.855	0.823	0.792	0.763	0.735	0.683	0.636	0.592	0.552	
7	5	0.822	0.784	0.747	0.713	0.681	0.621	0.567	0.519	0.476	
8	6	0.790	0.746	0.705	0.666	0.630	0.564	0.507	0.456	0.410	
9	7	0.760	0.711	0.665	0.623	0.583	0.513	0.452	0.400	0.354	
10	8	0.731	0.677	0.627	0.582	0.540	0.467	0.404	0.351	0.305	
11	9	0.703	0.645	0.592	0.544	0.500	0.424	0.361	0.308	0.263	
12	10	0.676	0.614	0.558	0.508	0.463	0.386	0.322	0.270	0.227	
13	11	0.650	0.585	0.527	0.475	0.429	0.350	0.287	0.237	0.195	
14	12	0.625	0.557	0.497	0.444	0.397	0.319	0.257	0.208	0.168	
15	13	0.601	0.530	0.469	0.415	0.368	0.290	0.229	0.182	0.145	
16	14	0.577	0.505	0.442	0.388	0.340	0.263	0.205	0.160	0.125	
17	15	0.555	0.481	0.417	0.362	0.315	0.239	0.183	0.140	0.108	
18	16	0.534	0.458	0.394	0.339	0.292	0.218	0.163	0.123	0.093	
19	17	0.513	0.436	0.371	0.317	0.270	0.198	0.146	0.108	0.080	
20	18	0.494	0.416	0.350	0.296	0.250	0.180	0.130	0.095	0.069	
21	19	0.475	0.396	0.331	0.277	0.232	0.164	0.116	0.083	0.060	
22	20	0.456	0.377	0.312	0.258	0.215	0.149	0.104	0.073	0.051	
23											

For the two-year investment, we read down the 10% column and across row 4. We multiply 0.826 (computed as 0.909/1.10 = 0.826) by $5,000 and get $4,130, which confirms our earlier computation of $4,132 (the difference is due to rounding in the present-value table). Using the table, we can compute the present value of any single future amount.

Present Value of an Annuity

Return to Exhibit B-8 on page 650. That investment provided the investor with only a single future receipt ($5,000 at the end of two years). *Annuity investments* provide multiple receipts of an equal amount at fixed intervals over the investment's duration.

Consider an investment that promises *annual* cash receipts of $10,000 to be received at the end of each of three years. Assume that you demand a 12% return on your investment. What is the investment's present value? That is, what would you pay today to acquire the investment? The investment spans three periods, and you would pay the sum of three present values. The computation follows.

Year	Annual Cash Receipt	Present Value of $1 at 12% (Exhibit B-9)	Present Value of Annual Cash Receipt
1	$10,000	0.893	$ 8,930
2	10,000	0.797	7,970
3	10,000	0.712	7,120
Total present value of investment............................			$24,020

The present value of this annuity is $24,020. By paying this amount today, you will receive $10,000 at the end of each of the three years while earning 12% on your investment.

EXHIBIT B-10
Present Value of Annuity of $1

	A	B	C	D	E	F	G	H	I	J	K
1					Present Value of Annuity of $1						
2	Period	4%	5%	6%	7%	8%	10%	12%	14%	16%	
3	1	0.962	0.952	0.943	0.935	0.926	0.909	0.893	0.877	0.862	
4	2	1.886	1.859	1.833	1.808	1.783	1.736	1.690	1.647	1.605	
5	3	2.775	2.723	2.673	2.624	2.577	2.487	2.402	2.322	2.246	
6	4	3.630	3.546	3.465	3.387	3.312	3.170	3.037	2.914	2.798	
7	5	4.452	4.329	4.212	4.100	3.993	3.791	3.605	3.433	3.274	
8	6	5.242	5.076	4.917	4.767	4.623	4.355	4.111	3.889	3.685	
9	7	6.002	5.786	5.582	5.389	5.206	4.868	4.564	4.288	4.039	
10	8	6.733	6.463	6.210	5.971	5.747	5.335	4.968	4.639	4.344	
11	9	7.435	7.108	6.802	6.515	6.247	5.759	5.328	4.946	4.608	
12	10	8.111	7.722	7.360	7.024	6.710	6.145	5.650	5.216	4.833	
13	11	8.760	8.306	7.887	7.499	7.139	6.495	5.938	5.453	5.029	
14	12	9.385	8.863	8.384	7.943	7.536	6.814	6.194	5.660	5.197	
15	13	9.986	9.394	8.853	8.358	7.904	7.103	6.424	5.842	5.342	
16	14	10.563	9.899	9.295	8.745	8.244	7.367	6.628	6.002	5.468	
17	15	11.118	10.380	9.712	9.108	8.559	7.606	6.811	6.142	5.575	
18	16	11.652	10.838	10.106	9.447	8.851	7.824	6.974	6.265	5.669	
19	17	12.166	11.274	10.477	9.763	9.122	8.022	7.120	6.373	5.749	
20	18	12.659	11.690	10.828	10.059	9.372	8.201	7.250	6.467	5.818	
21	19	13.134	12.085	11.158	10.336	9.604	8.365	7.366	6.550	5.877	
22	20	13.590	12.462	11.470	10.594	9.818	8.514	7.469	6.623	5.929	
23											

This example illustrates repetitive computations of the three future amounts, a time-consuming process. One way to ease the computational burden is to add the three present values of $1 (0.893 + 0.797 + 0.712) and multiply their sum (2.402) by the annual cash receipt ($10,000) to obtain the present value of the annuity ($10,000 × 2.402 = $24,020).

An easier approach is to use a present-value-of-an-annuity table. Exhibit B-10 shows the present value of $1 to be received periodically for a given number of periods. The present value of a three-period annuity at 12% is 2.402 (the junction of row 5 and the 12% column). Thus, $10,000 received annually at the end of each of three years, discounted at 12%, is $24,020 ($10,000 × 2.402), which is the present value.

Using Present Value to Compute the Fair Value of Investments

Recall that, at the end of each year, investors are required to adjust the portfolio of non-strategic investments to fair values. Some types of investments (publicly traded shares and bonds) have quoted prices in active markets. Determining fair value for these investments is easy: merely obtain the quoted price from the financial media (usually the Internet or the *Globe and Mail* on the year-end). Other types of non-traditional investments (e.g., notes, non-publicly traded bonds or shares, contracts, annuities) may not have daily quoted market prices in active markets. Therefore, the company may use financial models that predict expected cash flows from these investments over a period of time and discount those cash flows back to the balance sheet date.

Using Microsoft Excel to Calculate Present Value

While tables such as Exhibits B-9 and B-10 are helpful, they are limited to the interest rates in the columns or the periods of time in the rows. Using a computer program like Microsoft Excel provides an infinite range of interest rates and periods. For that reason, most business people solve present-value problems quickly and easily using Excel rather than tables.

- *To compute the present value of a single payment*, the following formula applies:

$$= \text{Payment}/(1 + i)^n$$
$$\text{where } i = \text{interest rate}$$
$$n = \text{number of period}$$

- In Excel, we use the ^ symbol to indicate the exponent. To illustrate, suppose you are expecting to receive a $500,000 payment four years from now, and suppose that market interest rates are 8%. You would enter the following formula in Excel:

$$= 500000/(1.08)^4$$

You should calculate a present value of $367,514.93 (rounded to $367,515).

- *To compute the present value of an annuity (stream of payments)*, open an Excel spreadsheet to a blank cell. Click the insert function button (f_x). Then select the "Financial" category from the drop-down box. The following box will appear:

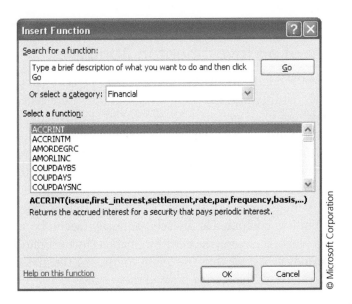

Scroll down the function list and select "PV." A description of the PV function will display beneath the function list, along with the following line: **PV (rate, nper, pmt, fv, type)**. Double-click PV, and the following box will appear:

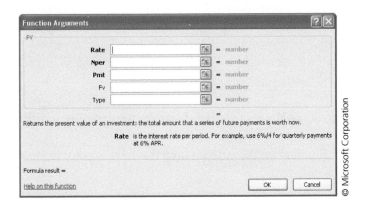

Enter the interest rate, the number of periods, and the payment (as a negative number). The present value of the annuity will appear at the bottom of the box after the "=" sign.

To illustrate, notice that we have assumed an investment that is expected to return $20,000 per year for 20 years and a market interest rate of 8%. The net present value of this annuity (rounded to the nearest cent) is $196,362.95, computed with Excel as follows:

MyLab Accounting

Try It in Excel: Net Present Value

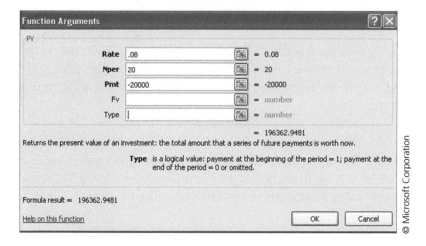

Present Value of an Investment in Bonds

The present value of a bond—its market price—is the present value of the future principal amount at maturity plus the present value of the future stated interest payments. The principal is a *single amount* to be received by the investor and paid by the debtor at maturity. The interest is an *annuity* because it occurs periodically.

Let's compute the present value of 9% five-year bonds of Air Canada from the standpoint of an investor. The face value of the bonds is $100,000, and the face interest rate is 9% annually. Because bonds typically pay interest twice per year, these bonds pay 4 1/2% semi-annually. At issuance, the market interest rate is assumed to be 10% annually, but it is computed at 5% semi-annually (again, because the bonds pay interest twice a year). Therefore, the effective (market) interest rate for each of the 10 semi-annual periods is 5%. We thus use 5% in computing the present value of the maturity and of the interest. The market price of these bonds is $96,149, as follows:

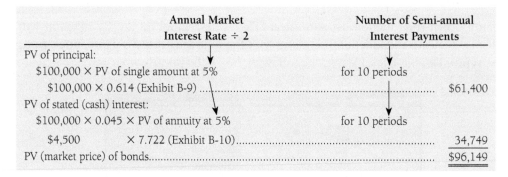

	Annual Market Interest Rate ÷ 2	Number of Semi-annual Interest Payments	
PV of principal:			
$100,000 × PV of single amount at 5%		for 10 periods	
$100,000 × 0.614 (Exhibit B-9)			$61,400
PV of stated (cash) interest:			
$100,000 × 0.045 × PV of annuity at 5%		for 10 periods	
$4,500 × 7.722 (Exhibit B-10)			34,749
PV (market price) of bonds			$96,149

The fair value of the Air Canada bonds on the investor's balance sheet would be $96,149.*

We discuss accounting for these bonds from the debtor's point of view in Chapter 7.

---

*The process of estimating fair value using discounted cash flow models is similar for all types of investments.

STOP + THINK (B-3)

What would the present value of $5,000 be at the end of eight years if the interest was 5%?

Summary of IFRS-ASPE Differences

Concepts	IFRS	ASPE
Non-strategic investments (p. 636)	These investments are reported at fair value, with unrealized and realized gains and losses reported in net income (short-term investments), unless the company elects to report them in other comprehensive income (short-term and long-term investments).	These investments are reported at fair value, with unrealized and realized gains and losses reported in net income.
Strategic investments (a) Investments subject to significant influence (p. 639)	A company shall apply the equity method to account for these investments.	A company may choose to apply either the equity method or the cost method. If the share investments are quoted in an active market, then the fair value method replaces the cost method as an option, with any changes in fair value reported through net income.
(b) Investments in controlled subsidiaries (p. 641)	A company shall consolidate its financial statements with those of its subsidiaries.	A company may choose to account for its subsidiaries using the cost method, the equity method, or the consolidation method. If share investments are quoted in an active market, then the fair value method replaces the cost method, with any changes in fair value reported through net income.
Amortization of the discount or premium relating to long-term investments in bonds (p. 644)	The effective-interest method must be used to amortize discounts and premiums.	The straight-line method or the effective-interest method may be used to amortize discounts and premiums.

SUMMARY

SUMMARY OF LEARNING OBJECTIVES

LEARNING OBJECTIVE	SUMMARY
❶ **Analyze** and **report** non-strategic investments	Non-strategic investments are initially recorded at cost and subsequently reported on the balance sheet at fair value. Any changes in value are recorded through net income (profit or loss, short-term investments) or under "other comprehensive income" (short-term or long-term investments). The cost method is used for investments where the market price is not available.

2 Analyze and report strategic investments

If the company (investor) owns between 20% and 50% of the voting shares of the investee and exercises significant influence over the investee, the equity method is used to account for the investment. This means that the investor recognizes their share of the investee's net income as their own. The investor's share of dividends is treated as a return of investment. If the company (investor) owns more than 50% of the investee's shares and exercises control over the investee, the financial statements of the investee are consolidated (combined) with those of the investor. The result is as if the parent and subsidiary are one company. Goodwill and Non-controlling interest are two accounts that only a consolidated entity would have. Goodwill results when a company pays more for the subsidiary company than the fair value of the subsidiary's net assets. Non-controlling interest occurs when a company buys less than 100% of the company they control.

3 **Analyze** and **report** long-term investment in bonds

When a company buys a long-term investment in bonds, they are recorded at the price paid. When there is a premium or discount, the bonds are amortized to account for interest revenue and the bond's carrying amount. These bonds are reported on the balance sheet at its amortized cost.

4 **Report** investing activities on the statement of cash flows

Buying and selling long-term investments in shares and bonds are reported under investing activities.

5 **Explain** the impact of the time value of money on certain types of investments

Time value of money refers to the fact that money earns interest over time, and it plays a key role in measuring the value of certain long-term investments as well as long-term debt. Interest is the cost of using money. The difference between your original (present) investment and the future value of the investment is the amount of interest revenue you will earn.

MyLab Accounting

END-OF-CHAPTER SUMMARY PROBLEM

Suppose Parent Company paid $85,000 for all of the common shares of Subsidiary Company, and Parent owes Subsidiary $20,000 on a note payable.

Requirements:

Compete the following consolidation worksheet.

	A	B	C	D	E	F	G
1		Parent Corporation	Subsidiary Corporation	Eliminations		Parent and Subsidiary Consolidated Amounts	
1				Debit	Credit		
2	**Assets**						
3	Cash	7,000	4,000				
4	Note receivable from Subsidiary		20,000				
5	Investment in Subsidiary	85,000					
6	Other assets	108,000	99,000				
7	Total	200,000	123,000				
8	**Liabilities and Shareholders' Equity**						
9	Accounts payable	15,000	8,000				
10	Notes payable	20,000	30,000				
11	Common shares	120,000	60,000				
12	Retained earnings	45,000	25,000				
13	Total	200,000	123,000				
14							

ANSWER

	A	B	C	D	E	F	G
1		Parent Corporation	Subsidiary Corporation	Eliminations		Parent and Subsidiary Consolidated Amounts	
				Debit	Credit		
2	**Assets**						
3	Cash	7,000	4,000			11,000	
4	Note receivable from Subsidiary		20,000		(a) 20,000		
5	Investment in Subsidiary	85,000			(b) 85,000		
6	Other assets	108,000	99,000			207,000	
7	Total	200,000	123,000			218,000	
8	**Liabilities and Shareholders' Equity**						
9	Accounts payable	15,000	8,000			23,000	
10	Notes payable	20,000	30,000	(a) 20,000		30,000	
11	Common shares	120,000	60,000	(b) 60,000		120,000	
12	Retained earnings	45,000	25,000	(b) 25,000		45,000	
13	Total	200,000	123,000	105,000	105,000	218,000	
14							

REVIEW

MyLab Accounting

Make the grade with MyLab Accounting: The Quick Quiz questions, Short Exercises, Exercises, and Problems (Group A) marked with a ⊕ can be found on MyLab Accounting. You can practise them as often as you want, and most feature step-by-step guided instructions to help you find the right answer.

QUICK QUIZ (ANSWERS APPEAR ON THE LAST PAGE OF THIS CHAPTER.)

1. A company's investment in less than 1% of GE's shares, ⊕ which it expects to hold for two years and then sell, is which type of investment?
   a. Strategic
   b. Equity
   c. Non-strategic
   d. Consolidation

2. DuBois Corporation purchased a non-strategic investment ⊕ in 1,000 shares of Scotiabank (BNS) for $31 per share. On the next balance sheet date, BNS is quoted at $35 per share. DuBois's *balance sheet* should report

   a. unrealized loss of $4,000.
   b. unrealized gain of $31,000.
   c. investments of $31,000.
   d. investments of $35,000.

3. Use the DuBois Corporation data in question 2. The ⊕ company reports changes in fair value through net income DuBois's *income statement* should report
   a. unrealized gain of $4,000.
   b. unrealized loss of $4,000.
   c. investments of $31,000.
   d. nothing because DuBois hasn't sold the investment.

4. Use the DuBois Corporation data in question 2. DuBois sold the Scotiabank shares for $40,000 the following year. DuBois's *income statement* should report
   a. unrealized gain of $4,000.
   b. gain on sale of $9,000.
   c. gain on sale of $5,000.
   d. investments of $40,000.

5. Alexander Moving & Storage Inc. paid $100,000 for 20% of the common shares of Sellers Ltd. Sellers earned net income of $50,000 and paid dividends of $25,000. Alexander accounts for the investment using the equity method. The carrying value of Alexander's investment in Sellers is
   a. $100,000.
   b. $105,000.
   c. $125,000.
   d. $150,000.

6. Tarrant Inc. owns 80% of Rockwall Corporation, and Rockwall owns 80% of Kaufman Company. During 2020, these companies' net incomes are as follows before any consolidations:
   • Tarrant, $100,000
   • Rockwall, $68,000
   • Kaufman, $40,000

   How much net income should Tarrant report for 2020?
   a. $100,000
   b. $164,000
   c. $180,000
   d. $204,000

7. TRULINE Inc. holds an investment in Manulife bonds that pay interest each June 30. TRULINE's *balance sheet* at December 31 should report
   a. interest receivable.
   b. interest payable.
   c. interest revenue.
   d. interest expense.

8. Consolidation accounting
   a. combines the accounts of the parent company and those of the subsidiary companies.
   b. eliminates all liabilities.
   c. reports the receivables and payables of the parent company only.
   d. All of the above.

9. On January 1, 2020, Vallée Bleue Ltée purchased $100,000 face value of the 7% bonds of Mail Frontier Inc. at 105. Interest is paid on January 1. The bonds mature on January 1, 2021. For the year ended December 31, 2020, Vallée Bleu received cash interest of
   a. $5,000.
   b. $6,000.
   c. $6,400.
   d. $7,000.

10. Return to Vallée Bleue's bond investment in question 9. Assume an effective interest rate of 6%. For the year ended December 31, 2020, Vallée Bleu earned interest revenue of
   a. $5,000.
   b. $6,300.
   c. $7,000.
   d. $7,700.

ACCOUNTING VOCABULARY

bond investments Bonds and notes are debt instruments that an investor intends to hold until maturity.   (p. 644)

consolidated statements Financial statements of the parent company plus those of majority-owned subsidiaries as if the combination were a single legal entity.   (p. 641)

controlling (majority) interest Ownership of more than 50% of an investee company's voting shares and can exercise control over the investee.   (p. 641)

equity method The method used to account for investments in which the investor has 20–50% of the investee's voting shares and can significantly influence the decisions of the investee.   (p. 639)

future value Measures the future sum of money that a given current investment is "worth" at a specified time in the future, assuming a certain interest rate.   (p. 648)

long-term investments Any investment that does not meet the criteria of a short-term investment; any investment that the investor expects to hold for longer than a year.   (p. 635)

majority interest Ownership of more than 50% of an investee company's voting shares.   (p. 641)

non-controlling interest A subsidiary company's equity that is held by shareholders other than the parent company.   (p. 643)

non-strategic investments Investments in which the investor owns less than 20% of the voting shares of the investee and is presumed to exercise no influence.   (p. 635)

parent company An investor company that owns more than 50% of the voting shares of a subsidiary company.   (p. 641)

present value The value on a given date of a future payment or series of future payments, discounted to reflect the time value of money.   (p. 649)

strategic investments Investments in which the investor owns more than 20% of the voting shares of the investee and is presumed to exercise either significant influence or control over the investee.   (p. 636)

subsidiary company An investee company in which a parent company owns more than 50% of the voting shares and can exercise control over the subsidiary.   (p. 641)

ASSESS YOUR PROGRESS

SHORT EXERCISES

SB-1 Assume Knowlton Holdings Ltd. completed these long-term non-strategic investment transactions during 2020:

LEARNING OBJECTIVE ❶

Analyze and report a non-strategic investment

2020		
Feb.	10	Purchased 300 shares of BCE, paying $25 per share.
		Knowlton intends to hold the investment for the indefinite future.
Dec.	1	Received a cash dividend of $0.36 per share on the BCE shares.
Dec.	31	Adjusted the BCE investment to its current fair value of $7,000.

1. Journalize Knowlton's investment transactions assuming the company reports any changes in fair value through other comprehensive income. Explanations are not required.
2. Show how to report the investment and any unrealized gain or loss on Knowlton's balance sheet at December 31, 2020. Ignore income tax.

SB-2 Use the data given in exercise SB-1. On May 19, 2021, Knowlton sold its investment in BCE shares for $26 per share.

LEARNING OBJECTIVE ❶

Account for the sale of a non-strategic investment

1. Journalize the sale. No explanation is required.
2. How does the gain or loss that you recorded here differ from the gain or loss that was recorded at December 31, 2020?

SB-3 Suppose on February 1, 2020, General Motors paid $41 million for a 40% investment in ABC Ltd., an auto parts manufacturer. Assume ABC earned net income of $6 million and paid cash dividends of $2 million during 2020.

LEARNING OBJECTIVE ❷

Analyze and report a 40% investment in another company

1. What method should General Motors use to account for the investment in ABC? Give your reason.
2. Journalize these three transactions on the books of General Motors. Show all amounts in millions of dollars, and include an explanation for each entry.
3. Post to the Long-Term Investment T-account. What is its balance after all the transactions are posted?

SB-4 Use the data given in exercise SB-3. Assume that in November 2021, General Motors sold half its investment in ABC to Toyota. The sale price was $14 million. Compute General Motors's gain or loss on the sale.

LEARNING OBJECTIVE ❷

Account for the sale of an equity-method investment

SB-5 Answer these questions about consolidation accounting:

LEARNING OBJECTIVE ❷

Understand consolidated financial statements

1. Define *parent company*. Define *subsidiary company*.
2. How do consolidated financial statements differ from the financial statements of a single company?
3. Which company's name appears on the consolidated financial statements? How much of the subsidiary's shares must the parent own before reporting consolidated statements?

SB-6 Two accounts that arise from consolidation accounting are Goodwill and Non-Controlling Interest.

LEARNING OBJECTIVE ❷

Understand goodwill and non-controlling interest

1. What is *goodwill*, and how does it arise? Which company reports goodwill, the parent or the subsidiary? Where is goodwill reported?
2. What is non-controlling interest and which company reports it, the parent or the subsidiary? Where is non-controlling interest reported?

LEARNING OBJECTIVE ❸

Analyze and report a bond investment

SB-7 Suppose Prudential Bache (PB) buys $1,000,000 of CitiCorp bonds at a price of 101. The CitiCorp bonds pay cash interest at the annual rate of 7% and mature at the end of five years.

1. How much did PB pay to purchase the bond investment? How much will PB collect when the bond investment matures?
2. How much cash interest will PB receive each year from CitiCorp?
3. Will PB's annual interest revenue on the bond investment be more or less than the amount of cash interest received each year? Give your reason.
4. Compute PB's first-year interest revenue on this bond investment. Use the effective interest of 6.75% to amortize the investment.

LEARNING OBJECTIVE ❸

Record bond investment transactions

SB-8 Return to exercise SB-7, the Prudential Bache (PB) investment in CitiCorp bonds. Journalize the following on PB's books:

a. Purchase of the bond investment on January 2, 2020. PB expects to hold the investment to maturity.
b. Receipt of annual cash interest on December 31, 2020
c. Amortization of the bonds on December 31, 2020
d. Collection of the investment's face value at the maturity date on January 2, 2025. (Assume the receipt of 2024 interest and the amortization of bonds for 2024 have already been recorded, so ignore these entries.)

LEARNING OBJECTIVE ❺

Calculate present value

SB-9 Calculate the present value of the following amounts:

1. $10,000 at the end of five years at 8%
2. $10,000 a year at the end of the next five years at 8%

LEARNING OBJECTIVE ❺

Calculate the present value of an investment

SB-10 Arnold Financing leases airplanes to airline companies. Arnold has just signed a 10-year lease agreement that requires annual lease payments of $1,000,000. What is the present value of the lease using a 10% interest rate?

LEARNING OBJECTIVE ❹

Report investing activities on the statement of cash flows

SB-11 Companies divide their cash flows into three categories for reporting on the statement of cash flows.

1. List the three categories of cash flows in the order they appear on the statement of cash flows. Which category of cash flows is most closely related to this appendix?
2. Identify two types of transactions that companies report as cash flows from investing activities.

LEARNING OBJECTIVE ❺

Calculate present value

SB-12 Calculate the present value of the following amounts:

1. $12,000 at the end of five years at 10%
2. $12,000 a year at the end of the next five years at 10%

LEARNING OBJECTIVE ❺

Calculate the present value of an investment

SB-13 Chaplin Leasing leased a car to a customer. Chaplin will receive $150 a month for 60 months.

1. What is the present value of the lease if the annual interest rate in the lease is 12%? Use the PV function in Excel to compute the present value.
2. What is the present value of the lease if the car can likely be sold for $7,500 at the end of five years?

EXERCISES

LEARNING OBJECTIVE ❶

Record transactions for a non-strategic investment

EB-14 Journalize the following non-strategic investment transactions of Solomon Brothers Department Stores assuming the company reports changes in fair value through net income:

a. Purchased 400 shares of Royal Bank of Canada at $40 per share, with the intent of holding the shares in the near future
b. Received cash dividend of $0.50 per share on the Royal Bank of Canada investment
c. At year-end, adjusted the investment account to current fair value of $35 per share
d. Sold the shares for the market price of $30 per share

⊕ **EB-15** Dow-Smith Ltd. bought 3,000 common shares of Shoppers Drug Mart at $50.00, 600 common shares of Bank of Montreal (BMO) at $42.50, and 1,400 common shares of EnCana at $93.36, all as non-strategic investments. At December 31, TSX Online reports Shoppers's shares at $48.05, BMO's shares at $31.25, and EnCana's shares at $56.96. The company reports changes in fair value through other comprehensive income.

LEARNING OBJECTIVE ❶

Analyze and report non-strategic investments

Requirements

1. Determine the cost and the fair value of the long-term investment portfolio at December 31.
2. Record Dow-Smith's adjusting entry at December 31.
3. What would Dow-Smith report on its income statement and balance sheet for the information given? Make the necessary disclosures. Ignore income tax.

⊕ **EB-16** BlackBerry owns equity-method investments in several companies. Suppose BlackBerry paid $1,000,000 to acquire a 25% investment in Thai Software Company. Thai Software reported net income of $640,000 for the first year and declared and paid cash dividends of $420,000.

LEARNING OBJECTIVE ❷

Account for transactions under the equity method

1. Record the following in BlackBerry's journal: (a) purchase of the investment, (b) BlackBerry's proportion of Thai Software's net income, and (c) receipt of the cash dividends.
2. What is the ending balance in BlackBerry's investment account?

⊕ **EB-17** Without making journal entries, record the transactions of exercise EB-16 directly in the BlackBerry T-account, Long-Term Investment in Thai Software. Assume that after all the noted transactions took place, BlackBerry sold its entire investment in Thai Software for cash of $2,700,000. How much is BlackBerry's gain or loss on the sale of the investment?

LEARNING OBJECTIVE ❷

Analyze gains or losses on equity-method investments

⊕ **EB-18** Oaktree Financial Inc. paid $500,000 for a 25% investment in the common shares of eTrav Inc. For the first year, eTrav reported net income of $200,000 and at year-end declared and paid cash dividends of $100,000. On the balance sheet date, the fair value of Oaktree's investment in eTrav shares was $384,000.

LEARNING OBJECTIVE ❷

Apply the appropriate accounting method for a 25% investment

CT

Requirements

1. Using the facts provided, identify the method and explain why it would be appropriate for Oaktree Financial to use in accounting for its investment in eTrav.
2. Show everything that Oaktree would report for the investment and any investment revenue in its year-end financial statements.

⊕ **EB-19** Assume that on September 30, 2020, Manulife Financial paid 95.95 for 7% bonds of Hydro-Québec as a long-term bond investment. The effective interest rate was 8%. The maturity value of the bonds will be $20,000 on September 30, 2025. The bonds pay interest on March 31 and September 30.

LEARNING OBJECTIVE ❸

Analyze and report bond investment transactions

Requirements

1. What method should Manulife use to account for its investment in the Hydro-Québec bonds?
2. Using the effective interest method of amortizing the bonds, journalize all of Manulife's transactions on the bonds for 2020.
3. Show how Manulife would report everything related to the bond investment on its balance sheet at December 31, 2020.

⊕ **EB-20** Brinkman Corp. purchased ten $1,000, 5% bonds of General Electric Corporation when the market rate of interest was 4%. Interest is paid annually on the bonds, and the bonds will mature in six years. Compute the price Brinkman paid (the present value) on the bond investment.

LEARNING OBJECTIVE ❺

Calculate the present value of a bond investment

EB-21 Alpha Inc., owns Beta Corp. The two companies' individual balance sheets follow:

	A	B	C	D	E	F
1		Alpha Inc.	Beta Corporation	Eliminations Debit	Credit	Consolidated Amounts
2	**Assets**					
3	Cash	46,000	20,000			
4	Accounts receivable, net	75,000	52,000			
5	Note receivable from Alpha		29,000			
6	Inventory	56,000	80,000			
7	Investment in Beta	113,000				
8	Plant & equipment, net	283,000	97,000			
9	Other assets	29,000	13,000			
10	Total	602,000	291,000			
11	**Liabilities and Shareholders' Equity**					
12	Accounts payable	49,000	22,000			
13	Notes payable	148,000	33,000			
14	Other liabilities	78,000	123,000			
15	Common shares	112,000	80,000			
16	Retained earnings	215,000	33,000			
17	Total	602,000	291,000			
18						

Requirements

1. Prepare a consolidated balance sheet of Alpha, Inc. It is sufficient to complete the consolidation work sheet. Use Exhibit B-5 as a model.
2. What is the amount of shareholders' equity for the consolidated entity?

EB-22 During fiscal year 2020, Donuts 'R' Us Inc. reported net loss of $135.8 million. Donuts received $1.0 million from the sale of other businesses. Donuts made capital expenditures of $10.4 million and sold property, plant, and equipment for $7.3 million. The company purchased long-term investments at a cost of $12.2 million and sold other long-term investments for $2.5 million.

Requirements

1. Prepare the investing activities section of the Donuts 'R' Us statement of cash flows.
2. Identify the items that would help Donuts 'R' Us determine whether the company is growing or shrinking.

EB-23 At the end of the year, Blue Chip Properties Ltd.'s statement of cash flows reported the following for investment activities:

	A	B	C	D
1	**Blue Chip Properties Ltd.** Consolidated Statement of Cash Flows (Partial)			
2	**Cash Flows from Investing Activities**			
3	Notes receivable collected	$ 3,110,000		
4	Purchases of short-term investments	(3,457,000)		
5	Proceeds from sales of equipment	1,409,000*		
6	Proceeds from sales of investments (cost of $450,000)	461,000		
7	Expenditures for property, plant, and equipment	(1,761,000)		
8	Net cash used by investing activities	$ (238,000)		
9				

*Cost $5,100,000; Accumulated depreciation, $3,691,000

Requirement

For each item listed, make the journal entry that placed the item on Blue Chip's statement of cash flows.

EB-24 Which option is better: receive $100,000 now or $20,000, $25,000, $30,000, $25,000, and $20,000, respectively, over the next five years?

LEARNING OBJECTIVE ⑤

Calculate the present value of competing investments

Requirements

1. Assuming a 5% interest rate, which investment opportunity would you choose?
2. If you could earn 10%, would your choice change?

EB-25 Big-Box Retail Corporation reported shareholders' equity on its balance sheet at December 31, 2020, as follows:

LEARNING OBJECTIVE ①

Explain and analyze accumulated other comprehensive income

Big-Box Retail Corporation
Balance Sheet (Partial)
December 31, 2020

	millions
Shareholders' Equity:	
Common shares, $0.10	
800 million shares authorized, 300 million shares issued	$1,113
Retained earnings	6,250
Accumulated other comprehensive income (loss)	(?)

Requirements

1. What one component that was discussed in this appendix is included in accumulated other comprehensive income?
2. For the component of accumulated other comprehensive income, describe the event that can cause a *positive* balance. Also describe the event that can cause a negative balance for each component.
3. At December 31, 2019, Big-Box's accumulated other comprehensive loss was $53 million. Then, during 2020, Big-Box had an unrealized loss of $16 million on non-strategic investments. Assume Big-Box chooses to record any changes in fair value through other comprehensive income. What was Big-Box's balance of accumulated other comprehensive income (loss) at December 31, 2020?

PROBLEMS (GROUP A)

PB-26A Winnipeg Exchanges Ltd. completed the following long-term investment transactions during 2020:

LEARNING OBJECTIVES ①②

Analyze and report various long-term investment transactions on the balance sheet and income statement

2020		
May	12	Purchased 20,000 shares, which make up 35% of the common shares of Fellingham Corporation at a total cost of $370,000
July	9	Received annual cash dividend of $1.26 per share on the Fellingham investment
Sept.	16	Purchased 800 common shares of Tomassini Inc. as a non-strategic investment, paying $41.50 per share
Oct.	30	Received cash dividend of $0.30 per share on the Tomassini investment
Dec.	31	Received annual report from Fellingham Corporation. Net income for the year was $510,000.

At year-end the current fair value of the Tomassini shares is $30,600. The fair value of the Fellingham shares is $652,000. The company reports changes in fair value through other comprehensive income.

Requirements

1. Using the facts provided, determine the methods used to record each of the investments and what basis you used to make that decision.
2. Show what Winnipeg Exchanges Ltd. would report on its year-end balance sheet and income statement for these investment transactions. Ignore income tax.

LEARNING OBJECTIVES ①②

Analyze and report non-strategic and equity-method investments

PB-27A The beginning balance sheet of New Technology Corporation included the following:

Long-Term Investment in MSC Software (equity-method investment)	$619,000

New Technology completed the following investment transactions during the year 2020:

Mar. 16		Purchased 2,000 shares of ATI Inc. as a long-term non-strategic investment, paying $12.25 per share
May 21		Received cash dividend of $0.75 per share on the ATI investment
Aug. 17		Received cash dividend of $81,000 from MSC Software
Dec. 31		Received annual report from MSC Software. Net income for the year was $550,000. Of this amount, New Technology's proportion is 22%.

At year-end, the fair values of New Technology's investments are ATI, $25,700, and MSC, $700,000. The company reports any changes in fair value through other comprehensive income.

Requirements

1. Record the transactions in the journal of New Technology Corporation.
2. Post entries to the T-account for Long-Term Investment in MSC and determine its balance at December 31, 2020.
3. Show how to report the Long-Term Non-strategic Investment and the Long-Term Investment in MSC accounts on New Technology's balance sheet at December 31, 2020.

LEARNING OBJECTIVE ②

Analyze consolidated financial statements

PB-28A This problem demonstrates the dramatic effect that consolidation accounting can have on a company's ratios. ABC Company owns 100% of ABC Credit Corporation, its financing subsidiary. ABC's main operations consist of manufacturing automotive products. ABC Credit Corporation mainly helps people finance the purchase of automobiles from ABC and its dealers. The two companies' individual balance sheets are adapted and summarized as follows (amounts in billions):

	ABC (Parent)	ABC Credit (Subsidiary)
Total assets	$94.8	$179.0
Total liabilities	$68.4	$164.7
Total shareholders' equity	26.4	14.3
Total liabilities and equity	$94.8	$179.0

Requirements

1. Compute the debt ratio of ABC Company considered alone.
2. Determine the consolidated total assets, total liabilities, and shareholders' equity of ABC Company after consolidating the financial statements of ABC Credit into the totals of ABC, the parent company.

3. Recompute the debt ratio of the consolidated entity. Why do companies prefer not to consolidate their financing subsidiaries into their own financial statements?

PB-29A Insurance companies and pension plans hold large quantities of bond investments. Prairie Insurance Corp. purchased $600,000 of 5% bonds of Eaton Inc. for 104.5 on March 1, 2020, when the effective interest rate was 4%. These bonds pay interest on March 1 and September 1 each year. They mature on March 1, 2025. At February 28, 2021, the market price of the bonds is 103.5.

LEARNING OBJECTIVE ❸

Analyze and report a bond investment

Requirements

1. Journalize Prairie's purchase of the bonds as a long-term investment on March 1, 2020 (to be held to maturity), receipt of cash interest and amortization of the bond investment on September 1, 2020, and accrual of interest revenue and amortization at February 28, 2021. Use the effective-interest method for amortizing the bond investment.
2. Show all financial statement effects of this long-term bond investment on Prairie Insurance Corp.'s balance sheet and income statement at February 28, 2021.

PB-30A Annual cash flows from two competing investment opportunities are given. Each investment opportunity will require the same initial investment at the end of each year.

LEARNING OBJECTIVE ❺

Explain the impact of the time value of money on valuation of investments

| | Investment | |
Year	A	B
1.................................	$10,000	$ 8,000
2.................................	8,000	8,000
3.................................	6,000	8,000
	$24,000	$24,000

Requirement

Using the information in the question, assume a 12% interest rate and determine the investment opportunity that should be chosen.

PB-31A Zeta, Inc., owns Theta Corp. These two companies' individual balance sheets follow:

LEARNING OBJECTIVE ❷

Prepare a consolidated balance sheet

	A	B	C	D	E	F
1		Zeta Inc.	Theta Corporation	Eliminations Debit	Credit	Consolidated Amounts
2	**Assets**					
3	Cash	48,000	18,000			
4	Accounts receivable	82,000	58,000			
5	Note receivable from Zeta		33,000			
6	Inventory	54,000	83,000			
7	Investment in Theta	119,000				
8	Plant & equipment, net	288,000	98,000			
9	Other assets	29,000	11,000			
10	Total	620,000	301,000			
11	**Liabilities and Shareholders' Equity**					
12	Accounts payable	49,000	35,000			
13	Notes payable	152,000	23,000			
14	Other liabilities	78,000	124,000			
15	Common shares	107,000	82,000			
16	Retained earnings	234,000	37,000			
17	Total	620,000	301,000			
18						

Requirements

1. Prepare a consolidated balance sheet of Zeta, Inc. It is sufficient to complete the consolidation work sheet. Use Exhibit B-5 as a model.
2. What is the amount of shareholders' equity for the consolidated entity?

LEARNING OBJECTIVE ④

Use the statement of cash flows

PB-32A Excerpts from Smart Pro Inc.'s statement of cash flows appear as follows:

	A	B	C	D
1	**Smart Pro Inc.** Consolidated Statement of Cash Flows (Partial, Adapted) For the Years Ended December 31			
2	*(in millions)*	**2020**	**2019**	
3	Cash and cash equivalents, beginning of year	$ 2,976	$ 3,695	
4	Net cash provided by operating activities	8,654	12,827	
5	Cash flows provided by (used for) investing activities:			
6	Additions to property, plant, and equipment	(7,309)	(6,674)	
7	Acquisitions of other companies	(883)	(2,317)	
8	Purchases of investments	(7,141)	(17,188)	
9	Sales of investments	15,138	16,144	
10	Net cash (used for) investing activities	(195)	(10,035)	
11	Cash flows provided by (used for) financing activities:			
12	Borrowing	329	215	
13	Repayment of long-term debt	(10)	(46)	
14	Proceeds from issuance of shares	762	797	
15	Repurchase of common shares	(4,008)	(4,007)	
16	Payment of dividends to shareholders	(538)	(470)	
17	Net cash (used for) financing activities	(3,465)	(3,511)	
18	Net increase (decrease) in cash and cash equivalents	4,994	(719)	
19	Cash and cash equivalents, end of year	$ 7,970	$ 2,976	
20				

Source: Based on Smart Pro Inc. – Annual Report.

Requirement

As the chief executive officer of Smart Pro Inc., your duty is to write the management letter to your shareholders to explain Smart Pro's investing activities during 2020. Compare the company's level of investment with the preceding year, and indicate the major way the company financed its investments during 2020. Net income for 2020 was $1,291 million.

LEARNING OBJECTIVE ②

Analyze consolidated financial statements

PB-33A Spindler Motor Company (Spindler) owns 100% of Spindler Motor Credit Corporation (SMCC), its financing subsidiary. Spindler's main operations consist of manufacturing automotive products. SMCC mainly helps people finance the purchase of automobiles from Spindler and its dealers. The two companies' individual balance sheets are adapted and summarized as follows (amounts in billions):

	Spindler (Parent)	SMCC (Subsidiary)
Total assets	$85.1	$169.2
Total liabilities	$65.3	$155.9
Total shareholders' equity	19.8	13.3
Total liabilities and equity	$85.1	$169.2

Assume that SMCC's liabilities include $1.3 billion owed to Spindler, the parent company.

Requirements

1. Compute the debt ratio of Spindler Motor Company considered alone.
2. Determine the consolidated total assets, total liabilities, and shareholders' equity of Spindler Motor Company after consolidating the financial statements of SMCC into the totals of Spindler, the parent company.
3. Recompute the debt ratio of the consolidated entity. Why do companies prefer not to consolidate their financing subsidiaries into their own financial statements?

PROBLEMS (GROUP B)

PB-34B Homestead Financial Corporation owns numerous investments in the shares of other companies. Homestead Financial completed the following long-term investment transactions:

LEARNING OBJECTIVES ❶❷

Analyze and report various long-term investment transactions on the balance sheet and income statement

2020		
May	1	Purchased 8,000 shares, which make up 25% of the common shares of Mars Company at total cost of $450,000
Sept.	15	Received a cash dividend of $1.40 per share on the Mars investment
Oct.	12	Purchased 1,000 common shares of Mercury Corporation as a non-strategic investment, paying $22.50 per share
Dec.	14	Received a cash dividend of $0.75 per share on the Mercury investment
	31	Received annual report from Mars Company. Net income for the year was $350,000.

At year-end the current fair value of the Mercury shares is $19,200. The fair value of the Mars shares is $740,000. The company reports changes in fair value through net income.

Requirements

1. Using the facts provided, determine the methods used to record each of the investments and what basis you used to make that decision.
2. Show what Homestead Financial will report on its year-end balance sheet and income statement for these investments. Ignore income tax.

PB-35B The beginning balance sheet of Dealmaker Securities Limited included the following:

LEARNING OBJECTIVES ❶❷

Analyze and report non-strategic and equity-method investments

Long-Term Investments in Affiliates (equity-method investments).............................. $409,000

Dealmaker completed the following investment transactions during the year:

Feb.	16	Purchased 10,000 shares of BCM Software common shares as a long-term non-strategic investment, paying $9.25 per share
May	14	Received cash dividend of $0.82 per share on the BCM investment
Oct.	15	Received cash dividend of $29,000 from an affiliated company
Dec.	31	Received annual reports from affiliated companies. Their total net income for the year was $620,000. Of this amount, Dealmaker's proportion is 25%.

The fair values of Dealmaker's investments are BCM, $89,000, and affiliated companies, $947,000. The company reports changes in fair value through other comprehensive income.

Requirements

1. Record the transactions in the journal of Dealmaker Securities.
2. Post entries to the Long-Term Investments in Affiliates T-account, and determine its balance at December 31.
3. Show how to report Long-Term Non-strategic Investments and Long-Term Investments in Affiliates on Dealmaker's balance sheet at December 31.

PB-36B Financial institutions hold large quantities of bond investments. Suppose Sun Life Financial purchases $500,000 of 6% bonds of General Components Corporation for 88 on January 1, 2020, when the effective interest rate is 8%. These bonds pay interest on January 1 and July 1 each year. They mature on January 1, 2028. At December 31, 2020, the market price of the bonds is 90.

Requirements

1. Journalize Sun Life's purchase of the bonds as a long-term investment on January 1, 2020 (to be held to maturity), receipt of cash interest and amortization of the bond investment on July 1, 2020, and accrual of interest revenue and amortization at December 31, 2020. Use the effective-interest method for amortizing the bond investment.
2. Show all financial statement effects of this long-term bond investment on Sun Life's balance sheet and income statement at December 31, 2020.

PB-37B Annual cash flows from two competing investment opportunities are given. Each investment opportunity will require the same initial investment.

	Investment	
Year	X	Y
1	$15,000	$10,000
2	10,000	10,000
3	5,000	10,000
	$30,000	$30,000

Requirement

Using the information in the question, assume a 10% interest rate and determine the investment opportunity that should be chosen.

PB-38B This problem demonstrates the dramatic effect that consolidation accounting can have on a company's ratios. Snider Motor Company (Snider) owns 100% of Snider Motor Credit Corporation (SMCC), its financing subsidiary. Snider's main operations consist of manufacturing automotive products. SMCC mainly helps people finance the purchase of automobiles from Snider and its dealers. The two companies' individual balance sheets are adapted and summarized as follows (amounts in billions):

	Snider (Parent)	SMCC (Subsidiary)
Total assets	$78.8	$163.1
Total liabilities	$63.8	$155.2
Total shareholders' equity	15.0	7.9
Total liabilities and equity	$78.8	$163.1

Assume that SMCC's liabilities include $1.6 billion owed to Snider, the parent company.

Requirements

1. Compute the debt ratio of Snider Motor Company considered alone.
2. Determine the consolidated total assets, total liabilities, and shareholders' equity of Snider Motor Company after consolidating the financial statements of SMCC into the totals of Snider, the parent company.
3. Recompute the debt ratio of the consolidated entity. Why do companies prefer not to consolidate their financing subsidiaries into their own financial statements?

LEARNING OBJECTIVE ➍

Use the statement of cash flows

PB-39B Marine Transport Ltd.'s statement of cash flows, as adapted, appears as follows:

	A	B	C	D
1	**Marine Transport Ltd.** Consolidated Statement of Cash Flows For the Years Ended December 31 (Stated in thousands of Canadian dollars)			
2		**2020**	**2019**	
3	**Cash flows from (used in):**			
4	**Operating activities:**			
5	Net earnings	$ 192,833	$ 114,676	
6	Items not involving cash:			
7	Depreciation and amortization	127,223	111,442	
8	Amortization of other liabilities	(897)	(868)	
9	Amortization of hedge settlements	1,400	1,427	
10	Net realized loss on cash flow hedge	18	—	
11	Loss on derecognition of property and equipment and			
12	ship parts	32,773	394	
13	Stock-based compensation expense	20,058	21,205	
14	Future income tax expense	41,775	46,635	
15	Unrealized foreign exchange loss (gain)	13,813	(346)	
16	Decrease in non-cash working capital	112,069	43,707	
17		541,065	338,272	
18	**Financing activities:**			
19	Increase in long-term debt	141,178	418,581	
20	Repayment of long-term debt	(156,516)	(132,559)	
21	Decrease in obligations under capital lease	(356)	(480)	
22	Share issuance costs	—	(10)	
23	Shares repurchased	(21,250)	—	
24	Issuance of common shares	1,551	—	
25	Increase in other assets	(20,897)	(27,830)	
26	Increase in non-cash working capital	(3,000)	(1,071)	
27		(59,290)	256,631	
28	**Investing activities:**			
29	Ship additions	(191,437)	(438,906)	
30	Ship disposals	1,975	3,822	
31	Other property and equipment additions	(24,639)	(43,590)	
32	Other property and equipment disposals	13,819	1,611	
33		(200,282)	(477,063)	
34				
35	Cash flow from operating, financing, and investing activities	281,493	117,840	
36	Effect of exchange rate on cash	(5,452)	37	
37	Net change in cash	276,041	117,877	
38	Cash, beginning of year	377,517	259,640	
39	Cash, end of year	$ 653,558	$ 377,517	
40				
41	Cash is defined as cash and cash equivalents.			
42				

Requirement

As a member of an investment club, you have been asked to review Marine Transport's major investing activities during 2020. Compare the company's level of investment with the previous year, and indicate how the company financed its investments during 2020.

PB-40B Randall Motor Company (Randall) owns 100% of Randall Motor Credit Corporation (RMCC), its financing subsidiary. Randall's main operations consist of manufacturing automotive products. RMCC mainly helps people finance the purchase of automobiles from Randall

LEARNING OBJECTIVE ➋

Analyze consolidated financial statements

and its dealers. The two companies' individual balance sheets are adapted and summarized as follows (amounts in billions):

	Randall (Parent)	RMCC (Subsidiary)
Total assets	$80.6	$164.8
Total liabilities..	$63.9	$155.4
Total shareholders' equity..	16.7	9.4
Total liabilities and equity..	$80.6	$164.8

Assume that RMCC's liabilities include $1.6 billion owed to Randall, the parent company.

Requirements

1. Compute the debt ratio of Randall Motor Company considered alone.
2. Determine the consolidated total assets, total liabilities, and shareholders' equity of Randall Motor Company after consolidating the financial statements of RMCC into the totals of Randall, the parent company.
3. Recompute the debt ratio of the consolidated entity. Why do companies prefer not to consolidate their financing subsidiaries into their own financial statements?

APPLY YOUR KNOWLEDGE

DECISION CASES

This section's material reflects CPA enabling competencies, including:

I   Professional and ethical behaviour

II   Problem-solving and decision-making

III   Communication

IV   Self-management

V   Teamwork and leadership

Based on Chartered Professional Accountant standards

LEARNING OBJECTIVE ❷

Make an investment decision

LEARNING OBJECTIVES ❶❷❸

Make an investment sale decision

Case 1. Infografix Corporation's consolidated sales for 2020 were $26.6 million and expenses totaled $24.8 million. Infografix operates worldwide and conducts 37% of its business outside Canada. During 2020, Infografix reported the following items in its financial statements (amounts in millions):

Unrealized holding on non-strategic investments	(32.8)

As you consider an investment in Infografix shares, some concerns arise. Answer the following questions:

1. What do the parentheses around the dollar amounts signify?
2. Is this item reported as an asset, liability, shareholders' equity, revenue, or expense? Are they normal-balance accounts, or are they contra accounts?
3. Is this item reason for rejoicing or sorrow at Infografix? Are Infografix's emotions about this item deep or only moderate? Why?
4. Did Infografix include this item in net income? Did it include this item in retained earnings? In the final analysis, how much net income did Infografix report for 2020?
5. Should these items scare you away from investing in Infografix shares? Why or why not?

Case 2. Cathy Talbert is the general manager of Barham Ltd., which provides data-management services for physicians in the Regina, Saskatchewan, area. Barham is having a rough year. Net income trails projections for the year by almost $75,000. This shortfall is especially important—Barham plans to issue shares early next year and needs to show investors that the company can meet its earnings targets.

Barham holds several investments purchased a few years ago. Even though investing in shares is outside Barham's core business of data-management services, Talbert thinks these investments may hold the key to helping the company meet its net income goal for the year. She is considering what to do with the following investments:

1. Barham owns 50% of the common shares of Prairie Office Systems, which provides the business forms that Barham uses. Prairie Office Systems has lost money for the past two years but still has a retained earnings balance of $550,000. Talbert thinks she can get Prairie's treasurer to declare a $160,000 cash dividend, half of which would go to Barham.

2. Barham owns a bond investment with a 4% coupon rate and an annual interest payment. The bond was purchased eight years ago for $293,000. The purchase price represents a discount from the bonds' maturity value of $400,000 based on an effective rate of 8%. These bonds mature two years from now, and their current market value is $380,000. Ms. Talbert has checked with a Scotiabank investment representative and Talbert is considering selling the bonds. A charge of 1% commission would be made on the sale transaction.

3. Barham owns 5,000 Royal Bank of Canada (RBC) shares valued at $53 per share. One year ago, RBC was worth only $28 per share. Barham purchased the RBC shares for $37 per share. The company reports any changes in fair value through net income. Talbert wonders whether Barham should sell the RBC shares.

Requirement

Evaluate all three actions as a way for Barham Ltd. to generate the needed amount of income. Recommend the best way for Barham to achieve its net income goal.

ETHICAL DECISIONS

Media One owns 15% of the voting shares of Online Inc. The remainder of the Online shares are held by numerous investors with small holdings. Austin Cohen, president of Media One and a member of Online's board of directors, heavily influences Online's policies.

Under the fair-value method of accounting for investments, Media One's net income increases as it receives dividend revenue from Online. Media One pays President Cohen a bonus, computed as a percentage of Media One's net income. Therefore, Cohen can control his personal bonus to a certain extent by influencing Online's dividends.

A recession occurs in 2020, and Media One's income is low. Cohen uses his power to have Online pay a large cash dividend. The action requires Online to borrow in order to pay the dividend.

Requirements

1. In getting Online to pay the large cash dividend, is Cohen acting within his authority as a member of the Online board of directors? Are Cohen's actions ethical? Whom can his actions harm?

2. Discuss how using the equity method of accounting for investment would decrease Cohen's potential for manipulating his bonus.

FOCUS ON FINANCIAL STATEMENT ANALYSIS

Dollarama Inc.

Dollarama's financial statements are given in Appendix A.

1. Does Dollarama have any subsidiaries? How can you tell?
2. Is Dollarama expanding or contracting its operations? How can you tell?
3. Did Dollarama's goodwill suffer any impairment during the year? How can you tell?

LEARNING OBJECTIVE ❷

Analyze investments, consolidated statements, and international operations

MyLab Accounting

CHECK YOUR WORK

STOP + THINK ANSWERS

STOP + THINK (B-1)

Microsport would receive cash interest of $10,800 ($120,000 × .09) on December 31, 2023.

STOP + THINK (B-2)

The company spent most of its cash acquiring other companies.

STOP + THINK (B-3)

Using the table in Exhibit B-9, the present value at the end of eight years at 5% interest would be $3,385 ($5,000 × 0.677).

QUICK QUIZ ANSWERS

1. *c*
2. *d (1,000 shares × $35 = $35,000)*
3. *a ($35,000 − $31,000 = $4,000)*
4. *c [$40,000 − (1,000 shares × $35) = $5,000]*
5. *b [$100,000 + 0.20 ($50,000 − $25,000) = $105,000]*
6. *c ($100,000 + 0.80 [$68,000 + 0.80($40,000)]*
   = $180,000)
7. *a*
8. *a*
9. *d (100,000 × 0.07 = $7,000)*
10. *b ($105,000 × 0.06 = 6,300;*
    $7,000 − $6,300 = $700
    Interest income = $7,000 − $700 = $6,300)

Summary of Differences Between International Financial Reporting Standards and Accounting Standards for Private Enterprises

Canada has two main sets of generally accepted accounting principles: the International Financial Reporting Standards (IFRS) that must be applied by publicly accountable enterprises, and the Accounting Standards for Private Enterprises (ASPE) that are applied by most other Canadian companies. The following table provides a chapter-by-chapter summary of the IFRS-ASPE differences that appear in this textbook. There are many more differences between the two sets of standards, but they are left to be discussed in senior accounting courses.

CHAPTER 1

Summary of IFRS-ASPE Differences

Concepts	IFRS	ASPE
The income statement (p. 8)	This financial statement is called the statement of profit or loss.	This financial statement is called the income statement.
Changes in retained earnings during an accounting period (p. 10)	These changes are reported in the statement of changes in owners' equity.	These changes are reported in the statement of retained earnings.
The balance sheet (p. 11)	This financial statement is called the statement of financial position.	This financial statement is called the balance sheet.
The cash flow statement (p. 15)	This financial statement is called the statement of cash flows.	This financial statement is called the cash flow statement.
Application of IFRS and ASPE (p. 20)	Publicly accountable enterprises or those enterprises planning to become one must apply IFRS.	Private enterprises have the option of applying IFRS, but almost all apply ASPE, which is simpler and less costly for these smaller enterprises.
Historical-cost assumption (p. 23)	Certain assets and liabilities are permitted to be recorded at their fair values rather than being kept on the books at their historical costs.	With rare exceptions, assets and liabilities are carried at their historical costs for as long as the company owns or owes them.

CHAPTER 6

Summary of IFRS-ASPE Differences

Concepts	IFRS	ASPE
Depreciation (p. 283)	This concept is called depreciation.	This concept is called amortization.
Significant components of an item of property, plant, or equipment (p. 298)	Significant components shall be depreciated separately.	Significant components are amortized separately only when it is practical to do so.
Impairment (p. 298)	A company shall assess at the end of each reporting period whether there are any signs that an asset may be impaired. Irrespective of any signs of impairment, a company must annually review goodwill and intangible assets with indefinite useful lives for impairment.	A company shall test an asset for impairment whenever events or circumstances indicate its carrying amount may not be recoverable.
	If an impaired asset subsequently increases in value, a company may reverse all or part of any previous write-down but not on goodwill.	A company may not reverse any write-downs, even if an impaired asset subsequently increases in value.
Revaluation (p. 299)	A company may choose to use the revaluation model to measure its property, plant, and equipment.	A company must use the cost method; no revaluation is permitted.

CHAPTER 7

Summary of IFRS-ASPE Differences

Concepts	IFRS	ASPE
Differences between income tax expense and income tax payable (p. 342)	Accounted for as deferred income taxes.	Accounted for as future income taxes.
Provisions and contingent liabilities (p. 344)	A contingent liability is recorded as a provision when it is probable that an outflow of economic benefits will be required to settle the liability. *Probable* is generally considered to mean that an outflow is *more likely than not* to occur.	A contingent liability is recorded as a liability when it is likely that an outflow of economic benefits will be required to settle the liability. *Likely* is generally considered to be a higher threshold to meet than *probable*, so fewer contingent liabilities will be recorded under ASPE than under IFRS.
Government remittances (p. 346)	No separate disclosure of these liabilities is required.	Government remittances (other than income taxes) such as sales taxes, Employment Insurance, and Canada Pension Plan payable must be disclosed separately, either on the balance sheet or in the notes.
Amortization of discounts and premiums (p. 352)	The effective-interest method must be used to amortize discounts and premiums.	The straight-line method is available as an amortization option.
Finance leases (p. 365)	Leases that transfer substantially all the risks and rewards incidental to the ownership of assets to the lessee are called finance leases.	The equivalent term is capital leases. There are no differences in accounting for these leases.

CHAPTER 8

Summary of IFRS-ASPE Differences

Concept	IFRS	ASPE
Accumulated other comprehensive income (p. 399)	Included as a component of shareholders' equity.	No accounting or reporting of this component is required.
Statement of changes in shareholders' (or owners') equity (p. 413)	Companies must report this statement.	Companies must report only a statement of retained earnings, which contains only a subset of the information reported in the statement of changes in shareholders' equity.

CHAPTER 9

Summary of IFRS-ASPE Differences

Concepts	IFRS	ASPE
Classification of interest paid and interest and dividends received (p. 449)	Interest paid may be classified as either an operating activity or a financing activity.	Interest paid must be classified as an operating activity.
Classification of interest and dividends received (p. 449)	Interest and dividends received may be classified as either operating activities or investing activities.	Interest and dividends received must be classified as operating activities.
Classification of dividends paid (p. 449)	Dividends paid may be classified as either an operating activity or a financing activity. *Note: Once a classification scheme has been chosen for each of the above items, it must be used consistently thereafter.*	Dividends paid must be classified as a financing activity.

APPENDIX B

Summary of IFRS-ASPE Differences

Concepts	IFRS	ASPE
Non-strategic investments (p. 636)	These investments are reported at fair value, with unrealized and realized gains and losses reported in net income (short-term investments), unless the company elects to report them in other comprehensive income (short-term and long-term investments).	These investments are reported at fair value, with unrealized and realized gains and losses reported in net income or other comprehensive income.
Strategic investments (a) Investments subject to significant influence (p. 639)	A company shall apply the equity method to account for these investments.	A company may choose to apply either the equity method or the cost method. If the share investments are quoted in an active market, then the fair value method replaces the cost method as an option, with any changes in fair value reported through net income.
(b) Investments in controlled subsidiaries (p. 641)	A company shall consolidate its financial statements with those of its subsidiaries.	A company may choose to account for its subsidiaries using the cost method, the equity method, or the consolidation method. If share investments are quoted in an active market, then the fair value method replaces the cost method, with any changes in fair value reported through net income.
Amortization of the discount or premium relating to long-term investments in bonds (p. 644)	The effective-interest method must be used to amortize discounts and premiums.	The straight-line method or the effective-interest method may be used to amortize discounts and premiums.

Check Figures

CHAPTER 1

S1-1	NCF*
S1-2	a. $300,000 b. 200,000 c. 100,000
S1-3	NCF
S1-4	NCF
S1-5	NCF
S1-6	Net income $70
S1-7	R/E, end $260
S1-8	Total assets $140,000
S1-9	CB, Dec. 31, 2020, $19,000
S1-10	NCF
S1-11	NCF
S1-12	NCF
E1-13	NCF
E1-14	NCF
E1-15	NCF
E1-16	Telus Total assets $16,987 mil.
E1-17	2. $2,997.8 mil. 3. $1,836.4 mil.
E1-18	1. No net loss 2. No net loss 3. Net loss of $1 mil.
E1-19	1. Total assets $840,000 2. SE $400,000
E1-20	NCF
E1-21	R/E $25 mil.
E1-22	1. Net inc. before tax $9 mil. 2. Dividends $3 mil.
E1-23	Net cash provided by operations $360 thou. End Cash $125,000
E1-24	R/E, July 31, 2020, $5,900
E1-25	Total assets $44,100
E1-26	Net cash provided by operations $11,100. End Cash $8,100
E1-27	NCF
E1-28	NCF
P1-29A	1. Net inc. $28,000
P1-30A	Chain Inc.
P1-31A	1. Total assets $99,000
P1-32A	1. Total assets $160,000

P1-33A	1. Net inc. $86,000 2. R/E, end. $116,000 3. Total assets $180,000
P1-34A	1. Net decrease in cash $41 mil.
P1-35A	1. b. $2,400 thou. g. $5,700 thou. m. $2,600 thou. s. $17,400 thou.
P1-36A	1. Total assets $760 mil.
P1-37B	1. Net inc. $0.8 mil.
P1-38B	Electric Inc. ending assets $3,389 mil. Water Corp. repurchase of shares $20 mil. Gas Limited expenses $10,036 mil.
P1-39B	1. Total assets $114,000
P1-40B	2. Total assets $199,000
P1-41B	1. Net inc. $282,500 2. R/E, end. $540,700 3. Total assets $679,400
P1-42B	1. Net increase in cash $34,000
P1-43B	1. b. $5,850 thou. g. $15,400 thou. n. $3,670 thou. v. $43,490 thou.
P1-44B	1. Total assets $710 mil.
DC1	NCF
DC2	1. Net inc. $0; Total assets $70,000
DC3	Total assets $213,500
ED1	NCF
ED2	NCF
ED3	NCF
FOFSA	1. Net earnings of $519.4 mil. is 16.6% increase 3. Total resources: $1,934.3 mil. Amt. owed $2,186.7 mil. Equity ($252.4) mil. (deficit)

CHAPTER 2

S2-1	NCF
S2-2	a. $12,000 b. $2,000
S2-3	Cash bal. $23,000
S2-4	NCF

---

*NCF = No Check Figure.

S2-5	NCF
S2-6	2. A/P bal. $2,000
S2-7	2. Cash bal. $100
	A/R bal. $400, Service Rev. bal. $500
	3. Total assets $500
S2-8	T/B total $398 mil. Net income, $31 mil.
S2-9	1. $95,000
	2. $39,000
	3. $38,000
	4. $56,000
S2-10	T/B total $70,900
S2-11	NCF
S2-12	Total debits $160,000
E2-13	Cash $10,000
	B/S Total assets $270,000
E2-14	NCF
E2-15	NCF
E2-16	NCF
E2-17	2. a. $68,300 b. $5,000 c. $11,000
	d. $57,050 ($50,000 + $7,050) e. $7,050
E2-18	NCF
E2-19	NCF
E2-20	2. T/B total $32,200
	3. Total assets $30,700
E2-21	Cash bal. $10,700; Owing $30,600
E2-22	1. T/B total $71,200 2. Net inc. $14,300
E2-23	T/B total $94,200
E2-24	Cash bal. $4,200
E2-25	1. T/B total $27,500
	2. Net income $8,500
E2-26	1. T/B out of balance by $1,900
	2. Total assets $43,000, Total liabilities $12,100,
	Net inc. $5,100
E2-27	2. $24,500
	3. $43,300
	4. $23,100
E2-28	4. T/B total $14,400
E2-29	a. Cash paid $85,000
	b. Cash collections $52,000
	c. Cash paid on a note payable $17,000
E2-30	1. T/B out of balance by $2,200
	2. T/B total $118,200
	3. Total assets $111,500, Total liabilities
	$71,800, Net inc. $12,400
E2-31	NCF
P2-32A	Total assets $300,000, Total liabilities $150,000,
	Net inc. $30,000
P2-33A	1. Net inc. $8,900
	3. Total assets 23,700

P2-34A	3. Cash bal. $7,700; A/P bal. $5,500
P2-35A	2. Total assets $56,500
P2-36A	3. Cash bal. $10,800; Amt. owed $35,600
P2-37A	3. T/B total $35,000
	4. Net inc. $2,205
P2-38A	T/B total $116,800
P2-39B	Total assets $292,000
	Net inc. $33,000
P2-40B	1. Net inc. $16,400 3. Total assets $73,900
P2-41B	3. Cash bal. $32,500; A/P bal. $5,200
P2-42B	3. b. Total assets $56,400
P2-43B	3. Cash bal. $26,300; Amt. owed $30,000
P2-44B	3. T/B total $29,300
	4. Net inc. $7,290
P2-45B	T/B total $174,600
DC1	1. T/B total $27,900
	2. Net inc. $6,400
DC2	Net inc. $3,000; Total assets $21,000
ED1	NCF
ED2	NCF
ED3	NCF
FOFSA	Task 1. 3. 4. Cash $1,600.6 mil; A/R $15.4 mil.;
	Inventories $490.9 mil.; A/P $228.4 mil
	Task 2 NCF

CHAPTER 3

S3-1	a. Net inc. $50 mil.
	b. Ending cash $90 mil.
S3-2	NCF
S3-3	NCF
S3-4	1. Prepaid Rent bal. $2,000
	2. Supplies bal. $500
S3-5	3. $20,000 Carrying amount
S3-6	Income statement, $42,000,000; Balance sheet
	$2,000,000
S3-7	2. Interest Payable Dec. 31 bal. $1,500
S3-8	2. Interest Receivable Dec. 31 bal. $1,500
S3-9	NCF
S3-10	Prepaid Rent: a. $6,000 b. $0; Rent Expense:
	a. $0 b. $6,000.
S3-11	NCF
S3-12	Net inc. $3,500 thou.; R/E $4,800 thou. Total
	assets $97,900 thou.
S3-13	Retained earnings $4,800 thou.
S3-14	a. 1.24 b. 0.69

S3-15	NCF
E3-16	2. Sales $4,100; Operating expenses $800
E3-17	a. Net Inc. $10,000 b. Net Inc. $80,000
E3-18	1. Interest expense $0.4 mil.
E3-19	NCF
E3-20	NCF
E3-21	NCF
E3-22	2. Net inc. overstated by $18,600
E3-23	NCF
E3-24	Carrying amount $48,000
E3-25	Sales Revenue $15,700
E3-26	Net inc. $4,000 thou.; Total assets $22,200 thou.; R/E $6,800 thou.
E3-27	Sales rev. $20,900 mil.; Insurance expense $330 mil; other operating expense $4,200 mil.
E3-28	Mountain B/S: Unearned service rev. $3,000; Squamish I/S: Consulting expense $9,000
E3-29	NCF
E3-30	Net Inc. $1,200 thou. Dec. 31, 2020, bal. of R/E $2,700 thou.
E3-31	NCF
E3-32	1. Total assets $39,100 2. Current ratio Current Yr. 1.26 Debt ratio Current Yr. 0.48
E3-33	1. 2020 Current ratio 2.0; Debt ratio 0.40; 2019 Current ratio 1.88; Debt ratio 0.35; 2018 Current ratio 1.33; Debt ratio 0.29
E3-34	7. Net inc. $1,200; Total assets $12,800; R/E $200
E3-35	2019: 1.868; 2020: 2.174
E3-36	a. Net inc. $108,000 b. Total assets $158,000 c. Total liabilities $13,000 d. Total shareholders' equity $145,000
E3-37	2019 Current ratio 1.82; 2020 Current ratio 2.06
E3-38	Total assets $59,200
P3-39A	1. $27 mil. 3. End. rec. $6 mil. 4. End. Payable $8 mil.
P3-40A	2. Cash basis—loss $700, Accrual basis—inc. $3,240
P3-41A	NCF
P3-42A	a. Insurance Exp. $3,100 d. Supplies Exp. $6,600
P3-43A	2. Net inc. $6,000; Total assets $54,000; R/E $15,000
P3-44A	2. Total assets $68,600; Net inc. $4,100; Total Liabilities $7,400
P3-45A	1. Net inc. $39,200; Total assets $47,000; 2. Debt ratio 0.549

P3-46A	2. March 31, 2020 bal. of R/E $47,300
P3-47A	1. Total assets $83,300 2. Current ratio 2020, 1.60, Debt ratio 2020, 0.32
P3-48A	1. Current ratio 2020, 1.69; 2. Debt ratio 2020, 0.574
P3-49B	1. $15; 3. End. rec. $5; 4. End payable $6
P3-50B	2. Cash basis—loss $2,700, Accrual basis—inc. $1,100
P3-51B	NCF
P3-52B	c. Supplies Exp. $11,400 f. Insurance Exp. $2,700
P3-53B	2. Net inc. $19,800; Total assets $61,600; R/E $36,200
P3-54B	2. Total assets $30,400; Net inc. $25,500; Total liabilities $14,700
P3-55B	1. Net inc. $78,600; Total assets $109,000 2. Debt ratio 0.42
P3-56B	2. Dec. 31, 2020 bal. of R/E $16,800
P3-57B	1. Total assets $55,000 2. Current ratio 2020, 1.71; Debt ratio 0.42
P3-58B	1. 2020, Current ratio 1.36, 2. Debt ratio 0.681
DC1	1. $2,000 3. Current ratio 1.748
DC2	Net inc. $7,000, Total assets $32,000
DC3	1. $260,000 2. Shareholder Equity $148,000
ED1	NCF
ED2	1. Overstate $26,000
ED3	NCF
FOFSA	Task 1 5. 2018: Current ratio 0.79; Debt ratio 1.13 Task 2 2. Deprec. Expense, $57.9 mil. Task 3 NCF

CHAPTER 4

S4-1	NCF
S4-2	3. Bad debt expense $2.1 mil.
S4-3	NCF
S4-4	Adj. bal. $3,005
S4-5	NCF
S4-6	$1,000 stolen
S4-7	2. A/R, net $62,500
S4-8	4. Dr Bad debt exp. $15,000
S4-9	1. A/R bal. $184,000 2. Allowance for Uncollectible Accounts $16,500 3. A/R, net $167,500
S4-10	d. Bad debt exp. $12,000
S4-11	3. A/R, net $123,000
S4-12	b. Dr Cash $93,600
S4-13	3. $102,667

S4-14	c. Dr Cash $6,480
S4-15	a. Notes rec. $6,000; Interest rec. $280
	b. Interest rev. $280
	c. Nothing to report
	d. Interest rev. $200
S4-16	1. 0.95 2. 24 days
S4-17	2. Net Inc. $4,424 thou. 3. 1.60
E4-18	Bookkeeper stole $1,000
E4-19	NCF
E4-20	Adj. bal. $1,150
E4-21	Adj. bal. $1,780
E4-22	NCF
E4-23	A/R, net $91,000
E4-24	3. A/R, net $49,500
E4-25	2. A/R, net $52,800
E4-26	3. A/R, net $224,850
E4-27	Bad debt exp. $150; Write-offs $148
E4-28	Dec. 31 Dr Interest rec. $1,326
E4-29	I/S: Interest rev. $750 for 2019 and $250 for 2020
E4-30	NCF
E4-31	1. a. 1.89 b. 53 days
E4-32	1. 10 days
E4-33	Expected net inc. with bank card $129,800
E4-34	a. $28 mil. b. $11,148 mil.
P4-35A	Adj. bal. $6,090
P4-36A	1. Adj. bal. $2,242.16
P4-37A	4. Allowance for Uncollectible Accounts $318; A/R $4,517
	5. I/S: Bad debt. exp. $380
P4-38A	3. A/R, net: 2020, $212,800; 2019, $207,800
P4-39A	2. Corrected ratios: Current 1.48; Acid-test 0.75;
	3. Net inc., corrected $84,000
P4-40A	2. 12/31/20 Note rec. $25,000; Interest rec. $82
P4-41A	1. ratios: a. 1.98 b. 1.14 c. 31 days
P4-42B	Adj. bal. $5,960
P4-43B	1. Adj. bal. $8,239
P4-44B	5. I/S: Bad debt. exp. $335 thou.
P4-45B	3. A/R, net: 2020, $102,200; 2016 $107,300
P4-46B	2. Corrected ratios: Current 1.32; Acid-test 0.78
	3. Net inc., corrected $76,000
P4-47B	2. 12/31/20 Note rec. $20,000; Interest rec. $247
P4-48B	1. 2020 ratios: a. 1.87 b. 0.87 c. 35 days
DC1	Net inc. $223,000
DC2	2020: Days' sales in rec. 26 days; Cash collections $1,456 thou.

ED1	NCF
FOFSA	1. Adj. bal. $662.1 mil.
	2. Customers owed $15,263 thou. (2018) and $15,386 (2017)
	3. Collected $3,266,088 thous.
	5. A/R turnover = 213
	Days in receivables = 1.71 days
	Acid-test ratio = 0.09

CHAPTER 5

S5-1	NCF
S5-2	GP $160,000
S5-3	1. a. COGS: Weighted-Avg. $3,760; b. FIFO $3,740
S5-4	Net inc.: Weighted-Avg. $3,060; FIFO $3,100
S5-5	Inc. tax exp: Weighted-Avg. $551; FIFO $558
S5-6	NCF
S5-7	COGS $421,000
S5-8	GP% 0.321; Inv. TO 3.0 times
S5-9	c. COGS $1,190 mil. d. GP $510 mil.
S5-10	1. Correct GP $5.7 mil.
	2. Correct GP $5.1 mil.
S5-11	NCF
S5-12	2. $90,000 3. GP $50,000
E5-13	3. GP $1,100 thou.
E5-14	2. GP $3,790
E5-15	1. COGS: a. $1,730 b. $1,760 c. $1,710
E5-16	$12.50
E5-17	2. Net inc. $132
E5-18	1. GP: FIFO $0.2 mil.;
	Weighted-avg. $0.6 mil.
E5-19	NCF
E5-20	NCF
E5-21	GP $45,000
E5-22	a. $475 c. $56 f. $2 g. $3;
	Myers (net loss) $(136) mil.
E5-23	Myers GP% 0.125; Inv. TO 17.9 times
E5-24	GP $16.3 bil.; GP% 29.7; Inv. TO 5.3 times
E5-25	Net inc.: 2020 $65,000; 2019 $69,000
E5-26	1. Ending inv. $1,320 COGS $2,890;
	2. Ending inv. $1,347 COGS $2,863;
	3. Ending Inv. $1,410 COGS $2,800
E5-27	4. COGS $2,863
E5-28	1. COGS $2,843
	2. GP $2,843
E5-29	COGS $3,010

E5-30	1. A/R $4,900
E5-31	NCF
E5-32	1. COGS $150,410; 2. COGS $152,750
E5-33	GP 2020, $8.3 thou.; GP% 0.202, Inv. TO 3.7 times
P5-34A	2. COGS $3,546; GP $2,595
P5-35A	2. Inv. ending bal. $700,000 3. Net inc. $603,000
P5-36A	1. (a) GP $2,409 Ending Inv. $2,437 (b) GP $2,400 Ending Inv. $2,428
P5-37A	1. COGS: Weighted-Avg. $7,290; FIFO $7,200 3. Net inc. $2,457
P5-38A	1. GP: Weighted-Avg. $60,286; FIFO $60,785
P5-39A	NCF
P5-40A	1. Chocolate Treats: GP% 12.5%; Inv. TO 17.9 times
P5-41A	1. Net inc. each yr. $2 mil.
P5-42A	2. GP $1,595
P5-43B	2. COGS $3,417; GP $3,279
P5-44B	2. Inv. ending bal. $1,750,000 3. Net inc. $1,448,400
P5-45B	1. (a) GP $1,173 Ending inv. $340 (b) GP $1,169 Ending Inv. $336
P5-46B	1. COGS: Weighted-Avg. $40,678; FIFO $40,530 3. Net inc. $11,028
P5-47B	1. GP: Weighted-Avg. $291,571; FIFO $299,500
P5-48B	NCF
P5-49B	1. 2020: TC Motors: GP% 24.7%; Inv. TO 8.0 times; X-Country Trucks: GP% 33.8%; Inv. TO 45.4 times
P5-50B	1. Net inc. (thou): 2021, $150; 2020, $320; 2019, $50
P5-51B	2. GP $1,188
DC1	1. Net inc.: FIFO $370,300, Weighted-avg. $364,161
DC2	NCF
ED1	NCF
ED2	NCF
FOFSA	Task 1 3. Purchases $1,989,753 thou. 4. 2018: GP% 39.8%; Inv. TO 4.1 times Task 2 3. Cash payments $1,959,877 thou.

CHAPTER 6

S6-1	2. Carrying amount $29,893 mil.
S6-2	NCF
S6-3	Building cost $56,000
S6-4	Net inc. overstated

S6-5	2. Carrying amount: SL $21 mil.; UOP $22 mil.; DDB $15 mil.
S6-6	a. SL $4 mil. b. UOP $2 mil. c. DDB none
S6-7	a. SL 1.25 mil. b. UOP 3.5 mil. c. DDB 2.857,143 mil.
S6-8	Dep'n. Exp. $12,000
S6-9	1. $13,000
S6-10	NCF
S6-11	1. Goodwill $19.7 mil.
S6-12	1. Net inc. $2,100,000
S6-13	Net cash provided by investing $6 mil.
S6-14	ROA 15%
S6-15	ROA 2019 17.7%, ROA 2020 18%
S6-16	NCF
S6-17	GW 4.8 mil.
S6-18	a. Equip. loss $40,000
E6-19	Land $283,000, Building $3,820,000
E6-20	Machine cost 1 $25,000; 2 $41,700; 3 $33,300
E6-21	NCF
E6-22	2. Building, net $737,160
E6-23	Yr 1: SL $9,000, UOP $7,200, DDB $19,980
E6-24	I/S: Dep. Exp.–building $6,000; B/S: Building net $194,000
E6-25	1. ROA 2020 5.96%; 2019 5.4%
E6-26	Dep'n yr. 12, $55,833
E6-27	Loss on sale $2,200
E6-28	Carrying amount $140,800
E6-29	NCF
E6-30	Amort. yr. 3, $200,000
E6-31	NCF
E6-32	1. Cost of goodwill $17,000,000
E6-33	NCF
E6-34	NCF
E6-35	1. ROA 2020 4.75%; 2019 0.3%
E6-36	NCF
E6-37	5,600 hours
E6-38	Sale price $20.2 mil.
E6-39	Expected net inc. for 2020, $21,426
E6-40	2022 Effects on: 2. Equip. $50,000 under; 3. Net inc. $50,000 over; 4. Equity $50,000 under
P6-41A	1. Land $296,600; Land Improve. $103,800; Warehouse $1,241,000
P6-42A	2. A/Dep.–Building. $105,000; A/Dep.-Equip. $338,000

P6-43A	Dec. 31 Dep. Exp.–Motor Carrier Equip. $58,667; Dep. Exp.–Building. $1,050
P6-44A	NCF
P6-45A	Dep. SL $44,000; UOP 2024, $33,000, DDB, 2024, $11,104
P6-46A	1. Carrying amount $41,497 thou. 3. PPE bal. $68,406; A/Dep. bal. $26,909; Long term investment bal. $108,302
P6-47A	Part 1. 2. Goodwill $1.2 mil. Part 2. 2. Net inc. $3,720,000
P6-48A	1. Loss on sale $0.1 mil. 2. PP&E, net $0.7 mil.
P6-49A	1. ROA 2020 6.62%; 2019 5.61%
P6-50A	2. Loss on sale $257 mil.
P6-51B	1. Land $143,450; Land Improve. $86,000; Garage $654,000
P6-52B	2. A/Dep.–Building. $52,000; A/Dep.–Equip. $437,500
P6-53B	Dec. 31 Dep. Exp.–Comm. Equip. $4,000; Dep. Exp.–Televideo Equip. $1,333
P6-54B	NCF
P6-55B	Dep. SL $9,000; UOP 2021, $9,720; DDB, 2021, $4,741
P6-56B	1. Carrying amount $2,131 mil.; 3. Premises and Equip. bal. $5,941; A/Dep. bal. $3,810
P6-57B	Part 1. 2. Goodwill $5,500; Part 2. 3. Amort. $300,000
P6-58B	1. Gain on sale $0.02 bil. 2. PPE net $7.26 bil.
P6-59B	1. ROA 2020 8.34%; 2019 8.08%
P6-60B	2. Loss on sale $304 mil.
DC1	1. Net inc.: LPF $142,125; BA $128,250
ED1	NCF
ED2	NCF
FOFSA	4. Proportion of PP&E used up in 2018, 42.4%

CHAPTER 7

S7-1	Salaries payable $1,666
S7-2	Salaries exp. $2000
S7-3	2. Est. Warranty pay. bal. $50,000
S7-4	Warranty exp. $60,000
S7-5	1. 2020, A/P TO = 9; Days pay. outstanding = 41 days
S7-6	a. $897,500; b. $551,875
S7-7	NCF
S7-8	b. 10/31/2020, Interest exp. $313

S7-9	2. 07/31/2020, Interest exp. $3,915
S7-10	3. 07/31/2020, Interest exp. $3,915; 01/31/2021 Interest exp. $3,934
S7-11	1. $9,400; 2. $10,000 on July 1, 2030; 3. $325; 4. $355
S7-12	b. 12/31/2020, Int. exp. $375
S7-13	1. Leverage ratio: Best Buy 2.45, Walmart 2.54; Debt ratio: Best Buy 0.59 Walmart 0.61
S7-14	Leverage ratio 2.5; Debt ratio 0.60; Time interest earned ratio 3.73 times
S7-15	Total liabilities $501,000
E7-16	2. Warranty exp. $9,000; Est. Warranty Pay. $7,600
E7-17	Unearned subscription rev. $1,000
E7-18	Salaries payable $13,656
E7-19	3. 2020, Interest exp. $1,250; 2021, $1,750
E7-20	2. 2020, Leverage ratio 1.90; Debt ratio 0.47
E7-21	2. Debt ratio 0.76
E7-22	Company B: Current ratio 1.89; Debt ratio 0.60; Leverage ratio 2.48; Times interest earned ratio 7.2 times
E7-23	d. Total current liabilities $154,713
E7-24	c. 12/31/2020, Interest exp. $2,625
E7-25	4. Annual interest exp. straight-line $15,800
E7-26	1. 01/31/2021 Bond carrying amount $372,811
E7-27	1. 06/30/2020 Bond carrying amount $553,125
E7-28	01/01/2020 Bond Carrying amount $287,041
E7-29	2. 2020, Leverage ratio 2.0; Debt ratio 0.50
E7-30	Sobeys: Current 1.00; Debt 0.51; Times interest earned 9.50 times
E7-31	Company F: Current ratio 2.10; Debt ratio 0.59; Leverage ratio 2.45; Times interest earned ratio 6.3 times
E7-32	2. Leverage ratio 1.42; Debt ratio 0.30
E7-33	1. 2020, Current ratio 1.17; Debt ratio 0.571
E7-34	5. 3/15/2022 Bond Carrying amount $97,632
E7-35	Plan A, EPS $4.12
P7-36A	e. Note pay. due in 1 year $20,000; Interest pay. $6,000
P7-37A	12/31/2020, Warranty Expense $3,800; 4/30/2021 Interest exp. $1,500
P7-38A	2. Interest pay. $30,000; Bonds pay. $4,500,000
P7-39A	4. Interest pay. $5,667; Bonds pay. net $194,250
P7-40A	2. Bonds pay. net $583,800; 3. a. $24,900; b. $24,000
P7-41A	2. Alternative 1, EPS $13.38

P7-42A	3. 12/31/2023 Bond carrying amt. $589,001
P7-43A	1. 12/31/2022 Bond Carrying amt. $474,920; 3. Bond pay. net $472,352
P7-44A	NCF
P7-45A	2. Leverage ratio 1.36, Debt ratio 0.26
P7-46A	2. Carrying amt. $553,000; 3. Time interest earned ratio 4.3 times
P7-47A	c. Interest expense $66,667
P7-48B	e. Long term notes pay. due in 1 year $20,000; Interest pay. $2,083
P7-49B	12/31/2020 Warranty expense $18,000; 6/30/2021 Interest exp. $9,000
P7-50B	1. a. Bonds pay. $1,000,000; c. Interest pay. $20,000
P7-51B	4. Interest pay. $7,000; Notes pay. net $289,000
P7-52B	2. $95,200; 3. a. $4,600; b. $4,000
P7-53B	2.12/31/2023 Bond carrying amt. $483,439
P7-54B	NCF
P7-55B	2. Leverage ratio 2.63; Debt ratio 0.62
P7-56B	2. Bonds pay. carrying amt. $313,000 3. Times interest earned ratio 2.7 times
P7-57B	2. Interest pay. $26,250; Bonds pay. $4,500,000
DC1	1. Debt ratio 0.82; ROA 1.5%; 2. Leverage ratio 5.71; ROE 8.6%; 3. Debt ratio 0.92; ROA 0.1%
DC2	EPS Plan A $4.78; Plan B $4.54; Plan C $4.63
ED1	NCF
ED2	NCF
ED3	NCF
FOFSA	NCF

CHAPTER 8

S8-1	NCF
S8-2	NCF
S8-3	NCF
S8-4	NCF
S8-5	1. $1.80 3. $5,650 profit
S8-6	NCF
S8-7	Total SE $1,246 thou.
S8-8	a. $585 thou. b. $3,011 thou. c. $4,257 thou.
S8-9	NCF
S8-10	R/E increased $50,000
S8-11	1. $150,000 4. Pref. $450,000

S8-12	2. No effect
S8-13	Carrying amount per share $61.60
S8-14	2. Decrease SE $49,500,000
S8-15	ROA 1.5%; ROE 3.9%
S8-16	Total SE $2,010,000
E8-17	1. ROA 9.3%; ROE 26%
E8-18	2. Total SE $92,500
E8-19	Total SE $143,000
E8-20	Total contributed capital $1,045,000
E8-21	SE $(29) deficit
E8-22	Overall increase in SE $19,100
E8-23	NCF
E8-24	Total SE $4,300 mil.
E8-25	3. 564 mil. shares 4. $136 mil.
E8-26	2019: Pref. $24,000; Com. $26,000
E8-27	2. Total SE $8,134,000
E8-28	a. Decrease SE $80 mil. e. Increase SE $3,000
E8-29	Total SE $2,755 mil.
E8-30	1. $10.90 2. $10.77
E8-31	1. ROA 10.2%; ROE 18%
E8-32	1. ROA 4.1%; ROE 11.7%
E8-33	b. Issued 500 shares
E8-34	Div. $1,407 mil.
E8-35	Total SE $65 mil.
P8-36A	NCF
P8-37A	2. Total SE $207,500
P8-38A	Total SE $663,000
P8-39A	NCF
P8-40A	Total SE $7,680,000
P8-41A	4. $22,500
P8-42A	2. Total SE $95,800
P8-43A	NCF
P8-44A	1. Total assets $559,000, Total SE $296,000 2. ROA 20.1%; ROE 34.9%
P8-45A	1. $806 mil. 2. $5 per share 3. $10 per share 4. 7.8%
P8-46B	NCF
P8-47B	2. Total SE $323,800
P8-48B	Total SE $540,000
P8-49B	NCF
P8-50B	Total SE $4,126,000
P8-51B	4. $183,700
P8-52B	2. Total SE $132,800

P8-53B	NCF
P8-54B	1. Total assets $568,000, Total SE $312,000 2. ROA 16.4%; ROE 26.1%
P8-55B	1. $537 mil. 2. $3.01 per share 3. $3.77 per share 4. 8%
DC1	3. Total SE: Plan 1, $220,000 Plan 2, $230,000
DC2	NCF
ED1	NCF
ED2	NCF
ED3	NCF
FOFSA	Task 1 NCF Task 2 379,050 common shares 2. Avg. share price $47.03 Task 3 NCF Task 4 2018: ROA 29.3%; ROE (683.4)%

CHAPTER 9

S9-1	NCF
S9-2	NCF
S9-3	Net cash oper. $70,000
S9-4	NCF
S9-5	Net cash oper. $54,000
S9-6	Net cash oper. $54,000 Net increase in cash $53,000
S9-7	Net cash oper. $56,000 Net increase in cash $15,900
S9-8	a. $60,000; b. $20,000
S9-9	a. New borrowing $10,000 b. Issuance $8,000 c. Dividends $146,000
E9-10	NCF
E9-11	NCF
E9-12	NCF
E9-13	Net cash oper. ($32,000)
E9-14	Net cash oper. ($80,000)
E9-15	Net cash oper. $111,100 Net increase in cash $11,100
E9-16	NCF
E9-17	a. Cash proceeds of sale $46,000; b. Cash dividends $26,000
E9-18	1. Gain on sale of property and equipment $120 thou. 2. LT debt issued $240 thou.
E9-19	a. $23,996 c. $3,577 f. $626
E9-20	Total assets $317,400
P9-21A	NCF

P9-22A	1. Net inc. $51,667 2. Total assets $396,667 3. Net cash oper. $(49,000) Net increase in cash $90,000
P9-23A	Net cash oper. $63,200 Net increase in cash $16,000 Non-cash inv. and fin. $160,000
P9-24A	Net cash oper. $76,900 Net (decrease) in cash $(4,100) Non-cash inv. and fin. $101,000
P9-25A	Net cash oper. $80,000 Net increase in cash $12,300
P9-26B	NCF
P9-27B	1. Net inc. $157,333 2. Total assets $340,333 3. Net cash oper. $81,000 Net increase in cash $191,000
P9-28B	Net cash oper. $74,500 Net (decrease) in cash $(5,700) Non-cash inv. and fin. $290,400
P9-29B	Net cash oper. $68,700 Net increase in cash $16,300 Non-cash inv. and fin. $30,000
P9-30B	Net cash oper. $90,600 Net increase in cash $13,100
DC1	1. Net cash oper. $132 thou. Net (decrease) in cash $(46) thou.
DC2	NCF
ED1	NCF
ED2	NCF
FOFSA	NCF

APPENDIX 9A

S9A-1	Net cash oper. $110,000 Net (decrease) in cash $(20,000)
S9A-2	Net cash oper. $13,000
S9A-3	Net cash oper. $13,000 Net increase in cash $12,000
S9A-4	a. $699,000 b. $326,000
S9A-5	a. $68,000 b. $134,000
E9A-6	NCF
E9A-7	NCF
E9A-8	Net cash oper. $21,000
E9A-9	NCF
E9A-10	Net cash oper. $102,000 Net increase in cash $29,000

E9A-11   a. $50,000 b. $113,000

E9A-12   (in thousands) a. $24,637; b. $18,134; c. $3,576; d. $530; e. $73; f. $1,294

P9A-13A   Net cash oper. $95,700
Net (decrease) in cash $(2,700)
Non-cash inv. and fin. $79,400

P9A-14A   1. Net inc. $51,667
2. Total assets $396,667
3. Net cash oper. ($49,000)
Net increase in cash $90,000

P9A-15A   Net cash oper. $80,000
Net increase in cash $12,300

P9A-16A   Net cash oper. $55,800
Net (decrease) in cash $(2,000)
Non-cash inv. and fin. $99,100

P9A-17A   Net cash oper. $73,200
Net increase in cash $20,000
Non-cash inv. and fin. $19,000

P9A-18B   Net cash oper. $30,000
Net increase in cash $7,600
Non-cash inv. and fin. $142,800

P9A-19B   1. Net inc. $157,333
2. Total assets $340,333
3. Net cash oper. $81,000
Net increase in cash $191,000

P9A-20B   Net cash oper. $90,600
Net increase in cash $13,100

P9A-21B   Net cash oper. $77,200
Net (decrease) in cash $(4,600)
Non-cash inv. and fin. $83,200

P9A-22B   Net cash oper. $40,400
Net increase in cash $4,100
Non-cash inv. and fin. $48,300

CHAPTER 10

S10-1   2020 Net inc. increase 9.2%

S10-2   2020 Sales trend 107%

S10-3   2020 Cash 2.13%

S10-4   Net inc. Porterfield 6.21%

S10-5   2020 Current ratio 1.37

S10-6   2020 Allstott Inc. Quick ratio 1.18

S10-7   a. 28.4 times; 12.9 days b. 9 days c. 2.6 times d. −118 days

S10-8   1. 80.8% 2. 6.5

S10-9   a. 7.74% b. 1.369 c. 13.2% d. 4.77 e. 50.6%

S10-10   1. EPS $4.85; P/E 16

S10-11   a. $3,855 thou. d. $873 thou.

S10-12   a. $562 thou. d. $3,768 thou. e. $1,294 thou.

E10-13   2020 WC increase 26.8%

E10-14   Net inc. decreased 5.8%

E10-15   Yr.4 Net inc. trend 47%

E10-16   Current assets 24.6%; Total liabilities 41.7%

E10-17   Net inc. 2020 20.1%, 2019 20.0%

E10-18   NCF

E10-19   a. 1.67 b.0.83 c. 4.4 times d. 9.5 times e. 38 days

E10-20   2020 ratios: a. 2.07 b. 0.91 c. 0.47 d. 4.13

E10-21   2020 ratios: Return on net sales 0.098; ROA. 0.132; ROE 0.151; EPS 0.67

E10-22   2020 ratios: P/E 17.3; Div. yield. 0.014; BV per common share $6

E10-23   Total liab. & S/H equity $20,000 mil.

E10-24   Net inc. $720 mil.

E10-25   2020 Net inc. $168,000

P10-26A   4. 2020 17.3%

P10-27A   1. Net inc. 10.7%, Current assets 77.1%

P10-28A   NCF

P10-29A   1. Current ratio 1.74; 2. a. Current ratio 1.84

P10-30A   1. 2020 a. 1.96 f. 255 k. 17

P10-31A   Video a. 0.60 b. 2.16 c. 100 d. 0.68 f. 0.196

P10-32A   NCF

P10-33A   1. 2020 a. 1.46 d. 7.61 g. 83 days

P10-34B   4. 2020 14.6%

P10-35B   1. Net inc. 5.3%, Current assets 75%

P10-36B   NCF

P10-37B   1. Current ratio 1.54; 2. a. Current ratio 1.44

P10-38B   1. 2020 a. 1.94 f. 256 k. 13

P10-39B   Thrifty a. 0.78 b. 2.32 c. 40 d. 0.41 f. 0.349

P10-40B   NCF

P10-41B   1. 2020 a. 1.96 d. 5.95 g. 67 days

DC1   NCF

DC2   NCF

DC3   NCF

ED1   NCF

ED2   NCF

FOF   1. Net inc. trend 2018 108%
3. Net inc. 2018 16%; 2017 15%

APPENDIX B

SB-1   2. Unrealized loss on invest. $500
LT investment at fair value $7,000

SB-2   1. Other comprehensive income $800

SB-3	3. LT investment bal. $42.6 mil.
SB-4	Loss on sale $7.3 mil.
SB-5	NCF
SB-6	NCF
SB-7	2. Cash Interest $70,000 4. Interest revenue $68,175
SB-8	c. Dr. Interest Revenue $1,825
SB-9	1. PV $6,810 2. PV $39,930
SB-10	PV $6,145,000
SB-11	NCF
SB-12	1. PV $7,452 2. PV $45,492
SB-13	1. PV $6,743.26 2. PV $10,871.63
EB-14	d. Loss on sale $2,000
EB-15	2. Other comprehensive income $63,560 3. LT investments $242,644
EB-16	2. Invest. end. bal. $1,055,000
EB-17	Gain on sale $1,645,000
EB-18	2. Long term investment at equity $525,000
EB-19	3. Interest rec. $350; LT investment in bonds $19,224
EB-20	PV of bond investment $10,521
EB-21	2. Shareholders' equity $327,000
EB-22	Net cash used inv. $(11.8) mil.
EB-23	NCF
EB-24	1. PV of investment at 5%, $103,890 2. PV of investment at 10%, $90,855

EB-25	Accum. other comprehensive loss Dec 31, 2020, $(69) mil.
PB-26A	2. B/S LT invest. at equity $523,300, I/S Equity method invest. rev. $178,500, Div. Rev. $240, Other comprehensive income $2,600
PB-27A	2. LT invest. in MSC bal. $659,000
PB-28A	3. Consolidated debt ratio 0.898
PB-29A	2. B/S LT investment in bonds $622,031; I/S Interest rev. $25,031
PB-30A	Choose Investment A, PV $19,578
PB-31A	2. Shareholders' equity $341,000
PB-32A	NCF
PB-33A	3. Consolidated debt ratio 0.917
PB-34B	2. B/S LT invest. at equity $526,300, I/S Equity method invest. rev. $87,500, Div rev. $750, Other income (loss) $(3,300)
PB-35B	2. LT invest. in Affil. bal. $535,000
PB-36B	2. LT invest. in bonds $445,304; Int. rev. $35,304
PB-37B	Choose Investment X, PV $25,650
PB-38B	3. Consolidated debt ratio 0.935
PB-39B	NCF
PB-40B	3. Consolidated debt ratio 0.929
DC1	NCF
DC2	2. Gain on sale $4,872 3. Gain on sale $125,000
ED1	NCF
FOFSA	NCF

accelerated depreciation method A depreciation method that writes off a relatively larger amount of the asset's cost nearer the start of its useful life than the straight-line method does. (p. 288)

account The record of the changes that have occurred in a particular asset, liability, or element of shareholders' equity during a period. (p. 56)

account format A balance sheet format that lists assets on the left side and liabilities above shareholders' equity on the right side. (p. 129)

account payable A liability for goods or services purchased on credit and backed by the general reputation and credit standing of the debtor. (p. 336)

accounting An information system that measures and records business activities, processes data into reports, and reports results to decision makers. (p. 3)

accounting equation Assets = Liabilities + Owners' Equity. Provides the foundation for the double-entry method of accounting. (p. 11)

Accounting Standards for Private Enterprises (ASPE) Canadian accounting standards that specify the *generally accepted accounting principles* applicable to *private enterprises* that are required to follow *GAAP* and choose not to apply *IFRS*. (p. 8)

accounts payable turnover (T/O) A liquidity ratio that measures the number of times per year a company was able to repay its accounts payable in full. Calculated by dividing the cost of goods sold by the average accounts payable balance for the year. (pp. 362, 539)

accounts receivable turnover Measures a company's ability to collect cash from credit customers. To compute accounts receivable turnover, divide net credit sales by average net accounts receivable. (p. 538)

accrual An adjustment related to revenues earned or expenses incurred prior to any cash or invoice changing hands. (p. 120)

accrual accounting A basis of accounting that records transactions based on whether a business has acquired an asset, earned revenue, taken on a liability, or incurred an expense, regardless of whether cash is involved. (p. 109)

accrued expense An expense that has been incurred but not yet paid or invoiced. (p. 120)

accrued revenue A revenue that has been earned but not yet collected or invoiced. (p. 122)

accumulated depreciation The account showing the sum of all depreciation expense from the date of acquiring a capital asset. (p. 119)

acid-test ratio Ratio of the sum of cash plus short-term investments plus net current receivables to total current liabilities. Tells whether the entity can pay all its current liabilities if they come due immediately. Also called the *quick ratio*. (pp. 202, 537)

adjusted trial balance A list of all the ledger accounts with their adjusted balances. (p. 126)

aging-of-receivables method A way to estimate bad debts by analyzing accounts receivable according to the length of time they have been receivable from the customer. Also called the *balance-sheet approach* because it focuses on accounts receivable. (p. 190)

allowance for bad debts Another name for *allowance for uncollectible accounts*. (p. 190)

allowance for doubtful accounts Another name for *allowance for uncollectible accounts*. (p. 190)

allowance for uncollectible accounts A contra account, related to accounts receivable, that holds the estimated amount of collection losses. (p. 190)

allowance method A method of recording collection losses based on estimates of how much money the business will not collect from its customers. (p. 190)

amortization Allocation of the cost of an intangible asset with a finite life over its useful life. (p. 301)

asset A resource owned or controlled by a company as a result of past events and from which the company expects to receive future economic benefits. (p. 11)

asset turnover The dollars of sales generated per dollar of assets invested. Net sales divided by Average total assets. (p. 542)

auditor An accountant who provides an independent opinion on whether an entity's financial statements have been prepared in accordance with generally accepted accounting principles. (p. 17)

bad debt expense A cost to the seller of extending credit to customers. Arises from a failure to collect an account receivable in full. (p. 189)

balance sheet Reports a company's financial position as at a specific date. In particular, it reports a company's assets, liabilities, and owners' equity. Also called the *statement of financial position*. (p. 11)

bank collections Collections of money by the bank on behalf of a depositor. (p. 182)

bank reconciliation A document explaining the reasons for the difference between a depositor's records and the bank's records about the depositor's cash. (p. 181)

bank statement Document showing the beginning and ending balances of a particular bank account and listing the month's transactions that affected the account. (p. 180)

benchmarking The comparison of a company to a standard set by other companies, with a view toward improvement. (p. 527)

board of directors Group elected by the shareholders to set policy for a corporation and to appoint its officers. (p. 6)

bond discount Excess of a bond's face (par) value over its issue price. (p. 348)

bond investments Bonds and notes are debt instruments that an investor intends to hold until maturity. (p. 644)

bond premium Excess of a bond's issue price over its face value. (p. 348)

bonds payable Groups of notes payable issued to multiple lenders called *bondholders*. (p. 347)

book value (of a share) Amount of owners' equity on the company's books for each share of its stock. (p. 409)

book value per common share Common shareholders' equity divided by the number of common shares outstanding. The recorded amount for each common share outstanding. (p. 546)

brand name A distinctive identification of a product or service. Also called a *trademark* or *trade name*. (p. 302)

capital expenditure Expenditure that increases an asset's capacity or efficiency, or extends its useful life. Capital expenditures are debited to an asset account. Also called *betterments*. (p. 282)

carrying amount The historical cost of an asset net of its accumulated depreciation. (p. 13)

carrying amount (of a capital asset) The asset's cost minus accumulated depreciation. (p. 119)

cash conversion cycle The number of days it takes to convert cash into inventory, inventory to receivables, and receivables back into cash, after paying off payables. Days inventory outstanding + days sales outstanding − days payables outstanding. (p. 539)

cash equivalents Investments such as term deposits, guaranteed investment certificates, or high-grade government securities that are considered so similar to cash that they are combined with cash for financial disclosure on the balance sheet. (pp. 178, 446)

cash-basis accounting Accounting that records only transactions in which cash is received or paid. (p. 109)

chairperson Elected by a corporation's board of directors, usually the most powerful person in the corporation. (p. 398)

chart of accounts List of a company's accounts and their account numbers. (p. 69)

cheque Document instructing a bank to pay the designated person or business the specified amount of money. (p. 179)

classified balance sheet A balance sheet that shows current assets separate from long-term assets, and current liabilities separate from long-term liabilities. (p. 129)

closing entries Entries that transfer the revenue, expense, and dividend balances from these respective accounts to the Retained Earnings account. (p. 136)

common-size financial statements A financial statement that reports only percentages (no dollar amounts). (p. 527)

comparability Investors like to compare a company's financial statements from one year to the next. Therefore, a company must consistently use the same accounting method each year. (pp. 21, 248)

consolidated statements Financial statements of the parent company plus those of majority-owned subsidiaries as if the combination were a single legal entity. (p. 641)

contingent liability A possible obligation that arises from past events and whose existence will be confirmed only by the occurrence or non-occurrence of one or more uncertain future events not wholly within the control of the company. (p. 345)

contra account An account that always has a companion account and whose normal balance is opposite that of the companion account. (p. 119)

controlling (majority) interest Ownership of more than 50% of an investee company's voting shares and can exercise control over the investee. (p. 641)

copyright Exclusive right to reproduce and sell a book, musical composition, film, other work of art, or computer program. Issued by the federal government, copyrights extend 50 years beyond the author's life. (p. 301)

corporation An incorporated business owned by one or more *shareholders*, which according to the law is a legal "person" separate from its owners. (p. 6)

cost of goods sold Cost of the inventory the business has sold to customers. Also called *cost of sales*. (p. 231)

credit The right side of an account. (p. 70)

creditor The party to whom money is owed. (p. 195)

cumulative preferred shares Preferred shares whose owners must receive all dividends in arrears plus the current year's dividend before the corporation can pay dividends to the common shareholders. (p. 407)

current asset An asset that is expected to be converted to cash, sold, or consumed during the next 12 months, or within the business's normal operating cycle if longer than a year. (p. 11)

current liability A debt due to be paid within one year or within the entity's operating cycle if the cycle is longer than a year. (p. 14)

current portion of long-term debt The amount of the principal that is payable within one year. Also called *current instalment of long-term debt*. (p. 343)

current ratio Current assets divided by current liabilities. Measures a company's ability to pay current liabilities with current assets. (pp. 138, 535)

date of declaration The date on which the Board of Directors declares a dividend to shareholders. (p. 404)

date of payment The date on which a dividend is actually paid to shareholders. (p. 405)

date of record The date on which a person must be recorded as a shareholder in order to receive a dividend. (p. 405)

days payable outstanding (DPO) Another way of expressing the accounts payable turnover ratio, this measure indicates how many days it will take to pay off the accounts payable balance in full. Calculated by dividing the *accounts payable turnover* into 365. (pp. 362, 539)

days' inventory outstanding Calculated as 365 days divided by inventory turnover. Indicates how many days it takes to sell inventory. (pp. 251, 538)

days' sales in receivables Ratio of average net accounts receivable to one day's sales. Indicates how many days' sales remain in Accounts Receivable awaiting collection. Also called the *collection period* and *days sales outstanding*. (pp. 203, 539)

debentures Unsecured bonds—bonds backed only by the good faith of the borrower. (p. 348)

debit The left side of an account. (p. 70)

debt ratio Ratio of total liabilities to total assets. States the proportion of a company's assets that is financed with debt. (pp. 139, 540)

debtor The party who owes money.   (p. 195)

deferral An adjustment related to a transaction for which a business has received or paid cash in advance of delivering or receiving goods or services.   (p. 115)

deferred income tax liability The amount of income taxes payable in future periods as a result of differences between accounting income and taxable income in current and prior periods. Under ASPE, this is known as a *future income tax liability.*   (p. 342)

deficit The term used when *retained earnings* is a negative balance.   (pp. 10, 404)

deposits in transit A deposit recorded by the company but not yet recorded by its bank.   (p. 181)

depreciable cost The cost of a tangible asset minus its estimated residual value.   (p. 285)

depreciation An expense to recognize the portion of a capital asset's economic benefits that has been used up during an accounting period.   (pp. 118, 283)

direct method A method of determining cash flows from operating activities in which all cash receipts and cash payments from operating activities are directly reported on the statement of cash flows.   (p. 450)

disclosure A company's financial statements should report enough information for users to make informed decisions about the company.   (p. 248)

dividend yield Ratio of dividends per share to the share's market price per share. Tells the percentage of a share's market value that the company returns to shareholders as dividends.   (p. 546)

double-diminishing-balance (DDB) method An accelerated depreciation method that computes annual depreciation by multiplying the asset's decreasing carrying amount by a constant percentage, which is two times the straight-line rate.   (p. 288)

double-entry system An accounting system that uses debits and credits to record the dual effects of each business transaction.   (p. 69)

doubtful account expense Another name for *bad debt expense.*   (p. 189)

earnings per share (EPS) Amount of a company's net income per outstanding common share.   (pp. 360, 544)

electronic funds transfer System that transfers cash by electronic communication rather than by paper documents.   (p. 178)

entire period Length of time during which beginning inventory and purchases are taken into account when calculating unit cost.   (p. 241)

equity method The method used to account for investments in which the investor has 20–50% of the investee's voting shares and can significantly influence the decisions of the investee.   (p. 639)

estimated residual value Expected cash value of an asset at the end of its useful life. Also called *scrap value* or *salvage value.*   (p. 284)

estimated useful life Length of service that a business expects to get from an asset. May be expressed in years, units of output, kilometres, or other measures.   (p. 284)

ethical standards Standards that govern the way we treat others and the way we restrain our selfish desires. They are shaped by our cultural, socioeconomic, and religious backgrounds.   (p. 25)

expense A cost incurred to purchase the goods and services a company needs to run its business on a day-to-day basis. The opposite of revenue.   (p. 9)

face value of bond The principal amount payable by the issuer. Also called *maturity value.*   (p. 347)

fair value The amount that a business could sell an asset for, or the amount that a business could pay to settle a liability.   (p. 24)

fair value (of a share) The price that a willing buyer would pay a willing seller to acquire a share.   (p. 409)

faithful representation A fundamental qualitative characteristic of accounting information. Information is a faithful representation if it is complete, neutral, accurate, and reflects the economic substance of the underlying transaction or event.   (p. 20)

finance lease Under IFRS, a lease that transfers substantially all the risks and rewards incidental to ownership of assets to the lessee.   (p. 365)

financial accounting The branch of accounting that provides information for managers inside a business and for decision makers outside the business.   (p. 5)

financial statements The reports that companies use to convey the financial results of their business activities to various user groups, which can include managers, investors, creditors, and regulatory agencies.   (p. 2)

financing activities Activities that result in changes in the size and composition of a company's contributed equity and borrowings.   (pp. 15, 448)

first-in, first-out (FIFO) cost method Inventory costing method by which the first costs into inventory are the first costs out to cost of goods sold. Ending inventory is based on the costs of the most recent purchases.   (p. 242)

FOB (free on board) destination The inventory is included in the books of the seller.   (p. 234)

FOB (free on board) shipping point The inventory is included in the books of the buyer.   (p. 234)

franchises and licences Privileges granted by a private business or a government to sell a product or service in accordance with specified conditions.   (p. 302)

free cash flow A measure of how much cash a company has available to pursue new business opportunities. Calculated by deducting capital expenditures from cash flow from operating activities.   (p. 464)

future value Measures the future sum of money that a given current investment is "worth" at a specified time in the future, assuming a certain interest rate.   (p. 648)

gain A type of income other than revenue that results in an increase in economic benefits to a company, and usually occurs outside the course of the company's ordinary business activities.   (p. 8)

generally accepted accounting principles (GAAP) The guidelines of financial accounting, which specify the standards for how accountants must record, measure, and report financial information.   (p. 7)

going-concern assumption The assumption that an entity will continue operating normally for the foreseeable future.   (p. 22)

goodwill Excess of the cost of an acquired company over the sum of the market values of its net assets (assets minus liabilities).   (p. 302)

gross margin Another name for *gross profit*. (p. 233)

gross profit Sales revenue minus cost of goods sold. Also called *gross margin*. (p. 233)

gross profit percentage Gross profit divided by net sales revenue. Also called the *gross margin percentage*. (p. 250)

historical-cost assumption Holds that assets should be recorded at their actual cost, measured on the date of purchase as the amount of cash paid plus the dollar value of all non-cash consideration (other assets, privileges, or rights) also given in exchange. (p. 22)

horizontal analysis Study of percentage changes over time through comparative financial statements. (p. 519)

income Consists of a company's *revenues* and *gains*. (p. 8)

income statement The financial statement that measures a company's operating performance for a specified period of time. In particular, it reports income, expenses, and net income. Also called the *statement of profit or loss*. (p. 8)

indirect method A method of determining cash flows from operating activities in which net income is adjusted for non-cash transactions, any deferrals or accruals of past or future operating cash receipts or payments, and items of income or expense associated with investing or financing cash flows. (p. 450)

intangible assets Long-lived assets with no physical form that convey a special right to current and expected future benefits. (p. 279)

interest The borrower's cost of renting money from a lender. Interest is revenue for the lender and expense for the borrower. (p. 195)

interest-coverage ratio Another name for the *times-interest-earned ratio*. (pp. 364, 540)

International Financial Reporting Standards (IFRS) International accounting standards that specify the *generally accepted accounting principles* which must be applied by *publicly accountable enterprises* in Canada and over 100 other countries. (p. 7)

inventory turnover Ratio of cost of goods sold to average inventory. Indicates how rapidly inventory is sold. (pp. 250, 537)

investing activities Activities that include the purchase and sale of long-term assets and other investments that result in cash inflows or outflows related to resources used for generating future income and cash flows. (pp. 15, 448)

journal The chronological accounting record of an entity's transactions. (p. 73)

lease Rental agreement in which the tenant (lessee) agrees to make rent payments to the property owner (lessor) in exchange for the use of the asset. (p. 365)

ledger The book of accounts and their balances. (p. 73)

lessee Tenant in a lease agreement. (p. 365)

lessor Property owner in a lease agreement. (p. 365)

leverage Earning more income on borrowed money than the related interest expense, thereby increasing the earnings for the owners of the business. Also called *trading on the equity*. (p. 543)

leverage ratio Shows the ratio of a company's total assets to total shareholders' equity. It is an alternative way of expressing how much debt a company has used to fund its assets, or in other words, how much leverage it has used. (pp. 363, 543)

liability An obligation (or debt) owed by a company, which it expects to pay off in the future using some of its assets. (p. 13)

limited liability No personal obligation of a shareholder for corporation debts. A shareholder can lose no more on an investment in a corporation's shares than the cost of the investment. (p. 397)

line of credit A method of short-term borrowing that provides a company with as-needed access to credit up to a maximum amount specified by its lender. (p. 336)

liquidity A measure of how quickly an asset can be converted to cash. The higher an asset's liquidity, the more quickly it can be converted to cash. (pp. 11, 129)

long-term asset Another term for *non-current asset*. (p. 13)

long-term investments Any investment that does not meet the criteria of a short-term investment; any investment that the investor expects to hold for longer than a year. (p. 635)

long-term liability Another term for *non-current liability*. (p. 14)

loss A type of expense that results in a decrease in economic benefits to a company, and usually occurs outside the course of the company's ordinary business activities. The opposite of a gain. (p. 9)

lower-of-cost-and-net-realizable-value (LCNRV) rule Requires that an asset be reported in the financial statements at whichever is lower—its historical cost or its net realizable value. (p. 248)

majority interest Ownership of more than 50% of an investee company's voting shares. (p. 641)

management accounting The branch of accounting that generates information for the internal decision makers of a business, such as top executives. (p. 5)

market interest rate Interest rate that investors demand for loaning their money. Also called *effective interest rate*. (p. 349)

market price (of a bond) The price investors are willing to pay for a bond. It is equal to the present value of the principal payments plus the present value of the interest payments. (p. 348)

market price (of a share) The price that a willing buyer would pay a willing seller to acquire a share. (p. 403)

material Accounting information is material if it is significant enough in nature or magnitude that omitting or misstating it could affect the decisions of an informed user. (p. 21)

maturity date The date on which a debt instrument must be paid. (p. 195)

mortgage A *term loan* secured by real property, such as land and buildings. (p. 365)

multi-step income statement An income statement that contains subtotals to highlight important relationships between revenues and expenses. (p. 130)

net assets Another name for *owners' equity*. (p. 14)

net earnings Another name for *net income*. (p. 10)

net income The excess of a company's total income over its total expenses. (p. 10)

net loss Occurs when a company's total expenses exceed its total income. (p. 10)

net profit Another term for *net income*. (p. 10)

net realizable value (NRV) The amount a business could get if it sold the inventory less the costs of selling it. (p. 248)

net working capital Current assets – current liabilities. Measures the ease with which a company will be able to use its current assets to pay off its current liabilities.   (p. 138)

non-cash operating working capital account A current asset or current liability account that derives from an operating activity and is not included in cash and cash equivalents.   (p. 454)

non-controlling interest A subsidiary company's equity that is held by shareholders other than the parent company.   (p. 643)

non-current asset Any asset that is not classified as a current asset.   (p. 11)

non-current liability A liability a company expects to pay off beyond one year from the balance sheet date.   (p. 14)

non-strategic investments Investments in which the investor owns less than 20% of the voting shares of the investee and is presumed to exercise no influence.   (p. 635)

nonsufficient funds (NSF) cheque A cheque for which the payer's bank account has insufficient money to pay the cheque. NSF cheques are cash receipts that turn out to be worthless.   (p. 182)

obsolescence Occurs when an asset becomes outdated or no longer produces revenue for the company.   (p. 284)

operating activities Activities that comprise the main revenue-producing activities of a company, and generally result from the transactions and other events that determine net income.   (pp. 15, 448)

operating lease A lease in which the risks and rewards of asset ownership are not transferred to the lessee.   (p. 365)

outstanding cheques Cheques issued by the company and recorded on its books but not yet paid by its bank.   (p. 181)

owners' equity The company owners' remaining interest in the assets of the company after deducting all its liabilities.   (p. 14)

par value shares Shares of stock that have a value assigned to them by articles of the corporation.   (p. 400)

parent company An investor company that owns more than 50% of the voting shares of a subsidiary company.   (p. 641)

partnership An unincorporated business with two or more parties as co-owners, with each owner being a partner in the business.   (p. 5)

patent A federal government grant giving the holder the exclusive right for 20 years to produce and sell an invention.   (p. 301)

payroll Employee compensation, a major expense of many businesses.   (p. 339)

periodic inventory system An inventory system in which the business does not keep a continuous record of the inventory on hand. Instead, at the end of the period, the business makes a physical count of the inventory on hand and applies the appropriate unit costs to determine the cost of the ending inventory.   (p. 234)

permanent accounts Assets, liabilities, and shareholders' equity accounts, which all have balances that carry forward to the next fiscal year.   (p. 136)

perpetual inventory system An inventory system in which the business keeps a continuous record for each inventory item to show the inventory on hand at all times.   (p. 234)

physical wear and tear Occurs when the usefulness of the asset deteriorates.   (p. 284)

post-employment benefits A special type of employee benefits that do not become payable until after a person has completed employment with the company. They include such things as pension benefits, medical and dental insurance, and prescription drug benefits.   (p. 366)

posting Transferring amounts from the journal to the ledger.   (p. 73)

preferred shares Shares that give their owners certain advantages, such as the priority to receive dividends before the common shareholders and the priority to receive assets before the common shareholders if the corporation liquidates.   (p. 400)

present value The value on a given date of a future payment or series of future payments, discounted to reflect the time value of money.   (p. 649)

president Chief executive officer in charge of managing the day-to-day operations of a corporation.   (p. 398)

pretax accounting income Income before tax on the income statement; the basis for computing income tax expense.   (p. 341)

price/earnings ratio (multiple) Ratio of the market price of a common to the company's earnings per share. Measures the value that the stock market places on $1 of a company's earnings.   (p. 545)

principal The amount borrowed by a debtor and lent by a creditor.   (p. 195)

private enterprise An entity that has not issued and does not plan to issue shares or debt on public markets.   (p. 7)

proprietorship An unincorporated business with a single owner, called the proprietor.   (p. 5)

provision Under IFRS, a present obligation of uncertain timing or amount that is recorded as a liability because it is probable that economic resources will be required to settle it.   (p. 344)

publicly accountable enterprises (PAEs) Corporations that have issued or plan to issue shares or debt in a public market.   (p. 7)

purchase allowance A decrease in the cost of purchases because the seller has granted the buyer a discount (an allowance) from the amount owed.   (p. 236)

purchase discount A decrease in the cost of purchases earned by making an early payment to the vendor.   (p. 236)

purchase return A decrease in the cost of purchases because the buyer returned the goods to the seller.   (p. 236)

quick ratio Another name for *acid-test ratio*.   (pp. 202, 537)

receivables Monetary claims against a business or an individual, acquired mainly by selling goods or services and by lending money.   (p. 187)

relevance A fundamental qualitative characteristic of accounting information. Information is relevant if it has predictive value, confirmatory value, or both, and is *material*.   (p. 20)

remittance advice An optional attachment to a cheque (sometimes a perforated tear-off document and sometimes capable of being electronically scanned) that indicates the payer, date, and purpose of the cash payment. The remittance advice is often used as the source document for posting cash receipts or payments.   (p. 179)

report format A balance sheet format that lists assets at the top, followed by liabilities and then shareholders' equity.   (p. 129)

repurchased shares A corporation's own shares that it has issued and later reacquired.   (p. 403)

retained earnings Represent the accumulated net income of a company since the day it started business, less any net losses and dividends declared during this time.   (p. 10)

return on assets (ROA) Measures how profitably management has used the assets that shareholders and creditors have provided the company.   (pp. 304, 410, 543)

return on common shareholders' equity Net income minus preferred dividends, divided by average common shareholders' equity. A measure of profitability. Also called *return on equity (ROE)*.   (p. 543)

return on equity (ROE) Net income divided by average total assets. This ratio measures how profitably management has used the assets that shareholders and creditors have provided the company.   (p. 411)

return on net sales Ratio of net income to net sales. A measure of profitability. Also called *return on sales*.   (p. 542)

revenue Consists of amounts earned by a company in the course of its ordinary, day-to-day business activities. The vast majority of a company's revenue is earned through the sale of its primary goods and services.   (p. 8)

sales discount Percentage reduction of sale price by the seller as an incentive for early payment before the due date. A typical way to express a sales discount is "2/10, n/30." This means the seller will grant a 2% discount if the invoice is paid within 10 days, or the full amount is due within 30 days.   (p. 238)

sales returns and allowances Merchandise returned for credit or refunds for services provided.   (p. 238)

sales tax payable The amount of HST, GST, and provincial sales tax owing to government bodies.   (p. 338)

separate-entity assumption Holds that the business activities of the reporting entity are separate from the activities of its owners.   (p. 22)

serial bonds Bonds that mature in instalments over a period of time.   (p. 348)

shareholder A party who owns shares of a corporation.   (p. 6)

shareholders' equity Another term for *owners' equity*.   (p. 14)

shares Legal units of ownership in a corporation.   (p. 6)

short-term notes payable Notes payable due within one year.   (p. 337)

single-step income statement Lists all revenues together and all expenses together; there is only one step in arriving at net income.   (p. 130)

specific identification cost method Inventory costing method based on the specific cost of particular units of inventory.   (p. 240)

stable-monetary-unit assumption Holds that regardless of the reporting currency used, financial information is always reported under the assumption that the value of the currency is stable, despite the fact that its value does change due to economic factors such as inflation.   (p. 22)

stated interest rate Interest rate printed on the bond certificate that determines the amount of cash interest the borrower pays and the investor receives each year. Also called the *coupon rate* or *contract interest rate*.   (p. 348)

stated value An arbitrary amount assigned by a company to a share of its stock at the time of issue.   (p. 400)

statement of cash flows Reports cash receipts and cash payments classified according to the entity's major activities: operating, investing, and financing.   (p. 15)

statement of changes in shareholders' equity Reports the changes in all categories of shareholders' equity during the period.   (p. 413)

statement of financial position Another name for the *balance sheet*.   (p. 11)

statement of retained earnings Summary of the changes in the retained earnings of a corporation during a specific period.   (p. 10)

stock dividend A proportional distribution by a corporation of its own shares to its shareholders.   (p. 405)

stock split An increase in the number of authorized, issued, and outstanding shares of stock coupled with a proportionate reduction in the share's book value.   (p. 407)

straight-line (SL) method Depreciation method in which an equal amount of depreciation expense is assigned to each year of asset use.   (p. 285)

strategic investments Investments in which the investor owns more than 20% of the voting shares of the investee and is presumed to exercise either significant influence or control over the investee.   (p. 636)

subsidiary company An investee company in which a parent company owns more than 50% of the voting shares and can exercise control over the subsidiary.   (p. 641)

tangible long-lived assets Also called property, plant, and equipment.   (p. 279)

taxable income The basis for computing the amount of tax to pay the government.   (p. 341)

temporary accounts Revenue, expense, and dividend accounts, which do not have balances that carry forward to the next fiscal year.   (p. 136)

term The length of time from inception to maturity.   (p. 195)

term bonds Bonds that all mature at the same time for a particular issue.   (p. 348)

term loan A long-term loan at a stated interest rate, typically from a single lender such as a bank, which must be repaid over a specified number of years. Usually secured by specific assets of the borrower, often the ones acquired using the loan proceeds.   (p. 365)

Timeliness The need to report accounting information to users in time for it to influence their decisions.   (p. 21)

times-interest-earned ratio Ratio of income from operations to interest expense. Measures the number of times that operating income can cover interest expense. Also called the *interest-coverage ratio*.   (pp. 364, 540)

trademark, trade name A distinctive identification of a product or service. Also called a *brand name*.   (p. 302)

trading on the equity Another name for *leverage*.   (p. 544)

transaction An event that has a financial impact on a business and that can be reliably measured.   (p. 56)

trend percentages A form of horizontal analysis that indicates the direction a business is taking. (p. 523)

trial balance A list of all the ledger accounts with their balances. (p. 79)

uncollectible account expense Another name for bad debt expense. (p. 189)

understandability The need to clearly and concisely classify and present financial information so that reasonably knowledgeable and diligent users of the the information can understand it. (p. 21)

underwriter Organization that purchases the bonds from an issuing company and resells them to its clients or sells the bonds for a commission, agreeing to buy all unsold bonds. (p. 348)

unearned revenue A liability that arises when a business receives cash from a customer prior to providing the related goods or services. (pp. 117, 342)

units-of-production (UOP) method Depreciation method by which a fixed amount of depreciation is assigned to each unit of output produced by the plant asset. (p. 287)

verifiability The ability to check financial information for accuracy, completeness, and reliability. (p. 21)

vertical analysis Analysis of a financial statement that reveals the relationship of each statement item to a specified base, which is the 100% figure. (p. 524)

weighted-average-cost method Inventory costing method based on the average cost of inventory for the period. Weighted-average cost is determined by dividing the cost of goods available by the number of units available. Also called the *average cost method.* (p. 240)

working capital Current assets minus current liabilities; measures a business's ability to meet its short-term obligations with its current assets. Also called *net working capital.* (p. 534)